VIDEO CLIP

Practical Application
of Conservation

VIDEO CLIP

Sociodramatic Play
(social pretend play)

VIDEO CLIP

Bullying

VIDEO CLIP

Scaffolding

VIDEO CLIP

Relational Aggression

VIDEO CLIP

Physical Growth

VIDEO CLIP

Self Awareness

VIDEO CLIP

Reactive Aggression

VIDEO CLIP

Deductive Reasoning

VIDEO CLIP

Gender Consistency

VIDEO CLIP

Human Aggression:
Bandura's Bobo Doll
CLASSIC MODULE

VIDEO CLIP

Egocentrism

VIDEO CLIP

Parten's Play
Categories

VIDEO CLIP

Physical Growth

VIDEO CLIP

Invincibility Fable

VIDEO CLIP

Rough and Tumble Play

VIDEO CLIP

Mental Age Testing
CLASSIC MODULE

VIDEO CLIP

Imaginary Audience

VIDEO CLIP

Self Awareness

VIDEO CLIP

Neglected Child

Child Development

THIRD EDITION

Robert S. Feldman

University of Massachusetts, Amherst

PEARSON

Prentice
Hall

Upper Saddle River, New Jersey 07458

Library of Congress Cataloging-in-Publication Data

Feldman, Robert S. (Robert Stephen), [date]
  Child development / Robert S. Feldman. — 3rd ed.
    p.   cm.
  Includes bibliographical references and index.
  ISBN 0-13-182961-0
  1. Child development.   2. Child psychology.   3. Adolescence.   4. Adolescent psychology.
  I. Title.

HQ767.9.F43   2003
305.231—dc21

2003044013

Editor-in-Chief: *Leah Jewell*
Executive Acquisitions Editor: *Jennifer Gilliland*
Editorial Assistant: *Blythe Ferguson*
AVP/Director of Production and Manufacturing: *Barbara Kittle*
Director of Marketing: *Beth Mejia*
Executive Marketing Manager: *Sheryl Adams*
Editor-in-Chief, Development: *Rochelle Diogenes*
Development Editor: *Roberta Lewis*
Managing Editor: *Joanne Riker*
Project Manager: *Maureen Richardson*
Prepress and Manufacturing Manager: *Nick Sklitsis*
Prepress and Manufacturing Buyer: *Tricia Kenny*
Creative Design Director: *Leslie Osher*
Line Art Manager: *Guy Ruggiero*
Interior and Cover Design: *Ximena Tamvakopoulos*
Electronic Illustrations: *Maria Piper*
Director, Image Resource Center: *Melinda Reo*
Photo Research Supervisor: *Beth Boyd*
Image Permission Supervisor: *Michelina Viscusi*
Photo Researcher: *Toni Michaels/PhotoFind LLC*

Acknowledgments for copyrighted material may be found beginning
on p. 544, which constitutes an extension of this copyright page.

This book was set in 10/13 Minion by Interactive Composition Corp.
and was printed by R. R. Donnelley. The cover was printed by Phoenix Color Corp.

© 2004, 2001, 1998 by Pearson Education, Inc.
Upper Saddle River, NJ 07458

Printed in the United States of America
10   9   8   7   6   5   4   3   2   1

ISBN 0-13-182961-0

Pearson Education Ltd., *London*
Pearson Education Australia PTY, Limited, *Sydney*
Pearson Education Singapore, Pte. Ltd
Pearson Education North Asia Ltd, *Hong Kong*
Pearson Education Canada, Ltd., *Toronto*
Pearson Educación de Mexico, S.A. *de C.V.*
Pearson Education—Japan, *Tokyo*
Pearson Education Malaysia, Pte. Ltd
Pearson Education, Upper Saddle River, *New Jersey*

To my children

Brief Contents

Contents

3 The Start of Life: Genetics and Prenatal Development 54

Birth and the Newborn Infant   94

BRIDGES

7 Social and Personality Development in Infancy 198

9 Cognitive Development in the Preschool Years   258

10 Social and Personality Development in the Preschool Years   290

● B R I D G E S ●

PART 4 / MIDDLE CHILDHOOD

11 Physical Development in Middle Childhood   320

12 Cognitive Development in Middle Childhood 344

13 Social and Personality Development in Middle Childhood 380

PART 5 / ADOLESCENCE

15 Cognitive Development in Adolescence 438

16 Social and Personality Development in Adolescence 468

B R I D G E S

Preface

hild development is a unique field of study. Unlike other disciplines, each of us has experience with its subject matter in very personal ways. It is not just a discipline that deals with ideas and concepts and theories but one that above all has at its heart the forces that have made each of us who we are.

This third edition of *Child Development* seeks to capture the discipline in a way that sparks and nurtures and shapes readers' interest. It is meant to excite students about the field, to draw them into its way of looking at the world, and to mold their understanding of developmental issues. By exposing readers to both the current content and the promise inherent in child and adolescent development, the text is designed to keep interest in the discipline alive long after students' formal study of the field has ended.

Overview

Child Development provides a broad overview of the field of development. It covers the full range of childhood and adolescence, from the moment of conception through the end of adolescence. The text furnishes a broad, comprehensive introduction to the field, covering basic theories and research findings, as well as highlighting current applications outside the laboratory. It covers childhood and adolescence chronologically, encompassing the prenatal period, infancy and toddlerhood, the preschool years, middle childhood, and adolescence. Within these periods, it focuses on physical, cognitive, and social and personality development.

The book seeks to accomplish the following four major goals:

- First and foremost, the book is designed to provide a broad, balanced overview of the field of child development. It introduces readers to the theories, research, and applications that constitute the discipline, examining both the traditional areas of the field as well as more recent innovations.

  The book pays particular attention to the applications developed by child and adolescent development specialists. While not slighting theoretical material, the text emphasizes what we know about development across childhood and adolescence, rather than focusing on unanswered questions. It demonstrates how this knowledge may be applied to real-world problems.

  In sum, the book highlights the interrelationships among theory, research, and application, accentuating the scope and diversity of the field. It also illustrates how child developmentalists use theory, research, and applications to help solve significant social problems.

- The second major goal of the text is to explicitly tie development to students' lives. Findings from the study of child and adolescent development have a significant degree of relevance to students, and this text illustrates how these findings can be applied in a meaningful, practical sense. Applications are presented in a contemporaneous framework, including current news items, timely world events, and contemporary uses of child development that draw readers into the field. Numerous descriptive scenarios and vignettes reflect everyday situations in people's lives, explaining how they relate to the field.

  For example, each chapter begins with an opening prologue that provides a real-life situation relating to the chapter subject area. All chapters also have a "Becoming an Informed Consumer of Development" section, which explicitly suggests ways to apply developmental findings to students' experience. These sections portray how these findings can be applied in a practical, hands-on way. Each chapter also includes a feature called "From Research to Practice" that discusses ways that developmental research is being used to answer the problems that society faces.

In addition, most chapters feature an interview, under the heading "Careers in Child Development," with a person working in a profession related to the chapter's topic. These interviews illustrate how a background in child development can be beneficial in a variety of vocations.

Finally, there are numerous questions in figure and photo captions asking readers to take the perspective of people in a variety of professions that make use of child development, including health care professionals, educators, and social workers.

- The third goal of this book is to highlight both the commonalties and the diversity of today's multicultural society. Consequently, every chapter has at least one "Developmental Diversity" section. These features explicitly consider how cultural factors relevant to development both unite and diversify our contemporary, global society. In addition, the book incorporates material relevant to diversity throughout every chapter.

- Finally, the fourth goal of the text is one that underlies the other three: making the field of child development engaging, accessible, and interesting to students. Child development is a joy both to study and to teach because so much of it has direct, immediate meaning to our lives. Because all of us are involved in our own developmental paths, we are tied in very personal ways to the content areas covered by the book. *Child Development,* then, is meant to engage and nurture this interest, planting a seed that will develop and flourish throughout readers' lifetimes.

To accomplish this fourth goal, the book is "user-friendly." Written in a direct, conversational voice, it replicates as much as possible a dialogue between author and student. The text is meant to be understood and mastered on its own, without the intervention of an instructor. To that end, it includes a variety of pedagogical features. Each chapter contains a "Looking Ahead" overview that sets the stage for the chapter, a running glossary, a detailed summary, an epilogue containing critical thinking questions, and a list of key terms and concepts. In addition, each chapter has several "Review and Apply" sections. The "Review" provides an enumeration of the key concepts, and the "Applying Child Development" section asks questions that promote and test critical thinking and applications of the material.

The Philosophy Behind the Book

Child Development blends and integrates theory, research, and applications. It is *not* an applied development book, focused solely on techniques for translating the knowledge base of development into answers to societal problems. Nor is it a theory-oriented volume, concentrating primarily on the field's abstract theories. Instead, the focus of the text is on the scope and breadth of human development during childhood and adolescence. The strategy of concentrating on the scope of the field permits the text to examine both the traditional core areas of the field and evolving, nontraditional areas of development.

Furthermore, the book focuses on the here-and-now, rather than attempting to provide a detailed historical record of the field. Although it draws on the past where appropriate, it does so with a view toward delineating the field as it now stands and the directions in which it is evolving. Similarly, while providing descriptions of classic studies, the emphasis is more on current research findings and trends.

Overall, then, *Child Development* provides a broad overview of child and adolescent development, integrating the theory, research, and applications of the discipline. It is meant to be a book that readers will want to keep in their own personal libraries, one that they will take off the shelf when considering problems related to that most intriguing of questions: How do people get to be the way they are?

Specific Features

- *Chapter-opening prologues.* Each chapter begins with a short vignette, describing an individual or situation that is relevant to the basic developmental issues being addressed in the chapter. For instance, the chapter on birth describes a premature birth, and the chapter on cognitive development in adolescence provides an account of a teenager who has overcome considerable odds to achieve success.

PROLOGUE: Giant Steps

 routine prenatal test brought Jennifer and Brian Buchkovich horrifying news: Their unborn baby, Ethan, was afflicted with spina bifida, a failure of the spine to close over the spinal cord. The birth defect, which affects 2,000 children a year, usually leads to paralysis and cognitive delays. But doctors offered the Windber, Pennsylvania, couple a glimmer of hope—an experimental operation designed to reduce the damage and to eliminate or delay the need for

- *Looking Ahead sections.* These opening sections orient readers to the topics to be covered, bridging the opening prologue with the remainder of the chapter and providing orienting questions.

- *From Research to Practice.* Each chapter includes a box that focuses on the ways in which research in child development can be used in terms of both everyday child-rearing issues and public policy. For instance, these boxes include discussions on the consequences of infant child care, teaching children desired behavior, and the use of antidepressants to treat childhood psychological problems.

○— FROM RESEARCH TO PRACTICE —○

Cyberspace: Adolescents Online

Students at McClymonds High School in Oakland, California, have a mission: In conjunction with local entomologists, they are creating an online collection of insects in the neighborhood. By placing their "collection" on the World Wide Web, they expect to provide a long-term resource for local residents. (Harmon, 1997)

he widespread availability of the Internet and the World Wide Web is likely to produce significant changes in the lives of many adolescents. Easy access to far-reaching information and contacts is likely to bring benefits and, at the same time, dangers that are both real and virtual.

The educational promise of the Internet is significant.

Despite the substantial benefits of the Internet, its use also has a downside. Claims that cyberspace is overrun with pornog-

- *Developmental Diversity.* Every chapter has at least one "Developmental Diversity" box highlighting issues relevant to the multicultural society in which we live. Examples include discussions of the cultural dimensions of motor development, the adjustment of children from immigrant families, multicultural education, and overcoming gender and racial barriers to achievement.

● DEVELOPMENTAL DIVERSITY ●

Preschools Around the World: Why Does the United States Lag Behind?

In France and Belgium, access to preschool is a legal right. In Sweden and Finland, preschoolers whose parents work have child care provided, if it is wanted. Russia has an extensive system of state-run *yasli-sads,* nursery schools and kindergartens, attended by 75 percent of children aged 3 to 7 in urban areas.

In contrast, the United States has no coordinated national policy on preschool education—or on the care of children in

as the age of students rises. Thus college and high school teachers are paid the most, while preschool and elementary school teachers are paid the least.)

Preschools also differ significantly from one country to another according to the views that different societies hold of the purpose of early childhood education (Lamb et al., 1992). For instance, in a cross-country comparison of preschools in China, Japan, and the United States, researchers found that parents in the three countries view the purpose of preschools very differently. Whereas parents in China tend to see preschools primarily as a way of giving children a good start academically, Japanese

---

- *Becoming an Informed Consumer of Development.* Every chapter includes information on specific uses that can be derived from research conducted by developmental investigators. For instance, the text provides concrete information on exercising an infant's body and senses, keeping preschoolers healthy, increasing children's competence, and choosing a career.

- *Careers in Child Development.* Many chapters include an interview with a person working in a field that uses the findings of child and adolescent development. Among those interviewed are a school nurse, a special education teacher, and a child care provider.

● CAREERS IN CHILD DEVELOPMENT ●

Valerie Patterson

Education: . . . .   Western Washington University, Bellingham: B.A. in psychology; City University, Tacoma, Washington: M.A. in special education

Position: . . . .   Special education teacher, Sajhalie Junior High School, Federal Way, Washington

Home: . . . .   Sumner, Washington

Individualized attention and close communication with parents have helped create a welcoming environment for students with special needs at Sajhalie Junior High School in Federal Way, Washington, according to special education teacher Valerie

---

- *Child.Links. Child.Links* are marginal icons indicating material related to a page on the World Wide Web. Readers can refer to the page number on the *Child Development* Companion Website page, where hot links are provided to the relevant Web sites. In addition, video clip icons indicate relevant observational video segments on the CD-ROM accompanying the book.

brother or sister. For most college students, if the birth happened before they reached the age of 3, they can remember virtually nothing about it (Sheingold & Tenney, 1982).

However, more recent research shows surprising retention in infants. For example, Nancy Myers and her colleagues exposed a group of 6-month-old children to an unusual series of events in a laboratory, such as intermittent periods of light and dark and unusual sounds. When the children were later tested at the age of 1½ years or 2½ years, they demonstrated clear evidence that they had some memory of their participation in the earlier experience. Their behavior, such as reaching for things, reflected their earlier participation. They also seemed more familiar with the testing situation itself, showing more willingness to remain in a potentially unnerving situation than a control group of same-age children (N. A. Myers, Clifton, & Clarkson, 1987; see also Jusczyk & Hohne, 1997; Mandler & McDonough, 1995).

Such findings are consistent with evidence that the physical record of a memory in the brain appears to be relatively permanent, suggesting that memories, even from infancy, may

- *Review and Apply sections*. Interspersed throughout each chapter are several short recaps of the chapter's main points, followed by questions designed to provoke critical thinking and applications of the material to child development. In each section, at least one question asks readers to take the perspective of someone working in an occupation that relies on findings of child development, including the fields of health care, education, and social work.

Review

- During the preschool period, the body grows steadily in height and weight, with individual differences varying widely around the average.
- Preschool children's bodies change in shape and structure, as well as size, becoming more slender and long-limbed and developing body proportions generally similar to adults'.
- The brain grows at a very fast rate during the preschool years, due largely to an increase in cell interconnections and the amount of myelin, and lateralization becomes more pronounced.

- *Running Glossary*. Key terms are defined in the margins of the page on which the term is presented.

- *End-of-chapter material*. Each chapter ends with a detailed summary and a list of key terms and concepts. This material is designed to help students study and retain the information in the chapter. A short epilogue includes critical thinking questions relating to the prologue at the opening of the chapter. Because the opening prologue serves as a case study that foreshadows a topic the chapter will address, the thought-provoking end-of-chapter questions provide a way of tying the chapter together. They also illustrate how the concepts addressed in the chapter can be applied to the real-world situation described in the opening prologue.

- *Bridges*. A Bridges section follows each major part of the book. These sections tie together coverage of the previous period of childhood to the subsequent period, acting as a conceptual link between the various stages of childhood and adolescence.

What's New in This Edition?

Reflecting the importance of providing a firm foundation for students embarking on the study of child development, two new chapters have been added to the beginning of the book. The first chapter includes newly expanded coverage of the scope of the field and its historical building blocks. Chapter 2 focuses on the major theoretical perspectives and on research methods and strategies. These two chapters offer students an engaging introduction to the field, laying the groundwork for their future study—and mastery—of the discipline.

A considerable number of new topics and areas have been added to the third edition. A sampling of topics that have been either newly included or expanded also illustrates the scope of the revision; they include new material on the contextual perspective, the chronosystem, the number of genes in humans, fetal alcohol effects, nonorganic failure to thrive, affordances, epigenetic theory, cultural differences in autobiographical memories, "tough" and "cool" popular children, racial differences in puberty, efficacy of virginity pledges, and MAMA cycles. In addition, a wealth of contemporary research is cited in this edition. Hundreds of new research citations have been added, most from the last few years.

Furthermore, several entirely new features have been added to the third edition. As mentioned earlier, each chapter contains *Child.Links* that direct readers to the *Child Development* Web site, where they will be directed to specific sites relevant to the topic being discussed. In addition, every chapter now ends with an epilogue that includes critical thinking questions regarding the chapter prologue, tying the material in the chapter together.

One of the most significant innovations in the new edition is an increased emphasis on helping students understand the link between various careers and findings from child development. This is accomplished in several ways. First, every *Applying Child Development* section includes at least one critical thinking question to be considered from the perspective of someone in a profession such as education, health provider, or social worker. Second, many of the photo and figure captions ask questions relevant to professionals who make use of child development. Finally, most chapters include an interview with someone who works in a career that relies on the field of child development. These interviews bring alive child development and demonstrate to students the importance of the field.

Instructor and Student Supplements to accompany *Child Development, Third Edition*

The Third Edition's supplements package has gone through extensive revision and refinement to provide you and your students with the best teaching and learning materials, both in print and in media formats.

Print and Media Supplements for the Instructor

NEW Prentice Hall's Observations in Child Developmental Psychology   Created by David Daniel and packaged FREE with every new text, this CD-ROM brings to life more than 30 key concepts discussed in the narrative of the text. Students get to view each video twice: once with an introduction to the concept being illustrated and again with commentary describing what is taking place at crucial points in the video. Whether your course has an observation component or not, this CD-ROM provides your students the opportunity to see children in action. These videos are also available on the Instructor's Resource CD-ROM, described below, for use in lecture presentations.

Instructor's Resource Manual   Created by Elaine Cassel, each chapter in the manual includes the following resources: Learning objectives; lecture suggestions and discussion topics; classroom activities, demonstrations, and exercises; out-of-class assignments and projects; multimedia resources; video resources; transparencies masters; and handouts. Designed to make your lectures more effective and to save you preparation time, this extensive resource gathers together the most effective activities and strategies for teaching your child development course.

Test Item File   Created by Deanna Nekovei of Texas A&M University, Kingsville, this test bank contains over 3,500 multiple choice, true/false, and short answer essay questions. Each question references the section and page number in the text, provides an easy, moderate or difficult key for level of difficulty, and lists the question type of factual, conceptual or applied.

NEW Prentice Hall's Test Generator   Available on one dual-platform CD-ROM, this test generator program provides instructors "best in class" features in an easy to use program. Using the TestGen Wizard you can create tests, easily select questions with drag-and-drop or point and click functionality, add or modify test questions using the built in Question Editor, and print tests in a variety of formats. The program comes with full technical support and telephone "Request a Test" service.

NEW Instructor's Resource CD-ROM   This valuable, time-saving supplement provides you with electronic version of a variety of teaching resources all in one place so that you may customize your lecture notes and media presentations. This CD-ROM includes PowerPoint

Slides customized to the third edition, electronic versions of the artwork in the text chapters, electronic version of the Overhead Transparencies, electronic files for the Instructor Resource Manual and the Test Item File as well as clips from Prentice Hall's Observations in Child Development CD-ROM formatted for in-class presentation.

PowerPoint Slides for Child Development, Third Edition   Each chapter's presentations highlight the key points covered in the text. Provided in two versions—one with the chapter graphics and one without—to give you flexibility in preparing your lectures. Available on the Instructor's Resource CD-ROM or on Prentice Hall's Psychology Central website described below.

***NEW* Prentice Hall's Child Development Transparencies, 2004**   Designed to be used in large lecture settings, this set of over 130 full-color transparencies includes illustrations from the text as well as images from a variety of other sources. Available in acetate form, online at Psychology Central or on the Instructor's Resource CD-ROM.

***NEW* Psychology Central Website at www.prenhall.com/psychology**   Password protected for instructor's use only, this site allows you online access to all of Prentice Hall's Psychology supplements. You'll find a multitude of resources for teaching Developmental Psychology. From this site you can download any of the key supplements available for *Child Development*, third edition including the following: Instructor's Resource Manual, Test Item File, PowerPoint Slides, chapter graphics and electronic versions of the Child Development Transparencies, 2004. Contact your Prentice Hall representative for the User ID and Password to access this site.

Online Course Management with WebCT, BlackBoard, or CourseCompass   FREE upon adoption of the text, instructors interested in using online course management have their choice of options. Each course comes preloaded with text specific quizzing and testing material and can be fully customized for your course. Contact your Prentice Hall representative or visit **www.prenhall.com/demo** for more information.

Video Support for Children and Their Development

Films for the Humanities and Sciences   A wealth of full-length videos from the extensive library of *Films for the Humanities and Sciences*, on a variety of topics in developmental psychology, are available to qualified adopters. Contact your Prentice Hall representative for a list of videos.

ABC News/Prentice Hall Video Libraries   Consisting of brief segments from award-winning news programs such as *Good Morning America, Nightline, 20/20* and *World News Tonight,* these videos discuss current issues and are a great way to launch your lectures.

NEW Developmental Psychology, 2004
NEW Issues in Child and Adolescent Development, 2002
Human Development, Series IV

***NEW* Lecture Launcher Video for Developmental Psychology**   Adopters can receive this new videotape that includes short clips covering all major topics in developmental psychology. The videos have been carefully selected from the *Films for Humanities and Sciences* library, and edited to provide brief and compelling video content for enhancing your lectures. Contact your Prentice Hall representative for a full list of video clips on this tape.

Print and Media Supplements for the Student

***NEW* Prentice Hall's Observations in Child Developmental Psychology**   Created by David Daniel and packaged *FREE* with every new text, this CD-ROM brings to life more than

VIDEO CLIP

Little Albert
CLASSIC MODULE

30 key concepts discussed in the narrative of the text. Students get to view each video twice: once with an introduction to the concept being illustrated and again with commentary describing what is taking place at crucial points in the video. Whether your course has an observation component or not, this CD-ROM provides your students the opportunity to see children in action.

Study Guide   Written by Mark P. Rittman of Cuyahoga Community College, this student study guide helps students master the core concepts presented in each chapter. For each chapter, this study guide provides an outline, learning objectives, key terms and concepts review, a guided review, and practice multiple choice and essay questions.

Companion Website at www.prenhall.com/feldman   Authored by Pamela Anderson and Deborah Bobek of Tufts University, this online study guide allows students to review each chapter's material, take practice tests, research topics for course projects and more! The third edition's companion Website includes the following resources for each chapter: Chapter objectives, interactive lectures, five different types of quizzes that provide immediate, text-specific feedback and coaching comments, WebEssays, WebDestinations, NetSearch, and *NEW* FlashCards. Access to the Website is free and unrestricted to all students.

NEW The Prentice Hall Guide to Evaluating Online Resources with Research Navigator: Psychology, 2004   This guide provides students with a hands-on introduction to the Internet, teaches students how to critically evaluate online resources and guides students through the research process for three different types of research projects using *Research Navigator*. Access to *Research Navigator*, a customized research database for students of psychology described below, comes FREE with this guide!

Research Navigator™   Research Navigator features three exclusive databases full of source material, including:

- **EBSCO's ContentSelect Academic Journal Database** organized by subject, each subject contains 50–100 of the leading academic journals for that discipline. Instructors and students can search the online journals by keyword, topic, or multiple topics. Articles include abstract and citation information and can be cut, pasted, emailed, or saved for later use.

- **The New York Times Search-by-Subject One Year Archive** organized by subject and searchable by keyword, or multiple keywords. Instructors and students can view the full text of the article.

- **Link Library** organized by subject, offers editorially selected "best of the web" sites. Link libraries are continually scanned and kept up to date providing the most relevant and accurate links for research assignments.

  To see for yourself how this resource works, take a tour at www.researchnavigator.com, or ask your local Prentice Hall representative for more details.

Supplementary Texts

Contact your Prentice Hall representative to package any of these supplementary texts with *Child Development, Third Edition:*

Twenty Studies that Revolutionized Child Psychology by Wallace E. Dixon, Jr.
Presenting the seminal research studies that have shaped modern developmental psychology, this brief text provides an overview of the environment that gave rise to each study, its experimental design, its findings, and its impact on current thinking in the discipline.

Human Development in Multicultural Context: A Book of Readings by Michele A. Paludi. This compilation of readings highlights cultural influences in developmental psychology.

The Psychology Major: Careers and Strategies for Success by Eric Landrum (Idaho State University) and Stephen Davis (Emporia State University). This 176-page paperback provides valuable information on career options available to psychology majors, tips for improving academic performance, and a guide to the APA style of research reporting.

Acknowledgments

I am grateful to the following reviewers who provided a wealth of comments, criticism, and encouragement:

Carolyn Cooper, Longwood College; Angie Cranor, University of North Carolina at Greensboro; Thomas Fitzpatrick, SUNY Rockland; Eugene Geist, Ohio University; Sarah DeHaas, Juniata College; Penny Hauser-Cram, Boston College; Denis Hatter, Otterbein College; Jean V. Kizer, Mississippi State University; Jacqueline Lerner, Tufts University; Laura Levine, Central Connecticut State University; Terry McNabb, Coe College; Sandra Panetta, Arapahoe Community College; Ratna Raj, Cerro Coso Community College; Denise Hatter, Otterbein College; Lynne Rompelman, Concordia University; and Mary Wilson, North Essex Community College; Dr. Marc Alcorn, University of Northern Colorado; Prof. Lori Beasley, University of Central Oklahoma; Patricia Jarvis, Ph.D., Illinois State University; Prof. Kevin Keating, Broward Community College; Dr. Judith Levine, State University of New York, Farmingdale; Prof. Joann Nelson, South Illinois University; Dean Schroeder, Laramie County Community College; and Dr. Robert Schultz, Fulton-Montgomery Community College.

Many others deserve a great deal of thanks. I am indebted to the many people who provided me with a superb education, first at Wesleyan University and later at the University of Wisconsin. Specifically, Karl Scheibe played a pivotal role in my undergraduate education, and the late Vernon Allen acted as mentor and guide through my graduate years. It was in graduate school that I learned about development, being exposed to such experts as Ross Parke, John Balling, Joel Levin, Herb Klausmeier, and Frank Hooper.

My education continued when I became a professor. I am especially grateful to my colleagues at the University of Massachusetts, who make the university such as wonderful place in which to teach and do research.

Several people played central roles in the development of this book. Edward Murphy brought a keen intelligence and editorial eye to the process, and the book has been greatly strengthened by his input. Christopher Poirier provided research assistance, and I am thankful for his help on this and on other projects for which he provided welcomed, if often unacknowledged, help. Most of all, John Graiff was essential in juggling and coordinating the multiple aspects of writing this book, and I am very grateful for the central role he played.

I am also grateful to the superb Prentice Hall team that was instrumental in the development of this book. Jennifer Gilliland oversaw the project, always providing support and direction. I am grateful for her enthusiasm, intelligence, and creativity. Roberta Lewis, development editor, provided excellent advice and suggestions, improving the text significantly. On the production end of things, Maureen Richardson, production supervisor, and Toni Michaels, photo editor, helped give the book its distinctive look. Finally, I'd like to thank my new marketing manager, Sheryl Adams, on whose skills I'm counting. It's a privilege to be part of this world-class team.

I also wish to acknowledge the members of my family, who play such a pivotal role in my life. My brother, Michael; my sisters-in-law and brothers-in-law; my nieces and nephews—all make up an important part of my life. In addition, I am always indebted to the older generation of my family, who led the way in a manner I can only hope to emulate. I will always be obligated to Ethel Radler, Harry Brochstein, and the late Mary Vorwerk. Most of all, the list is headed by my father, the late Saul Feldman, and my terrific mother, Leah Brochstein.

In the end, it is my immediate family who deserve the greatest thanks. My three terrific kids, Jonathan, Joshua, and Sarah, are my pride and joy. And ultimately my wife, Katherine Vorwerk, provides the love and grounding that makes everything worthwhile. I thank them, with all my love.

Robert S. Feldman
University of Massachusetts, Amherst

About the Author

Robert S. Feldman is a professor at the University of Massachusetts in Amherst, where he is director of undergraduate studies in psychology. A recipient of the College Distinguished Teacher Award, he has also served as a Hewlett Teaching Fellow and Senior Online Teaching Fellow.

Professor Feldman was educated as an undergraduate at Wesleyan University, from which he graduated with high honors, and received his M.S. and Ph.D. degrees from the University of Wisconsin in Madison, where he specialized in social and developmental psychology.

Among his more than 100 books, chapters, and articles, he has edited *Development of Nonverbal Behavior in Children* (Springer-Verlag) and *Applications of Nonverbal Behavioral Theory and Research* (Erlbaum) and co-edited *Fundamentals of Nonverbal Behavior* (Cambridge University Press). He is the recipient of grants from the National Institute of Mental Health and the National Institute of the Disabilities and Rehabilitation Research, which have supported his research on the development of nonverbal behavior in children. A past Fulbright lecturer and research scholar, he is a Fellow of the American Psychological Association and of the American Psychological Society.

During the course of nearly two decades as a college instructor, he has taught both undergraduate and graduate courses at Mount Holyoke College, Wesleyan University, and Virginia Commonwealth University, in addition to the University of Massachusetts.

Professor Feldman is a music lover, an enthusiastic pianist, and an excellent cook. He has three children, and he and his wife, a psychologist, live in Amherst, Massachusetts, in a home overlooking the Holyoke mountain range.

Child Development

1

An Introduction to Child
Development

PROLOGUE: The New Worlds of Childhood

When Elizabeth Carr's class was learning how an egg combines with sperm in the mother's body to create a child, she felt compelled to interrupt.

"I piped up to say that not all babies are conceived like that and explained about sperm and eggs and petri dishes," said Elizabeth, the first child in the United States born through in vitro fertilization.

Because her mother's landmark pregnancy was documented in great detail by a film crew, Elizabeth has seen pictures of the egg and sperm that united to become her, the petri dish where she was conceived, and the embryonic blob of cells that grew into the bubbly young woman who now plays field hockey and sings in the school chorus. . . .

Elizabeth said that her parents—whose egg and sperm joined in a petri dish at the Jones Institute for Reproductive Medicine in Norfolk, Virginia—have always made it clear that she was created differently from other children. Although she said she had faced taunts of "test-tube baby" or "weirdo" a few times at school, she said she had never felt resentful about her conception.

"I'm so grateful that they went through all this to have me. . . . Now I'm just a normal [daughter] trying to keep my room clean." (Rosenthal, 1996, pp. A1, B8)

Elizabeth Carr, the first "test-tube" baby.

3

LOOKING AHEAD ▶

Welcome to the new world of childhood—or rather, just one of many new worlds. Issues ranging from so-called test tube babies to the consequences of poverty on development to the effects of culture and race raise significant developmental concerns. Underlying these are even more fundamental issues: How do children develop physically? How does their understanding of the world grow and change over time? And how do our personalities and our social world develop as we move from birth through adolescence?

Each of these questions, and many others we'll encounter throughout this book, are central to the field of child development. Consider, for example, the range of approaches that different specialists in child development might take when considering the story of Elizabeth Carr:

- Child development researchers who investigate behavior at the level of biological processes might determine if Elizabeth's functioning prior to birth was affected by her conception outside the womb.

- Specialists in child development who study genetics might examine how the biological endowment from Elizabeth's parents affects her later behavior.

- For child development specialists who investigate the ways thinking changes over the course of childhood, Elizabeth's life might be examined in terms of how her understanding of the nature of her conception changed as she grew older.

- Other researchers in child development who focus on physical growth might consider whether her growth rate differed from children conceived more traditionally.

- Child development experts who specialize in the social world of children might look at the ways that Elizabeth interacted with other children and the kinds of friendships she developed.

Although their interests take many forms, all these specialists in child development share one concern: understanding the growth and change that occur during the course of childhood and adolescence. Taking many differing approaches, developmentalists study how both our biological inheritance from our parents and the environment in which we live jointly affect our behavior.

Some researchers in child development focus on explaining how our genetic background can determine not only how we look but also how we behave and how we relate to others—that is, matters of personality. These professionals explore ways to identify how much of our potential as human beings is provided—or limited—by heredity. Other child development specialists look to the environment in which we are raised, exploring ways in which our lives are shaped by the world that we encounter. They investigate the extent to which we are shaped by our early environments and how our current circumstances influence our behavior in both subtle and obvious ways.

Whether they focus on heredity or environment, all child development specialists hope that their work will ultimately inform and support the efforts of professionals whose careers are devoted to improving the lives of children. Practioners in fields ranging from education to health care to social work draw on the findings of child development researchers, using their research findings to advance children's welfare.

In this chapter, we orient ourselves to the field of child development. We begin with a discussion of the scope of the discipline, illustrating the wide array of topics it covers and the range of ages it examines, from the moment of conception through the end of adolescence. We also survey the foundations of the field and examine the key issues and questions that underlie child development. Finally, we consider where the child development field is likely to go in the future. After reading this chapter, you will be able to answer these questions:

- **What is child development?**
- **What is the scope of the field?**
- **What are the key issues and questions in the field of child development?**
- **What is the future of child development likely to hold?**

An Orientation to Child Development

Have you ever marveled at the way an infant tightly grips your finger with tiny, perfectly formed hands? Or at how a preschooler methodically draws a picture? Or at the way an adolescent can make involved decisions about whom to invite to a party?

If you've ever wondered about such things, you are asking the kinds of questions that scientists in the field of child development pose. **Child development** is the scientific study of the patterns of growth, change, and stability that occur from conception through adolescence.

Although the definition of the field seems straightforward, the simplicity is somewhat misleading. To understand what child development is actually about, we need to look beneath the various parts of the definition.

In its study of growth, change, and stability, child development takes a *scientific* approach. Like members of other scientific disciplines, researchers in child development test their assumptions about the nature and course of human development by applying scientific methods. As we'll see in the next chapter, they develop theories about development, and they use methodical, scientific techniques to validate the accuracy of their assumptions systematically.

Child development focuses on *human* development. Although some specialists in the field study the course of development in nonhuman species, the vast majority examine growth and change in people. Some seek to understand universal principles of development, while others focus on how cultural, racial, and ethnic differences affect the course of development. Still others aim to understand the unique aspects of individuals, looking at the traits and characteristics that differentiate one person from another. Regardless of approach, however, all child developmentalists view development as a continuing process throughout childhood and adolescence.

As developmental specialists focus on the ways people change and grow during their lives, they also consider stability in children's and adolescents' lives. They ask in which areas and in what periods people show change and growth and when and how their behavior reveals consistency and continuity with prior behavior.

Finally, although child development focuses on childhood and adolescence, the process of development persists throughout *every* part of people's lives, beginning with the moment of conception and continuing until death. Developmental specialists assume that in some ways people continue to grow and change right up to the end of their lives, while in other respects their behavior remains stable. At the same time, these specialists believe that no particular, single period of life governs all development. Instead, they believe that every period of life contains the potential for both growth and decline in abilities and that individuals maintain the capacity for substantial growth and change throughout their lives.

Child development   The field that involves the scientific study of the patterns of growth, change, and stability that occur from conception through adolescence

Characterizing Child Development: The Scope of the Field

Clearly, the definition of child development is broad and the scope of the field is extensive. Consequently, professionals in child development cover several quite diverse areas, and a typical developmentalist specializes in two ways: topical area and age range.

Topical Areas in Child Development.   The field of child development includes three major topics or approaches:

- Physical development
- Cognitive development
- Social and personality development

An individual in the child development field might specialize in a particular one of these topical areas. For example, some developmentalists focus on **physical development,** examining the ways in which the body's makeup—the brain, nervous system, muscles, and senses and the need for food, drink, and sleep—helps determine behavior. For example, one specialist in physical development might examine the effects of malnutrition on the pace of growth in children, while another might look at how sexual maturation proceeds during adolescence.

Other developmental specialists examine **cognitive development,** seeking to understand how growth and change in intellectual capabilities influence a person's behavior. Cognitive developmentalists examine learning, memory, problem solving, and intelligence. For example, specialists in cognitive development might want to see how intellectual abilities change over the course of childhood or if cultural differences exist in the factors to which children attribute their academic successes and failures.

Finally, some developmental specialists focus on personality and social development. **Personality development** is the study of stability and change in the enduring characteristics that differentiate one person from another. **Social development** is the way in which individuals' interactions with others and their social relationships grow, change, and remain stable over the course of life. A developmentalist interested in personality development might ask whether there are stable, enduring personality traits throughout the life span, while a specialist in social development might examine dating patterns during adolescence. Personality and social developmentalists also focus on emotional development throughout childhood and adolescence. (The major approaches are summarized in Table 1-1.)

Age Ranges and Individual Differences.   As they specialize in chosen topical areas, child developmentalists typically look at particular age ranges. They usually divide childhood and adolescence into broad age ranges: the prenatal period (the period from conception to birth), infancy and toddlerhood (birth to age 3), the preschool period (ages 3 to 6), middle childhood (ages 6 to 12), and adolescence (ages 12 to 20).

Although most child developmentalists accept these broad periods, the age ranges themselves are in many ways arbitrary. Although some periods have one clear-cut boundary (infancy begins with birth, the preschool period ends with entry into public school, and adolescence starts with sexual maturity), others don't.

For instance, consider the separation between middle childhood and adolescence, which usually occurs around the age of 12. Because the boundary is based on a biological change, the onset of sexual maturation, which varies greatly from one individual to another, the specific age of entry into adolescence varies from one person to the next.

In short, there are substantial individual differences in the timing of events in people's lives. In part, this is a biological fact of life: People mature at different rates and reach developmental milestones at different points. However, environmental factors also play a significant role in determining the age at which a particular event is likely to occur. For example, the typical age at which people become romantically involved with members of the opposite sex

Physical development   Development involving the body's physical makeup, including the brain, nervous system, muscles, and senses and the need for food, drink, and sleep

Cognitive development   Development involving the ways that growth and change in intellectual capabilities influence a person's behavior

Personality development   Development involving the ways that the enduring characteristics that differentiate one person from another change over the life span

Social development   The way in which individuals' interactions with others and their social relationships grow, change, and remain stable over the course of life

TABLE 1-1   APPROACHES TO CHILD DEVELOPMENT

Orientation	Defining Characteristics	Examples of Questions Asked*
Physical development	Examines how brain, nervous system, muscles, sensory capabilities, and needs for food, drink, and sleep affect behavior	What determines the sex of a child? (3) What are the long-term consequences of premature birth? (4) What are the benefits of breast-feeding? (5) What are the consequences of early or late sexual maturation? (14)
Cognitive development	Examines intellectual abilities, including learning, memory, problem solving, and intelligence	What are the earliest memories that can be recalled from infancy? (6) What are the consequences of watching television? (9) Are there benefits to bilingualism? (12) Are there ethnic and racial differences in intelligence? (12) How does an adolescent's egocentrism affect his or her view of the world? (15)
Personality and social development	Examines enduring characteristics that differentiate one person from another and how interactions with others and social relationships grow and change over the life span	Do newborns respond differently to their mothers than to others? (4) What is the best procedure for disciplining children? (10) When does a sense of gender develop? (10) How can we promote cross-race friendships? (13) What are the causes of adolescent suicide? (16)

*Numbers in parentheses indicate in which chapter the question is addressed.

varies substantially from one culture to another, depending in part on the way that male–female relationships are viewed in a given culture.

It is important to keep in mind, then, that when developmental specialists discuss age ranges, they are talking about averages—the times when people, on average, reach particular milestones. Some children will reach the milestone earlier, some later, and many—in fact, most—will reach it just around the time of the average. Such variation becomes noteworthy only when children show substantial deviation from the average. For example, parents whose child begins to speak at a much later age than average might decide to have their son or daughter evaluated by a speech therapist.

Furthermore, as children grow older, they become more likely to deviate from the average and exhibit individual differences. In very young children, a good part of developmental change is genetically determined and unfolds automatically, making development fairly similar in different children. But as children age, environmental factors become more potent, leading to greater variability and individual differences as time passes.

The Links Between Topics and Ages.   Each of the broad topical areas of child development—physical, cognitive, and social and personality development—plays a role throughout childhood and adolescence. Consequently, some developmental experts focus on physical development during the prenatal period and others on what occurs during adolescence. Some might specialize in social development during the preschool years, while others look at social relationships in middle childhood. And still others might take a broader approach, looking at cognitive development through every period of childhood and adolescence (and beyond).

This wedding of two children in India is an example of how environmental factors can play a significant role in determining the age when a particular event is likely to occur.

— DEVELOPMENTAL DIVERSITY —

How Culture, Ethnicity, and Race Influence Development

South American Mayan mothers are certain that almost constant contact between themselves and their infant children is necessary for good parenting, and they are physically upset if contact is not possible. They are shocked when they see a North American mother lay her infant down, and they attribute the baby's crying to the poor parenting of the North American. (Morelli et al., 1992)

Two views of parenting are at odds in this passage. Is one right and the other wrong? Probably not, if we take into consideration the cultural context in which the mothers are operating. In fact, different cultures and subcultures have their own views of appropriate and inappropriate child rearing, just as they have different developmental goals for children (Francasso et al., 1997; Greenfield, 1995, 1997).

Specialists in child development must take into consideration broad cultural factors, such as an orientation toward individualism or collectivism. In addition, they must also take into account finer ethnic, racial, socioeconomic, and gender differences if they are to achieve an understanding of how people change and grow throughout the life span. If these specialists succeed in doing so, not only can they achieve a better understanding of human development, but they may also be able to derive more precise applications for improving the human social condition.

Efforts to understand how diversity affects development have been hindered by difficulties in finding an appropriate vocabulary. For example, members of the research community—as well as society at large—have sometimes used terms such as *race* and *ethnic group* in inappropriate ways. *Race* is a biological concept, which should be employed to refer to classifications based on physical and structural characteristics of species. In contrast, *ethnic group* and *ethnicity* are broader terms, referring to cultural background, nationality, religion, and language.

The concept of race has proved particularly problematic. Although it formally refers to biological factors, race has taken on substantially more meanings—many of them inappropriate—that range from skin color to religion to culture. Moreover, the concept of race is exceedingly imprecise; depending on how it is defined, there are between 3 and 300 races, and no race is biologically pure. Furthermore, the fact that 99.9 percent of humans' genetic makeup is identical in all humans makes the question of race seem comparatively insignificant (Angier, 2000; Betancourt & Lopez, 1993; Carpenter, 2000).

In addition, there is little agreement about which names best reflect different races and ethnic groups. Should the term *African*

The face of the United States is changing as the proportion of children from different backgrounds is increasing.

American—which has geographical and cultural implications—be preferred over *black,* which focuses primarily on skin color? Is *Native American* preferable to *Indian*? Is *Hispanic* more appropriate than *Latino*? And how can researchers accurately categorize people with multiethnic backgrounds? The choice of category has important implications for the validity and usefulness of research. The choice even has political implications. For example, the decision to permit people to identify themselves as "multiracial" on U.S. government forms and in the 2000 U.S. Census was highly controversial (Evinger, 1996; Jones, 1994).

As the proportion of minorities in U.S. society continues to increase, it becomes crucial to take the complex issues associated with human diversity into account in order to fully understand development (Fowers & Richardson, 1996). In fact, it is only by looking for similarities and differences among various ethnic, cultural, and racial groups that developmental researchers can distinguish principles of development that are universal from ones that are culturally determined. In the years ahead, then, it is likely that child development will move from a discipline that primarily focuses on children with North American and European backgrounds to one that encompasses the development of children around the globe.

Society's view of childhood and what is appropriate to ask of children has changed through the ages. These children worked full time in mines in the early 1900s.

The variety of topical areas and age ranges studied within the field of child development means that specialists from many diverse backgrounds and areas of expertise consider themselves child developmentalists. Psychologists who study behavior and mental processes, educational researchers, geneticists, and physicians are only some of the people who specialize and conduct research in child development. Furthermore, developmentalists work in a variety of settings, including university departments of psychology, education, human development, and medicine, as well as nonacademic settings as varied as human service agencies and child care centers.

The diversity of specialists working under the broad umbrella of child development brings a variety of perspectives and intellectual richness to the field of child development. In addition, it permits the research findings of the field to be used by practitioners in a wide array of applied professions. Teachers, nurses, social workers, child care providers, and social policy experts all rely on the findings of child development to make decisions about how to improve children's welfare.

Cohort Influences on Development: Developing With Others in a Social World.

Bob, born in 1947, is a baby boomer. He was born soon after the end of World War II, when an enormous bulge in the birthrate occurred as soldiers returned to the United States from overseas. He was an adolescent at the height of the civil rights movement and the beginning of protests against the Vietnam War. His mother, Leah, was born in 1922; she is part of the generation that passed its childhood and teenage years in the shadow of the Great Depression. Bob's son, Jon, was born in 1975. Now starting a career after graduating from college and newly married, he is a member of what has been called Generation X.

These people are in part products of the social times in which they live. Each belongs to a particular **cohort,** a group of people born at around the same time in the same place. Such major social events as wars, economic upturns and depressions, famines, and epidemics (like the one related to the AIDS virus) work similar influences on members of a particular cohort.

Normative Influences on Development.
People who are members of a cohort are subject to particular normative events. **Normative events** are events that occur in a similar way for most individuals in a group. Normative events may be biologically, socially, or culturally determined. For example, reaching puberty at the start of adolescence is a normative event because it happens to everyone at roughly the same period of life. Similarly, entry into formal education in public schools typically occurs around the age of 5 or 6 in Western cultures.

Cohort A group of people born at around the same time in the same place

Normative events Events that occur in a similar way for most individuals in a group

There are several classes of normative events. *Normative history-graded influences* are biological and environmental influences associated with a particular historical moment. For instance, children who lived in New York City shared both biological and environmental challenges due to the terrorist attack on the World Trade Center towers that occurred on September 11, 2001. Their development is going to be affected by this normative history-graded event.

Normative history-graded influences contrast with *normative age-graded influences,* which are biological and environmental influences that are similar for individuals in a particular age group, regardless of when or where they were raised. For example, biological events such as menopause are universal events that occur at relatively the same time throughout all societies. Similarly, a sociocultural event such as graduation from high school can be considered a normative age-graded influence because it occurs at the end of the teenage years for most adolescents in the United States.

Development is also affected by *normative sociocultural-graded influences,* which include ethnicity, social class, subcultural membership, and other factors. For example, sociocultural-graded influences will be considerably different for immigrant children who speak English as a second language than for children born in the United States who speak English as their first language.

Finally, nonnormative life events also influence development. *Nonnormative life events* are specific, atypical events that occur in a particular person's life at a time when such events do not happen to most people. For instance, the experience of Elizabeth Carr, who grew up with the knowledge that she was the first person in the United States to be conceived using in vitro fertilization, constitutes a nonnormative life event. In addition, children can create their own nonnormative life events. For instance, a high school girl who enters and wins a national science competition produces a nonnormative life event for herself. In a very real sense, she is actively constructing her own environment, thereby participating in her own development.

R E V I E W *&* A P P L Y

Review

- Child development, a scientific approach to understanding human growth and change from conception to adolescence, encompasses physical, cognitive, and social and personality development.

- Developmentalists typically divide childhood and adolescence into the prenatal period (from conception to birth), infancy and toddlerhood (birth to age 3), the preschool period (ages 3 to 6), middle childhood (ages 6 to 12), and adolescence (ages 12 to 20).

- Membership in a cohort, based on age and place of birth, subjects people to influences related to historical events. People are also subject to normative age-graded influences, normative sociocultural-graded influences, and nonnormative life events.

Applying Child Development

- What are some environmental factors that might influence the timing of a child's development?

- *From an educator's perspective:* How would a student's cohort membership affect his or her readiness for school?

Children: Past, Present, and Future

Children have been the target of study from the time that humans have walked the planet. Parents are endlessly fascinated by their children, and the growth displayed throughout childhood and adolescence is a source of both curiosity and wonderment.

But it is relatively recent in the course of history that children have been studied from a scientific vantage point. Even a brief look at how the field of child development has developed shows that there has been considerable growth in the way that children are viewed.

Early Views of Children

Although it is hard to imagine, some scholars believe that there was a time when childhood didn't even exist, at least in the minds of adults. According to Philippe Ariès, who studied paintings and other forms of art, children in medieval Europe were not given any special status before 1600. Instead, they were viewed as miniature, somewhat imperfect adults. They were dressed in adult clothing and not treated specially in any significant way. Childhood was not seen as a stage qualitatively different from adulthood (Ariès, 1962).

Although the view that children during the Middle Ages were seen simply as miniature adults may be somewhat exaggerated—Ariès's arguments were based primarily on art depicting the European aristocracy, a very limited sample of Western culture—it is clear that childhood had a considerably different meaning than it does now. Moreover, the idea that childhood could be studied systematically did not take hold until later.

During medieval times in Europe, children were thought of as miniature, although imperfect, adults. This view of childhood was reflected in how children were dressed—identically as adults.

Baby Biographies.   Among the first instances in which children were methodically studied came in the form of *baby biographies,* which were popular in the late 1700s in Germany. Observers—typically parents—tried to trace the growth of a single child, recording the physical and linguistic milestones achieved by their child.

But it was not until Charles Darwin, who developed the theory of evolution, that observation of children took a more systematic turn. Darwin was convinced that understanding the development of individuals within a species could help identify how the species itself had developed. He made baby biographies more scientifically respectable by producing one of his own, recording his own son's development during his first year.

A wave of baby biographies were produced following publication of Darwin's book. Furthermore, other historical trends were helping propel the development of a new scientific discipline focusing on children. Scientists were discovering the mechanisms behind conception, and geneticists were beginning to unlock the mysteries of heredity. Philosophers were arguing about the relative influences of nature (heredity) and nurture (influences in the environment).

Focus on Childhood.   In addition, as the adult labor pool increased, children were not needed as a source of inexpensive labor, paving the way for laws that protected children from exploitation. The advent of more universal education meant that children were separated from adults for more of the day, and educators sought to identify better ways of teaching children. Advances in psychology led people to focus on the ways that events that had occurred during childhood influenced them during their adult lives. As a consequence of these significant social changes, child development became recognized as a field of its own.

The 20th Century: Child Development as a Discipline.   Several figures became central to the emerging field of child development. For example, Alfred Binet, a French psychologist, not only pioneered work on children's intelligence but also investigated memory and mental calculation. G. Stanley Hall pioneered the use of questionnaires to illuminate children's thinking and behavior. He also wrote the first book that targeted adolescence as a distinct period of development—aptly titled *Adolescence* (Hall, 1904/1916).

Contributions of Women.   Even though prejudice hindered women in their pursuit of academic careers, they made significant contributions to the discipline of child development during the early part of the 1900s. For example, Leta Stetter Hollingworth was one of the first psychologists to focus on child development (Denmark & Fernandez, 1993; Hollingworth, 1943/1990).

During the first decades of the 1900s, one emerging trend that had enormous impact on our understanding of children's development was the rise of large-scale, systematic, and ongoing investigations of children and their development throughout the life span. For example, the Stanford Studies of Gifted Children began in the early 1920s and continue today. Similarly, the Fels Research Institute Study and the Berkeley Growth and Guidance Studies helped identify the nature of change in children's lives as they became older. Using a normative approach, they studied large numbers of children in order to determine the nature of normal growth (Dixon & Lerner, 1999).

The women and men who built the foundations of child development shared a common goal: to scientifically study the nature of growth, change, and stability throughout childhood and adolescence. They brought the field to where it is today.

Today's Key Issues and Questions: Child Development's Underlying Themes

Today, several key issues and questions dominate the field of child development. Among the major issues (summarized in Table 1-2) are the nature of developmental change, the

TABLE 1-2 MAJOR ISSUES IN CHILD DEVELOPMENT	
Issue	**Explanation**
Continuous change versus discontinuous change	In continuous change, development is gradual: The achievements at one level build on the previous one. The underlying developmental processes driving the change remain the same over the course of the life span. In contrast, discontinuous change occurs in distinct steps or stages, with each stage bringing about behavior that is assumed to be qualitatively different from that seen at earlier stages.
Critical and sensitive periods	A critical period is a specific time during development when a particular event has its greatest consequences. Although early developmental psychologists placed great emphasis on the importance of critical periods, more recent thinking suggests that in may areas, individuals may be more flexible than was first thought, particularly in the areas of personality and social development. As a result, developmentalists now refer instead to *sensitive periods* in which organisms are particularly susceptible to certain kinds of stimuli in their environments.
Life span approaches versus focus on particular periods	Earlier developmental psychologists studying the life span focused primarily on infancy and adolescence. Current thinking sees the entire life span as important for a number of reasons, including the discovery that developmental growth and change continue throughout every part of life.
Nature–nurture issue	Nature refers to traits, abilities, and capabilities that are inherited from one's parents. It encompasses any factor that is produced by the predetermined unfolding of genetic information. Nurture involves the environmental influences that shape behavior. Some may be biological, while others are more social. Some influences are a result of larger society-level factors, such as the socioeconomic opportunities available to members of minority groups.

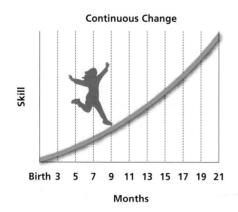

FIGURE 1-1   TWO APPROACHES TO DEVELOPMENTAL CHANGE

The two approaches to development are continuous change, which is gradual, with achievements at one level building on those of previous levels, and discontinuous change, which occurs in distinct steps or stages.

importance of critical and sensitive periods, life span approaches versus more focused approaches, and the nature–nurture issue.

Continuous Change Versus Discontinuous Change.

One of the primary issues challenging child developmentalists is whether development proceeds in a continuous or discontinuous fashion (illustrated in Figure 1-1). In **continuous change,** development is gradual, with achievements at one level building on those of previous levels. Continuous change is quantitative; the basic underlying developmental processes that drive change remain the same over the course of the life span. Continuous change, then, produces changes that are a matter of degree but not kind.

In contrast, **discontinuous change** occurs in distinct steps or stages. Each stage brings about behavior that is assumed to be qualitatively different from behavior at earlier stages. Consider the example of cognitive development. We'll see in Chapter 2 that some cognitive developmentalists suggest that our thinking changes in fundamental ways as children develop and that such development is not just a matter of quantitative change but also one of qualitative change.

Most developmentalists agree that taking an either-or position on the continuous-versus-discontinuous issue is inappropriate. Although many types of developmental change are continuous, others are clearly discontinuous (Flavell, 1994; Rutter et al., 1997; van Geert, 1998).

Critical and Sensitive Periods: Gauging the Impact of Environmental Events.

If a woman comes down with a case of rubella (German measles) in the 11th week of pregnancy, the consequences for the child she is carrying are likely to be devastating: They include the potential for blindness, deafness, and heart defects. However, if she comes down with the same strain of rubella in the 30th week of pregnancy, damage to the child is unlikely.

The differing outcomes of the disease in the two periods demonstrate the concept of critical periods. A **critical period** is a specific time during development when a particular event has its greatest consequences. Critical periods occur when the presence of certain kinds of environmental stimuli are necessary for development to proceed normally.

Although early specialists in child development placed great emphasis on the importance of critical periods, more recent thinking suggests that in many realms, individuals may be more flexible than was first thought, particularly in the domains of cognitive, personality, and social development. In these areas, there is a significant degree of *plasticity,* the degree to which a developing behavior or physical structure is modifiable. For instance, rather than suffering permanent damage from a lack of certain kinds of early social experiences, there is increasing evidence that children can use later experiences to help overcome earlier deficits.

Consequently, developmentalists are now more likely to speak of **sensitive periods** rather than critical periods. In a sensitive period, organisms are particularly susceptible to certain kinds of stimuli in their environment. In contrast to a critical period, however, the absence of

Continuous change   Gradual development in which achievements at one level build on those of previous levels

Discontinuous change   Development that occurs in distinct steps or stages, with each stage bringing about behavior that is assumed to be qualitatively different from behavior at earlier stages

Critical period   A specific time during development when a particular event has its greatest consequences

Sensitive period   A specific time when organisms are particularly susceptible to certain kinds of stimuli in their environment

those stimuli during a sensitive period does not always produce irreversible consequences (Barinaga, 2000; Hol, Van den Berg, Van Ree, & Spruijt, 1999; R. A. Thompson & Nelson, 2001).

Life Span Approaches Versus a Focus on Particular Periods. On what part of the life span should child developmentalists focus their attention? For early developmentalists, the answers tended to be infancy and adolescence. Most attention was clearly concentrated on those two periods, largely to the exclusion of other parts of childhood.

Today, however, the story is different. The entire period encompassing conception through adolescence is now regarded as important, for several reasons. One is the discovery that developmental growth and change continue during every stage of life.

Furthermore, an important part of every person's environment is the other people in the person's social environment. To understand the social influences on children of a given age, we need to understand the people who are in large measure providing those influences. For instance, to understand development in infants, we need to unravel the effects of their parents' age on their social environment. It is likely that a 15-year-old mother will present parental influences of a very different sort from those presented by a 37-year-old mother. Consequently, infant development is in part an outgrowth of adult development.

The Relative Influence of Nature and Nurture on Development. One of the enduring questions of child development involves how much of people's behavior is due to their genetically determined nature and how much is due to nurture, the physical and social environment in which a child is raised. This issue, which has deep philosophical and historical roots, has dominated much work in child development.

In this context, *nature* refers to traits, abilities, and capacities that are inherited from one's parents. It encompasses any factor that is produced by the predetermined unfolding of genetic information—a process known as **maturation.** These genetic, inherited influences are at work as we move from the one-cell organism that is created at the moment of conception to the billions of cells that make up a fully formed human. Nature influences whether our eyes are blue or brown, whether we have thick hair throughout life or eventually go bald, and how good we are at athletics. Nature allows our brains to develop in such a way that we can read the words on this page.

In contrast, *nurture* refers to the environmental influences that shape behavior. Some of these influences may be biological, such as the impact of a pregnant mother's use of cocaine on her unborn child or the amounts and kinds of food available to children. Other environmental influences are more social, such as the ways parents discipline their children and the effects of peer pressure on an adolescent. Finally, some influences are a result of larger, society-level factors, such as the socioeconomic circumstances in which people find themselves.

If our traits and behavior were determined solely by either nature or nurture, there would probably be little debate regarding the issue. However, for most critical behaviors, this is hardly the case. Take, for instance, one of the most controversial arenas: intelligence. As we'll consider in detail in Chapter 12, the question of whether intelligence is determined primarily by inherited, genetic factors—nature—or is shaped by environmental factors—nurture—has caused lively and often bitter arguments. Largely because of its social implications, the issue has spilled out of the scientific arena and into the realm of politics and social policy.

Implications for Child Rearing and Social Policy. Consider the implications of the nature-versus-nurture issue: If the extent of one's intelligence is primarily determined by heredity and consequently is largely fixed at birth, then efforts to improve intellectual performance later in life may be doomed to failure. In contrast, if intelligence is primarily a result of environmental factors, such as the amount and quality of schooling and stimulation to which

Maturation The process of the predetermined unfolding of genetic information

one is exposed, then we would expect that an improvement in social conditions could bring about an increase in intelligence.

The extent of social policy affected by ideas about the origins of intelligence illustrates the significance of issues that involve the nature–nurture question. As we address it in relation to several topical areas throughout this book, keep in mind that specialists in child development reject the notion that behavior is the result solely of either nature or nurture. Instead, the question is one of degree.

Furthermore, the interaction of genetic and environmental factors is complex, in part because certain genetically determined traits have not only a direct influence on children's behavior but an indirect influence in shaping children's *environments* as well. For example, a child who is consistently cranky and who cries a great deal—a trait that may be produced by genetic factors—may influence her environment by making her parents so highly responsive to her insistent crying that they rush to comfort her whenever she cries. Their responsivity to the child's genetically determined behavior consequently becomes an environmental influence on her subsequent development.

In sum, the question of how much of a given behavior is due to nature and how much to nurture is a challenging one. Ultimately, we should consider the two sides of the nature–nurture issue as opposite ends of a continuum, with particular behaviors falling somewhere in the middle. We can say something similar about the other controversies that we have considered. For instance, continuous versus discontinuous development is not an either-or proposition; some forms of development fall toward the continuous end of the continuum, while others lie closer to the discontinuous end. In short, few statements about development involve either-or absolutes.

The Future of Child Development

We've examined the foundations of the field of child development, along with the key issues and questions that underlie the discipline. But what lies ahead? Several trends appear likely to emerge:

- As research in development continues to be amassed, the field will become increasingly specialized. New areas of study and perspectives will emerge.

- The explosion in information about genes and the genetic foundations of behavior will influence all spheres of child development. Increasingly, developmentalists will link work across biological, cognitive, and social domains, and the boundaries between different subdisciplines will be blurred.

- The increasing diversity of the population of the United States in terms of race, ethnicity, language, and culture will lead the field to focus greater attention on issues of diversity.

- A growing number of professionals in a variety of fields will make use of child development's research and findings. Educators, social workers, nurses and other health care providers, genetic counselors, toy designers, child care providers, cereal manufacturers, social ethicists, and members of dozens of other professions, will all draw on the field of child development.

- Work on child development will increasingly influence public interest issues. Discussion of many of the major social concerns of our time, including violence, prejudice and discrimination, poverty, changes in family life, child care, schooling, and even terrorism, can be informed by research in child development. Consequently, child developmentalists are likely to make important contributions to 21st-century society (Diener et al., 1999; Zigler & Finn-Stevenson, 1999). (For one example of the current contributions of work in child development, see the *From Research to Practice* box.)

Preventing Violence in Children

When other children were hearing fairy tales, Garland Hampton heard bedtime stories about the day Uncle Robert killed two Milwaukee police officers, or the time Grandma, with both barrels, blew away the father of two of her children back in '62. By the time he was 9, he had seen his mother kill her boyfriend.

Now, at 15, locked up in the County Jail and awaiting trial on murder charges, Garland is still enough of a child that he is afraid he might cry when darkness falls.

But he is old enough to have had a nasty past of his own, too: at 10, there was trouble about stolen bicycles; at 12, he was picked up for shooting and wounding a gang rival; at 14, for carrying a .357 Magnum and a bag of cocaine, and now, gunning down a fellow gang member. Prosecutors say he is an adolescent menace to society, who must pay for his sins like a man.

Garland just says he is scared. (Terry, 1994, p. A1)

*G*arland's descent into violence is representative of the lives of too many children and adolescents in the United States today. Many observers have called the level of violence nothing less than an epidemic. In fact, surveys find that violence and crime rank as the issue of greatest concern to most U.S. citizens (S. N. Hart, Brassard, & Karlson, 1996; Mehran, 1997). How can we explain the level of violence? How do people learn to be violent? How can we control and remedy aggression? And how can we discourage violence from occurring in the first place?

Child development has sought to answer such questions from several different perspectives. The examples that follow show some of the many ways in which the field seeks concrete solutions to pressing social problems.

- *Explaining the roots of violence.* Some child developmentalists have looked at how early behavior problems may be associated with later difficulties in controlling aggression. For instance, Avashlom Caspi and colleagues are examining how a lack of control in early childhood is associated with later conduct disorders and antisocial behavior during adolescence (see Caspi et al., 1995).

- *Dealing effectively with acts of aggression.* According to psychologist Arnold Goldstein (1994) of Syracuse University's Center for Research on Aggression, schoolteachers and school administrators must be on the lookout for even mild forms of aggression, such as bullying and sexual harassment.

Unless such forms of aggression are checked, they are likely to endure and to escalate into more blatant forms.

Such "minor" forms of aggression are many. Name-calling, threats, thefts, extortion of lunch money, spreading of rumors, and racial and gender-based slurs can all have psychological and academic consequences. And major forms of aggression can have even more profound consequences—and are becoming increasingly commonplace. For instance, gun violence is seen in almost two thirds of all high schools and around a quarter of junior high schools around the United States.

To deal with such aggression, Goldstein has implemented a program that teaches students to "unlearn" aggression. Assuming that aggression is initially learned as a strategy—often successful—for dealing with conflict, the program teaches moral reasoning and new ways of controlling anger and handling conflict without aggression (Azar & McCarthy, 1994; Goldstein, 1994).

- *Seeking to prevent violence and other forms of juvenile delinquency.* Some developmental experts have designed violence prevention programs based on the assumption that families, peers, schools, and the community as a whole must be taken into account.

For instance, the Yale Child Welfare Research Program provided a randomly chosen group of poor families with child care, medical care, and parent education regarding child development for the 17 months following the birth of their first child. The families also received home visits to help them obtain food and housing and to offer general advice. Ten years later, their children had better school attendance and were rated less aggressive by their teachers than children in families who did not participate in the program. In addition, these children were less likely than nonparticipants, in the eyes of their mothers, to stay out all night, steal, or be cruel to animals. According to developmental psychologist Edward Zigler, the program was also cost-effective: For each of the children in the program, the annual cost of remedial and support services was more than $1,000 lower than for those in the control group (Zigler, 1994; Zigler & Finn-Stevenson, 1999).

As these examples illustrate, developmental researchers are making progress in dealing with the violence that is increasingly part of modern society. Furthermore, violence is just one example of the areas in which experts in child development are contributing their skills for the betterment of human society. As we'll see throughout this book, the field has much to offer.

BECOMING AN INFORMED CONSUMER OF DEVELOPMENT

Assessing Information on Child Development

If you immediately comfort crying babies, you'll spoil them.
If you let babies cry without comforting them, they'll be untrusting and clingy as adults.

Spanking is one of the best ways to discipline your child.
Never hit your child.

If a marriage is unhappy, children are better off if their parents divorce than if they stay together.
No matter how difficult a marriage is, parents should avoid divorce for the sake of their children.

There is no lack of advice on the best way to raise a child or, more generally, to lead one's life. From best-sellers with titles such as *The No-Cry Sleep Solution* to magazine and newspaper columns that provide advice on every imaginable topic, each of us is exposed to tremendous amounts of information.

Yet not all advice is equally valid. The mere fact that something is in print, on television, or on an Internet Web site does not automatically make it legitimate or accurate. Fortunately, some guidelines can help distinguish when recommendations and suggestions are reasonable and when they are not. Here are a few:

- Consider the source of the advice. Information from established, respected organizations such as the American Medical Association, the American Psychological Association, and the American Academy of Pediatrics is likely to be the result of years of study, and its accuracy is probably high.

- Evaluate the credentials of the person providing advice. Information coming from established, acknowledged researchers and experts in a field is likely to be more accurate than that coming from a person whose credentials are obscure.

- Understand the difference between anecdotal evidence and scientific evidence. Anecdotal evidence is based on one or two instances of a phenomenon, haphazardly discovered or encountered; scientific evidence is based on careful, systematic procedures.

- Keep cultural context in mind. Although an assertion may be valid in some contexts, it may not be true in all. For example, it is typically assumed that providing infants the freedom to move about and exercise their limbs facilitates their muscular development and mobility. Yet in some cultures, infants spend most of their time closely bound to their mothers with no apparent long-term damage (H. Kaplan & Dove, 1987; Tronick, Thomas, & Daltabuit, 1994).

- Don't assume that because many people believe something, it is necessarily true. Scientific evaluation has often proved that some of the most basic presumptions about the effectiveness of various techniques are invalid. For instance, consider DARE, the Drug Abuse Resistance Education antidrug program that is used in about half the school systems in the United States. DARE is designed to prevent the spread of drugs through lectures and question-and-answer sessions run by police officers. Careful evaluation, however, finds no evidence that the program is effective in reducing drug use (Lyman et al., 1999).

In short, the key to evaluating information relating to child development is to maintain a healthy dose of skepticism. No source of information is invariably, unfailingly accurate. By keeping a critical eye on the statements you encounter, you'll be in a better position to determine the very real contributions made by child developmentalists in understanding how we change and grow over the course of childhood and adolescence.

REVIEW & APPLY

Review

- Early historical views of children built the foundations of child development today.

- Four important issues in child development are continuity versus discontinuity in development, the importance of critical periods, whether to focus on certain periods or on the entire period of childhood, and the nature–nurture issue. Each is best seen not as an either-or choice but as a continuum, along which aspects of development can be placed.

- Developmental researchers are making progress in dealing with many pressing social issues, such as violence, school attendance, and juvenile delinquency.

Applying Child Development

- Are there aspects of physical development (such as in the area of athletics) that appear to be subject to discontinuous change? Can continuous change account for such instances of development?

- *From a caregiver's perspective:* Can you think of physical, cognitive, or socioemotional changes the development of which may be subject to sensitive periods?

What is child development?

- Child development is a scientific approach to questions about growth, change, and stability that occur from conception to adolescence.

What is the scope of the field?

- The scope of the field encompasses physical, cognitive, and social and personality development at all ages from conception through adolescence.

- Culture—both broad and narrow—is an important issue in child development. Many aspects of development are influenced not only by broad cultural differences but also by ethnic, racial, and socioeconomic differences within a particular culture.

- Every person is subject to normative history-graded influences, normative age-graded influences, normative sociocultural-graded influences, and nonnormative life events.

What are the key issues and questions in the field of child development?

- Four key issues in child development are (1) whether developmental change is continuous or discontinuous, (2) whether development is largely governed by critical or sensitive periods during which certain influences or experiences must occur for development to be normal, (3) whether to focus on certain particularly important periods in human development or on the entire life span, and (4) the nature–nurture controversy, which focuses on the relative importance of genetic versus environmental influences.

What is the future of child development likely to hold?

- Future trends in the field are likely to include increasing specialization, the blurring of boundaries between different areas, increasing attention to issues involving diversity, and an increasing influence on public interest issues.

EPILOGUE

 his chapter introduced the growing field of child development. We have reviewed the broad scope of the field, touching on the wide range of topics that child developmentalists may address, and have discussed the key issues and questions that have shaped the field since its inception.

Before proceeding to the next chapter, take a few minutes to reconsider the prologue of this chapter—about the case of Elizabeth Carr, the first American to be born through in vitro fertilization. Based on what you now know about child development, answer the following questions:

1. What are some of the potential benefits, and the costs, of the type of conception—in vitro fertilization—that was carried out for Elizabeth's parents?

2. What are some questions that developmentalists who study either physical, cognitive, or personality and social development might ask about the effects on Elizabeth of being conceived via in vitro fertilization?

3. The creation of complete human clones—exact genetic replicas of an individual—is still in the realm of science fiction, but the theoretical possibility does raise some important questions. For example, what would be the psychological consequences of being a clone?

4. If clones could actually be produced, how might it help scientists understand the relative impact of heredity and environment on development?

KEY TERMS AND CONCEPTS

child development (p. 5)

physical development (p. 6)

cognitive
   development (p. 6)

personality
   development (p. 6)

social development (p. 6)

cohort (p. 9)

normative events (p. 9)

continuous change (p. 13)

discontinuous
   change (p. 13)

critical period (p. 13)

sensitive period (p. 13)

maturation (p. 14)

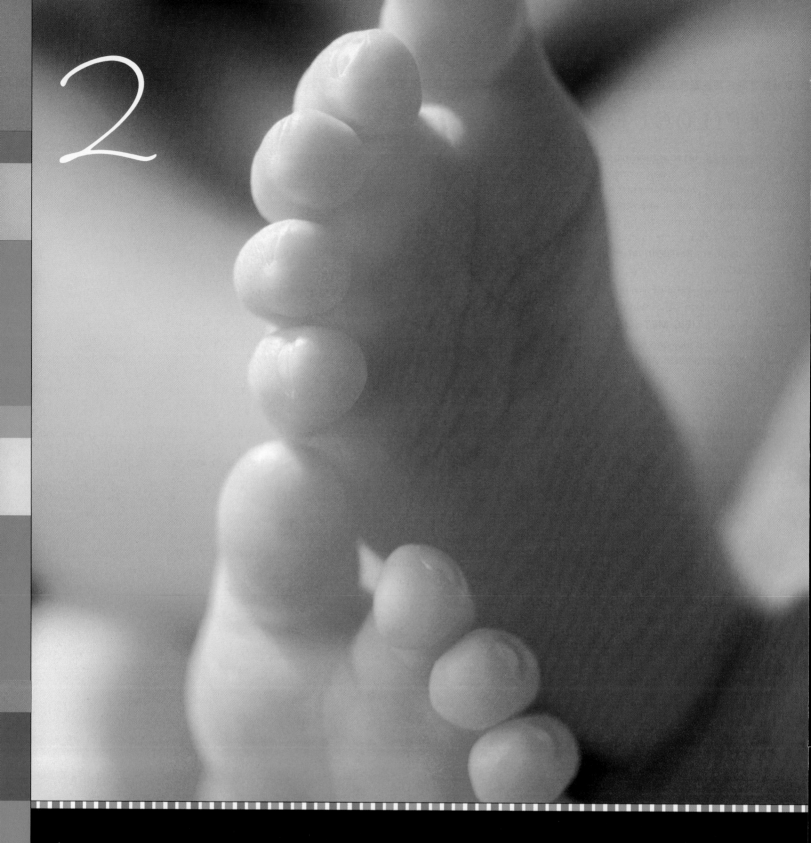

2

Theoretical Perspectives and Research

PROLOGUE: Family Bonds

It was just after the birth of their fourth son that Julia Burke's husband, Thomas, died in the terrorist attack that leveled the World Trade Center. For close to a year afterward, she had tried to shield her children from the devastation of the attack, never letting them see images of the towers collapsing.

Then, just before the first anniversary of her husband's death, she returned with her family to the site of the attack. The two oldest boys remembered the buildings; they had made frequent visits to see their father in his office on the 104th floor.

As they walked around what had become known as Ground Zero, now leveled and awaiting rebuilding, Burke's son Brian picked up something that looked like a piece of tile. He told his mother that he thought it might be from the cafeteria near his father's office. He carefully slid the remnant into her purse for safekeeping.

Thomas Burke and his family before he died in the World Trade Center terrorist attack.

For the Burke children, this visit was a way of keeping the memory of their father alive. "This was where he was the last time he was alive," said Burke's widow. "It's the closest thing we can get to that. This is sacred ground. It's part of our history now—part of our family history." (Brzezinski, 2002)

LOOKING AHEAD

For the Burke children, the death of their father raises a number of significant developmental issues. How much of the incident will they remember when they are older? How will life in a single-parent home affect their development? Will their relationship with others be affected by their experience? More generally, how will the terrorist attack affect their future development?

The ability to answer these questions depends on the accumulated findings from literally thousands of developmental research studies. These studies have looked at questions ranging from brain development to the nature of social relationships to the way in which cognitive abilities grow throughout childhood and adolescence. The common challenge of these studies is to pose and answer questions of interest in development.

Like all of us, child developmentalists ask questions about people's bodies, minds, and social interactions—and about how these aspects of human life change as people age. But to the natural curiosity that we all share, developmental scientists add one important ingredient that makes a difference in how they ask—and try to answer—questions. This ingredient is the scientific method. This structured but straightforward way of looking at phenomena elevates questioning from mere curiosity to purposeful learning. With this powerful tool, developmentalists are able not only to ask good questions but also to begin to answer them systematically.

In this chapter, we consider the way in which developmentalists ask and answer questions about the world. We begin with a discussion of the broad perspectives used in understanding children and their behavior. These perspectives provide broad approaches from which to view the development along multiple dimensions. We then turn to the basic building blocks of the science of child development: research. We describe the major types of research that developmentalists perform to pursue their research and get answers to their questions. Finally, we focus on two important issues in developmental research: One is how to choose research participants so that results can be applied beyond the study setting, and the other is the central issue of ethics.

In sum, after reading this chapter, you will be able to answer these questions:

● **What are the major perspectives on child development?**

● **What is the scientific method, and how does it help answer questions about child development?**

● **What are the major research strategies and challenges?**

Perspectives on Children

When Roddy McDougall said his first word, his parents were elated—and relieved. They had anticipated the moment for what seemed a long time; most of the children of his age had already uttered their first word. In addition, his grandparents had weighed in with their concerns, his grandmother going so far as to suggest that he might be suffering from some sort of developmental delay, although that was based solely on a "feeling" she had. But the moment Roddy spoke, his parents' and grandparents' anxieties fell away, and they all simply experienced great pride in Roddy's accomplishment.

The concerns Roddy's relatives felt were based on their vague conceptions of how a normal child's development proceeds. Each of us has established ideas about the course of development, and we use them to make judgments and develop hunches about the meaning of children's behavior. Our experience orients us to certain types of behavior that we see as particularly important. For some people, it may be when a child says his or her first word; for others, it may be the way a child interacts with others.

Like laypersons, child developmentalists have developed their own set of broad perspectives on childhood. Unlike laypersons, though, the perspectives used by developmentalists are more focused and precise, and they encompass one or more **theories,** explanations and predictions concerning phenomena of interest. A theory provides a framework for understanding the relationships among an organized set of facts or principles (Lerner, 2002).

We'll consider five major perspectives used in child development: the psychodynamic, behavioral, cognitive, contextual, and evolutionary perspectives. Each emphasizes somewhat different aspects of development that steer inquiry in particular directions. Furthermore, each perspective continues to evolve and change, as befits a growing and dynamic discipline.

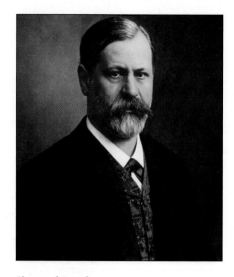

Sigmund Freud

The Psychodynamic Perspective: Focusing on Internal Forces

When Janet was 6 months old, she was involved in a bloody automobile accident—or so her parents tell her, since she has no conscious recollection of it. Now, however, at age 24, she is having difficulty maintaining relationships, and her therapist is seeking to determine whether her current problems are a result of the early accident.

Looking for such a link might seem a bit far-fetched, but to proponents of the **psychodynamic perspective,** it is not so improbable. Advocates of the psychodynamic perspective believe that behavior is motivated by inner forces, memories, and conflicts of which a person has little awareness or control. The inner forces, which may stem from one's childhood, continually influence behavior throughout the life span.

Freud's Psychoanalytic Theory.
The psychodynamic perspective is most closely associated with Sigmund Freud and his psychoanalytic theory. Freud, who lived from 1856 to 1939, was a Viennese physician whose revolutionary ideas ultimately had a profound effect not just on the fields of psychology and psychiatry but on Western thought in general (Masling & Bornstein, 1996).

Freud's **psychoanalytic theory** suggests that unconscious forces act to determine personality and behavior. To Freud, the *unconscious* is a part of the personality about which a person is unaware. It contains infantile wishes, desires, demands, and needs that are hidden, because of their disturbing nature, from conscious awareness. Freud suggested that the unconscious is responsible for a good part of our everyday behavior.

According to Freud, everyone's personality has three aspects: id, ego, and superego. The **id** is the raw, unorganized, inborn part of personality that is present at birth. It represents primitive drives related to hunger, sex, aggression, and irrational impulses. The id operates according to the *pleasure principle,* in which the goal is to maximize satisfaction and reduce tension.

The **ego** is the part of personality that is rational and reasonable. The ego acts as a buffer between the real world outside of us and the primitive id. The ego operates on the *reality principle,* in which instinctual energy is restrained in order to maintain the safety of the individual and help integrate the person into society.

Finally, Freud proposed that the **superego** represents a person's conscience, incorporating distinctions between right and wrong. It develops around age 5 or 6 and is learned from an individual's parents, teachers, and other significant figures.

In addition to providing an account of the various parts of the personality, Freud also suggested the ways in which personality developed during childhood. He argued that **psychosexual development** occurred as children passed through a series of stages, in which

Theories Explanations and predictions concerning phenomena of interest, providing a framework for understanding the relationships among an organized set of facts or principles

Psychodynamic perspective The approach to the study of development that states behavior is motivated by inner forces, memories, and conflicts of which a person has little awareness or control

Psychoanalytic theory The theory proposed by Freud that suggests that unconscious forces act to determine personality and behavior

Id According to Freud, the raw, unorganized, inborn part of personality that is present at birth

Ego According to Freud, the part of personality that is rational and reasonable

Superego According to Freud, the aspect of personality that represents a person's conscience, incorporating distinctions between right and wrong

Psychosexual development According to Freud, a series of stages that children pass through in which pleasure, or gratification, is focused on a particular biological function and body part

	TABLE 2-1	FREUD'S AND ERIKSON'S THEORIES		
Approximate Age	**Freud's Stages of Psychosexual Development**	**Major Characteristics of Freud's Stages**	**Erikson's Stages of Psychosocial Development**	**Positive and Negative Outcomes of Erikson's Stages**
Birth to 12–18 months	Oral	Interest in oral gratification from sucking, eating, mouthing, biting	Trust vs. mistrust	*Positive:* Feelings of trust from environmental support *Negative:* Fear and concern regarding others
12–18 months to 3 years	Anal	Gratification from expelling and withholding feces; coming to terms with society's controls relating to toilet training	Autonomy vs. shame and doubt	*Positive:* Self-sufficiency if exploration is encouraged *Negative:* Doubts about self, lack of independence
3 to 5–6 years	Phallic	Interest in the genitals; coming to terms with Oedipal conflict, leading to identification with same-sex parent	Initiative vs. guilt	*Positive:* Discovery of ways to initiate actions *Negative:* Guilt from actions and thoughts
5–6 years to adolescence	Latency	Sexual concerns largely unimportant	Industry vs. inferiority	*Positive:* Development of sense of competence *Negative:* Feelings of inferiority, no sense of mastery
Adolescence to adulthood (Freud) Adolescence (Erikson)	Genital	Reemergence of sexual interests and establishment of mature sexual relationships	Identity vs. role diffusion	*Positive:* Awareness of uniqueness of self, knowledge of role to be followed *Negative:* Inability to identify appropriate roles in life
Early adulthood (Erikson)			Intimacy vs. isolation	*Positive:* Development of loving, sexual relationships and close friendships *Negative:* Fear of relationships with others
Middle adulthood (Erikson)			Generativity vs. stagnation	*Positive:* Sense of contribution to continuity of life *Negative:* Trivialization of one's activities
Late adulthood (Erikson)			Ego integrity vs. despair	*Positive:* Sense of unity in life's accomplishments *Negative:* Regret over lost opportunities of life

pleasure, or gratification, was focused on a particular biological function and body part. As illustrated in Table 2-1, he suggested that pleasure shifted from the mouth (the *oral stage*) to the anus (the *anal stage*) and eventually to the genitals (the *phallic stage* and the *genital stage*).

According to Freud, if children are unable to gratify themselves sufficiently during a particular stage, or conversely, if they receive too much gratification, fixation may occur. **Fixation** is behavior reflecting an earlier stage of development due to an unresolved conflict. For instance, fixation at the oral stage might produce an adult unusually absorbed in oral activities—eating, talking, or chewing gum. Freud also argued that fixation was represented through symbolic sorts of oral activities, such as the use of "biting" sarcasm.

Fixation Behavior reflecting an earlier stage of development

Psychosocial development The approach to the study of development that encompasses changes in the understanding individuals have of their interactions with others, of others' behavior, and of themselves as members of society

Erikson's Psychosocial Theory. Psychoanalyst Erik Erikson, who lived from 1902 to 1994, provided an alternative psychodynamic view in his theory of psychosocial development, which emphasizes our social interaction with other people. In Erikson's view, society and culture both challenge and shape us. **Psychosocial development** encompasses changes in our interactions with and understandings of one another, as well as in our knowledge and understanding of ourselves as members of society (Erikson, 1963).

Erikson's theory suggests that developmental change occurs throughout our lives in eight distinct stages (see Table 2-1). The stages emerge in a fixed pattern and are similar for all people.

Erikson argues that each stage presents a crisis or conflict that the individual must resolve. Although no crisis is ever fully resolved, making life increasingly complicated, the individual must at least address the crisis of each stage sufficiently to deal with demands made during the next stage of development.

Unlike Freud, who regards development as relatively complete by adolescence, Erikson suggests that growth and change continue throughout the life span. For instance, he suggests that during middle adulthood, people pass through the *generativity-versus-stagnation stage,* in which their contributions to family, community, and society can produce either positive feelings about the continuity of life or a sense of stagnation and disappointment about what they are passing on to future generations.

Assessing the Psychodynamic Perspective.   It is hard for us to grasp the full significance of psychodynamic theories, represented by Freud's psychoanalytic theory and Erikson's theory of psychosocial development. Freud's introduction of the notion that unconscious influences affect behavior was a monumental accomplishment, and the fact that it seems at all reasonable to us shows how extensively the idea of the unconscious has pervaded thinking in Western cultures. In fact, work by contemporary researchers studying memory and learning suggests that we carry with us memories of which we are not consciously aware that have a significant impact on our behavior. The example of Janet, who was in a car accident when she was a baby, demonstrates one application of psychodynamically based thinking and research (L. L. Jacoby & Kelley, 1992; Kihlstrom, 1987; Mitchell, 1998; Westen, 1990).

Some of the most basic principles of Freud's psychoanalytic theory have been called into question, however, because they have not been validated by subsequent research. In particular, the notion that people pass through stages in childhood that determine their adult personalities has little definitive research support. In addition, because much of Freud's theory was based on a limited population of upper-middle-class Austrians living during a strict, puritanical era, its application to broad, multicultural populations is questionable. Finally, because Freud's theory focuses primarily on male development, it has been criticized as sexist and may be interpreted as devaluing women. For such reasons, many developmentalists question Freud's theory (Brislin, 1993; Crews, 1993; Guthrie & Lonner, 1986).

Erikson's view that development continues throughout the life span is important and has received considerable support. However, the theory also has its drawbacks. Like Freud's theory, it focuses more on men's than women's development, and it is also vague in some respects. Furthermore, as is the case with psychodynamic theories in general, it is difficult to make definitive predictions about a given individual's behavior using the theory. In sum, then, the psychodynamic perspective provides good descriptions of past behavior but imprecise predictions of future behavior (T. F. Hetherington & Weinberger, 1993; Whitbourne et al., 1992; Zauszniewski & Martin, 1999).

Erik Erikson

The Behavioral Perspective: Focusing on External Forces

When Elissa Sheehan was 3, a large brown dog bit her, and she needed dozens of stitches and several operations. From the time she was bitten, she broke into a sweat whenever she saw a dog and in fact never enjoyed being around any pet.

To a child development specialist using the behavioral perspective, the explanation for Elissa's behavior is straightforward: She has a learned fear of dogs. Rather than looking inside the organism at unconscious processes, the **behavioral perspective** suggests that the keys to understanding development are observable behavior and outside stimuli in the environment. If we know the stimuli, we can predict the behavior.

Behavioral theories reject the notion that people universally pass through a series of stages. Instead, people are assumed to be affected by the environmental stimuli to which they happen to be exposed. Developmental patterns, then, are personal, reflecting a particular set of

Behavioral perspective The approach to the study of development that suggests that the keys to understanding development are observable behavior and outside stimuli in the environment

John B. Watson

VIDEO CLIP

Little Albert
CLASSIC MODULE

environmental stimuli, and behavior is the result of continuing exposure to specific factors in the environment. Furthermore, developmental change is viewed in quantitative, rather than qualitative, terms. For instance, behavioral theories hold that advances in problem-solving capabilities as children age are largely a result of greater mental *capacities* rather than changes in the *kind* of thinking that children are able to bring to bear on a problem.

Classical Conditioning: Stimulus Substitution.   "Give me a dozen healthy infants, well-formed, and my own specified world to bring them up in and I'll guarantee to take any one at random and train him to become any type of specialist I might select—doctor, lawyer, artist, merchant-chief, and yes, even beggar-man and thief, regardless of his talents, penchants, tendencies, abilities . . . " (J. B. Watson, 1925, p. 14).

With these words, John B. Watson, one of the first American psychologists to advocate a behavioral approach, summed up the behavioral perspective. Watson, who lived from 1878 to 1958, believed strongly that we could gain a full understanding of development by carefully studying the stimuli that make up the environment. In fact, he argued that by effectively controlling a person's environment, it was possible to produce virtually any behavior.

As we will consider further in Chapter 4, **classical conditioning** occurs when an organism learns to respond in a particular way to a neutral stimulus that normally does not evoke that type of response. For instance, if a dog is repeatedly exposed to the pairing of two stimuli, such as the sound of a bell and the presentation of meat, it may learn to react to the bell alone in the same way it reacts to the meat—by salivating and wagging its tail with excitement. Dogs don't typically respond to bells in this way; the behavior is a result of stimulus substitution.

The same process of classical conditioning explains how we learn emotional responses. In the case of dog-bite victim Elissa Sheehan, for instance, one stimulus has been substituted for another: Elissa's unpleasant experience with a particular dog (the initial stimulus) has been transferred to other dogs and to pets in general.

Operant Conditioning.   In addition to classical conditioning, other types of learning derive from the behavioral perspective. In fact, the learning approach that probably has had the greatest influence is operant conditioning. **Operant conditioning** is a form of learning in which a voluntary response is strengthened or weakened by its association with positive or negative consequences.

In operant conditioning, formulated and championed by psychologist B. F. Skinner (1975), who lived from 1904 to 1990, individuals learn to act deliberately on their environments in order to bring about desired consequences. In a sense, then, children *operate* on their environments to bring about a desired state of affairs.

Whether or not children will seek to repeat a behavior depends on whether it is followed by reinforcement. *Reinforcement* is the process by which a stimulus is provided that increases the probability that a preceding behavior will be repeated. Hence a student is apt to work harder in school if he or she receives good grades, workers are likely to labor harder at their jobs if their efforts are tied to pay increases, and people are more apt to buy lottery tickets if they are reinforced by winning at least occasionally. In addition, *punishment,* the introduction of an unpleasant or painful stimulus or the removal of a desirable stimulus, will decrease the probability that a preceding behavior will occur in the future.

Behavior that is reinforced, then, is more likely to be repeated in the future, whereas behavior that receives no reinforcement or is punished is likely to be discontinued or, in the language of operant conditioning, *extinguished*. Principles of operant conditioning are used in **behavior modification,** a formal technique for promoting the frequency of desirable behaviors and decreasing the incidence of unwanted ones. Behavior modification has been used in a variety of situations, ranging from teaching severely retarded people the rudiments of language to helping people stick to diets (Berigan & Deagle, 1999; D. L. Katz, 2001; Sulzer-Azaroff & Mayer, 1991).

Classical conditioning A type of learning in which an organism responds in a particular way to a neutral stimulus that normally does not bring about that type of response

Operant conditioning A form of learning in which a voluntary response is strengthened or weakened, depending on its association with positive or negative consequences

Behavior modification A formal technique for promoting the frequency of desirable behaviors and decreasing the incidence of unwanted ones

B. F. Skinner

Social-Cognitive Learning Theory: Learning Through Imitation.   Beavis and Butt-head, cartoon characters formerly on MTV, discuss how enjoyable it is to set fires. On at least one occasion, one of them lights the other's hair on fire using matches and an aerosol spray can. Not long after seeing the show, 5-year-old Austin Messner set his bed on fire with a cigarette lighter, starting a blaze that killed his younger sister.

Cause and effect? We can't know for sure, but it certainly seems possible, especially looking at the situation from the perspective of social-cognitive learning theory. According to developmental psychologist Albert Bandura (1977, 1994), a significant amount of learning is explained by **social-cognitive learning theory,** an approach that emphasizes learning by observing the behavior of another person, called a *model.*

We don't need to experience the consequences of a behavior ourselves to learn it. Social-cognitive learning theory holds that when we see the behavior of a model being rewarded, we are likely to imitate that behavior. For instance, in one classic experiment, children who were afraid of dogs were exposed to a model, nicknamed the "Fearless Peer," who was seen playing happily with a dog (Bandura, Grusec, & Menlove, 1967). After exposure, the children who had previously been afraid were more likely to approach a strange dog than children who had not seen the model.

Bandura (1986) suggests that social-cognitive learning proceeds in four steps. First, an observer must pay attention and perceive the most critical features of a model's behavior. Second, the observer must successfully recall the behavior. Third, the observer must reproduce the behavior accurately. Finally, the observer must be motivated to learn and carry out the behavior. Rather than learning's being a matter of trial and error, as it is with operant conditioning, in social-cognitive learning theory, behavior is learned through observation.

According to social-cognitive learning theory, observation of television programs such as *Jackass* can produce significant amounts of learning—not all of it positive.

Assessing the Behavioral Perspective.   The behavioral perspective has had an important influence in the field of child development. Work using the perspective has made significant contributions, ranging from techniques for educating children with severe mental retardation to identifying procedures for curbing aggression.

At the same time, there are controversies regarding the behavioral perspective. For example, although they are part of the same general behavioral perspective, classical and operant conditioning, on the one hand, and social learning theory, on the other, disagree in some basic ways. Both classical and operant conditioning consider learning in terms of external stimuli

Social-cognitive learning theory An approach to the study of development that emphasizes learning by observing the behavior of another person, called a model

and responses, in which the only important factors are the observable features of the environment. In such an analysis, people and other organisms are "black boxes"; nothing that occurs inside the box is understood—or much cared about, for that matter.

To social learning theorists, such an analysis is an oversimplification. They argue that what makes people different from rats and pigeons is mental activity, in the form of thoughts and expectations. A full understanding of people's development, they maintain, cannot occur without moving beyond external stimuli and responses.

In many ways, social learning theory has come to predominate in recent decades over classical and operant conditioning theories. In fact, another perspective that focuses explicitly on internal mental activity has become enormously influential. This is the cognitive approach, which we consider next.

The Cognitive Perspective: Examining the Roots of Understanding

When 3-year-old Jake is asked why it sometimes rains, he answers, "So the flowers can grow." When his 11-year-old sister Lila is asked the same question, she responds, "Because of evaporation from the surface of the earth." And when their cousin Ajima, who is studying meteorology in her high school science class, considers the same question, her extended answer includes a discussion of cumulonimbus clouds, the Coriolis effect, and synoptic charts.

To a developmental theorist using the cognitive perspective, the difference in the sophistication of the answers is evidence of a different degree of knowledge and understanding, or cognition. The **cognitive perspective** focuses on the processes that allow people to know, understand, and think about the world.

The cognitive perspective emphasizes how people internally represent and think about the world. By using this perspective, developmental researchers hope to understand how children and adults process information and how their ways of thinking and understanding affect their behavior. They also seek to learn how cognitive abilities change as people develop, the degree to which cognitive development represents quantitative and qualitative growth in intellectual abilities, and how different cognitive abilities are related to one another (Salthouse, 1998).

Piaget's Theory of Cognitive Development.   No single person has had a greater impact on the study of cognitive development than Jean Piaget. A Swiss psychologist who lived from 1896 to 1980, Piaget proposed that all people passed in a fixed sequence through a series of universal stages of cognitive development. He suggested that not only did the quantity of information increase in each stage, but the quality of knowledge and understanding changed as well. His focus was on the change in cognition that occurred as children moved from one stage to the next (Piaget, 1952, 1962, 1983).

Although we'll consider Piaget's theory in detail beginning in Chapter 6, we can get a broad sense of it now by looking at some of its main features. Piaget suggested that human thinking is arranged into *schemes*, organized mental patterns that represent behaviors and actions. In infants, such schemes represent concrete behavior—a scheme for sucking, for reaching, and for each separate behavior. In older children, the schemes become more sophisticated and abstract. Schemes are like intellectual computer software that directs and determines how data from the world are looked at and dealt with (Achenbach, 1992).

Piaget suggests that children's *adaptation*—his term for the way in which children respond and adjust to new information—can be explained by two basic principles. **Assimilation** is the process in which people understand an experience in terms of their current stage of cognitive development and way of thinking. In contrast, **accommodation** refers to changes in existing ways of thinking in response to encounters with new stimuli or events.

Assimilation occurs when people use their current ways of thinking about and understanding the world to perceive and understand a new experience. For example, a young child who has not yet learned to count will look at two rows of buttons, each containing the same

---

Cognitive perspective The approach to the study of development that focuses on the processes that allow people to know, understand, and think about the world

Assimilation The process in which people understand an experience in terms of their current stage of cognitive development and way of thinking

Accommodation The process that changes existing ways of thinking in response to encounters with new stimuli or events

number of buttons, and say that a row in which the buttons are closely spaced together has fewer buttons in it than a row in which the buttons are more spread out. The experience of counting buttons, then, is *assimilated* to already existing schemes that contain the principle "bigger is more."

Later, however, when the child is older and has had sufficient exposure to new experiences, the content of the scheme will undergo change. In understanding that the quantity of buttons is identical whether they are spread out or closely spaced, the child has *accommodated* to the experience. Assimilation and accommodation work in tandem to bring about cognitive development.

Assessing Piaget's Theory. Piaget was without peer in influencing our understanding of cognitive development, and he is one of the towering figures in child development. He provided masterful descriptions of how intellectual growth proceeds during childhood— descriptions that have stood the test of literally thousands of investigations. By and large, then, Piaget's broad view of the sequence of cognitive development is accurate (Zigler & Gilman, 1998).

However, the specifics of the theory, particularly in terms of change in cognitive capabilities over time, have been called into question. For instance, some cognitive skills clearly emerge earlier than Piaget suggested. Furthermore, the universality of Piaget's stages has been disputed. A growing amount of evidence suggests that the emergence of particular cognitive skills occurs according to a different timetable in non-Western cultures. And in every culture, some people never seem to reach Piaget's highest level of cognitive sophistication: formal, logical thought (Rogoff & Chavajay, 1995).

Ultimately, the greatest criticism leveled at the Piagetian perspective is that cognitive development is not necessarily as discontinuous as Piaget's stage theory suggests. Remember that Piaget argued that growth proceeded in four distinct stages in which the quality of cognition differed from one stage to the next. However, many developmental researchers argue that growth is considerably more continuous. These critics have suggested an alternative perspective, known as the information processing approaches; these focus on the processes that underlie learning, memory, and thinking throughout childhood.

Information Processing Approaches. Information processing approaches have become an important alternative to Piagetian approaches. **Information processing approaches** to cognitive development seek to identify the ways individuals take in, use, and store information.

Information processing approaches grew out of developments in the electronic processing of information, particularly as carried out by computers. They assume that even complex behavior such as learning, remembering, categorizing, and thinking can be broken down into a series of individual, specific steps.

In stark contrast to Piaget's view that thinking undergoes qualitative advances as children age, information processing approaches assume that development is marked more by quantitative advances. Our capacity to handle information changes with age, as does our processing speed and efficiency. Furthermore, information processing approaches suggest that as people age, we are better able to control the nature of processing, and that we can change in the strategies we choose to process information.

Assessing the Information Processing Approaches. As we'll see in future chapters, information processing approaches have become a central part of our understanding of development. At the same time, they do not offer a complete explanation for behavior. For example, information processing approaches have paid little attention to behavior such as creativity, in which the most profound ideas are often developed in a seemingly nonlogical, nonlinear manner. In addition, they do not take into account the social context in which development takes place.

Information processing approaches Approaches to the study of cognitive development that seek to identify the ways individuals take in, use, and store information

Cognitive neuroscience approaches Approaches to the study of cognitive development that focus on how brain processes are related to cognitive activity

Contextual perspective The perspective that considers the relationship between individuals and their physical, cognitive, personality, social, and physical worlds

Bioecological approach The perspective suggesting that different levels of the environment simultaneously influence every biological organism

Cognitive Neuroscience Approaches.   Among the most recent additions to the array of approaches taken by child developmentalists, **cognitive neuroscience approaches** look at cognitive development through the lens of brain processes.

Rather than simply assuming that there are hypothetical or theoretical cognitive structures related to thinking, cognitive neuroscientists seek to identify actual locations and functions within the brain that are related to different types of cognitive activity. For example, using sophisticated brain scanning techniques, cognitive neuroscientists have demonstrated that thinking about the meaning of a word activates different areas of the brain than thinking about how the word sounds when spoken.

The Contextual Perspective: Taking a Broad Approach to Development

Although child developmentalists often consider the course of development in terms of physical, cognitive, and personality and social factors by themselves, such a categorization has one serious drawback: In the real world, none of these broad influences occurs in isolation from any other. Instead, there is a constant, ongoing interaction between the different types of influence.

The **contextual perspective** considers the relationship between individuals and their physical, cognitive, personality, and social worlds. It suggests that a child's unique development cannot be properly viewed without seeing the child enmeshed within a complex social and cultural context. We'll consider two major theories that fall into this category, Bronfenbrenner's bioecological approach and Vygotsky's sociocultural theory.

Bronfenbrenner's Bioecological Approach to Development.   Psychologist Urie Bronfenbrenner (1989, 2000) originated the **bioecological approach,** which suggests that there are five levels of the environment that simultaneously influence every biological organism. Bronfenbrenner argues that we cannot fully understand development without considering how a person fits into each of these levels (illustrated in Figure 2-1):

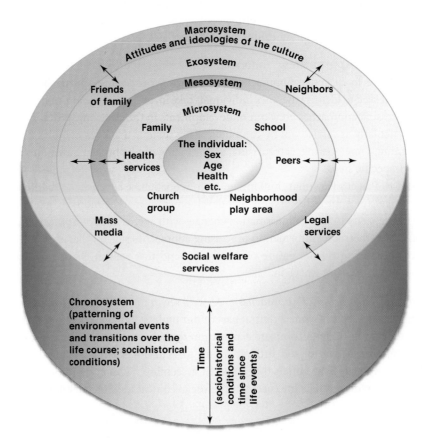

FIGURE 2-1   BRONFENBRENNER'S APPROACH TO DEVELOPMENT

Urie Bronfenbrenner's bioecological approach to development offers five levels of the environment that simultaneously influence individuals: the macrosystem, exosystem, mesosystem, microsystem, and chronosystem.

(*Source:* Adapted from Bronfenbrenner & Morris, 1998)

- The *microsystem* is the everyday, immediate environment in which children lead their daily lives. Homes, caregivers, friends, and teachers are all part of the microsystem. But the child is not just a passive recipient of influences in the microsystem. Instead, children actively help construct the microsystem, shaping the immediate world in which they live. The microsystem is the level at which most traditional work in child development has been directed.

- The *mesosystem* provides connections between the various aspects of the microsystem. Like links in a chain, the mesosystem binds children to parents, students to teachers, employees to bosses, friends to friends. It acknowledges the direct and indirect influences that bind us to one another, such as those that affect a mother who has a bad day at the office and then is short-tempered with her daughter at home.

- The *exosystem* represents broader influences, encompassing social institutions such as local government, the community, schools, places of worship, and the local media. Each of these larger institutions of society can have an immediate, and major, impact on personal development, and each affects how the microsystem and mesosystem operate. For example, the quality of a school will affect a child's cognitive development and can have long-term consequences.

- The *macrosystem* represents the larger cultural influences on an individual. Society in general, governments, religious systems, political thought, and other broad, encompassing factors are components of the macrosystem. Children are both part of a broader culture (such as Western culture) and at the same time influenced by their membership in a particular subculture (for instance, Mexican American subculture).

- Finally, the *chronosystem* underlies all of the other systems. It involves the way in which the passage of time, including historical events (such as the terrorist attacks in September 2001) and more gradual historical changes (such as changes in the number of women who work outside the home) affect children's development.

The bioecological approach provides several advantages. For one thing, it emphasizes the interconnectedness of the influences on development. Because the various levels are related to one another, a change in one part of the system affects other parts of the system. For instance, a parent's loss of a job (involving the mesosystem) has an impact on a child's microsystem (Bronfenbrenner, 2000; Bronfenbrenner & Morris, 1998).

Conversely, changes on one environmental level may make little difference if other levels are not also changed. For instance, improving the school environment may have a negligible effect on academic performance if children receive little support for academic success in their home environment. Similarly, the bioecological approach illustrates that the influences among different family members are multidirectional. Parents don't just influence their child's behavior—the child also influences the parents' behavior.

Finally, the bioecological approach stresses the importance of broad cultural factors that affect development. Researchers in child development increasingly look at how membership in cultural and subcultural groups influences behavior.

The Influence of Culture.   Consider, for instance, whether you agree that children should be taught that their classmates' assistance is indispensable to getting good grades in school or that they should definitely plan to continue their fathers' business or that children should follow their parents' advice in determining their career plans. If you have been raised in the most widespread North American culture, you would likely disagree with all three statements, since they violate the premises of *individualism*, the dominant Western philosophy that emphasizes personal identity, uniqueness, freedom, and the worth of the individual.

By contrast, if you were raised in a traditional Asian culture, it is considerably more likely that you will agree with the three statements. Why? The statements reflect the value orientation known as collectivism. *Collectivism* is the notion that the well-being of the group

Sociocultural theory An approach that emphasizes how cognitive development proceeds as a result of social interactions between members of a culture

is more important than that of the individual. People raised in collectivistic cultures tend to emphasize the welfare of the groups to which they belong, sometimes even at the expense of their own personal well-being.

The individualism–collectivism spectrum is one of several dimensions along which cultures differ, and it illustrates differences in the cultural contexts in which people operate. Such broad cultural values play an important role in shaping the ways people view the world and behave (de Mooij, 1998; Dent-Read & Zukow-Goldring, 1997; U. Kim et al., 1994).

Assessing the Bioecological Approach. Although Bronfenbrenner considers biological influences an important component of the bioecological approach, ecological influences are central to the theory. In fact, some critics argue that the perspective pays insufficient attention to biological factors. Still, the bioecological approach is of considerable importance to child development, suggesting as it does the multiple levels at which the environment affects children's development. (Also see the *Careers in Child Development* box, which describes someone whose work involves looking at children and their parents, taking the contextual perspective into account.)

Vygotsky's Sociocultural Theory. To Russian child developmentalist Lev Semenovich Vygotsky, a full understanding of development was impossible without taking into account the culture in which children develop. Vygotsky's **sociocultural theory** emphasizes how cognitive development proceeds as a result of social interactions between members of a culture (Beilin, 1996; Bonk & Kim, 1998; Daniels, 1996; Vygotsky, 1926/1997, 1930–1935/1978; Wertsch & Tulviste, 1992).

Vygotsky, who lived from 1896 to 1934, argued that children's understanding of the world is acquired through their problem-solving interactions with adults and other children. As children play and cooperate with others, they learn what is important in their society and at the same time advance cognitively in their understanding of the world. Consequently, to understand the course of development, we must consider what is meaningful to members of a given culture.

Assessing Vygotsky's Theory. Sociocultural theory has become increasingly influential, despite Vygotsky's death seven decades ago. The reason is the growing acknowledgment of the

According to Vygotsky, through play and cooperation with others, children can develop cognitively in their understanding of the world and learn what is important in society.

CAREERS IN CHILD DEVELOPMENT

Sue Ferguson

Education:	University of Oregon, Eugene: B.A. in elementary education, M.A. in early childhood curriculum and instruction
Position:	Family advocate with Head Start at the Bellevue Community College Early Learning, Family, and Child Care Center
Home:	Kirkland, Washington

*n*owadays, child care providers are far more than the group babysitters they were in the past. Today, they seek to carefully individualize their treatment of children to enhance their development, according to Sue Ferguson, a family advocate at the Bellevue Community College Early Learning, Family, and Child Care Center. The center serves approximately 200 children from ages 6 months to 6 years, as well as their parents.

"We don't teach to a group anymore," Ferguson explains. "We have to learn each child's interest and help the child develop that interest. For example, if one child shows interest in rolling a ball, the teacher will make sure that that activity is available throughout the day," Ferguson adds. "If a child pulls himself or herself up and tries to stand, there will be more activities for the child along those lines. We don't provide teacher-picked examples; we allow the children to develop their own interests."

Infants as young as 6 months are given individualized attention, according to Ferguson, and they are allowed to lead the direction of their development. In addition, parents are informed regarding their child's development.

"Many, many sensory activities are available," Ferguson notes, "as well as materials for them to experience what the teacher may bring to class."

A new study, instituted in 2002 by Bellevue in collaboration with the University of Washington, involves the videotaping of parents. These tapes are then played back for the infants while the parent is away.

"The study will continue for more than a year, but some early results appear to indicate that infants do feel more comfortable in group care if they see their parents," she adds.

"We don't teach to a group anymore. We have to learn each child's interest and help the child develop that interest."

central importance of cultural factors in development. Children do not develop in a cultural vacuum. Instead, their attention is directed by society to certain areas, and as a consequence, they develop particular kinds of skills that are an outcome of their cultural environment. Vygotsky was one of the first developmentalists to recognize and acknowledge the importance of culture, and as today's society becomes increasingly multicultural, sociocultural theory is helping us understand the rich and varied influences that shape development (Matusov & Hayes, 2000; Reis, Collins, & Berscheid, 2000).

Sociocultural theory is not without its critics, however. Some suggest that Vygotsky's strong emphasis on the role of culture and social experience led him to ignore the effects of biological factors on development. In addition, his perspective seems to minimize the role that individuals can play in shaping their own environment.

Evolutionary perspective   The theory that seeks to identify behavior that is the result of our genetic inheritance from our ancestors

The Evolutionary Perspective: Our Ancestors' Contributions to Behavior

One increasingly influential approach is the evolutionary perspective, the final developmental perspective that we will consider. The **evolutionary perspective** seeks to identify behavior that is the result of our genetic inheritance from our ancestors (Bjorklund & Pellegrini, 2000; Geary & Bjorklund, 2000).

Evolutionary approaches grow out of the groundbreaking work of Charles Darwin. In 1859, Darwin argued in *On the Origin of Species* that a process of natural selection creates traits in a species that are adaptive to its environment. Using Darwin's arguments, evolutionary approaches contend that our genetic inheritance not only determines such physical traits as skin color and eye color but certain personality traits and social behaviors as well. For instance, as we'll discuss further in future chapters, some evolutionary developmentalists suggest that people's levels of shyness or sociability are influenced by genetic factors (Plomin & McClearn, 1993).

The evolutionary perspective draws heavily on the field of *ethology,* which examines the ways in which our biological makeup influences our behavior. According to *ethological theories,* development is heavily influenced by biological and evolutionary factors.

A primary proponent of ethological approaches was Konrad Lorenz (1903–1989), who discovered that newborn geese are genetically programmed to become attached to the first moving object they see after birth. His work, which demonstrated the importance of biological determinants in influencing behavior patterns, ultimately led developmentalists to consider the ways in which human behavior might reflect inborn genetic patterns.

As we'll consider later in this chapter, the evolutionary perspective encompasses one of the fastest growing areas within the field of child development: behavioral genetics. *Behavioral genetics* studies the effects of heredity on behavior. Behavioral geneticists seek to understand how we might inherit certain behavioral traits and how the environment influences whether we actually display such traits. It also considers how genetic factors may produce psychological disorders such as schizophrenia (T. J. Bouchard, 1994; R. Freedman, Adler, & Leonard, 1999; Lander & Schork, 1994; Mowry, Nancarrow, & Levinson, 1997).

Although the evolutionary perspective is increasingly visible in the field of child development, it has been subjected to considerable criticism. Some developmentalists are concerned

Konrad Lorenz, seen here with geese imprinted to him, considered the ways in which behavior reflects inborn genetic patterns.

that because of its focus on genetic and biological aspects of behavior, the evolutionary perspective pays insufficient attention to the environmental and social factors involved in producing children's and adults' behavior. Other critics argue that there is no good way to experimentally test theories derived from the evolutionary approach. Still, the evolutionary approach has stimulated a significant amount of research on how our biological inheritance influences our traits and behaviors (Baltes, 1987; Bjorklund, 1997a; Dent-Read & Zukow-Goldring, 1997; L. B. Leonard, 1998; Plomin & Caspi, 1998).

Why "Which Perspective Is Right?" Is the Wrong Question

We have considered five major perspectives on development: psychodynamic, behavioral, cognitive, contextual, and evolutionary—summarized in Table 2-2. It would be natural to wonder which of them provides the most accurate account of child development.

TABLE 2-2 MAJOR PERSPECTIVES ON CHILD DEVELOPMENT			
Perspective	**Key Ideas About Human Behavior and Development**	**Major Proponents**	**Example**
Psychodynamic	Behavior throughout life is motivated by inner, unconscious forces, stemming from childhood, over which we have little control.	Sigmund Freud, Erik Erikson	This view might suggest that an adolescent who is overweight has a fixation in the oral stage of development.
Behavioral	Development can be understood by studying observable behavior and environmental stimuli.	John B. Watson, B. F. Skinner, Albert Bandura	In this perspective, an overweight adolescent might be seen as not being rewarded for good nutritional and exercise habits.
Cognitive	Emphasis is on how changes or growth in the ways people know, understand, and think about the world affect behavior.	Jean Piaget	This view might suggest that an overweight adolescent hasn't learned effective ways to stay at a healthy weight and doesn't value good nutrition.
Contextual	Behavior is determined by the relationship between individuals and their physical, cognitive, personality, social, and physical worlds.	Lev Vygotsky, Urie Bronfenbrenner	In this perspective, an adolescent may become overweight because of a family environment in which food and meals are unusually important and intertwined with family rituals.
Evolutionary	Behavior is the result of genetic inheritance from our ancestors: Traits and behavior that are adaptive for promoting the survival of our species have been inherited through natural selection.	Konrad Lorenz; influenced by early work of Charles Darwin	This view might suggest that an adolescent might have a genetic tendency toward obesity because extra fat helped family ancestors survive in times of famine.

For several reasons, this is not an entirely appropriate question. For one thing, each perspective emphasizes somewhat different aspects of development. For instance, the psychodynamic approach emphasizes emotions, motivational conflicts, and unconscious determinants of behavior. In contrast, behavioral perspectives emphasize overt behavior, paying far more attention to what people *do* than what goes on inside their heads, which is deemed largely irrelevant. The cognitive perspective takes quite the opposite tack, looking more at what people *think* than at what they do. Finally, while the contextual perspective focuses on the interaction of environmental influences, the evolutionary perspective focuses on how inherited biological factors underlie development.

Each perspective is based on its own premises and focuses on different aspects of development. Furthermore, the same developmental phenomenon can be looked at from a number of perspectives simultaneously. In fact, some child developmentalists use an *eclectic* approach, drawing on several perspectives simultaneously (Lewkowicz & Lickliter, 2002).

We can think of the different perspectives as analogous to a set of maps of the same general geographical area. One map may contain detailed depictions of roads; another map may show topographical features; another may show political subdivisions, such as cities, towns, and counties; and still another may highlight particular points of interest, such as scenic areas and historical landmarks. Each of the maps is accurate, but each provides a different point of view and way of thinking. No one map is "complete," but by considering them together, we can come to a fuller understanding of the area.

In the same way, the various theoretical perspectives provide different ways of looking at development. Considering them together paints a full portrait of the myriad ways human beings change and grow over the course of their lives. However, not all theories and claims derived from the various perspectives are accurate. How do we choose among competing explanations? The answer is *research,* which we consider in the final part of this chapter.

REVIEW & APPLY

Review

- The psychodynamic perspective looks primarily at the influence of internal, unconscious forces on development.

- The behavioral perspective focuses on external, observable behaviors as the key to development.

- The cognitive perspective focuses on mental activity.

- The contextual perspective focuses on the relationship between individuals and the social context in which they lead their lives.

- Finally, the evolutionary perspective seeks to identify behavior that is a result of our genetic inheritance from our ancestors.

Applying Child Development

- What examples of human behavior have you seen that seem as though they may have been inherited from our ancestors? Why do you think they are inherited?

- *From the perspective of an educator:* How might the kind of social learning that comes from viewing television influence children's behavior?

The Scientific Method and Research

The Egyptians had long believed that they were the most ancient race on earth, and Psamtik [king of Egypt in the 7th century B.C.], driven by intellectual curiosity, wanted to prove that flattering belief. Like a good researcher, he began with a hypothesis: If children had no opportunity to learn a language from older people around them, they would spontaneously speak the primal, inborn language of humankind—the natural language of its most ancient people—which, he expected to show, was Egyptian.

To test his hypothesis, Psamtik commandeered two infants of a lower-class mother and turned them over to a herdsman to bring up in a remote area. They were to be kept in a sequestered cottage [and] properly fed and cared for but were never to hear anyone speak so much as a word. The Greek historian Herodotus, who tracked the story down and learned what he calls "the real facts" from priests of Hephaestus in Memphis, says that Psamtik's goal "was to know, after the indistinct babblings of infancy were over, what word they would first articulate."

The experiment, he tells us, worked. One day, when the children were two years old, they ran up to the herdsman as he opened the door of their cottage and cried out "*Becos!*" Since this meant nothing to him, he paid no attention, but when it happened repeatedly, he sent word to Psamtik, who at once ordered the children brought to him. When he too heard them say it, Psamtik made inquiries and learned that *becos* was the Phrygian word for bread. He concluded that, disappointingly, the Phrygians were an older race than the Egyptians. (M. Hunt, 1993, pp. 1–2)

With the perspective of several thousand years, we can easily see the shortcomings—both scientific and ethical—in Psamtik's approach. Yet his procedure represents an improvement over mere speculation and as such is sometimes regarded as the first developmental experiment in recorded history (M. Hunt, 1993).

Theories and Hypotheses: Posing Developmental Questions

Questions such as those raised by Psamtik lie at the heart of the study of child development. Is language innate? What are the effects of malnutrition on later intellectual performance? How do infants form relationships with their parents, and does participation in day care disrupt such relationships? Why are adolescents susceptible to peer pressure?

To resolve such questions, specialists in child development rely on the scientific method. The **scientific method** is the process of posing and answering questions using careful, controlled techniques that include systematic, orderly observation and the collection of data. As shown in Figure 2-2, the scientific method involves three major steps: (1) identifying questions of interest, (2) formulating an explanation, and (3) carrying out research that either lends support to the explanation or refutes it.

> **Scientific method** The process of posing and answering questions using careful, controlled techniques that include systematic, orderly observation and the collection of data

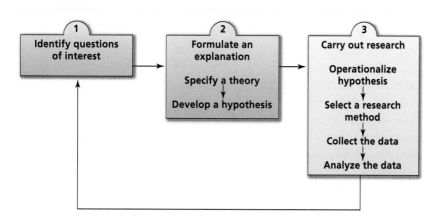

FIGURE 2-2   THE SCIENTIFIC METHOD

A cornerstone of research, the scientific method is used by psychologists as well as researchers from all other scientific disciplines.

Theories: Framing Broad Explanations

The first step in the scientific method, the identification of questions of interest, begins when an observer puzzles over some aspect of behavior. Perhaps it is an infant who cries when she is picked up by a stranger, or a child who is doing poorly in school, or an adolescent who engages in risky behavior. Developmentalists, like all of us, start with questions about such everyday aspects of behavior, and—also like all of us—they seek to determine answers to these questions.

However, it is the way that developmental researchers try to find answers that differentiates them from more casual observers. Developmental researchers formulate *theories,* broad explanations and predictions about phenomena of interest. Using one of the major perspectives that we discussed earlier, researchers develop more specific theories. In fact, all of us develop theories about development, based on our experience, folklore, and articles in magazines and newspapers. For instance, many people theorize that there is a crucial bonding period between parent and child immediately after birth, which is a necessary ingredient in forming a lasting parent–child relationship. Without such a bonding period, they assume, the parent–child relationship will be forever compromised (Furnham & Weir, 1996).

Whenever we employ such explanations, we are developing our own theories. However, the theories in child development are different. Whereas our own personal theories are built on unverified observations that are developed haphazardly, developmentalists' theories are more formal, based on a systematic integration of prior findings and theorizing. These theories allow developmental researchers to summarize and organize prior observations and to move beyond existing observations to draw deductions that may not be immediately apparent.

Hypotheses: Specifying Testable Predictions

Although the development of theories provides a general approach to a problem, it is only the first step. In order to determine the validity of a theory, developmental researchers must test it scientifically. To do that, they develop hypotheses, based on their theories. A **hypothesis** is a prediction stated in a way that permits it to be tested. For instance, someone who subscribes to the general theory that bonding is a crucial ingredient in the parent–child relationship might derive the more specific hypothesis that adopted children whose adoptive parents never had the chance to bond with them immediately after birth may ultimately have less secure relationships with their adoptive parents. Others might derive other hypotheses, such as that effective bonding occurs only if it lasts for a certain length of time or that bonding affects the mother–child relationship but not the father–child relationship. (In case you're wondering, as we'll discuss in Chapter 4, these particular hypotheses have *not* been upheld; there are no long-term reactions to the separation of parent and child immediately after birth, even if the separation lasts several days, and there is no difference in the strength of bonds with mothers and bonds with fathers.)

Choosing a Research Strategy: Answering Questions

Once researchers have formed a hypothesis, they must develop a strategy for testing its validity. The first step is to state the hypothesis in a way that will allow it to be tested. **Operationalization** is the process of translating a hypothesis into specific, testable procedures that can be measured and observed.

For example, a researcher interested in testing the hypothesis that "being evaluated leads to anxiety" might operationalize "being evaluated" as a teacher's giving a grade to a student or in terms of a child's commenting on a friend's athletic skills. Similarly, "anxiety" could be operationalized in terms of responses on a questionnaire or as measurements of biological reactions by an electronic instrument.

The choice of how to operationalize a variable often reflects the kind of research that is to be conducted. There are two major categories of research: correlational research and

Hypothesis   A prediction stated in a way that permits it to be tested

Operationalization   The process of translating a hypothesis into specific, testable procedures that can be measured and observed

experimental research. **Correlational research** seeks to identify whether an association or relationship between two factors exists. As we'll see, correlational research cannot be used to determine whether one factor causes changes in the other. For instance, correlational research could tell us if there is an association between the number of minutes a mother and her newborn child are together immediately after birth and the quality of the mother–child relationship when the child reaches 2 years of age. Such correlational research indicates whether the two factors are *associated* or *related* to one another but not whether the initial contact caused the relationship to develop in a particular way (Schutt, 2001).

In contrast, **experimental research** is designed to discover *causal* relationships between various factors. In experimental research, researchers deliberately introduce a change in a situation in order to see the consequences of that change. For instance, a researcher conducting an experiment might vary the number of minutes that mothers and children interact immediately following birth in an attempt to see whether the amount of bonding time affects the mother–child relationship.

Because experimental research is able to answer questions of causality, it represents the heart of developmental research. However, some research questions cannot be answered through experiments, for either technical or ethical reasons. In fact, a great deal of pioneering developmental research—such as that conducted by Piaget and Vygotsky—employed correlational techniques. Consequently, correlational research remains an important tool in the developmental researcher's toolbox.

Correlational Studies

As we've noted, correlational research examines the relationship between two variables to determine whether they are associated, or *correlated*. For instance, researchers interested in the relationship between televised aggression and subsequent behavior have found that children who watch a substantial amount of aggression on television—murders, crime, shootings, and the like—tend to be more aggressive than those who watch only a little. In other words, as we'll discuss in greater detail in Chapter 10, viewing of aggression and actual aggression are strongly associated, or correlated, with one another (Center for Communication and Social Policy, 1998).

But does this mean we can conclude that the viewing of televised aggression *causes* the more aggressive behavior of the viewers? Not at all. Consider some of the other possibilities: It might be that being aggressive in the first place makes children more likely to choose to watch violent programs. In such a case, then, it is the aggressive tendency that causes the viewing behavior, not the other way around.

Or consider another possibility. Suppose that children who are raised in poverty are more likely to behave aggressively *and* to watch higher levels of aggressive television than those raised in more affluent settings. In this case, it is socioeconomic status that causes *both* the

Correlational research Research that seeks to identify whether an association or relationship between two factors exists

Experimental research Research designed to discover causal relationships between various factors

FIGURE 2-3 FINDING A CORRELATION

Finding a correlation between two factors does not imply that one factor *causes* the other factor to vary. For instance, suppose that a study found that viewing television programs with high levels of aggression is correlated with actual aggression in children. The correlation might reflect at least three possibilities: (a) watching television programs containing high levels of aggression causes aggression in viewers; (b) children who behave aggressively choose to watch television programs with high levels of aggression; or (c) some third factor, such as a child's socioeconomic status, leads to both high viewer aggression and choosing to watch television programs with high viewer aggression.

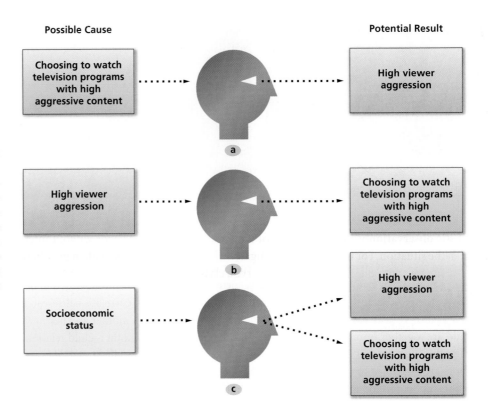

aggressive behavior and the television viewing. (The various possibilities are illustrated in Figure 2-3).

In short, finding that two variables are correlated proves nothing about causality. Although it is possible that the variables are linked causally, this is not necessarily the case.

Nevertheless, correlational studies can provide important information. For instance, as we'll see in later chapters, we know from correlational studies that the closer the genetic link between two people, the more highly associated their intelligence. We have learned that the more parents speak to their young children, the more extensive the children's vocabularies. And we know from correlational studies that the better the nutrition that infants receive, the fewer cognitive and social problems they experience later (B. Hart & Risley, 1995; Plomin, 1994b; Pollitt et al., 1993).

The Correlation Coefficient. The strength and direction of a relationship between two factors is represented by a mathematical score, called a *correlation coefficient,* that ranges from $+1$ to -1. A positive correlation indicates that as the value of one factor increases, it can be predicted that the value of the other will also increase. For instance, if we find that the more calories children eat, the better their school performance, and the fewer calories children eat, the worse their school performance, we have found a positive correlation. (Higher values of the factor "calories" are associated with higher values of the factor "school performance," and lower values of the factor "calories" are associated with lower values of the factor "school performance.") The correlation coefficient, then, would be indicated by a positive number, and the stronger the association between calories and school performance, the closer the number would be to $+1$.

In contrast, a correlation coefficient with a negative value informs us that as the value of one factor increases, the value of the other factor declines. For example, suppose we found that the greater the number of hours adolescents spend using instant messaging on their computers, the worse their academic performance. Such a finding would result in a negative correlation, ranging between 0 and -1. More instant messaging is associated with lower performance, and less instant messaging is associated with better performance. The stronger the association between instant messaging and school performance, the closer the correlation coefficient will be to -1.

Finally, it is possible that two factors are unrelated to one another. For example, it is unlikely that we would find a correlation between school performance and shoe size. In this case, the lack of a relationship would be indicated by a correlation coefficient close to 0.

It is important to reiterate what we noted earlier: Even if the correlation coefficient involving two variables is very strong, there is no way we can know whether one factor *causes* another factor to vary. It simply means that the two factors are associated with one another in a predictable way.

Types of Correlational Studies. There are several types of correlational studies. **Naturalistic observation** is the observation of a naturally occurring behavior without intervention in the situation. For instance, an investigator who wishes to learn how often preschool children share toys with one another might observe a classroom over a 3-week period, recording how often the preschoolers spontaneously share with one another. The key point about naturalistic observation is that the investigator simply observes the children without interfering with the situation in any way (P. A. Adler & Adler, 1994; Blasko, Kazmerski, Corty, & Kallgren, 1998; Erlandson et al., 1993).

While naturalistic observation has the advantage of identifying what children do in their "natural habitat," there is an important drawback to the method: Researchers are unable to exert control over factors of interest. For instance, in some cases, researchers might find so few naturally occurring instances of the behavior of interest that they are unable to draw any conclusions at all. In addition, children who know they are being watched may modify their behavior as a result of the observation. Consequently, their behavior may not be representative of how they would behave if they were not being watched.

Increasingly, naturalistic observation employs *ethnography*, a method borrowed from the field of anthropology and used to investigate cultural questions. In ethnography, a researcher's goal is to understand a culture's values and attitudes through careful, extended examination. Typically, researchers using ethnography act as *participant observers*, living for a period of weeks, months, or even years in another culture. By carefully observing everyday life and conducting in-depth interviews, researchers are able to obtain a deep understanding of life in another culture (Fetterman, 1998).

Although ethnographic studies provide a fine-grained view of everyday behavior in another culture, they suffer from several drawbacks. As mentioned, the presence of a participant observer may influence the behavior of the individuals being studied. Furthermore, because only a small number of individuals are studied, it may be hard to generalize the findings to people in other cultures. Finally, ethnographers may misinterpret and misconceive what they are observing, particularly in cultures that are very different from their own (Hammersley, 1992).

Case studies involve extensive, in-depth interviews with a particular individual or small group of individuals. They often are used not just to learn about the individual being interviewed but also to derive broader principles or draw tentative conclusions that might apply to others. For example, case studies have been conducted on children who display unusual genius and on children who have spent their early years in the wild without human contact. These case studies have provided important information to researchers and have suggested hypotheses for future investigation (L. T. Goldsmith, 2000; Hebert, 1998; Lane, 1976).

Using **diaries**, participants are asked to keep a record of their behavior on a regular basis. For example, a group of adolescents may be asked to record each time they interact with friends for more than 5 minutes, thereby providing a way to track their social behavior.

In **survey research**, a group of people chosen to represent some larger population are asked questions about their attitudes, behavior, or thinking on a given topic. For instance,

Naturalistic observation is used to examine a situation in its natural habitat without interference of any sort. What are some disadvantages of naturalistic observation?

Naturalistic observation   Studies in which researchers observe some naturally occurring behavior without intervening or making changes in the situation

Case studies   Extensive, in-depth interviews with a particular individual or small group of individuals

Diaries   A research technique in which participants are asked to keep a record of their behavior on a regular basis

Survey research   Research in which a group of people chosen to represent some larger population are asked questions about their attitudes, behavior, or thinking on a given topic

surveys have been conducted about parents' use of punishment on their children and on attitudes toward breast-feeding. From the responses, inferences are drawn regarding the larger population represented by the individuals being surveyed.

Experiments: Determining Cause and Effect

In an **experiment,** an investigator, called an *experimenter,* typically devises two different experiences for *participants,* or *subjects.* These two different experiences are called treatments. A **treatment** is a procedure applied by an investigator. One group of participants receives one of the treatments, while another group of participants receives either no treatment or an alternative treatment. The group receiving the treatment is known as the **treatment group** (sometimes called the *experimental group*), while the no-treatment or alternative-treatment group is called the **control group.**

Although the terminology may seem daunting at first, there is an underlying logic to it that helps sort it out. Think in terms of a medical experiment in which the aim is to test the effectiveness of a new drug. In testing the drug, we wish to see if the drug successfully *treats* the disease. Consequently, the group that receives the drug would be called the *treatment* group. In comparison, another group of participants would not receive the drug treatment. Instead, they would be part of the no-treatment *control* group.

Similarly, suppose we wish to explore the consequences of exposure to movie violence on viewers' subsequent aggression. We might take a group of adolescents and show them a series of movies that contain a great deal of violent imagery. We would then measure their subsequent aggression. This group would constitute the treatment group. But we would also need another group—a control group. To fulfill this need, we might take a second group of adolescents, show them movies that contain no aggressive imagery, and then measure their subsequent aggression. This would be the control group.

By comparing the amount of aggression displayed by members of the treatment and control groups, we would be able to determine if exposure to violent imagery produces aggression in viewers. And this is just what a group of researchers found: Running an experiment of this very sort, psychologist Jacques-Philippe Leyens and colleagues at the University of Louvain in Belgium found that the level of aggression rose significantly for the adolescents who had seen the movies containing violence (Leyens et al., 1975).

Designing an Experiment.   The central feature of this experiment—and all other experiments—is the comparison of the consequences of different treatments. The use of both treatment and control groups allows researchers to rule out the possibility that something other than the experimental manipulation produced the results found in the experiment. For instance, if a control group was not used, experiments could not be certain that some other factor, such as the time of day the movies were shown, the need to sit still during the movie, or even the mere passage of time, produced the changes that were observed. By employing a control group, then, experimenters can draw accurate conclusions about causes and effects.

The formation of treatment and control groups represents the independent variable in an experiment. The **independent variable** is the variable that researchers manipulate in the experiment. In contrast, the **dependent variable** is the variable that researchers measure in an experiment and expect to change as a result of the experimental manipulation. (One way to remember the difference: A hypothesis predicts how a dependent variable *depends* on the manipulation of the independent variable.) In an experiment studying the effects of taking a drug, for instance, manipulating whether participants receive or don't receive a drug is the independent variable. Measurement of the effectiveness of the drug or no-drug treatment is the dependent variable.

To consider another example, let's take the Belgian study of the consequences of observing filmed aggression on future aggression. In this experiment, the independent variable is the *level of aggressive imagery* viewed by participants—determined by whether they viewed films

Experiment   A process in which an investigator, called an experimenter, devises two different experiences for subjects or participants

Treatment   A procedure applied by an experimental investigator based on two different experiences devised for subjects or participants

Treatment group   The group in an experiment that receives the treatment

Control group   The group in an experiment that receives either no treatment or an alternative treatment

Independent variable   The variable in an experiment that is manipulated by researchers

Dependent variable   The variable in an experiment that is measured and is expected to change as a result of the experimental manipulation

containing aggressive imagery (the treatment group) or devoid of aggressive imagery (the control group). The dependent variable in the study? It was what the experimenters expected to vary as a consequence of viewing a film: the *aggressive behavior* shown by participants after they had viewed the films and measured by the experimenters. Every experiment has an independent and dependent variable.

Random Assignment.   One critical step in the design of experiments is to assign participants to different treatment groups. The procedure that is used is known as random assignment. In *random assignment,* participants are assigned to different experimental groups or "conditions" on the basis of chance and chance alone. By using this technique, the laws of statistics ensure that personal characteristics that might affect the outcome of the experiment are divided proportionally among the participants in the different groups. In other words, the groups are equivalent to one another in terms of the personal characteristics of the participants. Equivalent groups achieved by random assignment allow an experimenter to draw conclusions with confidence.

Given the advantage of experimental research—that it provides a means of determining causality—why aren't experiments always used? The answer is that there are some situations that a researcher, no matter how ingenious, simply cannot control. And there are some situations that it would be unethical to control, even if it were possible. For instance, no researcher would be able to assign different groups of infants to parents of high and low socioeconomic status in order to learn the effects of such status on subsequent development. Similarly, we cannot control what a group of children watch on television throughout their childhood years in order to learn if childhood exposure to televised aggression leads to aggressive behavior later in life. Consequently, in situations in which experiments are logistically or ethically impossible, developmentalists employ correlational research.

Choosing a Research Setting.   Deciding where to conduct a study may be as important as determining what to do. In the Belgian experiment on the influence of exposure to media aggression, the researchers used a real-world setting—a group home for boys who had been convicted of juvenile delinquency. They chose this **sample,** the group of participants chosen for the experiment, because it was useful to have adolescents whose normal level of aggression was relatively high and because they could incorporate showing the films into the everyday life of the home with minimal disruption.

Using a real-world setting like the one in the aggression experiment is the hallmark of a field study. A **field study** is a research investigation carried out in a naturally occurring setting. Field studies may be carried out in preschool classrooms, at community playgrounds, on school buses, or on street corners. Field studies capture behavior in real-life settings, and research participants may behave more naturally than they would if they were brought into a laboratory.

Sample   A group of participants chosen for an experiment

Field study   A research investigation carried out in a naturally occurring setting

Developmentalists work in such diverse settings as in a laboratory preschool on a college campus and in human service agencies.

Laboratory study   A research investigation conducted in a controlled setting explicitly designed to hold events constant

Field studies may be used in both correlational studies and experiments. Field studies typically employ naturalistic observation, the technique we discussed earlier in which researchers observe some naturally occurring behavior without intervening or making changes in the situation. For instance, a researcher might examine behavior in a child care center, view the groupings of adolescents in high school corridors, or observe elderly adults in a senior center.

However, it often is difficult to run an experiment in real-world settings, where it is hard to exert control over the situation and environment. Consequently, field studies are more typical of correlational designs than experimental designs, and most developmental research experiments are conducted in laboratory settings. A **laboratory study** is a research investigation

○— D E V E L O P M E N T A L   D I V E R S I T Y —○

Choosing Research Participants Who Represent the Diversity of Children

In order for child development to represent the full range of humanity, its research must incorporate children of different races, ethnicities, cultures, genders, and other categories. However, although the field of child development is increasingly concerned with issues of human diversity, its actual progress in this domain has been slow, and in some ways, it has actually regressed.

For instance, between 1970 and 1989, only 4.6 percent of the articles published in *Developmental Psychology,* one of the premier journals of the discipline, focused on African American participants. Moreover, the number of published studies involving African American participants of all ages actually declined over that 20-year period (S. Graham, 1992; MacPhee, Kreutzer, & Fritz, 1994).

Even when minority groups are included in research, the particular participants may not represent the full range of variation that actually exists within the group. For example, African American infants used in a research study might well be disproportionally upper- and middle-class, because parents in higher socioeconomic groups may be more likely to have the time and transportation capabilities to bring their infants into a research center. In contrast, African Americans (as well as members of other groups) who are relatively poor will face more hurdles when it comes to participating in research.

Something is amiss when a science that seeks to explain children's behavior—as is the case with child development—disregards significant groups of individuals. Child developmentalists are aware of this issue, and they have become increasingly sensitive to the importance of using participants who are fully representative of the general population (Rogler, 1999).

In order to understand development in all children, researchers must include participants in their studies that represent the diversity of humanity.

conducted in a controlled setting explicitly designed to hold events constant. The laboratory may be a room or building designed for research, as in a university's psychology department. The ability to control the settings in laboratory studies enables researchers to learn more clearly how their treatments affect participants.

REVIEW & APPLY

Review

- Theories in child development are systematically derived explanations of facts or phenomena. Theories suggest hypotheses, which are predictions that can be tested.

- Experimental research seeks to discover cause-and-effect relationships through the use of a treatment group and a control group. Correlational studies examine relationships between factors without demonstrating causality.

- Research studies may be conducted in laboratories, where conditions can be controlled effectively, or in field settings, where participants are subject to natural conditions.

Applying Child Development

- Formulate a theory about one aspect of child development and a hypothesis that relates to it.

- *From an educator's perspective:* Why might you criticize theories that are supported only by data collected from laboratory studies, rather than from field studies? Would such criticism be valid?

Research Strategies and Challenges

Developmental researchers typically focus on one of two approaches to research: theoretical research or applied research. The two approaches are in fact complementary.

Theoretical and Applied Research: Complementary Approaches

Theoretical research is designed specifically to test some developmental explanation and expand scientific knowledge, while **applied research** is meant to provide practical solutions to immediate problems. For instance, if we were interested in the processes of cognitive change during childhood, we might carry out a study of how many digits children of various ages can remember after one exposure to multidigit numbers—a theoretical approach. Alternatively, we might focus on how children learn by examining ways in which elementary school instructors can teach children to remember information more easily. Such a study would represent applied research, because the findings are applied to a particular setting and problem.

Often the distinctions between theoretical and applied research are blurred. For instance, is a study that examines the consequences of ear infections in infancy on later hearing loss theoretical or applied research? Because such a study may help illuminate the basic processes involved in hearing, it can be considered theoretical. But to the extent that the study helps us

Theoretical research Research designed specifically to test some developmental explanation and expand scientific knowledge

Applied research Research meant to provide practical solutions to immediate problems

FROM RESEARCH TO PRACTICE

Using Research to Improve Public Policy

Do children benefit from preschool?

What is the best approach to reducing the number of unwed teenage girls who become mothers?

Does research support the legalization of marijuana?

Should preschoolers diagnosed with attention deficit hyperactivity disorder receive drugs to treat their condition?

Will a series of national educational achievement tests improve scholastic performance?

Each of these questions represents a major national policy issue that can be answered appropriately in only one way: by considering the results of relevant research studies. By conducting controlled studies, developmental researchers have made a number of important contributions in a variety of areas. Consider, for instance, some of the ways that various types of research findings have been used to improve public policy (Lorion et al., 1996; Marshall, 2000; Susman-Stillman et al., 1996):

- *Determining the right questions.* Research findings can provide a means of determining what questions to ask in the first place. For example, studies of children's caregivers have led policymakers to question whether the benefits of infant day care are outweighed by possible deterioration in parent–child bonds.

- *Writing legislation and laws that improve the lives of children.* A good deal of legislation has been passed based on findings from developmental researchers. For example, research

revealing that children with developmental disabilities benefit from exposure to children without special needs ultimately led to the passage of national legislation mandating that children with disabilities be placed in regular school classes as much as possible.

- *Developing effective intervention programs.* Research has often helped policymakers and other professionals determine how to implement programs designed to improve the lives of children, adolescents, and adults. Research has shaped programs designed to reduce the incidence of unsafe sex among teenagers, to increase the level of prenatal care for pregnant mothers, and to raise class attendance rates in school-age children. The common thread among such programs is that many of the details of the programs are built on basic research findings.

- *Evaluating public policy programs.* Once a public policy has been implemented, it is necessary to determine whether it has been effective and successful in accomplishing its goals. To do this, researchers employ formal evaluation techniques, developed from basic research procedures. For instance, researchers have continually scrutinized the Head Start preschool program, which has received massive federal funding, to ensure that it is effective in improving children's academic performance.

Developmentalists have worked hand in hand with policymakers, and the resulting research findings have had a substantial impact on public policies, creating potential benefits for all of us.

understand how to prevent hearing loss in children and how various medicines may ease the consequences of the infection, it may be considered applied research (Lerner, Fisher, & Weinberg, 2000).

In short, even the most applied research can help advance our theoretical understanding of a particular topical area, and theoretical research can provide concrete solutions to a range of practical problems. In fact, as discussed in the accompanying *From Research to Practice* box, research of both a theoretical and an applied nature has played a significant role in shaping and resolving a variety of public policy questions.

Measuring Developmental Change

For developmental researchers, the question of how people grow and change throughout the life span is central to their discipline. Consequently, one of the thorniest research issues they face concerns the measurement of change and differences over age and time. To solve this problem, researchers have developed three major strategies: longitudinal research, cross-sectional research, and cross-sequential research.

Longitudinal Studies: Measuring Individual Change.

If you were interested in learning how a child's moral development changes between the ages of 3 and 5, the most direct approach would be to take a group of 3-year-olds and follow them until they were 5, testing them periodically.

Such a strategy illustrates longitudinal research. In **longitudinal research,** the behavior of one or more study participants is measured as they age. Longitudinal research measures change over time. By following many individuals over time, researchers can understand the general course of change across some period of life.

The granddaddy of longitudinal studies, which has become a classic, is a study of gifted children begun by Lewis Terman more than 75 years ago. In the study—which is still ongoing—a group of 1,500 children with high IQs were tested about every 5 years. Now in their 80s, the participants—who call themselves "Termites"—have provided information on everything from intellectual accomplishment to personality and longevity (Friedman et al., 1995; Lippa, Martin, & Friedman, 2000; L. M. Terman & Oden, 1959).

Longitudinal research has also provided great insight into language development. For instance, by tracing how children's vocabularies increase on a day-by-day basis, researchers have been able to understand the processes that underlie the human ability to become competent in using language.

Longitudinal studies can provide a wealth of information about change over time (J. Bullock, 1995; Elder, 1998). However, they have several drawbacks. For one thing, they require a tremendous investment of time, because researchers must wait for participants to become older. Furthermore, there is a significant possibility of participant *attrition,* or loss, over the course of the research. Participants may drop out of a study, move away, or become ill or even die as the research proceeds.

Finally, participants who are observed or tested may become "test-wise" and perform better each time they are assessed as they become more familiar with the procedure. Even if the observations of participants in a study are not terribly intrusive (such as simply recording, over a lengthy period of time, vocabulary increases in infants and preschoolers), experimental participants may be affected by the repeated presence of an experimenter or observer.

Consequently, despite the benefits of longitudinal research, particularly its ability to look at change within individuals, developmental researchers often turn to other methods in conducting research. The alternative they choose most often is the cross-sectional study.

Cross-Sectional Studies.

Let's return to the issue of moral development in children 3 to 5 years of age. Instead of using a longitudinal approach and following the same children over several years, we might conduct the study by simultaneously looking at three groups of children: 3-year-olds, 4-year-olds, and 5-year-olds.

Such an approach typifies cross-sectional research. In **cross-sectional research,** people of different ages are compared at the same point in time. Cross-sectional studies provide information about differences in development between different age groups.

Cross-sectional research is considerably more economical in terms of time than longitudinal research: Participants are tested at just one point in time. For instance, Terman's study might conceivably have been completed 75 years ago if Terman had simply looked at a group of gifted 5-year-olds, 10-year-olds, 15-year-olds, and so forth, all the way through a group of 80-year-olds. Because the participants would not be periodically tested, there would be no chance that they would become test-wise, and problems of participant attrition would not occur. Why, then, would anyone choose to use a procedure other than cross-sectional research?

Longitudinal research Research in which the behavior of one or more individuals is measured as the subjects age

Cross-sectional research Research in which people of different ages are compared at the same point in time

Cross-sectional research allows researchers to compare representatives of different age groups at the same time.

Cross-sequential studies Studies in which researchers examine members of a number of different age groups at several points in time

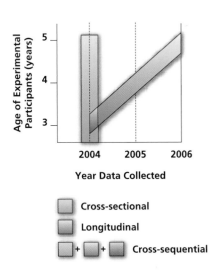

FIGURE 2-4
RESEARCH TECHNIQUES FOR STUDYING DEVELOPMENT

In a *cross-sectional study,* 3-, 4- and 5-year-olds are compared at a similar point in time (2004). In *longitudinal research,* a set of participants who are 3 years old in 2004 are studied when they are 4 years old (in 2005) and when they are 5 years old (in 2006). Finally, a *cross-sequential study* combines cross-sectional and longitudinal techniques; here, a group of 3-year-olds would be compared initially in 2004 with 4- and 5-year-olds but would also be studied 1 and 2 years later, when they themselves were 4 and 5 years old. Although the graph does not illustrate this, researchers carrying out this cross-sequential study might also choose to retest the children who were 4 and 5 in 2004 for the next 2 years. What advantages do the three kinds of studies offer?

The answer is that cross-sectional research brings its own set of difficulties. We can start with cohort effects. Recall that every person belongs to a particular *cohort,* the group of people born at around the same time in the same place. If we find that people of different ages vary along some dimension, it may be due to differences in cohort membership, not age per se.

Consider a concrete example: If we find in a correlational study that people who are 15 years old perform better on a test of intelligence than those who are 75 years old, there are several explanations. Although the finding may be due to decreased intelligence in older people, it may also be attributable to cohort differences. The group of 75-year-olds may have had less formal education than the 15-year-olds, because members of the older cohort were less likely to finish high school and attend college than members of the younger one. Or perhaps the members of the older group performed less well because as infants they received less adequate nutrition than members of the younger group. In short, we cannot fully rule out the possibility that differences we find between people of different age groups in cross-sectional studies are due to cohort differences.

Cross-sectional studies may also suffer from *selective dropout* in that participants in some age groups are more likely to quit participating in a study than others. For example, suppose a study of cognitive development in preschoolers includes a lengthy assessment of cognitive abilities. It is possible that young preschoolers would find the task more difficult and demanding than older preschoolers. As a result, the younger preschoolers would be more likely to discontinue participation in the study than the older preschoolers. If the least competent young preschoolers are the ones who drop out, then the remaining sample of participants in the study will consist of the more competent young preschoolers—together with a broader and more representative sample of older preschoolers. Clearly, the results of such a study would be questionable (S. A. Miller, 1998).

Finally, cross-sectional studies have a more basic disadvantage: They are unable to inform us about changes in individuals or groups. Although we can establish differences related to age, we cannot fully determine if such differences are related to change over time.

Cross-Sequential Studies.   Because both longitudinal and cross-sectional studies have drawbacks, researchers have turned to some compromise techniques. Among the most frequently employed are cross-sequential studies, which are essentially a combination of longitudinal and cross-sectional studies.

In **cross-sequential studies,** researchers examine a number of different age groups at several points in time. For instance, an investigator interested in children's moral behavior might begin a cross-sequential study by examining the behavior of three groups of children, who were either 3 years old, 4 years old, or 5 years old at the time the study begins. (This is no different from the way a cross-sectional study would be done.)

However, the study wouldn't stop there but would continue for the next several years. During this period, each of the research participants would be tested annually. Thus the 3-year-olds would be tested at ages 3, 4, and 5; the 4-year-olds at ages 4, 5, and 6; and the 5-year-olds at ages 5, 6, and 7. Such an approach combines the advantages of longitudinal and cross-sectional research and also permits developmental researchers to tease out the consequences of age *change* versus age *difference.* (The major research techniques for studying development are summarized in Figure 2-4.)

Ethics and Research: The Morality of Research

Return, for a moment, to the "study" conducted by Egyptian King Psamtik in which two children were removed from their mothers and held in isolation in an effort to learn about the

BECOMING AN INFORMED CONSUMER OF DEVELOPMENT

Critically Evaluating Developmental Research

"Study Shows Adolescent Suicide Reaches New Peaks."
"Genetic Basis Found for Children's Obesity."
"New Research Points to Cure for Sudden Infant Death Syndrome."

We've all seen headlines like these, which at first glance seem to herald important, meaningful discoveries. But before we accept the findings, it is important to think critically about the research on which the headlines are based. Among the most important questions that we should consider are the following:

- Is the study grounded in theory, and what are the underlying hypotheses about the research? Research should flow from theoretical foundations, and hypotheses should be logical and based on some underlying theory. Only by considering the results in terms of theory and hypotheses can we determine how successful the research has been.

- Is this an isolated research study, or does it fit into a series of investigations addressing the same general problem? A one-time study is far less meaningful than a series of studies that build upon one another. By placing research in the context of

other studies, we can be much more confident regarding the validity of the findings of a new study.

- Who took part in the study, and how far can we generalize the results beyond the participants? As we discussed earlier in the chapter, conclusions about the meaning of research can only be generalized to people who are similar to the participants in a study.

- Was the study carried out appropriately? Although it is often difficult to know the details of a study from media summaries, it is important to learn as much as possible about who did the study and how it was done. For instance, did it include appropriate control groups, and are the researchers who conducted it reputable? One clue that a study meets these criteria and is well done is if the findings reported in the media are based on a study published in a major journal such as *Developmental Psychology, Adolescence, Child Development,* or *Science*. Each of these journals is carefully edited, and only the best, most rigorous research is reported in them.

- Were the participants studied long enough to draw reasonable developmental implications? A study that purports to study long-term development should encompass a reasonably long time frame. Furthermore, developmental implications beyond the age span studied should not be drawn.

---

roots of language. Clearly, such an experiment raises blatant ethical concerns, and nothing like it would ever be done today.

But sometimes ethical issues are more subtle. For instance, in seeking to understand the roots of aggressive behavior, U.S. government researchers proposed holding a conference to examine possible genetic roots of aggression. Based on work conducted by biopsychologists and geneticists, some researchers had begun to raise the possibility that genetic markers might be found that would allow the identification of children as being particularly prone to violence. In such cases, it might be possible to track these violence-prone children and provide interventions that might reduce the likelihood of later violence.

Critics objected strenuously, however. They argued that such identification might lead to a self-fulfilling prophecy. Children labeled as violence-prone might be treated in a way that would actually *cause* them to be more aggressive than if they hadn't been so labeled. Ultimately, under intense political pressure, the conference was canceled (R. Wright, 1995).

To help researchers deal with such ethical problems, the major organizations of developmentalists, including the Society for Research in Child Development and the American Psychological Association, have developed comprehensive ethical guidelines for researchers. Among the basic principles that must be followed are those involving freedom from harm, informed consent, the use of deception, and maintenance of subjects' privacy (American Psychological Association, 1992; Sales & Folkman, 2000).

Freedom From Harm.   Researchers must protect participants from physical and psychological harm. Their welfare, interests, and rights come before those of researchers. In research, subjects' rights always come first (Sieber, 1998).

Informed Consent.   Consent must be obtained from subjects before their participation in a study. If they are above the age of 7, participants must voluntarily agree to be in a study. For those under 18, their parents or guardians must also provide consent.

The requirement for informed consent raises some difficult issues. Suppose, for instance, that researchers wish to learn the psychological consequences of abortion on adolescents. Although they may be able to obtain the consent of an adolescent who has had an abortion, the researchers may need to get her parents' permission as well, because she is a minor. But suppose the adolescent hasn't told her parents that she has had an abortion. In such a case, the mere request for permission from the parents would violate the privacy of the adolescent, leading to a breach of ethics.

Use of Deception.   Although deception to disguise the true purpose of an experiment is permissible, any experiment that uses deception must undergo careful scrutiny by an independent panel before it is conducted. Suppose that we want to know the reaction of subjects to success and failure. It is ethical to tell subjects that they will be playing a game when the true purpose is actually to observe how they respond to doing well or poorly on the task. However, such a procedure is ethical only if it causes no harm to participants, has been approved by a review panel, and ultimately includes a full debriefing, or explanation, for participants when the study is over.

Maintenance of Privacy.   Subjects' privacy must be maintained. If they are videotaped during the course of a study, for example, they must give their permission for the videotapes to be viewed. Furthermore, access to the tapes must be carefully restricted.

Review

- Developmentalists typically focus on either applied or theoretical research.

- Researchers measure age-related change using longitudinal studies (same participants at different ages), cross-sectional studies (different-age participants at one time), and cross-sequential studies (different-age participants at several times).

- Critical ethical guidelines include such issues as the prevention of harm to participants, informed consent, the use of deception, and privacy.

Applying Child Development

- What problems might affect a study of age-related changes in attitudes toward the police conducted at a single time among a cross section of children aged 5, 10, 15, and 20?

- *From the perspective of a health care provider:* Are there some special circumstances involving adolescents, who are not legally adults, that would justify allowing them to participate in a study without obtaining their parents' permission?

LOOKING **BACK**

○ **What are the major perspectives on child development?**

- Five major theoretical perspectives guide the study of child development: the psycho-dynamic, behavioral, cognitive, contextual, and evolutionary perspectives.

- The psychodynamic perspective is exemplified by the psychoanalytic theory of Freud and the psychosocial theory of Erikson. Freud focused attention on the unconscious and on stages through which children must pass successfully to avoid harmful fixations. Erikson identified eight distinct stages of development, each characterized by a conflict, or crisis, to work out.

- The behavioral perspective typically concerns stimulus–response learning, exemplified by classical conditioning, the operant conditioning of Skinner, and Bandura's social-cognitive learning theory.

- The cognitive perspective focuses on the processes that allow people to know, under-stand, and think about the world. For example, Piaget identified developmental stages through which all children are assumed to pass. Each stage involves qualitative differences in thinking. In contrast, information processing approaches attribute cognitive growth to quantitative changes in mental processes and capacities. Cognitive neuroscientists seek to identify locations and functions within the brain that are related to different types of cognitive activity.

- The contextual perspective stresses the interrelatedness of developmental areas and the importance of broad cultural factors in human development. Bronfenbrenner's ecologi-cal approach focuses on the microsystem, mesosystem, exosystem, macrosystem, and chronosystem. Vygotsky's sociocultural theory emphasizes the central influence on cognitive development exerted by social interactions between members of a culture.

- The evolutionary perspective attributes behavior to genetic inheritance from our ances-tors, contending that genes determine not only traits such as skin color and eye color but certain personality traits and social behaviors as well.

○ **What is the scientific method, and how does it help answer questions about child development?**

- The scientific method is the process of posing and answering questions using careful, con-trolled techniques that include systematic, orderly observation and the collection of data.

- Theories are broad explanations of facts or phenomena of interest, based on a systematic integration of prior findings and theories. Hypotheses are theory-based predictions that can be tested. Operationalization is the process of translating a hypothesis into specific, testable procedures that can be measured and observed.

- Researchers test hypotheses by correlational research (to determine if two factors are associated) and experimental research (to discover cause-and-effect relationships).

- Correlational studies use naturalistic observation, case studies, diaries, and survey re-search to investigate whether certain characteristics of interest are associated with other characteristics. Correlational studies lead to no direct conclusions about cause and effect.

- Typically, experimental research studies are conducted on participants in a treatment group, who receive the experimental treatment, and participants in a control group, who do not. Following the treatment, differences between the two groups can help the experimenter determine the effects of the treatment. Experiments may be conducted in a laboratory or in a real-world setting.

○ **What are the major research strategies and challenges?**

- Theoretical research is designed specifically to test some developmental explanation and expand scientific knowledge, whereas applied research is meant to provide practical solutions to immediate problems.

- To measure change at different ages, researchers use longitudinal studies of the same participants over time, cross-sectional studies of different-age participants conducted at one time, and cross-sequential studies of different-age participants at several points in time.

- Ethical guidelines for research include the protection of participants from harm, informed consent of participants, limits on the use of deception, and the maintenance of privacy.

EPILOGUE

his chapter examined the way developmentalists use theory and research to understand child development. We reviewed the broad approaches to children, examining the theories that each has produced. In addition, we looked at the ways in which research is conducted.

Before proceeding to the next chapter, think about the prologue of this chapter, about the Burke children, whose father was killed in the terrorist attack on the World Trade Center. Based on what you now know about theories and research, answer the following questions:

1. How might child developmentalists from the psychodynamic, behavioral, cognitive, contextual, and evolutionary perspectives explain how the children would be affected by the terrorist attack and the death of their father? What differences might there be in the questions that would interest them and the studies they might wish to conduct?

2. Formulate one hypothesis using either the behavioral or cognitive perspective about the effects on television viewers of witnessing the immediate aftermath of the terrorist attack.

3. Design a correlational study to test the hypothesis you generated in response to question 2.

4. Try to design an experimental study to test the hypothesis in question 2.

KEY TERMS AND CONCEPTS

theories (p. 23)

psychodynamic
    perspective (p. 23)

psychoanalytic
    theory (p. 23)

id (p. 23)

ego (p. 23)

superego (p. 23)

psychosexual
    development (p. 23)

fixation (p. 24)

psychosocial
    development (p. 24)

behavioral
    perspective (p. 25)

classical
   conditioning (p. 26)
operant
   conditioning (p. 26)
behavior
   modification (p. 26)
social-cognitive learning
   theory (p. 27)
cognitive
   perspective (p. 28)
assimilation (p. 28)
accommodation (p. 28)
information processing
   approaches (p. 29)
cognitive neuroscience
   approaches (p. 30)
contextual
   perspective (p. 30)

bioecological
   approach (p. 30)
sociocultural theory (p. 32)
evolutionary
   perspective (p. 34)
scientific method (p. 37)
hypothesis (p. 38)
operationalization (p. 38)
correlational
   research (p. 39)
experimental
   research (p. 39)
naturalistic
   observation (p. 41)
case studies (p. 41)
diaries (p. 41)
survey research (p. 41)
experiment (p. 42)

treatment (p. 42)
treatment group (p. 42)
control group (p. 42)
independent
   variable (p. 42)
dependent variable (p. 42)
sample (p. 43)
field study (p. 43)
laboratory study (p. 44)
theoretical
   research (p. 45)
applied research (p. 45)
longitudinal
   research (p. 47)
cross-sectional
   research (p. 47)
cross-sequential
   studies (p. 48)

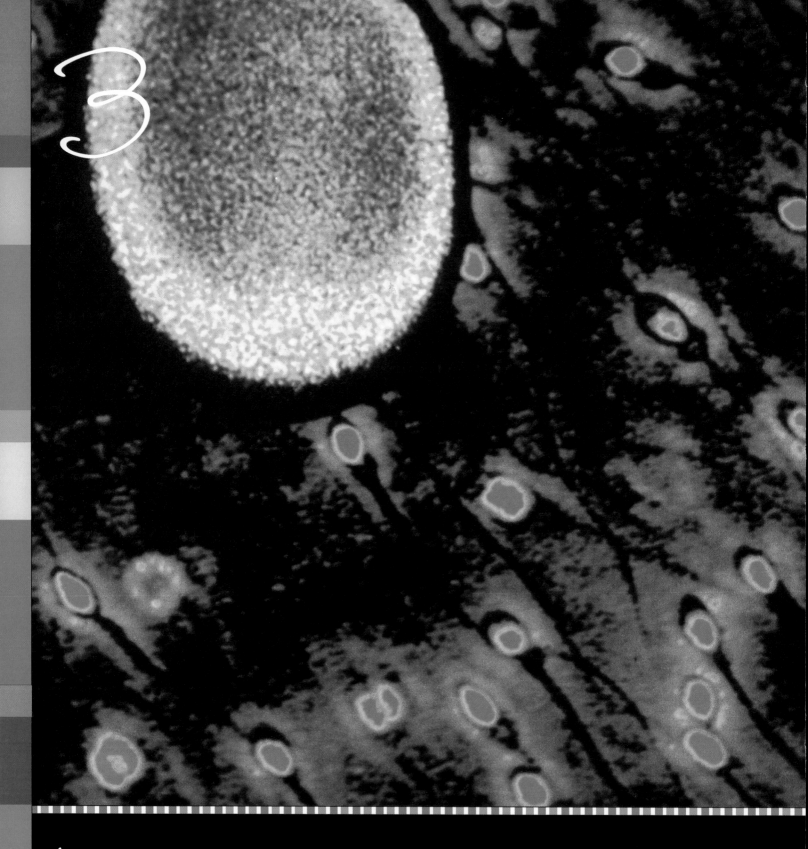

3

The Start of Life

PROLOGUE: Giant Steps

routine prenatal test brought Jennifer and Brian Buchkovich horrifying news: Their unborn baby, Ethan, was afflicted with spina bifida, a failure of the spine to close over the spinal cord. The birth defect, which affects 2,000 children a year, usually leads to paralysis and cognitive delays. But doctors offered the Windber, Pennsylvania, couple a glimmer of hope—an experimental operation designed to reduce the damage and to eliminate or delay the need for a surgically implanted shunt to drain excess fluid from the brain. The hitch: The surgery would have to be performed while Ethan was still inside Jennifer's womb. ("Giant Steps," 2000, p. 117)

Ethan Buchkovich and family

LOOKING **AHEAD** ▶

The Buchkoviches took the risk, and it appears to have paid off: Although Ethan has shown some developmental delays, he's just a bit behind schedule.

Operations on unborn children are becoming nearly routine as scientists learn more about the course of development prior to birth. In this chapter, we'll examine what developmental researchers and other scientists have learned about ways that heredity and the environment work in tandem to create and shape human beings. We begin with the basics of heredity, the genetic transmission of characteristics from biological parents to their children, by examining how we receive our genetic endowment. We'll consider a burgeoning area of study, behavioral genetics, that specializes in the consequences of heredity on behavior. We'll also discuss what happens when genetic factors cause development to go awry and how such problems are dealt with through genetic counseling and the brave new world of cloning and genetic engineering.

Next, we'll turn to a discussion of the interaction of heredity and environment. We'll consider the relative influence of genes and environment on a variety of characteristics, including physical traits, intelligence, and even personality.

Finally, we'll focus on the very first stage of development, prenatal growth and change. We'll see that prenatal growth begins at the moment of conception and review some of the alternatives available to couples who find it difficult to conceive. We'll also talk about the stages of the prenatal period and examine both the dangers and the promise of growth in the prenatal environment.

In sum, after reading this chapter, you will be able to answer these questions:

- **What is our basic genetic endowment, and how can human development go awry?**
- **How do the environment and genetics work together to determine human characteristics?**
- **Which human characteristics are significantly influenced by heredity?**
- **What happens during the prenatal stages of development?**
- **What are the threats to the fetal environment, and what can be done about them?**

Heredity

We humans begin the course of our lives simply. Like individuals from tens of thousands of other species, we start as a single cell, a tiny speck probably weighing no more than one twenty-millionth of an ounce. But from this humble beginning, human development follows its own unique path, accomplishing a journey that leads to the flowering of humankind's vast potential.

What determines the process that transforms the single cell into something that we can more easily identify as a person? The answer is the human *genetic code,* transmitted at the moment of conception from the mother and father and embedded in that single first cell.

Genes and Chromosomes: The Code of Life

Gene The basic unit of genetic information

DNA (deoxyribonucleic acid) The substance that genes are composed of that determines the nature of every cell in the body and how it will function

Our genetic code is stored and communicated in our **genes,** the basic units of genetic information. Genes are the biological equivalent of software that programs the future development of all parts of the body's "hardware."

Humans have some 30,000 genes. All genes are composed of specific sequences of **DNA (deoxyribonucleic acid)** molecules. They are arranged in specific locations and in a specific

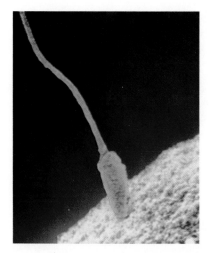

(a) Conception

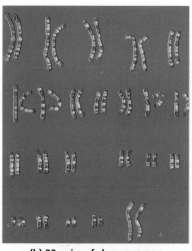

(b) 23 pairs of chromosomes

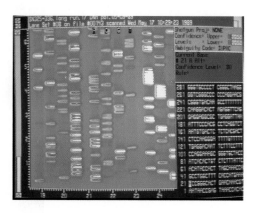

(c) A map of gene sequences

FIGURE 3-1   GENES AND CHROMOSOMES

At the moment of conception (a), humans receive 23 pairs of chromosomes, half from the mother and half from the father (b). These chromosomes contain thousands of genes, some of which are shown in the computer-generated map in (c).

order along rod-shaped portions of DNA—46 **chromosomes** that are organized in 23 pairs. A child's mother and father each provide one of the two chromosomes in each of the 23 pairs. At the moment of conception, or fertilization, the 23 maternal and 23 paternal chromosomes unite within a single new cell, called a **zygote.** The 46 chromosomes in the new zygote contain the genetic blueprint that will guide cell activity for the rest of the individual's life (Celera Genomics, 2001; Pennisi, 2000; see Figure 3-1). Through a process called *mitosis,* which accounts for the replication of most types of cells, nearly all the cells of the body will contain the same 46 chromosomes as the zygote.

Specific genes in precise locations on the chromosomes determine the nature and functioning of every cell in the body. For instance, genes determine which cells will ultimately become part of the heart and which will become part of the muscles of the leg. Genes also establish how different parts of the body will function—how rapidly the heart will beat or how much strength a muscle will have.

If each parent provides just 23 chromosomes, where does the potential for the vast diversity of human beings come from? The answer resides primarily in the nature of the processes that underlie the cell division of the gametes. When **gametes**—the sex cells, sperm and ova—are formed in the adult human body in a process called *meiosis,* each gamete receives one of the two chromosomes that make up each of the 23 pairs. Because for each of the 23 pairs it is largely a matter of chance which member of the pair is contributed, there are 2^{23}, or some 8 million, different combinations possible. Furthermore, other processes, such as random transformations of particular genes, add to the variability of the genetic brew. The ultimate outcome: tens of *trillions* of possible genetic combinations.

With so many possible genetic mixtures provided by heredity, there is no likelihood that someday you'll bump into a genetic duplicate of yourself—with one exception: an identical twin.

Multiple Births: Two—or More—for the Genetic Price of One.   Although it doesn't seem surprising when dogs and cats give birth to several offspring at one time, in humans multiple births are cause for comment. They should be: Less than 3 percent of all pregnancies produce twins, and the odds are much slimmer for three or more children.

Why do multiple births occur? Some occur when a cluster of cells in the ovum splits off within the first 2 weeks after fertilization. The result is two genetically identical zygotes,

Chromosomes   Rod-shaped portions of DNA that are organized in 23 pairs

Zygote   The new cell formed by the process of fertilization

Gametes   The sex cells from the mother and father that form a new cell at conception

Monozygotic and dizygotic twins present opportunities to learn about the relative contributions of heredity and situational factors. What kinds of things can psychologists learn from studying twins?

which, because they come from the same original zygote, are called *monozygotic.* **Monozygotic twins** are twins who are genetically identical. Any differences in their future development can be attributed only to environmental factors, since genetically they are exactly the same.

There is a second, and actually more common, mechanism that produces multiple births. In these cases, two separate ova are fertilized by two separate sperm at roughly the same time. Twins produced in this fashion are known as **dizygotic twins.** Because they are the result of two separate ovum–sperm combinations, they are no more genetically similar than two siblings born at different times.

Of course, not all multiple births produce only two babies. Triplets, quadruplets, and even more births are produced by either (or both) of the mechanisms that yield twins. Thus triplets may be some combination of monozygotic, dizygotic, or trizygotic.

Although the chances of having a multiple birth are typically slim, the odds rise considerably when couples use fertility drugs to improve the probability they will conceive a child. For example, 1 in 10 couples using fertility drugs has dizygotic twins, compared to an overall figure of 1 in 86 for Caucasian couples in the United States. Older women, too, are more likely to have multiple births, and multiple births are also more common in some families than in others. The increased use of fertility drugs and the rising average age of mothers giving birth has meant that multiple births have increased in the past 25 years (Lang, 1999; see Figure 3-2).

There are also racial, ethnic, and national differences in the rate of multiple births, probably due to inherited differences in the likelihood that more than one ovum will be released at a time. One out of 70 African American couples has a dizygotic birth, compared with the 1 out of 86 figure for white American couples (V. Vaughan, McKay, & Behrman, 1979; R. Wood, 1997).

Mothers carrying multiple children run a higher-than-average risk of premature delivery and birth complications. Consequently, these mothers must be particularly concerned about their prenatal care.

Boy or Girl? Establishing the Sex of the Child.   Recall that there are 23 matched pairs of chromosomes. In 22 of these pairs, each chromosome is similar to the other member of its pair. The one exception is the 23rd pair, which is the one that determines the sex of the child.

Monozygotic twins   Twins who are genetically identical

Dizygotic twins   Twins who are produced when two separate ova are fertilized by two separate sperm at roughly the same time

U.S. Birth of Twins per 1,000 Women

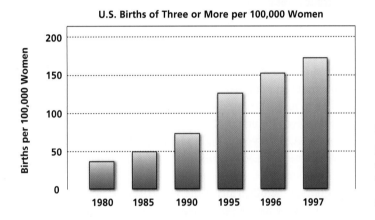

U.S. Births of Three or More per 100,000 Women

FIGURE 3-2   RISING MULTIPLE

Multiple births have increased significantly over the past 25 years. What are some of the reasons for this phenomenon?

(*Source:* J. A. Martin & Park, 1999)

In females, the 23rd pair consists of two matching, relatively large X-shaped chromosomes, appropriately identified as XX. In males, by contrast, the members of the pair are dissimilar. One consists of an X-shaped chromosome, but the other is a smaller Y-shaped chromosome. This pair is identified as XY. Since a female's 23rd pair of chromosomes are both Xs, an ovum will always carry an X chromosome. A male's 23rd pair is XY, so each sperm could carry either an X or a Y chromosome.

If the sperm contributes an X chromosome when it meets an ovum (which, remember, will always contribute an X chromosome), the child will have an XX pairing on the 23rd chromosome and will be a female. If the sperm contributes a Y chromosome, the result will be an XY pairing—a male (see Figure 3-3).

It is clear from this process that the father's sperm determines the gender of the child. This fact is leading to the development of techniques that will allow parents to increase the chances of specifying the gender of their child. In one new technique, lasers measure the DNA in sperm. By identifying and discarding sperm that harbor the unwanted sex chromosome, the chances of having a child of the desired sex increase dramatically (Belkin, 1999; Hayden, 1998).

Of course, procedures for choosing a child's sex raise ethical and practical issues. For example, in cultures that value one gender over the other, might there be a kind of gender discrimination prior to birth? Furthermore, a shortage of children of the less preferred sex might ultimately emerge. Many questions remain, then, before sex selection becomes routine.

The Basics of Genetics: The Mixing and Matching of Traits

What determined the color of your hair? Why are you tall or short? What made you suscepti-ble to hay fever? And why do you have so many freckles? To answer these questions, we need

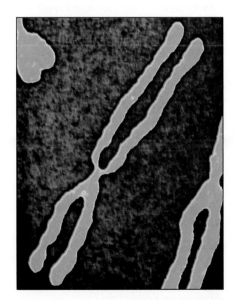

Not only is the X chromosome important in determining gender, but it is also the site of genes controlling other aspects of development.

Female   Male

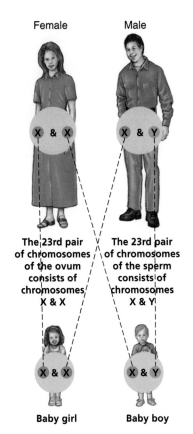

X & X   X & Y

The 23rd pair   The 23rd pair
of chromosomes   of chromosomes
of the ovum   of the sperm
consists of   consists of
chromosomes   chromosomes
X & X   X & Y

X & X   X & Y

Baby girl   Baby boy

FIGURE 3-3   DETERMINING SEX

When an ovum and sperm meet at the moment of fertilization, the ovum is certain to provide an X chromosome, while the sperm will provide either an X or a Y chromosome. If the sperm contributes its X chromosome, the child will have an XX pairing on the 23rd chromosome and will be a girl. If the sperm contributes a Y chromosome, the result will be an XY pairing—a boy. Does this mean that girls are more likely to be conceived than boys?

(CW)

Dominant trait   The one trait that is expressed when two competing traits are present

Recessive trait   A trait that is present in an organism but is not expressed

Genotype   The underlying combination of genetic material present (but not outwardly visible) in an organism

Phenotype   An observable trait; the trait that is actually seen

Homozygous   Inheriting from parents similar genes for a given trait

Heterozygous   Inheriting from parents different forms of a gene for a given trait

---

to consider the basic mechanisms involved in the way that the genes we inherit from our parents transmit information.

We can start by examining the discoveries of an Austrian monk, Gregor Mendel, in the mid-1800s. In a series of simple yet convincing experiments, Mendel cross-pollinated pea plants that always produced yellow seeds with pea plants that always produced green seeds. The result was not, as one might guess, a plant with a combination of yellow and green seeds or with yellow-green seeds. Instead, all of the resulting plants had yellow seeds. At first it appeared that the green-seeded plants had had no influence.

However, additional research on Mendel's part proved that this was not true. He bred together plants from the new, yellow-seeded generation that had resulted from his original cross-breeding of the green- and yellow-seeded plants. The consistent result was a ratio of three quarters yellow seeds to one quarter green seeds.

Why did this 3-to-1 ratio of yellow to green seeds appear so consistently? It was Mendel's genius to provide an answer. Based on his experiments with pea plants, he argued that when two competing *traits,* such as a green or yellow coloring of seeds, were both present, only one could be expressed. The one that was expressed was called a **dominant trait.** Meanwhile, the other trait remained present in the organism, although it was not expressed (displayed). This was called a **recessive trait.** In the case of Mendel's original pea plants, the offspring plants received genetic information from both the green- and yellow-seeded parents. However, the yellow trait was dominant, and consequently, the recessive green trait did not assert itself.

Keep in mind, however, that genetic material relating to both parent plants is present in the offspring, even though it cannot be seen. The genetic information is known as the organism's genotype. A **genotype** is the underlying combination of genetic material present (but outwardly invisible) in an organism. In contrast, a **phenotype** is the observable trait, the trait that actually is seen.

Although the offspring of the yellow-seeded and green-seeded pea plants all have yellow seeds (i.e., they have a yellow-seeded phenotype), the genotype consists of genetic information relating to both parents.

And what is the nature of the information in the genotype? To answer that question, let's turn from peas to people. In fact, the principles are the same not just for plants and humans but for the majority of species.

Recall that parents transmit genetic information to their offspring via the chromosomes they contribute through the gamete they provide during fertilization. Some of the genes form pairs called *alleles,* genes governing traits that may take alternate forms, such as hair or eye color. A child's allele may contain similar or dissimilar genes from each parent. If the child receives similar genes, he or she is said to be **homozygous** for the trait. If the child receives different forms of the gene from its parents, he or she is said to be **heterozygous.** In the case of heterozygous alleles, the dominant characteristic is expressed. However, if the child happens to receive a recessive allele from each parent and therefore lacks a dominant characteristic, the child will display the recessive characteristic.

Transmission of Genetic Information in Humans.   We can see this process at work in humans by considering the transmission of *phenylketonuria (PKU),* an inherited disorder in which a child is unable to make use of phenylalanine, an essential amino acid present in proteins found in milk and other foods. If left untreated, PKU allows phenylalanine to build up to toxic levels, causing brain damage and mental retardation.

PKU is produced by a single allele, or pair of genes. As shown in Figure 3-4, we can label each gene of the pair with a *P* if it carries a dominant gene, which causes the normal production of phenylalanine, or a *p* if it carries the recessive gene that produces PKU. In cases in which neither parent is a PKU carrier, both the mother's and the father's pairs of genes are the dominant form, symbolized as *PP.* Consequently, no matter which member of the pair is

a

Mother   Father

P P   P P

Does not carry recessive PKU gene   Does not carry recessive PKU gene

Mother contributes either P or P   Father contributes either P or P

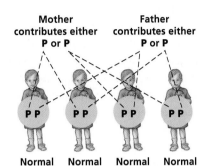

P P   P P   P P   P P

Normal   Normal   Normal   Normal

Result: No child can inherit PKU

b

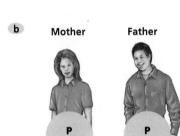

Mother   Father

P p   P P

Carries recessive PKU gene   Does not carry recessive PKU gene

Mother contributes either P or p   Father contributes either P or P

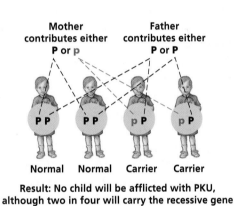

P P   P P   p P   p P

Normal   Normal   Carrier   Carrier

Result: No child will be afflicted with PKU, although two in four will carry the recessive gene

c

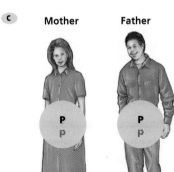

Mother   Father

P p   P p

Carries recessive PKU gene   Carries recessive PKU gene

Mother contributes either P or p   Father contributes either P or p

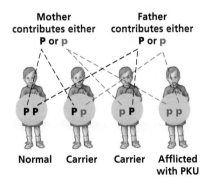

P P   P p   p P   p p

Normal   Carrier   Carrier   Afflicted with PKU

Result: One in four children will inherit two dominant genes and will not have PKU; two in four will inherit one recessive gene and not be afflicted with PKU but will carry the recessive gene; and one in four will have PKU

FIGURE 3-4 PKU PROBABILITIES

PKU, a disease that causes brain damage and mental retardation, is produced by a single pair of genes inherited from one's mother and father. If neither parent carries a gene for the disease (a), a child cannot develop PKU. Even if one parent carries the recessive gene but the other doesn't (b), the child cannot inherit the disease. However, if both parents carry the recessive gene (c), there is a one in four chance that the child will have PKU.

Gregor Mendel's pioneering experiments on pea plants provided the foundation for the study of genetics.

contributed by the mother and father, the resulting pair of genes in the child will be *PP*, and the child will not have PKU.

However, consider what happens if one of the parents has a recessive *p* gene. In this case, which we can symbolize as *Pp*, the parent will not have PKU, since the normal *P* gene is dominant. But the recessive gene can be passed down to the child. This is not so bad: If the child has only one recessive gene, he or she will not suffer from PKU. But what if both parents carry a recessive *p* gene? In this case, although neither parent has the disorder, it is possible for the child to receive a recessive gene from both parents. The child's genotype for PKU then will be *pp*, and he or she will have the disorder.

Remember, though, that even children whose parents both have the recessive gene for PKU have only a 25 percent chance of inheriting the disorder. Due to the laws of probability, 25 percent of children with *Pp* parents will receive the dominant gene from each parent (these children's genotype would be *PP*), and 50 percent will receive the dominant gene from one parent and the recessive gene from the other (their genotypes would be either *Pp* or *pP*). Only the unlucky 25 percent who receive the recessive gene from each parent and end up with the genotype *pp* will suffer from PKU.

The transmission of PKU illustrates the basic principles of how genetic information passes from parent to child. However, in some respects, the case of PKU is simpler than most cases of genetic transmission. Relatively few traits are governed by a single pair of genes. Instead, most traits are the result of polygenic inheritance. In **polygenic inheritance,** a combination of multiple gene pairs is responsible for the production of a particular trait.

Furthermore, some genes come in several alternate forms, and still others act to modify the way that particular genetic traits (produced by other alleles) are displayed. Genes also vary in terms of their *reaction range,* the potential degree of variability in the actual expression of a trait due to environmental conditions. And some traits, such as blood type, are produced by genes in which neither member of a pair of genes can be classified as purely dominant or recessive. Instead, the trait is expressed in terms of a combination of the two genes—as in type AB blood.

A number of recessive genes, called **X-linked genes,** are located only on the X chromosome. Recall that in females, the 23rd pair of chromosomes is an XX pair, while in males it is an XY pair. One result is that males have a higher risk for a variety of X-linked disorders, since males lack a second X chromosome that might counteract the genetic information that produces the disorder. For example, males are significantly more apt to have red-green color blindness, a disorder produced by a set of genes on the X chromosome.

Similarly, *hemophilia,* a blood disorder, is produced by X-linked genes. Hemophilia has been a recurrent problem in the royal families of Europe, as illustrated in Figure 3-5, which shows the inheritance of hemophilia in some of the descendants of Queen Victoria of Great Britain.

Polygenic inheritance   Inheritance in which a combination of multiple gene pairs is responsible for the production of a particular trait

X-linked genes   Genes that are considered recessive and located only on the X chromosome

FIGURE 3-5   INHERITING HEMOPHILIA

Hemophilia, a blood clotting disorder, has been an inherited problem throughout the royal families of Europe, as illustrated by the descendants of Queen Victoria of Britain.

(*Source:* Adapted from Kimball, 1983)

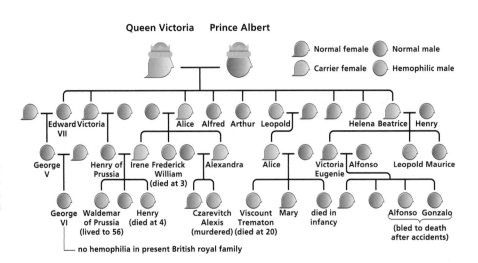

The Human Genome: Cracking the Genetic Code.   Mendel's achievements in recognizing the basics of genetic transmission of traits were trailblazing. However, they mark only the beginning of our understanding of the ways that particular sorts of characteristics are passed on from one generation to the next.

The most recent milestone in understanding genetics was reached in early 2001, when molecular biologists succeeded in mapping the specific sequence of genes on each chromosome. This accomplishment stands as one of the most important moments in the history of genetics and, for that matter, all of biology (Celera Genomics, 2001).

The mapping of the gene sequence has already provided important advances in our understanding of genetics. For instance, the number of human genes, long thought to be 100,000, has been revised downward to 30,000—not many more than organisms that are far less complex (see Figure 3-6). Furthermore, scientists have discovered that 99.9 percent of the gene sequence is shared by all humans, indicating that many of the differences that seemingly separate people—such as race—are, literally, only skin-deep. The mapping of the human genome will also help in the identification of particular disorders to which a given individual is susceptible (Carpenter, 2000; Celera Genomics, 2001; D. H. Levy, 2000).

The mapping of the human gene sequence is supporting the rapidly burgeoning field of behavioral genetics. As the name implies, **behavioral genetics** studies the effects of heredity on behavior. Rather than simply examining stable, unchanging characteristics such as hair or eye color, behavioral genetics takes a broader approach, considering how our personality and behavioral habits are affected by genetic factors. Behavioral genetics merges the interests of psychologists, who focus on the causes of behavior, with those of geneticists, who focus on the processes that permit the transmission of characteristics through heredity (Dick & Rose, 2002; McGuffin, Riley, & Plomin, 2001).

The promise of behavioral genetics is substantial. For one thing, researchers working in the field have gained a better understanding of the specifics of the genetic code that underlie human behavior and development. Such advances have provided knowledge of the workings of genetics at a molecular and chemical level. Furthermore, scientists are learning how various behavioral difficulties, including psychological disorders such as schizophrenia, may have a genetic basis (Conklin & Iacono, 2002; see Table 3-1).

Even more important, researchers are seeking to identify how genetic defects may be remedied (Peltonen & McKusick, 2001; Plomin & Rutter, 1998). To understand how that possibility

APPROXIMATE NUMBERS OF GENES

FIGURE 3-6   UNIQUELY HUMAN?

Once thought to contain more than 100,000 genes, humans actually have about 30,000 genes, making them not much more genetically complex than some primitive species.

(*Source:* Celera Genomics, 2001)

Estimated percentage of each creature's total genes found in humans are indicated by the dotted line.

Behavioral genetics   The study of the effects of heredity on behavior

TABLE 3-1 CURRENT UNDERSTANDING OF THE GENETIC BASIS OF SELECTED BEHAVIORAL DISORDERS AND TRAITS	
Behavioral Trait	**Current Ideas of Genetic Basis**
Huntington's disease	Huntington gene has been identified.
Early onset (familial) Alzheimer's disease	Three distinct genes have been identified.
Fragile X mental retardation	Two genes have been identified.
Late-onset Alzheimer's disease	One allele has been associated with increased risk.
Attention-deficit hyperactivity disorder	Three locations related to the genetics involved with the neurotransmitter dopamine may contribute.
Dyslexia	Relationships to two locations, on chromosomes 6 and 15, have been suggested.
Schizophrenia	There is no consensus, but links to numerous chromosomes, including 1, 5, 6, 10, 13, 15, and 22, have been reported.

(*Source:* Adapted from McGuffin, Riley, & Plomin, 2001)

might come about, we need to consider the ways in which genetic factors, which normally cause development to proceed so smoothly, may falter.

Inherited and Genetic Disorders: When Development Goes Awry

PKU is just one of several disorders that may be inherited. Like a bomb that is harmless until its fuse is lit, a recessive gene responsible for a disorder may be passed on unknowingly from one generation to the next, revealing itself only when, by chance, it is paired with another recessive gene. It is only when two recessive genes come together like a match and a fuse that the gene will express itself and a child will inherit the genetic disorder.

But there is another way that genes are a source of concern: In some cases, genes become physically damaged. For instance, genes may break down due to wear-and-tear or chance events occurring during the cell division processes of meiosis and mitosis. Sometimes genes, for no known reason, spontaneously change their form, a process called *spontaneous mutation.* Alternatively, certain environmental factors, such as exposure to X-rays, may produce a malformation of genetic material. When such damaged genes are passed on to a child, the results can be disastrous in terms of future physical and cognitive development.

In addition to PKU, which occurs once in 10,000 to 20,000 births, other inherited and genetic disorders include the following:

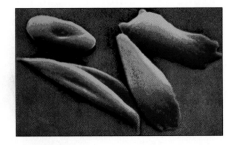

Sickle-cell anemia, named for the presence of misshapen red blood cells, is carried in the genes of 1 in 10 African Americans.

Down syndrome A disorder produced by the presence of an extra chromosome on the 21st pair; formerly referred to as mongolism

Fragile X syndrome A disorder that occurs when a particular gene is injured on the X chromosome, resulting in mild to moderate mental retardation

Sickle-cell anemia A blood disorder that gets its name from the shape of the red blood cells in those who have it

Tay-Sachs disease A disorder for which there is no treatment that produces blindness, muscle degeneration, and early death

Klinefelter's syndrome A disorder resulting from the presence of an extra X chromosome that produces underdeveloped genitals, extreme height, and enlarged breasts

- *Down syndrome.* As noted earlier, most people have 46 chromosomes, arranged in 23 pairs. One exception is individuals with **Down syndrome,** a disorder produced by the presence of an extra chromosome on the 21st pair. Once referred to as mongolism, Down syndrome is the most frequent cause of mental retardation. It occurs in about 1 out of 500 births, although the risk is much greater in mothers who are unusually young or old (J. Carr, 1995; Cicchetti & Beeghly, 1990).

- *Fragile X syndrome.* **Fragile X syndrome** occurs when a particular gene is injured on the X chromosome. The result is mild to moderate mental retardation.

- *Sickle-cell anemia.* Around one tenth of the African American population carries genes that produce sickle-cell anemia, and 1 African American in 400 actually has the disease. **Sickle-cell anemia** is a blood disorder that gets its name from the shape of the red blood cells in those who have it. Symptoms include episodes of pain in which red blood cells clump in the blood vessels, poor appetite, stunted growth, and yellowish eyes. People afflicted with the most severe form of the disease rarely live beyond childhood. However, for those with less severe cases, medical advances have produced significant increases in life expectancy (Leary, 1995).

- *Tay-Sachs disease.* Occurring mainly in Jews of eastern European ancestry and French Canadians, **Tay-Sachs disease** usually causes death before its victims reach school age. There is no treatment for the disorder, which produces blindness and muscle degeneration prior to death.

- *Klinefelter's syndrome.* One male out of every 400 is born with **Klinefelter's syndrome,** the presence of an extra X chromosome. The resulting XXY complement produces underdeveloped genitals, extreme height, and enlarged breasts. Klinfelter's syndrome is one of a number of genetic abnormalities that result from receiving the improper number of sex chromosomes. For instance, there are disorders produced by an extra Y chromosome (XYY), a missing second chromosome (called *Turner syndrome*), and three X chromosomes (XXX). Such disorders are typically characterized by problems relating to sexual characteristics and by intellectual deficits (K. Sorensen, 1992; Sotos, 1997).

It is important to keep in mind that the mere fact that a disorder has genetic roots does not mean that environmental factors do not also play a role (Moldin & Gottesman, 1997). Consider, for instance, sickle-cell anemia, which primarily afflicts people of African descent. Because the disease can be fatal in childhood, we'd expect that those who suffer from it would be unlikely to live long enough to pass it on. And this does seem to be true, at least in the United States: Compared with parts of West Africa, the incidence in the United States is much lower.

But why shouldn't the incidence of sickle-cell anemia also be gradually reduced for people in West Africa? This question proved puzzling for many years until scientists determined that carrying the sickle-cell gene increases immunity to malaria, which is a common disease in West Africa (Allison, 1954). This heightened immunity meant that people with the sickle-cell gene had a genetic advantage (in terms of resistance to malaria) that offset, to some degree, the disadvantage of being a carrier of the sickle-cell gene.

The lesson of sickle-cell anemia is that genetic factors are intertwined with environmental considerations and can't be looked at in isolation. Furthermore, we need to remember that although we've been focusing on inherited factors that can go awry, in the vast majority of cases, the genetic mechanisms with which we are endowed work quite well. Overall, around 95 percent of children born in the United States are healthy and normal. For the 250,000 or so who are born with some sort of physical or mental disorder, appropriate intervention often can help treat and in some cases cure the problem.

Moreover, due to advances in behavioral genetics, genetic difficulties can increasingly be forecast, anticipated, and planned for before a child's birth. Recall, for example, Ethan Buchkovich, described in the chapter prologue, whose parents not only learned about his spina bifida before his birth but were even able to take steps before he was born to reduce the severity of his condition. In fact, as scientists' knowledge regarding the specific location of particular genes expands, predictions of what the genetic future may hold are becoming increasingly exact, as we discuss next (Plomin & Rutter, 1998).

Prenatal Assessment and Genetic Counseling: Predicting Future Development

> The last thing Joey Paulowsky needs is another bout with cancer. Only 7 years old, the Dallas native has already fought off leukemia, and now his family worries that Joey could be hit again. The Paulowsky family carries a genetic burden—a rare form of inherited cancer of the thyroid. Deborah, his mother, found a lump in her neck six years ago, and since then one family member has died of the cancer and 10 others have had to have their thyroids removed. "Do I have cancer?" Joey asks his mother. "Will it hurt?" The Paulowskys will know the answer next month, when the results of a genetic test will show whether their son carries the family's fateful mutation. (Brownlee, Cook, & Hardigg, 1994, p. 59)

The answer will be delivered by a member of a field that just a few decades ago was nonexistent: genetic counseling. **Genetic counseling** focuses on helping people deal with issues relating to inherited disorders.

Genetic counselors use a variety of data in their work. For instance, couples contemplating having a child may seek to determine the risks involved in a future pregnancy. In such a case, a counselor will take a thorough family history, seeking any familial incidence of birth defects that might indicate a pattern of recessive or X-linked genes. In addition, the counselor will take into account factors such as the age of the mother and father and any previous abnormalities in other children they may have already had.

Typically, genetic counselors suggest a thorough physical examination. Such an exam may identify physical abnormalities that potential parents may have and not be aware of. In addition, samples of blood, skin, and urine may be used to isolate and examine specific chromosomes. Possible genetic defects, such as the presence of an extra sex chromosome, can be identified by assembling a *karyotype,* a chart containing enlarged photos of each of the chromosomes.

Prenatal Testing.   If the woman is already pregnant, there are a variety of techniques to assess the health of her unborn child (see Table 3-2 for a list of currently available tests). For

Genetic counseling The discipline that focuses on helping people deal with issues relating to inherited disorders

TABLE 3-2   FETAL DEVELOPMENT MONITORING TECHNIQUES

Technique	Description
Amniocentesis	Done between the 15th and 18th week of pregnancy, this procedure examines a sample of the amniotic fluid, which contains fetal cells. Recommended if either parent carries Tay-Sachs, spina bifida, sickle-cell, Down syndrome, muscular dystrophy, or Rh disease.
Chorionic villus sampling (CVS)	Done at 8 to 11 weeks, either transabdominally or transcervically, depending on where the placenta is located. Involves inserting a needle (abdominally) or a catheter (cervically) into the substance of the placenta but staying outside the amniotic sac and removing 10 to 15 milligrams of tissue. This tissue is manually cleaned of maternal uterine tissue and then grown in culture, and a karyotype is made, as with amniocentesis.
Embryoscopy	Examines the embryo or fetus during the first 12 weeks of pregnancy by means of a fiber-optic endoscope inserted through the cervix. Can be performed as early as week 5. Access to the fetal circulation may be obtained through the instrument, and direct visualization of the embryo permits the diagnosis of malformations.
Fetal blood sampling (FBS)	Performed after 18 weeks of pregnancy by collecting a small amount of blood from the umbilical cord for testing. Used to detect Down syndrome and most other chromosome abnormalities in the fetuses of couples who are at increased risk of having an affected child. Many other diseases can be diagnosed using this technique.
Sonoembryology	Used to detect abnormalities in the first trimester of pregnancy. Involves high-frequency transvaginal probes and digital image processing. In combination with ultrasound, can detect more than 80 percent of all malformations during the second trimester.
Sonogram	Uses ultrasound to produce a visual image of the uterus, fetus, and placenta.
Ultrasound	Uses very high frequency sound waves to detect structural abnormalities or multiple pregnancies, measure fetal growth, judge gestational age, and evaluate uterine abnormalities. Also used as an adjunct to other procedures such as amniocentesis.

Amniocentesis   The process of identifying genetic defects by examining a small sample of fetal cells drawn by a needle inserted into the amniotic fluid surrounding the unborn fetus

Chorionic villus sampling (CVS)   A test used to find genetic defects that involves taking samples of hairlike material that surrounds the embryo

example, in **amniocentesis,** a small sample of fetal cells is drawn through a tiny needle inserted into the amniotic fluid surrounding the unborn fetus. By analyzing the fetal cells, technicians can identify a variety of genetic defects. In addition, they can determine the sex of the child. Although there is always a danger to the fetus in such an invasive procedure, amniocentesis is generally safe when carried out between the 12th and 16th week of pregnancy.

An additional test, **chorionic villus sampling (CVS),** can be employed even earlier. The test involves taking small samples of hairlike material that surrounds the embryo. CVS can be done between the 8th and 11th week of pregnancy. However, because it is riskier than amniocentesis and can identify fewer genetic problems, its use is relatively infrequent.

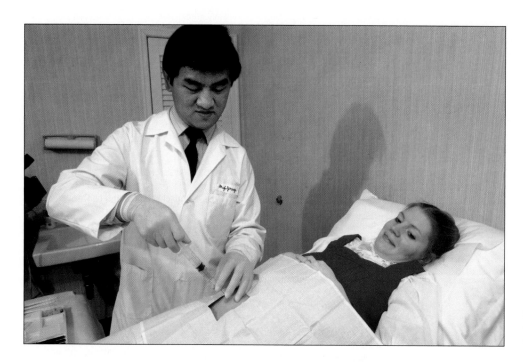

In amniocentesis, a sample of fetal cells is withdrawn from the amniotic sac and used to identify a number of genetic defects.

Other tests that are less invasive and therefore less risky are also possible. For instance, the unborn child may be examined through **ultrasound sonography,** in which high-frequency sound waves are used to bombard the mother's womb. These waves produce a rather indistinct but useful image of the unborn baby, whose size and shape can then be assessed. Repeated use of ultrasound sonography as the pregnancy progresses can reveal developmental patterns.

After the various tests are complete and all possible information is available, the couple will meet with the genetic counselor again. Typically, counselors avoid giving specific recommendations. Instead, they lay out the facts and, if fetal defects are found, present various options, ranging from doing nothing to taking more drastic steps, such as terminating the pregnancy through abortion. Ultimately, it is the parents who must decide what course of action to follow.

Genetic Testing in the Larger Population.   The newest role of genetic counselors involves testing people to identify whether they themselves, rather than their children, are susceptible to future disorders because of genetic abnormalities. For instance, *Huntington's disease,* a devastating, always fatal disorder marked by tremors and intellectual deterioration, typically does not appear until people reach their 40s. However, genetic testing can identify much earlier whether a person carries the flawed gene that produces Huntington's disease. Presumably, people's knowledge that they carry the gene can help them prepare themselves for the future (van 't Spijker & ten Kroode, 1997).

In addition to Huntington's disease, more than 450 disorders can be predicted on the basis of genetic testing (see Table 3-3). Although such testing may bring welcome relief from future worries if the results are negative, positive results may produce just the opposite effect. In fact, genetic testing raises difficult practical and ethical questions (Haederle, 1999; Holtzman et al., 1997; Kenen et al., 2000; Meiser & Dunn, 2000; Painter, 1997).

Suppose, for instance, that a person who thought she was susceptible to Huntington's disease was tested in her 20s and found that she did not carry the defective gene. Obviously, she would experience tremendous relief. But suppose she found that she did carry the flawed gene and was therefore going to get the disease. She might well experience depression and remorse. In fact, some studies show that 10 percent of people who find they have the flawed gene that leads to Huntington's disease never fully recover emotionally (Groopman, 1998; G. Hamilton, 1998; R. Nowak, 1994a).

Ultrasound sonography   A process in which high-frequency sound waves scan the mother's womb to produce an image of the unborn baby, whose size and shape can then be assessed

TABLE 3-3   SOME CURRENTLY AVAILABLE DNA-BASED GENE TESTS

Disease	Description
Adult polycystic kidney disease	Kidney failure and liver disease
Alpha-1-antitrypsin deficiency	Emphysema and liver disease
Alzheimer's disease	Late-onset variety of senile dementia
Amyotrophic lateral sclerosis (Lou Gehrig's disease)	Progressive motor function loss leading to paralysis and death
Ataxia telangiectasia	Progressive brain disorder resulting in loss of muscle control and cancers
Breast and ovarian cancer (inherited)	Early-onset tumors of breasts and ovaries
Charcot-Marie-Tooth	Loss of feeling in ends of limbs
Congenital adrenal hyperplasia	Hormone deficiency; ambiguous genitalia and male pseudohermaphroditism
Cystic fibrosis	Thick mucus accumulations in lungs and chronic infections in lungs and pancreas
Duchenne muscular dystrophy (Becker muscular dystrophy)	Severe to mild muscle wasting, deterioration, weakness
Dystonia	Muscle rigidity, repetitive twisting movements
Factor V-Leiden	Blood-clotting disorder
Fanconi anemia, group	Anemia, leukemia, skeletal deformities
Fragile X syndrome	Mental retardation
Gaucher disease	Enlarged liver and spleen, bone degeneration
Hemophilia A and B	Bleeding disorders
Hereditary nonpolyposis colon cancer[a]	Early-onset tumors of colon and sometimes other organs
Huntington's disease	Progressive neurological degeneration, usually beginning in midlife
Myotonic dystrophy	Progressive muscle weakness
Neurofibromatosis, type 1	Multiple benign nervous system tumors that can be disfiguring; cancers
Phenylketonuria	Progressive mental retardation due to missing enzyme; correctable by diet
Prader Willi/Angelman syndromes	Decreased motor skills, cognitive impairment, early death
Sickle-cell disease	Blood cell disorder; chronic pain and infections
Spinal muscular atrophy	Severe, usually lethal progressive muscle-wasting disorder in children
Spinocerebellar ataxia, type 1	Involuntary muscle movements, reflex disorders, explosive speech
Tay-Sachs disease	Seizures, paralysis; fatal neurological disease of early childhood
Thalassemias	Anemias

[a]These are susceptibility tests that provide only an estimated risk for developing the disorder.

(*Source:* Human Genome Project, 1998)

— FROM RESEARCH TO PRACTICE —

A Small Step by ANDi: Genetic Engineering, Gene Therapy, and Cloning

In all ways he looks like an ordinary rhesus monkey. But in one respect, this monkey is unique: He is the first genetically modified primate. Named ANDi (for "Inserted DNA" in reverse), the monkey was the recipient of a gene taken from jellyfish. Scientists inserted the gene into monkey eggs and fertilized the modified eggs with monkey sperm in the lab. Ultimately, three baby monkeys were born, one of which—ANDi—included the new gene in his DNA (W. S. Chan et al., 2001).

ANDi is the result of genetic engineering. He joins the fruit flies, rabbits, sheep, and cows that now carry genes from other species. Other genetically engineered animals have been produced that are exact genetic replicas, or *clones,* of members of the same species (Kolata, 1998; Lanza et al., 2001; Pennisi & Vogel, 2000).

The technological advance that ANDi represents takes us one step farther down the road toward genetic engineering in humans. Genetic engineering has the potential to go beyond the kind of prenatal surgery used in the case of Ethan Buchkovich described in the chapter prologue to allow scientists to correct genetic flaws well before an individual is born.

Genetic engineering is likely to revolutionize medicine in the 21st century. Already, some forms of gene therapy are being used to correct genetic defects in humans after they are born. In *gene therapy,* genes that are targeted to correct a particular disease are injected into a patient's bloodstream. When the genes arrive at the site of the defective genes that are causing the disease, their presence leads to the production of chemicals that can treat the problem. For instance, in the case of cancer, corrective genes might be engineered to produce proteins that could kill tumor cells. In other cases, new genes can be added to make up for missing or ineffective cells (Kmiec, 1999; Levy, 2000).

The list of diseases currently being treated through gene therapy is still relatively short, although the number is growing. For instance, experiments using gene therapy are now being employed for cystic fibrosis, hemophilia, rheumatoid arthritis, AIDS, and several other diseases. When such treatments will move from the experimental to the routine, however, remains to be seen (Begley, 1998).

Advances in genetic engineering promise to make gene therapy even more useful. In a process called *germ-line gene therapy,* genetic modifications can correct problems not only for unborn

The first patient ever to receive gene therapy was Ashanti De Silva, a 4-year-old with a rare, inherited disease called **severe combined immunodeficiency (SCID),** which caused her immune system to shut down. Consequently, she was continually susceptible to a huge number of infections. To remedy the situation, scientists removed some white blood cells from Ashanti's immune system and inserted non-diseased copies of the defective gene. Five years later, Ashanti was a normal 9-year-old with no immune-system problems (W. F. Anderson, 1995).

In a feat of genetic engineering, ANDi (for inserted DNA in reverse) is a Rhesus monkey containing the gene of a jellyfish.

individuals but for future generations as well. In germ-line gene therapy, scientists might "harvest" defective cells soon after conception, removing them from the fertilized egg within the mother and placing them in a test-tube culture. Gene therapy could be employed to correct the defects in the cells. Next, one of the corrected cells—a slightly altered clone of the initial cells—could be returned to the mother. In a more extreme possibility, cells from one parent might be altered genetically to remove any defects, and this clone could then be permitted to grow. The result would be a clone, genetically identical to the parent except for the lack of the genetic defect. Obviously, such possibilities raise serious ethical questions (Wilmut, 1998; Zanjani & Anderson, 1999).

Will the technology that is making gene therapy possible lead to the ultimate science-fiction feat: cloning a complete human being? Some scientists are beginning to think so, for use in such cases as when a husband and wife who are both infertile wish to clone themselves in order to have genetically related children. Although important technological hurdles remain to be overcome before cloning will be routine, the confidence of researchers appears to have spurred political leaders to think about the ethical and moral consequences of cloning. Most Americans oppose the cloning of human embryos, and laws limiting human cloning have already been enacted (Gordon, 1999; Saad, 2002; Stolberg, 2001).

Genetic testing is clearly a complicated issue. It rarely provides a simple yes or no answer as to whether an individual will be susceptible to a disorder. Instead, it typically presents a range of probabilities. In some cases, the likelihood of actually becoming ill depends on the type of environmental stressors to which a person is exposed. Personal differences also affect a given person's susceptibility to a disorder (Holtzman et al., 1997; Patenaude, Guttmacher, & Collins, 2002).

As our understanding of genetics continues to grow, researchers and medical practitioners have moved beyond testing and counseling to actively working to change flawed genes. The possibilities for genetic intervention and manipulation increasingly border on what once was science fiction—as we consider in the accompanying *From Research to Practice* box about cloning.

REVIEW & APPLY

Review

- In humans, the male sex cell (the sperm) and the female sex cell (the ovum) each provide the developing baby with 23 chromosomes.

- A genotype is the underlying combination of genetic material present in an organism but not visible; a phenotype is the visible trait, the expression of the genotype.

- The field of behavioral genetics, a combination of psychology and genetics, studies the effects of genetics on behavior.

- Several inherited and genetic disorders are due to damaged or mutated genes.

- Genetic counselors use a variety of data and techniques to advise future parents of possible genetic risks to their unborn children.

Applying Child Development

- What are some ethical and philosophical questions surrounding the issue of genetic counseling? Might it sometimes be unwise to know ahead of time about possible genetically linked disorders that might afflict your child or yourself?

● *From the perspective of a health care provider:* How might the study of identical twins who were separated at birth help determine the effects of genetic and environmental factors on a medical disorder? How might you design such a study?

The Interaction of Heredity and Environment

Like many other parents, Jared's mother, Leesha, and his father, Jamal, tried to figure out which one of them their new baby resembled more. He seemed to have Leesha's big, wide eyes and Jamal's generous smile. As he grew, Jared grew to resemble his mother and father even more. His hair grew in with a hairline just like Leesha's, and his teeth, when they came, made his smile resemble Jamal's even more. He also seemed to act like his parents. For example, he was a charming little baby, always ready to smile at people who visited the house—just like his friendly, jovial dad. He seemed to sleep like his mom, which was lucky, since Jamal was an extremely light sleeper who could do with as little as 4 hours a night, while Leesha liked a regular 7 or 8 hours.

Were Jared's ready smile and regular sleeping habits something he just luckily inherited from his parents? Or did Jamal and Leesha provide a happy and stable home that encouraged these welcome traits? What causes our behavior, nature or nurture? Is behavior produced by inherited, genetic influences, or is it triggered by factors in the environment?

The simple answer is: There is no simple answer.

The Role of the Environment in Determining the Expression of Genes: From Genotypes to Phenotypes

As developmental research accumulates, it is becoming increasingly clear that to view behavior as due to *either* genetic *or* environmental factors is inappropriate. A given behavior is not caused by genetic factors alone, nor is it caused solely by environmental forces. Instead, as we first discussed in Chapter 1, the behavior is the product of some combination of the two (Rutter et al., 1997).

For instance, consider **temperament,** patterns of arousal and emotionality that represent consistent and enduring characteristics in an individual. Suppose we found—as increasing evidence suggests is the case—that a small percentage of children are born with temperaments that produce an unusual degree of physiological reactivity. Having a tendency to shrink from anything unusual, such infants react to novel stimuli with a rapid increase in heartbeat and unusual excitability of the limbic system of the brain. Such heightened reactivity to stimuli at the start of life, which seems to be linked to inherited factors, is also likely to cause children, by the time they are 4 or 5, to be considered shy by their parents and teachers. But not always; some of them behave indistinguishably from their peers at the same age (Kagan & Snidman, 1991; McCrae et al., 2000).

What makes the difference? The answer seems to be the environment in which the children are raised. Children whose parents encourage them to be outgoing by arranging new opportunities for them may overcome their shyness. In contrast, children raised in a stressful environment marked by marital discord or a prolonged illness may be more likely to retain their shyness later in life (Joseph, 1999; Kagan, Arcus, & Snidman, 1993; Pedlow et al., 1993). Jared, described earlier, may have been born with an easy temperament, which was easily reinforced by his caring parents.

Such findings illustrate that many traits reflect **multifactorial transmission,** meaning that they are determined by a combination of both genetic and environmental factors. In

Temperament Patterns of arousal and emotionality that are consistent and enduring characteristics in an individual

Multifactorial transmission The determination of traits by a combination of both genetic and environmental factors in which a genotype provides a range within which a phenotype may be expressed

multifactorial transmission, a genotype provides a particular range within which a phenotype may achieve expression. For instance, people with a genotype that permits them to gain weight easily may never be slim, no matter how much they diet. They may be *relatively* slim, given their genetic heritage, but they may never be able to get beyond a certain degree of thinness (Faith, Johnson, & Allison, 1997). In many cases, then, it is the environment that determines the way in which a particular genotype will be expressed as a phenotype (Plomin, 1994a; Wachs, 1992, 1993, 1996).

On the other hand, certain genotypes are relatively unaffected by environmental factors. In such cases, development follows a preordained pattern, relatively independent of the specific environment in which a person is raised. For instance, research on pregnant women who were severely malnourished during famines caused by World War II found that their children were, on average, unaffected physically or intellectually as adults (Z. Stein et al., 1975). Similarly, no matter how much health food people eat, they are not going to grow beyond certain genetically imposed limitations in height. Little Jared's hairline was probably very little affected by any actions on the part of his parents.

Ultimately, of course, it is the unique interaction of inherited and environmental factors that determines people's patterns of development. As Jerome Kagan and colleagues (1993, p. 209) write:

> No human quality, psychological or physiological, is free of the contribution of events both within and outside the organism. . . . Every psychological quality is like a pale gray fabric woven from thin black threads, which represent biology, and thin white ones, which represent experience. But it is not possible to detect any quite black or white threads in the gray cloth.

The more appropriate question, then, is *how much* of the behavior is caused by genetic factors and *how much* by environmental factors. (See, for example, the range of possibilities for the determinants of intelligence illustrated in Figure 3-7.)

Answering the Nature–Nurture Riddle

Developmental researchers have used several strategies to try to resolve the question of the degree to which traits, characteristics, and behavior are produced by genetic or environmental factors. In seeking a resolution, they have turned to studies involving both nonhuman species and humans (Collins et al., 2000; Plomin, 1994a; Wahlsten & Gottlieb, 1997).

Nature ➤➤➤				Nurture
Intelligence is provided entirely by genetic factors; environment plays no role. Even a highly enriched environment and excellent education make no difference.	Although largely inherited, intelligence is affected by an extremely enriched or deprived environment.	Intelligence is affected both by a person's genetic endowment and environment. A person genetically predisposed to low intelligence may perform better if raised in an enriched environment or worse in a deprived environment. Similarly, a person genetically predisposed to higher intelligence may perform worse in a deprived environment or better in an enriched environment.	Although intelligence is largely a result of environment, genetic abnormalities may produce mental retardation.	Intelligence depends entirely on the environment. Genetics plays no role in determining intellectual success.

Possible Causes

FIGURE 3-7   POSSIBLE CAUSES OF INTELLIGENCE

Intelligence may be explained by a range of possible causes, spanning the nature–nurture continuum. Which of these explanations do you find most convincing, given the evidence discussed in this chapter?

Nonhuman Studies: Controlling Both Genetics and Environment.   One approach to understanding the relative contribution of heredity and environment makes use of animals. It is relatively simple to develop breeds of animals that are genetically similar to one another in terms of specific traits. The people who raise Butterball turkeys for Thanksgiving do it all the time, producing turkeys that grow especially rapidly so that they can be brought to market inexpensively. Similarly, strains of laboratory animals can be bred to share similar genetic backgrounds.

By observing animals with similar genetic backgrounds in different environments, scientists can determine, with reasonable precision, the effects of specific kinds of environmental stimulation. Conversely, researchers can examine groups of animals that have been bred to have significantly *different* genetic backgrounds on particular traits. Then by exposing such animals to identical environments, they can determine the role that genetic background plays.

Of course, the drawback to using nonhumans as research subjects is that we can't be sure how well the findings we obtain can be generalized to people. Still, the opportunities that animal research offers are substantial.

Human Studies: Exploiting Genetic Similarities and Dissimilarities.   Obviously, researchers can't control either the genetic backgrounds or the environments of humans in the way they can with nonhumans. However, nature has conveniently provided the potential to carry out various kinds of "natural experiments" in the form of twins.

Recall that monozygotic twins share an identical genetic code. Because their inherited backgrounds are precisely the same, any variations in their behavior must be due entirely to environmental factors.

In a world devoid of ethics, it would be rather simple for researchers to make use of identical twins to draw unequivocal conclusions about the roles of nature and nurture. For instance, by separating identical twins at birth and placing them in totally different environments, researchers could assess the impact of environment unambiguously. Obviously, ethical considerations make this impossible. However, there are a number of cases in which identical twins are put up for adoption at birth and are raised in substantially different environments. Such instances allow us to draw fairly confident conclusions about the relative contributions of genetics and environment (Bailey et al., 2000; T. J. Bouchard & Pedersen, 1999).

Still, the data from monozygotic twins raised in different environments are not always without bias. Adoption agencies typically take the characteristics (and wishes) of birth mothers into account when they place babies in adoptive homes. For instance, children tend to be placed with families of the same race and religion. Consequently, even when monozygotic twins are placed in different adoptive homes, there are often similarities in the two home environments. The consequence is that researchers can't always unambiguously attribute differences in behavior to genetics or environment.

Dizygotic twins, too, present opportunities to learn about the relative contributions of heredity and situational factors. Recall that dizygotic twins are genetically no more similar than siblings in a family born at different times. It is possible to compare behavior within pairs of dizygotic twins with that of pairs of monozygotic twins (who are genetically identical). If monozygotic twins are more similar on a particular trait, on average, than dizygotic twins, we can assume that genetics plays an important role in determining the expression of that trait (e.g., P. Schulman, Keith, & Seligman, 1993).

Still another approach is to study people who are totally unrelated to one another and who therefore have dissimilar genetic backgrounds but share an environmental background. For instance, a family that adopts, at the same time, two very young unrelated children will probably provide them with quite similar environments throughout their childhood. In this case, similarities in the children's characteristics and behavior can be attributed with some confidence to environmental influences (N. L. Segal, 1993, 2000).

Finally, developmental researchers have examined groups of people in light of their degree of genetic similarity. For instance, if we find a high association on a particular trait between biological parents and their children but a weaker association between adoptive parents and their children, we have evidence for the importance of genetics in determining the expression of that trait. On the other hand, if there is a stronger association on a trait between adoptive parents and their children than between biological parents and their children, we have evidence for the importance of the environment in determining that trait. In general, when a particular trait tends to occur at similar levels among genetically similar individuals but tends to vary more among genetically more distant individuals, we can assume that genetics plays an important role in the development of that trait (Rowe, 1994).

Developmental researchers have used all these approaches, and more, to study the relative impact of genetic and environmental factors. What have they found? Before turning to their specific findings, it is important to restate the general conclusion resulting from decades of research: Virtually all traits, characteristics, and behaviors are the joint result of the combination and interaction of nature and nurture. Like love and marriage and horses and carriages, genetic and environmental factors work in tandem, creating the unique individual that each of us is and will become.

Physical Traits: Family Resemblances

Some traits—like curly hair—have a clear genetic component.

When patients entered the examining room of Dr. Cyril Marcus, they didn't realize that sometimes they were actually being treated by his identical twin brother, Dr. Stewart Marcus. So similar in appearance and manner were the twins that even longtime patients were fooled by this admittedly unethical behavior, which occurred in a bizarre case made famous in the film *Dead Ringers.*

Monozygotic twins are merely the most extreme example of the fact that the more genetically similar two people are, the more likely they are to share physical characteristics. Tall parents tend to have tall children, and short ones tend to have short children. Obesity, which is defined as being more than 20 percent above the average weight for a given height, also has a strong genetic component. For example, in one study, pairs of identical twins were put on diets that contained an extra 1,000 calories a day and ordered not to exercise. Over a 3-month period, the twins gained almost identical amounts of weight. Moreover, different pairs of twins varied substantially in how much weight they gained, with some pairs gaining almost three times as much weight as other pairs (C. Bouchard et al., 1990).

Other, less obvious physical characteristics also show strong genetic influences. For instance, blood pressure, respiration rates, and even the age at which life ends are more similar in closely related individuals than in those who are less genetically similar (Jost & Sontag, 1944; Price & Gottesman, 1991; T. Sorensen et al., 1988).

Intelligence: More Research, More Controversy

No other issue involving the relative influence of heredity and environment has generated more research than the topic of intelligence. Why? The main reason is that intelligence, generally measured in terms of an IQ score, is a core human characteristic. IQ is strongly related to success in scholastic endeavors and somewhat less strongly to other types of achievement.

Let's first consider the degree to which intelligence is related to genetic factors. The answer is unambiguous: Genetics plays a significant role in intelligence. Both overall intelligence and specific subcomponents of intelligence (such as spatial skills, verbal skills, and memory) show strong effects for heredity (Cardon & Fulker, 1993; McGue et al., 1993; Rowe, 1999). As can be seen in Figure 3-8, the closer the genetic link between two individuals, the greater the correspondence of their overall IQ scores.

Not only is genetics an important influence on intelligence, but the impact also increases with age. For instance, as fraternal (dizygotic) twins move from infancy to adolescence, their

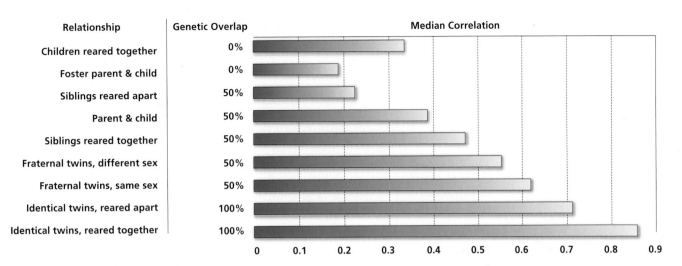

Relationship	Genetic Overlap	Median Correlation

FIGURE 3-8   GENETICS AND IQ

The closer the genetic link between two individuals, the greater the correspondence between their IQ scores. Why do you think there is a sex difference in the fraternal twins figures? Might there be other sex differences in other sets of twins or siblings not shown on this chart?

(*Source:* T. J. Bouchard & McGue, 1981)

IQ scores become less similar. In contrast, the IQ scores of identical (monozygotic) twins become increasingly similar over the course of time. These opposite patterns suggest the intensifying influence of inherited factors with increasing age (N. Brody, 1993; McGue et al., 1993; Wilson, 1983).

Although it is clear that heredity plays an important role in intelligence, investigators are much more divided on the question of how to quantify that role. Perhaps the most extreme view is held by psychologist Arthur Jensen (1969), who argues that as much as 80 percent of intelligence is a result of the influence of heredity. Others have suggested more modest figures, ranging from 50 to 70 percent. It is critical to keep in mind that such figures are averages across large groups of people, and any particular individual's degree of inheritance cannot be predicted from these averages (see Devlin, Daniels, & Roeder, 1997; Herrnstein & Murray, 1994).

It is important to keep in mind that although heredity clearly plays an important role in intelligence, environmental factors are profoundly influential. Even the most extreme estimates of the role of genetics still allow for environmental factors to play a significant role. In fact, in terms of public policy for maximizing people's intellectual success, the issue is not whether primarily hereditary or environmental factors underlie intelligence. Instead, we should be asking what can be done to maximize the intellectual development of each individual (T. J. Bouchard, 1997; Scarr & Carter-Saltzman, 1982; Storfer, 1990).

Genetic and Environmental Influences on Personality: Born to Be Outgoing?

Although it seems reasonable to most people that such characteristics as skin color and eye color are inherited, the notion that personality characteristics are affected by genetic factors seems less credible. However, increasing evidence supports the conclusion that at least some personality traits have at least some genetic components (J. Cohen, 1999; Plomin & Caspi, 1998; Rowe, 1994).

For example, neuroticism and extroversion are among the personality factors that have been linked most directly to genetic factors. The term *neuroticism,* when considered in the context of personality, refers to the degree of moodiness, touchiness, or sensitivity an individual characteristically displays. In other words, neuroticism reflects emotional reactivity. *Extroversion* is the degree to which a person seeks to be with others, to behave in an outgoing manner, and generally to be sociable (Bergeman et al., 1993; Loehlin, 1992; Plomin, 1994b). For instance, Jared, the baby described earlier in this chapter, may have inherited a tendency to be outgoing from his extroverted father, Jamal.

How do we know which personality traits reflect genetics? Some evidence comes from examination of genes. For instance, surprising evidence suggests that a specific gene partly determines *risk-taking behavior.* According to two teams of researchers, a novelty-seeking gene affects the production of the brain chemical dopamine, making some people more prone than others to seek out novel situations and to take risks (Benjamin et al., 1996; Ebstein et al., 1996).

Other evidence for the role of genetics in the determination of personality traits comes from studies of twins. For instance, in one large-scale study, personality psychologist Auke Tellegen and colleagues (1988) studied the personality traits of hundreds of pairs of twins. Because a good number of the twins were genetically identical but had been raised apart, it was possible to determine with some confidence the influence of genetic factors.

Tellegen found that certain traits reflected the contribution of genetics considerably more than others. As you can see in Figure 3-9, social potency (the tendency to be a masterful, forceful leader who enjoys being the center of attention) and traditionalism (strict endorsement of rules and authority) are strongly associated with genetic factors.

Other research has revealed genetic influences on other, less central personality traits. For example, a person's political attitudes, religious interests and values, and even attitudes toward human sexuality seem to have genetic components (Lykken et al., 1993; Olson et al., 2001).

Clearly, genetic factors play a role in determining personality. At the same time, the environment in which a child is raised affects personality development. For example, some parents encourage high activity levels, seeing activity as a manifestation of independence and intelligence. Other parents may encourage lower levels of activity on the part of their children, feeling that more passive children will get along better in society. Part of these parental

"The good news is that you will have a healthy baby girl. The bad news is that she is a congenital liar."

FIGURE 3-9   INHERITING TRAITS

These traits are among the personality factors that are related most closely to genetic factors. The higher the percentage, the greater the degree to which the trait reflects the influence of heredity. Do these figures mean that "leaders are born, not made"? Why or why not?

(*Source:* Tellegen et al., 1988)

Trait	%
Social potency	61%
A person high in this trait is masterful, a forceful leader who likes to be the center of attention.	
Traditionalism	60%
Follows rules and authority, endorses high moral standards and strict discipline.	
Stress reaction	55%
Feels vulnerable and sensitive and is given to worries and is easily upset.	
Absorption	55%
Has a vivid imagination readily captured by rich experience; relinquishes sense of reality.	
Alienation	55%
Feels mistreated and used, that "the world is out to get me."	
Well-being	54%
Has a cheerful disposition, feels confident and optimistic.	
Harm avoidance	50%
Shuns the excitement of risk and danger, prefers the safe route even if it is tedious.	
Aggression	48%
Is physically aggressive and vindictive, has taste for violence and is "out to get the world."	
Achievement	46%
Works hard, strives for mastery, and puts work and accomplishment ahead of other things.	
Control	43%
Is cautious and plodding, rational and sensible, likes carefully planned events.	
Social closeness	33%
Prefers emotional intimacy and close ties, turns to others for comfort and help.	

attitudes is culturally determined; parents in the United States may encourage higher activity levels, while parents in Asian cultures may encourage greater passivity. In both cases, children's personalities will be shaped in part by their parents' attitudes.

Clearly, both genetic and environmental factors have consequences for a child's personality, illustrating once again the critical interplay between nature and nurture. Furthermore, the way in which nature and nurture interact can be reflected not just in the behavior of individuals but also in the very foundations of a culture, as we see next.

DEVELOPMENTAL DIVERSITY

Cultural Differences in Physical Arousal: Might a Culture's Philosophical Outlook Be Determined by Genetics?

The Buddhist philosophy, an inherent part of many Asian cultures, emphasizes harmony and peacefulness and suggests that one should seek the eradication of human desire. In contrast, some of the traditional philosophies of Western civilization, such as those of Martin Luther and John Calvin, accentuate the importance of controlling the anxiety, fear, and guilt that are thought to be basic parts of the human condition.

Could such philosophical approaches reflect, in part, genetic factors? That is the controversial suggestion made by developmental psychologist Jerome Kagan and his colleagues (1993). They speculate that the underlying temperament of a given society, determined genetically, may predispose people in that society toward a particular philosophy.

Kagan bases his admittedly speculative suggestion on well-confirmed findings that show clear differences in temperament between Caucasian and Asian children. For instance, one study that compared 4-month-old infants in China, Ireland, and the United States found several relevant differences. In comparison to the Caucasian American babies and the Irish babies, the Chinese babies had significantly lower motor activity, irritability, and vocalization (see Table 3-4).

Kagan and colleagues (1994) suggest that the Chinese, who enter the world temperamentally calmer, may find Buddhist philosophical notions of serenity more in tune with their natural inclinations. In contrast, Westerners, who are emotionally more volatile and tense and who report higher levels of guilt, are more likely to be attracted to philosophies that articulate the necessity of controlling the unpleasant feelings that they are more apt to encounter in their everyday experience.

It is important to note that this does not mean that one philosophical approach is necessarily better or worse than the other. Nor does it mean that either of the temperaments from which the philosophies are thought to spring is superior or inferior to the other. Similarly, we must keep in mind that any single individual within a culture can be more or less temperamentally volatile and that the range of temperaments found even within a particular culture is vast. Finally, as we noted in our initial discussion of temperament, environmental conditions can have a significant effect on the portion of a person's temperament that is not genetically determined.

Still, the notion that the very basis of culture—its philosophical traditions—may be affected by genetic factors is intriguing. More research is necessary to determine just how the unique interaction of heredity and environment within a given culture may produce a framework for viewing and understanding the world.

TABLE 3-4   MEAN BEHAVIORAL SCORES FOR CAUCASIAN AMERICAN, IRISH, AND CHINESE 4-MONTH-OLD INFANTS

Behavior	American	Irish	Chinese
Motor activity score	48.6	36.7	11.2
Crying (in seconds)	7.0	2.9	1.1
Fretting (% trials)	10.0	6.0	1.9
Vocalizing (% trials)	31.4	31.1	8.1
Smiling (% trials)	4.1	2.6	3.6

(*Source:* Kagan, Arcus, & Snidman, 1993)

Psychological Disorders: The Roles of Genetics and Environment

Lori Schiller began to hear voices when she was a teenager in summer camp. Without warning, the voices screamed "You must die! Die! Die!" She ran from her bunk into the darkness, where she thought she could get away. Camp counselors found her screaming as she jumped wildly on a trampoline. "I thought I was possessed," she said later. (Bennett, 1992, p. A1)

In a sense, she was possessed: possessed with schizophrenia, one of the severest types of psychological disorder. Normal and happy through childhood, Schiller's world took a tumble during adolescence as she increasingly lost her hold on reality. For the next two decades, she would be in and out of institutions, struggling to ward off the ravages of the disorder.

What was the cause of Schiller's mental disorder? Increasing evidence suggests that schizophrenia is brought about by genetic factors. The disorder runs in families, with some families showing an unusually high incidence. Moreover, the closer the genetic links between someone with schizophrenia and another family member, the more likely it is that the other person will also develop schizophrenia. For instance, a monozygotic twin has close to a 50 percent risk of developing schizophrenia when the other twin develops the disorder (see Figure 3-10). By contrast, a niece or nephew of a person with schizophrenia has less than a 5 percent chance of developing the disorder (Gottesman, 1991, 1993; Prescott & Gottesman, 1993).

However, these data also illustrate that genetics alone does not influence the development of the disorder. If genetics were the sole cause, the risk for an identical twin would be 100 percent. Consequently, other factors account for the disorder, ranging from structural abnormalities in the brain to a biochemical imbalance (R. E. Gur & Chin, 1999; Iacono & Grove, 1993; Z. W. Wang et al., 1993).

It also seems that even if individuals harbor a genetic predisposition toward schizophrenia, they are not destined to develop the disorder. Instead, they may inherit an unusual sensitivity to stress in the environment. If stress is low, schizophrenia will not occur. But if stress is sufficiently strong, it will lead to schizophrenia. On the other hand, for someone with a strong genetic predisposition toward the disorder, even relatively weak environmental stressors may

FIGURE 3-10   THE GENETICS OF SCHIZOPHRENIA

The psychological disorder of schizophrenia has clear genetic components. The closer the genetic links between someone with schizophrenia and another family member, the more likely it is that the other person will also develop schizophrenia.

(*Source:* Gottesman, 1991)

Lifetime Risk of Developing Schizophrenia (percent)

Group	Risk
General population	1%
Spouses of patients	2%
First cousins	2%
Uncles/aunts	2%
Nephews/nieces	4%
Grandchildren	5%
Half-siblings	6%
Children	13%
Siblings	9%
Siblings with 1 parent with schizophrenia	17%
Dizygotic twins	17%
Parents	6%
Monozygotic twins	48%

Degree of Risk: 0 10 20 30 40 50

lead to schizophrenia (Bergen et al., 1998; Gottesman, 1991; Norman & Malla, 2001; Paris, 1999).

Several other psychological disorders have been shown to be related, at least in part, to genetic factors. For instance, major depression, alcoholism, autism, and attention deficit hyperactivity disorder have significant inherited components (Roy et al., 1999; Rutter et al., 1993; Shields, 1973).

The example of schizophrenia and other genetically related psychological disorders also illustrates a fundamental principle regarding the relationship between heredity and environment, one that underlies much of our previous discussion. Specifically, the role of genetics is often to produce preparedness for a future course of development. When and whether a certain behavioral characteristic will actually be displayed depends on the nature of the environment (B. Cooper, 2001). Thus although a predisposition for schizophrenia may be present at birth, typically people do not show the disorder until adolescence—if at all.

Similarly, certain other kinds of traits are more likely to be displayed as the influence of parents and other socializing factors declines. For example, adopted children may, early in their lives, display traits that are relatively similar to their adoptive parents' traits, given the overwhelming influence of the environment on young children. But as they get older and their parents' influence declines, genetically influenced traits may begin to manifest themselves as unseen genetic factors begin to play a greater role (Caspi & Moffitt, 1991, 1993; Loehlin, 1992).

Can Genes Influence Environment?

According to developmental psychologist Sandra Scarr (1992, 1993), the genetic endowment provided to children by their parents not only determines their genetic characteristics but also actively influences their environment. Scarr suggests three ways a child's genetic predisposition might influence his or her environment.

Children may display **active genotype–environment effects** by focusing on the aspects of their environment that are most congruent with their genetically determined abilities. At the same time, they pay less attention to the aspects of the environment that are less compatible with their genetic endowment. For instance, two girls may be reading the same school bulletin board. One may notice the sign advertising tryouts for Little League baseball, while her less coordinated but more musically endowed friend might be more apt to spot the notice recruiting students for an after-school chorus. In each case, the child is attending to the aspects of the environment in which her genetically determined abilities can flourish.

In some cases, there are **passive genotype–environment effects,** in which *parents'* genes are associated with the environment in which children are raised. For example, a particularly sports-oriented parent, who has genes that promote good physical coordination, may provide many opportunities for a child to play sports.

There are also **evocative genotype–environment effects,** in which a child's genes elicit a particular type of environment. For instance, an infant's demanding behavior may cause parents to be more attentive to the infant's needs than they would be if the infant were less demanding. Or a child who is genetically inclined to be well coordinated may play ball with anything in the house so often that his parents notice and then decide that he should have some sports equipment.

In sum, determining whether behavior is primarily attributable to nature or nurture is a bit like shooting at a moving target. Not only are behaviors and traits a joint outcome of genetic and environmental factors, but the relative influence of genes and environment for specific characteristics also shifts over the course of people's lives. Although the pool of genes we inherit at birth sets the stage for our future development, the constantly shifting scenery and the other characters in our lives determine just how our development eventually plays out.

Developmental psychologist Sandra Scarr argues that children's genetic characteristics actively influence and shape their environment.

Active genotype–environment effects Situations in which children focus on the aspects of their environment that are most congruent with their genetically determined abilities

Passive genotype–environment effects Situations in which parents' genes are associated with the environment in which children are raised

Evocative genotype–environment effects Situations in which a child's genes elicit a particular type of environment

R E V I E W & A P P L Y

Review

- Human characteristics and behavior are a joint outcome of genetic and environmental factors.

- Genetic influences have been identified in physical characteristics, intelligence, personality traits and behaviors, and psychological disorders.

- There is some speculation that entire cultures may be predisposed genetically toward certain types of philosophical viewpoints and attitudes.

Applying Child Development

- Consider the personality characteristics that you believe you inherited from one or both of your parents. If you had grown up in a different environment, how might those characteristics be different?

- *From an educator's perspective:* Some people have used the proven genetic basis of intelligence to argue against strenuous educational efforts on behalf of individuals with below-average IQs. Does this viewpoint make sense based on what you have learned about heredity and environment? Why or why not?

Prenatal Growth and Change

VIDEO CLIP

Prenatal Development

Robert accompanied Lisa to her first appointment with the midwife. The midwife checked the results of tests done to confirm the couple's own positive home pregnancy test. "Yep, you're going to have a baby," she confirmed, speaking to Lisa. "You'll need to set up monthly visits for the next six months, then more frequently as your due date approaches. You can get this prescription for prenatal vitamins filled at any pharmacy, and here are some important guidelines about diet and exercise. You don't smoke, do you? That's good." Then she turned to Robert, "How about you? Do you smoke?" After giving lots of instructions and advice, she left the couple feeling slightly dazed but ready to do whatever was necessary to have a healthy baby.

From the moment of conception, development proceeds relentlessly. As we've seen, many aspects are guided by the complex set of genetic guidelines inherited from the parents. Of course, prenatal growth, like all development, is also influenced from the start by environmental factors (Leavitt & Goldson, 1996). As we'll see, both parents, like Lisa and Robert, can take part in providing a good prenatal environment.

Fertilization: The Moment of Conception

When most of us think about the facts of life, we tend to focus on the events that cause a male's sperm cells to begin their journey toward a female's ovum. Yet the act of sex that brings about the potential for conception is both the consequence and the start of a long string of events that precede and follow **fertilization,** or conception, the joining of sperm and ovum to create the single-celled zygote from which each of us began our lives.

Fertilization   The process by which a sperm and an ovum—the male and female gametes, respectively—join to form a single new cell

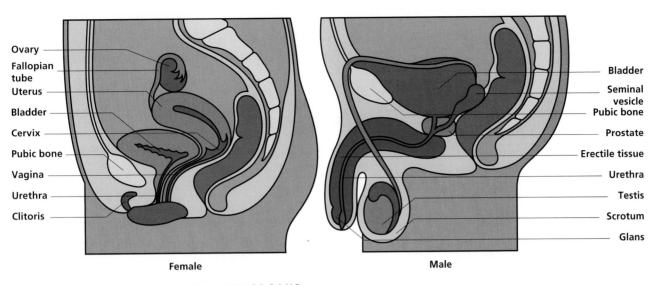

Female

Male

FIGURE 3-11   ANATOMY OF THE SEX ORGANS

The basic anatomy of the sexual organs is illustrated in these cutaway side views.

Both the male's sperm and the female's ovum come with a history of their own. Females are born with around 400,000 ova located in the two ovaries (see Figure 3-11 for the basic anatomy of the female and male sex organs). However, the ova do not mature until the female reaches puberty. From that point until she reaches menopause, the female will ovulate about every 28 days. During ovulation, an egg is released from one of the ovaries and pushed by minute hair cells through the fallopian tube toward the uterus. If the ovum meets a sperm in the fallopian tube, fertilization takes place (Aitken, 1995).

Sperm, which look a little like microscopic tadpoles, have a shorter life span. They are created by the testicles at a rapid rate: An adult male typically produces several hundred million sperm a day. Consequently, the sperm ejaculated during sexual intercourse are of considerably more recent origin than the ovum toward which they are heading.

When sperm enter the vagina, they begin a winding journey that takes them through the cervix, the opening into the uterus, and into the fallopian tube, where fertilization may take place. However, only a tiny fraction of the 300 million cells that are typically ejaculated during sexual intercourse ultimately survive the arduous journey. That's usually OK, though: It takes only one sperm to fertilize an ovum, and each sperm and ovum contains all the genetic data necessary to produce a new human.

Alternative Routes to Pregnancy: Giving Nature a Boost

For some couples, conception presents a major challenge. In fact, some 15 percent of couples suffer from **infertility,** the inability to conceive after 12 to 18 months of trying to become pregnant.

In men, infertility is a result of producing too few sperm. In other cases, infertility is a result of the age of the parents (the older the parents, the more likely infertility will occur; see Figure 3-12). Use of illicit drugs or cigarettes and previous bouts of sexually transmitted diseases also increase infertility (Gibbs, 2002).

Whatever the cause of infertility, there are several approaches that provide alternative paths to conception (Colon, 1997; M. Rosenthal, 1998). Some difficulties can be corrected through the use of drugs or surgery. Another option may be **artificial insemination,** a procedure in which a man's sperm is placed directly into a woman's vagina by a physician. In some situations, the woman's husband provides the sperm, while in others it is an anonymous donor from a sperm bank.

Infertility   The inability to conceive after 12 to 18 months of trying to become pregnant

Artificial insemination   A process of fertilization in which a man's sperm is placed directly into a woman's vagina by a physician

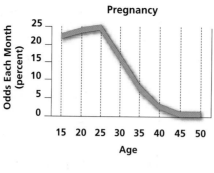

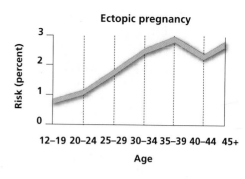

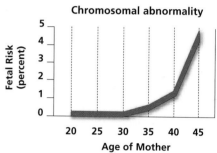

FIGURE 3-12   OLDER WOMEN AND RISKS OF PREGNANCY

Not only does the rate of infertility increase as women get older, but the risk of chromosomal abnormality increases as well.

(*Source:* Reproductive Medicine Associates of New Jersey, 2002)

In other cases, fertilization takes place outside of the mother's body. **In vitro fertilization (IVF)** is a procedure in which some of a woman's ova are removed from her ovaries, and a man's sperm are used to fertilize the ova in a laboratory. Once conception occurs, the fertilized egg or eggs are then implanted in a woman's uterus. Similarly, *gamete intrafallopian transfer (GIFT)* and *zygote intrafallopian transfer (ZIFT)* are procedures in which an egg and sperm or a fertilized egg is implanted in a woman's fallopian tubes. In IVF, GIFT, and ZIFT, implantation is done either in the woman who provided the donor eggs or in a **surrogate mother,** a woman who agrees to carry the child to term. Surrogate mothers may also be used in cases in which the mother is unable to conceive; the surrogate mother is artificially inseminated by a father and agrees to give up rights to the infant (van Balen, 1998).

In vitro fertilization (IVF)   A procedure in which a woman's ova are removed from her ovaries and a man's sperm are used to fertilize the ova in a laboratory

Surrogate mother   A woman who agrees to carry a child to term if the mother who provides the donor eggs is unable to conceive

"I'm their real child, and you're just a frozen embryo thingy they bought from some laboratory."

The use of a surrogate mother presents a variety of ethical and legal issues, as well as many emotional concerns. In some cases, surrogate mothers have refused to give up the child after its birth, while in others, the surrogate mother has sought to have a role in the child's life. In such cases, the rights of the mother, the father, the surrogate mother, and ultimately the baby are in conflict.

How do children conceived using emerging reproductive technologies such as in vitro fertilization fare? Research shows that they do quite well. In fact, one study found that the quality of parenting in families who have used such techniques may even be superior to that in families with naturally conceived children. Furthermore, the later psychological adjustment of children conceived using in vitro fertilization and artificial insemination is no different from that of children conceived using natural techniques (van Balen, 1998; Hahn & Di Pietro, 2001).

The Stages of the Prenatal Period: The Onset of Development

The prenatal period consists of three phases: the germinal, embryonic, and fetal stages. They are summarized in Table 3-5.

The Germinal Stage: Fertilization to 2 Weeks.   In the **germinal stage,** the first—and shortest—stage of the prenatal period, the zygote begins to divide and grow in complexity during the first 2 weeks following conception. During the germinal stage, the fertilized egg (now called a *blastocyst*) travels toward the *uterus,* where it becomes implanted in the organ's wall, which is rich in nutrients. The germinal stage is characterized by methodical cell division, which gets off to a quick start: Three days after fertilization, the organism consists of some 32 cells, and by the next day, the number doubles. Within a week, it is made up of 100 to 150 cells, and the number rises with increasing rapidity.

In addition to increasing in number, the cells of the organism become increasingly specialized. For instance, some cells form a protective layer around the mass of cells, while others begin to establish the rudiments of a placenta and umbilical cord. When fully developed, the **placenta** serves as a conduit between the mother and fetus, providing nourishment and oxygen via the *umbilical cord.* In addition, waste materials from the developing child are removed through the umbilical cord.

Germinal stage   The first—and shortest—stage of the prenatal period, which takes place during the first 2 weeks following conception

Placenta   A conduit between the mother and fetus, providing nourishment and oxygen via the umbilical cord

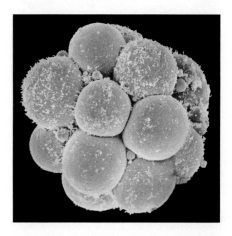

The germinal stage of the prenatal period gets off to a fast start. Here the embryo has divided into 16 cells just days after fertilization.

TABLE 3-5 STAGES OF THE PRENATAL PERIOD		
GERMINAL	EMBRYONIC	FETAL
Fertilization to 2 Weeks	**2 Weeks to 8 Weeks**	**8 Weeks to Birth**
The germinal stage is the first and shortest, characterized by methodical cell division and the attachment of the organism to the wall of the uterus. Three days after fertilization, the zygote consists of 32 cells, a number that doubles by the next day. Within a week, the zygote multiplies to 100 to 150 cells. The cells become specialized, with some forming a protective layer around the zygote.	The zygote is now designated an embryo. The embryo develops three layers, which ultimately form a different set of structures as development proceeds. The layers are as follows: Ectoderm: Skin, sense organs, brain, spinal cord Endoderm: Digestive system, liver, respiratory system Mesoderm: Muscles, blood, circulatory system At 8 weeks, the embryo is 1 inch long.	The fetal stage formally starts when the differentiation of the major organs has occurred. Now called a fetus, the individual grows rapidly as length increases 20 times. At 4 months, the fetus weighs an average of 4 ounces; at 7 months, 3 pounds; and at the time of birth, the average child weighs just over 7 pounds.

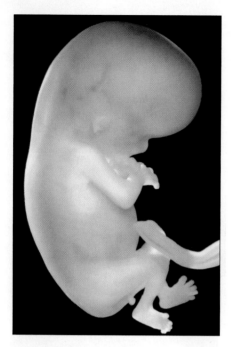

The fetal stage begins at 8 weeks following conception.

Embryonic stage The period in prenatal development from 2 to 8 weeks following fertilization, during which significant growth occurs in the major organs and body systems

Fetal stage The stage of prenatal development that begins at about 8 weeks after conception and continues until birth

Fetus A developing child, from 8 weeks after conception until birth

The Embryonic Stage: 2 Weeks to 8 Weeks.   By the end of the germinal period—just 2 weeks after conception—the organism is firmly secured to the wall of the mother's uterus. At this point, the child is called an *embryo*. The **embryonic stage** is the period from 2 to 8 weeks following fertilization. One of the highlights of this stage is the development of the major organs and basic anatomy.

At the beginning of the embryonic stage, the developing child has three distinct layers, each of which will ultimately form a different set of structures as development proceeds. The outer layer of the embryo, the *ectoderm*, will form skin, hair, teeth, sense organs, and the brain and spinal cord. The *endoderm*, the inner layer, produces the digestive system, liver, pancreas, and respiratory system. Sandwiched between the ectoderm and endoderm is the *mesoderm*, from which the muscles, bones, blood, and circulatory system are forged. Every part of the body is formed from these three layers.

If you were looking at an embryo at the end of the embryonic stage, you might be hard pressed to identify it as human. Only an inch long, an 8-week-old embryo has what appear to be gills and a tail-like structure. But a closer look reveals several familiar features. Rudimentary eyes, nose, lips, and even teeth can be recognized, and the embryo has stubby bulges that will form arms and legs.

The Fetal Stage: 8 Weeks to Birth.   It is not until the final period of prenatal development, the fetal stage, that the developing child becomes instantly recognizable. The **fetal stage** starts at about 8 weeks after conception and continues until birth. The fetal stage formally starts when the differentiation of the major organs has occurred.

Now called a **fetus,** the developing child undergoes astoundingly rapid change during the fetal stage. For instance, it increases in length some 20 times, and its proportions change dramatically. At 2 months, around half the fetus is what will ultimately be its head; by 5 months, the head accounts for just over a quarter of its total size (see Figure 3-13). The fetus also increases in weight substantially. At 4 months, the fetus weighs an average of about 4 ounces; at 7 months, it weighs about 3 pounds; and at the time of birth, the average child weighs just over 7 pounds.

At the same time, the developing child is rapidly becoming more complex. Organs become more differentiated and start to work. By 3 months, for example, the fetus swallows and urinates. In addition, the interconnections between the different parts of the body become more complex and integrated. Arms develop hands; hands develop fingers; fingers develop nails.

As this is happening, the fetus makes itself known to the outside world. In the earliest stages of pregnancy, mothers may be unaware that they are pregnant. As the fetus becomes

FIGURE 3-13
BODY PROPORTIONS

During the fetal period, the proportions of the body change dramatically. At 2 months, the head represents about half the fetus, but by the time of birth, it is one quarter of its total size.

| 1/2 | 3/8 | 1/4 |

| 2 months after conception | 5 months after conception | Newborn |

increasingly active, however, most mothers cannot help but take notice. By 4 months, a mother can feel the movement of her child, and several months later, others can feel the baby's kicks through the mother's abdomen.

During the fetal stage, the fetus develops a wide repertoire of different types of activities (Smotherman & Robinson, 1996). In addition to the kicks that alert its mother to its presence, the fetus can turn, do somersaults, cry, hiccup, clench its fist, open and close its eyes, and suck its thumb. It also is capable of hearing and can even respond to sounds that it hears repeatedly (Lecanuet, Granier-Deferre, & Busnel, 1995). For instance, researchers Anthony De Casper and Melanie Spence (1986) asked a group of pregnant mothers to read aloud the Dr. Seuss story *The Cat in the Hat* two times a day during the latter months of pregnancy. Three days after the babies were born, they appeared to recognize the story they had heard, responding more to it than to another story that had a different rhythm.

Just as no two adults are alike, no two fetuses are the same. Although development during the prenatal period follows the broad patterns outlined here, there are significant differences in the specific nature of individual fetuses' behavior. Some fetuses are exceedingly active, while others are more sedentary. (The more active fetuses will probably be more active infants as well.) Some have relatively quick heart rates, while others' heart rates are slower, with the typical range varying between 120 and 160 beats per minute (Lecanuet et al., 1995; Smotherman & Robinson, 1996).

Such differences in fetal behavior are due in part to genetic characteristics inherited at the moment of fertilization. Other kinds of differences, though, are brought about by the nature of the environment in which the child spends its first 9 months of life. As we will see, there are numerous ways in which the prenatal environment of infants affects their development, in good ways and bad.

As with adults, there are broad differences in the nature of fetuses. Some are very active while others are more reserved, and these characteristics can continue after birth.

Miscarriage

A *miscarriage*—also known as a *spontaneous abortion*—occurs when pregnancy ends before the developing child is able to survive outside the mother's womb. The embryo detaches from the wall of the uterus and is expelled.

Some 15 to 20 percent of all pregnancies end in miscarriage, usually in the first several months of pregnancy. Many occur so early that the mother is not even aware she was pregnant and may not even know she has suffered a miscarriage. Typically, miscarriages are attributable to some sort of genetic abnormality.

In *abortion*, a mother voluntarily chooses to terminate her pregnancy. Some 1.2 million abortions occur annually in the United States, and worldwide, the number is estimated at 46 million. Abortion involves a complex set of physical, psychological, legal, and ethical issues that have serious consequences for all parties involved (Alan Guttmacher Institute, 1999).

The Prenatal Environment: Threats to Development

According to the Siriono people of South America, if a pregnant woman eats the meat of certain kinds of animals, she runs the risk of having a child who may act and look like those animals. According to opinions offered on daytime television talk shows such as the Oprah Winfrey show, a pregnant mother should avoid getting angry in order to spare her child from entering the world with anger (Cole, 1992).

Such views are largely the stuff of folklore, although there is some evidence that a mother's anxiety during pregnancy may affect the sleeping patterns of the fetus prior to birth. Furthermore, certain aspects of mothers' and fathers' behavior, both before and after conception, can produce lifelong consequences for the child. Some consequences show up immediately, but many possible problems aren't apparent before birth. Other problems, more insidious, may not appear until years after birth (Couzin, 2002; Groome et al., 1995).

Some of the most profound consequences are brought about by teratogenic agents. A **teratogen** is an environmental agent such as a drug, chemical, virus, or other factor that

Teratogen   A factor that produces a birth defect

produces a birth defect. Although it is the job of the placenta to keep teratogens from reaching the fetus, the placenta is not entirely successful at this, and probably every fetus is exposed to some teratogens.

The timing and quantity of exposure to a teratogen are crucial. At some phases of prenatal development, a certain teratogen may have only a minimal impact. At other periods, however, the same teratogen may have profound consequences. Furthermore, different organ systems are vulnerable to teratogens at different times during development. For example, the brain is most susceptible from 15 to 25 days after conception, while the heart is most vulnerable from 20 to 40 days following conception (see Figure 3-14; Bookstein et al., 1996; Needleman & Bellinger, 1994).

Mother's Diet. Most of our knowledge of the environmental factors that affect the developing fetus comes from the study of the mother. For instance, as the midwife pointed out in the example of Lisa and Robert, a mother's diet plays an important role in bolstering the development of the fetus. A mother who eats a varied diet high in nutrients is apt to have fewer complications during pregnancy, an easier labor, and a generally healthier baby than a mother whose diet is restricted in nutrients (J. L. Brown, 1987; Morgane et al., 1993; Rizzo et al., 1997; Waugh & Bulik, 1999).

The problem of diet is of immense global concern, with 800 million hungry people in the world. Even worse, nearly 30 percent of the world's population suffers from some form of

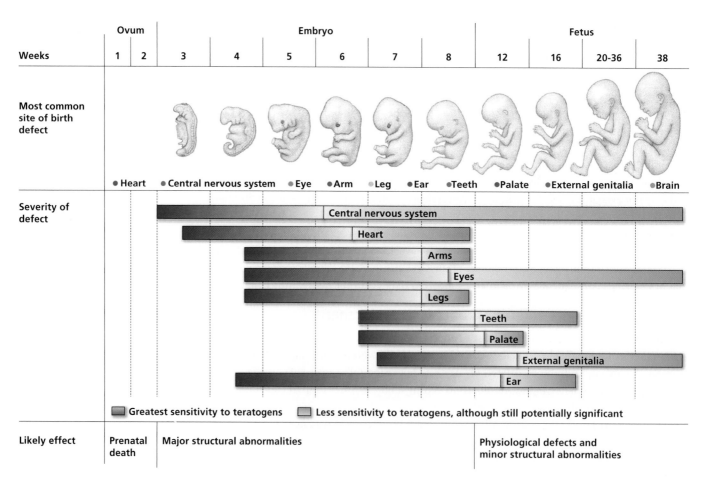

FIGURE 3-14   TERATOGEN SENSITIVITY

Depending on their state of development, various parts of the body vary in their sensitivity to teratogens.

(*Source:* K. L. Moore, 1998)

malnutrition. Clearly, restrictions in diet that bring about hunger on such a massive scale affect millions of children born to women living in those conditions (World Food Summit, 2002).

Fortunately, there are ways to counteract the types of maternal malnourishment that affect prenatal development. Dietary supplements given to mothers can reverse some of the problems produced by a poor diet (Crosby, 1991; Prentice, 1991). Furthermore, research shows that babies who were malnourished as fetuses but who are subsequently raised in enriched environments can overcome some of the effects of their early malnourishment (Grantham-McGregor et al., 1994). However, the reality is that few of the world's children whose mothers were malnourished before their birth are apt to find themselves in enriched environments after birth (Garber, 1981; Ricciuti, 1993; Zeskind & Ramey, 1981).

Mother's Age.   With a great deal of medical help from her physicians, a 63-year-old woman gave birth in 1997. At the time, she was the oldest woman ever known to have become a mother. Most of the media attention, which was substantial, focused on the medical ethics of the case and the potential psychological difficulties for a child whose mother would be so atypically old.

However, the mother's advanced age probably had physical effects on her and her child as well. Women who give birth when over the age of 30 are at greater risk for a variety of pregnancy and birth complications than younger ones. For instance, they are more apt to give birth prematurely, and their children are more likely to have low birthweights. By the time they are 42 years old, 90 percent of a woman's eggs are no longer normal (Cnattingius, Berendes, & Forman, 1993; Gibbs, 2002; Vercellini et al., 1993).

Furthermore, older mothers are considerably more likely to give birth to children with Down syndrome, a form of mental retardation. About 1 of every 100 babies born to mothers over 40 has Down syndrome; for mothers over 50, the incidence increases to 25 percent, or 1 in 4 (Gaulden, 1992). However, some researchers argue that older mothers are not automatically at risk for more pregnancy problems. For instance, one study found that when women in their 40s who had not experienced health difficulties were considered, they were no more likely to have prenatal problems than those in their 20s (Ales, Druzin, & Santini, 1990).

The risks involved in pregnancy are greater not only for unusually old mothers but for atypically young women as well. Women who become pregnant during adolescence—a phenomenon that accounts for 20 percent of all pregnancies—are more likely to have premature deliveries. Furthermore, the mortality rate of infants born to adolescent mothers is double that for mothers in their 20s.

Mother's Prenatal Support.   Keep in mind, though, that the higher mortality rate for babies of adolescent mothers reflects more than just physiological problems related to the mothers' young age. Heightened mortality is also a consequence of adverse social and economic factors. Many teenage mothers do not have enough money or social support, a situation that prevents them from getting good prenatal care and parenting support after the baby is born. Poverty or social circumstances may even have set the stage for the adolescent to become pregnant in the first place.

Mother's Illness.   Depending on when it strikes, an illness in a pregnant woman can have devastating consequences. For instance, the onset of *rubella* (German measles) in the mother prior to the 11th week of pregnancy is likely to cause serious consequences in the baby, including blindness, deafness, heart defects, or brain damage. In later stages of a pregnancy, however, adverse consequences of rubella become increasingly less likely.

Several other diseases may affect a developing fetus, again depending on when the illness is contracted. For instance, *chickenpox* may produce birth defects, and *mumps* may increase the risk of miscarriage.

Some sexually transmitted diseases such as *syphilis* can be transmitted directly to the fetus, who will be born suffering from the disease. In some cases, sexually transmitted diseases such as *gonorrhea* are communicated to the child as it passes through the birth canal to be born.

AIDS (acquired immune deficiency syndrome) is the newest, and probably the deadliest, of the diseases to affect a newborn. Mothers who have the disease or who are merely carriers of the virus may pass it on to their fetuses through the blood that reaches the placenta. If the fetuses contract the disease—and some 30 percent of infants born to mothers with AIDS are born with the virus—they face a devastating path. Many have birth abnormalities, including small, misshapen faces; protruding lips; and brain deterioration. Ninety percent experience neurological symptoms exemplified by intellectual delays and deficits and loss of motor coordination, facial expressions, and speech. Because AIDS causes a breakdown of the immune system, these babies are extremely susceptible to infection. The long-term prognosis for infants born with AIDS is grim: Although drugs such as AZT may stave off the symptoms of the disease, AIDS babies rarely survive beyond infancy ("AIDS and Mental Health," 1994; Chin, 1994; Frenkel & Gau, 1994).

Mother's Drug Use. A mother's use of many kinds of drugs—both legal and illegal—poses serious risks to the unborn child. Even over-the-counter remedies for common ailments can have surprisingly injurious consequences. For instance, aspirin taken for a headache can lead to bleeding in the fetus. Moreover, impairments in the physical development of 4-year-olds have been linked to the frequent use of aspirin during pregnancy (H. M. Barr et al., 1990; Griffith, Azuma, & Chasnoff, 1994).

Even drugs prescribed by medical professionals have sometimes had disastrous consequences. In the 1950s, many women who were advised to take *thalidomide* for morning sickness during their pregnancies gave birth to children with stumps instead of arms and legs. Although the physicians who prescribed the drug did not know it at the time, thalidomide inhibited the growth of limbs that would normally have occurred during the first 3 months of pregnancy.

Some drugs taken by mothers cause difficulties in their children literally decades after they were taken. As recently as the 1970s, the artificial hormone *DES (diethylstilbestrol)* was frequently prescribed to prevent miscarriage. Only later was it found that the daughters of mothers who took DES stood a much higher than normal chance of developing a rare form of vaginal or cervical cancer and had more difficulties during their pregnancies (Herbst, 1981). Sons of the mothers who had taken DES had their own problems, including a higher than average rate of reproductive difficulties (Herbst, 1981).

Illicit drugs may pose even greater risks to the prenatal environment. For one thing, the quality and purity of drugs purchased illegally vary significantly, so drug users can never be quite sure what specifically they are ingesting. Furthermore, the effects of some commonly used illicit drugs can be particularly devastating (De Cristofaro & La Gamma, 1995; Visscher, Bray, & Kroutil, 1999).

Consider the use of *marijuana*. One of the most commonly used illegal drugs—millions of people in the United States have admitted trying it—marijuana used during pregnancy can restrict the oxygen that reaches the fetus. Its use can lead to infants who are irritable, nervous, and easily disturbed (Cornelius, Day, Richardson, & Taylor, 1999; Feng, 1993).

During the early 1990s, *cocaine* use by pregnant women led to an epidemic of thousands of so-called crack babies. Cocaine produces an intense restriction of the arteries leading to the fetus, causing a significant reduction in the flow of blood and oxygen. This process increases the risks of fetal death.

At birth, children whose mothers were addicted to cocaine may themselves be addicted to the drug and may have to suffer through the agonies of withdrawal. Even if not addicted, they may be born with significant problems. They are often shorter and weigh less than average, and they may have serious respiratory problems, visible birth defects, or seizures. They behave quite differently from other infants: Their reactions to stimulation are muted, but once they start to cry, it may be hard to soothe them (Alessandri, Bendersky, & Lewis, 1998; Andrews, Francis, & Riese, 2000; Bendersky & Lewis, 1998; L. T. Singer et al., 2000).

It is difficult to determine the long-term effects of mothers' cocaine use in isolation, because such drug use is often accompanied by poor prenatal care and impaired nurturing following birth (B. J. Myers et al., 1992; G. A. Richardson & Day, 1994). In fact, in many cases, it is the poor caregiving by mothers who use cocaine that results in children's problems, rather than exposure to the drug. Treatment of children exposed to cocaine consequently requires not only that the child's mother stop using the drug but also that the level of care the mother or other caregivers provide to the infant be improved ("Cocaine Before Birth," 1998).

Mother's Use of Alcohol, Tobacco, and Caffeine.   A pregnant woman who reasons that having a drink every once in a while or smoking an occasional cigarette has no appreciable effect on her unborn child is in all likelihood kidding herself: Increasing evidence suggests that even small amounts of alcohol and nicotine can disrupt development of the fetus.

Mothers' use of alcohol can have profound consequences for the unborn child. The children of alcoholics, who consume substantial quantities of alcohol during pregnancy, are at the greatest risk. Approximately 1 out of every 750 infants is born with **fetal alcohol syndrome (FAS),** a disorder that may include below-average intelligence and sometimes mental retardation, delayed growth, and facial deformities. FAS is now the primary preventable cause of mental retardation (Able & Sokol, 1987; Feng, 1993; Steinhausen & Spohr, 1998; Streissguth, Randels, & Smith, 1991).

Even mothers who use smaller amounts of alcohol during pregnancy place their children at risk. **Fetal alcohol effects (FAE)** is a condition in which children display some, although not all, of the problems of fetal alcohol syndrome due to their mothers' consumption of alcohol during pregnancy (Streissguth, 1997).

Children who do not have FAE may still be affected by their mothers' use of alcohol. Studies have found that maternal consumption of an average of just two alcoholic drinks a day during pregnancy is associated with lower intelligence in their offspring at age 7. Other research concurs, suggesting that relatively small quantities of alcohol taken during pregnancy can have future adverse effects on children's behavior and psychological functioning (R. G. Barr et al., 1991; C. H. Johnson et al., 2001; Korkman et al., 1998; Shriver & Piersel, 1994). Furthermore, the consequences of alcohol ingestion during pregnancy are long-lasting. For example, one study found that the success of 14-year-olds on a test involving spatial and visual reasoning was related to their mothers' alcohol consumption during pregnancy. The more the mothers reported drinking, the less accurately their children responded (E. Hunt et al., 1995).

Because of the risks associated with alcohol, physicians today counsel pregnant women (and even those who are trying to become pregnant) to avoid drinking any alcoholic beverages. In addition, they caution against another practice proven to have an adverse effect on an unborn child: smoking.

Smoking produces several consequences, none good. For starters, smoking reduces the oxygen content and increases the carbon monoxide of the mother's blood, which quickly reduces the oxygen available to the fetus. In addition, the nicotine and other toxins in cigarettes slow the respiration rate of the fetus and speed up its heart.

The ultimate result is an increased possibility of miscarriage and a higher likelihood of death during infancy. In fact, recent estimates suggest that smoking by pregnant women leads to 115,000 miscarriages and the deaths of 5,600 babies in the United States alone each year (Di Franza & Lew, 1995; Feng, 1993; Mills, 1999; Ness et al., 1999).

Smokers are twice as likely as nonsmokers to have babies with an abnormally low birthweight, and smokers' babies tend to be shorter, on average, than those of nonsmokers. Furthermore, women who smoke during pregnancy are 50 percent more likely to have mentally retarded children (Dejin-Karlsson et al., 1998; Drews et al., 1996; Fried & Watkinson, 1990).

Fetal alcohol syndrome (FAS) A disorder caused by the mother's consumption of substantial quantities of alcohol during pregnancy, potentially resulting in mental retardation and delayed growth in the child

Fetal alcohol effects (FAE) A condition in which children display some, although not all, of the problems of fetal alcohol syndrome due to the mother's consumption of alcohol during pregnancy

Although the risks are not fully proven, some studies show that large quantities of caffeine—which is found in coffee, tea, some sodas, and chocolate—can hurt a fetus. Consequently, mothers should moderate their intake of caffeine in any of its forms (Fortier, Marcoux, & Beaulac-Baillargeon, 1993).

Do Fathers Affect the Prenatal Environment?   It would be easy to reason that once the father has done his part in the sequence of events leading to fertilization, he would have no role in the *prenatal* environment of the fetus. In fact, developmental researchers have in the past generally shared this view, and there is little research investigating fathers' influence on the prenatal environment.

However, it is becoming increasingly clear that fathers' behavior may well influence the prenatal environment. Consequently, as the example of Lisa and Robert's visit to midwife described earlier in the chapter showed, health practitioners are applying the research to suggest ways fathers can support healthy prenatal development.

For instance, a father-to-be should avoid smoking. Secondhand smoke from a father's cigarettes may affect the mother's health, which in turn influences her unborn child. The greater the level of a father's smoking, the lower the birthweight of his children. Similarly, a father's use of alcohol and illegal drugs such as cocaine can not only lead to chromosomal damage that may affect the fetus at conception but may also affect the prenatal environment by creating stress in the mother and generally producing an unhealthy environment (J. Campbell et al., 1992; D. H. Rubin et al., 1986; Wakefield et al., 1998).

○— BECOMING AN INFORMED CONSUMER OF DEVELOPMENT —○

Optimizing the Prenatal Environment

If you are contemplating ever having a child, you may be overwhelmed, at this point in the chapter, by the number of things that can go wrong. Don't be. Although both genetics and the environment pose their share of risks, in the vast majority of cases, pregnancy and birth proceed without mishap. Moreover, there are several things that women can do—both before and during pregnancy—to optimize the probability that pregnancy will progress smoothly. Among them are the following:

- First, women should have nonemergency X-rays only during the first 2 weeks after their menstrual periods. Second, women should be vaccinated against rubella (German measles) at least 3, and preferably 6, months before getting pregnant. Finally, women who are planning to become pregnant should avoid the use of birth control pills at least 3 months before trying to conceive, because of disruptions to hormone production caused by the pills.

- Eat well before, during, and after pregnancy. Pregnant mothers are, as the old saying goes, eating for two. This means that it is more essential than ever to eat regular, well-balanced meals.

- Don't use alcohol or other drugs. The evidence is clear that many drugs pass directly to the fetus and may cause birth defects. It is also clear that the more one drinks, the greater the risk to the fetus. The best advice, whether you are already pregnant or planning to have a child, is not to use *any* drug unless so directed by a physician. If you are planning to get pregnant, encourage your partner to avoid using alcohol or other drugs, too.

- Monitor caffeine intake. Although it is still unclear whether caffeine produces birth defects, it is known that the caffeine found in coffee, tea, chocolate, and some sodas can pass to the fetus, acting as a stimulant. Because of this, you probably shouldn't drink more than a few cups of coffee a day.

- Whether pregnant or not, don't smoke. This holds true for mothers, fathers, and anyone else in the vicinity of the pregnant mother, since research suggests that smoke in the fetal environment can affect birthweight.

- Exercise regularly. In most cases, women can continue to exercise, particularly exercises involving low-impact routines. But extreme exercise should be avoided, especially on very hot or very cold days. "No pain, no gain" isn't applicable during pregnancy (J. E. Brody, 1994a; Warrick, 1991).

REVIEW & APPLY

Review

- Fertilization joins one sperm and one ovum to start the journey of prenatal development. Some couples, however, need medical intervention to help them conceive. Among the alternate routes to conception are artificial insemination and in vitro fertilization (IVF).

- The prenatal period consists of three stages: germinal, embryonic, and fetal.

- The prenatal environment significantly influences the development of the baby. The diet, age, prenatal support, and illnesses of mothers can affect their babies' health and growth.

- Mothers' use of drugs, alcohol, tobacco, and caffeine can adversely affect the health and development of the unborn child. Fathers' and others' behaviors (e.g., smoking) can also affect the health of the unborn child.

Applying Child Development

- Studies show that "crack babies" who are now entering school have significant difficulty dealing with multiple stimuli and forming close attachments. How might both genetic and environmental influences have combined to produce these results?

- *From a health care provider's perspective:* In addition to avoiding smoking, do you think there are other steps fathers might take to help their unborn children develop normally in the womb? What are they, and how might they affect the environment of the unborn child?

LOOKING BACK

- **What is our basic genetic endowment, and how can human development go awry?**

- A child receives 23 chromosomes from each parent. These 46 chromosomes provide the genetic blueprint that will guide cell activity for the rest of the individual's life.

- Gregor Mendel discovered an important genetic mechanism that governs the interactions of dominant and recessive genes and their expression in alleles. Traits such as hair color and eye color and the presence of phenylketonuria (PKU) are alleles and follow this pattern.

- Genes may become physically damaged or may spontaneously mutate. If damaged genes are passed on to the child, the result can be a genetic disorder.

- Behavioral genetics, which studies the genetic basis of human behavior, focuses on personality characteristics and behaviors and on psychological disorders such as schizophrenia. Researchers are now discovering how to remedy certain genetic defects through gene therapy.

- Genetic counselors use data from tests and other sources to identify potential genetic abnormalities in women and men who plan to have children. Recently, they have begun testing individuals for genetically based disorders that may eventually appear in the individuals themselves.

⊙ **How do the environment and genetics work together to determine human characteristics?**

• Behavioral characteristics are often determined by a combination of genetics and environment. Genetically based traits represent a potential, called the genotype, which may be affected by the environment and is ultimately expressed in the phenotype.

• To work out the different influences of heredity and environment, researchers use nonhuman studies and human studies, particularly of twins.

⊙ **Which human characteristics are significantly influenced by heredity?**

• Virtually all human traits, characteristics, and behaviors are the result of the combination and interaction of nature and nurture. Many physical characteristics show strong genetic influences. Intelligence contains a strong genetic component but can be significantly influenced by environmental factors.

• Some personality traits, including neuroticism and extroversion, have been linked to genetic factors, and even attitudes, values, and interests have a genetic component. Some personal behaviors may be genetically influenced through the mediation of inherited personality traits.

• The interaction between genetic and environmental effects has been classified into three types: active genotype–environment effects, passive genotype–environment effects, and evocative genotype–environment effects.

⊙ **What happens during the prenatal stages of development?**

• Achieving the union of a sperm and an ovum at the moment of fertilization, which begins the process of prenatal development, can be difficult for some couples. Infertility, which occurs in some 15 percent of couples, can be treated by drugs, surgery, artificial insemination, and in vitro fertilization.

• The germinal stage (fertilization to 2 weeks) is marked by rapid cell division and specialization and the attachment of the zygote to the wall of the uterus. During the embryonic stage (2 to 8 weeks), the ectoderm, the mesoderm, and the endoderm begin to grow and specialize. The fetal stage (8 weeks to birth) is characterized by a rapid increase in complexity and differentiation of the organs. The fetus becomes active and most of its systems operational.

⊙ **What are the threats to the fetal environment, and what can be done about them?**

• Factors in the mother that may affect the unborn child include diet, age, illnesses, and drug, alcohol, tobacco, and caffeine use. The behaviors of fathers and others in the environment may also affect the health and development of the unborn child.

EPILOGUE

 n this chapter, we discussed the basics of heredity and genetics, including the way in which the code of life is transmitted across generations through DNA. We also saw how genetic transmission can go wrong and discussed ways in which genetic disorders can be treated—and perhaps prevented—through new interventions such as genetic counseling and gene therapy.

One important theme in this chapter has been the interaction between hereditary and environmental factors in the determination of a number of human traits. While we have encountered a number of surprising instances in which heredity plays a part—including in the development of personality traits and even personal preferences and tastes—we have also seen that heredity alone is virtually never the sole factor in any complex trait. Environment nearly always plays an important role.

Finally, we reviewed the main stages of prenatal growth—germinal, embryonic, and fetal—and examined threats to the prenatal environment and ways to optimize that environment for the fetus.

Before moving on, return to the prologue of this chapter—about Ethan Buchkovich, who was operated on before birth—and answer the following questions.

1. When parents decide whether to choose prenatal surgery for their baby, what criteria should be applied to balance the risk of surgery against the risk of a birth defect such as spina bifida?

2. A gene—or a genetic susceptibility—for spina bifida may one day be discovered. If a couple learned that a baby conceived by them would have a 20 percent chance of being born with the disorder, what issues would they have to face in deciding whether to start or continue a pregnancy? Would the issues be different if the chances were 50 percent?

3. If a genetic test exists that can reveal whether an infant is likely to be born with a genetic disorder, do parents have a responsibility to undergo that test? Why or why not?

4. How does gene therapy differ from prenatal surgery? What hopes does gene therapy hold for couples like the Buchkoviches faced with the likelihood of a serious genetic defect in their infant?

5. Based on what you know about genetics and prenatal development, how might a disorder like spina bifida occur in an infant? If it is carried in a recessive gene, how would it express itself? Which layer of the embryo is apparently affected in the development of spina bifida: the ectoderm, mesoderm, or endoderm?

KEY TERMS AND CONCEPTS

genes (p. 56)

DNA (deoxyribonucleic acid) (p. 56)

chromosomes (p. 57)

zygote (p. 57)

gametes (p. 57)

monozygotic twins (p. 58)

dizygotic twins (p. 58)

dominant trait (p. 60)

recessive trait (p. 60)

genotype (p. 60)

phenotype (p. 60)

homozygous (p. 60)

heterozygous (p. 60)

polygenic inheritance (p. 62)

X-linked genes (p. 62)

behavioral genetics (p. 63)

Down syndrome (p. 64)

fragile X syndrome (p. 64)

sickle-cell anemia (p. 64)

Tay-Sachs disease (p. 64)

Klinefelter's syndrome (p. 64)

genetic counseling (p. 65)

amniocentesis (p. 66)

chorionic villus sampling (CVS) (p. 66)

ultrasound sonography (p. 67)

temperament (p. 71)

multifactorial transmission (p. 71)

active genotype–environment effects (p. 79)

passive genotype–environment effects (p. 79)

evocative genotype–environment effects (p. 79)

fertilization (p. 80)

infertility (p. 81)

artificial insemination (p. 81)

in vitro fertilization (IVF) (p. 82)

surrogate mother (p. 82)

germinal stage (p. 83)

placenta (p. 83)

embryonic stage (p. 84)

fetal stage (p. 84)

fetus (p. 84)

teratogen (p. 85)

fetal alcohol syndrome (FAS) (p. 89)

fetal alcohol effects (FAE) (p. 89)

4

Birth and the Newborn Infant

PROLOGUE: A Tiny Life

amara Nussbaum* entered this world weighing 12.5 ounces, the weight of three sticks of butter plus a pat. She had M&M-size kneecaps. Her thighs, the size of an adult's thumb, splayed out like frogs' legs on a platter when she was held in the palm of a hand. At 365 grams, her birthweight was 135 grams shy of what is thought to be the minimum weight necessary for a baby to have any hope at all of survival.

The first time he saw her, Mohamed Tata, a neonatologist at City Hospital, looked for some signal from the premature baby that she was ready to join the fight for life. She didn't have the lung power to cry, but she had enough muscle tone to squirm. What worked most immediately in her favor the day she was born was her skin. Plum red and dusted with downy fetal hair, it appeared tough enough to hold warmth in and keep infection out. He took her strong

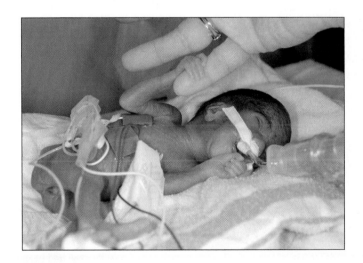

Tamara Nussbaum

skin as that signal, and unleashed the arsenal of technology available in today's neonatal intensive care units, or NICUs. It was a split-second judgment call that he knew full well could result in a child who would never walk, talk, or eat by herself. Or his call could result in a child with a pretty normal life, perhaps needing only a pair of glasses or a specialized school reading program. (Brink, 1998, p. 60)

*Names have been changed to protect privacy.

LOOKING AHEAD ▶

So far, it appears that Dr. Tata's call was right. Tamara is developing fairly normally, although with the developmental delays that characterize many children who are born prematurely.

Every birth is tinged with a combination of excitement and some degree of anxiety. In the vast majority of cases, delivery goes smoothly, and it is an amazing and joyous moment. Yet the wonder experienced at birth is far overshadowed by the extraordinary nature of newborns themselves. They enter the world with a surprising array of capabilities, ready from the first moments of life outside the womb to respond to the world and the people in it.

In this chapter, we'll examine the events that lead to the delivery and birth of a child and take an initial look at the newborn. We first consider labor and delivery, exploring how the process usually proceeds, as well as several alternative approaches.

We next examine some of the possible complications of birth. Problems that can occur range from premature births to infant mortality. Finally, we consider the extraordinary range of capabilities of newborns. We'll look not only at their physical and perceptual abilities but also at the way they enter the world with the ability to learn and with skills that help form the foundations of their future relationships with others.

After reading this chapter, you will be able to answer these questions:

- What is the normal process of labor?
- What complications can occur at birth, and what are their causes, effects, and treatments?
- What capabilities does the newborn have?

Birth

Her head was cone-shaped at the top. Although I knew this was due to the normal movement of the head bones as she came through the birth canal and that this would change in a few days, I was still startled. She also had some blood on the top of her head and was damp, a result of the amniotic fluid in which she had spent the last 9 months. There was some white, cheesy substance over her body, which the nurse wiped off just before she placed her in my arms. I could see a bit of downy hair on her ears, but I knew that this too would disappear before long. Her nose looked a little as if she had been on the losing end of a fistfight: It was squashed into her face, flattened by its trip through the birth canal. But as she seemed to fix her eyes on me and grasped my finger, it was clear that she was nothing short of perfect. (Adapted from Brazelton, 1983)

For those of us accustomed to thinking of newborns in the images of baby food commercials, this portrait of a typical newborn may be surprising. Yet most **neonates**—the term used for newborns—are born resembling this one. Make no mistake, however: Despite their temporary blemishes, babies are a welcome sight to their parents from the moment of their birth.

The neonate's outward appearance is caused by a variety of factors in its journey from the mother's uterus down the birth canal and out into the world. We can trace its passage, beginning with the release of the chemicals that initiate the process of labor.

Neonate   A newborn

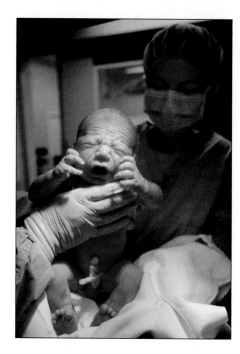

The image of newborns portrayed in commercials differs dramatically from reality.

Labor: Launching the Process of Birth

About 266 days after conception, for the average mother, a protein called *corticotropin-releasing hormone (CRH)* triggers the release of hormones and the process that leads to birth. One critical hormone is *oxytocin,* which is released by the mother's pituitary gland. When the concentration of oxytocin becomes high enough, the mother's uterus begins periodic contractions (Nathanielsz, 1996; R. Smith, 1999).

During the prenatal period, the uterus, which is composed of muscle tissue, slowly expands as the fetus grows. Although for most of the pregnancy it is inactive, after the 4th month, it occasionally contracts in order to ready itself for the eventual delivery. These spasms, called *Braxton-Hicks contractions,* are sometimes called "false labor," due to the fact that they do not necessarily signify that the baby will be born soon.

When birth is actually imminent, the uterus begins to contract intermittently. Its increasingly intense contractions act as if it were a vise, opening and closing to force the head of the fetus against the *cervix,* the neck of the uterus that separates it from the vagina. Eventually, the force of the contractions becomes strong enough to propel the fetus slowly down the birth canal until it enters the world as a newborn (Mittendorf et al., 1990).

Labor proceeds in three stages (see Figure 4-1). In the *first stage of labor,* the uterine contractions initially occur around every 8 to 10 minutes and last about 30 seconds. As labor proceeds, the contractions occur more frequently and last longer. Toward the end of labor, the contractions may occur every 2 minutes and last almost 2 minutes. As the contractions increase to their greatest intensity, during the period known as *transition,* the mother's cervix opens fully, eventually expanding enough to allow the baby's head (the widest part of the body) to pass through.

This first stage of labor is the longest. Its duration varies significantly, depending on the mother's age, race, ethnicity, number of prior pregnancies, and a variety of other factors involving both the fetus and the mother. Typically, labor takes 16 to 24 hours for firstborn children, but there are wide variations. Births of subsequent children usually involve shorter periods of labor.

During the *second stage of labor,* which typically lasts around 90 minutes, the baby's head emerges further from the mother with each contraction, increasing the size of the vaginal

Stage 1

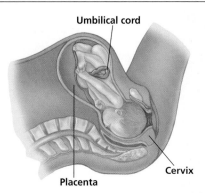

Umbilical cord

Placenta

Cervix

Uterine contractions initially occur every 8 to 10 minutes and last 30 seconds. Toward the end of labor, contractions may occur every 2 minutes and last as long as 2 minutes. As the contractions increase, the cervix, which separates the uterus from the vagina, becomes wider, eventually expanding to allow the baby's head to pass through.

Stage 2

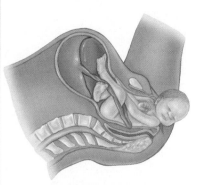

The baby's head starts to move through the cervix and birth canal. Typically lasting around 90 minutes, the second stage ends when the baby has completely left the mother's body.

Stage 3

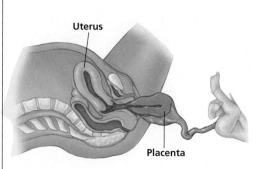

Uterus

Placenta

The child's umbilical cord (still attached to the neonate) and the placenta are expelled from the mother. This stage is the quickest and easiest, taking just a few minutes.

FIGURE 4-1   **THE THREE STAGES OF LABOR**

opening. Because the area between the vagina and rectum must stretch a good deal, an incision called an **episiotomy** is sometimes made to increase the size of the opening of the vagina. However, this practice has been increasingly criticized in recent years as potentially causing more harm than good, and the number of episiotomies has fallen drastically over the past decade (Goldberg et al., 2002).

The second stage of labor ends when the baby has completely left the mother's body. The *third stage of labor* occurs when the umbilical cord (still attached to the neonate) and the placenta are expelled from the mother. This stage is the quickest and easiest, taking just a few minutes.

The nature of a woman's reactions to labor reflect, in part, cultural factors. Although there is no evidence that the physiological aspects of labor differ among women of different cultures, expectations about labor and interpretations of its pain do vary significantly from one culture to another (Scopesi, Zanobini, & Carossino, 1997).

For instance, there is a kernel of truth to popular stories of pregnant women in certain societies putting down the tools with which they are tilling their fields, stepping aside and giving birth, and immediately returning to work with their neonates wrapped and bundled on their backs. Accounts of the !Kung people in Africa describe the woman in labor sitting calmly beside a tree and without much ado—or assistance—successfully giving birth to a child and quickly recovering. By contrast, many societies regard childbirth as dangerous, and some even view it much like an illness. Such cultural perspectives color the way people in a given society view the experience of childbirth (Cole, 1992; Maiden, 1997).

Birth: From Fetus to Neonate

The exact moment of birth occurs when the fetus, having left the uterus through the cervix, passes through the vagina to emerge fully from its mother's body. In most cases, babies automatically make the transition from taking in oxygen via the placenta to using their lungs to breathe air. Consequently, as soon as they are outside the mother's body, most newborns spontaneously cry. This helps them clear their lungs and breathe on their own.

What happens next varies from situation to situation and from culture to culture. In Western cultures, health care workers are almost always on hand to assist with the birth. In the United States, 99 percent of births are attended by professional health care workers, but

Episiotomy An incision sometimes made during childbirth to increase the size of the opening of the vagina to allow the baby to pass

worldwide only about 50 percent of births have professional health care workers in attendance (United Nations, 1990).

The Apgar Scale.   In most cases, the newborn infant first undergoes a quick visual inspection. Parents may be counting fingers and toes, but trained health care workers look for something more. Typically, they employ the **Apgar scale,** a standard measurement system that looks for a variety of indications of good health (see Table 4-1). Developed by physician Virginia Apgar in 1953, the scale directs attention to five basic qualities, recalled most easily by using the letters of Apgar's name as a guide: *appearance* (color), *pulse* (heart rate), *grimace* (reflex irritability), *activity* (muscle tone), and *respiration* (respiratory effort).

Using the scale, health care workers assign the newborn a score ranging from 0 to 2 on each of the five qualities, producing an overall score that can range from 0 to 10. The vast majority of children score 7 or above. The 10 percent of neonates who score under 7 require help to start breathing. Newborns who score under 4, like Tamara Nussbaum, described at the beginning of the chapter, need immediate lifesaving intervention.

Although low Apgar scores may indicate problems or birth defects that were already present in the fetus, the process of birth itself may sometimes cause difficulties. Among the most profound are those relating to a temporary deprivation of oxygen.

At various junctures during labor, the fetus may not get sufficient oxygen. This can happen for any of a number of reasons. For instance, the umbilical cord may get wrapped around the neck of the fetus. The cord can also be pinched during a prolonged contraction, thereby cutting off the supply of oxygen that flows through it.

Lack of oxygen for a few seconds is not particularly harmful to the fetus, but deprivation for any longer time may cause serious harm. A restriction of oxygen, or **anoxia,** lasting a few minutes can produce brain damage as brain cells die. Furthermore, anoxia can lead to such an increase in blood pressure that bleeding occurs in the brain.

Physical Appearance and Initial Encounters.   After assessing the newborn's health, health care workers next deal with the remnants of the child's passage through the birth canal. You'll recall the description of the thick, greasy substance (like cheese) that covers the newborn. This material, called *vernix,* smoothes the passage through the birth canal; it is no longer

Apgar scale   A standard measurement system that looks for a variety of indications of good health in newborns

Anoxia   A restriction of oxygen to the baby, lasting a few minutes during the birth process, which can produce brain damage

	TABLE 4-1 APGAR SCALE			

A score is given for each sign at 1 minute and 5 minutes after the birth. If there are problems with the baby, an additional score is given at 10 minutes. A score of 7–10 is considered normal, whereas 4–7 might require some resuscitative measures, and a baby with an Apgar score of 3 or below requires immediate resuscitation.

	Sign	0 Points	1 Point	2 Points
A	Appearance (skin color)	Blue-gray, pale all over	Normal, except for extremities	Normal over entire body
P	Pulse	Absent	Below 100 bpm	Above 100 bpm
G	Grimace (reflex irritability)	No response	Grimace	Sneezes, coughs, pulls away
A	Activity (muscle tone)	Absent	Arms and legs flexed	Active movement
R	Respiration	Absent	Slow, irregular	Good, crying

(*Source:* Apgar, 1953)

Bonding Close physical and emotional contact between parent and child during the period immediately following birth, argued by some to affect later relationship strength

needed once the child is born and is quickly cleaned away. Newborns' bodies are also covered with a fine, dark fuzz known as *lanugo;* this soon disappears. The newborn's eyelids may be puffy due to an accumulation of fluids during labor, and the newborn may have blood or other fluids on parts of its body.

After being cleansed, the newborn is usually returned to the mother and the father, if he is present. The everyday and universal occurrence of childbirth makes it no less miraculous to parents, and most cherish this time to make their first acquaintance with their child.

However, the importance of the initial encounter between parent and child has become a matter of considerable controversy. Some psychologists and physicians argued in the 1970s and early 1980s that **bonding,** the close physical and emotional contact between parent and child during the period immediately following birth, was a crucial ingredient for forming a lasting relationship between parent and child. Their arguments were based in part on research conducted on nonhuman species such as ducklings. This work showed that there was a critical period just after birth when organisms showed a particular readiness to learn, or *imprint,* from other members of their species who happened to be present (Lorenz, 1957).

According to the concept of bonding applied to humans, a critical period begins just after birth and lasts only a few hours. During this period, actual skin-to-skin contact between mother and child supposedly leads to deep, emotional bonding (de Chateau, 1980; Klaus & Kennell, 1976). The corollary to this assumption is that if circumstances prevent such contact, the bond between mother and child will forever be lacking in some way. Because medical practices prevalent at the time often left little opportunity for sustained mother and child physical contact immediately after birth, the concept was received with alarm and generated a substantial amount of public attention (Eyer, 1992).

There was just one problem: Scientific evidence for the notion was lacking. When developmental researchers carefully reviewed the research literature, they found little support for the idea. Although it does appear that mothers who have early physical contact with their babies are more responsive to them than those who don't have such contact, the difference lasts only a few days. Furthermore, although parents may experience concern, anxiety, and even disappointment, there are no lingering reactions to separations immediately following birth, even for those that extend for several days. Such news is reassuring to parents like Tamara Nussbaum's mother, whose children must receive immediate, intensive medical attention just after birth. It is also comforting to parents who adopt children and are not present at all at their births (Eyer, 1994; Lamb, 1982a; Redshaw, 1997).

Approaches to Childbirth: Where Medicine and Attitudes Meet

Ester Iverem knew herself well enough to know that she didn't like the interaction she had with medical doctors. So she opted for a nurse-midwife at Manhattan's Maternity Center where she was free to use a birthing stool and to have her husband, Nick Chiles, by her side. When contractions began, Iverem and Chiles went for a walk, stopping periodically to rock—a motion, she says, "similar to the way children dance when they first learn how, shifting from foot to foot." That helped her work through the really powerful contractions.

"I sat on the birthing chair [a Western version of the traditional African stool, which lies low to the ground and has an opening in the middle for the baby to come through] and Nick was sitting right behind me. When the midwife said 'Push!' the baby's head just went 'pop!' and out he came." Their son, Mazi (which means "Sir" in Ibo) Iverem Chiles, was placed on Ester's breast while the midwives went to prepare for his routine examination. (Knight, 1994, p. 122)

For something as natural as giving birth, which occurs throughout the nonhuman animal world apparently without much thought, parents in the Western world have developed a

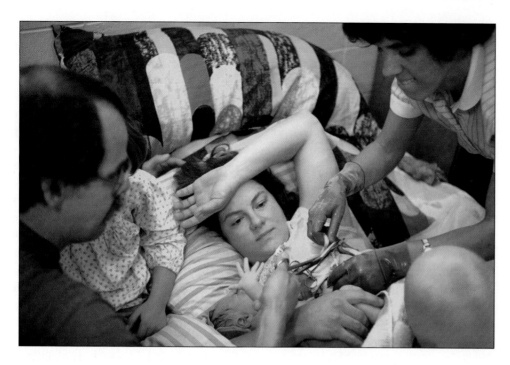

A midwife helps in this home delivery.

variety of strategies—and some very strong opinions. Should the birth take place in a hospital or in the home? Should a physician, a nurse, or a midwife assist? Is the father's presence desirable? Should siblings and other family members be on hand to participate in the birth?

Most of these questions cannot be answered definitively, primarily because the choice of childbirth techniques often comes down to a matter of values and opinions. No single

BECOMING AN INFORMED CONSUMER OF DEVELOPMENT

Dealing With Labor

Every woman who is soon to give birth has some fear of labor. Most have heard gripping tales of extended, 48-hour labors or vivid descriptions of the pain that accompanies labor. Still, most mothers would agree that the rewards of giving birth are worth the effort.

There is no single right or wrong way to deal with labor. However, experts suggest several strategies that can help make the process as positive as possible (Salmon, 1993):

- Be flexible. Although you may have carefully worked out beforehand a scenario about what to do during labor, don't feel an obligation to follow through exactly. If one strategy is ineffective, turn to another.

- Communicate with your health care providers. Let them know what you are experiencing. They may be able to suggest ways to deal with what you are encountering.

- Remember that labor is, well, laborious. Expect that you may become fatigued, but realize that as the final stages of labor occur, you may well get a second wind.

- Accept your partner's support. If a spouse or other partner is present, allow that person to make you comfortable and provide support. Research has shown that women who are supported by a spouse or partner have a more comfortable birth experience (Bader, 1995).

- Be realistic and honest about your reactions to pain. Even if you had planned an unmedicated delivery, realize that you may find the pain difficult to tolerate. At that point, consider the use of drugs. Above all, don't feel that asking for pain medication is a sign of failure. It isn't.

- Focus on the big picture. Keep in mind that labor is part of a process that ultimately leads to an event unmatched in the joy it can bring.

procedure will be effective for all mothers and fathers, and no conclusive research evidence has proved that one procedure is significantly more effective than another. As we'll see, there is a wide variety of issues and options involved.

The abundance of choices is due largely to a reaction to traditional medical practices that had been prevalent in the United States until the early 1970s. Before that time, the typical procedure went something like this: A woman in labor was placed in a room with many other women, all of whom were in various stages of childbirth and some of whom were screaming in pain. Fathers and other family members were not allowed to be present. Just before delivery, the woman was rolled into a delivery room, where the birth took place. Often she was so drugged that she was not aware of the birth at all.

Physicians argued that such procedures were necessary to ensure the health of the newborn and the mother. However, critics charged that alternatives were available that would not only maximize the medical well-being of the participants in the birth but also represent an emotional and psychological improvement as well (Pascoe, 1993).

Alternative Birthing Procedures.   Not all mothers give birth in hospitals, and not all births follow a traditional course. Among the major alternatives to traditional birthing practices are the following (J. J. Mathews & Zadek, 1991; M. Smith, 1990):

In Lamaze classes, parents are taught relaxation techniques to prepare for childbirth and to reduce the need for anesthetics.

- Lamaze birthing techniques. The Lamaze method has achieved widespread popularity in the United States. Based on the writings of Dr. Fernand Lamaze (1970), the method makes use of basic psychological techniques involving relaxation training. Typically, mothers-to-be participate in a series of weekly training sessions in which they learn exercises that help them relax various parts of the body on command. A "coach," most typically the father, is trained along with the future mother. The training allows women to cope with painful contractions with a relaxation response, rather than by tensing up, which may make the pain more acute. In addition, the women learn to focus on a relaxing stimulus, such as a tranquil scene in a picture. The goal is to learn how to deal positively with pain and to relax at the onset of a contraction.

  Does the procedure work? Most mothers, as well as fathers, report that a Lamaze birth is a very positive experience. They enjoy the sense of mastery that they gain over the process of labor, a feeling of control over what can be a formidable experience (Bing, 1983; M. C. Mackey, 1990; Wideman & Singer, 1984). However, we can't be sure that parents who choose the Lamaze method aren't already more highly motivated about the experience of childbirth than parents who do not choose the technique. It is therefore possible that the accolades they express after Lamaze births are due to their initial enthusiasm and not to the Lamaze procedures themselves.

  Although it is not possible to pinpoint definitively the specific consequences of Lamaze preparation for childbirth, one thing is certain: Participation in Lamaze procedures, as well as other so-called *natural childbirth techniques* in which the emphasis is on educating the parents about the process of birth and minimizing the use of drugs, is relatively rare among members of lower income groups, including many members of ethnic minorities. Parents in these groups may not have the transportation, time, or financial resources to attend childbirth preparation classes. The result is that women in lower income groups tend to be less prepared for the events of labor and consequently may suffer more pain and anguish during childbirth (Ball, 1987).

- The Leboyer method. Consider the abrupt transition faced by a neonate. Accustomed to floating in a pool of warm water (the amniotic fluid) for 9 months, hearing only muffled sounds and seeing light only dimly, the newborn is violently thrust into a very different world outside the mother. How might this transition be facilitated?

According to French physician Frederick Leboyer (1975) (pronounced "luh-bwah-YAY"), the optimal approach is to maintain the environment of the womb as long as possible after birth. Under Leboyer's method, delivery rooms are kept softly lighted and hushed. As soon as the baby is born, it is placed on the mother's stomach and then floated in a pool of warm water. The umbilical cord is not cut immediately after birth, as is traditionally done to compel the baby to breathe on its own. Instead, the cord is left intact, allowing the neonate to acclimate gradually to an air-breathing world.

Although the Leboyer technique gained some popularity in the early 1980s, today only one remnant is seen frequently: Newborns are often placed on the warmth of the mother's stomach just after birth.

- Family birthing centers. When Jill Rakovich became pregnant for the third time, she and her husband, Milos, decided they wanted to find a less forbidding locale than the traditional delivery room. They had both found this setting uncomfortable and grim when their two older children were born.

  After researching the possibilities, Jill discovered a family birthing center located close to a nearby hospital. The center consisted of rooms decorated like homey bedrooms. Unlike the typical forbidding hospital room, these looked warm and inviting, although they also were supplied with several pieces of medical equipment. When labor began, Jill and Milos went to the birthing center and settled into one of the rooms. Labor proceeded smoothly, and as her husband watched, Jill gave birth to their third child.

  The decision to use a birthing center is becoming increasingly common. In the majority of cases, labor and delivery are uneventful, permitting births to occur in the relatively relaxed, homelike setting the birthing center provides. In the event of complications, equipment is at hand. Supporters of birthing centers suggest that they provide a more comfortable and less stressful environment than a hospital room, offering a setting that may facilitate labor and delivery (Eakins, 1986).

  Because of the popularity of the philosophy behind birthing centers, many hospitals have opened birthing rooms of their own. The increasing prevalence of birthing centers reflects the view that childbirth is a natural part of life that should not be rigidly isolated

Family birthing centers, looking more like bedrooms than traditional delivery rooms, produce a more relaxed and less intimidating atmosphere than that typically found in hospitals.

from its other aspects. Rather than medical events that involve a passive patient and a dictatorial physician, labor and delivery are now typically viewed as participatory experiences involving the mother, the father, other family members, and care providers acting jointly.

This philosophy also has implications for the choice of care provider. In place of a traditional *obstetrician*, a physician who specializes in delivering babies, some parents are turning

"Midwifery treats pregnancy as a normal part of life, instead of as a set of potential problems."

CAREERS IN CHILD DEVELOPMENT

Mary Lou Singleton

Education: . . . . **Grinnell College, Grinnell, Iowa: B.A. in psychology; licensed by the New Mexico Department of Public Health to practice midwifery**

Position: . . . . **Midwife**

Home: . . . . **Albuquerque, New Mexico**

In today's world of high-tech medicine, it seems surprising that the ancient profession of midwifery still plays a needed role in one of the most basic of human events: the birth of a child.

According to Mary Lou Singleton, who initially wanted to become an obstetrician but changed her mind when she read about midwifery in an anthropology course, the practice involves much more than merely attending to the birth.

"I provide complete prenatal care, but my focus is on the emotional and psychosocial aspects of the pregnancy," she explains. "I usually schedule an hour per visit, and I use the first ten minutes to check blood pressure and run some basic tests. The remainder of the time we discuss motherhood and the pregnancy itself.

"Midwifery treats pregnancy as a normal part of life, instead of as a set of potential problems. A normal, healthy woman who becomes pregnant should be treated as a normal, healthy, pregnant woman," she adds.

In the course of a pregnancy, Singleton conducts approximately 10 prenatal visits to the mother's home.

"I visit about once a month until the twenty-eighth week of pregnancy, then once every other week until the thirty-sixth week, and then weekly until I get the call," she says.

Armed with a beeper and cell phone, as well as her "birth bag," containing items such as a fetoscope to monitor the baby's heart rate and a birthing tub for the comfort of the mother, Singleton makes sure that she's ready when the call comes. She also makes sure that traditional medicine is available if needed.

"I have backup physicians at two of the local hospitals who are always available for consultation if needed or if there is a risk situation," she says.

According to Singleton, the process of home birth with a midwife makes the event more family-oriented and allows the mother to bond immediately with her child. "Birth is a family event, not a medical event. When it happens, the whole family should be able to participate in it," says Singleton.

"Everyone should have complete faith in the mother's ability to go through with the birth in this way. Letting her feel that faith is the best kind of support for a woman in labor," Singleton says.

to a *midwife,* a childbirth attendant who stays with the mother throughout labor and delivery. Midwives—often nurses specializing in childbirth—are used primarily for pregnancies in which no complications are expected. Although the use of midwives is increasing in the United States, they are employed in only a minority of births (De Clercq, 1992). In contrast, midwives help deliver some 80 percent of babies in other parts of the world. Moreover, in countries at all levels of economic development, many births successfully take place at home. For instance, more than a third of all births in the Netherlands occur at home (Treffers et al., 1990).

Which setting and care provider are optimal? In the majority of cases, it does not make a great deal of difference. Naturally, arrangements for care should be made thoughtfully and in advance, and backup medical help should be on call. If a birth is to occur outside a traditional hospital, such a hospital should be within a reasonable distance. Furthermore, for pregnancies that stand a high risk of complications—such as those of women whose previous deliveries have been difficult—a hospital setting is preferable (Rusting, 1990). In addition to choosing the setting and who will attend the birth, parents face other birthing decisions. One major area of decision making concerns how to deal with the pain of childbirth.

Pain and Childbirth.   Any woman who has delivered a baby will agree that childbirth is painful. But how painful, exactly, is it?

The question is largely unanswerable. One reason is that pain is a subjective, psychological phenomenon that cannot be easily measured. No one is able to answer the question of whether one person's pain is "greater" or "worse" than someone else's pain, although some studies have tried to quantify it. For instance, in one survey, women were asked to rate the pain they experienced during labor on a 1-to-5 scale, with 5 being the most painful. Nearly half (44 percent) said "5," and an additional quarter said "4" (L. Yarrow, 1992).

Furthermore, because pain is usually a sign that something is wrong in one's body, we have learned to react to pain with fear and concern. Yet during childbirth, pain is actually a signal that the body is working appropriately—that the contractions that are meant to propel the baby through the birth canal are doing their job. Consequently, the experience of pain during labor is difficult for women in labor to interpret, thereby potentially increasing their anxiety and making the contractions seem even more painful.

Ultimately, the nature of every woman's delivery depends on a complex series of factors. These factors encompass such variables as how much preparation and support she has before and during delivery, her culture's view of pregnancy and delivery, and the specific nature of the delivery itself (Davis-Floyd, 1994; Di Matteo & Kahn, 1997; Walker & O'Brien, 1999).

Use of Anesthesia and Pain-Reducing Drugs.   Among the greatest advances of modern medicine is the ongoing discovery of drugs that reduce pain. However, the use of medication during childbirth is a practice that holds both benefits and pitfalls (Shute, 1997).

About a third of women who receive treatment for pain do so in the form of *epidural anesthesia,* which produces numbness from the waist down. Traditional epidurals produce an inability to walk and in some cases prevent women from helping to push the baby out during delivery. However, a newer form of epidural, known as a *walking epidural* or *dual spinal-epidural,* uses smaller needles and a system for administering continuous doses of anesthetic. It permits women to move about more freely during labor and has fewer side effects than traditional epidural anesthesia.

It is clear that drugs hold the promise of greatly reducing and even eliminating pain associated with labor. However, pain reduction comes at a cost: The stronger the drug, the greater its effects on the fetus and neonate. Because of the small size of the fetus relative to the mother,

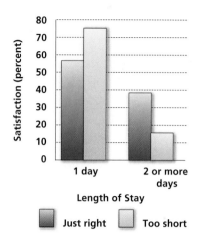

FIGURE 4-2   LONGER IS BETTER

Mothers are most satisfied with their medical care if they stay longer following a birth than if they are discharged after only a day. However, some medical insurance companies are now pushing for a reduction to a stay of only 24 hours following a birth. What arguments might a health care professional use against such a reduction?

(*Source:* D. L. Finkelstein, Harper, & Rosenthal, 1998)

drug doses that might have only a minimal effect on the mother can have a magnified effect on the fetus.

Many studies have demonstrated the results of the use of anesthesia during delivery. Some consequences are immediate: Anesthetics may temporarily depress the flow of oxygen to the fetus and slow labor. In addition, newborns whose mothers have been anesthetized are less physiologically responsive and show poorer motor control during the first days of life after birth (Douglas, 1991; S. H. Halpern et al., 1998; Walker & O'Brien, 1999).

However, most research suggests that drugs, as they are currently employed during labor, produce only minimal risks to the fetus and neonate (Shute, 1997). Guidelines issued by the American College of Obstetricians and Gynecologists (2002) suggest that a woman's request for pain relief at any stage of labor should be honored and that the proper use of minimal amounts of drugs for pain relief is reasonable and has no significant effect on a child's later well-being.

Postdelivery Hospital Stay: Deliver, Then Depart?   When New Jersey mother Diane Mensch was sent home from the hospital just a day after the birth of her third child, she still felt exhausted. But her insurance company insisted that 24 hours was sufficient time to recover, and it refused to pay for more. Three days later, her newborn was back in the hospital, suffering from jaundice. Mensch is convinced that the problem would have been discovered and treated sooner had she and her newborn been allowed to remain in the hospital longer (Begley, 1995).

Mensch's experience is not atypical. The average hospital stay following normal births decreased from 3.9 days in the 1970s to 2 days in the 1990s, prompted in large part by medical insurance companies, who advocated hospital stays of only 24 hours following birth in order to reduce costs.

However, medical care providers have fought against this trend, believing that there are definite risks involved, both for mothers and for their newborns. For instance, mothers may begin to bleed if they tear tissue injured during childbirth. It is also riskier for newborns to be discharged prematurely from the intensive medical care that hospitals can provide. Furthermore, mothers are more satisfied with their medical care when they stay longer (D. L. Finkelstein, Harper, & Rosenthal, 1998; see Figure 4-2).

In accordance with these views, the American Academy of Pediatrics states that women should stay in the hospital no less than 48 hours after giving birth, and the U.S. Congress has passed legislation mandating a minimum insurance coverage of 48 hours for childbirth (American Academy of Pediatrics, 1995).

REVIEW & APPLY

Review

- In the first stage of labor, contractions increase in frequency, duration, and intensity until the baby's head is able to pass through the cervix. In the second stage, the baby moves through the cervix and birth canal and leaves the mother's body. In the third stage, the umbilical cord and placenta emerge.

- Immediately after birth, birthing attendants usually examine the neonate using a measurement system such as the Apgar scale.

- Many birthing options are available to parents today. They may weigh the advantages and disadvantages of anesthetic drugs during birth, and they may choose alternatives to traditional hospital birthing, including the Lamaze method, the Leboyer method, the use of a birthing center, and the use of a midwife.

Applying Child Development

- Why might cultural differences exist in expectations and interpretations of labor? What implications would such cultural differences have for how women are prepared for childbirth?

- *From a health care worker's perspective:* Whereas 99 percent of U.S. births are attended by professional medical workers or birthing attendants, this is the case in only about half of births worldwide. What do you think are some causal factors and implications of this statistic?

Birth Complications

In addition to the usual complimentary baby supplies that most hospitals bestow on new mothers, the maternity nurses at Greater Southeast Hospital have become practiced in handing out "grief baskets."

Inside are items memorializing one of [Washington, D.C.'s] grimmest statistics— an infant mortality rate that's more than twice the national average. The baskets contain a photograph of the dead newborn, a snip of its hair, the tiny cap it wore, and a yellow rose. (P. Thomas, 1994, p. A14)

The infant mortality rate in Washington, D.C., capital of the richest country in the world, is 14.9 deaths per 1,000 births, exceeding the rate of countries such as Hungary, Cuba, Kuwait, and Costa Rica. Overall, the United States ranks 26th among industrialized countries, with 7.3 deaths for every 1,000 live births (Eberstadt, 1994; National Center for Health Statistics, 2000; Singh & Yu, 1995; see Figure 4-3).

Why is infant survival less likely in the United States than in other, less developed countries? To answer this question, we need to consider the nature of the problems that can occur during labor and delivery.

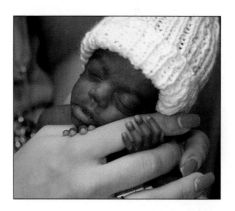

Preterm infants stand a much greater chance of survival today than they did even a decade ago.

Preterm Infants: Too Soon, Too Small

Like Tamara Nussbaum, whose birth was described in the chapter prologue, some 6 to 7 percent of infants are born earlier than normal. **Preterm infants,** or premature infants, are born less than 38 weeks after conception. Because they have not had time to develop fully as fetuses, preterm infants are at high risk for illness and death (Jeng, Yau, & Teng, 1998).

The extent of danger faced by preterm babies largely depends on the child's weight at birth, which has great significance as an indicator of the extent of the baby's development. Although the average newborn weighs around 3,400 grams (about 7½ pounds), **low-birthweight infants** weigh less than 2,500 grams (around 5½ pounds). Although only 7 percent of all newborns in the United States fall into the low-birthweight category, they account for the majority of newborn deaths (Gross, Spiker, & Haynes, 1997).

Although most low-birthweight infants are preterm, some are small-for-gestational-age babies. **Small-for-gestational-age infants** are infants who, because of delayed fetal growth,

Preterm infants Infants born less than 38 weeks after conception (also known as premature infants)

Low-birthweight infants Infants who weigh less than 2,500 grams (around 5½ pounds)

Small-for-gestational-age infants Infants who, because of delayed fetal growth, weigh 90 percent (or less) of the average weight of infants of the same gestational age

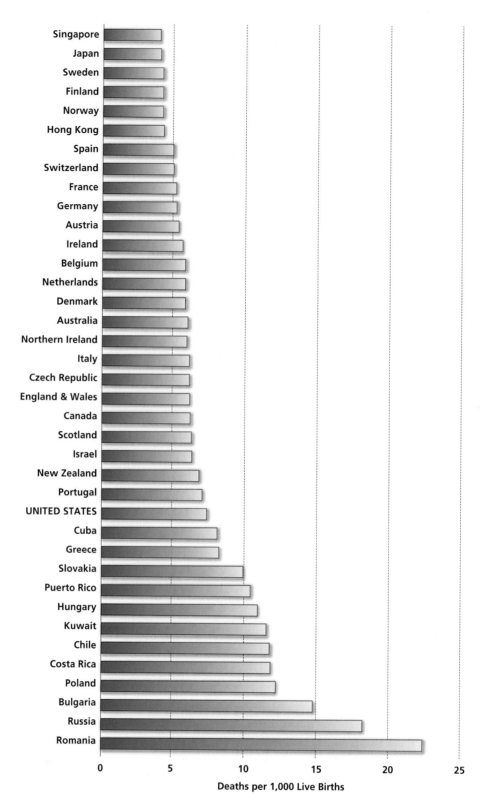

FIGURE 4-3   INTERNATIONAL INFANT MORTALITY

Although the United States has greatly reduced its infant mortality rate since 1965, it currently ranks 26th among industrialized countries. What are some of the reasons for this infant mortality ranking?

(*Source:* National Center for Health Statistics, 2000)

weigh 90 percent (or less) of the average weight of infants of the same gestational age. Small-for-gestational-age infants are sometimes also preterm but may not be (Meisels & Plunkett, 1988; Shiono & Behrman, 1995).

If the degree of prematurity is not too great and weight at birth is not extremely low, the threat to the child's well-being is relatively minor. In such cases, the main treatment may be to keep the baby in the hospital to gain weight. Additional weight is critical because fat layers help prevent chilling in neonates, who are not particularly efficient at regulating body temperature.

Newborns who are born more prematurely and who have significantly below-average birthweights face a tougher road. For them, simply staying alive is a major task. For instance, low-birthweight infants are highly vulnerable to infection. Furthermore, because their lungs have not had time to develop completely, premature babies have problems taking in sufficient oxygen. As a consequence, they may experience *respiratory distress syndrome (RDS),* with potentially fatal consequences.

To deal with RDS, low-birthweight infants are often placed in incubators, enclosures in which temperature and oxygen content are controlled. The exact amount of oxygen is carefully monitored. Too low a concentration of oxygen will not provide relief, and too high a concentration can damage the delicate retinas of the eyes, leading to permanent blindness.

The immature development of preterm neonates makes them unusually sensitive to stimuli in their environment. They can easily be overwhelmed by the sights, sounds, and sensations they experience, and their breathing may be interrupted or their heart rates may slow. Furthermore, they are often unable to move smoothly; their arm and leg movements are uncoordinated, causing them to jerk about and appear startled. Such behavior is quite disconcerting to parents (Doussard-Roosevelt et al., 1997; Field, 1990).

Despite the difficulties they experience at birth, the majority of preterm infants eventually develop normally in the long run. However, the tempo of development often proceeds more slowly for preterm children compared to children born at full term, and more subtle problems sometimes emerge later. For example, by the end of their first year, only 10 percent of prematurely born infants display significant problems, and only 5 percent are seriously disabled. By the age of 6, however, approximately 38 percent have mild problems that call for special educational interventions. For instance, some preterm children show learning disabilities, behavior disorders, or lower-than-average IQ scores. Others have difficulties with physical coordination. Still, around 60 percent of preterm infants are free of even minor problems (Arseneault et al., 2002; Farel et al., 1998; Nadeau et al., 2001).

Very-Low-Birthweight Infants: The Smallest of the Small. The story is less positive for the most extreme cases of prematurity—very-low-birthweight infants. **Very-low-birthweight infants** weigh less than 1,250 grams (around 2¼ pounds) or, regardless of weight, have been in the womb less than 30 weeks.

Not only are very-low-birthweight infants tiny, some fitting easily in the palm of the hand like little Tamara Nussbaum, but they also hardly seem even to belong to the same species as full-term newborns. Their eyes may be fused shut, and their earlobes may look like flaps of skin on the sides of their heads. Their skin is a darkened red color, whatever their race.

Very-low-birthweight babies are in grave danger from the moment they are born, due to the immaturity of their organ systems. Until about two decades ago, these babies would not have survived outside the womb. However, medical advances have led to a higher chance of survival, pushing the **age of viability,** the point at which an infant can survive prematurely, to about 22 weeks after conception—some 4 months earlier than the term of a normal delivery. Of course, the longer the period of development beyond conception, the greater a newborn's chances of survival. A baby born earlier than 25 weeks has less than a 50–50 chance of survival (see Figure 4-4).

The physical and cognitive problems experienced by low-birthweight and preterm babies are even more pronounced in very-low-birthweight infants, with astonishing financial consequences. A 3-month stay in an incubator in an intensive care unit can run into the hundreds

Very-low-birthweight infants Infants who weigh less than 1,250 grams (around 2¼ pounds) or, regardless of weight, have been in the womb less than 30 weeks

Age of viability The point at which an infant can survive a premature birth

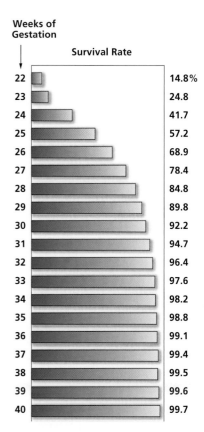

Weeks of Gestation

Survival Rate	
22	14.8%
23	24.8
24	41.7
25	57.2
26	68.9
27	78.4
28	84.8
29	89.8
30	92.2
31	94.7
32	96.4
33	97.6
34	98.2
35	98.8
36	99.1
37	99.4
38	99.5
39	99.6
40	99.7

FIGURE 4-4   SURVIVAL AND GESTATIONAL AGE

Chances of a fetus surviving greatly improve after about 28 weeks. Rates shown are the percentages of babies born in the United States after specified lengths of gestation who survive the first year of life. Rates are based on data collected from 1989 to 1991.

(*Source:* National Center for Health Statistics, 1997).

of thousands of dollars, and about half of these newborns ultimately die, despite massive medical intervention (H. G. Taylor et al., 2000).

Even if a very-low-birthweight preterm infant survives, the medical costs can continue to mount. For instance, one estimate suggests that the average monthly cost of medical care for such infants during the first 3 years of life may be 3 to 50 times higher than the medical costs for a full-term child. Such astronomical costs have raised ethical debates about the expenditure of substantial financial and human resources in cases in which a positive outcome may be unlikely (Kraybill, 1998; M. Prince, 2000; Wallace et al., 1995).

As medical capabilities progress, the age of viability is likely to be pushed even earlier. Developmental researchers, however, are formulating new strategies for dealing with preterm infants in the hope of improving their lives. Furthermore, emerging evidence suggests that high-quality care can provide protection from some of the risks associated with prematurity and that in fact by the time they reach adulthood, premature babies may be little different from other adults (Hack et al., 2002).

Research also shows that preterm infants who receive more responsive, stimulating, and organized care are apt to show more positive outcomes than children whose care is not as good. Some of these interventions are quite simple. For example, "kangaroo care," in which infants are held, skin to skin, against their parents' chests, appears to be effective in promoting the development of preterm infants. Massaging preterm infants several times a day triggers a complex chemical reaction that assists infants in their efforts to survive (R. S. Feldman et al., 2002; Field, 2000, 2001; Picard, Del Dotto, & Breslau, 2000).

Causes of Preterm and Low-Birthweight Deliveries.   Although half of preterm and low-birthweight births are unexplained, several known causes account for the remainder. In some cases, difficulties relating to the mother's reproductive system cause such births. For instance, mothers carrying twins have unusual stress placed on them, which can lead to premature labor. In fact, most multiple births are preterm to some degree (Cooperstock et al., 1998; Paneth, 1995; Radetsky, 1994).

In other cases, preterm and low-birthweight babies are a result of the immaturity of the mother's reproductive system. Young mothers—under the age of 15—are more prone to deliver prematurely than older ones. In addition, a woman who has not had much time between pregnancies is more likely to deliver a preterm or low-birthweight infant than a woman whose reproductive system has had a chance to recover from a prior delivery (Du Plessis, Bell, & Richards, 1997).

Finally, factors that affect the general health of the mother, such as nutrition, level of medical care, amount of stress in the environment, and economic support, are all related to prematurity and low birthweight. Rates of preterm births differ between racial groups, not because of race per se but because members of racial minorities have disproportionately lower incomes. For instance, the percentage of low-birthweight infants born to African American mothers is double that for Caucasian American mothers (E. Carlson & Hoem, 1999; S. E. Cohen, 1995; National Center for Health Statistics, 1993; Radetsky, 1994; J. A. Stein, Lu, & Gelberg, 2000). The factors associated with increased risk of low birthweight are summarized in Table 4-2.

Postmature Babies: Too Late, Too Large

One might imagine that a baby who spends extra time in the womb might have some advantages, given the opportunity to continue growth undisturbed by the outside world. Yet the reality is different. **Postmature infants**—those still unborn 2 weeks after the mother's due date—face several risks.

For example, the blood supply from the placenta may become insufficient to nourish the still-growing fetus adequately. Consequently, the blood supply to the brain may be decreased,

Postmature infants Infants still unborn 2 weeks after the mother's due date

TABLE 4-2	FACTORS ASSOCIATED WITH INCREASED RISK OF LOW BIRTHWEIGHT

I. Demographic Risks
  A. Age (less than 17; over 34)
  B. Race (minority)
  C. Low socioeconomic status
  D. Unmarried
  E. Low level of education

II. Medical Risks Predating Pregnancy
  A. Parity (0 or more than 4)
  B. Low weight for height
  C. Genitourinary anomalies or surgery
  D. Selected diseases such as diabetes or chronic hypertension
  E. Nonimmune status for selected infections such as rubella
  F. Poor obstetric history, including previous low-birthweight infant or multiple spontaneous abortions
  G. Maternal genetic factors (such as low weight at own birth)

III. Medical Risks in Current Pregnancy
  A. Multiple pregnancy
  B. Poor weight gain
  C. Short interpregnancy interval
  D. Low blood pressure
  E. Hypertension, preeclampsia, or toxemia
  F. Selected infections such as asymptomatic bacteriuria, rubella, or cytomegalovirus
  G. First- or second-trimester bleeding

H. Placental problems such as placenta previa or abruptio placentae
I. Severe morning sickness
J. Anemia or abnormal hemoglobin
K. Severe anemia in a developing baby
L. Fetal anomalies
M. Incompetent cervix
N. Spontaneous premature rupture of membrane

IV. Behavioral and Environmental Risks
  A. Smoking
  B. Poor nutritional status
  C. Alcohol and other substance abuse
  D. DES exposure and other toxic exposure, including occupational hazards
  E. High altitude

V. Health Care Risks
  A. Absent or inadequate prenatal care
  B. Iatrogenic prematurity

VI. Evolving Concepts of Risks
  A. Stress, both physical and psychosocial
  B. Uterine irritability
  C. Events triggering uterine contractions
  D. Cervical changes detected before onset of labor
  E. Selected infections such as mycoplasma or chlamydia trachomatis
  F. Inadequate plasma volume expansion
  G. Progesterone deficiency

(*Source:* Adapted from Committee to Study the Prevention of Low Birthweight, 1985)

leading to the potential of brain damage. Similarly, labor becomes riskier (for both the child and the mother) as a fetus who may be equivalent in size to a 1-month-old infant has to make its way through the birth canal (Boylan, 1990; K. M. Shea, Wilcox, & Little, 1998).

In some ways, difficulties involving postmature infants are more easily prevented than those involving preterm babies, since medical practitioners can induce labor artificially if the pregnancy continues too long. Not only can certain drugs bring on labor, but physicians also have the option of performing cesarean deliveries, a form of delivery we consider in the *From Research to Practice* box.

Infant Mortality and Stillbirth: The Tragedy of Premature Death

The joy that accompanies the birth of a child is completely reversed when a newborn dies. The relative rarity of their occurrence makes infant deaths even harder for parents to bear.

Cesarean Delivery: Intervening in the Process of Birth

As Elena entered her 18th hour of labor, the obstetrician who was monitoring her progress began to look concerned. She told Elena and her husband, Pablo, that the fetal monitor revealed that the fetus's heart rate had begun to fall after each contraction. After trying some simple remedies, such as repositioning Elena on her side, the obstetrician came to the conclusion that the fetus was in distress. She told them that the baby should be delivered immediately, and to accomplish that, she would have to carry out a cesarean delivery.

Elena became one of the almost 1 million mothers in the United States who have a cesarean delivery each year. In a **cesarean delivery** (sometimes known as a cesarean section or "c-section"), the baby is surgically removed from the uterus rather than allowed to travel through the birth canal.

Cesarean deliveries occur most frequently when the fetus shows distress of some sort. For instance, if the fetus appears to be in danger, as indicated by a sudden rise or drop in its heart rate or if blood is seen coming from the mother's vagina during labor, a cesarean may be performed. In addition, mothers over

the age of 40 are more likely to have cesarean deliveries than younger ones (Dulitzki et al., 1998; W. M. Gilbert, Nesbitt, & Danielsen, 1999).

Cesarean deliveries are also sometimes used if the baby is in *breech position,* with its feet rather than its head in the birth canal. Breech position births, which occur in about 1 out of 25 births, place the baby at risk because the umbilical cord is more likely to be compressed, depriving the baby of oxygen. Cesarean deliveries are also more likely in *transverse position* births, in which the baby lies crosswise in the uterus, or when the baby's head is so large that it has trouble moving through the birth canal.

The routine use of **fetal monitors,** devices that measure the baby's heartbeat during labor, has contributed to a soaring rate of cesarean deliveries. Almost 25 percent of all children in the United States are born in this way, up some 500 percent from the early 1970s (National Center for Health Statistics, 1993b). What benefits have resulted from this increase?

According to critics, very few. Other countries have substantially lower rates of cesarean deliveries (see Figure 4-5), and there is no association between successful birth consequences and the rate of cesarean deliveries. In addition, cesarean deliveries carry dangers. The procedure involves major surgery, and recovery can be lengthy, particularly when compared to a normal delivery. In addition, the risk of maternal infection is higher with cesarean

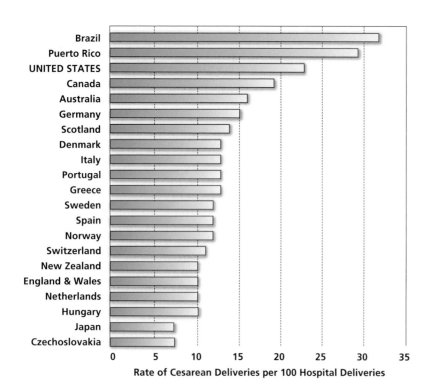

Rate of Cesarean Deliveries per 100 Hospital Deliveries

FIGURE 4-5
CESAREAN DELIVERIES

The rate at which cesarean deliveries are performed varies substantially from one country to another. How would health care workers explain the high rate in the United States compared to other countries?

(*Source:* Notzon, 1990, p. 3287)

deliveries (J. Fisher, Astbury, & Smith, 1997; Koroukian, Trisel, & Rimm, 1998).

Finally, a cesarean delivery presents some risks for the baby. Although cesarean babies are spared the stresses of passing though the birth canal, their relatively easy passage into the world may deter the normal release of certain stress-related hormones, such as catecholamines, into the newborn's bloodstream. Because these hormones help prepare the neonate to deal with the stress of the world outside the womb, their absence may be detrimental to the newborn child. In fact, research indicates that babies who have not experienced labor due to a cesarean delivery are more prone to initial breathing problems upon birth than those who experience at least some labor prior to being born via a cesarean delivery. Finally, mothers who deliver by cesarean are less satisfied with the birth experience, although their dissatisfaction does not influence the quality of mother–child interactions (Durik, Hyde, & Clark, 2000; Hales, Morgan, & Thurnau, 1993).

Due in part to the increase in cesarean deliveries that results from the use of fetal monitors, medical authorities currently recommend avoiding their routine use. These experts cite research evidence that the outcomes are no better for newborns who have been monitored than for those who have not been monitored. Medical personnel have also noticed that monitors tend to indicate fetal distress when there is none—false alarms—with disquieting regularity (Albers & Krulewitch, 1993; Levano et al., 1986). Monitors can, however, still play a crucial role in high-risk pregnancies and in cases of preterm and postmature babies.

Sometimes a child does not even live beyond its passage through the birth canal. **Stillbirth,** the delivery of a child who is not alive, occurs in less than 1 delivery out of 100. Sometimes the death is detected before labor begins. In this case, labor is typically induced, or physicians may carry out a cesarean delivery in order to remove the body from the mother as soon as possible. In other cases of stillbirth, the baby dies during its travels through the birth canal.

Infant mortality is defined as death within the first year of life. In 2001, the overall rate in the United States was 6.9 deaths per 1,000 live births, having fallen from 8.5 deaths per 1,000 live births during the 1990s. However, infant mortality is a major health issue among minorities, with the rate for infants of black mothers 2.5 times those of non-Hispanic white or Hispanic mothers (MacDorman et al., 2002).

Whether the death is a stillbirth or occurs after the child is born, the loss of a baby is a tragic event. The impact on parents is significant: They move through the same stages of grief and mourning as they experience when an older loved one dies. In fact, the cruel juxtaposition of the first dawning of life and an unnaturally early death may make the death particularly difficult to accept and deal with. Depression is a common aftermath (Finkbeiner, 1996; McGreal, Evans, & Burrows, 1997; J. A. Murray et al., 2000).

Cesarean delivery A birth in which the baby is surgically removed from the uterus rather than traveling through the birth canal

Fetal monitor A device that measures the baby's heartbeat during labor

Stillbirth Delivery of a child that is not alive; occurs in less than 1 delivery out of 100

Infant mortality Death within the first year of life

Postpartum Depression: From the Heights of Joy to the Depths of Despair

She had been overjoyed when she found out that she was pregnant and had spent the months of her pregnancy happily preparing for her baby's arrival. The birth was routine, the baby a healthy, pink-cheeked boy. But only a few days after her son's birth, she sank into the depths of depression. Constantly crying, confused, feeling incapable of caring for her child, she was experiencing unshakable despair.

The diagnosis: a classic case of postpartum depression. *Postpartum depression,* a period of deep depression following the birth of a child, affects some 10 percent of all new mothers. Although it takes several forms, its main symptom is an enduring, deep feeling of sadness and unhappiness, lasting in some cases for months or even years. In about 1 in 500 cases, the symptoms are even worse, evolving into a total break with reality. In extremely rare instances, postpartum depression may turn deadly. For example, a mother in Texas who was charged

DEVELOPMENTAL DIVERSITY

Overcoming Racial and Cultural Differences in Infant Mortality

The general decline in the infant mortality rate in the United States over the past several decades masks significant racial differences. In particular, African American babies are more than twice as likely to die before the age of 1 than white babies. Such differences are largely the result of socioeconomic factors; the poverty rate among African American women is significantly greater than for Caucasian women, resulting in poorer prenatal care. As a consequence, the percentage of low-birthweight births—the factor most closely linked to infant mortality—is significantly greater among African American mothers than mothers of other racial groups (see Figure 4-6; G. J. Duncan & Brooks-Gunn, 2000; National Center for Health Statistics, 1998; Stolberg, 1999).

But it is not just members of particular racial groups in the United States who suffer from poor mortality rates. As mentioned earlier, the overall U.S. rate of infant mortality is higher than the rate in many other countries. For example, the mortality rate in the United States is almost double that of Japan, which has the lowest mortality rate of any country in the world.

What makes the United States fare so poorly in terms of newborn survival? One answer is that the United States has a higher rate of low-birthweight and preterm deliveries than many other countries. In fact, when U.S. infants are compared to infants of the same weight who are born in other countries, the differences in mortality rates disappear (Paneth, 1995; Wilcox et al., 1995).

Although overall infant mortality rates have declined in the United States, there are significant differences in mortality among members of different racial and socioeconomic groups.

Another reason for the higher U.S. mortality rate relates to economic diversity. The United States has a higher proportion of people living in poverty than many other countries. Because people in lower economic categories are less likely to have adequate medical care and tend to be less healthy, the relatively high

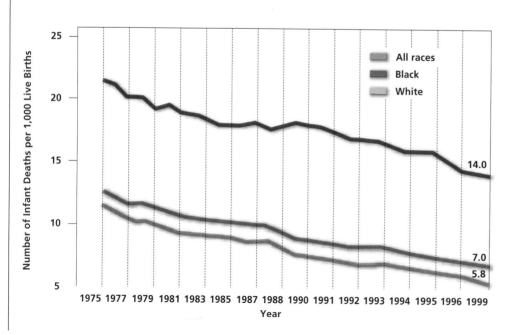

FIGURE 4-6   RACE AND INFANT MORTALITY

Although infant mortality is dropping for both African American and white children, the death rate is still more than twice as high for African American children. These figures show the number of deaths in the first year of life for every 1,000 live births. Taking the perspective of a social worker, what might be done to reduce this high rate of infant mortality?

(*Sources:* National Center for Health Statistics, 2002; Health Resources and Services Administration, 1998)

proportion of economically deprived individuals in the United States has an impact on the overall mortality rate (Aved et al., 1993; Terry, 2000).

Furthermore, many countries do a significantly better job providing prenatal care to mothers-to-be than the United States. For instance, low-cost and even free care, both before and after delivery, is often available in other countries. Paid maternity leave is frequently provided to pregnant women, lasting in some cases as long as 51 weeks (see Table 4-3). Such opportunities for maternity leave are important: Mothers who spend more time on maternity leave may have better mental health and higher quality interactions with their infants (R. Clark et al., 1997; Hyde et al., 1995).

Furthermore, in certain European countries, women receive a comprehensive package of services involving general practitioner, obstetrician, and midwife. Pregnant women receive many privileges, such as transportation benefits for visits to health care providers. In Norway, pregnant women may be given living expenses for up to 10 days so that they can be close to a hospital when it is time to give birth. And when their babies are born, new mothers receive, for just a small payment, the assistance of trained home helpers (C. A. Miller, 1987; Morice, 1998).

In the United States, the story is very different. The lack of national health care insurance or a national health policy means that prenatal care is often haphazardly provided to the poor. About 1 out of every 6 pregnant women has insufficient prenatal care. Some 20 percent of white women and close to 40 percent of African American women who are pregnant receive no prenatal care early in their pregnancies. Five percent of white mothers and 11 percent of African American mothers do not see a health care provider until the last 3 months of pregnancy; some never see a health care provider at all. In fact, the percentage of pregnant women in the United States who receive virtually no prenatal care actually increased in the 1990s (J. L. Johnson, Primas, & Coe, 1994; Mikhail, 2000; National Center for Health Statistics, 1993; P. Thomas, 1994).

The ultimate outcome of the deficiency in prenatal services to women with low incomes is the higher likelihood of death for their infants. Yet this unfortunate state of affairs can be changed if greater support is provided. A start would be to ensure that all economically disadvantaged pregnant women have access to free or inexpensive high-quality medical care from the very beginning of pregnancy. Furthermore, barriers that prevent poor women from receiving such care should be reduced. For instance, programs can be developed that help pay for transportation to a health facility or for the care of older children while the mother is making a health care visit (Aved et al., 1993).

Finally, programs that provide basic education for all mothers-to-be are of paramount importance. Increasing the level of understanding of the potential risks involved in childbearing could prevent many problems before they actually occur (Carnegie Task Force, 1994; Fangman et al., 1994).

TABLE 4-3	MATERNITY LEAVE POLICIES GUARANTEED BY LAW	
Country	**Number of Weeks Allowed**	**Portion of Salary Replaced**
Canada	17–18	55% for 15 weeks
China	13	100%
Columbia	12	100%
Egypt	7	100%
France	16–26	100%
Germany	14	100%
Iraq	9	100%
Italy	20	80%
Japan	14	60%
Mexico	12	100%
Morocco	12	100%
Netherlands	16	100%
Nigeria	12	50%
Sweden[a]	66	14 weeks, 100%; 1 year, 75%
United Kingdom	14–18	90%
United States	12	0%

[a]For both parents combined.

(*Source:* International Labor Organization, 1998)

with drowning all five of her children in a bathtub said that postpartum depression led to her actions (Walther, 1997; Yardley, 2001).

For mothers who suffer from postpartum depression, the symptoms are often bewildering. The onset of depression usually comes as a complete surprise. Certain mothers do seem more likely to become depressed, such as those who have been clinically depressed at some point in the past or who have depressed family members. Furthermore, women who are unprepared for the range of emotions that follow the birth of a child—some positive, some negative—may be more prone to depression. Finally, postpartum depression may be triggered by the pronounced swings in hormone production that occur after birth (V. Hendrick, Altshuler, & Suri, 1998; Mauthner, 1999; L. Murray & Cooper, 1997; Swendsen & Mazure, 2000).

Whatever the cause, it is clear that maternal depression leaves its marks on the infant. As we'll see later in the chapter, babies are born with impressive social capacities, and they are highly attuned to the moods of their mothers. When depressed mothers interact with their infants, they are likely to display little emotion and to act detached and withdrawn. This lack of responsiveness leads infants to display fewer positive emotions and to withdraw from contact not only with their mothers but with other adults as well. Maternal depression can also have a negative effect on marital relations and other family members' mental health (Boath, Pryce, & Cox, 1998; T. Jacobsen, 1999; M. K. Weinberg & Tronick, 1996).

REVIEW & APPLY

Review

- Largely because of low birthweight, preterm infants may have substantial difficulties after birth and later in life.

- Very-low-birthweight infants are in special danger because of the immaturity of their organ systems.

- Preterm and low-birthweight deliveries can be caused by health, age, and pregnancy-related factors in the mother. Income (and because of its relationship with income, race) is also an important factor.

- Cesarean deliveries are performed with postmature babies or when the fetus is in distress, in the wrong position, or unable to progress through the birth canal.

- Infant mortality rates can be affected by the availability of inexpensive health care and good education programs for mothers-to-be.

- Postpartum depression affects about 10 percent of new mothers.

Applying Child Development

- What are some ethical considerations relating to the provision of intensive medical care to very-low-birthweight babies? Do you think such interventions should be routine practice? Why or why not?

- *From an educator's perspective:* Why do you think the United States lacks educational and health care policies that could reduce infant mortality rates overall and among poorer people? What arguments would you make to change this situation?

The Competent Newborn

Relatives gathered around the infant car seat and its occupant, Kaita Castro. Born just 2 days ago, this is Kaita's first day home from the hospital with her mother. Kaita's nearest cousin, 4-year-old Tabor, seems uninterested in the new arrival. "Babies can't do anything fun. They can't even do anything at all," he says.

Kaita's cousin Tabor is partly right. There are many things babies cannot do. Neonates arrive in the world incapable of caring for themselves, for example. Why are human infants born so dependent, while members of other species seem to arrive much better equipped for their lives?

In one sense, we are all born too soon. The size of the brain of the average newborn is just one quarter what it will be at adulthood. In comparison, the brain of the macaque monkey, which is born after just 24 weeks of gestation, is 65 percent of its adult size. Because of the relative puniness of the infant human brain, some observers have suggested that we are propelled out of the womb some 6 to 12 months sooner than we ought to be.

In reality, evolution probably knew what it was doing: If we stayed inside our mothers' bodies much longer than we do, our head would be so large that we'd never manage to get through the birth canal (Gould, 1977; Kotre & Hall, 1990; Schultz, 1969).

The relatively underdeveloped brain of the human newborn helps explain the infant's apparent helplessness. Because of this, the earliest views of newborns focused on the things that they could not do, comparing them rather unfavorably to older members of the human species.

Today, however, such beliefs have taken a back seat to more favorable views of the neonate. As developmental researchers have begun to understand more about the nature of newborns, they have come to the realization that infants enter this world with an astounding array of capabilities in all domains of development, physical, cognitive, and social.

Physical Competence: Meeting the Demands of a New Environment

The world faced by a neonate is remarkably different from the one it experienced in the womb. Consider, for instance, the significant changes in functioning that Kaita Castro encountered as she began the first moments of life in her new environment (summarized in Table 4-4).

Newborns enter the world preprogrammed to find, take in, and digest food in the form of the rooting, sucking, and swallowing reflexes.

TABLE 4-4   KAITA CASTRO'S FIRST ENCOUNTERS UPON BIRTH

1. As soon as she is through the birth canal, Kaita automatically begins to breathe on her own despite no longer being attached to the umbilical cord that provided precious air in the womb.

2. Reflexes—unlearned, organized involuntary responses that occur in the presence of stimuli—begin to take over. Sucking and swallowing reflexes permit Kaita immediately to ingest food.

3. The rooting reflex, which involves turning in the direction of a source of stimulation, guides Kaita toward potential sources of food that are near her mouth, such as her mother's nipple.

4. Kaita begins to cough, sneeze, and blink—reflexes that help her avoid stimuli that are potentially bothersome or hazardous.

5. Her senses of smell and taste are highly developed. Physical activities and sucking increase when she smells peppermint. Her lips pucker when a sour taste is placed on her lips.

6. Objects with colors of blue and green seem to catch Kaita's attention more than other colors, and she reacts sharply to loud, sudden noises. She will also continue to cry if she hears other newborns cry but will stop if she hears a recording of her own voice crying.

Reflexes Unlearned, organized involuntary responses that occur automatically in the presence of certain stimuli

VIDEO CLIP

Reflexes

Kaita's most immediate task was to bring sufficient air into her body. Inside her mother, air was delivered through the umbilical cord, which also provided a means for taking away carbon dioxide. The realities of the outside world are different: Once the umbilical cord was cut, Kaita's respiratory system needed to begin its lifetime's work.

For Kaita, the task was automatic. As noted earlier, most newborn babies begin to breathe on their own as soon as they are exposed to air. The ability to breathe immediately is a good indication that the respiratory system of the neonate is reasonably well developed, despite its lack of breathing rehearsal in the womb.

Neonates emerge from the uterus more practiced in other types of physical activities. For example, newborns such as Kaita show several **reflexes**—unlearned, organized involuntary responses that occur automatically in the presence of certain stimuli. Some of these reflexes are well rehearsed, having been present for several months before birth. The *sucking reflex* and the *swallowing reflex* permit Kaita to begin right away to ingest food. The *rooting reflex,* which involves turning in the direction of a source of stimulation (such as a light touch) near the mouth, is also related to eating. It guides the infant toward potential sources of food that are near its mouth, such as a mother's nipple.

Not all of the reflexes that are present at birth lead the newborn to seek out desired stimuli such as food. For instance, Kaita can cough, sneeze, and blink—reflexes that help her to avoid stimuli that are potentially bothersome or hazardous.

Kaita's sucking and swallowing reflexes, which help her consume her mother's milk, are coupled with the newfound ability to digest nutrients. The neonate's digestive system initially produces feces in the form of *meconium,* a greenish-black material that is a remnant of the neonate's days as a fetus.

Because the liver, a critical component of the digestive system, does not always work effectively at first, almost half of all newborns develop a distinctly yellowish tinge to their bodies and eyes. This change in color is a symptom of *neonatal jaundice.* It is most likely to occur in preterm and low-weight neonates, and it is typically not dangerous. Treatment most often consists of placing the baby under fluorescent lights or administering medicine.

Sensory Capabilities: Experiencing the World

Just after Kaita was born, her father was certain that she looked directly at him. Did she, in fact, see him?

This is a hard question to answer for several reasons. For one thing, when sensory experts talk of "seeing," they mean both a sensory reaction due to the stimulation of the visual sensory organs and an interpretation of that stimulation (the distinction, as you might recall from an introductory psychology class, between sensation and perception). Furthermore, as we'll discuss further when we consider sensory capabilities during infancy in Chapter 5, it is tricky, to say the least, to pinpoint the specific sensory skills of newborns who lack the ability to explain what they are experiencing.

Still, we do have some answers to the question of what newborns are capable of seeing and, for that matter, questions about their other sensory capabilities. For example, it is clear that neonates such as Kaita can see to some extent. Although their visual acuity is not fully developed, newborns pay active attention to certain types of information in their environment (Haith, 1991a; C. Moore, 1999).

For instance, neonates pay closest attention to portions of scenes in their field of vision that are highest in information, such as objects that sharply contrast with the rest of their environment. Furthermore, infants can discriminate different levels of brightness. There is even evidence suggesting that newborns have a sense of size constancy. They seem aware that objects stay the same size even though the size of the image on the retina varies with distance (Slater & Johnson, 1998; Slater, Mattock, & Brown, 1990).

Not only can newborn babies distinguish different colors, but they seem to prefer particular ones. For example, they are able to distinguish between red, green, yellow, and blue, and they take more time staring at blue and green objects, suggesting a partiality for those colors (R. J. Adams, Mauer, & Davis, 1986).

Newborns are also clearly capable of hearing. They react to certain kinds of sounds, showing startle reactions to loud, sudden noises, for instance. They also exhibit familiarity with certain sounds. For example, a crying newborn will continue to cry when it hears other newborns crying. If the baby hears a recording of its own crying, however, it is more likely to stop crying, as if recognizing the familiar sound (Dondi, Simion, & Caltran, 1999; G. B. Martin & Clark, 1982).

As with vision, however, the degree of auditory acuity is not as great as it will be later. The auditory system is not completely developed. Moreover, amniotic fluid, which is initially trapped in the middle ear, must drain out before the newborn can fully hear (Reinis & Goldman, 1980).

In addition to sight and hearing, the other senses also function quite adequately in the newborn. It is obvious that newborns are sensitive to touch. For instance, they respond to stimuli such as the hairs of a brush, and they are aware of puffs of air so weak that adults cannot notice them. The senses of smell and taste are also well developed. Newborns suck and increase other physical activity when the odor of peppermint is placed near the nose. They also pucker their lips when a sour taste is placed on them and respond with appropriate facial expressions to other tastes as well. Such findings clearly indicate that the senses of touch, smell, and taste are not only present at birth but reasonably sophisticated (Marlier, Schaal, & Soussignan, 1998; Mistretta, 1990).

In one sense, the sophistication of the sensory systems of newborns such as Kaita is not surprising. After all, the typical neonate has had 9 months to prepare for his or her encounter with the outside world. As noted in Chapter 3, human sensory systems begin their development well before birth. Furthermore, some researchers suggest that the passage through the birth canal places babies in a state of heightened sensory awareness, preparing them for the world that they are about to encounter for the first time (Bornstein & Lamb, 1992b).

Starting at birth, infants are able to distinguish colors and even show preferences for particular ones.

Early Learning Capabilities

One-month-old Michael Samedi was on a car ride with his family when a thunderstorm suddenly began. The storm rapidly became violent, and flashes of lightning were quickly followed by loud thunderclaps. Michael was clearly disturbed and began to sob. With each new thunderclap, the pitch and fervor of his crying increased. Unfortunately, before very long it wasn't just the sound of the thunder that would raise Michael's anxiety; the sight of the lightning alone was enough to make him cry out in fear. In fact, even as an adult, Michael feels his chest tighten and his stomach churn at the mere sight of lightning.

Classical Conditioning. The source of Michael's fear is classical conditioning, a basic type of learning first identified by Ivan Pavlov (and first discussed in Chapter 2). In **classical conditioning,** an organism learns to respond in a particular way to a neutral stimulus that normally does not bring about that type of response.

Pavlov discovered that by repeatedly pairing two stimuli, such as the sound of a bell and the arrival of meat, he could make hungry dogs learn to respond (in this case by salivating) not only when the meat was presented but even when the bell was sounded without the presence of meat (Pavlov, 1927).

The key feature of classical conditioning is stimulus substitution, in which a stimulus that doesn't naturally bring about a particular response is paired with a stimulus that does

VIDEO CLIP

Pavlov's Classical Conditioning
CLASSIC MODULE

Classical conditioning A type of learning in which an organism responds in a particular way to a neutral stimulus that normally does not bring about that type of response

Operant conditioning   A form of learning in which a voluntary response is strengthened or weakened, depending on its association with positive or negative consequences

Habituation   The decrease in the response to a stimulus that occurs after repeated presentations of the same stimulus

evoke that response. Repeatedly presenting the two stimuli together results in the second stimulus's taking on the properties of the first. In effect, the second stimulus is substituted for the first.

One of the earliest examples of the power of classical conditioning in shaping human emotions was demonstrated in the case of an 11-month-old infant known by researchers as "Little Albert" (J. B. Watson & Rayner, 1920). Although he initially adored furry animals and showed no fear of rats, Little Albert learned to fear them when, during a laboratory demonstration, a loud noise was sounded every time he played with a cute and harmless white rat. In fact, the fear generalized to other furry objects, including rabbits and even a Santa Claus mask. (By the way, such a demonstration would be considered unethical today, and it would never be conducted.)

Infants are capable of learning very early through classical conditioning. For instance, 1- and 2-day-old newborns who are stroked on the head just before being given a drop of a sweet-tasting liquid soon learn to turn their heads and suck at the head-stroking alone (Blass, Ganchrow, & Steiner, 1984). Clearly, classical conditioning is in operation from the time of birth.

Operant Conditioning.   But classical conditioning is not the only mechanism through which infants learn; they also respond to operant conditioning. As noted in Chapter 2, **operant conditioning** is a form of learning in which a voluntary response is strengthened or weakened, depending on its association with positive or negative consequences. In operant conditioning, infants learn to act deliberately on their environments in order to bring about some desired consequence. An infant who learns that crying in a certain way is apt to bring her parents' immediate attention is displaying operant conditioning.

Like classical conditioning, operant conditioning functions from the earliest days of life. For instance, researchers have found that even newborns readily learn through operant conditioning to keep sucking on a nipple when it permits them to continue hearing their mothers read a story or to listen to music (Butterfield & Siperstein, 1972; De Casper & Fifer, 1980; Lipsitt, 1986).

VIDEO CLIP

Habituation/
Dishabituation

Habituation.   Probably the most primitive form of learning is demonstrated by the phenomenon of habituation. **Habituation** is the decrease in the response to a stimulus that occurs after repeated presentations of the same stimulus.

Habituation in infants relies on the fact that the presentation of a novel stimulus typically produces an *orienting response*, in which the infant quiets, becomes attentive, and experiences a slowed heart rate. When the novelty wears off due to repeated exposure to the stimulus, the infant no longer reacts with an orienting response. However, when a new and different stimulus is presented, the infant once again reacts with an orienting response. When this happens, we can say that the infant has learned to recognize the original stimulus and to distinguish it from others.

Habituation occurs in every sensory system, and researchers have studied it in several ways. One is to examine changes in sucking, which stops temporarily when a new stimulus is presented. This reaction is not unlike that of an adult who temporarily puts down her knife and fork when a dinner companion makes an interesting statement to which she wishes to pay particular attention. Other measures of habituation include changes in heart rate, respiration rate, and the length of time an infant looks at a particular stimulus.

The development of habituation is linked to physical and cognitive maturation. It is present at birth and becomes more pronounced over the first 12 weeks of infancy. Difficulties involving habituation may be a signal of developmental problems (Braddock, 1993; Rovee-Collier, 1987; Tamis-LeMonda & Bornstein, 1993).

TABLE 4-5	THREE BASIC PROCESSES OF LEARNING	
Type	**Description**	**Example**
Classical conditioning	A situation in which an organism learns to respond in a particular way to a neutral stimulus that normally does not bring about that type of response	A hungry baby stops crying when her mother picks her up because she has learned to associate being picked up with subsequent feeding.
Operant conditioning	A form of learning in which a voluntary response is strengthened or weakened, depending on its positive or negative consequences	An infant who learns that smiling at his parents brings positive attention may smile more often.
Habituation	The decrease in the response to a stimulus that occurs after repeated presentations of the same stimulus	A baby who showed interest and surprise at first seeing a novel toy may show no interest after seeing the same toy several times.

Are There Limits on Learning?   Although the three basic processes of learning that we've considered—classical conditioning, operant conditioning, and habituation (summarized in Table 4-5)—are all present at birth, they initially face considerable constraints. According to researchers Marc Bornstein and Michael Lamb (1992a), three factors limit the success of learning during infancy. One is the *behavioral state* of the infant. In order for learning to occur, infants must be in a sufficiently attentive state to sense, perceive, and recognize the relationship between various stimuli and responses. Without at least a minimal level of attentiveness, learning will not be possible (Papousek & Bernstein, 1969).

Natural constraints on learning are a second limiting factor. Not all behaviors are physically possible for an infant, and infants' perceptual systems, which are not fully developed at birth, may not be sufficiently refined to respond to, or even notice, a particular stimulus. Consequently, certain types of classical and operant conditioning that are possible with older individuals are ineffective with infants.

Finally, *motivational constraints* may limit learning. In order for learning to occur, the response involved must not be so taxing on infants that they are unmotivated to respond. If the response is too demanding, learning may fail to appear, not because the infants haven't learned an association between a stimulus and a response, but because they just don't have the energy or skills to proceed (Rovee-Collier, 1987).

Despite these limitations, infants show great capacities for learning. But just how far do the capabilities of infants extend beyond the basic learning processes? Research on social competence in infants illustrates just how competent infants are in another important regard.

Social Competence: Responding to Others

Soon after Kaita was born, her older brother looked down at her in her crib and opened his mouth wide, pretending to be surprised. Kaita's mother, looking on, was amazed when it appeared that Kaita imitated his expression, opening her mouth as if *she* were surprised.

Researchers registered surprise of their own when they first found that newborns did indeed have the capability to imitate others' behavior. Although infants were known to have all the muscles in place to produce facial expressions related to basic emotions, the actual appearance of such expressions was assumed to be largely random.

However, research beginning in the late 1970s suggested a different conclusion. For instance, developmental researchers demonstrated that when exposed to an adult modeling a

Developmental psychologist Tiffany Field carried out pioneering work on infants' facial expressions.

behavior that the infant already performed spontaneously, such as opening the mouth or sticking out the tongue, the newborn was apt to imitate the behavior (Meltzoff & Moore, 1977).

Even more exciting were findings from a series of studies conducted by developmental psychologist Tiffany Field and her colleagues (Field, 1982; Field et al., 1984; Field & Walden, 1982). They initially showed that infants could discriminate between such basic facial expressions as happiness, sadness, and surprise. They then exposed newborns to an adult model with a happy, sad, or surprised facial expression. The results were clear: The newborns produced a reasonably accurate imitation of the adult's expression (see Figure 4-7).

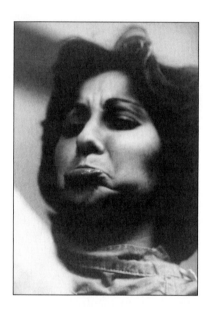

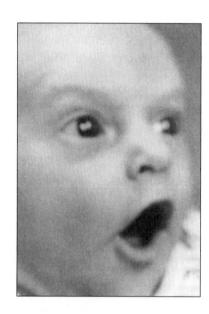
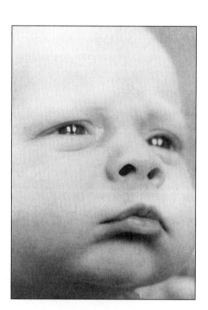

FIGURE 4-7   NONVERBAL IMITATION

It is clear that this newborn infant is imitating the happy, surprised, and sad expressions of the adult model. How might a day care worker use facial expressions to help determine the needs of an infant?

(*Source:* Courtesy of Dr. Tiffany Field)

TABLE 4-6	FACTORS THAT ENCOURAGE SOCIAL INTERACTION BETWEEN FULL-TERM NEWBORNS AND THEIR PARENTS

Full-Term Newborn	Parent
Has organized states	Helps regulate infant's states
Attends selectively to certain stimuli	Provides these stimuli
Behaves in ways interpretable as specific communicative intent	Searches for communicative intent
Responds systematically to parent's acts	Wants to influence newborn, feel effective
Acts in temporally predictable ways	Adjusts actions to newborn's temporal rhythms
Learns from and adapts to parent's behavior	Acts repetitively and predictably

(*Source:* Eckerman & Oehler, 1992)

Subsequent research, conducted just minutes after birth and in a variety of cultures, has shown that all normal newborns have the ability to imitate. Imitative skills are more than a mere curiosity. Effective social interaction with others relies in part on the ability to react to other people in an appropriate manner and to understand the meaning of others' emotional states. Consequently, a newborn's ability to imitate provides the infant with an important foundation for social interaction later in life (Meltzoff & Moore, 1999; Nadel & Butterworth, 1999; R. D. Phillips et al., 1990; Walker-Andrews & Dickson, 1997).

Several other aspects of newborns' behavior also act as forerunners for more formal types of social interaction that they will develop as they grow. As shown in Table 4-6, certain characteristics of neonates mesh with parental behavior to help produce a social relationship between child and parent, as well as social relationships with others (Eckerman & Oehler, 1992).

For example, newborns cycle through various **states of arousal,** different degrees of sleep and wakefulness, ranging from deep sleep to great agitation. Although these cycles are disrupted immediately after birth, they quickly become more regularized. Caregivers become involved when they seek to aid the infant in transitions from one state to another. For instance, a father who rhythmically rocks his crying daughter in an effort to calm her is engaged in a joint activity that is a prelude to future social interactions of different sorts. Similarly, newborns tend to pay particular attention to their mothers' voices (Hepper, Scott, & Shahidullah, 1993). In turn, parents and others modify their speech when talking to infants, using a different pitch and tempo than they use with older children and adults (De Casper & Fifer, 1980; Fernald, 1984; Trainor, Austin, & Desjardins, 2000).

The ultimate outcome of the social interactive capabilities of the newborn infant, and the responses such behavior brings about from parents, is to pave the way for future social interactions. Just as the neonate shows remarkable skills on a physical and perceptual level, its social capabilities are no less sophisticated.

States of arousal   Different degrees of sleep and wakefulness through which newborns cycle, ranging from deep sleep to great agitation

R E V I E W   *&*   A P P L Y

Review

● Neonates are in many ways helpless, but studies of what they *can* do, rather than what they *can't* do, have revealed some surprising capabilities.

- Newborns' respiratory and digestive systems begin to function at birth. Babies have an array of reflexes to help them eat, swallow, find food, and avoid unpleasant stimuli.

- Newborns' sensory competence includes the ability to distinguish objects in the visual field and to see color differences, the ability to hear and to discern familiar sounds, and sensitivity to touch, odors, and tastes.

- The processes of classical conditioning, operant conditioning, and habituation demonstrate infants' learning capabilities.

- Infants develop the foundations of social competence early.

Applying Child Development

- Developmental researchers no longer view the neonate as a helpless, incompetent creature but rather as a remarkably competent, developing human being. *From a child care worker's perspective:* What do you think are some implications of this change in viewpoint for methods of child rearing and child care?

- According to this chapter, classical conditioning relies on stimulus substitution. *From an educator's perspective:* Can you think of examples of the use of classical conditioning on adults in everyday life, in such areas as entertainment, advertising, or politics?

- **What is the normal process of labor?**

  - In the first stage of labor, contractions occur about every 8 to 10 minutes, increasing in frequency, duration, and intensity until the mother's cervix expands. In the second stage of labor, which lasts about 90 minutes, the baby begins to move through the cervix and birth canal and ultimately leaves the mother's body. In the third stage of labor, which lasts only a few minutes, the umbilical cord and placenta are expelled from the mother.

  - After it emerges, the newborn, or neonate, is usually inspected for irregularities, cleaned, and returned to its mother and father.

  - Parents-to-be have a variety of choices regarding the setting for the birth, medical attendants, and whether or not to use pain-reducing medication. Sometimes medical intervention, such as cesarean delivery, becomes necessary.

- **What complications can occur at birth, and what are their causes, effects, and treatments?**

  - Preterm, or premature, infants, born less than 38 weeks following conception, generally have low birthweight, which can cause chilling, vulnerability to infection, respiratory distress syndrome, and hypersensitivity to environmental stimuli. They may even show adverse effects later in life, including slowed development, learning disabilities, behavior disorders, below-average IQ scores, and problems with physical coordination.

- Very-low-birthweight infants are in special danger because of the immaturity of their organ systems. However, medical advances have pushed the age of viability of the infant back to about 24 weeks following conception.

- Postmature babies, who spend extra time in their mothers' womb, are also at risk. However, physicians can artificially induce labor or perform a cesarean delivery to address this situation. Cesarean deliveries are performed when the fetus is in distress, in the wrong position, or unable to progress through the birth canal.

- The infant mortality rate in the United States is higher than the rate in many other countries and higher for low-income families than for higher income families.

- Postpartum depression, an enduring, deep feeling of sadness, affects about 10 percent of new mothers. In severe cases, its effects can be harmful to the mother and the child, and medical intervention is required.

● **What capabilities does the newborn have?**

- Human newborns quickly master breathing through the lungs, and they are equipped with reflexes to help them eat, swallow, find food, and avoid unpleasant stimuli. Their sensory capabilities are also sophisticated.

- From birth, infants learn through classical conditioning, operant conditioning, and habituation. Newborns are able to imitate the behavior of others, a capability that helps them form social relationships and facilitates the development of social competence.

EPILOGUE

 ur discussion in this chapter focused on the processes of labor and birth. We considered the birthing options that are available to parents and the complications that can arise during the birthing process. We discussed treatments and interventions and examined the grim topics of stillbirth and infant mortality.

We concluded with a discussion of the surprising capabilities of newborns and their early development of social competence.

Before we move on to a more detailed discussion of infants' physical development, return for a moment to the case of the very premature Tamara Nussbaum, discussed in the prologue. Using your understanding of the issues discussed in this chapter, answer the following questions.

1. Tamara Nussbaum was born at 25 weeks from the time of conception. Why was the fact that she was born alive so surprising? Can you discuss her birth in terms of the "age of viability"?

2. How useful would the Apgar scale be in cases such as Tamara's? What procedures and activities were most likely set into motion immediately after her birth?

3. What dangers was Tamara subject to immediately after birth because of her extreme prematurity? What dangers would be likely to continue into her childhood?

4. What ethical considerations affect the decision of whether the high costs of medical interventions for extremely premature babies are justifiable? Who should pay those costs?

KEY TERMS AND CONCEPTS

neonate (p. 96)
episiotomy (p. 98)
Apgar scale (p. 99)
anoxia (p. 99)
bonding (p. 100)
preterm infants (p. 107)
low-birthweight
    infants (p. 107)
small-for-gestational-age
    infants (p. 107)

very-low-birthweight
    infants (p. 109)
age of viability (p. 109)
postmature
    infants (p. 110)
cesarean
    delivery (p. 113)
fetal monitor (p. 113)
stillbirth (p. 113)
infant mortality (p. 113)

reflexes (p. 118)
classical conditioning
    (p. 119)
operant conditioning
    (p. 120)
habituation (p. 120)
states of arousal (p. 123)

In Part 1, we began our examination of child and adolescent development, starting with conception and continuing through the process of birth. We looked at a few of the things that can go wrong during gestation and birth, but mostly we saw how, in the vast majority of instances, the complex business of forming new life proceeds flawlessly.

Our discussion featured an introduction to some of the broad themes in the field of human development, including especially the importance of critical periods and the nature–nurture controversy. We will revisit these themes frequently as we continue our consideration of human development, looking next at development during infancy. The first 2 years of life, for example, are a sensitive period during which we are best able to learn our native language.

We examined how parents pass along a range of instinctual behaviors, traits, and capabilities to their children through their genes and chromosomes. As we explore the rest of childhood and adolescence, we'll notice the importance of genetics again and again, and we'll explore the complex interaction of genetics and environment. For example, in Part 2, we'll discuss the ways that a baby's inborn temperament can affect the child's family environment, showing the links among physical, cognitive, and social development.

We saw how well equipped human infants are from the moment of birth—and even before. In the next part of the book, we'll see how babies' reflexes not only help them survive through infancy but also help them learn and form attachments with the people who love them.

What we encountered more than anything else as we stepped into the field of child development was a sense of wonder at the way in which the process of life begins and unfolds. As we move into our consideration of infancy in Part 2, we'll see how physical, cognitive, and social and personality development work together to form individuals during infancy. And we'll continue to be awestruck with the transformations that humans undergo as they proceed through life. ■

5

Physical Development in Infancy

PROLOGUE: Sensing the World

It's Tuesday afternoon at the Epsteins' Philadelphia apartment. Seven-month-old Ana Natalia is sitting up, smiling, waiting for her favorite midafternoon activities: snack time, featuring a lovely sweet-potato purée, accompanied by a gentle back rub. When her mother, Lucia, puts some world music on the CD player, Ana Natalia arches her 15-pound body in delight. Life doesn't get any better than cool tunes, good food and a massage. (Raymond, 2000, p. 16)

Infancy is a time of remarkable growth as children become increasingly engaged with the world around them.

LOOKING AHEAD ▶

Even infants know the pleasures that the senses offer. In a remarkable way, they engage the world on a variety of levels, responding to the stimulation of taste, sound, touch, sight, and several other modalities.

The ability of infants to take in and respond to the world around them is among a variety of dramatic physical attainments that characterize infancy. In this chapter, we consider the nature of physical development during the period of infancy, which starts at birth and continues until the second birthday. We begin by discussing the pace of growth during infancy, noting obvious changes in height and weight but also less apparent changes in the nervous system. We also consider how infants quickly develop stable patterns in which their basic activities, such as sleeping, eating, and attending to the world, take on some degree of order.

Our discussion then turns to motor development, the development of skills that will eventually allow an infant to roll over, take a first step, and pick up a pin from the floor—skills that ultimately form the basis of later, even more complex behaviors. We start with basic, genetically determined reflexes and consider how even these may be modified through experience. We also discuss the nature and timing of the development of particular physical skills, look at whether their emergence can be speeded up, and consider the importance of early nutrition to their development.

Finally, we explore the development of the senses during infancy. We investigate how several individual sensory systems operate, and we look at how infants sort out data from the sense organs and transform it into meaningful information.

In sum, after reading this chapter, you will be able to answer these questions:

- **How do the human body and nervous system develop?**
- **Does the environment affect the pattern of development?**
- **What developmental tasks must infants undertake in this period?**
- **What is the role of nutrition in physical development?**
- **What sensory capabilities do infants possess?**

Growth and Stability

The average newborn weighs just over 7 pounds, which is probably less than the weight of the average Thanksgiving turkey. Its length is a mere 20 inches, shorter than a loaf of French bread. It is helpless; if left to fend for itself, it could not survive.

VIDEO CLIP

Physical Growth

Yet after just a few years, the story is very different. Babies are much larger, they are mobile, and they become increasingly independent. How does this growth happen? We can answer this question first by describing the changes in weight and height that occur over the first 2 years of life and then by examining some of the principles that underlie and direct that growth.

Physical Growth: The Rapid Advances of Infancy

Over the first 2 years of a human's life, growth occurs at a rapid pace (see Figure 5-1). By the age of 5 months, the average infant's birthweight has doubled to around 15 pounds. By the first birthday, the infant's weight has tripled to about 22 pounds. Although the pace of weight gain slows during the second year, it still continues to increase. By the end of the second year, the average child weighs four times as much as at birth. These numbers are averages, but there is considerable variation among infants. Ana Natalia Epstein, described in the chapter prologue, for example, is within the normal range, even though her weight at 7 months is only about 15 pounds. Height and weight measurements, which are taken regularly during physician visits during a baby's first year, provide a way to spot problems in development.

The weight gains of infancy are matched by increases in length. By the end of the first year, the typical baby stands about 30 inches tall, an average increase from birth of almost a foot. Children generally reach a height of 3 feet by their second birthday.

Not all parts of an infant's body grow at the same rate. For instance, as we saw first in Chapter 3, at birth the head accounts for one quarter of the newborn's entire body size. During the first 2 years of life, the rest of the body begins to catch up. By the age of 2, the baby's head is only one fifth of its body length, and by adulthood, it is only one eighth (see Figure 5-2).

The disproportionately large size of an infant's head at birth is an example of one of the major principles governing growth: the cephalocaudal principle, which relates to the direction of growth. The **cephalocaudal principle** states that growth follows a pattern that begins with head and upper body parts and then proceeds to the rest of the body. The word *cephalocaudal* is derived from Greek and Latin roots meaning "head-to-tail." The cephalocaudal growth principle means that we develop visual abilities (located in the head) well before we master the ability to walk (closer to the end of the body). The cephalocaudal principle operates both prenatally and postnatally.

Three other principles (summarized in Table 5-1) help explain the patterns by which growth occurs. The **proximodistal principle** states that development proceeds from the center of the body outward. Based on the Latin words for "near" and "far," the proximodistal principle means that the trunk of the body grows before the extremities of the arms and legs. Similarly, it is only after growth has occurred in the arms and legs that the fingers and toes can grow. Furthermore, the development of the ability to use various parts of the body also follows the proximodistal principle. For instance, the effective use of the arms precedes the ability to use the hands.

Another major principle of growth concerns the way complex skills build on simpler ones. The **principle of hierarchical integration** states that simple skills typically develop separately and independently. Later, however, these simple skills are integrated into more complex ones. Thus the relatively complex skill of grasping something in the hand cannot be mastered until the developing infant learns how to control and integrate the movements of the individual fingers.

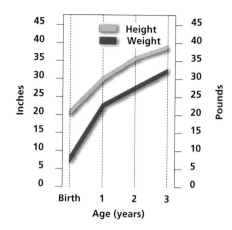

FIGURE 5-1   HEIGHT AND WEIGHT GROWTH

Although the greatest increases in height and weight occur during the first year of life, children continue to grow rapidly throughout infancy and toddlerhood.

Cephalocaudal principle   The principle that growth follows a pattern that begins with the head and upper body parts and then proceeds down to the rest of the body

Proximodistal principle   The principle that development proceeds from the center of the body outward

Principle of hierarchical integration   The principle that simple skills typically develop separately and independently but are later integrated into more complex skills

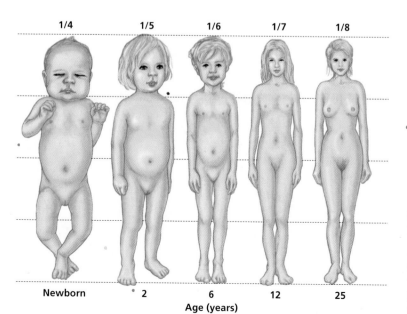

FIGURE 5-2   DECREASING PROPORTIONS

At birth, the head represents one quarter of the neonate's body size. By adulthood, the head is only one eighth the size of the body. How might a midwife explain why the neonate's head is so large?

TABLE 5-1	THE MAJOR PRINCIPLES GOVERNING GROWTH		
Cephalocaudal Principle	**Proximodistal Principle**	**Principle of Hierarchical Integration**	**Principle of the Independence of Systems**
Growth follows a pattern that begins with the head and upper body parts and then proceeds to the rest of the body. Based on Greek and Latin roots meaning "head-to-tail."	Development proceeds from the center of the body outward. Based on the Latin words for "near" and "far."	Simple skills typically develop separately and independently. Later they are integrated into more complex skills.	Different body systems grow at different rates.

Principle of the independence of systems
The principle that different body systems grow at different rates

Neuron The basic nerve cell of the nervous system

The last major principle of growth is the **principle of the independence of systems,** which suggests that different body systems grow at different rates. This principle means that growth in one system does not necessarily imply that growth is occurring in others. For instance, Figure 5-3 illustrates the patterns of growth for three very different systems: body size, which we've already discussed; the nervous system; and sexual characteristics. As you can see, both the rate and the timing of these different aspects of growth are independent (Bornstein & Lamb, 1992; Bremner, Slater, & Butterworth, 1997).

The Nervous System and Brain: The Foundations of Development

When Rina was born, she was the first baby among her parents' circle of friends. These young adults marveled at the infant, oohing and aahing at every sneeze and smile and whimper, trying to guess at their meaning. Whatever feelings, movements, and thoughts Rina was experiencing, they were all brought about by the same complex network: the infant's nervous system. The *nervous system* consists of the brain and the nerves that extend throughout the body.

Neurons are the basic cells of the nervous system. Figure 5-4 shows the structure of an adult neuron. Like all cells in the body, neurons have a cell body containing a nucleus. But unlike other cells, neurons have a distinctive ability: They can communicate with other cells, using a cluster of fibers called *dendrites* at one end. Dendrites receive messages from other cells. At their opposite end, neurons have a long extension called an *axon,* the part of the neuron that carries messages destined for other neurons. Neurons do not actually touch one

FIGURE 5-3 **MATURATION RATES**

Different body systems mature at different rates. For instance, the nervous system is highly developed during infancy, while the development of body size is considerably less developed. The development of sexual characteristics lags even more, maturing at adolescence. What are the implications of this delay in the development of sexuality?

(*Source:* Bornstein & Lamb, 1992a, p. 135)

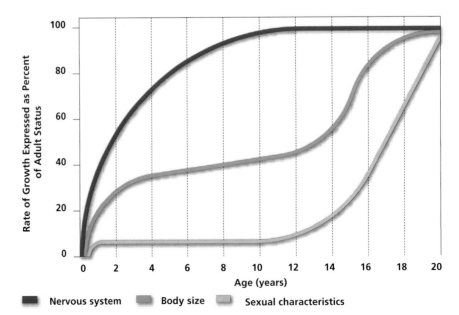

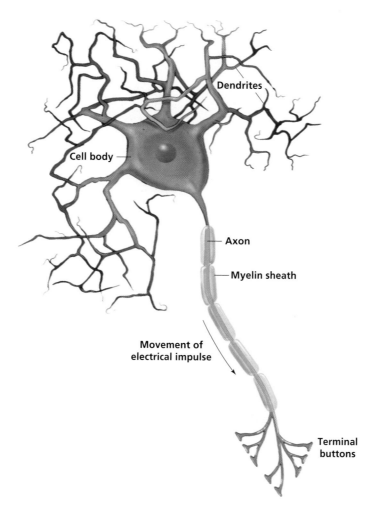

FIGURE 5-4   **THE NEURON**

The basic element of the nervous system, the neuron is comprised of a number of components.

(*Source:* Van de Graaf, 2000, p. 339)

another. Rather, they communicate with other neurons by means of chemical messengers, *neurotransmitters,* that travel across the small gaps, known as **synapses,** between neurons.

Although estimates vary, infants are born with between 100 and 200 billion neurons. In order to reach this number, neurons multiply at an amazing rate prior to birth. In fact, at some points in prenatal development, cell division creates some 250,000 additional neurons every minute.

At birth, most neurons in an infant's brain have relatively few connections to other neurons. During the first 2 years of life, however, a baby's brain will establish billions of new connections between neurons. Furthermore, the network of neurons becomes increasingly complex, as illustrated in Figure 5-5. The intricacy of neural connections continues to increase throughout life. In fact, in adulthood, a single neuron is likely to have a minimum of 5,000 connections to other neurons or other body parts.

Babies are actually born with more neurons than they need. In addition, although synapses are formed throughout life, based on our changing experiences, the billions of new synapses infants form during the first 2 years are also more numerous than necessary. What happens to the extra neurons and synaptic connections?

We can liken the changes that the brain undergoes in its development after birth to the actions of a farmer who, in order to strengthen the vitality of a fruit tree, prunes away unnecessary branches. In the same way, the ultimate capabilities of the brain are brought about in part by a "pruning down" of unnecessary neurons. Neurons that do not become interconnected with other neurons as the infant's experience of the world increases become unnecessary. They eventually die out, increasing the efficiency of the nervous system.

VIDEO CLIP

Synaptic Development

Synapse   The gap at the connection between neurons through which neurons chemically communicate with one another

FIGURE 5-5 **NEURON NETWORKS**

Over the first 2 years of life, networks of neurons become increasingly complex and interconnected.

| Birth | 1 Month | 3 Months | 15 Months | 24 Months |

Similarly, other connections between neurons are strengthened as a result of their use during the baby's experiences. If a baby's experiences do not stimulate certain nerve connections, these, like unused neurons, are eliminated—a process called *synaptic pruning*. The result of synaptic pruning is to allow established neurons to build more elaborate communication networks with other neurons. Unlike most other aspects of growth, then, the development of the nervous system proceeds most effectively through the loss of cells (M. H. Johnson, 1998; Kolb, 1989, 1995).

After birth, neurons continue to increase in size. In addition to growth in dendrites, the axons of neurons become coated with **myelin,** a fatty substance that, like the insulation on an electric wire, provides protection and speeds the transmission of nerve impulses. So even though many neurons are lost, the increasing size and complexity of the remaining ones contributes to impressive brain growth. A baby's brain triples its weight during the first 2 years of life, and it reaches more than three quarters of its adult weight and size by the age of 2.

As they grow, a baby's neurons also move around, becoming arranged by function. Some move into the **cerebral cortex,** the upper layer of the brain, while others move to *subcortical levels,* which are below the cerebral cortex. The subcortical levels, which regulate such fundamental activities as breathing and heart rate, are the most fully developed at birth. As time passes, however, the cells in the cerebral cortex, which are responsible for higher order processes such as thinking and reasoning, become more developed and interconnected.

Brain development, much of which unfolds automatically because of genetically predetermined patterns, is also strongly susceptible to environmental influences. **Plasticity,** the degree to which a developing structure or behavior is modifiable due to experience, is relatively great for the brain. For instance, as we've seen, an infant's sensory experience affects both the size of individual neurons and the structure of their interconnections. Consequently, compared with those brought up in more enriched environments, infants raised in severely restricted settings are likely to show differences in brain structure and weight (Gottlieb, 1991; Kolb, 1995; Rosenzweig & Bennett, 1976).

Work with nonhumans has been particularly illuminating in revealing the nature of the brain's plasticity. For instance, some studies have compared rats raised in an unusually visually stimulating environment to those raised in more typical and less interesting cages. Results of such research show that areas of the brain associated with vision are both thicker and heavier for the rats reared in enriched settings (J. E. Black & Greenough, 1986; Cynader, 2000).

On the other side of the coin, environments that are unusually barren or in some way restricted may impede the brain's development. Again, work with nonhumans provides some intriguing data. In one study, kittens were fitted with goggles that restricted their vision so that they could view only vertical lines. When the cats grew up and had their goggles removed, they were unable to see horizontal lines, although they saw vertical lines perfectly well.

Myelin   A fatty substance that helps insulate neurons and speeds the transmission of nerve impulses

Cerebral cortex   The upper layer of the brain

Plasticity   The degree to which a developing structure or behavior is modifiable due to experience

Analogously, kittens whose goggles restricted their vision of vertical lines early in life were effectively blind to vertical lines during their adulthood, although their vision of horizontal lines was accurate (Hirsch & Spinelli, 1970).

However, when goggles are placed on older cats who have lived relatively normal lives as kittens, such results are not seen after the goggles are removed. The conclusion is that there is a sensitive period for the development of vision. As noted in Chapter 1, a **sensitive period** is a specific but limited time, usually early in an organism's life, during which the organism is particularly susceptible to environmental influences relating to some particular facet of development. A sensitive period may be associated with a behavior—such as the development of full vision—or with the development of a structure of the body, such as the configuration of the brain.

The existence of sensitive periods raises several important issues. For one thing, it suggests that unless an infant receives a certain level of early environmental stimulation during a sensitive period, the infant may suffer damage or fail to develop capabilities that can never be fully remedied. If this is true, providing successful later intervention for such children may prove to be particularly challenging.

The opposite question also arises: Does an unusually high level of stimulation during sensitive periods produce developmental gains beyond what a more commonplace level of stimulation would provide?

Such questions have no simple answers. Determining how unusually impoverished or enriched environments affect later development is one of the central questions addressed by developmental researchers seeking to maximize opportunities for children. In the meantime, many developmentalists suggest that there are many simple ways parents and caregivers can provide a stimulating environment that will encourage healthy brain growth. Cuddling, talking and singing to, and playing with babies all help enrich their environment (Lafuente et al., 1997; Lamb, 1994).

Integrating the Bodily Systems: The Life Cycles of Infancy

Most of the humorous "new baby" greeting cards in your local greeting card shop feature jokes about infants' bodily cycles and the difficulty new parents have in adjusting to these irregular events. Indeed, in the first days of life, infants show a jumble of different behavioral patterns. The most basic activities—sleeping, eating, crying, attending to the world—are controlled by a variety of bodily systems. Although each of these individual behavioral patterns

Sensitive period A specific but limited time, usually early in an organism's life, during which the organism is particularly susceptible to environmental influences relating to some particular facet of development

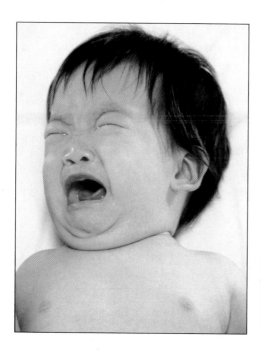 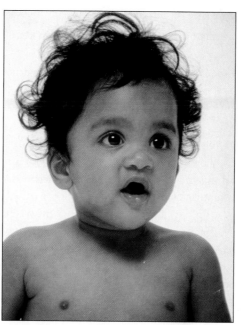

Infants cycle through various states, including crying and alertness. These states are integrated through bodily rhythms.

Rhythms   Repetitive, cyclical patterns of behavior

State   The degree of awareness an infant displays to both internal and external stimulation

may be functioning effectively, it takes some time and effort for infants to integrate the separate systems. In fact, one of the neonate's major missions is to make its individual behaviors work in harmony (Ingersoll & Thoman, 1999; Thoman, 1990; Thoman & Whitney, 1990).

Rhythms and States.   One of the most important ways that behavior becomes integrated is through the development of various body **rhythms,** repetitive, cyclical patterns of behavior. Some rhythms are immediately obvious, such as the change from wakefulness to sleep. Others are more subtle but still easily noticeable, such as breathing and sucking patterns. Still other rhythms may require careful observation to be noticed. For instance, newborns may go through periods in which they jerk their legs in a regular pattern every minute or so. Although some of these rhythms are apparent just after birth, others emerge slowly over the first year as the nervous system becomes more integrated (Groome et al., 1997; Robertson, 1982; Thelen, 1979).

One of the major body rhythms is that of an infant's **state,** the degree of awareness it displays to both internal and external stimulation. As can be seen in Table 5-2, such states include various levels of wakeful behaviors, such as alertness, fussing, and crying, and different levels of sleep as well. Each change in state brings about an alteration in the amount of stimulation required to get the infant's attention (Balaban, Snidman, & Kagan, 1997; Brazelton, 1973; Karmel, Gardner, & Magnano, 1991; Thoman & Whitney, 1990).

Some of the different states that infants experience produce changes in electrical activity in the brain. These changes are reflected in different patterns of electrical *brain waves,* which

TABLE 5-2   PRIMARY BEHAVIORAL STATES

States	Characteristics	Percentage of Time When Alone in State
Awake States		
Alertness	Attentive or scanning, the infant's eyes are open, bright, and shining.	6.7
Nonalert waking	Eyes are usually open but dull and unfocused. Varied, but typically high motor activity.	2.8
Fussing	Fussing is continuous or intermittent, at low levels.	1.8
Crying	Intense vocalizations occurring singly or in succession.	1.7
Transition States Between Sleep and Waking		
Drowsiness	Infant's eyes are heavy-lidded but open and close slowly. Low level of motor activity.	4.4
Daze	Open but glassy and immobile eyes. State occurs between episodes of alertness and drowsiness. Low level of activity.	1.0
Sleep–wake transition	Behaviors of both wakefulness and sleep are evident. Generalized motor activity; eyes may be closed, or they open and close rapidly. State occurs when baby is awakening.	1.3
Sleep States		
Active sleep	Eyes closed; uneven respiration; intermittent rapid eye movements. Smiles, frowns, grimaces, mouthing, sucking, sighs, and sigh-sobs also occur.	50.3
Quiet sleep	Eyes are closed, and respiration is slow and regular. Motor activity is limited to occasional startles, sigh-sobs, or rhythmic mouthing.	28.1
Transitional Sleep State		
Active–quiet transition sleep	During this state, which occurs between periods of active sleep and quiet sleep, the eyes are closed and there is little motor activity. Infant shows mixed behavioral signs of active sleep and quiet sleep.	1.9

(*Source:* Adapted from Thoman & Whitney, 1990)

Infants sleep in spurts, often making them out of sync with the rest of the world.

can be measured by a device called an *electroencephalogram,* or *EEG.* Starting at 3 months before birth, these brain wave patterns are relatively irregular. However, by 3 months after birth, a more mature pattern emerges, and the brain waves stabilize (Parmelee & Sigman, 1983).

Sleep: Perchance to Dream?   At the beginning of infancy, the major state that occupies a baby's time is sleep—much to the relief of exhausted parents, who often regard sleep as a welcome respite from caregiving responsibilities. On average, newborn infants sleep some 16 to 17 hours a day. However, there are wide variations. Some sleep more than 20 hours, while others sleep as little as 10 hours a day (Parmelee, Wenner, & Schulz, 1964).

Even though infants sleep a lot, you probably shouldn't ever wish to "sleep like a baby," despite popular wisdom. For one thing, the sleep of infants comes in fits and starts. Rather than covering one long stretch, sleep initially comes in spurts of around 2 hours, followed by periods of wakefulness. Because of this, infants are out of sync with the rest of the world, for whom sleep comes at night and wakefulness during the day (Groome et al., 1997).

Luckily for their parents, infants eventually settle into a more adultlike pattern. After a week, babies sleep a bit more at night and are awake for slightly longer periods during the day. Typically, by the age of 16 weeks, infants begin to sleep as much as 6 continuous hours at night, and daytime sleep falls into regular naplike patterns. Most infants sleep through the night by the end of the first year, and the total amount of sleep they need each day is down to about 15 hours (Thoman & Whitney, 1989).

Hidden beneath the supposedly tranquil sleep of infants is another cyclic pattern. During periods of sleep, infants' heart rates increase and become irregular, their blood pressure rises, and they begin to breathe more rapidly (Montgomery-Downs & Thoman, 1998). Sometimes, although not always, their closed eyes begin to move in a back-and-forth pattern, as if they were viewing an action-packed scene. This period of active sleep is similar, although not identical, to the **rapid eye movement (REM) sleep** that is found in older children and adults and is associated with dreaming.

At first, this active, REM-like sleep takes up around half of an infant's sleep, compared with just 20 percent of an adult's sleep (see Figure 5-6). However, the quantity of active sleep quickly declines and, by the age of 6 months, amounts to just one third of total sleep time (Coons & Guilleminault, 1982; Sandyk, 1994).

Rapid eye movement (REM) sleep   The period of sleep in older children and adults that is associated with dreaming

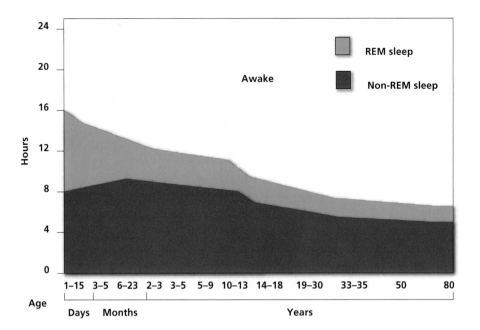

FIGURE 5-6   REM SLEEP OVER THE LIFE SPAN

As we age, the proportion of REM sleep increases as the proportion of non-REM sleep declines. In addition, the total amount of sleep falls as we get older. How would a child care worker use an infant's sleep pattern to plan the child's day?

(*Source:* Adapted from Roffwarg, Muzio, & Dement, 1966)

The appearance of active sleep periods that are similar to REM sleep in adults raises the intriguing question of whether infants dream during those periods. No one knows the answer, although it seems unlikely. First of all, young infants do not have much to dream about, given their relatively limited experiences. Furthermore, the brain waves of sleeping infants appear to be qualitatively different from those of adults who are dreaming. It is not until the baby reaches 3 or 4 months of age that the wave patterns become similar to those of dreaming adults, suggesting that young infants are not dreaming during active sleep—or at least are not doing so in the same way as adults do (McCall, 1979; Parmelee & Sigman, 1983).

Then what is the function of REM sleep in infants? Although we don't know for certain, some researchers think it provides a means for the brain to stimulate itself—a process called *autostimulation* (Roffwarg, Muzio, & Dement, 1966). Stimulation of the nervous system would be particularly important in infants, who spend so much time sleeping and relatively little in alert states.

Although the patterns that infants show in their wakefulness–sleep cycles seem largely preprogrammed by genetic factors, environmental influences also play a part. For instance, both long- and short-term stressors in infants' environments can affect their sleep patterns. When environmental circumstances keep babies awake, sleep, when at last it comes, is apt to be less active (and quieter) than usual (Goodlin-Jones, Burnham, & Anders, 2000; L. F. Halpern, MacLean, & Baumeister, 1995).

The Effects of the Environment.   Furthermore, cultural practices affect the sleep patterns of infants. For example, among the Kipsigis of Africa, infants sleep with their mothers at night and are allowed to nurse whenever they wake. In the daytime, they accompany their mothers during daily chores, often napping while strapped to their mothers' backs. As a result of these practices, Kipsigi infants do not sleep through the night until much later than babies in Western societies, and for the first 8 months of life, they seldom sleep longer than 3 hours at a stretch. In comparison, 8-month-old infants in the United States may sleep as long as 8 hours at a time (Anders & Taylor, 1994; Boismier, 1977; Cole, 1992; Super & Harkness, 1982).

SIDS: The Unanticipated Killer.   For a tiny percentage of infants, the rhythm of sleep is interrupted by a deadly affliction: sudden infant death syndrome. **Sudden infant death syndrome (SIDS)** is a disorder in which seemingly healthy infants die in their sleep. Put to bed for a nap or for the night, the infant simply never wakes up.

Sudden infant death syndrome (SIDS) The unexplained death of a seemingly healthy baby

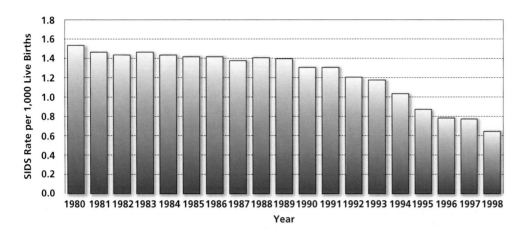

FIGURE 5-7 **DECLINING RATES OF SIDS**

In the United States, SIDS rates have dropped dramatically since 1980 as parents have become more informed and put babies to sleep on their backs instead of their stomachs. Why is this important information for parents and other child care providers to know and understand?

(*Sources:* Centers for Disease Control and Prevention; National Center for Health Statistics)

No known cause has been found to explain SIDS, which strikes about 1 in 1,000 infants in the United States each year. Although it seems to occur when the normal patterns of breathing during sleep are interrupted, scientists have been unable to discover why that might happen. It is clear that infants don't smother or choke; they die a peaceful death, simply ceasing to breathe.

No means for preventing the syndrome have been found. However, as more parents have become aware of guidelines from the American Academy of Pediatrics, which suggests that babies sleep on their backs rather than on their sides or stomachs, the number of deaths from SIDS has decreased significantly (see Figure 5-7). Still, SIDS is the leading cause of death in children under the age of 1 year (Mendelowitz, 1998).

Certain factors are associated with an increased risk of SIDS. For instance, boys and African Americans are at greater risk. In addition, low birthweight and low Apgar scores at birth are associated with SIDS, as is having a mother who smokes during pregnancy. Some evidence also suggests that a brain defect that affects breathing may produce SIDS. In a small number of cases, child abuse may be the actual cause; some researchers contend that abuse may actually account for a relatively high number of deaths. Still, there is no clear-cut factor that explains why some infants die from the syndrome. SIDS occurs in children of every race and socioeconomic group and in children who have had no apparent health problems (Byard & Krous, 1999; Hauck & Hunt, 2000; Mendelowitz, 1998; Milerad et al., 1998; D. Rosen, 1997).

Because parents are unprepared for the death of an infant from SIDS, the event is particularly devastating. Parents often feel guilt, fearing that they were neglectful or somehow contributed to their child's death. Such guilt is unwarranted, since nothing has been identified so far that can prevent SIDS.

REVIEW & APPLY

Review

- The major principles of growth are the cephalocaudal principle, the proximodistal principle, the principle of hierarchical integration, and the principle of the independence of systems.

- The development of the nervous system first entails the development of billions of neurons and interconnections among them. Later the numbers of both neurons and connections decrease as a result of the infant's experiences.

- Brain plasticity, the susceptibility of a developing organism to environmental influences, is relatively high.

- Researchers have identified sensitive periods during the development of body systems and behaviors—limited periods when the organism is particularly susceptible to environmental influences.

- Babies integrate their individual behaviors by developing rhythms—repetitive, cyclical patterns of behavior. A major rhythm relates to the infant's state—the awareness it displays to internal and external stimulation.

Applying Child Development

- What are some cultural influences on infants' daily patterns of behavior that operate in the culture of which you are a part? How do these patterns differ from the influences of other cultures (either in or outside the United States) of which you are aware?

- Research indicates that there is a sensitive period during childhood for normal language acquisition. Persons deprived of normal language stimulation as babies and children may never use language with the same skill as others who were not so deprived. *From a speech therapist's perspective:* For babies who are born deaf, what are the implications of this research finding, particularly with regard to signed languages?

Motor Development

Suppose you were hired by a genetic engineering firm to redesign newborns and were charged with replacing the current version with a new, more mobile one. The first change you'd probably consider in carrying out this (luckily fictitious) job would be in the conformation and composition of the baby's body.

The shape and proportions of newborn babies are simply not conducive to easy mobility. Their heads are so large and heavy that young infants lack the strength to raise them. Because their limbs are short in relation to the rest of the body, their movements are further impeded. Furthermore, their bodies are mainly fat, with a limited amount of muscle; the result is that they lack strength (Illingworth, 1973).

Fortunately, it doesn't take long before infants begin to develop a remarkable amount of mobility. In fact, even at birth, they have an extensive repertoire of behavioral possibilities brought about by innate reflexes, and their range of motor skills grows rapidly during the first 2 years of life.

Reflexes: Our Inborn Physical Skills

When her father pressed 3-day-old Christina's palm with his finger, she responded by tightly winding her small fist around his finger and grasping it. When he moved his finger upward, she held on so tightly that it seemed he might be able to lift her completely off her crib floor.

The Basic Reflexes. In fact, her father was right: Christina probably could have been lifted in this way. The reason for her resolute grip was activation of one of the dozens of reflexes with which infants are born. **Reflexes** are unlearned, organized involuntary responses that occur automatically in the presence of certain stimuli. As we first noted in Chapter 4, when we discussed reflexes relating to the intake of food, newborns enter the world with an expansive repertoire of behavioral patterns that when activated help them adapt to their new surroundings and serve to protect them.

Reflexes Unlearned, organized involuntary responses that occur automatically in the presence of certain stimuli

(a)

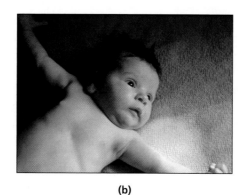
(b)

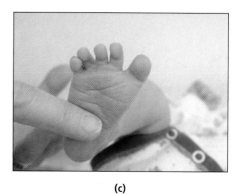
(c)

Infants show (a) the rooting and grasping reflexes, (b) the startle reflex, and (c) the Babinski reflex.

As we can see from the list in Table 5-3, many reflexes clearly represent behavior that has survival value, helping to ensure the well-being of the infant. For instance, the *swimming reflex* makes a baby who is lying face down in a body of water paddle and kick in a sort of swimming motion. The obvious consequence of such behavior is to help the baby move from danger and survive until a caregiver can come to its rescue. Similarly, the *eye-blink reflex* seems designed to protect the eye from too much direct light, which might damage the retina.

Given the protective value of many reflexes, it might seem beneficial for them to remain with us for our entire lives. In fact, some do: The eye-blink reflex remains functional throughout the full life span. On the other hand, quite a few reflexes, such as the swimming reflex, disappear after a few months. Why should this be the case?

Most researchers attribute the gradual disappearance of reflexes to the increase in voluntary control over behavior that occurs as infants become more able to control their muscles. In addition, it may be that reflexes form the foundation for future, more complex behaviors. As these more intricate behaviors become well learned, they subsume the earlier reflexes (Minkowski, 1967; Myklebust & Gottlieb, 1993; Touwen, 1984).

TABLE 5-3	SOME BASIC REFLEXES IN INFANTS		
Reflex	**Approximate Age of Disappearance**	**Description**	**Possible Function**
Rooting reflex	3 weeks	Tendency to turn the head toward things that touch the cheek	Food intake
Stepping reflex	2 months	Movement of legs when held upright with feet touching the floor	Preparation for independent locomotion
Swimming reflex	4–6 months	Tendency to paddle and kick in a sort of swimming motion when lying face down in a body of water	Avoidance of danger
Moro reflex	6 months	Activated when support for the neck and head is suddenly removed: the arms thrust outward and then appear to grasp onto something	Protection from falling
Babinski reflex	8–12 months	Fanning the toes in response to a stroke on the outside of the foot	Unknown
Startle reflex	Remains in different form	In response to a sudden noise, flinging out the arms, arching the back, and spreading the fingers	Protection
Eye-blink reflex	Remains	Rapid shutting and opening of eye on exposure to direct light	Protection of the retina
Sucking reflex	Remains	Tendency to suck at things that touch the lips	Food intake
Gag reflex	Remains	Clearing its throat of obstructions	Prevention of choking

It may even be that the use of reflexes stimulates parts of the brain responsible for more complex behaviors. For example, some researchers argue that exercise of the stepping reflex helps the brain's cortex later develop the ability to walk. As evidence, developmental psychologist Philip R. Zelazo and his colleagues conducted a study in which they gave 2-week-old infants practice in walking for four sessions of 3 minutes each over a 6-week period. The results showed that the children who had the walking practice actually began to walk unaided several months earlier than those who had had no such practice. These researchers suggest that the training produced stimulation of the stepping reflex, which in turn led to stimulation of the brain's cortex, readying the infant earlier for independent locomotion (N. A. Zelazo et al., 1993; P. R. Zelazo, 1998).

Do these findings suggest that parents should make out-of-the-ordinary efforts to stimulate their infant's reflexes? Probably not. Although the evidence shows that intensive practice may produce an earlier appearance of certain motor activities, there is no evidence that the activities are performed qualitatively any better in practiced infants than in unpracticed infants. Furthermore, even when early gains are found, they do not seem ultimately to produce an adult who is more proficient in motor skills.

In fact, structured exercise may do more harm than good: According to the American Academy of Pediatrics (1988), structured exercise for infants may lead to muscle strain, fractured bones, and dislocated limbs, consequences that far outweigh the unproven benefits that may come from the practice.

The Universality of Reflexes.   Although reflexes are, by definition, genetically determined and common to all infants, there are actually some cultural variations in the ways they are displayed. For instance, consider the *Moro reflex* (often called the "startle response"), which is activated when support for the neck and head is suddenly removed. The Moro reflex consists of the infant's arms thrusting outward and then appearing to seek to grasp onto something. Most scientists feel that the Moro reflex represents a leftover response that we humans have inherited from our nonhuman ancestors. The Moro reflex is an extremely useful behavior for monkey babies, who travel about by clinging to their mothers' backs. If they lose their grip, they fall down unless they are able to grasp quickly onto their mothers' fur in a Moro-like reflex (Prechtl, 1982).

Although the Moro reflex is found in all humans, it appears with significantly different vigor in different children. Some differences reflect cultural and ethnic variations. For instance, Caucasian infants show a pronounced response to situations that produce the Moro reflex. Not only do they fling out their arms, but they also cry and respond in a generally agitated manner. In contrast, Navajo babies react to the same situation much more calmly. Their arms do not flail out as much, and they cry only rarely (D. G. Freedman, 1979).

In some cases, reflexes can serve as helpful diagnostic tools for pediatricians. Because reflexes emerge and disappear on a regular timetable, their absence or presence at a given point of infancy can provide a clue that something may be amiss in an infant's development. (Even for adults, physicians include reflexes in their diagnostic bags of tricks, as anyone knows who has had a knee tapped with a rubber mallet to see if the lower leg jerks forward.)

Although some reflexes may be remnants from our prehuman past and seemingly have little usefulness in terms of survival today, they may still serve a very contemporary function. According to some developmental researchers, some reflexes may promote caregiving and nurturance on the part of adults in the vicinity. For instance, Christina's father, who found his daughter gripping his finger tightly when he pressed her palm, probably cares little that she is simply responding with an innate reflex. Instead, he will more likely view his daughter's action as responsiveness to him, a signal perhaps of increasing interest and affection on her part. As we will see in Chapter 7 when we discuss the social and personality development of infants, such apparent responsiveness can help cement the growing social relationship between an infant and its caregivers (S. M. Bell & Ainsworth, 1972; Belsky, Rovine, & Taylor, 1984).

Motor Development in Infancy: Landmarks of Physical Achievement

> Josh's parents had intimations that his first steps would not be too far in the future. He was able to drag himself up and, clutching the side of chairs and tables, progress slowly around the living room. But one day, when Josh suddenly lunged forward toward the center of the room, taking one awkward step after another away from the safety of the furniture, his parents were still taken by surprise. Despite the appearance that he was about to keel over at any second, Josh tottered all the way across the room, finally reaching the other side. Not quite knowing how to stop, he toppled over, landing in a happy heap. It was a moment of pure glory.

Probably no physical changes are more obvious—or more eagerly anticipated—than the increasing array of motor skills that babies acquire during infancy. Most parents can remember their child's first steps with a sense of pride and awe at how quickly she changed from a helpless infant, unable even to roll over, into a person who could navigate quite effectively in the world.

Gross Motor Skills. Even though the motor skills of newborn infants are not terribly sophisticated compared with the attainments that will soon appear, infants are nevertheless able to accomplish some kinds of movement. For instance, when placed on their stomach, they wiggle their arms and legs and may try to lift their heavy head. As their strength increases, they are able to push hard enough against the surface on which they are resting to propel their body in various directions. They often end up moving backward rather than forward, but by the age of 6 months, they become rather accomplished at moving themselves in particular directions. These initial efforts are the forerunners of crawling, in which babies coordinate the motions of their arms and legs to propel themselves forward. Crawling appears typically between the ages of 8 and 10 months (Adolph, 1997; Adolph, Vereijken, & Denny, 1998). (Figure 5-8 provides a summary of some of the milestones of normal motor development.)

This 5-month-old girl demonstrates her gross motor skills.

Walking comes later. At around the age of 9 months, most infants are able to walk by supporting themselves on furniture, and half of all infants can walk well by the end of their first year of life.

At the same time infants are learning to move around, they are perfecting the ability to remain in a stationary sitting position. At first, babies cannot remain seated upright without support. But they quickly master this ability, and most are able to sit without support by the age of 6 months.

Fine Motor Skills. As infants are perfecting their gross motor skills, such as sitting upright and walking, they are also making advances in their fine motor skills (see Table 5-4). For instance, by the age of 3 months, infants show some ability to coordinate the movements of their limbs (Thelen, 1994).

Furthermore, although infants are born with a rudimentary ability to reach toward an object, this ability is neither very sophisticated nor very accurate, and it disappears around the age of 4 weeks. A different and more precise form of reaching reappears at 4 months. It takes some time for infants to coordinate successful grasping after they reach out, but in fairly short order they are able to reach out and hold on to an object of interest (Berthier, 1996; Mathew & Cook, 1990; Rochat & Goubet, 1995).

By 4 months of age, infants are able to reach toward an object with some degree of precision.

The sophistication of fine motor skills continues to grow. By the age of 11 months, infants are able to pick up off the ground objects as small as marbles—presenting care providers with issues of safety, since the place such objects often go next is the mouth. By the time they are 2 years old, children can carefully hold a cup, bring it to their lips, and take a drink without spilling a drop.

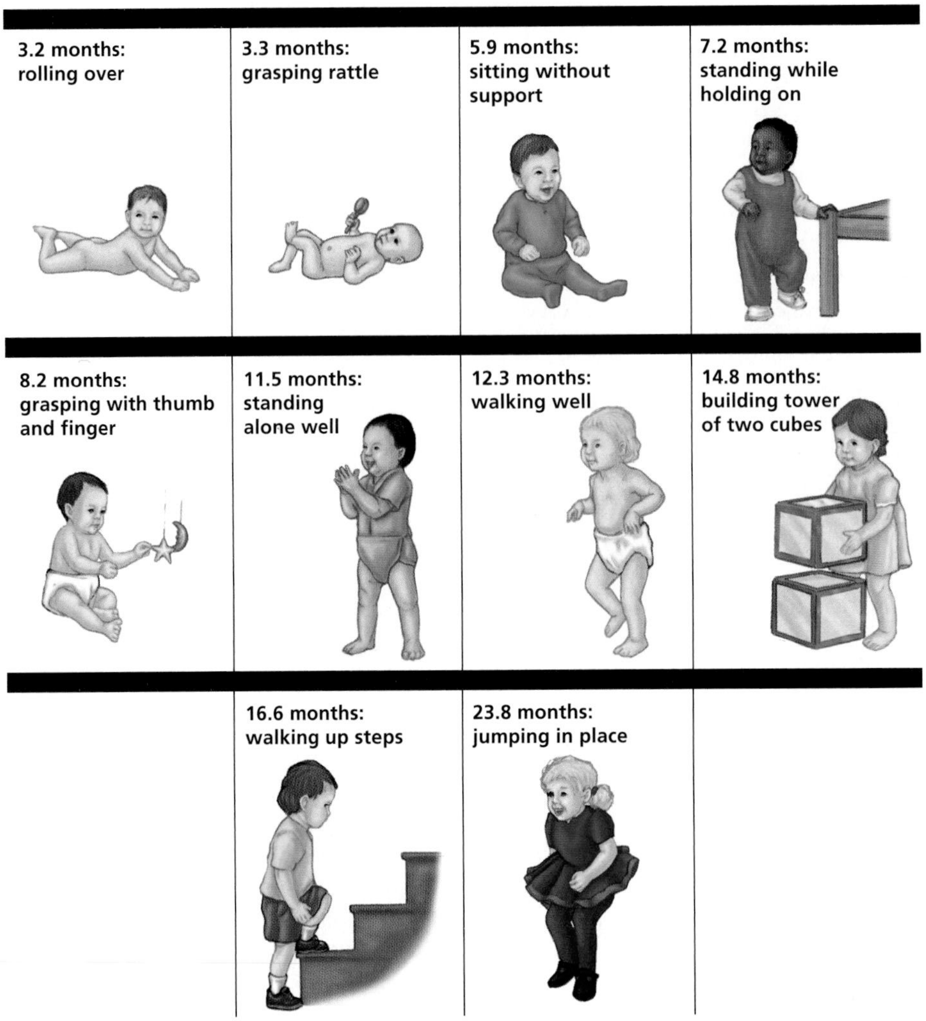

FIGURE 5-8   MILESTONES OF MOTOR DEVELOPMENT

Fifty percent of children are able to perform each skill at the month indicated in the figure. However, the specific time at which each skill appears varies widely. For example, one quarter of children are able to walk well at 11.1 months; by 14.9 months, 90 percent of children are walking well. How is knowledge of such average benchmarks helpful and potentially harmful to parents?

(*Source:* Frankenburg et al., 1992a)

TABLE 5-4 MILESTONES OF FINE MOTOR DEVELOPMENT	
Approximate Age (months)	**Skill**
3	Opens hand prominently
3.5	Grasps rattle
8.5	Grasps with thumb and finger
11	Holds crayon adaptively
14	Builds tower of two cubes
16	Places pegs in board
24	Imitates strokes on paper
33	Copies circle

(*Source:* Adapted from Frankenburg et al., 1992b)

Grasping, like other motor advances, follows a sequential developmental pattern in which simple skills are combined into more sophisticated ones. For example, infants first begin picking things up with their whole hand. As they get older, they use a *pincer grasp,* where thumb and index finger meet to form a circle. The pincer grasp allows for considerably more precise motor control.

Developmental Norms: Comparing the Individual to the Group.   It is important to keep in mind that the timing of the milestones that we have been discussing is based on norms. **Norms** represent the average performance of a large sample of children of a given age. They permit comparisons between a particular child's performance on a particular behavior and the average performance of the children in the norm sample.

For instance, one of the most widely used techniques to determine infants' normative standing is the **Brazelton Neonatal Behavioral Assessment Scale (NBAS),** a measure designed to determine infants' neurological and behavioral responses to their environment.

The NBAS provides a supplement to the traditional Apgar test (discussed in Chapter 4) that is given immediately following birth. Taking about 30 minutes to administer, the NBAS includes 27 separate categories of responses that cover four general aspects of infants' behavior: interactions with others (such as alertness and cuddliness), motor behavior, physiological control (such as the ability to be soothed after being upset), and responses to stress (Brazelton, 1973, 1990; Brazelton, Nugent, & Lester, 1987; Davis & Emory, 1995).

Although the norms provided by scales such as the NBAS are useful in making broad generalizations about the timing of various behaviors and skills, they must be interpreted with caution. Because norms are averages, they mask substantial individual differences in the times when children attain various achievements. For example, some children, like Josh, whose first steps were described earlier, may be ahead of the norm. Other perfectly normal children may be a bit behind the norm. They may also hide the fact that the sequence in which various behaviors are achieved may differ somewhat from one child to another.

Furthermore, norms are useful only to the extent that they are based on data from a large, heterogeneous, culturally diverse sample of children. Unfortunately, many of the norms on which developmental researchers have traditionally relied have been based on groups of infants who are predominantly Caucasian and from the middle and upper socioeconomic strata (e.g., Gesell, 1946).

This limitation would not be critical if no differences existed in the timing of development in children from different cultural, racial, and social groups. But they do. For example, as a group, African American babies show more rapid motor development than Caucasian babies throughout infancy. Moreover, there are significant variations related to cultural factors, as we discuss in the *Developmental Diversity* box (Brazelton, 1991; Keefer et al., 1991; Rosser & Randolph, 1989; E. E. Werner, 1972).

Nutrition in Infancy: Fueling Motor Development

> Rosa sighed as she sat down to nurse the baby—*again*. She had fed 4-week-old Juan about every hour today, yet he still seemed hungry. Some days it seemed like all she did was breast-feeding. "Well, he must be going through a growth spurt," she decided as she settled into her favorite rocking chair and put the baby to her nipple.

The rapid physical growth that occurs during infancy is fueled by the nutrients that infants receive. Without proper nutrition, infants such as Juan not only cannot reach their physical potential but may suffer cognitive and social consequences as well (Pollitt, 1994; Pollitt et al., 1994, 1996).

Malnutrition.   *Malnutrition,* the condition of having an improper amount and balance of nutrients, produces several results, none good. Children who are malnourished begin to show

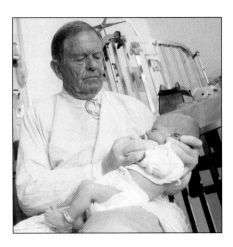

T. Berry Brazelton devised the Brazelton Neonatal Behavioral Assessment Scale (NBAS), which measures infants' neurological and behavioral responses.

Norms   The average performance of a large sample of children of a given age

Brazelton Neonatal Behavioral Assessment Scale (NBAS)   A measure designed to determine infants' neurological and behavioral responses to their environment

DEVELOPMENTAL DIVERSITY

The Cultural Dimensions of Motor Development

Among the Ache people, who live in the rain forest of South America, infants face an early life of physical restriction. Because the Ache lead a nomadic existence, living in a series of tiny camps in the rain forest, open space is at a premium. Consequently, for the first few years of life, infants spend nearly all their time in direct physical contact with their mothers. Even when they are not physically touching their mothers, they are permitted to venture no more than a few feet away.

Infants among the Kipsigis people, who live in a more open environment in rural Kenya, Africa, lead quite a different existence. Their lives are filled with activity and exercise. Parents seek to teach their children to sit up, stand, and walk from the earliest days of infancy. For example, very young infants are placed in shallow holes in the ground designed to keep them in an upright position. Parents begin to teach their children to walk starting at the 8th week of life. The infants are held with their feet touching the ground as they are pushed forward.

Clearly, the infants in these two societies lead very different lives (H. Kaplan & Dove, 1987; Super, 1976). But do the relative lack of early motor stimulation for Ache infants and the efforts of the Kipsigis to encourage motor development really matter?

The answer is both yes and no. It's yes in that Ache infants tend to show delayed motor development, relative both to Kipsigis infants and to children raised in Western societies. Although their social abilities are no different, Ache children tend to begin walking at around 23 months, about a year later than the typical child in the United States. In contrast, Kipsigis children, who are encouraged in their motor development, learn to sit up and walk several weeks earlier, on average, than U.S. children.

In the long run, however, the differences between Ache, Kipsigis, and Western children disappear. By late childhood, there is no evidence of differences in overall motor skills among Ache, Kipsigis, and Western children.

Variations in the timing of motor skills seem to depend in part on parental expectations of the "appropriate" schedule for the emergence of specific skills. For instance, one study examined the motor skills of infants who lived in a single city in England whose mothers varied in ethnic origin. English, Jamaican, and Indian mothers' expectations were first assessed regarding several markers of their infants' motor skills. The Jamaican mothers expected their infants to sit and walk significantly earlier than the English and Indian mothers, and the actual emergence of these activities was in line with their expectations. The source of the Jamaican infants' earlier mastery seemed to lie in the treatment of the children by their parents. For instance, Jamaican mothers gave their children practice in stepping quite early in infancy (Hopkins & Westra, 1989, 1990).

In sum, the time at which specific motor skills appear is in part determined by cultural factors. Activities that are an intrinsic part of a culture are more apt to be intentionally taught to infants in that culture, leading to the potential of their earlier emergence (Nugent, Lester, & Brazelton, 1989).

It is not surprising that children in a given culture who are expected by their parents to master a particular skill and who are taught components of that skill from an early age are more likely to be proficient in that skill earlier than children from other cultures with no such expectations and no such training. The larger question, however, is whether the earlier emergence of a basic motor behavior in a given culture has lasting consequences for specific motor skills and for achievements in other domains. On this issue, the jury is still out (Bloch, 1989).

What is clear, however, is that there are certain genetically determined constraints on how early a skill can emerge. It is physically impossible for 1-month-old infants to stand and walk, regardless of the encouragement and practice they may get in their culture. Parents who are eager to accelerate their infants' motor development, then, should be cautioned not to hold overly ambitious goals. In fact, they might well ask themselves whether it matters if an infant acquires a motor skill a few weeks earlier than its peers.

The most reasonable answer is no. Although some parents may take pride in a child who walks earlier than other babies (just as some parents may be concerned over a delay of a few weeks), in the long run, the timing of this activity will probably make no difference.

a slower growth rate by the age of 6 months. By the time they reach the age of 2 years, their height and weight are only 95 percent of the height and weight of children in the more industrialized countries.

Furthermore, children who have been chronically malnourished during infancy later score lower on IQ tests and tend to do less well in school. These effects may linger even if the

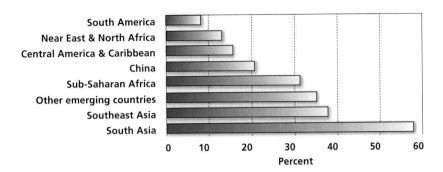

FIGURE 5-9
UNDERWEIGHT CHILDREN

In developing countries, the number of underweight children under the age of 5 years is substantial.

(*Source:* World Food Council, 1992, tab. 2, p. 8)

children's diet has improved substantially (D. E. Barrett & Frank, 1987; Grantham-McGregor, Ani, & Fernald, 2001).

The problem of malnutrition is greatest in underdeveloped countries, where almost 10 percent of infants are severely malnourished. In the Dominican Republic, 13 percent of children under 3 years of age are underweight, and 21 percent have stunted growth. In other areas, the problem is even worse. In South Asia, for example, almost 60 percent of all children are underweight. Overall, in developing countries, one third of children under age 5 are stunted (World Food Council, 1992; see Figure 5-9).

Problems of malnourishment are not restricted to developing countries, however. In the United States, the richest country in the world, some 14 million children live in poverty, which puts them at risk for malnutrition. In fact, although overall poverty rates are no worse than they were 20 years ago, the poverty rate for children under the age of 3 has increased. One quarter of families who have children 2 years old and younger live in poverty. And as we can see in Figure 5-10, the rates are even higher for African American and Hispanic families and for single-parent families (Carnegie Task Force, 1994; G. J. Duncan & Brooks-Gunn, 2000; Einbinder, 2000).

Although these children rarely become severely malnourished, due to adequate social safety nets, they remain susceptible to *undernutrition,* in which there is some deficiency in diet. In fact, some surveys find that as many as a quarter of 1- to 5-year-old children in the United States have diets that fall below the minimum caloric intake recommended by nutritional experts. Although the consequences are not as severe as those of malnutrition,

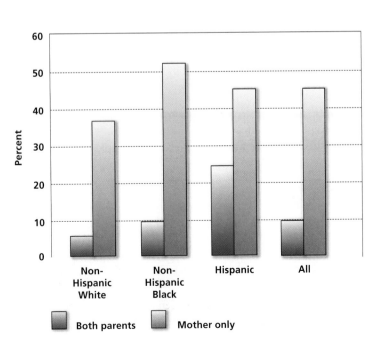

FIGURE 5-10   **CHILDREN LIVING IN POVERTY**

The incidence of poverty among children under the age of 3 is particularly high in minority and single-parent households. (Figures shown are only for single mothers and not fathers because 97 percent of all children under 3 who live with a single parent live with their mothers; only 3 percent live with their fathers.) From the perspective of a social worker or educator, what are the implications of growing up in poverty?

(*Source:* National Center for Children in Poverty, Joseph L. Mailman School of Public Health, Columbia University)

Marasmus A disease characterized by the cessation of growth

Kwashiorkor A disease in which a child's stomach, limbs, and face swell with water

Nonorganic failure to thrive A disorder in which infants stop growing due to a lack of stimulation and attention as the result of inadequate parenting

undernutrition also has long-term costs. For instance, cognitive development later in childhood is affected by even mild to moderate undernutrition (Pollitt et al., 1996; Sigman, 1995; U.S. Bureau of the Census, 1992).

Severe malnutrition during infancy may lead to several disorders. Malnutrition during the first year can produce **marasmus,** a disease in which infants stop growing. Attributable to a severe deficiency in proteins and calories, marasmus causes the body to waste away and ultimately results in death. Older children are susceptible to **kwashiorkor,** a disease in which a child's stomach, limbs, and face swell with water. To a casual observer, it appears that a child with kwashiorkor is actually chubby. However, this is an illusion: The child's body is in fact struggling to make use of the few nutrients that are available.

In some cases, infants who receive sufficient nutrition act as though they have been deprived of food. Looking as though they suffer from marasmus, they are underdeveloped, listless, and apathetic. The real cause, though, is emotional: They lack sufficient love and emotional support. In such cases, known as **nonorganic failure to thrive,** children stop growing not for biological reasons but due to a lack of stimulation and attention from their parents. Usually occurring by the age of 18 months, nonorganic failure to thrive can be reversed through intensive parent training or by placing children in a foster home where they can receive emotional support.

Obesity. It is clear that malnourishment during infancy has potentially disastrous consequences for an infant. Less clear, however, are the effects of *obesity,* defined as weight greater than 20 percent above the average for a given height. For one thing, there appears to be no correlation between obesity during infancy and obesity at the age of 16 years. (There is an association between obesity after the age of 6 and adult weight, however.)

Furthermore, although some research suggests that overfeeding during infancy may lead to the creation of unnecessary fat cells, which remain in the body throughout life, it is not clear that an abundance of fat cells necessarily leads to adult obesity. In fact, genetic factors are an important determinant of obesity (C. Bouchard et al., 1990; Fabsitz, Carmelli, & Hewitt, 1992).

In sum, obesity during infancy is not a major concern. However, the societal view that "a fat baby is a healthy baby" is not necessarily correct either. Rather than focusing on their infant's weight, parents should concentrate on providing appropriate nutrition. At least during the period of infancy, concerns about weight need not be central as long as infants are provided with an appropriate diet.

Although everyone agrees on the importance of receiving proper nutrition during infancy, just how to reach that goal is a source of controversy. Because infants are not born with the ability to eat or digest solid food, at first they exist solely on a liquid diet. But just what should that liquid be—a mother's breast milk or a formula of commercially processed cow's milk with vitamin additives? The answer has changed more than once during the past century.

Breast or Bottle?

Half a century ago, if a mother asked her pediatrician whether breast-feeding or bottle-feeding was better, she would have received a simple and clear-cut answer: Bottle-feeding was

 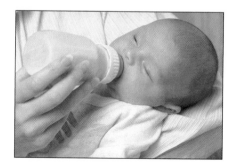

Breast or bottle? Although infants receive adequate nourishment from breast- or bottle-feeding, most authorities agree that "breast is best."

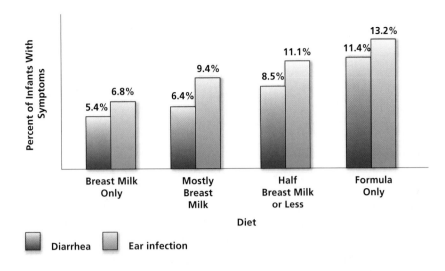

FIGURE 5-11   **BREAST MILK ADVANTAGES**

One of the advantages to breast milk is that it contains all the nutrients necessary for growth; it also appears to offer some degree of immunity to a variety of childhood diseases. What social changes in the U.S. might encourage more mothers to breast-feed?

(*Source:* Data from Scariati, Grummer-Strawn, & Fein, 1997, tab. 3)

the preferred method. Starting around the 1940s, the general belief among child care experts was that breast-feeding was an obsolete method that put children unnecessarily at risk.

With bottle-feeding, the argument went, parents could keep track of the amount of milk their baby was receiving and could thereby ensure that the child was taking in sufficient nutrients. In contrast, mothers who breast-fed their babies could never be certain just how much milk their infants were getting. Furthermore, use of the bottle was said to help mothers keep their feedings to a rigid schedule of one bottle every 4 hours, at that time the recommended procedure.

Today, however, a mother would get a very different answer to the same question. Child care authorities agree that for the first 12 months of life, there is no better food for an infant than breast milk (American Academy of Pediatrics, 1997). Breast milk not only contains all the nutrients necessary for growth but also seems to offer some degree of immunity to a variety of childhood diseases, such as respiratory illnesses, ear infections, diarrhea, and allergies (see Figure 5-11). Breast milk is more easily digested than cow's milk or formula, and it is sterile, warm, and convenient for the mother to dispense. There is even some evidence that breast milk may enhance cognitive growth, leading to higher adult intelligence (Mortensen et al., 2002; Rogan & Gladen, 1993).

Breast-feeding also offers significant emotional advantages for both mother and child. Most mothers report that the experience of breast-feeding brings about feelings of well-being and intimacy with their infants, perhaps because of the production of endorphins in mothers' brains. Breast-fed infants are also more responsive to their mothers' touch and their mother's gaze during feeding, and they are calmed and soothed by the experience. As we'll see in Chapter 7, this mutual responsiveness may lead to healthy social development (Epstein, 1993; Gerrish & Mennella, 2000; Lavelli & Poli, 1998).

Breast-feeding may even hold health-related advantages for mothers. For instance, research suggests that women who breast-feed may have lower rates of ovarian cancer and breast cancer prior to menopause. Furthermore, the hormones produced during breast-feeding help shrink the uterus following birth, enabling the mothers' bodies to return more quickly to a prepregnancy state. These hormones may also inhibit ovulation, reducing (but not eliminating) the chance of becoming pregnant and thereby helping to space the birth of additional children (Altemus et al., 1995; Herbst, 1994; Ross & Yu, 1994).

Obviously, breast-feeding is not the solution to every problem faced by infants, and the millions of individuals who have been raised on formula should not be concerned that they have suffered irreparable harm. In fact, recent research suggests that infants fed enriched formula show better cognitive development than those using traditional formula. But it does continue to be clear that the popular slogan used by groups advocating the use of breast-feeding is right on target: "Breast is best" (Birch et al., 2000).

"I forgot to say I was breast-fed."

Social Patterns in Breast-Feeding.   Although it has several advantages, only about half of all new mothers in the United States breast-feed. This is a decline from the peak reached in 1982, when almost two thirds of all new mothers breast-fed their babies. Although recent figures suggest that breast-feeding may once again be on the rise, the decline that occurred in the 1980s was significant (Ross Laboratories, 1993; Ryan, 1997).

Issues of age, social status, and race influence the decision whether to breast-feed. The rates of breast-feeding are highest among women who are older, better educated, and of higher socioeconomic status and who have social or cultural support. Moreover, there are ethnic and racial group differences. For instance, breast-feeding among Caucasian mothers in the United States occurs at a rate almost double that for African American mothers (Health Resources and Services Administration, 1993; Mahoney & James, 2000; Richardson & Champion, 1992; Thiel de Bocanegra, 1998).

If authorities are in agreement about the benefits of breast-feeding, why in so many cases do women not breast-feed? In some cases, they can't. Some women have difficulties producing milk, while others are taking some type of medicine or have an infectious disease such as AIDS that could be passed on to their infants through breast milk. Sometimes infants are too ill to nurse successfully. And in many cases of adoption, where the birth mother is unavailable after giving birth, the adoptive mother has no choice but to bottle-feed.

In other cases, the decision not to breast-feed is based on practical considerations. Women who hold jobs outside the home may not have sufficiently flexible schedules to breast-feed their infants. This problem is particularly true with less affluent women, who may have less control over their schedules. Such problems may also account for the lower rate of breast-feeding among mothers of lower socioeconomic status, who may lack social support for breast-feeding (Arlotti et al., 1998).

Education is also an issue: Some women simply do not receive adequate information and advice regarding the advantages of breast-feeding and choose to use formula because it seems an appropriate choice. Indeed, some hospitals may inadvertently encourage the use of formula by including it in the gift packets new mothers receive as they leave the hospital.

In developing countries, the use of formula is particularly problematic. Because formula often comes in powdered form that must be mixed with water, local pollution of the water supply can make formula particularly dangerous. In poverty-stricken areas, parents may dilute formula too much because they can't afford to buy the proper amounts, leading to problems with infant malnutrition or undernutrition.

Educational, social, and cultural support for breast-feeding is particularly important. For instance, physicians need to educate their patients about the importance of the practice and to provide specific information on just how to breast-feed. Although breast-feeding is a natural act, mothers require a bit of practice to learn how to hold the baby properly, position the nipple correctly, and deal with such potential problems as nipple soreness.

Introducing Solid Foods: When and What?

Although pediatricians agree that breast milk is the ideal initial food, at some point infants require more nutriments than breast milk alone can provide. The American Academy of Pediatrics (1997) suggests that babies can start solids at around 6 months, although solid foods aren't needed until 9 to 12 months of age.

Solid foods are introduced into an infant's diet gradually, one at a time. Most often cereal comes first, followed by strained fruits. Vegetables and other foods are typically introduced next, although the order varies significantly from one infant to another.

The timing of *weaning*, the cessation of breast- or bottle-feeding, varies greatly. In developed countries such as the United States, weaning frequently occurs as early as 3 or 4 months. On the other hand, in certain subcultures within the United States, breast-feeding may continue for 2 or 3 years. The American Academy of Pediatrics (1997) recommends that infants be fed breast milk for the first 12 months.

Infants generally start eating solid foods at around 4 to 6 months, gradually working their way up to a variety of foods.

R E V I E W & A P P L Y

Review

- Reflexes are universal, genetically acquired physical behaviors.
- During infancy, children achieve a series of landmarks in their physical development on a generally consistent schedule, with some individual and cultural variations.
- Training and cultural expectations affect the timing of the development of motor skills.
- Nutrition strongly affects physical development. Malnutrition can slow growth, affect intellectual performance, and cause diseases such as marasmus and kwashiorkor. The victims of undernutrition also suffer negative effects.
- The advantages of breast-feeding are numerous, including nutritional, immunological, emotional, and physical benefits for the infant and physical and emotional benefits for the mother.

Applying Child Development

- What advice might you give a friend who is concerned about the fact that her infant is still not walking at 14 months when every other baby she knows started walking by the first birthday? What should be done, if anything, to help a child's development of walking skills?
- *From an educator's perspective:* Given that malnourishment negatively affects physical growth, how can it also harm IQ scores and school performance? How might malnourishment affect education in third-world countries? In the United States?

Sensation   The stimulation of the sense organs

Perception   The sorting out, interpretation, analysis, and integration of stimuli involving the sense organs and brain

The Development of the Senses

According to William James (1890/1950), one of the "founding fathers" of psychology, the world of the infant is a "blooming, buzzing confusion." Was he right? In this case, James's wisdom failed him. The newborn's world does lack the clarity and stability that we can distinguish as adults, but day by day the world grows increasingly comprehensible as the infant's ability to sense and perceive the environment develops. As we saw in the case of Ana Natalia Epstein, described at the start of the chapter, babies appear to thrive in an environment enriched by pleasing sensations.

The processes that underlie infants' understanding of the world around them are sensation and perception. **Sensation** is the stimulation of the sense organs, and **perception** is the sorting out, interpretation, analysis, and integration of stimuli involving the sense organs and the brain. Thus sensation is the responsiveness of the sense organs to stimulation, while perception is the interpretation of that stimulation. Sorting out infants' capabilities in the realm of sensation and perception presents a challenge to the ingenuity of investigators (D. G. K. Nelson et al., 1995).

Visual Perception: Seeing the World

From the time of Lee Eng's birth, everyone who met him felt that he gazed at them intently. His eyes seemed to meet those of visitors. They seemed to bore deeply and knowingly into the faces of people who were looking at him.

How good in fact was Lee's vision, and what, precisely, could he make out of his environment? Quite a bit. According to some estimates, a newborn's distance vision ranges from 20/200 to 20/600, which means that an infant cannot discern visual material beyond 20 feet that an adult with normal vision is able to see from a distance of between 200 and 600 feet (Haith, 1991b).

These figures indicate that infants' distance vision is some 10 to 30 times poorer than the average adult's, perhaps suggesting that the vision of infants is inadequate. However, looking at the figures from a different perspective suggests a revised interpretation: The vision of newborns provides the same degree of distance acuity as the uncorrected vision of many adults who wear eyeglasses or contact lenses. (If you wear glasses or contact lenses, remove them to get a sense of what an infant can see of the world). Furthermore, infants' distance vision grows increasingly acute. By 6 months of age, the average infant's vision is already 20/20—in other words, identical to that of adults (Aslin, 1987; Simons, 1993).

A neonate's view of the world is limited to 8 to 14 inches. Objects beyond that distance are fuzzy.

A month after birth, newborns' vision has improved, but still lacks clarifying detail.

By three months, objects are seen with clarity.

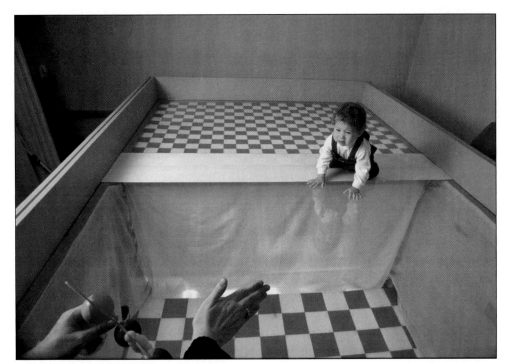

FIGURE 5-12   VISUAL CLIFF

The "visual cliff" experiment examines the depth perception of infants. Most infants in the age range of 6 to 14 months cannot be coaxed to cross the cliff, apparently responding to the fact that the patterned area seems to drop several feet.

Other visual abilities grow rapidly. For instance, *binocular vision*, the ability to combine the images coming to each eye to see depth and motion, is achieved at around 14 weeks. Before then, infants do not integrate the information from each eye.

 Depth perception is a particularly useful ability, as illustrated in a classic study by developmental psychologists Eleanor Gibson and Richard Walk (1960) in which infants were placed on a sheet of heavy glass. A checkered pattern appeared under half of the glass sheet, making it seem that the infant was on a stable floor. However, in the middle of the glass sheet, the pattern dropped down several feet, forming an apparent "visual cliff." The question Gibson and Walk asked was whether infants would willingly crawl across the cliff when called by their mother (see Figure 5-12).

The results were unambiguous. Most of the infants in the study, who ranged in age from 6 to 14 months, could not be coaxed over the apparent cliff. Clearly, the ability to perceive depth had already developed in most of them by that age. On the other hand, these findings did *not* show that infants were afraid of falling. Their heart rates slowed when placed at the visual cliff; fear would have been indicated by a faster heart rate. It is only later, when they become more mobile, that infants start to experience a fear of falling. Furthermore, the visual cliff research does not permit us to know whether infants are responding to depth itself or merely to the *change* in visual stimuli that occurs when they are moved from a lack of depth to depth (Bertenthal, Campos, & Kermoian, 1994; Campos, Langer, & Krowitz, 1970).

Infants also show clear visual preferences that are present from birth. For example, when given a choice, infants reliably prefer to look at stimuli that include patterns than to look at simpler stimuli (see Figure 5-13). How do we know? Developmental psychologist Robert Fantz (1963) created a classic test. He built a chamber in which babies could lie on their back and see pairs of visual stimuli above them. Fantz could determine which of the stimuli the infants were looking at by observing the reflections of the stimuli in their eyes.

Fantz's work was the impetus for a great deal of research on the preferences of infants, most of which points to a critical conclusion: Infants are genetically preprogrammed to prefer particular kinds of stimuli. For instance, just minutes after birth, they show preferences for certain colors, shapes, and configurations of various stimuli. They prefer curved over straight lines, three-dimensional figures to two-dimensional ones, and human faces to nonfaces. Such

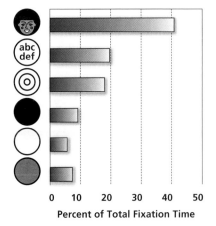

FIGURE 5-13   PREFERRING COMPLEXITY

In a classic experiment, researcher Robert Fantz found that 2- and 3-month-old infants preferred to look at more complex stimuli than simple ones.

(*Source:* Adapted from Fantz, 1961, p. 72)

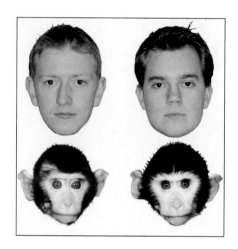

FIGURE 5-14
DISTINGUISHING FACES

Examples of faces used in a study that found that 6-month-old infants distinguished human or monkey faces equally well, whereas 9-month-olds were less adept at distinguishing monkey faces than human faces.

(*Source:* Pascalis, de Haan, & Nelson, 2002, p. 1322)

capabilities may be a reflection of the existence of highly specialized cells in the brain that react to stimuli of a particular pattern, orientation, shape, and direction of movement (Csibra et al., 2000; Hubel & Wiesel, 1979; Rubenstein, Kalakanis, & Langlois, 1999).

However, genetics is not the sole determinant of infant visual preferences. Just a few hours after birth, infants have already learned to prefer their own mother's face to other faces. Similarly, between the ages of 6 and 9 months, infants become more adept at distinguishing between the faces of humans, while they become less able to distinguish faces of members of other species (see Figure 5-14). Such findings provide another clear piece of evidence of how heredity and environmental experiences are woven together to determine an infant's capabilities (Hood, Willen, & Driver, 1998; Mondloch et al., 1999; Pascalis et al., 2002).

Auditory Perception: The World of Sound

What is it about a mother's lullaby that helps soothe a crying, fussy baby? Some clues emerge when we look at the capabilities of infants in the realm of auditory sensation and perception.

It is clear that infants hear from the time of birth—and even before. As noted in Chapter 4, the ability to hear begins prenatally. Even in the womb, the fetus responds to sounds outside of its mother. Furthermore, infants are born with preferences for particular sound combinations. For example, an infant can more easily discern a blend of musical tones if the underlying frequencies of the tones are related as simple mathematical proportions than if the relationship between tones is a more complex combination (Schellenberg & Trehub, 1996).

Because they have had some practice in hearing before birth, it is not surprising that infants have reasonably good auditory perception after they are born. In fact, for certain very high and very low frequencies, infants are actually more sensitive to sound than adults—and this sensitivity seems to increase during the first 2 years of life. On the other hand, infants are initially less sensitive than adults to middle-range frequencies. Eventually, however, their capabilities in the middle range improve over time (Fenwick & Morrongiello, 1991; L. A. Werner & Marean, 1996).

It is not entirely clear what leads to the improvement during infancy in sensitivity to sounds, although it may be related to the maturation of the nervous system. More puzzling is why, after infancy, children's ability to hear very high and low frequencies gradually declines. One explanation may be that exposure to high levels of noise may diminish capacities at the extreme ranges (Kryter, 1983; B. A. Schneider, Trehub, & Bull, 1980; Trehub et al., 1988, 1989).

In addition to the ability to detect sound, infants need several other abilities in order to hear effectively. For instance, *sound localization* permits infants to pinpoint the direction from which a sound is emanating. Compared to adults, infants have a slight handicap in this task because effective sound localization requires the use of the slight difference in the times at which a sound reaches our two ears. Because infants' heads are smaller than those of adults, the difference in timing of the arrival of sound at the two ears is less than it is in adults.

However, despite the potential limitation brought about by smaller head size, infants' sound localization abilities are actually fairly good even at birth, and they reach adult levels of success by the age of 1 year (Clifton, 1992; Litovsky & Ashmead, 1997). Interestingly, the improvement is not steady: Although we don't know why, the accuracy of sound localization actually declines between birth and 2 months of age but then begins to increase (Aslin, 1987; B. A. Schneider, Bull, & Trehub, 1988; Trehub et al., 1989).

Infant discrimination of groups of different sounds, in terms of their patterns and other acoustical characteristics, is also quite good. For instance, the change of a single note in a six-tone melody can be detected by infants as young as 6 months old. They also react to changes in musical key (Trehub, Thorpe, & Morrongiello, 1985). In sum, they listen with a keen ear to the melodies of lullabies sung to them by their mothers and fathers.

Even more important to their ultimate success in the world, young infants are capable of making the fine discriminations that their future understanding of language will require

(Bijeljac-Babic, Bertoncini, & Mehler, 1993). For instance, in one classic study, a group of 1- to 4-month-old infants sucked on synthetic nipples that activated a recording of a person saying "ba" every time they sucked (Eimas et al., 1971). At first, their interest in the sound made them suck vigorously. Soon, though, they became acclimated to the sound (through the process of *habituation,* discussed in Chapter 4) and sucked with less energy. On the other hand, when the experimenters changed the sound to "pa," the infants immediately showed new interest and sucked with greater vigor once again. The clear conclusion: Infants as young as 1 month old could make the distinction between the two similar sounds (Eimas et al., 1971; J. C. Goodman & Nusbaum, 1994; J. L. Miller & Eimas, 1995).

Even more intriguing, young infants are able to discriminate certain characteristics that differentiate one language from another. By the age of 4½ months, infants are able to discriminate their own names from similar-sounding words. By the age of 5 months, they can distinguish the difference between English and Spanish passages, even when the two are similar in meter, number of syllables, and speed of recitation. In fact, some evidence suggests that even 2-day-olds show a preference for the language spoken by the people around them over other languages (Bahrick & Pickens, 1988; Best, 1994; Mandel, Jusczyk, & Pisoni, 1995; Moon, Cooper, & Fifer, 1993).

Given their ability to discriminate a difference in speech as slight as the difference between two consonants, it is not surprising that infants can distinguish different people on the basis of voice. In fact, from an early age, they show clear preferences for some voices over others. For instance, in one experiment, newborns were allowed to suck a synthetic nipple that turned on a recording of a human voice reading a story. The infants sucked significantly longer when the voice was that of their mother than when the voice was that of a stranger (De Casper & Fifer, 1980; Fifer, 1987).

How do such preferences arise? One hypothesis is that prenatal exposure to the mother's voice is the key. As support for this conjecture, researchers point to the fact that newborns do not show a preference for their father's voice over other male voices. Furthermore, newborns prefer listening to melodies sung by their mother before they were born to melodies that were not sung before birth. It seems, then, that the prenatal exposure to their mother's voice—although muffled by the liquid environment of the womb—helps shape infants' listening preferences (De Casper & Prescott, 1984; Panneton, 1985).

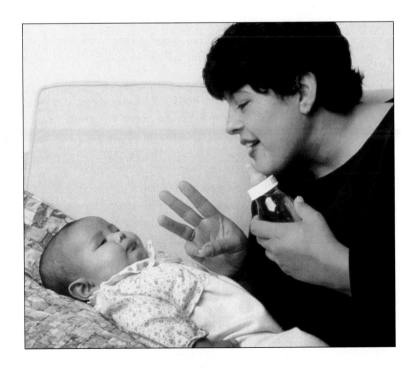

By the age of 4 months, infants are able to discriminate their own names from other, similar-sounding words.

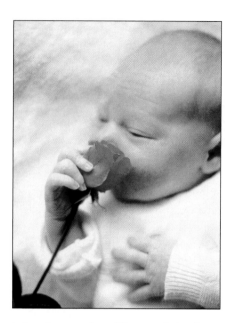

Infants' sense of smell is so well developed that they can distinguish their mothers on the basis of smell alone.

Smell and Taste

What do infants do when they smell a rotten egg? Pretty much what adults do—crinkle their nose and generally look unhappy. On the other hand, the scent of bananas and butter produces a pleasant reaction on the part of infants (Steiner, 1979).

The sense of smell is so well developed, even among very young infants, that at least some 12- to 18-day-old babies can distinguish their mother on the basis of smell alone. For instance, in one experiment, infants were exposed to the smell of gauze pads worn under the arms of adults the previous evening. Infants who were being breast-fed were able to distinguish their mother's scent from that of other adults. However, not all infants could do this: Those who were being bottle-fed were unable to make the distinction. Moreover, both breast-fed and bottle-fed infants were unable to distinguish their fathers on the basis of odor (R. H. Porter, Bologh, & Malkin, 1988; R. H. Porter & Winberg, 1999; Soussignan et al., 1997).

Taste, like smell, shows surprising sophistication during infancy. Some reactions are well developed at birth, such as disgust over bitter tastes. At the same time, infants seem to have an innate sweet tooth—even before they have teeth: Very young infants smile when a sweet-tasting liquid is placed on their tongue. They also suck harder at a bottle if it is sweetened. Since breast milk has a sweet taste, it is possible that this preference may be part of our evolutionary heritage, retained because it offered a survival advantage. Infants who preferred sweet tastes may have been more likely to ingest sufficient nutrients and to survive than those who did not (Porges & Lipsitt, 1993; Rosenstein & Oster, 1988; Steiner, 1979).

Infants also develop taste preferences based on what their mother drank while they were in the womb. For instance, one study found that women who drank carrot juice while pregnant had children who had a preference for the taste of carrots during infancy (Mennella, 2000).

Sensitivity to Pain and Touch

When Eli Rosenblatt was 8 days old, he participated in the ancient Jewish ritual of circumcision. As he lay nestled in his father's arms, the foreskin of his penis was removed. Although Eli shrieked in what seemed to his anxious parents as pain, he soon settled down and went back to sleep. Others who had watched the ceremony assured his parents, with great authority, that at Eli's age babies don't really experience pain, at least not in the same way that adults do.

Were Eli's relatives accurate in saying that young infants don't experience pain? In the past, many medical practitioners would have agreed. In fact, because they assumed that infants didn't experience pain in truly bothersome ways, many physicians routinely carried out medical procedures, and even some forms of surgery, without the use of painkillers or anesthesia. Their argument was that the risks from the use of anesthesia outweighed the potential pain that the young infants experienced.

(CW) **Contemporary Views on Infant Pain.**   Today, however, it is widely acknowledged that infants are born with the capacity to experience pain. Obviously, no one can be sure if the experience of pain in children is identical to that in adults, any more than we can tell if an adult friend who complains of a headache is experiencing pain that is more or less severe than our own pain when we have a headache.

What we do know is that pain produces signs of distress in infants, such as a rise in heartbeat, sweating, facial expressions indicative of discomfort, and changes in the intensity and tone of crying (C. C. Johnston, 1989). Such evidence indicates that infants do experience pain.

There also seems to be a developmental progression in reactions to pain. For example, a newborn infant who has her heel pricked for a blood test responds with signs of distress, but it takes her several seconds to show the response. In contrast, only a few months later, the same procedure brings a much more immediate response. It is possible that the delayed reaction in infants is produced by the relatively slower transmission of information within the newborn's nervous system (Anand & Hickey, 1987, 1992; Axia, Bonichini, & Benini, 1995; F. L. Porter, Porges, & Marshall, 1988).

— FROM RESEARCH TO PRACTICE —

Should Male Infants Be Circumcised?

It is a routine practice in both the Jewish and Islamic faiths: circumcision of male infants soon after birth, a procedure in which the skin covering the end of the penis is removed. But are there medical reasons to perform the practice?

According to the American Academy of Pediatrics (2000), the answer is no. Admittedly, some minor health benefits are associated with circumcision, including a slightly lower risk of urinary tract infections and sexually transmitted diseases (including AIDS), a lower risk of cancer of the penis (a disease for which the risk is already very low), and easier genital hygiene.

However, these minor benefits have to be weighed against the risks involved in circumcision. As in any surgery, there is a small risk of complications, such as bleeding, infection, irritation, and botched surgery. It is also possible—although hard to substantiate—that circumcision reduces sexual pleasure.

After analyzing the risks and benefits, the academy determined that the benefits are not sufficient to recommend that all boys be routinely circumcised—or that the practice be avoided. Instead, the decision to have male infants circumcised must rest on religious, social, and cultural traditions. For example, some parents may choose circumcision because they want their child to look like the other males in the family, all of whom are circumcised. Or the practice may be an ingrained tradition or a matter of religious practice. The point is that such decisions are not medical but cultural and psychological (American Academy of Pediatrics, 1999a; Springen, 2000).

What is clear, though, is that if a male baby is to be circumcised, painkillers should be used. Local anesthetics can be injected prior to the operation, and topical creams can also be used. The pain of circumcision can—and should—be avoided.

In addition, research with rats suggests that exposure to pain in infancy may lead to a permanent rewiring of the nervous system that results in greater sensitivity to pain during adulthood. Such findings indicate that infants who must undergo extensive, painful medical treatments and tests may be unusually sensitive to pain when older (Ruda et al., 2000).

In response to increasing support for the notion that infants experience pain and that its effects may be long-lasting, medical experts now endorse the use of anesthesia and painkillers during surgery for even the youngest infants. According to the American Academy of Pediatrics (2000), painkilling drugs are appropriate in most types of surgery—including, as we consider in the *From Research to Practice* box, the practice of circumcision.

Responding to Touch.   It clearly does not take the sting of pain to get an infant's attention. Recall how much Ana Natalia Epstein, the baby described in the chapter prologue, enjoyed her afternoon massage. Even the youngest infants respond to gentle touches, such as a soothing caress, which can calm a crying, fussy infant (Stack & Muir, 1992).

In fact, touch is one of the most highly developed sensory systems in a newborn. It is also one of the first to develop; there is evidence that by 32 weeks after conception, the entire body is sensitive to touch. Furthermore, several of the basic reflexes present at birth, such as the rooting reflex, require touch sensitivity to operate: An infant must sense a touch near the mouth in order to seek automatically a nipple to suck (Haith, 1986).

Infants' abilities in the realm of touch are particularly helpful in their efforts to explore the world. Several theorists have suggested that one of the ways children gain information about the world is through touching. For instance, at the age of 6 months, infants are apt to place almost any object in their mouth, apparently taking in data about its configuration from their sensory responses to the feel of it in the mouth (Ruff, 1989).

In addition, touch plays an important role in an organism's future development, for it triggers a complex chemical reaction that assists infants in their efforts to survive. For example, gentle massage stimulates the production of certain chemicals in an infant's brain that instigate growth. Periodic massage is also helpful in treating several kinds of medical conditions,

Touch is one of the most highly developed sensory systems from the time of birth.

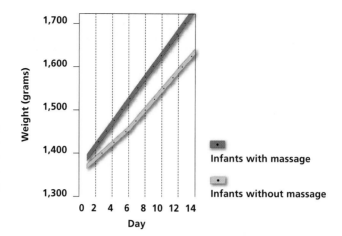

FIGURE 5-15   EFFECT OF MASSAGE ON WEIGHT GAIN

The weight gain of premature infants who were systematically massaged is greater than those who did not receive the massage. How can this phenomenon be explained, and what implications does it have for parents and health care workers?

(*Source:* American Academy of Pediatrics)

including premature delivery and the effects of prenatal exposure to AIDS or cocaine. Furthermore, massage is beneficial for infants and even older children whose mothers are depressed and for those who suffer from burns, cancer, asthma, and a variety of other medical conditions (Field, 1995a, 1995b, 1999; Hernandez-Reif et al., 1999; Schanberg et al., 1993).

In one study that illustrates the benefits of massage, a group of preterm infants who were massaged for 15 minutes three times a day gained weight some 50 percent faster than a group of preterm infants of the same age who were not stroked (see Figure 5-15). The massaged infants were also more active and more responsive to stimuli. Ultimately, the preterm infants who were massaged were discharged earlier from the hospital, and the costs of their medical care were significantly lower than for infants in the unmassaged group (Field, 1988, 1995b).

Multimodal Perception: Combining Individual Sensory Inputs

When Eric Pettigrew was 7 months old, his grandparents presented him with a squeaky rubber doll. As soon as he saw it, he reached out for it, grasped it in his hand, and listened as it squeaked. He seemed delighted with the gift.

One way of considering Eric's sensory reaction to the doll is to focus on each of the senses individually: what the doll looked like to Eric, how it felt in his hand, and what it sounded like. In fact, this approach has dominated the study of sensation and perception in infancy.

However, let's consider another approach: We might examine how the various sensory responses are integrated with one another. Instead of looking at each individual sensory response, we could consider how the responses work together and are combined to produce Eric's ultimate reaction. The **multimodal approach to perception** considers how information that is collected by various individual sensory systems is integrated and coordinated.

Although the multimodal approach is a relatively recent innovation in the study of how infants understand their sensory world, it raises some fundamental issues about the development of sensation and perception. For instance, some researchers argue that sensations are initially integrated with one another in the infant, while others maintain that the infant's sensory systems are initially separate and that brain development leads to increasing integration (De Gelder, 2000; Lickliter & Bahrick, 2000; P. C. Quinn & Eimas, 1996).

We do not know yet which view is correct. However, it does appear that by an early age, infants are able to relate what they have learned about an object through one sensory channel to what they have learned about it through another. For instance, even 1-month-old infants are able to recognize by sight objects that they have previously held in their mouths but never seen (Meltzoff, 1981; Streri & Spelke, 1988). Clearly, some cross-talk between various sensory channels is already possible a month after birth.

The success of infants at multimodal perception is another example of the sophisticated perceptual abilities of infants, which continue to grow throughout the period of infancy. Such

Multimodal approach to perception The approach that considers how information that is collected by various individual sensory systems is integrated and coordinated

BECOMING AN INFORMED CONSUMER OF DEVELOPMENT

Exercising Your Infant's Body and Senses

We've seen how the experiences infants encounter as they grow are reflected in their motor and sensory development. For instance, recall how cultural expectations and environments affect the age at which various physical milestones, such as the first step, occur. Does this suggest that parents are well advised to try to accelerate their infants' timetables?

Although experts disagree, most feel that such acceleration yields little advantage. No data suggest that a child who walks at 10 months ultimately has any advantage over one who walks at 15 months.

Nevertheless, parents should ensure that their infants receive sufficient physical and sensory stimulation. There are several specific ways to accomplish this goal:

- Carry a baby in different positions—in a backpack, in a frontpack, or in a football hold with the infant's head in the palm of your hand and its feet lying on your arm.

- Let infants explore their environment. Don't contain them too long in a barren environment. Let them crawl or wander around—after first making the environment "childproof" by removing dangerous objects.

- Engage in "rough-and-tumble" play. Wrestling, dancing, and rolling around on the floor—if not violent—are activities that are fun and that stimulate older infants' motor and sensory systems.

- Let babies touch their food and even play with it. Infancy is too early to start teaching table manners.

- Provide toys that stimulate the senses, particularly those that can stimulate more than one sense at a time. For example, brightly colored, textured toys with movable parts are enjoyable and help hone infants' senses.

---

perceptual growth is aided by infants' discovery of **affordances,** the action possibilities that a given situation or stimulus provides. For example, infants learn that they might potentially fall when walking down a steep ramp—in other words, the ramp affords the possibility of falling. Such knowledge is crucial as infants make the transition from crawling to walking. Similarly, infants learn that an object shaped in a certain way can slip out of their hands if not grasped correctly. For example, Eric is learning that his toy has several affordances: He can grab it and squeeze it, listen to it squeak, and even chew comfortably on it if he is teething (Adolph, 1997; Adolph, Eppler, & Gibson, 1993; McCarty & Ashmead, 1999).

Affordances The action possibilities that a given situation or stimulus provides

REVIEW & APPLY

Review

- Sensation refers to the activation of the sense organs by external stimuli. Perception is the analysis, interpretation, and integration of sensations.

- Infants' sensory abilities are surprisingly well developed at or shortly after birth. Their perceptions help them explore and begin to make sense of the world.

- Very early, infants can see depth and motion, distinguish colors and patterns, localize and discriminate sounds, and recognize the sound and smell of their mother.

- Infants are sensitive to pain and touch, and most medical authorities now subscribe to procedures, including anesthesia, that minimize infants' pain.

- Infants also have a keen ability to integrate information from more than one sense.

Applying Child Development

- Are the processes of sensation and perception always linked? Is it possible to sense without perceiving? To perceive without sensing? How?

- Persons who are born without the use of one sense often develop unusual abilities in one or more other senses. *From an educator's perspective:* What are the implications for educating children who are lacking in a particular sense?

LOOKING **BACK**

⊙ **How do the human body and nervous system develop?**

- Human babies grow rapidly in height and weight, especially during the first 2 years of life.

- Major principles that govern human growth include the cephalocaudal principle, the proximodistal principle, the principle of hierarchical integration, and the principle of the independence of systems.

- The nervous system contains a huge number of neurons, more than will be needed as an adult. For neurons to survive and become useful, they must form interconnections with other neurons based on the infant's experience of the world. Connections and neurons that are not used are eliminated as an infant develops.

⊙ **Does the environment affect the pattern of development?**

- Brain development, largely predetermined genetically, also contains a strong element of plasticity—a susceptibility to environmental influences.

- Many aspects of development occur during sensitive periods when the organism is particularly susceptible to environmental influences.

⊙ **What developmental tasks must infants undertake in this period?**

- One of the primary tasks of the infant is the development of rhythms—cyclical patterns that integrate individual behaviors. An important rhythm pertains to the infant's state—the degree of awareness it displays to stimulation.

- Reflexes are unlearned, automatic responses to stimuli that help newborns survive and protect themselves. Some reflexes also have value as the foundation for future, more conscious behaviors.

- The development of gross and fine motor skills proceeds along a generally consistent timetable in normal children, with substantial individual and cultural variations.

⊙ **What is the role of nutrition in physical development?**

- Adequate nutrition is essential for physical development. Malnutrition and undernutrition affect physical aspects of growth and may also affect IQ and school performance.

- Breast-feeding has distinct advantages over bottle-feeding, including the nutritional completeness of breast milk, its provision of a degree of immunity to certain childhood diseases, and its easy digestibility. In addition, breast-feeding offers significant physical and emotional benefits to both child and mother.

● **What sensory capabilities do infants possess?**

• Sensation, the stimulation of the sense organs, differs from perception, the interpretation and integration of sensed stimuli.

• Infants' visual and auditory perception are rather well developed, as are the senses of smell and taste. Infants use their highly developed sense of touch to explore and experience the world. In addition, touch plays an important role in the individual's future development, which is only now being understood.

EPILOGUE

In this chapter, we discussed the nature and pace of infants' physical growth and the pace of less obvious growth in the brain and nervous system and in the regularity of infants' patterns and states.

We next looked at motor development, the development and uses of reflexes, the role of environmental influences on the pace and shape of motor development, and the importance of nutrition.

We closed the chapter with a look at the senses, observing how sophisticated the infant's ability is to use the senses and to combine data from multiple sensory sources.

Think back for a moment to the prologue of this chapter, about 7-month-old Ana Natalia Epstein's encounters with a variety of sensory stimuli, and answer these questions:

1. How do researchers find out whether various forms of sensory stimulation are pleasurable to infants? Do you think there is a danger of overinterpretation of infants' reactions?

2. Are the reactions that a baby produces in response to a piece of music or a backrub examples of sensation or perception? Why? How would a researcher explore this question?

3. Which principle or principles of growth (cephalocaudal, proximodistal, hierarchical integration, independence of systems) might underlie the development of the senses?

4. In addition to her physical development, do you think Ana Natalia's home environment might affect other aspects of her development, such as her intellectual and social development? If so, in what ways?

KEY TERMS AND CONCEPTS

cephalocaudal principle (p. 131)
proximodistal principle (p. 131)
principle of hierarchical integration (p. 131)
principle of the independence of systems (p. 132)
neuron (p. 132)
synapse (p. 133)
myelin (p. 134)

cerebral cortex (p. 134)
plasticity (p. 134)
sensitive period (p. 135)
rhythms (p. 136)
state (p. 136)
rapid eye movement (REM) sleep (p. 137)
sudden infant death syndrome (SIDS) (p. 138)
reflexes (p. 140)
norms (p. 145)

Brazelton Neonatal Behavioral Assessment Scale (NBAS) (p. 145)
marasmus (p. 148)
kwashiorkor (p. 148)
nonorganic failure to thrive (p. 148)
sensation (p. 152)
perception (p. 152)
multimodal approach to perception (p. 158)
affordances (p. 159)

6

Cognitive Development in Infancy

PROLOGUE: Paige

aige Arbeiter was a 2-pound 7-ounce preemie when she earned the nickname "Little Houdini" six years ago. A day and a half after delivery, she pulled the tube off her face to breathe on her own. And she dazzled her intensive-care nurses by inching across her incubator to hang a tiny foot out the door.

When Paige went home after six weeks, her parents noticed that loud noises didn't faze her. The pediatrician told them repeatedly not to worry, but when Paige was 10 months old they took her to New York's Long Island Jewish Speech and Hearing Center for tests. The verdict: she was nearly deaf in both ears.

"Most people we told said, 'Oh, you caught it so early, she'll be just fine,'" her mom recalls. "But we learned we'd missed a very important period in her speech and language development." (Cowley, 2000b, p. 12)

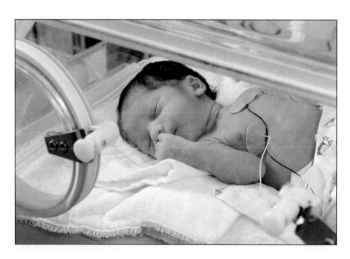

Language development can be affected by a variety of factors, such as premature birth, as illustrated by the case of Paige Arbeiter.

With the help of an ear implant that improves her hearing and with speech therapy, Paige now counts to 10, but her overall language proficiency lags far behind that of other children her age.

Why is early exposure to language critical to subsequent language development? To answer that question, developmental researchers have focused on cognitive development during the first 2 years of life—the topic of this chapter. We examine the work of developmental researchers who seek to understand and explain the enormous strides that infants make in their understanding of the world and their ability to communicate with others.

We begin by discussing the work of Swiss psychologist Jean Piaget, whose theory of developmental stages served as a highly influential impetus for a considerable amount of research on cognitive development. We'll look at both the limitations and the contributions of this important developmental theorist.

We then turn to the basic processes by which cognitive growth occurs. After considering how learning takes place, we examine memory in infants and the ways in which infants process, store, and retrieve information. We discuss the controversial issue of the recollection of events that occurred during infancy. We also address individual differences in intelligence.

Finally, we consider language, the medium by which we all communicate with others. We look at the roots of language in prelinguistic speech and trace the milestones indicating the development of language skills in the progression from a baby's first words to phrases and sentences. We also look at the characteristics of communication addressed to infants and examine some surprising universals in the nature of such communication across different cultures.

In sum, after reading this chapter, you'll be able to answer these questions:

- **What are the fundamental features of Piaget's theories of cognitive development?**
- **How do infants process information?**
- **How is infant intelligence measured?**
- **By what processes do children learn to use language?**
- **How do children influence adults' language?**

Piaget's Approach to Cognitive Development

Olivia's dad is wiping up the mess around the base of her high chair for the third time today. Lately, 14-month-old Olivia seems to take great delight in dropping food from the high chair. She also drops toys, spoons, anything, it seems, just to watch how it hits the floor. It's almost as if she is experimenting to see what kind of noise or what size splatter is produced by each different thing she drops.

Swiss psychologist Jean Piaget (1896–1980) would probably have agreed that Olivia is conducting her own series of experiments to learn more about the workings of her world. Piaget's views of the ways infants learn can be summed up in a simple equation: *action = knowledge.* He argued that infants do not acquire knowledge from facts communicated by others or through sensation and perception. Instead, Piaget suggested that knowledge is the product of direct motor behavior. Although many of his basic explanations and propositions have been challenged by subsequent research, as we'll discuss later, the view that in significant ways infants learn by doing remains unquestioned (Bullinger, 1997; Piaget, 1952, 1962, 1983).

Key Elements of Piaget's Theory

As first noted in Chapter 2, Piaget's theory is based on a *stage approach* to development. He assumed that all children pass through a series of four universal stages—sensorimotor, preoperational, concrete operational, and formal operational—in a fixed order from birth through adolescence. He also suggested that movement from one stage to the next occurred when a child reaches an appropriate level of physical maturation *and* is exposed to relevant types of experience. Without such experience, children are assumed to be incapable of reaching their cognitive potential. Furthermore, in contrast to approaches to cognition that focus on changes in the *content* of children's knowledge about the world, Piaget argued that it was critical to also consider the changes in the *quality* of children's knowledge and understanding as they move from one stage to another.

For instance, as they develop cognitively, infants experience changes in their understanding about what can and cannot occur in the world. Consider a baby who participates in an experiment during which she is exposed to an impossible event. Through some clever trickery with mirrors, she sees three identical versions of her mother all at the same time. A 3-month-old infant shows no disturbance over the multiple apparitions and in fact will interact happily with each. However, by 5 months of age, the child becomes quite agitated at the sight of multiple mothers. Apparently by this time the child has figured out that she has but one mother, and viewing three at a time is thoroughly alarming (T. G. R. Bower, 1977). To Piaget, such reactions indicate that a baby is developing a mastery of underlying principles regarding the way the world operates.

Piaget believed that the basic building blocks of the way we understand the world are mental structures called **schemes,** organized patterns of functioning, that adapt and change with mental development. Although at first schemes are related to physical, or sensorimotor, activity, as children develop, their schemes move to a mental level, reflecting thought. Schemes are similar to computer software: They direct and determine how data from the world, such as new events or objects, are considered and dealt with (Achenbach, 1992).

Handed a new cloth book, for example, a baby will touch it, mouth it, and perhaps try to tear it or bang it on the floor. To Piaget, each of these actions may represent a scheme, and they are the infant's way of gaining knowledge and understanding of this new object. Adults, by contrast, would use a different scheme upon encountering the book. Rather than picking it up and putting it in their mouths or banging it on the floor, they would probably be drawn to the letters on the page, seeking to understand the book through the meaning of the printed words—a very different approach.

Piaget suggested that two principles underlie the growth in children's schemes: assimilation and accommodation. **Assimilation** is the process by which people understand an experience in terms of their current stage of cognitive development and way of thinking. Assimilation occurs, then, when a stimulus or event is acted on, perceived, and understood in accordance with existing patterns of thought. For example, an infant who tries to suck on any toy in the same way is assimilating the objects to her existing sucking scheme. Similarly, a child who encounters a flying squirrel at a zoo and calls it a "bird" is assimilating the squirrel to her existing scheme of "bird."

In contrast, when we make changes in our existing ways of thinking, understanding, or behaving in response to encounters with new stimuli or events, **accommodation** has taken place. For instance, when a child modifies the way he sucks on a toy according to the particular shape of the toy, he is accommodating his sucking scheme to the special characteristics of

Swiss psychologist Jean Piaget

Scheme   An organized pattern of sensorimotor functioning

Assimilation   The process in which people understand an experience in terms of their current stage of cognitive development and way of thinking

Accommodation   Changes in existing ways of thinking that occur in response to encounters with new stimuli or events

Sensorimotor stage Piaget's initial major stage of cognitive development, which can be broken down into six substages

the toy. In the same way, a child who sees a flying squirrel and calls it "a bird with a tail" is beginning to accommodate to new knowledge, modifying her scheme of "bird."

Piaget believed that the earliest schemes are primarily limited to the reflexes with which we are all born, such as sucking and rooting. Infants start to modify these simple early schemes almost immediately, through the processes of assimilation and accommodation, in response to their sensorimotor exploration of the environment. Schemes quickly become more sophisticated as infants become more advanced in their motor capabilities—to Piaget, a signal of the potential for more advanced cognitive development. Because the sensorimotor stage of development begins at birth and continues until the child is about 2 years old, we consider it here in detail. (We'll discuss development during the other stages in future chapters.)

The Sensorimotor Period: Charting the Course of Early Cognitive Growth

Piaget suggests that the **sensorimotor stage,** the initial major stage of cognitive development, can be broken down into six substages. These are summarized in Table 6-1, and we'll consider them in more detail. However, it is important to keep in mind that although the specific substages of the sensorimotor period may at first appear to unfold with great regularity, as infants

TABLE 6-1 PIAGET'S SIX SUBSTAGES OF THE SENSORIMOTOR STAGE

Substage	Age	Description	Example
Substage 1: Simple reflexes	0–1 month	During this period, the various reflexes that determine the infant's interactions with the world are at the center of its cognitive life.	The sucking reflex causes the infant to suck at anything placed in its lips.
Substage 2: First habits and primary circular reactions	1–4 months	At this age, infants begin to coordinate what were separate actions into single, integrated activities.	An infant might combine grasping an object while sucking on it or staring at something while touching it.
Substage 3: Secondary circular reactions	4–8 months	During this period, infants take major strides in shifting their cognitive horizons beyond themselves and begin to act on the outside world.	A child who repeatedly picks up a rattle in her crib and shakes it in different ways to see how the sound changes is demonstrating her ability to modify her cognitive scheme about shaking rattles.
Substage 4: Coordination of secondary circular reactions	8–12 months	In this stage, infants begin to use more calculated approaches to producing events, coordinating several schemes to generate a single act. They achieve object permanence during this stage.	An infant will push one toy out of the way to reach another toy that is lying, partially exposed, under it.
Substage 5: Tertiary circular reactions	12–18 months	At this age, infants develop what Piaget regards as the deliberate variation of actions that bring desirable consequences. Rather than just repeating enjoyable activities as in Substage 4, infants appear to carry out miniature experiments to observe the consequences.	A child will drop a toy repeatedly, varying the position from which he drops it, carefully observing each time to see where it falls.
Substage 6: Beginnings of thought	18–24 months	The major achievement of Substage 6 is the capacity for mental representation or symbolic thought. Piaget argued that only at this stage can infants imagine where objects that they cannot see might be.	Children can even plot in their heads unseen trajectories of objects, so if a ball rolls under a piece of furniture, they can figure out where it is likely to emerge on the other side.

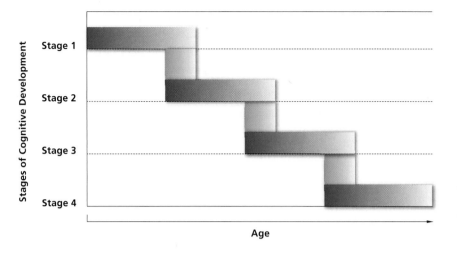

reach a particular age and smoothly proceed into the next substage, the reality of cognitive development is somewhat different. First, the age at which infants actually reach a particular stage varies a good deal among different children. The exact timing of a stage reflects an interaction between the infant's level of physical maturation and the nature of the social environment in which the child is being raised. Consequently, although Piaget contended that the order of the substages does not change from one child to the next, he admitted that the timing can and does vary to some degree.

Furthermore, Piaget argued that development is a more gradual process than the demarcation of different stages might seem to imply. Specifically, infants do not go to sleep one night in one substage and wake up the next morning in the next one. Instead, there is a rather steady shift in behavior as a child moves toward the next stage of cognitive development. Infants also pass through periods of transition, in which some aspects of their behavior reflect the next higher stage while other aspects indicate their current stage (see Figure 6-1).

Substage 1: Simple Reflexes. The first substage of the sensorimotor period, *simple reflexes*, encompasses the first month of life. During this time, the various inborn reflexes, described in Chapters 4 and 5, are at the center of a baby's cognitive life, determining the nature of her interactions with the world. For example, the sucking reflex causes the infant to suck at anything placed in her lips. This sucking behavior, according to Piaget, provides the newborn with information about objects—information that paves the way to the next substage of the sensorimotor period.

At the same time, some of the reflexes become modified as a result of the infant's experience with the nature of the world. For instance, an infant who is being breast-fed but also receives supplemental bottles may start to change the way he sucks, depending on whether the nipple is on a breast or a bottle.

Substage 2: First Habits and Primary Circular Reactions. The second substage of the sensorimotor period, *first habits and primary circular reactions*, occurs from 1 to 4 months of age. In this period, infants begin to coordinate what were separate actions into single, integrated activities. For instance, an infant might combine grasping an object while sucking on it or staring at something while touching it.

If an activity engages a baby's interests, she may repeat it over and over, simply for the sake of continuing to experience it. This repetition of a chance motor event helps the baby start building cognitive schemes through a process known as a **circular reaction.** *Primary circular reactions* are schemes reflecting an infant's repetition of interesting or enjoyable actions, just for the enjoyment of doing them. Piaget referred to these schemes as *primary* because the

Circular reaction An activity that permits the construction of cognitive schemes through the repetition of a chance motor event

Goal-directed behavior Behavior in which several schemes are combined and coordinated to generate a single act to solve a problem

activities they involve focus on the infant's own body. Thus when an infant first puts his thumb in his mouth and begins to suck, it is a mere chance event. However, when he repeatedly sucks his thumb in the future, it represents a primary circular reaction, which he is repeating because the sensation of sucking is pleasurable.

Substage 3: Secondary Circular Reactions.   Substage 3, *secondary circular reactions,* occurs from 4 to 8 months of age. During this period, infants take major strides in shifting their cognitive horizons beyond themselves and begin to act on the outside world. For instance, infants now seek to repeat enjoyable events in their environment, if they happen to produce them through chance activities. A child who repeatedly picks up a rattle in her crib and shakes it in different ways to see how the sound changes is demonstrating her ability to modify her cognitive scheme about shaking rattles. She is engaging in what Piaget calls secondary circular reactions.

Secondary circular reactions are schemes regarding repeated actions that bring about a desirable consequence. The major difference between primary circular reactions and secondary circular reactions is whether the infant's activity is focused on the infant and his own body (primary circular reactions) or whether it involves actions relating to the world outside (secondary circular reactions).

During the third substage, the degree of vocalization increases substantially as infants come to notice that if they make noises, other people around them will respond with noises of their own. Similarly, infants begin to imitate the sounds made by others. Vocalization becomes a secondary circular reaction that ultimately helps lead to the development of language and the formation of social relationships.

Substage 4: Coordination of Secondary Circular Reactions.   One of the major leaps forward in terms of cognitive development comes as infants move through the next substage, *coordination of secondary circular reactions,* which lasts from around 8 months to 12 months. Before this stage, behavior involved direct action on objects. When something happened by chance that caught an infant's interest, she attempted to repeat the event using a single scheme. However, in Substage 4, infants begin to use more calculated approaches to producing events. They employ **goal-directed behavior,** in which several schemes are combined and coordinated to generate a single act to solve a problem. For instance, they will push one toy

Piaget suggests that infants increasingly seek to repeat enjoyable events by acting on their environment.

out of the way to reach another toy that is lying, partially exposed, under it. They also begin to anticipate upcoming events. For instance, Piaget tells of his son Laurent, who at 8 months "recognizes by a certain noise caused by air that he is nearing the end of his feeding, and instead of insisting on drinking to the last drop, he rejects his bottle" (1952, pp. 248–249).

Infants' newfound purposefulness, their ability to use means to attain particular ends, and their skill in anticipating future circumstances owe their appearance in part to the developmental achievement of object permanence that emerges in Substage 4. **Object permanence** is the realization that people and objects exist even when they cannot be seen. It is a simple principle, but its mastery has profound consequences.

Consider, for instance, 7-month-old Chu, who has yet to learn the idea of object permanence. Chu's father shakes a rattle in front of him, then takes the rattle and places it under a blanket. To Chu, who has not mastered the concept of object permanence, the rattle no longer exists. He will make no effort to look for it.

Several months later, when he is in Substage 4, the story is quite different (see Figure 6-2). This time, as soon as his father places the rattle under the blanket, Chu tries to toss the cover aside, eagerly searching for the rattle. Chu clearly has learned that the object continues to exist even when it cannot be seen. For the infant who achieves an understanding of object permanence, then, out of sight is decidedly not out of mind.

The attainment of object permanence extends not only to inanimate objects but to people too. It gives Chu the security that his father and mother still exist even when they have left the room. This awareness is likely a key element in the development of social attachments, which we consider in Chapter 7. The recognition of object permanence also feeds infants' growing assertiveness: As they realize that an object taken away from them doesn't just cease to exist but is merely somewhere else, their only-too-human reaction may be to want it back—and quickly.

Although the understanding of object permanence emerges in Substage 4, it is only a rudimentary understanding. It takes several months for the concept to be fully comprehended, and infants continue for several months to make certain kinds of errors relating to object permanence. For instance, they are often fooled when a toy is hidden first under one blanket and then under a second blanket. In seeking out the toy, Substage 4 infants most often turn to the first hiding place, ignoring the second blanket under which the toy is currently located, even if the hiding was done in plain view.

Object permanence The realization that people and objects exist even when they cannot be seen

VIDEO CLIP
Object Permanence

Before Object Permanence

After Object Permanence

FIGURE 6-2
OBJECT PERMANENCE

Before an infant has understood the idea of object permanence, he will not search for an object that has been hidden right before his eyes. But several months later, he will search for it, illustrating that he has attained object permanence. Why would the concept of object permanence be important to a caregiver?

Substage 5: Tertiary Circular Reactions. Substage 5, *tertiary circular reactions,* is reached at around the age of 12 months and extends to 18 months. As the name of the stage indicates, during this period infants develop what Piaget labeled *tertiary circular reactions,* schemes regarding the deliberate variation of actions that bring desirable consequences. Rather than just repeating enjoyable activities, as they do with secondary circular reactions, infants appear to carry out miniature experiments to observe the consequences.

For example, Piaget observed his son Laurent dropping a toy swan repeatedly, varying the position from which he dropped it, carefully observing each time to see where it fell. Instead of just repeating the action each time (as in a secondary circular reaction), Laurent made modifications in the situation to learn about their consequences. As you may recall from our discussion of research methods in Chapter 2, this behavior represents the essence of the scientific method: An experimenter varies a situation in a laboratory to learn the effects of the variation. To infants in Substage 5, the world is their laboratory, and they spend their days leisurely carrying out one miniature experiment after another. Olivia, the baby described earlier who enjoyed dropping things from her high chair, is another little scientist in action.

What is most striking about infants' behavior during Substage 5 is their interest in the unexpected. Unanticipated events are treated not only as interesting but also as something to be explained and understood. Infants' discoveries can lead to newfound skills, some of which may cause a certain amount of chaos, as Olivia's dad realized while cleaning up around her high chair.

Substage 6: Beginnings of Thought. The final stage of the sensorimotor period, *beginnings of thought,* lasts from around 18 months to 2 years. The major achievement of Substage 6 is the capacity for mental representation, or symbolic thought. A **mental representation** is an internal image of a past event or object. Piaget argued that by this stage, infants can imagine where objects that they cannot see might be. They can even plot in their heads unseen trajectories of objects, so if a ball rolls under a piece of furniture, they can figure out where it is likely to emerge on the other side.

Because of children's new abilities to create internal representations of objects, their understanding of causality also becomes more sophisticated. For instance, consider Piaget's description of his son Laurent's efforts to open a garden gate:

> Laurent tries to open a garden gate but cannot push it forward because it is held back by a piece of furniture. He cannot account either visually or by any sound for the cause that prevents the gate from opening, but after having tried to force it he suddenly seems to understand; he goes around the wall, arrives at the other side of the gate, moves the armchair which holds it firm, and opens it with a triumphant expression. (Piaget, 1954, p. 296)

The attainment of mental representation also permits another important development: the ability to pretend. Using the skill of what Piaget refers to as **deferred imitation,** in which a person who is no longer present is imitated, children are able to pretend that they are driving a car, feeding a doll, or cooking dinner long after they have witnessed such scenes played out in reality. To Piaget, deferred imitation provided clear evidence that children form internal mental representations.

Appraising Piaget: Support and Challenges

Most developmental researchers would probably agree that in many significant ways, Piaget's descriptions of how cognitive development proceeds during infancy are quite accurate (P. L. Harris, 1983, 1987). Yet there is substantial disagreement over the validity of the theory and many of its specific predictions.

Mental representation An internal image of a past event or object

Deferred imitation An act in which a person who is no longer present is imitated by children who have witnessed a similar act

With the attainment of the cognitive skill of deferred imitation, children are able to imitate people and scenes they have witnessed in the past.

Let's start with what is clearly correct about the Piagetian approach. Piaget was a masterful reporter of children's behavior, and his descriptions of growth during infancy remain a monument to his powers of observation. Furthermore, literally thousands of studies have supported Piaget's view that children learn much about the world by acting on objects in their environment. Finally, the broad outlines sketched out by Piaget of the sequence of cognitive development and the increasing cognitive accomplishments that occur during infancy are generally accurate (Gratch & Schatz, 1987).

On the other hand, specific aspects of the theory have come under increasing scrutiny—and criticism—in the decades since Piaget carried out his pioneering work. For example, some researchers question the stage conception that forms the basis of Piaget's theory. Although, as noted earlier, even Piaget acknowledged that children's transitions between stages are gradual, critics contend development proceeds in a much more continuous fashion. Rather than showing major leaps of competence at the end of one stage and the beginning of the next, improvement comes in more gradual increments, growing step by step, skill by skill.

For instance, developmental researcher Robert Siegler (1995) suggests that cognitive development proceeds not in stages but in "waves." According to him, children don't one day drop a mode of thinking and the next take up a new form. Instead, there is an ebb and flow of cognitive approaches that children use to understand the world. One day children may use one form of cognitive strategy, whereas another day they may choose a less advanced strategy, moving back and forth over a period of time. Although one strategy may be used most frequently at a given age, children still may have access to alternative ways of thinking. Siegler thus sees cognitive development as in constant flux.

Other critics dispute Piaget's notion that cognitive development is grounded in motor activities. Some developmental specialists charge that such a view ignores the importance of the sophisticated sensory and perceptual systems that are present from a very early age in infancy—systems about which Piaget knew little, since so much of the research illustrating their sophistication was done much more recently (Butterworth, 1994). Some research studies have also involved children born without arms and legs (due to their mothers' unwitting use of teratogenic drugs during pregnancy, as described in Chapter 3). Critics of Piaget point out that these studies show that such children display normal cognitive development, despite their lack of practice with motor activities (Decarrie, 1969).

To bolster their views, Piaget's critics also point to studies that cast doubt on Piaget's view that infants are incapable of mastering the concept of object permanence until they are close to a year old. For instance, some work suggests that younger infants may not appear to understand object permanence because the techniques used to test their abilities are too insensitive (Baillargeon & De Vos, 1991; Munakata et al., 1997).

It may be that a 4-month-old doesn't search for a rattle hidden under a blanket because she hasn't learned the motor skills necessary to do the searching—not because she doesn't understand that the rattle still exists. Similarly, the apparent inability of young infants to comprehend object permanence may reflect more about their memory deficits than their lack of understanding of the concept: The memories of young infants may be poor enough that they simply do not recall the earlier concealment of the toy. In fact, when more age-appropriate tasks were employed, some researchers found indications of object permanence in children as young as 3½ months (Baillargeon, 1987; Mandler, 1990; Spelke, 1991).

Other types of behavior likewise seem to emerge earlier than Piaget suggested. For instance, recall the ability of neonates to imitate basic facial expressions of adults just hours after birth, as we discussed in Chapter 4. The presence of such skill at such an early age contradicts Piaget's view that initially infants are able to imitate only behavior that they see in others, using parts of their own body that they can plainly view, such as their hands and feet. In fact, facial imitation suggests that humans are born with a basic capability for imitating others' actions, a capability that depends on certain kinds of environmental experiences (Meltzoff & Moore, 1989), but one that Piaget believed develops later in infancy.

Some of the most powerful evidence against Piaget's views emerges from work with children in non-Western cultures. For instance, some evidence suggests that cognitive skills emerge among children in non-Western cultures on a different timetable from children living in Europe and the United States. Infants raised in the Ivory Coast, in Africa, for example, reach the various substages of the sensorimotor period at an earlier age than infants reared in France (Dasen et al., 1978). This is not altogether surprising, since parents in the Ivory Coast tend to emphasize motor skills more heavily than parents in Western societies, thereby providing greater opportunity for practice of those skills (Dasen et al., 1978; Rogoff & Chavajay, 1995).

Piaget's Enduring Achievements.   Despite these problems regarding Piaget's view of the sensorimotor period, even his most passionate critics concede that he has provided us with a masterful description of the broad outlines of sensorimotor development during infancy. His failings seem to be in underestimating the capabilities of younger infants and in his claims that sensorimotor skills develop in a consistent, fixed pattern. Still, his influence has been enormous, and although the focus of many contemporary developmental researchers has shifted to newer information processing approaches, which we discuss next, Piaget remains a towering and pioneering figure in the field of development (Fischer & Hencke, 1996; Roth, Slone, & Dar, 2000; Scholnick et al., 1999; Siegler, 1994).

R E V I E W   &   A P P L Y

Review

● Jean Piaget's theory of human cognitive development involves a succession of stages through which children progress from birth to adolescence.

● As humans move from one stage to another, the way they understand the world changes.

- The sensorimotor stage, from birth to about 2 years, involves a gradual progression through simple reflexes, single coordinated activities, interest in the outside world, purposeful combinations of activities, manipulation of actions to produce desired outcomes, and symbolic thought.

- Piaget is respected as a careful observer of children's behavior and a generally accurate interpreter of the way human cognitive development proceeds.

Applying Child Development

- Name some examples of the principles of assimilation and accommodation at work in child development. *From an educator's perspective:* How might these principles function in adult human learning?

- In general, what are some implications for child-rearing practices of Piaget's observations about the ways children gain an understanding of the world? *From a caregiver's perspective:* Would you use the same approaches in child rearing for a child growing up in a non-Western culture? Why or why not?

Information Processing Approaches to Cognitive Development

At the age of 3 months, Amber Nordstrom breaks into a smile as her brother Marcus stands over her crib, picks up a doll, and makes a whistling noise through his teeth. In fact, Amber never seems to tire of Marcus's efforts at making her smile, and soon whenever Marcus appears and simply picks up the doll, her lips begin to curl into a smile.

Clearly, Amber remembers Marcus and his humorous ways. But how does she remember him? And how much else can Amber remember?

To answer questions such as these, we need to diverge from the road that Piaget laid out for us. Rather than seeking to identify the universal, broad milestones in cognitive development through which all infants pass, as Piaget tried to do, we must consider the specific processes by which individual babies acquire and use the information to which they are exposed. We need, then, to focus less on the qualitative changes in infants' mental lives and consider more closely their quantitative capabilities.

Information processing approaches to cognitive development seek to identify the way that individuals take in, use, and store information (Siegler, 1998). According to these approaches, the quantitative changes in infants' abilities to organize and manipulate information represent the hallmarks of cognitive development.

Taking this perspective, cognitive growth is characterized by increasing sophistication, speed, and capacity in information processing. Earlier, we compared Piaget's idea of schemes to computer software, which directs the computer in how to deal with data from the world. Information processing approaches focus on the types of "mental programs" that people use when they seek to solve problems (Mehler & Dupoux, 1994; Reyna, 1997). These approaches use a model that seeks to identify the way that individuals take in, use, and solve problems.

Information processing approaches   Models that seek to identify the way that individuals take in, use, and store information

Encoding, Storage, and Retrieval: The Foundations of Information Processing

Information processing has three basic aspects: encoding, storage, and retrieval (see Figure 6-3). *Encoding* is the process by which information is initially recorded in a form usable to memory. Infants and children—indeed, all people—are exposed to a massive amount of information; if they tried to process it all, they would be overwhelmed. Consequently, they encode selectively, picking and choosing the information to which they will pay attention.

Even if someone has been exposed to the information initially and has encoded it in an appropriate way, there is still no guarantee that he will be able to use it in the future. Information must also have been stored in memory adequately. *Storage* refers to the maintenance of material saved in memory. Finally, success in using the material in the future depends on retrieval processes. *Retrieval* is the process by which material in memory storage is located, brought into awareness, and used.

We can use our comparison to computers again here. Information processing approaches suggest that the processes of encoding, storage, and retrieval are analogous to different parts of a computer. Encoding can be thought of as a computer's keyboard, through which one inputs information; storage is the computer's hard drive, where information is stored; and retrieval is analogous to a computer's screen, where information is displayed. Only when all three processes—encoding, storage, and retrieval—are operating can information be processed.

In some cases, encoding, storage, and retrieval are relatively automatic, while in other cases they are deliberate. *Automatization* is the degree to which an activity requires attention. Processes that require relatively little attention are automatic; processes that require relatively large amounts of attention are controlled. For example, activities that are automatic for you but required your full attention at first include walking, eating with a fork, and reading.

Automatic mental processes help children in their initial encounters with the world by enabling them to easily and "automatically" process information in particular ways. For instance, by the age of 5, children automatically encode information in terms of frequency. Without a lot of attention to counting or tallying, they become aware, for example, of how often they have encountered various people, permitting them to differentiate familiar from unfamiliar people (Hasher & Zacks, 1984).

Furthermore, without intending to and without being aware of it, infants and children develop a sense of how often different stimuli are found together simultaneously. This permits them to develop an understanding of *concepts,* categorizations of objects, events, or people that share common properties. For example, by encoding the information that four legs, a wagging tail, and barking are often found together, we learn very early in life to understand the concept of "dog." Children—as well as adults—are rarely aware of how they learn such concepts, and they are often unable to articulate the features that distinguish one concept (such as "dog") from another (such as "cat"). Instead, learning tends to occur automatically.

Some of the things we learn automatically are unexpectedly complex. For example, infants have the ability to learn subtle statistical patterns and relationships; these results are consistent

FIGURE 6-3
INFORMATION PROCESSING

Information processing is the process by which information is encoded, stored, and retrieved.

FIGURE 6-4
MICKEY MOUSE MATH

Researcher Karen Wynn found that 5-month-olds like Michelle Follet, pictured here, reacted differently according to whether the number of Mickey Mouse statuettes they saw represented correct or incorrect addition. Do you think this ability is unique to humans? How would an educator explain the uniqueness of this ability?

with a growing body of research showing that the mathematical skills of infants are surprisingly sophisticated. For instance, infants as young as 5 months are able to calculate the outcome of simple addition and subtraction problems. In a study by developmental psychologist Karen Wynn, infants first were shown an object—a 4-inch-high Mickey Mouse statuette (see Figure 6-4). A screen was then raised, hiding the statuette. Next the experimenter showed the infants a second, identical Mickey Mouse and then placed it behind the same screen. Finally, depending on the experimental condition, one of two outcomes occurred. In the "correct addition" condition, the screen dropped, revealing the two statuettes (analogous to $1 + 1 = 2$). But in the "incorrect addition" condition, the screen dropped to reveal just one statuette (analogous to the incorrect $1 + 1 = 1$).

Because infants look longer at unexpected occurrences than at expected ones, the researchers examined the pattern of infants' gazes in the different conditions. In support of the notion that infants can distinguish between correct and incorrect addition, the infants in the experiment gazed longer at the incorrect result than at the correct one. In a similar procedure, infants looked longer at incorrect subtraction problems than at correct ones. The conclusion: Infants have rudimentary mathematical skills (Simon, Hespos, & Rochat, 1995; Wynn, 1992, 1995, 2000).

The results of this research suggest that infants have an innate ability to comprehend certain basic mathematical functions and statistical patterns. This inborn proficiency is likely to form the basis for learning more complex mathematics and statistical relationships later in life, as well as paving the way for language acquisition (Marcus et al., 1999; Mix, Huttenlocher, & Levine, 2001, 2002; Wynn, 2000).

We turn now to several aspects of information processing, focusing on memory and individual differences in intelligence.

Memory During Infancy

Simona Young was fated to spend her infancy with virtually no human contact. For up to 20 hours each day, she was left alone in a crib in a squalid Romanian orphanage. Cold bottles of milk were propped above her small body, which she would clutch to get nourishment. She would rock back and forth, rarely feeling any soothing touch or

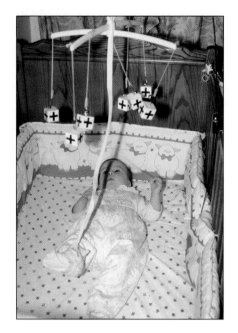

FIGURE 6-5   EARLY SIGNS OF MEMORY

Infants who had learned the association between a moving mobile and kicking showed surprising recall ability if they were exposed to a reminder.

hearing words of comfort. Alone in her bleak surroundings, she would rock back and forth for hours on end.

Simona's story, however, has a happy ending. After being adopted by a Canadian couple when she was two, Simona's life is now filled with the usual activities of childhood involving friends, classmates, and above all, a loving family. In fact, now, at age six, she can remember almost nothing of her miserable life in the orphanage. It is as if she has entirely forgotten the past. (Blakeslee, 1995, p. C1)

How likely is it that Simona truly remembers nothing of her infancy? And if she ever does recall her first 2 years of life, how accurate will her memories be? To answer these questions, we need to consider the qualities of memory that exist during infancy.

Memory Capabilities in Infancy.   Certainly, infants have **memory** capabilities, defined as the process by which information is initially recorded, stored, and retrieved. As we've seen, the ability of infants to distinguish new stimuli from old, as illustrated by habituation, implies that some memory of the old must be present. Unless the infants had some memory of an original stimulus, it would be impossible for them to recognize that a new stimulus differed from the earlier one (Newcombe, Drummey, & Lie, 1995).

However, infants' capability to habituate and show other basic forms of learning tells us little about how age brings about changes in the capacities of memory and in its fundamental nature. Do infants' memory capabilities increase as they get older? The answer is clearly affirmative. In one study, infants were taught that they could move a mobile hanging over the crib by kicking (see Figure 6-5). It took only a few days for 2-month-old infants to forget their training, but 6-month-old infants still remembered for as long as 3 weeks (Rovee-Collier, 1993, 1999).

Furthermore, infants who were later prompted to recall the association between kicking and moving the mobile showed evidence that the memory continued to exist even longer. Infants who had received just two training sessions lasting 9 minutes each still recalled about a week later, as illustrated by the fact that they began to kick when placed in the crib with the mobile. Two weeks later, however, they made no effort to kick, suggesting that they had forgotten entirely.

But they hadn't: When the babies saw a reminder—a moving mobile—their memories were apparently reactivated. In fact, the infants could remember the association, following prompting, for as long as an additional month (Sullivan, Rovee-Collier, & Tynes, 1979). Other evidence confirms these results, suggesting that hints can reactivate memories that at first seem lost and that the older the infant, the more effective such prompting is (Hayne & Rovee-Collier, 1995; Rovee-Collier & Gerhardstein, 1997; Rovee-Collier & Hayne, 1987).

Is the nature of memory in infants different from that in older children and adults? Some researchers suggest that memory during infancy is dependent on particular neurological systems in the brain—specifically, the hippocampus—and that memory in later life involves additional structures of the brain (C. A. Nelson, 1995).

Other researchers suggest, however, that information is processed similarly throughout the life span even though the particular information changes and different parts of the brain may be used. According to memory expert Carolyn Rovee-Collier (1999), people, regardless of their age, gradually lose memories, although, just like babies, they may regain them if reminders are provided. Moreover, the more times a memory is retrieved, the more enduring the memory becomes.

The Duration of Memories.   Although the processes that underlie memory retention and recall seem similar throughout the life span, the quantity of information stored and recalled does differ markedly as infants develop. Older infants can retrieve information more

Memory   The process by which information is initially recorded, stored, and retrieved

rapidly and remember it longer. But just how long? Can memories from infancy be recalled, for example, when babies become grownups?

Researchers disagree on the age from which memories can be retrieved. Older research supports the notion of **infantile amnesia,** the lack of memory for experiences that occurred prior to 3 years of age. For instance, consider whether you can recall the birth of a younger brother or sister. For most college students, if the birth happened before they reached the age of 3, they can remember virtually nothing about it (Sheingold & Tenney, 1982).

However, more recent research shows surprising retention in infants. For example, Nancy Myers and her colleagues exposed a group of 6-month-old children to an unusual series of events in a laboratory, such as intermittent periods of light and dark and unusual sounds. When the children were later tested at the age of 1½ years or 2½ years, they demonstrated clear evidence that they had some memory of their participation in the earlier experience. Their behavior, such as reaching for things, reflected their earlier participation. They also seemed more familiar with the testing situation itself, showing more willingness to remain in a potentially unnerving situation than a control group of same-age children (N. A. Myers, Clifton, & Clarkson, 1987; see also Jusczyk & Hohne, 1997; Mandler & McDonough, 1995).

Such findings are consistent with evidence that the physical record of a memory in the brain appears to be relatively permanent, suggesting that memories, even from infancy, may be enduring. However, memories may not be easily, or accurately, retrieved. For example, memories are susceptible to interference from other, newer information, which may displace or block out the older information, thereby preventing its recall.

Furthermore, recall of memories is sensitive to the context in which the memories were initially formed. If changes have occurred in the context relating to the initial memories, recall may be difficult. In addition, language plays a key role in determining the way in which memories from early in life can be recalled: Older children and adults may be able to report memories only by using the vocabulary that they had available at the time of the initial event, when the memories were stored. Because their vocabulary at the time of initial storage may have been quite limited, they are unable to describe the event later in life, even though it is actually in their memory (S. A. Adler, Gerhardstein, & Rovee-Collier, 1998; Bauer et al., 2000; Simcock & Hayne, 2002).

The question of how well memories formed during infancy are retained in adulthood remains not fully answered. Although infants' memories may be highly detailed and can be enduring if the infants experience repeated reminders, it is still not clear how accurate those memories remain over the course of the life span. In fact, research shows that early memories are susceptible to misrecollection if people are exposed to related contradictory information following the initial formation of the memory. Not only does such new information potentially impair recall of the original material, but the new material may be inadvertently incorporated into the original memory, thereby corrupting its accuracy (Bauer, 1996; Du Breuil, Garry, & Loftus, 1998; Fivush, 1995).

In sum, the data suggest that at least theoretically, it is possible for memories to remain intact from a very young age—if subsequent information does not interfere with them. This is a big "if," because most memories are likely to involve experiences that are somehow related to subsequent experiences and therefore susceptible to interference. Ultimately, it may be that the validity of recollections of memories from infancy needs to be evaluated on a case-by-case basis.

The Cognitive Neuroscience of Memory. Some of the most exciting research on the development of memory is coming from studies of the neurological basis of memory. Advances in brain scan technology, as well as studies of adults with brain damage, suggest that

Infantile amnesia The lack of memory for experiences that occurred before age 3

there are two separate systems involved with long-term memory. These two systems, called explicit memory and implicit memory, retain different sorts of information. *Explicit memory* is memory that is conscious and can be recalled intentionally. In comparison, *implicit memory* is memory that is recalled unconsciously. Implicit memory consists of motor skills, habits, and activities that can be remembered without conscious cognitive effort, such as how to ride a bike or climb a staircase.

Explicit and implicit memory emerge at different rates and involve different parts of the brain. Earliest memories seem to be implicit, and they involve the cerebellum and brain stem. The forerunner of explicit memory involves the hippocampus, but true explicit memory doesn't emerge until the second half of the first year. When explicit memory does emerge, it involves an increasing number of areas of the cortex of the brain (Vargha-Khadem et al., 1997).

Individual Differences in Intelligence: Is One Infant Smarter Than Another?

Maddy Rodriguez is a bundle of curiosity and energy. At 6 months of age, she cries heartily if she can't reach a toy, and when she sees a reflection of herself in a mirror, she gurgles and seems, in general, to find the situation quite amusing.

Jared Lynch, at 6 months, is a good deal more inhibited than Maddy. He doesn't seem to care much when a ball rolls out of his reach, and he loses interest in it rapidly. And unlike Maddy, when he sees himself in a mirror, he pretty much ignores the reflection.

As anyone who has observed more than one baby can tell you, not all infants are alike. Some are full of energy and life, apparently displaying a natural-born curiosity, while others seem, by comparison, somewhat less interested in the world around them. Does this mean that such infants differ in intelligence?

Answering questions about how and to what degree infants vary in their underlying intelligence is not easy. Although it is clear that different infants show significant variations in their behavior, the issue of just what types of behavior may be related to cognitive ability is complicated. Interestingly, the examination of individual differences between infants was the initial approach taken by developmental specialists to understand cognitive development, and such issues still represent an important focus in the field.

What Is Infant Intelligence?   Before we can address whether and how infants may differ in intelligence, we need to consider what is meant by the term *intelligence*. Educators, psychologists, and other experts on development have yet to agree on a general definition of intelligent behavior, even among adults. Is it the ability to do well in scholastic endeavors? Proficiency in business negotiations? Competence in navigating across treacherous seas, such as that shown by peoples of the South Pacific, who have no knowledge of Western navigational techniques?

Defining intelligence in infants is even more problematic than with adults. Is it the speed with which a new task is learned through classical or operant conditioning? How fast a baby becomes habituated to a new stimulus? The age at which an infant learns to crawl or walk? Furthermore, even if we are able to identify particular behaviors that seem validly to differentiate one infant from another in terms of intelligence during infancy, we need to address a further, and probably more important, issue: How well do measures of infant intelligence relate to eventual adult intelligence?

Clearly, such questions are not simple, and no simple answers have been found. However, developmental specialists have devised several approaches (summarized in Table 6-2) to illuminate the nature of individual differences in intelligence during infancy.

Determining what is meant by intelligence in infants represents a major challenge for developmentalists.

TABLE 6-2	APPROACHES USED TO DETECT DIFFERENCES IN INTELLIGENCE DURING INFANCY

Approach	Description
Developmental quotient	Formulated by Arnold Gesell, the developmental quotient is an overall developmental score that relates to performance in four domains: motor skills (balance and sitting), language use, adaptive behavior (alertness and exploration), and personal and social skills (feeding and dressing).
Bayley Scales of Infant Development	Developed by Nancy Bayley, the Bayley Scales of Infant Development evaluate an infant's development from 2 to 42 months. The Bayley Scales focus on two areas: mental abilities (senses, perception, memory, learning, problem solving, and language) and motor abilities (fine and gross motor skills).
Visual recognition memory measurement	Measures of visual recognition memory, the memory of and recognition of a stimulus that has been previously seen, also relate to intelligence. The more quickly an infant can retrieve a representation of a stimulus from memory, the more efficient, presumably, is that infant's information processing.

Developmental Scales. Developmental psychologist Arnold Gesell (1946) formulated the earliest measure of infant development, which was designed to screen out abnormally developing babies from those with typical development. Gesell based his scale on examinations of hundreds of babies. He compared their performance at different ages to learn what behaviors were most common at a particular age. Any infant who varied significantly from the norms of a given age was considered to be developmentally delayed or advanced.

Following the lead of researchers who sought to quantify intelligence through a specific score (known as an *intelligence quotient,* or IQ), Gesell developed a developmental quotient, or DQ. The **developmental quotient** is an overall developmental score that relates to performance in four domains: motor skills (e.g., balance and sitting), language use, adaptive behavior (such as alertness and exploration), and personal and social skills (for example, feeding and dressing).

Later researchers have created other developmental scales. For instance, Nancy Bayley (1969) developed one of the most widely used measures for infants. The **Bayley Scales of Infant Development** evaluate an infant's development from 2 to 42 months. The Bayley Scales focus on two areas: mental abilities and motor abilities. The mental scale focuses on the senses, perception, memory, learning, problem solving, and language, while the motor scale evaluates fine and gross motor skills (see Table 6-3). Like Gesell's approach, the Bayley yields a developmental quotient (DQ). A child who scores at an average level—meaning average performance for other children at the same age—receives a score of 100 (Bayley, 1969; M. M. Black & Matula, 1999; Gagnon & Nagle, 2000).

The virtue of approaches such as those taken by Gesell and Bayley is that they provide a good snapshot of an infant's current developmental level. Using these scales, we can tell in an objective manner whether a particular infant falls behind or is ahead of others of the same age. They are particularly useful in identifying infants who are substantially behind their peers and who therefore need immediate special attention (Culbertson & Gyurke, 1990).

On the other hand, except in extreme cases, such scales are not very good at all in predicting a child's future course of development. A child whose development at the age of 1 year is relatively slow, as identified by these measures, does not necessarily display slow development

Developmental quotient An overall developmental score that relates to performance in four domains: motor skills, language use, adaptive behavior, and personal and social skills

Bayley Scales of Infant Development A measure that evaluates an infant's development from 2 to 42 months

TABLE 6-3	SAMPLE ITEMS FROM THE BAYLEY SCALES OF INFANT DEVELOPMENT	
Age	**Mental Scale**	**Motor Scale**
2 months	Turns head to sound Reacts to disappearance of face	Holds head erect/steady for 15 seconds Sits with support
6 months	Lifts cup by handle Looks at pictures in book	Sits alone for 30 seconds Grasps foot with hands
12 months	Builds tower of 2 cubes Turns pages of book	Walks with help Grasps pencil in middle
17–19 months	Imitates crayon stroke Identifies objects in photo	Stands alone on right foot Walks up stairs with help
23–25 months	Matches pictures Imitates a 2-word sentence	Laces 3 beads Jumps distance of 4 inches
38–42 months	Names 4 colors Uses past tense Identifies gender	Copies circle Hops twice on 1 foot Walks down stairs, alternating feet

Source: From the *Bayley Scales of Infant Development* Copyright © 1993 by The Psychological Corporation. Reproduced by permission. "Bayley Scales of Infant Development" is a registered trademark of The Psychological Corporation.

at age 5, 12, or 25. The association between most measures of behavior during infancy and adult intelligence, then, is minimal (Di Lalla et al., 1990; Molfese & Acheson, 1997; L. S. Siegel, 1989).

Because of the difficulties in using developmental scales to obtain measures of infant intelligence that are related to later intelligence, investigators have turned in the past decade to other techniques that may help assess intelligence in a meaningful way. Some have proved to be quite useful.

Information Processing Approaches to Individual Differences in Intelligence.
When we speak of intelligence in everyday parlance, we often differentiate between "quick" individuals and those who are "slow." Actually, according to research on the speed of information processing, such terms hold some truth. Contemporary approaches to infant intelligence suggest that the speed with which infants process information may correlate most strongly with later intelligence, as measured by IQ tests administered during adulthood (Rose & Feldman, 1997; Sigman, Cohen, & Beckwith, 1997).

How can we tell if a baby is processing information quickly or not? Most researchers use *habituation tests.* Infants who process information efficiently ought to be able to learn about stimuli more quickly. Consequently, we would expect that they would turn their attention away from a given stimulus more rapidly than those who are less efficient at information processing, leading to the phenomenon of habituation. Similarly, measures of **visual recognition memory,** the memory and recognition of a stimulus that has been previously seen, also relate to IQ. The more quickly an infant can retrieve a representation of a stimulus from memory, the more efficient, presumably, is that infant's information processing (Canfield et al., 1997; Tamis-LeMonda & Bornstein, 1993).

Research using an information processing framework is clear in suggesting a relationship between information processing and cognitive abilities: Measures of how quickly infants lose interest in stimuli that they have previously seen, as well as their responsiveness to new

Visual recognition memory The memory and recognition of a stimulus that has been previously seen

stimuli, correlate moderately well with later measures of intelligence. Infants who are more efficient information processors during the 6 months following birth tend to have higher intelligence scores between 2 and 12 years of age, as well as higher scores on other measures of cognitive competence (S. A. Rose & Feldman, 1995; Sigman et al., 1997; Slater, 1995).

Other research suggests that abilities related to the *multimodal approach to perception,* which we considered in Chapter 5, may offer clues about later intelligence. For instance, the information processing skill of cross-modal transference is associated with intelligence. **Cross-modal transference** is the ability to identify a stimulus that has previously been experienced through only one sense by using another sense. For instance, a baby who is able to recognize by sight a screwdriver that she has previously only touched but not seen is displaying cross-modal transference. Research has found that the degree of cross-modal transference displayed by an infant at age 1—which requires a high level of abstract thinking—is associated with intelligence scores several years later (S. A. Rose et al., 1991; S. A. Rose & Ruff, 1987; Spelke, 1987).

> **Cross-modal transference** The ability to identify, using another sense, a stimulus that has previously been experienced only through one sense

Although information processing efficiency and cross-modal transference abilities during infancy relate moderately well to later IQ scores, we need to keep in mind two qualifications. First, even though there is an association between early information processing capabilities and later measures of IQ, the correlation is only moderate in strength. Other factors, such as the degree of environmental stimulation, also play a crucial role in determining adult intelligence. Consequently, we should not assume that intelligence is somehow permanently fixed in infancy.

Second, and perhaps even more important, intelligence measured by traditional IQ tests relates to a particular type of intelligence that emphasizes abilities that lead to academic but not artistic or professional success. Consequently, predicting that a child may do well on IQ tests later in life is not the same as predicting that the child will be successful later in life.

Still, the relatively recent finding that an association exists between efficiency of information processing and later IQ scores has changed how we view the consistency of cognitive development throughout the life span. Whereas the earlier reliance on scales such as the Bayley led to the misconception that little continuity existed, the more recent information processing approaches suggest that cognitive development unfolds in a more orderly, continuous manner from infancy to the later stages of life.

Assessing Information Processing Approaches.   In considering information processing perspectives on cognitive development during infancy, we've seen an approach that is very different from Piaget's. Rather than focusing on broad explanations of the *qualitative* changes that occur in infants' capabilities, as Piaget does, information processing looks at *quantitative* change. Piaget sees cognitive growth occurring in fairly sudden spurts; information processing sees more gradual, step-by-step growth. (Think of the difference between a track-and-field runner leaping hurdles and a slow but steady marathon racer.)

Because information processing researchers consider cognitive development in terms of a collection of individual skills, they are often able to use more precise measures of cognitive ability, such as processing speed and memory recall, than proponents of Piaget's approach. Still, the very precision of these individual measures makes it harder to get an overall sense of the nature of cognitive development, something at which Piaget was a master. It's as if information processing approaches focus more on the individual pieces of the puzzle of cognitive development, while Piagetian approaches focus more on the whole puzzle.

Ultimately, both Piagetian and information processing approaches are essential to our understanding of cognitive development in infancy. Coupled with advances in the biochemistry of the brain and theories that consider the effects of social factors on learning and cognition (which we'll discuss in the next chapter), the two approaches will continue to help us paint a full picture of cognitive development.

⊶ BECOMING AN INFORMED CONSUMER OF DEVELOPMENT ⊶

What Can You Do to Promote Infants' Cognitive Development?

All parents want their children to reach their full cognitive potential, but sometimes efforts to reach this goal take a bizarre path. For instance, some parents spend hundreds of dollars enrolling in workshops with titles such as "How to Multiply Your Baby's Intelligence" and buying books with titles such as *How to Teach Your Baby to Read* (Sharpe, 1994).

Do such efforts ever succeed? Although some parents swear they do, there is no scientific support for the effectiveness of such programs. For example, despite the many cognitive skills of infants, no infant can actually read. Furthermore, "multiplying" a baby's intelligence is impossible, and such organizations as the American Academy of Pediatrics and the American Academy of Neurology have denounced programs that claim to do so.

On the other hand, certain things can be done to promote cognitive development in infants. The following suggestions, based on findings of developmental researchers, offer a starting point (Meyerhoff & White, 1986; M. Schulman, 1991; Schwebel, Maher, & Fagley, 1990):

- *Give infants the opportunity to explore the world.* As Piaget suggests, children learn by doing, and they need the opportunity to explore and probe their environment. Make sure the environment contains a variety of toys, books, and other sources of stimulation.

- *Be responsive to infants both verbally and nonverbally.* Try to speak *with* babies, not *at* them. Ask questions, listen to their responses, and provide further communication.

- *Read to your infants.* Although they may not understand the meaning of your words, they will respond to your tone of voice and the intimacy provided by the activity. Reading together also begins to create a lifelong reading habit.

- *Keep in mind that you don't have to be with an infant 24 hours a day.* Just as infants need time to explore their world on their own, parents and other caregivers need time off from child care activities.

- *Don't push infants, and don't expect too much too soon.* Your goal should not be to create a genius; it should be to provide a warm, nurturing environment that will allow an infant to reach his or her potential.

One important way to encourage cognitive development in infants is to read to them.

Helen Shwe

Education: . . . . **University of Rochester: B.A. in cognitive science; Stanford University: M.A. and Ph.D. in developmental psychology**

Position: . . . . **Toy Designer and Consultant**

Home: . . . . **Redwood City, California**

Toys have traditionally been provided to children for entertainment, but over the years it has become apparent that what were once considered mere playthings have become important components of a child's development. As a result, toy researchers and designers, like Helen Shwe, are designing toys not only for specific age groups but also to encourage development.

"First you have to decide on the age group for whom the toy is targeted and make sure that the range is not too broad," explains Shwe, who is a consultant to a number of toy designers. "Because their cognitive and social development changes so much, you have to keep their interest. A three-year-old is very different from a four-year-old."

While color, texture, and shape are most important for very young children, according to Shwe, toy designs for older children consider the social aspect.

"At around age three, you try to have a toy that will allow multiple children to play with it," Shwe notes. "A toy that will encourage social interaction and cooperation. Fantasy and pretend play is popular, and you would want to bring some of that into the design.

"For example, a social action toy will allow children to compose a song together. One would push a button to add one phrase, and the other child would add another musical phrase."

One area of toy design that has grown quickly over the past several years has been the incorporation of technology into toys.

"Today, more than fifty percent of toys have some type of electronics or technology," Shwe points out. "Technology toys have refreshed content in that a parent can connect to a Web site and download new content for the toy as the child grows," she adds.

Although the combination of developmental psychologists and high technology can provide some interesting and sophisticated playthings for children, Shwe notes that there will always be room for more traditional toys.

"There is definitely room for both types of toys," she asserts, "because they foster different abilities."

"Because their cognitive and social development changes very much, you have to keep their interest. A three-year-old is very different from a four-year-old."

R E V I E W & A P P L Y

Review

● Information processing approaches consider quantitative changes in children's abilities to organize and use information. Cognitive growth is regarded as the increasing sophistication of encoding, storage, and retrieval.

- Infants clearly have memory capabilities from a very early age, although the duration and accuracy of such memories are unresolved questions.

- Traditional measures of infant intelligence focus on behavioral attainments, which can help identify developmental delays or advances but are not strongly related to measures of adult intelligence.

- Information processing approaches to assessing intelligence rely on variations in the speed and quality with which infants process information.

Applying Child Development

- What information from this chapter could you use to refute the claims of books or educational programs that promise to help parents multiply their babies' intelligence or instill advanced intellectual skills in infants? *From an educator's perspective:* Based on valid research, what approaches would you use for intellectual development of infants?

- In what ways is the use of such developmental scales as Gesell's or Bayley's helpful? In what ways is it dangerous? *From a nurse's perspective:* How would you maximize the helpfulness and minimize the danger if you were advising a parent?

The Roots of Language

Vicki and Dominic were engaged in a friendly competition over whose name would be the first word their baby, Maura, said. "Say 'mama,'" Vicki would coo before handing Maura over to Dominic for a diaper change. Grinning, he would take her and coax, "No, say 'daddy.'" Both parents ended up losing—and winning—when Maura's first word sounded more like "baba" and seemed to refer to her bottle.

Mama. No. Cookie. Dad. Joe. Most parents can remember their baby's first word, and no wonder. It's an exciting moment. When an infant utters his or her first word, no matter what it is, it marks the start of a transformation: from an entity seemingly not so different from animals of many other species to an entity who can now use a skill that is, arguably, unique to human beings.

But those initial words are just the first and most obvious manifestations of language. Many months earlier, infants began using language to comprehend the world around them. How does this linguistic ability develop? What pattern or sequence does language development follow? And how does the use of language mark a transformation in the cognitive world of infants and their parents? We consider these questions, and others, as we address the development of language during the first years of life.

The Fundamentals of Language: From Sounds to Symbols

Language, the systematic, meaningful arrangement of symbols, provides the basis for communication. But it does more than this: It is closely tied to the way infants think and understand the world. It enables them to reflect on people and objects and to convey their thoughts to others.

Language has several formal characteristics that must be mastered as linguistic competence is developed (M. Barrett, 1999), including the following:

- *Phonology.* Phonology refers to the basic sounds of language, called *phonemes,* that can be combined to produce words and sentences. For instance, the *a* in *mat* and the *a* in *mate* represent two different phonemes in English. Although English employs just 40 phonemes

---

Language A systematic, meaningful arrangement of symbols that provides a basis for communication

to create every word in the language, other languages have as many as 85 phonemes—and some as few as 15 (Akmajian, Demers, & Harnish, 1984).

- *Morphemes.* A morpheme is the smallest language unit that has meaning. Some morphemes are complete words, while others add information necessary for interpreting a word, such as the endings -*s* for plural and -*ed* for past tense.

- *Semantics.* Semantics are the rules that govern the meaning of words and sentences. As their knowledge of semantics develops, children are able to understand the subtle distinction between "Ellie was hit by a car" (an answer to the question of why Ellie has not been in school for the past week) and "A car hit Ellie" (used to announce an emergency situation).

In considering the development of language, we need to distinguish between linguistic *comprehension,* the understanding of speech, and linguistic *production,* the use of language to communicate. One principle underlies the relationship between the two: Comprehension precedes production. An 18-month-old may be able to understand a complex series of directions ("Pick up your coat from the floor and put it on the chair by the fireplace") but may not yet have strung more than two words together when speaking for herself. Comprehension, then, begins earlier than production, and throughout infancy, comprehension increases at a faster rate than production. For instance, during infancy, comprehension expands at a rate of 22 new words a month, while production increases at a rate of about 9 new words a month, once infants start talking. Other forms of language ability show the same pattern, with comprehension consistently preceding production (Benedict, 1979; Jusczyk, 1997; Tincoff & Jusczyk, 1999; see Figure 6-6).

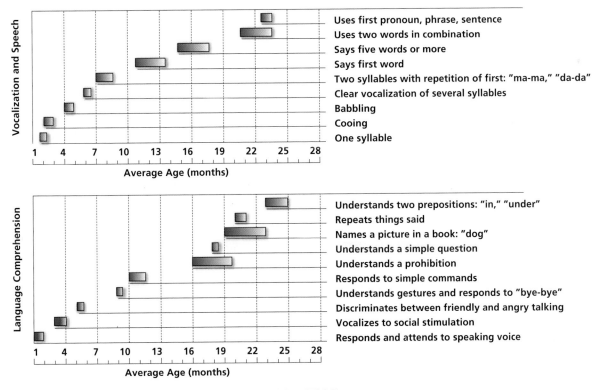

FIGURE 6-6   COMPREHENSION BEFORE PRODUCTION

Throughout infancy, the comprehension of speech precedes the production of speech.

(*Source:* Adapted from Bornstein & Lamb, 1992a)

Although we tend to think of language in terms of the production of words and then groups of words, infants can begin to communicate linguistically well before they say their first word.

Prelinguistic Communication.

Consider the following "dialogue" between a mother and her 3-month-old child (C. E. Snow, 1977):

INFANT: [*smiles*]

MOTHER: Oh, what a nice little smile! Yes, isn't that pretty? There now. There's a nice little smile.

INFANT: [*burps*]

MOTHER: What a nice wind as well! Yes, that's better, isn't it? Yes. Yes.

INFANT: [*vocalizes*]

MOTHER: Yes! There's a nice noise.

Although we tend to think of language in terms of the production first of words and then of groups of words, infants actually begin to communicate linguistically well before they say their first word. Spend 24 hours with even a very young infant and you will hear a variety of sounds: cooing, crying, gurgling, murmuring, and assorted other noises. These sounds, although not meaningful in themselves, play an important role in linguistic development, paving the way for true language (Bloom, 1993). It is this very early period of linguistic development that Paige Arbeiter, whom we met in the chapter prologue, appears to have missed almost entirely.

 Prelinguistic communication is communication through sounds, facial expressions, gestures, imitation, and other nonlinguistic means. When a father responds to his daughter's "ah" with an "ah" of his own and then the daughter repeats the sound and the father responds once again, they are engaged in prelinguistic communication. Clearly, the "ah" sound has no particular meaning. However, its repetition, which mimics the give-and-take of conversation, teaches the infant something about turn-taking (Dromi, 1993).

Babbling.

The most obvious manifestation of prelinguistic communication is babbling. **Babbling,** making speechlike but meaningless sounds, starts at the age of 2 or 3 months and continues until around the age of 1 year. When they babble, infants repeat the same vowel sound over and over, changing the pitch from high to low (as in "ee-ee-ee," repeated at different pitches). After the age of 5 months, the sounds of babbling begin to expand, reflecting the addition of consonants (such as "bee-bee-bee-bee").

Prelinguistic communication Communication through sounds, facial expressions, gestures, imitation, and other nonlinguistic means

Babbling Making speechlike but meaningless sounds

Babbling is a universal phenomenon, accomplished in the same way in all cultures. While they are babbling, infants spontaneously produce all of the sounds found in every language, not just the language they hear people around them speaking. Furthermore, careful observational research finds that babies babble more with the right side of their mouths than their left side, suggesting that babbling may involve areas of the brain that have been shown in older children and adults to be central to the production of language (Holowka & Petitto, 2002).

In fact, as discussed in the *From Research to Practice* box, even deaf children display their own form of babbling: Infants who cannot hear and who are exposed to sign language babble with their hands instead of their voices (Cormier, Mauk, & Repp, 1998; Locke, 1994; Petitto & Marentette, 1991).

Babbling follows a progression from sounds that are the simplest to make to more complex sounds. Furthermore, although initially exposure to a particular language does not seem to influence babbling, experience eventually does make a difference. By the age of 6 months, babbling differs according to the language to which infants are exposed (Blake & Boysson-Bardies, 1992). The difference is so noticeable that even untrained listeners can distinguish between babbling infants who have been raised in cultures in which French, Arabic, or Cantonese is spoken (Boysson-Bardies, Sagart, & Durand, 1984; Boysson-Bardies & Vihman, 1991; Locke, 1983; Oller et al., 1997; Vihman, 1991).

Babbling may be the most obviously languagelike achievement of early infancy, but there are other indications of prelinguistic speech. For instance, consider 5-month-old Marta, who spies her red ball just beyond her reach. After reaching for it and finding that she is unable to get to it, she makes a cry of anger that alerts her parents that something is amiss, and her mother hands it to her. Communication, albeit prelinguistic, has occurred.

Four months later, when Marta faces the same situation, she no longer bothers to reach for the ball and doesn't respond in anger. Instead, she holds out her arm in the direction of the ball and with great purpose seeks to catch her mother's eye. When her mother sees the behavior, she knows just what Marta wants. Clearly, Marta's communicative skills—although still prelinguistic—have taken a leap forward.

Even these prelinguistic skills are supplanted in just a few months when the gesture gives way to a new communicative skill: producing an actual word. Marta's parents clearly hear her say "ball."

First Words. When a mother and father first hear their child say "Mama" or "Dada," or even "baba," the first word spoken by Maura, the baby described earlier in this section, it is hard to be anything but delighted. But their initial enthusiasm may be dampened a bit when they find that the same sound is used to ask for a cookie, a doll, and a tattered old blanket.

First words are generally spoken somewhere around the age of 10 to 14 months but may occur as early as 9 months. Linguists differ on just how to recognize that a first word has actually been uttered. Some say it is when an infant clearly understands words and can produce a sound that is close to a word spoken by adults, such as a child who uses "mama" for any request she may have. Other linguists use a stricter criterion for the first word; they restrict it to cases in which children give a clear, consistent name to a person, event, or object. In this view, "mama" counts as a first word only if it is consistently applied to the same person, seen in a variety of situations and doing a variety of things, and is not used to label other people (Bornstein & Tamis-LeMonda, 1989; Hollich et al., 2000; Kamhi, 1986).

Although there is disagreement over when we can say a first word has been uttered, no one disputes that once an infant starts to produce words, the rate of increase in vocabulary is rapid. By the age of 15 months, the average child has a vocabulary of 10 words. The child's vocabulary methodically expands until the one-word stage of language development ends at around 18 months. Around that time, a sudden spurt in vocabulary occurs. In just a short period—a few weeks somewhere between 16 and 24 months of age—a child's vocabulary

Babbling is universal, done in the same way across all cultures.

FROM RESEARCH TO PRACTICE

Do Gestures Hold the Key to Understanding the Origins of Human Language?

One chimp sits in the group, contentedly eating fruit in her natal African forest. As she does, a second, younger chimp approaches, but not too close, and extends her hand in a cupping gesture. She is asking the first chimp to share the food. Another chimp, this one at a research center outside Atlanta, eyes a banana just beyond reach, outside and to the left of his cage. When a scientist approaches, the chimp gestures with his right hand, extending it in what's called a whole-hand point, looking back and forth between the scientist and the banana: would you mind passing the chow, big guy? (Begley, 1999, p. 56)

As language goes, these examples are not all that sophisticated. But gestures such as these may provide clues to understanding how language evolved in human beings and how infants use gestures to make themselves understood.

Researchers have begun to extend findings from studies of chimps to studies of human infants who can neither hear nor speak. According to an increasing body of research on such deaf-mute children, language based on gestures may be innate in the human brain. Going even further, some scientists argue that language may have evolved directly from the use of hand gestures (Azar, 2000; Corballis, 1999; Hickok, Bellugi, & Klima, 2001).

Evidence for this theory comes from several sources. For one thing, blind children gesture in much the same way that sighted children do, suggesting that the use of gestures is a natural part of development. Second, research shows that gesturing follows a set of sophisticated rules that are similar to the rules of verbal language. In fact, children who are deaf have invented numerous forms of sign language, and their gestural babbling is analogous to the verbal babbling of children who can speak. Furthermore, as shown in Figure 6-7, the areas of the brain that are activated during the production of hand gestures are similar to

VIDEO CLIP

Teaching Sign Language

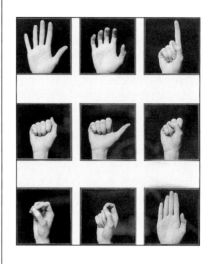

Deaf infants who are exposed to sign language do their own type of babbling, related to the use of signs.

the areas activated during speech production (Corballis, 2000; Mayberry & Nicoladis, 2001; Senghas & Coppola, 2001).

The theory that gestures form a kind of sophisticated silent language helps explain the relatively quick evolution of spoken language in humans. According to fossil evidence, the ability to speak—signaled by the emergence of vocal tracts—did not develop until around 150,000 years ago; we also know that civilizations with spoken language emerged around 5,000 years ago. The time span between the emergence of vocal tracts and the use of spoken language is remarkably quick—the blink of an eye in evolutionary terms. However, if humans had already developed a sophisticated use of gestures that included the formal attributes of language, the quick leap to a spoken language begins to make sense.

The idea that spoken language evolved from gestural languages remains a theory. Still, it does help explain the universal nature of gesturing, and it also helps us understand how human babies develop the ability to use the spoken word.

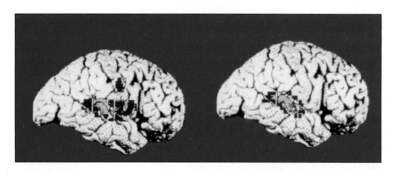

FIGURE 6-7   BROCA'S AREA

Areas of the brain that are activated during speech are similar to the areas activated during the production of hand gestures.

(*Source:* Krantz, 1999)

TABLE 6-4 THE FIRST WORDS CHILDREN UNDERSTAND AND SPEAK

Category	Comprehension Percentage	Production Percentage
1. Nominals (words referring to things)	56	61
Specific (people, animals, objects)	17	11
General (words referring to all members of a category)	39	50
Animate (objects)	9	13
Inanimate (objects)	30	37
Pronouns (e.g., *this, that, they*)	1	2
2. Action words	36	19
Social action games (e.g., peek-a-boo)	15	11
Events (e.g., *eat*)	1	—
Locatives (locating or putting something in specific location)	5	1
General action and inhibitors (e.g., *don't touch*)	15	6
3. Modifiers	3	10
Status (e.g., *all gone*)	2	4
Attributes (e.g., *big*)	1	3
Locatives (e.g., *outside*)	0	2
Possessives (e.g., *mine*)	1	1
4. Personal and social words	5	10
Assertions (e.g., *yes*)	2	9
Social expressive (e.g., *bye-bye*)	4	1

Note: Percentage refers to percentage of children who include this type of word among their first 50 words.
(*Source:* Adapted from Benedict, 1979)

typically increases from 50 to 400 words (E. Bates, Bretherton, & Snyder, 1988; Fernald et al., 1989; Gleitman & Landau, 1994).

As you can see from the list in Table 6-4, the first words in children's early vocabularies typically refer to objects and things, both animate and inanimate. Most often they refer to people or objects who constantly appear and disappear ("Mama"), to animals ("kitty"), or to temporary states ("wet"). These first words are often **holophrases,** one-word utterances that stand for a whole phrase whose meaning depends on the particular context in which they are used. For instance, a youngster may use the holophrase "ma" to mean, depending on the context, "I want to be picked up by Mom" or "I want something to eat, Mom" or "Where's Mom?" (E. Clark, 1983; Dromi, 1987; K. Nelson, 1981).

Culture has an effect on the types of first words spoken. For example, North American English-speaking infants are more apt to use nouns initially, whereas Chinese Mandarin-speaking infants use more verbs than nouns (Tardif, 1996).

First Sentences. When Aaron was 19 months old, he heard his mother coming up the back steps, as she did every day just before dinner. Aaron turned to his father and distinctly said, "Ma come." In stringing those two words together, Aaron took a giant step in his language development.

The increase in vocabulary that comes at around 18 months is accompanied by another accomplishment: the linking together of individual words into sentences that convey a single thought. Although there is a good deal of variability in the time at which children first create two-word phrases, it is generally around 8 to 12 months after they say their first word.

Holophrases One-word utterances that stand for a whole phrase, whose meaning depends on the particular context in which they are used

By the age of two, most children use two-word phrases, such as "ball play."

Telegraphic speech   Speech in which words not critical to the message are left out

Underextension   The overly restrictive use of words, common among children just mastering spoken language

The linguistic advance represented by two-word combinations is important because the linkage not only provides labels for things in the world but also indicates the relationships between them. For instance, the combination may declare something about possession ("Mama key") or recurrent events ("Dog bark"). Interestingly, most early sentences don't represent demands or even necessarily require a response. Instead, they are often merely comments and observations about events occurring in the child's world (Halliday, 1975; Slobin, 1970).

Two-year-olds using two-word combinations tend to employ particular sequences that are similar to the ways in which adult sentences are constructed. For instance, sentences in English typically follow a pattern in which the subject of the sentence comes first, followed by the verb, and then the object ("Josh threw the ball"). Children's speech most often uses a similar order, although not all the words are initially included. Consequently, a child might say "Josh threw" or "Josh ball" to indicate the same thought. What is significant is that the order is typically not "threw Josh" or "ball Josh" but rather the usual order of English, which makes the utterance much easier for an English speaker to comprehend (R. Brown, 1973; Hirsh-Pasek & Michnick-Golinkoff, 1996; Maratsos, 1983).

Although the creation of two-word sentences represents an advance, the language used by children is still by no means adultlike. As we've just seen, 2-year-olds tend to leave out words that aren't critical to the message, similar to the way we might write a telegram for which we were paying by the word. For that reason, their talk is often called **telegraphic speech.** Rather than saying, "I showed you the book," a child using telegraphic speech might say, "I show book." "I am drawing a dog" might become "Drawing dog" (see Table 6-5).

Beginning to Master Spoken Language.   Early language has other characteristics that differentiate it from the language used by adults. For instance, consider Sarah, who refers to the blanket she sleeps with as "blankie." When her Aunt Ethel gives her a new blanket, Sarah refuses to call the new one a "blankie," restricting the word to her original blanket.

Sarah's inability to generalize the label of "blankie" to blankets in general is an example of **underextension,** using words too restrictively, which is common among children just mastering spoken language. Underextension occurs when language novices think that a word refers to a specific instance of a concept instead of to all examples of the concept (Caplan & Barr, 1989).

TABLE 6-5   CHILDREN'S IMITATION OF SENTENCES SHOWING DECLINE OF TELEGRAPHIC SPEECH

	Eve, 25.5 Months	Adam, 28.5 Months	Helen, 30 Months	Ian, 31.5 Months	Jimmy, 32 Months	June, 35.5 Months
I showed you the book.	I show book.	(I show) book.	C	I show you the book.	C	Show you the book.
I am very tall.	(My) tall.	I (very) tall.	I very tall.	I'm very tall.	Very tall.	I very tall.
It goes in a big box.	Big box.	Big box.	In big box.	It goes in the box.	C	C
I am drawing a dog.	Drawing dog.	I draw dog.	I drawing dog.	Dog.	C	C
I will read the book.	Read book.	I will read book.	I read the book.	I read the book.	C	C
I can see a cow.	See cow.	I want see cow.	C	Cow.	C	C
I will not do that again.	Do-again.	I will that again.	I do that.	I again.	C	C

C = correct imitation.

(*Source:* Adapted from R. Brown & Fraser, 1963)

As infants like Sarah grow more adept with language, the opposite phenomenon some-times occurs. In **overextension,** words are used too broadly, overgeneralizing their meaning. For example, when Sarah refers to buses, trucks, and tractors as "cars," she is guilty of over-extension, making the assumption that any object with wheels must be a car. Although overextension reflects speech errors, it also shows that advances are occurring in the child's thought processes: The child is beginning to develop general mental categories and concepts (Behrend, 1988).

Infants also show individual differences in the style of language they use. For example, some use a **referential style,** in which language is used primarily to label objects. Others tend to use an **expressive style,** in which language is used primarily to express feelings and needs about oneself and others (E. Bates et al., 1994; K. Nelson, 1996).

Language styles reflect, in part, cultural factors. For example, mothers in the United States label objects more frequently than Japanese mothers do, encouraging a more referential style of speech. In contrast, mothers in Japan are more apt to speak more about social interactions, encouraging a more expressive style of speech (Fernald & Morikawa, 1993).

The Origins of Language Development: The Learning Theory Approach. The immense strides in language development during the preschool years raise a fundamental question: How does proficiency in language come about? Linguists are deeply divided on how to answer this question.

One response comes from the basic principles of learning. According to the **learning theory approach,** language acquisition follows the basic laws of reinforcement and condition-ing discussed in Chapter 2. For instance, a child who articulates the word "da" may be hugged and praised by her father, who jumps to the conclusion that she is referring to him. This reac-tion reinforces the child, who is more likely to repeat the word. In sum, the learning theory perspective on language acquisition suggests that children learn to speak by being rewarded for making sounds that approximate speech. Through the process of *shaping,* language becomes more and more similar to adult speech (Skinner, 1957).

There's a problem, though, with the learning theory approach. It doesn't seem to explain adequately how readily children acquire the rules of language. For instance, novice users of language are reinforced not only when they use grammatically impeccable language but also when they make errors. Parents are apt to be just as responsive if their child says, "Why the dog won't eat?" as they are if the child phrases the question more correctly ("Why won't the dog eat?"). Both forms of the question are understood correctly, and both elicit the same response; reinforcement is provided for both correct and incorrect language usage. Under such circumstances, learning theory is hard put to explain how children learn to speak properly.

Still other problems exist with learning theory explanations. For instance, research shows that children are able to move beyond specific utterances they have heard and produce novel phrases, sentences, and constructions. Furthermore, children can apply rules to nonsense words. In one study, 4-year-old children heard the nonsense verb *pilk* in the sentence "The bear is pilking the horse." Later, when asked what was happening to the horse, they responded by placing the nonsense verb in the correct tense and voice: "He's getting pilked by the bear."

The Nativist Approach. Such conceptual difficulties with the learning theory approach have led to the development of an alternative known as the nativist approach, championed by the linguist Noam Chomsky (1968, 1978, 1991, 1999). The **nativist approach** argues that there is a genetically determined, innate mechanism that directs the development of language. According to Chomsky, people are born with an innate capacity to use language, which emerges, more or less automatically, as they mature.

Overextension The overly broad use of words, overgeneralizing their meaning

Referential style A speaking style in which language is used primarily to label objects

Expressive style A speaking style in which language is used primarily to express feel-ings and needs about oneself and others

Learning theory approach The perspective that language acquisition follows the basic laws of reinforcement and conditioning

Nativist approach The perspective that a genetically determined, innate mechanism directs language development

Language acquisition device (LAD) A neural system of the brain hypothesized to permit understanding of language

Infant-directed speech A type of speech directed toward infants, characterized by short, simple sentences

Chomsky's analysis of different languages suggests that all the world's languages share a similar underlying structure, which he calls *universal grammar*. In this view, the human brain is wired with a neural system called the **language acquisition device (LAD)** that both permits the understanding of language structure and provides a set of strategies and techniques for learning the particular characteristics of the language to which a child is exposed. In this view, language is uniquely human, made possible by a genetic predisposition to both comprehend and produce words and sentences (Lillo-Martin, 1997; Lust, Suner, & Whitman, 1995; M. A. Nowak, Komarova, & Niyogi, 2001).

Support for Chomsky's nativist approach comes from work of Anthony Monaco and colleagues (2002), who identified a specific gene related to speech production. If this finding is supported by subsequent work, it provides strong evidence for an evolutionary basis to language (Wade, 2001).

Like the learning theory approach, the view that language represents an innate ability unique to humans has its critics. For instance, some researchers argue that certain primates are able to learn at least the basics of language, an ability that calls into question the uniqueness of the human linguistic capacity. Other critics suggest that we must identify mechanisms other than either a language acquisition device or learning theory principles if we are to fully understand the processes that underlie language development (MacWhinney, 1991; Savage-Rumbaugh et al., 1993).

The Interactionist Approach. Given that neither the learning theory nor the nativist perspective provides an explanation that is fully supported by research, some theorists have turned to a theory that combines both schools of thought. The *interactionist perspective* suggests that language development is produced through a combination of genetically determined predispositions and environmental events.

The interactionist perspective accepts that innate factors shape the broad outlines of language development. However, interactionists also argue that the specific course of language development is determined by the language to which children are exposed and the reinforcement they receive for using language in particular ways. Social factors are considered key to development, since the motivation provided by one's membership in a society and culture and one's interactions with others lead to the use of language and the growth of language skills.

Just as there is support for some aspects of learning theory and nativist positions, the interactionist perspective also has some support. We don't know which of these positions will ultimately provide the best explanation. More likely, different factors play different roles at different times during childhood. The full explanation for language acquisition, then, remains to be found.

Speaking to Children: The Language of Infant-Directed Speech

Say the following sentence aloud: "Do you like the apple dumpling?"

Now pretend that you are going to ask the same question of an infant, and speak it as you would for the child's ears.

Chances are several things happened when you translated the phrase for the infant. First of all, the wording probably changed, and you may have said something like, "Does baby like the apple dumpling?" At the same time, the pitch of your voice probably rose, your general intonation most likely had a singsong quality, and you probably separated your words carefully.

Infant-directed speech, also known as "motherese," includes the use of short, simple sentences and is spoken using a pitch higher than that used with older children and adults.

Infant-Directed Speech. The shift in your language was due to an attempt to use what has been called **infant-directed speech,** a style of speech directed toward infants. This type of speech pattern was previously called *motherese* because it was assumed that it applied only to

DEVELOPMENTAL DIVERSITY

Is Infant-Directed Speech Similar in All Cultures?

Do mothers in the United States, Sweden, and Russia speak the same way to their infants?

In some respects, they do. Although the words themselves differ across languages, the way the words are spoken is quite similar. According to a growing body of research, there are basic similarities across cultures in the nature of infant-directed speech (Grieser & Kuhl, 1988; Papousek & Papousek, 1991; Rabain-Jamin & Sabeau-Jouannet, 1997).

Consider, for instance, the comparison in Table 6-6 of the major characteristics of speech directed at infants used by native speakers of English and Spanish. Of the 10 most frequent features, 6 are common to both: exaggerated intonation, high pitch, lengthened vowels, repetition, lower volume, and instructional emphasis (i.e., heavy stress on certain key words, such as emphasizing the word *ball* in the sentence, "No, that's a *ball*") (Blount, 1982). Similarly, mothers in the United States, Sweden, and Russia all exaggerate and elongate the pronunciation of the three vowel sounds of "ee," "ah," and "oh" when speaking to infants in similar ways, despite differences in the languages in which the sounds are used (Kuhl et al., 1997).

Even deaf mothers use a form of infant-directed speech: When communicating with their infants, deaf mothers use signed language at a significantly slower tempo than when communicating with adults, and they frequently repeat the signs (Masataka, 1996, 1998, 2000; Swanson, Leonard, & Gandour, 1992).

The cross-cultural similarities in infant-directed speech are so great, in fact, that they appear in some facets of language specific to particular types of interactions. For instance, evidence comparing American English, German, and Mandarin Chinese

speakers shows that in each of the languages, pitch rises when a mother is attempting to get an infant's attention or produce a response, and pitch falls when she is trying to calm an infant (Papousek & Papousek, 1991).

Why do we find such similarities across very different languages? One hypothesis is that the characteristics of infant-directed speech activate innate responses in infants. As we have noted, infants seem to prefer infant-directed speech over adult-directed speech, suggesting that their perceptual systems may be more responsive to such characteristics. Another explanation is that infant-directed speech facilitates language development, providing cues as to the meaning of speech before infants have developed the capacity to understand the meaning of words (Fernald, 1989; Fernald & Kuhl, 1987; C. Fisher & Tokura, 1996; Kuhl et al., 1997).

Despite the similarities in the style infant-directed speech across diverse cultures, there are some important cultural differences in the *quantity* of speech that infants hear from their parents. For example, although the Gusii of Kenya care for their infants in an extremely close physical way, they speak to them less than American parents do (Le Vine et al., 1994).

TABLE 6-6 THE MOST COMMON FEATURES OF INFANT-DIRECTED SPEECH

English	Spanish
1. Exaggerated intonation	1. Exaggerated intonation
2. Breathiness	2. Repetition
3. High pitch	3. High pitch
4. Repetition	4. Instructional
5. Lowered volume	5. Attentionals
6. Lengthened vowel	6. Lowered volume
7. Creaky voice	7. Raised volume
8. Instructional	8. Lengthened vowel
9. Tenseness	9. Fast tempo
10. Falsetto	10. Personal pronoun substitution

(*Source:* Adapted from Blount, 1982)

mothers. However, that assumption was wrong, and the gender-neutral term *infant-directed speech* is now used more frequently.

Infant-directed speech is characterized by short, simple sentences. Pitch becomes higher, the range of frequencies increases, and intonation is more varied. Words are repeated, and topics are restricted to items that are assumed to be comprehensible to infants, such as concrete objects in the baby's environment.

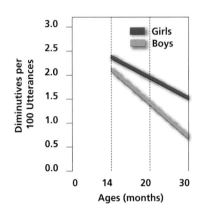

FIGURE 6-8   DIMINISHING DIMINUTIVES

Although adults' use of diminutives toward both male and female infants declines as the infants age, they are consistently used more often in speech directed at females. What would an educator make of the cultural significance of this?

(*Source:* Gleason et al., 1991)

Sometimes infant-directed speech includes amusing sounds that are not even words, imitating the prelinguistic speech of infants. In other cases, it has little formal structure but is similar to the kind of telegraphic speech that infants use as they develop their own language skills.

Infant-directed speech changes as children become older. Around the end of the first year, infant-directed speech takes on more adultlike qualities. Sentences become longer and more complex, although individual words are still spoken slowly and deliberately. Pitch is also used to focus attention on particularly important words.

Infant-directed speech plays an important role in infants' acquisition of language. Newborns prefer such speech to regular language, a fact that suggests that they may be particularly receptive to it. Furthermore, some research suggests that unusually extensive exposure to infant-directed speech early in life is related to the comparatively early utterance of first words and earlier linguistic competence in other areas (R. P. Cooper & Aslin, 1990, 1994; Gogate, Bahrick, & Watson, 2000; Hampson & Nelson, 1993).

Gender Differences.   To a girl, a bird is a *birdie,* a blanket a *blankie,* and a dog a *doggy.* To a boy, a bird is a *bird,* a blanket a *blanket,* and a dog a *dog.*

At least that's what parents of boys and girls appear to think, as illustrated by the language they use toward their sons and daughters. Virtually from the time of birth, the language parents employ with their children differs depending on the child's sex, according to research conducted by developmental psychologist Jean Berko Gleason (1987; Gleason et al., 1991).

Gleason found that by the age of 32 months, girls hear twice as many diminutives (words such as *kitty* or *dolly* instead of *cat* or *doll*) as boys hear. Although the use of diminutives declines with increasing age, their use consistently remains higher in speech directed at girls than in that directed at boys (see Figure 6-8).

Parents are also more apt to respond differently to children's requests depending on the child's gender. For instance, when turning down a child's request, mothers are likely to respond with a firm no to a male child but to soften the blow to a female child by providing a diversionary response ("Why don't you do this instead?") or by somehow making the refusal less direct. Consequently, boys tend to hear firmer, clearer language, while girls are exposed to warmer phrases, often referring to inner emotional states (Perlmann & Gleason, 1990).

Do such differences in language directed at boys and girls during infancy affect their behavior as adults? Although there is no direct evidence that plainly supports such an association, it is clear that men and women use different sorts of language as adults. For instance, as adults, women tend to use more tentative, less assertive language than men. While we don't know if these differences are a reflection of early linguistic experiences, such findings are certainly intriguing (Leaper, Anderson, & Sanders, 1998; Matlin, 1987; Tannen, 1991).

R E V I E W *&* A P P L Y

Review

- Before they speak, infants understand many adult utterances and engage in several forms of prelinguistic communication, including the use of facial expressions, gestures, imitation, and babbling.

- Children typically produce their first words between 10 and 14 months and rapidly increase their vocabularies from that point on, especially during a spurt at about 18 months.

- Children's language development proceeds through a pattern of holophrases, two-word combinations, and telegraphic speech.

- Learning theorists believe that basic learning processes account for language development, whereas Noam Chomsky and his followers argue that humans have an innate language capacity. The interactionists suggest that language is a consequence of both environmental and innate factors.

- When talking to infants, adults of all cultures tend to use infant-directed speech.

Applying Child Development

- What are some ways in which children's linguistic development reflects their acquisition of new ways of interpreting and dealing with their world?

- What are some implications of differences in the ways adults speak to boys and girls? *From an educator's perspective:* How might such speech differences contribute to later differences not only in speech but also in attitudes?

LOOKING **BACK**

- ⬤ **What are the fundamental features of Piaget's theories of cognitive development?**

- Jean Piaget's stage theory asserts that children pass through stages of cognitive development in a fixed order. The stages represent changes not only in the quantity of infants' knowledge but in the quality of that knowledge as well.

- According to Piaget, all children pass gradually through the four major stages of cognitive development (sensorimotor, preoperational, concrete operational, and formal operational) and their various substages when the children are at an appropriate level of maturation and are exposed to relevant types of experiences.

- In the Piagetian view, children's understanding grows through assimilation of their experiences into their current way of thinking or through accommodation of their current way of thinking to their experiences.

- During the sensorimotor period (birth to about 2 years), with its six substages, infants progress from the use of simple reflexes through the development of repeated and integrated actions that gradually increase in complexity to the ability to generate purposeful effects from their actions. By the end of the sixth substage of the sensorimotor period, infants are beginning to engage in symbolic thought.

- ⬤ **How do infants process information?**

- Information processing approaches to the study of cognitive development seek to learn how individuals receive, organize, store, and retrieve information. Such approaches differ from Piaget's by considering quantitative changes in children's abilities to process information.

- Infants have memory capabilities from their earliest days, although the accuracy of infant memories is a matter of debate.

● **How is infant intelligence measured?**

- Traditional measures of infant intelligence, such as Gesell's developmental quotient and the Bayley Scales of Infant Development, focus on average behavior observed at particular ages in large numbers of children.

- Information processing approaches to assessing intelligence rely on variations in the speed and quality with which infants process information.

● **By what processes do children learn to use language?**

- Prelinguistic communication involves the use of sounds, gestures, facial expressions, imitation, and other nonlinguistic means to express thoughts and states. Prelinguistic communication prepares the infant for speech.

- Infants typically produce their first words between the ages of 10 and 14 months. At around 18 months, children typically begin to link words together into primitive sentences that express single thoughts. Beginning speech is characterized by the use of holophrases, telegraphic speech, underextension, and overextension.

- The learning theory approach to language acquisition assumes that adults and children use basic behavioral processes—such as conditioning, reinforcement, and shaping—in language learning. A different approach proposed by Chomsky holds that humans are genetically endowed with a language acquisition device that permits them to detect and use the principles of universal grammar that underlie all languages.

● **How do children influence adults' language?**

- Adult language is influenced by the children to whom it is addressed. Infant-directed speech takes on characteristics, surprisingly invariant across cultures, that make it appealing to infants and probably encourage language development.

- Adult language also exhibits differences based on the gender of the child to whom it is directed, which may have effects that emerge later in life.

EPILOGUE

 n this chapter, we looked at infants' cognitive development from the perspective of Jean Piaget, focusing on the substages of the sensorimotor stage through which infants pass in the first 2 years of life. We also looked at a different perspective on infant development based on information processing theory. We examined infant learning, memory, and intelligence, and we concluded the chapter with a look at language.

Look back at the prologue to this chapter, about Paige Arbeiter, an infant with a hearing disorder, and answer the following questions:

1. Paige's hearing disorder was not properly diagnosed until she was 10 months old. What elements of linguistic development did Paige probably miss?

2. Do you think a child who misses the first year of linguistic development because of a disorder and then completely recovers from the disorder will learn to speak? In what ways will his development be different from others'? Why?

3. Do you think Paige, who could apparently make sounds despite her imperfect hearing, babbled verbally during her first year? Did she babble in any other way? Why?

4. If Paige had been raised by deaf parents who used sign language, do you think Paige would have developed sign language as a normal aspect of her development?

5. Do hearing children raised by deaf parents learn to use sign language through the same process as other children learn to speak? Do you think such children also develop spoken language? Why?

KEY TERMS AND CONCEPTS

scheme (p. 165)
assimilation (p. 165)
accommodation (p. 165)
sensorimotor stage (p. 166)
circular reaction (p. 167)
goal-directed behavior
    (p. 168)
object permanence (p. 169)
mental representation
    (p. 170)
deferred imitation (p. 170)
information processing
    approaches (p. 173)
memory (p. 176)

infantile amnesia
    (p. 177)
developmental
    quotient (p. 179)
Bayley Scales of Infant
    Development (p. 179)
visual recognition
    memory (p. 180)
cross-modal transference
    (p. 181)
language (p. 184)
prelinguistic
    communication (p. 186)
babbling (p. 186)

holophrases (p. 189)
telegraphic speech
    (p. 190)
underextension (p. 190)
overextension (p. 191)
referential style (p. 191)
expressive style (p. 191)
learning theory
    approach (p. 191)
nativist approach (p. 191)
language acquisition
    device (LAD) (p. 192)
infant-directed
    speech (p. 192)

7

Social and Personality Development in Infancy

PROLOGUE: The Velcro Chronicles

It was during the windy days of March that the problem in the child care center first arose. Its source: 10-month-old Russell Ruud. Otherwise a model of decorum, Russell had somehow learned how to unzip the Velcro chin strap to his winter hat. He would remove the hat whenever he got the urge, seemingly oblivious to the potential health problems that might follow.

But that was just the start of the real difficulty. To the chagrin of the teachers in the child care center, not to speak of the children's parents, soon other children were following his lead, removing their own caps at will.

Russell's mother, made aware of the anarchy at the child care center—and of the other parents' distress over Russell's behavior—pleaded innocent. "I never showed Russell how to unzip the Velcro," claimed his mother, Judith Ruud, an economist with the Congressional Budget Office in Washington, D.C. "He learned by trial and error, and the other kids saw him do it one day when they were getting dressed for an outing" (Goleman, 1993, C10).

By then, though, it was too late for excuses: Russell, it seems, was an excellent teacher. Keeping the children's

Infants not only learn desirable behaviors, but less positive ones (like shoe removal techniques), through observation of their more "expert" peers.

hats on their heads proved to be no easy task. Even more ominous was the thought that if the infants could master the Velcro straps on their hats, would they soon be unfastening the Velcro straps on their shoes and removing *them*?

LOOKING **AHEAD** ▶

Russell's behavior embodies what recent research suggests is a heretofore unsuspected outcome of infants' participation in child care: the acquisition of new skills and abilities from more "expert" peers. Infants, as we will see, have an amazing capacity to learn from other children, and their interactions with others can play a central role in their developing social and emotional worlds.

In this chapter, we consider social and personality development in infancy. We begin by examining the emotional lives of infants, considering which emotions they feel and how well they can decode others' emotions. We also consider how infants use others to shape their own reactions and how they view their own mental life and that of others.

We then turn to a consideration of infants' social relationships. We look at how they forge bonds of attachment and the ways they interact with family members and peers.

Finally, we cover the characteristics that differentiate one infant from another. We'll discuss differences in the way children are treated depending on their gender. We'll consider the nature of family life as the 21st century begins and discuss how it differs from earlier eras. The chapter closes with a look at the advantages and disadvantages of infant child care outside the home, a child care option that today's families increasingly employ.

In short, after reading this chapter, you will be able to answer these questions:

- **What sort of emotional lives do infants have?**
- **What sort of mental lives do infants have?**
- **What is attachment in infancy, and how does it relate to the future social competence of individuals?**
- **What roles do other people play in infants' social development?**
- **What sorts of individual differences do infants display?**
- **Is day care beneficial or harmful for infants?**

Forming the Roots of Sociability

Germaine smiles when he catches a glimpse of his mother. Tawanda looks angry when her mother takes away the spoon that she is playing with. Sydney scowls when a loud plane flies overhead.

A smile. A look of anger. A scowl. The emotions of infancy are written all over a baby's face. Yet do infants experience emotions in the same way that adults do? When do they become capable of understanding what others are experiencing emotionally? And how do they use others' emotional states to make sense of their environment? We consider these questions as we seek to understand how infants develop emotionally and socially.

Emotions in Infancy: Do Infants Experience Emotional Highs and Lows?

Anyone who spends any time at all around infants knows that they display facial expressions that seem indicative of their emotional states. In situations in which we expect them to be happy, they seem to smile; when we might assume they are frustrated, they show anger; and when we might expect them to be unhappy, they look sad.

In fact, these basic facial expressions are remarkably similar across the most diverse cultures. Whether we look at babies in India, the United States, or the jungles of New Guinea, the

FIGURE 7-1   UNIVERSALS IN FACIAL EXPRESSIONS

In every culture, infants show similar facial expressions relating to basic emotions. Do you think such expressions are similar in nonhuman animals?

expression of basic emotions is the same (see Figure 7-1). Furthermore, the nonverbal expression of emotion, called *nonverbal encoding,* is fairly consistent throughout the life span. These consistencies have led researchers to conclude that we are born with the capacity to display basic emotions (Camras, Malatesta, & Izard, 1991; Ekman & O'Sullivan, 1991; R. S. Feldman, 1982; Izard et al., 1995).

Infants appear to display a fairly wide range of emotional expressions. According to research on what mothers see in their children's nonverbal behavior, almost all think that by the age of 1 month, their babies have expressed interest and joy. In addition, 84 percent of mothers think their infants have expressed anger, 75 percent surprise, 58 percent fear, and 34 percent sadness. Research using the Maximally Discriminative Facial Movement Coding System (MAX), developed by psychologist Carroll Izard, also finds that interest, distress, and disgust are present at birth and that other emotions emerge over the next few months (W. Johnson et al., 1982; Sroufe, 1996; see Figure 7-2).

Although infants display similar *kinds* of emotions, the *degree* of emotional expressiveness varies between infants. In fact, reliable differences in expressiveness are found between children in different cultures, even during infancy. For example, developmental psychologist Linda Camras and colleagues (1998) have found that at the age of 11 months, Chinese infants are generally less expressive than European, American, and Japanese infants (Eisenberg et al., 2000).

Experiencing Emotions.   Does the capability of infants to express emotions nonverbally in a consistent, reliable manner mean that they actually *experience* emotions, and if they do, is the experience similar to that of adults? These questions are not easy to answer.

The fact that children display nonverbal expressions in a manner similar to that of adults does not necessarily mean that the actual experience is identical. In fact, if the nature of such displays is innate, or inborn, it is possible that facial expressions can occur without any

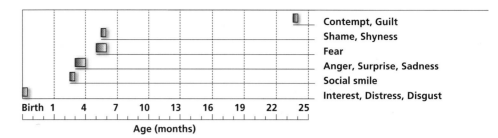

FIGURE 7-2   EMERGENCE OF EMOTIONAL EXPRESSIONS

Emotional expressions emerge at roughly these times. Keep in mind that expressions in the first few weeks after birth do not necessarily reflect particular inner feelings.

accompanying emotional experience. Nonverbal expressions, then, might be emotionless in young infants, in much the same way that your knee reflexively jerks forward when a physician taps it, without the involvement of emotions (Soussignan et al., 1997).

However, most developmental researchers think otherwise: They argue that the nonverbal expressions of infants represent emotional experiences. In fact, developmental psychologist Carroll Izard suggests in his **differential emotions theory** that emotional expressions not only reflect emotional experiences but also help regulate the emotions themselves. Izard suggests that infants are born with an innate repertoire of emotional expressions, reflecting basic emotional states. As infants and children grow older, they expand and modify these basic expressions and become more adept at controlling their nonverbal behavioral expressions. Furthermore, Izard suggests that in addition to becoming able to express nonverbally a wider variety of emotions, we also become able to internally experience more differentiated emotions (K. A. Buss & Goldsmith, 1998; Camras et al., 1991; Izard & Malatesta, 1987).

In sum, infants do appear to experience emotions, although the range of emotions at birth is fairly restricted. However, as they get older, infants both display and experience a wider range of increasingly complex emotions (Fox, 1994; Messinger, 2002; Sroufe, 1996).

VIDEO CLIP

Stranger Anxiety

Stranger Anxiety and Separation Anxiety. "She used to be such a friendly baby," thought Erika's mother. "No matter whom she encountered, she had a big smile. But now I don't know what's happened. Almost the day she turned seven months old, she began to react to strangers as if she were seeing a ghost. Her face crinkles up with a frown, and she either turns away or stares at them with suspicion. And she doesn't want to be left with anyone she doesn't already know. It's as if she has undergone a personality transplant."

What happened to Erika is in fact quite typical. By the end of the first year, infants often develop both stranger anxiety and separation anxiety. **Stranger anxiety** is the caution and wariness displayed by infants when encountering an unfamiliar person. Such anxiety typically appears in the second half of the first year.

What brings on stranger anxiety? One basic cause is the increased cognitive abilities of infants, allowing them to separate the people they know from the people they don't know. The same cognitive advances that allow them to respond so positively to the people with whom they are familiar also give them the ability to recognize people who are unfamiliar. Furthermore, between 6 and 9 months, infants begin trying to make sense of their world. When something happens that they can't make sense of—such as the appearance of an unknown person—they experience fear. It's as if an infant has a question but is unable to answer it (Ainsworth, 1973; Kagan, Kearsley, & Zelazo, 1978).

Although stranger anxiety is common after the age of 6 months, significant differences exist between children. Some infants, particularly those who have a lot of experience with strangers, tend to show less anxiety than those whose experience with strangers is limited. Furthermore, not all strangers evoke the same reaction. For instance, infants tend to show less anxiety with female strangers than with male strangers. In addition, they react more positively to strangers who are children than to strangers who are adults, perhaps because their size is less intimidating (Brooks & Lewis, 1976; R. A. Thompson & Limber, 1990).

Differential emotions theory Izard's theory that emotional expressions reflect emotional experiences and help in the regulation of emotion itself

Stranger anxiety The caution and wariness displayed by infants when encountering an unfamiliar person

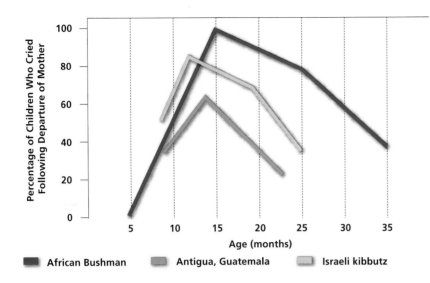

African Bushman   Antigua, Guatemala   Israeli kibbutz

FIGURE 7-3
SEPARATION ANXIETY

Separation anxiety, the distress displayed by infants when their usual care provider leaves their presence, is a universal phenomenon beginning around the age of 7 or 8 months. It peaks around the age of 14 months and then begins to decline. Does separation anxiety have survival value for humans?

(*Source:* Kagan, Kearsley, & Zelazo, 1978)

Separation anxiety is the distress displayed by infants when a customary care provider departs. Separation anxiety, which is universal across cultures, usually begins at about 7 or 8 months (see Figure 7-3). It peaks around 14 months and then decreases. Separation anxiety is largely attributable to the same reasons as stranger anxiety. Infants' growing cognitive skills allow them to ask questions with no readily apparent answers: "Why is my mother leaving?" "Where is she going?" and "Will she come back?"

Stranger anxiety and separation anxiety represent important social progress. They reflect both cognitive advances and the growing emotional and social bonds between infants and their caregivers—bonds that we'll consider later in the chapter when we discuss infants' social relationships.

Smiling.   As Luz lay sleeping in her crib, her mother and father caught a glimpse of the most beautiful smile crossing her face. Her parents were sure that Luz was having a pleasant dream. Were they right?

Probably not. The earliest smiles expressed during sleep probably have little meaning, although no one can be absolutely sure. However, by 3 to 12 weeks it is clear that babies begin to smile reliably at the sight of stimuli that please them, including toys, mobiles, and—to the delight of parents—people. The first smiles tend to be relatively indiscriminate, as infants first begin to smile at the sight of almost anything they find amusing. However, as they get older, they become more selective in their smiles.

A baby's smile in response to another person, rather than to nonhuman stimuli, is considered a **social smile.** As babies get older, their social smiles become directed toward particular individuals, not just anyone (Wolff, 1963). By the age of 18 months, social smiling directed more toward mothers and other caregivers becomes more frequent than smiling directed toward nonhuman objects. Moreover, if an adult is unresponsive to a child, the amount of smiling decreases. In short, by the end of the second year, children are quite purposefully using smiling to communicate their positive emotions, and they are sensitive to the emotional expressions of others (Carvajal & Iglesias, 2000; Fogel et al., 2000; Messinger & Fogel, 1998).

Decoding Others' Facial and Vocal Expressions.   You may recall from Chapter 4 that neonates are able to imitate adults' facial expressions, a capability that is apparent even minutes after birth (Kaitz et al., 1988; Reissland, 1988). Although their imitative abilities certainly do not imply that they can understand the meaning of others' facial expressions, such imitation does pave the way for *nonverbal decoding* abilities, which begin to emerge fairly soon.

VIDEO CLIP

Separation Anxiety

When infants smile at a person, rather than a nonhuman stimulus, they are displaying a social smile.

Separation anxiety   The distress displayed by infants when a customary care provider departs

Social smile   Smiling in response to other individuals

Using these abilities, infants can interpret others' facial and vocal expressions that carry emotional meaning (Slater & Butterworth, 1997; Walker-Andrews, 1997).

Infants seem to be able to discriminate vocal expressions of emotion at a slightly earlier age than they discriminate facial expressions. Although relatively little attention has been given to infants' perception of vocal expressions, it does appear that they are able to discriminate happy and sad vocal expressions at the age of 5 months (Soken & Pick, 1999; Walker-Andrews & Lennon, 1991).

Scientists know more about the *sequence* in which nonverbal facial decoding ability progresses. In the first 6 to 8 weeks, infants' visual precision is sufficiently limited that they cannot pay much attention to others' facial expressions. But they soon begin to discriminate among different facial expressions of emotion and even seem to be able to respond to differences in type and intensity of emotion conveyed by facial expressions (Lamb, Morrison, & Malkin, 1987; C. A. Nelson, 1987).

By the time they reach the age of 4 months, infants may already have begun to understand the emotions that lie behind the facial and vocal expressions of others. How do we know this? One important clue comes from a study in which 7-month-old infants were shown a pair of facial expressions relating to joy and sadness and simultaneously heard a vocalization representing either joy (a rising tone of voice) or sadness (a falling tone of voice). The infants paid more attention to the face that matched the tone, suggesting that they had at least a rudimentary understanding of the emotional meaning of facial expressions and voice tones (R. D. Phillips et al., 1990; Soken & Pick, 1999; Walker-Andrews, 1997).

In sum, infants learn early both to produce and to decode emotions. Such abilities play an important role not only in helping them experience their own emotions but also, as we see next, in using others' emotions to understand the meaning of ambiguous social situations.

Social Referencing: Feeling What Others Feel

VIDEO CLIP

Social Referencing

> Twenty-three-month-old Stephania watches as her older brother, Eric, and his friend Chen argue loudly with each other and begin to wrestle. Uncertain of what is happening, Stephania glances at her mother. Her mother, though, wears a smile, knowing that Eric and Chen are just playing. On seeing her mother's reaction, Stephania smiles too, mimicking her mother's facial expression.

Like Stephania, most of us have been in situations in which we feel uncertain. In such cases, we sometimes turn to others to see how they are reacting. This reliance on others, known as social referencing, helps us decide what an appropriate response ought to be.

Social referencing is the intentional search for information about others' feelings to help explain the meaning of uncertain circumstances and events. Social referencing is used to clarify the meaning of a situation by reducing our uncertainty about what is occurring.

Social referencing first tends to occur around the age of 8 or 9 months. It is a fairly sophisticated social ability: Infants need it not only to understand the significance of others' behavior, such as their facial expressions, but also to realize that others' behavior has meaning with reference to specific circumstances (W. D. Rosen, Adamson, & Bakeman, 1992; Walden & Ogan, 1988).

Facial Expressions.   Infants make particular use of facial expressions in their social referencing, the way Stephania did when she noticed her mother's smile. For instance, in one study, infants were given an unusual toy to play with. The amount of time they played with it depended on their mothers' facial expressions. When their mothers displayed disgust, they played with it significantly less than when their mothers appeared pleased. Furthermore, when given the opportunity to play with the same toy later, the infants revealed lasting consequences of their mothers' earlier behavior, despite the mothers' now neutral-appearing facial reactions (Hornik & Gunnar, 1988).

Social referencing The intentional search for information about others' feelings to help make sense of uncertain circumstances and events

Two Explanations of Social Referencing.   Although it is clear that social referencing begins fairly early in life, researchers are still not certain *how* it operates. Consider one possibility: It may be that observing someone else's facial expression brings about the emotion the expression represents. That is, an infant who views someone looking sad may come to feel sad herself, and her behavior may be affected. On the other hand, it may be that viewing another's facial expression simply provides information. In this case, the infant does not experience the particular emotion represented by another's facial expression; she simply uses the display as data to guide her own behavior.

Both explanations for social referencing have received support, and so we still don't know which is correct. What we do know is that social referencing is most likely to occur when a situation breeds uncertainty and ambiguity. Furthermore, infants who reach the age when they are able to use social referencing become quite upset if they receive conflicting nonverbal messages from their mothers and fathers. Mixed messages, then, are a real source of stress for an infant (Camras & Sachs, 1991; Hirshberg, 1990; Hirshberg & Svejda, 1990; Walden & Baxter, 1989).

The Development of Self: Do Infants Know Who They Are?

> Elysa, 8 months old, crawls past the full-length mirror that hangs on a door in her parents' bedroom. She barely pays any attention to her reflection as she moves by. But her cousin Brianna, who is almost 2 years old, stares at herself in the mirror as she passes and laughs as she sees, and then rubs, a smear of jelly on her forehead.

Perhaps you have had the experience of catching a glimpse of yourself in a mirror and noticing a hair out of place. You probably reacted by attempting to push the unruly hair back into place. Your reaction shows more than that you care about how you look. It implies that you have a sense of yourself, the awareness and knowledge that you are an independent social entity to which others react and which you attempt to present to the world in ways that reflect favorably on you.

However, we are not born with the knowledge that we exist independently from others and the larger world. Although it is difficult to demonstrate, the youngest infants do not seem to have a sense of themselves as individuals. They do not recognize likenesses of themselves, whether in photos or in mirrors, and they show no evidence of being able to distinguish themselves from other people (Gallup, 1977).

The roots of **self-awareness,** knowledge that one exists separately from the rest of the world, begin to grow at around the age of 12 months. We know this from a simple but ingenious experimental technique known as the *mirror-and-rouge task*. In it, an infant's nose is secretly colored with a dab of red rouge, and the infant is seated in front of a mirror. If infants touch their noses or attempt to wipe off the rouge, we have evidence that they have at least some knowledge of their physical characteristics. For them, this awareness is one step in developing an understanding of themselves as independent objects. For instance, Brianna, in the example at the beginning of this section, showed her awareness of her independence when she tried to rub the jam off her forehead.

Although some infants as young as 12 months seem startled on seeing the rouge spot, for most a reaction does not occur until between 17 and 24 months of age. It is also around this age that children begin to show awareness of their own capabilities. For instance, infants who participate in experiments when they are between the ages of 23 and 25 months sometimes begin to cry if the experimenter asks them to imitate a complicated sequence of behaviors involving toys, although they readily accomplish simpler sequences. According to developmental psychologist Jerome Kagan (1981), their reaction suggests that they are conscious that they lack the capability to carry out difficult tasks and are unhappy about it—a reaction that provides a clear indication of self-awareness (Asendorpf, Warkentin, & Baudonniere, 1996; Legerstee, 1998).

VIDEO CLIP

Self Awareness

Self-awareness Knowledge that one exists separately from the rest of the world

Research suggests that this 18-month-old is exhibiting a clearly developed sense of self.

In sum, by the age of 18 to 24 months, infants have developed at least the rudiments of awareness of their own physical characteristics and capabilities, and they understand that their appearance is stable over time. Although it is not clear how far this awareness extends, it is becoming increasingly evident that—as we discuss next—infants have not only a basic understanding of themselves but also the beginnings of an understanding of how the mind operates—what has come to be called a "theory of mind" (Legerstee, Anderson, & Schaffer, 1998; P. Mitchell & Riggs, 1999; C. Moore, 1996).

Theory of Mind: Infants' Perspectives on the Mental Lives of Others—and Themselves

VIDEO CLIP

Theory of Mind

What are infants' thoughts about thinking? According to developmental psychologist John Flavell, infants begin to understand certain things about the mental processes of themselves and others at quite an early age. Flavell has investigated children's **theory of mind,** their knowledge and beliefs about the mental world. Theories of mind are the explanations that children use to explain how others think. For instance, cognitive advances during infancy permit older infants to come to see people in very different ways from how they view other objects. They learn to see others as *compliant agents,* beings similar to themselves who behave under their own power and who have the capacity to respond to infants' requests (Flavell, Green, & Flavell, 1995; Rochat, 1999). Eighteen-month-old Chris, for example, has come to realize that he can ask his father to play a favorite game.

In addition, children's capacity to understand intentionality and causality grows during infancy. They begin to understand that others' behaviors have some meaning and that the behaviors they see people enacting are designed to accomplish particular goals, in contrast to the "behaviors" of inanimate objects (S. A. Gelman & Kalish, 1993; Golinkoff, 1993; Parritiz, Mangelsdorf, & Gunnar, 1992).

By the age of 2, infants begin to demonstrate the rudiments of empathy. **Empathy** is an emotional response that corresponds to the feelings of another person. At 24 months of age, infants sometimes comfort others or show concern for them. In order to do this, they need to be aware of others' emotional states. Further, during their second year, infants begin to use deception, both in games of "pretend" and in outright attempts to fool others. A child who plays "pretend" and who uses falsehoods must be aware that others hold beliefs about the world—beliefs that can be manipulated. In short, by the end of infancy, children have developed the

Theory of mind   Children's knowledge and beliefs about their mental world

Empathy   An emotional response that corresponds to the feelings of another person

rudiments of their own personal theory of mind. It helps them understand the actions of others, and it affects their own behavior (K. Lee & Homer, 1999; Zahn-Waxler, Robinson, & Emde, 1992).

R E V I E W *&* A P P L Y

Review

- Infants appear to express and to experience emotions, which broaden in range to reflect increasingly complex emotional states.

- Infants from different cultures use similar facial expressions to express basic emotional states.

- Infants begin to experience stranger anxiety at about 6 months and separation anxiety at around 8 months of age.

- The ability to decode the nonverbal facial and vocal expressions of others develops early in infants. The use of nonverbal decoding to clarify situations of uncertainty and determine appropriate responses is called *social referencing*.

- Infants develop self-awareness, the knowledge that they exist separately from the rest of the world, after about 12 months of age.

- By the age of 2, children have developed the rudiments of a theory of mind.

Applying Child Development

- If the facial expressions that convey basic emotions are similar across cultures, how do such expressions arise? Can you think of facial expressions that are culture-specific? How do they arise?

- In what situations do adults rely on social referencing to work out appropriate responses? *From a social worker's perspective:* How might social referencing be used to influence parents' behavior toward their children?

Forging Relationships

> Louis Moore became the center of attention on the way home [from the hospital]. His father brought Martha, aged five, and Tom, aged three, to the hospital with him when Louis and his mother were discharged. Martha rushed to see "her" new baby and ignored her mother. Tom clung to his mother's knees in the reception hall of the hospital.
>
> A hospital nurse carried Louis to the car.... The two older children immediately climbed over the seat and swamped mother and baby with their attention. Both children stuck their faces into his, smacked at him, and talked to him. They soon began to fight over him with loud voices. The loud argument and the jostling of his mother upset Louis and he started to cry. He let out a wail that came like a shotgun blast into the noisy car. The children quieted immediately and looked with awe at this new infant. His insistent wails drowned out their bickering. He had already asserted himself

Attachment The positive emotional bond that develops between a child and a particular individual

in their eyes. Martha's lip quivered as she watched her mother attempt to comfort Louis, and she added her own soft cooing in imitation of her mother. Tom squeezed even closer to his mother, put his thumb in his mouth, and closed his eyes to shut out the commotion. (Brazelton, 1983, p. 48)

The arrival of a newborn brings a dramatic change to a family's dynamics. No matter how welcome a baby's birth, it causes a fundamental shift in the roles that people play within the family. Mothers and fathers must start to build a relationship with their infant, and older children must adjust to the presence of a new member of the family and build their own alliance with their infant brother or sister.

Although the process of social development during infancy is neither simple nor automatic, it is crucial: The bonds that grow between infants and their parents, family, and others provide the foundation for a lifetime's worth of social relationships.

Attachment: Forming Social Bonds

 The most important form of social development that takes place during infancy is attachment. **Attachment** is the positive emotional bond that develops between a child and a particular individual. Children who become attached to a given person feel pleasure when they are with the person and are comforted by the person's presence at times of distress. The nature of our attachment during infancy affects how we relate to others throughout the rest of our lives (Fraley, 2002; C. Hamilton, 2000; Waters, Weinfield, & Hamilton, 2000).

Social Bonds with the Animal Kingdom. To understand attachment, the earliest researchers turned to the bonds that form between parents and children in the nonhuman animal kingdom. For instance, ethologist Konrad Lorenz (1965) observed newborn goslings, who have an innate tendency to follow their mother, the first moving object to which they are typically exposed after birth. Lorenz found that goslings whose eggs were raised in an incubator and who viewed him just after hatching would follow his every movement, as if he were their mother. He labeled this process *imprinting:* behavior that takes place during a critical period and involves attachment to the first moving object that is observed.

The bonds that children forge with others play a crucial role in their lives.

Lorenz's findings suggested that attachment was based on biologically determined factors, and other theorists agreed. For instance, Freud suggested that attachment grew out of a mother's ability to satisfy a child's oral needs.

It turns out, however, that the ability to provide food and other physiological needs may not be as crucial as Freud and other theorists first thought. In a classic study, psychologist Harry Harlow gave infant monkeys the choice of cuddling one of two artificial "monkeys"—a wire one that provided food or a soft terry cloth one that was warm but did not provide food (see Figure 7-4). Their preference was clear: They would spend most of their time clinging to the cloth monkey, although they made occasional expeditions to the wire monkey to nurse. Harlow suggested that the preference for the warm cloth monkey provided *contact comfort* (Harlow & Zimmerman, 1959).

Harlow's work clearly illustrates that food alone is insufficient to bring about attachment. Furthermore, given that the monkey's preference for the soft cloth "mothers" developed some time after birth, these findings are consistent with the research showing little support for the existence of a critical bonding period between human mothers and infants immediately following birth.

Human Attachment.

The earliest work on human attachment, which is still highly influential, was carried out by John Bowlby (1951). Bowlby's theorizing about attachment had a biological basis, although it was supplemented by observations of emotionally disturbed children with whom he worked in a London clinic. Consequently, his is an *epigenetic theory,* a developmental theory that stresses the reciprocal interaction between genes and the environment.

In Bowlby's view, attachment is based primarily on infants' needs for safety and security—their genetically determined motivation to avoid predators. As they develop, infants come to learn that their safety is best provided by a particular individual. This realization ultimately leads to the development of a special relationship with that individual, who is typically the mother. Bowlby suggests that this single relationship is qualitatively different from the bonds formed with others, including the father—a suggestion that, as we'll see later, has been a source of some subsequent dispute.

Bowlby also argues that attachment—which has its roots in the desire to seek the protective security of the mother—is critical in allowing an infant to explore the world. According to his view, having a strong, firm attachment provides a kind of home base. As children become more independent, they can progressively roam farther from their secure base.

Measuring Attachment: The Strange Situation.

Developmental psychologist Mary Ainsworth (1973; Ainsworth et al., 1978) built on Bowlby's theorizing to develop a widely used experimental technique to measure attachment. The **Ainsworth Strange Situation** consists of a sequence of staged episodes that illustrate the strength of attachment between a child and (typically) his or her mother. The Strange Situation follows this general eight-step pattern: (1) The mother and baby enter an unfamiliar room; (2) the mother sits down, leaving the baby free to explore; (3) an adult stranger enters the room and converses first with the mother and then with the baby; (4) the mother exits the room, leaving the baby alone with the stranger; (5) the mother returns, greeting and comforting the baby, and the stranger leaves; (6) the mother departs again, leaving the baby alone; (7) the stranger returns; and (8) the mother returns and the stranger leaves (Ainsworth et al., 1978).

Infants' reactions to the various aspects of the Strange Situation vary considerably, depending on the nature of their attachment to their mothers. One-year-olds show three major patterns—securely attached, avoidant, and ambivalent (summarized in Table 7-1). Children who have a **secure attachment pattern** use the mother as the kind of home base that Bowlby described. These children seem at ease in the Strange Situation as long as their mothers are present. They explore independently, returning to her occasionally. Although they may or may not appear upset when she leaves, securely attached children immediately go to her when she

FIGURE 7-4
MONKEY MOTHERS MATTER

Harlow's research showed that monkeys preferred the warm, soft "mother" over the wire "monkey" that provided food. What lessons can an infant caregiver learn from this research?

VIDEO CLIP

Nature of Development of Affection–Harlow's Monkeys
CLASSIC MODULE

Ainsworth Strange Situation A sequence of staged episodes that illustrate the strength of attachment between a child and (typically) his or her mother

Secure attachment pattern A style of attachment in which children use the mother as a kind of home base and are at ease when she is present; when she leaves, they become upset, and they go to her as soon as she returns

Label	Seeking Proximity with Caregiver	Maintaining Contact with Caregiver	Avoiding Proximity with Caregiver	Resisting Contact with Caregiver	Crying
TABLE 7-1 CLASSIFICATIONS OF INFANT ATTACHMENT					
Secure	High	High (if distressed)	Low	Low	Low (pre-separation), high or low (separation), low (reunion)
Avoidant	Low	Low	High	Low	Low (pre-separation), high or low (separation), low (reunion)
Ambivalent	High	High (often pre-separation)	Low	High	Occasionally (pre-separation), high (separation), moderate to high (reunion)

(*Source:* Waters, 1978)

returns and seek contact. Most children—about two-thirds—fall into the securely attached category.

In contrast, children with an **avoidant attachment pattern** do not seek proximity to the mother, and after she has left, they typically do not seem distressed. Furthermore, they seem to avoid her when she returns. It is as if they are indifferent to her behavior. Some 20 percent of 1-year-old children are in the avoidant category.

Finally, children with an **ambivalent attachment pattern** display a combination of positive and negative reactions to their mothers. Initially, ambivalent children are in such close contact with the mother that they hardly explore their environment. They appear anxious even before the mother leaves, and when she does leave, they show great distress. But upon her return, they show ambivalent reactions, seeking to be close to her but also hitting and kicking, apparently in anger. About 12 percent of 1-year-olds fall into the ambivalent classification (Cassidy & Berlin, 1994).

A subsequent expansion of Ainsworth's work suggests that there is a fourth category: disorganized-disoriented. Children who have a **disorganized-disoriented attachment pattern** show inconsistent and often contradictory behavior, such as approaching the mother when she returns but not looking at her. Their confusion suggests that they may be the least securely attached children of all (Egeland & Farber, 1984; Mayseless, 1996; O'Connor, Sigman, & Brill, 1987).

A child's attachment style would be of only minor consequence were it not for the fact that the nature of the attachment between infants and their mothers has significant consequences for relationships at later stages of life. For example, boys who are securely attached at the age of 1 year show fewer psychological difficulties at older ages than avoidant or ambivalent children do. Similarly, children who are securely attached as infants tend to be more

In this illustration of the strange situation, the infant first explores the playroom on his own, as long as his mother is present. But when she leaves, he begins to cry. On her return, however, he is immediately comforted and stops crying. The conclusion: he is securely attached.

socially and emotionally competent later, and others view them more positively. Adult romantic relationships are associated with the kind of attachment style developed during infancy (B. A. Schneider, Atkinson, & Tardif, 2001).

However, we cannot say that children who do not have a secure attachment style during infancy invariably experience difficulties later in life or that those with a secure attachment at age 1 always have good adjustment later on. In fact, some evidence suggests that children with avoidant and ambivalent attachment—as measured by the Strange Situation—do quite well (M. Lewis, 1998; M. Lewis, Feiring, & Rosenthal, 2000; Vondra & Barnett, 1999; Weinfield, Sroufe, & Egeland, 2000).

Producing Attachment: The Roles of the Mother and Father

> As 5-month-old Annie cries passionately, her mother comes into the room and gently lifts her from her crib. After just a few moments, as her mother rocks Annie and speaks softly, Annie's cries cease, and she cuddles in her mother's arms. But the moment her mother places her back in the crib, Annie begins to wail again, leading her mother to pick her up once again.

The pattern is familiar to most parents. The infant cries, the parent reacts, and the child responds in turn. Such seemingly insignificant sequences as these, repeatedly occurring in the lives of infants and parents, help pave the way for the development of relationships between children, their parents, and the rest of the social world. We'll consider how each of the major caregivers and the infant play a role in the development of attachment.

Mothers and Attachment.   Sensitivity to their infants' needs and desires is the hallmark of mothers of securely attached infants. Such a mother tends to be aware of her child's moods, and she takes into account her child's feelings as they interact. She is also responsive during face-to-face interactions, provides feeding "on demand," and is warm and affectionate to her infant (Ainsworth, 1993; De Wolff & van IJzendoorn, 1997; Howes, Galinsky, & Kontos, 1998).

It is not just a matter of responding in *any* fashion to their infants' signals that separates mothers of securely attached and insecurely attached children. Mothers of secure infants tend to provide the appropriate level of response. In fact, research has shown that overly responsive mothers are just as likely to have insecurely attached children as underresponsive mothers. In contrast, mothers whose communication involves *interactional synchrony,* in which caregivers respond to infants appropriately and both caregiver and child match emotional states, are more likely to produce secure attachment (Belsky, Rovine, & Taylor, 1984; Kochanska, 1998).

The research showing the correspondence between mothers' sensitivity to their infants and the security of the infants' attachment is consistent with Ainsworth's arguments that attachment depends on how mothers react to their infants' social overtures. Ainsworth suggests that mothers of securely attached infants respond rapidly and positively to their infants. For example, Annie's mother responds quickly to her cries by cuddling and comforting her. In contrast, the way for mothers to produce insecurely attached infants, according to Ainsworth, is to ignore their behavioral cues, to behave inconsistently with them, and to ignore or reject their social efforts.

But how do mothers know how to respond to their infants' cues? One answer is that they learn from their own mothers. For instance, mothers tend to have attachment styles that are similar to those developed by their infants. In fact, some research finds substantial stability in attachment patterns from one generation to the next (Benoit & Parker, 1994).

In part, mothers' (and others') behavior toward infants is a reaction to the children's ability to provide effective cues. A mother may not be able to respond effectively to a child whose own behavior is unrevealing, misleading, or ambiguous. The kinds of signals an infant sends may in part determine how successful the mother will be in responding.

Avoidant attachment pattern   A style of attachment in which children do not seek proximity to the mother; after the mother has left, they seem to avoid her when she returns, as if angered by her behavior

Ambivalent attachment pattern   A style of attachment in which children display a combination of positive and negative reactions to their mothers; they show great distress when the mother leaves, but upon her return, they may simultaneously seek close contact but also hit and kick her

Disorganized-disoriented attachment pattern   A style of attachment in which children show inconsistent, often contradictory behavior, such as approaching the mother when she returns but not looking at her

Many Ainsworth, who devised the Strange Situation to measure attachment.

Fathers and Attachment.   Up to now, we've barely touched on one of the key players involved in the upbringing of a child: the father. In fact, if you looked at the early theorizing and research on attachment, you'd find little mention of the father and his potential contributions to the life of the infant (Russell & Radojevic, 1992; Tamis-LeMonda & Cabrera, 1999).

There are at least two reasons for this omission. First, John Bowlby, who provided the initial theory of attachment, suggested that there was something unique about the mother–child relationship. He believed that the mother was uniquely equipped, biologically, to provide sustenance for the child, and he concluded that this capability led to the development of a special relationship between mothers and their children. Second, the early work on attachment was influenced by the traditional social views of the time, which considered it "natural" for the mother to be the primary caregiver, while the father's role was to work outside the home to provide a living for his family.

Several factors led to the demise of this view. One was that societal norms changed, and fathers began to take a more active role in child-rearing activities. More important, it became increasingly clear from research findings that despite social norms that relegated fathers to secondary child-rearing roles, some infants formed their primary initial relationship with their fathers (Goossens & van IJzendoorn, 1990; Lamb, 1982b; Volling & Belsky, 1992).

In addition, a growing body of research showed the critical importance of fathers' demonstrations of love for their children, revealed by fathers' nurturance, warmth, affection, support, and concern. In fact, certain kinds of psychological disorders, such as substance abuse and depression, have been found to be related more to fathers' than mothers' behavior. In short, evidence of the importance of fathers' behavior has been growing (Rohner, 1998; Tamis-LeMonda & Cabrera, 1999).

Other research reveals that infants may develop strong attachment relationships with multiple individuals simultaneously. For example, one study found that although most infants formed their first primary relationship with one person, around one third had multiple relationships, and it was difficult to determine which attachment was primary. Furthermore, by the time the infants were 18 months old, most had formed multiple relationships. In sum, infants may develop attachments not only to their mothers but to a variety of other individuals as well (Fox, Kimmerly, & Schafer, 1991; K. S. Rosen & Burke, 1999; Silverstein & Auerbach, 1999).

Are There Differences in Attachment to Mothers and Fathers?   Although infants are fully capable of forming attachments to both mother and father—as well as other

The differences in the ways that fathers and mothers play with their children occur even in families in which the father is the primary caregiver. Based on this observation, how does culture affect attachment?

individuals—the nature of attachment between infants and mothers, on the one hand, and infants and fathers, on the other hand, is not identical. For example, when they are in unusually stressful circumstances, most infants prefer to be soothed by their mothers than by their fathers (Cox et al., 1992; Lamb, 1977; Pipp, Easterbrooks, & Brown, 1993).

One reason for qualitative differences in attachment involves the differences in what fathers and mothers do with their children. Mothers spend a greater proportion of their time feeding and directly nurturing their children. In contrast, fathers spend more time, proportionally,

─● DEVELOPMENTAL DIVERSITY ●─

Does Attachment Differ Across Cultures?

Recall that the work on attachment was initially inspired by John Bowlby's observations of the biologically motivated efforts of the young of other species to seek safety and security. From these observations, Bowlby suggested that seeking attachment was a biological universal, one that we should find not only in other species but among humans as well. Such reasoning suggests that we should see attachment strivings in all humans, regardless of their culture.

However, research has brought this contention into question. For example, one study of German infants showed that most fell into the avoidant category. Other studies, conducted in Israel and Japan, have found a smaller proportion of infants who were more securely attached than in the United States. Finally, comparisons of Chinese and Canadian children show that Chinese children are more inhibited than Canadians in the Strange Situation (X. Chen et al., 1998; Grossmann et al., 1982; Sagi, 1990; Takahashi, 1986).

Other cross-cultural analyses confirm not only that there are differences in the proportions of infants who fall into the various attachment categories but also that subcultural differences exist even within particular societies (Sagi, van IJzendoorn, & Kroonenberg, 1991; Sagi, Donnell et al., 1994; Sagi, van IJzendoorn et al., 1995; Rothbaum et al., 2000). Do such findings suggest that we should abandon the notion that attachment is a universal biological tendency?

Not necessarily. On the one hand, it is possible that Bowlby's claim that the desire for attachment is universal was too strongly stated. On the other hand, most of the data on attachment have been obtained by using the Ainsworth Strange Situation, which may not be the most appropriate measure in non-Western cultures. For example, Japanese parents seek to avoid separation and stress during infancy, and they don't strive to foster independence to the same degree as parents in many Western societies. Because of their relative lack of prior experience in separation, then, Japanese infants placed in the Strange Situation may experience unusual stress, producing the appearance of less secure attachment in Japanese children. If a different measure of attachment were used, one that might be

Japanese parents seek to avoid separation and stress during infancy and do not foster independence. As a result, Japanese children often have the appearance of being less securely attached according to the Strange Situation, but using other measurement techniques they may well score higher in attachment.

administered later in infancy, more Japanese infants could likely be classified as secure (Mizuta et al., 1996; Nakagawa, Lamb, & Miyaki, 1992; Vereijken, Riksen-Walraven, & Kondo-Ikemura, 1997).

More recent approaches view attachment not as entirely biologically determined but rather as susceptible to cultural norms and expectations. Cross-cultural and within-cultural differences in attachment reflect the nature of the measure employed. Specifically, some developmental specialists suggest that attachment should be viewed as a general tendency that is modifiable according to how actively caregivers in a society seek to instill independence in their children. Consequently, secure attachment may be seen earliest in cultures that promote independence but may be delayed in societies in which independence is a less important cultural value (Harwood, Miller, & Irizarry, 1995; Rothbaum et al., 2000).

Mutual regulation model The model in which infants and parents learn to communicate emotional states to one another and to respond appropriately

playing with infants. Almost all fathers do contribute to child care: Surveys show that 95 percent say they perform some child care tasks every day. But on average they still do less than mothers. For instance, 30 percent of fathers with wives who work do 3 or more hours of daily child care. In comparison, 74 percent of employed married mothers spend that amount of time every day in child care activities (Grych & Clark, 1999; L. Jacobsen & Edmondson, 1993; Kazura, 2000).

Furthermore, the nature of fathers' play with their babies is often quite different from that of mothers'. Fathers engage in more physical, rough-and-tumble activities with their children. In contrast, mothers play traditional games such as peekaboo and games with more verbal elements (Lamb, 1986; Parke, 1990, 1996).

These differences in the ways that fathers and mothers play with their children occur even in the minority of families in the United States in which the father is the primary caregiver. Moreover, the differences occur in very diverse cultures: Fathers in Australia, Israel, India, Japan, Mexico, and even in the Aka Pygmy tribe in central Africa all engage more in play than in caregiving, although the amount of time they spend with their infants varies widely. For instance, Aka fathers spend more time caring for their infants than members of any other known culture, holding and cuddling their babies at a rate some five times higher than anywhere else in the world (Bronstein, 1999; De Loache & Gottlieb, 2000; Lamb, 1987; Roopnarine, 1992).

These similarities and differences in child-rearing practices across different societies raise an important question: How does culture affect attachment?

Infant Interactions: Developing Relationships

Research on attachment is clear in showing that infants may develop multiple attachment relationships and that the specific individuals with whom the infant is primarily attached may change over the course of time. These variations in attachment highlight the fact that the development of relationships is an ongoing process, not only during infancy but throughout our lifetime.

Which processes underlie the development of relationships during infancy? One answer comes from studies that examine how parents interact with their children. For instance, in almost all cultures, mothers behave in typical ways with their infants. They tend to exaggerate their facial and vocal expressions—the nonverbal equivalent of the infant-directed speech that they use when they speak to infants (discussed in Chapter 6). Similarly, they often imitate their infants' behavior, responding to distinctive sounds and movements by repeating them. There are even types of games, such as peekaboo, itsy-bitsy spider, and patty-cake, that are nearly universal (Field, 1979, 1990; Kochanska, 1997).

According to the **mutual regulation model,** infants and parents learn to communicate emotional states to one another and to respond appropriately. For instance, both infant and parent act jointly to regulate turn-taking behavior, with one individual waiting until the other completes a behavioral act before starting another. Consequently, at the age of 3 months, infants and their mothers have about the same influence on each other's behavior. Interestingly, by the age of 6 months, infants have more control over turn-taking, although by the age of 9 months both partners once again become roughly equivalent in terms of mutual influence (Cohn & Tronick, 1988, 1989; Tronick, 1998).

One of the ways infants and parents signal each other when they interact is through facial expressions. As we saw earlier in this chapter, even very young infants are able to read, or decode, the facial expressions of their caregivers, and they react to those expressions (Anisfeld, 1996; Camras et al., 1991; Lelwica & Haviland, 1983).

For example, an infant whose mother, during an experiment, displays a stony, immobile facial expression reacts by making a variety of sounds, gestures, and facial expressions of her own in response to such a puzzling situation—and possibly to elicit some new response from her mother. Infants also show more happiness themselves when their mothers appear happy, and they look at their mothers longer. Conversely, infants are apt to respond with sad looks and to turn away when their mothers display unhappy expressions (Termin & Izard, 1988).

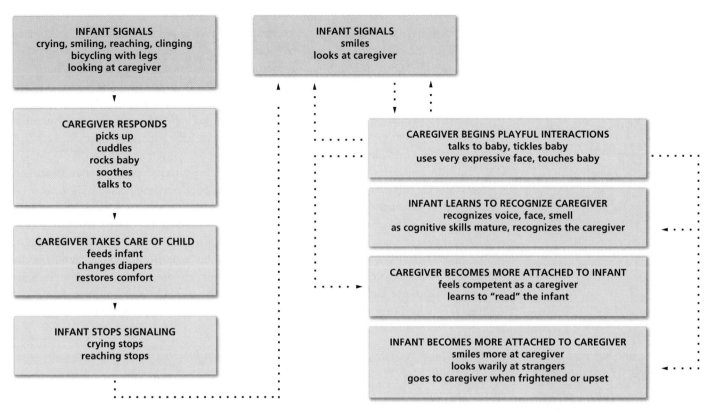

FIGURE 7-5   SEQUENCE OF INFANT–CAREGIVER INTERACTION

The actions and reactions of caregivers and infants influence each other in complex ways. Would this be a pattern that a social worker might also observe, and use, in terms of adult–adult interactions?

(*Sources:* S. M. Bell & Ainsworth, 1972; Tomlinson-Keasey, 1985)

In short, the development of attachment in infants does not merely represent a reaction to the behavior of the people around them. Instead, there is a process of **reciprocal socialization,** in which infants' behaviors invite further responses from parents and other caregivers. In turn, the caregivers' behaviors bring about a reaction from the child, continuing the cycle. Recall the example of Annie, the baby who kept crying to be picked up when her mother put her in her crib. Ultimately, the actions and reactions of parents and child lead to an increase in attachment, forging and strengthening bonds between infants and caregivers. Figure 7-5 summarizes the sequence of infant–caregiver interaction (Ainsworth & Bowlby, 1991; S. M. Bell & Ainsworth, 1972; Bradley & Caldwell, 1995; Egeland, Pianta, & O'Brien, 1993).

Infants' Sociability With Peers: Infant–Infant Interaction

How sociable are infants with other children? Although it is clear that they do not form "friendships" in the traditional sense, they do react positively to the presence of peers from early in life, and they engage in rudimentary forms of social interaction (Field, 1990).

Infants' sociability is expressed in several ways. From the earliest months of life, infants smile, laugh, and vocalize while looking at their peers. They show more interest in peers than in inanimate objects and pay greater attention to other infants than they do to a mirror image of themselves (Legerstee et al., 1998). They also begin to show preferences for people with whom they are familiar over people they do not know. For example, studies of identical twins show that twins exhibit a higher level of social behavior toward each other than toward an unfamiliar infant (Field, 1981, 1990; Field & Roopnarine, 1982; Fogel, 1980).

Infant's level of sociability generally rises with age. Nine- to 12-month-olds mutually present and accept toys, particularly if they know each other. They also play social games, such as

Reciprocal socialization A process in which infants' behaviors invite further responses from parents and other caregivers, which in turn bring about further responses from the infants

peekaboo or crawl-and-chase (Endo, 1992; Vincze, 1971). Such behavior is important, as it serves as a foundation for future social exchanges in which children will try to elicit responses from others and then offer reactions to those responses (C. Brownell, 1986; Howes, 1987). These kinds of exchanges are important to learn because they continue even into adulthood. For example, someone who says, "Hi, what's up?" may be trying to elicit a response to which he or she can then reply.

Finally, as infants age, they begin to imitate each other, as well as their parents. Such imitation serves a social function and can also be a powerful teaching tool. For example, recall the story of 10-month-old Russell Ruud in the prologue to this chapter, who showed the other children in his child care center how he could remove his hat by unfastening its Velcro straps and soon had others following his lead (Gergely, Bekkering, & Király, 2002; Mueller & Vandell, 1979).

According to Andrew Meltzoff, a developmental psychologist at the University of Washington, Russell's ability to impart this information is only one example of how so-called expert babies are able to teach skills and information to other infants. According to the research of Meltzoff and his colleagues, the abilities learned from the "experts" are retained and later utilized to a remarkable degree. Moreover, learning by exposure starts early in life. For example, recent evidence shows that even 6-week-old infants perform delayed imitation of a novel stimulus to which they have earlier been exposed, such as an adult's sticking the tongue out

"Basically the Help Me Grow program goal is to provide health and developmental services, so when the children are three they are healthy and ready to start school."

CAREERS IN CHILD DEVELOPMENT

Joyce Meyers

Education: . . . . **Capital University, Columbus, Ohio: B.S.W.**
Position: . . . . **Social worker and service coordinator for the Help Me Grow program, Knox County Health Department, Mount Vernon, Ohio**
Home: . . . . **Mount Vernon, Ohio**

Not all newborns and infants have access to the proper care needed for good development or the opportunity to participate in a preschool. For those who don't, social workers like Joyce Meyers of the Help Me Grow program make sure that as many of them as possible receive the best care and attention available.

"We live in a small county that is mostly rural," says Meyers, who carries a caseload of 46 children, "and many of the issues we deal with involve poverty, inadequate parenting skills, and lack of education."

Meyers tries to assess a child's home situation and identify what the problems are. She then refers the parents to the appropriate service organization to address the specific problems.

"When we initially go into the home, we make two or three visits, for a comprehensive assessment," she explains. "We try to identify the issues that need to be addressed. But we have to be cautious because in some cases there are so many issues that the parent may be overwhelmed. We then have to determine the top-priority issues."

Parenting education is provided in the home as well as in classes available at a local health center.

"We also make sure the parents have a health care provider for themselves and their children. If not, we will find one for them," Meyers points out. "Basically, the goal of the Help Me Grow program is to provide health and developmental services so that when the children reach the age of three, they are healthy and ready to start preschool."

the side of the mouth (R. G. Barr & Hayne, 1999; Hanna & Meltzoff, 1993; Meltzoff & Moore, 1994, 1999).

Finding that infants learn new behaviors, skills, and abilities due to exposure to other children has several implications. For one thing, it suggests that interactions between infants provide more than social benefits; they may have an impact on children's future cognitive development as well. For example, there is evidence that the number of siblings—and whether those siblings are older or younger—affects a child's cognitive development (D. B. Downey, 2001; Rodgers, 2001; Zajonc, 2001).

In addition, exposure to other infants illustrates a possible benefit that infants derive from participation in child care centers (which we consider later in this chapter). The opportunity to learn from their peers may prove to be a lasting advantage for infants in group child care settings.

R E V I E W & A P P L Y

Review

- Attachment, the positive emotional bond between an infant and a significant individual, relates to a person's later social competence as an adult.

- By the amount of emotion they display nonverbally, infants help determine the nature and quality of their caregivers' responses to them.

- Infants and the persons with whom they interact engage in reciprocal socialization as they mutually adjust to one another's interactions.

- Infants react differently to other children than to inanimate objects, and gradually they engage in increasing amounts of peer social interaction.

Applying Child Development

- In what sort of society might the attachment style labeled "avoidant" be encouraged by cultural attitudes toward child rearing? In such a society, would characterizing the infant's consistent avoidance of its mother as anger be an accurate interpretation?

- Does the importance of infants' early attachment to primary caregivers have social policy implications relating to working parents? *From a social worker's perspective:* Do current policies reveal societal assumptions pertaining to the different roles of mothers and fathers?

Differences Among Infants

Lincoln was a difficult baby, his parents both agreed. For one thing, it seemed like they could never get him to sleep at night. He cried at the slightest noise, a problem since his crib was near the windows facing a busy street. Worse yet, once he started crying, it seemed to take forever to calm him down again. One day, his mother, Aisha, was telling her mother-in-law, Mary, about the challenges of being Lincoln's mom. Mary recalled that her own son, Lincoln's father, Malcom, had been much the same way. "He was my first child, and I thought this was how all babies acted. So we just kept trying

Personality The assortment of enduring characteristics that differentiate one individual from another

Erikson's theory of psychosocial development The theory that considers how individuals come to understand themselves and the meaning of others' behavior—and their own

Trust-versus-mistrust stage According to Erikson, the period during which infants develop a sense of trust or mistrust, largely depending on how well their needs are met by their caregivers

Autonomy-versus-shame-and-doubt stage The period during which, according to Erikson, toddlers (aged 18 months to 3 years) develop independence and autonomy if they are allowed the freedom to explore or come to feel shame and self-doubt if they are restricted and overprotected

Temperament Patterns of arousal and emotionality that are consistent and enduring characteristics of an individual

According to Erikson, children from 18 months to 3 years develop independence and autonomy if parents encourage exploration and freedom, within safe boundaries. What does Erikson theorize if children are restricted and overly protected at this stage?

different ways until we found out how he worked. I remember we put his crib all over the apartment until we finally found out where he could sleep, and it ended up being in the hallway for a long time. Then his sister, Maleah, came along, and she was so quiet and easy, I didn't know what to do with my extra time!"

As the story of Lincoln's family shows, babies are not all alike, and neither are their families. In fact, as we'll see, some of the differences among people seem to be present from the moment we are born. The differences among infants include overall personality and temperament and differences in the lives they lead—differences based on their gender, the nature of their family, and the ways in which they are cared for.

Personality Development: The Characteristics That Make Infants Unique

The origins of **personality,** the assortment of enduring characteristics that differentiate one individual from another, stem from infancy. From birth onward, infants begin to exhibit unique, stable traits and behaviors that ultimately lead to their growing into distinct individuals (Caspi, 2000; Kagan, 2000; Pipp-Siegel & Foltz, 1997).

According to psychologist Erik Erikson, whose approach to personality development we first discussed in Chapter 2, infants' early experiences are responsible for shaping one of the key aspects of their personalities: whether they will be basically trusting or mistrustful.

Erikson's theory of psychosocial development considers how individuals come to understand themselves and the meaning of others' behavior—and their own (Erikson, 1963). The theory suggests that developmental change occurs throughout people's lives in eight distinct stages, the first of which occurs in infancy.

According to Erikson, during the first 18 months of life, we pass through the **trust-versus-mistrust stage.** During this period, infants develop a sense of trust or mistrust, depending largely on how well their needs are met by their caregivers. Mary's attention to Malcom's needs, in our example, probably helped him develop a basic sense of trust in the world. Erikson suggests that if infants are able to develop trust, they experience a sense of hope, which permits them to feel as if they can fulfill their needs successfully. By contrast, feelings of mistrust lead infants to see the world as harsh and unfriendly, and they may have later difficulties in forming close bonds with others.

During the end of infancy, children enter the **autonomy-versus-shame-and-doubt stage,** which lasts from around 18 months to 3 years. During this period, children develop independence and autonomy if parents encourage exploration and freedom, within safe boundaries. However, if children are restricted and overly protected, they come to feel shame, self-doubt, and unhappiness.

Erikson argues that personality is shaped primarily by infants' experiences. However, as we discuss next, other developmentalists concentrate on consistencies of behavior that are present at birth, even before the experiences of infancy. These consistencies are viewed as largely genetically determined and as providing the raw material of personality.

Temperament: Stabilities in Infant Behavior

Sarah's parents thought there must be something wrong. Unlike her older brother, Josh, who had been so active as an infant that he seemed never to be still, Sarah was much more placid. She took long naps and was easily soothed on those relatively rare occasions when she became agitated. What could be producing her extreme calm?

The most likely answer is that the difference between Sarah and Josh reflected a difference in temperament. As we first discussed in Chapter 3, **temperament** encompasses patterns of arousal and emotionality that are consistent and enduring characteristics of an individual (Rothbart, Ahadi, & Evans, 2000).

Temperament refers to *how* children behave, as opposed to *what* they do or *why* they do it. Infants show temperamental differences in general disposition from the time of birth, largely due initially to genetic factors, and temperament tends to be fairly stable well into adolescence. But temperament is not fixed and unchangeable: Child-rearing practices can modify temperament significantly. In fact, some children show little consistency in temperament from one age to another (Lemery et al., 1999; McCrae et al., 2000; Rothbart & Bates, 1998; Rothbart, Derryberry, & Hershey, 2000).

Temperament is reflected in several dimensions of behavior. One central dimension is *activity level,* which reflects the degree of overall movement. Some babies (like Sarah and Maleah, in the earlier example) are relatively placid, and their movements are slow and almost leisurely. In contrast, the activity level of other infants (like Josh) is quite high, with strong, restless movements of the arms and legs.

Another important dimension of temperament is the nature and quality of an infant's mood and in particular a child's *irritability*. Like Lincoln, who was described in the example at the beginning of this section, some infants are easily disturbed and cry easily, while others are relatively easygoing. Irritable infants fuss a great deal, and they are easily upset. They are also difficult to soothe when they do begin to cry. Such irritability is relatively stable: Researchers find that infants who are irritable at birth remain irritable at age 1, and even at age 2 they are still more easily upset than infants who were not irritable just after birth (Reese, 1987; Worobey & Bajda, 1989). The various aspects of temperament are identified in Table 7-2.

Categorizing Temperament: Easy, Difficult, and Slow-to-Warm Babies.   Because temperament can be viewed along so many dimensions, some researchers have asked whether there are broader categories that can be used to describe children's overall behavior. According to Alexander Thomas and Stella Chess (1977, 1980), who carried out a large-scale study of a

TABLE 7-2 DIMENSIONS OF TEMPERAMENT	
Dimension	**Definition**
Activity level	Proportion of active time periods to inactive time periods
Approach–withdrawal	Response to a new person or object, based on whether the child accepts the new situation or withdraws from it
Adaptability	How easily the child is able to adapt to changes in his or her environment
Quality of mood	Contrast of the amount of friendly, joyful, and pleasant behavior with unpleasant, unfriendly behavior
Attention span and persistence	Amount of time the child devotes to an activity and effect of distraction on that activity
Distractibility	Degree to which stimuli in the environment alter behavior
Rhythmicity (regularity)	Regularity of basic functions such as hunger, excretion, sleep, and wakefulness
Intensity of reaction	Energy level or reaction of the child's response
Threshold of responsiveness	Intensity of stimulation needed to elicit a response

(*Source:* A. Thomas, Chess, & Birch, 1968)

group of infants that has come to be known as the New York Longitudinal Study, babies can be described according to one of several profiles:

- **Easy babies** have a positive disposition. Their body functions operate regularly, and they are adaptable. They are generally positive, showing curiosity about new situations, and their emotions are moderate or low in intensity. This category applies to the largest number of infants, about 40 percent.

- **Difficult babies** have more negative moods and are slow to adapt to new situations. When confronted with a new situation, they tend to withdraw. About 10 percent of infants belong in this category.

- **Slow-to-warm babies** are inactive, showing relatively calm reactions to their environment. Their moods are generally negative, and they withdraw from new situations, adapting slowly. Approximately 15 percent of infants are slow to warm.

The remaining 35 percent cannot be consistently categorized. These children show a variety of combinations of characteristics. For instance, one infant may have relatively sunny moods but react negatively to new situations, or another may show little stability of any sort in terms of general temperament.

The Consequences of Temperament: Does Temperament Matter?   One obvious question to emerge from the findings of the relative stability of temperament is whether a particular kind of temperament is beneficial. The answer seems to be that no single type of temperament is invariably good or bad. Instead, children's long-term adjustment depends on the **goodness of fit** of their particular temperament and the nature and demands of the environment in which they find themselves. For instance, children with a low activity level and low irritability may do particularly well in an environment in which they are left to explore on their own and are allowed largely to direct their own behavior. In contrast, high-activity-level, highly irritable children may do best with more assertive guidance, which permits them to channel their energy in particular directions (Mangelsdorf et al., 1990; Strelau, 1998; A. Thomas & Chess, 1977, 1980). Mary, the grandmother in the earlier example, found ways to adjust the environment for her son, Malcom. Malcom and Aisha may need to do the same for their own son, Lincoln.

Some research does suggest that certain temperaments are generally more adaptive than others. For instance, researchers found that difficult children were more likely to show behavior problems by school age than those who were classified in infancy as easy children (A. Thomas, Chess, & Birch, 1968). But not all difficult children experience problems. The key determinant seems to be the way parents react to their infant's difficult behavior. If they react by showing anger and inconsistency—responses that their child's difficult, demanding behavior readily evokes—the child is ultimately more likely to experience behavior problems. By contrast, parents who display more warmth and consistency in their responses are more likely to have children who avoid later problems (Belsky, Fish, & Isabella, 1991; Teerikangas et al., 1998).

Furthermore, temperament seems to be at least weakly related to infants' attachment to their adult caregivers. For example, infants vary considerably in how much emotion they display nonverbally. Some are "poker-faced," showing little expressivity, while others' reactions tend to be much more easily decoded. More expressive infants may provide more easily discernible cues to others, thereby easing the way for caregivers to be more successful in responding to their needs and facilitating attachment (R. S. Feldman & Rimé, 1991; Goldsmith & Harman, 1994; Seifer, Schiller, & Sameroff, 1996).

Cultural differences also have a major influence on the consequences of a particular temperament. For instance, children who would be described as "difficult" in Western cultures

Easy babies   Babies who have a positive disposition; their body functions operate regularly, and they are adaptable

Difficult babies   Babies who have negative moods and are slow to adapt to new situations; when confronted with a new situation, they tend to withdraw

Slow-to-warm babies   Babies who are inactive, showing relatively calm reactions to their environment; their moods are generally negative, and they withdraw from new situations, adapting slowly

Goodness of fit   The notion that development is dependent on the degree of match between children's temperament and the nature and demands of the environment in which they are being raised

actually seem to have an advantage in the East African Masai culture. The reason? Mothers offer their breast to their infants only when they fuss and cry; therefore, the irritable, more difficult infants are apt to receive more nourishment than the more placid, easy infants. Particularly when environmental conditions are bad, as during a drought, difficult babies may have an advantage (M. W. de Vries, 1984).

Recent approaches to temperament grow out of the framework of behavioral genetics that we discussed in Chapter 3. For instance, Arnold Buss and Robert Plomin (1984) argue that temperamental characteristics represent inherited traits that are fairly stable during childhood and across the entire life span. These traits are seen as making up the core of personality and playing a substantial role in future development.

Gender: Boys in Blue, Girls in Pink

From the moment of birth, girls and boys are treated differently. Their parents send out different kinds of birth announcements. They are dressed in different clothes and wrapped in different-colored blankets. They are given different toys (Bridges, 1993; Coltrane & Adams, 1997).

Parents play with them differently. From birth on, fathers tend to interact more with sons than daughters, while mothers interact more with daughters (Leaper, Anderson, & Sanders, 1998; Parke & Sawin, 1980). Because, as we noted earlier in the chapter, mothers and fathers play in different ways (with fathers typically engaging in more physical, rough-and-tumble activities and mothers in traditional games such as peekaboo), male and female infants are clearly exposed to different styles of activity and interaction from their parents (V. J. Grant, 1994; Lamb, 1986; Parke, 1990; Power & Parke, 1982).

The behavior exhibited by girls and boys is interpreted in very different ways by adults. For instance, in one experiment, researchers showed adults a video of an infant whose name was given as either "John" or "Mary" (Condry & Condry, 1976). Although it was the same baby performing a single set of behaviors, adults perceived "John" as adventurous and inquisitive, while "Mary" was seen as fearful and anxious. Clearly, adults view the behavior of children through the lens of gender. **Gender** refers to the sense of being male or female. The term *gender* is often used to mean the same thing as *sex*, but the two are not actually the same. *Sex* typically refers to sexual anatomy and sexual behavior, while *gender* refers to the perception of maleness or femaleness. All cultures prescribe *gender roles* for males and females, but these roles differ greatly from one culture to another.

Gender Differences.   Although to some extent boys and girls live in at least partially different worlds due to their gender, there is a considerable amount of argument over both the extent and causes of such gender differences. Some gender differences are fairly clear from the time of birth. For example, male infants tend to be more active and fussier than female infants. Boys' sleep tends to be more disturbed than that of girls. Boys grimace more, although no gender difference exists in the overall amount of crying. There is also some evidence that male newborns are more irritable than female newborns, although the findings are inconsistent (W. O. Eaton & Enns, 1986; S. Phillips, King, & Du Bois, 1978).

Differences among male and female infants, however, are generally minor. In fact, in most ways, infants seem so similar that usually adults cannot discern whether a baby is a boy or a girl, as the "John" and "Mary" video research shows. Furthermore, it is important to keep in mind that there are much larger differences among individual boys and among individual girls than there are, on average, between boys and girls (Unger & Crawford, 1999).

Gender Roles.   Gender differences emerge more clearly as children age and become increasingly influenced by the gender roles that society sets out for them. For instance, by the age of 1 year, infants are able to distinguish between males and females. Girls at this age prefer

Gender   The sense of being male or female

Parents of girls who play with toys related to activities typically associated with boys are apt to be less concerned than parents of boys who play with toys typically associated with girls.

to play with dolls or stuffed animals, while boys seek out blocks and trucks. Often, of course, these are the only options available to them, due to the choices their parents and other adults have made in the toys they provide (Caldera & Sciaraffa, 1998; Poulin-Dubois et al., 1994; Serbin et al., 2001; Servin, Bohlin, & Berlin, 1999).

Children's preferences for certain kinds of toys are reinforced by their parents, although parents of boys are more apt to be concerned about their child's choosing "girls'" toys than parents of girls are about preferences for "boys'" toys. For example, 1-year-old boys receive more positive reactions for playing with transportation and building toys than girls of the same age do. Moreover, the amount of reinforcement boys receive for playing with toys that society deems appropriate increases with age. Yet girls who play with toys regarded by society as "masculine" are less discouraged for their behavior than boys who play with toys regarded as "feminine" (Eisenberg et al., 1985; Fagot & Hagan, 1991).

By the time they reach the age of 2, boys behave more independently and less compliantly than girls. Much of this behavior can be traced to parental reactions to earlier behavior. For instance, when a child takes his or her first steps, parents tend to react differently, depending on the child's gender: Boys are encouraged more to go off and explore the world, while girls are hugged and kept close. In general, all kinds of exploratory behavior tend to be encouraged more in boys than in girls. It is hardly surprising, then, that by the age of 2, girls tend to show less independence and greater compliance (Brooks-Gunn & Matthews, 1979; Fagot, 1978; Kuczynski & Kochanska, 1990).

Societal encouragement and reinforcement do not, however, completely explain differences in behavior between boys and girls. For example, as we'll discuss further in Chapter 10, one study examined girls who were exposed before birth to abnormally high levels of androgen, a male hormone, because their mothers unwittingly took a drug containing the hormone while pregnant. Later, these girls were more likely to play with toys stereotypically preferred by boys (such as cars) and less likely to play with toys stereotypically associated with girls (such as dolls). Although there are many alternative explanations for these results—you can probably think of several yourself—one possibility is that exposure to male hormones affected the brain development of the girls, leading them to favor toys that involve certain kinds of preferred skills (S. C. Levine et al., 1999; Mealey, 2000).

Infant Child Care: Assessing the Consequences

Should infants be placed in group child care settings, such as the one described in the chapter prologue, where Russell Ruud was leading the Velcro revolt? For many parents, there is little choice: Economic reality or the desire to maintain a career requires that their children be left in the care of others for a portion of the day, typically in an infant child care setting. In fact, recent figures indicate that almost 30 percent of preschool children whose mothers work outside the home spend their days in child care centers (see Figure 7-6), and, overall, more than 80 percent of infants are cared for by people other than their mothers during their first year of life. The majority of these infants begin child care outside the home before the age of 4 months and are enrolled for almost 30 hours per week (National Institute of Child Health and Human Development, 1997a). Do such arrangements have discernible effects on infant development?

The answer is reassuring. According to the findings of a large study supported by the National Institute of Child Health and Human Development (NICHD), high quality child care outside the home produces only minor differences from home care in most respects and may even enhance certain aspects of development. For example, most research finds little or no difference in the strength or nature of parental attachment bonds of infants who have been in high quality child care and infants raised solely by their parents. However, the research found that infants are less secure when they are placed in low quality child care, if they are placed in multiple-child care arrangements, or if their mothers are relatively insensitive and unresponsive (NICHD, 1997b, 1999, 2002).

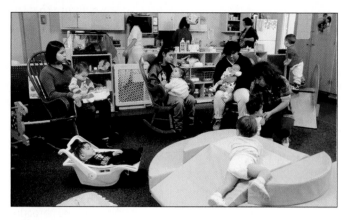

High quality infant child care seems to produce only minor differences from home care in most respects, and some aspects of development may even be enhanced. What aspects of development might be enhanced by participation in infant child care outside the home?

The study also found an unexpected gender difference: Boys who experienced high levels of care and girls who had minimal amounts of care were somewhat less apt to be securely attached—although the meaning of this finding is unclear. Overall, though, there is little evidence that even extensive and continuous enrollment in child care outside the home is related to undesirable outcomes.

In fact, various studies have found clear benefits from participation in child care outside the home. For instance, children who participate in Early Head Start—a program that serves at-risk infants and toddlers in high quality child care centers—are later better able to solve problems, pay greater attention to others, and use language more effectively than poor children who do not participate in the programs. In addition, their parents (who are also involved in the program) benefit from their participation. Participating parents talk and read more to their children and are less likely to spank them ("Early Head Start," 2001).

In addition to the direct benefits from child care outside the home, there are indirect ones. For example, although parental employment itself has been shown to have little effect on children's later functioning, children in lower income households and those whose mothers are single may actually benefit from the higher income produced by parental employment (E. Harvey, 1999).

It is important to note, however, that not all research on group child care provides such good news. Some studies on the outcomes of infant child care centers have yielded mixed or even negative results, finding lower attachment on the part of children in child care. Still other research shows virtually no difference between children receiving care from their mothers and those receiving nonmaternal care. Ultimately, more research is needed on just who makes use of child care and how it is used by members of different segments of society if we are to fully understand its consequences (Belsky & Rovine, 1988; Hungerford, Brownell, & Campbell, 2000; Erel, Oberman, & Yirmiya, 2000).

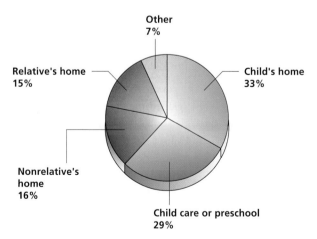

Other
7%

Relative's home
15%

Child's home
33%

Nonrelative's home
16%

Child care or preschool
29%

FIGURE 7-6   WHERE ARE CHILDREN CARED FOR?

Most children spend their days at home, but almost 30 percent of children younger than 5 years of age whose mothers work outside the home spend their days in child care centers.

(*Sources*: U.S. Bureau of the Census, 1997; Health Resources and Services Administration, 1998)

In sum, differences in behavior between boys and girls begin in infancy and—as we will see in future chapters—continue throughout childhood (and beyond). Although gender differences have complex causes, representing some combination of innate, biologically related factors and environmental factors, they play a profound role in the social and emotional development of infants.

Family Life in the 21st Century

A look back at television shows of the 1950s (such as *Leave It to Beaver*) finds a world of families portrayed in a way that today seems oddly old-fashioned and quaint: mothers and fathers, married for years, and their good-looking children making their way in a world that seems to have few, if any, serious problems.

Even in the 1950s, such a view of family life was overly romantic and unrealistic. Today, however, it is broadly inaccurate, representing only a minority of families in the United States. A quick review tells the story:

- The number of single-parent families has increased dramatically in the past two decades, and the number of two-parent households has declined. Some 27 percent of all families

---

BECOMING AN INFORMED CONSUMER OF DEVELOPMENT

Choosing the Right Infant Care Provider

If there is one finding that emerges with crystal clarity from research conducted on the consequences of infant child care programs, it is that benefits occur only when child care is of high quality. But what distinguishes high quality child care from low caliber programs? The American Psychological Association suggests that parents consider the following questions in choosing a program (Committee on Children, Youth and Families, 1994; NICHD, 2002; Zigler & Styfco, 1994):

- Are there enough providers? A desirable ratio is one adult for every three infants, although one to four can be adequate.

- Are groups of manageable size? Even with several providers, no group should have more than eight infants.

- Has the center complied with all governmental regulations, and is it licensed?

- Do the people providing the care seem to like what they are doing? What is their motivation? Is child care just a temporary job, or is it a career? Are they well trained and experienced? Do they seem happy in the job, or is offering child care just a way to earn money?

- What do the caregivers do during the day? Do they spend their time playing with, listening and talking to, and paying attention to the children? Do they seem genuinely interested in the children, rather than merely going through the motions of caring for them?

- Are the children safe and clean? Does the environment allow infants to move around safely? Are the equipment and furniture in good repair? Do the providers adhere to the highest levels of cleanliness? After changing a baby's diaper, do providers wash their hands?

- Do the caregivers demonstrate a knowledge of the basics of infant development and an understanding of how normal children develop? Do they seem alert to signs that development may depart from normal patterns?

- Is the environment happy and cheerful? Child care is not just a babysitting service—for the time an infant is there, it is the child's whole world. You should feel fully comfortable and confident that the child care center is a place where your infant will be treated as an individual.

In addition to following these guidelines, you may contact the National Association for the Education of Young Children, from which you may be able to get the name of a resource and referral agency in your area. Write (enclosing a self-addressed, stamped envelope) to NAEYC Information Service, 1834 Connecticut Avenue NW, Washington, DC 20009; or call (800) 424-2460.

with children are headed by single parents. Sixty-five percent of African American children and 37 percent of Hispanic children live in single-parent households (Federal Interagency Forum on Child and Family Statistics, 2000; U.S. Bureau of the Census, 2001a).

- The average size of families is shrinking. Today, on average, there are 2.6 persons per household, compared to 2.8 in 1980. The number of people living in nonfamily households (without any relatives) is close to 30 million.

- In 1960, 5 percent of all births in the United States were to unmarried mothers; in 2000, 33 percent of births were to unmarried mothers.

- Every minute, an adolescent in the United States gives birth.

- Fifty-five percent of women with infants work at full- or part-time jobs.

- More than 5 million children under the age of 3 are cared for by other adults while their parents work, and more than half of mothers of infants work outside the home.

- One in 6 children lives in poverty in the United States. The rates are even higher for African American and Hispanic families and for single-parent families of young children. More children under 3 live in poverty than older children, adults, or the elderly do (Einbinder, 2000).

Many of these statistics are disheartening. At the very least, they suggest that infants are being raised in environments in which substantial stressors are present, factors that make an unusually difficult task of raising children, which is never easy even under the best circumstances.

But society is adapting to the new realities of family life. Several kinds of social support exist for the parents of infants, and new institutions are evolving to help in their care. One example is the growing array of child care arrangements available to help working parents, discussed in the *From Research to Practice* box on page 223. Some guidelines for parents who choose group child care are presented in the *Becoming an Informed Consumer of Development* box.

REVIEW & APPLY

Review

- According to Erikson, during infancy individuals move from the trust-versus-mistrust stage of psychosocial development to the autonomy-versus-shame-and-guilt stage.

- Temperament encompasses enduring levels of arousal and emotionality that are characteristic of an individual.

- Gender differences become more pronounced as infants age.

- Child care outside of the home can have neutral, positive, or negative effects on the social development of children, depending largely on its quality.

- Research on the effects of child care must take into account the varying quality of different child care settings and the social characteristics of the parents who use child care.

Applying Child Development

- What are some social implications of the changes in family life described in this chapter? What sorts of family policies might be instituted to address these changes?

● *From an educator's perspective:* Why does society frown less on girls playing with "boys'" toys than boys playing with "girls'" toys? Should our educational institutions try to address this situation, and if so, in what ways?

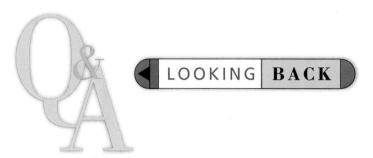

LOOKING BACK

● **What sort of emotional lives do infants have?**

- Infants display a variety of facial expressions, which are similar across cultures and appear to reflect basic emotional states.

- By the end of the first year, infants often develop both stranger anxiety, wariness around an unknown person, and separation anxiety, distress displayed when a customary care provider departs.

- Early in life, infants develop the capability of nonverbal decoding: determining the emotional states of others based on their facial and vocal expressions.

- Through social referencing, infants from the age of 8 or 9 months use the expressions of others to clarify ambiguous situations and learn appropriate reactions to them.

● **What sort of mental lives do infants have?**

- Infants begin to develop self-awareness at about the age of 12 months.

- They also begin to develop a theory of mind—knowledge and beliefs about how they and others think.

● **What is attachment in infancy, and how does it relate to the future social competence of individuals?**

- Attachment, a strong, positive emotional bond that forms between an infant and one or more significant persons, is a crucial factor in enabling individuals to develop social relationships.

- Infants display one of four major attachment patterns: securely attached, avoidant, ambivalent, and disorganized-disoriented. Research suggests an association between an infant's attachment pattern and his or her adult social and emotional competence.

● **What roles do other people play in infants' social development?**

- Mothers' interactions with their babies are particularly important for social development. Mothers who respond effectively to their babies' social overtures appear to contribute to the babies' ability to become securely attached.

- Through a process of reciprocal socialization, infants and caregivers interact and affect one another's behavior, which strengthens their mutual relationship.

- From an early age, infants engage in rudimentary forms of social interaction with other children, and their level of sociability increases as they age.

● **What sorts of individual differences do infants display?**

- The origins of personality, the enduring characteristics that differentiate one individual from another, arise during infancy.

- Temperament encompasses the levels of arousal and emotionality that are characteristic of an individual. Temperamental differences underlie the broad classification of infants into easy, difficult, and slow-to-warm categories.

- As infants age, gender differences become more pronounced, mostly due to environmental influences. Differences are accentuated by parental expectations and behavior.

● **Is day care beneficial or harmful for infants?**

- Day care, which has expanded in response to the changing nature of the family, can be beneficial to the social development of children, fostering social interaction and cooperation, if it is of high quality.

EPILOGUE

 n this chapter, we looked at the ways in which infants develop as social individuals, decoding and encoding emotions using social referencing and a theory of mind. We considered the attachment patterns that infants display and their potential long-term effects. We examined personality, taking a close look at Erik Erikson's theory of psychosocial development. We also discussed temperament and explored the nature and causes of gender differences. We concluded with a discussion of infant day care.

Return to the prologue of this chapter, about Russell Ruud's Velcro discovery, and answer the following questions:

1. Is this episode evidence of self-awareness on the part of Russell or his child care companions? Why or why not?

2. What role do you think social referencing might have played in this scenario? If Russell's care providers had reacted with obvious negativity, would this have stopped the other children from imitating Russell?

3. How does this story relate to the sociability of infants?

4. Can we form any opinion about Russell's personality based on this event? Why or why not?

5. Do you think Russell's actions might have brought a different response from his adult care providers if he had been a girl? Would the response from his peers have been different? Why or why not?

KEY TERMS AND CONCEPTS

differential emotions
  theory (p. 202)
stranger anxiety (p. 202)
separation anxiety
  (p. 203)
social smile (p. 203)
social referencing (p. 204)

self-awareness (p. 205)
theory of mind
  (p. 206)
empathy (p. 206)
attachment (p. 208)
Ainsworth Strange
  Situation (p. 209)

secure attachment
  pattern (p. 209)
avoidant attachment
  pattern (p. 211)
ambivalent
  attachment
  pattern (p. 211)

In Part 2, we looked at various aspects of infants' development. We discussed the ways in which they grow physically, examining their remarkably rapid progress from largely instinctual beings to individuals with a range of complex physical and motor abilities. We'll see next how preschoolers use their physical skills to further their explorations of the world and as the basis for building even more complex skills.

Turning to infants' cognitive development, we encountered Piaget and the notion of stages of development, as well as some alternative views. We evaluated how well these views explain the amazing growth in learning, memory, and especially language that infants experience—and adults witness with awe. Language development is far from complete as children become preschoolers, however. In Part 3, we'll see that children experience amazing progress in language, at the same time as they continue learning about the world around them.

We also examined social and personality development. We looked at personality and temperament and observed that gender differences are a matter of both genes and environment. We saw how infants begin to develop as social beings, moving from interactions with their parents to relations with other adults and children. Next we'll see how, as preschoolers, children continue to expand their social circles through play and friendships.

Above all, we continued to marvel at the rate of infants' progress, and we got a preview of the ways in which factors that date from infancy continue to influence the individual into adulthood. In subsequent parts of the book, we'll see, for example, that temperament and personality remain uncannily constant, that infant attachment patterns can have lasting effects, and that the earliest social influences can define gender roles for life. As we proceed, keep in mind that the seeds of our future appear in many cases to be present in our earliest beginnings. ■

8

Physical Development in the Preschool Years

PROLOGUE: Aaron

aron, a wildly energetic preschooler who has just turned 3, was trying to stretch far enough to reach the bowl of cookies that he spied sitting on the kitchen counter. Because the bowl was just beyond his grasp, he pushed a chair from the kitchen table over to the counter and climbed up.

Because he still couldn't reach the cookies from the chair, Aaron climbed onto the kitchen counter and crawled over to the cookie bowl. He pried the lid off the jar, thrust his hand in, pulled out a cookie, and began to munch on it.

But not for long. His curiosity getting the better of him, he grabbed another cookie and began to work his body along the counter toward the sink. He climbed in, twisted the cold water faucet to the "on" position, and happily splashed in the cold water.

The preschool period is an exciting time for children and a challenging one for parents.

Aaron's father, who had left the room for only a moment, returned to find Aaron sitting in the sink, soaked, with a contented smile on his face.

Consider how far Aaron has come from his infancy. Just a few years earlier, he could not even lift his head. Now he's able to move with great assurance, pushing furniture, opening jars, turning knobs, and climbing on chairs. Of course, such advances in mobility also pose new challenges to parents, who must bring a new level of vigilance in order to prevent injuries, the greatest threat to preschoolers' physical well-being. (Think what would have happened if Aaron had turned on the hot water, rather than the cold, when he reached the sink.)

The preschool period is an exciting time in children's lives. In one sense, the preschool years mark a time of preparation: a period spent anticipating and getting ready for the start of a child's formal education, through which society will begin the process of passing on its intellectual tools to a new generation.

But it is a mistake to take the label "preschool" too literally. The years between 3 and 6 are hardly a mere way station in life, an interval spent waiting for the next, more important period to start. Rather, the preschool years are a time of tremendous change and growth as physical, intellectual, and social development proceeds at a rapid pace.

In this chapter, we focus on the physical changes that occur during the preschool years. We begin by considering the nature of growth during those years. We discuss the rapid changes in the body's weight and height, as well as developmental changes in the brain and its neural byways. We also consider some intriguing findings relating to the ways the brain functions in terms of gender and culture.

Next, we focus on health and wellness in the preschool years. After discussing the nutritional needs of preschoolers, we examine the risk of illness and injury that they face. We also look at the grimmer side of some children's lives: child abuse and psychological maltreatment.

The chapter ends with a discussion of the development of gross and fine motor skills. We consider the significant changes that occur during the preschool period in motor performance and what these changes allow children to accomplish. We also look at the impact of being right- or left-handed and discuss how artistic abilities develop during the preschool years.

After reading this chapter, you'll be able to answer the following questions:

- What changes in the body and the brain do children experience in the preschool years?
- What are the nutritional needs of preschool children, and what causes obesity?
- What threats to their health and wellness do preschool children experience?
- What are child abuse and psychological maltreatment, what factors contribute to them, and can anything be done about them?
- In what ways do children's gross and fine motor skills develop during the preschool years?
- How do handedness and artistic expression develop during these years?

Physical Growth

It is an unseasonably warm spring day at the Cushman Hill Preschool, one of the first nice days after a long winter. The children in Mary Scott's class have happily left their winter coats in the classroom for the first time this spring, and they are excitedly playing outside. Jessie plays a game of catch with Germaine, and Sarah and Molly are climbing up the slide. Craig and Marta chase one another, while Jesse and Bernstein try, with gales of giggles, to play leapfrog. Virginia and Ollie sit across from each other on the teeter-totter, successively bumping it so hard into the ground that they both are in danger of being knocked off. Erik, Jim, Scott, and Paul race around the perimeter of the playground, running for the sheer joy of it.

These same children, now so active and mobile, were unable even to crawl or walk just a few years earlier. Just how far they have developed is apparent when we look at the specific changes they have undergone in their size, shape, and physical abilities.

The Growing Body

Two years after birth, the average child in the United States weighs 25 to 30 pounds and is close to 36 inches tall—around half the height of the average adult. Children grow steadily during the preschool period, and by the time they are 6 years old, they weigh, on average, about 46 pounds and stand 46 inches tall (see Figure 8-1).

VIDEO CLIP

Physical Growth

Individual Differences in Height and Weight.   These averages mask great individual differences in height and weight. For instance, 10 percent of 6-year-olds weigh 55 pounds or more, and 10 percent weigh 36 pounds or less. Furthermore, average differences in height and weight between boys and girls increase during the preschool years. Although at age 2 the differences are relatively small, by the age of 6, boys begin to be taller and heavier, on average, than girls.

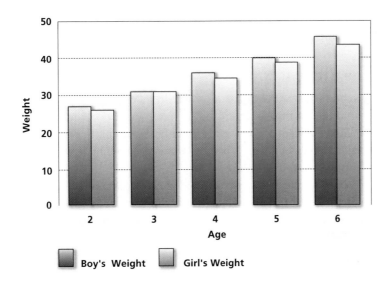

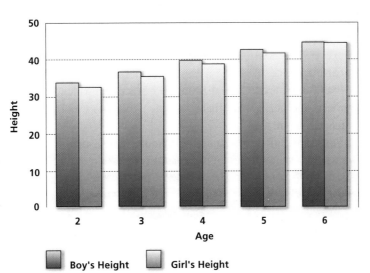

FIGURE 8-1   **GAINING HEIGHT AND WEIGHT**

The preschool years are marked by steady increases in height and weight. The figures show the median point for boys and girls at each age, in which 50 percent of children in each category are above this height or weight level and 50 percent are below it.

(*Source:* National Center for Health Statistics, 2000)

Lateralization The process whereby certain functions are located more in one hemisphere of the brain than in the other

Furthermore, profound differences in height and weight exist between children in economically developed countries and those in developing countries. The better nutrition and health care received by children in developed countries translates into significant differences in growth. For instance, the average Swedish 4-year-old is as tall as the average 6-year-old in Bangladesh (United Nations, 1990).

Differences in height and weight reflect economic factors within the United States as well. For instance, children in families whose income is below the poverty level are more likely to be short than children raised in affluent homes (D. E. Barrett & Frank, 1987; Ogden et al., 2002).

Changes in Body Shape and Structure.   If we compare the bodies of a 2-year-old and a 6-year-old, we find that the bodies vary not only in height and weight but also in shape. During the preschool years, boys and girls become less chubby and roundish and more slender. They begin to burn off some of the fat they have carried from their infancy, and they no longer have a potbellied appearance. Their arms and legs lengthen, and the size relationship between the head and the rest of the body becomes more adultlike. In fact, by the time children reach 6 years of age, their proportions are quite similar to those of adults.

The changes in size, weight, and appearance we see during the preschool years are only the tip of the iceberg. Internally, other physical changes are occurring as well. Children grow stronger as their muscle size increases and their bones become sturdier. The sense organs continue their development. For instance, the *eustachian tube* in the ear, which carries sounds from the external part of the ear to the internal part, moves from a position that is almost parallel to the ground at birth to a more angular position. This change sometimes leads to an increase in the frequency of earaches during the preschool years.

The Growing Brain

The brain grows at a faster rate than any other part of the body. Two-year-olds have brains that are about three quarters the size and weight of an adult brain. By age 5, a child's brain weighs 90 percent of the average adult brain weight. In comparison, the average 5-year-old's total body weight is just 30 percent of average adult body weight (Lowrey, 1986; Nihart, 1993; Schuster & Ashburn, 1986).

Why does the brain grow so rapidly? An important reason is an increase in the number of interconnections among cells, as we saw in Chapter 5. These interconnections allow for more complex communication between neurons—and also permit the rapid growth of the cognitive skills that we'll discuss in Chapter 9.

By the end of the preschool period, some parts of the brain have undergone particularly significant growth. For example, the *corpus callosum,* a bundle of nerve fibers that connect the two hemispheres of the brain, becomes considerably thicker, developing as many as 800 million individual fibers that help coordinate brain functioning between the two hemispheres (Branch & Heller, 1998).

Lateralization.   The two halves of the brain also begin to become increasingly differentiated and specialized. **Lateralization,** the process in which certain functions become localized more in one hemisphere than the other, becomes more pronounced during the preschool years (see Figure 8-2).

For almost all right-handed individuals and a majority of left-handed people, the left hemisphere concentrates on tasks that necessitate verbal competence, such as speaking, reading, thinking, and reasoning. The right hemisphere develops its own strengths, especially in nonverbal areas such as comprehension of spatial relationships, recognition of patterns and drawings, music, and emotional expression (Fiore & Schooler, 1998; McAuliffe & Knowlton, 2001; Zaidel, 1994).

Each of the two hemispheres also begins to process information in a slightly different manner. Whereas the left hemisphere considers information sequentially, one piece of data at a

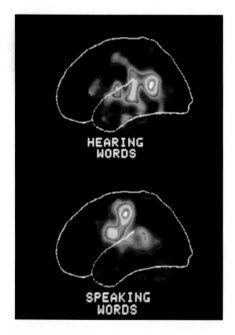

FIGURE 8-2   BRAIN ACTIVITY

This series of PET scans of the brain shows that activity in the right or left hemisphere of the brain differs according to the task in which a person is engaged. How might educators use this finding in their approach to teaching?

time, the right hemisphere processes information in a more global manner, reflecting on it as a whole (Gazzaniga, 1983; Leonard et al., 1996; Springer & Deutsch, 1989).

Despite the specialization of the hemispheres, we need to keep in mind that in most respects the two hemispheres act in tandem. They are interdependent, and the differences between the two are minor. Furthermore, the fact that each hemisphere specializes in certain tasks does not mean that it alone functions in any particular area. In fact, each hemisphere can perform most of the tasks of the other. For example, the right hemisphere does some language processing and plays an important role in language comprehension (Beeman & Chiarello, 1998; Knecht et al., 2000).

In addition, many individual differences exist in the nature of lateralization. For example, many of the 10 percent of people who are left-handed or ambidextrous (able to use both hands interchangeably) have language centered in the right hemisphere or have no specific language center (Banich & Nicholas, 1998).

Left- and Right-Brain Interactions.   In evaluating findings relating to the lateralization of the brain, it is important to keep in mind that the two halves of the brain do not work in

DEVELOPMENTAL DIVERSITY

Are Gender and Culture Related to the Brain's Structure?

Among the most controversial findings relating to the specialization of the hemispheres of the brain is evidence that lateralization is related to gender and culture. For instance, starting during the first year of life and continuing in the preschool years, boys and girls show some hemispheric differences associated with lower body reflexes and the processing of auditory information (Grattan et al., 1992; Shucard et al., 1981). Furthermore, males clearly tend to show greater lateralization of language in the left hemisphere; among females, however, language is more evenly divided between the two hemispheres (R. C. Gur et al., 1982). Such differences may help explain why—as we'll see in the next chapter—females' language development proceeds at a more rapid pace during the preschool years than males' language development.

We still don't know the source of the difference in lateralization between females and males. One explanation is genetic: that female and male brains are predisposed to function in slightly different ways. This view is supported by data suggesting that there are minor structural differences between males' and females' brains. For instance, a section of the corpus callosum is proportionally larger in women than in men. Furthermore, studies conducted among other species, such as primates, rats, and hamsters, have found size and structural differences in the brains of males and females (Hammer, 1984; Highley et al., 1999; Witelson, 1989).

Before we accept a genetic explanation for the differences between female and male brains, we need to consider an equally plausible alternative: It may be that verbal abilities emerge earlier in girls because girls receive greater encouragement for verbal skills than boys do. For instance, some evidence suggests that even as infants, girls are spoken to more than boys. Such higher levels of verbal stimulation may produce growth in particular areas of the brain that does not occur in boys. Consequently, environmental factors rather than genetic ones may lead to the gender differences we find in brain lateralization.

Even more tentative is evidence that suggests that the culture in which one is raised may be related to brain lateralization. For instance, native speakers of Japanese process information related to vowel sounds primarily in the left hemisphere of the brain. In comparison, North and South Americans and Europeans—as well as people of Japanese ancestry who learn Japanese as a second language—process vowel sounds primarily in the brain's right hemisphere.

The explanation for this cultural difference in processing of vowels seems to rest on the nature of the Japanese language. Specifically, the Japanese language allows for the expression of complex concepts using only vowel sounds. Consequently, a specific type of brain lateralization may develop while learning and using Japanese at a relatively early age (Tsunoda, 1985).

This explanation, which is speculative, does not rule out the possibility that some type of subtle genetic difference may also be at work in determining the difference in lateralization. Once again, then, we find that teasing out the relative impact of heredity and environment is a challenging task.

Myelin Protective insulation that surrounds parts of neurons

isolation from one another. The two hemispheres are interdependent, and information of no matter what sort is typically processed simultaneously, to at least some degree, by both hemispheres.

Furthermore, the brain has remarkable resiliency. If the hemisphere that specializes in a particular type of information is damaged, the other hemisphere may take up the slack. For instance, when young children suffer brain damage to the left side of the brain (which specializes in verbal processing) and initially lose language capabilities, the linguistic deficits are often not permanent. In such cases, the right side of the brain pitches in and may be able to compensate substantially for the damage to the left hemisphere (Hoptman & Davidson, 1994; Kempler et al., 1999).

The Links Between Brain Growth and Cognitive Development. Neuroscientists are just beginning to understand the ways in which brain development is related to the cognitive development that we'll consider in Chapter 9. For example, there are periods during childhood in which the brain shows unusual growth spurts, and these periods are linked to advances in cognitive abilities. One study that measured electrical activity in the brain throughout the life span found unusual spurts at between 18 and 24 months, a time when language abilities increase rapidly. Other spurts occurred around other ages when cognitive advances are particularly intense (Fischer & Rose, 1995; see Figure 8-3).

Other research has suggested that increases in **myelin,** the protective insulation that surrounds parts of neurons, may be related to preschooler's growing cognitive capabilities. For example, increases in myelin of the reticular formation, an area of the brain associated with attention and concentration, is completed by the time children are about 5. This may be associated with children's growing attention span as they approach school age. The improvement in memory that occurs during the preschool years may also be associated with increased myelin in the hippocampus, an area associated with memory (Paus et al., 1999; Rolls, 2000).

We do not yet know the direction of causality (does brain development produce cognitive advances, or do cognitive accomplishments fuel brain development?). However, it is clear that increases in our understanding of the physiological aspects of the brain will eventually have important implications for parents and teachers.

Sensory Development

The increasing development of the brain permits improvements in the senses during the preschool period. For instance, brain maturation leads to better control of eye movements

FIGURE 8-3
BRAIN GROWTH SPURT

According to one study, electrical activity in the brain has been linked to advances in cognitive abilities at various stages of life. In this graph, activity increases dramatically between 18 and 24 months, a period during which language rapidly develops.

(*Source:* Fischer & Rose, 1995)

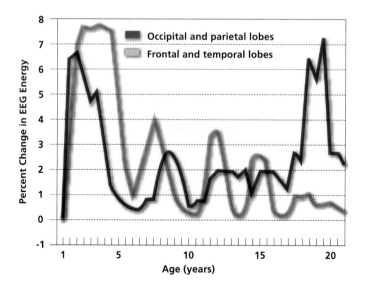

FIGURE 8-4 SENSORY DEVELOPMENT

Preschool-age children who view this odd vegetable-fruit-bird combination focus on the components that make it up. Not until they reach middle childhood do they begin to look at the figure as a whole in addition to its parts.

(*Source:* Elkind, 1978)

and focusing. Still, preschoolers' eyes are not as capable as they will be in later stages of development. Specifically, preschool-age children are unable to easily and precisely scan groupings of small letters, as is required when reading small print. Consequently, preschoolers who start to read often focus on just the initial letter of a word and guess at the rest—leading, as you might expect, to relatively frequent errors. It is not until they are approximately 6 years of age that children can effectively focus and scan. Even at this point, however, they still don't have the capabilities of adults (Aslin, 1987; Rayner & Pollatsek, 1989; Vurpillot, 1968; Willows, Kruk, & Corcos, 1993).

Preschool-age children also begin a gradual shift in the way they view objects made up of multiple parts. For instance, consider the rather unusual vegetable-fruit-bird combination shown in Figure 8-4. Rather than identifying it as a bird, as most adults do, preschool-age children see the figure in terms of the parts that make it up ("carrots" and "cherries" and "a pear"). Not until they reach middle childhood, about the age of 7 or 8, do they begin to look at the figure in terms of both its overall organization and its parts ("a bird made of fruit").

Preschoolers' judgments of objects may reflect the way in which their eyes move when perceiving figures (Zaporozhets, 1965). Until the age of 3 or 4, preschoolers devote most of their looking to the insides of two-dimensional objects they are scanning, concentrating on the internal details and largely ignoring the perimeter of the figure. In contrast, 4- and 5-year-olds begin to look more at the surrounding boundaries of the figure, and at 6 and 7 years of age, they look at the outside systematically, with far less scanning of the inside. The result is a greater awareness of the overall organization of the figure.

Of course, vision is not the only sense that improves during the preschool period. For instance, *auditory acuity,* or the sharpness of hearing, improves as well. However, because hearing is more fully developed at the start of the preschool period, the improvement is not as significant as with vision.

One area in which preschoolers' auditory acuity does show some deficits is in their ability to isolate specific sounds when many sounds are heard simultaneously (Moores & Meadow-Orlans, 1990). This deficiency may account for why some preschoolers are easily distracted by competing sounds in group situations such as classrooms.

Sleep

No matter how tired they may be, some active preschoolers find it difficult to make the transition from the excitement of the day to settling down for a night's rest. This may lead to friction between caregivers and preschoolers over bedtime. Children may object to being told to sleep, and it may take them some time before they are able to fall asleep.

Nightmare A vivid bad dream, usually occurring toward morning

Night terror An intense physiological arousal that causes a child to awaken in a state of panic

Although most children settle down fairly easily and drift off into sleep, for some sleep presents a real problem. As many as 20 to 30 percent of preschoolers experience difficulties lasting more than an hour in getting to sleep. Furthermore, they may wake in the night and call to their parents for comfort (Lozoff, Wolf, & Davis, 1985).

Once they do get to sleep, most preschoolers sleep fairly soundly through the night. However, between 10 and 50 percent of children aged 3 to 5 experience nightmares, with the frequency higher in boys than girls. **Nightmares** are vivid bad dreams, usually occurring toward morning. Although an occasional nightmare is no cause for concern, when they occur repeatedly and cause a child anxiety during waking hours, they may be indicative of a problem (Mindell & Cashman, 1995).

Night terrors produce intense physiological arousal and cause a child to wake up in an intense state of panic. After waking from a night terror, children are not easily comforted, and they cannot say why they are so disturbed and cannot recall having a bad dream. But the following morning, they cannot remember anything about the incident. Night terrors are much less frequent than nightmares, occurring in just 1 to 5 percent of children (Bootzin et al., 1993).

R E V I E W & A P P L Y

Review

- During the preschool period, the body grows steadily in height and weight, with individual differences varying widely around the average.
- Preschool children's bodies change in shape and structure, as well as size, becoming more slender and long-limbed and developing body proportions generally similar to adults'.
- The brain grows at a very fast rate during the preschool years, due largely to an increase in cell interconnections and the amount of myelin, and lateralization becomes more pronounced.
- The senses, especially vision and hearing, improve during the preschool years.

Applying Child Development

- If a child is reported to be "at the 10th percentile in height and weight," what does this mean? Is it cause for concern? How about the 90th percentile?
- *From a health care worker's perspective:* How might biology and environment combine to affect the physical growth of a child adopted as an infant from a developing country and reared in a more industrialized one?

Health and Wellness

For the average child in the United States, a runny nose due to the common cold is the most frequent—and happily, the most severe—health problem during the preschool years. In fact, the majority of children in the United States are quite healthy during this period. The major threats to health and wellness come not from disease but, as we'll see, from injuries due to accidents.

Nutrition: Eating the Right Foods

Nutritional needs change during the preschool years. Because the rate of growth during this period is slower than during infancy, preschoolers need less food to maintain their growth. The change in food consumption may be so noticeable that parents sometimes worry that their preschooler is not eating enough. However, children tend to be quite adept at maintaining an appropriate intake of food, if they are provided with nutritious meals. In fact, anxiously encouraging children to eat more than they seem to want naturally may lead them to increase their food intake beyond an appropriate level.

Ultimately, some children's food consumption can become so high as to lead to **obesity,** which is defined as a body weight more than 20 percent above the average weight for a person of a given age and height. The prevalence of obesity among older preschoolers has increased significantly over the past 20 years. (We'll discuss the causes of obesity in Chapter 11.)

How do parents ensure that their children have good nutrition without turning mealtimes into a tense, adversarial situation? In most cases, the best strategy is to make sure that a variety of foods, low in fat and high in nutritional content, is available. Foods that have a relatively high iron content are particularly important: Iron deficiency anemia, which causes chronic fatigue, is one of the prevalent nutritional problems in developed countries such as the United States. High-iron foods include dark green vegetables (such as broccoli), whole grains, and some kinds of meat (Ranade, 1993).

Of course, preschool children, like adults, will not find all foods equally appealing, and children should be given the opportunity to develop their own natural preferences. As long as their overall diet is adequate, no single food is indispensable.

Providing preschoolers with a variety of foods helps ensure good nutrition.

Minor Illnesses of Preschoolers

The average preschooler has seven or eight minor colds and other minor respiratory illnesses in each of the years from ages 3 to 5 (Denny & Clyde, 1983). Although the sniffles and coughs that are the symptoms of such illnesses are certainly distressing to children, the unpleasantness is usually not severe, and the illnesses usually last only a few days.

Actually, such minor illnesses may offer some unexpected benefits: Not only may they help children build up immunity to more severe illnesses to which they may be exposed in the future, but they may also provide some emotional benefits. Specifically, some researchers argue that minor illness permits children to understand their bodies better. It may also permit them to learn coping skills that will help them deal more effectively with more severe diseases in the future. Furthermore, it gives them the ability to understand better what others who are sick are going through. This ability to put oneself in another's shoes, known as empathy, may teach children to be more sympathetic and better caretakers (Kalish, 1996; Parmelee, 1986; G. E. A. Solomon & Cassimatis, 1999).

Major Illnesses

The preschool years were not always a period of relatively good health. Before the discovery of vaccines and the routine immunization of children, the preschool period was a dangerous time. Even today, this period is risky in many parts of the world, as well as in certain lower socioeconomic segments of the U.S. population. In fact, probably because of a combination of the lack of a national health care policy and complacency on the part of government officials, the proportion of children immunized in the United States has fallen during some portions of the last two decades—at the same time as it has been rising in many third-world countries (B. C. Williams, 1990).

Why does the United States, the richest nation in the world, provide less than ideal health care for its children? Culture provides a major part of the answer. The U.S. cultural tradition is that children are the complete responsibility of their parents, not of the government or of other individuals. What this means is that socioeconomic factors prevent some children from getting good health care and that members of minority groups, which tend to have less disposable income, suffer from inferior care (see Figure 8-5).

In other cultures, however, child rearing is regarded more as a shared, collective responsibility. Until the United States gives greater priority to the health of its children, the country will continue to lag behind in the effectiveness of its child care (Clinton, 1996).

Obesity A body weight more than 20 percent higher than the average weight for a person of a given age and height

BECOMING AN INFORMED CONSUMER OF DEVELOPMENT

Keeping Preschoolers Healthy

There's no way around it: Even the healthiest preschooler occasionally gets sick. Social interactions with others ensure that illnesses are going to be passed from one child to another. However, some diseases are preventable, and others can be minimized if simple precautions are taken:

- Preschoolers should eat a well-balanced diet containing the proper nutrients, particularly foods with sufficient protein. (The recommended energy intake for children aged 2 to 4 is about 1,300 calories a day; for those aged 4 to 6, it is around 1,700 calories a day.) Because preschoolers' stomachs are small, they may need to eat as often as five to seven times a day.

- Children should get as much sleep as they wish. Being run-down from lack of either nutrition or sleep makes children more susceptible to illness.

- Children should avoid contact with others who are ill. Although they may not understand the concept of germs and contagion (Solomon & Cassimatis, 1999), children should be told to wash their hands after playing with other kids who are obviously sick.

- Ensure that children follow an appropriate schedule of immunizations. As illustrated in Table 8-1, current recommendations are that a child should have received nine different vaccines and other preventive medicines in five to seven separate visits to the doctor.

- Finally, if a child does get ill, remember this: Minor illnesses during childhood sometimes provide immunity to more serious illnesses later on.

TABLE 8-1 RECOMMENDED CHILDHOOD IMMUNIZATION SCHEDULE

Vaccines are listed under routinely recommended ages. Bars indicate range of recommended ages for immunization. Any dose not given at the recommended age should be given as a "catch-up" immunization at any subsequent visit when indicated and feasible. Ovals indicate vaccines to be given if previously recommended doses were missed or given earlier than the recommended minimum age.

| Vaccine | Birth | Age in Months | | | | | | | | Age in Years | | |
		1	2	4	6	12	15	18	24	4–6	11–12	14–18
Hepatitis B		Hep B #1										
			Hep B #2			Hep B #3					Hep B	
Diphtheria, tetanus, pertussis			DTaP	DTaP	DTaP		DTaP			DTaP	Td	
H. influenzae, type b			Hib	Hib	Hib	Hib						
Inactivated polio			IPV	IPV		IPV				IPV		
Pneumococcal conjugate			PCV	PCV	PCV	PCV						
Measles, mumps, rubella						MMR				MMR	MMR	
Varicella						Var					Var	
Hepatitis A										Hep A—in selected areas		

Approved by the Advisory Committee on Immunization Practices, the American Academy of Pediatrics, and the American Academy of Family Physicians. For additional information about the vaccines listed here, visit the National Immunization Program home page at www.cdc.gov/nip or call the National Immunization Hotline at (800) 232-2522 (English) or (800) 232-0233 (Spanish). (*Source:* American Academy of Pediatrics, 2000)

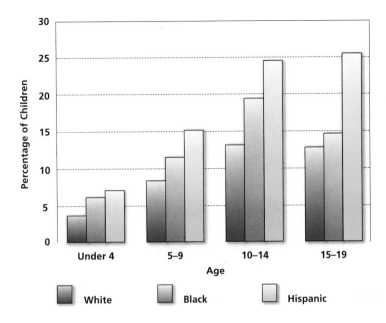

FIGURE 8-5   CHILDREN WITH NO PHYSICIAN VISITS IN THE PAST YEAR

In every age group, more black and Hispanic children than white children did not have a single visit to a physician during the previous year. From a social worker's perspective, what could you do to help minority children have better access to health care?

(*Source:* Health Resources and Services Administration, 2001)

Cancer and AIDS.   The most frequent major illness to strike preschoolers is cancer, particularly in the form of leukemia. Leukemia causes the bone marrow to produce an excessive amount of white blood cells, inducing severe anemia and, potentially, death. Although just two decades ago a diagnosis of leukemia was the equivalent of a death sentence, today the story is quite different. Due to advances in treatment, more than 70 percent of victims of childhood leukemia survive (American Cancer Society, 1993).

One childhood disease that presents a more discouraging picture is childhood AIDS, or acquired immune deficiency syndrome. Children with this disease face many difficulties. For instance, even though there is virtually no risk of spreading the disease through everyday contact, children with AIDS may be shunned by others. Furthermore, because their parents may suffer from the disease themselves—children with AIDS typically have contracted the disease prenatally from their mothers—there are often severe disruptions in the family due to a parent's death. On the other hand, the number of cases of AIDS in children is declining due to increasing use of drugs that reduce prenatal transmission from mothers to children (Centers for Disease Control and Prevention, 1997; Frenkel & Gaur, 1994).

Reactions to Hospitalization.   For ill preschoolers who must spend time in the hospital, the experience is quite difficult. The most frequent reaction of 2- to 4-year-olds is anxiety, most typically brought about by the separation from their parents. At slightly older ages, preschoolers may become upset because they interpret their hospitalization, on some level, as desertion or rejection by their family. Their anxiety may result in the development of new fears, such as fear of the dark or of hospital staff (S. E. Taylor, 1991).

One of the ways that hospitals deal with the anxieties of young patients is to allow a parent to stay for lengthy periods of time with the child or even, in some cases, permitting parents to spend the night on a cot in the child's room. But it does not have to be a parent who can alleviate a child's fears; research has shown that assigning children a "substitute mother," a nurse or other care provider who is supportive and nurturing, can go a long way toward reducing children's concerns (Branstetter, 1969).

Emotional Illness.   Although physical illness is typically a minor problem during the preschool years, an increasing number of children are being treated with drugs for emotional disorders. In fact, the use of drugs such as antidepressants and stimulants doubled or even tripled between 1991 and 1995 (see Figure 8-6).

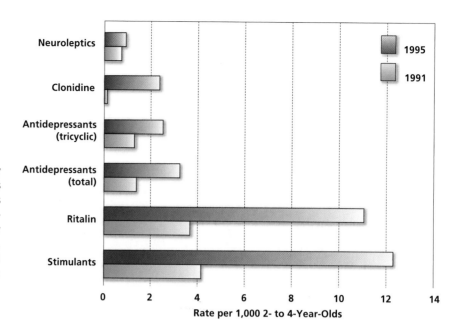

FIGURE 8-6   NUMBERS OF PRESCHOOL CHILDREN TAKING MEDICATION FOR BEHAVIORAL PROBLEMS

Although there is no clear explanation why the use of stimulants and antidepressants has increased among children, some experts believe medication is being used as a quick-fix solution for behavior problems that may in fact be normal difficulties in growing up. From an educator's perspective, how would you go about determining the extent of a behavioral problem in a child?

(*Source:* Zito et al., 2000)

It is not clear why the incidence of emotional illness has skyrocketed. Rather than reflecting an actual increase, some experts believe that parents and preschool teachers may be seeking a quick fix for behavior problems that may in fact represent normal difficulties (Colino, 2002; Pear, 2000; Zito et al., 2000).

Injuries: Playing It Safe

The greatest risk that preschoolers face comes not from illness or nutritional problems but from accidents: Children have twice the chance of dying from an injury than from an illness before the age of 10. In fact, children in the United States have a 1-in-3 likelihood every year of receiving an injury that requires medical attention (National Safety Council, 1989).

The danger of injuries during the preschool years is in part a result of high levels of physical activity. A 3-year-old might think that it is perfectly reasonable to climb on an unsteady chair to get something that is out of reach, and a 4-year-old might enjoy holding on to a low tree branch and swinging her legs up and down. At the same time, children lack the judgment to know that their activities may hold some danger, and they are less likely than older children to be careful.

Accident Risk.   In fact, some children are more apt to take risks than others, and such preschoolers are more likely to be injured than their more cautious peers. Boys, who are both more active than girls and tend to take more risks, have a higher rate of injuries. Ethnic differences, probably due to differences in cultural norms about how closely children need to be supervised, can also be seen in accident rates. Asian American children in the United States, who tend to be supervised particularly strictly by their parents, have one of the lowest accident rates for children. Economic factors also play a role. Children raised under conditions of poverty in urban areas, whose inner-city neighborhoods may contain more hazards than more affluent areas, are twice as likely to die of injuries than children living in affluence.

The range of dangers that preschoolers face is wide. Injuries come from falls, burns from stoves and fires, drowning in bathtubs indoors and standing water outdoors, and suffocation in places such as abandoned refrigerators. Auto accidents also account for a large number of injuries.

Lead Poisoning Risk.   Children also face injuries from poisonous substances such as household cleaners and lead paint. For example, 14 million children are at risk for *lead poisoning* due to exposure to potentially toxic levels of lead. Although there are stringent restrictions on the

Preschoolers' high level of physical activity and their curiosity increase the risk of injury.

amount of lead permitted in paint and gasoline, lead is found on painted walls and window frames—particularly in older homes; in gasoline; in ceramics; in lead-soldered pipes; and in trace amounts in dust and water. People who live in areas of substantial air pollution due to automobile and truck traffic may also be exposed to high levels of lead. The U.S. Department of Health and Human Services has called lead poisoning the most hazardous health threat to children under the age of 6 (Duncan & Brooks-Gunn, 2000; Lanphear, 1998).

Poor children are particularly susceptible to lead poisoning, and the results of poisoning tend to be worse for them than for children from more affluent families. Children living in poverty are more apt to reside in housing that contains peeling and chipping lead paint or to live near heavily trafficked urban areas with high levels of air pollution. At the same time, many families living in poverty may be less stable and unable to provide consistent opportunities for intellectual stimulation that might serve to offset some of the cognitive problems caused by the poisoning (P. G. Harvey et al., 1984; Tesman & Hills, 1994).

Even tiny amounts of lead can permanently harm children. Exposure to lead has been linked to lower intelligence, problems in verbal and auditory processing, and both hyperactivity and distractibility. High lead levels have also been linked to higher levels of antisocial behavior, including aggression and delinquency in school-age children (see Figure 8-7). At yet higher levels of exposure, lead poisoning results in illness and death (Y. Finkelstein, Markowitz, & Rosen, 1998; Leviton et al., 1993; Needleman et al., 1996).

Reducing the Risks.   Although we can never completely prevent exposure to dangerous substances such as lead, accidents, and injuries, the risks can be reduced. Poisons, medicines, household cleaners, and other potentially dangerous substances can be removed from the house or kept under lock and key, and parents can strap their children into car seats whenever they take them along for a ride. Because drowning can occur in just a few inches of water and in a short time, young children should never be left unattended in the bathtub. Finally, children can be taught basic safety rules from the earliest age. Ultimately, adults need to concentrate on "injury control" rather than focusing on preventing "accidents," which implies a random act in which no one is at fault (Garbarino, 1988; J. R. Mathews et al., 1987).

Child Abuse and Psychological Maltreatment: The Grim Side of Family Life

In one sense, she was just another statistic: Elisa Izquierdo—born 1989, died 1995. But her death put a face on what some experts call a public health epidemic of child abuse—and a system of protection that often fails those most in need.

The facts of Elisa's case are nothing less than horrifying. Conceived in a homeless shelter, she was probably a victim of abuse from the earliest years of her life. Her mother, estranged from her father, was a crack cocaine addict who somehow became convinced that her daughter had been put under a spell and harbored evil spirits. With twisted logic, Elisa's mother tried to batter the supposed evil out of Elisa through years of beatings and violations of every part of her body. The abuse culminated one November evening with her mother forcing Elisa to eat feces, mopping the floor with her head, and throwing her against a concrete wall. When Elisa was found by authorities, there was no part of her body that was not cut or bruised. (N. Bernstein & Bruni, 1995; van Biema, 1995)

At least five children are killed by their parents or caregivers every day, and 140,000 others are physically injured every year. Overall, each year more than 3 million children in the United States are the victims of **child abuse,** the physical or psychological maltreatment or neglect of children. Violence claims the lives of at least 2,000 children annually. The abuse takes several forms, ranging from actual physical abuse to psychological mistreatment (U.S. Advisory Board on Child Abuse and Neglect, 1995; Briere et al., 1996; Children's Bureau, 1998; English, 1998; see Figure 8-8).

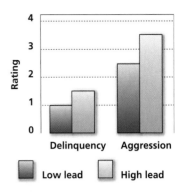

FIGURE 8-7   THE CONSEQUENCES OF LEAD POISONING

High levels of lead have been linked to higher levels of antisocial behavior, including aggression and delinquency in school-age children. What roles can social workers and health care workers play in preventing lead poisoning among children?

(*Source:* Needleman et al., 1996)

The urban environment in which poor children often live make them especially susceptible to lead poisoning.

Child abuse   The physical or psychological maltreatment or neglect of children

FIGURE 8-8   *CHILD ABUSE*

Although neglect is the most frequent form of abuse, other types of abuse are also prevalent. How can caregivers and educators, as well as health care and social workers, take the lead in identifying child abuse before it becomes serious?

(*Source:* Health Resources and Services Administration, 2001)

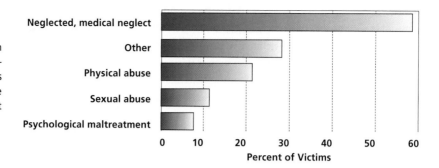

Physical Abuse.   Why does physical abuse occur? Most parents certainly don't intend to abuse their children. In fact, most parents who abuse their children later express bewilderment and dismay at their own behavior.

One reason for child abuse is the vague demarcation between permissible and impermissible forms of physical violence. Societal folklore says that spanking is not merely acceptable but often necessary and desirable. For example, one survey found that almost half of mothers with children under 4 years of age had spanked their child in the previous week, and close to 20 percent of mothers believe it is appropriate to spank a child less than 1 year of age. Furthermore, there are some group differences in perceptions of spanking: males and African Americans show more support for spanking than females and whites. Furthermore, most people believe that spanking is more appropriate for preschool-age children than for older children (Flynn, 1998; Socolar & Stein, 1995, 1996).

Unfortunately, the line between "spanking" and "beating" is not clear, and spankings begun in anger can escalate easily into abuse. Furthermore, despite common wisdom, the use of physical punishment of any sort is *not* recommended by child care experts, according to the American Academy of Pediatrics (1998). (For a guide to when punishment crosses the line into abuse, see Table 8-2.)

Many other societies do not differentiate between acceptable violence and abuse as we do in the United States. For instance, Sweden outlaws *any* form of physical punishment directed

---

 TABLE 8-2   WHAT ARE THE WARNING SIGNS OF CHILD ABUSE?

Because child abuse is typically a secret crime, identifying the victims of abuse is particularly difficult. Still, there are several signs that indicate that a child is the victim of violence (Robbins, 1990):

- Visible, serious injuries that have no reasonable explanation

- Bite or choke marks

- Burns from cigarettes or immersion in hot water

- Feelings of pain for no apparent reason

- Fear of adults or care providers

- Inappropriate attire in warm weather (long sleeves, long pants, high-necked garments)—possibly to conceal injuries to the neck, arms, and legs

- Extreme behavior—highly aggressive, extremely passive, or extremely withdrawn

- Fear of physical contact

If you suspect that a child is a victim of aggression, it is your responsibility to act. Call your local police or the department of social services in your city or state, or call the National Child Abuse Hotline in Washington, DC, at (800) 422-4453. Talk to a teacher or a member of the clergy. Remember, by acting decisively, you can literally save someone's life.

toward a child. In many other countries, such as China, social norms work against the use of physical punishment, and its use is rare. In contrast, the values of personal freedom and responsibility prevalent in the United States help foster a social climate in which high levels of aggression toward children occur (Durrant, 1999; Kessen, 1979).

Child Abuse and Privacy of Child Care.   Another factor that leads to high rates of abuse is the privacy with which child care is conducted in Western societies. Unlike cultures in which child rearing is seen as the joint responsibility of several people and even society as a whole, in most Western cultures—and particularly in the United States—children are raised in private, isolated households. Furthermore, parents of abused children often have unrealistically high expectations regarding children's abilities to be compliant at a particular age. Their children's failure to meet these unrealistic expectations may provoke abuse (L. Peterson, 1994).

Finally, abuse inflicted on children is often associated with violence that the abusers themselves have suffered as children. According to the **cycle-of-violence hypothesis,** the abuse and neglect that children suffer predispose them as adults to abuse and neglect their own children (Maxfield & Widom, 1996).

The cycle-of-violence hypothesis suggests that victims of abuse have learned from their childhood experiences that violence is an appropriate and acceptable form of discipline. Violence is consequently perpetuated from one generation to another, as each generation learns to behave abusively through its participation in an abusive, violent family (Ney, Fung, & Wickett, 1993; Straus & Gelles, 1990).

Although there are many cases in which abusive parents have themselves suffered abuse as children, being abused as a child does not inevitably lead to abuse of one's own children. In fact, statistics show that only about one third of people who were abused or neglected as children abuse their own children; the remaining two thirds of people abused as children do not turn out to be child abusers (Cicchetti, 1996; Strauss & McCord, 1998).

Although child abuse can occur in any household regardless of economic well-being or the social status of the parents, it is most frequent in families living in stressful environments. Conditions of poverty, single-parent households, and families with higher than average levels of marital conflict create such environments. Stepfathers are more likely to commit abuse against stepchildren than genetic fathers are against their own offspring. Child abuse is also related to the presence of violence between spouses (Emery & Laumann-Billings, 1998; Kotch et al., 1999).

Children with certain characteristics are more prone to be the victims of child abuse. Abused children are more likely to be fussy, resistant to control, and not readily adaptable to new situations. Keep in mind that labeling children as being at higher risk for receiving abuse does not make them responsible for their abuse; the family members who carry out the abuse are at fault (Ammerman & Patz, 1996; Gelles & Cornell, 1990; Putnam, 1995).

Psychological Maltreatment and Child Neglect.   Children may also be the victims of psychological maltreatment. Unlike physical abuse, in which children suffer actual bodily injury and punishment, **psychological maltreatment** occurs when parents or other caregivers harm children's behavioral, cognitive, emotional, or physical functioning. Psychological maltreatment may occur through either overt behavior or neglect (S. N. Hart, Brassard, & Karlson, 1996).

For example, abusive parents may frighten, belittle, or humiliate their children, thereby intimidating and harassing them. Children may be made to feel like disappointments or failures, or they may be constantly reminded that they are a burden to their parents. Parents may tell their children that they wish they had never had children and specifically that they wish that their children had never been born. Children may be threatened with abandonment or even death. In other instances, older children may be exploited. They may be forced to seek employment and then to give their earnings to their parents.

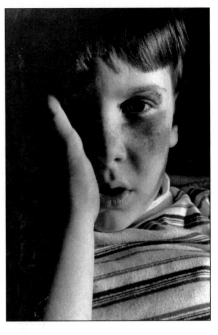

Each year, more than 3 million children in the United States are victims of child abuse.

Cycle-of-violence hypothesis The theory that abuse and neglect that children suffer predispose them as adults to abuse and neglect their own children

Psychological maltreatment Harm to children's behavioral, cognitive, emotional, or physical functioning caused by parents or other caregivers verbally, through their actions, or through neglect

In other cases of psychological maltreatment, the abuse takes the form of neglect. In **child neglect,** parents ignore their children or are emotionally unresponsive to them. In such cases, children may be given unrealistic responsibilities or may be left to fend for themselves.

No one is certain how much psychological maltreatment occurs each year because data separating psychological maltreatment from other types of abuse are not routinely gathered. However, it is clear that profound neglect that involves children who are unsupervised or uncared for is the most frequent form of psychological maltreatment (B. Hewitt, 1997).

The lack of trustworthy statistics for psychological maltreatment stems from obstacles that stand in the way of unambiguously identifying cases. Most maltreatment occurs in the privacy of people's homes. Furthermore, psychological maltreatment typically causes no physical damage, such as bruises or broken bones, to alert physicians, teachers, and other authorities. Despite the fact that some professionals—such as teachers, social workers, and health care workers—are mandated by law in some jurisdictions to report suspected abuse, many cases of psychological maltreatment are not identified because of its ambiguity.

What are the consequences of psychological maltreatment? Although some children are sufficiently resilient to survive the abuse and grow into psychologically healthy adults, in many cases, lasting damage results. For example, psychological maltreatment has been associated with low self-esteem, lying, misbehavior, and underachievement in school. In extreme cases, it can produce criminal behavior, aggression, and murder. In other instances, children who have been psychologically maltreated become depressed and even commit suicide (Leiter & Johnsen, 1997; Repetti, Taylor, & Seeman, 2002; R. C. Solomon & Serres, 1999).

Resilience: Overcoming the Odds

Not all children succumb to the mistreatment and abuse that life dishes out to them. In fact, some do surprisingly well, considering the types of problems they have encountered. What enables some children to overcome stress and trauma that may scar others for life?

Resilience refers to the ability to overcome circumstances that place a child at high risk for psychological or physical damage. Children's potentially negative reactions to difficult circumstances—such as extremes of poverty, prenatal stress, or homes that are racked with violence or other forms of social disorder—can be reduced or, in certain cases, eliminated.

According to developmental psychologist Emmy Werner (1995), resilient children have temperaments that evoke positive responses from a wide variety of caregivers. They tend to be affectionate, easygoing, and good-natured. They are easily soothed as infants, and they are able to elicit care from the most nurturant people in any environment they find themselves in. In short, because of their pleasant temperaments, they are able to evoke whatever support is present in a given setting. In a sense, then, resilient children are able to create their own environments by drawing out behavior in others that is necessary for their own development.

Similar traits are associated with resilience in older children. The most resilient school-age children are those who are socially pleasant, are outgoing, and have good communication skills. They tend to be relatively intelligent, and they are independent, feeling that they can shape their own fate and are not dependent on others or on luck (Eisenberg et al., 1997; E. E. Werner, 1993, 1995; E. E. Werner & Smith, 1992).

The characteristics of resilient children suggest ways to improve the prospects of children who are at risk from a variety of developmental threats. For instance, in addition to decreasing their exposure to factors that put them at risk in the first place, we need to increase their competence and teach them ways to deal with their situation. In fact, programs that have been successful in helping especially vulnerable children have a common thread: They provide competent and caring adult models who can teach the children problem-solving skills and help them communicate their needs to people who are in a position to help them (Heller et al., 1999; E. M. Hetherington & Blechman, 1996; Wyman et al., 1999).

Child neglect Ignoring one's children or being emotionally unresponsive to them

Resilience The ability to overcome circumstances that place a child at high risk for psychological or physical damage

CAREERS IN CHILD DEVELOPMENT

David S. Kurtz

Education: . . . . University of California, Irvine: B.S. in biology and B.A. in psychology; California State University, Fullerton: M.A. in experimental psychology; California School of Professional Psychology, Los Angeles: M.A. and Ph.D. in clinical psychology

Position : . . . . Associate director of the Childhelp Los Angeles Center

Home : . . . . Glendale, California

What is it like to pick up the phone and hear the voice of an abused child reaching out for help? David Kurtz knows.

For most of his 8 years with the Childhelp Los Angeles Center, Kurtz worked in crisis intervention. He was one of the many counselors working the phones at the National Child Abuse Hotline located at Childhelp.

Currently the associate director of the center, Kurtz still finds occasion to provide help and support via the phone lines.

"Those who call us with a child abuse issue may be the parents of an abused child, a neighbor who has witnessed child abuse, or an adult who was a victim of abuse twenty or thirty years ago," says Kurtz. "But children who call in, or people who represent them, are given priority. They are put at the front of the line.

"For younger children, the caller is usually a sibling or an adult who is representing the abused child," he says, adding that there are also occasions when a parent may call about his or her own frustrations with a very young child.

"We often explore developmental issues when parents call us," he notes. "Often we find that a significant part of parents' frustration is attributable to their unrealistic expectations of what children are capable of doing at a given age.

"An example of this is a highly frustrated woman who called us after returning from a grocery-shopping trip with her child. She had a very strong impulse to slap the child, and she was afraid she would lose control. The child kept pulling items off the shelves at the store, and she was convinced the child was doing it intentionally to upset her.

"When we asked how old the child was, she said ten months. We explained that her child was much too young to be acting intentionally in that way and that the child was not trying to get at her. Clearly, this parent was not alone. Many parents who have to deal with some sort of disciplinary issue would benefit from a better understanding of child development."

Kurtz emphasizes the importance of establishing as trusting a relationship as possible with the stressed people who are looking for help on this issue. "When people call, it's essential to build a rapport with them. The general policy at the Hotline is that the counselors do not give their names, but with children we make an exception," he says. "A child is going to be very, very scared and will be dealing with confused feelings of shame, guilt, and fear that the abuser—who is usually a close family member—is going to get into trouble."

"Often we find that a significant part of parents' frustration is attributable to their unrealistic expectations of what children are capable of doing at a given age."

Review

- Nutritional needs change during the preschool years, with children needing less food to maintain growth.

- Illness in preschoolers is generally mild, and injury presents a far greater health risk during this period than illness.

- Abuse may be physical or psychological, is associated with both social and personal factors, and can have long-term effects.

- According to the cycle-of-violence hypothesis, child abuse may be perpetuated from one generation to the next because persons who were abused as children show a tendency to be abusers as adults.

- Resilience is a personal characteristic that permits some children to avoid damage from environments of risk.

Applying Child Development

- What are some ways that increased understanding of issues relating to the physical development of preschoolers might help parents and caregivers in their care of children?

- *From a social worker's perspective:* If a society's emphasis on family privacy contributes to the prevalence of child abuse, what sorts of social policies regarding privacy do you think are appropriate? Why?

Motor Development

Anya sat in the sandbox at the park, chatting with the other parents and playing with her two children, 5-year-old Nicholai and 13-month-old Sofia. While she chatted, she kept a close eye on Sofia, who would still put sand in her mouth sometimes if she wasn't stopped. Today, however, Sofia seemed content to run the sand through her hands and try to put it into a bucket. Nicholai, meanwhile, was busy with two other boys, rapidly filling and emptying the other sand buckets to build an elaborate sand city, which they would then destroy with toy trucks.

When children of different ages gather at a playground, it's easy to see that preschool children have come a long way in their motor development since infancy. Both their gross and their fine motor skills have become increasingly fine-tuned. Sofia, for example, is still mastering putting sand into a bucket, while her brother, Nicholai, uses that skill easily as part of his larger goal of building a sand city.

Gross Motor Skills

 By the time they are 3, children have mastered a variety of skills: jumping, hopping on one foot, skipping, and running. By 4 and 5, their skills have become more refined as they have gained ever greater control over their muscles. For instance, at 4 they can throw a ball with

During the preschool years, children grow in both gross and fine motor skills.

enough accuracy that a friend can catch it, and by age 5 they can toss a ring and have it land on a peg 5 feet away. Five-year-olds can learn to ride bikes, climb ladders, and ski downhill—activities that all require considerable coordination (J. E. Clark & Humphrey, 1985). Table 8-3 summarizes major gross motor skills that emerge during the preschool years.

Activity Level.   The advances in gross motor skills may be related to brain development and myelination of neurons in areas of the brain related to balance and coordination. Another reason motor skills develop at such a rapid clip during the preschool years is that children spend a great deal of time practicing them. During this period, the general level of activity is extraordinarily high: Preschoolers seem to be perpetually in motion. In fact, the activity level is higher at age 3 than at any other point in the entire life span (W. O. Eaton & Yu, 1989; Poest et al., 1990).

Despite generally high activity levels, there are also significant variations between children. Some differences are related to inherited temperament. Due to temperamental factors, children who are unusually active during infancy tend to continue in this way during the preschool years, while those who are relatively docile during infancy generally remain fairly docile during those years. Furthermore, monozygotic (identical) twins tend to show more

TABLE 8-3 MAJOR GROSS MOTOR SKILLS IN EARLY CHILDHOOD		
3-Year-Olds	**4-Year-Olds**	**5-Year-Olds**
Cannot turn or stop suddenly or quickly	Have more effective control of stopping, starting, and turning	Can start, turn, and stop effectively in games
Can jump a distance of 15 to 24 inches	Can jump a distance of 24 to 33 inches	Can make a running jump of 28 to 36 inches
Can ascend a stairway unaided, alternating the feet	Can descend a long stairway alternating the feet, if supported	Can descend a long stairway alternating the feet
Can hop, using an irregular series of jumps with some variations added	Can hop four to six steps on one foot	Can easily hop a distance of 16 feet
(*Source:* Corbin, 1973)		

similar activity levels than dizygotic twins, a fact that suggests the importance of genetics in determining activity level (Goldsmith & Gottesman, 1981).

Of course, genetics is not the sole determinant of preschoolers' activity levels. Environmental factors, such as a parent's style of discipline and, more broadly, a particular culture's view of what is appropriate and inappropriate behavior, also play a role. Some cultures are fairly lenient in allowing preschoolers to play vigorously, while others are considerably more restrictive.

Ultimately, a combination of genetic and environmental factors determines just how active a child will be. But the preschool period generally represents the most active time of the child's entire life.

Gender Differences in Gross Motor Skills.   Girls and boys differ in several aspects of gross motor coordination. In part, this difference is produced by variations in muscle strength, which is somewhat greater in boys than in girls. For instance, boys can typically throw a ball better and jump higher. Furthermore, boys' overall activity levels are generally greater than girls' (W. O. Eaton & Yu, 1989; Pelligrini & Smith, 1998).

Although they are not as strong as boys and have lower overall activity levels, girls generally surpass boys in tasks that involve the coordination of their arms and legs. For instance, at the age of 5, girls are better than boys at performing jumping jacks and balancing on one foot (Cratty, 1979).

The differences between preschoolers on some tasks involving gross motor skills are due to a number of factors. In addition to genetically determined differences in strength and activity levels, social factors likely play a role. As we will discuss further in Chapter 10, gender increasingly determines the sorts of activities that are seen by society as appropriate for girls and appropriate for boys. For instance, if the games that are considered acceptable for preschool boys tend to involve gross motor skills more than the games deemed appropriate for girls, boys will have more practice in gross motor activities and ultimately be more proficient in them than girls (Golombok & Fivush, 1994; Yee & Brown, 1994).

Regardless of their gender, however, children typically show significant improvement in their gross motor skills during the preschool years. Such improvement permits them by the time they are 5 to climb ladders, play follow-the-leader, and snowboard with relative ease.

Fine Motor Skills

At the same time that gross motor skills are developing, children are progressing in their ability to use fine motor skills, which involve smaller, more delicate body movements. Fine motor skills encompass such varied activities as using a fork and spoon, cutting with scissors, tying one's shoelaces, and playing the piano.

The skills involved in fine motor movements require a good deal of practice, as anyone knows who has watched a 4-year-old struggling painstakingly to copy letters of the alphabet. Yet fine motor skills show clear developmental patterns (see Table 8-4). At the age of 3, children can undo their clothes when they go to the bathroom, they can put a simple jigsaw puzzle together, and they can fit blocks of different shapes into matching holes. However, they do not show much polish in accomplishing such tasks; for instance, they may try to force puzzle pieces into place.

By the age of 4, their fine motor skills are considerably better. For example, they can fold paper into triangular designs and print their name with a crayon. And by the time they are 5, most children are able to hold and manipulate a thin pencil properly.

Another aspect of muscular skills—one that parents of toddlers often find most problematic—is bowel and bladder control. As we discuss in the *From Research to Practice* box, the timing and nature of toilet training is a controversial issue.

TABLE 8-4	FINE MOTOR SKILLS IN EARLY CHILDHOOD	
3-Year-Olds	**4-Year-Olds**	**5-Year-Olds**
Cuts paper	Folds paper into triangles	Folds paper into halves and quarters
Pastes using finger	Prints name	Draws triangle, rectangle, circle
Builds bridge with three blocks	Strings beads	Uses crayons effectively
Draws ○ and +	Copies X	Creates clay objects
Draws doll	Builds bridge with five blocks	Copies letters
Pours liquid from pitcher without spilling	Pours from various containers	Copies two short words
Completes simple jigsaw puzzle	Opens and positions clothespins	

Handedness: Separating Righties From Lefties

How do preschoolers decide which hand to hold the pencil in as they work on their copying and other fine motor skills? For many, their choice was established soon after birth.

By the end of the preschool years, most children show a clear preference for the use of one hand over the other—the development of **handedness.** Actually, some signals of future handedness are seen early in infancy, when infants may show a preference for one side of the body over the other. By the age of 7 months, some infants seem to favor one hand by grabbing more with it than the other. Many children, however, show no preference until the end of the preschool years (Michel, 1981; D. S. Ramsay, 1980; Saudino & McManus, 1998).

By the age of 5, most children display a clear tendency to use one hand over the other, with 90 percent being right-handed and 10 percent left-handed. More boys than girls are left-handed.

Much speculation has been devoted to the meaning of handedness, fueled in part by longstanding myths about the sinister nature of left-handedness. (The word *sinister* itself is derived from a Latin word meaning "on the left.") In Islamic cultures, for instance, the left hand is generally used when going to the toilet, and it is considered uncivilized to serve food with that hand. In Christian art, portrayals of the devil often show him as left-handed.

However, there is no scientific basis for myths that suggest that there is something wrong with being left-handed. In fact, some evidence exists that left-handedness may be associated with certain advantages. For example, a study of 100,000 students who took the Scholastic Assessment Test (SAT) showed that 20 percent in the highest-scoring category were left-handed, double the proportion of left-handed people in the general population. Such gifted individuals as Michelangelo, Leonardo da Vinci, Benjamin Franklin, and Pablo Picasso were left-handed (B. Bower, 1985).

Although some educators of the past tried to force left-handed children to use the right hand, particularly when learning to write, thinking has changed. Most teachers now encourage children to use whichever hand they prefer. Still, most left-handed people will agree that the design of desks, scissors, and most other everyday objects favors the right-handed. In fact, the world is so "right biased" that it may prove to be a dangerous place for lefties: Left-handed

Handedness A clear preference for the use of one hand over the other

○— **FROM RESEARCH TO PRACTICE** —○

Potty Wars: When—and How—Should Children Be Toilet-Trained?

Ann Wright, of University Park, Maryland, woke up on a sweltering night in June at 3 a.m., her head spinning as she reenacted the previous day's parenting trauma: She and her husband, Oliver, had told their 4-year-old daughter, Elizabeth, on Thursday night that it was time for her to stop using her pull-up training pants. For the next 18½ hours, the girl had withheld her urine, refusing to use the toilet.

"We had been talking to her for months about saying goodbye to the pull-ups, and she seemed ready," says Wright. "But on the day of the big break she refused to sit on the toilet. Two hours before she finally went, she was crying and constantly moving, clearly uncomfortable."

Eventually the child wet herself. (Gerhardt, 1999)

Few child care issues raise so much concern among parents as toilet training. And on few issues are there so many opposing opinions from experts and laypersons. Often the various viewpoints are played out in the media and even take on political overtones. On the one hand, for instance, the well-known pediatrician T. Berry Brazelton (1997; Brazelton et al., 1999) suggests a flexible approach to

Among the signs that a child is ready to give up diapers is evidence that he or she is able to follow directions and can get to the bathroom and undress on his or her own.

toilet training, advocating that it be put off until the child shows signs of readiness. On the other hand, psychologist John Rosemond, known primarily for his media advocacy of a conservative, traditional stance to child rearing, argues for a more rigid approach, saying that toilet training should be done early and quickly.

What is clear is that the age at which toilet training takes place has been rising over the past few decades. For example, in 1957, fully 92 percent of children were toilet trained by the age of 18 months. In 1999, only 25 percent were toilet trained at that age, and just 60 percent at 36 months. Two percent were still not toilet-trained at the age of 4 (Goode, 1999).

The current guidelines of the American Academy of Pediatrics support Brazelton's position, suggesting that there is no single time to begin toilet training and that training should begin only when children show that they are ready. Children have no bladder or bowel control until the age of 12 months and only slight control for 6 months after that. Although some children show signs of readiness for toilet training between 18 and 24 months, some are not ready until 30 months or older (American Academy of Pediatrics, 1999b; Stadtler, Gorski, & Brazelton, 1999).

The signs of readiness include staying dry at least 2 hours at a time during the day or waking up dry after naps; regular and predictable bowel movements; an indication, through facial expressions or words, that urination or a bowel movement is about to occur; the ability to follow simple directions; the ability to get to the bathroom and undress alone; discomfort with soiled diapers; asking to use the toilet or potty chair; and the desire to wear underwear. Furthermore, children must be ready not only physically but also emotionally, and if they show strong signs of resistance to toilet training, like Elizabeth in our example, toilet training should be put off (American Academy of Pediatrics, 1999b).

Even after children are toilet-trained during the day, it often takes months or years before they are able to achieve control at night. Around three quarters of boys and most girls are able to stay dry after the age of 5 years.

Complete toilet training eventually occurs in almost all children as they mature and attain greater control over their muscles. However, delayed toilet training can be a cause for concern if a child is upset about it or if it makes the child a target of ridicule from siblings or peers. In such cases, several types of treatments have proved effective. In particular, treatments in which children are rewarded for staying dry or are awakened by a battery device that senses when they have wet the bed are often effective (American Psychiatric Association, 1994; Wagner, Smith, & Norris, 1988).

people have more accidents and are at greater risk of dying younger than right-handed people (Coren & Halpern, 1991; Ellis & Engh, 2000).

Art: The Picture of Development

It is a basic feature of many kitchens: the refrigerator covered with recent art created by the children of the house. Yet the art that children create is far more important than mere kitchen decoration. Developmentalists suggest that art plays an important role in honing fine motor skills, as well as in several other aspects of development.

At the most basic level, the production of art involves practice with tools such as paint-brushes, crayons, pencils, and markers. As preschoolers learn to manipulate these tools, they gain motor control skills that will help them as they learn to write.

But art also teaches several important lessons. For example, children learn the importance of planning, restraint, and self-correction. When 3-year-olds pick up a brush, they tend to swish it across the page, with little thought of the ultimate product. By the time they are 5, however, children spend more time thinking about and planning the final product. They are more likely to have a goal in mind when they start out, and when they are finished, they examine their creation to see how successful they have been. Older children will also produce the same artwork over and over, seeking to overcome their previous errors and improve the final product.

According to developmental psychologist Howard Gardner (1980), the rough, unformed art of preschoolers represents the equivalent of linguistic babbling in infants. He argues that the random marks that young preschoolers make contain all the building blocks of more sophisticated creations that will be produced later.

Other researchers suggest that children's art proceeds through a series of stages during the preschool years (Kellogg, 1970). The first is the *scribbling* stage, in which the end product appears to be random scrawls across a paper. But this is not the case: Instead, scribbles can be categorized, consisting of 20 distinct types, such as horizontal lines and zigzags.

The *shape* stage, which is reached around the age of 3, is marked by the appearance of shapes such as squares and circles. In this stage, children draw shapes of various sorts, as well as X's and plus signs. After reaching this stage, they soon move into the *design* stage, which is characterized by the ability to combine more than one simple shape into a more complex one.

Finally, children enter the *pictorial* stage between the ages of 4 and 5. At this point, drawings begin to approximate recognizable objects (see Figure 8-9).

The depiction of recognizable real-world objects, known as representational art, may appear to be a substantial advance over previous art, and adults often strongly encourage its

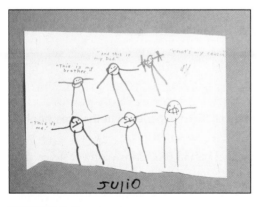 

FIGURE 8-9   ART OF DEVELOPMENT

As preschoolers enter the pictorial stage between the ages of 4 and 5, their drawings begin to approximate recognizable objects.

creation. However, in some respects this change to representational art is regrettable, for it marks a shift in focus away from an interest in form and design. Because form and design are important and in some ways essential, a focus on representation may ultimately have disadvantages. As the great artist Pablo Picasso once remarked, "It has taken me a whole lifetime to learn to draw like children" (Winner, 1986, 1989).

Review

- Gross motor development advances rapidly during the preschool years, a time of uniquely high activity levels.

- Gender differences in gross motor development emerge during this period, with boys excelling in activities involving strength and girls in those involving coordination. Fine motor skills, producing smaller, more delicate movements and requiring practice, begin to advance in this period.

- By the end of the preschool years, most children have developed handedness.

- The development of artistic expression follows a fairly regular pattern, progressing through the scribbling, shape, design, and pictorial stages.

Applying Child Development

- Do you think environmental influences can overcome the strength advantages of boys and the coordination advantages of girls? Would this be desirable? Why or why not?

- How might culture influence activity level in children? *From an educator's perspective:* What might the long-term effects be on children influenced in this way?

- **What changes in the body and the brain do children experience in the preschool years?**

- Children's physical growth during the preschool period proceeds steadily. Differences in height and weight reflect individual differences, gender, and economic status.

- In addition to gaining height and weight, the body of the preschooler undergoes changes in shape and structure. Children grow more slender, and their bones and muscles strengthen.

- Brain growth is particularly rapid during the preschool years, with the number of inter-connections among cells and the amount of myelin around neurons increasing greatly. Through the process of lateralization, the two halves of the brain begin to specialize in somewhat different functions. However, despite lateralization, the two hemispheres function as a unit and in fact differ only slightly.

- There is some evidence that the structure of the brain differs by gender and culture. For instance, boys and girls show some hemispheric differences in lower body reflexes, the processing of auditory information, and language. Furthermore, some studies suggest that such structural features as the processing of vowel sounds may show cultural differences.

- Brain development permits improvements in sensory processing during the preschool years, including better control of eye movements and focusing and improved visual perception and auditory acuity.

- Although most children sleep well at night, sleep presents real difficulties for some. Sleep-related problems include nightmares and night terrors.

○ **What are the nutritional needs of preschool children, and what causes obesity?**

- Preschoolers need less food than they did in the early years. Primarily, they require balanced nutrition. If parents and caregivers provide a good variety of healthful foods, children will generally achieve an appropriate intake of nutrients.

- Obesity is caused by both genetic and environmental factors. One strong environmental influence appears to be parents and caregivers, who may substitute their own interpretations of their children's food needs for the children's internal tendencies and controls.

○ **What threats to their health and wellness do preschool children experience?**

- Children in the preschool years generally experience only minor illnesses, but they are susceptible to some dangerous diseases, including childhood leukemia and AIDS.

- In the economically developed world, immunization programs have largely controlled most life-threatening diseases during these years. This is not the case, however, in economically disadvantaged sectors of the world.

- Preschool children are at greater risk from accidents than from illness or nutritional problems. The danger is due partly to children's high activity levels and partly to environmental hazards, such as lead poisoning.

○ **What are child abuse and psychological maltreatment, what factors contribute to them, and can anything be done about them?**

- Child abuse may take physical forms, but it may also be more subtle. Psychological mal-treatment may involve neglect of parental responsibilities, emotional negligence, intimidation or humiliation, unrealistic demands and expectations, or exploitation of children.

- Child abuse occurs with alarming frequency in the United States and other countries, especially in stressful home environments. Firmly held notions regarding family privacy and norms that support the use of physical punishment in child rearing contribute to the high rate of abuse.

- The cycle-of-violence hypothesis points to the likelihood that persons who were abused as children may turn into abusers as adults.

- Resilience is a personal characteristic that permits some children at risk for abuse to overcome their dangerous situations. Resilient children tend to be affectionate and easygoing, able to elicit a nurturant response from people in their environment.

⦿ **In what ways do children's gross and fine motor skills develop during the preschool years?**

- Gross motor skills advance rapidly during the preschool years, a time when the activity levels of children are at their peak. Genetic and cultural factors determine how active a given child will be.

- During these years, gender differences in gross motor skill levels begin to emerge clearly, with boys displaying greater strength and activity levels and girls showing greater coordination of arms and legs. Both genetic and social factors probably play a role in determining these differences.

- Fine motor skills also develop during the preschool years, with increasingly delicate movements being mastered through extensive practice.

⦿ **How do handedness and artistic expression develop during these years?**

- Handedness asserts itself, with the great majority of children showing a clear preference for the right hand by the end of the preschool years.

- The meaning of handedness is unclear, but the right-handed have certain practical advantages because of the "right bias" of the world.

- The development of artistic expression progresses during the preschool years through the scribbling, shape, design, and pictorial stages. Artistic expression entails the development of important related skills, including planning, restraint, and self-correction.

EPILOGUE

 e saw in this chapter the enormous physical changes that accompany the move from infancy into the preschool years. Beginning with the growth of their bodies, both in weight and height, preschoolers make enormous physical strides. Although they face threats to their health from sickness and accidental injury, for the most part children are healthy, energetic, inquisitive, and mastering an impressive list of physical accomplishments during the preschool years.

Before we move on to a discussion of children's cognitive development, turn back to this chapter's prologue, which describes Aaron's excursion across the kitchen counter and into the sink (with a stop along the way at the cookie jar). Consider these questions:

1. Why, specifically, do you think Aaron climbed up on the counter? Was it merely to get a cookie?

2. What gross and fine motor skills were involved in Aaron's journey across the counter and into the sink?

3. What dangers did Aaron face in this incident?

4. What could Aaron's father, who had left the room for only a moment, have done to prevent Aaron from climbing into the sink?

KEY TERMS AND CONCEPTS

lateralization (p. 234)

myelin (p. 236)

nightmare (p. 238)

night terror (p. 238)

obesity (p. 239)

child abuse (p. 243)

cycle-of-violence
   hypothesis (p. 245)

psychological
   maltreatment (p. 245)

child neglect (p. 246)

resilience (p. 246)

handedness (p. 251)

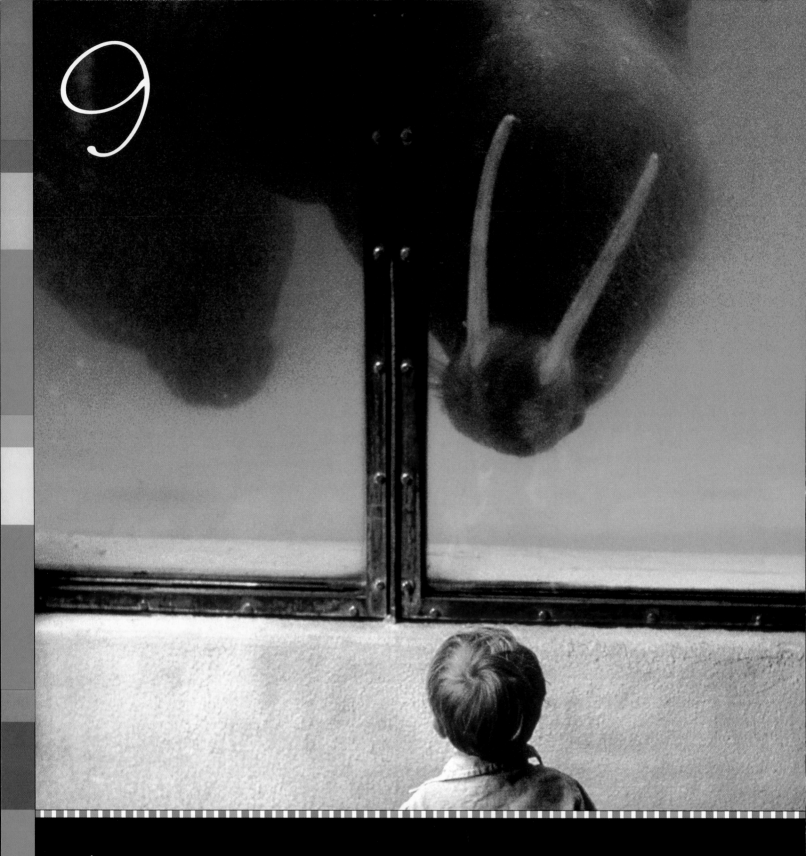

9

Cognitive Development
in the Preschool Years

PROLOGUE: The Long Goodbye

he night before my younger child, Will, started kindergarten, neither he nor I could sleep. Mingled with his excitement was, I imagined, concern over some of the worries that he had expressed to my husband and me: Would he be smart enough? Would he be able to read? Would there be enough time at school to play? Similar doubts haunted my own dreams . . .; I wondered whether I should have left Will in preschool for another year (with an August birthday, he would be one of the youngest in his class), whether his skills would be as advanced as the other children's, whether his teacher would appreciate his charms, tolerate his mishaps, and love him no matter what, as we do—and how I would survive without a little one at my heels.

The next morning, I helped Will get dressed in the new outfit that we had bought weeks earlier and carefully laid out the night before. To avoid last-minute panic, I'd packed his favorite lunch and his backpack the night before. After

The first day of school is emotional for both children and their parents.

a photo session, we set off together. Although he clutched my hand on the walk to the classroom, Will lined up with his classmates as if he had been doing it for years, and trotted into the class with nary a backward glance. (Fishel, 1993, p. 165)

259

LOOKING AHEAD ▶

The experience of attending school for the first time produces a combination of apprehension, exhilaration, and anticipation in preschoolers—and in their parents. It marks the start of an intellectual, as well as social, journey that will continue for many years and shape the development of the children in significant ways.

In this chapter, we focus on the cognitive and linguistic growth that occurs during the preschool years. We begin by examining the major approaches to cognitive development, including Piaget's theory, information processing approaches, and the increasingly influential view of cognitive development of Russian developmental psychologist Lev Vygotsky that takes culture into account.

We then turn to the important advances in language development that occur during the preschool years. We consider several different explanations for the rapid increase in language abilities that characterizes the preschool period and consider the effects that poverty has on language development.

Finally, we discuss two of the major factors that influence cognitive development during the preschool years: schooling and television. We consider the different types of child care and preschool programs, and we end with a discussion of how exposure to television affects preschool viewers.

After reading this chapter, you'll be able to answer the following questions:

- How does Piaget interpret cognitive development during the preschool years?

- How do information processing approaches and Vygotsky's theory explain cognitive development?

- How do children's linguistic abilities develop in the preschool years, and what is the importance of early linguistic development?

- What kinds of preschool educational programs are available in the United States, and what effects do they have?

- What effects does television have on preschoolers?

Intellectual Development

Three-year-old Sam was talking to himself. As his parents listened with amusement from another room, they could hear him using two very different voices. "Find your shoes," he said in a low voice. "Not today. I'm not going. I hate the shoes," he said in a higher-pitched voice. The lower voice answered, "You are a bad boy. Find the shoes, bad boy." The higher voiced response was "No, no, no."

Sam's parents realized that he was playing a game with his imaginary friend, Gill. Gill was a bad boy who often disobeyed his mother, at least in Sam's imagination. In fact, according to Sam's musings, Gill often was guilty of the very same misdeeds for which his parents blamed Sam.

In some ways, the intellectual sophistication of 3-year-olds is astounding. Their creativity and imagination leap to new heights, their language is increasingly sophisticated, and they reason and think about the world in ways that would have been impossible even a few months earlier. But what underlies the dramatic advances in intellectual development that start in the preschool years and continue throughout that period? We can consider several approaches, starting with a look at Piaget's findings on the cognitive changes that occur during the preschool years.

Piaget's Stage of Preoperational Thinking

The Swiss psychologist Jean Piaget, whose stage approach to cognitive development we discussed in Chapter 6, saw the preschool years as a time of both stability and great change. He suggests that the preschool years fit entirely into a single stage of cognitive development—the preoperational stage—which lasts from the age of 2 years until around 7 years.

During the **preoperational stage,** children's use of symbolic thinking grows, mental reasoning emerges, and the use of concepts increases. Children become better at representing events internally, and they grow less dependent on the use of direct sensorimotor activity to understand the world around them. Yet they are still not capable of **operations:** organized, formal, logical mental processes. It is only at the end of the preoperational stage that the ability to carry out operations comes into play.

According to Piaget, a key aspect of preoperational thought is **symbolic function,** the ability to use a mental symbol, a word, or an object to stand for or represent something that is not physically present. For example, during this stage, preschoolers can use a mental symbol for a car (the word *car*), and they likewise understand that a small toy car is representative of the real thing. Because of their ability to use symbolic function, children have no need for direct experience with an actual car to understand its basic purpose and use.

The Relation Between Language and Thought.   Symbolic function is at the heart of one of the major advances that occurs in the preoperational period: the increasingly sophisticated use of language. As we discuss later in this chapter, children make substantial progress in language skills during the preschool period.

Piaget suggests that language and thinking are inextricably intertwined and that the advances in language that occur during the preschool years offer several improvements over the type of thinking that is possible during the earlier sensorimotor period. For instance, thinking embedded in sensorimotor activities is relatively slow, since it depends on actual movements of the body that are bound by human physical limitations. In contrast, the use of symbolic thought allows preschoolers to represent actions symbolically, permitting much greater speed.

Even more important, the use of language allows children to think beyond the present to the future. Consequently, rather than being grounded in the immediate here-and-now, preschoolers can imagine future possibilities through language.

Do the increased language abilities of preschoolers lead to increased thinking proficiency, or vice versa? This question—whether thought determines language or language determines thought—is one of the most enduring and most controversial in the field of psychology and development. Piaget's answer is that language grows out of cognitive advances, rather than the other way around. He argues that improvements during the earlier sensorimotor period are necessary for language development and that continuing growth in cognitive ability during the preoperational period provides the foundation for language ability. Consequently, Piaget suggests that language development is based on the development of more sophisticated modes of thinking—and not the other way around.

Centration: What You See Is What You Think.   Place a dog mask on a cat and what do you get? According to 3- and 4-year-old preschoolers, a dog. To them, a cat with a dog mask ought to bark like a dog, wag its tail like a dog, and eat dog food. In every respect, the cat has been transformed into a dog (R. de Vries, 1969).

Piaget suggests that the root of this belief is centration, a key element and limitation, of the thinking of children in the preoperational period. **Centration** is the process of concentrating on one limited aspect of a stimulus and ignoring other aspects.

Preoperational stage   According to Piaget, the stage that lasts from ages 2 to 7 during which children's use of symbolic thinking grows, mental reasoning emerges, and the use of concepts increases

Operations   Organized, formal, logical mental processes

Symbolic function   According to Piaget, the ability to use a mental symbol, a word, or an object to represent something that is not physically present

Centration   The process of concentrating on one limited aspect of a stimulus and ignoring other aspects

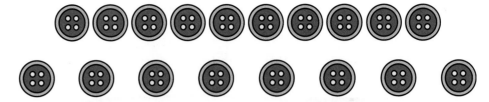

FIGURE 9-1   WHICH ROW CONTAINS MORE BUTTONS?

When preschoolers are shown these two rows and asked the question of which row has more buttons, they usually respond that the lower row of buttons contains more, because it looks longer. They answer in this way even though they know quite well that 10 is greater than 8. Do you think an educator could teach preschoolers to answer correctly?

Preschoolers are unable to consider all available information about a stimulus. Instead, they focus on superficial, obvious elements that are within their sight. These external elements come to dominate preschoolers' thinking, leading to inaccuracy in thought.

For example, consider what preschoolers say when they are shown two rows of buttons, one with 10 buttons that are closely spaced together, and the other with 8 buttons spread out to form a longer row (see Figure 9-1). If asked which of the rows contains more buttons, children who are 4 or 5 usually choose the row that looks longer, rather than the one that actually contains more buttons. This occurs in spite of the fact that children this age know quite well that 10 is more than 8.

The cause of the children's mistake is that the visual image dominates their thinking. Rather than taking into account their understanding of quantity, they focus on appearance. To a preschooler, appearance is everything. Preschoolers' focus on appearances might be related to another aspect of preoperational thought, the lack of conservation.

Conservation: Learning That Appearances Are Deceiving.   Consider the following scenario:

> Four-year-old Jaime is shown two drinking glasses of different shapes. One is short and broad; the other, tall and thin. A teacher half-fills the short, broad glass with apple juice. The teacher then pours the juice into the tall, thin glass. The juice fills the tall glass almost to the brim. The teacher asks Jaime a question: Is there more juice in the second glass than there was in the first?

If you view this as an easy task, so do children like Jaime. They have no trouble answering the question. However, they almost always get the answer wrong.

Most 4-year-olds respond that there is more apple juice in the tall, thin glass than there was in the short, broad one. In fact, if the juice is poured back into the shorter glass, they are quick to say that there is now less juice than there was in the taller glass (see Figure 9-2).

FIGURE 9-2   WHICH GLASS CONTAINS MORE?

Most 4-year-old children believe that the amount of liquid in these two glasses differs because of the differences in the containers' shapes, even though they may have seen equal amounts of liquid being poured into each.

The reason for the error in judgment is that children of this age have not mastered conservation. **Conservation** is the knowledge that quantity is unrelated to the arrangement and physical appearance of objects. During the preoperational period, preschoolers are unable to understand that changes in one dimension (such as appearance) do not necessarily mean that other dimensions (such as quantity) are changed.

Children who do not yet understand the principle of conservation feel quite comfortable in asserting that the amount of liquid changes as it is poured between glasses of different sizes. They simply are unable to realize that the transformation in appearance does not imply a transformation in quantity.

The inability to conserve manifests itself in several ways during the preoperational period. For example, if 5-year-olds are shown a row of checkers and asked to build a row that is "the same," the row they typically build will be identical in length—but it may vary in the number of checkers. Similarly, if shown two rows of checkers, each with the same number of checkers, but one with the checkers more spread out, children in the preoperational stage will reason that the two rows are not equal.

The lack of conservation also manifests itself in children's understanding of area, as illustrated by Piaget's cow-in-the-field problem (Piaget, Inhelder, & Szeminska, 1948/1960). In the problem, two equally sized sheets of green paper, representing two grassy fields, are shown to a child, and a toy cow is placed in each field. Next, a toy barn is placed in each field, and children are asked which cow has more grass to eat. The typical—and, so far, correct—response is that the cows have the same amount.

In the next step, a second toy barn is placed in each field. But in one field, the barns are placed adjacent to one another, while in the second field, they are separated from one another. Children who have not mastered conservation usually say that the cow in the field with the adjacent barns has more grass to eat than the cow in the field with the separated barns. In contrast, children who can conserve answer, correctly, that the amount available is identical. (Some other conservation tasks are shown in Figure 9-3).

Why do children in the preoperational stage make errors on tasks that require conservation? Piaget suggests that the main reason is that their tendency toward centration prevents them from focusing on the relevant features of the situation. Furthermore, they cannot follow the sequence of transformations that accompanies changes in the appearance of a situation.

Incomplete Understanding of Transformation. Children in the preoperational period are unable to understand the notion of transformation. **Transformation** is the process in which one state is changed into another. For instance, adults know that if a pencil that is held upright is allowed to fall down, it goes through a series of successive positions until it reaches its final, horizontal resting spot (see Figure 9-4 on page 265). In contrast, children in the preoperational period are unable to envision or recall the successive transformations that the pencil followed in moving from the upright to the horizontal position. If asked to reproduce the sequence in a drawing, they draw the pencil upright and lying down, with nothing in between. Basically, they ignore the intermediate steps.

Similarly, a preoperational child who sees several worms during a walk in the woods may believe that they are all the same worm. The reason: She views each sighting in isolation and is unable to reconstruct the transformation it would take for the worm to move quickly from one sighting to the next and realize that worms can't perform that transformation.

Egocentrism: The Inability to Take Others' Perspectives. Another hallmark of the preoperational period is egocentric thinking. **Egocentric thought** is thinking that does not take the viewpoints of others into account. Preschoolers do not understand that others have different perspectives from their own. Egocentric thought takes two forms: the lack of awareness that others see things from a different physical perspective and the failure to realize that others may hold thoughts, feelings, and points of view that differ from theirs. (Note what

VIDEO CLIP

Conservation

VIDEO CLIP

Practical Application of Conservation

Conservation The knowledge that quantity is unrelated to the arrangement and physical appearance of objects

Transformation The process whereby one state is changed into another

Egocentric thought Thinking that does not take the viewpoints of others into account

Type of Conservation	Modality	Change in Physical Appearance	Average Age at Which Invariance Is Grasped
Number	Number of elements in a collection 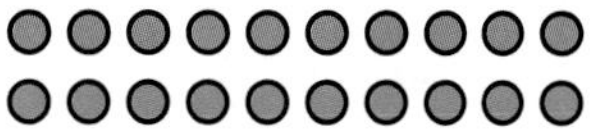	Rearranging or dislocating elements 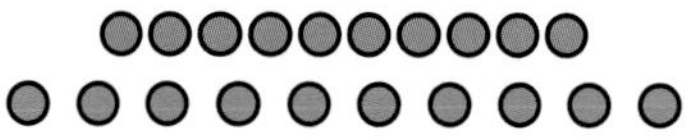	6–7 years
Substance (mass)	Amount of a malleable substance (e.g., clay or liquid) 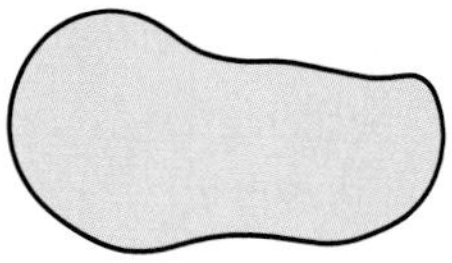	Altering shape 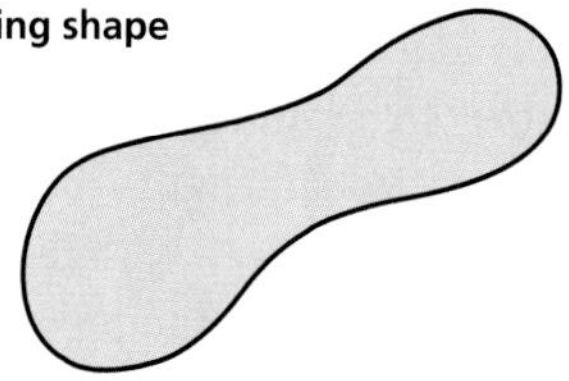	7–8 years
Length	Length of a line or object 	Altering shape or configuration 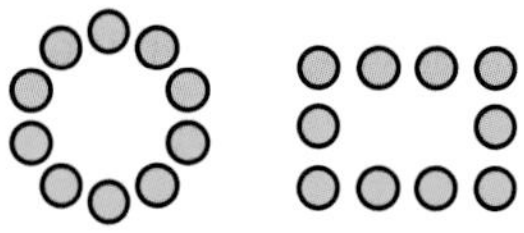	7–8 years
Area	Amount of surface covered by a set of plane figures 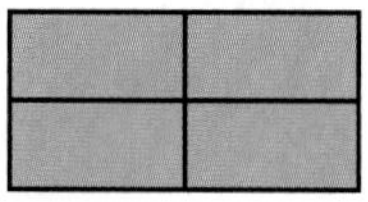	Rearranging the figures 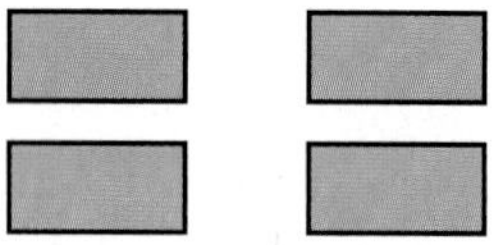	8–9 years
Weight	Weight of an object 	Altering shape 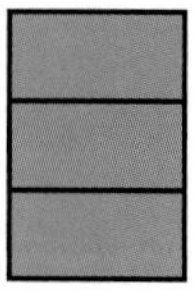	9–10 years
Volume	Volume of an object (in terms of water displacement) 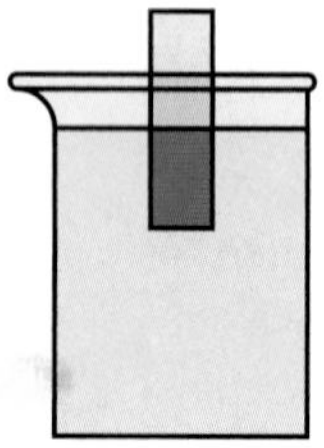	Altering shape 	14–15 years

FIGURE 9-3   COMMON TESTS OF CHILDREN'S UNDERSTANDING OF THE PRINCIPLE OF CONSERVATION

From the perspective of an educator, why would a knowledge of a child's level of conservation be important?

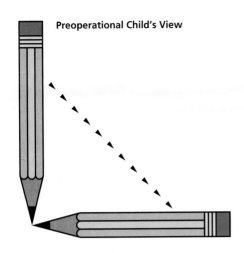

Preoperational Child's View

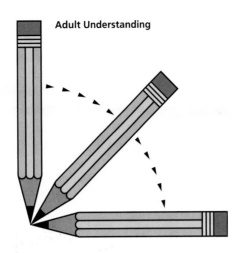

Adult Understanding

FIGURE 9-4   THE FALLING PENCIL

Children in Piaget's preoperational stage do not understand that as a pencil falls from the upright to the horizontal position, it moves through a series of intermediary steps. Instead, they think that there are no intermediate steps in the change from the upright to horizontal position.

egocentric thought does *not* imply: that preoperational children intentionally think in a selfish or inconsiderate manner.)

Egocentric thinking underlies children's lack of concern over their nonverbal behavior and the impact it has on others. For instance, a 4-year-old who is given an unwanted gift of socks when he was expecting something more desirable may frown and scowl as he opens the package, unaware that his face can be seen by others and may reveal his true feelings about the gift (R. S. Feldman, 1992).

Egocentrism lies at the heart of several types of behavior during the preoperational period. For instance, preschoolers may talk to themselves, even in the presence of others, and at times they simply ignore what others are telling them. Rather than being a sign of eccentricity, such behavior illustrates the egocentric nature of preoperational children's thinking: the lack of awareness that their behavior acts as a trigger to others' reactions and responses. Consequently, a considerable amount of verbal behavior on the part of preschoolers has no social motivation behind it but is meant for the preschoolers' own consumption.

Similarly, egocentrism can be seen in hiding games with children during the preoperational stage. In a game of hide-and-seek, 3-year-olds may attempt to hide by covering their faces with a pillow—even though they remain in plain view. Their reasoning is that if they cannot see others, others cannot see them. They assume that others share their view.

The Emergence of Intuitive Thought.   Because Piaget labeled the preschool years the "preoperational period," it is easy to assume that this is a period of marking time, waiting for the more formal emergence of operations. However, the preoperational period is far from idle. Cognitive development proceeds steadily, and in fact several new types of ability emerge. A case in point: the development of intuitive thought.

Intuitive thought refers to preschoolers' use of primitive reasoning and their avid acquisition of knowledge about the world. From about age 4 through age 7, children's curiosity blossoms. They constantly seek out the answers to a wide variety of questions.

At the same time, children may act as if they are authorities on particular topics, feeling certain that they have the correct—and final—word on an issue. If pressed, they are unable to back up their reasoning, and they are inattentive to how they know what they know. In other words, their intuitive thought leads them to believe that they know answers to all kinds of questions, but there is little or no logical basis for this confidence in their understanding of the way the world operates.

By contrast, the intuitive thinking that children display in the late stages of the preoperational period has certain qualities that prepare them for more sophisticated forms of reasoning. For example, by the end of the preoperational stage, preschoolers begin to understand the notion of functionality. *Functionality* refers to the concept that actions, events, and outcomes

Intuitive thought Thinking that reflects preschoolers' use of primitive reasoning and their avid acquisition of knowledge about the world

are related to one another in fixed patterns. For instance, preschoolers come to understand that pushing harder on the pedals makes a bicycle move faster or that pressing a button on a remote control makes the television change channels.

Furthermore, children begin to show an awareness of the concept of identity in the later stages of the preoperational period. *Identity* is the understanding that certain things stay the same, regardless of changes in shape, size, and appearance. For instance, knowledge of identity allows one to understand that a lump of clay contains the same amount of clay regardless of whether it is clumped into a ball or stretched out like a snake. Comprehension of identity is necessary for children to develop an understanding of conservation, the ability to understand that quantity is not related to physical appearances, as we discussed earlier. Piaget regarded children's development of conservation as a skill that marks the transition from the preoperational period to the next stage, concrete operations, which we will discuss in Chapter 12.

Evaluating Piaget's Approach to Cognitive Development.   Piaget, a masterful observer of children's behavior, provides a detailed portrait of preschoolers' cognitive abilities. His rich description of how children view the world is simply unmatched by most other accounts of cognitive development. The broad outlines of his approach provide us with a useful means of thinking about the advances in cognitive ability that occur during the preschool years (Siegal, 1997).

However, it is important to consider Piaget's approach to cognitive development within the appropriate historical context and in light of more recent research findings. Recall, as we discussed in Chapter 6, that his theory is based on extensive observations of relatively few children. Despite his insightful and groundbreaking observations, recent experimental investigations suggest that in certain regards, Piaget underestimated children's capabilities.

Take Piaget's views of how children in the preoperational period understand numbers. He contends that preschoolers' thinking is seriously handicapped, as evidenced by their performance on tasks involving conservation and *reversibility,* the understanding that a transformation can be reversed to return something to its original state. Yet more recent experimental work suggests otherwise. For instance, developmental psychologist Rochel Gelman (1982) has found that children as young as 3 can readily discern the difference between rows of two and three toy animals, regardless of the animals' spacing. Furthermore, older children are able to note differences in number, performing tasks such as identifying which of two numbers is larger and indicating that they understand some rudiments of addition and subtraction problems (Sophian, Garyantes, & Chang, 1997; Wynn, 1992).

Based on such evidence, Gelman (1982) concludes that children have an innate ability to count, one akin to the ability to use language that some theorists see as universal and genetically determined. Such a conclusion is clearly at odds with Piagetian notions, which suggest that children's numerical abilities do not blossom until after the preoperational period.

Some developmentalists (particularly those who favor the information processing approach, as we'll see later in the chapter) also believe that cognitive skills develop in a more continuous manner than Piaget's stage theory implies. Rather than thoughts changing in quality, as Piaget argues, critics of Piaget suggest that developmental changes are more quantitative in nature. The underlying processes that produce cognitive skill are regarded by such critics as undergoing only minor changes with age (Case, 1991; Gelman & Baillargeon, 1983).

There are further difficulties with Piaget's view of cognitive development. His contention that conservation does not emerge until the end of the preoperational period and in some cases even later has not stood up to careful experimental scrutiny. For instance, performance on conservation tasks can be improved by providing preoperational children with certain kinds of training and experiences. The mere possibility of enhancing performance argues against the Piagetian view that children in the preoperational period have not reached a level of cognitive maturity that would permit them to understand conservation (Field, 1987; Siegler, 1995).

Clearly, children are more capable at an earlier age than Piaget's account would lead us to believe. Why did Piaget underestimate children's cognitive abilities? One answer is that this questioning of children used language that was too difficult to allow children to answer in a way that would provide a true picture of their skills. In addition, as we've seen, Piaget tended to concentrate on preschoolers' *deficiencies* in thinking, focusing his observations on children's lack of logical thought. In contrast, more recent theorists have focused more on children's competence. By shifting the question, they have found increasing evidence for a surprising degree of competence in preschoolers.

Information Processing Approaches to Cognitive Development

Even as an adult, Paco has clear recollections of his first trip to a farm, when he was 3 years old. He was visiting his godfather, who lived in Puerto Rico, and the two of them went to a nearby farm. Paco recounts seeing what seemed like hundreds of chickens, and he clearly recalls his fear of the pigs, who seemed huge, smelly, and frightening. Most of all he recalls the thrill of riding on a horse with his godfather.

That Paco has a clear memory of his farm trip is not surprising: Most people have unambiguous, and seemingly accurate, memories dating as far back as the age of 3. But are the processes used to form memories during the preschool years similar to those that operate later in life? More broadly, what general changes in the processing of information occur during the preschool years?

Information processing approaches view the changes that occur in children's cognitive abilities during the preschool years as analogous to the way a computer program becomes more sophisticated as a programmer modifies it on the basis of experience. These approaches focus on changes in the kinds of "mental programs" that children invoke when approaching problems. In fact, for many child developmentalists, information processing approaches represent the dominant, most comprehensive, and ultimately most accurate explanation of how children develop cognitively (Mehler & Dupoux, 1994; Siegler, 1994).

We'll focus on two domains that highlight the approach taken by information processing theorists: understanding of numbers and memory development during the preschool years.

Preschoolers' Understanding of Numbers.   As we saw earlier, one of the flaws critics have noticed in Piaget's theory is that preschoolers have a greater understanding of numbers than Piaget thought. Researchers using information processing approaches to cognitive development have found increasing evidence for the sophistication of preschoolers' understanding of numbers. The average preschooler is able not only to count but also to do so in a fairly systematic and consistent manner (Siegler, 1998).

For instance, Rochel Gelman (1982; Gelman & Gallistel, 1978) suggests that preschoolers follow a number of principles in their counting. When shown a group of several items, they know they should assign just one number to each item and that each item should be counted only once. Moreover, even when they get the *names* of numbers wrong, they are consistent in their usage. For instance, a 4-year-old who counts three items as "one, three, seven" will say "one, three, seven" when counting another group of different items. And if asked how many there are, she will probably say that there are seven items in the group.

In short, preschoolers may demonstrate a surprisingly sophisticated understanding of numbers, although their understanding is not totally firm. Still, by the age of 4, most are able to carry out simple addition and subtraction problems by counting, and they are able to compare different quantities quite successfully (Donlan, 1998).

Memory: Recalling the Past.   Think back to your own earliest memory. If you are like Paco, described earlier, and most other people, it is probably of an event that occurred after

How specific and accurate will these pre-schoolers' memories of this event be in the future?

the age of 3. According to Katherine Nelson (1989, 1992), **autobiographical memory,** memory of particular events from one's own life, achieves little accuracy until after 3 years of age. Accuracy then increases gradually and slowly throughout the preschool years (see also Gathercole, 1998).

Preschool children's recollections of events that happened to them are sometimes, but not always, accurate. For instance, 3-years-olds can remember fairly well central features of routine occurrences, such as the sequence of events involved in eating at a restaurant. In addition, preschoolers are typically accurate in their responses to open-ended questions, such as "What rides did you like best at the amusement park?" (G. S. Goodman & Reed, 1986; K. Nelson, 1986; D. W. Price & Goodman, 1990).

One determinant of the accuracy of preschoolers' memories is how soon they are assessed. Unless an event is particularly vivid or meaningful, it is unlikely to be remembered at all. Moreover, not all autobiographical memories last into later life. For instance, Will, the 5-year-old described in the prologue to this chapter, may remember the first day of kindergarten 6 months or a year later, but later in his life, he might not remember that day at all.

Furthermore, memories are affected by cultural factors. For example, early childhood memories of Chinese college students are more likely to be unemotional and reflect activities involving social roles, whereas U.S. college students' earliest memories are more emotionally elaborate and focus on specific events (Q. Wang, 2001).

Not only do preschoolers' autobiographical memories fade, but they may not be particularly accurate. For example, if an event happens often, it may be hard to remember one specific time it happened. Preschoolers' memories of familiar events are often organized in terms of **scripts,** broad representations in memory of events and the order in which they occur. For example, a young preschooler might represent eating in a restaurant in terms of a few steps: talking to a waitress, getting the food, and eating. With age, the scripts become more elaborate: getting in the car, being seated at the restaurant, ordering, waiting for the food to come, eating, ordering dessert, and paying for the food. Because events that are frequently repeated tend to be melded into scripts, particular instances of a scripted event are recalled with less accuracy than those that are unscripted in memory (Farrar & Goodman, 1992; Fivush, Kuebli, & Clubb, 1992).

Preschoolers' inability to understand complex causal relationships also lead to inaccurate autobiographical memories. Furthermore, as we consider next, their memories are susceptible to the suggestions of others. This is a special concern when children are called on to testify in legal situations, such as when abuse is suspected, as discussed in the *From Research to Practice* box.

Information Processing Theories in Perspective

According to information processing approaches, cognitive development consists of gradual improvements in the ways people perceive, understand, and remember information. With age and practice, preschoolers process information more efficiently and with greater sophistication, and they are able to handle increasingly complex problems. In the eyes of proponents of information processing approaches, it is these quantitative advances in information processing—and not the qualitative changes suggested by Piaget—that constitute cognitive development (Case & Okamoto, 1996; Goswami, 1998; Chen & Siegler, 2000).

Support and Criticism. For supporters of information processing approaches, the reliance on well-defined processes that can be tested, with relative precision, by research is one of the perspective's most important features. Rather than relying on concepts that are somewhat vague, such as Piaget's notions of assimilation and accommodation, information processing approaches provide a comprehensive, logical set of concepts.

For instance, dramatic changes in the nature of attention occur as preschoolers grow older: They have longer attention spans, can monitor and plan what they are attending to more

Autobiographical memory Memory of particular events from one's own life

Scripts Broad representations in memory of events and the order in which they occur

— FROM RESEARCH TO PRACTICE —

Children's Eyewitness Testimony: Memory on Trial

I was looking and then I didn't see what I was doing and it got in there somehow. . . . The mousetrap was in our house because there's a mouse in our house. . . . The mousetrap is down in the basement, next to the firewood. . . . I was playing a game called "Operation" and then I went downstairs and said to Dad, "I want to eat lunch," and then it got stuck in the mousetrap. . . . My daddy was down in the basement collecting firewood. . . . [My brother] pushed me [into the mousetrap]. . . . It happened yesterday. The mouse was in my house yesterday. I caught my finger in it yesterday. I went to the hospital yesterday. (Ceci & Bruck, 1993, p. A23)

Despite the detailed account by this 4-year-old boy of his encounter with a mousetrap and subsequent trip to the hospital, there's a problem: The incident never happened, and the memory is entirely false.

The 4-year-old's explicit recounting of a mousetrap incident that had not actually occurred was the product of a study on children's memory. Each week for 11 weeks, the 4-year-old boy was told, "You went to the hospital because your finger got caught in a mousetrap. Did this ever happen to you?"

The first week, the child quite accurately said, "No. I've never been to the hospital." But by the second week, the answer changed to, "Yes, I cried." In the third week, the boy said, "Yes. My mom went to the hospital with me." By the eleventh week, the answer had expanded to the quote above (Ceci & Bruck, 1993).

The embellishment of a completely false incident is characteristic of the fragility and inaccuracy of memory in young children. Young children may recall things quite mistakenly, but with great conviction, contending that events occurred that never really happened and forgetting events that did occur.

Furthermore, children's memories are susceptible to the suggestions of adults asking them questions. This is particularly true of preschoolers, who are considerably more vulnerable to suggestion than either adults or school-age children. Preschoolers are also more prone to make inaccurate inferences about the reasons behind others' behavior and less able to draw appropriate conclusions based on their knowledge of a situation (Bruck & Ceci, 1999; Ceci & Huffman, 1997; Loftus, 1997; W. C. Thompson, Clarke-Stewart, & Lepore, 1997).

Of course, preschoolers recall many things accurately; as we discussed earlier in the chapter, children as young as 3 recall some events in their lives without distortion. However, not all recollections are accurate, and some events that are recalled with seeming accuracy never actually occurred.

The error rate for children is further heightened when the same question is asked repeatedly (Cassel, Roebers, & Bjorklund, 1996). Furthermore, false memories—of the type reported by the 4-year-old who "remembered" going to the hospital after his finger was caught in a mousetrap—may in fact be more persistent than actual memories (Brainerd, Reyna, & Brandse, 1995).

In addition, when questions are highly suggestive (i.e., when questioners attempt to lead a person to particular conclusions), children are more apt to make mistakes in recall (Ackil & Zaragoza, 1998; Ceci & Huffman, 1997). For instance, consider the following excerpt, which presents an extreme example of a preschool child being questioned. It comes from an actual case involving a teacher, Kelly Michaels, who was accused of sexually molesting children in a preschool:

Social worker: Don't be so unfriendly. I thought we were buddies last time.

Child: Nope, not any more.

Social worker: We have gotten a lot of other kids to help us since I last saw you. . . . Did we tell you that Kelly is in jail?

Child: Yes. My mother already told me.

Social worker: Did I tell you that this is the guy (*pointing to the detective*) that arrested her? . . . Well, we can get out of here real quick if you just tell me what you told me the last time, when we met.

Child: I forgot.

Social worker: No you didn't. I know you didn't.

Child: I did! I did!

Social worker: I thought we were friends last time.

Child: I'm not your friend any more!

Social worker: How come?

Child: Because I hate you!

Social worker: You have no reason to hate me. We were buddies when you left.

Child: I hate you now!

Social worker: Oh, you do not, you secretly like me, I can tell.

Child: I hate you.

Social worker: Oh, come on. We talked to a few more of your buddies. And everyone told me about the nap room, and the bathroom stuff, and the music room stuff, and the choir stuff, and the peanut butter stuff, and everything. . . . All your buddies [talked]. . . . Come on, do you want to help us out? Do you want to keep her in jail? I'll let you hear your voice and play with the tape recorder; I need your help again. Come on. . . . Real quick, will you just tell me what happened with the wooden spoon? Let's go.

Child: I forgot.

Detective: Now listen, you have to behave.

Social worker: Do you want me to tell him to behave? Are you going to be good boy, huh? While you are here, did he [the detective] show you his badge and his handcuffs? (Ceci & Bruck, 1993, pp. 422–423)

Clearly, the interview is filled with leading questions, not to mention social pressure to conform ("all your buddies talked"), bribery ("I'll let you hear your voice and play with the tape recorder"), and even implicit threats ("did the detective show you his badge and handcuffs?").

How can children be questioned to produce the most accurate recollections? One way is to question them as soon as possible after an event has occurred. The longer the time between the event and the questioning, the less reliable children's recollections are. Furthermore, specific questions are answered more accurately than general ones. Asking the questions outside of a courtroom is also preferable, as the courtroom setting can be intimidating and frightening (Ceci & Bruck, 1995; Poole & Lamb, 1998; Saywitz & Nathanson, 1993; see Table 9-1).

Although some experts have advocated the use of anatomically correct dolls, on which children can point out where they have or may have experienced inappropriate contact, careful research has not been supportive of the technique. In fact, in some instances, children, using anatomically correct dolls, have claimed that they have touched other people in places that are wholly implausible—as when a child claimed to have touched a female's penis (Bruck et al., 1995; Wolfner, Faust, & Dawes, 1993). A study on the use of anatomical dolls found that preschoolers who had not been abused nevertheless described behaviors that are associated

The conviction of preschool teacher Kelly Michaels for sexually molesting several preschool children may have been the result of leading questions posed to the children.

with sexual abuse (Geddie, Dawson, & Weunsch, 1998). Based on this research, the use of anatomically correct dolls does not appear to be the best way to interview preschool-age children (Bruck, Ceci, & Francoeur, 2000).

Ultimately, no foolproof way exists to test the accuracy of children's recollections. Testimony needs to be evaluated on a case-by-case basis, and judges must ensure that children are questioned in a low-key, nonthreatening manner by impartial questioners (Bruck, Ceci, & Hembrooke, 1998; B. N. Gordon, Baker-Ward, & Ornstein, 2001).

TABLE 9-1   ELICITING ACCURATE RECOLLECTIONS FROM CHILDREN
Recommended Practice
• Play dumb: Interviewer: Now that I know you a little better, tell me why you are here today.
• Ask follow-up questions: Child: Bob touched my private. Interviewer: Tell me everything about that.
• Encourage children to describe events: Interviewer: Tell me everything that happened at Bob's house from the beginning to the end.
• Avoid suggesting that interviewers expect descriptions of particular kinds of events.
• Avoid offering rewards or expressing disapproval.
(*Source:* Poole & Lamb, 1998)

effectively, and become increasingly aware of their cognitive limitations. As we discussed earlier in this chapter, these advances may be due to brain development. Such increasing attentional abilities place some of Piaget's findings in a different light. For instance, increased attention allows older children to attend to both the height *and* the width of tall and short glasses into which liquid is poured. This permits them to understand that the amount of liquid in the glasses stays the same when it is poured back and forth. Preschoolers, in contrast, are unable to attend to both dimensions simultaneously and thus are less able to conserve (J. A. Hudson, Sosa, & Shapiro, 1997; P. H. Miller & Seier, 1994; P. H. Miller, Woody-Ramsey, & Aloise, 1991).

Proponents of information processing theory have also been successful in focusing on important cognitive processes to which alternative approaches have traditionally shown relatively little concern, such as memory and attention. They suggest that information processing provides a clear, logical, and full account of cognitive development.

Yet information processing approaches have their detractors, who raise significant points. For one thing, the focus on a series of single, individual cognitive processes leaves out of consideration some important factors that appear to influence cognition. For instance, information processing theorists pay relatively little attention to social and cultural factors—a deficiency that Vygotsky's approach, which we'll consider next, attempts to remedy.

An even more important criticism is that information processing approaches "lose the forest for the trees." In other words, information processing approaches pay so much attention to the detailed, individual sequence of processes that comprise cognitive processing and development that they never adequately paint a whole, comprehensive picture of cognitive development—which Piaget clearly did quite well.

Influence of Information Processing Approaches.   Developmentalists using information processing approaches have responded to such criticisms. They contend that their model of cognitive development has the advantage of being precisely stated and capable of leading to testable hypotheses. They also argue that there is far more research supporting their approach than there is for alternative theories of cognitive development. In short, they suggest that their approach provides a more accurate account than any other.

Information processing approaches have been highly influential over the past several decades. They have inspired a tremendous amount of research that has helped explain how children develop cognitively. Furthermore, it is clear that the information processing perspective will continue to be an important guide to understanding how children make such remarkable cognitive strides as they develop.

Vygotsky's View of Cognitive Development: Taking Culture Into Account

> As her daughter watches, a member of the Chilcotin Indian tribe prepares a salmon for dinner. When the daughter asks a question about a small detail of the process, the mother takes out another salmon and repeats the entire process. According to the tribal view of learning, understanding and comprehension can come only from grasping the total procedure, and not from learning about the individual subcomponents of the task. (Tharp, 1989)

The Chilcotin view of how children learn about the world contrasts with the prevalent view of Western society, which assumes that only by mastering the separate parts of a problem can one fully comprehend it. Do differences in the ways particular cultures and societies approach problems influence cognitive development? According to Russian developmental psychologist Lev Vygotsky, who lived from 1896 to 1934, the answer is a clear yes.

Focusing on Social and Cultural Factors.   In an increasingly influential view, Vygotsky argues that the focus of cognitive development should be on a child's social and cultural

Russian developmental psychologist Lev Vygotsky proposed that the focus of cognitive development should be on a child's social and cultural world, as opposed to the Piagetian approach, which concentrates on individual performance.

world. Instead of concentrating on individual performance, as Piagetian and many alternative approaches do, Vygotsky focuses on the social aspects of development and learning. He holds that cognitive development proceeds as a result of social interactions in which partners jointly work to solve problems. Because of the assistance that such adult and peer partners provide, children gradually grow intellectually and begin to function on their own (Vygotsky, 1978, 1926/1997; Wertsch & Tulviste, 1992).

Vygotsky contends that the nature of the partnership that adults and peers provide is determined largely by cultural and societal factors. For instance, culture and society establish the institutions, such as preschools and playgroups—and the kindergarten that young Will, introduced in the chapter prologue, is about to enter; these promote development by providing opportunities for cognitive growth. Furthermore, by emphasizing particular tasks, culture and society shape the nature of specific cognitive advances. Unless we look at what is important and meaningful to members of a given society, we may seriously underestimate the nature and level of cognitive abilities that will ultimately be attained (Belmont, 1995; Tappan, 1997).

Societal expectations about gender also play a role in how children come to understand the world. For example, one study conducted at a science museum found that parents provided more detailed scientific explanations to boys than to girls at museum displays. Such differences in level of explanation may lead to more sophisticated understanding of science in boys and may ultimately produce later gender differences in science learning (K. Crowley et al., 2001).

Vygotsky's approach is quite different from that of Piaget. Where Piaget looked at developing children and saw junior scientists, working by themselves to develop an independent understanding of the world, Vygotsky saw cognitive apprentices, learning from master teachers the skills that are important in the child's culture. In Vygotsky's view, children's cognitive development is dependent on interaction with others. Vygotsky argued that it was only through partnership with other people—peers, parents, teachers, and other adults—that children could fully develop their knowledge, thinking processes, beliefs, and values (Fernyhough, 1997; Kitchener, 1996).

The Zone of Proximal Development.   Vygotsky proposed that children's cognitive abilities increase through exposure to information that resides within the child's zone of proximal development. The **zone of proximal development (ZPD)** is the level at which a child can *almost* perform a task independently but can complete the task with the assistance of someone more competent. When appropriate instruction is offered within the ZPD, children are able to increase their understanding and master new tasks. For cognitive development to occur, then, new information must be presented—by parents, teachers, or more skilled peers—within the child's zone of proximal development. For example, a preschooler might not be able to figure out by himself how to get a handle to stick on the clay pot he's building, but he could do it with some advice from his child care teacher (Blank & White, 1999; Rogoff, 1990; Steward, 1995).

The concept of the zone of proximal development suggests that even though two children might be able to achieve the same amount without help, if one child receives aid, he or she may improve substantially more than the other. The greater the improvement that comes with help, the larger the zone of proximal development (see Figure 9-5).

Scaffolding.   The assistance provided by others has been termed scaffolding (D. Wood, Bruner, & Ross, 1976). **Scaffolding** is the support for learning and problem solving that encourages independence and growth. To Vygotsky, the process of scaffolding not only helps children solve specific problems but also aids in the development of their overall cognitive abilities.

Scaffolding takes its name from the scaffolds that are put up to aid in the construction of a building and removed once the building is complete. In education, scaffolding involves, first of all, helping children think about and frame a task in an appropriate manner. In addition, a

VIDEO CLIP

Scaffolding

Zone of proximal development (ZPD) According to Vygotsky, the level at which a child can *almost,* but not fully, comprehend or perform a task without assistance

Scaffolding The support for learning and problem solving that encourages independence and growth

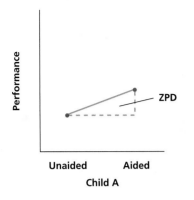 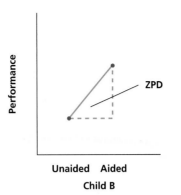

FIGURE 9-5   SAMPLE ZONES OF PROXIMAL DEVELOPMENT (ZPDs) FOR TWO CHILDREN

Although the two children's performance is similar when working at a task without aid, the second child benefits more from aid and therefore has a larger ZPD. Is there any way to measure a child's ZPD? Can it be enlarged?

parent or teacher is likely to provide clues to task completion that are appropriate to the child's level of development and also likely to model behavior that can lead to completion of the task (Radziszewska & Rogoff, 1988; Rogoff, 1995). As in construction, the scaffolding that more competent people provide, which facilitates the completion of identified tasks, is removed once children are able to solve a problem on their own. For example, after suggesting some ideas for different ways to make a handle for a clay pot, the teacher might leave the child alone to try out the handle he likes best.

In some societies, parental support for learning differs by gender. In one study, Mexican mothers were found to provide more scaffolding than fathers. A possible explanation is that mothers may be more aware of their children's cognitive abilities than fathers are (Tamis-LeMonda & Cabrera, 2002; Tenenbaum & Leaper, 1998).

Shaping by Culture.   The aid that more accomplished individuals provide to learners comes in the form of cultural tools. *Cultural tools* are actual, physical items (pencils, paper, calculators, computers, and so forth), as well as an intellectual and conceptual framework for solving problems. The intellectual and conceptual framework available to learners includes the language that is used in a culture, its alphabetical and numbering schemes, its mathematical and scientific systems, and even its religious systems. These cultural tools provide a structure that can be used to help children define and solve specific problems, as well as an intellectual point of view that encourages cognitive development.

For example, consider how people talk about distance. In cities, distance is usually measured in blocks ("the store is about 15 blocks away"). To a child from a rural background, such a unit of measurement is meaningless, and more meaningful distance-related terms may be used—for example, yards, miles, practical approximations such as "a stone's throw," or references to known distances and landmarks ("about half the way to town"). To make matters more complicated, "how far" questions are sometimes answered in terms not of distance but of time ("it's about 15 minutes to the store"), which will be understood variously to refer to walking or riding time, depending on context—and if riding time, to different forms of riding (oxcart, bicycle, bus, train, automobile, airplane), again depending on cultural context. Obviously, the nature of the tools available to children to solve problems and perform tasks is highly dependent on the culture in which they live.

Evaluating Vygotsky's Contributions.   Vygotsky's view—that the specific nature of cognitive development can be understood only by taking cultural and social context into account—has become increasingly influential in recent years. In some ways, this is surprising, in light of the fact that Vygotsky died more than six decades ago at the young age of 37 (van der Veer & Valsiner, 1991, 1994).

Several factors explain Vygotsky's growing influence. One is that until fairly recently, he was largely unknown to developmentalists. His writings are only now becoming widely disseminated in the United States due to the growing availability of good English translations. In fact, for most of the 20th century, Vygotsky was not widely known even in his native land. His work was banned for some time, and not until the breakup of the Soviet Union in 1991 did it become freely available in the former Soviet republics. Thus Vygotsky, long hidden from his fellow developmentalists, emerged onto the scene only long after his death.

Even more important, though, is the quality of Vygotsky's ideas. They represent a consistent theoretical system and help explain a growing body of research attesting to the importance of social interaction in promoting cognitive development. The idea that children's comprehension of the world is an outcome of their interactions with their parents, peers, and other members of society is both appealing and well supported by research findings. It is also consistent with a growing body of multicultural and cross-cultural research, which finds evidence that cognitive development is shaped, in part, by cultural factors (Beilin, 1996; Daniels, 1996).

Of course, not every aspect of Vygotsky's theorizing has been supported, and he can be criticized for a lack of precision in his conceptualization of cognitive growth. For instance, such broad concepts as the zone of proximal development are not terribly precise, and they do not always lend themselves to experimental tests (Wertsch, 1999).

Furthermore, Vygotsky was largely silent on how basic cognitive processes such as attention and memory develop and how children's natural cognitive capabilities unfold. Because of his emphasis on broad cultural influences, he did not focus on how individual bits of information are processed and synthesized. These processes, which must be taken into account if we are to have a complete understanding of cognitive development, are more directly addressed by information processing theories.

Still, Vygotsky's melding of the cognitive and social worlds of children has been an important advance in our understanding of cognitive development. One can only imagine what his impact would have been if he had lived a longer life. (See Table 9-2 for a comparison of Piaget's theory, information processing theories, and Vygotskian approaches.)

TABLE 9-2	COMPARISON OF PIAGET'S THEORY, INFORMATION PROCESSING THEORIES, AND VYGOTSKY'S APPROACH TO COGNITIVE DEVELOPMENT		
	Piaget	**Information Processing**	**Vygotsky**
Key concepts	Stages of cognitive development; qualitative growth from one stage to another	Gradual, quantitative improvements in attention, perception, understanding, and memory	Culture and social context drive cognitive development
Role of stages	Heavy emphasis	No specific stages	No specific stages
Importance of social factors	Low	Low	High
Educational perspective	Children must have reached a given stage of development for specific types of educational interventions to be effective	Education is reflected in gradual increments in skills	Education is very influential in promoting cognitive growth; teachers serve as facilitators

R E V I E W *&* A P P L Y

Review

- According to Piaget, children in the preoperational stage develop symbolic function, a qualitative change in their thinking that is the foundation of further cognitive advances.

- Preoperational children use intuitive thought to explore and draw conclusions about the world, and their thinking begins to encompass the important notions of functionality and identity.

- Recent developmentalists, while acknowledging Piaget's gifts and contributions, take issue with his emphasis on children's limitations and his underestimation of their capabilities.

- Proponents of information processing approaches argue that quantitative changes in children's processing skills largely account for their cognitive development.

- Vygotsky believes that children develop cognitively within a context of culture and society through such processes as scaffolding, the temporary support that children need to help them frame and complete tasks.

Applying Child Development

- In your view, how do thought and language interact in preschoolers' development? How do children who have been deaf from birth think?

- *From an educator's perspective:* If children's cognitive development is dependent on interactions with others, what obligations does society have regarding such social settings as preschools and neighborhoods?

The Growth of Language

I tried it out and it was very great!
    This is a picture of when I was running through the water with Mommy.
    Where you are going when I go to the fireworks with Mommy and Daddy?
    I didn't know creatures went on floats in pools.
    We can always pretend we have another one.
    And the teacher put it up on the counter so no one could reach it.
    I really want to keep it while we're at the park.
    You need to get your own ball if you want to play "hit the tree."
    When I grow up and I'm a baseball player, I'll have my baseball hat, and I'll put it
on, and I'll play baseball. (Schatz, 1994, p. 179)

Listen to Ricky at the age of 3. In addition to recognizing most letters of the alphabet, printing the first letter of his name, and writing the word *hi*, he is readily capable of producing the complex sentences just quoted.

During the preschool years, children's language skills reach new heights of sophistication. Children begin the period with reasonable linguistic capabilities, though with significant gaps in both comprehension and production. However, by the end of the preschool years, they can hold their own with adults, both comprehending and producing language that has many of the qualities of adults' language. How does this transformation occur?

Syntax The combining of words and phrases to form meaningful sentences

Fast mapping The process in which new words are associated with their meaning after only a brief encounter

Grammar The system of rules that determine how thoughts can be expressed

Private speech Spoken language that is not intended for others and is commonly used by children during the preschool years

Language Advances During the Preschool Years

The two-word utterances of the 2-year-old soon increase in both number of words and scope. Indeed, language blooms so rapidly between the late 2s and the mid-3s that researchers have yet to understand the exact pattern. What is clear is that sentence length increases at a steady pace, and the ways in which children at this age combine words and phrases to form sentences—known as **syntax**—doubles each month. By the time a preschooler is 3, the various combinations reach into the thousands (Oller, 1999; Pinker, 1994; Wheeldon, 1999). For an example of one child's growth in the use of language, see Table 9-3.

Fast Mapping.   In addition to producing sentences of increasing complexity, children make enormous leaps in the number of words they use. By age 6, the average child has a vocabulary of around 14,000 words. This means that preschoolers acquire vocabulary at a rate of around 10 new words a day (E. Clark, 1983). They manage this feat through a process known as **fast mapping,** in which new words are associated with their meaning after only a brief encounter (Fenson et al., 1994).

By the age of 3, preschoolers routinely use plurals and possessive forms of nouns (such as *boys* and *boy's*), employ the past tense (adding *-ed* at the ends of words), and use articles (*the* and *a*). They can ask and answer complex questions ("Where did you say my book is?" "Those are trucks, aren't they?").

Preschoolers' skills extend to the appropriate formation of words that they have never before encountered. For example, in one classic experiment, preschool children were shown cards with drawings of a cartoonlike bird, such as the ones shown in Figure 9-6. The experimenter told the children that the figure was a "wug," and then showed them a card with two of the cartoon figures. "Now there are two of them," the children were told, and they were then asked to supply the missing word in the sentence, "There are two _____" (the answer to which, as *you* no doubt know, is "wugs") (Berko, 1958).

Not only did the children demonstrate that they knew rules about forming the plural of nouns but also that they understood possessive forms of nouns and the third-person singular and past-tense forms of verbs—all for words that they never had previously encountered, since they were nonsense words with no real meaning.

This is a wug.

Now there is another one. There are two of them. There are two _____ .

FIGURE 9-6   APPROPRIATE FORMATION OF WORDS

Even though preschoolers—like the rest of us—are unlikely to have ever before encountered a wug, they are able to produce the appropriate word to fill in the blank (which, for the record, is *wugs*).

(*Source:* Adapted from Berko, 1958)

Learning Grammar.   Preschoolers also learn what *cannot* be said as they acquire the principles of grammar. **Grammar** is the system of rules that determine how thoughts can be expressed. For instance, preschoolers come to learn that "I am sitting" is correct, while the similarly structured "I am knowing" is incorrect. Although they still make frequent mistakes of one sort or another, 3-year-olds follow the principles of grammar most of the time. Some errors are very noticeable—such as the use of *mens* and *catched*—but these errors are actually quite rare, occurring between 0.5 and 8 percent of the time. Put another way, more than 90 percent of the time young preschoolers are correct in their grammatical constructions (de Villiers & de Villiers, 1992; Guasti, 2002; Pinker, 1994).

Private Speech.   In even a short visit to a preschool, you're likely to notice some children talking to themselves during play periods. A child might be reminding a doll that the two of them are going to the grocery store later, or another child, while playing with a toy racing car, might speak of an upcoming race. In some cases, the talk is sustained, as when a child, working on a puzzle, says things like, "This piece goes here. . . . Uh-oh, this one doesn't fit. . . . Where can I put this piece? . . . This can't be right."

Some developmentalists suggest that **private speech,** speech by children that is directed to themselves, performs an important function. For instance, Vygotsky suggests that private speech is used as a guide to behavior and thought. By communicating with themselves through private speech, children are able to try out ideas, acting as their own sounding boards. In this way, private speech facilitates children's thinking and helps them control their behavior.

TABLE 9-3   GROWING SPEECH CAPABILITIES

Over the course of just a year, the sophistication of the language of a boy named Adam increased amazingly, as these speech samples show.

Age	Sentences Produced
2 years, 3 months:	Play checkers. Big drum. I got horn. A bunny-rabbit walk.
2 years, 4 months:	See marching bear go? Screw part machine. That busy bulldozer truck.
2 years, 5 months:	Now put boots on. Where wrench go? Mommy talking bout lady. What that paper clip doing?
2 years, 6 months:	Write a piece of paper. What that egg doing? I lost a shoe. No, I don't want to sit seat.
2 years, 7 months:	Where piece a paper go? Ursula has a boot on. Going to see kitten. Put the cigarette down. Dropped a rubber band. Shadow has hat just like that. Rintintin don't fly, Mommy.
2 years, 8 months:	Let me get down with the boots on. Don't be afraid a horses. How tiger be so healthy and fly like kite? Joshua throw like a penguin.
2 years, 9 months:	Where Mommy keep her pocketbook? Show you something funny. Just like turtle make mud pie.
2 years, 10 months:	Look at that train Ursula brought. I simply don't want put in chair. You don't have paper. Do you want little bit, Cromer? I can't wear it tomorrow.
2 years, 11 months:	That birdie hopping by Missouri in bag. Do want some pie on your face? Why you mixing baby chocolate? I finish drinking all up down my throat. I said why not you coming in? Look at that piece of paper and tell it. Do you want me tie that round? We going turn light on so you can't see.
3 years, 0 months:	I going come in fourteen minutes. I going wear that to wedding. I see what happens. I have to save them now. Those are not strong mens. They are going sleep in wintertime. You dress me up like a baby elephant.
3 years, 1 month:	I like to play with something else. You know how to put it back together. I gon' make it like a rocket to blast off with. I put another one on the floor. You went to Boston University? You want to give me some carrots and some beans? Press the button and catch it, sir. I want some other peanuts. Why you put the pacifier in his mouth? Doggies like to climb up.
3 years, 2 months:	So it can't be cleaned? I broke my racing car. Do you know the light wents off? What happened to the bridge? When it's got a flat tire it's need a go to the station. I dream sometimes. I'm going to mail this so the letter can't come off. I want to have some espresso. The sun is not too bright. Can I have some sugar? Can I put my head in the mailbox so the mailman can know where I are and put me in the mailbox? Can I keep the screwdriver just like a carpenter keep the screwdriver?

(*Source:* Pinker, 1994)

(Have you ever said to yourself, "Take it easy" or "Calm down" when trying to control your anger over some situation?) In Vygotsky's view, then, private speech ultimately serves an important social function, allowing children to solve problems and reflect on difficulties they encounter (Winsler, Diaz, & Montero, 1997). He suggests further that private speech is a forerunner to the internal dialogues that we use when we reason with ourselves during thinking.

Pragmatics The aspect of language relating to communicating effectively and appropriately with others

Social speech Speech directed toward another person and meant to be understood by that person

In addition, private speech may foster the development of preschoolers' pragmatic abilities. **Pragmatics** is the aspect of language relating to communicating effectively and appropriately with others. The development of pragmatic abilities permits children to understand the basics of conversations—turn-taking, sticking to a topic, and acceptable subjects of conversation according to the conventions of society. When children are taught that the appropriate response to receiving a gift is "Thank you" or that they should use different language in various settings (on the playground with their friends versus in the classroom with their teacher), they are learning the pragmatics of language.

Social Speech. The preschool years also mark an increase in social speech. **Social speech** is speech directed toward another person and meant to be understood by that person. Before the age of 3, children may seem to be speaking only for their own entertainment, apparently uncaring whether anyone else can understand. However, during the preschool years, children begin to direct their speech to others, wanting others to listen and becoming frustrated when they cannot make themselves understood. As a result, they begin to adapt their speech to others through pragmatics, as just noted. Recall that Piaget contended that most speech during the preoperational period was egocentric: Preschoolers were seen as taking little account of the effect their speech was having on others. However, more recent experimental evidence suggests that children are somewhat more adept in taking others into account than Piaget initially suggested.

Poverty and Language Development

The language that preschoolers hear at home has profound implications for future cognitive success, according to results of a landmark study by psychologists Betty Hart and Todd Risley (1995). The researchers studied the language used over a 2-year period by a group of parents of varying levels of affluence as they interacted with their children. Their examination of some 1,300 hours of everyday interactions between parents and children produced several major findings:

- The rate at which language was addressed to children varied significantly according to the economic level of the family. As can be seen in Figure 9-7, the greater the affluence of the parents, the more they spoke to their children.

- In a typical hour, parents classified as professionals spent almost twice as much time interacting with their children as parents receiving welfare assistance.

FIGURE 9-7 **DIFFERENT LANGUAGE EXPOSURES**

Parents at differing levels of affluence provide different language experiences. Professional parents and working parents address more words to their children, on average, than parents on welfare. Why do you think this is so?

(*Source:* B. Hart & Risley, 1995, p. 239)

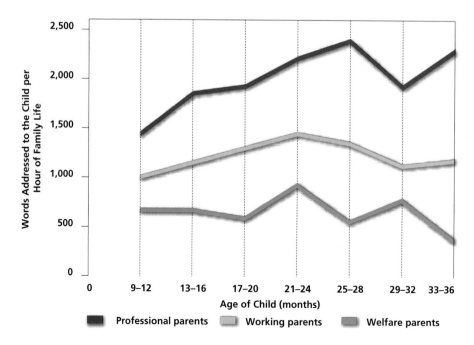

- By the age of 4, children in families with parents classified as professionals were likely to have been exposed to some 13 million more words than those in families receiving welfare assistance.

- The kind of language used in the home differed among the various types of families. Children in families receiving welfare assistance were apt to hear prohibitions ("no" or "stop," for example) twice as frequently as those in families with parents classified as professionals.

Ultimately, the study found that the type of language to which children were exposed was associated with their performance on tests of intelligence. The greater the number and variety of words children heard, for instance, the better their performance at age 3 on a variety of measures of intellectual achievement.

Although the findings are correlational and therefore cannot be interpreted in terms of cause and effect, they clearly suggest the importance of early exposure to language, in terms of both quantity and variety. They also suggest that intervention programs that teach parents to speak to their children more often and use more varied language may be useful in alleviating some of the potentially damaging consequences of poverty.

The research is also consistent with an increasing body of evidence that family income and poverty have powerful consequences for children's general cognitive development and behavior. By the age of 5, children raised in poverty tend to have lower IQ scores and perform less well on other measures of cognitive development than children raised in affluence. Furthermore, the longer children live in poverty, the more severe the consequences. Poverty not only reduces the educational resources available to children but also has such negative effects on *parents* that it limits the psychological support they can provide their families. In short, the consequences of poverty are substantial and long-lasting (Bornstein & Bradley, 2003; C. T. Ramey & Ramey, 1998; Whitehurst & Fischel, 2000).

R E V I E W & A P P L Y

Review

- In the preschool years, substantial linguistic advances are made in sentence length, vocabulary, syntax, and the use of forms such as plurals and possessives.

- Another linguistic development is a gradual shift from private to social speech.

- Economic factors in the home have a significant influence on language development. Children raised in affluence hear a greater quantity and variety of language from their parents than children of poverty.

Applying Child Development

- In what ways might adults use private speech? What functions does it serve?

- *From a social worker's perspective:* What do you think are the underlying reasons for differences between poor and more affluent households in the use of language, and how do such language differences affect a family's social interactions?

Schooling and Society

It's a Thursday afternoon at Unitel Studio on Ninth Avenue, where *Sesame Street* is taping its nineteenth season. Hanging back in the wings is a newcomer on the set, a compact young woman with short blonde hair named Judy Sladky. Today is her screen test. Other performers come to New York aspiring to be actresses, dancers, singers, comedians. But Sladky's burning ambition is to be Alice, a shaggy mini-mastodon who will make her debut later this season as the devoted baby sister of Aloysius Snuffle-upagus, the biggest creature on the show. (Hellman, 1987, p. 50)

Ask almost any preschooler, and she or he will be able to identify Snuffle-upagus, as well as Big Bird, Bert, Ernie, and a host of other characters as the members of the cast of *Sesame Street,* the most successful television show in history targeted at preschoolers, with a daily audience in the millions.

However, preschoolers do more than watch TV. Many spend a good portion of their day involved in some form of child care setting outside their own homes, designed, in part, to enhance their cognitive development. What are the consequences of these activities? We turn now to a consideration of how early childhood education and television are related to preschool development.

Early Childhood Education: Taking the *Pre-* out of the Preschool Period

The term *preschool period* is something of a misnomer: Almost three quarters of children in the United States are enrolled in some form of care outside the home, much of which is designed either explicitly or implicitly to teach skills that will enhance intellectual, as well as social, abilities (see Figure 9-8). There are several reasons for this increase, but one major factor is the rise in the number of families in which both parents work outside the home. For instance, a high proportion of fathers work outside the home, and close to 60 percent of women with children under age 6 are employed, most of them full time (Borden, 1998; L. A. Gilbert, 1994; Tamis-LeMonda & Cabrera, 2002).

However, there is another reason, less tied to the practical considerations of child care: Developmental psychologists have found increasing evidence that children can benefit substantially from involvement in some form of educational activity before they enroll in formal schooling, which typically takes place at age 5 or 6 in the United States. When compared to children who stay at home and have no formal educational involvement, those children enrolled in *good* preschools enjoy clear cognitive and social benefits (Clarke-Stewart, 1993; Haskins, 1989; McCartney, 1984).

The Varieties of Early Education.   The approaches taken to early education vary greatly. Some outside-the-home care for children is little more than babysitting, while other options are designed to promote intellectual and social advances. Let's take a closer look at three of the latter type.

FIGURE 9-8   CARE OUTSIDE THE HOME

Approximately 75 percent of children in the United States are enrolled in some form of care outside the home—a trend that is the result of more parents being employed full time. Evidence suggests that children can benefit from early childhood education. What role might a caregiver provide that can help the educational development of a child?

(*Source:* National Center for Education Statistics, 1997)

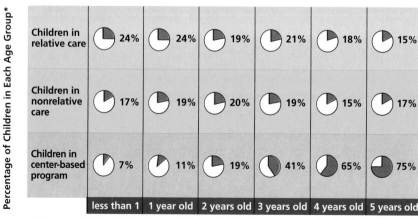

Percentage of Children in Each Age Group*	less than 1	1 year old	2 years old	3 years old	4 years old	5 years old
Children in relative care	24%	24%	19%	21%	18%	15%
Children in nonrelative care	17%	19%	20%	19%	15%	17%
Children in center-based program	7%	11%	19%	41%	65%	75%

*Columns do not add up to 100 because some children participated in more than one type of day care.

Child care centers typically provide care for children all day, while their parents are at work. (Child care centers were once referred to as day care centers. However, because a significant number of parents work nonstandard schedules and therefore require care for their children at times other than during the day, the preferred label is now *child care centers*.)

Although many child care centers were first established as safe, warm environments where children could be cared for and could interact with other children, today their purpose tends to be broader, aimed at providing some form of intellectual stimulation. Still, their primary purpose tends to be more social and emotional than cognitive.

Some child care is provided in family child care centers, small operations run in private homes. Because such centers are often unlicensed, the quality of care can be uneven, and parents should investigate carefully before enrolling their children. In contrast, providers of center-based care, which is offered in institutions such as schools, community centers, and churches and synagogues, are licensed and regulated by governmental authorities. Because teachers in such programs are more often trained professionals than those who provide family child care, the quality of care is often higher and more stable.

Preschools, also known as **nursery schools,** are more explicitly designed to provide intellectual and social experiences for children. Because they tend to be more limited in their schedules, typically providing care for only 3 to 5 hours a day, preschools mainly serve children from the middle and higher socioeconomic levels.

Like child care centers, preschools vary enormously in the activities they provide. Some emphasize social skills, while others focus on intellectual development. Some do both. For instance, Montessori preschools, which use a method developed by Italian educator Maria Montessori, employ a carefully designed set of materials to create an environment that fosters sensory, motor, and language development.

School child care is provided by some local school systems in the United States. Almost half the states fund pre-kindergarten programs for 4-year-olds, often targeted at disadvantaged children. Because they are typically staffed by better trained teachers than less regulated child care centers, school child care programs are often of higher quality than other early education alternatives.

The Effectiveness of Child Care.   How effective are early education programs? According to developmental psychologist Alison Clarke-Stewart, who has studied the issue extensively, preschoolers enrolled in child care centers show intellectual development that at least matches that of children at home and often is better. For instance, some studies find that child care preschoolers are more verbally fluent, show memory and comprehension advantages, and achieve higher IQ scores than at-home children. Other studies find that early and long-term participation in child care is particularly helpful for children from impoverished home environments or who are otherwise at risk (Clarke-Stewart, 1993; Peisner-Feinberg et al., 2001; S. L. Ramey, 1999).

Similar advantages are found in social development. Children in high-quality programs tend to be more self-confident, independent, and knowledgeable about the social world in which they live than those who do not participate. On the other hand, not all the outcomes of outside-the-home care are positive: Children in child care have been found to be less polite, less compliant, less respectful of adults, and sometimes more competitive and aggressive than their peers (J. E. Bates et al., 1991; Belsky, Steinberg, & Walker, 1982; National Institute of Child Health and Human Development, 2001a, 2001b).

It is important to keep in mind that not all early childhood care programs are equally effective. As we observed of infant child care in Chapter 7, one key factor is program *quality:* High-quality care provides intellectual and social benefits, while low-quality care is not only unlikely to furnish benefits but may actually harm children (V. E. Lee, Loeb, & Lubeck, 1998; C. T. Ramey & Ramey, 1999).

Child care center A place that provides care for children while their parents are at work

Preschool (nursery school) A child care facility designed to provide intellectual and social experiences for youngsters

School child care A child care facility provided by some local school systems in the United States

"I didn't realize how much I needed to get away from that day-care grind."

The Quality of Child Care.   How can we define "high quality"? Several characteristics are important; they are analogous to those that pertain to infant child care (see Chapter 7). For example, high-quality facilities have well-trained care providers. Furthermore, both the overall size of the group and the ratio of care providers to children are critical. Single groups should not have more than 14 to 20 children, and there should be no more than five to ten 3-year-olds or seven to ten 4- or 5-year-olds per caregiver. Finally, the curriculum of a child care facility should not be left to chance but should be carefully planned out and coordinated among the teachers (Cromwell, 1994; National Research Council, 1991; Scarr, 1997).

No one knows how many programs in the United States can be considered "high quality," but there are many fewer than desirable. In fact, the United States lags behind almost every other industrialized country in the quality of child care, as well as in its quantity and affordability (Ripple et al., 1999; Scarr, 1998; Zigler & Finn-Stevenson, 1995).

Preparing for Academic Pursuits: Does Head Start Truly Provide a Head Start?
Although many programs designed for preschoolers focus primarily on social and emotional factors, some programs are geared primarily toward promoting cognitive gains and preparing preschoolers for the more formal instruction they will experience when they start kindergarten. In the United States, the best-known program designed to promote future academic success is Head Start. Born in the 1960s when the United States declared its War on Poverty, the program has served over 13 million children and their families. Although it was designed to serve the "whole child," including children's physical health, self-confidence, social responsibility, and social and emotional development, the program has been scrutinized most closely in relation to the goal of improving cognitive processes (Ripple et al., 1999; Zigler & Styfco, 1994; Zigler, Styfco, & Gilman, 1993).

Whether Head Start is seen as successful or not depends on the lens through which one is looking. If, for instance, the program is expected to provide long-term increases in IQ scores, it is a disappointment. Although graduates of Head Start programs tend to show immediate IQ gains, these increases do not last. But it is clear that preschoolers who participate in Head Start are more ready for future schooling than those who do not. Furthermore, graduates of Head Start programs have better future school adjustment than their peers, and they are less likely to be in special education classes or to be retained in grade. Finally, some research suggests that ultimately Head Start graduates show higher academic performance at the end of high school, although the gains are modest (Currie & Thomas, 1995; Galper, Wigfield, & Seefeldt, 1997; S. L. Ramey, 1999).

DEVELOPMENTAL DIVERSITY

Preschools Around the World: Why Does the United States Lag Behind?

In France and Belgium, access to preschool is a legal right. In Sweden and Finland, preschoolers whose parents work have child care provided, if it is wanted. Russia has an extensive system of state-run *yasli-sads,* nursery schools and kindergartens, attended by 75 percent of children aged 3 to 7 in urban areas.

In contrast, the United States has no coordinated national policy on preschool education—or on the care of children in general. There are several reasons for this. For one, decisions about education have traditionally been left to the states and local school districts. For another, the United States has no tradition of teaching preschoolers, unlike other countries in which preschool-age children have been enrolled in formal programs for decades. Finally, the status of preschools in the United States has been traditionally low. Preschool and nursery school teachers are the lowest paid of all teachers. (Teacher salaries increase as the age of students rises. Thus college and high school teachers are paid the most, while preschool and elementary school teachers are paid the least.)

Preschools also differ significantly from one country to another according to the views that different societies hold of the purpose of early childhood education (Lamb et al., 1992). For instance, in a cross-country comparison of preschools in China, Japan, and the United States, researchers found that parents in the three countries view the purpose of preschools very differently. Whereas parents in China tend to see preschools primarily as a way of giving children a good start academically, Japanese parents view them primarily as a way of giving children the opportunity to be members of a group. In the United States, in comparison, parents regard the primary purpose of preschools as making children more independent and self-reliant, although obtaining a good academic start and having group experience are also important (Huntsinger et al., 1997; Tobin, Wu, & Davidson, 1989; see Figure 9-9).

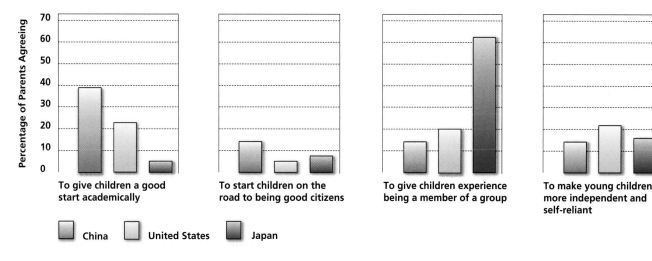

FIGURE 9-9   **THE PURPOSE OF PRESCHOOL**

To parents in China, Japan, and the United States, the main purpose of preschools is very different. Whereas parents in China see preschools mainly as a way of giving children a good start academically, parents in Japan see them primarily as a means of giving children the experience of being a member of a group. In contrast, parents in the United States view preschools as a way of making children more independent, although obtaining a good academic start and group experience are also important. As a preschool educator, how would you interpret these findings?

(*Source:* Adapted from Tobin, Wu & Davidson, 1989)

The most recent comprehensive evaluations of early intervention programs suggest that as a group they can provide significant benefits and that government funds invested early in life may ultimately lead to a reduction in future costs. For instance, compared with children who did not participate in early intervention programs, participants in various programs showed gains in emotional or cognitive development, better educational outcomes, increased economic self-sufficiency, reduced levels of criminal activity, and improved health-related behaviors. Although not every program produced all these benefits and not every child benefited to the same extent, the results of the evaluations suggest that the potential benefits of early intervention can be substantial (F. A. Campbell et al., 2001; Wigfield et al., 1999; Schnur & Belanger, 2000).

Despite evidence supporting the effectiveness of early interventions in general, Head Start remains controversial. Some researchers suggest that the costs of Head Start—which, because of its intensity, is a relatively expensive form of child care—could be better spent on other forms of child care. For instance, developmentalist Sandra Scarr (1996, 1998) suggests that low-income preschool children may be better off spending more time in less costly programs than participating part time in Head Start programs. (For more on preschools from the perspective of a preschool teacher, see *Careers in Child Development*.)

"For children to fully understand what is going on, the information you provide has to be meaningful for them."

● CAREERS IN CHILD DEVELOPMENT ●

Roberto Recio Jr.

Education: . . . . **Daley College, Chicago: A.A. in early childhood education**
Position: . . . . **Head teacher, Christopher House Uptown preschool**
Home: . . . . **Chicago**

For Robert Recio, head teacher at the Christopher House Uptown preschool in Chicago, each day offers new challenges as he seeks to enhance children's development.

Recio tries to be more of a role model, guide, and facilitator than a teacher, he says. "I try to prepare the environment to provide stimulating and challenging material. For children to fully understand what is going on, the information you provide has to be meaningful for them. If it's not relevant, they won't be motivated and will not get it."

Recio, who along with two assistants is responsible for 20 children aged 3 to 5, uses hands-on approaches to learning.

"The other day we were talking about fishing, so I went to the market and bought an actual fish and brought it in the next day," Recio says. "You should have seen the smiles on their faces as they were touching it and smelling it. Most of these children have never seen a real fish. We later used it in an art project making prints with it."

Recio is constantly interacting with the children and challenging them, even when doing chores.

"When they set tables for lunch, I will ask them how many utensils need to be used. Or when setting up chairs, I will put out fewer than the number of children we have, and I'll have them figure out how many more are needed," he explains.

While math, science, and art are all covered in Recio's class on a daily basis, one additional area he feels is particularly important is making the children aware of the diversity within their community.

"We have a lot of cultural diversity in our class," he notes. At the same time, he adds, "I like to have them understand that we are all the same inside."

"Say, Dad, think you could wrap it up? I have a long day tomorrow."

Are We Pushing Children Too Hard and Too Fast?   Not everyone agrees that programs that seek to enhance academic skills during the preschool years are a good thing. In fact, according to developmental psychologist David Elkind (1984, 1988), U.S. society tends to push children so rapidly that they begin to feel stress and pressure at a young age.

Elkind argues that academic success is largely dependent on factors out of parents' control, such as inherited abilities and a child's rate of maturation. Consequently, children of a particular age cannot be expected to master educational material without taking their current level of cognitive development into account. In short, children require **developmentally appropriate educational practice,** which is education that is based on both typical development and the unique characteristics of a given child (Bredekamp, 1987; Cromwell, 1994).

Elkind argues that parents should provide a relaxed environment in which learning is encouraged, but not pushed, in order to reduce pressure on children. Although appealing, Elkind's idea is not without its critics. For instance, some educators have argued that pushing children is largely a phenomenon of the middle and higher socioeconomic levels, possible only if parents are relatively affluent. For poorer children, whose parents may have neither substantial resources available to push their children nor the easy ability to create an environment that promotes learning, the benefits of formal programs that promote learning are likely to outweigh their drawbacks.

Television: Learning From the Media

Television plays a central role in many U.S. households. In fact, it is one of the most potent and widespread stimuli to which children are exposed, with the average preschooler watching more than 21 hours of TV a week. More than a third of households with children 2 to 7 years of age say that the television is on "most of the time" in their homes. In comparison, these children spend only three quarters of an hour reading on the average day (Bryant & Bryant, 2001; V. J. Rideout et al., 1999; J. P. Robinson & Bianchi, 1997; see Figure 9-10).

Controlling TV Exposure.   Despite the introduction of a number of high-quality educational programs over the past decade, many children's programs are not of high quality or are not appropriate for a preschool audience. Accordingly, the American Academy of Pediatrics (1999) recommends that exposure to television should be limited. It suggests that children watch *no* television until the age of 2 and after that no more than 1 to 2 hours of quality programming a day.

Developmentally appropriate educational practice   Education that is based on both typical development and the unique characteristics of a given child

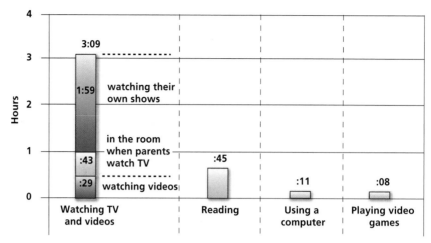

Times are presented in hours: minutes. Numbers cannot be summed to calculate children's total media use time because they may have used more than one medium at a time. Reading includes amount of time children are read to.

FIGURE 9-10   TELEVISION TIME

Although 2- to 7-year-olds spend more time reading than playing video games or using a computer, they spend considerably more time watching television. As an educator, how would you instill interest in children to read more?

(*Source:* V. J. Rideout et al., 1999)

What are the limits of preschoolers' "television literacy"? When they do watch television, preschool children often do not fully understand the plots of the stories they are viewing, particularly in longer programs. They are unable to recall significant story details after viewing a program, and the inferences they make about the motivations of characters are limited and often erroneous. Moreover, preschool children may have difficulty separating fantasy from reality in television programming (Rule & Ferguson, 1986; J. C. Wright et al., 1994).

Nevertheless, some kinds of information are likely to be understood relatively well by children. For instance, preschoolers are able to decode the facial expressions they see on television. Perhaps this is related to the fact that the television shows viewed most frequently by children include surprisingly high rates of nonverbal displays of emotion. However, the emotional displays that children view on TV differ from what they find in the everyday, nontelevised world. On TV, certain emotions (such as happiness and sadness) are displayed considerably more frequently than others (for instance, fear and disgust) (Coats & Feldman, 1995; Houle & Feldman, 1991).

In short, the world to which preschoolers are exposed on TV is imperfectly understood and unrealistic. As they get older and their information processing capabilities improve, preschoolers' understanding of the material they see on television improves. They remember things more accurately, and they become better able to focus on the central message of a show. This suggests that the powers of the medium of television may be harnessed to bring about cognitive gains—exactly what the producers of *Sesame Street* set out to do (L. E. Levine & Waite, 2000; D. G. Singer & Singer, 2000; Weisinger, 1998).

***Sesame Street:* A Teacher in Every Home?**   *Sesame Street* is, without a doubt, the most popular educational program for children in the United States. Almost half of all preschoolers in the United States watch the show, and it is broadcast in almost 100 different countries and in 13 foreign languages. Characters like Big Bird and Elmo have become familiar throughout the world, to both adults and preschoolers (Bickham, Wright, & Huston, 2000; Liebert & Sprafkin, 1988).

BECOMING AN INFORMED CONSUMER OF DEVELOPMENT

Promoting Cognitive Development in Preschoolers: From Theory to the Classroom

We have considered the notion that one focus of the preschool period should be on promoting future academic success, and we have also discussed the alternative view that pushing children too hard academically may be hazardous to their well-being.

There is, however, a middle ground. Drawing on research conducted by developmental psychologists who examine cognitive development during the preschool years (E. Reese & Cox, 1999), we can make several suggestions for parents and preschool teachers who wish to improve the academic readiness of children without creating undue stress. Among them are the following:

- Both parents and teachers should be aware of the stage of cognitive development, with its capabilities and limitations, that each individual child has reached. Unless they are aware of a child's current level of development, it will be impossible to provide appropriate materials and experiences.

- Instruction should be at a level just slightly higher than each student's current level of cognitive development. With too little novelty, children will be bored; with too much, they will be confused.

- Instruction should be individualized as much as possible. Because children of the same age may be at different levels of cognitive development, curriculum materials that are prepared individually stand a better chance of success.

- Opportunities for social interaction—both with other students and with adults—should be provided. By receiving feedback from others and observing how others react in given situations, preschoolers learn new approaches and new ways of thinking about the world.

- Let students make mistakes. Cognitive growth often flows from confronting and correcting errors.

- Because cognitive development can occur only when children have achieved the appropriate level of maturation, preschoolers should not be pushed too far ahead of their current state of cognitive development.

- Read to children. Children learn from hearing stories read to them, and it can motivate them to learn to read themselves.

Sesame Street was devised with the express purpose of providing an educational experience for preschoolers. Its specific goals include teaching letters and numbers, increasing vocabulary, and teaching preliteracy skills.

Has *Sesame Street* achieved its goals? Most evidence suggests that it has. Formal evaluations of the show find that preschoolers living in lower income households who watch the show are better prepared for school, and they perform significantly higher on several measures of verbal and mathematics ability at ages 6 and 7 than those who do not watch it. Furthermore, viewers of *Sesame Street* spend more time reading than nonviewers. And by the time they are 6 and 7, viewers of *Sesame Street* and other educational programs tend to be better readers and to be judged more positively by their teachers (Huston & Wright, 1995).

Sesame Street does have its critics, however. Some educators claim that the frenzied pace at which different scenes are shown makes viewers less receptive to the traditional forms of teaching that they will experience when they begin school. However, careful evaluations of the program find no evidence that viewing *Sesame Street* leads to a decline in the enjoyment of traditional schooling. Indeed, the most recent findings regarding *Sesame Street* and informative programs like it show quite positive outcomes for viewers (J. C. Wright et al., 2001).

REVIEW & APPLY

Review

- Enrollments are on the rise in many different kinds of preschool programs, primarily due to increased numbers of families in which both parents work outside the home.

- Preschool programs can be beneficial if they are of high quality, with trained staff, good curriculum, proper group sizes, and low student–staff ratios.

- With the exception of the successful Head Start program, the U.S. government pays little attention to preschool education, in contrast with many other countries.

- The effects of television on preschoolers are mixed, with benefits from some programs and clear disadvantages due to other aspects of viewing.

Applying Child Development

- Do you think that children with certain personality or cognitive characteristics might benefit more from preschool programs than children with different characteristics? What sorts of characteristics might make a difference?

- *From the perspective of an educator:* Should the United States develop a more encouraging and more supportive preschool policy? If so, what sort of policy? If not, why not?

LOOKING BACK

- **How does Piaget interpret cognitive development during the preschool years?**

- During the stage that Piaget has described as *preoperational,* children are not yet able to engage in organized, formal, logical thinking. However, their development of symbolic function permits quicker and more effective thinking as they are freed from the limitations of sensorimotor learning.

- According to Piaget, children in the preoperational stage engage in intuitive thought for the first time, actively applying rudimentary reasoning skills to the acquisition of world knowledge.

- **How do information processing approaches and Vygotsky's theory explain cognitive development?**

- A different approach to cognitive development is taken by proponents of information processing theories, who focus on preschoolers' storage and recall of information and on quantitative changes in information processing abilities (such as attention).

- Lev Vygotsky proposed that the nature and progress of children's cognitive development are dependent on the children's social and cultural context.

- **How do children's linguistic abilities develop in the preschool years, and what is the importance of early linguistic development?**

- Children rapidly progress from two-word utterances to longer, more sophisticated expressions that reflect their growing vocabularies and emerging grasp of grammar.

- The development of linguistic abilities is affected by socioeconomic status. The result can be lowered linguistic—and ultimately academic—performance by poorer children.

○ **What kinds of preschool educational programs are available in the United States, and what effects do they have?**

• The United States lacks a coordinated national policy on preschool education. The major federal initiative in U.S. preschool education has been the Head Start program, which has yielded mixed, although promising, results.

• Early childhood educational programs—center-based, school-based, or preschool—can lead to cognitive and social advances.

○ **What effects does television have on preschoolers?**

• The effects of television are mixed. On the one hand, preschoolers' sustained exposure to emotions and situations that are not representative of the real world have raised concerns. On the other hand, preschoolers can derive meaning from such targeted programs as *Sesame Street,* which are designed to bring about cognitive gains.

EPILOGUE

 n this chapter, we looked at children in the preschool years. We discussed cognitive development from the Piagetian perspective, with its description of the characteristics of thought in the preoperational stage, and from the perspective of information processing theorists and Lev Vygotsky. We then discussed the burst in linguistic ability that occurs during the preschool years and the influence of television on preschoolers' development. We concluded with a discussion of preschool education and its effects.

Return to the prologue, which describes Will's preparation for his first day of kindergarten, and answer the following questions:

1. According to Piaget, what sorts of understandings—and limitations to his understandings—will Will have as he enters school?

2. Can you discuss from an information processing perspective the likely course of Will's cognitive development during his preschool years? What most likely changed as he progressed toward kindergarten, and why?

3. In what ways is kindergarten likely to affect Will's sense of the pragmatics of language that govern communications with others?

4. To what aspects of the school "culture" that Will is joining do Vygotsky's theories apply? What features of the typical kindergarten program would a follower of Vygotsky emphasize?

KEY TERMS AND CONCEPTS

preoperational stage (p. 261)
operations (p. 261)
symbolic function (p. 261)
centration (p. 261)
conservation (p. 263)
transformation (p. 263)
egocentric thought (p. 263)
intuitive thought (p. 265)

autobiographical memory (p. 268)
scripts (p. 268)
zone of proximal development (ZPD) (p. 272)
scaffolding (p. 272)
syntax (p. 276)
fast mapping (p. 276)
grammar (p. 276)

private speech (p. 276)
pragmatics (p. 278)
social speech (p. 278)
child care center (p. 281)
preschool (nursery school) (p. 281)
school child care (p. 281)
developmentally appropriate educational practice (p. 285)

10

Social and Personality Development in the Preschool Years

PROLOGUE: Feeling His Mother's Pain

When Alison Gopnik got home from the lab one day, she was overcome with the feeling that she was a lousy teacher, an incompetent scientist and a bad mother. A student had argued with a grade, a grant proposal had been rejected and the chicken legs she'd planned for dinner were still in the freezer. So the University of California, Berkeley, developmental psychologist collapsed on the couch and started to cry. Her son, almost 2, sized up the situation like a little pro. He dashed to the bathroom, fumbled around for what he needed and returned with Band-Aids—which he proceeded to stick all over his sobbing (and now startled) mother, figuring that eventually he would find the place that needed patching. (Begley, 2000, p. 25)

A child's ability to understand others' emotions begins to grow during the preschool years.

LOOKING **AHEAD** ▶

Like most 2-year-olds, Gopnik's son could not only share his mother's pain but was able to find a way to try to soothe it. During the preschool years, children's ability to understand others' emotions begins to grow, and it colors their relationships with others.

In this chapter, we address social and personality development during the preschool period, a time of enormous growth and change. We begin by examining how preschool-age children continue to form a sense of self, focusing on how they develop their self-concepts. We especially examine issues of self relating to gender, a central aspect of children's views of themselves and others.

Preschoolers' social lives are the focus of the next part of the chapter. We look at how children play with one another, examining the various types of play. We consider how parents and other authority figures use discipline to shape children's behavior.

Finally, we examine two key aspects of preschool-age children's social behavior: moral development and aggression. We consider how children develop a notion of right and wrong and how that development can lead them to be helpful to others. We also look at the other side of the coin—aggression—and examine the factors that lead preschool-age children to behave in a way that hurts others. We end on an optimistic note: considering how we may help preschool-age children to be more moral and less aggressive individuals.

In sum, after reading this chapter, you will be able to answer the following questions:

- How do preschool-age children develop a concept of themselves?
- How do children develop a sense of racial identity and gender?
- In what sorts of social relationships and play do preschoolers engage?
- What sorts of disciplinary styles do parents employ, and what effects do they have?
- How do children develop a moral sense?
- How does aggression develop in preschool-age children?

Forming a Sense of Self

Although the question "Who am I?" is not explicitly posed by most preschool-age children, it underlies a considerable amount of development during the preschool years. During this period, children wonder about the nature of the self, and the way they answer the "Who am I?" question may affect them for the rest of their lives.

Psychosocial Development: Resolving the Conflicts

Mary-Alice's preschool teacher raised her eyebrows slightly when the 4-year-old took off her coat. Mary-Alice, usually dressed in well-matched play suits, was a medley of prints. She had on a pair of flowered pants, along with a completely clashing plaid top. The outfit was accessorized with a striped headband, socks in an animal print, and Mary-Alice's polka-dotted rain boots. Mary-Alice's mom gave a slightly embarrassed shrug. "Mary-Alice got dressed all by herself this morning," she explained as she handed over a bag containing spare shoes, just in case the rain boots became uncomfortable during the day.

Psychoanalyst Erik Erikson might well have praised Mary-Alice's mother for helping Mary-Alice develop a sense of initiative (if not of fashion). The reason: Erikson (1963) suggested that during the preschool years, children face a key conflict relating to psychosocial development that involves the development of initiative.

As we discussed in Chapter 7, **psychosocial development** encompasses changes both in the understandings individuals have of themselves as members of society and in their comprehension of the meaning of others' behavior. Erikson suggests that throughout life, society and culture present particular challenges, which shift as people age. Erikson suggests that people pass through eight distinct stages, each of which necessitates resolution of a crisis or conflict. Our experiences as we try to resolve these conflicts lead us to develop ideas about ourselves that can last for the rest of our lives.

In the early part of the preschool period, children are ending the autonomy-versus-shame-and-doubt stage, which lasts from around 18 months to 3 years. In this period, children either become more independent and autonomous if their parents encourage exploration and freedom or experience shame and self-doubt if they are restricted and overprotected.

The preschool years largely encompass the **initiative-versus-guilt stage,** which lasts from around age 3 to age 6. It is during this period that children's views of themselves undergo major change as preschool-age children face conflicts between, on the one hand, the desire to act independently of their parents and, on the other hand, the guilt that comes from the unintended consequences of their actions. In essence, preschool-age children come to realize that they are persons in their own right, and they begin to make decisions and to shape the kinds of persons that they will become.

Parents, such as Mary-Alice's mother, who react positively to this transformation toward independence can help their children resolve the opposing feelings that are characteristic of this period. By providing their children with opportunities to act self-reliantly while still giving them direction and guidance, parents can support and encourage their children's initiative. Conversely, parents who discourage their children's efforts to seek independence may contribute to a sense of guilt that persists throughout their lives and also affects their self-concept, which begins to develop during this period.

Self-Concept in the Preschool Years: Thinking About the Self

If you ask preschool-age children to specify what makes them different from other kids, they readily respond with answers like "I'm a good runner" or "I like to color" or "I'm a big girl." Such

Psychosocial development According to Erikson, development that encompasses changes both in the understandings individuals have of themselves as members of society and in their comprehension of the meaning of others' behavior

Initiative-versus-guilt stage According to Erikson, the period during which children aged 3 to 6 years experience conflict between independence of action and the sometimes negative results of that action

VIDEO CLIP

Self Awareness

The view of the self that preschoolers develop depends in part on the culture in which they grow up.

answers relate to **self-concept**—their identity or their set of beliefs about what they are like as individuals (J. D. Brown, 1998; Pipp-Siegel & Foltz, 1997; Tesser, Felson, & Suls, 2000).

The statements that describe children's self-concepts are not necessarily accurate. In fact, preschool children typically overestimate their skills and knowledge across all domains of expertise. Consequently, their view of the future is quite rosy: They expect to win the next game they play, to beat all opponents in an upcoming race, to write great stories when they grow up. Even when they have just experienced failure at a task, they are likely to expect to do well in the future. This optimistic view is held, in part, because they have not yet started to compare themselves and their performance against others (Damon & Hart, 1988; Ruble, 1983; Stipek & Hoffman, 1980).

Preschool-age children also begin to develop a view of self that reflects the way their particular culture considers the self. For example, many Asian societies tend to have a **collectivistic orientation,** promoting the notion of interdependence. People in such cultures tend to regard themselves as parts of a larger social network in which they are interconnected with others. In contrast, children in Western cultures are more likely to develop an independent view of the self, reflecting an **individualistic orientation** that emphasizes personal identity and the uniqueness of the individual. They are more apt to see themselves as self-contained and autonomous, in competition with others for scarce resources. Consequently, children in Western cultures are more likely to focus on their uniqueness and what sets them apart from others—what makes them special.

Such views pervade a culture, sometimes in subtle ways. For instance, one well-known saying in Western cultures states that "the squeaky wheel gets the grease." Preschoolers who are exposed to this perspective come to understand that they should seek to get the attention of others by standing out and making their needs known. Children in Asian cultures, by contrast, are exposed to a different perspective; they are told that "the nail that stands out gets pounded down." This perspective suggests to preschoolers that they should attempt to blend in and refrain from making themselves distinctive (Markus & Kitayama, 1991; K. H. Rubin, 1998; Triandis, 1995).

Preschoolers' developing self-concepts can also be affected by their culture's attitudes toward various racial and ethnic groups (see the *Developmental Diversity* box).

Gender Identity: Developing Femaleness and Maleness

Boys' awards: Best Thinker, Most Eager Learner, Most Imaginative, Most Enthusiastic, Most Scientific, Best Friend, Mr. Personality, Hardest Worker, Best Sense of Humor
Girls' awards: All-Around Sweetheart, Sweetest Personality, Cutest, Best Sharer, Best Artist, Most Generous, Best Manners, Best Helper, Most Creative

What's wrong with this picture? To one parent, whose daughter received one of the girls' awards during a kindergarten graduation ceremony, quite a bit. While the girls were getting pats on the back for their pleasing personalities, the boys were receiving awards for their intellectual and analytic skills (Deveny, 1994).

Such a situation is not rare: Girls and boys often live in very different worlds. Differences in the ways males and females are treated begin at birth, continue during the preschool years, and as we'll see later, extend into adolescence and beyond (Coltrane & Adams, 1997; Maccoby, 1999).

The Beginnings of Gender Identity.   Gender, the sense of being male or female, is well established by the time children reach the preschool years. By the age of 2, children consistently label themselves and those around them as male or female (Fagot & Leinbach, 1993; Poulin-Dubois et al., 1994; Signorella, Bigler & Liben, 1993).

One way gender is manifested is in play. During the preschool years, boys spend more time than girls in rough-and-tumble play, while girls spend more time than boys in organized games

Self-concept A person's identity or set of beliefs about what one is like as an individual

Collectivistic orientation A philosophy that promotes the notion of interdependence

Individualistic orientation A philosophy that emphasizes personal identity and the uniqueness of the individual

DEVELOPMENTAL DIVERSITY

Developing Racial and Ethnic Awareness

The preschool years mark an important turning point for children. Their answer to the question of who they are begins to take into account their racial and ethnic identity.

For most preschool-age children, racial awareness comes relatively early. Certainly, even infants are able to distinguish different skin colors; their perceptual abilities allow for such color distinctions quite early in life. However, it is only later that children begin to attribute meaning to different racial characteristics. By the time they are 3 or 4 years of age, preschool-age children distinguish between African Americans and whites and begin to understand the significance that society places on racial membership (Bigler & Liben, 1993; H. W. Harris, Blue, & Griffin, 1995; Sheets & Hollins, 1999).

At the same time, some preschool-age children start to experience ambivalence over the meaning of their racial and ethnic identity. Some preschoolers experience **race dissonance,** the

phenomenon in which minority children indicate preferences for majority values or people. For instance, some studies find that as many as 90 percent of African American children, when asked about their reactions to drawings of black and white children, react more negatively to the drawings of black children than to those of white children. However, these negative reactions did not translate into lower self-esteem for the African American subjects. Instead, their preferences appear to be a result of the powerful influence of the dominant white culture, rather than a disparagement of their own racial characteristics (N. Holland, 1994).

Ethnic identity emerges somewhat later. For instance, in one study of Mexican American ethnic awareness, preschoolers displayed only a limited knowledge of their ethnic identity. However, as they became older, their understanding of their racial background grew in both magnitude and complexity. In addition, preschoolers who were bilingual, speaking both Spanish and English, were most apt to be aware of their racial identity (Bernal, 1994).

---

and role-playing. Furthermore, boys begin to play more with boys, and girls play more with girls, a trend that increases during middle childhood. Actually, girls begin the process of preferring same-sex playmates a little earlier than boys. Girls first have a clear preference for interacting with other girls at age 2, while boys don't show much preference for same-sex partners until age 3 (Benenson, 1994; Boyatzis, Mallis, & Leon, 1999; Braza et al., 1997; Fagot, 1991).

Such same-sex preferences appear in many cultures. For instance, studies of kindergartners in mainland China reveal no examples of mixed-gender play. Similarly, gender "outweighs" ethnic variables when it comes to play: A Hispanic boy would rather play with a white boy than with a Hispanic girl (Fishbein & Imai, 1993; C. L. Martin, 1993; Shepard, 1991; P. J. Turner, Gervai, & Hinde, 1993; Whiting & Edwards, 1988).

Gender Expectations.   Preschool-age children also begin to hold expectations about appropriate behavior for girls and boys. In fact, their expectations about gender-appropriate behavior are even more rigid and gender-stereotyped than those of adults and may be less flexible during the preschool years than at any other point in life. For instance, beliefs in gender stereotypes become more pronounced up to age 5 and have already started to become somewhat less rigid by age 7, although they never disappear altogether. In fact, the content of gender stereotypes held by preschoolers is similar to that held traditionally by adults in the same society (Golombok & Fivush, 1994; Urberg, 1982; Yee & Brown, 1994).

And what is the nature of preschoolers' gender expectations? Like adults, preschoolers expect that males are more apt to have traits involving competence, independence, forcefulness, and competitiveness. In contrast, females are viewed as more likely to have traits such as warmth, expressiveness, nurturance, and submissiveness. Although these are *expectations* and say nothing about the way that men and women actually behave, such expectations provide the lens through which preschool-age children view the world. Preschoolers' views and expectations affect their own behavior as well as the way they interact with peers and adults (Durkin & Nugent, 1998; Signorella et al., 1993).

Race dissonance The phenomenon in which minority children indicate preferences for majority values or people

The prevalence and strength of preschoolers' gender expectations and the differences in behavior between boys and girls have proved puzzling. Why should gender play such a powerful role during the preschool years (as well as during the rest of the life span)? Developmentalists have proposed several explanations.

Biological Perspectives on Gender. Recall that *gender* relates to the sense of being male or female, while *sex* refers to the physical characteristics that differentiate males and females. It would hardly be surprising to find that the biological characteristics associated with sex might themselves lead to gender differences, and this has in fact been shown to be true.

Hormones are one such biological characteristic. Some research has focused on girls whose mothers had taken drugs that contained high levels of *androgens* (male hormones) to treat medical problems they had before they realized that they were pregnant. These androgen-exposed girls are more likely to display behaviors associated with male stereotypes than their sisters who were not exposed to androgens (Money & Ehrhardt, 1972). Androgen-exposed girls preferred boys as playmates and spent more time than other girls playing with toys associated with the male role, such as cars and trucks. Similarly, boys prenatally exposed to unusually high levels of female hormones are apt to display more behaviors that are stereotypically female than is usual (Berenbaum & Hines, 1992; Hines & Kaufman, 1994).

Moreover, as we first noted in Chapter 8, some research suggests that biological differences exist in the structure of female and male brains. For instance, part of the corpus callosum, the bundle of nerves that connects the hemispheres of the brain, is proportionally larger in women than in men (Whitelson, 1989). To some theoreticians, evidence such as this suggests that gender differences may be produced by biological factors (Benbow, Lubinski, & Hyde, 1997).

Before accepting such contentions, however, it is important to note that alternative explanations abound. For example, it may be that the corpus callosum is proportionally larger in women as a result of certain kinds of experiences that influence brain growth in particular ways. If this is true, environmental experience produces biological change, and not the other way around.

Other developmentalists see gender differences as reflecting the goal of survival of the species through reproduction. Basing their work on an evolutionary approach, these theorists suggest that our male ancestors who showed more stereotypically masculine qualities, such as forcefulness and competitiveness, may have been able to attract females who were able to provide them with hardy offspring. Females who excelled at stereotypically feminine tasks, such as nurturing, may have been valuable partners because they could increase the likelihood that children would survive the dangers of childhood (Geary, 1998).

As in other domains that involve the interaction of inherited biological characteristics and environmental influences, it is difficult to attribute behavioral characteristics unambiguously to biological factors. Because of this problem, we must consider other explanations for gender differences.

Psychoanalytic Perspectives. You may recall from Chapter 2 that Freud's psychoanalytic theory suggests that we move through a series of stages related to biological urges. To Freud, the preschool years encompass the *phallic stage*, in which the focus of a child's pleasure relates to genital sexuality.

Freud argued that the end of the phallic stage is marked by an important turning point in development: the Oedipal conflict. According to Freud, the *Oedipal conflict* occurs at around the age of 5, when the anatomical differences between males and females become particularly evident. Boys begin to develop sexual interests in their mothers, viewing their fathers as rivals. As a consequence, boys conceive a desire to kill their fathers—just as Oedipus did in the ancient Greek tragedy. However, because they view their fathers as all-powerful, boys develop a fear of retaliation, which takes the form of *castration anxiety*. To overcome this fear, boys repress their desires for their mothers and instead begin to identify with their fathers, attempting to be as similar to them as possible. **Identification** is the process in which children attempt to be similar to their parent of the same sex, incorporating the parent's attitudes and values.

Girls, according to Freud, go through a different process. They begin to feel sexual attraction toward their fathers and experience *penis envy*—a view that not unexpectedly has led to accusations that Freud viewed women as inferior to men. To resolve their penis envy, girls ultimately identify with their mothers, attempting to be as similar to them as possible.

In the cases of both boys and girls, the ultimate result of identifying with the same-sex parent is that the children adopt their parents' gender attitudes and values. In this way, says Freud, society's expectations about the ways females and males "ought" to behave are perpetuated into new generations.

If you are like many people, you may find it difficult to accept Freud's elaborate explanation of gender differences. So do most developmentalists, who believe that gender development is best explained by other mechanisms. In part, they base their criticisms of Freud on the lack of scientific support for his theories. For example, children learn gender stereotypes much earlier than the age of 5. Furthermore, this learning occurs even in single-parent households. However, some aspects of psychoanalytic theory have been supported, such as findings indicating that preschool-age children whose same-sex parents support sex-stereotyped behavior tend to demonstrate that behavior also. Still, far simpler processes can account for this phenomenon, and many developmentalists have searched for explanations of gender differences other than Freud's (Maccoby, 1980; Mussen, 1969).

Social Learning Approaches.   According to social learning approaches, children learn gender-related behavior and expectations from their observation of others. In this view, children watch the behavior of their parents, teachers, siblings, and even peers. Their observation of the rewards that these others attain for acting in a gender-appropriate manner leads them to conform to such behavior themselves (Rust et al., 2000).

Books and the media, and in particular television and video games, also play a role in perpetuating traditional views of gender-related behavior from which preschoolers may learn. For instance, television shows typically define female characters in terms of their relationships with males. Furthermore, females are more apt to appear with males, whereas female–female relationships are relatively uncommon. Also, females appear as victims far more often than males do (Dietz, 1998; Turner-Bowker, 1996; J. C. Wright et al., 1995). Television also presents men and women in traditional gender roles. For instance, analyses of the most popular television shows find that male characters outnumber female characters by 2 to 1. Furthermore, women are much less likely to be illustrated as decision makers or productive individuals and more likely to be portrayed as characters interested in romance, home, and family. Such models, according to social learning theory, are apt to have a powerful influence on preschoolers' definitions of appropriate behavior (Browne, 1998; Van den Berg & Streckfuss, 1992).

In some cases, learning of social roles does not involve models but occurs more directly. For example, most of us have heard preschool-age children being told by their parents to act like a "little girl" or "little man." What this generally means is that girls should behave politely and courteously or that boys should be tough and stoic—traits associated with society's traditional stereotypes of men and women. Such direct training sends a clear message about the behavior expected of a preschool-age child (Witt, 1997).

Cognitive Approaches.   In the view of some theorists, the desire to form a clear sense of identity leads children to establish a **gender identity,** a perception of themselves as male or female. To do this, they develop a **gender schema,** a cognitive framework that organizes information relevant to gender (G. D. Levy, Barth, & Zimmerman, 1998; Lobel et al., 2000; C. L. Martin, 2000).

Gender schemas are developed early in life, forming a lens through which preschoolers view the world. For instance, preschoolers use their increasing cognitive abilities to develop

According to social learning approaches, children observe the behavior of adults of the same sex as themselves and come to imitate it.

Identification The process in which children attempt to be similar to their parent of the same sex, incorporating the parent's attitudes and values

Gender identity The perception of oneself as male or female

Gender schema A cognitive framework that organizes information relevant to gender

Gender constancy The fact that people are permanently males or females, depending on fixed, unchangeable biological factors

Androgynous Encompassing characteristics thought typical of both sexes

VIDEO CLIP

Gender Consistency

"rules" about what is right and what is inappropriate for males and females. Thus some girls decide that wearing pants is inappropriate for a female and apply the rule so rigidly that they refuse to wear anything but dresses. Or a preschool boy may reason that since makeup is typically worn by females, it is inappropriate for him to wear makeup even when he is in a play and all the other boys and girls are wearing it.

According to *cognitive-developmental theory,* proposed by Lawrence Kohlberg (1966), this rigidity is in part an outcome of changes in preschoolers' understanding of gender. Initially, gender schemas are influenced by erroneous beliefs about sex differences. Specifically, young preschoolers believe that sex differences are based not on biological factors but on differences in appearance or behavior. Employing this view of the world, a girl may reason that she can be a father when she grows up, or a boy may think he could turn into a girl if he put on a dress and tied his hair in a ponytail. However, by the time they reach the age of 4 or 5, children develop an understanding of **gender constancy,** the fact that people are permanently males or females, depending on fixed, unchangeable biological factors.

Although research has supported the notion that the understanding of gender constancy changes during the preschool period, it has been less supportive of the idea that this understanding is the source of gender-related behavior. In fact, the appearance of gender schemas occurs well before children understand gender constancy. Even young preschool-age children assume that certain behaviors are appropriate and others are not on the basis of stereotypic views of gender (Bussey & Bandura, 1992; Maccoby, 1990; Warin, 2000).

Can we reduce the objectionable consequences of viewing the world in terms of gender schemas? According to Sandra Bem (1987), one way is to encourage children to be **androgynous,** adopting gender roles that encompass characteristics thought typical of both sexes. For instance, parents and caregivers can encourage preschool children to devise a gender schema through which they see males as assertive (typically viewed as a male-appropriate trait) but at the same time warm and tender (usually viewed as female-appropriate traits). Similarly, girls might be encouraged to see the female role as both empathic and tender (typically seen as female-appropriate traits) and competitive, assertive, and independent (typical male-appropriate traits).

Like the other approaches to gender development (summarized in Table 10-1), the cognitive perspective does not imply that differences between the two sexes are in any way

TABLE 10-1	FOUR APPROACHES TO GENDER DEVELOPMENT	
Perspective	**Key Concepts**	**Applying the Concepts to Preschool Children**
Biological	Our ancestors who behaved in ways that are now stereotypically feminine or masculine may have been more successful in reproducing. Brain differences may lead to gender differences.	Girls may be genetically "programmed" by evolution to be more expressive and nurturing, while boys are "programmed" to be more competitive and forceful. Hormone exposure before birth has been linked to both boys' and girls' behaving in ways typically expected of the other gender.
Psychoanalytic	Gender development is the result of identification with the same-sex parent, achieved by moving through a series of stages related to biological urges.	Girls and boys whose parents of the same sex behave in stereotypically masculine or feminine ways are likely to do so, too, perhaps because they identify with those parents.
Social learning	Children learn gender-related behavior and expectations from their observation of others' behavior.	Children notice that other children and adults are rewarded for behaving in ways that conform to standard gender stereotypes—and sometimes punished for violating those stereotypes.
Cognitive	Through the use of gender schemas, developed early in life, preschoolers form a lens through which they view the world. They use their increasing cognitive abilities to develop "rules" about what is appropriate for males and females.	Preschoolers are more rigid in their rules about proper gender behavior than people at other ages, perhaps because they have just developed gender schemas that don't yet permit much variation from stereotypical expectations.

improper or inappropriate. Instead, it suggests that preschoolers should be taught to treat others as individuals. Furthermore, preschoolers need to learn the importance of fulfilling their own talents, acting as individuals and not as representatives of a particular gender.

R E V I E W & A P P L Y

Review

- According to Erikson's psychosocial development theory, preschool-age children move from the autonomy-versus-shame-and-doubt stage to the initiative-versus-guilt stage.

- During the preschool years, children develop their self-concepts, beliefs about themselves that they derive from their own perceptions, their parents' behaviors, and society.

- Racial and ethnic awareness begins to form in the preschool years.

- Gender awareness also develops in the preschool years. Explanations of this phenomenon include biological, psychoanalytical, social learning, and cognitive approaches.

Applying Child Development

- What are the distinctions among gender differences, gender expectations, and gender stereotypes? How are they related?

- *From a child care provider's perspective:* How would you relate Erikson's stages of trust-versus-mistrust, autonomy-versus-shame-and-doubt, and initiative-versus-guilt to the issue of secure attachment?

Friends and Family: Preschoolers' Social Lives

When Juan was 3, he had his first best friend, Emilio. Juan and Emilio, who lived in the same apartment building in San Jose, were inseparable. They played incessantly with toy cars, racing them up and down the apartment hallways until some of the neighbors began to complain about the noise. The boys pretended to read to one another, and sometimes they slept over at each other's home—a big event for a 3-year-old. Neither boy seemed more joyful than when he was with his "best friend"—the term each used of the other.

An infant's family can provide nearly all the social contact he or she needs. As preschoolers, however, many children, like Juan and Emilio, begin to discover the joys of friendship with their peers. Although they may expand their social circles considerably, parents and family nevertheless remain very influential in the lives of preschoolers. Let's take a look at both of these sides of preschoolers' social development, friends and family.

The Development of Friendships

Before the age of 3, most social activity involves simply being in the same place at the same time, without real social interaction. However, at around the age of 3, children begin to develop real friendships like Juan and Emilio's. Peers come to be seen not as miniature, less powerful adults but as individuals who hold some special qualities and rewards. While

As preschoolers get older, their conception of friendship evolves and the quality of their interactions changes.

preschoolers' relations with adults reflect children's needs for care, protection, and direction, their relations with peers are based more on the desire for companionship, play, and entertainment.

Furthermore, as they get older, preschoolers' conception of friendship gradually evolves. With age, they come to view friendship as a continuing state, a stable relationship that has meaning beyond the immediate moment and that bears implications for future activity (J. R. Harris, 1998, 2000; J. Snyder, Horsch, & Childs, 1997).

The quality of interactions that children have with friends changes during the preschool period. The focus of friendship in 3-year-olds is the enjoyment of carrying out shared activities—doing things together and playing jointly, as when Juan and Emilio played with their toy cars in the hallway. Older preschoolers, however, pay more attention to abstract concepts such as trust, support, and shared interests (Park, Lay, & Ramsay, 1993). Playing together, however, remains an important part of all preschoolers' friendships. Like friendships, play patterns change during the preschool years.

Playing by the Rules: The Work of Play

In Minka Arafat's class of 3-year-olds, Minnie bounces her doll's feet on the table as she sings softly to herself. Josh pushes his toy car across the floor, making motor noises. Sarah chases Abdul around and around the perimeter of the room.

Play is more than what children of preschool age do to pass the time. Instead, play serves an important purpose: helping preschoolers develop socially, cognitively, and physically (Pellegrini & Smith, 1998; Power, 1999).

Categorizing Play. At the beginning of the preschool years, children engage in **functional play**—simple, repetitive activities typical of 3-year-olds. Functional play may involve objects, such as dolls or cars, or repetitive muscular movements like skipping, jumping, or rolling and unrolling a piece of clay. Functional play, then, involves doing something for the sake of being active, rather than with the aim of creating some end product (K. H. Rubin, Fein, & Vandenberg, 1983).

As children get older, functional play declines. By the time they are 4, children become involved in a more sophisticated form of play. In **constructive play,** children manipulate objects to produce or build something. A child who builds a house out of Legos or puts a puzzle together is involved in constructive play: He or she has an ultimate goal—to produce something. Such play is not necessarily aimed at creating something novel; children may repeatedly build a house of blocks, let it fall into disarray, and then rebuild it.

Constructive play permits children to test their developing physical and cognitive skills and to practice their fine muscle movements. They gain experience in solving problems about the ways and the sequences in which things fit together. They also learn to cooperate with others—a development we observe as the social nature of play shifts during the preschool period. Consequently, it is important for adults who care for preschoolers to provide a variety of toys that allow for both functional and constructive play (Edwards, 2000; Fromberg & Bergen, 1998; Power, 1999; Tegano et al., 1991).

VIDEO CLIP

Parten's Play Categories

Functional play Play that involves simple, repetitive activities typical of 3-year-olds

Constructive play Play in which children manipulate objects to produce or build something

Parallel play Action in which children play with similar toys, in a similar manner, but do not interact with each other

Onlooker play Action in which children simply watch others at play but do not actually participate themselves

The Social Aspects of Play. If two preschoolers are sitting at a table side by side, each putting a different puzzle together, are they engaged jointly in play? According to pioneering work done by Mildred Parten (1932), the answer is yes. She suggests that these preschoolers are engaged in **parallel play,** in which children play with similar toys, in a similar manner, but do not interact with each other. Parallel play is typical for children during the early preschool years. Preschoolers also engage in another form of play, a highly passive one: onlooker play. In **onlooker play,** children simply watch others at play but do not actually participate themselves. They may look on silently, or they may make comments of encouragement or advice.

In parallel play, children play with similar toys, in a similar manner, but don't necessarily interact with one another.

As they get older, however, preschool-age children engage in more sophisticated forms of social play that involve a greater degree of interaction. In **associative play,** two or more children actually interact with one another by sharing or borrowing toys or materials, although they do not do the same thing. In **cooperative play,** children genuinely play with one another, taking turns, playing games, or devising contests. (The various types of play are summarized in Table 10-2.)

Associative play   Play in which two or more children interact by sharing or borrowing toys or materials, although they do not do the same thing

Cooperative play   Play in which children genuinely interact with one another, taking turns, playing games, or devising contests

⚙ TABLE 10-2	PRESCHOOLERS' PLAY	
Type of Play	**Description**	**Examples**
Functional play	Simple, repetitive activities typical of 3-year-olds. May involve objects or repetitive muscular movements.	Moving dolls or cars repetitively. Skipping, jumping, rolling or unrolling a piece of clay.
Constructive play	More sophisticated play in which children manipulate objects to produce or build something. Developed by age 4, constructive play lets children test physical and cognitive skills and practice fine muscle movements.	Building a doll house or car garage out of Legos, putting together a puzzle, making an animal out of clay.
Parallel play	Children use similar toys in a similar manner at the same time but do not interact with each other. Typical of children during the early preschool years.	Children sitting side by side, each playing with his or her own toy car, putting together his or her own puzzle, or making an individual clay animal.
Onlooker play	Children simply watch others at play but do not actually participate. They may look on silently or make comments of encouragement or advice. Common among preschoolers and helpful when a child wishes to join a group already at play.	One child watches as a group of others play with dolls, cars, or clay; build with Legos; or work on a puzzle together.
Associative play	Two or more children interact, sharing or borrowing toys or materials, although they do not do the same thing.	Two children, each building his or her own Lego garage, may trade bricks back and forth.
Cooperative play	Children genuinely play with one another, taking turns, playing games, or devising contests.	A group of children working on a puzzle may take turns fitting in the pieces. Children playing with dolls or cars may take turns making the dolls talk or may agree on rules to race the cars.

VIDEO CLIP

Rough and Tumble Play

VIDEO CLIP

Sociodramatic Play
(social pretend play)

Although associative and cooperative play do not typically become prevalent until children reach the end of the preschool years, the amount and kinds of social experience children have had significantly influences the nature of play. For instance, children who have had substantial preschool experience are apt to engage in more social forms of behavior, such as associative and cooperative play, fairly early in the preschool years than those with less experience (Roopnarine, Johnson, & Hooper, 1994).

Furthermore, solitary and onlooker play continue in the later stages of the preschool period. There are simply times when children prefer to play by themselves. And when newcomers join a group, one strategy for becoming part of the group—often successful—is to engage in onlooker play, waiting for an opportunity to join the play more actively (Howes, Unger, & Seidner, 1989; Hughes, 1995; P. K. Smith, 1978).

The nature of pretend or make-believe play also changes during the preschool period. In some ways, pretend play becomes increasingly *unrealistic* as preschoolers change from using only realistic objects to using less concrete ones. Thus at the start of the preschool period, children may pretend to listen to a radio only if they actually have a plastic radio that looks realistic. Later, however, they are more likely to use an entirely different object, such as a large cardboard box, as a pretend radio (Bornstein et al., 1996; Corrigan, 1987).

Russian developmentalist Lev Vygotsky (1930–1935/1978) argued that pretend play, particularly if it involves social play, is an important means for expanding preschool-age children's cognitive skills. Through make-believe play, children are able to "practice" activities that are a part of their particular culture and broaden their understanding of the way the world functions.

Children's cultural backgrounds also result in different styles of play. For example, comparisons of Korean Americans and Anglo-Americans find that Korean American children engage in a higher proportion of parallel play than their Anglo-American counterparts, while Anglo-American preschoolers are involved in more pretend play (Haight et al., 1999; Farver, Kim, & Lee-Shin, 1995; Farver & Lee-Shin, 2000; see Figure 10-1).

Preschoolers' Theory of Mind: Understanding What Others Are Thinking

One reason behind the developmental changes in children's play is the continuing development of preschoolers' theory of mind. As we first discussed in Chapter 7, *theory of mind* refers to knowledge and beliefs about the mental world. Using their theory of mind, children are able to come up with explanations for how others think and the reasons for their behaving in the way they do.

During the preschool years, children become more and more able to see the world from others' perspectives. Even children as young as 2 are able to understand that others have emotions, like Alison Gopnik's son, whose efforts to soothe his mother's pain were described

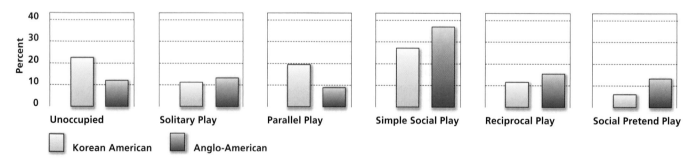

FIGURE 10-1   **COMPARING PLAY COMPLEXITY**

An examination of Korean American and Anglo-American preschoolers' play complexity finds clear differences in patterns of play. How would a child care provider explain this conclusion?

(*Source:* Adapted from Farver, Kim, & Lee-Shin, 1995)

in the chapter prologue. By the age of 3 or 4, preschoolers can distinguish between mental phenomena and physical actuality. For instance, 3-year-olds know that they can imagine something that is not physically present, such as a pretend animal, and that others can do the same. They can also pretend that something has happened and react as if it really had occurred. And they know that others have the same capability (Cadinu & Kiesner, 2000; Flavell, Flavell, & Green, 2001; Wellman, Cross, & Watson, 2001).

Preschool-age children also understand that people have motives and reasons for their behavior. A child at this age can understand that his mother is angry because she was late for an appointment, even if the child himself hasn't seen her be late. Furthermore, by the age of 4, preschool-age children's understanding that people can be fooled and that they can be mistaken by physical reality becomes surprisingly sophisticated. This increase in understanding helps children become more socially skilled (Nguyen & Frye, 1999; A. C. Watson et al., 1999).

What factors are involved in the emergence of theory of mind? Certainly, brain maturation and the development of language skills play a role. In particular, the ability to understand the meaning of words such as *think* and *know* is important in helping preschool-age children understand the mental life of others.

Opportunities for social interaction and make-believe play are also critical in promoting the development of theory of mind. For example, preschool-age children with older siblings (who provide high levels of social interaction) have more sophisticated theories of mind than those without older siblings (Ruffman et al., 1998; J. K. Watson, 2000).

Cultural factors also play an important role in the development of theory of mind. For example, children in more industrialized Western cultures may be more likely to regard others' behavior as due to the kinds of people they are, seeing it as a function of their personal traits and characteristics. In contrast, children in non-Western cultures may see others' behavior as produced by forces that are less under their personal control, such as unhappy gods or bad fortune (Lillard, 1998).

As we have seen, preschooler's family situations can influence their theory of mind. In fact, families provide a major influence on all aspects of preschoolers' development. What is family life like for today's young children?

Preschoolers' Family Lives

> Four-year-old Benjamin was watching TV while his mom cleaned up after dinner. After a while, he wandered in and grabbed a towel, saying, "Mommy, let me help you do the dishes." Surprised by this unprecedented behavior, she asked him, "Where did you learn to do dishes?"
>
> "I saw it on *Leave It to Beaver,*" he replied, "Only it was the dad helping. Since we don't have a dad, I figured I'd do it."

For an increasing number of preschool-age children, life does not mirror what we see in reruns of *Leave It to Beaver.* For instance, children are increasingly likely to live with only one parent. In 1960, less than 10 percent of all children under the age of 18 lived with one parent; by 1989, almost a quarter lived in a single-parent household. In fact, in the 1990s, almost 50 percent of all children experienced their parents' divorce and lived with one parent for an average of 5 years (Carnegie Task Force, 1994).

Still, for most children, the preschool years are not a time of upheaval and turmoil. Instead, the period encompasses a growing interaction with the world at large. As we've seen, for instance, preschoolers begin to develop genuine friendships with other children in which close ties emerge. Preschoolers tend to develop friendships when parents provide a warm, supportive home environment. A good deal of research finds that strong, positive relationships between parents and children encourage children's relationships with others (Howes, Galinsky, & Kontos, 1998; Sroufe, 1994). How do parents nurture that relationship? See the *From Research to Practice* box.

— ○ FROM RESEARCH TO PRACTICE ○ —

Effective Parenting: Teaching Children Desired Behavior

While she thinks no one is looking, Maria goes into her brother Alejandro's bedroom, where he has been saving the last of his Halloween candy. Just as she takes his last Reese's Peanut Butter Cup, the children's mother walks into the room and immediately takes in the situation.

 f you were Maria's mother, which of the following reactions seems most reasonable?

1. Tell Maria that she must go to her room and stay there for the rest of the day and that she is going to lose access to her favorite blanket, the one she sleeps with every night and during naps.

2. Mildly tell Maria that what she did was not such a good idea and that she shouldn't do it in the future.

3. Explain why her brother Alejandro was going to be upset and tell her that she must go to her room for an hour as punishment.

4. Forget about it and let the children sort it out themselves.

Each of these four alternative responses represents one of the major parenting styles identified by Diana Baumrind (1971, 1980) and updated by Eleanor Maccoby and Maccoby Martin, & Jacklin (1981). **Authoritarian parents** are controlling, punitive, rigid, and cold. Their word is law, and they value strict, unquestioning obedience from their children. They do not tolerate expressions of disagreement.

Permissive parents, in contrast, provide lax and inconsistent feedback. They require little of their children, and they don't see themselves as holding much responsibility for how their children turn out. They place little or no limits or controls on their behavior.

Authoritative parents are firm, setting clear and consistent limits. Although they tend to be relatively strict, like authoritarian parents, they are loving and emotionally supportive. They also try to reason with their children, giving explanations for why they should behave in a particular way and communicating the rationale for any punishment they may impose. Authoritative parents encourage their children to be independent.

Finally, **uninvolved parents** show virtually no interest in their children, displaying indifferent, rejecting behavior. They are detached emotionally and see their role as no more than feeding, clothing, and providing shelter for their child. In its most extreme form, uninvolved parenting results in *neglect,* a form of child abuse. (The four patterns are summarized in Table 10-3.)

Children with authoritative parents tend to be well adjusted, in part because the parents are supportive and take the time to explain things. What are the consequences of parents who are too permissive? Too authoritarian? Too uninvolved?

Does the particular style of discipline that parents use result in differences in children's behavior? The answer is very much yes—although, as you might expect, there are many exceptions.

Children of authoritarian parents tend to be withdrawn, showing relatively little sociability. They are not very friendly, often behaving uneasily around their peers. Girls who are raised by authoritarian parents are especially dependent on their parents, and boys are unusually hostile.

Permissive parents have children who in many ways share the undesirable characteristics of children of authoritarian parents. Children with permissive parents tend to be dependent and moody, and they are low in social skills and self-control.

Children of authoritative parents fare best. They are generally independent, friendly with their peers, self-assertive, and cooperative. They have a strong motivation to achieve, and they are typically successful and likable. They regulate their own behavior effectively, in terms of both their relationships with others and emotional self-regulation.

Authoritarian parents Parents who are controlling, punitive, rigid, and cold and whose word is law; they value strict, unquestioning obedience from their children and do not tolerate expressions of disagreement

Permissive parents Parents who provide lax and inconsistent feedback and require little of their children

Authoritative parents Parents who are firm, setting clear and consistent limits, but try to reason with their children, explaining why they should behave in a particular way

Uninvolved parents Parents who show virtually no interest in their children, displaying indifferent, rejecting behavior

TABLE 10-3   PARENTAL DISCIPLINE STYLES

Parenting Style	Nature of Demands and Responsiveness to Children	Characteristics	Relationship With Child
Authoritarian	High demands; low responsiveness	Controlling, punitive, rigid, cold	Parents' word is law; they value strict, unquestioning obedience from their child. They do not tolerate expressions of disagreement.
Authoritative	High demands; high responsiveness	Firm, setting clear and consistent limits	They are relatively strict but emotionally supportive; they encourage independence. They try to reason with their child and give the rationale for an imposed punishment.
Permissive	Low demands; high responsiveness	Lax and inconsistent feedback	They require little of their child, and they don't see themselves as holding much responsibility for how their child turns out. They place little or no limits or control on their child's behavior.
Uninvolved	Low demands; low responsiveness	Displaying indifferent, rejecting behavior	They are detached emotionally and see their role as only providing food, clothing, and shelter. In its extreme form, this parenting style results in neglect, a form of child abuse.

(*Sources:* Baumrind, 1971; Maccoby & Martin, 1983)

Some authoritative parents also display several characteristics that have come to be called *supportive parenting,* including parental warmth, proactive teaching, calm discussion during disciplinary episodes, and interest and involvement in children's peer activities. Children whose parents engage in such supportive parenting show better adjustment and are protected from the consequences of later adversity (Bullock, 2000; Kaufmann et al., 2000; Pettit, Bates, & Dodge, 1997; Snowden & Christian, 1999).

Children of parents with uninvolved parenting styles are the worst off. Their parents' lack of involvement disrupts their emotional development considerably, leading them to feel unloved and emotionally detached, and affects their physical and cognitive development as well.

Clearly, authoritative, supportive parents appear to be the most likely to produce successful children. But other parenting approaches are not always less effective. For instance, a significant number of children of authoritarian and permissive parents develop quite successfully. Moreover, parents are not entirely consistent: Although the authoritarian, permissive, authoritative, and uninvolved patterns describe general styles, sometimes parents switch from their dominant mode to one of the others. For instance, when a child darts into the street, even the most permissive parent is likely to react in a harsh, authoritarian manner, laying down strict demands about safety. In such cases, authoritarian styles may be most effective (Deater-Deckard & Dodge, 1997; Holden & Miller, 1999; Janssens & Dekovic, 1997).

Furthermore, the findings regarding child-rearing styles are chiefly applicable to Western societies. The style of parenting that is most successful may depend quite heavily on the norms of a particular culture—and what parents in a particular culture are taught regarding appropriate child-rearing practices (Papps et al., 1995; K. H. Rubin, 1998).

For example, the Chinese concept of *chiao shun* suggests that parents should be strict, firm, and in tight control of their children's behavior. Parents are seen to have a duty to train their children to adhere to socially and culturally desirable standards of behavior, particularly those manifested in good school performance. Children's acceptance of such an approach to discipline is seen as a sign of parental respect (Chao, 1994).

Parents in China are typically highly directive with their children, pushing them to excel and controlling their behavior to a considerably greater degree than parents typically do in Western countries. And it works: Children of Asian parents tend to be quite successful, particularly academically (L. Steinberg, Dornbusch, & Brown, 1992).

In contrast, U.S. parents are generally advised to use authoritative methods and explicitly to avoid authoritarian measures. Interestingly, it wasn't always this way. Until World War II, the point of view that dominated the advice literature was authoritarian, apparently founded on Puritan religious influences that suggested that children had "original sin" or that they needed to have their will broken in order to learn to obey (Smuts & Hagen, 1985).

In short, the child-rearing practices that parents are urged to follow reflect cultural perspectives about the nature of children, as well as about the appropriate role of parents. No single parenting pattern or style, then, is likely to be universally appropriate or invariably to produce successful children. Instead, cultural context must be taken into account (Bornstein, 2002; Bornstein et al., 1998; C. H. Hart et al., 1998).

R E V I E W *&* A P P L Y

Review

- In the preschool years, children develop their first true friendships on the basis of personal characteristics, trust, and shared interests.

- The character of preschoolers' play changes over time, growing more sophisticated, interactive, and cooperative and relying increasingly on social skills.

- There are several distinct child-rearing styles, including authoritarian, permissive, authoritative, and uninvolved.

- Child-rearing styles show strong cultural influences.

Applying Child Development

- What cultural and environmental factors in the United States may have contributed to the shift in the dominant child-rearing style from authoritarian to authoritative since World War II? Is another shift under way?

- *From an educator's perspective:* How might the styles and strategies of preschool-age children's play, such as parallel play and onlooker play, be mirrored in adult life in realms of interaction other than play?

Moral Development and Aggression

During snack time at preschool, playmates Jan and Meg inspected the goodies in their lunch boxes. Jan found two appetizing cream-filled cookies. Meg's snack offered less tempting carrot and celery sticks. As Jan began to munch on one of her cookies, Meg looked at the cut-up vegetables and burst into tears. Jan responded to Meg's distress by offering her companion one of her cookies, which Meg gladly accepted. Jan was able to put herself in Meg's place, understand Meg's thoughts and feelings, and act compassionately. (L. G. Katz, 1989, p. 213)

In this short scenario, we see many of the key elements of morality as it is played out among preschool-age children. Changes in children's views of morality and their helpfulness to others are an important element of growth during the preschool years.

Yet at the same time these changes are occurring, the degree and nature of aggressive behavior displayed by preschoolers are also changing. We can consider the development of morality and aggression as two sides of the coin of human conduct.

Developing Morality: Following Society's Rights and Wrongs

Moral development refers to the maturation of people's sense of justice, of what is right and wrong, and their behavior in connection with such issues. Moral development reflects changes in children's reasoning about morality, their attitudes toward moral transgressions, and their actions when facing moral issues. Developmentalists have evolved several approaches for studying moral development (Grusec & Kuczynski, 1997; Langford, 1995).

Piaget's View of Moral Development.   Child psychologist Jean Piaget was one of the first to study questions of moral development. He suggested that moral development, like cognitive development, proceeds in stages (Piaget, 1932). The earliest stage is a broad form of moral thinking known as **heteronomous morality,** in which rules are seen as invariant and

Moral development The maturation of people's sense of justice, of what is right and wrong, and their behavior in connection with such issues

Heteronomous morality The stage of moral development in which rules are seen as invariant and unchangeable

unchangeable. During this stage, which lasts from about age 4 through age 7, children play games rigidly, assuming that there is one and only one way to play and that every other way is wrong. At the same time, though, preschool-age children may not fully grasp game rules. Consequently, a group of children may be playing together, with each child playing according to a slightly different set of rules. Nevertheless, they enjoy playing with others. Piaget suggests that every child may "win" such a game, because winning is equated with having a good time, as opposed to truly competing with others.

Heteronomous morality is ultimately replaced by two later stages of morality: incipient cooperation and autonomous cooperation. In the *incipient cooperation stage,* which lasts from around age 7 to age 10, children's games become more clearly social. Children actually learn the formal rules of games, and they play according to this shared knowledge. Consequently, rules are still seen as largely unchangeable. There is a "right" way to play the game, and children play according to these formal rules.

It is not until the *autonomous cooperation stage,* which begins at about age 10, that children become fully aware that formal game rules can be modified if the people who play them agree. The later transition into more sophisticated forms of moral development—which we will consider in Chapter 15—also is reflected in school-age children's understanding that rules of law are created by people and are subject to change according to the will of people.

Preschoolers' reasoning about rules and issues of justice differ according to the moral stage each child has reached. For instance, consider the following two stories (Piaget, 1932, p. 122):

> A little boy who is called John is in his room. He is called to dinner. He goes into the dining room. But behind the door there was a chair, and on the chair there was a tray with fifteen cups on it. John couldn't have known there was all this behind the door. He goes in, the door knocks against the tray, bang go the fifteen cups, and they all get broken!

> Once there was a little boy whose name was Marcello. One day when his mother was out he tried to get some jam out of the cupboard. He climbed up on to a chair and stretched out his arm. But the jam was too high up and he couldn't reach it and have any. But while he was trying to get it he knocked over a cup. The cup fell down and broke.

Piaget found that a preschool child in the heteronomous morality stage judges the child who broke the 15 cups worse than the one who broke just one. In contrast, children who have moved beyond the heteronomous morality stage consider the child who broke the one cup naughtier. What accounts for the difference? Children in the heteronomous morality stage do not take *intention* into account.

Children in the heteronomous stage of moral development also believe in immanent justice. **Immanent justice** is the notion that rules that are broken earn immediate punishment. Preschool children believe that if they do something wrong, they will be punished instantly—even if no one sees them carrying out their misdeeds. In contrast, older children understand that punishments for misdeeds are determined and meted out by people. Children who have moved to the incipient cooperation stage and beyond have come to notice that authority figures make judgments about the severity of a transgression and that they take intentionality into account in determining the nature of the penalty to be imposed.

Evaluating Piaget's Approach to Moral Development.

Recent research suggests that although Piaget was on the right track in his description of how moral development proceeds, his approach suffers from the same problem we encountered in his theory of cognitive development. Specifically, Piaget underestimated the age at which children's moral skills are honed.

It is now clear that preschool-age children understand the notion of intentionality by about age 3, and this allows them to make judgments based on intent at an earlier age than Piaget supposed. Specifically, when presented with moral questions that emphasize intent,

Piaget believed that at the heteronomous morality stage, this child would feel that the degree to which she had done the wrong thing is directly related to the number of items broken.

Immanent justice The notion that rules that are broken earn immediate punishment

preschool children judge someone who is intentionally bad as more naughty than someone who is unintentionally bad but who creates more objective damage. Moreover, by the age of 4, they judge intentional lying as wrong (Bussey, 1992; Yuill & Perner, 1988).

Social Learning Approaches to Morality. Social learning approaches to moral development stand in stark contrast to Piaget's approach. Whereas Piaget emphasizes how limitations in preschoolers' cognitive development lead to particular forms of moral *reasoning,* social learning approaches focus more on how the environment in which preschoolers operate produces **prosocial behavior,** helping behavior that benefits others (Eisenberg et al., 1999).

Social learning approaches build on the behavioral approaches that we first discussed in Chapter 2. They acknowledge that some instances of children's prosocial behavior stem from situations in which they have received positive reinforcement for acting in a morally appropriate way. For instance, when Claire's mother tells her she has been a "good girl" for sharing a box of candy with her brother Dan, Claire's behavior has been reinforced. As a consequence, she is more likely to engage in sharing behavior in the future.

Modeling. Social learning approaches go a step further, arguing that not all prosocial behavior has to be directly performed and subsequently reinforced for learning to occur. According to social learning approaches, children also learn moral behavior more indirectly, by observing the behavior of others, called *models* (Bandura, 1977). Children imitate models who receive reinforcement for their behavior and ultimately learn to perform the behavior themselves. For example, when Claire's friend Jake watches Claire share her candy with her brother and hears Claire praised for her behavior, Jake is more likely to engage in sharing behavior himself at some later point.

Quite a few studies illustrate the power of models, and of social learning more generally, in producing prosocial behavior in preschool-age children. For example, experiments have shown that children who view someone behaving generously or unselfishly are apt to follow the model's example, subsequently behaving in a generous or unselfish manner themselves when put in a similar situation (Y. Kim & Stevens, 1987; Midlarsky & Bryan, 1972). The opposite also holds true: If a model behaves selfishly, children who observe such behavior tend to behave more selfishly themselves (Grusec, 1982, 1991; Staub, 1977).

Not all models are equally effective in producing prosocial responses. For instance, preschoolers are more apt to model the behavior of warm, responsive adults than of adults who appear colder. Furthermore, models viewed as highly competent or high in prestige are more effective than others (Bandura, 1977; M. R. Yarrow, Scott, & Waxler, 1973).

Children do more than simply mimic unthinkingly behavior that they see rewarded in others. By observing moral conduct, they are reminded of society's norms about the importance of moral behavior, as conveyed by parents, teachers, and other powerful authority figures. They notice the connections between particular situations and certain kinds of behavior. This increases the likelihood that similar situations will elicit similar behavior in the observer.

Consequently, modeling paves the way for the development of more general rules and principles in a process called **abstract modeling.** Rather than always modeling the particular behavior of others, older preschoolers begin to develop generalized principles that underlie the behavior that they observe. After observing repeated instances in which a model is rewarded for acting in a morally desirable way, children begin the process of inferring and learning the general principles of moral conduct (Bandura, 1991).

Empathy and Moral Behavior. According to some developmentalists, **empathy**—the understanding of what another individual feels—lies at the heart of some kinds of moral behavior. Think back to the example in this chapter's prologue, of Alison Gropnik's son who

Prosocial behavior Helping behavior that benefits others

Abstract modeling The process in which modeling paves the way for the development of more general rules and principles

Empathy The understanding of what another individual feels

used Band-Aids to try to heal whatever was making his mother cry. For her son to understand that Alison needed comforting, it was necessary for him to feel empathy with her unhappiness. Although he may have been confused about the source of her pain, Alison's son realized that she seemed hurt and warranted sympathy.

The roots of empathy grow early. One-year-old infants cry when they hear other infants crying. By 2 and 3, toddlers will offer gifts and spontaneously share toys with other children and adults, even if they are strangers (Radke-Yarrow, Zahn-Waxler, & Chapman, 1983; Stanjek, 1978; Zahn-Waxler & Radke-Yarrow, 1990).

During the preschool years, empathy continues to grow. Some theorists believe that increasing empathy—as well as other positive emotions, such as sympathy and admiration—leads children to behave in a more moral fashion. In addition, some negative emotions—such as anger at an unfair situation or shame over previous transgressions—may also promote moral behavior (Damon, 1988; Farver & Branstetter, 1994; P. A. Miller & Jansen op de Haar, 1997).

The notion that negative emotions may promote moral development is one that Freud first suggested in his theory of psychoanalytic personality development. Recall from Chapter 2 that Freud argued that a child's *superego,* the part of the personality that represents societal dos and don'ts, is developed through resolution of the Oedipal conflict. Children come to identify with their same-sex parent, incorporating that parent's standards of morality, in order to avoid unconscious guilt raised by the Oedipal conflict.

Whether or not we accept Freud's account of the Oedipal conflict and the guilt it produces—and, as noted earlier, most developmentalists do not—it is consistent with more recent findings. These suggest that preschoolers' attempts to avoid experiencing negative emotions sometimes lead them to act in more moral, helpful ways. For instance, one reason children help others is to avoid the feelings of personal distress that they experience when they are confronted with another person's unhappiness or misfortune (Eisenberg & Fabes, 1991).

"Have you been a moral child?"

Aggression and Violence in Preschoolers: Sources and Consequences

> Four-year-old Duane could not contain his anger and frustration anymore. Although he usually was mild-mannered, when Eshu began to tease him about the split in his pants and kept it up for several minutes, Duane finally snapped. Rushing over to Eshu, Duane pushed him to the ground and began to hit him with his small, closed fists. Because he was so distraught, Duane's punches were not terribly effective, but they were severe enough to hurt Eshu and bring him to tears before the preschool teachers could intervene.

Although violence of this sort is relatively rare among preschool-age children, aggression is not uncommon. The potential for verbal hostility, shoving matches, kicking, and other forms of aggression is present throughout the preschool period, although the degree to which aggression is acted out changes as children become older.

Aggression is intentional injury or harm to another person (Berkowitz, 1993). Infants don't act aggressively; it is hard to contend that their behavior is *intended* to hurt others, even if they inadvertently manage to do so. But by the time they reach preschool age, children demonstrate true aggression.

During the early preschool years, some of the aggression is addressed at attaining a desired goal, such as getting a toy away from another person or using a particular space occupied by another person. Consequently, in some ways the aggression is inadvertent, and minor scuffles may in fact be a typical part of early preschool life. It is the rare child who does not demonstrate at least an occasional act of aggression.

Extreme and sustained aggression, however, is cause for concern. In most children, aggression diminishes as they move through the preschool years. Typically, the frequency and average length of episodes of aggressive behavior decline over this period (E. M. Cummings, Iannotti, & Zahn-Waxler, 1989).

Advances in personality and social development contribute to the decline in aggression. Throughout the preschool years, children are increasingly able to control the emotions that they are experiencing. **Emotional self-regulation** is the capability to adjust emotions to a desired state and level of intensity. Starting at age 2, children are able to talk about their feelings and to engage in strategies to regulate them. As they get older, they develop more effective strategies, learning to cope more effectively with negative emotions. In addition to their increasing self-control, children are also, as we've seen, developing sophisticated social skills. Most learn to use language to express their wishes, and they become increasingly able to negotiate with others (Eisenberg & Zhou, 2000).

Although a decline in aggression is typical, some children remain aggressive throughout the preschool period. Furthermore, aggression is a relatively stable characteristic: The most aggressive preschoolers tend to be the most aggressive children during the school-age years, and the least aggressive preschoolers tend to be the least aggressive school-age children (Ialongo, Vaden-Kiernan, & Kellam, 1998; Kellam et al., 1998; K. H. Rosen, 1998; Tremblay, 2001).

Boys typically show higher levels of overt aggression than girls. However, although girls show lower levels of physical aggression, they may be just as aggressive, but in different ways from boys. Girls are more likely to practice **relational aggression,** which is nonphysical aggression that is intended to hurt another person's psychological well-being. Such aggression may be demonstrated through name-calling, withholding friendship, or simply saying mean, hurtful things that make the recipient feel bad (Simmons, 2002).

The Roots of Aggression.   How can we explain the aggression of preschoolers? Some theoreticians suggest that to behave aggressively is an instinct, part and parcel of the human condition. For instance, Freud's psychoanalytic theory suggests that we all have a death drive, which leads us to act aggressively toward others as we turn our inward hostility outward

---

VIDEO CLIP

Relational Aggression

VIDEO CLIP

Reactive Aggression

Aggression   Intentional injury or harm to another person

Emotional self-regulation   The capability to adjust one's emotions to a desired state and level of intensity

Relational aggression   Nonphysical aggression that is intended to hurt another person's psychological well-being

Aggression, both physical and verbal, is present throughout the preschool period.

(Freud, 1920). According to ethologist Konrad Lorenz (1966, 1974), an expert in animal behavior, animals—including humans—share a fighting instinct that stems from primitive urges to preserve territory, maintain a steady supply of food, and weed out weaker animals.

Similar arguments are made by evolutionary theorists and *sociobiologists,* scientists who consider the biological roots of social behavior. They argue that aggression leads to reproductive success, increasingly the likelihood that one's genes will be passed on to future generations. Furthermore, aggression may help strengthen the species and its gene pool as a whole. Ultimately, then, aggressive instincts promote the survival of one's genes to pass on to future generations (McKenna, 1983; M. J. Reiss, 1984).

Although instinctual explanations of aggression are logical, most developmentalists believe they are not the whole story (Bandura, 1978). Not only do instinctual explanations fail to take into account the increasingly sophisticated cognitive abilities that humans develop as they get older, but they also have relatively little experimental support. Moreover, they provide little guidance in determining when and how children, as well as adults, will behave aggressively, other than noting that aggression is an inherent part of the human condition. Consequently, developmentalists have turned to other approaches to explain aggression and violence.

Social Learning Approaches to Aggression.   The day after Duane lashed out at Eshu, Lynn, who had watched the entire scene, got into an argument with Ilya. They verbally bickered for a while, and suddenly Lynn balled her hand into a fist and tried to punch Ilya. The preschool teachers were stunned: It was rare for Lynn to get upset, and she had never displayed aggression before.

Is there a connection between the two events? Most of us would answer yes, particularly if we subscribed to the view, suggested by social learning approaches, that aggression is largely a learned behavior. Social learning approaches to aggression contend that aggression is based on prior learning. To understand the causes of aggressive behavior, then, we should look at the system of rewards and punishments that exists in a child's environment.

Social learning approaches to aggression emphasize how social and environmental conditions teach individuals to be aggressive. They grow out of behavioral perspectives, which suggest that aggressive behavior is learned through direct reinforcement. For instance, preschool-age children may learn that they can continue to play with the most desirable toys by declining aggressively their classmates' requests for sharing. In the parlance of traditional learning theory, they have been reinforced for acting aggressively, and they are more likely to behave aggressively in the future.

Learning Aggression Through Models.   But social learning approaches suggest that reinforcement also comes in less direct ways. A good deal of research suggests that exposure to aggressive models leads to increased aggression, particularly if the observers are themselves angered, insulted, or frustrated. For example, Albert Bandura and his colleagues illustrated the power of models in a classic study of preschool-age children (Bandura, Ross, & Ross, 1963). One group of children watched a film of an adult playing aggressively and violently with a Bobo doll (a large, inflated plastic dummy that always returns to an upright position after being pushed down). In comparison, children in another condition watched a film of an adult playing sedately with a set of Tinkertoys (see Figure 10-2). Later the preschool-age children were allowed to play with a number of toys, which included both the Bobo doll and the Tinkertoys. But first the children were led to feel frustration by being refused the opportunity to play with a favorite toy.

Consistent with social learning approaches, the preschool-age children modeled the behavior of the adult. Those who had seen the aggressive model playing with the Bobo doll were considerably more aggressive than those who had watched the calm, unaggressive model playing with the Tinkertoys.

Later research has supported this early study, and it is clear that exposure to aggressive models increases the likelihood that aggression on the part of observers will follow (Farver et al., 1997). These findings have profound consequences, particularly for children who live in

VIDEO CLIP

Human Aggression:
Bandura's Bobo Doll
CLASSIC MODULE

FIGURE 10-2   MODELING AGGRESSION

This series of photos is from Albert Bandura's classic Bobo doll experiment, designed to illustrate social learning of aggression. The photos clearly show how the adult model's aggressive behavior (in the first row) is imitated by children who had viewed the aggressive behavior (second and third rows).

communities in which violence is prevalent. For instance, one survey conducted in a city public hospital found that one child in every 10 under the age of 6 reported having witnessed a shooting or stabbing. Other research indicates that one third of the children in some urban neighborhoods have seen a homicide and that two thirds have seen a serious assault (Farver & Frosch, 1996; Groves et al., 1993; Osofsky, 1995).

Even children who are not witnesses to real-life violence—the majority of preschool-age children—are typically exposed to aggression via the medium of television, particularly in light of the high levels of viewing in which most preschool-age children engage. The average preschooler watches 3 hours of television each day, and even children whose parents don't own television sets watch from 1 to 2 hours a day at friends' homes (Condry, 1989).

Although television has a clear impact on cognitive development, as we discussed in Chapter 9, it has other, and perhaps even more important, consequences for frequent viewers. In particular, because it contains so much violent content (see Figure 10-3), the medium can have a powerful influence on the subsequent aggressive behavior of viewers (Huesmann, Moise, & Podolski, 1997; Liebert & Sprafkin, 1988; Sanson & di Muccio, 1993; W. Wood, Wong, & Chachere, 1991).

Programs such as the *Mighty Morphin Power Rangers* and *Pokémon* are watched by millions of preschoolers, who later imitate violent behavior during play. This is no surprise, given social learning theory. But does the playful enactment of aggression later turn into the real thing, producing children (and later adults) who demonstrate more actual—and ultimately deadly—aggression?

It is hard to answer the question definitively, primarily because no true experiments outside laboratory settings have been conducted. Although it is clear that laboratory observation of aggression on television leads to higher levels of aggression, evidence showing that real-world viewing of aggression is associated with subsequent aggressive behavior is correlational. (Think, for a moment, of how we might conduct a true experiment involving children's viewing habits. It would require that we control children's viewing of television in their homes for

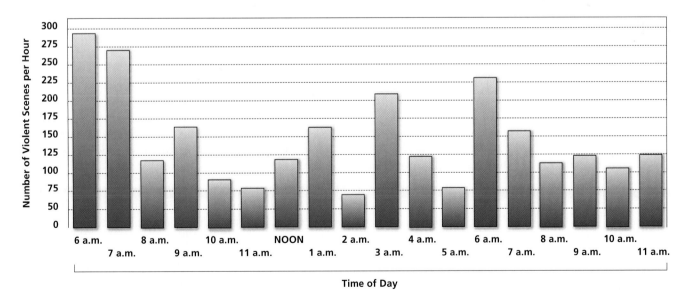

FIGURE 10-3   TELEVISED ACTS OF VIOLENCE

A survey of the violence shown on the major TV networks and several cable channels in Washington, DC. on one particular weekday found acts of violence during every time period. From the perspective of an educator, do you think depictions of violence on TV should be regulated? Why or why not?

(*Source:* Center for Media and Public Affairs, 1995)

Social learning explanations of aggression suggest that children seeing aggression on television can prompt them to act aggressively.

extended periods, exposing some to a steady diet of violent shows and others to nonviolent ones—something that most parents would not agree to.)

Despite the fact that the results are primarily correlational and therefore inconclusive, the weight of research evidence is clear in suggesting that observation of televised aggression does lead to subsequent aggression. For example, in one longitudinal study, children's preferences for violent television shows at age 8 were related to the seriousness of criminal convictions by age 30 (Huesmann, 1986). Other evidence supports the notion that observation of media violence can lead to a greater readiness to act aggressively and to an insensitivity to the suffering of victims of violence (Bushman & Geen, 1990; Comstock & Strasburger, 1990; Gadow & Sprafkin, 1993; Kremar & Greene, 2000; Linz, Donnerstein, & Penrod, 1989).

Fortunately, the same principles of social learning theory that lead preschoolers to learn aggression from television suggest ways to reduce the negative influence of the medium. For instance, children can be explicitly taught critical viewing skills that influence their interpretation of televised models. In such training, they are taught that violence is not representative of the real world, that the viewing of violence is objectionable, and that they should refrain from imitating the behavior they have seen on television (Eron & Huesmann, 1985; Farhi, 1995; Huesmann et al., 1983; Zillman, 1993).

Furthermore, just as exposure to aggressive models leads to aggression, observation of *nonaggressive* models can *reduce* aggression. Preschoolers don't learn from others only how to be aggressive; they can also learn how to avoid confrontation and to control their aggression, as we'll discuss later.

Cognitive Approaches to Aggression: The Thoughts Behind Violence.

Two children, waiting for their turn in a game of kickball, inadvertently knock into one another. One child's reaction is to apologize; the other's is to shove, saying angrily, "Cut it out."

Despite the fact that each child bears the same responsibility for the minor event, very different reactions result. The first child interprets the event as an accident, while the second sees it as a provocation and reacts with aggression.

The cognitive approach to aggression suggests that the key to understanding moral development is to examine preschoolers' interpretations of others' behavior and of the environmental context in which a behavior occurs. According to developmental psychologist Kenneth Dodge and his colleagues (Dodge & Coie, 1987; Dodge & Crick, 1990), some children are more prone than others to assume that actions are aggressively motivated. They are unable to pay attention to the appropriate cues in a situation and unable to interpret the behaviors in a given situation accurately. Instead, they assume—often erroneously—that what is happening is related to others' hostility. Subsequently, in deciding how to respond, they base their behavior on their inaccurate interpretation of behavior. In sum, they may behave aggressively in response to a situation that never in fact existed.

Although the cognitive approach to aggression provides a description of the process that leads some children to behave aggressively, it is less successful in explaining how certain children come to be inaccurate preceivers of situations in the first place. Furthermore, it fails to explain why such inaccurate perceivers so readily respond with aggression and why they assume that aggression is an appropriate and even desirable response.

On the other hand, cognitive approaches to aggression are useful in pointing out a means to reduce aggression: By teaching preschool-age children to be more accurate interpreters of a situation, we can induce them to be less prone to view others' behavior as motivated by hostility and consequently less likely to respond with aggression themselves. The guidelines in the *Becoming an Informed Consumer of Development* box are based on the various theoretical perspectives on aggression and morality that we've discussed in this chapter.

●— BECOMING AN INFORMED CONSUMER OF DEVELOPMENT —●

Increasing Moral Behavior and Reducing Aggression in Preschool-Age Children

Based on our discussions of moral development and the roots of aggression, we can identify several methods for encouraging preschoolers' moral conduct and reducing the incidence of aggression. Among the most practical and readily accomplished are the following (J. Bullock, 1988):

- Provide opportunities for preschool-age children to observe others acting in a cooperative, helpful, prosocial manner. Furthermore, encourage them to interact with peers in joint activities in which they share a common goal. Such cooperative activities can teach the importance and desirability of working with and helping others.

- Do not ignore aggressive behavior. Parents and teachers should intervene when they see aggression in preschoolers and send a clear message that aggression is an unacceptable means for resolving conflicts.

- Help preschoolers devise alternative explanations for others' behavior. This is particularly important for children who are prone to aggression and who may be apt to view others' conduct as more hostile than it actually is. Parents and teachers should help such children see that the behavior of their peers has several possible interpretations.

- Monitor preschoolers' television viewing, particularly the violence that they view. There is good evidence that observation of televised aggression increases children's levels of aggression. At the same time, encourage preschoolers to watch particular shows that are designed to increase the level of moral conduct, such as *Sesame Street, Mr. Rogers's Neighborhood,* and *Barney.*

- Help preschoolers understand their feelings. When children become angry—and there are times when almost all children do—they need to learn how to deal with their feelings in a constructive manner. Tell them *specific* things they can do to improve the situation ("I see you're really angry with Jake for not giving you a turn. Don't hit him, but tell him you want a chance to play with the game.")

- Explicitly teach reasoning and self-control. Preschoolers can understand the rudiments of moral reasoning, and they should be reminded why certain behaviors are desirable. For instance, explicitly saying, "If you take all the cookies, others will have no dessert," is preferable to saying, "Good children don't eat all the cookies."

REVIEW & APPLY

Review

- Piaget believed that preschoolers are in the heteronomous morality stage of moral development.

- Social learning approaches to moral development emphasize the importance of reinforcement for moral actions and the observation of models of moral conduct. Psychoanalytic and other theories focus on children's empathy with others and their wish to help others so that they can avoid unpleasant feelings themselves.

- Aggression typically declines in frequency and duration as children become more able to regulate their emotions and to use language to negotiate disputes.

- Ethologists and sociobiologists regard aggression as an innate human characteristic, while proponents of social learning and cognitive approaches focus on learned aspects of aggression.

Applying Child Development

- If high-prestige models of behavior are particularly effective in influencing moral attitudes and actions, are there implications for individuals in such industries as sports, advertising, and entertainment?

- *From an educator's perspective:* If television and aggression are ever conclusively linked, what will be the implications for education?

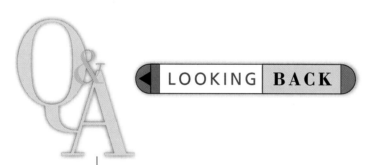

LOOKING BACK

- **How do preschool-age children develop a concept of themselves?**

- According to Erik Erikson, preschool-age children are initially in the autonomy-versus-shame-and-doubt stage (18 months to 3 years), in which they develop independence and mastery over their physical and social worlds or else feel shame, self-doubt, and unhappiness. Later, in the initiative-versus-guilt stage (ages 3 to 6), preschool-age children face conflicts between the desire to act independently and the guilt that comes from the unintended consequences of their actions.

- Preschoolers' self-concepts are formed partly from their own perceptions and estimations of their characteristics, partly from their parents' behavior toward them, and partly from cultural influences.

- **How do children develop a sense of racial identity and gender?**

- Preschool-age children form racial attitudes largely in response to their environment, including parents and other influences. Gender differences emerge early in the preschool years as children form expectations—which generally conform to social stereotypes— about what is appropriate and inappropriate for each sex.

- The strong gender expectations held by preschoolers are explained in different ways by different theorists. Some point to genetic factors as evidence for a biological explanation of gender expectations. Freud's psychoanalytic theories use a framework based on the subconscious. Social learning theorists focus on environmental influences, including parents, teachers, peers, and the media, while cognitive theorists propose that children form gender schemas, cognitive frameworks that organize information that the children gather about gender.

In what sorts of social relationships and play do preschoolers engage?

- Preschool social relationships begin to encompass genuine friendship, which takes on a dimension of stability and trust.

- Older preschoolers engage in more constructive play than functional play. They also engage in more associative and cooperative play than younger preschoolers, who do more parallel and onlooker playing.

What sorts of disciplinary styles do parents employ, and what effects do they have?

- Disciplinary styles differ both individually and culturally. In the United States and other Western societies, parents' styles tend to be mostly authoritarian, permissive, uninvolved, or authoritative, the last regarded as the most effective.

- Children of authoritarian and permissive parents may develop dependence, hostility, and low self-control, while children of uninvolved parents may feel unloved and emotionally detached. Children of authoritative parents tend to be more independent, friendly, self-assertive, and cooperative.

How do children develop a moral sense?

- Piaget believed that preschool-age children are in the heteronomous morality stage of moral development, characterized by a belief in external, unchangeable rules of conduct and sure, immediate punishment for all misdeeds.

- In contrast, social learning approaches to morality emphasize interactions between environment and behavior in moral development in which models of behavior play an important role in development.

- Some developmentalists believe that a child's development of empathy, which begins early in life, underlies many kinds of moral behavior. Other emotions, including the negative emotions of anger and shame, may also promote moral behavior.

How does aggression develop in preschool-age children?

- Aggression, which involves intentional harm to another person, begins to emerge in the preschool years. As children age and improve their language skills, acts of aggression typically decline in frequency and duration.

- Some ethologists, such as Konrad Lorenz, believe that aggression is simply a biological fact of human life, a belief held also by many sociobiologists, who focus on competition within species to pass genes on to the next generation.

- Social learning theorists focus on the role of the environment, including models of behavior and social reinforcement.

- The cognitive approach to aggression emphasizes the role of interpretations of the behaviors of others in determining aggressive or nonaggressive responses.

EPILOGUE

 n this chapter, we examined the social and personality development of preschool-age children, including their development of self-concept. We looked at the social relationships of preschool-age children and the changing nature of play. We considered typical styles of parental discipline and their effects later in life. We discussed the development of a moral sense from several developmental perspectives, and we concluded with a discussion of aggression.

Reread the prologue to this chapter, about Alison Gopnik's 2-year-old son, and answer the following questions:

1. In what ways do the actions of Alison Gopnik's son indicate that he is developing a theory of mind?

2. Is Erikson's framework of moral development helpful in interpreting the boy's actions in this instance? Why or why not?

3. Do you think the boy's reaction would have been different if his father had collapsed on the couch after a bad day instead of his mother? Why or why not? Can you think of a hypothesis to test based on this question? Could an experiment be devised to examine the hypothesis?

4. How might social learning approaches to morality and the concept of empathy explain the son's actions in helping his mother?

5. Can you discuss the boy's actions in terms of emotional self-regulation?

KEY TERMS AND CONCEPTS

psychosocial development (p. 293)
initiative-versus-guilt stage (p. 293)
self-concept (p. 294)
collectivistic orientation (p. 294)
individualistic orientation (p. 294)
race dissonance (p. 295)
identification (p. 297)
gender identity (p. 297)
gender schema (p. 297)

gender constancy (p. 298)
androgynous (p. 298)
functional play (p. 300)
constructive play (p. 300)
parallel play (p. 300)
onlooker play (p. 300)
associative play (p. 301)
cooperative play (p. 301)
authoritarian parents (p. 304)
permissive parents (p. 304)
authoritative parents (p. 304)

uninvolved parents (p. 304)
moral development (p. 306)
heteronomous morality (p. 306)
immanent justice (p. 307)
prosocial behavior (p. 308)
abstract modeling (p. 308)
empathy (p. 308)
aggression (p. 310)
emotional self-regulation (p. 310)
relational aggression (p. 310)

BRIDGES

In Part 3, we extended our discussion of physical, cognitive, and social and personality development into the preschool years. We saw that these years bring great improvements in children's motor skills, thinking, and language and in their social awareness and development of morality.

Children begin the preschool years as somewhat wobbly toddlers with few words at their command. They emerge with an array of skills for sports and games, learning, communicating, and making new friends. These skills will all help them as they enter the next period of their lives, the school years. For example, in the next part of the book we'll see how important friendships become to children during their school years.

We discussed many theories of cognitive and social development and encountered some of the groundbreaking ideas—and great controversies—associated with such giants in the field of development as Piaget, Vygotsky, Freud, and Erikson. All of these theorists stressed the importance of early developments as a foundation for later growth, whether in cognitive skills or personality development. As we go on, we'll see several ways in which our early experiences, even as babies, can affect us at later stages of life. For example, in Part 4, we'll explore how children's sociocultural environments during the preschool years might relate to their success in school.

Overall, we continued our observation of the amazing strides that children make as they become increasingly independent. As they move into middle childhood—the part of the life span that we will discuss in Part 4—we will continue to see the flowering of the remarkable cognitive and linguistic endowment of humans. We'll also take note of school-age children's equally remarkable capacity for social functioning. ∎

11

Physical Development in Middle Childhood

PROLOGUE: Suzanne McGuire

 t was a hot summer day in Atlanta, the kind when most adults are moving slowly through the heavy, humid air. But not 8-year-old Suzanne McGuire. She is a study in motion as she rounds the corner from third base to home plate, a look of triumph on her face.

A few moments earlier, she was waiting for the pitcher to throw the ball. At her first and second turns at bat, Suzanne had struck out, and she was still feeling unhappy and a bit humiliated by her performance.

Now, though, the pitch looked perfectly positioned, and she swung at it with a combination of confidence and high hope. As if by magic, the bat connected with the ball, lobbing it in a lazy arc well beyond the left fielder. It was a home run—and it created a moment that she would never forget.

Middle childhood is a period of significant physical, cognitive, and social change.

LOOKING AHEAD

Suzanne McGuire has come a long way from the preschooler she was only a few years earlier, for whom running quickly in a coordinated fashion was a challenge and successfully hitting an incoming pitch an impossibility.

Middle childhood is characterized by a procession of moments such as these, as children's physical, cognitive, and social skills ascend to new heights. In this chapter, we focus on the physical aspects of middle childhood, both in typical children and in children with special needs. Beginning at age 6 and continuing to the start of adolescence at around age 12, middle childhood is often referred to as the "school years" because it marks the beginning of formal education for most children. Sometimes the physical and cognitive growth that occurs during middle childhood is gradual; other times it is sudden; but always it is remarkable.

We begin our consideration of middle childhood by examining physical and motor development. We discuss how children's bodies change and the twin problems of malnutrition and—the other side of the coin—childhood obesity. Next we turn to motor development. We discuss the growth of gross and fine motor skills and the role that physical competence plays in children's lives. We also discuss threats to children's safety, including a new one that enters the home through the personal computer.

Finally, the chapter ends with a discussion of some of the special needs that affect the sensory and physical abilities of exceptional children. It concludes by focusing on the question of how children with special needs should be integrated into society.

In sum, after reading this chapter, you will be able to answer the following questions:

○ In what ways do children grow during the school years, and what factors influence their growth?

○ What are the nutritional needs of school-age children, and what are some causes and effects of improper nutrition?

○ What sorts of health threats do school-age children face?

○ What are the characteristics of motor development during middle childhood, and what advantages do improved physical skills bring?

○ What safety threats affect school-age children, and what can be done about them?

○ What sorts of special needs manifest themselves in the middle childhood years, and how can they be met?

The Growing Body

Cinderella, dressed in yella,
Went upstairs to kiss her fellah
But she made a mistake and kissed a snake.
How many doctors did it take?
One, two, . . .

While the other girls chanted the classic jump-rope rhyme, Kat proudly displayed her newly developed ability to jump backward. In second grade, Kat was starting to get quite good at jumping rope. In first grade, she had not been able to master it. But over the summer, she had spent many hours practicing, and now that practice seemed to be paying off.

As Kat is gleefully experiencing, middle childhood is the time when children make great physical strides, mastering all kinds of new skills as they grow bigger and stronger. How does this progress occur?

Physical Development

Slow and steady.

If three words could characterize the nature of growth during middle childhood, it would be these. Especially when compared to the swift growth during the first 5 years of life and the remarkable growth spurt characteristic of adolescence, middle childhood is relatively tranquil. But the body has not shifted into neutral. Physical growth continues, although at a more stately pace than it did during the preschool years.

Height and Weight Changes.   While they are in elementary school, children in the United States grow, on average, 2 to 3 inches a year. By the age of 11, the average height for girls is 4 feet 10 inches and the average height for boys is slightly shorter at 4 feet 9½ inches. This is the only time during the life span when girls are, on average, taller than boys. This height difference reflects the slightly more rapid physical development of girls, who start their adolescent growth spurt around the age of 10.

Weight gain follows a similar pattern. During middle childhood, both boys and girls gain around 5 to 7 pounds a year. Weight also becomes redistributed. As the rounded look of "baby fat" disappears, children's bodies become more muscular, and their strength increases.

Average height and weight increases disguise significant individual differences, as anyone who has seen a line of fourth graders walking down a school corridor has doubtless noticed. It is not unusual to see children of the same age who are 6 or 7 inches apart in height.

Cultural Patterns of Growth.   Most children in North America receive sufficient nutrients to grow to their full potential. In other parts of the world, however, inadequate nutrition and disease take their toll, producing children who are shorter and who weigh less than they would if they had sufficient nutrients. The discrepancies can be dramatic: Children in poorer areas of cities such as Calcutta, Hong Kong, and Rio de Janeiro are smaller than their counterparts in affluent areas of the same cities.

Variations of 6 inches in height between children of the same age are not unusual and well within the normal range.

VIDEO CLIP

Physical Growth

Children in poorer areas of cities, such as these youngsters in Calcutta, are shorter and weigh less than those raised in more affluent places.

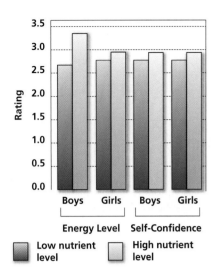

FIGURE 11-1
NUTRITIONAL BENEFITS

Children who received higher levels of nutrients had more energy and felt more self-confident than those whose nutritional intake was lower. How might a social worker use this information?

(*Source:* Adapted from Barrett & Radke-Yarrow, 1985)

"Can Johnny come out and eat?"

In the United States, most variations in height and weight are the result of different people's unique genetic inheritance, including factors relating to racial and ethnic background. For instance, children from Asian and Pacific Island backgrounds tend to be shorter, on average, than those of northern and central European heritage (Meredith, 1971). However, even within particular racial and ethnic groups there is significant variation between individuals. Furthermore, we cannot attribute racial and ethnic differences solely to inherited factors, because dietary customs and variations in levels of affluence may also contribute to the differences.

Nutrition: Links to Overall Functioning

The level of nutrition children experience during their lives significantly affects many aspects of their behavior. For instance, longitudinal studies over many years in Guatemalan villages show that children's nutritional backgrounds are related to several dimensions of social and emotional functioning at school age. Children who had received more nutrients were more involved with their peers, showed more positive emotion, had less anxiety, and had more moderate activity levels than their peers who had received less adequate nutrition (Barrett & Frank, 1987; see Figure 11-1).

Not only does good nutrition promote the growth of strong bones, but it is also related to the development of healthy teeth. During middle childhood, the majority of adult teeth replace the primary teeth of early childhood. Starting at around the age of 6, the primary teeth fall out at the rate of about four per year until the age of 11.

Nutrition is also linked to cognitive performance. For instance, in one study, children in Kenya who were well nourished performed better on a test of verbal abilities and on other cognitive measures than those who had mild to moderate undernutrition. Other research suggests that malnutrition may influence cognitive development by dampening children's curiosity, responsiveness, and motivation to learn (J. L. Brown & Pollitt, 1996; McDonald et al., 1994; Ricciuti, 1993; Sigman et al., 1989).

Although undernutrition and malnutrition clearly lead to physical, social, and cognitive difficulties, in some cases *overnutrition*—the intake of too many calories—presents problems of its own, particularly when it leads to childhood obesity.

Childhood Obesity

When Ruthellen's mother asks if she would like a piece of bread with her meal, Ruthellen replies that she'd better not have any—she thinks she may be getting fat. Ruthellen, who is of normal weight and height, is 6 years old.

Although height can be of concern to both children and parents during middle childhood, maintaining the appropriate weight is an even greater worry for some. In fact, concern about weight can border on an obsession, particularly among girls. For instance, many 6-year-old girls worry about becoming "fat," and some 40 percent of 9- and 10-year-olds are trying to lose weight. Why? Their concern is most often the result of the American preoccupation with being slim, which permeates every sector of society (Schreiber et al., 1996).

In spite of this widely held view that thinness is a virtue, however, increasing numbers of children are becoming obese. *Obesity* is defined as body weight that is more than 20 percent above the average for a person of a given age and height. By this definition, 13 percent of U.S. children are obese—a proportion that has tripled since the 1960s (Brownlee, 2002; J. Steinberg, 1996; Troiano et al., 1995).

Genetic Factors. Obesity is caused by a combination of genetic and social characteristics. Particular inherited genes predispose certain children to be overweight. For example, adopted

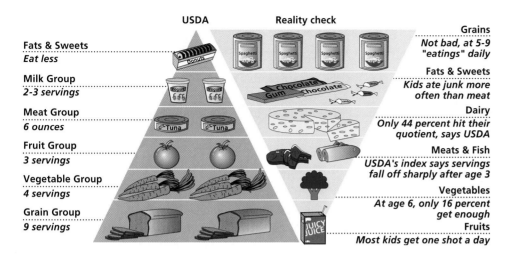

FIGURE 11-2 BALANCED DIET?

Studies have found that the diet of children is almost the opposite of that recommended by the U.S. Department of Agriculture—a situation that can lead to an increase in obesity. The typical 10-year-old is 10 pounds heavier than a decade ago. As a health care provider, what suggestions would you make to the parents of overweight children?

(*Sources:* NPD Group, 2002; U.S. Department of Agriculture, 1999)

children tend to have weights that are more similar to those of their birth parents than those of their adoptive parents (Whitaker et al., 1997; Zhang et al., 1994).

Social Factors.   Social factors also enter into children's weight problems. For example, parents who are particularly controlling and directive regarding their children's eating may produce children who lack internal controls to regulate their own food intake (K. D. Brownell & Rodin, 1994; Faith, Johnson, & Allison, 1997; S. L. Johnson & Birch, 1994).

Poor diet can also contribute to obesity. Despite their knowledge that certain foods are necessary for a balanced, nutritious diet, most children eat too few fruits and vegetables and more fats and sweets than recommended (see Figure 11-2).

Another important social factor that determines obesity is exercise—or rather, the lack of exercise. School-age children, by and large, tend to engage in relatively little exercise and are not particularly fit (Wolf et al., 1993). For instance, around 40 percent of boys aged 6 to 12 are unable to do more than one pull-up, and another 25 percent can't do any. Furthermore, school fitness surveys reveal that children in the United States have shown little or no improvement in the amount of exercise they get, despite national efforts to increase the level of fitness of school-age children. From the ages of 6 to 18, boys decrease their physical activity by 24 percent and girls by 36 percent (B. Murray, 1996a; Ungrady, 1992).

Why, when our visions of childhood include children running happily on school playgrounds, playing sports, and chasing one another in games of tag, is the actual level of exercise relatively low? One answer is that many kids are inside their homes, watching television or using computers.

The correlation between television viewing and obesity is significant: The more television children watch, the more likely they are to be overweight, for several reasons. For one thing, television viewing is a sedentary activity; few people engage in vigorous exercise while watching TV. Another factor is that children tend to snack while watching television, thereby increasing their caloric intake beyond nutritional need. Finally, frequent exposure to food commercials may entice habitual television viewers to be overly interested in food and eating (Gable & Lutz, 2000; Gortmaker et al., 1996; Harrell et al., 1997).

Computer use also has the potential to lead to obesity, for some children's greatest exercise is the clicking of a computer's mouse. If children spend a considerable amount of time in front of a computer screen, their cyberactivities may act as a substitute for more vigorous activities.

Treatment Strategies.   Regardless of the causes of childhood obesity, treatment is tricky, because creating too strong a concern about food and dieting must be avoided. In most cases,

BECOMING AN INFORMED CONSUMER OF DEVELOPMENT

Keeping Children Fit

Here is a brief portrait of a contemporary American: Sam works all week at a desk and gets no regular physical exercise. On weekends he spends many hours sitting in front of the TV, often snacking on sodas and sweets. Both at home and at restaurants, his meals feature high-calorie, fat-saturated foods. (J. Segal & Segal, 1992, p. 235)

Although this sketch could apply to many adult men and women, Sam is actually a 6-year-old. He is one of many school-age children in the United States who get little or no regular exercise and who are consequently physically unfit and at risk for obesity and other health problems.

However, several approaches can be taken to encourage children to become more physically active (O'Neill, 1994; Squires, 1991):

- Make exercise fun. If children are to build the habit of exercising, they must find it enjoyable. Activities that keep children on the sidelines or that are overly competitive may give children with inferior skills a lifelong distaste for exercise.

- Be an exercise role model. Children who see that exercise is a regular part of the lives of their parents, teachers, or adult friends may come to think of fitness as a regular part of their lives, too.

- Gear activities to the child's physical level and motor skills. For instance, use child-size equipment that can make participants feel successful.

- Encourage children to find an exercise partner. It could be a friend, a sibling, or a parent. Exercising can involve a variety of activities, such as roller skating or hiking, but almost all activities are carried out more eagerly in the company of another person.

- Start slowly. Sedentary children who haven't habitually engaged in physical activity should start off gradually. For instance, they could start with 5 minutes of exercise a day, 7 days a week. Over 10 weeks, they could move toward a goal of 30 minutes of exercise 3 to 5 days a week.

- Urge participation in organized sports activities, but do not push too hard. Not every child is athletically inclined, and pushing too hard for involvement in organized sports may backfire. Make participation and enjoyment the goals of such activities, not winning.

the goal of treatment for obesity is to temporarily maintain a child's current weight through an improved diet and increased exercise, rather than actually seeking to lose weight. In time, obese children's normal growth in height will result in their weight's becoming more normal. Some tips for easing sedentary kids into a more active lifestyle are presented in the *Becoming an Informed Consumer of Development* box.

Health During Middle Childhood

Imani was miserable. Her nose was running, her lips were chapped, and her throat was sore. Although she had been able to stay home from school and spend the day watching old reruns on TV, she still felt that she was suffering mightily.

Despite her misery, Imani's situation is not so bad. She'll get over the cold in a few days and be no worse for having experienced it. In fact, she may be a little better off, for she is now immune to the specific cold germs that made her ill in the first place.

Imani's cold may end up being the most serious illness that she gets during middle childhood. For most children, this is a period of robust health, and most of the ailments they do contract tend to be mild and brief. Routine immunizations during childhood have produced a considerably lower incidence of the life-threatening illnesses that 50 years ago claimed the lives of a significant number of children.

However, illness is not uncommon. For instance, more than 90 percent of children are likely to have at least one serious medical condition over the 6-year period of middle childhood,

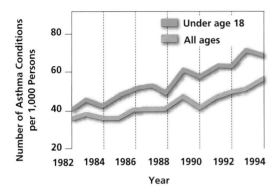

FIGURE 11-3   RISING RATES OF ASTHMA

Since the early 1980s, the rate of asthma among children has almost doubled. A number of factors explain the rise, including increased air pollution and better means of detecting the disease.

(*Source:* National Center for Health Statistics, 1997)

according to the results of one large survey. And although most children have short-term illnesses, about one in nine has a chronic, persistent condition, such as repeated migraine headaches (Starfield, 1991; Starfield et al., 1984). And some illnesses are actually becoming more prevalent.

Asthma.   Asthma is among the diseases that have shown a significant increase in prevalence in recent decades. **Asthma** is a chronic condition characterized by periodic attacks of wheezing, coughing, and shortness of breath. More than 5 percent of U.S. children suffer from the disorder, and worldwide there are 150 million sufferers (Doyle, 2000; Vogel, 1997; see Figure 11-3).

Asthma occurs when the airways leading to the lungs constrict, partially blocking the passage of air. Because the airways are obstructed, more effort is needed to push air through them, making breathing more difficult. As air is forced through the obstructed airways, it makes the whistling sound called wheezing.

Not surprisingly, children are often exceedingly frightened by asthma attacks, and the anxiety and agitation produced by their breathing difficulties may actually make the attack worse. In some cases, breathing becomes so difficult that further physical symptoms develop, including sweating, an increased heart rate, and—in the most severe cases—blueness in the face and lips due to a lack of oxygen.

Asthma attacks are triggered by a variety of factors. Among the most common are respiratory infections (such as colds or flu), allergic reactions to airborne irritants (such as pollution, cigarette smoke, dust mites, and animal dander and excretions), stress, and exercise. Sometimes even a sudden change in air temperature or humidity is enough to bring on an attack.

Although asthma can be serious, treatment is increasingly effective for those who suffer from the disorder. Some children who experience frequent asthma attacks use a small aerosol container with a special mouthpiece to spray drugs into the lungs. Other patients take tablets or receive injections (Klinnert, McQuaid, & Gavin, 1997).

One of the most puzzling questions about asthma is why more and more children are suffering from it. Some researchers suggest that increasing air pollution has led to the rise; others believe that cases of asthma that might have been missed in the past are being identified more accurately. Still others have suggested that exposure to "asthma triggers," such as dust, may be increasing because new buildings are more weatherproof—and therefore less drafty—than old ones, and consequently the flow of air within them is more restricted.

Finally, poverty may play an indirect role. Children living in poverty have a higher incidence of asthma than other children, probably due to poorer medical care and less sanitary living conditions. For instance, poor youngsters are more likely than more affluent ones to be exposed to triggering factors that are associated with asthma, such as dust mites, cockroach feces and body parts, and rodent feces and urine (Nossiter, 1995).

Asthma   A chronic condition characterized by periodic attacks of wheezing, coughing, and shortness of breath

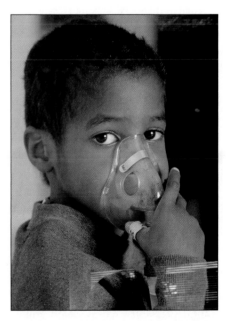

The incidence of asthma, a chronic respiratory condition, has increased dramatically over the past several decades.

Psychological Disorders.   Jackson had always been a quiet child and had, since his days as a toddler, seemed less exuberant than most other children. But when his third-grade teacher called his parents to report that Jackson seemed increasingly withdrawn from his classmates and had to be coaxed into going out to the playground, the parents thought they might have a serious problem on their hands. They took Jackson to a psychologist, who diagnosed Jackson as suffering from *childhood depression.*

For years, people neglected the symptoms of childhood depression, and even today, parents and teachers may overlook its presence. In part, their neglect is due to the fact that its symptoms are not entirely consistent with the ways adults express depression. Rather than

○— FROM RESEARCH TO PRACTICE —○

Orange-Flavored Prozac: The Growing Use of Antidepressants to Treat Childhood Psychological Problems

Andrew Crittendon was only 7 when an inexplicable bleakness descended on him. "I lost interest in everything," he recalls. "I just sat in my room and thought about how horrible life was." Andrew's mother, Beverly, started to worry when a trip to Six Flags Great Adventure didn't lift his spirits, and her concern turned to terror when the child started talking about suicide. Dr. Graham Emslie, the Dallas-based psychiatrist who diagnosed Andrew's depression, offered to enroll him in a study of Prozac. "I didn't care what they did," Andrew says, "as long as there was a chance it would make me feel better." It did—and he stayed on the drug for four years. At 11, he discovered he no longer needed it. Andrew is now a six-foot-tall ninth grader with his sights set on a career in filmmaking. "I'm really one of the happiest people I know," he says. (M. Crowley, 1997, p. 73)

The use of Prozac has become a popular—if controversial—treatment for a variety of childhood psychological disorders. In 1996 alone, some 200,000 prescriptions were written for children between the ages of 6 and 12, an increase of close to 300 percent over the previous year (Strauch, 1997).

Surprisingly, though, until early in 2003, the drug had not been approved by governmental regulators for use by children. In fact, very few antidepressant drugs have received approval for use by children or adolescents. Still, because the drugs had received approval for adult use, it is perfectly legal for physicians to write prescriptions for it for children (FDA, 2003).

Proponents of the increased use of Prozac, as well as other antidepressants such as Zoloft and Paxil, for children suggest that depression and other psychological disorders can be treated successfully using drug therapies. In many cases, more traditional nondrug therapies, which largely employ verbal methods, are ineffective. In such cases, drugs can provide the only form of relief. Furthermore, at least one clinical test has shown that the drugs are effective with children (Emslie et al., 1997, 1999).

Critics contend that there is little evidence in support of the long-term effectiveness of antidepressants in children. Even worse, no one knows the consequences of the use of antidepressants on the developing brain or any of the other possible long-term consequences of their use by children. Little is known about the correct dosages for children of given ages. Finally, some observers suggest that the use of special children's versions of the drugs, in orange- or mint-flavored syrups, might lead to overdoses or perhaps even encourage the use of illegal drugs (Strauch, 1997).

Although the use of antidepressant drugs to treat children is controversial, what is clear is that childhood depression and other psychological disorders remain a significant problem for many children. Experts suggest that between 2 and 5 percent of school-age children suffer from childhood depression. In some children it is particularly severe: About 1 percent are so depressed that they express suicidal ideas (P. Cohen et al., 1993; Larsson & Melin, 1992). Furthermore, some 8 to 9 percent of children suffer from *anxiety disorders,* in which they experience intense, uncontrollable anxiety about situations that most people would not find bothersome. For instance, some children have strong fears about specific stimuli—such as germs or school—while others have bouts of generalized anxiety, the source of which they cannot pinpoint (G. A. Bernstein & Borchardt, 1991; Ollendick et al., 1996; Silverman & Ginsburg, 1998; Wenner, 1994).

Childhood psychological disorders must not be ignored. Not only are the disorders disruptive during childhood, but those who suffer from psychological problems as children are at risk for future disorders during adulthood (Alloy et al., 1996; Kazdin, 1990; Mash & Barkley, 1998).

being manifested in a profound sadness or hopelessness, a negative outlook on life, and, in extreme cases, suicidal thoughts, as adult depression is, childhood depression may instead be characterized by the expression of exaggerated fears, clinginess, or avoidance of everyday activities. In older children, childhood depression may lead to sulking, school problems, and even acts of delinquency (J. Mitchell et al., 1988; Prieto, Cole, & Tageson, 1992; Wenar, 1994).

It is important to keep in mind that all children are occasionally sad, and short periods of unhappiness should not be mistaken for childhood depression. The distinguishing characteristics of childhood depression are its depth, which can be truly profound, and its duration, which can extend for days or even weeks (Bandura et al., 1999; Besseghini, 1997).

Like adult depression, childhood depression can be treated effectively through a variety of approaches. In addition to psychological counseling, drugs are sometimes prescribed, although their use is controversial (see the *From Research to Practice* box). Whatever treatment is chosen, it is important that childhood depression not be ignored, particularly because children who are depressed are at risk for mood disorders during adulthood (Alloy, Acocella, & Bootzin, 1996; Kazdin, 1990; Warner et al., 1999).

REVIEW & APPLY

Review

- During middle childhood, height and weight increase gradually, and the body loses its baby fat.

- Differences in average height and weight relate partly to affluence and poverty.

- Nutrition is important not only for its contribution to physical growth but also because it affects many aspects of social, emotional, and cognitive functioning.

- Obesity in children, which can be caused by genetic and social factors, can be a serious problem.

- The health of children in middle childhood is generally good, with few concerns for worries.

Applying Child Development

- What are some aspects of U.S. culture that may contribute to fitness and nutritional problems among school-age children?

- *From a health care provider's perspective:* Under what circumstances would you recommend the use of a growth hormone? Is shortness primarily a physical or a cultural problem?

Motor Development and Safety

When my son's friend Owen was 9 years old, everybody at school knew the shameful truth about him: He was a whiz at math but a lousy football player.

Nobody was more aware of this than Owen. "He knew he wasn't as good at sports as the others," says his mother, Cheryl. "It really got him down. Even when we told him, You have to get out there, you have to try, as soon as he made a mistake, he would just walk away. Owen's schoolwork was good, so he felt okay about himself. But because he didn't play sports, he didn't have as many friends as most kids did."

Then one day, just after he turned 10, when Owen happened to be at a nearby mall, he saw a demonstration of a martial art called tae kwon do. "That's what I want to do," he immediately told his mother. "Can you sign me up?"

He now takes lessons several times a week, and according to Cheryl, the changes are remarkable. "Owen's mood has improved, he's sleeping better, he's even better about doing homework," she says. "And when he got his yellow belt, he was over the moon." (Heath, 1994, pp. 127–128)

During middle childhood, children's athletic abilities play an important role in determining how they see themselves, as well as how they are viewed by others. This is also a time when such physical proficiencies develop substantially.

Motor Skills: Continuing Improvement

Watching a schoolyard softball player pitch a ball past a batter to the catcher or a third-grade runner reach the finish line in a race, it is hard not to be struck by the huge strides that children have made since the more awkward days of preschool. Both gross and fine motor skills improve significantly during the middle childhood years.

Gross Motor Skills. One important improvement in gross motor skills is in the realm of muscle coordination. For instance, most school-age children can readily learn to ride a bike, ice-skate, swim, and skip rope, skills that earlier they could not perform well (Cratty, 1986; see Figure 11-4).

Do boys and girls differ in their motor skills? Traditionally, developmentalists contended that gender differences in gross motor skills become increasingly pronounced during these years, with boys outperforming girls (Espenschade, 1960). However, more recent research casts some doubt on this claim. When comparisons are made between boys and girls who regularly take part in similar activities such as softball, gender variations in gross motor skills are found to be minimal (E. G. Hall & Lee, 1984).

During middle childhood, children master many types of skills that earlier they could not perform well, such as riding a bike, ice-skating, swimming, and skipping rope. Is this true for children in all cultures?

6 Years	7 Years	8 Years	9 Years	10 Years	11 Years	12 Years
Girls superior in accuracy of movement; boys superior in more forceful, less complex acts. Can throw with the proper weight shift and step. Acquire the ability to skip.	Can balance on one foot with eyes closed. Can walk on a 2-inch-wide balance beam without falling off. Can hop and jump accurately into small squares (hopscotch). Can correctly execute a jumping-jack exercise.	Can grip objects with 12 pounds of pressure. Can engage in alternate rhythmical hopping in a 2-2, 2-3, or 3-3 pattern. Girls can throw a small ball 33 feet; boys can throw a small ball 59 feet. The number of games participated in by both sexes is the greatest at this age.	Girls can jump vertically 8.5 inches over their standing height plus reach; boys can jump vertically 10 inches. Boys can run 16.6 feet per second and throw a small ball 41 feet; girls can run 16 feet per second and throw a small ball 41 feet.	Can judge and intercept directions of small balls thrown from a distance. Both girls and boys can run 17 feet per second.	Boys can achieve standing broad jump of 5 feet; girls can achieve standing broad jump of 4.5 feet.	Can achieve high jump of 3 feet.

FIGURE 11-4 GROSS MOTOR SKILLS DEVELOPED BETWEEN THE AGES OF 6 AND 12 YEARS

Why would it be important that a social worker be aware of this period of development?

(*Source:* Adapted from Cratty, 1979, p. 222)

What accounts for the discrepancy in earlier observations? Performance differences were probably found because of differences in motivation and expectations. Society told girls that they would do worse than boys in sports, and the girls' performance reflected that message.

Today, however, society's message has changed, at least officially. For instance, the American Academy of Pediatrics (1999) suggests that boys and girls should engage in the same sports and games and that they can do so together in mixed-gender groups. There is no reason to separate the sexes in physical exercise and sports until puberty, when the smaller size of females begins to make them more susceptible to injury in contact sports.

Fine Motor Skills. Typing at a computer keyboard, writing in cursive with pen or pencil, drawing detailed pictures—these are just some of the accomplishments that depend on improvements in fine motor coordination that occur during early and middle childhood. Children 6 and 7 years old are able to tie their shoes and fasten buttons; by age 8, they can use each hand independently; and by 11 and 12, they can manipulate objects with almost as much dexterity as they will have in adulthood.

One of the reasons for advances in fine motor skills is that the amount of myelin in the brain increases significantly between the ages of 6 and 8 (Lecours, 1982). *Myelin* provides protective insulation around parts of nerve cells. Because increased levels of myelin raise the speed at which electrical impulses travel between neurons, messages can reach muscles more rapidly and control them better.

Fine motor skills, such as typing on a keyboard, improve during early and middle childhood.

The Social Benefits of Physical Competence. Is Matt, a fifth grader who is a clear standout on his Saturday morning soccer team, more popular as a result of his physical talents?

He may well be. According to a long history of research on the topic, school-age children who perform well physically are often more accepted and better liked by their peers than those who perform less well (Branta, Lerner, & Taylor, 1997; Pintney, Forlands, & Freedman, 1937).

However, the link between physical competence and popularity is considerably stronger for boys than for girls. The reason for this sex difference most likely relates to differing societal standards for appropriate male and female behavior. Despite the increasing evidence that girls and boys do not differ substantially in athletic performance, a lingering "physical toughness" standard still exists for males but not for females. Regardless of age, males who are bigger, stronger, and more physically competent are seen as more desirable than those who are smaller, weaker, and less physically competent. In contrast, standards for females are less supportive of physical success. In fact, women receive less admiration for physical prowess than men do throughout the life span. Although these societal standards may be changing, with women's participation in sports activities becoming more frequent and valued, gender biases remain (Burn, 1996).

Although the social desirability of athletically proficient boys increases throughout elementary school and continues into secondary school, at some point the positive consequences of motor ability begin to diminish. Presumably, other traits become increasingly important in determining social attractiveness—some of which we'll discuss in Chapter 13.

Furthermore, it is difficult to sort out the extent that advantages from exceptional physical performance are due to actual athletic competence, as opposed to being a result of earlier maturation. Boys who physically mature at a more rapid pace than their peers or who happen to be taller, heavier, and stronger tend to perform better at athletic activities due to their relative size advantage. Consequently, it may be that early physical maturity is ultimately of greater consequence than physical skills per se.

Still, it is clear that athletic competence and motor skills in general play a notable role in school-age children's lives. However, it is important to help children avoid overemphasizing the significance of physical ability. Participation in sports should be fun, not something that separates one child from another or raises children's and parents' anxiety levels. In fact, some forms of organized sports, such as Little League baseball, are sometimes criticized for the emphasis they may place on winning at any cost. When children feel that success in sports is the sole goal, the pleasure of playing the game is diminished, particularly for children who are not naturally athletic and do not excel.

In sum, the goals of participation in sports and other physical activities should be to maintain physical fitness, to learn physical skills, and to become comfortable with one's body. And children should have fun in the process.

Threats to Children's Safety, Online and Off

The increasing independence and mobility of school-age children give rise to new safety issues. In fact, the rate of injury for children increases between the ages of 5 and 14 (see Figure 11-5). Furthermore, boys are more apt to be injured than girls, probably because their overall level of physical activity is greater (Schor, 1987).

Accidents. The most frequent source of injury to children is automobile accidents. Auto crashes annually kill 5 out of every 100,000 children between the ages 5 and 9. Fires and burns, drowning, and gun-related deaths follow in frequency (Health Resources and Services Administration, 1993).

The increased mobility of school-age children leads to other accidents. For instance, children who regularly walk to school on their own, many traveling such a distance alone for the

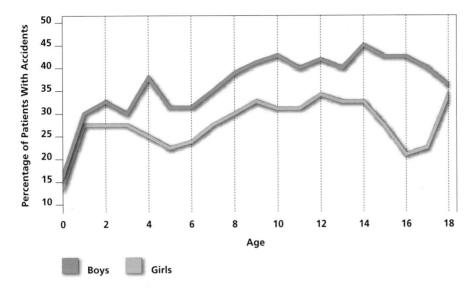

FIGURE 11-5 COMPARATIVE INJURY RATES BETWEEN GIRLS AND BOYS

As children become more independent and more mobile, their rate of injury increases.

(*Source:* Schor, 1987)

first time in their lives, face the risk of being hit by cars and trucks. Because of their lack of experience, they may misjudge distances when calculating just how far they are from an oncoming vehicle. Bicycle accidents also pose a risk, particularly as children venture out onto busy roads (Thomson et al., 1998).

Two ways to reduce motion-related injuries considerably are to use seat belts consistently inside the car and to wear appropriate protective gear outside. Bicycle helmets have significantly reduced head injuries, and their use is now mandatory in many localities. Similar protection is available for other activities; for example, knee and elbow pads have proved to be important sources of injury reduction for roller-blading and skateboarding (American Academy of Pediatrics, 1990).

Some injuries occur during organized sports activities—most often because of differences in participants' size. Younger players, outweighed and outperformed by older children, are often injured during organized games. Many such injuries could be avoided if games were limited to players of approximately the same weight, age, and skill level.

Safety in Cyberspace. The newest threat to the safety of school-age children comes from a source that just a decade ago was unheard of: the Internet and the World Wide Web. Although claims that cyberspace is overrun with pornography and child molesters are clearly exaggerated, it is true that cyberspace makes available material that many parents find objectionable (Lohr, 1995, 1996).

Although computer software developers are working on programs that will block particular computer sites, most experts feel that the most reliable safeguard is close supervision by parents. According to the National Center for Missing and Exploited Children (2002), a nonprofit organization that works with the U.S. Department of Justice, parents should warn their children never to provide personal information, such as home addresses or telephone numbers, to people on public computer "bulletin boards" or in chat rooms. In addition, children should not be allowed to hold face-to-face meetings with people they meet via computer, at least not without a parent present.

We do not yet have statistics that provide a true sense of the risk presented by exposure to cyberspace. But certainly a potential hazard exists, and parents must offer their children guidance in the use of this computer resource. It would be erroneous to think that just because children are in the supposed safety of their own rooms, logged on to home computers, they are truly safe. (Online safety rules for children are presented in Table 11-1.)

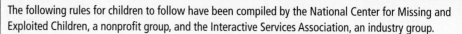

TABLE 11-1 ONLINE SAFETY RULES

The following rules for children to follow have been compiled by the National Center for Missing and Exploited Children, a nonprofit group, and the Interactive Services Association, an industry group.

- Do not give personal information such as your address, telephone number, parent's work address or telephone number, or the name and location of your school.

- Tell your parents if something that you come across online makes you feel uncomfortable.

- Never agree to get together with someone you "meet" online without your parents' permission. If your parents agree to the meeting, be sure the meeting is in a public place and that you bring them along.

- Never respond to messages or bulletin board items that are suggestive, obscene, belligerent, threatening, or make you feel uncomfortable. Give a copy of such messages to your parents and have them forward it to your Internet service provider.

- Never send pictures of yourself or any other personal material to a friend you meet online without telling your parents first.

- Follow the rules that your parents set for your online activities.

- There are places on the Internet that are for adults only. If you find yourself in one of those areas, LEAVE and go to one of the cool places on the Internet for kids.

(*Source:* National Center for Missing and Exploited Children, 1994)

R E V I E W & A P P L Y

Review

- School-age children experience continuing improvement in gross motor skills.

- Fine motor skills improve steadily during middle childhood, with children developing near-adult levels of coordination by the end of the period.

- Physical competence plays a large part in school-age children's lives and social success.

- Threats to safety in middle childhood include accidents that can result from increased independence and mobility and, increasingly, children's unsupervised access to cyberspace.

Applying Child Development

- How would you design an experiment to examine the roots of gender differences in gross motor skills? What impediments would there be to conducting such an experiment?

- *From an educator's perspective:* Do you think using blocking software or computer chips to screen potentially offensive content on the Internet is a practical idea? A good idea? Are such controls the best way to keep children safe in cyberspace?

Children With Special Needs

Dusty Nash, an angelic-looking blond child of seven, awoke at five one recent morning in his Chicago home and proceeded to throw a fit. He wailed. He kicked. Every muscle in his 50-pound body flew in furious motion. Finally, after about 30 minutes,

Dusty pulled himself together sufficiently to head downstairs for breakfast. While his mother bustled about the kitchen, the hyperkinetic child pulled a box of Kix cereal from the cupboard and sat on a chair.

But sitting still was not in the cards this morning. After grabbing some cereal with his hands, he began kicking the box, scattering little round corn puffs across the room. Next he turned his attention to the TV set, or rather, the table supporting it. The table was covered with checkerboard Con-Tact paper, and Dusty began peeling it off. Then he became intrigued with the spilled cereal and started stomping it to bits. At this point his mother interceded. In a firm but calm voice she told her son to get the stand-up dustpan and broom and clean up the mess. Dusty got out the dustpan but forgot the rest of the order. Within seconds he was dismantling the plastic dustpan, piece by piece. His next project: grabbing three rolls of toilet paper from the bathroom and unraveling them around the house. (Wallis, 1994, p. 43)

It was only 7:30 A.M.

Dusty—who has been diagnosed with attention deficit hyperactivity disorder (ADHD)—is one of millions of children who are classified as having *special needs*. Although every child has different specific capabilities, children with special needs differ significantly from typical children in terms of physical attributes or learning abilities. Furthermore, their needs present major challenges for both care providers and teachers.

We turn now to the most prevalent exceptionalities that affect children of normal intelligence: sensory difficulties, learning disabilities, and attention deficit disorders. (We will consider the special needs of children who are significantly below and above average in intelligence in Chapter 12.)

Sensory Difficulties

Anyone who has temporarily lost a pair of eyeglasses or a contact lens has had a glimpse of how difficult even rudimentary, everyday tasks must be for people with sensory impairments. To function with less than typical vision, hearing, or speech can be a tremendous challenge (M. C. Wang, Reynolds, & Walberg, 1996).

Visual problems.   **Visual impairment,** difficulties in seeing that may include blindness or partial sightedness, can be considered in either a legal or an educational sense. The definition of legal impairment is quite straightforward: Blindness is visual acuity of less than 20/200 after correction (meaning the inability to see even at 20 feet what a typical person can see at 200 feet), while *partial sightedness* is visual acuity of less than 20/70 after correction.

Even when the legal limits of impairment are not reached, however, visual impairment in an educational sense can be present. For one thing, the legal criterion pertains solely to distance vision, whereas most educational tasks require close-up vision. In addition, the legal definition does not consider abilities in the perception of color, depth, and light—all of which might influence a student's educational success. About one student in 1,000 requires special education services relating to a visual impairment.

Although most severe visual problems are identified fairly early, it sometimes happens that an impairment goes undetected. Furthermore, visual problems can emerge gradually as children develop physiologically and changes occur in the visual apparatus of the eye. Parents must be aware of the signals of visual problems in their children. Frequent eye irritation (redness, sties, or infection), continual blinking and facial contortions when reading, holding reading material unusually close to the face, difficulty in writing, and frequent headaches, dizziness, or burning eyes are some of the signs of visual problems.

Auditory Problems.   Another relatively frequent special need relates to **auditory impairment.** Auditory impairments can cause academic problems, and they can produce

---

Visual impairment Difficulties in seeing that may include blindness or partial sightedness

Auditory impairment A special need that involves the loss of hearing or some aspect of hearing

social difficulties as well, since considerable peer interaction takes place through informal conversation. Hearing loss, which affects 1 to 2 percent of the school-age population, is not simply a matter of not hearing enough. Rather, auditory problems can vary along a number of dimensions (L. K. Harris, Van Zandt, & Rees, 1997; U.S. Department of Education, 1987).

In some cases of hearing loss, only a limited range of frequencies, or pitches, is affected. For example, the loss may be great at pitches in the normal speech range yet minor in other frequencies, such as those of very high or low sounds. In addition, a child may require different levels of amplification at different frequencies. For this reason, a hearing aid that indiscriminately amplifies all frequencies equally may be ineffective.

The age of onset of a hearing loss is critical in determining the degree to which a child can adapt to the impairment. If the loss of hearing occurs in infancy, the effects will probably be much more severe than if it occurs after the age of 3. The reason relates to the critical role that hearing plays in the development of language. Children who have had little or no exposure to the sound of language are unable to understand or produce oral language themselves. On the other hand, loss of hearing after a child has learned language will not have serious consequences on subsequent linguistic development.

Severe and early loss of hearing is also associated with difficulties in abstract thinking. Because hearing-impaired children may have limited exposure to language, abstract concepts that can be understood fully only through the use of language may be less well understood than concrete concepts that can be illustrated visually (Fischgrund, 1996; Hewett & Forness, 1974).

Speech Problems.   Auditory difficulties are sometimes accompanied by speech impairments. A speech impairment is one of the most public types of exceptionality: Every time the child speaks aloud, the impairment is obvious to listeners. In fact, the definition of **speech impairment** suggests that speech is impaired when it deviates so much from the speech of others that it calls attention to itself, interferes with communication, or produces maladjustment in the speaker (Van Riper, 1972). In other words, if a child's speech sounds impaired, it probably is. Speech impairments are present in around 3 to 5 percent of the school-age population (U.S. Department of Education, 1987).

Stuttering, which entails substantial disruption in the rhythm and fluency of speech, is the most common speech impairment. Despite a great deal of research on the topic, no single cause has been identified. Although occasional stuttering is relatively normal in young children—and also sometimes occurs in normal adults—chronic stuttering can be a severe problem. Not only does stuttering hinder communication, but it can produce embarrassment and stress in children, who may become inhibited from conversing with others and speaking aloud in class.

Parents and teachers can adopt several strategies for dealing with stuttering. For starters, attention should not be drawn to the stuttering, and children should be given sufficient time to finish what they begin to say, no matter how protracted the statement becomes. It does not help stutterers to finish their sentences for them or otherwise correct their speech. Finally, stuttering can be helped through speech therapy (Onslow, 1992).

Learning Disabilities: Discrepancies Between Achievement and Capacity to Learn

Some 2.6 million school-age children in the United States are officially labeled as having learning disabilities. **Learning disabilities** are characterized by difficulties in the acquisition and use of listening, speaking, reading, writing, reasoning, or mathematical abilities (see Table 11-2). An ill-defined grab-bag category, learning disabilities are typically diagnosed when there is a

---

Speech impairment Speech that deviates so much from the speech of others that it calls attention to itself, interferes with communication, or produces maladjustment in the speaker

Stuttering Substantial disruption in the rhythm and fluency of speech; the most common speech impairment

Learning disabilities Difficulties in the acquisition and use of listening, speaking, reading, writing, reasoning, or mathematical abilities

---

TABLE 11-2   IDENTIFYING LEARNING DISABILITIES

The following items can be indicators of learning difficulties.

Types of Problems	Examples
Poor reading habits	Losing one's place frequently
	Jerking head from side to side
	Expressing insecurity by crying or refusing to read
	Holding the book inches from the face
	Showing tension while reading—reading in a high-pitched voice, biting lips, fidgeting
Word recognition errors	Omitting a word (e.g., "He came to the park" is read "He came to park")
	Inserting a word (e.g., "He came to the [beautiful] park")
	Substituting a word for another (e.g., "He came to the pond")
	Reversing letters or words (e.g., "The dog ate fast" is read "The dog fast ate")
	Not attempting to read an unknown word by breaking it into familiar units
	Reading slowly and laboriously, less than 30 words per minute
Comprehension errors	Not recalling basic facts (e.g., cannot answer questions taken directly from a passage)
	Not recalling sequence (e.g., cannot explain the order of events in a story)
	Not recalling main theme (e.g., cannot give the main idea of a story)

(*Source:* Adapted from Meece, 1997, p. 400)

---

discrepancy between children's actual academic performance and their apparent potential to learn (Hallahan, Kauffman, & Lloyd, 2000; Wong, 1996).

Such a broad definition encompasses a wide and heterogeneous variety of difficulties. For instance, some children suffer from *dyslexia,* a reading disability that can result in the misperception of letters during reading and writing, unusual difficulty in sounding out letters, confusion between left and right, and difficulties in spelling. Although the causes are not fully understood, one likely explanation is that dyslexia is produced by a problem in the part of the brain responsible for breaking words into the sound elements that make up language (Shaywitz, 1996).

In addition to disabilities that are related to reading, there are also mathematical disabilities. Mathematical disabilities encompass difficulties in counting, making calculations, and recalling basic arithmetic facts.

The causes of learning disabilities are not well understood. Although they are generally attributed to some form of brain dysfunction, probably due to genetic factors, some experts suggest that they are produced by such environmental causes as poor early nutrition or allergies (Castles et al., 1999; C. Mercer, 1992).

Attention Deficit Hyperactivity Disorder.   **Attention deficit hyperactivity disorder (ADHD)** is marked by inattention, impulsiveness, a low tolerance for frustration, and a great deal of inappropriate activity. Although all children show such traits some of the time, for those diagnosed with ADHD such behavior is common and interferes with their home and school functioning (Barkley, 1997, 1998b; Sandberg, 2002; Silver, 1999).

Attention deficit hyperactivity disorder (ADHD) A learning disability marked by inattention, impulsiveness, a low tolerance for frustration, and a great deal of inappropriate activity

Seven-year-old Dusty Nash's high energy level and short attention span are due to attention deficit hyperactivity disorder (ADHD), which occurs in 3 to 5 percent of the school-age population.

Although it is hard to know how many children have the disorder, most estimates put the number at 3.8 million Americans under the age of 18. Children with ADHD are physically active, are easily distracted, have difficulty staying on task and working toward goals, and have limited self-control. A child with ADHD can be a whirlwind of activity, exhausting the energy and patience of parents, teachers, and even peers. Dusty Nash, whose early morning escapades were described at the start of this section, is typical of children diagnosed with ADHD (Barkley, 1998a, 1998b; Nigg, 2001; Whalen et al., 2002).

Treatment of children with ADHD has been a source of considerable controversy. Because it has been found that doses of Ritalin or Dexedrine (which, paradoxically, are stimulants) reduce activity levels in hyperactive children, many physicians routinely prescribe drug treatment (J. Marx, 1999; Rief, 1995).

Although in many cases such drugs are effective in increasing attention span and compliance, in some cases the side effects are considerable, and the long-term health consequences of such treatment are unclear. Furthermore, although in the short run drugs often help scholastic performance, the long-term evidence for continued improvement is mixed. Drugs are prescribed far more frequently in the United States than in other countries, suggesting that they may be overprescribed (Hallahan et al., 2000; Marshall, 2000; Zernike & Petersen, 2001).

What are the most common signs of ADHD? Although it is often difficult to distinguish between children who simply have a high level of activity and those with ADHD, some of the most common symptoms include persistent difficulty in finishing tasks, following instructions, and organizing work; inability to watch an entire television program; frequent interruption of others; and a tendency to jump into a task before hearing all the instructions. A child who is suspected of having ADHD should be evaluated by a specialist. (Parents can receive information and support from the Center for Hyperactive Child Information, P.O. Box 66272, Washington, DC 20035.)

Least restrictive environment The setting most similar to that of children without special needs

Mainstreaming An educational approach in which exceptional children are integrated as much as possible into the traditional educational system and are provided with a broad range of educational alternatives

Full inclusion The integration of all students, even those with the most severe disabilities, into regular classes and all other aspects of school and community life

DEVELOPMENTAL DIVERSITY

Mainstreaming and Full Inclusion of Children With Special Needs

Are exceptional children best served by providing specialized services that separate them from their peers who do not have special needs, or do they benefit more from being integrated with their peers to the fullest extent?

If you had asked that question three decades ago, the answer would have been simple: Exceptional children were assumed to do best when removed from their regular classes and placed in a class taught by a special-needs teacher. Such classes often accommodated a hodgepodge of afflictions (emotional difficulties, severe reading problems, and physical disabilities such as multiple sclerosis). In addition, they kept students segregated from the regular educational process.

However, that changed when Congress passed Public Law 94-142, the Education for All Handicapped Children Act, in the mid-1970s. The intent of the law was to ensure that children with special needs received a full education in the **least restrictive environment,** the setting most similar to that of children without special needs (Yell, 1995).

In practice, the law has meant that children with special needs must be integrated into regular classrooms and regular activities to the greatest extent possible, as long as doing so is educationally beneficial. Children are to be isolated from the regular classroom only for subjects that are specifically affected by their exceptionality; for all other subjects, they are to be taught with nonexceptional children in regular classrooms. Of course, some children with severe handicaps still need a mostly or entirely separate education, depending on the extent of their

condition. But the goal of the law is to integrate exceptional children and typical children to the fullest extent possible (Yell, 1995).

This educational approach to special education, designed to end the segregation of exceptional students as much as possible, has come to be called mainstreaming. In **mainstreaming,** exceptional children are integrated as much as possible into the traditional educational system and are provided with a broad range of educational alternatives (Hocutt, 1996).

Mainstreaming was meant to provide a mechanism to equalize the opportunities available to all children. The ultimate objective of mainstreaming was to ensure that all persons, regardless of ability or disability, had—to the greatest extent possible—opportunities to choose their goals on the basis of a full education, enabling them to obtain a fair share of life's rewards (Fuchs & Fuchs, 1994).

To some extent, the benefits extolled by proponents of mainstreaming have been realized. However, classroom teachers must receive substantial support in order for mainstreaming to be effective. It is not easy to teach a class in which students' abilities vary greatly (T. Daly & Feldman, 1994; Kauffman, 1993; Scruggs & Mastropieri, 1994).

The benefits of mainstreaming have led some professionals to promote an alternative educational model known as full inclusion. **Full inclusion** is the integration of all students, even those with the most severe disabilities, into regular classes. In such a system, separate special education programs would cease to operate. Full inclusion is controversial, and it remains to be seen how widespread the practice will become (Hocutt, 1996; Kavale & Forness, 2000; B. Siegel, 1996).

Mainstreaming of exceptional children into traditional educational systems has provided opportunities that were previously denied.

"Information goes home every day on the progress of their children. We try to talk with parents on what the child did over the weekend to help us prepare for the coming week."

← CAREERS IN CHILD DEVELOPMENT →

Valerie Patterson

Education: . . . . Western Washington University, Bellingham: B.A. in psychology; City University, Tacoma, Washington: M.A. in special education

Position: . . . . Special education teacher, Sajhalie Junior High School, Federal Way, Washington

Home: . . . . Sumner, Washington

Individualized attention and close communication with parents have helped create a welcoming environment for students with special needs at Sajhalie Junior High School in Federal Way, Washington, according to special education teacher Valerie Patterson. Patterson presides over a class of nine students, aged 12 to 16, with moderate to severe disabilities. In addition to herself, Patterson has four paraeducators who assist in giving the students essential one-on-one attention.

To better provide for the needs of each student, educators and parents conduct a comprehensive assessment before school begins, Patterson notes.

"Each year, we meet with the parents of the students and prepare an individualized education plan, or IEP, setting up specific goals and objectives for each student," she explains. "We then add in specific skills, such as dealing with money, time management, following schedules—anything that is relative to the real world.

"The IEP can also be changed as the child progresses," she adds, "and as the child becomes more independent, we go back to the IEP for the next step."

According to Patterson, parents are constantly kept in touch through the progress reports on IEP goals and daily communication logs.

"We have an open-door policy for parents—they can come in at any time," Patterson says. "Information goes home every day on the progress of their children. We try to talk with parents on what their child did over the weekend to help us prepare for the coming week."

Since Sajhalie Junior High operates under a full-inclusion policy, every attempt is made to integrate special-needs students with the general student body.

"The whole class goes to an integrated physical education class," Patterson points out. "In addition, some kids attend other classes, and everyone eats in the cafeteria together."

◉ R E V I E W & A P P L Y ◉

Review

- Visual impairments can affect many aspects of life, including education. Auditory impairments can affect the development of language, learning, and social relationships.

- Speech impairments can impede effective oral communication and can have serious social consequences.

- Learning disabilities include difficulties in the acquisition and use of listening, speaking, reading, writing, reasoning, or mathematical abilities.

- Attention deficit hyperactivity disorder is marked by inattention, impulsiveness, a low tolerance for frustration, and very high activity levels.

- Mainstreaming and full inclusion can benefit children by emphasizing strengths instead of weaknesses and promoting social interaction skills.

Applying Child Development

- If hearing is associated with abstract thinking, how do people who were born deaf think?

- *From an educator's perspective:* What are the advantages of mainstreaming and full inclusion? What challenges do they present? Are there situations in which you would not support mainstreaming and full inclusion?

In what ways do children grow during the school years, and what factors influence their growth?

- The middle childhood years are characterized by slow and steady growth, with children gaining, on average, about 5 to 7 pounds per year and 2 to 3 inches. Weight is redistributed as baby fat disappears.

- In part, growth is genetically determined, but societal factors such as affluence, dietary habits, nutrition, and disease also contribute significantly.

What are the nutritional needs of school-age children, and what are some causes and effects of improper nutrition?

- Adequate nutrition is important because of its contributions to growth, health, social and emotional functioning, and cognitive performance.

- Obesity is partially influenced by genetic factors but is also associated with children's failure to develop internal controls over eating, overindulgence in sedentary activities such as television viewing, and lack of physical exercise.

What sorts of health threats do school-age children face?

- The health of children in the school years is generally good, and few health problems arise. However, the incidence of some diseases that affect children, such as asthma, is increasing.

- School-age children can suffer from psychological disorders as well as physical ones, including childhood depression. Because childhood depression can lead to adult mood disorders or even to suicide, it should be taken seriously.

● **What are the characteristics of motor development during middle childhood, and what advantages do improved physical skills bring?**

- During the middle childhood years, great improvements occur in gross motor skills. Cultural expectations probably underlie most gross motor skill differences between boys and girls. Fine motor skills also develop rapidly.

- Physical competence is important for a number of reasons, some of which relate to self-esteem and confidence. Physical competence also brings social benefits during this period, especially for males.

● **What safety threats affect school-age children, and what can be done about them?**

- Threats to safety in middle childhood relate mainly to children's increasing independence and mobility. Accidents account for most injuries, especially those related to automobiles, other vehicles (such as bicycles and skateboards), and sports. In most cases, the use of proper protective gear can greatly reduce injuries.

- An emerging area of potential danger for children is cyberspace. Unsupervised access to the Internet and the World Wide Web may permit children to explore offensive areas and come into contact with people who might take advantage of them.

● **What sorts of special needs manifest themselves in the middle childhood years, and how can they be met?**

- Visual, auditory, and speech impairments, as well as other learning disabilities, can lead to academic and social problems and must be handled with sensitivity and appropriate assistance.

- Learning disabilities, characterized by difficulties in the acquisition and use of listening, speaking, reading, writing, reasoning, or mathematical abilities, affect a small proportion of the population. Although the causes of learning disabilities are not well understood, some form of brain dysfunction seems to be involved.

- Children with attention deficit hyperactivity disorder exhibit another form of special need. ADHD is characterized by inattention, impulsiveness, failure to complete tasks, lack of organization, and excessive amounts of uncontrollable activity. Treatment of ADHD with drugs is controversial because of unwanted side effects and doubts about long-term consequences.

- Children with exceptionalities are generally placed today in the least restrictive environment, typically the regular classroom. Mainstreaming and full inclusion can benefit exceptional students by permitting them to focus on strengths and gain useful skills of social interaction.

EPILOGUE

hysical development during middle childhood has been the focus of this chapter. Beginning with a look at how children's height and weight increases during this period, we then examined gross and fine motor development, considering the importance of physical competence. Finally, we discussed children with special needs in the areas of sensory and physical abilities.

Before leaving this chapter, return for a moment to the description of Suzanne McGuire's home run in the prologue. Consider the following questions:

1. What kinds of physical abilities permitted Suzanne to play baseball? How had these abilities changed as she moved from the preschool period into middle childhood? What abilities does she probably still lack, given her developmental stage?

2. What advice would you have given Suzanne's parents regarding modeling and competition to encourage Suzanne to engage in physical exercise?

3. How can the ideas of fun and competition be reconciled in sports? Can organized competitive sports be fun for both physically competent and less competent individuals? Why or why not?

4. If children have special needs that reduce their physical abilities, should they be encouraged to participate in sports with other children, and if so, under what circumstances should that participation occur?

KEY TERMS AND CONCEPTS

asthma (p. 327)
visual impairment (p. 335)
auditory impairment
   (p. 335)
speech impairment (p. 336)

stuttering (p. 336)
learning disabilities (p. 336)
attention deficit
   hyperactivity disorder
   (ADHD) (p. 337)

least restrictive
   environment (p. 338)
mainstreaming (p. 338)
full inclusion (p. 338)

12

Cognitive Development in Middle Childhood

PROLOGUE: La-Toya Pankey and *The Witches*

here are few books in La-Toya Pankey's apartment on 102nd Street near Amsterdam Avenue in Manhattan, and even fewer places for an 8-year-old girl to steal away to read them.

There is no desk, no bookshelf, no reading lamp or even a bureau in La-Toya's small room, one of only two bedrooms in the apartment she shares with seven other people: her mother, her five sisters, and her infant brother.

At night, there is little light, save a couple of bare bulbs mounted on the peeling, beige walls. And there are few places to sit, except a lone, wooden chair at a battered kitchen table, which La-Toya must wait her turn to occupy.

Yet there was La-Toya, on a rainy evening earlier this month, leaning against that table and reading aloud, flawlessly, to her mother from the Roald Dahl classic *The Witches*,

La-Toya Pankey

which she had borrowed from the makeshift library in her third-grade classroom. (J. Steinberg, 1997, p. B1)

It was a significant moment for La-Toya. It marked a shift from the first-grade-level books that she had previously chosen to read to a far more challenging one, written at a grade level two years higher than her own.

Middle childhood is characterized by a procession of moments such as these as children's cognitive skills ascend to new heights. In this chapter, we consider the cognitive advances made by children during middle childhood. After beginning with Piaget's explanation for intellectual development, we turn to information processing approaches. We discuss the development of memory and how memory can be improved.

Next we turn to the important strides that occur in language development during the middle childhood years. We focus on increases in linguistic skill and examine the consequences of bilingualism, the use of more than one language to communicate. We then discuss schooling and the ways in which society transmits knowledge, beliefs, values, and wisdom to a new generation. We consider such topics as how children explain their academic performance and how teachers' expectations can affect student achievement.

Finally, the chapter ends by focusing on intelligence. It highlights what developmentalists mean when they speak of intelligence, how intelligence is related to school success, and the ways in which children differ from one another in terms of intelligence.

In sum, after reading this chapter, you will be able to answer the following questions:

- In what ways do children develop cognitively during the years of middle childhood?
- How does language develop during the middle childhood period, and what special circumstances pertain to children for whom English is not the first language?
- What trends are affecting schooling worldwide and in the United States?
- What kinds of subjective factors contribute to academic outcomes?
- How can intelligence be measured, what are some issues in intelligence testing, and how are children who fall outside the normal range of intelligence educated?

Intellectual and Language Development

Jared's parents were delighted when he came home from kindergarten one day and explained that he had learned why the sky was blue. He talked about the earth's atmosphere—although he didn't pronounce the word correctly—and how tiny bits of moisture in the air reflected the sunlight. Although his explanation had rough edges (he couldn't quite grasp what the atmosphere was), he still had the general idea, and that, his parents felt, was quite an achievement for their 5-year-old.

Fast-forward 6 years. Jared, now 11, had already spent an hour laboring over his evening's homework. After completing a two-page worksheet on multiplying and dividing fractions, he had begun work on his U.S. Constitution project. He was taking notes for his report, which would explain what political factions had been involved in the writing of the document and how the Constitution had been amended since its creation.

Jared is not alone in having made vast intellectual advances during middle childhood. During this period, children's cognitive abilities broaden, and they become increasingly able to understand and master complex skills. At the same time, though, their thinking is still not fully adultlike.

What are the advances, and the limitations, in thinking during childhood? Several perspectives explain what goes on cognitively during middle childhood.

Piagetian Approaches to Cognitive Development

Let's return for a moment to Jean Piaget's view of the preschooler, which we considered in Chapter 9. From Piaget's perspective, the preschooler thinks *preoperationally*. This type of thinking is largely egocentric, and preoperational children lack the ability to use *operations*—organized, formal, logical mental processes.

The Rise of Concrete Operational Thought.   All this changes, according to Piaget, during the concrete operational period, which coincides with the school years. The **concrete operational stage,** which occurs between 7 and 12 years of age, is characterized by the active and appropriate use of logic. Concrete operational thought involves applying *logical operations* to concrete problems. For instance, when children in the concrete operational stage are confronted with a conservation problem (such as determining whether the amount of liquid poured from one container to another container of a different shape stays the same), they use cognitive and logical processes to answer, no longer being influenced solely by appearance. Consequently, they easily—and correctly—solve conservation problems. Because they are less egocentric, they can take multiple aspects of a situation into account, an ability known as **decentering.** Jared, the sixth-grader described at the beginning of this section, was using his decentering skills to consider the views of the different factions involved in creating the U.S. Constitution.

The shift from preoperational thought to concrete operational thought does not happen overnight, of course. During the 2 years before children move firmly into the concrete operational period, they shift back and forth between preoperational and concrete operational thinking. For instance, they typically pass through a period when they can answer conservation problems correctly but can't articulate why they did so. When asked to explain the reasoning behind their answers, they may respond with an unenlightening, "Because."

However, once concrete operational thinking is fully engaged, children show several cognitive advances. For instance, they attain the concept of *reversibility*, which is the notion that processes that transform a stimulus can be reversed, returning it to its original form. Grasping reversibility permits children to understand that a ball of clay that has been squeezed into a long, snakelike rope can be returned to its original state. More abstractly, it allows school-age children to understand that if 3 + 5 equals 8, then 5 + 3 also equals 8—and later during the period, that 8 − 3 equals 5.

Concrete operational thinking also permits children to understand such concepts as the relationship between time and speed. For instance, consider the problem shown in Figure 12-1,

Concrete operational stage The period of cognitive development between 7 and 12 years of age, characterized by the active and appropriate use of logic

Decentering The ability to take multiple aspects of a situation into account

FIGURE 12-1   SAMPLE PROBLEM IN CONCRETE OPERATIONAL THINKING

After being told that the two cars traveling Routes 1 and 2 start and end their journeys in the same amount of time, children who are just entering the concrete operational period still reason that the cars are traveling at the same speed. Later, however, they reach the correct conclusion that the car traveling the longer route must be moving at a higher speed if it starts and ends its journey at the same time as the car traveling the shorter route.

Cognitive development makes substantial advances in middle childhood.

in which two cars start and finish at the same points in the same amount of time but travel different routes. Children who are just entering the concrete operational period reason that the cars are traveling at the same speed. However, between the ages of 8 and 10, children begin to draw the right conclusion: that the car traveling the longer route must be moving faster if it arrives at the finish point at the same time as the car traveling the shorter route.

Despite the advances that occur during the concrete operational stage, children still experience one critical limitation in their thinking. They remain tied to concrete, physical reality. Furthermore, they are unable to understand truly abstract or hypothetical questions or ones that involve formal logic.

Piaget in Perspective: Piaget Was Right—and Wrong.   As we learned in our prior consideration of Piaget's views in Chapters 6 and 9, researchers following in Piaget's footsteps have found much to cheer about, as well as much to criticize.

Piaget was a virtuoso observer of children, and his many books contain pages of brilliant, careful observations of children at work and play. Furthermore, his theories have powerful educational implications, and many schools employ principles derived from his views to guide the nature and presentation of instructional materials (Flavell, 1985, 1996; Siegler & Ellis, 1996).

In some ways, then, Piaget's approach was quite successful in describing cognitive development (Lourenco & Machado, 1996). At the same time, though, critics have raised compelling and seemingly legitimate grievances about his approach. As we have noted before, many researchers argue that Piaget underestimated children's capabilities, in part because of the limited nature of the miniexperiments he conducted. When a broader array of experimental tasks is used, children show less consistency within stages than Piaget would predict (Bjorklund, 1997; Siegler, 1994).

Furthermore, Piaget seems to have misjudged the age at which children's cognitive abilities emerge. As might be expected from our earlier discussions of Piaget's stages, increasing evidence suggests that children's capabilities emerge earlier than Piaget envisioned. Some children show evidence of a form of concrete operational thinking before the age of 7, the time at which Piaget suggested these abilities first appear.

The opposite phenomenon also seems to occur: Cross-cultural research implies that some children never leave the preoperational stage, failing to master conservation and to develop concrete operations. For example, pioneering work by Patricia Greenfield (1966) found that among the Wolof children in Senegal, a West African country, only half of children aged 10 to 13 understood conservation of liquid. Studies in other non-Western areas such as the jungles of New Guinea and Brazil and remote villages in Australia confirmed her findings: When a broad sample of children are studied—children who have had very different experiences from the western European children on whom Piaget based his theory—not everyone reaches the concrete operational stage (Dasen, 1977). It appears, then, that Piaget's claims that his stages provided a universal description of cognitive development were exaggerated.

Still, we cannot dismiss the Piagetian approach. Although some early cross-cultural research seemed to imply that children in certain cultures never left the preoperational stage, failing to master conservation and to develop concrete operations, more recent research suggests otherwise. For instance, with proper training in conservation, children in non-Western cultures who do not conserve can readily learn to do so. For instance, in one study, urban Australian children—who develop concrete operations on the same timetable as Piaget suggested—were compared to rural Aborigine children, who typically do not demonstrate an understanding of conservation at the age of 14 (Dasen, Ngini, & Lavallée, 1979). When the rural Aborigine children were given training, they showed conservation skills similar to their urban counterparts, although with a time lag of around 3 years (see Figure 12-2).

Furthermore, when children are interviewed by researchers from their own culture, who know the language and customs of the culture well and who use reasoning tasks that are related to domains important to the culture, the children are considerably more likely to display concrete operational thinking (Jahoda, 1983; Nyiti, 1982). Ultimately, such research suggests that Piaget was right when he argued that concrete operations were universally achieved during middle childhood. Although school-age children in some cultures may differ from Westerners in the demonstration of certain cognitive skills, the most probable explanation of the difference is that the non-Western children have had different sorts of experiences from those that permit children in Western societies to perform well on Piagetian measures of

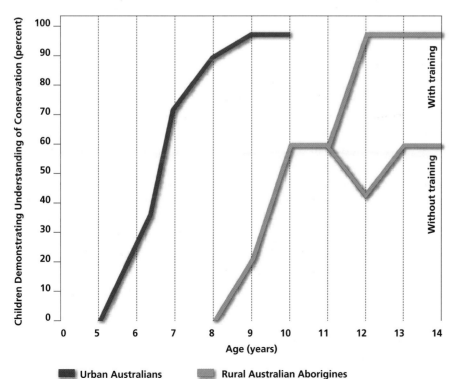

FIGURE 12-2 UNDERSTANDING OF CONSERVATION AMONG URBAN AND ABORIGINAL AUSTRALIAN CHILDREN

Rural Australian Aborigine children trail their urban counterparts in the development of their understanding of conservation. With training, they later catch up, but without training, around half of 14-year-old Aborigines do not understand conservation. What types of teaching programs might an educator provide to help the development of conservation?

(*Source:* Adapted from Dasen, Ngini, & Lavallée, 1979)

Memory The process by which information is recorded, stored, and retrieved

Metamemory An understanding about the processes that underlie memory that emerges and improves during middle childhood

conservation and concrete operations. The progress of cognitive development, then, cannot be understood without looking at the nature of a child's culture (Beilin & Pufall, 1992; Berry et al., 1992; Jahoda & Lewis, 1988; Mishra, 1997).

Information Processing in Middle Childhood

It is a significant achievement for first graders to learn basic math tasks, such as addition and subtraction of single-digit numbers, as well as the spelling of simple words such as *dog* and *run.* But by the time they reach the sixth grade, children are able to work with fractions and decimals, like the fractions worksheet that Jared, the boy in the example at the start of this section, completed for his sixth-grade homework. They can also spell such words as *exhibit* and *residence.*

According to *information processing approaches,* children become increasingly sophisticated in their handling of information. Like computers, they can process more data as the size of their memories increases and the "programs" they use to process information become increasingly sophisticated (Kuhn et al., 1995).

Memory. As we saw in Chapter 6, **memory** in the information processing model is the ability to encode, store, and retrieve information. For a child to remember a piece of information, the three processes must all function properly. Through *encoding,* the child initially records the information in a form usable to memory. Children who were never taught that 5 + 6 equals 11 or who didn't pay attention when they were exposed to this fact will never be able to recall it. They never encoded the information in the first place.

But mere exposure to a fact is not enough; the information also has to be *stored.* In our example, the information that 5 + 6 equals 11 must be placed and maintained in the memory system. Finally, proper functioning of memory requires that material that is stored in memory must be *retrieved.* Through retrieval, material in memory storage is located, brought into awareness, and used.

During middle childhood, short-term memory capacity improves significantly. For instance, children are increasingly able to hear a string of digits ("1-5-6-3-4") and then repeat the string in reverse order ("4-3-6-5-1"). At the start of the preschool period, they can remember and reverse only about two digits; by the beginning of adolescence, they can perform the task with as many as six digits. In addition, they use more sophisticated strategies for recalling information, which can be improved with training (Ardila & Rosselli, 1994; Bjorklund et al., 1994; Halford et al., 1994; Roodenrys, Hulme, & Brown, 1993).

Memory capacity may shed light on another issue in cognitive development. Some developmental psychologists suggest that the difficulty children experience in solving conservation problems during the preschool period may stem from memory limitations (Siegler & Richards, 1982). They argue that young children may simply be unable to recall all the necessary pieces of information that enter into the correct solution of conservation problems.

Metamemory, an understanding about the processes that underlie memory, also emerges and improves during middle childhood. By the time children enter first grade, they have a general notion of what memory is, and they are able to understand that some people have better memories than others (Lewis & Mitchell, 1994; W. Schneider & Pressley, 1989).

School-age children's understanding of memory becomes more sophisticated as they grow older and increasingly engage in *control strategies*—conscious, intentionally used tactics to improve cognitive processing. For instance, school-age children are aware that rehearsal, the repetition of information, is a useful strategy for improving memory, and they increasingly employ it over the course of middle childhood. Similarly, they progressively make more effort to organize material into coherent patterns, a strategy that permits them to recall it better. For instance, when faced with remembering a list including cups, knives, forks, and plates, older school-age children are more likely to group the items into coherent patterns—cups and plates, forks and knives—than children just entering the school-age years (M. L. Howe & O'Sullivan, 1990; Pressley & Van Meter, 1993; Weed, Ryan, & Day, 1990).

Memory requires three steps: encoding, storing, and retrieving material.

Improving Memory.   Can children be trained to be more effective in the use of control strategies? The answer is decidedly yes. School-age children can be taught to apply particular strategies, although such teaching is not a simple matter. For instance, children need to know not only how to use a memory strategy but also when and where to use it most effectively (O'Sullivan, 1993).

One example of an innovative technique is the keyword strategy, which can help students learn the vocabulary of a foreign language, the capitals of the states, or other information in which two sets of words or labels are paired. In the *keyword strategy,* one word is paired with another that sounds like it. For instance, in learning foreign-language vocabulary, a foreign word is paired with a common English word that has a similar sound. The English word is the keyword. Thus to learn the Spanish word for duck (*pato,* pronounced "pot-o"), the keyword might be *pot;* for the Spanish word for horse (*caballo,* pronounced "cob-eye-yo"), the keyword might be *eye.* Once the keyword is chosen, children then form a mental image of the two words interacting. For instance, a student might use an image of a duck taking a bath in a pot to remember the word *pato* or a horse with bulging eyes to remember the word *caballo* (Pressley, 1987; Pressley & Levin, 1983).

Other memory strategies include *rehearsal,* consistent repetition of information that children wish to remember; *organization,* which is placing material into categories (such as coastal states or types of food); and *cognitive elaboration,* in which mental images are linked with information that someone wants to recall. For example, in trying to remember where Cape Cod is on a map of Massachusetts, an 8-year-old might think of a muscle-bound Pilgrim to link the image of the shape of Cape Cod (which looks something like a flexing, curved arm) with its location. Whatever memory strategies children use, they use such strategies more often and more effectively as they get older.

Vygotsky's Approach to Cognitive Development and Classroom Instruction

Recall from Chapter 9 that Russian developmentalist Lev Vygotsky proposed that cognitive advances occur through exposure to information within a child's *zone of proximal development (ZPD).* The ZPD is the level at which a child can almost, but not quite, understand or perform a task unassisted.

Vygotsky's approach has been particularly influential in the development of several classroom practices based on the proposition that children should actively participate in their educational experiences (e.g., Holzman, 1997). Consequently, classrooms are seen as places where children should have the opportunity to experiment and try out new activities (Vygotsky, 1926/1997).

Specifically, Vygotsky suggests that education should focus on activities that involve interaction with others. Both child–adult and child–child interactions can provide the potential for cognitive growth. Yet the nature of the interactions must be carefully structured to fall within each individual child's ZPD.

Several noteworthy educational innovations have borrowed heavily from Vygotsky's work. For example, *cooperative learning,* in which children work together in groups to achieve a common goal, incorporates several aspects of Vygotsky's theory. Students working in cooperative groups benefit from the insights of others, and if they get off onto the wrong track, they may be brought back to the correct course by others in their group. However, not every peer is equally helpful to members of a cooperative learning group: As Vygotsky's approach would imply, individual children benefit most when at least some of the other members of the group are more competent at the task and can act as experts (Azmitia, 1988; Karpov & Haywood, 1998; Slavin, 1995).

Reciprocal teaching is another educational practice that reflects Vygotsky's approach to cognitive development. *Reciprocal teaching* is a technique to teach reading comprehension strategies. Students are taught to skim the content of a passage, raise questions about its

Students working in cooperative groups benefit from the insights of others.

central point, summarize the passage, and predict what will happen next. A key to this technique is its reciprocal nature. In the beginning, teachers lead students through the comprehension strategies. Gradually, students progress through their zones of proximal development, taking more and more control over use of the strategies, until the students are able to take on a teaching role. The method has shown impressive success in raising reading comprehension levels, particularly for students experiencing reading difficulties (Lysynchuk, Pressley, & Vye, 1990; Brown & Campione, 1994; Palincsar & Klenk, 1992).

Language Development: What Words Mean

If you listen to what school-age children say to one another, their speech, at least at first hearing, sounds not too different from that of adults. However, the apparent similarity is deceiving. The linguistic sophistication of children, particularly at the start of the school-age period, still requires refinement.

Mastering the Mechanics of Language.   Vocabulary continues to increase during the school years. Although children know thousands of words, they continue to add new words to their vocabularies at a fairly rapid clip. For instance, the average 6-year-old has a vocabulary of 8,000 to 14,000 words, and vocabulary grows by another 5,000 words between the ages of 9 and 11.

Furthermore, school-age children's mastery of grammar improves. For instance, the use of the passive voice is rare during the early school-age years (as in "The dog was walked by Jon," as opposed to the active voice "Jon walked the dog"), and children of 6 and 7 infrequently use conditional sentences such as "If Sarah sets the table, I will wash the dishes." However, over the course of middle childhood, the use of both passive voice and conditional sentences increases. In addition, children's understanding of *syntax,* the rules for combining words and phrases to form sentences, grows during middle childhood.

By the time they reach first grade, most children pronounce words quite accurately. However, certain *phonemes,* units of sound, remain troublesome. For instance, the ability to pronounce *j, v, th,* and *zh* sounds develops later than the ability to pronounce other phonemes.

School-age children also may have difficulty decoding sentences when the meaning depends on *intonation,* or tone of voice. For example, consider the sentence "George gave a book to David and he gave one to Bill." If the word *he* is emphasized, the meaning is "George gave a book to David and David gave a different book to Bill." But if the intonation emphasizes the word *and,* the meaning changes to "George gave a book to David and George also gave a book to Bill." School-age children cannot easily sort out subtleties such as these (Moshman, Glover, & Bruning, 1987; Woolfolk, 1993).

Children also become more competent during the school years in their use of *pragmatics,* the rules governing the use of language to communicate in a social context. Pragmatics concern children's ability to use appropriate and effective language in a given social setting.

For example, although children are aware of the rules of conversational turn-taking at the start of the early childhood period, their use of these rules is sometimes primitive. Consider the following conversation between 6-year-olds Yonnie and Max:

Yonnie: My dad drives a FedEx truck.
   Max: My sister's name is Molly.
Yonnie: He gets up really early in the morning.
   Max: She wet her bed last night.

Later, however, conversations show more give-and-take, with the second child actually responding to the comments of the first. For instance, this conversation between 11-year-olds Mia and Josh reflects a more sophisticated mastery of pragmatics:

Mia: I don't know what to get Claire for her birthday.
Josh: I'm getting her earrings.
Mia: She already has a lot of jewelry.
Josh: I don't think she has that much.

Metalinguistic Awareness.   One of the most significant developments in middle childhood is the increasing metalinguistic awareness of children. **Metalinguistic awareness** is an understanding of one's own use of language. By the time children are 5 or 6, they understand that language is governed by rules. Whereas in the early years they learn and comprehended these rules implicitly, during middle childhood children come to understand them more explicitly (Kemper & Vernooy, 1994).

Metalinguistic awareness helps children achieve comprehension when information is fuzzy or incomplete. For instance, when preschoolers are given ambiguous or nuclear information,

Metalinguistic awareness   An understanding of one's own use of language

The increase in metalinguistic skills during middle childhood allows children to enter into the give-and-take of conversation more successfully.

Bilingualism The ability to speak two languages

they rarely ask for clarification, and they tend to blame themselves if they do not understand. By the time they reach the age of 7 or 8, children realize that miscommunication may be due to factors attributable not only to themselves but to the person communicating with them as well. Consequently, school-age children are more likely to ask for clarifications of information that is unclear to them (Beal & Belgrad, 1990; Kemper & Vernooy, 1994).

How Language Promotes Self-Control.   The growing sophistication of their language helps school-age children control their behavior. For instance, in one experiment, children were told that they could have one marshmallow treat if they chose to eat one immediately but two treats if they waited. Most of the children, who ranged in age from 4 to 8, chose to wait, but the strategies they used while waiting differed significantly.

The 4-year-olds often chose to look at the marshmallows while waiting, a strategy that was not terribly effective. In contrast, 6- and 8-year-olds used language to help them overcome temptation, although in different ways. The 6-year-olds spoke and sang to themselves, reminding themselves that if they waited, they would get more treats in the end. The 8-year-olds focused on aspects of the marshmallows that were not related to taste, such as their appearance, which helped them wait.

Bilingualism

> For picture day at New York's P.S. 217, a neighborhood elementary school in Brooklyn, the notice to parents was translated into five languages. That was a nice gesture, but insufficient: More than 40 percent of the children are immigrants whose families speak any one of twenty-six languages, ranging from Armenian to Urdu. (Leslie, 1991, p. 56)

From the smallest towns to the biggest cities, the voices with which children speak are changing. In seven states, including Texas, New York, and Colorado, more than a quarter of the students are not native English speakers. In fact, English is the second language for more than 32 million Americans. **Bilingualism**—the use of two languages—is growing increasingly common (Health Resources and Services Administration, 1993; see Figure 12-3).

Children with little or even no English proficiency present a challenge to educators. One approach to educating non-English speakers is *bilingual education*, in which children are initially taught in their native language while at the same time learning English. With bilingual instruction, students are able to develop a strong foundation in basic subject areas using their native language. The ultimate goal of most bilingual education programs is to shift instruction into English.

An alternative approach is to immerse students in English, teaching solely in that language. To proponents of this approach, initially teaching students in a language other than English hinders students' efforts to learn English and slows their integration into society.

FIGURE 12-3 **THE TOP 10 LANGUAGES OTHER THAN ENGLISH SPOKEN IN THE UNITED STATES**

These figures show the number of U.S. residents over the age of 5 who speak a language other than English at home. With increases in the number and variety of languages spoken in the United States, what types of approaches might an educator use to meet the needs of bilingual students?

(*Source:* Health Resources and Services Administration, 1993)

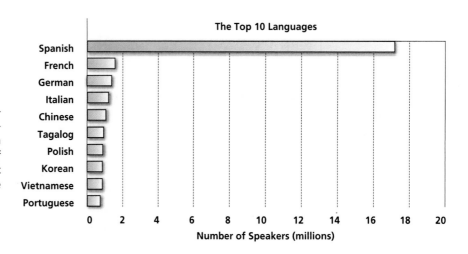

Bilingual education, in which children are initially taught in their native language while at the same time learning English, is one approach to educating non-English speakers.

The two quite different approaches have been highly politicized, with some politicians arguing in favor of "English only" laws. Still, the psychological research is clear in suggesting that knowing more than one language offers several cognitive advantages. For instance, speakers of two languages show greater cognitive flexibility. Because they have a wider range of linguistic possibilities to choose from as they assess a situation, they can solve problems with greater creativity and versatility. Furthermore, some research suggests that learning in one's native tongue is associated with higher self-esteem in minority students (Romaine, 1994; S. C. Wright & Taylor, 1995).

Bilingual students often have greater metalinguistic awareness, understanding the rules of language more explicitly. They may even score higher on tests of intelligence, according to some research. For example, one survey of French- and English-speaking schoolchildren in Canada found that bilingual students scored significantly higher on both verbal and nonverbal tests of intelligence than those who spoke only one language (Bochner, 1996; Genesee, 1994; Lambert & Peal, 1972; Ricciardelli, 1992).

Finally, because many linguists contend that universal processes underlie language acquisition, as we noted in Chapter 6, instruction in the native language may enhance instruction in a second language. In fact, as we discuss next, many educators believe that second-language learning should be a regular part of elementary schooling for *all* children (Kecskes & Papp, 2000; Lindholm, 1991; Perozzi & Sanchez, 1992; Yelland, Pollard, & Mercuri, 1993).

REVIEW & APPLY

Review

- According to Piaget, school-age children are in the concrete operational stage, characterized by the application of logical processes to concrete problems.

- Information processing approaches focus on quantitative improvements in memory and in the sophistication of the mental programs that the school-age child can handle.

- Vygotsky's approach holds that children in the school years should have the opportunity to experiment and participate actively with their colleagues in their educational experiences.

- The memory processes—encoding, storage, and retrieval—come under increasing control during the school years, and the development of metamemory improves cognitive processing and memorization.

- Language development is characterized by improvements in vocabulary, syntax, and pragmatics, by the growth of metalinguistic awareness, and by the use of language as a self-control device.

- Bilingualism can produce improvements in cognitive flexibility, metalinguistic awareness, and even intelligence test performance.

Applying Child Development

- Do you think adults use language as a self-control device? How?

- *From an educator's perspective:* Do you think that if Piaget had done his research in a different culture, he might have developed a theory of stages involving cognitive achievements and tasks that children in Western cultures would have difficulty accomplishing without explicit instruction? Why?

Schooling: The Three *R*s (and More) of Middle Childhood

As the eyes of the six other children in his reading group turned to him, Glenn shifted uneasily in his chair. Reading had never come easily to him, and he always felt anxious when it was his turn to read aloud. But as his teacher nodded in encouragement, he plunged in, hesitantly at first, then gaining momentum as he read the story about a mother's first day on a new job. He found that he could read the passage quite nicely, and he felt a surge of happiness and pride at his accomplishment. When he was done, he broke into a broad smile as his teacher said simply, "Well done, Glenn."

Small moments such as these, repeated over and over, make—or break—a child's educational experience. Schooling marks a time when society formally attempts to transfer to new generations its accumulated body of knowledge, beliefs, values, and wisdom. The success with which this transfer is managed determines, in a very real sense, the future fortunes of the world.

Schooling Around the World: Who Gets Educated?

In the United States, as in most developed countries, a primary school education is both a universal right and a legal requirement. Virtually all children are provided with a free education through the 12th grade.

Children in other parts of the world are not so fortunate. More than 160 million of the world's children do not have access to even a primary school education (World Conference on Education for All, 1990; International Literacy Institute, 2001). An additional 100 million children do not progress beyond a level comparable to our elementary school education, and close to a billion individuals (two thirds of them women) are illiterate throughout their lives (see Figure 12-4).

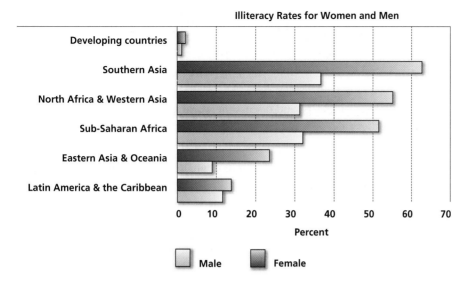

FIGURE 12-4   ILLITERACY RATES FOR WOMEN AND MEN

Although improvement has occurred over the past two decades, illiteracy remains a significant problem worldwide, particularly for women. Around the world, close to a billion people are illiterate throughout their lives.

(*Source:* UNESCO, 1998)

In almost all developing countries, fewer females than males receive formal education, a discrepancy found at every level of schooling. Even in developed countries, women lag behind men in their exposure to science and technical topics. These differences reflect widespread and deeply held cultural and parental biases that favor males over females. Educational levels in the United States are more nearly equal between men and women, and especially in the early years of school, boys and girls share equal access to educational opportunities.

What Makes Children Ready for School?

Many parents have a hard time deciding exactly when to enroll their children in school for the first time. Do children who are younger than most of the other children in their grade suffer as a result of the age difference? According to traditional wisdom, the answer is yes. Because younger children are assumed to be slightly less advanced developmentally than their peers, it has been assumed that such children would be at a competitive disadvantage. In some cases, teachers have recommended that students delay entry into kindergarten in order to cope better academically and emotionally.

However, more recent research has begun to dispel this view. According to a massive study conducted by developmental psychologist Frederick Morrison (1994), children who are among the youngest in first grade progress at the same rate as the oldest. Although they were slightly behind older first graders in reading, the difference was negligible. It was also clear that parents who chose to hold their children back in kindergarten, thereby ensuring that they would be among the oldest in first grade and after, were not doing their children a favor. These older children did no better than their younger classmates (De Angelis, 1994; F. J. Morrison, Smith, & Dow-Ehrensberger, 1995).

Other research even has identified some delayed negative reaction to delayed entry. For example, one longitudinal study examined adolescents whose entrance into kindergarten was delayed by a year. Even though many seemed to show no ill effects from the delay during elementary school, during adolescence a surprising number of these children had emotional and behavioral problems (Byrd, Weitzman, & Auinger, 1997).

In short, delaying children's entry into school does not necessarily provide an advantage and in some cases may actually be harmful. Ultimately, age per se is not a critical indicator of when children should begin school. Instead, the start of formal schooling is more reasonably tied to overall developmental readiness, the product of a complex combination of several factors. Family support is one of the factors that affects children's likelihood of success in school, as described the *Becoming an Informed Consumer of Development* box.

BECOMING AN INFORMED CONSUMER OF DEVELOPMENT

Creating an Atmosphere That Promotes School Success

What makes children succeed in school? Although there are many factors, some of which we'll be discussing in the next chapter, there are several practical steps that can be taken to maximize children's chances of success. Among them are these:

- *Promote a "literacy environment."* Parents should read to their children and familiarize them with books and reading. Adults should provide reading models so that children see that reading is an important activity in the lives of the adults with whom they interact.

- *Talk to children.* Discuss events in the news, talk about their friends, and share hobbies. Getting children to think about and discuss the world around them is one of the best preparations for school.

- *Provide a place for children to work.* This can be a desk, a corner of a table, or an area of a room. What's important is that it be a separate, designated area.

- *Encourage children's problem-solving skills.* To solve a problem, they should learn to identify their goal, what they know, and what they don't know; to design and carry out a strategy; and finally to evaluate their result.

Reading: Learning to Decode the Meaning Behind Words

The efforts of La-Toya Pankey (described in the chapter prologue) to improve her reading are no small matter, for there is no other task that is more fundamental to schooling than learning to read. Reading involves a significant number of skills, from low-level cognitive skills (the identification of single letters and associating letters with sounds) to higher level skills (matching written words with meanings located in long-term memory and using context and background knowledge to determine the meaning of a sentence).

Reading Stages.   Development of reading skill generally occurs in several broad and frequently overlapping stages (Chall, 1979; see Table 12-1). In *Stage 0,* which lasts from birth to the start of first grade, children learn the essential prerequisites for reading, including identification of the letters in the alphabet, sometimes writing their names, and reading a few very familiar words (such as their own names or *stop* on a stop sign).

Stage 1 brings the first real type of reading, but it is largely *phonological recoding.* At this stage, which usually encompasses the first and second grade, children can sound out words by

TABLE 12-1	DEVELOPMENT OF READING SKILLS	
Stage	**Age**	**Key Characteristics**
Stage 0	Birth to start of first grade	Learns prerequisites for reading, such as identification of the letters
Stage 1	First and second grades	Learns phonological recoding skills; starts reading
Stage 2	Second and third grades	Reads aloud fluently, but without much meaning
Stage 3	Third to eighth grade	Uses reading as a means for learning
Stage 4	Eighth grade and beyond	Understands reading in terms of reflecting multiple points of view

(*Source:* Based on Chall, 1979)

blending the letters together. Children also complete the job of learning the names of letters and the sounds that go with them.

In *Stage 2,* typically around second and third grades, children learn to read aloud with fluency. However, they do not attach much meaning to the words, because the effort involved in simply sounding out words is usually so great that relatively few cognitive resources are left over to process the meaning of the words. La-Toya's flawless reading of *The Witches* shows that she has reached at least this stage of reading development.

Stage 3 extends from fourth to eighth grades. Reading becomes a means to an end—in particular, a way to learn. Whereas earlier reading was an accomplishment in and of itself, now children use reading to learn about the world. However, understanding gained from reading is not complete. For instance, one limitation children have at this stage is that they are able to comprehend information only when it is presented from a single perspective.

In the final period, *Stage 4,* children are able to read and process information that reflects multiple points of view. This ability, which begins during the transition into high school, permits children to develop a far more sophisticated understanding of written material. This explains why great works of literature are not read at an earlier stage of education. It is not so much that younger children do not have the vocabulary to understand such works (although this is partially true); it is that they lack the ability to understand the multiple points of view that sophisticated literature presents.

Reading Approaches.   Educators have long been engaged in a debate regarding the most effective means of teaching reading. At the heart of this debate is a disagreement about the nature of the mechanisms by which information is processed during reading. According to proponents of *code-based approaches to reading,* reading should be taught by presenting the basic underlying skills. Code-based approaches emphasize the components of reading, such as the sounds of letters and their combinations—*phonics*—and how letters and sounds are combined to make words. They suggest that reading consists of processing the individual components of words, combining them into words, and then using the words to derive the meaning of written sentences and passages (Rayner et al., 2001).

In contrast, some educators argue that reading is taught most successfully by using a whole-language approach. In *whole-language approaches to reading,* reading is viewed as a natural process, similar to the acquisition of oral language. According to this view, children should learn to read through exposure to complete writing—sentences, stories, poems, lists, charts, and other real-life examples. Instead of being taught to painstakingly sound out words, children are encouraged to make guesses about the meanings of words based on the total context in which they appear. Through such a trial-and-error approach, children come to learn whole words and phrases at a time, gradually becoming proficient readers (S. Graham & Harris, 1997; L. Smith, 1992).

A growing body of evidence, based on careful research, suggests that code-based approach to reading instruction is superior to whole-language approaches. In fact, the National Reading Panel and National Research Council now support reading instruction using code-based approaches, signaling that an end may be near to the debate over which approach to teaching reading is more effective (Rayner et al., 2002).

Educational Trends: Beyond the Three *R*s

Schooling in the early 2000s is very different from what it was as recently as a decade ago. In fact, U.S. schools are experiencing a return to the educational fundamentals embodied in the traditional three *R*s (reading, 'riting, and 'rithmetic). This trend marks a departure from the 1970s and 1980s, when the emphasis was on socioemotional issues and on allowing students to choose study topics on the basis of their interests, instead of in accordance with a preset curriculum (Short & Talley, 1997).

Elementary school classrooms today also stress individual accountability, for both teachers and students. Teachers are more likely to be held responsible for their students' learning, and both students and teachers are more likely to be required to take tests, developed at the state or national level, to assess their competence.

Although by far the most schooling takes place in traditional classrooms, alternatives have also begun to spring up. For instance, dissatisfaction with public schools has led to the growth of home schooling, a phenomenon we discuss in the *From Research to Practice* box.

○— FROM RESEARCH TO PRACTICE —○

Home Schooling: Living Rooms as Classrooms

At 9:00 A.M. on a Wednesday, Damon Buchanan, 9 years old, sits on the couch going through one of his morning rituals: reading the horoscopes in the newspaper. In the kitchen, his brothers, Jacob, 7, and Logan, 4, are performing one of their "experiments," dropping action figures and Fisher-Price toys into glasses of water and then freezing them. Another day of school has begun.

For students like the Buchanan brothers, there is no distinction between their living room and the classroom because they are among the close to 1 million students who are home-schooled. *Home schooling* is a major educational phenomenon in which students are taught by their parents at home.

Parents have several motivations for schooling their children at home. Some parents feel that their children will thrive with the one-to-one attention that home schooling can bring, whereas they might get lost in a larger public school. Other parents are dissatisfied with the quality of instruction and teachers in their local public schools and feel that they can do a superior job at teaching. And some parents engage in home schooling for religious reasons, wishing to impart a particular religious ideology that would be impossible in a public school (Bauman, 2001).

Home schooling clearly works, in the sense that children who have been home-schooled generally do as well on standardized tests as students who have been educated traditionally. In addition, their acceptance rate into college appears to be no different from that of traditionally schooled children (Lattibeaudiere, 2000; Lauricella, 2001; Lines, 2001).

However, the apparent academic success of children schooled at home does not mean that home schooling per se is effective, since parents who choose to home-school their children may be more affluent or have the kind of well-structured family situation in which children would succeed no matter what kind of schooling they had. In contrast, parents in dysfunctional and disorganized families are unlikely to have the motivation or interest to home-school their children.

Home schooling, a growing educational practice, has both advantages and drawbacks.

Critics of home schooling argue that it has considerable drawbacks. For example, the social interaction involving groups of children that is inherent in classrooms in traditional schools is largely missing for home-schooled children. Learning in an at-home environment, while perhaps strengthening family ties, does not provide an environment that reflects the diversity of U.S. society, in which children must live once home schooling is done. Furthermore, even the best-equipped home is unlikely to have the sophisticated science and technology that are available at most schools. Finally, most parents do not have the preparation of well-trained teachers, and their teaching methods may be unsophisticated. Although parents may be successful in teaching subject areas in which their child is already interested, they may have more difficulty teaching subjects that their child seeks to avoid (Cai, Reeve, & Robinson, 2002; B. Murray, 1996b; Sharp, 1997).

Because home schooling is a relatively new phenomenon, few controlled experiments have been conducted examining its effectiveness. More research is needed to unambiguously determine to what extent home schooling is an effective means to educate children.

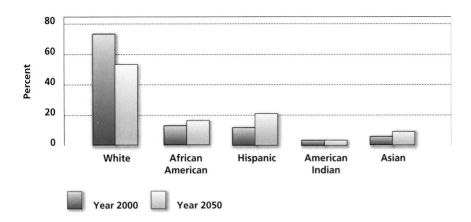

FIGURE 12-5   THE CHANGING FACE OF AMERICA

Current projections of the population makeup of the United States show that by the year 2050, the proportion of non-Hispanic whites will decline as the proportion of minority group members increases. What will be some of the impacts on social workers as the result of changing demographics?

(*Source:* U.S. Bureau of the Census, 2001b.)

Elementary schools are also paying increased attention to issues involving student diversity and multiculturalism. And with good reason: The demographic makeup of students in the United States is undergoing an extraordinary shift. For instance, the proportion of Hispanics will in all likelihood more than double in the next 50 years. Moreover, by the year 2050, non-Hispanic Caucasians will likely become a minority of the total population of the United States (U.S. Bureau of the Census, 2001b; see Figure 12-5). Consequently, educators have been increasingly serious about multicultural concerns.

Expectation Effects: How Teachers' Expectancies Influence Their Students

Suppose you were an elementary school teacher and were told that certain children in your class were expected to bloom intellectually in the coming year. Would you treat them differently from the children who were not so designated?

You probably would, according to the results of a classic but controversial study. Teachers do, in fact, treat children for whom they have expectations of improvement differently from those for whom they have no such expectations (R. Rosenthal & Jacobson, 1968). In the experiment, elementary school teachers were told at the beginning of a new school year that based on test results, five children in their classes would be likely to "bloom" in the upcoming year. In reality, however, the information was bogus: The names of the children had been picked at random, although the teachers didn't know that. At the end of the year, the children completed an intelligence test that was identical to one taken a year earlier. The results showed that clear differences existed in the intellectual growth of the so-called bloomers, compared with that of the other members of their classes. Those randomly designated as likely to make significant gains did, in fact, improve more than the other children.

When the findings of the experiment, reported in a book titled *Pygmalion in the Classroom,* were published, they caused an immediate stir among educators—and among the public at large. The reason for this furor was the implication of the results: If merely holding high expectations is sufficient to bring about gains in achievement, wouldn't holding low expectations lead to slowed achievement? And since teachers may sometimes hold low expectations for children from lower socioeconomic and minority backgrounds, did this mean that children from such backgrounds were destined to show low achievement throughout their educational careers?

Although the original experiment has been criticized on methodological and statistical grounds (R. Snow, 1969; Wineburg, 1987), enough new evidence has been amassed to make it clear that the expectations of teachers are communicated to their students and can in fact bring about the expected performance. The phenomenon has come to be called the **teacher expectancy effect**—the cycle of behavior in which a teacher transmits an expectation about a child and thereby actually brings about the expected behavior (Babad, 1992).

The expectations of parents and teachers have a significant effect on student performance.

Teacher expectancy effect   The phenomenon whereby an educator's expectations for a given child actually bring about the expected behavior

DEVELOPMENTAL DIVERSITY

Multicultural Education

Since the earliest period of formal education in the United States, classrooms have been populated by individuals from a broad range of backgrounds and experiences. Yet it is only relatively recently that variations in student backgrounds have been viewed as one of the major challenges—and opportunities—that educators face.

In fact, the diversity of background and experience in the classroom relates to a fundamental objective of education, which is to provide a formal mechanism to transmit the information a society deems important. As the famous anthropologist Margaret Mead (1942) once said, "In its broadest sense, education is the cultural process, the way in which each newborn human infant, born with a potentiality for learning greater than that of any other mammal, is transformed into a full member of a specific human society, sharing with the other members of a specific human culture" (p. 633).

Culture, then, can be thought of as a set of behaviors, beliefs, values, and expectations shared by members of a particular society. But although culture is often thought of in a relatively broad context (as in "Western culture" or "Asian culture"), it is also possible to focus on particular *subcultural* groups within a larger, more encompassing culture. For example, we can consider particular racial, ethnic, religious, socioeconomic, or even gender groups in the United States as manifesting characteristics of a subculture.

Membership in a cultural or subcultural group might be of only passing interest to educators were it not for the fact that students' cultural backgrounds have a substantial impact on the way that they—and their peers—are educated. In fact, in recent years, a considerable amount of thought has gone into establishing **multicultural education,** a form of education in which the goal is to help minority students develop competence in the culture of the majority group while maintaining positive group identities that build on their original cultures (Grant & Sleeter, 1986).

Cultural Assimilation or Pluralistic Society?   Multicultural education developed in part as a reaction to a **cultural assimilation model,** in which the goal of education is to assimilate individual cultural identities into a unique, unified American culture. In practical terms, this meant, for example, that non–English-speaking students were discouraged from speaking their native tongues and were totally immersed in English.

In the early 1970s, however, educators and members of minority groups began to suggest that the cultural assimilation model ought to be replaced by a **pluralistic society model.** According to this conception, American society is made up of diverse, coequal cultural groups that should preserve their individual cultural features.

The pluralistic society model grew in part from the belief that teachers, by discouraging children's use of their native tongues, denigrated their cultural heritages and lowered their self-esteem. Furthermore, because instructional materials inevitably feature

Pupils and teachers exposed to a diverse group can gain a better understanding of the world and greater sensitivity to the values and needs of others. What are some ways of developing greater sensitivity in the classroom?

culture-specific events and understandings, children who were denied access to their own cultural materials might never be exposed to important aspects of their backgrounds. For example, English-language texts rarely present some of the great themes that appear throughout Spanish literature and history (such as the search for the Fountain of Youth and the Don Juan legend). Hispanic students immersed in such texts might never come to understand important components of their own heritage.

Ultimately, educators began to argue that the presence of students representing diverse cultures enriched and broadened the educational experience of all students. Pupils and teachers exposed to people from different backgrounds could better understand the world and gain greater sensitivity to the values and needs of others.

Fostering a Bicultural Identity.   Today, most educators agree that the pluralistic society model is the most valid one for schooling and that minority children should be encouraged to develop a **bicultural identity.** They recommend that children be supported in maintaining their original cultural identities while they integrate themselves into the dominant culture. This view suggests that an individual can live as a member of two cultures, with two cultural identities, without having to choose one over the other (La Fromboise, Coleman, & Gerton, 1993).

Bicultural Education, Multicultural Education   However, the means of achieving the goal of biculturalism are far from clear. Consider, for example, children who enter a school speaking only Spanish. The traditional "melting pot" technique would be to immerse the children in classes taught in English while providing a crash course in English-language instruction (and little else) until the children demonstrate a suitable level of proficiency. Unfortunately, the traditional approach has a considerable drawback: Until the children master English, they fall further and further behind their peers who entered school already knowing English (First & Cardenas, 1986).

More contemporary approaches emphasize a bicultural strategy, in which children are encouraged to maintain simultaneous membership in more than one culture. In the case of Spanish-speaking children, for example, instruction begins in the child's native language and shifts as rapidly as possible to include English. Even after the children have mastered English, some instruction in the native language continues. At the same time, the school conducts a program of multicultural education for all students, in which teachers present material on the cultural backgrounds and traditions of all the students in the school. Such instruction is designed to enhance the self-image of speakers from both majority and minority cultures (Grant & Sleeter, 1986; S. C. Wright & Taylor, 1995).

Successful bicultural programs also attempt to bring aspects of multiple cultures into the context of everyday social interactions. In schools where many of the students speak a language other than English, for example, children are encouraged to use a variety of languages in their social relationships and to become equally adept at several languages.

Although most educational experts favor bicultural approaches, the general public does not always agree. For instance, the national "English only" movement mentioned earlier has as one of its goals the prohibition of school instruction in any language other than English. Whether such a perspective will prevail remains to be seen.

The teacher expectancy effect can be viewed as a special case of a broader concept known as the *self-fulfilling prophecy,* in which a person's expectation is capable of bringing about an outcome (M. Snyder, 1974). For instance, physicians have long known that providing patients with placebos (pills with no active ingredients) can sometimes "cure" them simply because the patients expect the medicine to work.

In the case of teacher expectancy effects, the basic explanation seems to be that teachers, after forming an initial expectation about a child's ability—often based inappropriately on such factors as previous school records, physical appearance, gender, or even race—transmit their expectation to the child through a complex series of verbal and nonverbal cues. These communicated expectations in turn indicate to the child what behavior is appropriate, and the child behaves accordingly (M. J. Harris & Rosenthal, 1986; S. Peterson & Bainbridge, 1999; R. Rosenthal, 1987, 1994; Wigfield et al., 1999).

Expectations are an omnipresent phenomenon in classrooms and are not the province of teachers alone. For instance, children develop their own expectations about their teacher's competence, based on rumors and other bits of information, and they communicate their expectations to the teacher. In the end, a teacher's behavior may be brought about in significant measure by children's expectations (R. S. Feldman & Prohaska, 1979; R. S. Feldman & Theiss, 1982; Jamieson et al., 1987).

Multicultural education   Education in which the goal is to help students from minority cultures develop competence in the culture of the majority group while maintaining positive group identities that build on their original cultures

Cultural assimilation model   The view of American society as a "melting pot" in which all cultures are amalgamated

Pluralistic society model   The concept that American society is made up of diverse, co-equal cultures that should preserve their individual features

Bicultural identity   The maintenance of one's original cultural identity while becoming integrated into the majority culture

Should Schools Teach Emotional Intelligence?

In many elementary schools, the hottest topic in the curriculum has little to do with the traditional three *Rs*. Instead, a significant educational trend for educators in many elementary schools throughout the United States is the use of techniques to increase students' **emotional intelligence,** the set of skills that underlie the accurate assessment, evaluation, expression, and regulation of emotions (Goleman, 1995; Mayer, 2001; Mayer, Salovey, & Caruso, 2000).

Psychologist Daniel Goleman (1995), who wrote a best-seller titled *Emotional Intelligence,* argues that emotional literacy should be a standard part of the school curriculum. He points to several programs that succeed in teaching students to manage their emotions more effectively. For instance, in one program, children are provided with lessons in empathy, self-awareness, and social skills. In another, children are taught about caring and friendship as early as first grade through exposure to stories.

Programs meant to increase emotional intelligence have not been met with universal acceptance. Critics suggest that the nurturance of emotional intelligence is best left to students' families and that schools ought to concentrate on more traditional curriculum matters. Others suggest that adding emotional intelligence to an already crowded curriculum may reduce time spent on academics. Finally, some critics argue that there is no well-specified set of criteria for what constitutes emotional intelligence, and consequently it is difficult to develop appropriate, effective curriculum materials (R. D. Roberts, Zeidner, & Matthews, 2001).

Still, most people consider emotional intelligence worthy of nurturance. It is clear that emotional intelligence is quite different from the traditional conceptions of intelligence that we'll consider in the next section of the chapter. The goal of emotional intelligence training is to produce people who are not only cognitively sophisticated but also able to manage their emotions effectively (M. Schulman & Mekler, 1994; Sleek, 1997).

R E V I E W *&* A P P L Y

Review

- Schooling in the United States, which is nearly universally available, has recently focused on the basic academic skills, student and teacher accountability, and multiculturalism.

- The development of reading skill generally occurs in several stages. Increasing research suggests that code-based (phonics) approaches are superior to whole-language approaches.

- Multicultural education is in transition from a melting pot model, based on cultural assimilation, to a pluralistic society model, in which coexisting cultures are respected for their unique contributions to the whole.

- The teacher expectancy effect causes teachers to hold and to communicate different expectations for different students, which can cause the students to fulfill those expectations.

- Emotional intelligence consists of the set of skills that underlie the accurate assessment, evaluation, expression, and regulation of emotions.

Applying Child Development

- Is an educational focus on the basic academic skills appropriate? What sorts of skills and abilities does the basics movement emphasize? What gets left out? What are the implications?

- *From an educator's perspective:* Should one goal of instruction be to foster cultural assimilation for children from other cultures? Why or why not?

Emotional intelligence   The set of skills that underlie the accurate assessment, evaluation, expression, and regulation of emotions

Intelligence: Determining Individual Strengths

"Why should you tell the truth?" "How far is Los Angeles from New York?" "A table is made of wood; a window is made of _____."

As 10-year-old Hyacinth sat hunched over her desk, trying to answer a long series of questions like these, she tried to guess the point of the test she was taking in her fifth-grade classroom. Clearly, the test didn't cover material that her teacher, Ms. White-Johnston, had talked about in class.

"What number comes next in this series: 1, 3, 7, 15, 31, _____?"

As she continued to work her way through the questions, she gave up trying to guess the rationale for the test. She'd leave that to her teacher, she sighed to herself. Rather than attempting to figure out what it all meant, she simply tried to do her best on the individual test items.

Hyacinth was taking an intelligence test. She might be surprised to learn that she was not alone in questioning the meaning and importance of the items on the test. Intelligence test items are painstakingly prepared, and intelligence tests show a strong relationship to success in school (for reasons we'll soon discuss). Many developmentalists, however, would admit to harboring their own doubts as to whether questions such as those on Hyacinth's test are entirely appropriate to the task of assessing intelligence.

Understanding just what is meant by the concept of intelligence has proved to be a major challenge for researchers interested in delineating what separates intelligent from unintelligent behavior. Although nonexperts have their own conceptions of intelligence (one survey found, for instance, that laypersons believe that intelligence consists of three components: problem-solving ability, verbal ability, and social competence), it has been more difficult for experts to concur (J. E. Davidson, 1990; M. J. A. Howe, 1997; Sternberg et al., 1981; R. A. Weinberg, 1989). Still, a general definition of intelligence is possible: **Intelligence** is the capacity to understand the world, think rationally, and use resources effectively when faced with challenges (D. Wechsler, 1975).

Part of the difficulty in defining intelligence stems from the many—and sometimes unsatisfactory—paths that have been followed over the years in the quest to distinguish more intelligent people from less intelligent ones. To understand how researchers have approached the task of devising batteries of assessments, called *intelligence tests,* we need to consider some of the historical milestones in the area of intelligence testing.

Intelligence Benchmarks: Differentiating the Intelligent from the Unintelligent

The Paris school system faced a problem at the turn of the 20th century: A significant number of children were not benefiting from regular instruction. Unfortunately, these children—many of whom we would now call mentally retarded—were generally not identified early enough to shift them to special classes. The French minister of instruction approached psychologist Alfred Binet with this problem and asked him to devise a technique for the early identification of students who might benefit from instruction outside the regular classroom.

Binet's Test.   Binet tackled his task in a thoroughly practical manner. His years of observing school-age children suggested to him that previous efforts to distinguish intelligent from unintelligent students—some of which were based on reaction time or keenness of sight—were off the mark. Instead, he launched a trial-and-error process in which items and tasks were administered to students who had been previously identified by teachers as being either "bright" or "dull." Tasks that the bright students completed correctly and the dull students failed to complete correctly were retained for the test. Tasks that did not discriminate between

The French educator Alfred Binet originated the intelligence test.

the two groups were discarded. The end result of this process was a test that reliably distinguished students who had previously been identified as fast or slow learners.

Binet's pioneering efforts in intelligence testing left three important legacies. The first was his pragmatic approach to the construction of intelligence tests. Binet did not have theoretical preconceptions about what intelligence was. Instead, he used a trial-and-error approach to psychological measurement that continues to serve as the predominant approach to test construction today. His definition of intelligence as *whatever his test measures* has been adopted by many modern researchers, and it is particularly popular among test developers, who respect the widespread utility of intelligence tests but wish to avoid arguments about the underlying nature of intelligence.

Our second inheritance from Binet stems from his focus on linking intelligence and school success. Binet's procedure for constructing an intelligence test ensured that intelligence—defined as performance on the test—and school success would be virtually one and the same. Thus Binet's intelligence test and today's tests that follow in Binet's footsteps have become reasonable indicators of the degree to which students possess attributes that contribute to successful school performance. Unfortunately, they do not provide particularly useful information regarding a vast number of other attributes that are largely unrelated to academic proficiency.

Finally, Binet developed a procedure of linking each intelligence test score with a **mental age,** the age of the children taking the test who, on average, achieved that score. For example, if a 6-year-old girl received a score of 30 on the test, and this was the average score received by 10-year-olds, her mental age would be considered 10 years. Similarly, a 15-year-old boy who scored a 90 on the test—thereby matching the mean score for 15-year-olds—would be assigned a mental age of 15 years.

Although assigning a mental age to students provides an indication of whether or not they are performing at the same level as their peers, it does not permit adequate comparisons between students of different **chronological (physical) ages.** By using mental age alone, for instance, it would be assumed that a 15-year-old responding with a mental age of 17 years would be as bright as a 6-year-old responding with a mental age of 8 years, when actually the 6-year-old would be showing a much greater *relative* degree of brightness.

Calculating IQ.   A solution to this problem comes in the form of the **intelligence quotient** or **IQ,** a score that takes into account a student's mental *and* chronological age. The traditional method of calculating an IQ score uses the following formula, in which MA stands for mental age and CA for chronological age:

$$\text{IQ score} = \frac{\text{MA}}{\text{CA}} \times 100$$

As a bit of trial-and-error with this formula demonstrates, people whose mental age is equal to their chronological age will always have an IQ of 100. Furthermore, if the chronological age exceeds the mental age—implying below-average intelligence—the score will be below 100; and if the chronological age is lower than the mental age—suggesting above-average intelligence—the score will be above 100.

Using this formula, we can return to our earlier example of a 15-year-old who scores at a 17-year-old mental age. This student's IQ is $17/15 \times 100$, or 113. In comparison, the IQ of a 6-year-old scoring at a mental age of 8 is $8/6 \times 100$, or 133—a higher IQ score than the 15-year-old's.

Although the basic principles behind the calculation of an IQ score still hold, scores today are calculated in a more mathematically sophisticated manner and are known as *deviation IQ scores.* The average deviation IQ score remains set at 100, but tests are now devised so that the degree of deviation from this score permits the calculation of the proportion of people who have similar scores. For instance, approximately two thirds of all people fall within 15 points of the average score of 100, achieving scores between 85 and 115. As scores rise or fall beyond

VIDEO CLIP

Mental Age Testing
CLASSIC MODULE

Mental age   The typical intelligence level found for people of a given chronological age

Chronological (physical) age   A person's age according to the calendar

Intelligence quotient (IQ)   A score that expresses the ratio between a person's mental and chronological ages

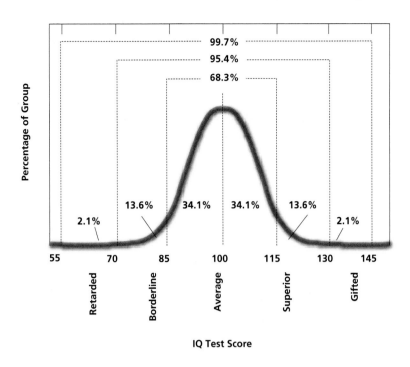

FIGURE 12-6 IQ SCORES

The most common and average IQ score is 100, with 68.3 percent of all people falling within 15 points of 100. About 95 percent of the population has scores that are within 30 points above or below 100; fewer than 3 percent score below 55 or above 145.

this range, the percentage of people in the same score category drops significantly (see Figure 12-6).

Measuring IQ: Present-Day Approaches to Intelligence

Since the time of Binet, tests of intelligence have become increasingly sophisticated in terms of the accuracy with which they measure IQ. However, most of them can still trace their roots to his original work in one way or another. For example, one of the most widely used tests, the **Stanford-Binet Intelligence Scale,** began as an American revision of Binet's original test. The test consists of a series of items that vary according to the age of the person being tested. For

Stanford-Binet Intelligence Scale A test that consists of a series of items that vary according to the age of the person being tested

A number of different tests are used to measure intelligence.

Wechsler Intelligence Scale for Children—Revised (WISC-IV) A test for children that provides separate measures of verbal and performance (nonverbal) skills, as well as a total score

Wechsler Adult Intelligence Scale—Revised (WAIS-III) A test for adults that provides separate measures of verbal and performance (nonverbal) skills, as well as a total score

Kaufman Assessment Battery for Children (K-ABC) A children's intelligence test permitting unusual flexibility in its administration

Fluid intelligence The ability to deal with new problems and situations

Crystallized intelligence The store of information, skills, and strategies that people have acquired through education and prior experiences and through their previous use of fluid intelligence

instance, young children are asked to answer questions about everyday activities or to copy complex figures. Older people are asked to explain proverbs, solve analogies, and describe similarities between groups of words. The test is administered orally, and test takers are given progressively more difficult problems until they are unable to proceed.

The **Wechsler Intelligence Scale for Children—Revised (WISC-IV)** and its adult version, the **Wechsler Adult Intelligence Scale—Revised (WAIS-III),** are two other widely used intelligence tests. The tests provide separate measures of verbal and performance (or nonverbal) skills, as well as a total score. As you can see from the sample items in Figure 12-7, the verbal tasks are traditional word problems testing skills such as understanding a passage, while typical nonverbal tasks are copying a complex design, arranging pictures in a logical order, and assembling objects. The separate portions of the test allow for easier identification of any specific problems a test taker may have. For example, significantly higher scores on the performance part of the test than on the verbal part may indicate difficulties in linguistic development.

The **Kaufman Assessment Battery for Children (K-ABC)** takes a different approach from the Stanford-Binet, WISC-IV, and WAIS-III. In it, children are tested on their ability to integrate different kinds of stimuli simultaneously and to use step-by-step thinking. A special virtue of the K-ABC is its flexibility. It allows the person giving the test to use alternative wording or gestures or even to pose questions in a different language in order to maximize a test taker's performance. This capability of the K-ABC makes it a more valid and more equitable test for children who are not native speakers of English.

What do the scores derived from IQ tests mean? For most children, IQ scores are reasonably good predictors of school performance. That's not surprising, given that the initial impetus for the development of intelligence tests was to identify children who were having difficulties in school (Sternberg & Grigorenko, 2002).

But when it comes to performance outside of academic spheres, the story is different. For instance, although people with higher IQ scores are apt to finish more years of schooling, once this is statistically controlled for, IQ scores are not closely related to income and later success in life. Furthermore, IQ scores are frequently inaccurate when it comes to predicting a particular individual's future success. For example, two people with different IQ scores may both finish their bachelor's degrees at the same college, and the person with the lower IQ might end up with a higher income and a more successful career. Because of these difficulties with traditional IQ scores, researchers have turned to alternative approaches to evaluating intelligence (McClelland, 1993).

Alternative Conceptions of Intelligence

The intelligence tests used most frequently in school settings today share an underlying premise: Intelligence is composed of a single, unitary mental ability factor. This one main attribute has commonly been called *g* (Spearman, 1927). The *g* factor is assumed to underlie performance on every aspect of intelligence, and it is the *g* factor that intelligence tests presumably measure.

However, many theorists dispute the notion that intelligence is unidimensional (M. Anderson, 1999; Neisser, 1999; Neisser et al., 1996). For example, some developmentalists suggest that in fact two kinds of intelligence exist: fluid intelligence and crystallized intelligence (Cattell, 1967, 1987). **Fluid intelligence** reflects information processing capabilities, reasoning, and memory. For example, a student asked to group a series of letters according to some criterion or to remember a set of numbers would be using fluid intelligence. In contrast, **crystallized intelligence** is the accumulation of information, skills, and strategies that people have learned through experience and can apply in problem-solving situations. A student would likely be relying on crystallized intelligence to solve a puzzle or deduce the solution to a mystery in which it was necessary to draw on past experience.

NAME	GOAL OF ITEM	EXAMPLE
VERBAL SCALE		
Information	Assess general information	How many nickels make a dime?
Comprehension	Assess understanding and evaluation of social norms and past experience	What is the advantage of keeping money in the bank?
Arithmetic	Assess math reasoning through verbal problems	If two buttons cost 15 cents, what will be the cost of a dozen buttons?
Similarities	Test understanding of how objects or concepts are alike, tapping abstract reasoning	In what way are an hour and a week alike?
PERFORMANCE SCALE		
Digit symbol	Assess speed of learning	Match symbols to numbers using key. 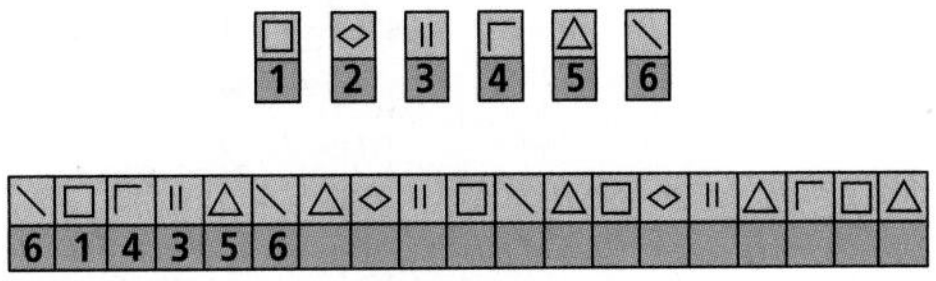
Picture completion	Visual memory and attention	Identify what is missing. 
Object assembly	Test understanding of relationship of parts to wholes	Put pieces together to form a whole. 

FIGURE 12-7   MEASURING INTELLIGENCE

The Wechsler Intelligence Scale for Children—Revised (WISC-IV) includes items such as these.

(*Source:* The Psychological Corporation. Copyright © 1990 by The Psychological Corporation. Reproduced by permission. All rights reserved.

Multiple Intelligences.   Other theorists divide intelligence into an even greater number of parts. For example, psychologist Howard Gardner's *theory of multiple intelligences* suggests that there are eight distinct intelligences, each relatively independent (see Table 12-2). Gardner (2000) suggests that these separate intelligences operate not in isolation but together, depending on the type of activity in which a person is engaged.

Interactive Intelligence.   The Russian psychologist Lev Vygotsky, whose approach to cognitive development we first discussed in Chapter 2, takes a very different approach to intelligence. He suggests that to assess intelligence, we should look not only at those cognitive processes that are fully developed but also at those that are currently being developed. To do this, Vygotsky contends that assessment tasks should involve cooperative interaction between the individual who is being assessed and the person who is doing the assessment—a process called *dynamic assessment.* In short, intelligence is seen as being reflected not only in how children can perform on their own but also in terms of how well they perform when helped by adults (A. L. Brown & Ferrara, 1999; Campione & Brown, 1987; J. S. Carlson & Wiedl, 1992; Daniels, 1996; Kozulin & Falik, 1995; Vygotsky, 1930–1935/1978).

The Processes of Intelligence.   Taking yet another approach, psychologist Robert Sternberg (1987, 1990) suggests that intelligence is best thought of in terms of information processing. In this view, the way in which people store material in memory and later use it to solve intellectual tasks provides the most precise conception of intelligence. Rather than focusing on the various subcomponents that make up the *structure* of intelligence, then, information processing approaches examine the *processes* that underlie intelligent behavior.

Researchers who have broken tasks and problems into their component parts have noted critical differences in the nature and speed of problem-solving processes between those who score high and those who score low on traditional IQ tests. For instance, when verbal problems such as analogies are broken into their component parts, it becomes clear that people with higher intelligence levels differ from others not only in the number of problems they are ultimately able to solve but in their method of solving the problems as well. People with high IQ scores spend more time on the initial stages of problem solving, retrieving relevant information from memory. In contrast, those who score lower on traditional IQ tests tend to spend less time on the initial stages, instead skipping ahead and making less informed guesses. The processes used in solving problems, then, may reflect important differences in intelligence (Deary & Stough, 1996; Sternberg, 1982, 1990).

Sternberg's work on information processing approaches to intelligence has led him to develop the **triarchic theory of intelligence.** According to this model, intelligence consists of three aspects of information processing: the componential element, the experiential element, and the contextual element. The *componential* aspect of intelligence reflects how efficiently people can process and analyze information. Efficiency in these areas allows people to infer relationships among different parts of a problem, solve the problem, and then evaluate their solution. People who are strong on the componential element score highest on traditional tests of intelligence (Sternberg, 1996).

The *experiential* element is the insightful component of intelligence. People who have a strong experiential element can easily compare new material with what they already know and can combine and relate facts that they already know in novel and creative ways. Finally, the *contextual* element of intelligence concerns practical intelligence, or ways of dealing with the demands of the everyday environment.

In Sternberg's view, people vary in the degree to which each of these three elements is present. Our level of success at any given task reflects the match between the task and our own specific pattern of strength on the three components of intelligence (Sternberg, 1985, 1991).

Triarchic theory of intelligence   The belief that intelligence consists of three aspects of information processing: the componential element, the experiential element, and the contextual element

TABLE 12-2   GARDNER'S EIGHT INTELLIGENCES

1. Musical intelligence (skills in tasks involving music). Case example:

   When he was 3, Yehudi Menuhin was smuggled into the San Francisco Orchestra concerts by his parents. The sound of Louis Persinger's violin so entranced the youngster that he insisted on a violin for his birthday and Louis Persinger as his teacher. He got both. By the time he was 10 years old, Menuhin was an international performer.

2. Bodily kinesthetic intelligence (skills in using the whole body or various portions of it in the solution of problems or in the construction of products or displays, exemplified by dancers, athletes, actors, and surgeons). Case example:

   Fifteen-year-old Babe Ruth played third base. During one game, his team's pitcher was doing poorly and Babe loudly criticized him from third base. Brother Mathias, the coach, called out, "Ruth, if you know so much about it, you pitch!" Babe was surprised and embarrassed because he had never pitched before, but Brother Mathias insisted. Ruth said later that at the very moment he took the pitcher's mound, he knew he was supposed to be a pitcher.

3. Logical mathematical intelligence (skills in problem solving and scientific thinking). Case example:

   Barbara McClintock won the Nobel Prize in medicine for her work in microbiology. She describes one of her breakthroughs, which came after thinking about a problem for half an hour . . . : "Suddenly I jumped and ran back to the [corn] field. At the top of the field [the others were still at the bottom] I shouted, 'Eureka, I have it!'"

4. Linguistic intelligence (skills involved in the production and use of language). Case example:

   At the age of 10, T. S. Elliot created a magazine called Fireside, to which he was the sole contributor. In a 3-day period during his winter vacation, he created eight complete issues.

5. Spatial intelligence (skills involving spatial configurations, such as those used by artists and architects). Case example:

   Navigation around the Caroline Islands is accomplished without instruments. . . . During the actual trip, the navigator must envision mentally a reference island as it passes under a particular star and from that he computes the number of segments completed, the proportion of the trip remaining, and any corrections in heading.

6. Interpersonal intelligence (skills in interacting with others, such as sensitivity to the moods, temperaments, motivations, and intentions of others). Case example:

   When Anne Sullivan began instructing the deaf and blind Helen Keller, her task was one that had eluded others for years. Yet just 2 weeks after beginning her work with Keller, Sullivan achieved a great success. In her words, "My heart is singing with joy this morning. A miracle has happened! The wild little creature of 2 weeks ago has been transformed into a gentle child."

7. Intrapersonal intelligence (knowledge of the internal aspects of oneself; access to one's own feelings and emotions). Case example:

   In her essay "A Sketch of the Past," Virginia Woolf displays deep insight into her own inner life through these lines, describing her reaction to several specific memories from her childhood that still, in adulthood, shock her: "Though I still have the peculiarity that I receive these sudden shocks, they are now always welcome; after the first surprise, I always feel instantly that they are particularly valuable. And so I go on to suppose that the shock-receiving capacity is what makes me a writer."

8. Naturalist intelligence (ability to identify and classify patterns in nature). Case example:

   In prehistoric periods, hunter-gatherers required naturalist intelligence in order to identify what types of plants were edible.

(*Source:* Adapted from Walters & Gardner, 1986)

Group Differences in IQ

A *jontry* is an example of a
  (a) rulpow
  (b) flink
  (c) spudge
  (d) bakwoe

If you were to encounter an item made up of nonsense words such as this on an intelligence test, your immediate—and quite legitimate—reaction would likely be to complain. How could a test that purports to measure intelligence include test items that incorporate meaningless terminology?

Yet for some people, the items actually used on traditional intelligence tests can appear equally nonsensical. To take a hypothetical example, suppose children living in rural areas were asked details about subways, while those living in urban areas were asked about the mating practices of sheep. In both cases, we would expect that the previous experiences of test takers would have a substantial effect on their ability to answer the questions. And if questions about such matters were included on an IQ test, the test could rightly be viewed as a measure of prior experience rather than intelligence.

Although the questions on traditional IQ tests are not so blatantly dependent on test takers' prior experiences, our examples, cultural background, and experience do have the potential to influence intelligence test scores. In fact, many educators suggest that traditional measures of intelligence are subtly biased in favor of white, upper- and middle-class students and against groups with different cultural experiences (Sternberg, 2001).

Explaining Racial Differences in IQ.   The issue of how cultural background and experience influence IQ test performance has led to considerable debate among researchers. The debate has been fueled by the finding that IQ scores of certain racial groups are consistently lower, on average, than the IQ scores of other groups. For example, the mean IQ score of African Americans tends to be about 15 points lower than the mean score of whites—although the measured difference varies a great deal, depending on the particular IQ test employed (e.g., Fish, 2001; Vance, Hankins, & Brown, 1988).

The question that emerges from such differences, of course, is whether they reflect actual differences in intelligence or are caused by bias in the intelligence tests themselves in favor of majority groups and against minorities. For example, if whites perform better on an IQ test than African Americans because of their greater familiarity with the language used in the test items, the test can hardly be said to provide a fair measure of the intelligence of African Americans. Similarly, an intelligence test written exclusively in African American vernacular English could not be considered an impartial measure of intelligence for whites.

The question of how to interpret differences between intelligence scores of different cultural groups lies at the heart of one of the major controversies in child development: To what degree is an individual's intelligence determined by heredity and to what degree by environment? The issue is important because of its social implications. For instance, if intelligence is primarily determined by heredity and is therefore largely fixed at birth, attempts to alter cognitive abilities later in life, such as schooling, will meet with limited success. On the other hand, if intelligence is largely environmentally determined, modifying social and educational conditions is a more promising strategy for bringing about increases in cognitive functioning (Sternberg & Grigorenko, 1996; Suzuki & Valencia, 1997).

***The Bell Curve* Controversy.**   Although investigations into the relative contributions to intelligence of heredity and environment have been conducted for decades, the smoldering debate became a raging fire with the publication in 1994 of a book by Richard J. Herrnstein and Charles Murray, titled *The Bell Curve.* In the book, Herrnstein and Murray argue that the average 15-point IQ difference between whites and African Americans is due primarily to heredity rather than environment. Furthermore, they argue that this IQ difference accounts for the higher rates of poverty, lower employment, and greater use of welfare among minority groups.

The conclusions reached by Herrnstein and Murray raised a storm of protest, and many researchers who examined the data reported in the book came to very different conclusions. Most developmentalists and psychologists responded by arguing that the differences between races in measured IQ can be explained by environmental factors. In fact, when various economic and social indicators are statistically taken into account simultaneously, mean IQ scores of black and white children turn out to be quite similar. For instance, children from similar middle-class backgrounds, whether African American or white, tend to have similar IQ scores (Brooks-Gunn, Klebanov, & Duncan, 1996; Nisbett, 1998).

Furthermore, critics maintained that there is little evidence to suggest that IQ is a cause of poverty and other social ills. In fact, some critics suggested, as mentioned earlier in this discussion, that IQ scores were unrelated in meaningful ways to later success in life (e.g., R. Jacoby & Glauberman, 1995; McClelland, 1993; Nisbett, 1994; Reifman, 2000; Sternberg, 1995, 1997; Sternberg & Wagner, 1993).

Finally, members of cultural and social minority groups may score lower than members of the majority group due to the nature of the intelligence tests themselves. It is clear that traditional intelligence tests may discriminate against minority groups who have not had exposure to the same environment as majority group members. Although certain IQ tests (such as the *System of Multicultural Pluralistic Assessment,* or *SOMPA*) have been designated as **culture-fair tests,** tests that are equally valid regardless of the cultural background of test takers, the reality is that no test can be completely without bias (Sandoval et al., 1998).

In short, most experts in the area of IQ were not convinced by *The Bell Curve*'s contention that differences in group IQ scores are largely determined by genetic factors. Still, we cannot put the issue to rest because it is impossible to design a definitive experiment that can determine the cause of differences in IQ scores between members of different groups. (Thinking about how such an experiment might be designed shows the futility of the enterprise: One cannot ethically assign children to different living conditions to find the effects of environment, nor would one wish to genetically control or alter intelligence levels in unborn children.)

In practical terms, however, it may ultimately be less important to know the absolute degree to which intelligence is determined by genetic and environmental factors than it is to learn how to improve children's living conditions and educational experiences. By enriching the quality of children's environments, we will be in a better position to permit all children to reach their full potential and to maximize their contributions to society, whatever their individual levels of intelligence (H. Gardner et al., 1994; Wachs, 1996; Wickelgren, 1999).

Falling Below and Above Intelligence Norms

Although Connie kept pace with her classmates in kindergarten, by the time she reached first grade she was academically the slowest in almost every subject. It was not that she didn't try but rather that it took her longer than other students to catch on to new material, and she regularly required special attention to keep up with the rest of the class.

Yet in some areas she excelled: When asked to draw or produce something with her hands, she not only matched her classmates' performance but exceeded it, producing beautiful work that was much admired by her classmates. Although the other students in the class felt that there was something different about Connie, they were hard-pressed to identify the source of the difference, and in fact they didn't spend much time pondering the issue.

Culture-fair tests Tests that are valid regardless of the test takers' cultural backgrounds

Connie's parents and teacher, though, knew what made her special. Extensive testing in kindergarten had shown that Connie's intelligence was well below normal, and she was officially classified as a special-needs student.

Below the Norm: Mental Retardation.   Approximately 1 to 3 percent of the school-age population is considered mentally retarded (U.S. Department of Education, 1987). Estimates vary because the most widely accepted definition of mental retardation is one that leaves a great deal of room for interpretation. According to the American Association on Mental Retardation (1992), **mental retardation** refers to "substantial limitations in present functioning" characterized by "significantly subaverage intellectual functioning, existing concurrently with related limitations in two or more of the following applicable adaptive skill areas: communication, self-care, home living, social skills, community use, self direction, health and safety, functional academics, leisure and work. Mental retardation manifests before age 18" (AAMR, 1992).

Although "subaverage intellectual functioning" can be measured in a relatively straightforward manner using standard IQ tests, it is more difficult to determine how to gauge limitations in "applicable adaptive skills." Ultimately, this imprecision leads to a lack of uniformity in the ways experts apply the label of "mental retardation." Furthermore, it has resulted in significant variation in the abilities of people who are categorized as mentally retarded. Accordingly, mentally retarded people range from those who can be taught to work and function with little special attention to those who are virtually untrainable and who never develop speech or such basic motor skills as crawling or walking (Matson & Mulick, 1991).

In addition, even when objective measures such as IQ tests are used to identify mentally retarded individuals, discrimination may occur against children from ethnically diverse backgrounds. Most traditional intelligence tests are standardized using white, English-speaking, middle-class populations. As a result, children from different cultural backgrounds may perform poorly on the tests not because they are retarded but because the tests use questions that are culturally biased in favor of majority group members. In fact, one classic study found that in one California school district, Mexican American students were 10 times more likely than whites to be placed in special education classes (J. R. Mercer, 1973). More recent findings show that nationally, twice as many African American students as white students are classified as mildly retarded, a difference that experts attribute primarily to cultural bias and poverty (Reschly, 1996; D. L. Terman et al., 1996).

Degrees of Retardation.   The vast majority of the mentally retarded—some 90 percent—have relatively minor levels of deficits. Classified with **mild retardation,** they score in the range of 50 or 55 to 70 on IQ tests. Typically, their retardation is not even identified before they reach school, although their early development is often slower than average. Once they enter elementary school, their retardation and their need for special attention usually become apparent, as it did with Connie, the first grader profiled at the beginning of this discussion. With appropriate training, these students can ultimately reach a third- to sixth-grade educational level, and although they cannot carry out complex intellectual tasks, they are able to hold jobs and function independently and successfully.

Intellectual and adaptive limitations become more apparent, however, at more extreme levels of mental retardation. People whose IQ scores range from around 35 or 40 to 50 or 55 are classified with **moderate retardation.** Accounting for 5 to 10 percent of those classified as mentally retarded, the moderately retarded display distinctive behavior early in their lives. They are slow to develop language skills, and their motor development is also affected. Regular schooling is usually not effective in training people with moderate retardation to acquire academic skills because generally they are unable to progress beyond the second-grade level. Still, they are capable of learning occupational and social skills, and they can learn to travel independently to familiar places. Typically, they require moderate levels of supervision.

At the most significant levels of retardation—in individuals with **severe retardation** (IQs ranging from around 20 or 25 to 35 or 40) and **profound retardation** (IQs below 20 or

Mental retardation   A significantly subaverage level of intellectual functioning that occurs with related limitations in two or more skill areas

Mild retardation   Retardation with IQ scores in the range of 50 or 55 to 70

Moderate retardation   Retardation with IQ scores from around 35 or 40 to 50 or 55

Severe retardation   Retardation with IQ scores that range from around 20 or 25 to 35 or 40

Profound retardation   Retardation with IQ scores below 20 or 25

The practice of mainstreaming places children with mental retardation in classes with typical children.

25)—the ability to function is severely limited. Usually, such people produce little or no speech, have poor motor control, and may need 24-hour nursing care. At the same time, though, some people with severe retardation are capable of learning basic self-care skills, such as dressing and eating, and they may even develop the potential to become partially independent as adults. Still, the need for relatively high levels of care continues throughout the life span, and most severely and profoundly retarded people are institutionalized for the majority of their lives.

Above the Norm: The Gifted and Talented.   Consider this situation:

> I was standing at the front of the room explaining how the earth revolves and how, because of its huge size, it is difficult for us to realize that it is actually round. All of a sudden, Spencer blurted out, "The earth isn't round." I curtly replied, "Ha, do you think it's flat?" He matter-of-factly said, "No, it's a truncated sphere." I quickly changed the subject. Spencer said the darndest things. (Payne et al., 1974, p. 94)

It sometimes strikes people as curious that the gifted and talented are considered to have a form of exceptionality. Yet, as the quote suggests, the 3 to 5 percent of school-age children who are gifted and talented present special challenges of their own.

Which students are considered to be **gifted and talented?** Because of the breadth of the term, little agreement exists among researchers on a single definition (Hoge, 1989). However, the federal government considers the term *gifted* to include "children who give evidence of high performance capability in areas such as intellectual, creative, artistic, leadership capacity, or specific academic fields, and who require services or activities not ordinarily provided by the school in order to fully develop such capabilities" (P.L. 97-35, sec. 582). Intellectual capabilities, then, represent only one type of exceptionality; unusual potential in areas outside the academic realm are also included in the concept. Gifted and talented children have so much potential that they, no less than students with low IQs, warrant special concern (Azar, 1995; Pfeiffer & Stocking, 2000; N. M. Robinson, Zigler, & Gallagher, 2000; Winner, 1997).

Although the stereotypic description of the gifted—particularly those with exceptionally high intelligence—would probably include characterizations such as "unsociable," "poorly adjusted," and "neurotic," such a view is far off the mark. In fact, most research suggests that highly intelligent people also tend to be outgoing, well adjusted, and popular (Field et al., 1998; A. W. Gottfried et al., 1994; Southern, Jones, & Stanley, 1993).

Gifted and talented Showing evidence of high performance capability in intellectual, creative, or artistic areas, in leadership capacity, or in specific academic fields

Acceleration The provision of special programs that allow gifted students to move ahead at their own pace, even if this means skipping to higher grade levels

Enrichment An approach whereby gifted students are kept at grade level but are enrolled in special programs and given individual activities to allow greater depth of study

For instance, one landmark long-term study of 1,500 gifted students that began in the 1920s found that the gifted did better in virtually every dimension studied. Not only were they smarter than average, but they were healthier, better coordinated, and psychologically better adjusted than their less intelligent classmates. Furthermore, their lives played out in ways that most people would envy. The subjects received more awards and distinctions, earned more money, and made many more contributions in art and literature than the average person. For instance, by the time they had reached the age of 40, they had collectively produced more than 90 books, 375 plays and short stories, and 2,000 articles, and they had registered more than 200 patents. Perhaps not surprisingly, they reported greater satisfaction with their lives than the nongifted (Sears, 1977; Shurkin, 1992; Terman & Oden, 1959).

Yet being gifted and talented is no guarantee of success in school, as we can see if we consider the particular components of the category. For example, the verbal abilities that allow the eloquent expression of ideas and feelings can equally permit the expression of glib and persuasive statements that happen to be inaccurate. Furthermore, teachers may sometimes misinterpret the humor, novelty, and creativity of unusually gifted children, considering their intellectual fervor to be disruptive or inappropriate. And peers are not always sympathetic: Some very bright children try to hide their intelligence in an effort to fit in better with other students (R. S. Feldman, 1982).

Educating the Gifted and Talented. Two main approaches to educating the gifted and talented have been devised: acceleration and enrichment (Feldhusen, Haeger, & Pellegrino, 1989). **Acceleration** allows gifted students to move ahead at their own pace, even if this means skipping to higher grade levels. The materials that students receive under acceleration programs are not necessarily different from what other students receive; they are simply provided at a faster pace than for the average student.

An alternative approach is **enrichment,** whereby gifted students are kept at grade level but are enrolled in special programs and given individual activities to allow greater depth of study on a given topic. In enrichment, the material provided to gifted students differs not only in the timing of its presentation but in its sophistication as well. Thus enrichment materials are designed to provide an intellectual challenge to the gifted student, encouraging higher order thinking.

Acceleration programs can be remarkably effective. Most studies have shown that gifted students who begin school even considerably earlier than their agemates do as well as or better than those who begin at the traditional age (Rimm & Lovance, 1992; Van Tassel-Baska, 1986). One of the best illustrations of the benefits of acceleration is the Study of Mathematically Precocious Youth, an ongoing program at Johns Hopkins University in Baltimore. In this program, seventh and eighth graders who have exceptional abilities in mathematics participate in a variety of special classes and workshops. The results have been nothing short of sensational, with students successfully completing college courses and sometimes even enrolling in college early. Some students have even graduated from college before the age of 18 (J. E. Brody & Benbow, 1987; Stanley & Benbow, 1983).

REVIEW & APPLY

Review

- The measurement of intelligence has traditionally been a matter of testing skills that promote academic success.

- Contemporary IQ tests include the Stanford-Binet Intelligence Scale, the Wechsler Intelligence Scale for Children—Revised (WISC-IV), the Wechsler Adult Intelligence Scale—Revised (WAIS-III), and the Kaufman Assessment Battery for Children (K-ABC).

- Recent theories of intelligence suggest that there may be several distinct intelligences or several components of intelligence that reflect different ways of processing information.

- U.S. educators are attempting to deal with substantial numbers of exceptional students whose intellectual and other skills are significantly lower or higher than normal.

Applying Child Development

- How do fluid intelligence and crystallized intelligence interact? Which of the two is likely to be more influenced by genetic factors and which by environmental factors? Why?

- *From an educator's perspective:* Does Howard Gardner's theory of multiple intelligences suggest that classroom instruction should be modified from an emphasis on the traditional three *R*s of reading, writing, and arithmetic?

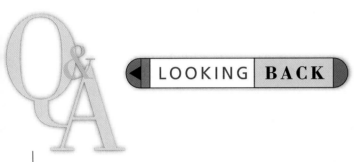

LOOKING BACK

- ◉ **In what ways do children develop cognitively during the years of middle childhood?**

- • According to Piaget, school-age children enter the concrete operational period and for the first time become capable of applying logical thought processes to concrete problems.

- • According to information processing approaches, children's intellectual development in the school years can be attributed to substantial increases in memory capacity and the sophistication of the "programs" children can handle.

- • Vygotsky recommends that students focus on active learning through child–adult and child–child interactions that fall within each child's zone of proximal development.

- ◉ **How does language develop during the middle childhood period, and what special circumstances pertain to children for whom English is not the first language?**

- • The language development of children in the school years is substantial, with improvements in vocabulary, syntax, and pragmatics. Children learn to control their behavior through linguistic strategies, and they learn more effectively by seeking clarification when they need it.

- • Bilingualism can be beneficial in the school years. Children who are taught all subjects in their first language with simultaneous instruction in English appear to experience few deficits and several linguistic and cognitive advantages.

- ◉ **What trends are affecting schooling worldwide and in the United States?**

- • Schooling, which is available to nearly all children in most developed countries, is not as accessible to children, especially girls, in many less developed countries.

- • The development of reading skill, which is fundamental to schooling, generally occurs in several stages. Research suggests that code-based (phonics) approaches are superior to whole-language approaches.

- Multiculturalism and diversity are significant issues in U.S. schools, where the melting pot society, in which minority cultures were assimilated to the majority culture, is being replaced by the pluralistic society, in which individual cultures maintain their own identities while participating in the definition of a larger culture.

⦾ **What kinds of subjective factors contribute to academic outcomes?**

- The expectancies of others, particularly teachers, can produce outcomes that conform to those expectancies by leading students to modify their behavior.

- Emotional intelligence is the set of skills that permit people to manage their emotions effectively.

⦾ **How can intelligence be measured, what are some issues in intelligence testing, and how are children who fall outside the normal range of intelligence educated?**

- Intelligence testing has traditionally focused on factors that differentiate successful academic performers from unsuccessful ones. The intelligence quotient, or IQ, reflects the ratio of a person's mental age to his or her chronological age. Other conceptualizations of intelligence focus on different types of intelligence or on different aspects of information processing.

- The question of whether there are racial differences in IQ, and how to explain those differences, is highly controversial.

- Children who are both above and below the norm benefit from special educational programs.

EPILOGUE

 n this chapter, we discussed children's cognitive development during the middle childhood years, tracing its development through the different lenses provided by Piaget, information processing approaches, and Vygotsky. We noted the increased capabilities that children develop during middle childhood in the areas of memory and language, both of which facilitate and support gains in many other areas.

We then looked at some aspects of schooling worldwide. We touched on such trends as the reemphasis on the academic basics, the great debate on reading instruction, and the changing picture for multicultural education and diversity.

Finally, we concluded the chapter with an examination of the controversial issue of intelligence: how it is defined, how it is tested, how IQ test differences are interpreted, and how children who fall significantly below or above the intellectual norm are educated and treated.

Look back to the prologue, about La-Toya Pankey's development of reading skills, and answer the following questions:

1. Judging from the cues provided in the prologue, how would you have estimated La-Toya's chances for academic success before you learned about her ability to read? Why?

2. If you wished to isolate the factors in La-Toya's genetic or environmental background that contributed to her interest and ability in reading, how would you proceed? Which factors would you examine? What questions would you ask?

3. Given her circumstances, what threats to academic accomplishment does La-Toya still face? What advantages does she seem to have?

4. Discuss La-Toya's situation in light of the premises of the authors of *The Bell Curve.* If La-Toya succeeds academically, outperforming students of higher socioeconomic status, how would the authors explain this phenomenon? How do you explain it?

KEY TERMS AND CONCEPTS

concrete operational stage
(p. 347)

decentering (p. 347)

memory (p. 350)

metamemory (p. 350)

metalinguistic awareness
(p. 353)

bilingualism (p. 354)

teacher expectancy effect
(p. 361)

multicultural education
(p. 363)

cultural assimilation model
(p. 363)

pluralistic society model
(p. 363)

bicultural identity (p. 363)

emotional intelligence
(p. 364)

intelligence (p. 365)

mental age (p. 366)

chronological (physical)
age (p. 366)

intelligence quotient (IQ)
(p. 366)

Stanford-Binet Intelligence
Scale (p. 367)

Wechsler Intelligence
Scale for Children—
Revised (WISC-IV) (p.
368)

Wechsler Adult
Intelligence Scale—
Revised (WAIS-III)
(p. 368)

Kaufman Assessment
Battery for Children
(K-ABC) (p. 368)

fluid intelligence (p. 368)

crystallized intelligence
(p. 368)

triarchic theory of
intelligence (p. 370)

culture-fair tests (p. 373)

mental retardation
(p. 374)

mild retardation
(p. 374)

moderate retardation
(p. 374)

severe retardation
(p. 374)

profound retardation
(p. 374)

gifted and talented
(p. 375)

acceleration (p. 376)

enrichment (p. 376)

13

Social and Personality Development in Middle Childhood

PROLOGUE: Playtime

 n a bright weekday afternoon, six boys are playing under the endless Nevada sky. Bryan and Christopher Hendrickson are third graders, 9-year-old twins, and as on so many afternoons, their garage is headquarters.

The twins, their younger brother, Andrew, and three friends pull two enormous boxes from the garage—one each from a recently purchased washer and dryer—and set to work transforming them.

"We're making our spaceship," says Bryan. "With guns included."

Why does the spaceship need guns?

"For evil, don't you know?" says Bryan. He sprays machine gun sounds.

As the sun sets, an ever-larger clan of kids, now including the twins' older sister, Lindsay, invades the backyard. The boxes become forts, the group divides in two, and a furious round of capture-the-stuffed-tiger ensues. . . .

Around 6 o'clock, mom Judy summons all the kids—now nearly a dozen—inside for dinner of pizza and juice. Later, the game resumes for another hour or so by moonlight

During middle childhood, play involves the development of fr[i]endships and social relationships.

before exhausting itself. Some children w[...]

Others are picked up by their parents. [...]

p. 56)

LOOKING AHEAD ▶

For Bryan and Christopher, afternoons like these represent more than just a way of passing time. They also pave the way for the formation of friendships and social relationships, a key developmental task during middle childhood.

In this chapter, we focus on social and personality development during middle childhood. It is a time when children's views of themselves undergo significant changes, they form new bonds with friends and family, and they become increasingly attached to social institutions outside the home.

We start our consideration of personality and social development during middle childhood by examining the changes that occur in the ways children see themselves. We discuss how they view their personal characteristics, and we examine the complex issue of self-esteem.

Next the chapter turns to relationships during middle childhood. We discuss the stages of friendship and the ways gender and ethnicity affect how and with whom children interact. We also examine how to improve children's social competence.

The last part of the chapter explores the central societal institution in children's lives: the family. We consider the consequences of divorce, self-care children, and the phenomenon of group care.

In sum, after reading this chapter, you will be able to answer the following questions:

- In what ways do children's views of themselves change during middle childhood?
- How does self-esteem affect behavior?
- What sorts of relationships and friendships are typical of middle childhood?
- What are the factors involved in popularity?
- How do sex and ethnicity affect friendships?
- How do today's diverse family and care arrangements affect children?

The Developing Self

Nine-year-old Karl Haglund is perched in his eagle's nest, a tree house built high in the willow that grows in his backyard. Sometimes he sits there alone among the tree's spreading branches, his face turned toward the sky, a boy clearly enjoying his solitude. . . .

This morning Karl is busy sawing and hammering. "It's fun to build," he says. "I started the house when I was 4 years old. Then when I was about 7, my dad built me this platform. 'Cause all my places were falling apart and they were crawling with carpenter ants. So we destroyed them and then built me a deck. And I built on top of it. It's stronger now. You can have privacy here, but it's a bad place to go when it's windy 'cause you almost get blown off." (Kotre & Hall, 1990, p. 116)

Karl's growing sense of competence is apparent as he describes how he and his father built his tree house. Conveying what psychologist Erik Erikson calls "industriousness," Karl's quiet pride in his accomplishment illustrates one of the ways in which children's views of themselves evolve.

According to Erik Erikson, middle childhood encompasses the industry-versus-inferiority stage, characterized by a focus on meeting the challenges presented by the world.

Psychosocial Development in Middle Childhood: Industry Versus Inferiority

According to Erikson, whose approach to psychosocial development we last discussed in Chapter 10, middle childhood encompasses the **industry-versus-inferiority stage.** Lasting from roughly age 6 to age 12, the industry-versus-inferiority stage is characterized by a focus on efforts to attain competence in meeting the challenges presented by parents, peers, school, and the complexities of the world.

As they move through middle childhood, children direct their energies not only to mastering what they are presented in school—an enormous body of information—but also to making a place for themselves in their social worlds. Success in this stage brings with it feelings of mastery and proficiency and a growing sense of competence, like those expressed by Karl when he talks about his building experience. Conversely, difficulties in this stage lead to feelings of failure and inadequacy. As a result, children may withdraw both from academic pursuits, showing less interest and motivation to excel, and from interactions with peers.

Children such as Karl may find that attaining a sense of industry during the middle childhood years has lasting consequences. For example, one study examined how childhood industriousness and hard work were related to adult behavior by following a group of 450 men over a 35-year period, starting in early childhood. The men who were most industrious and hardworking during childhood were most successful as adults, both in occupational attainment and in their personal lives. In fact, childhood industriousness was more closely associated with adult success than either intelligence or family background (Vaillant & Vaillant, 1981).

Understanding the Self: A New Response to "Who Am I?"

During middle childhood, children continue their efforts to answer the question "Who am I?" as they seek to understand the nature of the self. Although the question does not yet have the urgency it will assume in adolescence, elementary school children still seek to pin down their place in the world.

The Shift in Self-Understanding From the Physical to the Psychological.   Several changes in children's views of themselves during middle childhood illustrate the quest for

Industry-versus-inferiority stage   The period from ages 6 to 12 characterized by a focus on efforts to attain competence in meeting the challenges presented by parents, peers, school, and the complexities of the world

As children become older, they begin to characterize themselves in terms of their psychological attributes (such as being a responsible and nurturing individual) as well as their physical achievements.

self-understanding. For one thing, they begin to view themselves less in terms of external, physical attributes and more in terms of psychological traits (Aboud & Skerry, 1983; Marsh, Craven, & Debus, 1998).

For instance, 6-year-old Carey describes herself as "a fast runner and good at drawing"—both characteristics based in external activities relying on motor skills. In contrast, 11-year-old Meiping characterizes herself as "pretty smart, friendly, and helpful to my friends." Meiping's portrayal is based on psychological characteristics, inner traits that are more abstract than the younger child's descriptions. The use of inner traits to determine self-concept results from the child's increasing cognitive skills, a development that we discussed in Chapter 12.

In addition to shifting focus from external characteristics to internal, psychological traits, children's views of themselves become more differentiated. According to Erikson, children are seeking out endeavors in which they can be successfully industrious. As they get older, children discover that they may be good at some things and not so good at others. Ten-year-old Ginny, for instance, comes to understand that she is good at arithmetic but not very good at spelling; 11-year-old Alberto determines that he is good at softball but doesn't have the stamina to play soccer very well.

Children's self-concepts become divided into personal and academic spheres. In fact, as shown in Figure 13-1, self-concept in each of the four domains can be broken down even further. For instance, the nonacademic self-concept includes the components of physical appearance, peer relations, and physical ability. Academic self-concept is similarly divided by subject area. Research on students' self-concepts in English, mathematics, and nonacademic realms has found that the separate self-concepts are not always correlated, although there is overlap among them (Burnett, 1996; Marsh, 1990; Marsh & Holmes, 1990).

Social Comparison.   If someone asks you how good you are at math, how would you respond? Most of us would compare our performance to others who are roughly of the same age and educational level. It is unlikely that we'd answer the question by comparing ourselves either to Albert Einstein or to a kindergartner just learning about numbers.

Elementary school children begin to follow the same sort of reasoning when they seek to understand how able they are. Whereas earlier they tended to consider their abilities in terms of absolutes, now they begin to use social comparison processes to determine their levels of accomplishment during middle childhood (M. R. Weiss, Ebbeck, & Horn, 1997).

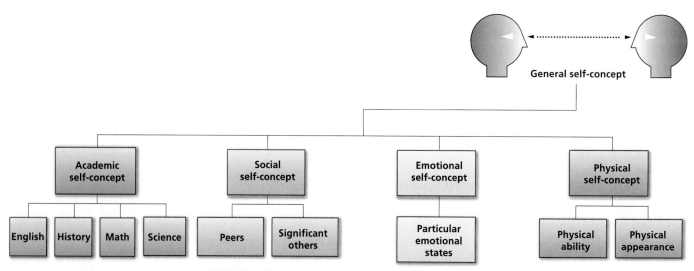

FIGURE 13-1   **LOOKING INWARD: THE DEVELOPMENT OF SELF**

As children get older, their views of themselves become more differentiated, comprising several personal and academic spheres. What cognitive changes make this possible?

(*Source:* Adapted from Shavelson, Hubner, & Stanton, 1976)

Social comparison is the desire to evaluate one's own behavior, abilities, expertise, and opinions by comparing them to those of others. According to a theory first suggested by psychologist Leon Festinger (1954), when concrete, objective measures of ability are lacking, people turn to *social reality* to evaluate themselves. Social reality refers to understanding that is derived from how others act, think, feel, and view the world.

But who provides the most adequate comparison? Generally, children compare themselves to persons who are similar along relevant dimensions. Consequently, when they cannot objectively evaluate their ability, children during middle childhood increasingly look to others who are similar to themselves (Ruble et al., 1989; Suls & Wills, 1991; J. Wood, 1989).

Downward Social Comparison. Although children typically compare themselves to similar others, in some cases—particularly when their self-esteem is at stake—they choose to make *downward social comparisons* with others who are obviously less competent or less successful (Pyszczynski, Greenberg, & La Prelle, 1985).

Downward social comparison protects self-image. By comparing themselves to those who are less able, children ensure that they will come out on top and thereby preserve an image of themselves as successful.

Downward social comparison helps explain why some students in elementary schools with low achievement levels are found to have stronger academic self-esteem than very capable students in schools with high achievement levels. The reason seems to be that students in the low-achievement schools observe others who are not doing terribly well academically, and they feel relatively good by comparison. In contrast, students in the high-achievement schools may find themselves competing with a more academically proficient group of students, and their perception of their performance may suffer in comparison. In some ways, then, it is better to be a big fish in a small pond than a small fish in a big one (Marsh & Parker, 1984).

Self-Esteem: Developing a View of Oneself

Children don't dispassionately view themselves just in terms of an itemization of physical and psychological characteristics. Instead, they make judgments about themselves as being good, or bad, in particular ways. **Self-esteem** is an individual's overall and specific positive and negative self-evaluation. Whereas self-concept reflects beliefs and cognitions about the self, self-esteem is more emotionally oriented (Baumeister, 1993; Davis-Kean & Sandler, 2001).

Self-esteem develops in important ways during middle childhood. As we've noted, children increasingly compare themselves to others, and as they do, they assess how well they measure up to society's standards. In addition, they increasingly develop their own internal standards of success, and they can see how well they compare to those.

One of the advances that occurs during middle childhood is an increasing differentiation of self-esteem. At the age of 7, most children have self-esteem that reflects a global, undifferentiated view of themselves. If their overall self-esteem is positive, they assume that they are relatively good at all things. Conversely, if their overall self-esteem is negative, they assume that they are inadequate at most things (Marsh & Shavelson, 1985; Harter, 1990b). As children progress into the middle childhood years, however, their self-esteem, like their self-concept, becomes differentiated: higher for some areas that they evaluate and lower for others.

Increase and Decline in Self-Esteem.   Generally, the self-esteem of most children tends to increase during middle childhood, with a brief decline around the age of 12. Although there are probably several reasons for the decline, the main one appears to be the school transition that typically occurs around this age: Students leaving elementary school and entering middle school and junior high school show a decline in self-esteem, which then gradually rises again (Eccles et al., 1989; Twenge & Campbell, 2001).

Children with chronically low self-esteem face a tough road, in part because their self-esteem becomes enmeshed in a cycle of failure that grows increasingly difficult to break.

Social comparison   Evaluation of one's own behavior, abilities, expertise, and opinions by comparing them to those of others

Self-esteem   An individual's overall and specific positive and negative self-evaluation

FIGURE 13-2   A CYCLE OF LOW SELF-ESTEEM

Because children with low self-esteem may expect to do poorly on a test, they may experience high anxiety and not work as hard as those with higher self-esteem. As a result, they actually do perform badly on the test, which in turn confirms their negative view of themselves. How would a teacher help such a student break this cycle?

Assume, for instance, that Harry, a student with chronically low self-esteem, is facing an important test. Because of his low self-esteem, he expects to do poorly. As a consequence, he is anxious—so anxious that he is unable to concentrate well and study effectively. Furthermore, he may decide not to study much because he figures that if he's going to do badly anyway, why bother studying?

Ultimately, of course, Harry's high anxiety and lack of effort bring about the result he expected: He does poorly on the test. This failure, which confirms Harry's expectation, reinforces his low self-esteem, and the cycle of failure continues (see Figure 13-2).

Promoting Self-Esteem.   Parents can help break the cycle of failure by promoting their children's self-esteem. The best way to do this is through the use of the *authoritative* child-rearing style that we discussed in Chapter 10. Authoritative parents are warm and emotionally supportive while still setting clear limits for their children's behavior. In contrast, other parenting styles have less positive effects on self-esteem. Parents who are highly punitive and controlling send a message to their children that they are untrustworthy and unable to make good decisions—a message that can undermine children's sense of adequacy—and highly indulgent parents can create a false sense of self-esteem in their children, which may ultimately be just as damaging to children (Damon, 1995).

Ethnicity and Self-Esteem.   If you were a member of a minority group whose members routinely experienced prejudice and discrimination, how might your self-esteem be affected?

For many decades, developmentalists hypothesized—and found supportive evidence for the notion—that members of minority groups would feel lower self-esteem than members of majority groups. In particular, the evidence seemed clear that African Americans had lower self-esteem than whites (Deutsch, 1967).

Some of the first evidence was found in a set of pioneering studies a generation ago, in which African American children were shown a black doll and a white doll (K. B. Clark & Clark, 1947). In the study, the children received a series of requests, including "Give me the doll that looks bad" and "Give me the doll that is a nice color." In every case, the African American children preferred white dolls over black ones. The interpretation drawn from the study was that the self-esteem of the African American children was low.

Subsequent research in the 1950s and 1960s supported the notion that children showed lower self-esteem as a consequence of being members of minority groups that were discriminated against. In fact, some research even suggested that members of minority groups preferred members of majority groups to members of their own groups and that they rejected membership in their own groups, showing a form of self-hatred due to minority group status (Milner, 1983).

DEVELOPMENTAL DIVERSITY

Are the Children of Immigrant Families Well Adjusted?

Immigration to the United States has undergone a significant rise in the past 30 years. More than 13 million children in the nation are either foreign-born or the children of immigrants—one fifth of the total population of children.

How well are these children of immigrants faring? Quite well. In fact, in some ways they are better off than their nonimmigrant peers. For example, they tend to have equal or better grades in school and better health-related adjustment than children whose parents were born in the United States. Psychologically, they also do quite well, showing similar levels of self-esteem to nonimmigrant children, although they do report feeling less popular and less in control of their lives (K. M. Harris, 2000; Kao, 2000; Kao & Tienda, 1995).

Why is the adjustment of immigrant children so generally positive? One answer is that often their socioeconomic status is relatively high. In spite of stereotypes that immigrant families come from lower social classes, many, in fact, are well educated and come to the United States seeking greater opportunities.

But socioeconomic status is only part of the story, for many immigrant children are not financially well off. However, they are often more highly motivated to succeed and place greater value on education than children in nonimmigrant families. In addition, many immigrant children come from societies that emphasize collectivism, and consequently they may feel more obligation and duty toward their family to succeed. Finally, having a strong cultural identity relating to their country of origin may prevent immigrant children from adopting undesirable behaviors—perceived as "American"—such as materialism or selfishness (Fuligni, Tseng, & Lam, 1999; M. A. Gibson & Bhachu, 1991).

In short, during the middle childhood years, children in immigrant families typically do quite well in the United States. The story is less clear, however, when immigrant children reach adolescence and adulthood. Although some research suggests that the longer an individual has been in the United States, the lower the level of adjustment, the findings are far from definitive. Research is just beginning to clarify the process by which adjustment changes over the course of the life span (Fulgini, 1998; Portes & Rumbaut, 2001).

Immigrant children tend to fare quite well in the United States, partly because many come from societies that emphasize collectivism and consequently may feel more obligation and duty to their family to succeed. What are some other cultural differences that can support the success of immigrant children?

In pioneering research conducted several decades ago, African American girls' preference for white dolls was viewed as an indication of low self-esteem. More recent evidence, however, suggest that white and African American children show little difference in self-esteem.

More recent theorizing, however, sheds a different light on the issue of self-esteem and racial group membership. According to *social identity theory,* members of a minority group are likely to accept the negative views held by a majority group only if they perceive that there is little realistic possibility of changing the power and status differences between the groups. If minority group members feel that prejudice and discrimination can potentially be reduced, and they blame society for the prejudice and not themselves, self-esteem should not differ between majority and minority groups (Abrams & Hogg, 1999; Tajfel, 1982; J. C. Turner & Onorato, 1999; M. E. Turner et al., 1992).

In fact, as group pride and ethnic awareness on the part of minority group members has grown, differences in self-esteem between members of different ethnic groups have narrowed. This trend has further been supported by an increased sensitivity to the importance of multiculturalism (Duckitt, 1994; Goodstein & Ponterotto, 1997; Harter, 1990a).

R E V I E W *&* A P P L Y

Review

- According to Erik Erikson, children in middle childhood are in the industry-versus-inferiority stage.

- In the middle childhood years, children begin to use social comparison and self-concepts based on psychological rather than physical characteristics.

- During the middle childhood years, self-esteem is based on comparisons with others and internal standards of success; if self-esteem is low, the result can be a cycle of failure.

Applying Child Development

- Give an example of the relationship between low self-esteem and the cycle of failure in an area other than academics. How might the cycle of failure be broken?

● *From an educator's perspective:* If industriousness is a more accurate predictor of future success than IQ, how might an individual's industriousness be improved? Should this be a focus of schooling?

Relationships: Building Friendship in Middle Childhood

In Lunch Room Number Two, Jamillah and her new classmates chew slowly on sandwiches and sip quietly on straws from cartons of milk. . . . Boys and girls look timidly at the strange faces across the table from them, looking for someone who might play with them in the schoolyard, someone who might become a friend.

For these children, what happens in the schoolyard will be just as important as what happens in the school. And when they're out on the playground, there will be no one to protect them. No child will hold back to keep from beating them at a game, humiliating them in a test of skill, or harming them in a fight. No one will run interference or guarantee membership in a group. Out on the playground, it's sink or swim. No one automatically becomes your friend. (Kotre & Hall, 1990, pp. 112–113)

As Jamillah and her classmates demonstrate, friendship comes to play an increasingly important role during middle childhood. Children grow progressively more sensitive to the importance of friends, and building and maintaining friendships becomes a large part of children's social lives.

The formation of friendships influences children's development in several ways. For instance, friendships provide children with information about the world and other people, as well as about themselves. Friends provide emotional support that allows children to respond more effectively to stress. They also provide support by helping children avoid being the target of aggression (Hodges et al., 1999).

Recall the Hendrickson twins described in the chapter prologue. They and their neighborhood friends are experiencing all of these benefits—and more. They are learning that friends can teach children how to manage and control their emotions and help them interpret their own emotional experiences. Friendships also provide a training ground for communicating and interacting with others, and they can foster intellectual growth. Finally, friendships allow children to practice their skills in forming close relationships with others—skills that will become increasingly important in their future lives (Asher & Parker, 1991; J. R. Harris, 1998; Hartup & Stevens, 1997; Nangle & Erdley, 2001).

Although friends and other peers become increasingly influential throughout middle childhood, their influence does not become greater than the influence of parents and other family members. Most developmentalists reject the argument that peers are the primary influence on psychological functioning, instead suggesting that it is a combination of factors that determines children's development during middle childhood (K. M. Harris, 2000; Vandell, 2000). For that reason, we'll talk more about the influence of family later in this chapter.

Stages of Friendship: Changing Views of Friends

During middle childhood, a child's conception of the nature of friendship undergoes some profound changes. According to developmental psychologist William Damon, a child's view of friendship passes through three distinct stages (Damon, 1977; Damon & Hart, 1988).

Stage 1: Basing Friendship on Others' Behavior.   In the first stage, which ranges from around 4 to 7 years of age, children see friends as others who like them and with whom they

Mutual trust is considered the centerpiece of friendship during middle childhood.

share toys and other activities. They view the children with whom they spend the most time as their friends. For instance, a kindergartner who was asked, "How do you know that someone is your best friend?" responded in this way:

> I sleep over at his house sometimes. When he's playing ball with his friends he'll let me play. When I slept over, he let me get in front of him in 4-squares. He likes me. (Damon, 1983, p. 140)

What children in this first stage don't do much of, however, is take others' personal qualities into consideration. For instance, they don't see their friendships as being based on their peers' unique positive personal traits. Instead, they use a very concrete approach to deciding who is a friend, dependent primarily on others' behavior. They like other children who share and with whom they can share, and they don't like those who don't share, who hit, or who don't play with them. In sum, in the first stage, friends are viewed largely in terms of presenting opportunities for pleasant interactions.

Stage 2: Basing Friendship on Trust. In the next stage, however, children's view of friendship becomes more complicated. Lasting from around age 8 to age 10, this stage covers a period in which children take others' personal qualities and traits into consideration, as well as the rewards they provide. But the centerpiece of friendship in this second stage is mutual trust. Friends are seen as those who can be counted on to help out when they are needed. This means that violations of trust are taken very seriously, and friends cannot make amends for such violations just by engaging in positive play, as they might at earlier ages. Instead, the expectation is that formal explanations and formal apologies must be provided before a friendship can be reestablished.

Stage 3: Basing Friendship on Psychological Closeness. The third stage of friendship begins toward the end of middle childhood, from 11 to 15 years of age. During this period, children begin to develop the view of friendship that they hold during adolescence. Although we'll discuss this perspective in detail in Chapter 16, the main criteria for friendship shift toward intimacy and loyalty. Friendship is characterized by psychological closeness, mutual disclosure, and exclusivity. By the time they reach the end of middle childhood, children seek out friends who will be loyal, and they come to view friendship not so much in terms of shared activities as in terms of the psychological benefits that friendship brings (Newcomb & Bagwell, 1995).

Children also develop clear ideas about which behaviors they seek in their friends and which they dislike. As can be seen in Table 13-1, fifth and sixth graders most enjoy others who invite them to participate in activities and who are helpful, both physically and psychologically. In contrast, displays of physical or verbal aggression, among other behaviors, are disliked.

Individual Differences in Friendship: What Makes a Child Popular?

Why is it that some children, like the Hendrickson twins described in the chapter prologue, are the schoolyard equivalent of the life of the party, while others are social isolates whose overtures toward their peers are dismissed or disdained?

Developmentalists have attempted to answer this question by examining individual differences in popularity, seeking to identify the reasons why some children climb the ladder of popularity while others remain firmly on the ground (Bigelow, Tesson, & Lewko, 1996; Bukowski & Cillessen, 1998).

Status Among School-Age Children: Establishing One's Position. Who's on top? Although school-age children are not likely to articulate such a question, the reality of children's friendships is that they exhibit clear hierarchies in terms of **status.** Status is the

Status The relative position of a person ascribed by other members of a group

TABLE 13-1	MOST-LIKED AND LEAST-LIKED BEHAVIORS THAT CHILDREN NOTE IN THEIR FRIENDS, IN ORDER OF IMPORTANCE

Most-Liked Behaviors	Least-Liked Behaviors
Having a sense of humor	Verbal aggression
Being nice or friendly	Expressions of anger
Being helpful	Dishonesty
Being complimentary	Being critical or criticizing
Inviting one to participate in games, etc.	Being greedy or bossy
Sharing	Physical aggression
Avoiding unpleasant behavior	Being annoying or bothersome
Giving one permission or control	Teasing
Providing instructions	Interfering with achievements
Loyalty	Unfaithfulness
Performing admirably	Violating of rules
Facilitating achievements	Ignoring others

(*Source:* Adapted from Zarbatany, Hartmann, & Rankin, 1990)

relative position of a person ascribed by other members of a group. Children who have higher status have greater access to available resources, such as games, toys, books, and information. In contrast, lower status children are more likely to follow the lead of children of higher status. Thinking back to the children in the chapter prologue, for example, when Bryan Hendrickson declared that the cardboard boxes would become spaceships, the other boys seemed willing to follow his direction.

Status and Popularity.   Status is an important determinant of children's friendships. High-status children tend to form friendships with higher status individuals, while lower status children are more likely to have friends of lower status. Status is also related to the number of friends a child has: Higher status children are more apt to have a greater number of friends than those of lower status. Consider, for example, the large group of friends that hang around the Hendrickson boys' house.

But it is not only the quantity of social interactions that separates high-status children from lower status children; the nature of their interactions is also different. Higher status children are more likely to be viewed as friends by other children. They are more likely to form cliques, groups that are viewed as exclusive and desirable, and they tend to interact with a greater number of other children. In contrast, children of lower status are more likely to play with younger or less popular children (Ladd, 1983).

In short, popularity is a reflection of children's status. School-age children who are mid to high in status are more likely to initiate and coordinate joint social behavior, making their general level of social activity higher than that of children low in social status (Erwin, 1993).

What Personal Characteristics Lead to Popularity?   Popular children share several personality characteristics. They are usually helpful, cooperating with others on joint projects. Again, consider the Hendrickson twins and their cooperative games with the cardboard boxes. Popular children are also funny, tending to have good senses of humor and to appreciate others' attempts at humor. Compared with children who are less popular, they are better able to understand others' emotional experiences by more accurately reading their nonverbal

A variety of factors lead some children to be unpopular and socially isolated from their peers.

behavior. They can also control their nonverbal behavior more effectively, thereby presenting themselves well. In short, popular children are high in **social competence,** the collection of individual social skills that permit individuals to perform successfully in social settings (R. S. Feldman, Philippot, & Custrini, 1991; R. S. Feldman, Tomasian, & Coats, 1999; Saarni, 1999).

Generally speaking, then, popular children are typically friendly, open, and cooperative. But some popular children have a very different profile. For example, one significant subgroup of popular boys displays an array of negative behaviors. Despite acting aggressive, being disruptive, and causing trouble, they are seen as cool and tough by their peers, and they are remarkably popular (Rodkin et al., 2000).

Social Problem-Solving Abilities.   Another factor that relates to children's popularity is their skill at social problem solving. **Social problem solving** refers to the use of strategies for solving social conflicts in ways that are satisfactory both to oneself and to others. Because social conflicts arise frequently among school-age children—even between the best of friends—successful strategies for dealing with them are an important element of social success (G. Downey et al., 1998; Laursen, Hartup, & Koplas, 1996; A. J. Rose & Asher, 1999).

According to developmental psychologist Kenneth Dodge (1985b; Dodge & Crick, 1990; Dodge & Price, 1994; Dodge et al., 1986), successful social problem solving proceeds through a series of steps that correspond to children's information processing strategies (see Figure 13-3). Dodge argues that the manner in which children solve social problems is a consequence of the decisions that they make at each point in the sequence.

By carefully delineating each of the stages, Dodge provides a means by which interventions can be targeted toward a specific child's deficits. For instance, some children routinely misinterpret the meaning of other children's behavior (Step 2) and then respond according to their misinterpretation.

Consider, for example, Frank, a fourth grader, who is playing a game with Bill. While playing the game, Bill begins to get angry because he is losing. If Frank mistakenly assumes that Bill is angry not because he is losing but because of something that Frank has done, Frank's misunderstanding may lead *him* to react with anger, making the situation more volatile. If Frank had interpreted the source of Bill's anger more accurately, Frank might have been able to behave in a more effective manner, thereby defusing the situation.

Generally, children who are popular are better at interpreting the meaning of others' behavior. Furthermore, they possess a wider inventory of techniques for dealing with social

Social competence   The collection of social skills that permit individuals to perform successfully in social settings

Social problem solving   The use of strategies for solving social conflicts in ways that are satisfactory both to oneself and to others

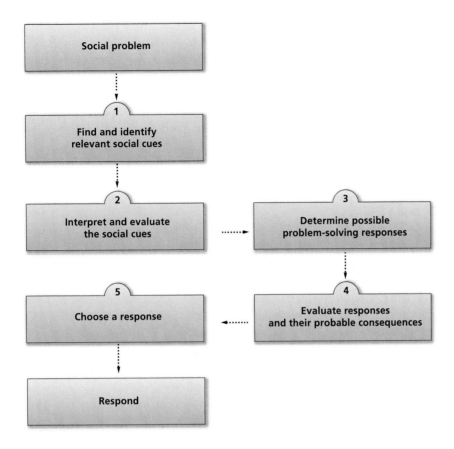

FIGURE 13-3   PROBLEM-SOLVING STEPS

Children's problem solving proceeds through several steps involving different information processing strategies. In what ways might an educator use children's problem-solving skills as a learning tool?

(*Source:* Adapted from Dodge, 1985.)

problems. In contrast, less popular children tend to be less effective at understanding the causes of others' behavior, and their strategies for dealing with social problems are more limited (A. J. Rose & Asher, 1999; Vitaro & Pelletier, 1991).

Teaching Social Competence.   Can anything be done to help unpopular children learn social competence? Happily, the answer appears to be yes. Several programs have been developed to teach children a set of social skills that seem to underlie general social competence. For example, in one experimental program, a group of unpopular fifth and sixth graders were taught the skills that underlie such abilities as holding a conversation with friends. They were taught ways to disclose material about themselves, to learn about others by asking questions, and to offer help and suggestions to others in a nonthreatening way. Compared with a group of children who did not receive such training, the children who were in the experiment interacted more with their peers, held more conversations, developed higher self-esteem, and—most critically—were more accepted by their peers than before training (Asher & Rose, 1997; Bierman & Furman, 1984).

Similarly, children in another program were taught to be more adept at decoding the meaning of facial expressions, thereby becoming more sensitive to others' emotions and moods. As a result of their training, some children in the program became noticeably better at making friends and getting along with their teachers (Nowicki & Oxenford, 1989).

Gender and Friendships: The Sex Segregation of Middle Childhood

Boys are idiots. Girls have cooties.

Those are the typical views offered by boys and girls regarding members of the opposite sex during the elementary school years. Avoidance of the opposite sex becomes quite pronounced during those years, to the degree that the social networks of most boys and girls

Though same-sex groupings dominate in middle childhood, when boys and girls do make occasional forays into each others' territory, there are often romantic overtones. Such behavior has been termed "border work."

consist almost entirely of same-sex groupings (P. A. Adler, Kless & Adler, 1992; Gottman, 1986; T. E. Lewis & Phillipsen, 1998). For example, the Hendrickson twins, described in the chapter prologue, spent much of the day with their all-boy group of friends before allowing their older sister and some other girls and boys to join them.

Interestingly, the segregation of friendships by sex occurs in almost all societies. In nonindustrialized societies, same-sex segregation may be the result of the types of activities that children engage in. For instance, in many cultures, boys are assigned one type of chore and girls another (Harkness & Super, 1985; Whiting & Edwards, 1988). Participation in different activities may not provide the whole explanation for sex segregation, however: Even children in more developed countries who attend the same schools and participate in many of the same activities tend to avoid members of the other sex.

Boys' Friendship Patterns. When boys and girls make occasional forays into the territory of the other sex, the action often has romantic overtones. For instance, girls may threaten to kiss a boy, or boys might try to lure girls into chasing them. Such behavior, termed "border work," helps emphasize the clear boundaries that exist between the sexes. In addition, it may pave the way for future interactions that do involve romantic or sexual interests when school-age children reach adolescence and cross-sex interactions become more socially endorsed (Beal, 1994; Thorne, 1986).

The lack of boy–girl interaction in the middle childhood years means that boys' and girls' friendships are restricted to members of their own sex. Furthermore, the nature of friendships within these two groups is quite different (Lansford & Parker, 1999).

Boys typically have larger networks of friends than girls, and they tend to play in groups, rather than pairing off. The status hierarchy is usually fairly blatant, with an acknowledged leader and members falling into particular levels of status. Because of the fairly rigid rankings that represent the relative social power of those in the group, known as the **dominance hierarchy,** members of higher status can safely question and oppose children lower in the hierarchy (Beal, 1994).

Boys tend to be concerned with their place in the status hierarchy, and they attempt to maintain their status and improve on it. This makes for a style of play known as *restrictive.* In restrictive play, interactions are interrupted when a child feels that his status is challenged. Thus a boy who feels that he is unjustly challenged by a peer of lower status may attempt to end the interaction by scuffling over a toy or otherwise behaving assertively. Consequently, boys' play tends to come in bursts, rather than in more extended, tranquil episodes (Benenson & Apostoleris, 1993; Boulton & Smith, 1990).

The language of friendship used among boys reflects their concern over status and challenge. For instance, consider this conversation between two boys who were good friends (Goodwin, 1990, p. 37):

Child 1: Why don't you get out of my yard?
Child 2: Why don't you *make* me get out the yard?
Child 1: I *know* you don't want that.
Child 2: You're not gonna make me get out the yard cuz you can't.
Child 1: Don't force me.
Child 2: You can't. Don't force me to hurt you [*snickers*].

Girls' Friendship Patterns. Friendship patterns among girls are quite different. Rather than having a wide network of friends, school-age girls focus on one or two "best friends" who are of relatively equal status. In contrast to boys, who seek out status differences, girls profess to avoid differences in status, preferring to maintain friendships at equal-status levels.

Conflicts among school-age girls are usually solved through compromise, by ignoring the situation, or by giving in, rather than by seeking to make one's own point of view prevail. In

Dominance hierarchy Rankings that represent the relative social power of the individuals in a group

sum, the goal is to smooth over disagreements, making social interaction easy and nonconfrontational (Goodwin, 1990).

According to developmental psychologist Carole Beal (1994), the motivation of girls to solve social conflict indirectly does not stem from a lack of self-confidence or from apprehension over the use of more direct approaches. In fact, when school-age girls interact with other girls who are not considered friends or with boys, they can be quite confrontational. However, among friends their goal is to maintain equal-status relationships—ones lacking a dominance hierarchy.

The language used by girls tends to reflect their view of relationships. Rather than blatant demands ("Give me the pencil"), girls are more apt to use language that is less confrontational and directive. Girls tend to use indirect forms of verbs, such as "Let's go to the movies" or "Would you want to trade books with me?" rather than "I want to go to the movies" or "Let me have these books" (Goodwin, 1980, 1990).

Promoting Friendships Across Racial and Ethnic Lines: Integration in and out of the Classroom

Are friendships color-blind? For the most part, the answer is no. Children's closest friendships tend to be with others of the same race. In fact, as children age, the number and depth of friendships outside their own racial group decline. By the time they are 11 or 12, it appears that African American children become particularly aware of and sensitive to the prejudice and discrimination directed toward members of their race, and they are more apt to make ingroup–outgroup distinctions (Bigler, Jones, & Lobliner, 1997; Hartup, 1983; Singleton & Asher, 1979).

For instance, when third graders from one longtime integrated school were asked to name a best friend, around one quarter of white children and two thirds of African American children chose a child of the other race. In contrast, by the time they reached 10th grade, less than 10 percent of whites and 5 percent of African Americans named a different-race best friend (Asher, Singleton, & Taylor, 1982; Singleton & Asher, 1979).

Nevertheless, although they may not choose each other as best friends, whites and African Americans—as well as members of other minority groups—can show a high degree of mutual acceptance. This pattern is particularly true in schools with ongoing integration efforts. This makes sense: A good deal of research supports the notion that contact between majority and minority group members can reduce prejudice and stereotyping (Gaertner et al., 1990; Kerner & Aboud, 1998; Wells & Crain, 1994).

As children age, the number of and depth of friendships outside their own racial group tend to decline. What are some ways in which schools can foster mutual acceptance?

Stopping the Torment: Dealing With Schoolyard Bullies

For some children, school represents a battleground in which they live in constant fear of being the victim of a bully. In fact, according to the National Association of School Psychologists, 160,000 U.S. schoolchildren stay home from school each day because they are afraid of being bullied (Bosworth, Espelage, & Simon, 1999; Juvonen & Graham, 2001).

Characteristics of Bullying Victims. The victims of bullies typically share several characteristics. Most often they are loners who are fairly passive. They often cry easily, and they tend to lack the social skills that might otherwise defuse a bullying situation with humor. But even children without these characteristics are bullied at some point in their school careers: Some 90 percent of middle school students report being bullied at some point in their time at school, beginning as early as the preschool years (Crick, Casas, & Ku, 1999; S. K. Egan & Perry, 1998; D. Schwartz et al., 1997).

Characteristics of Bullies. About 15 percent of students bully others at one time or another. About half of all bullies come from abusive homes—meaning, of course, that half don't.

VIDEO CLIP

Bullying

BECOMING AN INFORMED CONSUMER OF DEVELOPMENT

Increasing Children's Social Competence

Considering that building and maintaining friendships is of great importance in children's development, is there anything that parents and teachers can do to increase children's social competence?

The answer is a clear yes. Among the strategies that work are the following:

- Encourage social interaction. Teachers can devise ways in which children are led to take part in group activities, and parents can encourage membership in such groups as Brownies and Cub Scouts or participation in team sports.

- Teach listening skills to children. Show them how to listen carefully and respond to the underlying meaning of a communication as well as its overt content.

- Make children aware that people display emotions and moods nonverbally and that consequently they should pay attention to others' nonverbal behavior, as well as to what they are saying verbally.

- Teach conversational skills, including the importance of asking questions and self-disclosure. Encourage students to use "I" statements, in which they clarify their own feelings or opinions, and to avoid making generalizations about others.

- Don't ask children to choose teams or groups publicly. Instead, assign children randomly: It works just as well in ensuring a distribution of abilities across groups and avoids the public embarrassment of a situation in which some children are consistently chosen last.

They tend to watch more television containing violence, and they misbehave more at home and at school than nonbullies. When their bullying gets them into trouble, they may try to lie their way out of the situation, and they show little remorse for their victimization of others. Furthermore, bullies are more likely than their peers to break the law as adults. Although bullies are sometimes popular with other children, some ironically find themselves victims of bullying (Haynie et al., 2001; Kaltiala-Heino et al., 2000; Olweus, 1995).

Despite the prevalence of bullying, it is possible to stop the behavior. Victims of bullying can be taught skills that help them defuse difficult circumstances that might otherwise lead to being victimized. They can be taught to protect themselves by leaving situations in which bullying can occur. They also need to increase their tolerance, understanding that they should not get upset by a bully's taunts and realizing that they are not responsible for the bully's behavior (Garrity, Jens, & Porter, 1996; K. Sullivan, 2000).

Of course, changing the behavior of the bully is also a good way to address the problem. For instance, bullies and their classmates need to be taught the importance of creating a caring, warm environment. Social pressures can help by fostering the adoption of school norms in which bullying is not tolerated, by helping children develop positive social skills, and by encouraging bullies to keep their bullying in check (Seppa, 1996).

REVIEW & APPLY

Review

- Children's understanding of friendship changes from the sharing of enjoyable activities, through the consideration of personal traits that can meet their needs, to a focus on intimacy and loyalty.

- Friendships in childhood display status hierarchies. Improvements in social problem solving and social information processing can lead to better interpersonal skills and greater popularity.

- Boys and girls engage increasingly in same-sex friendships, with boys' friendships involving group relationships and girls' friendships characterized by equal-status pairings.

- Interracial friendships decrease in frequency as children age, but equal-status contacts among members of different races can promote mutual acceptance and appreciation.

- Many children are the victims of bullies during their school years, but both victims and bullies can be taught to reduce bullying.

Applying Child Development

- Do you think the stages of friendship are a childhood phenomenon, or do adults' friendships go through similar stages? Is there any stage of friendship that stands out more than others during middle childhood development?

- *From a social worker's perspective:* How might it be possible to decrease the segregation of friendships along racial lines? What factors would have to change in individuals or in society?

Home and School in Middle Childhood

Tamara's mother, Brenda, waited outside the door of Brenda's second-grade classroom for the end of the school day. Tamara came over to greet her mother as soon as she spotted her. "Mom, can Anna come over to play today?" Tamara asked. Brenda had been looking forward to having some time alone with Tamara, who had spent the last three days at her dad's house. But, Brenda reflected, Tamara hardly ever got to ask kids over after school, so she agreed to the request. Unfortunately, it turned out today wouldn't work for Anna's family, so they tried to find an alternate date. "How about Thursday?" Anna's mother suggested. Before Tamara could reply, her mother reminded her, "You'll have to ask your dad. You're at his house that night." Tamara's expectant face fell. "OK," she mumbled.

How will Tamara's adjustment be affected by splitting her time between the two homes where she lives with her divorced parents? What about the adjustment of her friend, Anna, whose parents live together but both work outside the home? These are just two of the questions we need to consider as we look at the ways that children's schooling and home life affect their lives during middle childhood.

Family: The Changing Home Environment

The original plot goes like this: First comes love. Then comes marriage. Then comes Mary with a baby carriage. But now there's a sequel: John and Mary break up. John moves in with Sally and her two boys. Mary takes the baby, Paul. A year later Mary meets Jack, who is divorced with three children. They get married. Paul, barely 2 years old, now has a mother, a father, a stepmother, a stepfather, and five stepbrothers and stepsisters—as well as four sets of grandparents (biological and step) and countless aunts and uncles. And guess what? Mary's pregnant again. (Kantrowitz & Wingert, 1990, p. 24)

We've already noted in earlier chapters the changes that have occurred in the structure of the family over the past few decades. With an increase in the number of parents who both work outside of the home, a soaring divorce rate, and a rise in single-parent families, the environment faced by children passing through middle childhood in the 21st century is very different from that of prior generations.

One of the basic challenges for children and their parents is to navigate the independence that increasingly characterizes children's behavior during middle childhood. During the period, children move from being almost completely controlled by their parents to increasingly controlling their own destinies—or at least their everyday conduct. Middle childhood, then, is a period of **coregulation.** Increasingly, parents provide broad guidelines for conduct, while children have control over their everyday behavior. For instance, parents may urge their daughter to buy a balanced, nutritious school lunch each day, but their daughter's decision to regularly buy pizza and two desserts is very much her own.

Family Life.   During the middle years of childhood, children spend significantly less time with their parents. Still, parents remain the major influence in their children's lives, and they are seen as providing essential assistance, advice, and direction (Furman & Buhrmester, 1992).

Siblings also have an important influence on children during middle childhood, for good and for bad. Although brothers and sisters can provide support, companionship, and a sense of security, they can also be a source of strife.

Sibling rivalry can occur, with siblings competing or quarreling with one another. Such rivalry can be most intense when siblings are similar in age and of the same gender (N. Howe & Ross, 1990). Parents may intensify sibling rivalry by being perceived as favoring one child over another. Such perceptions may or may not be accurate. For example, older siblings may be permitted more freedom, which the younger sibling may interpret as favoritism. In some cases, perceived favoritism not only leads to sibling rivalry but may also damage the self-esteem of the younger sibling (Ciricelli, 1995).

What about children who have no siblings? Although only children have no opportunity to develop sibling rivalry, they also miss out on the benefits that siblings can bring. Still, despite the stereotype that only children are spoiled and self-centered, the reality is that they are as well adjusted as children with brothers and sisters. In fact, in some ways only children are better adjusted, often having higher self-esteem and stronger motivation to achieve. This is particularly good news for parents in the People's Republic of China, where a strict one-child policy is in effect. In fact, Chinese only children often perform better than children with siblings (Falbo, 1992; Jiao, Ji, & Jing, 1996).

When Both Parents Work: How Do Children Fare?   In most cases, children whose parents both work full time outside of the home fare quite well. Children whose parents are loving, are sensitive to their children's needs, and provide appropriate substitute care typically develop no differently from children in families in which one of the parents does not work (Harvey, 1999; L. W. Hoffman, 1989).

The good adjustment of children whose mothers and fathers both work relates to the psychological adjustment of the parents, especially mothers. In general, women who are satisfied with their lives tend to be more nurturing with their children. When work provides a high level of satisfaction, then, mothers who work outside the home may be more psychologically supportive of their children. Thus it is not so much a question of whether a mother chooses to work full time, to stay at home, or to arrange some combination of the two. What matters is how satisfied she is with the choices she has made (Barnett & Rivers, 1992; L. A. Gilbert, 1994; Scarr, Phillips, & McCartney, 1989).

Although we might expect that children whose parents both work would spend comparatively less time with their parents than children with one parent at home full time, research suggests otherwise. Children with mothers and fathers who work full time spend essentially the

Coregulation   Joint control of children's behavior exercised by the parents and the children themselves

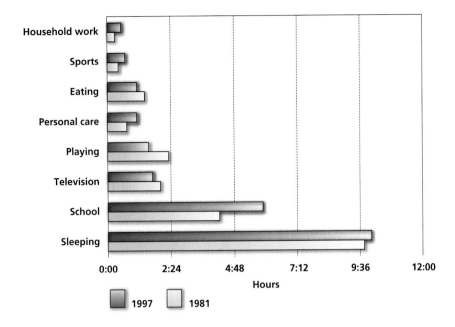

FIGURE 13-4 HOW KIDS SPEND THEIR TIME

Whereas the amount of time children spend on certain activities has remained constant over the years, the time spent on others, such as playing and eating, have shown significant changes. What might account for these changes?

(*Source:* Hofferth & Sandberg, 1998)

same amount of time with family, in class, with friends, and alone as children in families where one parent stays at home (Galambos & Dixon, 1984; M. H. Richards & Duckett, 1991, 1994).

What are children doing during the day? The activities that take the most time are sleeping and school. The next most frequent activities are watching television and playing, followed closely by personal care and eating. This has changed little over the past 20 years (see Figure 13-4). What has changed is the amount of time spent in supervised, structured settings. In 1981, about 40 percent of a child's day was free time; by the late 1990s, only 25 percent of a child's day was unscheduled (Hofferth & Sandberg, 1998). (For another view of what children do with their time, see the *From Research to Practice* box.)

Divorce. Having divorced parents, like Tamara, the second grader described earlier, is no longer very distinctive. Only around half the children in the United States spend their entire childhood living in the same household with both their parents. The rest will live in single-parent homes or with stepparents, grandparents, or other nonparental relatives, and some will end up in foster care.

How do children react to divorce? The answer depends on how soon you ask the question following the divorce. Immediately after a divorce, the reactions can be quite devastating. Both children and parents may show several types of psychological maladjustment for a period that may last from 6 months to 2 years. For instance, children may experience anxiety, depression, sleep disturbances, or phobias. Even though children most often live with their mothers following a divorce, the quality of the mother–child relationship declines in the majority of cases (Gottman, 1993; Holroyd & Sheppard, 1997; Wallerstein, Lewis, & Blakeslee, 2000).

During the early stage of middle childhood, children whose parents are divorcing often blame themselves for the breakup. By the age of 10, children feel pressure to choose sides, taking the position of either the mother or the father. They thereby experience some degree of divided loyalty (Shaw, Winslow, & Flanagan, 1999; Wallerstein & Blakeslee, 1989).

Although researchers agree that the short-term consequences of divorce can be quite disruptive, the longer-term consequences are less clear. Some researchers find the outcomes become less destructive 18 months to 2 years later, and most children begin to return to their predivorce state of psychological adjustment. For many children, there are minimal long-term consequences (E. M. Hetherington & Kelly, 2002).

However, some researchers suggest that the fallout from divorce lingers. For example, twice as many children of divorced parents require psychological counseling as children from intact

---

○— FROM RESEARCH TO PRACTICE —○

Home and Alone: What Do Children Do?

When 10-year-old Johnetta Colvin comes home after finishing a day at Martin Luther King Elementary School; the first thing she does is grab a few cookies and turn on the computer. She takes a quick look at her e-mail and then goes over to the television and typically spends the next hour watching. During commercials, she takes a look at her homework.

What she doesn't do is chat with her parents, neither of whom are there. She's home alone.

Johnetta is far from unique. Johnetta is a **self-care child,** the term for children who let themselves into their homes after school and wait alone until their parents return from work. Some 12 to 14 percent of children in the United States between the ages of 5 and 12 spend some time alone after school, without adult supervision (Berger, 2000; Lamorey, Robinson, & Rowland, 1998).

In the past, concern about self-care children centered on their lack of supervision and the emotional costs of being alone. In fact, such children were previously called *latchkey children,* raising connotations of sad, pathetic, and neglected children.

However, a new view of self-care children is emerging. According to sociologist Sandra Hofferth, given the hectic schedule of many children's lives, a few hours alone may provide a helpful period of decompression. Furthermore, it may provide the opportunity for children to develop a greater sense of autonomy (Hofferth & Sandberg, 2001).

Research has identified few differences between self-care children and children who return to homes with parents. Although some children report negative experiences while at home by themselves (such as loneliness), they seem emotionally undamaged by the experience. In addition, if they stay at home by themselves rather than "hanging out" unsupervised with friends, they may avoid involvement in activities that can lead to difficulties (Belle, 1999; Goyette-Ewing, 2000; Long & Long, 1983; Rodman & Cole, 1987).

In sum, the consequences of being a self-care child are not necessarily harmful. In fact, such children may develop an enhanced sense of independence and competence. Furthermore, the time spent alone provides an opportunity to work uninterrupted on homework and school or personal projects. Some findings even suggest that children with employed parents can have higher self-esteem because they feel they are contributing to the household in significant ways (L. W. Hoffman, 1989).

---

families. In addition, people who have experienced parental divorce are more at risk for experiencing divorce themselves later in life (Amato & Booth, 2001; Wallerstein et al., 2000).

How children react to divorce depends on several factors. One is the economic standing of the family the child is living with. In many cases, divorce brings a decline in both parents' standards of living. When this occurs, children may be thrown into poverty.

In other cases, the negative consequences of divorce are less severe because the divorce reduces hostility and anger in the home. If the predivorce household was overflowing with parental strife, the greater calm of a postdivorce household may be beneficial to children. This is particularly true for children who maintain a close, positive relationship with the parent with whom they do not live. For some children, then, experiencing a parental divorce is an improvement over living with parents who have an intact but unhappy marriage, high in conflict (Booth & Edwards, 1989; Cherlin, 1993; Davies & Cummings, 1994; Gelles, 1994; A. E. Gottfried & Gottfried, 1994).

Single-Parent Families. Almost one quarter of all children under the age of 18 in the United States live with only one parent. If present trends continue, almost three quarters of American children will spend some portion of their lives in a single-parent family before they are 18 years old. For minority children, the numbers are even higher: More than 60 percent of African American children and 35 percent of Hispanic children under the age of 18 live in single-parent homes (Demo & Acock, 1991; U.S. Bureau of the Census, 1994, 2000).

In most cases of single-parent households, no spouse was ever present (that is, the mother never married), the spouses have divorced, or the spouse is absent (see Figure 13-5). In the vast majority of cases, the single parent who is present is the mother.

Self-care children Children who let themselves into their homes after school and wait alone until their caretakers return from work; formerly known as *latchkey children*

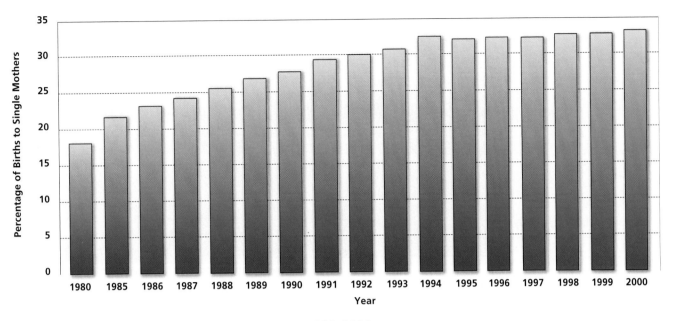

FIGURE 13-5   INCREASE OF SINGLE MOTHERS, 1980–2000

The percentage of mothers without spouses has increased significantly in recent decades. Do you think this trend has affected the approaches used by social workers?

(*Source:* National Center for Health Statistics, 2002)

What consequences are there for children living in homes with just one parent? This is a difficult question to answer. Much depends on whether a second parent was present earlier and the nature of the parents' relationship at that time. Furthermore, the economic status of the single-parent family plays a role in determining the consequences for children. Single-parent families are often less well off financially than two-parent families, and living in relative poverty has a negative impact on children (Gongla & Thompson, 1987; Gottman & Katz, 1989).

In sum, the impact of living in a single-parent family is not, by itself, negative or positive. Given the large number of single-parent households, the stigma once associated with such families has largely disappeared. The ultimate consequences for children depend on a variety of factors that accompany single parenthood, such as the economic status of the family, the amount of time that the parent is able to spend with the child, and the degree of stress in the household.

Living in Blended Families.   For many children, the aftermath of divorce includes the subsequent remarriage of one or both parents. In fact, more than 10 million households in the United States contain at least one spouse who has married more than once. More than 5 million remarried couples have at least one stepchild living with them in what have come to be called **blended families.** Overall, 17 percent of all children in the United States live in blended families (U.S. Bureau of the Census, 2001a).

Living in a blended family is challenging for the children involved. There is often a fair amount of *role ambiguity,* in which roles and expectations are unclear. Children may be uncertain about their responsibilities, how to behave to stepparents and stepsiblings, and how to make a host of decisions that have wide-ranging implications for their role in the family. For instance, a child in a blended family may have to choose which parent to spend each vacation and holiday with or to decide between the conflicting suggestions they have received from biological parent and stepparent (Cherlin, 1993; Dainton, 1993).

In many cases, however, school-age children in blended families often do surprisingly well. In comparison to adolescents, who have more difficulties, school-age children often

Based on current trends, almost three quarters of American children will spend some portion of their lives in a single-parent family. What are some possible consequences for a child raised in a single-parent household?

Blended family   A household consisting of a couple and at least one child from a prior relationship

Blended families result when previously married husbands and wives with children marry.

adjust relatively smoothly to blended arrangements, for several reasons. For one thing, the family's financial situation is often improved after a parent remarries. In addition, in a blended family, more people are available to share the burden of household chores. Finally, the simple fact that the family contains more individuals can increase the opportunities for social interaction (E. M. Hetherington & Clingempeel, 1992; E. M. Hetherington, Stanley-Hagan, & Anderson, 1989).

However, not all children adjust well to life in a blended family. Some find the disruption of routine and of established networks of family relationships difficult. For instance, a child who is used to having her mother's complete attention may find it difficult to observe her mother showing interest and affection to a stepchild. The most successful blending of families occurs when the parents support children's self-esteem and create a culture in which all family members feel included. Generally, the younger the children, the easier the transition is within a blended family (Buchanan, Maccoby, & Dornbusch, 1996).

Group Care: Orphanages in the 21st Century

The term *orphanage* evokes images of pitiful youngsters clothed in rags, eating porridge out of tin cups, and housed in huge, prisonlike institutions. The reality today is different. Even the term *orphanage* is rarely used, having been replaced by *group home* or *residential treatment center*. Typically housing a relatively small number of children, group homes are used for children whose parents are no longer able to care for them adequately.

Almost 100,000 children in the United States live in group homes, and three quarters enter as victims of neglect and abuse. Although most of them can be returned to their homes following intervention by social service agencies, the remaining one quarter are so psychologically damaged due to abuse or other causes that they are likely to remain there throughout childhood. Children who have developed severe problems, such as high levels of aggression or anger, have difficulty finding adoptive families, and in fact it is often difficult to find even temporary foster families who are able to cope with their emotional and behavior problems (Berrick, 1998; Carnegie Task Force, 1994; Roche, 2000).

Although some politicians have suggested that an increase in group care is a solution to complex social problems associated with unwed mothers who become dependent on welfare, experts in providing social services and psychological treatment are not so sure. For one thing, group homes cannot always consistently provide the support and love potentially available in a family setting. Moreover, group care is not cheap: It can cost some $40,000 per year to support a child in group care—about 10 times the cost of maintaining a child in foster care or on welfare (Fanshel, Finch, & Grundy, 1990, 1992; Roche, 2000).

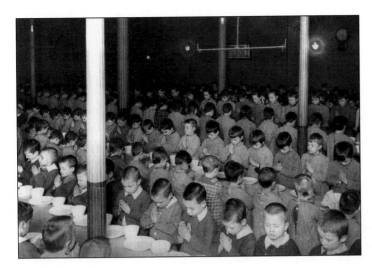

Although the orphanages of the early 1900s were crowded and institutional (left), today the equivalent, called group homes or residential treatment centers (right), are much more pleasant.

Other experts argue that group care is inherently neither good nor bad. Instead, the consequences of living away from one's family may be quite positive, depending on the particular characteristics of the staff of the group home and whether child and youth care workers are able to develop an effective, stable, and strong emotional bond with a specific child. On the other hand, if a worker is unable to form a meaningful relationship with a child in a group home, the results may well be unfavorable (McKenzie, 1997; Reddy & Pfeiffer, 1997; Shealy, 1995).

School: The Academic Environment

Where do children spend most of their time? During the school year, at least, children spend more of their day in the classroom than anywhere else. It is not surprising, then, that schools have a profound impact on children's lives, shaping and molding not only their ways of thinking but also the ways they view the world. We turn now to a number of critical aspects of schooling in middle childhood.

Attributions: How Children Explain Academic Success and Failure.   Most of us, at one time or another, have done poorly on a test. Think back to how you felt when you received a bad grade. Did you feel shame? Anger at the teacher? Fear of the consequences? According to psychologist Bernard Weiner (1985, 1994), your response in such situations is determined largely by the particular causes to which you attribute your failure. And the kinds of attributions you make ultimately determine how hard you strive to do well on future tests.

Weiner has proposed a theory of motivation based on people's **attributions,** their explanations for the reasons behind their behavior. He suggests that people attempt to determine the causes of their academic success or failure by considering three basic dimensions: (1) whether the cause is internal (dispositional) or external (situational), (2) whether the cause is stable or unstable, and (3) whether the cause is controllable or uncontrollable.

Consider, for instance, a student named Henry who gets a 98, the highest score in the class, on an exam. To what can he attribute his success? He might think it is a result of his ability, his effort in studying for the test, or the fact that he was rested and relaxed when he took the test. Because each of these factors is related to what Henry is or has done, they are internal attributions. But note how they differ on the other two dimensions: Ability is a stable, enduring factor, while study effort and degree of relaxation are both unstable and can fluctuate from one test to another. Finally, study effort and degree of relaxation differ from each other in

Attributions People's explanations for the outcomes of their behavior

terms of controllability: Whereas amount of effort is controllable, degree of relaxation may not be.

How people feel about their performance in a situation is a factor of the attributions they make for that performance. For example, the internal–external dimension can be linked to esteem-related emotions. When a success is attributed to internal factors, students tend to feel pride, but failure attributed to internal factors causes shame. The stability dimension determines future expectations about success and failure. Specifically, when students attribute success or failure to factors that are relatively stable and invariant, they are apt to expect similar performance in the future. In contrast, when they attribute performance to unstable factors such as effort or luck, their expectations about future performance are relatively unaffected.

Finally, the controllability dimension affects emotions that are directed toward others. If children feel that failure was due to factors within their control—such as lack of effort—they are apt to experience anger, at themselves and others; but if the failure was uncontrollable, they are likely to feel sadness.

Cultural Comparisons: Individual Differences in Attribution.   Not everyone comes to the same conclusions about the sources of success and failure. In fact, among the strongest influences on people's attributions are their race, ethnicity, and socioeconomic status. Because different experiences give us different perceptions about the ways things in the world fit together, it is not surprising that there are subcultural differences in how achievement-related behaviors are understood and explained.

One important difference is related to racial factors: African Americans are less likely than whites to attribute success to internal rather than external causes. Specifically, African American children sometimes feel that task difficulty and luck (external causes) are the major determinants of their performance outcomes. They may believe that even if they put in maximum effort, prejudice and discrimination will prevent them from succeeding (Friend & Neale, 1972; S. Graham, 1990, 1994; Ogbu, 1988).

Such an attributional pattern, one that overemphasizes the importance of external causes, can cause problems. Attributions to external factors reduce a student's sense of personal responsibility for success or failure. But when attributions are based on internal factors, they suggest that a change in behavior—such as increased effort—can bring about a change in success (Glasgow et al., 1997; S. Graham, 1986, 1990).

African Americans are not the only group susceptible to maladaptive attributional patterns. Women, for example, often attribute their unsuccessful performance to low ability, an

Doonesbury © 1988, G. B. Trudeau. Reprinted with permission of Universal Press Syndicate. All rights reserved.

uncontrollable factor. Ironically, though, they do not attribute successful performance to high ability but rather to factors outside their control. A belief in this pattern suggests the conclusion that even with future effort, success will be unattainable. Females who hold these views may be less inclined to expend the effort necessary to improve their rate of success (Dweck, 1991; Dweck & Bush, 1976; D. A. Phillips & Zimmerman, 1990; L. J. Nelson & Cooper, 1997).

DEVELOPMENTAL DIVERSITY

Cultural Differences in Attributions for Academic Performance: Explaining Asian Academic Success

Consider two students, Ben and Hannah, each performing poorly in school. Suppose you thought that Ben's poor performance was due to unalterable, stable causes, such as a lack of intelligence, while Hannah's was produced by temporary causes, such as a lack of hard work. Who would you think would ultimately do better in school?

If you are like most people, you'd probably predict that the outlook was better for Hannah. After all, Hannah could always work harder, but it is difficult for someone like Ben to develop higher intelligence.

According to psychologist Harold Stevenson, this reasoning lies at the heart of the superior school performance of Asian students, compared with students in the United States. Stevenson's research suggests that teachers, parents, and students in the United States are likely to attribute school performance to stable, internal causes, while people in Japan, China, and other East Asian countries are more likely to see temporary, situational factors as the cause of their performance. The Asian view, which stems in part from ancient Confucian writings, tends to accentuate the necessity of hard work and perseverance (Stevenson & Lee, 1990).

This cultural difference in attributional styles is displayed in several ways. For instance, surveys show that mothers, teachers, and students in Japan and Taiwan all believe strongly that students in a typical class tend to have the same amount of ability. In contrast, mothers, teachers, and students in the United States are apt to disagree, arguing that there are significant differences in ability among the various students (see Figure 13-6).

It is easy to imagine how such different attributional styles can influence teaching approaches. If, as in the United States, students and teachers seem to believe that ability is fixed and locked in, poor academic performance will be greeted with a sense of failure and reduced motivation to work harder to overcome it. In contrast, Japanese teachers and students are apt to see failure as a temporary setback, due to their lack of hard work. After making such an attribution, they are more apt to expend increased effort on future academic activities.

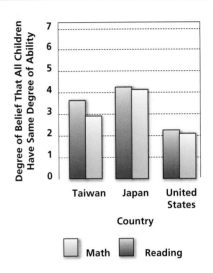

FIGURE 13-6   MOTHERS' BELIEFS IN CHILDREN'S ABILITY

Compared to mothers in Taiwan and Japan, U.S. mothers were less apt to believe that all children have the same degree of underlying, innate ability. Subjects responded using a 7-point scale, where 1 indicated "strongly disagree" and 7 indicated "strongly agree." What are the implications of this finding for educators in the United States?

(*Source:* Stevenson & Lee, 1990)

Some developmentalists have suggested that these different attributional orientations may explain the fact that Asian students frequently outperform American students in international comparisons of student achievement (Linn, 1997; Wheeler, 1998). Because Asian students tend to assume that academic success results from hard work, they may put greater effort into their schoolwork than American students, who believe that their inherent ability determines their performance. These arguments suggest that the attributional style of students and teachers in the United States might well be maladaptive. They also argue that the attributional styles taught to children by their parents may have a significant effect on their future success (Chao, 1996; C. Chen & Stevenson, 1995; M. J. Eaton & Dembo, 1997; Geary, 1996; Little & Lopez, 1997).

Review

- Self-care children may develop independence and enhanced self-esteem from their experience.

- The consequences of divorce depend on such factors as financial circumstances and the comparative levels of tension in the family before and after the divorce.

- The effects of being raised in a single-parent household depend on financial circumstances, the amount of parent–child interaction, and the level of tension in the family.

- Attributional patterns differ along individual, cultural, and gender dimensions.

Applying Child Development

- Politicians often speak of "family values." How does this concept relate to the diverse family situations covered in this chapter, including divorced parents, single parents, blended families, working parents, self-care children, and group care?

- *From a health care worker's perspective:* How might the development of self-esteem in middle childhood be affected by a divorce? Can constant hostility and tension between parents lead to a child's health problems?

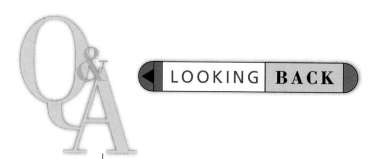

- **In what ways do children's views of themselves change during middle childhood?**

- According to Erik Erikson, children in the middle childhood years are in the industry-versus-inferiority stage, focusing on achieving competence and responding to a wide range of personal challenges.

- Children in the middle childhood years begin to view themselves in terms of psychological characteristics and to differentiate their self-concepts into separate areas. They use social comparison to evaluate their behavior, abilities, expertise, and opinions.

- **How does self-esteem affect behavior?**

- Children in these years are developing self-esteem; those with chronically low self-esteem can become trapped in a cycle of failure in which low self-esteem feeds on itself by producing low expectations and poor performance.

- **What sorts of relationships and friendships are typical of middle childhood?**

- Children's friendships display status hierarchies, and their understanding of friendship passes through stages, from a focus on mutual liking and time spent together through the consideration of personal traits and the rewards that friendship provides to an appreciation of intimacy and loyalty.

○ **What are the factors involved in popularity and unpopularity?**

• Popularity in children is related to traits that underlie social competence. Because of the importance of social interactions and friendships, developmental researchers have engaged in efforts to improve social problem-solving skills and the processing of social information.

○ **How do sex and ethnicity affect friendships?**

• Boys and girls in middle childhood increasingly prefer same-sex friendships. Male friendships are characterized by groups, status hierarchies, and restrictive play. Female friendships tend to involve one or two close relationships, equal status, and a reliance on cooperation.

• Cross-race friendships diminish in frequency as children age. Equal-status interactions among members of different racial groups can lead to improved understanding, mutual respect and acceptance, and a decreased tendency to stereotype.

○ **How do today's diverse family and care arrangements affect children?**

• Children in families in which both parents work outside the home generally fare well. Self-care children who fend for themselves after school may develop independence and a sense of competence and contribution.

• Immediately after a divorce, the effects on children in the middle childhood years can be serious, depending on the financial condition of the family and the hostility level between spouses before the divorce.

• The consequences of living in a single-parent family depend on the financial condition of the family and, if there had been two parents, the level of hostility that existed between them. Blended families present challenges to the child but can also offer opportunities for increased social interaction.

• Children in group care tend to have been victims of neglect and abuse. Many can be helped and placed with their own or other families, but about 25 percent of them will spend their childhood years in group care.

EPILOGUE

 n this chapter, we considered social and personality development in the middle childhood years and examined self-esteem. We discussed relationships and friendships, and we looked at the ways gender and race can affect friendships. We considered the changing nature of family arrangements and the effects of these changes on social and personality development. We concluded with a discussion of attributions of success and failure, expectancies, and emotional intelligence.

Return to the prologue—about Bryan and Christopher Hendrickson—and answer the following questions:

1. In what ways do the Hendrickson twins' activities exemplify Erikson's industry-versus-inferiority stage of development?

2. How does the children's play with the boxes differ from the way they would have played during the preschool years?

3. What would you expect is the basis of the friendship between the twins and the other kids in the prologue?

4. What educated guesses can you make about the popularity, status, and social competence of the twins based on the information in the prologue?

KEY TERMS AND CONCEPTS

industry-versus-inferiority
   stage (p. 383)
social comparison (p. 385)
self-esteem (p. 385)
status (p. 390)

social competence (p. 392)
social problem solving
   (p. 392)
dominance hierarchy
   (p. 394)

coregulation (p. 398)
self-care children (p. 400)
blended family (p. 401)
attributions (p. 403)

he growth of the body, the amazing strides in cognitive development and the use of language, and the changes in self-definition and social relationships during the middle childhood years have been the major topics of Part 4. We saw how children use their expanded physical and cognitive abilities to negotiate new ways of solving problems, understanding their role in the world, and dealing with other people more effectively. We observed the foundation of many future developments that will become more evident in adolescence and adulthood. In our discussion of adolescence, for example, we'll see that children's concepts of themselves continue to become more differentiated and that they develop varying levels of self-esteem for different areas of their lives.

We continued our consideration of the major developmental theorists— Piaget, Erikson, Vygotsky, and others—and their explanations of the key events and milestones that children experience during these years, and we extended our discussion of the influences that society exerts on children through phenomena associated with family life, divorce, schooling, popularity, and friendship. The major theorists will figure heavily in our discussion of adolescence, too, and we'll explore the pressures of society that adolescents face.

In brief, what we can see in the middle childhood period is a tremendous outward expansion of the individual, embarking on a personal redefinition process that will continue, with even more noticeable effects, in adolescence. We can uncover the roots of independence and self-determination in middle childhood, and we can appreciate the extent to which the individual and the social environment are intertwined in this period. As we move on into adolescence, we'll see how the relationships between individuals and the society in which they live become even more important. ■

14

Physical Development in Adolescence

CHAPTER OUTLINE

PHYSICAL MATURATION

Growth During Adolescence: The Rapid Pace of Physical and Sexual Maturation

Puberty: The Start of Sexual Maturation

Body Image: Reactions to Physical Changes in Adolescence

Nutrition and Food: Fueling the Growth of Adolescence

Brain Development and Thought: Paving the Way for Cognitive Growth

STRESS AND COPING

The Origins of Stress: Reacting to Life's Challenges

Meeting the Challenge of Stress

THREATS TO ADOLESCENTS' WELL-BEING

Illegal Drugs

Alcohol: Use and Abuse

Tobacco: The Dangers of Smoking

Sexually Transmitted Diseases

PROLOGUE: Picture of Health

 assie Harwood is the picture of good health. Ask her how she sees herself, and she pipes back: "Athletic, intelligent, and energetic." The 13-year-old honors student from Potomac, Maryland, loves soccer and lacrosse. She runs as fast and plays as hard as the boys in her class. Her three brothers joke that she eats more than anyone else in the house. Sure, she has the requisite posters of Leonardo Di Caprio on her bedroom wall. But next to Leo hang pictures of her real idol, U.S. Women's Soccer Team star Mia Hamm. The only supermodels in Cassie's room are those sporting milk mustaches. She has more than 100 of the popular "Got Milk?" ads plastered to her wall. "They're cool," says Cassie. "All that stuff with all the skinny models is just not me." (Clemetson, 1998, pp. 14, 16)

Cassie Harwood (left) and her soccer coach.

LOOKING **AHEAD** ▶

Cassie Harwood's positive outlook on life is no accident. With high-achieving parents who provide consistent encouragement to excel, she has developed into an adolescent success story.

Yet even Cassie—who faces few of the threats to her well-being that less fortunate adolescents must overcome—cannot avoid encountering the significant challenges that arise during adolescence. In this chapter and the ones that follow, we examine these challenges as we consider the basic issues and questions that underlie adolescence.

Adolescence is the developmental stage between childhood and adulthood. It begins and ends imprecisely, starting just before the teenage years and ending just after them. This imprecision reflects the nature of society's treatment of the period: Adolescents are considered to be no longer children but not yet adults. Clearly, though, adolescence is a time of considerable physical, cognitive, and social growth and change (L. W. Hoffman, 1996).

This chapter focuses on physical growth during adolescence. We begin by considering the extraordinary physical maturation that occurs during adolescence, triggered by the onset of puberty. We then discuss the consequences of early and late maturation and how they differ for males and females. We also consider nutrition during adolescence. After discussing the causes—and consequences—of obesity, we discuss eating disorders, which are surprisingly common during the period.

We then turn to stress and coping. We examine the causes of stress during adolescence, as well as the short- and long-term consequences of stress. We also discuss the ways in which people can cope with it.

The chapter concludes with a discussion of several of the major threats to adolescents' well-being. We'll focus on drug, alcohol, and tobacco use, as well as sexually transmitted diseases.

After reading this chapter, then, you'll be able to answer the following questions:

- ● **What physical changes do adolescents experience?**
- ● **What are the consequences of early and late maturation?**
- ● **What are the nutritional needs and concerns of adolescents?**
- ● **What are the effects of stress, and what can be done about it?**
- ● **What are some threats to the well-being of adolescents?**
- ● **What dangers do adolescent sexual practices present, and how can these dangers be avoided?**

Physical Maturation

For the male members of the Awa tribe, the beginning of adolescence is signaled by an elaborate and—to Western eyes—gruesome ceremony marking the transition from childhood to adulthood. First the boys are whipped for 2 or 3 days with sticks and prickly branches. Through the whipping, the boys atone for their previous infractions and honor tribesmen who were killed in warfare.

But that's just for starters. In the next phase of the ritual, sharpened sticks are punched into the boys' nostrils, producing a torrent of blood. Then adults force a 5-foot length of vine into the boys' throats, causing them to choke and vomit. Finally, deep cuts are made in the boys' genitals. Jeering onlookers poke at the cuts to make them bleed even more.

Adolescence The developmental stage between childhood and adulthood

Most of us probably feel gratitude that we did not have to endure such physical trials when we entered adolescence. But members of Western cultures do have their own rites of passage into adolescence, admittedly less fearsome, such as bar mitzvahs and bat mitzvahs at age 12 or 13 for Jewish boys and girls and confirmation ceremonies in many Christian denominations (Delaney, 1995; Dunham, Kidwell, & Wilson, 1986; Herdt, 1998).

Regardless of the nature of the ceremonies celebrated by various cultures, their underlying purpose tends to be similar from one culture to the next: symbolically celebrating the onset of the physical changes that take a child to the doorstep of adulthood.

Growth During Adolescence: The Rapid Pace of Physical and Sexual Maturation

The growth in height and weight during adolescence can be breathtaking. In only a few months, an adolescent can grow several inches and require a whole new wardrobe. In fact, in a period of only 4 years, boys and girls undergo a transformation, at least in physical appearance, from children to young adults.

The dramatic physical changes are evidence of the **adolescent growth spurt,** a period of very rapid growth in height and weight. During the adolescent growth spurt, height and weight increase as quickly as they did during infancy. On average, boys grow 4.1 inches a year and girls 3.5 inches a year. Some adolescents grow as much as 5 inches in a single year (Tanner, 1972).

The adolescent growth spurts begin at different times for boys and for girls. On average, girls start their spurts 2 years earlier than boys, and they complete them earlier as well. As you can see in Figure 14-1, girls begin their spurts around age 10, boys at about age 12. For about 2 years starting at age 11, girls tend to be a bit taller than boys. This soon changes, however: By the age of 13, boys, on average, are taller than girls—a state of affairs that persists for the remainder of the life span.

Puberty: The Start of Sexual Maturation

Like the growth spurt, **puberty,** the period during which the sexual organs mature, begins earlier for girls than for boys. Girls start puberty at around age 11 or 12, and boys begin at around age 13 or 14. However, there are wide variations among individuals. For example, some girls begin puberty as early as 7 or 8 or as late as 16 years of age.

Adolescent growth spurt   A period of very rapid growth in height and weight during adolescence

Puberty   The period of maturation during which the sexual organs mature

VIDEO CLIP

Physical Growth

Note the changes that have occurred in just a few years in these pre- and postpuberty photos of the same boy.

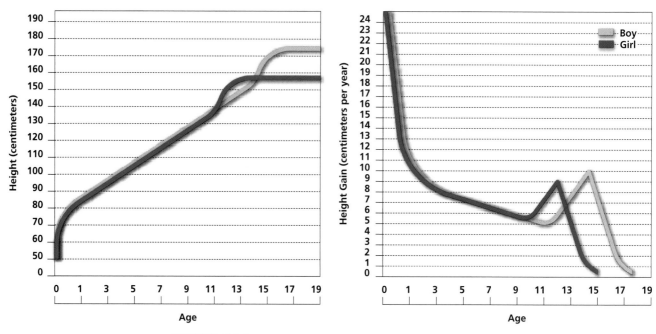

FIGURE 14-1   GROWTH PATTERNS

Patterns of growth are depicted in two ways. The figure on the left shows height at a given age, while the figure on the right shows the height *increase* that occurs from birth through the end of adolescence. Notice that girls begin their growth spurt around age 10; boys, about 2 years later. However, by the age of 13, boys tend to be taller than girls. Why is it important that educators be aware of the social consequences of being taller or shorter than average for boys and girls?

(*Source:* Adapted from Cratty, 1986)

Girls begin their growth spurt several years earlier than boys, leading to significant disparities in mixed-gender settings.

Menarche   The onset of menstruation

Puberty begins when the pituitary gland in the brain signals other glands in children's bodies to begin producing the sex hormones, androgens (male hormones) or estrogens (female hormones), at adult levels. The pituitary gland also signals the body to increase production of growth hormones that interact with the sex hormones to cause the growth spurt and puberty.

Puberty in Girls.   What triggers the start of puberty in girls? Although we know what happens when it begins, no one has yet identified the reason that it begins at a particular time. However, it is clear that environmental and cultural factors play a role. For example, **menarche,** the onset of menstruation and probably the most conspicuous signal of puberty in girls, varies greatly in different parts of the world. In poorer, developing countries, menstruation begins later than in more economically advantaged countries. Even in wealthier countries, girls in more affluent groups begin to menstruate earlier than less affluent girls (see Figure 14-2). Consequently, it appears that girls who are better nourished and healthier are more apt to start menstruation at an earlier age than those who suffer from malnutrition or chronic disease. In fact, some studies have suggested that weight or the proportion of fat to muscle in the body play a role in the timing of menarche. For example, in the United States, athletes with a low percentage of body fat may start menstruating later than less active girls (M. P. M. Richards, 1996; Vizmanos & Marti-Henneberg, 2000).

Other factors can affect the timing of menarche. For instance, environmental stress due to such factors as parental divorce or high levels of family conflict can bring about an early onset (Graber, Brooks-Gunn, & Warren, 1995; Hulanicka, 1999; K. Kim & Smith, 1999; K. Kim, Smith, & Palermiti, 1997).

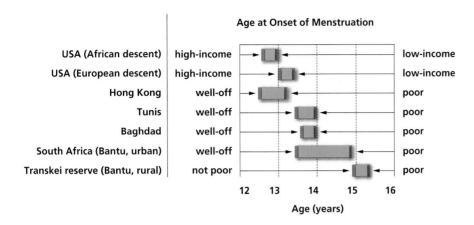

FIGURE 14-2   ONSET OF MENSTRUATION

The onset of menstruation occurs earlier in more economically advantaged countries than in poorer nations. But even in wealthier countries, girls living in more affluent circumstances begin to menstruate earlier than those living in less affluent situations.

(*Source:* Adapted from Eveleth & Tanner, 1976)

Over the past century, girls in the United States and other cultures have been entering puberty at earlier ages. Near the end of the 19th century, menstruation began, on average, around age 14 or 15, compared with today's 11 or 12. Other indictors of puberty, such as the age at which adult height and sexual maturity are reached, have also appeared at earlier ages, probably due to reduced disease and improved nutrition. The earlier start of puberty is an example of a significant **secular trend,** a statistical tendency observed over several generations.

Menstruation is just one of several changes in puberty that are related to the development of primary and secondary sex characteristics. **Primary sex characteristics** are associated with the development of the organs and structures of the body that are directly related to reproduction. In contrast, **secondary sex characteristics** are the visible signs of sexual maturity that do not involve the sex organs directly.

For instance, girls experience the development of primary sex characteristics through changes in the vagina and uterus as a result of maturation. Secondary sex characteristics include the development of breasts and pubic hair. Breasts begin to grow at around the age of 10, and pubic hair beings to appear at about age 11. Underarm hair appears about 2 years later.

For some girls, indications of puberty start unusually early. One out of 7 Caucasian girls develops breasts or pubic hair by age 8, and the figure is one out of 2 for African American girls. The reasons for this early onset of puberty—and the racial difference—are unclear, and the demarcation between normal and abnormal onset of puberty is a point of controversy among specialists (Endocrine Society, 2001; Lemonick, 2000).

Puberty in Boys.   Boys' sexual maturation follows a somewhat different course. In terms of primary sex characteristics, the penis and scrotum begin to grow at an accelerated rate around the age of 12, and they reach adult size about 3 or 4 years later. As boys' penises enlarge, the prostate gland and seminal vesicles, which produce semen (the fluid that carries sperm) also grow. This sets the stage for the first ejaculation, known as *spermarche* or *semenarche.* Spermarche usually occurs around the age of 13, although the body has already been producing sperm for more than a year. Initially, the semen contains relatively few sperm, but the amount of sperm increases significantly with age. At the same time, secondary sex characteristics develop. Pubic hair begins to grow around the age of 12, followed by the growth of underarm and facial hair. Finally, boys' voices deepen as the vocal cords become longer and the larynx larger. (Figure 14-3 summarizes the changes that occur in sexual maturation during early adolescence.)

The surge in production of hormones that triggers the start of adolescence may also lead to rapid swings in mood. For example, boys may have feelings of anger and annoyance that are associated with higher hormone levels. In girls, higher levels of hormones are associated with anger and depression (Buchanan, Eccles, & Becker, 1992; Hankin & Abramson, 2001; Stice, Presnell, & Bearman, 2001).

Secular trend   A statistical tendency observed over several generations

Primary sex characteristics   Characteristics that are associated with the development of the organs and structures of the body that directly relate to reproduction

Secondary sex characteristics   The visible signs of sexual maturity that do not involve the sex organs directly

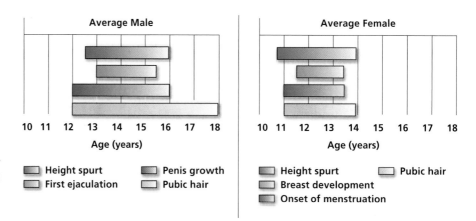

FIGURE 14-3   THE CHANGES OF SEXUAL MATURATION DURING ADOLESCENCE

Changes in sexual maturation occur for both males and females primarily during early adolescence.

(*Source:* Adapted from Tanner, 1978)

Body Image: Reactions to Physical Changes in Adolescence

Many parents notice that adolescents seem to suddenly develop a habit of spending inordinate amounts of time in the bathroom grooming and gazing at themselves. Unlike infants, who also undergo extraordinarily rapid growth, adolescents are well aware of what is happening to their bodies, and they may react with horror or joy. Few, though, are neutral about the changes they are witnessing (Mehran, 1997).

For instance, menarche produces several psychological consequences. In the past, Western society has emphasized the more negative aspects of menstruation, such as the potential of cramps and messiness, and girls tended to react to menarche with anxiety (Ruble & Brooks-Gunn, 1982). Today, however, society's view of menstruation tends to be more positive, in part because menstruation has been demystified and discussed more openly. (For instance, television commercials for tampons are commonplace.) As a consequence, menarche is typically accompanied by an increase in self-esteem, a rise in status, and greater self-awareness (Brooks-Gunn & Reiter, 1990; N. G. Johnson, Roberts, & Worell, 1999).

In some ways, a boy's first ejaculation is roughly equivalent to menarche in a girl. However, while girls generally tell their mothers about the onset of menstruation, boys rarely mention their first ejaculation to either their parents or their friends (J. H. Stein & Reiser, 1994). Why? One reason is that boys see the first ejaculation as an indication of their budding sexuality, an area about which they are quite uncertain and which they are therefore reluctant to discuss with others.

Menstruation and ejaculations generally occur privately, but changes in body shape and size are quite public. Consequently, teenagers entering puberty are frequently embarrassed by the changes that are occurring.

Girls, in particular, are often unhappy with their new bodies. This dissatisfaction is likely due to strong societal pressures regarding the ideal female shape, which frequently has little to do with the reality of mature women's bodies. Specifically, ideals of beauty in many Western countries call for an unrealistic thinness that is quite different from the actual shape of most women. Puberty brings a considerable increase in the amount of fatty tissue, as well as enlargement of the hips and buttocks—a far cry from the slenderness that society seems to demand (Attie & Brooks-Gunn, 1989; Tobin-Richards, Boxer, & Petersen, 1983; Unger & Crawford, 1999).

How children react to the onset of puberty depends, in part, on when it happens. Girls and boys who mature either earlier or later than most of their peers are especially affected by the timing of puberty.

Boys who mature early tend to be more successful in athletics and have a more positive self-concept. Explain why there can be a downside to early maturation.

Early Maturation.   For boys, early maturation is largely a plus. Early-maturing boys tend to be more successful at athletics, presumably because of their larger size. Furthermore, they tend to be more popular and to have a more positive self-concept.

The downside is that boys who mature early are more apt to have difficulties in school. They are more likely to become involved in delinquency and substance abuse because their larger size makes it more likely that they will seek out the company of older boys who may involve them in activities that are inappropriate for their age. Overall, though, the pluses seem to outweigh the minuses for early-maturing boys (Andersson & Magnusson, 1990; P. Duncan et al., 1985; Livson & Peskin, 1980).

The story is different for early-maturing girls. For them, the obvious changes in their bodies—such as the development of breasts—may lead them to feel uncomfortable and different from their peers (J. Lee, 1997; J. M. Williams & Currie, 2000). Moreover, because girls, in general, mature earlier than boys, early maturation tends to come at a very young age in the girl's life. Early-maturing girls may have to endure ridicule from their less mature classmates. Although girls who mature earlier tend to be sought after more as potential dates, they may not be socially ready to participate in the kind of dating situations that most girls deal with at a later age, and such situations may be psychologically challenging for early-maturing girls (Simmons & Blyth, 1987).

Whether girls face difficulties with early maturation depends in part on cultural norms and standards. For instance, in the United States, the notion of female sexuality is regarded with a degree of ambivalence. Consequently, the outcome of early maturation may be negative. In countries in which attitudes about sexuality are more liberal, the results of early maturation may be more positive. For example, in Germany, which has a more open view of sex, early-maturing girls have higher self-esteem than such girls in the United States. Furthermore, the consequences of early maturation vary even within the United States, depending on the views of girls' peer groups and on prevailing community standards regarding sex (Petersen, 2000; Silbereisen et al., 1989).

Late Maturation.   As with early maturation, the situation with late maturation is mixed, although in this case boys fare worse than girls. For instance, boys who are smaller and lighter than their more mature peers tend to be viewed as less attractive. Because of their smaller size, they are at a disadvantage when it comes to sports activities. Furthermore, because of the social convention that boys should be taller than their dates, the social lives of late-maturing boys may suffer. Ultimately, these difficulties may lead to a decline in self-concept. If this happens, the disadvantages of late maturation for boys could extend well into adulthood (Livson & Peskin, 1980; Mussen & Jones, 1957). Yet coping with the challenges of late maturation may actually help males in some ways. Late-maturing boys grow up to have certain positive qualities, such as assertiveness and insightfulness, and they are more creatively playful than early maturers.

The picture for late-maturing girls is a bit more complicated. Girls who mature later may be overlooked in dating and other mixed-sex activities during junior high and middle school, and they may have relatively low social status (Apter et al., 1981; Clarke-Stewart & Friedman, 1987). However, by the time they are in 10th grade and have begun to mature visibly, late-maturing girls' satisfaction with themselves and their bodies may be greater than that of early maturers. In fact, late-maturing girls may end up with fewer emotional problems. The reason? Late-maturing girls are more apt to fit the societal ideal of a slender, "leggy" body type than early maturers, who tend to look heavier in comparison (Petersen, 1988; Simmons & Blythe, 1987).

The Complexities of Early and Late Maturation.   In sum, the reactions to early and late maturation present a complex picture. Some developmentalists suggest that the concern over early and later maturation, and over the effects of puberty in general, may have been overemphasized in the past (Paikoff & Brooks-Gunn, 1990; Petersen & Crockett, 1985). Rather than focusing on the growth spurt and sexual maturation that occur during adolescence, they suggest that other factors, such as changes in peer groups, family dynamics, and

Anorexia nervosa   A severe and potentially life-threatening eating disorder in which individuals refuse to eat while denying that their behavior or skeletal appearance is out of the ordinary

particularly schools and other societal institutions, may be more pertinent in determining an adolescent's behavior. As we have seen repeatedly, we need to consider the complete constellation of factors affecting individuals in order to understand their development.

Nutrition and Food: Fueling the Growth of Adolescence

> A rice cake in the afternoon, an apple for dinner. That was Heather Rhodes's typical diet her freshman year at St. Joseph's College in Rensselaer, Indiana, when she began to nurture a fear (exacerbated, she says, by the sudden death of a friend) that she was gaining weight. But when Rhodes, now 20, returned home to Joliet, Illinois, for summer vacation a year and a half ago, her family thought she was melting away. "I could see the outline of her pelvis in her clothes . . . " says Heather's mother . . . , so she and the rest of the family confronted Heather one evening, placing a bathroom scale in the middle of the family room. "I told them they were attacking me and to go to hell," recalls Heather, who nevertheless reluctantly weighed herself. Her 5′7″ frame held a mere 85 pounds—down 22 pounds from her senior year in high school. "I told them they rigged the scale," she says. It simply didn't compute with her self-image. "When I looked in the mirror," she says, "I thought my stomach was still huge and my face was fat." (Sandler, 1994, p. 56)

Heather was suffering from a severe eating disorder known as anorexia nervosa.

Ordinarily, the rapid physical growth of adolescence is fueled by an increase in food consumption. Particularly during the growth spurt, adolescents eat substantial quantities of food, increasing their intake of calories dramatically. During the teenage years, the average girl requires some 2,200 calories a day, and the average boy 2,800.

Of course, not just any calories help nourish adolescents' growth. Several key nutrients are essential, including in particular calcium and iron. The calcium provided by milk aids bone growth and may prevent the later development of osteoporosis—thinning of bones—that affects 25 percent of women later in their lives. Similarly, iron is necessary to prevent iron-deficiency anemia, an ailment that is not uncommon among teenagers.

For most adolescents, the major nutritional issue is ensuring the consumption of a sufficient balance of appropriate foods. But for a substantial minority, nutrition can be a major concern and can create a real threat to health. Among the most prevalent problems are obesity and eating disorders like the one afflicting Heather Rhodes.

Obesity.   The most common nutritional concern during adolescence is obesity. Some 20 percent of adolescents are overweight, and 14 percent can be formally classified as obese (having a body weight that is more than 20 percent above average). The prevalence of obesity in adolescents has almost tripled in the past two decades (Office of the Surgeon General, 2001).

Although adolescents are obese for the same reasons as younger children, the psychological consequences may be particularly severe during a time of life when body image is of special concern. Furthermore, the potential health consequences of obesity during adolescence are also problematic. For instance, obesity taxes the circulatory system, increasing the likelihood of high blood pressure and diabetes. Finally, obese adolescents stand an 80 percent chance of becoming obese adults.

Anorexia Nervosa and Bulimia: The Frightening World of Eating Disorders.   The desire to avoid obesity sometimes becomes so strong that it turns into a problem. For instance, Heather Rhodes suffered from anorexia nervosa. **Anorexia nervosa** is a severe eating disorder in which individuals refuse to eat while denying that their behavior or their appearance, which may become skeletal, is out of the ordinary.

Anorexia is a severe psychological disorder; some 15 to 20 percent of its victims literally starve themselves to death. It primarily afflicts women between the ages of 12 and 40; those most susceptible are intelligent, successful, and attractive white adolescent girls from affluent

Obesity has become the most common nutritional concern during adolescence. In addition to issues of health, what are some psychological concerns about obesity in adolescence?

homes. Anorexia is also becoming a problem for more boys. About 10 percent of anorexics are male, and the percentage is increasing (Button, 1993; Crosscope-Happel et al., 2000; Hsu, 1990).

In the early stages, anorexics' lives become centered on food. Even though they eat little, they may go shopping often, collect cookbooks, talk about food, or cook huge meals for others. Although they may be incredibly thin, their body images are so distorted that they see their reflections in mirrors as disgustingly fat and keep trying to lose more and more weight. Even when they look like skeletons, they are unable to see what they have become.

Bulimia, another eating disorder, is characterized by binges on large quantities of food, followed by purges of the food through vomiting or the use of laxatives. Bulimics may eat an entire gallon of ice cream or a whole package of tortilla chips. But after such a binge, sufferers experience powerful feelings of guilt and depression, and they intentionally rid themselves of the food.

Although the weight of a person with bulimia remains fairly normal, the disorder is quite hazardous. The constant vomiting and diarrhea of the binge-and-purge cycles may produce serious lesions in the mouth and throat as well as a chemical imbalance that can lead to heart failure.

This young woman suffers from anorexia nervosa, a severe eating disorder in which people refuse to eat while denying that their behavior and appearance are out of the ordinary.

What Causes Eating Disorders?   The exact reasons for the occurrence of eating disorders are not clear, although several factors appear to be implicated. Dieting often precedes the development of eating disorders, as even normal-weight individuals are spurred on by societal standards of slenderness to seek to lower their weight. Furthermore, girls who mature earlier than their peers and who have a higher level of body fat are more susceptible to eating disorders during later adolescence. In addition, adolescents who are clinically depressed are more likely to develop eating disorders later (Cauffman & Steinberg, 1996; R. M. Gardner et al., 2000; Striegel-Moore, 1997).

Some theorists suggest that a biological cause lies at the root of both anorexia nervosa and bulimia. In fact, there appear to be genetic components to the disorders, and in some cases doctors have found hormonal imbalances in sufferers (Condit, 1990; Irwin, 1993; Treasure & Tiller, 1993).

Other attempts to explain the eating disorders emphasize psychological and social factors. For instance, some experts suggest that the disorders are a result of overdemanding parents or by-products of other family difficulties. Culture also plays a role. Anorexia nervosa, for instance, is found only in cultures that idealize slender female bodies. Because in most places such a standard does not hold, anorexia is not prevalent outside the United States. For instance, there is no anorexia in all of Asia, with two interesting exceptions: the upper classes of Japan and of Hong Kong, where Western influence is greatest. Furthermore, anorexia nervosa is a fairly recent disorder. It was not seen in the 17th and 18th centuries, when the ideal of the female body was a plump corpulence. The increasing number of boys with anorexia in the United States may be related to a growing emphasis on a muscular male physique that features little body fat (Keel, Leon, & Fulkerson, 2000; D. A. Miller, McCluskey-Fawcett, & Irving, 1993).

Anorexia nervosa and bulimia are most likely products of both biological and environmental causes. Consequently, treatment typically involves multiple approaches. For instance, both psychological therapy and dietary modifications are likely to be needed for successful treatment (S. Gilbert, 2000; K. J. Miller & Mizes, 2000; Porzelius, Dinsmore, & Staffelbach, 2001; Walsh & Devlin, 1998).

Brain Development and Thought: Paving the Way for Cognitive Growth

Continuing physical development of the body also means physical development of the brain. The number of neurons, the cells of the nervous system, continue to grow, and their interconnections become more complex (Thompson & Nelson, 2001).

Bulimia   An eating disorder that primarily afflicts adolescent girls and young women, characterized by binges on large quantities of food followed by purges of the food through vomiting or the use of laxatives

The prefrontal cortex, the area of the brain responsible for impulse control, is biologically immature during adolescence, leading to some of the risky and impulsive behavior associated with people in this age group.

One specific area of the brain that undergoes considerable development throughout adolescence is the prefrontal cortex, which is not fully developed until around the age of 20. The *prefrontal cortex* is the part of the brain that allows people to think, evaluate, and make complex judgments in a uniquely human way.

The prefrontal cortex is also the area of the brain that provides for impulse control. Rather than simply reacting to emotions such as anger or rage, an individual with a fully developed prefrontal cortex is able to inhibit the desire for action that stems from such emotions. During adolescence, the prefrontal cortex is biologically immature, and hence the ability to inhibit impulses is not fully developed. This biological fact leads to some of the risky and impulsive behaviors that are characteristic of adolescence, which we'll discuss later in the chapter (Nell, 2002; D. R. Weinberger, 2001).

REVIEW & APPLY

Review

- Adolescence is a period of rapid physical growth, including the changes associated with puberty. Girls typically begin their growth spurts and puberty about 2 years earlier than boys.

- Puberty can cause reactions in adolescents ranging from confusion to increased self-esteem.

- Early or late maturation can bring advantages and disadvantages, depending on one's sex, as well as emotional and psychological maturity.

- Adequate nutrition is essential in adolescence because of the need to fuel physical growth. Changing physical needs and environmental pressures can induce obesity and eating disorders.

- The two most common eating disorders are anorexia nervosa and bulimia. Both must be treated with a combination of physical and psychological therapies.

Applying Child Development

- How might societal and environmental influences contribute to the emergence of an eating disorder?

- *From an educator's perspective:* Why do you think the passage to adolescence is regarded in many cultures as a significant transition that calls for unique ceremonies?

Stress The physical response to events that threaten or challenge us

Stress and Coping

Few of us need much of an introduction to **stress,** the response to events that threaten or challenge us. Stress is a part of nearly everyone's existence, and most people's lives are crowded with events and circumstances, known as *stressors,* that produce threats to our well-being. Stressors need not be unpleasant events: Even the happiest events, such as obtaining admission to a sought-after college or graduating from high school, can produce stress for adolescents.

Stress produces several outcomes. The most immediate is typically a biological reaction, as certain hormones, secreted by the adrenal glands, cause a rise in heart rate, blood pressure, respiration rate, and sweating. In some situations, these immediate effects may be beneficial because they produce an "emergency reaction" in the sympathetic nervous system that prepares people to defend themselves from a sudden, threatening situation. A person challenged by a snarling, ferocious dog, for instance, would want all the bodily preparedness possible to deal with the emergency situation.

However, long-term, continuous exposure to stressors may result in a reduction of the body's ability to deal with stress. As stress-related hormones are constantly secreted, the heart, blood vessels, and other body tissues may deteriorate. As a consequence, people become more susceptible to diseases as their ability to fight off germs declines (S. Cohen, Tyrrell, & Smith, 1993; Kiecolt-Glaser & Glaser, 1986; Schneiderman, 1983).

The Origins of Stress: Reacting to Life's Challenges

Although stress is experienced long before adolescence, it becomes particularly wearing during the teenage years, and it can produce formidable costs (see Figure 14-4). Over the long run, the constant wear-and-tear caused by the physiological arousal that occurs as the body tries to fight off stress produces negative effects. For instance, headaches, backaches, skin rashes, indigestion, chronic fatigue, sleep disturbances, and even the common cold are stress-related illnesses (S. Cohen et al., 1993; Kiecolt-Glaser & Glaser, 1991; Reid et al., 2002).

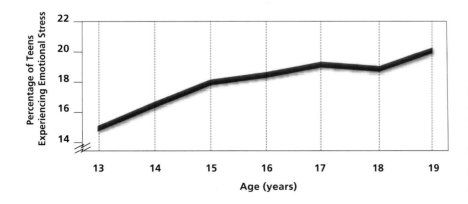

FIGURE 14-4 TEENAGE STRESS

Teenage students may experience stress concerning where they will work in the future and at what kind of job. What can health care workers look for as signs of stress among adolescents?

(*Source:* National Longitudinal Study of Adolescent Health, 2000)

TABLE 14-1   WILL STRESS IN YOUR LIFE PRODUCE ILLNESS?

Using the following scale, you can assess the degree of stress in your life. Take the stressor value given beside each event you have experienced, and multiply it by the number of occurrences over the past year (up to a maximum of four); then add up the scores.

87 Experienced the death of a spouse	49 Had a major change in amount of independence and responsibility
77 Got married	47 Had a major change in responsibilities at work
77 Experienced the death of a close family member	46 Experienced a major change in the use of alcohol
76 Got divorced	45 Revised personal habits
74 Experienced a marital separation from mate	44 Had trouble with school administration
68 Experienced the death of a close friend	43 Held a job while attending school
68 Experienced pregnancy or fathered a pregnancy	43 Had a major change in social activities
65 Had a major personal injury or illness	42 Had trouble with in-laws
62 Were fired from work	42 Had a major change in working hours or conditions
60 Ended a marital engagement or a steady relationship	42 Changed residence or living conditions
58 Had sexual difficulties	41 Had your spouse begin or cease work outside the home
58 Experienced a marital reconciliation with your mate	41 Changed your choice of major field of study
57 Had a major change in self-concept or self-awareness	41 Changed dating habits
56 Experienced a major change in the health or behavior of a family member	40 Had an outstanding personal achievement
54 Became engaged to be married	38 Had trouble with your boss
53 Had a major change in financial status	38 Had a major change in amount of participation in school activities
52 Took on a mortgage or loan of less than $10,000	37 Had a major change in type and/or amount of recreation
52 Had a major change in the use of drugs	36 Had a major change in church activities
50 Had a major conflict or change in values	34 Had a major change in sleeping habits
50 Had a major change in the number of arguments with your spouse	33 Took a trip or vacation
50 Gained a new family member	30 Had a major change in eating habits
50 Entered college	26 Had a major change in the number of family get-togethers
50 Changed to a new school	22 Were found guilty of minor violations of the law
50 Changed to a different line of work	

A total score of 1,435 or higher places you in a high-stress category. According to M. B. Marx, Garrity, & Bowers (1975), a high score increases the chances of experiencing a future stress-related illness, although it certainly does not guarantee it.

(*Source:* Adapted from Rahe & Arthur, 1978)

Psychosomatic disorders Medical problems caused by the interaction of psychological, emotional, and physical difficulties

Stress may also lead to **psychosomatic disorders,** medical problems caused by the interaction of psychological, emotional, and physical difficulties. For instance, ulcers, asthma, arthritis, and high blood pressure may—although not invariably—be produced or worsened by stress (C. A. Coleman, Friedman, & Burright, 1998; Lepore, Palsane, & Evans, 1991).

Stress may even cause more serious, even life-threatening illnesses. According to some research, the greater the number of stressful events a person experiences over the course of a year, the more likely he or she is to have a major illness (Coddington, 1984; Holmes & Rahe, 1967; see Table 14-1).

BECOMING AN INFORMED CONSUMER OF DEVELOPMENT

Coping with Stress

Although no single formula can cover all cases of stress, some general guidelines can help everyone cope with the stress that is part of life. Among them are the following (Greenglass & Burke, 1991; Holahan & Moos, 1987, 1990; R. M. Kaplan, Sallis, & Patterson, 1993; Sacks, 1993).

- Seek control over the situation producing the stress. Putting yourself in charge of a situation that is producing stress can take you a long way toward coping with it.

- Redefine the "threat" as a "challenge." Changing the definition of a situation can make it seem less threatening. "Look for the silver lining" isn't bad advice.

- Get social support. Almost any difficulty can be faced more easily with the help of others. Friends, family members, and even telephone hot lines staffed by trained counselors can provide significant support. (For help in identifying appropriate hot lines, the U.S. Public Health Service maintains a master toll-free number that can provide phone numbers and addresses of many national groups. Call 800-336-4794.)

- Use relaxation techniques. Procedures that reduce the physiological arousal brought about by stress can be particularly effective. A variety of techniques produce relaxation, such as transcendental meditation, Zen, yoga, progressive muscle relaxation, and even hypnosis; these have been shown to be effective in reducing stress. One that works particularly well, devised by physician Herbert Benson (1993), is illustrated in Table 14-2.

- If all else fails, keep in mind that a life without any stress at all would be a dull one. Stress is a natural part of life, and successfully coping with it can be a gratifying experience.

TABLE 14-2   HOW TO ELICIT THE RELAXATION RESPONSE

There are several approaches to eliciting the relaxation response. Here is one standard set of instructions:

Step 1. Pick a focus word or short phrase that's firmly rooted in your personal belief system. For example, a nonreligious individual might choose a neutral word like one or peace or love. A Christian person desiring to use a prayer could pick the opening words of Psalm 23, The Lord is my shepherd; a Jewish person could choose Shalom.

Step 2. Sit quietly in a comfortable position.

Step 3. Close your eyes.

Step 4. Relax your muscles.

Step 5. Breathe slowly and naturally, repeating your focus word or phrase silently as you exhale.

Step 6. Throughout, assume a passive attitude. Don't worry about how well you're doing. When other thoughts come to mind, simply say to yourself, "Oh, well," and gently return to the repetition.

Step 7. Continue for 10 to 20 minutes. You may open your eyes to check the time, but do not use an alarm. When you finish, sit quietly for a minute or so, at first with your eyes closed and later with your eyes open. Then do not stand for one or two minutes.

Step 8. Practice the technique once or twice a day.

Some general advice on regular practice of the relaxation response:

- Try to find 10 to 20 minutes in your daily routine; before breakfast is a good time.

- Sit comfortably.

- For the period you will practice, try to arrange your life so you won't have distractions. Put the phone on the answering machine, and ask someone else to watch the kids.

- Time yourself by glancing periodically at a clock or watch (but don't set an alarm). Commit yourself to a specific length of practice, and try to stick to it.

(*Source:* Benson, 1993)

Preventing School Violence

When two students went on a rampage at Littleton, Colorado's Columbine High School one bright April morning, the result was shocking. The gunmen, who targeted blacks and athletes, murdered 13 fellow students and a teacher, and they planted dozens of bombs around the school. As the two ran through the school, laughing, students hid in storage rooms, offices, and closets to escape the danger. At the end of the shooting spree, the gunmen took their own lives.

In retrospect, the signs of impending violence seemed obvious. One of the pair created a Web page containing death threats, and the two had made a video for a class that foreshadowed the massacre. One had a bedroom filled with Nazi and hate literature and explosives. Both had threatened fellow students, saying, "Just wait," to those who made fun of the black trenchcoats they wore as members of the "Trenchcoat Mafia." Minor disagreements with others turned into threats of violence. In a philosophy class, one spoke incessantly about purchasing a gun.

Still, no one could predict the direction their anger would take.

The Columbine shooting is one of a number of significant acts of violence that have occurred in U.S. schools. Since 1974, there have been about 100 incidents of school violence. The good news is that despite the public perception that school violence is on the upswing, in fact there has been a decline in overall violence. In fact, even in the year of the Columbine shooting, the number of deaths in school-related incidents dropped 40 percent from the previous year (J. Spencer, 2001).

Although statistically the likelihood of injury from a school shooting is tiny, and school is actually one of the safest places for children, adolescents still experience stress involving safety issues. For example, after a school shooting in Jonesboro, Arkansas, almost three quarters of respondents on a national survey said they felt that a shooting was "likely" or "very likely" in their own community.

Why do some students behave in violent ways? In an analysis of school shootings, the Federal Bureau of Investigation has identified several characteristics of individuals who are at risk for carrying out violence in schools. They include a low tolerance

Programs involving peer mediation are useful in curbing violence.

for frustration, poor coping skills, a lack of resiliency, failed love relationships, resentment over perceived injustices, depression, self-centeredness, and alienation (O'Toole, 2000).

According to psychologist Elliot Aronson (2000), students who carry out violence in schools have frequently been the targets of bullying or have been rejected in some way. He notes that there are tremendous status differences in schools, and students who have been taunted and humiliated by students of higher status (or by their parents or other adults) may lash out in frustration.

To respond to the potential of violence, many schools have taken significant steps to prevent a shooting. Some have installed metal detectors and security cameras and conduct surprise searches of student lockers. Others have a "zero tolerance" policy that mandates that students are suspended if they bring to school anything—even a penknife—that could potentially be used as a weapon. Some schools even make students wear identification tags and carry clear plastic backpacks.

Unfortunately, there is little evidence that such security measures are effective. What seems to work better are programs that moderate the cultures of schools. For instance, programs involving cooperative learning, peer mediation, and communication skills training appear to be helpful. In addition, teaching students, parents, and educators to take threats seriously is important; many students who become violent threaten to commit violence before they actually do. Ultimately, schools need to be places where students feel comfortable discussing their feelings and problems, rather than sources of alienation and rejection (Aronson, 2000; Mulvey & Cauffman, 2001; J. Spencer, 2001).

Before you start calculating whether you are overdue for a major illness, however, keep in mind some important limitations to the research. Not everyone who experiences high stress becomes ill, and the weights given to particular stressors probably vary from one person to the next. Furthermore, there is a kind of circularity to such enumerations of stressors: Because the research is correlational, it is possible that someone who has a major illness to begin with is more likely to experience some of the stressors on the list. For example, a person may have lost a job *because* of the effects of an illness, rather than developing an illness because of the loss of a job. Still, the list of stressors does provide a way to consider how most people react to various potentially stressful events in their lives. (For another aspect of stress during adolescence, see the *From Research to Practice* box.)

Meeting the Challenge of Stress

Some adolescents are better than others at **coping,** making efforts to control, reduce, or tolerate the threats and challenges that lead to stress. What is the key to successful coping?

Some individuals use *problem-focused coping,* by which they attempt to manage a stressful problem or situation by directly changing the situation to make it less stressful. For example, a high school student who is having academic difficulties may speak to his teachers and ask that they extend the deadlines for assignments, or a worker who is dissatisfied with her job assignment can ask that she be assigned other tasks.

Other adolescents employ *emotion-focused coping,* which involves the conscious regulation of emotion. For instance, a teenager who is having problems getting along with her boss in her after-school job may tell herself that she should look at the bright side: At least she has a job in the first place (Folkman & Lazarus, 1980, 1988).

Coping is also aided by the presence of *social support,* assistance and comfort supplied by others. Turning to others in the face of stress can provide both emotional support (in the form of a shoulder to cry on) and practical, tangible support (such as an advance of one's allowance) (Spiegel, 1993; Weigel et al., 1998).

Finally, even if adolescents don't consciously cope with stress, some psychologists suggest that they may unconsciously use defensive coping mechanisms that aid in stress reduction. *Defensive coping* involves the unconscious use of strategies that distort or deny the true nature of a situation. For instance, a person may deny the seriousness of a threat, trivialize a life-threatening illness, or tell himself that academic failure on a series of tests is unimportant. The problem with such defensive coping is that it does not deal with the reality of the situation but merely avoids or ignores the problem.

REVIEW & APPLY

Review

- Stress, which is healthy in small doses, can be harmful to body and mind if it is frequent or long-lasting.

- The body's immediate reactions to stress include a hormone-induced rise in heart rate, blood pressure, respiration rate, and sweating.

- Long-term exposure to stressors may cause deterioration in the heart, blood vessels, and other body tissues. Stress is linked to many common ailments.

- Strategies for coping with stress include problem-focused coping, emotion-focused coping, the use of social support, and defensive coping.

Coping   Efforts to control, reduce, or tolerate the threats and challenges that lead to stress

Applying Child Development

- In what circumstances can stress be an adaptive, helpful response? In what circumstances is it maladaptive?

- *From the perspective of a health care provider:* Are there periods of life that are relatively stress-free, or do people of all ages experience stress? Do stressors differ from age to age?

Threats to Adolescents' Well-Being

Like most parents, I had thought of drug use as something you worried about when your kids got to high school. Now I know that, on the average, kids begin using drugs at 11 or 12, but at the time that never crossed our minds. Ryan had just begun attending mixed parties. He was playing Little League. In the eighth grade, Ryan started getting into a little trouble—one time he and another fellow stole a fire extinguisher, but we thought it was just a prank. Then his grades began to deteriorate. He began sneaking out at night. He would become belligerent at the drop of a hat, then sunny and nice again. . . .

It wasn't until Ryan fell apart at 14 that we started thinking about drugs. He had just begun McLean High School, and to him, it was like going to drug camp every day. Back then, everything was so available. He began cutting classes, a common tip-off, but we didn't hear from the school until he was flunking everything. It turned out that he was going to school for the first period, getting checked in, then leaving and smoking marijuana all day. (Shafer, 1990, p. 82)

Ryan's parents learned all too soon that marijuana was not the only drug Ryan was using. As his friends later admitted, Ryan was what they called a "garbage head." He would try anything. Despite efforts to curb his use of drugs, he never succeeded in stopping. He died at the age of 16, hit by a passing car after wandering into the street while under the influence.

Although most cases of adolescent drug use produce far less extreme results, the use of drugs, as well as other kinds of substance use and abuse, represents a primary threat to health during adolescence, which otherwise is usually one of the healthiest periods of life. Although the extent of risky behavior is difficult to gauge, preventable problems such as drug, alcohol, and tobacco use, as well as sexually transmitted diseases, represent serious threats to adolescents' well-being.

Illegal Drugs

How common is illegal drug use during adolescence? Very. For instance, a recent annual survey of nearly 50,000 U.S. students shows that almost 40 percent of high school seniors and more than a third of eighth graders report having used marijuana within the past year. Furthermore, marijuana use over the prior 12 months has increased since 1995 for 10th and 12th graders but dropped slightly for eighth graders (L. D. Johnston, Bachman, & O'Malley, 2002; see Figure 14-5).

The use of other illegal drugs is on the rise. Although drug use by adolescents is less prevalent than it was during parts of the 1970s and 1980s, drug use began to rise during the early 1990s. Furthermore, usage rates for some illegal drugs, such as Ecstasy, increased considerably at the end of the 1990s and into the 21st century.

Why do adolescents use drugs? There are multiple reasons. Some relate to the perceived pleasurable experience drugs may provide and others to the escape from the pressures of everyday life that drugs temporarily permit. Some adolescents try drugs simply for the thrill

Marijuana use continues to be more prevalent among older adolescents.

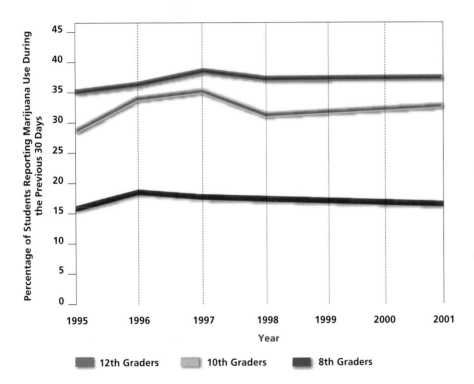

FIGURE 14-5 PERCENTAGE OF STUDENTS REPORTING MARIJUANA USE DURING THE PREVIOUS 30 DAYS

According to a recent annual survey, marijuana use over the last 12 months has increased since 1995 for 10th and 12th graders but dropped slightly for 8th graders. What do educators and health care workers need to be aware of when dealing with adolescent drug use?

(*Source:* L. D. Johnston, Bachman, & O'Malley, 2002)

of doing something illegal. The alleged drug use of well-known role models, such as movie star Robert Downey Jr., may also contribute. Finally, peer pressure plays a role: Adolescents, as we'll discuss in greater detail in Chapter 16, are particularly susceptible to the perceived standards of their peer groups (Bogenschneider et al., 1998; Jenkins, 1996; Petraitis, Flay, & Miller, 1995).

The use of illegal drugs is dangerous in several respects. For one thing, some drugs are addictive. **Addictive drugs** produce a biological or psychological dependence in users, leading to increasingly powerful cravings for them. When drugs produce a biological addiction, the body becomes so used to their presence that it is unable to function in their absence. Drugs can also

Addictive drugs Drugs that produce a biological or psychological dependence in users, leading to increasingly powerful cravings for them

produce a psychological addiction. In such cases, people grow to depend on drugs to cope with the everyday stress of life, often to the exclusion of other techniques.

In addition, if drugs are used as an escape, they may prevent adolescents from confronting—and potentially solving—the problems that led them to drug use in the first place. Finally, drugs may be dangerous because even casual users of less hazardous drugs can escalate to more dangerous forms of substance abuse. For instance, those who smoke marijuana are 85 times more likely to use cocaine than those who do not (B. M. Segal & Stewart, 1996; Toch, 1995).

"Many adolescents that we deal with do not believe that marijuana, and sometimes even cocaine, are harmful."

CAREERS IN CHILD DEVELOPMENT

Doreen Gail Branch

Education: . . . .   Howard University, Washington, DC: B.S. and M.A. in psychology
Position: . . . .   Substance abuse research associate, National Public Service Research Institute
Home: . . . .   Greenbelt, Maryland

People of many ages abuse alcohol, tobacco, and drugs, but one group that is particularly vulnerable to the allure of drugs is adolescents. In an effort to create effective preventive programs, Doreen Branch is working on a project with a community services coalition in Maryland's Prince George's County. The coalition serves adolescents between the ages of 12 and 18.

"We are currently looking at the community and how the different parts can band together to battle alcohol, tobacco, and other drug abuse, as well as problems associated with their use," says Branch.

One major goal of her work is to provide youth with alternatives to using drugs by introducing them to other activities. "Many people are familiar with midnight basketball programs," she says, "but our efforts go beyond them. For instance, one of the things we are developing is a tennis program that not only teaches tennis but also provides mentoring to at-risk adolescents." She notes that such programs emphasize that there are more interesting and more productive things to do with one's time than use drugs.

"We have to educate students on drugs, and we need to inform them of the dangers of even a little drug use. Many adolescents that we deal with do not believe that marijuana and sometimes even cocaine are harmful," Branch adds.

Branch is also studying how tobacco and alcohol manufacturers use advertising to influence teenagers. "One of the things that we are trying to do is to change local policies in terms of billboards that cater to the advertising of cigarettes and alcohol. Although many of these advertisements are in the poorest sections of town, all teenagers can be influenced by them," she notes.

One tactic she has used to deter drug use by adolescents has been to ask them to write, produce, and act in their own commercials on the dangers of drug and alcohol abuse. Another has been to provide funding for a large meeting, the "Kiamsha Youth Empowerment Conference." With some help from adult mentors, Maryland adolescents organized the meeting largely by themselves.

"The issues discussed at the conference included drugs, sex, violence, and spirituality," Branch reports. "The whole conference was planned and conducted by teenagers. They hit on a lot of issues that kids have to deal with, and—in part because it was planned by the adolescents themselves—it was a great success."

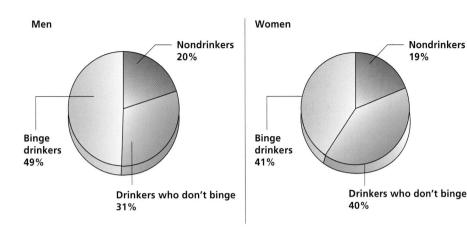

Men

Nondrinkers
20%

Binge
drinkers
49%

Drinkers who don't binge
31%

Women

Nondrinkers
19%

Binge
drinkers
41%

Drinkers who don't binge
40%

FIGURE 14-6   ALCOHOL CONSUMPTION AMONG COLLEGE STUDENTS

For men, binge drinking was defined as consuming five or more drinks in one sitting; for women, the total was four or more.

(*Source:* Wechsler et al., 2002)

Alcohol: Use and Abuse

Alcohol is the number one drug of choice for adolescents. Almost all adolescents experiment with alcohol, and more than 40 percent of college students say they've had 5 or more drinks within the past 2 weeks, and some 16 percent consume 16 or more drinks per week. High school students, too, are drinkers: Forty-one percent of ninth graders, and almost two thirds of 12th graders use alcohol (Center on Addiction and Substance Abuse, 2002).

Almost half of all college students drink heavily, engaging in *binge drinking* (see Figure 14-6). (Binge drinking is defined for men as drinking five or more drinks in one sitting; for women, who tend to weigh less and whose bodies absorb alcohol less efficiently, binge drinking is defined as four drinks in one sitting; H. Wechsler & Nelson, 2001; H. Wechsler et al., 2002.)

Such alcohol use is often dangerous. On an average day, four college students die from accidents that involve alcohol, and almost 200 women are raped or sexually assaulted by their dates after alcohol use (Hingson et al., 2002; National Advisory Council, 2002).

Why do adolescents begin drinking? Some believe it is the "adult" thing to do. For some—especially male athletes, whose rate of drinking tends to be higher than that of the adolescent general population—drinking is seen as a way of maintaining a "macho" image. Others drink for the same reason that people use drugs: It releases inhibitions and tension and reduces stress. Finally, some adolescents drink because of a *false consensus effect,* in which they assume that everyone is drinking a lot based on a few conspicuous examples (C. N. Carr, Kennedy, & Dimick, 1996; Pavis, Cunningham-Burley, & Amos, 1997).

In some cases, alcohol use becomes a habit that cannot be controlled. **Alcoholics,** for whom alcohol use has become a problem, learn to depend on alcohol and are unable to control their drinking. They also become increasingly immune to the effects of drinking and therefore need to consume ever-larger amounts to bring about the positive sensations they crave. Some drink throughout the day; others go on binges in which they consume huge quantities of alcohol (Morse & Flavin, 1992; National Institute on Alcohol Abuse and Alcoholism, 1990).

The reasons that some adolescents become alcoholics are not fully known. Genetics plays a role: Alcoholism runs in families (Schuckit, 1999). However, not all alcoholics have family members with alcohol problems. For those adolescents, alcoholism may be triggered by efforts to deal with environmental stress (Boyd, Howard, & Zucker, 1995; Bushman, 1993).

No matter what the origins of an adolescent's problems with alcohol or drugs, parents, teachers, and friends can help the teen find help—if they realize there is a problem. How can concerned friends and family members tell if an adolescent they know is having difficulties with alcohol or drugs? Some of the telltale signs are described in the *Becoming an Informed Consumer of Development* box.

About half of all college students engage in binge drinking.

Alcoholics   People who have learned to depend on alcohol and are unable to control their drinking

---

○— BECOMING AN INFORMED CONSUMER OF DEVELOPMENT —○

Hooked on Drugs or Alcohol?

Although it is not always easy to determine if an adolescent has a drug or alcohol abuse problem, there are some signals. Among them are the following (adapted from Franck & Brownstone, 1991, pp. 593–594):

Identification With the Drug Culture

- Drug-related magazines or slogans on clothing
- Conversation and jokes that are preoccupied with drugs
- Hostility discussing drugs
- Collection of beer cans

Signs of Physical Deterioration

- Memory lapses, short attention span, difficulty concentrating
- Poor physical coordination, slurred or incoherent speech
- Unhealthy appearance, indifference to hygiene and grooming
- Bloodshot eyes, dilated pupils

Dramatic Changes in School Performance

- Marked downturn in grades—not just from Cs to Fs but from As to Bs and Cs

- Assignments not completed
- Increased absenteeism or tardiness

Changes in Behavior

- Chronic dishonesty (lying, stealing, cheating); trouble with the police
- Changes in friends; evasiveness in talking about new ones
- Possession of large amounts of money
- Increasing and inappropriate anger, hostility, irritability, secretiveness
- Reduced motivation, energy, self-discipline, self-esteem
- Diminished interest in extracurricular activities and hobbies

If an adolescent—or anyone else, for that matter—fits any of these descriptors, help is probably needed. It is possible to get advice from a national hot line. For alcohol difficulties, call the National Council on Alcoholism at (800) 622–2255; for drug problems, call the National Institute on Drug Abuse at (800) 662–4357. In addition, those who need advice can find a local listing for Alcoholics Anonymous or Narcotics Anonymous in the telephone book. Finally, for help with alcohol and drug problems, contact the National Council on Alcoholism and Drug Dependence at 12 West 21st Street, New York, NY 10010.

Tobacco: The Dangers of Smoking

Most adolescents are well aware of the dangers of smoking, but many still indulge in it. Although recent figures show that, overall, a smaller proportion of adolescents smoke than in prior decades, the numbers remain substantial. Furthermore, within certain groups the numbers are increasing. For instance, smoking is more prevalent among girls, and in several countries, including Austria, Norway, and Sweden, the proportion of girls who smoke is higher than the proportion of boys. There are racial differences, as well: White children and children in lower socioeconomic status households are more likely to experiment with cigarettes and to start smoking earlier than African American children and children living in higher socioeconomic status households. Also, smoking among white males of high school age is significantly greater than among African American males in high school, although the differences have narrowed in recent years (Griesler & Kandel, 1998; Harrell et al., 1998; Stolberg, 1998).

 Adolescents smoke despite growing social sanctions against the habit. As the dangers of secondhand smoke become more apparent, many people look down on smokers. More places, including schools and places of business, have become "smoke-free," a trend that makes it increasingly difficult to find a place to smoke. Furthermore, the health dangers of smoking are hardly in dispute: Every package of cigarettes carries a warning that smoking is linked to a higher mortality rate, and even adolescents who smoke admit that they know the dangers.

Why, then, do adolescents begin to smoke and then maintain the habit? One reason is that smoking is still considered sexy and hip. Advertisements for cigarettes depict attractive

individuals smoking, and clever ads, such as the highly successful "Joe Camel" series, make an effective pitch to young males. In fact, before Joe Camel commercials were withdrawn from use, children as young as 6 could identify Joe Camel as readily as Mickey Mouse (Bartecchi, MacKenzie, & Schrier, 1995; Lipman, 1992; Ono, 1995; Urberg, Degirmencioglu, & Pilgrim, 1997).

There are other reasons, too. Nicotine, the active chemical ingredient of cigarettes, can produce biological and psychological dependency: Smoking produces a pleasant emotional state that smokers seek to maintain (R. Nowak, 1994b; Pomerleau & Pomerleau, 1989). Furthermore, exposure to parents and peers who smoke increases the chances that an adolescent will take up the habit (Botvin et al., 1994; Webster, Hunter, & Keats, 1994). Finally, smoking is sometimes seen as an adolescent rite of passage: Trying cigarettes is regarded as a sign of growing up. Although one or two cigarettes do not usually produce a lifetime smoker, it takes only a little more to start the habit. In fact, people who smoke as few as 10 cigarettes early in their lives stand an 80 percent chance of becoming habitual smokers (Bowen et al., 1991; Salber, Freeman, & Abelin, 1968; Stacy et al., 1992).

Sexually Transmitted Diseases

In the fall of 1990, Krista Blake was 18 and looking forward to her first year at Youngstown State University in Ohio. She and her boyfriend were talking about getting married. Her life was, she says, "basic, white-bread America." Then she went to the doctor, complaining about a backache, and found out she had the AIDS virus.

Blake had been infected with HIV, the virus that causes AIDS, two years earlier by an older boy, a hemophiliac. "He knew that he was infected, and he didn't tell me," she says. "And he didn't do anything to keep me from getting infected, either." (Becahy, 1992, p. 49)

Aids. Krista Blake, who later died from the disorder, was not alone: **Acquired immune deficiency syndrome (AIDS)** is one of the leading causes of death among young people. Because AIDS, which is caused by the human immunodeficiency virus (HIV), is spread primarily through sexual contact, it is classified as a **sexually transmitted disease (STD).** Although in the United States it began as a problem that primarily afflicted homosexuals, it has spread to other populations, including heterosexuals and intravenous drug users. Minorities have been

Acquired immune deficiency syndrome (AIDS) A sexually transmitted disease, produced by the human immunodeficiency virus (HIV), that has no cure and ultimately causes death

Sexually transmitted disease (STD) A disease that is spread through sexual contact

Krista Blake contracted AIDS at the age of 16. She later died from the disease.

○─ DEVELOPMENTAL DIVERSITY ─○

Selling Death: Pushing Smoking to the Less Advantaged

In Dresden, Germany, three women in miniskirts offer passers-by a pack of Lucky Strikes and a leaflet that reads: "You just got hold of a nice piece of America." Says a local doctor, "Adolescents time and again receive cigarettes at such promotions."

A Jeep decorated with the Camel logo pulls up to a high school in Buenos Aires. A woman begins handing out free cigarettes to 15- and 16-year-olds during their lunch recess.

At a video arcade in Taipei, free American cigarettes are strewn atop each game. At a disco filled with high school students, free packs of Salems are on each table. (Ecenbarger, 1993, p. 50)

If you are a cigarette manufacturer and you find that the number of people using your product is declining, what do you do? U.S. companies have sought to carve out new markets by turning to the least advantaged groups of people,

both at home and abroad. For instance, in the early 1990s, the R. J. Reynolds tobacco company designed a new brand of cigarettes it named Uptown. The advertising used to herald its arrival made clear who the target was: African Americans living in urban areas (M. Quinn, 1990). Because of subsequent protests, the tobacco company withdrew Uptown from the market.

In addition to seeking new converts in the United States, tobacco companies aggressively recruit adolescent smokers abroad. In many developing countries, the number of smokers is still low. Tobacco companies are seeking to increase this number through marketing strategies designed to hook adolescents on the habit by means of free samples (Sesser, 1993; Winter, 2001; see Figure 14-7).

The strategy is effective. For instance, in some Latin American cities, as many as 50 percent of teenagers smoke. According to the World Health Organization, smoking will prematurely kill some 200 million of the world's children and adolescents, and overall, 10 percent of the world's population will die because of smoking (Ecenbarger, 1993).

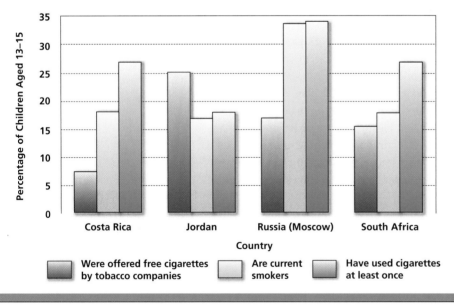

FIGURE 14-7   FINDING NEW SMOKERS

While the offering of cigarettes to minors in the United States is strictly controlled, tobacco companies are aggressively marketing their products overseas, primarily in developing countries.

(*Source:* World Health Organization & Centers for Disease Control, 1999)

particularly hard hit: African Americans and Hispanics account for some 40 percent of AIDS cases, although they make up only 18 percent of the population. Already, 25 million people have died due to AIDS, and the number of people living with the disease numbers more than 40 million worldwide (see Figure 14-8).

AIDS and Adolescent Behavior.   It is no secret how AIDS is transmitted—through the exchange of bodily fluids, including semen and blood. However, motivating teenagers to employ safer sex practices that can prevent its spread has proved difficult. One good sign is that the use of condoms during sexual intercourse has increased, and people are less likely to engage in casual sex with new acquaintances (Everett et al., 2000; Kalichman, 1998).

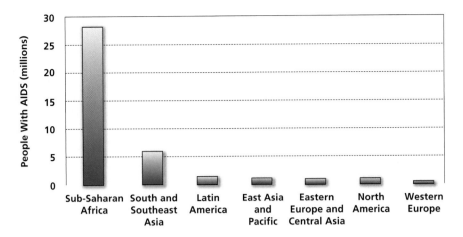

FIGURE 14-8 AIDS AROUND THE WORLD

The number of people carrying the AIDS virus varies substantially by geographic region. Most of the afflicted people are in Africa and South Asia.

(*Source:* UNAIDS & World Health Organization, 2001)

But the use of safer sex practices is far from universal. Adolescents, who—as we noted earlier in the chapter—are prone to engage in risky behavior due to feelings of invulnerability, are likely to believe that their chances of contracting AIDS are minimal. This is particularly true when adolescents perceive that their partner is "safe"—someone they know well and with whom they are involved in a relatively long-term relationship (Freiberg, 1998; Lefkowitz, Sigman, & Au, 2000; Serovich & Greene, 1997).

Unfortunately, unless an individual knows the complete sexual history and HIV status of a partner, unprotected sex remains risky. And learning a partner's complete sexual history is difficult. It is often inaccurately communicated because of embarrassment, a sense of privacy, or simple forgetfulness.

Short of celibacy, a solution regarded as improbable for many adolescents involved in relationships, there is no certain way to avoid AIDS. However, health experts suggest several strategies for making sex safer; these are listed in Table 14-3.

Other Sexually Transmitted Diseases. Although AIDS is the deadliest of sexually transmitted diseases, others are far more common (see Figure 14-9). In fact, one in four adolescents contracts an STD before graduating from high school. Following a single instance of unprotected sex with an infected partner, a teenage woman has a 1 percent chance of acquiring the virus that causes AIDS, a 30 percent chance of getting genital herpes, and a 50 percent chance of getting gonorrhea. Overall, around 2.5 million teenagers contract an STD each year. (Alan Guttmacher Institute, 1993a; Kaiser Family Foundation, 2002; Leary, 1996).

TABLE 14-3 SAFER SEX: PREVENTING THE TRANSMISSION OF AIDS

Health psychologists and educators have devised several guidelines to help prevent the spread of AIDS. Among them are the following:

- **Use condoms.** The use of condoms greatly reduces the risk of transmission of the virus that produces AIDS, which occurs through exposure to bodily fluids such as semen or blood.

- **Avoid high-risk behaviors.** Such practices as unprotected anal intercourse or sharing needles used for injecting drugs greatly increase the risk of AIDS.

- **Know your partner's sexual history.** Knowing your partner's sexual history can help you to evaluate the risks of sexual contact.

- **Consider abstinence.** Although not always a practical alternative, the only certain way of avoiding AIDS is to refrain from sexual activity altogether.

3 million teenagers, about 1 person in 8 aged 13–19 and about 1 in 4 of those who have had sexual intercourse, acquire an STD every year. Among the most common are the following:

Chlamydia: Chlamydia is more common among teenagers than among older men and women; in some studies, 10 to 29 percent of sexually active adolescent girls and 10 percent of teenage boys have been found to be infected with chlamydia.

Genital herpes: A viral disease that is incurable, often indicated first by small blisters or sores around the genitals. It is periodically contagious.

Trichomoniasis: An infection of the vagina or penis, caused by a parasite.

Gonorrhea: Adolescents aged 15–19 have higher rates of gonorrhea than sexually active men and women in any 5-year age group between 20 and 44.

Syphilis: Infectious syphilis rates more than doubled between 1986 and 1990 among females aged 15–19.

FIGURE 14-9 COMMON SEXUALLY TRANSMITTED DISEASES

Aside from AIDS, these are the most common sexually transmitted diseases (STDs) among adolescents.

(*Source:* Alan Guttmacher Institute, 1993a)

Although most adolescents are well aware of the importance of safer sex practices, their feelings of invulnerability sometimes lead them to believe that their chances of contracting a sexually transmitted disease are minimal—especially when they are well acquainted with their partner.

Chlamydia, a disease caused by a parasite, is the most common STD. Initially it has few symptoms, but later it causes burning urination and a discharge from the penis or vagina. It can lead to pelvic inflammation and even to sterility. Although not bacterial in origin, chlamydial infections can be treated successfully with antibiotics. Unfortunately, many adolescents are not aware of chlamydia, and those who have heard of it are typically unaware of the problems it causes (Nockels & Oakshott, 1999).

Another common STD is **genital herpes,** which is caused by a virus much like the one that produces cold sores around the mouth. The first symptoms of herpes are often small blisters or sores around the genitals; they may break open and become quite painful. Although the sores may heal after a few weeks, the disease often recurs after an interval, and the cycle repeats itself. When the sores reappear, the disease, for which there is no cure, is contagious.

Several other STDs are frequent among adolescents. *Trichomoniasis,* an infection in the vagina or penis, is caused by a parasite. Initially without symptoms, it can eventually cause a painful discharge. *Gonorrhea* and *syphilis* are the STDs that have been recognized for the longest time; cases were recorded by ancient historians. Until the advent of antibiotics, both diseases were deadly; today both can be treated quite effectively.

Chlamydia The most common sexually transmitted disease, caused by a parasite

Genital herpes A common sexually transmitted disease caused by a virus that produces blisters and sores

Even though many STDs are treatable, they remain a serious health concern. Furthermore, contracting an STD is not only an immediate problem during adolescence but could become a problem later in life too. Some diseases increase the chances of future infertility and cancer.

REVIEW & APPLY

Review

- Illegal drug use is prevalent among adolescents as a way to find pleasure, avoid pressure, or gain the approval of peers.

- The use of alcohol is also popular among adolescents, who often wish to appear adult, to lessen inhibitions, or to relieve stress.

- Despite the well-known dangers of smoking, adolescents often smoke to enhance their image or emulate adults.

- AIDS is the most serious of the sexually transmitted diseases, ultimately causing death. Safe sex practices or sexual abstinence can prevent AIDS, although adolescents often ignore these strategies.

- Adolescents also contract other sexually transmitted diseases, such as chlamydia, genital herpes, trichomoniasis, gonorrhea, and syphilis.

Applying Child Development

- How do adolescents' concerns about self-image and their perception that they are the center of attention contribute to smoking and alcohol use?

- *From a health care worker's perspective:* Why do adolescents' increased cognitive abilities, including the ability to reason and to think experimentally, fail to deter them from irrational behavior such as drug and alcohol abuse, tobacco use, and unsafe sex practices?

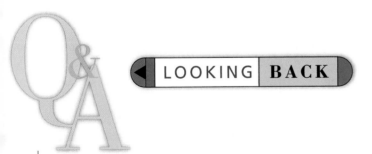

LOOKING BACK

● **What physical changes do adolescents experience?**

- The adolescent years are marked by a physical growth spurt that mirrors the rapid growth rate of infancy. Girls' growth spurts begin around age 10, about 2 years earlier than boys'.

- The most significant event during adolescence is the onset of puberty, which begins for most girls at around age 11 and for most boys at around age 13. As puberty commences, the body begins to produce male or female hormones at adult levels, the sex organs develop and change, menstruation and ejaculation begin, and other body changes occur.

- The timing of puberty is linked to cultural and environmental factors, as well as biological ones. Compared with the past, girls in the United States today experience menarche—the onset of menstruation—at the significantly younger age of 11 or 12, most likely because of better nutrition and overall health.

- The physical changes that accompany puberty, which adolescents usually experience with keen interest, often have psychological effects, which may involve an increase in self-esteem and self-awareness, as well as some confusion and uncertainty about sexuality.

○ **What are the consequences of early and late maturation?**

- Adolescents who mature either early or late may experience a variety of consequences. For boys, early maturation can lead to increased athleticism, greater popularity, and a more positive self-concept. Although early maturation can lead to increased popularity and an enhanced social life, girls may also experience embarrassment over the changes in their bodies that differentiate them from their peers. Furthermore, early physical maturation can lead both boys and girls into activities and situations for which they are not adequately prepared.

- Late maturation, because it results in smaller size, can put boys at a distinct physical and social disadvantage, which can affect self-concept and have lasting negative consequences. Girls who mature late may suffer neglect by their peers of both sexes, but ultimately they appear to suffer no lasting ill effects and may even benefit from late maturation.

○ **What are the nutritional needs and concerns of adolescents?**

- Even though most adolescents have no greater nutritional worries than fueling their growth with appropriate foods, some are obese or overweight and may suffer psychological and physical consequences. Furthermore, a substantial number are excessively concerned about obesity to the point of developing an eating disorder.

- Two major eating disorders that affect adolescent girls are anorexia nervosa—a refusal to eat because of a perception of being overweight—and bulimia—a cycle of binge eating followed by purges via vomiting or use of laxatives. Both biological and environmental factors appear to contribute to these disorders, and treatment typically involves psychological therapy and dietary changes.

○ **What are the effects of stress, and what can be done about it?**

- Moderate, occasional stress is biologically healthy, producing physical reactions that facilitate the body's defense against threats, but long exposure to stressors produces damaging physical and psychosomatic effects.

- Stress has been linked to many common ailments, including headaches, back pains, rashes, indigestion, and even the common cold. It has also been linked to psychosomatic disorders, such as ulcers, asthma, arthritis, and high blood pressure, and to more serious and even life-threatening illnesses.

- People cope with stress in a number of ways, including problem-focused coping, by which they attempt to modify the stressful situation, and emotion-focused coping, by which they attempt to regulate the emotional response to stress.

- Coping is aided by social support from others. Defensive coping, which is the unconscious resort to a strategy of denial, is less successful because it represents a failure to deal with the reality of the situation.

○ **What are some threats to the well-being of adolescents?**

- The use of illicit drugs is alarmingly prevalent among adolescents, who are motivated by pleasure-seeking, pressure avoidance, the desire to flout authority, or the imitation of role models.

- Drug use is dangerous not only because it can escalate and lead to addiction but also because adolescents' avoidance of underlying problems can have serious effects.

- Alcohol use is also prevalent among adolescents, who may view drinking as a way to lower inhibitions or to manifest adult behavior.

- Even though the dangers of smoking are well known and accepted by adolescents, tobacco use continues. Despite a reduction in smoking among adolescents in general, smoking within some groups has actually increased. Adolescents who smoke appear to be motivated by a desire to appear adult and "cool."

- Among the warning signs that an adolescent may have a problem with drugs or alcohol are identification with the drug culture, evidence of physical deterioration, dramatic declines in school performance, and significant changes in behavior.

● **What dangers do adolescent sexual practices present, and how can these dangers be avoided?**

- AIDS is one of the leading causes of death among young people, affecting minority populations with particular severity. Adolescent behavior patterns and attitudes, such as not inquiring about a partner's HIV or AIDS status and a belief in personal invulnerability, work against the use of safer sex practices that can prevent the disease.

- Other sexually transmitted diseases, including chlamydia, genital herpes, trichomoniasis, gonorrhea, and syphilis, occur frequently among the adolescent population and can also be prevented by adopting safer sex practices or abstinence.

EPILOGUE

In this chapter, we began our examination of adolescence, a period of great change in people's lives. We looked at the significant physical changes that adolescents undergo and at some of the risks that they face.

Before turning to the next chapter, return for the moment to the opening prologue of this one, about Cassie Harwood. In light of what you now know about adolescence, consider the following questions about her:

1. Given Cassie's characterization of herself as "athletic, intelligent, energetic," do you think she still might suffer from substantial stress? Why or why not?

2. Do you believe that Cassie's athletic interests make her more or less susceptible to the health-related risks that characterize adolescence? Why or why not?

3. Why do you think that Cassie has apparently avoided buying into to society's "ideal" of the appropriate body type?

4. What arguments would you use that could convince Cassie to avoid the typical health-related risks of adolescence?

KEY TERMS AND CONCEPTS

adolescence (p. 412)
adolescent growth spurt (p. 413)
puberty (p. 413)
menarche (p. 414)
secular trend (p. 415)
primary sex characteristics (p. 415)
secondary sex characteristics (p. 415)

anorexia nervosa (p. 418)
bulimia (p. 419)
stress (p. 421)
psychosomatic disorders (p. 422)
coping (p. 425)
addictive drugs (p. 427)
alcoholics (p. 429)

acquired immune deficiency syndrome (AIDS) (p. 431)
sexually transmitted disease (STD) (p. 431)
chlamydia (p. 434)
genital herpes (p. 434)

15

Cognitive Development in Adolescence

PROLOGUE: Against the Odds

 ecently, a student was shot dead by a classmate during lunch period outside Frank W. Ballou Senior High. It didn't come as much of a surprise to anyone at the school, in this city's most crime-infested ward. Just during the current school year, one boy was hacked by a student with an ax, a girl was badly wounded in a knife fight with another female student, five fires were set by arsonists, and an unidentified body was dumped next to the parking lot.

But all is quiet in the echoing hallways at 7:15 A.M., long before classes start on a spring morning. The only sound comes from the computer lab, where 16-year-old Cedric Jennings is already at work on an extra-credit project, a program to bill patients at a hospital. Later, he will work on his science-fair project, a chemical analysis of acid rain.

Students in inner-city, poor neighborhoods face extraordinary challenges.

He arrives every day this early and often doesn't leave until dark. The high-school junior with the perfect grades has big dreams: He wants to go to Massachusetts Institute of Technology. (Suskind, 1994, p. A1)

LOOKING AHEAD ▶

Cedric Jennings was one of a tiny group of students who had an average of B or better at their huge inner-city high school in Washington, DC. These achievers were a lonely group, the frequent target of threats and actual violence. Yet Cedric persevered, intent on getting a college education and succeeding academically and, ultimately, in life—something that he would ultimately accomplish.

Whether it is exemplified by the success and perseverance of students like Cedric Jennings or comes more easily, the intellectual growth that occurs during adolescence is impressive. In fact, by the end of the period, adolescents' cognitive proficiencies match those of adults in major respects.

In this chapter, we examine cognitive development during adolescence. The chapter begins with an examination of several theories that seek to explain cognitive development. We first consider the Piagetian approach, discussing the way in which adolescents use what Piaget calls formal operations to solve problems. We then turn to the increasingly influential information processing perspectives, which provide a different point of view. We consider the growth of metacognitive capabilities, through which adolescents become increasingly aware of their own thinking processes.

The chapter then turns to the development of moral reasoning and behavior. We consider two major approaches, both of which seek to explain the ways adolescents differ from one another in their moral judgments.

The chapter ends with an examination of school performance and career choices. After discussing the profound impact that socioeconomic status has on school achievement, we consider school performance and ethnicity. We close with a discussion of the ways in which adolescents make career choices.

After reading this chapter, then, you'll be able to answer the following questions:

- How does cognitive development proceed during adolescence?
- What aspects of cognitive development cause difficulties for adolescents?
- Through what stages does moral development progress during childhood and adolescence?
- What factors affect adolescent school performance?
- Who attends college, and how is the college experience different for men and women?
- How do adolescents make career choices, and what influence do ethnicity and gender have on career opportunities?

Intellectual Development

Mrs. Kirby smiled as she read a particularly creative paper. As part of her eighth-grade American government class every year, she asked students to write about what their lives would be like if the United States had not won its war for independence from Britain. She had tried something similar with her sixth graders, but many of them seemed unable to imagine anything different from what they already knew. By eighth grade, however, they were able to come up with some very interesting scenarios.

What is it that sets adolescents' thinking apart from that of younger children? One of the major changes is the ability to think beyond the concrete, current situation to what *might* happen or *could* be. Adolescents are able to keep in their heads a variety of abstract possibilities, and they can see issues in relative, as opposed to absolute, terms. Instead of viewing problems as having black-and-white solutions, they are capable of perceiving shades of gray (Keating, 1980, 1990).

As was the case with other stages of life, we can use several approaches to explain adolescents' cognitive development. We'll begin by returning to Piaget's theory, which has had a significant influence on how developmentalists think about thinking during adolescence.

Piagetian Approaches to Cognitive Development

Fourteen-year-old Aleigh is asked to solve a problem that anyone who has seen a grandfather's clock may have pondered: What determines the speed at which a pendulum moves back and forth? In the version of the problem that she is asked to solve, Aleigh is given a weight hanging from a string. She is told that she can vary several things: the length of the string, the weight of the object at the end of the string, the amount of force used to push the string, and the height to which the weight is raised in an arc before it is released.

Aleigh doesn't remember, but she was asked to solve the same problem when she was 8 years old as part of a longitudinal research study. At that time, she was in the concrete operational period, and her efforts to solve the problem were not very successful. She approached the problem haphazardly, with no systematic plan of action. For instance, she simultaneously tried to push the pendulum harder *and* shorten the length of the string *and* increase the weight on the string. Because she was varying so many factors at once, when the speed of the pendulum changed, she had no way of knowing which factor or factors made a difference.

Now, however, Aleigh is much more systematic. Rather than immediately beginning to push and pull at the pendulum, she stops a moment and thinks. Then, just like a scientist conducting an experiment, she varies only one factor at a time. By examining each variable separately and systematically, she is able to come to the correct solution: The length of the string determines the speed of the pendulum.

Using Formal Operations to Solve Problems. Aleigh's approach to the pendulum question, a problem devised by Piaget, illustrates that she has moved into the formal operational period of cognitive development (Piaget & Inhelder, 1958). The **formal operational stage** is the stage at which people develop the ability to think abstractly. Piaget suggested that people reach it at the start of adolescence, around the age of 12.

By bringing formal principles of logic to bear on problems they encounter, adolescents in the formal operational stage are able to consider problems in the abstract rather than only in concrete terms. They are able to test their understanding by systematically carrying out rudimentary experiments on problems and situations and observing what their experimental interventions bring about.

Adolescents in the formal operational stage use *hypotheticodeductive reasoning,* in which they start with a general theory about what produces a particular outcome and then deduce explanations for specific situations in which they see that particular outcome. Like scientists who form hypotheses, they can then test their theories. What distinguishes this kind of thinking from earlier cognitive stages is the ability to start with abstract possibilities and move to the concrete; in previous stages, children are tied to the concrete here-and-now. For example, at age 8, Aleigh just started moving things around to see what would happen in the pendulum problem, a concrete approach. At age 12, however, she started with the abstract idea that each variable—the string, the size of the weight, and so forth—should be tested separately.

In addition to using hypotheticodeductive reasoning, adolescents can employ propositional thought during the formal operational stage. *Propositional thought* is reasoning that uses abstract logic in the absence of concrete examples. For example, propositional thinking

VIDEO CLIP

Deductive Reasoning

Formal operational stage The stage at which people develop the ability to think abstractly

Like scientists who form hypotheses, adolescents in the formal operational stage use hypotheticodeductive reasoning. They start with a general theory about what produces a particular outcome and then deduce explanations for specific situations in which they see that particular outcome.

allows adolescents to understand that if certain premises are true, a conclusion must also be true. For example, consider the following:

All men are mortal.   *[premise]*
Socrates is a man.   *[premise]*
Therefore, Socrates is mortal.   *[conclusion]*

Not only can adolescents understand that if both premises are true, then so is the conclusion, but they are also capable of using similar reasoning when premises and conclusions are stated more abstractly, as follows:

All *A*s are *B*.   *[premise]*
C is an *A*.   *[premise]*
Therefore, *C* is a *B*.   *[conclusion]*

Although Piaget proposed that children enter the formal operational stage at the beginning of adolescence, you may recall that he also hypothesized that as with all the stages of cognitive development, full capabilities do not emerge suddenly, at one stroke. Instead, they gradually unfold through a combination of physical maturation and environmental experiences. According to Piaget, it is not until adolescents are around 15 years old that they are fully settled in the formal operational stage.

In fact, some evidence suggests that a sizable proportion of people hone their formal operational skills at a later age and in some cases never fully employ formal operational thinking at all. For instance, most studies show that only 40 to 60 percent of college students and adults achieve formal operational thinking completely, and some estimates run as low as 25 percent. But many of those adults who do not show formal operational thought in every domain are fully competent in *some* aspects of formal operations (Keating & Clark, 1980; Sugarman, 1988).

The use of formal operations may well differ for this Honduran adolescent from someone the same age raised in the United States.

Cultural Influences.   One of the reasons adolescents differ in their use of formal operations relates to the culture in which they were raised. For instance, people who live in isolated, scientifically unsophisticated societies and who have little formal education are less likely to perform at the formal operational level than formally educated persons living in more technologically sophisticated societies (Jahoda, 1980; Segall et al., 1990).

Does this mean that adolescents (and adults) from cultures in which formal operations tend not to emerge are incapable of attaining them? Not at all. A more probable conclusion is that the scientific reasoning that characterizes formal operations is not equally valued in all societies. If everyday life does not require or promote a certain type of reasoning, it is unreasonable to expect people to employ that type of reasoning when confronted with a problem (Gauvain, 1998; Greenfield, 1976; J. D. Shea, 1985).

The Consequences of Adolescents' Use of Formal Operations.   Adolescents' ability to reason abstractly, embodied in their use of formal operations, leads to a change in their everyday behavior. Whereas earlier they may have unquestioningly accepted rules and explanations set out for them, their increased abstract reasoning abilities may lead them to question their parents and other authority figures far more strenuously. Advances in abstract thinking also lead to greater idealism, which may make adolescents impatient with imperfections in institutions such as schools and the government.

In general, adolescents become more argumentative, sometimes for the sake of being argumentative. They enjoy using abstract reasoning to poke holes in others' explanations, and their increased abilities to think critically make them acutely sensitive to parents' and teachers' perceived shortcomings (Elkind, 1994).

Coping with the increased argumentativeness of adolescents can be challenging for parents, teachers, and other adults who deal with adolescents. But it also makes adolescents more interesting as they actively seek to understand the values and justifications that they encounter in their lives.

Evaluating Piaget's Approach.   Each time we've considered Piaget's theory in previous chapters, several concerns have cropped up. Let's summarize some of the issues here:

- Piaget suggests that cognitive development proceeds in universal, steplike advances that occur at particular stages. Yet we find significant differences in cognitive abilities from one person to the next, especially when we compare individuals from different cultures. Furthermore, we find inconsistencies even within the same individual. People may be able to accomplish some tasks that indicate they have reached a certain level of thinking but not others. If Piaget were correct, a person ought to perform uniformly well once she or he reaches a given stage (Siegler, 1994).

- The notion of stages proposed by Piaget suggests that cognitive abilities do not grow gradually or smoothly. Instead, the stage point of view implies that cognitive growth is typified by relatively rapid shifts from one stage to the next. In contrast, many developmentalists argue that cognitive development proceeds in a more continuous fashion, increasing not so much in qualitative leaps forward as in quantitative accumulations. They also contend that Piaget's theory is better at *describing* behavior at a given stage than *explaining* why the shift from one stage to the next occurs (Case, 1991; Gelman & Baillargeon, 1983).

- Because of the nature of the tasks Piaget employed to measure cognitive abilities, critics suggest that he underestimated the age at which certain capabilities emerge. It is now widely accepted that infants and children are more sophisticated at an earlier age than Piaget asserted (Bornstein & Sigman, 1986).

- Piaget had a relatively narrow view of what is meant by *thinking* and *knowing*. To Piaget, knowledge consists primarily of the kind of understanding displayed in the pendulum problem. However, as we discussed in Chapter 12, developmentalists such as Howard Gardner (2000) suggest that we have many kinds of intelligence, separate from and independent of one another.

- Finally, some developmentalists argue that formal operations do not represent the epitome of thinking and that more sophisticated forms of thinking do not actually emerge until early adulthood. For instance, developmental psychologist Giesela Labouvie-Vief

(1980, 1986) argues that the complexity of society requires thought that is not necessarily based on pure logic. Instead, a kind of thinking is required that is flexible, allows for interpretive processes, and reflects the fact that reasons behind events in the real world are subtle—something that Labouvie-Vief calls *postformal thinking.*

These criticisms and concerns regarding Piaget's approach to cognitive development have considerable merit. Nevertheless, Piaget made momentous contributions to our understanding of cognitive development, and his work remains highly influential. He was a brilliant observer of children's and adolescents' behavior, and his portrayal of children as actively constructing and transforming information about their world has had a substantial impact on the way we view children and their cognitive capabilities.

Piaget's theory has been the impetus for an enormous number of studies on the development of thinking capacities and processes, and it also spurred a good deal of classroom reform. Finally, his bold statements about the nature of cognitive development provided a fertile soil from which many opposing positions on cognitive development bloomed, such as the information processing perspective, to which we turn next (Demetriou, Shayer, & Efklides, 1993; Zigler & Gilman, 1998).

Information Processing Perspectives: Gradual Transformations in Abilities

To proponents of information processing approaches to cognitive development, growth in mental abilities proceeds gradually and continuously. Unlike Piaget's view that the increasing cognitive sophistication of the adolescent is a reflection of stagelike spurts, the *information processing perspective* sees changes in cognitive abilities as gradual transformations in the capacity to take in, use, and store information.

In this view, developmental advances are brought about by progressive changes in the ways people organize their thinking about the world, develop strategies for dealing with new situations, sort facts, and achieve advances in memory capacity and perceptual abilities (Burbules & Lin, 1988; Pressley & Schneider, 1997; Wellman & Gelman, 1992).

The cognitive strides made during adolescence are considerable. Although general intelligence, as measured by traditional IQ tests, remains stable, dramatic improvements evolve in the specific mental abilities that underlie intelligence. Verbal, mathematical, and spatial abilities increase. Memory capacity grows, and adolescents become more adept at effectively dividing their attention across more than one stimulus at a time—such as simultaneously studying for a biology test and listening to a music CD.

Furthermore, as Piaget noted, adolescents grow increasingly sophisticated in their understanding of problems, their ability to grasp abstract concepts and to think hypothetically, and their comprehension of the possibilities inherent in situations.

Adolescents know more about the world, too; their store of knowledge increases as the amount of material to which they are exposed grows and their memory capacity enlarges (Pressley, 1987). Taken as a whole, the mental abilities that underlie intelligence show a marked improvement during adolescence, peaking at around age 20.

According to information processing explanations of cognitive development during adolescence, one of the most important reasons for advances in mental abilities is the growth of metacognition. **Metacognition** is the knowledge that people have about their own thinking processes and their ability to monitor their own cognition. Although school-age children can use some metacognitive strategies, adolescents are much more adept at understanding their own mental processes.

For example, as adolescents improve their understanding of their memory capacity, they get better at gauging how long they need to study a particular kind of material to memorize it for a test. Furthermore, they can judge when they have fully memorized the material considerably more accurately than when they were younger. These improvements in metacognitive

Metacognition The knowledge that people have about their own thinking processes and their ability to monitor their cognition abilities permit adolescents to comprehend and master school material more effectively (Kuhn, 2000; Landine & Stewart, 1998; T. O. Nelson, 1994).

Yet advances in metacognition do not always produce positive results. For instance, metacognition may make adolescents particularly introspective and self-conscious—two hallmarks of the period that, as we see next, may produce a high degree of egocentrism.

Adolescents' Self-Absorption

Carlos is furious at his parents. He sees them as totally unfair because whenever he borrows their car, they insist that he call home and let them know where he is. Eleanor is angry at Molly because Molly, by chance, bought earrings just like hers, and Molly insists on sometimes wearing them to school. Lou is upset with his biology teacher, Ms. Sebastian, for giving a long, difficult midterm exam on which he didn't do well.

Each of these adolescents is furious, angry, or upset over what may seem like not-so-unreasonable behavior on the part of others. Why? One cause may lie in the egocentrism that sometimes dominates adolescents' thinking. **Adolescent egocentrism** is a state of self-absorption in which the world is viewed from one's own point of view. Egocentrism makes adolescents highly critical of authority figures such as parents and teachers, unwilling to accept criticism, and quick to find fault with others' behavior (Elkind, 1967, 1985; Rycek et al., 1998).

The kind of egocentrism we see in adolescence helps explain why adolescents sometimes perceive that they are the focus of everyone else's attention. In fact, adolescents may develop what has been called an **imaginary audience,** fictitious observers who pay as much attention to the adolescents' behavior as adolescents do themselves.

Because of adolescents' newly sophisticated metacognitive abilities, they readily imagine that others are thinking about them, and they may construct elaborate scenarios about others' thoughts. The imaginary audience is usually perceived as focusing on the one thing that adolescents think most about: themselves. Unfortunately, these scenarios may suffer from the same kind of egocentrism as the rest of their thinking. For instance, a student sitting in a class may be sure a teacher is focusing on her, and a teenager at a basketball game may just know that everyone around is focusing on the pimple on his chin.

Egocentrism leads to a second distortion in thinking: the notion that one's experiences are unique. Adolescents develop **personal fables,** the view that what happens to them is unique, exceptional, and shared by no one else. For instance, teenagers whose romantic relationships have ended may feel that no one has ever experienced the hurt they feel, that no one has ever been treated so badly, that no one can understand what they are going through.

Personal fables also may make adolescents feel invulnerable to the risks that threaten others (Klaczynski, 1997). For example, they may think that there is no need to use condoms during sex because in the personal fables they construct, pregnancy and sexually transmitted diseases such as AIDS only happen to other kinds of people, not to them. They may drive after drinking because their personal fables paint them as careful drivers, always in control. Much of adolescents' risk taking may well be traced to the personal fables they construct for themselves (Arnett, 1995; Dolcini et al., 1989; Greene et al., 2000; Lightfoot, 1997; Ponton, 1999).

Adolescent egocentrism A state of self-absorption in which the world is viewed from one's own point of view

Imaginary audience Fictitious observers who pay as much attention to adolescents' behavior as they do themselves

Personal fables The view held by some adolescents that what happens to them is unique, exceptional, and shared by no one else

VIDEO CLIP
Egocentrism

VIDEO CLIP
Invincibility Fable

VIDEO CLIP
Imaginary Audience

Adolescents' egocentrism leads to the belief that what happens to them is unique and to feelings of invulnerability—producing risky behavior.

R E V I E W & A P P L Y

Review

- Adolescence corresponds to Piaget's formal operations period, a stage characterized by abstract reasoning and an experimental approach to problems.

- According to the information processing perspective, the cognitive advances of adolescence are quantitative and gradual, involving improvements in many aspects of thinking and memory. Improved metacognition enables the monitoring of thought processes and of mental capacities.

- Adolescents are susceptible to adolescent egocentrism and the perception that their behavior is constantly observed by an imaginary audience. They also construct personal fables that stress their uniqueness and immunity to harm.

Applying Child Development

- When facing complex problems, do you think most adults spontaneously apply formal operations like those used to solve the pendulum problem? Why or why not?

- *From a social worker's perspective:* In what ways does adolescent egocentrism complicate adolescents' social and family relationships? Do adults entirely outgrow egocentrism and personal fables?

Moral Development

Your wife is near death from an unusual kind of cancer. One drug exists that the physicians think might save her—a form of radium that a scientist in a nearby city has recently developed. The drug, though, is expensive to manufacture, and the scientist is charging 10 times what the drug costs him to make. He pays $1,000 for the radium and charges $10,000 for a small dose. You have gone to everyone you know to borrow money, but you can get together only $2,500—one quarter of what you need. You've told the scientist that your wife is dying and asked him to sell it more cheaply or let you pay later. But the scientist has said, "No, I discovered the drug and I'm going to make money from it." In desperation, you consider breaking into the scientist's laboratory to steal the drug for your wife.

Should you do it?

Kohlberg's Theory of Moral Development

According to developmental psychologist Lawrence Kohlberg, the answer that children give to this question reveals central aspects of their sense of morality and justice. He suggests that people's responses to moral dilemmas such as this one reveal the stage of moral development they have attained—and also yields information about their general level of cognitive development (Colby & Kohlberg, 1987; Kohlberg, 1984).

Kohlberg contends that people pass through a series of stages in the evolution of their sense of justice and in the kind of reasoning they use to make moral judgments. Primarily due to cognitive characteristics that we discussed earlier, school-age children tend to think either in terms of concrete, unvarying rules ("It is always wrong to steal" or "I'll be punished if I steal") or in terms of the rules of society ("Good people don't steal" or "What if everyone stole?").

By the time they reach adolescence, however, individuals are able to reason on a higher level, typically having reached Piaget's stage of formal operations. They are capable of comprehending abstract, formal principles of morality, and they consider cases such as the one just presented in terms of broader issues of morality and of right and wrong ("Stealing may be justifiable if you are following your own standards of conscience").

Kohlberg suggests that moral development can best be understood within the context of a three-level sequence, which is further subdivided into six stages (see Table 15-1). At the lowest

TABLE 15-1 KOHLBERG'S SEQUENCE OF MORAL REASONING

KOHLBERG'S SEQUENCE		SAMPLE MORAL REASONING	
Level	Stage	In Favor of Stealing	Against Stealing
Level 1 Preconventional morality: At this level, the concrete interests of the individual are considered in terms of rewards and punishments.	**Stage 1** Obedience and punishment orientation: At this stage, people stick to rules in order to avoid punishment, and obedience occurs for its own sake.	"If you let your wife die, you will get in trouble. You'll be blamed for not spending the money to save her, and there'll be an investigation of you and the druggist for your wife's death."	"You shouldn't steal the drug because you'll get caught and sent to jail if you do. If you do get away, your conscience will bother you thinking how the police will catch up with you at any minute."
	Stage 2 Reward orientation: At this stage, rules are followed only for a person's own benefit. Obedience occurs because of rewards that are received.	"If you do happen to get caught, you could give the drug back and you wouldn't get much of a sentence. It wouldn't bother you much to serve a little jail term, if you have your wife when you get out."	"You may not get much of a jail term if you steal the drug, but your wife will probably die before you get out, so it won't do much good. If your wife dies, you shouldn't blame yourself; it isn't your fault she has cancer."
Level 2 Conventional morality: At this level, people approach moral problems as members of society. They are interested in pleasing others by acting as good members of society.	**Stage 3** "Good boy" morality: Individuals at this stage show an interest in maintaining the respect of others and doing what is expected of them.	"No one will think you're bad if you steal the drug, but your family will think you're an inhuman husband if you don't. If you let your wife die, you'll never be able to look anybody in the face again."	"It isn't just the druggist who will think you're a criminal; everyone else will, too. After you steal the drug, you'll feel bad thinking how you've brought dishonor on your family and yourself; you won't be able to face anyone again."
	Stage 4 Authority and social-order-maintaining morality: People at this stage conform to society's rules and consider that "right" is what society defines as right.	"If you have any sense of honor, you won't let your wife die just because you're afraid to do the only thing that will save her. You'll always feel guilty that you caused her death if you don't do your duty to her."	"You're desperate and you may not know you're doing wrong when you steal the drug. But you'll know you did wrong after you're sent to jail. You'll always feel guilty for your dishonesty and law-breaking."
Level 3 Postconventional morality: At this level, people use moral principles that are seen as broader than those of any particular society.	**Stage 5** Morality of contract, individual rights, and democratically accepted law: People at this stage do what is right because of a sense of obligation to laws that are agreed on by society. They perceive that laws can be modified as part of changes in an implicit social contract.	"You'll lose other people's respect, not gain it, if you don't steal. If you let your wife die, it will be out of fear, not out of reasoning. So you'll just lose self-respect and probably the respect of others, too."	"You'll lose your standing and respect in the community and violate the law. You'll lose respect for yourself if you're carried away by emotion and forget the long-range point of view."
	Stage 6 Morality of individual principles and conscience: At this final stage, a person follows laws because they are based on universal ethical principles. Laws that violate the principles are disobeyed.	"If you don't steal the drug, and if you let your wife die, you'll always condemn yourself for it afterward. You won't be blamed and you'll have lived up to the outside rule of the law, but you won't have lived up to your own standards of conscience."	"If you steal the drug, you won't be blamed by other people, but you'll condemn yourself because you won't have lived up to your own conscience and standards of honesty."

(*Source:* Adapted from Kohlberg, 1969)

level, *preconventional morality* (Stages 1 and 2), people follow unvarying rules based on rewards and punishments. For example, a child at the preconventional level might evaluate the moral dilemma in our story by saying that it was not worth stealing the drug because if you were caught, you would go to jail.

In the next level, that of *conventional morality* (Stages 3 and 4), people approach moral problems in terms of their own position as good, responsible members of society. Thus children who decide against stealing the drug because they think they would feel guilty or dishonest and those who decide in favor of stealing the drug because if they did nothing in this situation, they would be unable to face others, would be reasoning at the conventional level of morality.

Finally, individuals using *postconventional morality* (Level 3; Stages 5 and 6) invoke universal moral principles that are considered broader than the rules of the particular society in which they live. Students who feel that they would condemn themselves if they did not steal the drug because they would not be living up to their own moral principles would be reasoning at the postconventional level.

Kohlberg's theory proposes that people move through the periods of moral development in a fixed order and that they are unable to reach the highest stage until about the age of 13, due to deficits in cognitive development that are not overcome until then (Kurtines & Gewirtz, 1987). However, not everyone is presumed to reach the highest stages: Kohlberg has found that only about 25 percent of all adults rise above the fourth stage of his model, into the level of postconventional morality.

Unfortunately, although Kohlberg's theory provides a good account of the development of moral *judgments,* it is less adequate in predicting moral *behavior.* For example, one experiment found that 15 percent of students who reasoned at the postconventional level of morality—the highest category—cheated on a task, although they were not as prone to cheating as those at lower levels: Some 55 percent of those at the conventional level and 70 percent of those at the preconventional level also cheated (Kohlberg, 1975; Kupfersmid & Wonderly, 1980). Clearly, knowing what is morally right does not always mean acting that way (Killen & Hart, 1995).

Still, a good deal of research suggests that some aspects of moral conduct are clearly related to Kohlberg's levels of moral reasoning, although the results are often complex and not easy to interpret. For instance, children who reason at Stage 1 and Stage 3 tend to be the best behaved in school, while those who reason at Stage 2 are more apt to exhibit poor social behavior in school settings. Such findings suggest that we have not heard the last word on Kohlberg's stages (Rest et al., 1999; Thoma & Rest, 1999).

Gilligan's Theory of Moral Development

An aspect of Kohlberg's theory that has proved particularly problematic is the difficulty it has explaining *girls'* moral judgments. Because the theory initially was based largely on data from males, some researchers have argued that it does a better job describing boys' moral development than girls'.

In fact, psychologist Carol Gilligan (1982, 1987) has suggested an alternative account of the development of moral behavior in girls. She suggests that differences in the ways boys and girls are raised in our society lead to basic distinctions in how men and women view moral behavior. According to her, boys view morality primarily in terms of broad principles such as justice or fairness, while girls see it in terms of responsibility toward individuals and a willingness to sacrifice themselves to help specific individuals within the context of particular relationships. Compassion for individuals, then, is a more prominent factor in moral behavior for women than it is for men (Gilligan, Lyons, & Hammer, 1990).

Because Kohlberg's theory considers moral behavior largely in terms of principles of justice, it is inadequate in describing the moral development of females. This accounts for the surprising finding that women typically score at a lower level than men on tests of moral judgment using Kohlberg's stage sequence. In Gilligan's view, a female's morality is centered

Carol Gilligan argues that boys and girls view morality differently, with boys seeing it primarily in terms of broad principles and girls considering it in terms of personal relationships and responsibility toward individuals.

These students exemplify Gilligan's stage of moral development in which violence against others (as well as oneself) is viewed as immoral.

more on individual well-being than on moral abstractions, and the highest levels of morality are represented by compassionate concern for the welfare of others.

Gilligan views morality as developing among females in a three-stage process (summarized in Table 15-2). In the first stage, called "orientation toward individual survival," females first concentrate on what is practical and best for them, gradually making a transition from selfishness to responsibility, in which they think about what would be best for others. In the second stage, termed "goodness as self-sacrifice," females begin to think that they must sacrifice their

TABLE 15-2   GILLIGAN'S THREE STAGES OF MORAL DEVELOPMENT FOR WOMEN

Stage	Characteristics	Example
Stage 1 Orientation toward individual survival	Initial concentration is on what is practical and best for self. Gradual transition from selfishness to responsibility, which includes thinking about what would be best for others.	A first grader may insist on playing only games of her own choosing when playing with a friend.
Stage 2 Goodness as self-sacrifice	Initial view is that a woman must sacrifice her own wishes to what other people want. Gradual transition from "goodness" to "truth," which takes into account needs of both self and others.	Now older, the same girl may believe that to be a good friend, she must play the games her friend chooses, even if she herself doesn't like them.
Stage 3 Morality of nonviolence	A moral equivalence is established between self and others. Hurting anyone—including oneself—is seen as immoral. Most sophisticated form of reasoning, according to Gilligan.	The same girl may realize that both friends must enjoy their time together and look for activities that both of them can enjoy.

own wishes to what other people want, ultimately making the transition from "goodness" to "truth," in which they take into account their own needs plus those of others. Finally, in the third stage, "morality of nonviolence," women come to see that hurting anyone is immoral—including hurting themselves. This realization establishes a moral equivalence between themselves and others and represents, according to Gilligan, the most sophisticated level of moral reasoning.

Gilligan's sequence of stages is clearly quite different from Kohlberg's. However, some researchers have suggested that her rejection of Kohlberg's work is too sweeping and that gender differences are not as pronounced as first thought (Colby & Damon, 1987). For instance, some studies have found that both males and females use similar "justice" and "compassion" orientations in making moral judgments. Thus the question of how boys and girls differ in their moral orientations remains unsettled (Crandall et al., 1999; Perry & McIntire, 1995).

Review

- Kohlberg proposed three broad levels of moral development, encompassing six stages.

- The ability to make moral judgments does not invariably lead to moral behavior, but there is a relationship between moral reasoning and moral behavior.

- Psychologist Carol Gilligan found that females view morality in terms of responsibility and self-sacrifice on behalf of others, in contrast to the broad principles of justice that characterize males' moral reasoning.

Applying Child Development

- In what ways are cognitive development and moral development interrelated? What cognitive abilities underlie the stages of moral development described by Kohlberg and Gilligan?

- *From an educator's perspective:* Should moral development be taught in public schools?

School Performance and Cognitive Development

Do the advances that occur in metacognition, reasoning, and other cognitive abilities during adolescence translate into improvements in school performance? If we use students' grades as the measure of school performance, the answer is no. On average, students' grades decline during the course of schooling (Schulenberg, Asp, & Petersen, 1984; Simmons & Blyth, 1987).

The reasons for this decline are not entirely clear. Obviously, the nature of the material to which students are exposed becomes increasingly complex and sophisticated over the course of adolescence. But the growing cognitive abilities of adolescents might be expected to compensate for the increased sophistication of the material. Thus we need to look to other explanations to account for the grade decline.

One explanation seems to relate not to student performance but to teachers' grading practices. It turns out that teachers grade older adolescents more stringently than younger ones.

Consequently, even though students may be demonstrating greater competence as they continue with their schooling, their grades don't necessarily reflect the improvement because teachers are grading them more strictly (Simmons & Blyth, 1987).

The decline in grades may also reflect broader difficulties in educational achievement, particularly that of students in the United States. For example, over the past four decades, the U.S. high school graduation rate has slipped from first place in the world to 24th and now stands at 72 percent (Organization for Economic Cooperation and Development, 1998; see Figure 15-1).

Furthermore, the performance of students in the United States on math and science is poor when compared to that of students in other industrialized countries, and performance in geography is only average. There is no single reason for this gap in the educational achievement of U.S. students, but a combination of factors, such as less time spent in classes and less intensive instruction, are at work. For example, the broad diversity of the U.S. school population may affect performance relative to other countries, in which the population attending

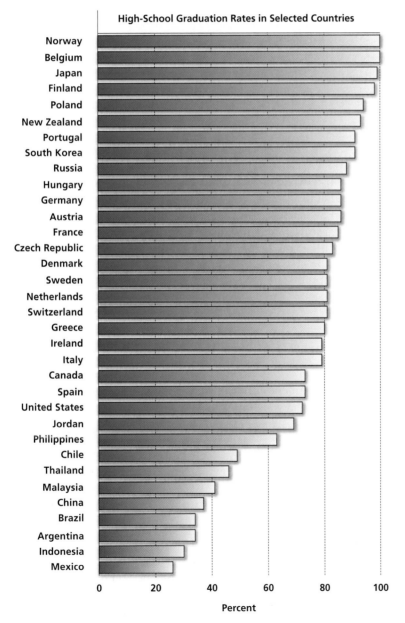

Note: The bars show the ratio of high-school graduates in 1996 to the population at the typical age of graduation in each country. The figures for Russia and Thailand are from 1997 and for Brazil from 1995. The figure for Belgium refers to the Flemish population only.

FIGURE 15-1   HIGH SCHOOL GRADUATION RATES: U.S. NO LONGER AT THE TOP OF THE CLASS

Although it once stood first in the percentage of the population who graduates from high school, the United States has dropped to 24th among industrialized countries.

(*Source:* Organization for Economic Cooperation and Development, 1998)

school is more homogeneous and affluent. As we discuss next, differences in socioeconomic status are reflected in school performance within the United States (Schemo, 2001; Stedman, 1997).

Socioeconomic Status and School Performance: Individual Differences in Achievement

Despite the ideal that all students are entitled to the same opportunity in the classroom, it is very clear that certain groups have more educational advantages than others. One of the most telling indicators of this reality is the relationship between educational achievement and socioeconomic status (SES).

Middle- and high-SES students, on average, earn higher grades, score higher on standardized tests of achievement, and complete more years of schooling than students from lower SES homes. Of course, this disparity does not start in adolescence; the same findings hold for children in lower grades. However, by the time students are in high school, the effects of socioeconomic status become even more pronounced (Garbarino & Asp, 1981).

Why do students from middle- and high-SES homes show greater academic success? There are several explanations, most involving environmental factors. For one thing, children living in poverty lack many of the advantages enjoyed by other children. Their nutrition and health may be less adequate. Often living in crowded conditions and attending inadequate schools, they may have few places to do homework. Their homes may lack the books and computers commonplace in more economically advantaged households.

Furthermore, parents living in poverty are less likely to be involved in their children's schooling—a factor that is related to school success. Poorer adolescents, who may live in impoverished areas of cities with high levels of violence, may also attend older and generally inadequate schools with run-down facilities and a higher incidence of violence. Taken together, these factors result in a less than optimal learning environment (C. R. Adams & Singh, 1998; N. K. Bowen & Bowen, 1999; Caldas & Bankston, 1997).

In short, students from impoverished backgrounds may be at a disadvantage from the day they begin their schooling. As they grow older, their school performance may continue to lag, and in fact their disadvantage may snowball. Because later school success builds heavily on basic skills presumably learned early in school, children who experience problems early may find themselves falling increasingly behind as adolescents (Huston, 1991; D. A. Phillips et al., 1994).

Ethnic and Racial Differences in School Achievement

Achievement differences between ethnic and racial groups are significant, and they paint a troubling picture of American education. For instance, data on school achievement indicate that on average, African American and Hispanic students tend to perform at lower levels, receive lower grades, and score lower on standardized tests of achievement than Caucasian students (see Table 15-3). In contrast, Asian American students tend to receive higher grades than Caucasian students (Dornbusch, Ritter, & Steinberg, 1992; National Center for Education Statistics, 2000a).

Socioeconomic Factors.   What is the source of these ethnic and racial differences in academic achievement? Much of the difference is due to socioeconomic factors: Because more African American and Hispanic families live in poverty, their economic disadvantage may be reflected in their school performance. In fact, when we take SES into account by comparing different ethnic and racial groups at the same socioeconomic level, achievement differences diminish (Luster & McAdoo, 1994; Meece & Kurtz-Costes, 2001; L. Steinberg, Dornbusch, & Brown, 1992).

But socioeconomic factors are not the full story. For instance, anthropologist John Ogbu (1988, 1992) argues that members of certain minority groups may perceive school success as

TABLE 15-3 PERFORMANCE ON TESTS OF ACHIEVEMENT

Reading 1998	4th Graders	8th Graders	12th Graders
National average	217	264	291
White	227	272	298
Black	194	243	270
Hispanic	196	244	275
Asian/Pacific Islander	225	271	289
American Indian	202	248	276
Mathematics 2000	**4th Graders**	**8th Graders**	**12th Graders**
National average	228	275	301
White	236	286	308
Black	205	247	274
Hispanic	212	253	283
Asian/Pacific Islander	232[a]	289	319
American Indian	216	255	293

[a]1996 figure.

(*Sources:* National Center for Education Statistics; National Assessment of Educational Progress.)

relatively unimportant. They may believe that prejudice in the workplace will stand in the way of their success no matter how much effort they expend. The conclusion is that hard work in school will have no eventual payoff.

Furthermore, Ogbu suggests that members of minority groups who enter a new culture voluntarily are more likely to be successful in school than those who are brought into a new culture against their will. For instance, he notes that Korean children who are the sons and daughters of voluntary immigrants to the United States tend to be, on average, quite successful in school. On the other hand, Korean children in Japan, whose parents were forced to immigrate during World War II and work as forced laborers, tend to do relatively poorly in school. The reason for the disparity? The process of involuntary immigration apparently leaves lasting scars, reducing the motivation to succeed in subsequent generations. Ogbu suggests that in the United States, the involuntary immigration as slaves of the ancestors of many African American students might be related to their motivation to succeed (Gallagher, 1994; Ogbu, 1992).

Attributions and Beliefs About Academic Success.   Another factor in the differential success of various ethnic and racial group members has to do with attributions for academic success. Students from many Asian cultures tend to view achievement as the consequence of temporary situational factors, such as how hard they work. In contrast, African American students are more apt to view success as the result of external causes over which they have no control, such as luck or societal biases. Students who subscribe to the belief that effort will lead to success and then expend that effort are more likely to do better in school than students who believe that effort makes little difference (Fuligni, 1997; Stevenson, Chen, & Lee, 1992; Stevenson & Stigler, 1992).

Ethnic disparities in adolescent performance may also be due to differences in adolescents' beliefs about the consequences of not doing well in school. Specifically, it may be that African American and Hispanic students tend to believe that they can succeed *despite* poor school

FROM RESEARCH TO PRACTICE

Cyberspace: Adolescents Online

Students at McClymonds High School in Oakland, California, have a mission: In conjunction with local entomologists, they are creating an online collection of insects in the neighborhood. By placing their "collection" on the World Wide Web, they expect to provide a long-term resource for local residents. (Harmon, 1997)

The widespread availability of the Internet and the World Wide Web is likely to produce significant changes in the lives of many adolescents. Easy access to far-reaching information and contacts is likely to bring benefits and, at the same time, dangers that are both real and virtual.

The educational promise of the Internet is significant. Through the Internet, students can tap into a vast array of information, ranging from library catalogs to government statistics to views of the landscape of Mars transmitted by cameras actually sitting on that planet. And adolescents are becoming increasingly familiar with computers, using them in a variety of ways (see Figure 15-2).

Although it is clear that the Internet is having an impact on education, it is not yet obvious how it will change education or whether the impact will be uniformly positive. For instance, schools must change their curricula to include specific instruction in a key skill for deriving value from the Internet: learning to sort through huge bodies of information to identify what is most useful and discard what is not. To obtain the full benefits of the Internet, then, students must obtain the ability to search, choose, and integrate information in order to create new knowledge (Oblinger & Rush, 1997).

Despite the substantial benefits of the Internet, its use also has a downside. Claims that cyberspace is overrun with

Racial disparities in computer access represent a major challenge to society.

pornography and child molesters may be exaggerated, but it is true that cyberspace makes available material that many parents and other adults find highly objectionable (Bremer & Rauch, 1998; Lohr, 1995; Staudenmeier, 1999).

The growing use of computers also presents a challenge involving race. Specifically, whites are significantly more likely than African Americans to have a computer at home. The results of one survey found that while 22 percent of whites reported using the World Wide Web in the past 6 months, only 17 percent of African Americans had done so. For people earning less than $40,000 a year, these disparities were even greater: More than twice as many whites as African-Americans report owing computers. These are wide disparities, and they suggest that African Americans may be at a disadvantage in terms of their access to computers. How society reduces these discrepancies is a matter of considerable importance (D. L. Hoffman & Novak, 1998).

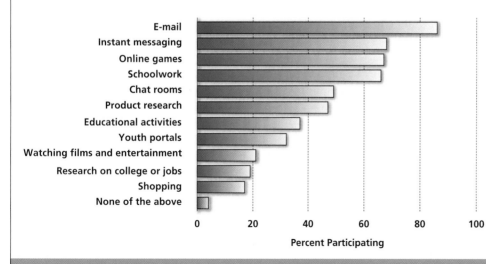

FIGURE 15-2   TEENAGE ONLINE ACTIVITY

Today, a large majority of teenagers use the Internet to communicate via e-mail and instant messaging, and many also use the new technology for education-related material and research. How will this trend affect the way educators will teach in the future?

(*Source:* Yankee Group Interactive Consumer Survey, 2001)

performance. This belief may cause them to put less effort into their studies. In contrast, Asian American students tend to believe that if they do not do well in school, they are unlikely to get good jobs and be successful. Asian Americans, then, are motivated to work hard in school by a fear of the consequences of poor academic performance (L. Steinberg et al., 1992). (For another aspect of adolescent behavior related to schooling, see the *From Research to Practice* box.)

Part-Time Work: Students on the Job

For most high school students, school is sandwiched between one or more part-time jobs. In fact, most 16- and 17-year-olds work at some sort of job, and 38 percent of 15-year-olds have regular employment during the school year (Employment Policies Institute, 2000).

Working offers several advantages. In addition to providing funds for recreational activities and sometimes necessities, it helps students learn responsibility, gives practice with the ability to handle money, and can help teach workplace skills.

However, there are also significant drawbacks to work. It may prevent students from participating in extracurricular activities, and it reduces the time available to do homework and to study for tests. Many jobs that are available to high school students are high on drudgery and low on transferable skills. Ultimately, the outcome of part-time work can be either positive or negative, depending on an individual student's circumstances (National Center for Education Statistics, 2001).

Dropping Out of School

Although most students complete high school, some half million students each year drop out prior to graduating. Adolescents who leave school do so for a variety of reasons. Some leave because of pregnancy or problems with the English language. Some leave for economic reasons, needing to support themselves or their families.

As shown in Figure 15-3, the dropout rate differs according to ethnicity. For instance, although the dropout rate for all ethnicities has been declining somewhat in recent decades, Hispanic and African American students are still more likely to leave high school before graduating than non-Hispanic white students. Not all minority groups show higher dropout rates, however: Asians, for instance, drop out at a lower rate than Caucasians (Canedy, 2001; National Center for Education Statistics, 2000b).

Twenty-three percent of students who live in households with the lowest 20 percent of income levels drop out. This rate is nearly eight times greater than the 3 percent of dropout

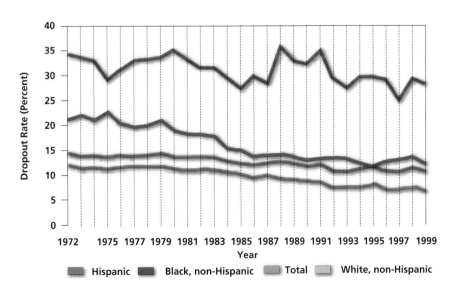

FIGURE 15-3   DROPOUT RATES AND ETHNICITY

In spite of the fact that dropout rates have been falling for all ethnic groups, Hispanic and African American students are still more likely not to graduate. How can social workers and educators work together to reduce high school dropout rates?

(*Source:* National Center for Education Statistics, 2000b)

students in households with incomes in the highest 20 percent. Because economic success is so dependent on education, dropping out often perpetuates a cycle of poverty (National Center for Education Statistics, 1997).

College: Pursuing Higher Education

For Enrico Vasquez, there was never any doubt: He was headed for college. Enrico, the son of a wealthy Cuban immigrant who had made a fortune in the medical supply business after fleeing Cuba 5 years before Enrico's birth, had had the importance of education constantly drummed into him by his family. In fact, the question was never *whether* he would go to college but what college he would be able to get into. As a consequence, Enrico found high school to be a pressure cooker: Every grade and extracurricular activity was evaluated in terms of its helping or hindering his chances of admission to a good college.

Armando Williams's letter of acceptance to Dallas County Community College is framed on the wall of his mother's apartment. To her, the letter represents nothing short of a miracle, an answer to her prayers. Growing up in a neighborhood infamous for its drugs and drive-by shootings, Armando had always been a hard worker and a "good boy," in his mother's view. But when he was growing up, she never even entertained the possibility of his making it to college. To see him reach this stage in his education fills her with joy.

Whether a student's enrollment seems almost inevitable or signifies a triumph over the odds, attending college is a significant accomplishment. Although students already enrolled may feel that college attendance is nearly universal, this is not the case at all: Nationwide, only a minority of high school graduates enter college.

Who Goes to College?

As in the U.S. population as a whole, U.S. college students are primarily white and middle class. Although nearly 69 percent of white high school graduates enter college, only 61 percent of African American and 47 percent of Hispanic graduates do so (see Figure 15-4). Even more striking, although the absolute number of minority students enrolled in college has increased, the overall *proportion* of the minority population that does enter college has *decreased* over

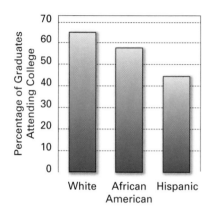

FIGURE 15-4   COLLEGE PARTICIPATION BY HIGH SCHOOL GRADUATES

The proportion of African Americans and Hispanics who enter college after graduating from high school is lower than the proportion of whites.

(*Source:* U.S. Bureau of the Census, 1998, 2000)

The diversity of students attending college is rising dramatically, although enrollment of minority students still lags proportionately to the enrollments of whites.

the past decade—a decline that most education experts attribute to changes in the availability of financial aid.

Furthermore, the proportion of students who enter college but ultimately never graduate is substantial. Only around 40 percent of those who start college finish 4 years later with a degree. Although about half of those who don't receive a degree in 4 years eventually do finish, the other half never obtain a college degree. For minorities, the picture is even worse: The national dropout rate for African American college students stands at 70 percent (Minorities in Higher Education, 1995).

These observations notwithstanding, the number of minority students attending college is rising dramatically, and minority students make up an increasingly larger proportion of the college population. Already at some colleges, such as the University of California at Berkeley, whites have shifted from the majority to the minority as what is traditionally called "minority" representation has increased significantly. These trends, reflecting changes in the ethnic composition of the United States, are significant, since higher education remains an important way for families to improve their economic well-being (Kates, 1995).

Gender and College Performance

> I registered for a calculus course my first year at DePauw. Even twenty years ago I was not timid, so on the very first day I raised my hand and asked a question. I still have a vivid memory of the professor rolling his eyes, hitting his head with his hand in frustration, and announcing to everyone, "Why do they expect me to teach calculus to girls?" I never asked another question. Several weeks later I went to a football game, but I had forgotten to bring my ID. My calculus professor was at the gate checking IDs, so I went up to him and said, "I forgot my ID but you know me, I'm in your class." He looked right at me and said, "I don't remember you in my class." I couldn't believe that someone who changed my life and whom I remember to this day didn't even recognize me. (Sadker & Sadker, 1994, p. 162)

Although such incidents of blatant sexism are less likely to occur today, prejudice and discrimination directed at women are still a fact of college life. For instance, the next time you are in class, consider the gender of your classmates and the subject matter of the class. Although men and women attend college in roughly equal numbers, there is significant variation in the classes they take. Classes in education and the social sciences, for instance, typically have a larger proportion of women than men; and classes in engineering, the physical sciences, and mathematics tend to have more men than women.

Even women who start out in mathematics, engineering, and the physical sciences are more likely than men to drop out. For instance, the attrition rate for all women in such fields during the college years is 2½ times greater than the rate for men. Ultimately, although white women make up 43 percent of the U.S. population, they earn just 22 percent of the bachelor of science degrees and 13 percent of the doctorates, and they hold only 10 percent of the jobs in physical science, math, and engineering. Nonwhite women, who hold "double minority" status, also hold fewer positions in science than nonwhite men (Cipra, 1991).

The differences in gender distribution and attrition rates across subject areas are no accident. They reflect the powerful influence of gender stereotypes that operate throughout the world of education and beyond. For instance, when women in their first year of college are asked to name a likely career choice, they are much less apt to choose careers that have traditionally been dominated by men, such as engineering or computer programming, and more likely to choose professions that have traditionally been populated by women, such as nursing and social work (Cooperative Institutional Research Program, 1990; Glick, Zion, & Nelson, 1988).

Male and female college students also have different expectations regarding their areas of competence. For instance, one survey asked first-year college students whether they were

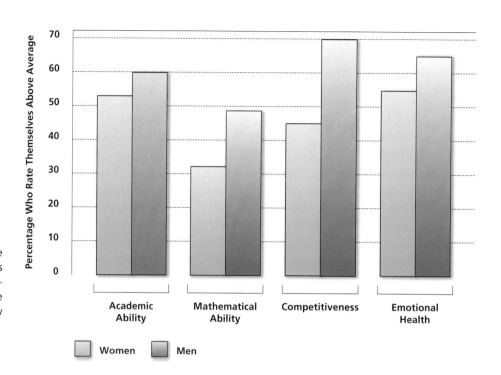

FIGURE 15-5

SELF-ASSESSMENTS IN VARIOUS CATEGORIES BY MALE AND FEMALE COLLEGE STUDENTS

During their first year of college, men are more likely than women to view themselves as above average in areas relevant to academic success. How can educators be made more aware of this problem, and how might it be addressed?

(*Source:* Sax et al., 2000)

Even though they may be unaware of it, both male and female professors treat men and women in their classes differently. For example, they typically call on men in class more frequently than women.

above or below average on a variety of traits and abilities. As can be seen in Figure 15-5, men were more likely than women to think of themselves as above average in overall academic and mathematical ability, competitiveness, and emotional health.

Both male and female college professors treat men and women differently in their classes, even though the different treatment is largely unintentional and the professors are unaware of their actions. For instance, professors call on men in class more frequently than women, and they make more eye contact with men than with women. Furthermore, male students are more likely to receive extra help from their professors than women. Finally, the male students often receive more positive reinforcement for their comments than female students—exemplified by the startling illustration in Table 15-4 (American Association of University Women, 1992; Epperson, 1988; Sadker & Sadker, 1994).

The different treatment of men and women in the college classroom has led some educators to argue in favor of single-sex colleges for women. They point to evidence that the rate of participation and ultimately the success of women in the sciences is greater for graduates of women's colleges than for graduates of coeducational institutions. Furthermore, some research suggests that women who attend same-sex colleges may show higher self-esteem than those attending coeducational colleges, although the evidence is not entirely consistent on this count (Mael, 1998; Miller-Bernal, 1993).

Why might women do better in single-sex colleges? One reason is that they receive more attention than they would in coeducational settings, where professors are affected, however inadvertently, by societal biases. In addition, women's colleges tend to have more female professors than coeducational institutions, and they thereby provide more role models for women. Finally, women attending women's colleges may receive more encouragement for participation in nontraditional subjects such as mathematics and science than those in coeducational colleges (Mael, 1998).

In fact, the effect of encouragement on women's mathematics achievement is illustrated by research involving women's expectations about mathematics performance, as discussed in the *Developmental Diversity* box.

TABLE 15-4 GENDER BIAS IN THE CLASSROOM

The course on the U.S. Constitution is required for graduation, and more than fifty students, approximately half male and half female, file in. The professor begins by asking if there are questions on next week's midterm. Several hands go up.

BERNIE: Do you have to memorize names and dates in the book? Or will the test be more general?

PROFESSOR: You do have to know those critical dates and people. Not every one but the important ones. If I were you, Bernie, I would spend time learning them. Ellen?

ELLEN: What kind of short-answer questions will there be?

PROFESSOR: All multiple choice.

ELLEN: Will we have the whole class time?

PROFESSOR: Yes, we'll have the whole class time. Anyone else?

BEN (calling out): Will there be an extra-credit question?

PROFESSOR: I hadn't planned on it. What do you think?

BEN: I really like them. They take some of the pressure off. You can also see who is doing extra work.

PROFESSOR: I'll take it under advisement. Charles?

CHARLES: How much of our final grade is this?

PROFESSOR: The midterm is 25 percent. But remember, class participation counts as well. Why don't we begin?

The professor lectures on the Constitution for twenty minutes before he asks a question about the electoral college. The electoral college is not as hot a topic as the midterm, so only four hands are raised. The professor calls on Ben.

BEN: The electoral college was created because there was a lack of faith in the people. Rather than have them vote for the president, they voted for the electors.

PROFESSOR: I like the way you think. (He smiles at Ben, and Ben smiles back.) Who could vote? (Five hands go up, five out of fifty.) Angie?

ANGIE: I don't know if this is right, but I thought only men could vote.

BEN (calling out): That was a great idea. We began going downhill when we let women vote. (Angie looks surprised but says nothing. Some of the students laugh, and so does the professor. He calls on Barbara.)

BARBARA: I think you had to be pretty wealthy, own property—

JOSH (not waiting for Barbara to finish, calls out): That's right. There was a distrust of the poor, who could upset the democracy. But if you had property, if you had something at stake, you could be trusted not to do something wild. Only property owners could be trusted.

PROFESSOR: Nice job, Josh. But why do we still have electors today? Mike?

MIKE: Tradition, I guess.

PROFESSOR: Do you think it's tradition? If you walked down the street and asked people their views of the electoral college, what would they say?

MIKE: Probably they'd be clueless. Maybe they would think that it elects the Pope. People don't know how it works.

PROFESSOR: Good, Mike. Judy, do you want to say something? (Judy's hand is at "half-mast," raised but just barely. When the professor calls her name, she looks a bit startled.)

JUDY (speaking very softly): Maybe we would need a whole new constitutional convention to change it. And once they get together to change that, they could change anything. That frightens people, doesn't it? (As Judy speaks, a number of students fidget, pass notes, and leaf through their books; a few even begin to whisper.)

(*Source:* Sadker & Sadker, 1994)

DEVELOPMENTAL DIVERSITY

Overcoming Gender and Racial Barriers to Achievement

When women take college classes in math, science, and engineering, they are more likely to do poorly than men who enter college with the same level of preparation and identical SAT scores. Strangely, however, this phenomenon does not hold true for other areas of the curriculum, where men and women perform at similar levels.

According to psychologist Claude Steele (1994), the reason has to do with women's acceptance of society's stereotypes about achievement in particular domains. Steele suggests that women are no strangers to society's dominant view that some subjects are more appropriate areas of study for women than others are. In fact, the pervasiveness of the stereotype makes women who attempt to achieve in traditionally "inappropriate" fields highly vulnerable.

Specifically, because of the strength and pervasiveness of such stereotypes, the performance of women seeking to achieve in nontraditional fields may be hindered as they are distracted by worries about the failure that society predicts for them. In some cases, a woman may decide that failure in a male-dominated field, because it would confirm societal stereotypes, would be so unpalatable that the struggle to succeed is not worth the effort. In that instance, the woman may not even try very hard.

But there is a bright side to Steele's analysis: If women can be convinced that societal stereotypes regarding achievement are invalid, their performance might well improve. And in fact, this is just what Steele found in a series of experiments he conducted at the University of Michigan and Stanford University (Steele, 1994).

In one study, male and female college students were told they would be taking two math tests: one in which there were gender differences—men supposedly performed better than women— and a second in which there were no gender differences. In reality, the tests were entirely similar, drawn from the same pool of difficult items. The reasoning behind the experimental manipulation was that women would be vulnerable to societal stereotypes on a test that they thought supported those stereotypes but would not be vulnerable on a test supposedly lacking gender differences.

Women choosing traditionally male fields such as math and science can overcome even long-standing societal stereotypes if they are convinced that others like them have been successful in these domains.

The results fully supported Steele's reasoning. When the women were told there were gender differences in the test, they greatly underperformed the men. But when they were told there were no gender differences, they performed virtually the same as the men.

In short, the evidence from this study and others clearly suggests that women are vulnerable to expectations regarding their future success, whether the expectations come from societal stereotypes or from information about the prior performance of women on similar tasks. More encouraging, the evidence suggests that if women can be convinced that others have been successful in given domains, they may overcome even long-standing societal stereotypes.

We should also keep in mind that women are not the only group susceptible to society's stereotyping. Members of minority groups, such as African Americans and Hispanic Americans, are also vulnerable to stereotypes about academic success. In fact, Steele suggests that African-Americans may "disidentify" with academic success by putting forth less effort on academic tasks and generally downgrading the importance of academic achievement. Ultimately, such disidentification may act as a self-fulfilling prophecy, increasing the chances of academic failure (Steele & Aronson, 1995; Osborne, 1997).

R E V I E W *&* A P P L Y

Review

- School success is related to socioeconomic status, with low-SES students achieving less academic success than others.

- Ethnicity also influences academic achievement and college attendance, due in part to SES differences and in part to a belief by some members of minority groups that hard work in school is unrelated to later career success.

- In college, women tend to choose and remain in different courses and majors than men. This is largely due to gender stereotypes that affect teachers' and students' expectations.

Applying Child Development

- What sorts of behaviors and attitudes on the part of supervisors and coworkers might hinder the advancement of women and minorities in the workplace?

- *From an educator's perspective:* Why might descendants of people who were forced to immigrate to a country be less successful academically than those who came voluntarily? What approaches might be used to overcome this obstacle?

Picking an Occupation: Choosing Life's Work

Some people know from childhood that they want to be physicians or actors or go into business, and they follow direct paths toward that goal. For others, the choice of a career is very much a matter of chance, of turning to the want ads and seeing what's available.

Regardless of how a career is chosen, it is unlikely to be the only career that people will have during the course of their lifetimes. As technology alters the nature of work at a rapid pace, changing careers at least once, and sometimes several times, is likely to be the norm in the 21st century.

Ginzberg's Three Periods

According to Eli Ginzberg (1972), people generally move through several stages in choosing a career. In the **fantasy period,** which lasts until around age 11, career choices are made—and discarded—without regard to skills, abilities, or available job opportunities. Instead, choices are made solely on the basis of what sounds appealing. Thus a child may decide that she wants to be a veterinarian, despite the fact that she is allergic to dogs and cats.

People begin to take practical considerations into account during the tentative period, which spans adolescence. During the **tentative period,** people begin to think in pragmatic terms about the requirements of various jobs and how their own abilities might fit with those requirements. They also consider their personal values and goals, exploring how well a particular occupation might satisfy them. Finally, in early adulthood, people enter the **realistic period,** in which they explore specific career options either through actual experience on the job or through training for a profession. They begin to narrow their choices to a few alternative careers and eventually make a commitment to a particular one.

Holland's Six Personality Types

Although the three stages make intuitive sense, the stage approach oversimplifies the process of choosing a career. Consequently, some researchers suggest that is more fruitful to examine

Fantasy period According to Ginzberg, the period of life when career choices are made—and discarded—without regard to skills, abilities, or available job opportunities

Tentative period The second stage of Ginzberg's theory, which spans adolescence, in which people begin to think in pragmatic terms about the requirements of various jobs and how their own abilities might fit with those requirements

Realistic period The stage in late adolescence and early adulthood during which people explore career options through job experience or training, narrow their choices, and eventually make a commitment to a career

the match between job-seekers' personality types and career requirements. For example, according to researcher John Holland (1973, 1987; Gottfredson & Holland, 1990), certain personality types match particularly well with certain careers. Specifically, he suggests that six personality types are important in career choice:

- *Realistic:* These people are down-to-earth, practical problem solvers who are physically strong, but their social skills are mediocre. They make good farmers, laborers, and truck drivers.

- *Intellectual:* Intellectual types are oriented toward the theoretical and the abstract. Although not particularly good with people, they are well suited to careers in math and science.

- *Social:* The traits associated with the social personality type are related to verbal skills and interpersonal relations. Social types are good at working with people and consequently make good salespersons, teachers, and counselors.

- *Conventional:* Conventional individuals prefer highly structured tasks. They make good clerks, secretaries, and bank tellers.

- *Enterprising:* These individuals are risk takers and take-charge types. They are good leaders and may be particularly effective as managers or politicians.

- *Artistic:* Artistic types use art to express themselves, and they often prefer the world of art to interactions with people. They are best suited to occupations involving art.

Of course, not everyone fits neatly into one particular personality type. Furthermore, there are certainly exceptions to the typology, with jobs being held successfully by people who don't have the predicted personality. Still, the theory forms the foundation of several instruments designed to assess the occupational options for which a given person is particularly suited (Randahl, 1991).

Gender and Career Choices: Women's Work

> WANTED: Full-time employee for small family firm. DUTIES: Including but not limited to general cleaning, cooking, gardening, laundry, ironing and mending, purchasing, bookkeeping and money management. Child care may also be required. HOURS: Avg. 55/wk but standby duty required 24 hours/day, 7 days/wk. Extra workload on holidays. SALARY AND BENEFITS: No salary, but food, clothing, and shelter provided at employer's discretion; job security and benefits depend on continued good will of employer. No vacation. No retirement plan. No opportunities for advancement. REQUIREMENTS: No previous experience necessary, can learn on the job. Only women need apply. (Unger & Crawford, 1992, p. 446.)

Just two decades ago, many women entering early adulthood assumed that this admittedly exaggerated job description matched the work for which they were best suited and to which they aspired: housewife. Even those women who sought work outside the home were relegated to certain professions. For instance, until the 1960s, employment ads in newspapers throughout the United States were almost always divided into two sections: "Help Wanted: Male" and "Help Wanted: Female." The men's job listings encompassed such professions as police officer, construction worker, and legal counsel; the women's listings were for secretaries, teachers, cashiers, and librarians.

The breakdown of jobs deemed appropriate for men and women reflected society's traditional view of what the two genders were best suited for. Traditionally, women were considered most appropriate for **communal professions,** occupations associated with relationships. In contrast, men were perceived as best suited for agentic professions. **Agentic professions** are associated with getting things accomplished. It is probably no coincidence that communal professions typically have lower status and lower salaries than agentic professions (Eagly & Steffen, 1984, 1986).

Communal professions Occupations associated with relationships

Agentic professions Occupations associated with getting things accomplished

CAREERS IN CHILD DEVELOPMENT

"You have to work on personal development before you can commit to something in the longer term."

Henry Klein

Education: . . . .   University of Pennsylvania, Philadelphia: B.A. in English, M.A. in sociology; Temple University, Philadelphia: Ph.D. in psychoeducational processes

Position: . . . .   Founder and director, American College and Career Counseling Center

Home: . . . .   Philadelphia, Pennsylvania

At one time or another, everyone has pondered the question of which career to pursue or whether to change a current job. For those facing that decision, there are people like Henry Klein. A former columnist who wrote for 20 years on careers and education for several Philadelphia newspapers, Klein has also published a book that answers questions about getting into college and staying in college.

In 1962, Klein founded the American College and Career Counseling Center in Philadelphia. Its purpose is to help people find professions that are right for them.

At Klein's center, career counseling, which lasts about five sessions, begins with a basic interview and proceeds to the point where the counselor and the client have identified specific companies to pursue and outlined concrete strategies for approaching them.

"Before people come to me for career counseling, I ask them to send me their résumés and, if they're close to graduation, copies of their transcripts," Klein explains. "I look through the transcript to find the strongest subject areas and try to get a baseline from that. I look for a particular trend in a field, and if there are no negatives, we go in that direction."

Although it is important to look at academic and work background, Klein points out that a person's character and development are equally important, perhaps even more so.

"A person with a fairly stable life, who hasn't moved around a lot or job-hopped, produces a trend in careers and vocations that we can use," he says. "You have to work on personal development before you can commit to something in the longer term.

"Even if you fell into the perfect job, your personal development might push you out sooner or later if you were not up to a long-term career commitment. You can't talk in terms of just one occupation; you have to think in terms of a career."

Although discrimination based on gender is far less blatant today than it was several decades ago—it is now illegal, for instance, to advertise a position specifically for a man or a woman—remnants of traditional gender role prejudice persist. As we discussed earlier in this chapter, women are less likely to be found in traditionally male-dominated professions such as engineering and computer programming. As shown in Figure 15-6, in 97 percent of the occupations for which data have been collected, women's weekly earnings are less than men's. In fact, women in many professions earn significantly less than men in identical jobs (Cooperative Institutional Research Program, 1990; U.S. Bureau of the Census, 2001b; Women's Bureau, 1998). Consequently, women even today expect to earn less than men, both when they start their careers and when they are at their peak. These expectations jibe with reality: On average, women earn 70 cents for every dollar that men earn. Moreover, women who are members of minority groups do even worse: African American women earn 62 cents for every dollar men make, while for Hispanic women the figure is 54 cents (Heckert & Wallis, 1998; Jackson, Gardner, & Sullivan, 1992; B. A. Martin, 1989; Women's Bureau, 1998).

Nevertheless, despite status and pay that are often lower than men's, more women are working outside the home than ever before. Between 1950 and 2000, the percentage of the

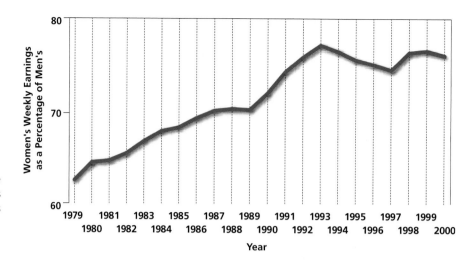

FIGURE 15-6   THE GENDER WAGE GAP

Women's weekly earnings as a percentage of men's has increased since 1979 but still is only slightly more than 75 percent and has remained steady in recent years.

(*Source:* U.S. Bureau of the Census, 2001b)

female population aged 16 and over in the U.S. labor force overall increased from around 35 percent to 60 percent. Today, women make up around 46 percent of the workforce. Almost all women expect to earn a living, and almost all do at some point in their lives. Furthermore, in about one half of U.S. households, women earn about as much as their husbands (Lewin, 1995; Women's Bureau, 2002).

In addition, opportunities for women are in many ways considerably greater today than they were in earlier years. Women are more likely to be physicians, lawyers, insurance agents, and bus drivers than they were in the past. However, within specific job categories, sex discrimination still occurs. For example, female bus drivers are more apt to have part-time school bus routes, while men hold better paying full-time routes in cities. Similarly, female

○— BECOMING AN INFORMED CONSUMER OF DEVELOPMENT —○

Choosing a Career

One of the greatest challenges people face in late adolescence is making a decision that will have lifelong implications: the choice of a career. Although there is no single correct choice—most people can be happy in any of several different jobs—the options can be daunting. Here are some guidelines for at least starting to come to grips with the question of what occupational path to follow.

- Systematically evaluate a variety of choices. Libraries and the Internet contain a wealth of information about potential career paths, and most colleges and universities have career centers that can provide occupational data and guidance.

- Know yourself. Evaluate your strengths and weaknesses, perhaps by completing a questionnaire at a college career center that can provide insight into your interests, skills, and values.

- Create a "balance sheet" listing the potential gains and losses that you will incur from a particular profession. First, list the

gains and losses that you will experience directly, and then list the gains and losses for others. Next, write down the projected social approval or disapproval you are likely to receive from others. By systematically evaluating a set of potential careers according to each of these criteria, you will be in a better position to compare different possibilities.

- "Try out" different careers through paid or unpaid internships. By experiencing a job firsthand, interns are able to get a better sense of what an occupation is truly like.

- Remember that if you make a mistake, you can change careers. In fact, people today increasingly change careers in early adulthood or even beyond. No one should feel locked into a decision made earlier in life. As we've seen throughout this book, people develop substantially as they age, and this development continues beyond adolescence to the entire life span. It is reasonable to expect that shifting values, interests, abilities, and life circumstances might make a different career more appropriate later in life than the one chosen in late adolescence.

pharmacists are more likely to work in hospitals, while men work in higher paying jobs in retail stores (England & McCreary, 1987; Unger & Crawford, 1999).

Women and minorities in high-status, visible professional roles still often hit what has come to be called the *glass ceiling*. The glass ceiling is an invisible barrier in an organization that prevents individuals from being promoted beyond a certain level because of discrimination. It operates subtly, and the people responsible for keeping the glass ceiling in place may not even be aware of how their actions perpetuate discrimination against women and minorities. For instance, a male supervisor in the oil exploration business may conclude that a particular task is "too dangerous" for a female employee. As a consequence of his decision, he may be preventing female candidates for the job from obtaining the experience they need to get promoted (Kilborne, 1995; Larwood, Szwajkowski, & Rose, 1988; A. M. Morrison & von Gilnow, 1990; R. A. Snyder et al., 1992).

Discrimination based on gender is less blatant than it once was, but it remains a potent force. However, strides have been made in many professions.

REVIEW & APPLY

Review

- According to Eli Ginzberg, people pass through three stages in considering careers: the fantasy period, the tentative period, and the realistic period.

- Other theories of career choice, such as John Holland's, attempt to match personality types to suitable careers.

- Gender influences career choice and attitudes and behaviors on the job. Traditionally, communal professions were considered more appropriate for women; the agentic professions, which pay more, were considered better suited for men.

Applying Child Development

- If it were proved that no link existed between academic success and later career success, would there be any justification for working hard in school? Why or why not?

- *From an educator's perspective:* Some people advocate same-sex (and even same-ethnicity) high schools and colleges as a way to combat the disadvantages of discrimination. Why might this be effective? What drawbacks do you see?

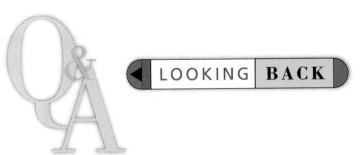

LOOKING BACK

- **How does cognitive development proceed during adolescence?**

  - Cognitive growth during adolescence is rapid, with gains in abstract thinking, reasoning, and the ability to view possibilities in relative rather than absolute terms.

  - Adolescence coincides with Piaget's formal operations period of development, when people begin to engage in abstract thought and experimental reasoning.

- According to information processing approaches, cognitive growth during adolescence is gradual and quantitative, involving improvements in memory capacity, mental strategies, and other aspects of cognitive functioning.

- Another major area of cognitive development is the growth of metacognition, which permits adolescents to monitor their thought processes and accurately assess their cognitive capabilities.

● **What aspects of cognitive development cause difficulties for adolescents?**

- Hand in hand with the development of metacognition is the growth of adolescent egocentrism, a self-absorption that makes it hard for adolescents to accept criticism and tolerate authority figures.

- Adolescents may play to an imaginary audience of critical observers, and they may develop personal fables, which emphasize the uniqueness of their experiences and supposed invulnerability to risks.

● **Through what stages does moral development progress during childhood and adolescence?**

- Adolescents develop morally as well as in other ways. According to Lawrence Kohlberg, people pass through three major levels and six stages of moral development as their sense of justice and their moral reasoning evolve.

- Kohlberg's levels of moral development are preconventional morality (motivated by rewards and punishments), conventional morality (motivated by social reference), and postconventional morality (motivated by a sense of universal moral principles)—a level that may be reached during adolescence but that many people never attain.

- Although Kohlberg's theory provides a good account of moral judgments, it is less adequate in predicting moral behavior.

- There appear to be gender differences in moral development not reflected in Kohlberg's work. Carol Gilligan has sketched out an alternative progression for girls, from an orientation toward individual survival through goodness as self-sacrifice to the morality of nonviolence.

● **What factors affect adolescent school performance?**

- School performance declines during the adolescent years. School achievement is linked with socioeconomic status, race, and ethnicity. Many academic achievement differences are due to socioeconomic factors, but other factors also play a part: attributional patterns regarding success factors and belief systems regarding the link between school success and success in life.

● **Who attends college, and how is the college experience different for men and women?**

- A larger proportion of white high school graduates enters and completes college than African American or Hispanic high school graduates. Nevertheless, minority students make up an increasingly larger proportion of the U.S. college population each year.

- The college experience differs for men and women. Differences are evident in courses and majors chosen and in expectations for financial success upon graduation. The differences appear to be attributable to gender stereotypes that operate in college to affect teachers' and students' expectations.

● **How do adolescents make career choices, and what influence do ethnicity and gender have on career opportunities?**

- According to Eli Ginzberg, people proceed through stages as they consider careers, from the fantasy period, in which dream choices are made without regard to practical factors, through the tentative period, which spans adolescence and involves pragmatic thought about job requirements and personal abilities and goals, to the realistic period of early adulthood, in which career options are explored through actual experience and training. Other theories of career choice, such as John Holland's, link personality characteristics and career options.

- Career choice and attitudes and behaviors on the job are influenced by gender. Traditionally, women have been associated with communal professions, which tend to be lower paid, and men with agentic professions, which pay better.

- Women and minorities in professional roles may find themselves hitting the "glass ceiling," an invisible barrier in an organization that prevents career advancement beyond a certain level because of conscious or unconscious discrimination.

EPILOGUE

 his chapter focused on the cognitive advances that occur during adolescence. We began by considering Piagetian and information processing approaches to cognitive development and then saw how adolescents' self-absorption occurs in part because of the state of their cognitive abilities. We then turned to moral development, focusing on moral reasoning and males' and females' different conceptions of morality. Finally, we looked at school performance and its relationship to cognitive development.

Before turning to the next chapter, return for the moment to the opening prologue of this one, about Cedric Jennings. In light of what you now know about adolescence, consider the following questions about Cedric:

1. Why do you think Cedric was able to overcome the deprivations and problems he faced to achieve academic success?

2. How might advances in Cedric's cognitive development have helped him meet the many challenges he faced?

3. Can you account for Cedric's achievements in terms of Piaget's theory? Can you account for it in terms of information processing approaches? Which approach seems most relevant and useful? Why?

4. Does Cedric's academic success imply that he has escaped the usual adolescent phenomena of egocentrism, belief in an imaginary audience, and personal fables? Why or why not?

KEY TERMS AND CONCEPTS

formal operational stage
  (p. 441)
metacognition (p. 444)
adolescent egocentrism
  (p. 445)

imaginary audience
  (p. 445)
personal fables (p. 445)
fantasy period (p. 461)
tentative period (p. 461)

realistic period (p. 461)
communal professions
  (p. 462)
agentic professions
  (p. 462)

16

Social and Personality Development in Adolescence

PROLOGUE: First Formal

Slim and dark, with a passing resemblance to actress Demi Moore, Leah is dressed up and ready to go to the first real formal dance of her life. True, the smashing effect of her short beaded black dress is marred slightly by the man's shirt she insists on wearing to cover her bare shoulders. And she is in a sulk. Her boyfriend, Sean Moffitt, is four minutes late, and her mother, Linda, refuses to let her stay out all night at a coed sleepover party after the dance.

When Sean arrives with his mother, Pam, Leah reluctantly sheds the work shirt. She greets Sean shyly, not sure he'll approve of that afternoon's makeover by hairdresser and manicurist. Sean, an easygoing youth with dimples and rosy cheeks, squirms in his tuxedo. Leah recombs his hair and makes him remove his earring. "None of the guys are wearing them to the dance," she declares. (She's wrong. A few moments later, their friends Melissa and Erik arrive, and Erik is wearing his earring.)

Leah's father, George, suggests a 2 A.M. curfew: Leah hoots incredulously. Sean pitches the all-nighter, stressing

In spite of the rebel stereotype, the majority of adolescents pass through the period in relative tranquility.

that the party will be chaperoned. Leah's mother has already talked to the host's mother, mortifying Leah with her off-hand comment that a coed sleepover seemed "weird." Rolling her eyes, Leah persists: "It's not like anybody's really going to sleep!" Sean asks his mother for another $20. "Why did the amount suddenly jump?" she asks, digging into her purse. (E. Graham, 1995, p. B1)

LOOKING **AHEAD** ▶

This snapshot of the life of 16-year-old Leah Brookner of Norwalk, Connecticut, provides a glimpse of some of the complex, interdependent relationships in which adolescents are involved. As Leah juggles parents, friends, and romantic partners, her life—like that of other adolescents—seems at times like an intricate jigsaw puzzle in which not all the pieces fit together perfectly.

Leah's life, which is focused around friends, parents, and school, is surprisingly typical. She is not a rebel, and she has good relations with her parents—as most of her peers have with theirs. Despite the reputation of adolescence as a time of confusion and rebellion, research shows that most people pass through the period without much turmoil. Although they may "try on" different roles and flirt with activities that their parents find objectionable, the majority of adolescents pass through the period in relative tranquillity (Petersen, 1988; L. Steinberg, 1993).

This is not to say that the transitions adolescents pass through are less than highly challenging. As we shall see in this chapter, in which we examine the personality and social developments of the period, adolescence brings about major changes in the ways in which individuals must deal with the world (Hersch, 1999; Takanishi, Hamburg, & Jacobs, 1997).

We begin by considering how adolescents form their views of themselves. We look at self-concept and self-esteem and at identity development. We also examine two major psychological difficulties, depression and suicide.

Next we discuss relationships during adolescence. We consider how adolescents reposition themselves within the family and how the influence of family members declines in some areas as peers take on new importance. We also examine the ways in which adolescents interact with their friends and at the determinants of popularity and rejection.

Finally, we consider dating and sexual behavior. We look at the role of dating in adolescents' lives, and we examine adolescents' sexual behavior and the standards that govern their sex lives. We conclude by looking at teenage pregnancy and at programs that seek to prevent unwanted pregnancy.

In sum, after reading this chapter, you will be able to answer the following questions:

- How does the development of self-concept, self-esteem, and identity proceed during adolescence?

- What dangers do adolescents face as they deal with the stresses of adolescence?

- How does the quality of relationships with family and peers change during adolescence?

- What are gender, race, and ethnic relations like in adolescence?

- What does it mean to be popular and unpopular in adolescence, and how do adolescents respond to peer pressure?

- What are the functions and characteristics of dating during adolescence?

- How does sexuality develop in the adolescent years?

- Why is teenage pregnancy more of a problem in the United States than in many other countries?

Identity: Asking "Who Am I?"

"Thirteen is a hard age, very hard. A lot of people say you have it easy, you're a kid, but there's a lot of pressure being 13—to be respected by people in your school, to be liked, always feeling like you have to be good. There's pressure to do drugs, too, so you try not to succumb to that. But you don't want to be made fun of, so you have to look cool. You gotta wear the right shoes, the right clothes—if you have Jordans, then it's all right."

—Carlos Quintana (1998, p. 66)

The thoughts of 13-year-old Carlos Quintana demonstrate a clear awareness—and self-consciousness—regarding his newly forming place in society and life. During adolescence, questions like "Who am I?" and "Where do I belong in the world?" begin to take on primary importance.

Why should issues of identity become so important during adolescence? One reason is that adolescents' intellectual capacities become more adultlike. They now understand and appreciate such abstract issues as the importance of establishing their position in society and the need to form a sense of themselves as individuals. They can now more easily see the linkages between their childhood identities and their future ones.

Another reason for the importance of identity during adolescence is that the dramatic physical changes during puberty make adolescents acutely aware of their own bodies and of the fact that other people are reacting to them in ways to which they are unaccustomed. Whatever the cause, adolescence often brings substantial changes in teenagers' self-concepts and self-esteem—in sum, their notions of their own identity.

Self-Concept: Characterizing the Self

Ask Geena to describe herself, and she says, "Others look at me as laid-back, relaxed, and not worrying too much. But really, I'm often nervous and emotional."

The fact that Geena distinguishes others' views of her from her own perceptions represents a developmental advance of adolescence. In childhood, Geena would have characterized herself according to a list of traits that would not differentiate her view of herself from others' perspectives. However, adolescents are able to make the distinction, and when they try to describe who they are, they take both their own and others' views into account (Harter, 1990b).

This broadening view of themselves is one aspect of adolescents' increasing discernment and perception in their understanding of who they are. The view of the self becomes more organized and coherent, and they can see various aspects of the self simultaneously. Furthermore, they look at the self from a psychological perspective, viewing traits not as concrete entities but as abstractions (G. R. Adams, Montemayor, & Gullotta, 1996). For example, teenagers are more likely than younger children to describe themselves in terms of their ideology (for example, saying something like "I'm an environmentalist") than in terms of physical characteristics (such as "I'm the fastest runner in my class.")

In some ways, however, the increasing differentiation of self-concept is a mixed blessing, especially during the earlier years of adolescence. At that time, adolescents may be troubled by the multiple aspects of their personalities. During the beginning of adolescence, for instance, teenagers may want to view themselves in a certain way ("I'm a sociable person and love to be with people"), and they may become concerned when their behavior is inconsistent with that view ("Even though I want to be sociable, sometimes I can't stand being around my friends and just want to be alone"). By the end of adolescence, however, teenagers accept the fact that different situations elicit different behaviors and feelings (Harter, 1990a; Pyryt & Mendaglio, 1994).

The self-concept of adolescents is sufficiently broad that they can distinguish between how they see themselves and how others see them. Why are issues of identity so important during adolescence?

Self-Esteem: Evaluating the Self

Knowing who you are and *liking* who you are two different things. Although adolescents become increasingly accurate in understanding who they are (their self-concept), this knowledge does not guarantee that they like themselves (their self-esteem) any better. In fact, their increasing accuracy in understanding themselves permits them to see themselves very clearly, warts and all.

The same cognitive sophistication that allows adolescents to differentiate various aspects of the self also leads them to evaluate those aspects in different ways (D. W. Chan, 1997; J. Cohen, 1999). For instance, an adolescent may have high self-esteem in terms of academic performance but lower self-esteem in terms of relationships with others. Or it may be just the opposite, as articulated by this adolescent:

> How much do I *like* the kind of person I am? Well, I like some things about me, but I don't like others. I'm glad that I'm popular since it's really important to me to have friends. But in school I don't do as well as the really smart kids. That's OK, because if you're too smart you'll lose your friends. So being smart is just not that important. Except to my parents. I feel like I'm letting them down when I don't do as well as they want. (Harter, 1990a, p. 364)

Gender Differences in Self-Esteem. What determines an adolescent's self-esteem? One factor is gender: Particularly during early adolescence, girls' self-esteem tends to be lower and more vulnerable than boys' (Byrne, 2000; Kling et al., 1999; Miyamoto et al., 2000).

One reason is that compared to boys, girls are more highly concerned about physical appearance and social success—in addition to academic achievement. Although boys are also concerned about these things, their attitudes are often more casual. Moreover, traditional societal messages may be interpreted as suggesting that female academic achievement is a roadblock to social success. Girls hearing such messages, then, are in a difficult bind: If they do well academically, they jeopardize their social success. No wonder that the self-esteem of adolescent

girls is more fragile than that of boys (Hess-Biber, 1996; Mendelson, White, & Mendelson, 1996; Unger & Crawford, 1999).

Socioeconomic Status in Self-Esteem.   Socioeconomic status (SES) and race also influence self-esteem. Adolescents of higher SES generally have higher self-esteem than those of lower SES, particularly during middle and late adolescence. It may be that the social status factors that especially enhance one's standing and self-esteem—such as having more expensive clothes or a car—become more conspicuous in the later periods of adolescence (Savin-Williams & Demo, 1983; Van Tassel-Baska, Olszewski-Kubilius, & Kulieke, 1994).

Race Differences in Self-Esteem.   Race also plays a role in self-esteem, although the findings are inconsistent. Early studies argued that minority status would lead to lower self-esteem. This finding led to the hypothesis—initially supported—that African Americans would have lower self-esteem than Caucasians. Researchers' explanations for this finding were straightforward: Societal prejudice would be incorporated into the self-concepts of the targets of the prejudice, making them feel disliked and rejected.

However, more recent research paints a different picture. Most findings now suggest that African Americans differ little from whites in their levels of self-esteem, and some findings even suggest that blacks may have higher self-esteem than whites. But the picture is mixed: Research also finds that Hispanics, Asians, and American Indians have *lower* levels of self-esteem than whites and blacks (Twenge & Crocker, 2002).

Why should this be? One explanation for the higher level of black self-esteem is that social movements in the African American community that bolster racial pride give support to African American adolescents. In fact, research finds that a stronger sense of racial identity is related to a higher level of self-esteem in African Americans and Hispanics (Gray-Little & Hafdahl, 2000; Lorenzo-Hernandez & Ouellette, 1998; Phinney, Lochner, & Murphy, 1990).

However, the confusing picture may be due to the fact that self-esteem is influenced not by race alone but by a complex combination of factors. So considering race alone, without other factors, may be too much of an oversimplification. For instance, some developmentalists have considered race and gender simultaneously, coining the term *ethgender* to refer to the joint influence of race and gender (Dukes & Martinez, 1994; Martinez & Dukes, 1991).

Research has revealed that minority status does not necessarily lead to low self-esteem. In fact, a strong sense of racial identity is tied to higher levels of self-esteem.

Identity-versus-identity-confusion stage
The period during which teenagers seek to determine what is unique and distinctive about themselves

CW

Identity Formation in Adolescence: Change or Crisis?

According to Erik Erikson (1963), whose theory we last discussed in Chapter 13, the search for identity inevitably leads some adolescents into substantial psychological difficulty as they encounter the adolescent identity crisis. Erikson's theory regarding this stage, which is summarized with his other stages in Table 16-1, suggests that adolescence is the time of the **identity-versus-identity-confusion stage.**

During the identity-versus-identity-confusion stage, teenagers seek to determine what is unique and distinctive about themselves. They strive to discover their particular strengths and weaknesses and the roles they can best play in their future lives. This discovery process often involves "trying on" different roles or choices, to see if they fit an adolescent's capabilities and self-concept. Through this process, adolescents seek to understand who they are by narrowing and making choices about their personal, occupational, sexual, and political commitments.

In Erikson's view, adolescents who stumble in their efforts to find a suitable identity may follow several dysfunctional courses. They may adopt socially unacceptable or deviant roles, or they may have difficulty forming and maintaining long-lasting close personal relationships later on in life. In general, their sense of self becomes "diffuse," failing to organize around a central, unified core identity.

By contrast, those who are successful in forging an appropriate identity set a course that provides a foundation for future psychosocial development. They learn their unique capabilities, and they develop an accurate sense of who they are. They are prepared to set out on a path that takes full advantage of what their unique strengths permit them to do (Archer & Waterman, 1994; Blustein, & Palladino, 1991; Kahn et al., 1985).

Societal Pressures and Reliance on Friends and Peers. Societal pressures are high during the identity-versus-identity-confusion stage, as any student knows who has been repeatedly asked by parents and friends "What's your major?" and "What are you going to do when you graduate?" Adolescents feel pressure to decide whether their post–high school plans include work or college and, if they choose work, which occupational track to follow. These are new choices, because up to this point in their development, U.S. society lays out a

---

TABLE 16-1   A SUMMARY OF ERIKSON'S STAGES

Stage	Approximate Age	Positive Outcomes	Negative Outcomes
1. Trust versus mistrust	Birth–1½ years	Feelings of trust from environmental support	Fear and concern regarding others
2. Autonomy versus shame and doubt	1½–3 years	Self-sufficiency if exploration is encouraged	Doubts about self, lack of independence
3. Initiative versus guilt	3–6 years	Discovery of ways to initiate actions	Guilt from actions and thoughts
4. Industry versus inferiority	6–12 years	Development of sense of competence	Feelings of inferiority, no sense of mastery
5. Identity versus identity confusion	Adolescence	Awareness of uniqueness of self, knowledge of role to be followed	Inability to identify appropriate roles in life
6. Intimacy versus isolation	Early adulthood	Development of loving, sexual relationships and close friendships	Fear of relationships with others
7. Generativity versus stagnation	Middle adulthood	Sense of contribution to continuity of life	Trivialization of one's activities
8. Ego-integrity versus despair	Late adulthood	Sense of unity in life's accomplishments	Regret over lost opportunities of life

(*Source:* Erikson, 1963)

During the identity-versus-identity-confusion stage, American teenagers seek to understand who they are by narrowing and making choices about their personal, occupational, sexual, and political commitments. Can this stage be applied to teenagers in other cultures? Why or why not?

universal educational track. However, the track ends at high school, and consequently, adolescents face difficult choices about which of several possible future paths they will follow (Kidwell et al., 1995).

During the identity-versus-identity-confusion period, adolescents increasingly rely on their friends and peers as sources of information. At the same time, their dependence on adults declines. As we discuss later in the chapter, this increasing dependence on the peer group enables adolescents to forge close relationships. It also helps them clarify their own identities as they compare themselves to others.

The importance of peers in helping adolescents define their identities and learn to form relationships points out a link between this stage of psychosocial development and the next stage Erikson proposed, known as intimacy versus isolation. It also relates to the subject of gender differences in identity formation. When Erikson developed his theory, he suggested that males and females move through the identity-versus-identity-confusion period differently. He argued that males were more likely to proceed through the social development stages in the order they are shown in Table 16-1, developing a stable identity before committing to an intimate relationship with another person. In contrast, he suggested that females reversed the order, seeking intimate relationships and then defining their identities through these relationships. These ideas largely reflect the social conditions at the time he was writing, when women were less likely to go to college or establish their own careers and instead often married early. Today, however, the experiences of boys and girls seem relatively similar during the identity-versus-confusion period.

Psychological Moratorium. Because of the pressures of the identity-versus-identity-confusion period, Erikson suggests that many adolescents pursue a "psychological moratorium." The *psychological moratorium* is a period during which adolescents take time off from the upcoming responsibilities of adulthood and explore various roles and possibilities. For example, many college students take a semester or year off to travel, work, or find some other way to examine their priorities.

However, many adolescents cannot, for practical reasons, pursue a psychological moratorium involving a leisurely exploration of various identities. Some adolescents, for economic reasons, must work part time after school and then take jobs immediately after graduation from high school. As a result, they have little time to experiment with identities and engage in

Identity achievement The status of adolescents who commit to a particular identity following a period of crisis during which they consider various alternatives

Identity foreclosure The status of adolescents who prematurely commit to an identity without adequately exploring alternatives

Moratorium The status of adolescents who may have explored various identity alternatives to some degree but have not yet committed themselves

Identity diffusion The status of adolescents who consider various identity alternatives but never commit to one or never consider identity options in any conscious way

a psychological moratorium. Does this mean that such adolescents will be psychologically damaged in some way? Probably not. In fact, the satisfaction that can come from successfully holding a part-time job while attending school may be a sufficient psychological reward to outweigh the inability to try out various roles.

Criticisms of Erikson's Theory.   One criticism that has been raised regarding Erikson's theory is that he uses male identity development as the standard against which to compare female identity. In particular, he saw males as developing intimacy only after they have achieved a stable identity, which is viewed as the normative pattern. To critics, Erikson's view is based on male-oriented concepts of individuality and competitiveness. In an alternative conception, psychologist Carol Gilligan has suggested that women develop identity through the establishment of relationships. In this view, a key component of a woman's identity is the building of caring networks between herself and others (Gilligan, Brown, & Rogers, 1990; Gilligan, 1982).

Marcia's Approach to Identity Development: Updating Erikson

Using Erikson's theory as a springboard, psychologist James Marcia (1966, 1980) suggests that identity can be seen in terms of four categories, called *statuses*. The identity statuses depend on whether each of two characteristics—crisis and commitment—is present or absent. *Crisis* is a period of identity development in which an adolescent consciously chooses between various alternatives and makes decisions. *Commitment* is psychological investment in a course of action or an ideology.

By conducting lengthy interviews with adolescents, Marcia proposed four categories of adolescent identity (see Table 16-2).

1. **Identity achievement.** Teenagers within this identity status have successfully explored and thought through who they are and what they want to do. Following a period of crisis during which they considered various alternatives, these adolescents have committed to a particular identity. Teens who have reached this identity status tend to be the most psychologically healthy, higher in achievement motivation and moral reasoning than adolescents of any other status.

2. **Identity foreclosure.** These are adolescents who have committed to an identity but did not do so by passing through a period of crisis in which they explored alternatives. Instead, they accepted others' decisions about what was best for them. Typical adolescents in this category are a son who enters the family business because it is expected of him and a daughter who decides to become a physician simply because her mother is one. Although foreclosers are not necessarily unhappy, they tend to have what can be called "rigid strength": Happy and self-satisfied, they also have a high need for social approval and tend to be authoritarian.

3. **Moratorium.** Although adolescents in the moratorium category have explored various alternatives to some degree, they have not yet committed themselves. As a consequence, they show relatively high anxiety and experience psychological conflict. But they are often lively and appealing, seeking intimacy with others. Adolescents of this status typically settle on an identity, but only after something of a struggle.

4. **Identity diffusion.** Some adolescents in this category consider various alternatives but never commit to one. Others in this group don't even get that far, not even considering their options in any conscious way. They tend to be flighty, shifting from one thing to the next. Although they may seem carefree, their lack of commitment impairs their ability to form close relationships. In fact, they are often socially withdrawn.

Teenagers who have successfully attained what James Marcia termed identity achievement tend to be the most psychologically healthy and higher in achievement motivation than adolescents of any other status.

It is important to note that adolescents are not necessarily stuck in one of the four categories. In fact, some move back and forth between moratorium and identity achievement in what has been called a "MAMA cycle" (from the initials of *moratorium, achievement,*

TABLE 16-2   MARCIA'S FOUR CATEGORIES OF ADOLESCENT IDENTITY DEVELOPMENT

The four categories in Marcia's theory of adolescent development are illustrated in this table, along with sample responses to the question, "Have you ever had any doubts about your religious beliefs?"

		COMMITMENT	
		Present	**Absent**
Exploration	**Present**	Identity achievement ("I've had plenty of doubts in the past, but for the most part I've resolved them.")	Moratorium ("I'm in a phase right now where I'm trying to figure it out. I just don't know where I stand.")
	Absent	Identity foreclosure ("I've known where I stand for as long as I can remember.")	Identity diffusion ("Sometimes I have doubts, and sometimes I'm pretty sure of where I stand. I guess I can't make up my mind.")

(*Source:* Marcia, 1980)

moratorium, achievement). Similarly, even though a forecloser may have settled on a career path during early adolescence with little active decision making, the person may reassess the choice later and move into another category. For some individuals, then, identity formation may take place beyond the period of adolescence. However, identity gels in the late teens and early 20s for most people (Kroger, 2000; Meeus, 1996; Waterman, 1982).

Cultural Identity

Although the path to forming an identity is difficult for all adolescents, it presents a particular challenge for members of racial and ethnic minority groups. One part of the problem stems from a set of contradictory societal values that we examined in Chapter 12. On the one hand, adolescents are told that society should be color-blind, that race and ethnic background should not matter in terms of opportunities and achievement. Based on a traditional *cultural assimilation model,* this view holds that individual cultural identities should be assimilated into a unified culture in the United States—the famous melting pot model.

On the other hand, the *pluralistic society model* suggests that U.S. society is made up of diverse, coequal cultural groups that should preserve their individual cultural features. The pluralistic society model grew in part from the belief that the cultural assimilation model denigrates the cultural heritage of minorities and lowers their self-esteem. According to this view, then, racial and ethnic factors become a central part of adolescents' identity and are not submerged in an attempt to assimilate into the majority culture.

There is a middle ground. Some observers suggest that identity in minority adolescents is facilitated by the formation of a *bicultural identity* in which adolescents draw from their own cultural identity while integrating themselves into the dominant culture. This view suggests that an individual can live as a member of two cultures, with two cultural identities, without having to choose one over the other (La Fromboise, Coleman, & Gerton, 1993). The choice of a bicultural identity is increasingly common. In fact, the number of individuals who think of themselves as belonging to more than one race is considerable, according to data from the 2000 U.S. census (Schmitt, 2001; see Figure 16-1).

Regardless of which path to identity a member of a minority group chooses, the process of identity formation is not likely to be simple. Racial and ethnic identity takes time to form, and for some individuals it may occur over a prolonged period. Still, the ultimate result can be the formation of a rich, multifaceted identity (Cross, 1991; R. E. Roberts et al., 1999; Tatum, 1997).

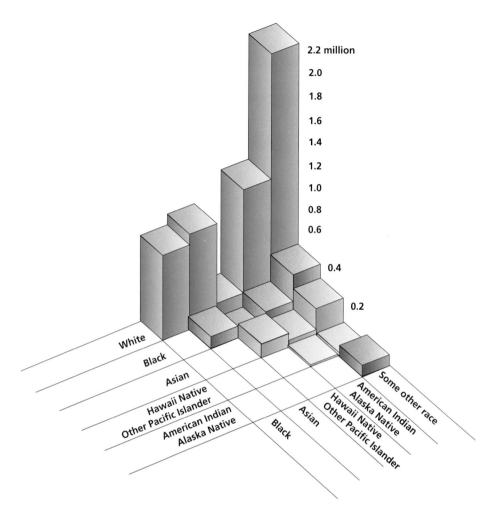

FIGURE 16-1 INCREASE IN BICULTURAL IDENTITY

On the 2000 census, almost 7 million people indicated they were multiracial. With the racial mix changing in the United States, what are the implications for social work in the future?

(*Source:* U.S. Bureau of the Census, 2000.)

Between 25 and 40 percent of girls and 20 to 35 percent of boys experience occasional episodes of depression during adolescence, although the incidence of major depression is far lower.

Depression and Suicide: Psychological Difficulties in Adolescence

Although by far the majority of teenagers weather the search for identity and the other challenges of the period without major psychological difficulties, some find adolescence particularly stressful. Some, in fact, experience severe psychological problems. Two of the most serious are adolescent depression and suicide (Besseghini, 1997).

Adolescent Depression. No one is immune from periods of sadness and bad moods, and adolescents are no exception. The end of a relationship, failure at an important task, the death of a loved one—all may produce profound feelings of sadness, loss, and grief. In situations such as these, depression is a fairly typical reaction.

How common are feelings of depression in adolescence? Although figures are hard to come by, some estimates suggest that 20 to 35 percent of boys and 25 to 40 percent of girls report having experienced depressed moods in the previous 6 months. Reports of feeling "sad and hopeless" are even higher: Almost two thirds of teenagers say they have experienced such feelings at one time or another. However, only a small minority of adolescents—about 3 percent—experience *major depression,* a full-blown psychological disorder in which depression is severe and lingers for long periods (Cicchetti & Toth, 1998; Culp, Clyman, & Culp, 1995).

Gender, ethnic, and racial differences also are found in depression rates. As is the case among adults, adolescent girls, on average, experience depression more often than boys. Furthermore, some studies have found that African American adolescents have higher rates of depression than white adolescents, although not all research supports this conclusion. Native Americans, too, appear to have higher rates of depression (Fleming & Offord, 1990; Nettles & Pleck, 1990; Stice, Presnell, & Bearman, 2001).

Depression has several causes. In cases of severe, long-term depression, biological factors are often involved. Some adolescents, for instance, seem to be genetically predisposed to experience depression (Brooks-Gunn, Petersen, & Compas, 1994; Ehlers, Frank, & Kupfer, 1988).

However, environmental and social factors relating to the extraordinary changes in the social lives of adolescents are also an important cause. An adolescent who experiences the death of a loved one, for example, or one who grows up with a depressed parent, is at a higher risk of depression. In addition, being unpopular, having few close friends, and experiencing rejection are associated with adolescent depression (Aseltine, Gore, & Colten, 1994; Hammond & Romney, 1995; Lau & Kwok, 2000).

One of the most puzzling questions about depression is why its incidence is higher among girls than boys. Hormones do not seem to be the reason. Little evidence links hormonal production in adolescent girls to depression (Lewinsohn et al., 1994; Nolen-Hoeksema & Girgus, 1994; Petersen, Sarigiani, & Kennedy, 1991).

Some psychologists speculate that stress is more pronounced for girls than for boys in adolescence, due to the many, sometimes contradictory, aspects of the traditional female gender role. Recall, for instance, the plight of the adolescent girl who was quoted in our discussion of self-esteem. Accepting traditional gender roles, she is worried both about doing well in school and about being popular. If she feels that academic success undermines her popularity, she is placed in a difficult bind.

There may be other causes of girls' generally higher levels of depression during adolescence. They may be more apt than boys to react to stress by turning inward, thereby experiencing a sense of helplessness and hopelessness. In contrast, boys more often react by externalizing the stress and acting more impulsively or aggressively, or by turning to drugs and alcohol (Hankin & Abramson, 2001).

Adolescent Suicide.   Elyssa Drazin was 16. Although her grades had gone down in the previous 6 months, she was still a pretty good student. Her social life had picked up over the last 2 years, and she had been involved with Hector Segool. In the past month, however, the relationship had cooled considerably, and Hector had told her he wanted to date other girls. Elyssa was devastated, and—as she wrote in a note that was found on her desk—she could not bear the thought of seeing Hector holding hands with another girl. She took a large quantity of sleeping pills and became one of the thousands of adolescents who take their own lives each year.

The rate of adolescent suicide in the United States has tripled in the past 30 years. In fact, one teenage suicide occurs every 90 minutes, for an annual rate of 12.2 suicides per 100,000 adolescents. Moreover, the reported rate may actually understate the true number of suicides; parents and medical personnel are often reluctant to report a death as suicide, preferring to label it an accident. Even with underreporting, suicide is the third most common cause of death in the 15-to-24-year-old age group, after accidents and homicide (Healy, 2001; C. S. Henry et al., 1993).

The rate of suicide is higher for boys than girls, although girls *attempt* suicide more frequently. Suicide attempts among males are more likely to result in death because of the methods they use: Boys tend to use more violent means, such as guns, while girls are more apt to choose the more peaceful strategy of drug overdose. Some estimates suggest that there are as many as 200 attempted suicides for every successful one (Berman & Jobes, 1991; D. Gelman, 1994; Hawton, 1986).

The reasons behind the increase in adolescent suicide in recent decades are unclear. The most obvious explanation is that the stress experienced by teenagers has increased, leading those who are most troubled to be more likely to commit suicide (Elkind, 1984). But why should stress have increased only for adolescents? The suicide rate for other segments of the population has remained fairly stable over the same time period. (And it's important to keep in mind that although the rate of suicide for adolescents has risen more than for other age groups, suicide is still more common among adults than it is among young people.)

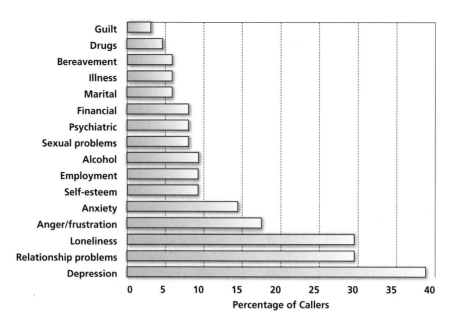

FIGURE 16-2
ADOLESCENT DIFFICULTIES

These problems were the ones most frequently cited by callers to a suicide prevention hot line who were contemplating suicide. What can health care workers and
educators do to help reduce suicidal feelings among adolescents?

(*Source:* Boston Samaritans, 1991)

Although an explanation for the increase in adolescent suicide has not been found, it is clear
that certain factors heighten the risk of suicide. One factor is depression. Depressed teenagers
who are experiencing a profound sense of hopelessness are at greater risk of committing suicide (although most deeply depressed individuals do not commit suicide). In addition, social
inhibition, perfectionism, and a high level of stress and anxiety are related to a greater risk of
suicide (Beautrais, Joyce, & Mulder, 1996; Huff, 1999; Lewinsohn, Rohde, & Seeley, 1994).

Some cases of suicide are associated with family conflicts and adjustment difficulties
(Pillay & Wassenaar, 1997). Others follow a history of abuse and neglect. The rate of suicide
among drug and alcohol abusers is also relatively high. As can be seen in Figure 16-2, teens
who called a hot line because they were thinking of killing themselves mentioned several
other factors as well (Brent et al., 1994; Garnefski & Arends, 1998; Lyon et al., 2000).

Some suicides appear to be caused by exposure to the suicide of others. In **cluster suicide,**
one suicide leads to attempts by others to kill themselves. For instance, some high schools
have experienced a series of suicides following a well-publicized case. As a result, many
schools have established crisis intervention teams to counsel students when one student
commits suicide (Hazell, 1993).

There are several warning signs that should sound an alarm regarding the possibility of
suicide, including these:

- Direct or indirect talk about suicide, such as "I wish I were dead" or "You won't have me to
worry about any longer"

- School difficulties, such as missed classes or a decline in grades

- Making arrangements as if preparing for a long trip, such as giving away prized possessions
or arranging for the care of a pet

- Writing a will

- Loss of appetite or excessive eating

- General depression, including a change in sleeping patterns, lethargy, and uncommunica-
tiveness

- Dramatic changes in behavior, such as a shy person suddenly acting outgoing

- Preoccupation with death in music, art, or literature

Cluster suicide   A situation in which one
suicide leads to attempts by others to kill
themselves

BECOMING AN INFORMED CONSUMER OF DEVELOPMENT

Deterring Adolescent Suicide

*I*f you suspect that an adolescent—or anyone else for that matter—is contemplating suicide, don't stand idly by. Act! Here are several suggestions:

- Talk to the person, listen without judging, and give the person an understanding forum in which to try to talk things through.

- Talk specifically about suicidal thoughts. Ask, "Do you have a plan?" "Have you bought a gun? Where is it?" "Have you stockpiled pills? Where are they?" The Public Health Service notes that "contrary to popular belief, such candor will not give a person dangerous ideas or encourage a suicidal act."

- Evaluate the situation, trying to distinguish between general upset and more serious danger, as when suicide plans *have* been made. If the crisis is acute, *do not leave the person alone.*

- Be supportive, let the person know you care, and try to break down his or her feelings of isolation.

- Take charge of finding help, without concern about invading the person's privacy. Do not try to handle the problem alone; get professional help immediately.

- Make the environment safe, removing from the premises (not just hiding) weapons such as guns, razors, scissors, medication, and other potentially dangerous household items.

- Do not keep suicide talk or threats secret; these are calls for help and warrant immediate action.

- Do not challenge, dare, or use verbal shock treatment. They can have tragic effects.

Contrary to popular belief, talking about suicide does not encourage it. In fact, it actually combats it by providing supportive feedback and breaking down the sense of isolation many suicidal people have.

- Make a contract with the person, getting a promise or commitment, preferably in writing, not to make any suicidal attempt until you have talked further.

- Beware of elevated moods and seemingly quick recoveries; sometimes they are illusory, reflecting the relief of finally deciding to commit suicide or the temporary release of talking to someone, though the underlying problems have not been resolved.

For immediate help with a suicide-related problem, call (800) 621-4000, a national hot line staffed with trained counselors.

REVIEW & APPLY

Review

- Self-concept during adolescence grows more differentiated as the view of the self becomes more organized, broader, and more abstract and takes account of the views of others.

- Self-esteem, too, grows increasingly differentiated as the adolescent develops the ability to place different values on different aspects of the self.

- Both Erikson's identity-versus-identity-confusion stage and Marcia's four identity statuses focus on the adolescent's struggle to determine an identity and a role in society.

- One of the dangers that adolescents face is depression, which affects girls more than boys.

- Suicide is the third most common cause of death among 15-to-24-year-olds.

Applying Child Development

- What are some consequences of the shift from reliance on adults to reliance on peers? Are there advantages? Dangers?

- *From a social worker's perspective:* Do you believe that all four of Marcia's identity statuses can lead to reassessment and different choices later in life? Are some statuses more likely than others to produce this type of rethinking? Why? Are there stages in Marcia's theory of development that may be more difficult to achieve for adolescents who live in poverty?

Relationships: Family and Friends

"Keep the Hell Out of My Room!" says a sign on Trevor's bedroom wall, just above an unmade bed, a desk littered with dirty T-shirts and candy wrappers, and a floor covered with clothes. Is there a carpet? "Somewhere," he says with a grin. "I think it's gold." Trevor is the third of four sons of Richard Kelson, 56, a retired truck driver, and his wife, JoAnn, 46, a medical tape transcriber. The family lives in a four-bedroom home across from Hunter Junior High School, where Trevor is in ninth grade. He spent the summer volunteering in a leadership-training program at the Sugar House Boys & Girls Club in Salt Lake City. "I guess it gives you a good feeling to help somebody else," he says. In off-hours, he played Nintendo with pal Andy Muhlestein, 15. "When we don't have anything else to do, and we're tired of playing videos," he says, "we sit around and talk about girls." (Fields-Meyer, 1995, p. 53)

The social world of adolescents is considerably wider than that of younger children. As adolescents' relationships with people outside the home grow increasingly important, their interactions with their families evolve and take on a new, and sometimes difficult, character (Collins, Gleason, & Sesma, 1997; Montemayor, Adams, & Gulotta, 1994).

Family Ties: Reassessing Relations With Relations

When Pepe Lizzagara entered junior high school, his relationship with his parents changed drastically. Although relations were quite good previously, by the middle of seventh grade, tensions grew. In Pepe's view, his parents always seemed to be "on his case." Instead of giving him more freedom, which he felt he deserved at age 13, they actually seemed to be getting more restrictive.

Pepe's parents would probably suggest that they were not the source of the tension in the household—Pepe was. From their point of view, Pepe, with whom they'd established what seemed to be a stable relationship throughout much of his childhood, suddenly seemed transformed. To his parents, Pepe presented novel and often bewildering behavior.

The Quest for Autonomy.   Parents are sometimes angered and even more frequently puzzled by adolescents' conduct. Children who have previously accepted their parents' judgments, declarations, and guidelines begin to question—and sometimes rebel against—their parents' views of the world.

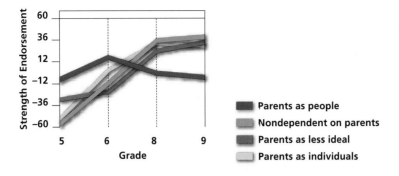

FIGURE 16-3   CHANGING VIEWS OF PARENTS

As adolescents become older, they come to perceive their parents in less idealized terms and more as individuals. What effect is this likely to have on family relations and how adolescents view education?

(*Source:* Adapted from L. Steinberg & Silverberg, 1986)

One reason for these clashes is the shift in the roles that both children and parents must deal with during adolescence. Adolescents increasingly seek **autonomy,** independence and a sense of control over their lives. Most parents intellectually realize that this shift is a normal part of adolescence, representing one of the primary developmental tasks of the period, and in many ways they welcome it as a sign of their children's growth. However, in many cases, the day-to-day realities of adolescents' increasing autonomy may prove difficult for them to deal with (Smetana, 1995).

In most families, teenagers' autonomy grows gradually over the course of adolescence. For instance, one study of changes in adolescents' views of their parents found that increasing autonomy led them to perceive parents less in idealized terms and more as persons in their own right. At the same time, adolescents came to depend more on themselves and to feel more like separate individuals (see Figure 16-3).

The increase in adolescent autonomy is reflected in the relationship between parents and teenagers. At the start of adolescence, the relationship tends to be asymmetrical: Parents hold most of the power and influence over the relationship. By the end of adolescence, however, power and influence have become more balanced, and parents and children end up in a more egalitarian relationship. Power and influence are shared, although parents typically retain the upper hand.

The degree of autonomy that is eventually achieved varies from one family to the next. Furthermore, cultural factors play an important role. In Western societies, which tend to value individualism, adolescents seek autonomy at a relatively early stage of adolescence. In contrast, Asian societies are *collectivistic;* they promote the idea that the well-being of the group is more important than that of the individual. In such societies, adolescents' aspirations to achieve autonomy are less pronounced (S. S. Feldman & Rosenthal, 1990; Kim et al., 1994).

Adolescents from different cultural backgrounds also vary in the degree of obligation to their family that they feel. Those in more collectivistic cultures tend to feel greater obligation to their families, in terms of expectations about their duty to provide assistance, show respect, and support their families in the future, than those from more individualistic societies (Fuligni, Tseng, & Lam, 1999; see Figure 16-4).

The Myth of the Generation Gap.

Teen movies often depict adolescents and their parents with totally opposing points of view about the world. For example, the parent of an environmentalist teen might turn out to own a polluting factory. These exaggerations are often funny because we assume there is a kernel of truth in them, in that parents and teenagers often don't see things the same way. According to this argument, there is a **generation gap,** a deep divide between parents and children in attitudes, values, aspirations, and worldviews.

The reality, however, is quite different. The generation gap, when it exists, is really quite narrow. Adolescents and their parents tend to see eye-to-eye in a variety of domains. Republican parents generally have Republican children; members of the Christian right have children

In collectivistic societies, the well-being of the group is promoted as more important than individual autonomy.

Autonomy   Having independence and a sense of control over one's life

Generation gap   A divide between parents and adolescents in attitudes, values, aspirations, and worldviews

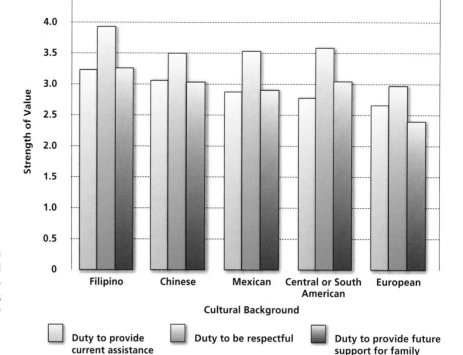

FIGURE 16-4 FAMILY OBLIGATIONS

Adolescents from Asian and Latin American groups feel a greater sense of respect and obligation toward their families than adolescents with European backgrounds. Does this attitude carry over into the classroom? If so, in what way?

(*Source:* Fuligni, Tseng, & Lam, 1999)

who espouse similar views; parents who advocate for abortion rights have children who are proabortion. On social, political, and religious issues, parents and adolescents tend to be in sync, and children's worries mirror those of their parents. Adolescents' concerns about society's problems (see Figure 16-5) are ones with which most adults would probably agree (Chira, 1994; PRIMEDIA/Roper, 1999; Youniss, 1989).

Similarly, there is typically no generation gap in the value that parents and adolescents place on the relationship they have with one another. As we observed in the chapter prologue about Leah's first formal dance, despite their quest for autonomy and independence, most adolescents have deep love, affection, and respect for their parents—reciprocating the feelings that their parents have for them. Although there are notable exceptions, with some parent–adolescent relationships marked by significant strife, the majority of relationships are more positive than negative. These positive relationships help adolescents avoid peer pressure (Gavin & Furman, 1996; Resnick et al., 1997; Shantz & Hartup, 1995).

Furthermore, even though adolescents spend decreasing amounts of time with their families in general, the amount of time they spend alone with each parent remains remarkably stable throughout adolescence (see Figure 16-6). In short, there is no evidence suggesting that family problems are worse during adolescence than at any other stage of development (Larson et al., 1996; L. Steinberg, 1990, 1993).

Parental Conflict in Adolescence

Although most adolescents get along with their parents most of the time, their relationships are not always sweetness and light. Parents and teens may hold similar attitudes about social and political issues, but they often hold different views on matters of personal taste such as music preferences and styles of dress., Also, as we've seen, parents and children may run into disagreements when children seek to achieve autonomy and independence. Consequently, parent–child conflicts are more likely to occur during adolescence, particularly during the early stages, although it's important to remember that not every family is affected to the same degree (Arnett, 1999; Laursen, Coy, & Collins, 1998; Sagrestano et al., 2000).

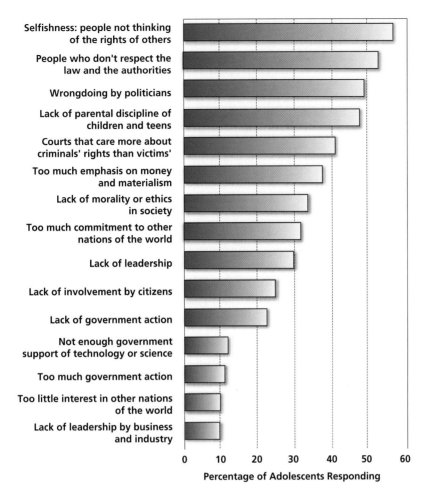

FIGURE 16-5 WHAT'S THE PROBLEM?

Adolescents' views of society's ills are ones with which their parents would be likely to agree.

(*Source:* PRIMEDIA/Roper, 1999)

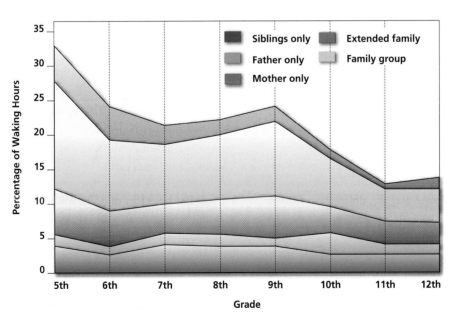

FIGURE 16-6 TIME SPENT BY ADOLESCENTS WITH THEIR PARENTS

Despite their quest for autonomy and independence, most adolescents have deep love, affection, and respect for their parents, and the amount of time they spend alone with each parent remains remarkably stable throughout the adolescent years.

(*Source:* Larson et al., 1996)

Difficulties in Early Adolescence. Why should strife be greater during early adolescence than at later stages of the period? According to developmental psychologist Judith Smetana, the reason involves differing definitions of, and rationales for, appropriate and inappropriate conduct. Parents may feel, for instance, that getting one's ear pierced in three places is inappropriate because society traditionally deems it inappropriate, whereas adolescents may view the issue in terms of personal choice (Smetana, 1988, 1989; Smetana, Yau, & Hanson, 1991).

Furthermore, the newly sophisticated reasoning of adolescents (discussed in Chapter 15) leads teenagers to think about parental rules in more complex ways. Arguments that were convincing to a school-age child ("Do it because I tell you to") are less compelling to an adolescent.

The argumentativeness and assertiveness of early adolescence may at first lead to an increase in conflict, but in many ways they play an important role in the evolution of parent–child relationships. Although parents may initially react defensively to the challenges that their children present and may grow inflexible and rigid, in most cases they eventually come to realize, simply, that their children are growing up.

Parents also come to see that their adolescent children's arguments are often compelling and not so unreasonable and that their daughter and sons can, in fact, be trusted with more freedom. Consequently, they become more yielding, allowing and eventually perhaps even encouraging independence. As this process occurs during the middle stages of adolescence, the combativeness of early adolescence declines.

Of course, this pattern does not apply for all adolescents. Although the majority of teenagers maintain stable relations with their parents throughout adolescence, as many as 20 percent pass through a fairly rough time (Dryfoos, 1990).

Cultural Differences in Parent–Child Conflicts.   Although parent–child conflicts are found in every culture, the amount of conflict seems lower in "traditional," preindustrial cultures. In fact, teenagers in traditional cultures also experience fewer mood swings and instances of risky behavior that are often seen during adolescence (Arnett, 1999; Schlegel & Barry, 1991).

Why? The answer may relate to the degree of independence that adolescents expect and adults permit. In more industrialized societies, in which the value of individualism is typically high, independence is an expected component of adolescence. Consequently, adolescents and their parents must negotiate the amount and timing of the adolescent's increasing independence—a process that often leads to strife.

In contrast, in more traditional societies, individualism is not valued as highly, and therefore adolescents are less inclined to seek out independence. With diminished independence seeking on the part of adolescents, the result is less parent–child conflict (Dasen, 2000).

Relationships With Peers: The Importance of Belonging

In the eyes of numerous parents, the most fitting symbol of adolescence is the telephone. For many of their sons and daughters, it appears to be an indispensable lifeline, sustaining ties to friends with whom they may have already spent many hours earlier in the day.

The seemingly compulsive need to communicate with friends demonstrates the role that peers play in adolescence. Continuing a trend that began in middle childhood, adolescents spend increasing amounts of time with their peers, and the importance of peer relationships grows as well. In fact, there is probably no period of life in which peer relationships are as important as they are in adolescence (Youniss & Haynie, 1992).

There are several reasons for the prominence of peers during adolescence. For one thing, peers provide the opportunity to compare and evaluate opinions, abilities, and even physical changes—a process called *social comparison*. Because physical and cognitive changes are so pronounced, especially during the early stages of puberty, adolescents turn increasingly to others who share, and consequently can shed light on, their own experiences (Paxton et al., 1999; Weiss, Ebbeck, & Horn, 1997).

Parents are unable to provide social comparison. Not only are they well beyond the changes that adolescents undergo, but adolescents' questioning of adult authority and their

Reference groups of peers provide norms for social comparison.

motivation to become more autonomous make parents, other family members, and adults in general inadequate and invalid sources of knowledge. Who is left to provide such information? Peers.

Finally, adolescence is a time of experimentation, of trying out new roles and conduct. Peers provide information about what roles and behaviors are most acceptable by serving as a reference group. A **reference group** is any group of people with whom one compares oneself.

Reference groups present a set of *norms*, or standards, against which adolescents can judge their social success. An adolescent need not even belong to a group for it to serve as a reference group. For instance, unpopular adolescents may find themselves belittled and rejected by members of a popular group yet use that more popular group as a reference group (Berndt, 1999).

Cliques and Crowds: Belonging to a Group.
Even if they do not belong to the group they use for reference purposes, adolescents are typically part of some identifiable group. In fact, one of the consequences of the increasing cognitive sophistication of adolescents is the ability to group others in more discriminating ways. Rather than defining people in concrete terms relating to what they do ("football players" or "musicians"), adolescents use more abstract terms packed with greater subtleties ("jocks" or "the artsy-craftsy crowd") (B. Brown, 1990; Montemayor et al., 1994).

What are the typical groups to which adolescence belong? There are actually two types: cliques and crowds. **Cliques** are groups of two to a dozen people whose members have frequent social interactions with one another. In contrast, **crowds** are larger, consisting of individuals who share particular characteristics but who may not interact with one another. For instance, "jocks" and "nerds" are representative of crowds found in many high schools.

Choice of membership in particular cliques and crowds is often determined by the degree of similarity with members of the group. One of the most important dimensions of similarity relates to substance use, adolescents tend to choose friends who use alcohol and other drugs to the same extent that they do. Their friends are also often similar in terms of their academic success, although this is not always true. For instance, during early adolescence, attraction to peers who are particularly well behaved seems to decrease while peers who behave more aggressively become more attractive (Bukowski, Sippola, & Newcomb, 2000; Hamm, 2000).

Reference group Any group of people with whom one compares oneself

Cliques Groups of 2 to 12 people whose members have frequent social interactions with one another

Crowds Larger groups than cliques, composed of individuals who share particular characteristics but who may not interact with one another

Sex cleavage Sex segregation in which boys interact primarily with boys and girls primarily with girls

Gender Relations. As children enter adolescence from middle childhood, their groups of friends are composed almost universally of same-sex individuals. Boys hang out with boys; girls hang out with girls. Technically, this sex segregation is called the **sex cleavage.**

However, the situation changes as members of both sexes enter puberty. Boys and girls experience the hormonal surge that marks puberty and causes the maturation of the sex organs. At the same time, societal pressures suggest that the time is appropriate for romantic involvement. These developments lead to a change in the ways adolescents view the opposite sex. Rather than seeing every member of the opposite sex as "annoying" and "a pain," boys and girls begin to regard each other with greater interest, in terms of both personality and sexuality.

When this change occurs, boys' and girls' cliques, which had previously moved along parallel but separate tracks, begin to converge. Adolescents begin to attend boy–girl dances or parties, although most of the time the boys still spend their time with boys and the girls with girls (Csikszentmihalyi & Larson, 1984). (Think back to your own early adolescence, and perhaps you'll recall dances with boys lined up on one side of the room and girls on the other.)

A little later, however, adolescents increasingly spend time with members of the opposite sex (Dunphy, 1963). New cliques emerge, composed of both males and females. Not everyone participates initially: Early on, the teenagers who are leaders of the same-sex cliques and who have the highest status pilot the way. Eventually, however, most adolescents find themselves in cliques that include boys and girls.

Cliques and crowds undergo yet another transformation at the end of adolescence: They become less powerful and may in fact succumb to the increased pairing off that occurs between males and females. Rather than the clique's being the center of adolescents' social lives, then, boy–girl interaction becomes the focus.

Popularity and Rejection: Being Liked or Disliked

Most adolescents have well-tuned antennae when it comes to determining who is popular and who is not. In fact, for some teenagers, concerns over popularity—or lack of it—may be a central focus of their lives. Think back, for example, to the girl quoted earlier in the chapter, who felt that having friends was more important than school success.

Actually, the social world of adolescents is not simply divided into popular and unpopular individuals; the differentiations are more complex (see Figure 16-7). For instance, some adolescents are controversial; in contrast to *popular* adolescents, who are mostly liked,

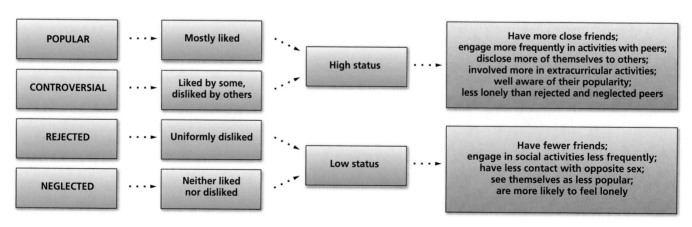

FIGURE 16-7
THE SOCIAL WORLD OF ADOLESCENCE

An adolescent's popularity can fall into one of four categories, depending on the opinions of his or her peers. Popularity is related to differences in status, behavior, and adjustment. From the perspective of an educator, how might popularity be related to the way that you teach?

DEVELOPMENTAL DIVERSITY

Race Segregation: The Great Divide of Adolescence

When Philip McAdoo, a [student] at the University of North Carolina, stopped one day to see a friend who worked on his college campus, a receptionist asked if he would autograph a basketball for her son. Because he was African American and tall, "she just assumed that I was on the basketball team," recounted McAdoo.

Jasme Kelly, an African American sophomore at the same college, had a similar story to tell. When she went to see a friend at a fraternity house, the student who answered the door asked if she was there to apply for the job of cook.

White students, too, find racial relations difficult and in some ways forbidding. For instance, Jenny Johnson, a white 20-year-old junior, finds even the most basic conversation with African American classmates difficult. She describes a conversation in which African American friends "jump at my throat because I used the word 'black' instead of African American. There is just such a huge barrier that it's really hard . . . to have a normal discussion." (Sanoff & Minerbrook, 1993, p. 58)

The pattern of race segregation found at the University of North Carolina is repeated over and over in schools and colleges throughout the United States: Even when they attend desegregated schools with a high proportion of minority students, people of different ethnicities and races interact very little. Moreover, even if they have a friend of a different ethnicity within the confines of a school, most adolescents don't interact with that friend outside of school (Du Bois & Hirsch, 1990).

It doesn't start out this way. During elementary school and even during early adolescence, there is a fair amount of integration among students of differing ethnicities. However, by middle and late adolescence, the amount of segregation is striking (Ennett & Bauman, 1996; M. B. Spencer, 1991; M. B. Spencer & Dornbusch, 1990; Shrum, Cheek, & Hunter, 1988).

Why should racial and ethnic segregation be the rule, even in schools that have been desegregated for some time? One reason is that minority students may actively seek support from others who share their minority status. Furthermore, by associating primarily with other members of their own minority group, they are able to affirm their own identity.

Other explanations for campus segregation are less positive. For instance, socioeconomic status differences between people of different races and ethnicities may keep integration at low

Adolescents who have had extensive interactions with members of different races are more likely to have friends of different races.

levels. Racial and ethnic differences tend to mirror SES differences: People from minority groups are overrepresented in lower SES groups (J. Coleman, 1961), just as people from the majority group are overrepresented in higher SES groups. Because cliques tend to have members of similar SES, they also display very little racial integration. It is possible, then, that apparent ethnic differences in interaction patterns are really due to SES characteristics and not to ethnicity per se.

Another explanation for the lack of interaction between members of different racial and ethnic groups relates to differences in academic performance. Because minority group members tend to experience less school success than members of the majority group, as we discussed in Chapter 13, it may be that ethnic and racial segregation is based not on ethnicity itself but on academic achievement.

Specifically, some students attend schools in which classes are assigned on the basis of students' prior levels of academic success. If minority group members experience less success, they may find themselves in classes with proportionally fewer majority group members. Similarly, majority students may be in classes with few minority students. Such class assignment practices, then, may inadvertently maintain and promote racial and ethnic segregation. This pattern would be particularly prevalent in schools where rigid academic tracking is practiced, with students assigned to "low," "medium," and "high" tracks depending on their prior achievement (Hallinan & Williams, 1989).

Finally, the lack of racial and ethnic interaction in school may reflect negative attitudes held by both majority and minority students. Minority students may feel that the white majority is prejudiced, discriminatory, and hostile, and they may prefer to stick to same-race groups. Conversely, majority students may assume that minority group members are antagonistic and unfriendly. Such mutually destructive attitudes reduce the likelihood that meaningful interaction can take place (N. Miller & Brewer, 1984; Phinney, Ferguson, & Tate, 1997).

Is the voluntary segregation along racial and ethnic lines found during adolescence inevitable? No. For instance, adolescents who have had extensive interactions with members of different races earlier in their lives are more likely to have friends of different races. Furthermore, schools that actively promote contact between members of different ethnicities in mixed-ability classes may create an environment in which cross-race friendships can flourish (Schofield & Francis, 1982).

Still, the task is daunting. Many societal pressures act to keep members of different races from interacting with one another. Furthermore, cliques may actively promote norms that discourage group members from crossing racial and ethnic lines to form new friendships.

Unpopular adolescents fall into several categories. Controversial adolescents are liked by some and disliked by others, rejected adolescents are uniformly disliked, and neglected adolescents are neither liked nor disliked.

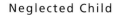
VIDEO CLIP

Neglected Child

Controversial adolescents Teenagers who are liked by some peers and disliked by others

Rejected adolescents Teenagers who are actively disliked and whose peers may react to them in an obviously negative manner

Neglected adolescents Children who receive relatively little attention from their peers in the form of either positive or negative interactions

controversial adolescents are liked by some and disliked by others. Furthermore, there are **rejected adolescents,** who are uniformly disliked, and **neglected adolescents,** who are neither liked nor disliked. In most cases, popular and controversial adolescents tend to be similar in that their overall status is higher, whereas rejected and neglected adolescents share a generally lower status.

Popular and controversial adolescents have more close friends, engage more frequently in activities with their peers, and disclose more about themselves to others than less popular students. They are also more involved in extracurricular school activities. In addition, they are well aware of their popularity, and they are less lonely than their less popular classmates (Englund et al., 2000; Franzoi, Davis, & Vasquez-Suson, 1994).

In contrast, the social world of rejected and neglected adolescents is considerably more negative. These young people have fewer friends, engage in social activities less frequently, and have less contact with the opposite sex. They see themselves—accurately, it turns out—as less popular, and they are more likely to feel lonely.

Conformity: Peer Pressure in Adolescence

Whenever Aldos Henry said he wanted to buy a particular brand of sneakers or a certain style of shirt, his parents complained that he was just giving in to peer pressure and told him to make up his own mind about things.

As they grow more confident of their own decisions, adolescents become less likely to conform to peers and parents.

In arguing with Aldos, his parents were subscribing to a view of adolescence that is quite prevalent in U.S. society: that teenagers are highly susceptible to **peer pressure,** the influence of one's peers to conform to their behavior and attitudes. Were his parents correct?

The research suggests that it all depends. In some cases, adolescents are indeed highly susceptible to the influence of their peers. For instance, when considering what to wear, whom to date, and what movies to see, adolescents are apt to follow the lead of their peers. But when it comes to many nonsocial matters, such as choosing a career path or trying to solve a problem, they are more likely to turn to an experienced adult (Phelan, Yu, & Davidson, 1994).

In short, particularly in middle and late adolescence, teenagers turn to those they see as experts on a given dimension (Young & Ferguson, 1979). If they have social concerns, they turn to the people most likely to be experts—their peers. If the problem is one about which parents or other adults are most likely to have expertise, teenagers tend to turn to them for advice and are most susceptible to their opinions.

Overall, then, it does not appear that susceptibility to peer pressure suddenly soars during adolescence. Instead, adolescence brings about a change in the choice of people to whom an individual conforms. Whereas children conform fairly consistently to their parents during childhood, in adolescence conformity shifts to include the peer group, in part because the pressures to conform increase.

Ultimately, however, adolescents conform less to both peers *and* adults as they develop increasing autonomy over their lives. As they grow in confidence and in the ability to make their own decisions, adolescents are more apt to remain independent and to reject pressures from others, no matter who those others are. Before they learn to resist the urge to conform to their peers, however, teenagers may get into trouble, often along with their friends (Crockett & Crouter, 1995; L. Steinberg, 1993).

Juvenile Delinquency: The Crimes of Adolescence

Although the vast majority of them are law-abiding citizens, adolescents, along with young adults, are more likely to commit crimes than any other age group. Some of the reasons for this state of affairs have to do with the definition of certain behaviors (such as drinking), which are illegal for adolescents but not for older individuals. But even when such crimes are disregarded, adolescents are disproportionately involved in violent crimes, such as murder, assaults, and rape, and property crimes involving theft, robbery, and arson.

Peer pressure The influence of one's peers to conform to their behavior and attitudes

Undersocialized delinquents Adolescent delinquents who are raised with little discipline or with harsh, uncaring parental supervision

Socialized delinquents Adolescent delinquents who know and subscribe to the norms of society and who are fairly normal psychologically

Although the number of violent crimes committed by U.S. adolescents in the 1990s declined, probably thanks to the strength of the economy, delinquency among some teenagers remains a significant problem (Office of Juvenile Justice and Delinquency Prevention, 2002; Pope & Bierman, 1999). Overall, a quarter of all serious violent crime involves an adolescent. Almost 20 percent of serious violent crimes are committed by adolescents, either alone or in groups. Another 8 percent are committed by adolescents in conjunction with older offenders.

Why do adolescents become involved in criminal activity? Some offenders are known as **undersocialized delinquents,** adolescents who are raised with little discipline or with harsh, uncaring parental supervision. These children have never been appropriately socialized and simply have not learned standards of conduct to regulate their own behavior. Undersocialized delinquents typically begin criminal activities at an early age, well before the onset of adolescence.

Undersocialized delinquents share several characteristics. They tend to be relatively aggressive and violent fairly early in life, characteristics that lead to rejection by peers and academic failure. They are also more likely to have been diagnosed with attention deficit disorder as children, and they tend to be less intelligent than average (Blau & Gullotta, 1995; B. Henry et al., 1996; Silverthorn & Frick, 1999).

Undersocialized delinquents often suffer from psychological difficulties and as adults fit a psychological pattern called *antisocial personality disorder*. They are relatively unlikely to be successfully rehabilitated, and many undersocialized delinquents end up living on the margins of society throughout their lives (D. O. Lewis et al., 1994; Lyman, 1996; Rönkä & Pulkkinen, 1995; Tate, Reppucci, & Mulvey, 1995).

But they are in the minority. Most adolescent offenders are socialized delinquents. **Socialized delinquents** know and subscribe to the norms of society; they are fairly normal psychologically. For them, transgressions committed during adolescence do not lead to a life of crime. Instead, most socialized delinquents pass through a period during adolescence when they engage in some petty crimes, but they do not continue lawbreaking into adulthood.

Socialized delinquents are typically highly influenced by their peers, and their delinquency often occurs in groups. In addition, some research suggests that parents of socialized delinquents supervise their children's behavior less closely than other parents (Dornbusch et al., 1985; Fletcher et al., 1995; Thornberry & Krohn, 1997; Windle, 1994).

Review

- The search for autonomy may cause a readjustment in relations between teenagers and their parents, but the generation gap is not as wide as is generally thought.

- Cliques and crowds serve as reference groups in adolescence and offer a ready means of social comparison. Sex cleavage gradually diminishes until boys and girls begin to pair off.

- Racial separation increases during adolescence, bolstered by socioeconomic status differences, different academic experiences, and mutually distrustful attitudes.

- Adolescents generally fall into one of four categories relating to popularity: popular, controversial, neglected, or rejected.

- Adolescents tend to conform to their peers in areas in which they regard their peers as experts and to adults in areas of perceived adult expertise.

● Adolescents are disproportionately involved in criminal activities, although most do not commit crimes. Those who do commit crimes can be categorized as undersocialized or socialized delinquents.

Applying Child Development

● How do the findings about conformity and peer pressure reported in this chapter relate to adolescents' developing cognitive abilities?

● *From a social worker's perspective:* In what ways do you think parents with different styles—authoritarian, authoritative, permissive, and uninvolved—tend to react to attempts to establish autonomy during adolescence? Are the styles of parenting different for a single parent? Are there cultural differences?

Dating, Sexual Behavior, and Teenage Pregnancy

> It took him almost a month, but Sylvester Chiu finally got up the courage to ask Jackie Durbin to go to the movies. It was hardly a surprise to Jackie, though. Sylvester had first told his friend Erik about his resolve to ask Jackie out, and Erik had told Jackie's friend Cynthia about Sylvester's plans. Cynthia, in turn, had told Jackie, who was primed to say yes when Sylvester finally did call.

Welcome to the complex world of dating, an important ritual of adolescence. We'll consider dating, as well as several other aspects of adolescents' relationships with one another, in the remainder of the chapter.

Dating: Boy Meets Girl in the 21st Century

By the time most girls are 12 or 13 and boys are 13 or 14, they begin to show an interest in dating. By the age of 16, more than 90 percent of teenagers have had at least one date, and by the end of high school, some three quarters of adolescents have dated someone steadily (Dickenson, 1975; McCabe, 1984).

The Functions of Dating.   Although on the surface dating may seem to be simply part of a pattern of courtship that can potentially lead to marriage, it actually serves other functions as well. For instance, dating is a way to learn how to establish intimacy with other individuals. Furthermore, it can provide entertainment and, depending on the status of the person one is dating, prestige. It even can be used to develop a sense of one's own identity (Sanderson & Cantor, 1995; Savin-Williams & Berndt, 1990; Skipper & Nass, 1966). For example, Leah Brookner and boyfriend Sean Moffitt, described in the chapter prologue, are definitely finding entertainment, and probably learning something about themselves, as they attend their first formal dance.

Just how well dating serves such functions, particularly the development of psychological intimacy, is an open question. What specialists in adolescence do know, however, is surprising: Dating in early and middle adolescence is not terribly successful at facilitating intimacy. On the contrary, dating is often a superficial activity in which the participants so rarely let down their guard that they never become truly close and never expose themselves emotionally to

Just how well dating serves to further such functions as the development of psychological intimacy is still an open question.

each other. Psychological intimacy may be lacking even when sexual activity is part of the relationship (Douvan & Adelson, 1966; Savin-Williams & Berndt, 1990).

True intimacy becomes more common during later adolescence. At that point, the dating relationship may be taken more seriously by both participants, and it may be seen as a way to select a mate and as a potential prelude to marriage.

Dating in Minority Groups. Cultural influences affect dating patterns among minority adolescents, particularly those whose parents have come to the United States from other countries. Minority parents may try to control their children's dating behavior in an effort to preserve the minority group's traditional values (M. B. Spencer & Dornbusch, 1990).

For example, Asian parents may be especially conservative in their attitudes and values, in part because they themselves may have had no experience of dating. (In many cases, the parents' marriage was arranged by others, and the entire concept of dating is unfamiliar.) They may insist that dating be conducted with chaperones or not at all. As a consequence, they may find themselves involved in substantial conflict with their children (Sung, 1985).

Sexual Relationships: Permissiveness With Affection

The maturation of the sexual organs during the start of adolescence opens a new range of possibilities in relations with others: sexuality. In fact, sexual behavior and thoughts are among the central concerns of adolescents. Almost all adolescents think about sex, and many think about it a good deal of the time (Kelly, 2001; Ponton, 2001).

Masturbation. For most adolescents, their initiation into sexuality comes from **masturbation,** sexual self-stimulation. Almost half of all adolescent boys and a quarter of adolescent girls report that they have engaged in masturbation. The frequency of masturbation shows a sex difference: Male masturbation is most frequent in the early teens and then begins to decline, while females begin more slowly and reach a maximum later (Oliver & Hyde, 1993; I. M. Schwartz, 1999).

Although masturbation is widespread, it may produce feelings of shame and guilt. There are several reasons for this. One is that adolescents may believe that masturbation signifies the inability to find a sexual partner—an erroneous assumption, since statistics show that three quarters of married men and nearly as many married women report masturbating between 10 and 24 times a year (M. Hunt, 1974). Another reason is the legacy of shame remaining from misguided past views. For instance, 19th-century physicians and clergy warned of horrible effects of masturbation, including "dyspepsia, spinal disease, headache, epilepsy, various kinds of fits . . . , impaired eyesight, palpitation of the heart, pain in the side and bleeding at the lungs, spasm of the heart, and sometimes sudden death" (Gregory, 1856). Suggested remedies included bandaging the genitals, covering them with a cage, tying the hands, male circumcision without anesthesia (so that it might better be remembered), and for girls, the administration of carbolic acid to the clitoris. One physician, J. W. Kellogg, believed that certain grains would be less likely to provoke sexual excitation—leading to his invention of corn flakes (M. Hunt, 1974; Michael et al., 1994).

The reality is different. Today, experts on sexual behavior view masturbation as a normal, healthy, and harmless activity (Leitenberg, Detzer, & Srebnik, 1993). In fact, some suggest that it provides a useful way to learn about one's own sexuality.

Sexual Intercourse. Although it may be preceded by many different types of sexual intimacy, including deep kissing, massaging, petting, and oral sex, sexual intercourse remains a major milestone in the perceptions of most adolescents. Consequently, the focus of researchers investigating sexual behavior has been on the act of intercourse.

The age at which adolescents first have sexual intercourse has been steadily declining for at least half a century. Overall, around half of adolescents begin having intercourse between the

Masturbation Sexual self-stimulation

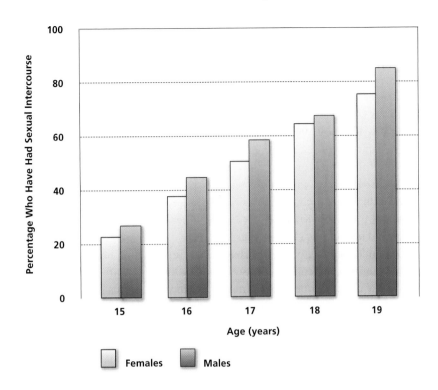

FIGURE 16-8   ADOLESCENTS AND SEXUAL ACTIVITY

The age at which adolescents have sexual intercourse for the first time is declining; today, 80 percent have sex before the age of 20.

(*Source:* Kantrowitz. & Wingert, 1999, p. 38)

ages of 15 and 18, and at least 80 percent have had sex before the age of 20 (see Figure 16-8). Some 7 percent of high school students report having had intercourse before the age of 13 (Centers for Disease Control & Prevention, 1998b; Seidman & Rieder, 1994).

Norms for Sexual Conduct.   Overall, sexual activities are taking place earlier during adolescence than they did in prior eras (Warren et al., 1997). This is in part a result of a change in societal norms governing sexual conduct. The prevailing norm several decades ago was the *double standard,* in which premarital sex was considered permissible for males but not for females. Women were told by society that "nice girls don't," while men heard that premarital sex was permissible—although they should be sure to marry virgins.

Today, however, the double standard has largely been supplanted by a new norm, called *permissiveness with affection.* According to this standard, premarital intercourse is viewed as permissible for both men and women if it occurs in the context of a long-term, committed, or loving relationship (Hyde, 1994; I. L. Reiss, 1960).

The demise of the double standard, however, is far from complete. Attitudes toward sexual conduct are typically more lenient for males than for females, even in relatively liberal cultures. And in some cultures, the standards for men and women are quite distinct. For example, in North Africa, the Middle East, and the majority of Asian countries, most women conform to societal norms suggesting that they abstain from sexual intercourse until they are married. In Mexico, where there are strict standards against premarital sex, males are also considerably more likely than females to have premarital sex (A. M. Johnson et al., 1992; Liskin, 1985; Spira et al., 1992). In comparison, in sub-Saharan Africa, women are more likely to have sexual intercourse prior to marriage, and intercourse is common among unmarried teenage women.

Sexual Orientation: Heterosexuality and Homosexuality

When we consider adolescents' sexual development, the most frequent pattern is *heterosexuality,* sexual attraction and behavior directed to the opposite sex. Yet some teenagers do not follow this path. Instead, some experience *homosexual* feelings, sexual attraction to members of their own sex.

At one time or another, around 20 to 25 percent of adolescent boys and 10 percent of adolescent girls have at least one same-sex sexual encounter. However, many fewer adolescents become exclusively homosexual. Although accurate figures are difficult to obtain, estimates range from a low of 1.1 percent to a high of 10 percent. Most experts believe that between 4 and 10 percent of men and women are exclusively homosexual during extended periods of their lives (Alan Guttmacher Institute, 1993b; Kinsey, Pomeroy, & Martin, 1948; McWhirter, Sanders, & Reinisch, 1990; Michael et al., 1994).

The difficulty in determining the proportion of people who are homosexual is due in part to the fact that homosexuality and heterosexuality are not completely distinct sexual orientations. Alfred Kinsey, a pioneer sex researcher, argued that sexual orientation should be viewed as a continuum on which "exclusively homosexual" is at one end and "exclusively heterosexual" at the other (Kinsey et al., 1948). In between are people who engage in both homosexual and heterosexual behavior.

Our understanding of sexual orientation is further complicated by confusion between sexual orientation and gender identity (Hunter & Mallon, 2000). Whereas sexual orientation relates to the object of one's sexual interests, *gender identity,* as noted in Chapter 10, is the gender a person believes he or she is psychologically. There is no relationship between sexual orientation and gender identity: A man who has a strong masculine gender identity may be attracted to other men. Furthermore, the extent to which men and women enact traditional "masculine" or "feminine" behavior is unrelated to their sexual orientation or gender identity.

The Causes of Sexual Orientation.   The factors that induce people to develop as heterosexual or homosexual are not well understood. Increasing evidence suggests that genetic and biological factors may play an important role. For instance, evidence from studies of twins shows that identical twins are more likely to both be homosexual than pairs of siblings who don't share their genetic makeup. Other research finds that various structures of the brain are different in homosexuals and heterosexuals, and hormone production also seems to be linked to sexual orientation (Berenbaum & Snyder, 1995; Gladue, 1994; Le Vay, 1993; Meyer-Bahlburg et al., 1995).

However, evidence of a biological cause is not yet conclusive, given that most findings are based on small samples (Byne & Parsons, 1994). Consequently, some researchers have suggested that family or peer environmental factors play a role. For example, Freud argued that homosexuality was the result of inappropriate identification with the opposite-sex parent (Freud, 1922/1959).

The difficulty with Freud's theoretical perspective and similar perspectives that followed is that there is no evidence to suggest that any particular family dynamic or child-rearing practice is consistently related to sexual orientation. Similarly, explanations based on learning theory, which suggest that homosexuality arises because of rewarding, pleasant homosexual experiences and unsatisfying heterosexual ones, do not appear to be a compelling answer (A. Bell & Weinberg, 1978; Golombok & Tasker, 1996; Isay, 1990).

In short, there is no accepted explanation of why some adolescents develop a heterosexual orientation and others a homosexual orientation. Most experts believe that sexual orientation develops out of a complex interplay of genetic, physiological, and environmental factors (Gladue, 1994).

Prejudice Due to Sexual Orientation.   What is clear is that adolescents who find themselves attracted to members of the same sex may face a more difficult time than other teens. U.S. society still harbors great ignorance and prejudice regarding homosexuality, persisting in the belief that people have a choice in the matter—which they do not. Gay and lesbian teens may be rejected by their family or peers or even harassed and assaulted if they are open about their orientation. The result is that adolescents who find themselves to

The stresses of adolescence are magnified for homosexuals, who often face societal prejudice. Eventually, however, most adolescents come to grips with their sexual orientation, as these students at a symposium exemplify.

be homosexual are at greater risk for depression, and suicide rates are significantly higher for homosexual adolescents than heterosexual adolescents (Henning-Stout, 1996; Remafedi et al., 1998).

Ultimately, though, most people are able come to grips with their sexual orientation. Once they are past adolescence, homosexuals have the same overall degree of mental and physical health as heterosexuals. Homosexuality is not considered a psychological disorder by any of the major psychological or medical associations, and all of them endorse efforts to reduce discrimination against homosexuals (Bersoff & Ogden, 1991; Herek, 1993; Patterson, 1994).

Teenage Pregnancy

Night has eased into day, but it is all the same for Tori Michel, 17. Her 5-day-old baby, Caitlin, has been fussing for hours, though she seems finally to have settled into the pink-and-purple car seat on the living-room sofa. "She wore herself out," explains Tori, who lives in a two-bedroom duplex in this St. Louis suburb with her mother, Susan, an aide to handicapped adults. "I think she just had gas."

Motherhood was not in Tori's plans for her senior year at Fort Zumwalt South High School—not until she had a "one-night thing" with James, a 21-year-old she met through friends. She had been taking birth-control pills but says she stopped after breaking up with a long-term boyfriend. "Wrong answer," she now says ruefully. (Gleick, Reed, & Schindehette, 1994, p. 40)

Feedings at 3:00 A.M., diaper changes, and visits to the pediatrician are not part of most people's vision of adolescence. Yet every year, tens of thousands of adolescents in the United States give birth. Figure 16-9 shows that although the birthrate for U.S. teenagers of different ethnic backgrounds has declined over the past four decades and is near record lows, about 5 percent of girls age 15 to 19 still become mothers each year (Darroch & Singh, 1999).

Despite the decline in teenage births, the problem remains severe, particularly when the rate of teenage pregnancy in the United States is compared to that in other industrialized countries, which is much lower. Although it might be suspected that the higher rates of pregnancy in the United States are due to more frequent or earlier sexual activity, that is not the case. For instance, there is little difference among industrialized countries in the age at which adolescents first have sexual intercourse.

What does differ is the use of birth control. Many adolescent pregnancies are unintended and happen because teenagers do not use effective contraceptives. Girls in the United States are much less likely to use contraception than teenagers in other countries. And even when they do use birth control, teenagers in the United States are less likely to use effective methods (Musick, 1993).

However, ineffective birth control is only part of the answer. An additional factor is that despite increasing rates of premarital sexual behavior, people in the United States remain

This 16-year-old mother and her child are representative of a major social problem: teenage pregnancy. Why is teenage pregnancy a greater problem in the United States than in other countries?

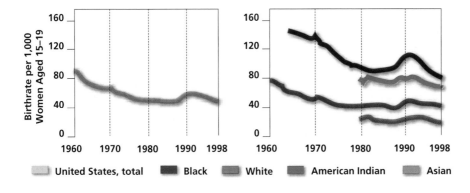

FIGURE 16-9 **TEENAGE BIRTHRATES**

The rate of teenagers giving birth in the United States declined significantly in the 1990s among all ethnic groups. What sorts of intervention have health care workers, social workers, and educators implemented to help reduce the rate of teenage pregnancies?

(*Source:* National Center for Health Statistics, 1998)

FROM RESEARCH TO PRACTICE

Taking the Pledge: Do Virginity Pledges Delay Premarital Sex Among Teenagers?

Does taking a pledge of virginity delay the incidence of premarital sex among teenagers?

Yes, at least under some circumstances. Recent research suggests that teenagers who make a public pledge to refrain from premarital sex delay intercourse significantly longer than those who do not make a public commitment. One study, sponsored by the National Institute of Child Health and Human Development, looked at 6,800 students from 141 schools in the United States. Adolescents who took a pledge to defer sexual intercourse until marriage delayed sex about 18 months longer than those who had never taken such a pledge. (Bearman & Bruckner, 2001).

But before those intent on delaying sexual intercourse until marriage begin printing up pledge cards, they need to keep in mind the limitations to pledges. First, the study examined only people who had voluntarily taken a public pledge; the results tell us nothing about whether people who are bullied through social pressure into making a pledge are more likely to remain virgins. Furthermore, the effectiveness of pledging depended on a student's age. For older adolescents, 18 years old and above, taking a pledge had no effect. Pledges were effective only for 16- and 17-year-olds.

Finally, the pledges were effective only when a *minority* of people in a school took such a pledge. When more than 30 percent took such a pledge, the effectiveness of the pledge diminished substantially. The reason for this somewhat surprising finding relates to why virginity pledges work in the first place: They offer adolescents a sense of identity, similar to the way joining a club does. When a minority of students take a virginity pledge, they feel part of a special group, and they are more likely to adhere to the norms of that group—in this case, remaining a virgin. In contrast, if a majority of students take a pledge of virginity, the pledge becomes less unique and adherence is less likely.

The study also examined whether breaking the pledge had an effect on pledgers' self-esteem. The answer: no. Despite previous research that found that girls who broke a virginity pledge had slightly lower self-esteem as a result, this study found that breaking the pledge had no effect on how teenagers viewed themselves (Bearman & Bruckner, 2001).

---

basically intolerant of premarital sex, and they are unwilling to provide sex education that includes information on contraception, which might reduce the rate of teenage pregnancies.

Consequently, sex education is more limited in the United States than in other industrialized countries. And because sex remains a contentious topic, with many political ramifications, effective sex education programs are difficult to develop and implement (Allen et al., 1997; Christopher, 1995; Rauch-Elnekave, 1994). Many pregnancy prevention efforts focus on abstinence, encouraging teens to avoid or delay having intercourse. The *From Research to Practice* box evaluates one popular strategy.

The results of an unintended pregnancy can be devastating to both mother and child. In comparison to earlier times, teenage mothers today are much less likely to be married. In a high percentage of cases, mothers care for their children without the help of the father (Coley & Chase-Lansdale, 1998; National Center for Health Statistics, 1998). Without financial or emotional support, a mother may have to abandon her own education, and consequently she may be relegated to unskilled, poorly paying jobs for the rest of her life. In other cases, she may develop a long-term dependence on welfare. An adolescent mother's physical and mental health may suffer as she faces unrelenting stress due to continual demands on her time (Ambuel, 1995; Barratt et al. 1996).

The children of teenage mothers also do not fare well when compared to children of older mothers. They are more likely to suffer from poor health and to show poorer school performance. Later, they are more likely to become teenage parents themselves, creating a cycle of pregnancy and poverty from which it is very difficult to escape (Carnegie Task Force, 1994; Furstenberg, Brooks-Gunn, & Morgan, 1987; N. Spencer, 2001).

●— CAREERS IN CHILD DEVELOPMENT —●

Name: Anne Marie La Corte

Education:	**St. Joseph's College, Standish, Maine: B.S. in professional arts; York Hospital, York, Pennsylvania: R.N.**
Position:	**School nurse, Voorhees High School, Glen Gardner, New Jersey**
Home:	**Washington, New Jersey**

Because adolescence is not only a time of great physical change but also one of major social and personality development, issues involving health come to the forefront during the high school years. And it is here that school nurses like Anne Marie La Corte stand ready to meet those needs.

The school year begins with making sure all entering freshman (ninth graders) are properly immunized and that all students who require medications are registered, according to La Corte, who is school nurse at Voorhees High School in Glen Gardner, New Jersey.

Serving approximately 1,100 students in grades 9–12, La Corte wears many hats in her role as school nurse.

"We have to be prepared to deal with a variety of emergency situations," she notes. "We have two defibrillators, which are available not only for the athletes but for the spectators as well. We also maintain a close relationship with the local emergency squad and work closely with school doctors."

In addition, issues of substance abuse, sexually transmitted diseases, teenage pregnancy, and mental health must be handled with sensitivity and discretion.

"It is absolutely crucial to have an open-door policy," La Corte says. "We have to be open, caring, and kind to have the students come in and talk to us.

"We provide pregnancy testing on an as-needed basis, as well as counseling to determine how to approach parents with the news," she added. "We also refer the student to liaison officers in the county public health department who can provide access to services and education. We also refer the student to a family physician, but we always maintain strict confidentiality with respect to the student."

One group of students who get more attention initially is the entering freshman class, who face a whole new environment.

"With the freshman, I sometimes have to act as a mother surrogate, just being there for them when they are stressed or uncertain about what to do," La Corte says. "For matters that are more serious, we have school-based counselors available who are part of the mental health program at local hospitals."

"It is absolutely critical to have an open door policy," La Corte said. "We have to be open, caring, and kind to have the students come in and talk to us."

● R E V I E W & A P P L Y ●

Review

● Dating in adolescence serves to provide intimacy, entertainment, and prestige.

● Masturbation, once viewed very negatively, is now generally regarded as a normal and harmless practice that continues into adulthood.

- Sexual intercourse is a major milestone that most people reach during adolescence. The age of first intercourse reflects cultural differences and has been declining for the past 50 years.

- Sexual orientation, which is most accurately viewed as a continuum rather than as separate categories, develops as the result of a complex combination of factors.

- Teenage pregnancy is a problem in the United States, with negative consequences for adolescent mothers and their children.

Applying Child Development

- Which factors in early and middle adolescence work against the achievement of true intimacy in dating?

- *From a health care worker's perspective*: How might the interplay of genetic, physiological, and environmental factors influence sexual orientation? Why is this information important to health care providers?

LOOKING **BACK**

- **How does the development of self-concept, self-esteem, and identity proceed during adolescence?**

  - During adolescence, self-concept differentiates to encompass others' views as well as one's own and to include multiple aspects simultaneously. Differentiation of self-concept can cause confusion as behaviors reflect a complex definition of the self.

  - Adolescents also differentiate their self-esteem, evaluating particular aspects of themselves differently.

  - According to Erik Erikson, adolescents are in the identity-versus-identity-confusion stage, seeking to discover their individuality and identity. They may become confused and exhibit dysfunctional reactions, and they may rely for help and information more on friends and peers than on adults.

  - James Marcia identifies four identity statuses that individuals may experience in adolescence and in later life: identity achievement, identity foreclosure, identity diffusion, and moratorium.

  - The formation of an identity is challenging for members of racial and ethnic minority groups, many of whom appear to be embracing a bicultural identity approach.

- **What dangers do adolescents face as they deal with the stresses of adolescence?**

  - Many adolescents have feelings of sadness and hopelessness, and some experience major depression. Biological, environmental, and social factors contribute to depression, and there are gender, ethnic, and racial differences in its occurrence.

- The rate of adolescent suicide is rising, with suicide now the third most common cause of death in the 15-to-24 age group.

⊙ **How does the quality of relationships with family and peers change during adolescence?**

- Adolescents' quest for autonomy often brings confusion and tension to their relationships with their parents, but the actual "generation gap" between parents' and teenagers' attitudes is usually small.

- Peers are important during adolescence because they provide social comparison and reference groups against which to judge social success. Relationships among adolescents are characterized by the need to belong.

⊙ **What are gender, race, and ethnic relations like in adolescence?**

- During adolescence, boys and girls begin to spend time together in groups and toward the end of adolescence to pair off.

- In general, segregation between people of different races and ethnicities increases in middle and late adolescence, even in schools with a diverse student body.

⊙ **What does it mean to be popular and unpopular in adolescence, and how do adolescents respond to peer pressure?**

- Degrees of popularity during adolescence include popular and controversial adolescents (on the high end of popularity) and neglected and rejected adolescents (on the low end).

- Peer pressure is not a simple phenomenon. Adolescents conform to their peers in areas of peer expertise and to adults in areas of adult expertise. As adolescents grow in confidence, their conformity to both peers and adults declines.

- Although most adolescents do not commit crimes, adolescents are disproportionately involved in criminal activities. Those who do commit crimes can be categorized as undersocialized or socialized delinquents.

⊙ **What are the functions and characteristics of dating during adolescence?**

- During adolescence, dating provides intimacy, entertainment, and prestige. Achieving psychological intimacy, difficult at first, becomes easier as adolescents mature, gain confidence, and take relationships more seriously.

⊙ **How does sexuality develop in the adolescent years?**

- For most adolescents, masturbation serves as the first step into sexuality. The age of first intercourse, which is now in the teens, has declined as the double standard has faded and the norm of permissiveness with affection has gained ground.

- Most people's sexual orientation is largely or entirely heterosexual, with between 4 and 10 percent of people being mostly or exclusively homosexual. Sexual orientation apparently develops out of a complex interplay of genetic, physiological, and environmental factors.

⊙ **Why is teenage pregnancy more of a problem in the United States than in many other countries?**

- In the United States, about 5 percent of girls under 20 give birth each year. The incidence of both contraception and sex education is comparatively low in the United States, a situation that contributes to the high rate of adolescent pregnancy.

EPILOGUE

e continued our consideration of adolescence in this chapter, discussing the highly important social and personality issues of self-concept, self-esteem, and identity. We looked at adolescents' relationships with family and peers and at gender, race, and ethnic relations during adolescence. Our discussion concluded with a look at dating, sexuality, and pregnancy.

Return to the prologue, in which we shared a moment in the life of 16-year-old Leah Brookner, who is about to head out to her first formal. In light of what you now know about adolescent social and personality development, consider the following questions:

1. In what ways does Leah appear to be dealing with the issues of self-concept, self-esteem, and identity?

2. How is she dealing with the issues of belonging and relationships with peers?

3. In what ways is Leah's behavior an example of the quest for autonomy? Is this evidence of a large generation gap in Leah's family?

4. What aspects of adolescent dating practices are evident in this scene? If Leah wants advice on dating or sexuality, is she more likely to seek it from her parents or her peers? Why?

KEY TERMS AND CONCEPTS

identity-versus-identity-confusion stage (p. 474)
identity achievement (p. 476)
identity foreclosure (p. 476)
moratorium (p. 476)
identity diffusion (p. 476)
cluster suicide (p. 480)

autonomy (p. 483)
generation gap (p. 483)
reference group (p. 487)
cliques (p. 487)
crowds (p. 487)
sex cleavage (p. 488)
controversial adolescents (p. 490)
rejected adolescents (p. 490)

neglected adolescents (p. 490)
peer pressure (p. 491)
undersocialized delinquents (p. 492)
socialized delinquents (p. 492)
masturbation (p. 494)

BRIDGES

Adolescence is the bridge between childhood and adulthood. In Part 5, we've seen how growth in different domains works together to help adolescents in the progression from child to adult. These developmental foundations that already have been laid continue to contribute to the enfolding of life as an adult.

The myth of adolescence in U.S. culture is that it is a time of emotional turmoil and intergenerational conflict. We've seen, however, that although making the transition to adulthood is challenging for everyone, reality often diverges from the myth of storm and stress.

Certainly, adolescents go through profound physical and cognitive changes. Physically, they experience extraordinary maturation with the onset of puberty, and they must cope with the sometimes uncomfortable changes associated with it. The developments of puberty, however, signal the start of their lives as sexually mature adults.

Adolescents' physical development is accompanied by cognitive advances that bring sophistication in the use of formal reasoning and abstract thought, as well as an increasing ability—and tendency—to question authority.

Teenagers' thoughts are often focused on themselves as they cross the bridge to adulthood. Maybe this helps them deal with one of the most important developmental tasks of the period: refining their view of themselves. We observed, for example, how adolescents use their increasingly sophisticated cognitive skills to differentiate their self-concept and self-esteem into component parts, a process they began during the school years and will continue throughout adulthood as people refine their views of themselves even further.

We discussed adolescents' relationships with peers and parents. The quest for autonomy, which is one of the hallmarks of adolescence, is eventually resolved, for most people, in the next phase of their lives, as young adults.

In sum, the story of childhood and adolescence provides the foundations for the remainder of the life span. As we age, life continues to present fresh challenges and opportunities as we continuously undergo and adjust to physical and cognitive changes and learn to relate to new social situations. Development persists throughout the remainder of life, building on the growth and accomplishments of childhood. ■

Glossary

Abstract modeling   The process in which modeling paves the way for the development of more general rules and principles (Ch. 10)

Acceleration   The provision of special programs that allow gifted students to move ahead at their own pace, even if this means skipping to higher grade levels (Ch. 12)

Accommodation   Changes in existing ways of thinking that occur in response to encounters with new stimuli or events (Ch. 2, 6)

Acquired immune deficiency syndrome (AIDS)   A sexually transmitted disease, produced by the human immunodeficiency virus (HIV), that has no cure and ultimately causes death (Ch. 14)

Active genotype–environment effects   Situations in which children focus on the aspects of their environment that are most congruent with their genetically determined abilities (Ch. 3)

Addictive drugs   Drugs that produce a biological or psychological dependence in users, leading to increasingly powerful cravings for them (Ch. 14)

Adolescence   The developmental stage between childhood and adulthood (Ch. 14)

Adolescent egocentrism   A state of self-absorption in which the world is viewed from one's own point of view (Ch. 15)

Adolescent growth spurt   A period of very rapid growth in height and weight during adolescence (Ch. 14)

Affordances   The action possibilities that a given situation or stimulus provides (Ch. 5)

Age of viability   The point at which an infant can survive a premature birth (Ch. 4)

Agentic professions   Occupations associated with getting things accomplished (Ch. 15)

Aggression   Intentional injury or harm to another person (Ch. 10)

Ainsworth Strange Situation   A sequence of staged episodes that illustrate the strength of attachment between a child and (typically) his or her mother (Ch. 7)

Alcoholics   People who have learned to depend on alcohol and are unable to control their drinking (Ch. 14)

Ambivalent attachment pattern   A style of attachment in which children display a combination of positive and negative reactions to their mothers; they show great distress when the mother leaves, but upon her return, they may simultaneously seek close contact but also hit and kick her (Ch. 7)

Amniocentesis   The process of identifying genetic defects by examining a small sample of fetal cells drawn by a needle inserted into the amniotic fluid surrounding the unborn fetus (Ch. 3)

Androgynous   Encompassing characteristics thought typical of both sexes (Ch. 10)

Anorexia nervosa   A severe and potentially life-threatening eating disorder in which individuals refuse to eat while denying that their behavior or skeletal appearance is out of the ordinary (Ch. 14)

Anoxia   A restriction of oxygen to the baby, lasting a few minutes during the birth process, which can produce brain damage (Ch. 4)

Apgar scale   A standard measurement system that looks for a variety of indications of good health in newborns (Ch. 4)

Applied research   Research meant to provide practical solutions to immediate problems (Ch. 2)

Artificial insemination   A process of fertilization in which a man's sperm is placed directly into a woman's vagina by a physician (Ch. 3)

Assimilation   The process in which people understand an experience in terms of their current stage of cognitive development and way of thinking (Ch. 2, 6)

Associative play   Play in which two or more children interact by sharing or borrowing toys or materials, although they do not do the same thing (Ch. 10)

Asthma   A chronic condition characterized by periodic attacks of wheezing, coughing, and shortness of breath (Ch. 11)

Attachment   The positive emotional bond that develops between a child and a particular individual (Ch. 7)

Attention deficit hyperactivity disorder (ADHD)   A learning disability marked by inattention, impulsiveness, a low tolerance for frustration, and a great deal of inappropriate activity (Ch. 11)

Attributions   People's explanations for the outcomes of their behavior (Ch. 13)

Auditory impairment   A special need that involves the loss of hearing or some aspect of hearing (Ch. 11)

Authoritarian parents   Parents who are controlling, punitive, rigid, and cold and whose word is law; they value strict, unquestioning obedience from their children and do not tolerate expressions of disagreement (Ch. 10)

Authoritative parents   Parents who are firm, setting clear and consistent limits, but try to reason with their children, explaining why they should behave in a particular way (Ch. 10)

Autobiographical memory   Memory of particular events from one's own life (Ch. 9)

Autonomy   Having independence and a sense of control over one's life (Ch. 16)

Autonomy-versus-shame-and-doubt stage   The period during which, according to Erikson, toddlers (aged 18 months to 3 years) develop independence and autonomy if they are allowed the freedom to explore or come to feel shame and self-doubt if they are restricted and overprotected (Ch. 7)

Avoidant attachment pattern   A style of attachment in which children do not seek proximity to the mother; after the mother has left, they seem to avoid her when she returns, as if angered by her behavior (Ch. 7)

Babbling   Making speechlike but meaningless sounds (Ch. 6)

Bayley Scales of Infant Development   A measure that evaluates an infant's development from 2 to 42 months (Ch. 6)

Behavior modification   A formal technique for promoting the frequency of desirable behaviors and decreasing the incidence of unwanted ones (Ch. 2)

Behavioral genetics   The study of the effects of heredity on behavior (Ch. 3)

Behavioral perspective   The approach to the study of development that suggests that the keys to understanding development are observable behavior and outside stimuli in the environment (Ch. 2)

Bicultural identity   The maintenance of one's original cultural identity while becoming integrated into the majority culture (Ch. 12)

Bilingualism   The ability to speak two languages (Ch. 12)

Bioecological approach   The perspective suggesting that different levels of the environment simultaneously influence every biological organism (Ch. 2)

Blended family   A household consisting of a couple and at least one child from a prior relationship (Ch. 13)

Bonding Close physical and emotional contact between parent and child during the period immediately following birth, argued by some to affect later relationship strength (Ch. 4)

Brazelton Neonatal Behavioral Assessment Scale (NBAS) A measure designed to determine infants' neurological and behavioral responses to their environment (Ch. 5)

Bulimia An eating disorder that primarily afflicts adolescent girls and young women, characterized by binges on large quantities of food followed by purges of the food through vomiting or the use of laxatives (Ch. 14)

Case studies Extensive, in-depth interviews with a particular individual or small group of individuals (Ch. 2)

Centration The process of concentrating on one limited aspect of a stimulus and ignoring other aspects (Ch. 9)

Cephalocaudal principle The principle that growth follows a pattern that begins with the head and upper body parts and then proceeds down to the rest of the body (Ch. 5)

Cerebral cortex The upper layer of the brain (Ch. 5)

Cesarean delivery A birth in which the baby is surgically removed from the uterus rather than traveling through the birth canal (Ch. 4)

Child abuse The physical or psychological maltreatment or neglect of children (Ch. 8)

Child care center A place that provides care for children while their parents are at work (Ch. 9)

Child development The field that involves the scientific study of the patterns of growth, change, and stability that occur from conception through adolescence (Ch. 1)

Child neglect Ignoring one's children or being emotionally unresponsive to them (Ch. 8)

Chlamydia The most common sexually transmitted disease, caused by a parasite (Ch. 14)

Chorionic villus sampling (CVS) A test used to find genetic defects that involves taking samples of hairlike material that surrounds the embryo (Ch. 3)

Chromosomes Rod-shaped portions of DNA that are organized in 23 pairs (Ch. 3)

Chronological (physical) age A person's age according to the calendar (Ch. 12)

Circular reaction An activity that permits the construction of cognitive schemes through the repetition of a chance motor event (Ch. 6)

Classical conditioning A type of learning in which an organism responds in a particular way to a neutral stimulus that normally does not bring about that type of response (Ch. 2, 4)

Cliques Groups of 2 to 12 people whose members have frequent social interactions with one another (Ch. 16)

Cluster suicide A situation in which one suicide leads to attempts by others to kill themselves (Ch. 16)

Cognitive development Development involving the ways that growth and change in intellectual capabilities influence a person's behavior (Ch. 1)

Cognitive neuroscience approaches Approaches to the study of cognitive development that focus on how brain processes are related to cognitive activity (Ch. 2)

Cognitive perspective The approach to the study of development that focuses on the processes that allow people to know, understand, and think about the world (Ch. 2)

Cohort A group of people born at around the same time in the same place (Ch. 1)

Collectivistic orientation A philosophy that promotes the notion of interdependence (Ch. 10)

Communal professions Occupations associated with relationships (Ch. 15)

Concrete operational stage The period of cognitive development between 7 and 12 years of age, characterized by the active and appropriate use of logic (Ch. 12)

Conservation The knowledge that quantity is unrelated to the arrangement and physical appearance of objects (Ch. 9)

Constructive play Play in which children manipulate objects to produce or build something (Ch. 10)

Contextual perspective The perspective that considers the relationship between individuals and their physical, cognitive, personality, social, and physical worlds (Ch. 2)

Continuous change Gradual development in which achievements at one level build on those of previous levels (Ch. 1)

Control group The group in an experiment that receives either no treatment or an alternative treatment (Ch. 2)

Controversial adolescents Teenagers who are liked by some peers and disliked by others (Ch. 16)

Cooperative play Play in which children genuinely interact with one another, taking turns, playing games, or devising contests (Ch. 10)

Coping Efforts to control, reduce, or tolerate the threats and challenges that lead to stress (Ch. 14)

Coregulation Joint control of children's behavior exercised by the parents and the children themselves (Ch. 13)

Correlational research Research that seeks to identify whether an association or relationship between two factors exists (Ch. 2)

Critical period A specific time during development when a particular event has its greatest consequences (Ch. 1)

Cross-modal transference The ability to identify, using another sense, a stimulus that has previously been experienced only through one sense (Ch. 6)

Cross-sectional research Research in which people of different ages are compared at the same point in time (Ch. 2)

Cross-sequential studies Studies in which researchers examine members of a number of different age groups at several points in time (Ch. 2)

Crowds Larger groups than cliques, composed of individuals who share particular characteristics but who may not interact with one another (Ch. 16)

Crystallized intelligence The store of information, skills, and strategies that people have acquired through education and prior experiences and through their previous use of fluid intelligence (Ch. 12)

Cultural assimilation model The view of American society as a "melting pot" in which all cultures are amalgamated (Ch. 12)

Culture-fair tests Tests that are valid regardless of the test takers' cultural backgrounds (Ch. 12)

Cycle-of-violence hypothesis The theory that abuse and neglect that children suffer predispose them as adults to abuse and neglect their own children (Ch. 8)

Decentering The ability to take multiple aspects of a situation into account (Ch. 12)

Deferred imitation An act in which a person who is no longer present is imitated by children who have witnessed a similar act (Ch. 6)

Dependent variable The variable in an experiment that is measured and is expected to change as a result of the experimental manipulation (Ch. 2)

Developmental quotient An overall developmental score that relates to performance in four domains: motor skills, language use, adaptive behavior, and personal and social skills (Ch. 6)

Developmentally appropriate educational practice   Education that is based on both typical development and the unique characteristics of a given child (Ch. 9)

Diaries   A research technique in which participants are asked to keep a record of their behavior on a regular basis (Ch. 2)

Differential emotions theory   Izard's theory that emotional expressions reflect emotional experiences and help in the regulation of emotion itself (Ch. 7)

Difficult babies   Babies who have negative moods and are slow to adapt to new situations; when confronted with a new situation, they tend to withdraw (Ch. 7)

Discontinuous change   Development that occurs in distinct steps or stages, with each stage bringing about behavior that is assumed to be qualitatively different from behavior at earlier stages (Ch. 1)

Disorganized-disoriented attachment pattern   A style of attachment in which children show inconsistent, often contradictory behavior, such as approaching the mother when she returns but not looking at her (Ch. 7)

Dizygotic twins   Twins who are produced when two separate ova are fertilized by two separate sperm at roughly the same time (Ch. 3)

DNA (deoxyribonucleic acid)   The substance that genes are composed of that determines the nature of every cell in the body and how it will function (Ch. 3)

Dominance hierarchy   Rankings that represent the relative social power of the individuals in a group (Ch. 13)

Dominant trait   The one trait that is expressed when two competing traits are present (Ch. 8)

Down syndrome   A disorder produced by the presence of an extra chromosome on the 21st pair; formerly referred to as mongolism (Ch. 3)

Easy babies   Babies who have a positive disposition; their body functions operate regularly, and they are adaptable (Ch. 7)

Ego   According to Freud, the part of personality that is rational and reasonable (Ch. 2)

Egocentric thought   Thinking that does not take the viewpoints of others into account (Ch. 9)

Embryonic stage   The period in prenatal development from 2 to 8 weeks following fertilization, during which significant growth occurs in the major organs and body systems (Ch. 3)

Emotional intelligence   The set of skills that underlie the accurate assessment, evaluation, expression, and regulation of emotions (Ch. 12)

Emotional self-regulation   The capability to adjust one's emotions to a desired state and level of intensity (Ch. 10)

Empathy   An emotional response that corresponds to the feelings of another person (Ch. 7, 10)

Enrichment   An approach whereby gifted students are kept at grade level but are enrolled in special programs and given individual activities to allow greater depth of study (Ch. 12)

Episiotomy   An incision sometimes made during childbirth to increase the size of the opening of the vagina to allow the baby to pass (Ch. 4)

Erikson's theory of psychosocial development   The theory that considers how individuals come to understand themselves and the meaning of others' behavior—and their own (Ch. 7)

Evocative genotype–environment effects   Situations in which a child's genes elicit a particular type of environment (Ch. 3)

Evolutionary perspective   The theory that seeks to identify behavior that is the result of our genetic inheritance from our ancestors (Ch. 2)

Experiment   A process in which an investigator, called an experimenter, devises two different experiences for subjects or participants (Ch. 2)

Experimental research   Research designed to discover causal relationships between various factors (Ch. 2)

Expressive style   A speaking style in which language is used primarily to express feelings and needs about oneself and others (Ch. 6)

Fantasy period   According to Ginzberg, the period of life when career choices are made—and discarded—without regard to skills, abilities, or available job opportunities (Ch. 15)

Fast mapping   The process in which new words are associated with their meaning after only a brief encounter (Ch. 9)

Fertilization   The process by which a sperm and an ovum—the male and female gametes, respectively—join to form a single new cell (Ch. 3)

Fetal alcohol effects (FAE)   A condition in which children display some, although not all, of the problems of fetal alcohol syndrome due to the mother's consumption of alcohol during pregnancy (Ch. 3)

Fetal alcohol syndrome (FAS)   A disorder caused by the mother's consumption of substantial quantities of alcohol during pregnancy, potentially resulting in mental retardation and delayed growth in the child (Ch. 3)

Fetal monitor   A device that measures the baby's heartbeat during labor (Ch. 4)

Fetal stage   The stage of prenatal development that begins at about 8 weeks after conception and continues until birth (Ch. 3)

Fetus   A developing child, from 8 weeks after conception until birth (Ch. 3)

Field study   A research investigation carried out in a naturally occurring setting (Ch. 2)

Fixation   Behavior reflecting an earlier stage of development (Ch. 2)

Fluid intelligence   The ability to deal with new problems and situations (Ch. 12)

Formal operational stage   The stage at which people develop the ability to think abstractly (Ch. 15)

Fragile X syndrome   A disorder that occurs when a particular gene is injured on the X chromosome, resulting in mild to moderate mental retardation (Ch. 3)

Full inclusion   The integration of all students, even those with the most severe disabilities, into regular classes and all other aspects of school and community life (Ch. 11)

Functional play   Play that involves simple, repetitive activities typical of 3-year-olds (Ch. 10)

Gametes   The sex cells from the mother and father that form a new cell at conception (Ch. 3)

Gender   The sense of being male or female (Ch. 7)

Gender constancy   The fact that people are permanently males or females, depending on fixed, unchangeable biological factors (Ch. 10)

Gender identity   The perception of oneself as male or female (Ch. 10)

Gender schema   A cognitive framework that organizes information relevant to gender (Ch. 10)

Gene   The basic unit of genetic information (Ch. 3)

Generation gap   A divide between parents and adolescents in attitudes, values, aspirations, and worldviews (Ch. 16)

Genetic counseling   The discipline that focuses on helping people deal with issues relating to inherited disorders (Ch. 3)

Genital herpes   A common sexually transmitted disease caused by a virus that produces blisters and sores (Ch. 14)

Genotype   The underlying combination of genetic material present (but not outwardly visible) in an organism (Ch. 3)

Germinal stage   The first—and shortest—stage of the prenatal period, which takes place during the first 2 weeks following conception (Ch. 3)

Gifted and talented   Showing evidence of high performance capability in intellectual, creative, or artistic areas, in leadership capacity, or in specific academic fields (Ch. 12)

Goal-directed behavior Behavior in which several schemes are combined and coordinated to generate a single act to solve a problem (Ch. 6)

Goodness of fit The notion that development is dependent on the degree of match between children's temperament and the nature and demands of the environment in which they are being raised (Ch. 7)

Grammar The system of rules that determine how thoughts can be expressed (Ch. 9)

Habituation The decrease in the response to a stimulus that occurs after repeated presentations of the same stimulus (Ch. 4)

Handedness A clear preference for the use of one hand over the other (Ch. 8)

Heteronomous morality The stage of moral development in which rules are seen as invariant and unchangeable (Ch. 10)

Heterozygous Inheriting from parents different forms of a gene for a given trait (Ch. 3)

Holophrases One-word utterances that stand for a whole phrase, whose meaning depends on the particular context in which they are used (Ch. 6)

Homozygous Inheriting from parents similar genes for a given trait (Ch. 3)

Hypothesis A prediction stated in a way that permits it to be tested (Ch. 2)

Id According to Freud, the raw, unorganized, inborn part of personality that is present at birth (Ch. 2)

Identification The process in which children attempt to be similar to their parent of the same sex, incorporating the parent's attitudes and values (Ch. 10)

Identity achievement The status of adolescents who commit to a particular identity following a period of crisis during which they consider various alternatives (Ch. 16)

Identity diffusion The status of adolescents who consider various identity alternatives but never commit to one or never consider identity options in any conscious way (Ch. 16)

Identity foreclosure The status of adolescents who prematurely commit to an identity without adequately exploring alternatives (Ch. 16)

Identity-versus-identity-confusion stage The period during which teenagers seek to determine what is unique and distinctive about themselves (Ch. 16)

Imaginary audience Fictitious observers who pay as much attention to adolescents' behavior as they do themselves (Ch. 15)

Immanent justice The notion that rules that are broken earn immediate punishment (Ch. 10)

In vitro fertilization (IVF) A procedure in which a woman's ova are removed from her ovaries and a man's sperm are used to fertilize the ova in a laboratory (Ch. 3)

Independent variable The variable in an experiment that is manipulated by researchers (Ch. 2)

Individualistic orientation A philosophy that emphasizes personal identity and the uniqueness of the individual (Ch. 10)

Industry-versus-inferiority stage The period from ages 6 to 12 characterized by a focus on efforts to attain competence in meeting the challenges presented by parents, peers, school, and the complexities of the world (Ch. 13)

Infant-directed speech A type of speech directed toward infants, characterized by short, simple sentences (Ch. 6)

Infant mortality Death within the first year of life (Ch. 4)

Infantile amnesia The lack of memory for experiences that occurred before age 3 (Ch. 6)

Infertility The inability to conceive after 12 to 18 months of trying to become pregnant (Ch. 3)

Information processing approaches Approaches to the study of cognitive development that seek to identify the ways individuals take in, use, and store information (Ch. 2, 6)

Initiative-versus-guilt stage According to Erikson, the period during which children aged 3 to 6 years experience conflict between independence of action and the sometimes negative results of that action (Ch. 10)

Intelligence The capacity to understand the world, think rationally, and use resources effectively when faced with challenges (Ch. 12)

Intelligence quotient (IQ) A score that expresses the ratio between a person's mental and chronological ages (Ch. 12)

Intuitive thought Thinking that reflects preschoolers' use of primitive reasoning and their avid acquisition of knowledge about the world (Ch. 9)

Kaufman Assessment Battery for Children (K-ABC) A children's intelligence test permitting unusual flexibility in its administration (Ch. 12)

Klinefelter's syndrome A disorder resulting from the presence of an extra X chromosome that produces underdeveloped genitals, extreme height, and enlarged breasts (Ch. 3)

Kwashiorkor A disease in which a child's stomach, limbs, and face swell with water (Ch. 5)

Laboratory study A research investigation conducted in a controlled setting explicitly designed to hold events constant (Ch. 2)

Language A systematic, meaningful arrangement of symbols that provides a basis for communication (Ch. 6)

Language-acquisition device (LAD) A neural system of the brain hypothesized to permit understanding of language (Ch. 6)

Lateralization The process whereby certain functions are located more in one hemisphere of the brain than in the other (Ch. 8)

Learning disabilities Difficulties in the acquisition and use of listening, speaking, reading, writing, reasoning, or mathematical abilities (Ch. 11)

Learning theory approach The perspective that language acquisition follows the basic laws of reinforcement and conditioning (Ch. 6)

Least restrictive environment The setting most similar to that of children without special needs (Ch. 11)

Longitudinal research Research in which the behavior of one or more individuals is measured as the subjects age (Ch. 2)

Low-birthweight infants Infants who weigh less than 2,500 grams (around 5½ pounds) (Ch. 4)

Mainstreaming An educational approach in which exceptional children are integrated as much as possible into the traditional educational system and are provided with a broad range of educational alternatives (Ch. 11)

Marasmus A disease characterized by the cessation of growth (Ch. 5)

Masturbation Sexual self-stimulation (Ch. 16)

Maturation The process of the predetermined unfolding of genetic information (Ch. 1)

Memory The process by which information is initially encoded, stored, and retrieved (Ch. 6, 12)

Menarche The onset of menstruation (Ch. 14)

Mental age The typical intelligence level found for people of a given chronological age (Ch. 12)

Mental representation An internal image of a past event or object (Ch. 6)

Mental retardation A significantly subaverage level of intellectual functioning that occurs with related limitations in two or more skill areas (Ch. 12)

Metacognition The knowledge that people have about their own thinking processes and their ability to monitor their cognition (Ch. 15)

Metalinguistic awareness An understanding of one's own use of language (Ch. 12)

Metamemory An understanding about the processes that underlie memory that emerges and improves during middle childhood (Ch. 12)

Mild retardation   Retardation with IQ scores in the range of 50 or 55 to 70 (Ch. 12)

Moderate retardation   Retardation with IQ scores from around 35 or 40 to 50 or 55 (Ch. 12)

Monozygotic twins   Twins who are genetically identical (Ch. 3)

Moral development   The maturation of people's sense of justice, of what is right and wrong, and their behavior in connection with such issues (Ch. 10)

Moratorium   The status of adolescents who may have explored various identity alternatives to some degree but have not yet committed themselves (Ch. 16)

Multicultural education   Education in which the goal is to help students from minority cultures develop competence in the culture of the majority group while maintaining positive group identities that build on their original cultures (Ch. 12)

Multifactorial transmission   The determination of traits by a combination of both genetic and environmental factors in which a genotype provides a range within which a phenotype may be expressed (Ch. 3)

Multimodal approach to perception   The approach that considers how information that is collected by various individual sensory systems is integrated and coordinated (Ch. 5)

Mutual regulation model   The model in which infants and parents learn to communicate emotional states to one another and to respond appropriately (Ch. 7)

Myelin   A fatty substance that helps insulate neurons and speeds the transmission of nerve impulses (Ch. 5, 8)

Nativist approach   The perspective that a genetically determined, innate mechanism directs language development (Ch. 6)

Naturalistic observation   Studies in which researchers observe some naturally occurring behavior without intervening or making changes in the situation (Ch. 2)

Neglected adolescents   Children who receive relatively little attention from their peers in the form of either positive or negative interactions (Ch. 16)

Neonate   A newborn (Ch. 4)

Neuron   The basic nerve cell of the nervous system (Ch. 5)

Night terror   Intense physiological arousal that cause a child to awaken in a state of panic (Ch. 8)

Nightmare   Vivid bad dreams, usually occurring toward morning (Ch. 8)

Nonorganic failure to thrive   A disorder in which infants stop growing due to a lack of stimulation and attention as the result of inadequate parenting (Ch. 5)

Normative events   Events that occur in a similar way for most individuals in a group (Ch. 1)

Norms   The average performance of a large sample of children of a given age (Ch. 5)

Obesity   A body weight more than 20 percent higher than the average weight for a person of a given age and height (Ch. 8)

Object permanence   The realization that people and objects exist even when they cannot be seen (Ch. 6)

Onlooker play   Action in which children simply watch others at play but do not actually participate themselves (Ch. 10)

Operant conditioning   A form of learning in which a voluntary response is strengthened or weakened, depending on its association with positive or negative consequence (Ch. 2, 4)

Operationalization   The process of translating a hypothesis into specific, testable procedures that can be measured and observed (Ch. 2)

Operations   Organized, formal, logical mental processes (Ch. 9)

Overextension   The overly broad use of words, overgeneralizing their meaning (Ch. 6)

Parallel play   Action in which children play with similar toys, in a similar manner, but do not interact with each other (Ch. 10)

Passive genotype–environment effects   Situations in which parents' genes are associated with the environment in which children are raised (Ch. 3)

Peer pressure   The influence of one's peers to conform to their behavior and attitudes (Ch. 16)

Perception   The sorting out, interpretation, analysis, and integration of stimuli involving the sense organs and brain (Ch. 5)

Permissive parents   Parents who provide lax and inconsistent feedback and require little of their children (Ch. 10)

Personal fables   The view held by some adolescents that what happens to them is unique, exceptional, and shared by no one else (Ch. 15)

Personality   The assortment of enduring characteristics that differentiate one individual from another (Ch. 7)

Personality development   Development involving the ways that the enduring characteristics that differentiate one person from another change over the life span (Ch. 1)

Phenotype   An observable trait; the trait that is actually seen (Ch. 3)

Physical development   Development involving the body's physical makeup, including the brain, nervous system, muscles, and senses and the need for food, drink, and sleep (Ch. 1)

Placenta   A conduit between the mother and fetus, providing nourishment and oxygen via the umbilical cord (Ch. 3)

Plasticity   The degree to which a developing structure or behavior is modifiable due to experience (Ch. 5)

Pluralistic society model   The concept that American society is made up of diverse, coequal cultures that should preserve their individual features (Ch. 12)

Polygenic inheritance   Inheritance in which a combination of multiple gene pairs is responsible for the production of a particular trait (Ch. 3)

Postmature infants   Infants still unborn 2 weeks after the mother's due date (Ch. 4)

Pragmatics   The aspect of language relating to communicating effectively and appropriately with others (Ch. 9)

Prelinguistic communication   Communication through sounds, facial expressions, gestures, imitation, and other nonlinguistic means (Ch. 6)

Preoperational stage   According to Piaget, the stage that lasts from ages 2 to 7 during which children's use of symbolic thinking grows, mental reasoning emerges, and the use of concepts increases (Ch. 9)

Preschool (nursery school)   A child care facility designed to provide intellectual and social experiences for youngsters (Ch. 9)

Preterm infants   Infants born less than 38 weeks after conception (also known as premature infants) (Ch. 4)

Primary sex characteristics   Characteristics that are associated with the development of the organs and structures of the body that directly relate to reproduction (Ch. 4)

Principle of hierarchical integration   The principle that simple skills typically develop separately and independently but are later integrated into more complex skills (Ch. 5)

Principle of the independence of systems   The principle that different body systems grow at different rates (Ch. 5)

Private speech   Spoken language that is not intended for others and is commonly used by children during the preschool years (Ch. 9)

Profound retardation   Retardation with IQ scores below 20 or 25 (Ch. 12)

Prosocial behavior   Helping behavior that benefits others (Ch. 10)

Proximodistal principle The principle that development proceeds from the center of the body outward (Ch. 5)

Psychoanalytic theory The theory proposed by Freud that suggests that unconscious forces act to determine personality and behavior (Ch. 2)

Psychodynamic perspective The approach to the study of development that states behavior is motivated by inner forces, memories, and conflicts of which a person has little awareness or control (Ch. 2)

Psychological maltreatment Harm to children's behavioral, cognitive, emotional, or physical functioning caused by parents or other caregivers verbally, through their actions, or through neglect (Ch. 8)

Psychosexual development According to Freud, a series of stages that children pass through in which pleasure, or gratification, is focused on a particular biological function and body part (Ch. 2)

Psychosocial development According to Erikson, development that encompasses changes both in the understandings individuals have of themselves as members of society and in their comprehension of the meaning of others' behavior (Ch. 2, 10)

Psychosomatic disorders Medical problems caused by the interaction of psychological, emotional, and physical difficulties (Ch. 14)

Puberty The period of maturation during which the sexual organs mature (Ch. 14)

Race dissonance The phenomenon in which minority children indicate preferences for majority values or people (Ch. 10)

Rapid eye movement (REM) sleep The period of sleep in older children and adults that is associated with dreaming (Ch. 5)

Realistic period The stage in late adolescence and early adulthood during which people explore career options through job experience or training, narrow their choices, and eventually make a commitment to a career (Ch. 15)

Recessive trait A trait that is present in an organism but is not expressed (Ch. 3)

Reciprocal socialization A process in which infants' behaviors invite further responses from parents and other caregivers, which in turn bring about further responses from the infants (Ch. 7)

Reference group Any group of people with whom one compares oneself (Ch. 16)

Referential style A speaking style in which language is used primarily to label objects (Ch. 6)

Reflexes Unlearned, organized involuntary responses that occur automatically in the presence of certain stimuli (Ch. 4, 5)

Rejected adolescents Teenagers who are actively disliked and whose peers may react to them in an obviously negative manner (Ch. 16)

Relational aggression Nonphysical aggression that is intended to hurt another person's psychological well-being (Ch. 10)

Resilience The ability to overcome circumstances that place a child at high risk for psychological or physical damage (Ch. 8)

Rhythms Repetitive, cyclical patterns of behavior (Ch. 5)

Sample A group of participants chosen for an experiment (Ch. 2)

Scaffolding The support for learning and problem solving that encourages independence and growth (Ch. 9)

Scheme An organized pattern of sensorimotor functioning (Ch. 6)

School child care A child care facility provided by some local school systems in the United States (Ch. 9)

Scientific method The process of posing and answering questions using careful, controlled techniques that include systematic, orderly observation and the collection of data (Ch. 2)

Scripts Broad representations in memory of events and the order in which they occur (Ch. 9)

Secondary sex characteristics The visible signs of sexual maturity that do not involve the sex organs directly (Ch. 14)

Secular trend A statistical tendency observed over several generations (Ch. 14)

Secure attachment pattern A style of attachment in which children use the mother as a kind of home base and are at ease when she is present; when she leaves, they become upset, and they go to her as soon as she returns (Ch. 7)

Self-awareness Knowledge that one exists separately from the rest of the world (Ch. 7)

Self-care children Children who let themselves into their homes after school and wait alone until their caretakers return from work; formerly known as *latchkey child* (Ch. 13)

Self-concept A person's identity or set of beliefs about what one is like as an individual (Ch. 10)

Self-esteem An individual's overall and specific positive and negative self-evaluation (Ch. 13)

Sensation The stimulation of the sense organs (Ch. 5)

Sensitive period A specific but limited time, usually early in an organism's life, during which the organism is particularly susceptible to environmental influences relating to some particular facet of development (Ch. 1, 5)

Sensorimotor stage Piaget's initial major stage of cognitive development, which can be broken down into six substages (Ch. 6)

Separation anxiety The distress displayed by infants when a customary care provider departs (Ch. 7)

Severe retardation Retardation with IQ scores that range from around 20 or 25 to 35 or 40 (Ch. 12)

Sex cleavage Sex segregation in which boys interact primarily with boys and girls primarily with girls (Ch. 16)

Sexually transmitted disease (STD) A disease that is spread through sexual contact (Ch. 14)

Sickle-cell anemia A blood disorder that gets its name from the shape of the red blood cells in those who have it (Ch. 3)

Slow-to-warm babies Babies who are inactive, showing relatively calm reactions to their environment; their moods are generally negative, and they withdraw from new situations, adapting slowly (Ch. 7)

Small-for-gestational-age infants Infants who, because of delayed fetal growth, weigh 90 percent (or less) of the average weight of infants of the same gestational age (Ch. 4)

Social-cognitive learning theory An approach to the study of development that emphasizes learning by observing the behavior of another person, called a model (Ch. 2)

Social comparison Evaluation of one's own behavior, abilities, expertise, and opinions by comparing them to those of others (Ch. 13)

Social competence The collection of social skills that permit individuals to perform successfully in social settings (Ch. 13)

Social development The way in which individuals' interactions with others and their social relationships grow, change, and remain stable over the course of life (Ch. 1)

Social problem solving The use of strategies for solving social conflicts in ways that are satisfactory both to oneself and to others (Ch. 13)

Social referencing The intentional search for information about others' feelings to help make sense of uncertain circumstances and events (Ch. 7)

Social smile Smiling in response to other individuals (Ch. 7)

Social speech Speech directed toward another person and meant to be understood by that person (Ch. 9)

Socialized delinquents Adolescent delinquents who know and subscribe to the norms of society and who are fairly normal psychologically (Ch. 16)

Sociocultural theory   An approach that emphasizes how cognitive development proceeds as a result of social interactions between members of a culture (Ch. 2)

Speech impairment   Speech that deviates so much from the speech of others that it calls attention to itself, interferes with communication, or produces maladjustment in the speaker (Ch. 11)

Stanford-Binet Intelligence Scale   A test that consists of a series of items that vary according to the age of the person being tested (Ch. 12)

State   The degree of awareness an infant displays to both internal and external stimulation (Ch. 5)

States of arousal   Different degrees of sleep and wakefulness through which newborns cycle, ranging from deep sleep to great agitation (Ch. 4)

Status   The relative position of a person ascribed by other members of a group (Ch. 13)

Stillbirth   Delivery of a child that is not alive; occurs in less than 1 delivery out of 100 (Ch. 4)

Stranger anxiety   The caution and wariness displayed by infants when encountering an unfamiliar person (Ch. 7)

Stress   The physical response to events that threaten or challenge us (Ch. 14)

Stuttering   Substantial disruption in the rhythm and fluency of speech; the most common speech impairment (Ch. 11)

Sudden infant death syndrome (SIDS)   The unexplained death of a seemingly healthy baby (Ch. 5)

Superego   According to Freud, the aspect of personality that represents a person's conscience, incorporating distinctions between right and wrong (Ch. 2)

Surrogate mother   A woman who agrees to carry a child to term if the mother who provides the donor eggs is unable to conceive (Ch. 3)

Survey research   Research in which a group of people chosen to represent some larger population are asked questions about their attitudes, behavior, or thinking on a given topic (Ch. 2)

Symbolic function   According to Piaget, the ability to use a mental symbol, a word, or an object to represent something that is not physically present (Ch. 9)

Synapse   The gap at the connection between neurons through which neurons chemically communicate with one another (Ch. 5)

Syntax   The combining of words and phrases to form meaningful sentences (Ch. 9)

Teacher expectancy effect   The phenomenon whereby an educator's expectations for a given child actually bring about the expected behavior (Ch. 12)

Tay-Sachs disease   A disorder for which there is no treatment that produces blindness, muscle degeneration, and early death (Ch. 3)

Telegraphic speech   Speech in which words not critical to the message are left out (Ch. 6)

Temperament   Patterns of arousal and emotionality that are consistent and enduring characteristics in an individual (Ch. 3, 7)

Tentative period   The second stage of Ginzberg's theory, which spans adolescence, in which people begin to think in pragmatic terms about the requirements of various jobs and how their own abilities might fit with those requirements (Ch. 15)

Teratogen   A factor that produces a birth defect (Ch. 3)

Theoretical research   Research designed specifically to test some developmental explanation and expand scientific knowledge (Ch. 2)

Theories   Explanations and predictions concerning phenomena of interest, providing a framework for understanding the relationships among an organized set of facts of principles (Ch. 2)

Theory of mind   Children's knowledge and beliefs about their mental world (Ch. 7)

Transformation   The process whereby one state is changed into another (Ch. 9)

Treatment   A procedure applied by an experimental investigator based on two different experiences devised for subjects or participants (Ch. 2)

Treatment group   The group in an experiment that receives the treatment (Ch. 2)

Triarchic theory of intelligence   The belief that intelligence consists of three aspects of information processing: the componential element, the experiential element, and the contextual element (Ch. 12)

Trust-versus-mistrust stage   According to Erikson, the period during which infants develop a sense of trust or mistrust, largely depending on how well their needs are met by their caregivers (Ch. 7)

Ultrasound sonography   A process in which high-frequency sound waves scan the mother's womb to produce an image of the unborn baby, whose size and shape can then be assessed (Ch. 3)

Underextension   The overly restrictive use of words, common among children just mastering spoken language (Ch. 6)

Undersocialized delinquents   Adolescent delinquents who are raised with little discipline or with harsh, uncaring parental supervision (Ch. 16)

Uninvolved parents   Parents who show virtually no interest in their children, displaying indifferent, rejecting behavior (Ch. 10)

Very-low-birthweight infants   Infants who weigh less than 1,250 grams (around 2¼ pounds) or, regardless of weight, have been in the womb less than 30 weeks (Ch. 4)

Visual impairment   Difficulties in seeing that may include blindness or partial sightedness (Ch. 11)

Visual recognition memory   The memory and recognition of a stimulus that has been previously seen (Ch. 6)

Wechsler Adult Intelligence Scale-Revised (WAIS-III)   A test for adults that provides separate measures of verbal and performance (nonverbal) skills, as well as a total score (Ch. 12)

Wechsler Intelligence Scale for Children-III (WISC-IV)   A test for children that provides separate measures of verbal and performance (nonverbal) skills, as well as a total score (Ch. 12)

X-linked genes   Genes that are considered recessive and located only on the X chromosome (Ch. 3)

Zone of proximal development (ZPD)   According to Vygotsky, the level at which a child can *almost*, but not fully, comprehend or perform a task without assistance (Ch. 9)

Zygote   The new cell formed by the process of fertilization (Ch. 3)

References

Able, E. L., & Sokol, R. J. (1987). Incidence of fetal alcohol syndrome and economic impact of FAS-related anomalies. *Drug and Alcohol Dependence, 19*, 51–70.

Aboud, F. E., & Skerry, S. A. (1983). Self and ethnic concepts in relations to ethnic constancy. *Canadian Journal of Behavioral Science, 15*, 14–26.

Abrams, D., & Hogg, M. A. (Eds.). (1999). *Social identity and social cognition*. Malden, MA: Blackwell.

Achenbach, T. A. (1992). Developmental psychopathology. In M. H. Bornstein & M. E. Lamb (Eds.), *Developmental psychology: An advanced textbook*. Hillsdale, NJ: Erlbaum.

Ackil, J. K., & Zaragoza, M. S. (1998). Memorial consequences of forced confabulation: Age differences in susceptibility to false memories. *Developmental Psychology, 34*, 1358–1372.

Adams, C. R., & Singh, K. (1998). Direct and indirect effects of school learning variables on the academic achievement of African American 10th graders. *Journal of Negro Education, 67*, 48–66.

Adams, G. R., Montemayor, R., & Gullotta, T. P. (Eds.). (1996). *Psychosocial development during adolescence*. Thousand Oaks, CA: Sage.

Adams, R. J., Mauer, D., & Davis, M. (1986). Newborns' discrimination of chromatic from achromatic stimuli. *Journal of Experimental Child Psychology, 41*, 267–281.

Adler, P. A., & Adler, P. (1994). Observational techniques. In N. K. Denzin & Y. S. Lincoln (Eds.), *Handbook of qualitative research*. Thousand Oaks, CA: Sage.

Adler, P. A., Kless, S. J., & Adler, P. (1992). Socialization to gender roles: Popularity among elementary school boys and girls. *Sociology of Education, 65*, 169–187.

Adler, S. A., Gerhardstein, P., & Rovee-Collier, C. K. (1998). Levels-of-processing effects in infant memory? *Child Development, 69*, 280–284.

Adolph, K. E. (1997). Learning in the development of infant locomotion. With commentary by B. I. Bertenthal, S. M. Boker, E. C. Goldfield, & E. J. Gibson. *Monographs of the Society for Research in Child Development, 62*, 238–251.

Adolph, K. E., Eppler, M. A., & Gibson, E. J. (1993). Crawling versus walking infants' perception of affordances for locomotion over sloping surfaces. *Child Development, 64*, 1158–1174.

Adolph, K. E., Vereijken, B., & Denny, M. A. (1998). Learning to crawl. *Child Development, 69*, 1299–1312.

AIDS and mental health, part II. (1994, February). *Harvard Mental Health Letter*, 1–4.

Ainsworth, M. D. S. (1973). The development of infant-mother attachment. In B. M. Caldwell & H. N. Ricciuti (Eds.), *Review of child development research* (Vol. 3). Chicago: University of Chicago Press.

Ainsworth, M. D. S. (1993). Attachment as related to mother-infant interaction. *Advances in Infancy Research, 8*, 1–50.

Ainsworth, M. D. S., & Bowlby, J. (1991). An ethological approach to personality development. *American Psychologist, 46*, 333–341.

Ainsworth, M. D. S., Blehar, M. C., Waters, E., & Wall, S. (1978). *Patterns of attachment: A psychological study of the Strange Situation*. Hillsdale, NJ: Erlbaum.

Aitken, R. J. (1995). The complexities of conception. *Science, 269*, 39–40.

Akmajian, A., Demers, R. A., & Harnish, R. M. (1984). *Linguistics*. Cambridge, MA: MIT Press.

Alan Guttmacher Institute. (1993a). *Report on viral sexual diseases*. Chicago: Author.

Alan Guttmacher Institute. (1993b). *Survey of male sexuality*. Chicago: Author.

Alan Guttmacher Institute. (1999). *Sharing responsibility: Women, society, and abortion worldwide*. New York: Author.

Albers, L. L., & Krulewitch, C. J. (1993). Electronic fetal monitoring in the United States in the 1980s. *Obstetrics and Gynecology, 82*, 8–10.

Ales, K. L., Druzin, M. L., & Santini, D. L. (1990). Impact of advanced maternal age on the outcome of pregnancy. *Surgery, Gynecology, and Obstetrics, 171*, 209–216.

Alessandri, S. M., Bendersky, M., & Lewis, M. (1998). Cognitive functioning in 8- to 18-month-old drug-exposed infants. *Developmental Psychology, 34*, 565–573.

Allen, J. P., Philliber, S., Herrling, S., & Kuperminc, G. P. (1997). Preventing teen pregnancy and academic failure: Experimental evaluation of a developmentally based approach. *Child Development, 64*, 729–742.

Allison, A. C. (1954). Protection afforded by sickle cell trait against subtertian malarial infection. *British Medical Journal, 1*, 290–294.

Alloy, L. B., Acocella, J., & Bootzin, R. R. (1996). *Abnormal psychology: Current perspectives*. New York: McGraw-Hill.

Altemus, M., Deuster, P. A., Galliven, E., Carter, C. S., & Gold, P. W. (1995). Suppression of hypothalmic pituitary adrenal axis responses to stress in lactating women. *Journal of Clinical Endocrinology and Metabolism, 80*, 2954–2959.

Amato, P. R., & Booth, A. (2001). The legacy of parents' marital discord: Consequences for children's marital quality. *Journal of Personality and Social Psychology, 81*, 627–638.

Ambuel, B. (1995). Adolescents, unintended pregnancy, and abortion: The struggle for a compassionate social policy. *Current Directions in Psychological Science, 4*, 1–5.

American Academy of Pediatrics. (1988). Infant exercise programs. *Pediatrics, 82*, 800–825.

American Academy of Pediatrics. (1989). Organized athletics for preadolescent children. *Pediatrics, 84*, 583–584.

American Academy of Pediatrics. (1990). Bicycle helmets. *Pediatrics, 85*, 229–230.

American Academy of Pediatrics. (1995). *Policy statement on length of hospital stay following birth*. Washington, DC: Author.

American Academy of Pediatrics. (1997). Breast-feeding and the use of human milk. *Pediatrics, 100*, 1035–1039.

American Academy of Pediatrics. (1998). Guidance for effective discipline. *Pediatrics, 101*, 723–728.

American Academy of Pediatrics. (1999a). *Circumcision: Information for parents*. Washington, DC: Author.

American Academy of Pediatrics. (1999b). Media education. *Pediatrics, 104*, 341–343.

American Academy of Pediatrics. (2000). *Recommended childhood immunization schedule, United States, January-December 2001*. Washington, DC: Author.

American Association of University Women. (1992). *How schools shortchange women: The AAUW report*. Washington, DC: Author.

American Association on Mental Retardation. (1992). *Mental retardation: Definition, classification, and systems of support*. Washington, DC: Author.

American Cancer Society. (1993). Cancer statistics, 1993. *Cancer Journal for Clinicians, 43*, 7–26.

American College of Obstetricians and Gynecologists. (2002). *Guidelines for perinatal care*. Washington, DC: Author.

American Psychiatric Association. (1994). *Diagnostic and statistical manual of mental disorders* (4th ed.). Washington, DC: Author.

American Psychological Association. (1992). *Ethical principles of psychologists and code of conduct*. Washington, DC: Author.

Ammerman, R. T., & Patz, R. J. (1996). Determinants of child abuse potential: Contribution of parent and child factors. *Journal of Clinical Child Psychology, 25*, 300–307.

Anand, K. J. S., & Hickey, P. R. (1987). Pain and its effect in the human neonate and fetus. *New England Journal of Medicine, 317*, 1321–1329.

Anand, K. J. S., & Hickey, P. R. (1992). Halothane-morphine compared with high-dose sufentanil for anesthesia and postoperative analgesia in neonatal cardiac surgery. *New England Journal of Medicine, 326*, 1–9.

Anders, T. F., & Taylor, T. (1994). Babies and their sleep environment. *Children's Environments, 11*, 123–134.

Anderson, M. (1999). *The development of intelligence*. Philadelphia: Psychology Press.

Anderson, R. N. (2001). United States life tables, 1998. In National Center for Health Statistics, *National vital statistics reports* (Vol. 48). Hyattsville, MD: Public Health Service.

Anderson, W. F. (1995, September). Gene therapy. *Scientific American*, 125–128.

Andersson, T., & Magnusson, D. (1990). Biological maturation in adolescence and the development of drinking habits and alcohol abuse among young males: A prospective longitudinal study. *Journal of Youth and Adolescence, 19*, 33–42.

Andrews, K., Francis, D. J., & Riese, M. L. (2000). Prenatal cocaine exposure and prematurity: Neurodevelopmental growth. *Journal of Developmental and Behavioral Pediatrics, 21*, 262–270.

Angier, N. (2000, August 22). Do races differ? Not really, genes show. *New York Times*, pp. S1, S6.

Anisfeld, M. (1996). Only tongue protrusion modeling is matched by neonates. *Developmental Review, 16*, 149–161.

Apgar, V. (1953). A proposal for a new method of evaluation in the newborn infant. *Current Research in Anesthesia and Analgesia, 32*, 260.

Apter, A., Galatzer, A., Beth-Halachmi, N., & Laron, Z. (1981). Self-image in adolescents with delayed puberty and growth retardation. *Journal of Youth and Adolescence, 10*, 501–505.

Archer, S. L., & Waterman, A. S. (1994). Adolescent identity development: Contextual perspectives. In C. B. Fisher & R. M. Lerner (Eds.), *Applied developmental psychology*. New York: McGraw-Hill.

Ardila, A., & Rosselli, M. (1994). Development of language, memory, and visuospatial ability in 5- to 12-year-old children using a neuropsychological battery. *Developmental Neuropsychology, 10*, 97–120.

Ariès, P. (1962). *Centuries of childhood*. New York: Knopf.

Arlotti, J. P., Cottrell, B. H., Lee, S. H., & Curtin, J. J. (1998). Breastfeeding among low-income women with and without peer support. *Journal of Community Health Nursing, 15*, 163–178.

Arnett, J. J. (1995). The young and reckless: Adolescent reckless behavior. *Current Directions in Psychological Science, 4*, 67–71.

Arnett, J. J. (1999). Adolescent storm and stress, reconsidered. *American Psychologist, 54*, 317–326.

Aronson, E. (2000). *Nobody left to hate: Teaching compassion after Columbine*. New York: Freeman.

Arseneault, L., Tremblay, R. E., Boulerice, B., & Saucier, J.-F. (2002). Obstetrical complications and violent delinquency: Testing two developmental pathways. *Child Development, 73,* 496–508.

Aseltine, R. H., Gore, S., & Colten, M. E. (1994). Depression and the social developmental context of adolescence. *Journal of Personality and Social Psychology, 67,* 252–263.

Asendorpf, J. B., Warkentin, V., & Baudonniere, P. (1996). Self-awareness and other-awareness II: Mirror self-recognition, social contingency awareness, and synchronic imitation. *Developmental Psychology, 32,* 313–321.

Asher, S. R., & Parker, J. G. (1991). The significance of peer relationship problems in childhood. In B. H. Schneider, G. Attili, J. Nadel, & R. P. Weisberg (Eds.), *Social competence in developmental perspective.* Amsterdam: Kluwer.

Asher, S. R., & Rose, A. J. (1997). Promoting children's social-emotional adjustment with peers. In P. Salovey & D. J. Sluyter (Eds.), *Emotional development and emotional intelligence: Educational implications.* New York: Basic Books.

Asher, S. R., Singleton, L. C., & Taylor, A. R. (1982). *Acceptance vs. friendship.* Paper presented at the meeting of the American Research Association, New York.

Aslin, R. N. (1987). Visual and auditory development in infancy. In J. D. Osofsky (Ed.), *Handbook of infant development* (2nd ed.). New York: Wiley.

Attie, I., & Brooks-Gunn, J. (1989). The development of eating problems in adolescent girls: A longitudinal study. *Developmental Psychology, 25,* 70–79.

Aved, B. M., Irwin, M. M., Cummings, L. S., & Findeisen, N. (1993). Barriers to prenatal care for low income women. *Western Journal of Medicine, 158,* 493–498.

Axia, G., Bonichini, S., & Benini, F. (1995). Pain in infancy: Individual differences. *Perceptual and Motor Skills, 81,* 142.

Azar, B. (1995, January). "Gifted" label stretches, it's more than high IQ. *Monitor on Psychology, 25.*

Azar, B. (2000, November). Hand-me-down skills. *Monitor on Psychology,* 64–66.

Azar, B., & McCarthy, K. (1994, October). Psychologists recommend vigilance against aggression. *Monitor on Psychology,* 45.

Azmitia, M. (1988). Peer interaction and problem solving: When are two heads better than one? *Child Development, 59,* 87–96.

Babad, E. (1992). Pygmalion—25 years after interpersonal expectations in the classroom. In P. D. Blanck (Ed.), *Interpersonal expectations: Theory, research and application.* Cambridge, England: Cambridge University Press.

Bader, A. P. (1995). Engrossment revisited: Fathers are still falling in love with their newborn babies. In J. L. Shapiro, M. J. Diamond, & M. Grenberg (Eds.), *Becoming a father.* New York: Springer.

Bahrick, L. E., & Pickens, J. N. (1988). Classification of bimodal English- and Spanish-language passages by infants. *Infant Behavior and Development, 11,* 277–296.

Bailey, J. M., Kirk, K. M., Zhu, G., Dunne, M. P., & Martin, N. G. (2000). Do individual differences in sociosexuality represent genetic or environmentally contingent strategies? Evidence from the Australian twin registry. *Journal of Personality and Social Psychology, 78,* 537–545.

Baillargeon, R. (1987). Object permanence in 3½- and 4½-month-old infants. *Developmental Psychology, 23,* 655–670.

Baillargeon, R., & De Vos, J. (1991). Object permanence in young infants: Further evidence. *Child Development, 62,* 1227–1246.

Balaban, M. T., Snidman, N., & Kagan, J. (1997). Attention, emotion, and reactivity in infancy and early childhood. In P. J. Lang, R. F. Simons, & M. T. Balaban (Eds.), *Attention and orienting: Sensory and motivational processes.* Mahwah, NJ: Erlbaum.

Ball, J. A. (1987). *Reactions to motherhood.* New York: Cambridge University Press.

Baltes, P. B. (1987). Theoretical propositions of life-span developmental psychology: On the dynamics between growth and decline. *Developmental Psychology, 23,* 611–626.

Bandura, A. (1977). *Social learning theory.* Englewood Cliffs, NJ: Prentice Hall.

Bandura, A. (1978). Social learning theory of aggression. *Journal of Communication, 28,* 12–29.

Bandura, A. (1986). *Social foundations of thought and action.* Englewood Cliffs, NJ: Prentice Hall.

Bandura, A. (1991). Social cognitive theory of moral thought and action. In W. M. Kurtines & J. L. Gewirtz (Eds.), *Handbook of moral behavior and development.* Hillsdale, NJ: Erlbaum.

Bandura, A. (1994). Social cognitive theory of mass communication. In J. Bryant & D. Zillmann (Eds.), *Media effects: Advances in theory and research.* Hillsdale, NJ: Erlbaum.

Bandura, A., Grusec, J. E., & Menlove, F. L. (1967). Vicarious extinction of avoidance behavior. *Journal of Personality and Social Psychology, 5,* 16–23.

Bandura, A., Pastorelli, C., Barbaranelli, C., & Caprara, G. V. (1999). Self-efficacy pathways to childhood depression. *Journal of Personality and Social Psychology, 76,* 258–269.

Bandura, A., Ross, D., & Ross, S. (1963). Vicarious extinction of avoidance behavior. *Journal of Personality and Social Psychology, 67,* 601–607.

Banich, M. T., & Nicholas, C. D. (1998). Integration of processing between the hemispheres in word recognition. In M. J. Beeman & C. Chiarello (Eds.), *Right hemisphere language comprehension: Perspectives from cognitive neuroscience.* Mahwah, NJ: Erlbaum.

Barinaga, M. (2000). A critical issue for the brain. *Science, 288,* 2116–2119.

Barkley, R. A. (1997). Behavioral inhibition, sustained attention, and executive functions: Constructing a unifying theory of ADHD. *Psychological Bulletin, 121,* 65–94.

Barkley, R. A. (1998a, September). Attention-deficit hyperactivity disorder. *Scientific American,* 66–71.

Barkley, R. A. (1998b). *Attention-deficit hyperactivity disorder: A handbook for diagnosis and treatment.* New York: Guilford Press.

Barnett, R. C., & Rivers, C. (1992). The myth of the miserable working woman. *Working Woman, 2,* 62–65, 83–85.

Barr, H. M., Streissguth, A. P., Darby, B. L., & Sampson, P. D. (1990). Prenatal exposure to alcohol, caffeine, tobacco, and aspirin: Effects on fine and gross motor performance in 4-year-old children. *Developmental Psychology, 26,* 339–348.

Barr, R. G., & Hayne, H. (1999). Developmental changes in imitation from television during infancy. *Child Development, 70,* 1067–1081.

Barr, R. G., Konner, M., Bakeman, R., & Adamson, L. (1991). Crying in !KungSan infants: A test of the cultural specificity hypothesis. *Developmental Medicine and Child Neurology, 33,* 601–610.

Barratt, M. S., Roach, M. A., Morgan, K. M., & Colbert, K. K. (1996). Adjustment to motherhood by single adolescents. *Family Relations, 45,* 209–215.

Barrett, D. E., & Frank, D. A. (1987). *The effects of undernutrition on children's behavior.* New York: Gordon & Breach.

Barrett, D. E., & Radke-Yarrow, M. R. (1985). Effects of nutritional supplementation on children's responses to novel, frustrating, and competitive situations. *American Journal of Clinical Nutrition, 42,* 102–120.

Barrett, M. (Ed.). (1999). *The development of language.* Philadelphia: Psychology Press.

Bartecchi, C. E., MacKenzie, T. D., & Schrier, R. W. (1995, May). The global tobacco epidemic. *Scientific American,* 44–51.

Bates, E., Bretherton, I., & Snyder, L. (1988). *From first words to grammar: Individual differences and dissociable mechanisms.* New York: Cambridge University Press.

Bates, E., Marchman, V., Thal, D., Fenson, L., Dale, P., Reznick, J. S., et al. (1994). Developmental and stylistic variation in the composition of the early vocabulary. *Journal of Child Language, 21,* 85–123.

Bates, J. E., Marvinney, D., Bennett, D. S., Dodge, K. A., Kelly, T., & Pettit, G. S. (1991, April). *Children's day care history and kindergarten adjustment.* Paper presented at the biennial meeting of the Society for Research in Child Development, Seattle.

Bauer, P. J. (1996). What do infants recall of their lives? Memory for specific events by 1- to 2-year-olds. *American Psychologist, 51,* 29–41.

Bauer, P. J., Wenner, J. A., Dropik, P. L., & Wewerka, S. S. (2000). Parameters of remembering and forgetting in the transition from infancy to early childhood. With commentary by Mark L. Howe. *Monographs of the Society for Research in Child Development, 65,* 4.

Bauman, K. J. (2001, March 29–31). *Home schooling in the United States: Trends and characteristics* (Working Paper No. 53). Paper presented at the annual meeting of the Population Association of American, Washington, DC.

Baumeister, R. F. (Ed.). (1993). *Self-esteem: The puzzle of low self-regard.* New York: Plenum.

Baumrind, D. (1971). Current patterns of parental authority. *Developmental Psychology Monographs, 4*(1, pt. 2).

Baumrind, D. (1980). New directions in socialization research. *Psychological Bulletin, 35,* 639–652.

Bayley, N. (1969). *Manual for the Bayley Scales of Infant Development.* New York: Psychological Corporation.

Bayley, N. (1993). *Bayley Scales of Infant Development (BSID-II)* (2nd ed.). San Antonio, TX: Psychological Corporation.

Beal, C. R. (1994). *Boys and girls: The development of gender roles.* New York: McGraw-Hill.

Beal, C. R., & Belgrad, S. L. (1990). The development of message evaluation skills in young children. *Child Development, 61,* 705–712.

Bearman, P. S, & Bruckner, H. (2001). Promising the future: Virginity pledges and first intercourse. *American Journal of Sociology, 106,* 859–912.

Beautrais, A. L., Joyce, P. R., & Mulder, R. T. (1996). Risk factors for serious suicide attempts among youths aged 13 through 24 years. *Journal of the American Academy of Child and Adolescent Psychiatry, 35,* 1174–1182.

Becahy, R. (1992, August 3). AIDS epidemic. *Newsweek,* p. 49.

Beeman, M. J., & Chiarello, C. (1998). Complementary right- and left-hemisphere language comprehension. *Current Directions in Psychological Science, 7,* 2–8.

Begley, S. (1995, July 10). Deliver, then depart. *Newsweek,* p. 62.

Begley, S. (1998, December 28). Into the gene pool: Ethical aspects of genetic research. *Newsweek,* p. 68.

Begley, S. (1999, March 15). Talking from hand to mouth. *Newsweek,* 56–58.

Begley, S. (2000). Wired for thought. *Newsweek* [Special issue: *Your Child*], 25–30.

Behrend, D. A. (1988). Overextensions in early language comprehension: Evidence from a signal detection approach. *Journal of Child Language, 15,* 63–75.

Beilin, H. (1996). Mind and meaning: Piaget and Vygotsky on causal explanation. *Human Development, 39,* 277–286.

Beilin, H., & Pufall, P. (Eds.). (1992). *Piaget's theory: Prospects and possibilities.* Hillsdale, NJ: Erlbaum.

Belkin, L. (1999, July 25). Getting the girl. *New York Times Magazine,* 26–35.

Bell, A., & Weinberg, M. S. (1978). *Homosexuality: A study of diversities among men and women.* New York: Simon & Schuster.

Bell, S. M., & Ainsworth, M. D. S. (1972). Infant crying and maternal responsiveness. *Child Development, 43,* 1171–1190.

Belle, D. (1999). The after-school lives of children: Alone and with others while parents work. Mahwah, NJ: Erlbaum.

Belmont, J. M. (1995). Discussion: A view from the empiricist's window. *Educational Psychologist, 30,* 99–102.

Belsky, J., Fish, M., & Isabella, R. (1991). Continuity and discontinuity in infant negative and positive emotionality: Family antecedents and attachment consequences. *Developmental Psychology, 27,* 421–431.

Belsky, J., & Rovine, M. (1988). Nonmaternal care in the first year of life and infant–parent attachment security. *Child Development, 59,* 157–167.

Belsky, J., Rovine, M., & Taylor, D. G. (1984). The Pennsylvania infant and family development project, III: The origins of individual differences in infant–mother attachment: Maternal and infant contributions. *Child Development, 55,* 718–728.

Belsky, J., Steinberg, L., & Walker, A. (1982). The ecology of day care: A critical review. *Child Development, 49,* 929–949.

Bem, S. (1987). Gender schema theory and its implications for child development: Raising gender-schematic children in a gender-schematic society. In M. R. Walsh (Ed.), *The psychology of women: Ongoing debates.* New Haven, CT: Yale University Press.

Benbow, C. P., Lubinski, D., & Hyde, J. S. (1997). Mathematics: Is biology the cause of gender differences in performance? In M. R. Walsh (Ed.), *Women, men, and gender: Ongoing debates.* New Haven, CT: Yale University Press.

Bendersky, M., & Lewis, M. (1998). Arousal modulation in cocaine-exposed infants. *Developmental Psychology, 34,* 555–564.

Benedict, H. (1979). Early lexical development: Comprehension and production. *Journal of Child Language, 6,* 183–200.

Benenson, J. F. (1994). Ages four to six years: Changes in the structures of play networks of boys and girls. *Merrill-Palmer Quarterly, 40,* 478–487.

Benenson, J. F., & Apostoleris, N. H. (1993, March). *Gender differences in group interaction in early childhood.* Paper presented at the biennial meeting of the Society for Research in Child Development, New Orleans.

Benjamin, J., Li, L., Patterson, C., Greenberg, B. D., Murphy, D. L. & Hamer, D. H. (1996). Population and familiar association between the D4 dopamine receptor gene and measures of novelty seeking. *Nature Genetics, 12,* 81–84.

Bennett, A. (1992, October 14). Lori Schiller emerges from the torments of schizophrenia. *Wall Street Journal,* pp. A1, A10.

Benoit, D., & Parker, K. C. H. (1994). Stability and transmission of attachment across three generations. *Child Development, 65,* 1444–1456.

Benson, H. (1993). The relaxation response. In D. Goleman & J. Guerin (Eds.), *Mind–body medicine: How to use your mind for better health.* Yonkers, NY: Consumer Reports.

Berenbaum, S. A., & Hines, M. (1992). Early androgens are related to sex-typed toy preferences. *Psychological Science, 3,* 202–206.

Berenbaum, S. A., & Snyder, E. (1995). Early hormonal influences on childhood sex-typed activity and playmate preferences: Implications for the development of sexual orientation. *Developmental Psychology, 31,* 31–42.

Bergeman, C., Chipuer, H., Plomin, R., Pedersen, N., McClearn, G. E., Nesselroade, J., et al. (1993). Genetic and environmental effects on openness to experience, agreeableness, and conscientiousness: An adoption/twin study. *Journal of Personality, 61,* 159–179.

Bergen, J., Hunt, G., Armitage, P., & Bashir, M. (1998). Six-month outcome following a relapse of schizophrenia. *Australian and New Zealand Journal of Psychiatry, 32,* 815–822.

Berger, L. (2000, April 11). What children do when home and alone. *New York Times,* p. F8.

Berigan, T. R., & Deagle, E. A., III. (1999). Treatment of smokeless tobacco addiction with bupropion and behavior modification. *Journal of the American Medical Association, 281,* 233.

Berko, J. (1958). The child's learning of English morphology. *Word, 14,* 150–177.

Berkowitz, L. (1993). *Aggression: Its causes, consequences, and control.* New York: McGraw-Hill.

Berman, A. L., & Jobes, D. A. (1991). *Adolescent suicide: Assessment and intervention.* Washington, DC: American Psychological Association.

Bernal, M. E. (1994, August). *Ethnic identity of Mexican American children.* Address at the annual meeting of the American Psychological Association, Los Angeles.

Berndt, T. J. (1999). Friends' influence on students' adjustment to school. *Educational Psychologist, 34,* 15–28.

Bernstein, G. A., & Borchardt, C. M. (1991). Anxiety disorders of childhood and adolescence: A critical review. *Journal of the Academy of Child and Adolescent Psychiatry, 30,* 519–532.

Bernstein, N., & Bruni, F. (1995, December 24). She suffered in plain sight, but alarms were ignored. *New York Times,* pp. 1, 22.

Berrick, J. D. (1998). When children cannot remain home: Foster family care and kinship care. *Future of Children, 8,* 72–87.

Berry, J. W., Poortinga, Y. H., Segall, M. H., & Dasen, P. R. (1992). *Cross-cultural psychology: Research and application.* New York: Cambridge University Press.

Bersoff, D. M. N., & Ogden, D. W. (1991). APA amicus curiae briefs: Furthering lesbian and gay male civil rights. *American Psychologist, 46,* 950–956.

Bertenthal, B. I., Campos, J. J., & Kermoian, R. (1994). An epigenetic perspective on the development of self-produced locomotion and its consequences. *Current Directions in Psychological Science, 3,* 140–145.

Berthier, N. E. (1996). Learning to reach: A mathematical model. *Developmental Psychology, 32,* 811–823.

Besseghini, V. H. (1997). Depression and suicide in children and adolescents. In G. Creastas, G. Mastorakos, & G. P. Choursos (Eds.), *Adolescent gynecology and endocrinology. Basic and clinical aspects.* New York: New York Academy of Sciences.

Best, C. T. (1994). The emergence of native-language phonological influences in infants: A perceptual assimilation model. In J. C. Goodman & H. C. Nusbaum (Eds.), *The development of speech perception: The transition from speech sounds to spoken words.* Cambridge, MA: MIT Press.

Betancourt, H., & Lopez, S. R. (1993). The study of culture, ethnicity, and race in American psychology. *American Psychologist, 48,* 1586–1596.

Bickham, D. S., Wright, J. C., & Huston, A. C. (2000). Attention, comprehension, and the educational influences of television. In D. G. Singer & J. L. Singer (Eds.). *Handbook of children and the media.* Thousand Oaks, CA: Sage.

Bierman, K. L., & Furman, W. (1984). The effects of social skills training and peer involvement on the social adjustment of preadolescents. *Child Development, 55,* 151–162.

Bigelow, B. J., Tesson, G., & Lewko, J. H. (1996). *Learning the rules: The anatomy of children's relationships.* New York: Guilford Press.

Bigler, R. S., Jones, L. C., & Lobliner, D. B. (1997). Social categorization and the formation of intergroup attitudes in children. *Child Development, 68,* 530–543.

Bigler, R. S., & Liben, L. S. (1993). A cognitive-development approach to racial stereotyping and reconstructive memory in Euro-American children. *Child Development, 64,* 1507–1518.

Bijeljac-Babic, R., Bertoncini, J., & Mehler, J. (1993). How do 4-day-old infants categorize multisyllabic utterances? *Developmental Psychology, 29,* 711–721.

Bing, E. D. (1983). *Dear Elizabeth Bing: We've had our baby.* New York: Pocket Books.

Birch, E. E., Garfield, S., Hoffman, D. R., Uauy, R., & Birch, D. G. (2000). A randomized controlled trail of early dietary supply of long-chain polyunsaturated fatty acids and mental development in term infants. *Developmental Medicine and Child Neurology, 42,* 174–181.

Bjorklund, D. F. (1997). In search of a metatheory of cognitive development (or Piaget is dead and I don't feel so good myself). *Child Development, 68,* 144–148.

Bjorklund, D. F., & Pellegrini, A. D. (2000). Child development and evolutionary psychology. *Child Development, 71,* 1687–1708.

Bjorklund, D. F., Schneider, W., Cassel, W. S., & Ashley, E. (1994). Training and extension of a memory strategy: Evidence of utilization deficiencies in the acquisition of an organizational strategy in high- and low-IQ children. *Child Development, 65,* 951–965.

Black, J. E., & Greenough, W. T. (1986). Induction of pattern in neural structure by experience: Implication for cognitive development. In M. E. Lamb, A. L. Brown, & B. Rogoff (Eds.), *Advances in developmental psychology* (Vol. 4). Hillsdale, NJ: Erlbaum.

Black, M. M., & Matula, K. (1999). *Essentials of Bayley Scales of Infant Development II assessment.* New York: Wiley.

Blake, J., & Boysson-Bardies, B. de. (1992). Patterns in babbling: A cross-linguistic study. *Journal of Child Language, 19,* 51–74.

Blakeslee, S. (1995, August 29). In brain's early growth, timetable may be crucial. *New York Times,* pp. C1, C3.

Blank, M., & White, S. J. (1999). Activating the zone of proximal development in school: Obstacles and solutions. In P. Lloyd & C. Fernyhough (Eds.), *Lev Vygotsky: Critical assessments: The zone of proximal development* (Vol. 3). New York: Routledge.

Blasko, D. G., Kazmerski, V. A., Corty, E. W., & Kallgren, C. A. (1998). Courseware for observational research (COR): A new approach to teaching naturalistic observation. *Behavior Research Methods, Instruments, and Computers, 30,* 217–222.

Blass, E. M., Ganchrow, J. R., & Steiner, J. E. (1984). Classical conditioning in newborn humans 2–48 hours of age. *Infant Behavior and Development, 7,* 223–235.

Bloch, H. (1989). On early coordinations of children and their future. In A. de Ribaupierre (Ed.), *Transition mechanisms in child development: The longitudinal perspective.* New York: Cambridge University Press.

Bloom, L. (1993). *The transition from infancy to language: Acquiring the power of expression.* New York: Cambridge University Press.

Blount, B. G. (1982). Culture and the language of socialization: Parental speech. In D. A. Wagner & H. W. Stevenson (Eds.), *Cultural perspectives on child development.* San Francisco: Freeman.

Blustein, D. L., & Palladino, D. E. (1991). Self and identity in late adolescence: A theoretical and empirical integration. *Journal of Adolescent Research, 6,* 437–453.

Boath, E. H., Pryce, A. J., & Cox, J. L. (1998). Postnatal depression: The impact on the family. *Journal of Reproductive and Infant Psychology, 16,* 199–203.

Bochner, S. (1996). The learning strategies of bilingual versus monolingual students. *British Journal of Educational Psychology, 66,* 83–93.

Bogenschneider, K., Wu, M.-Y., Raffaelli, M., & Tsay, J. C. (1998). Parent influences on adolescent peer orientation and substance use: The interface of parenting practices and values. *Child Development, 69,* 1672–1688.

Boismier, J. D. (1977). Visual stimulation and wake–sleep behavior in human neonates. *Developmental Psychology, 10,* 219–227.

Bonk, C. J., & Kim, K. A. (1998). Extending sociocultural theory to adult learning. In M. C. Smith & T. Pourchot (Eds.), *Adult learning and development: Perspectives from educational psychology.* Mahwah, NJ: Erlbaum.

Bookstein, F. L., Sampson, P. D., Streissguth, A. P., Barr, H. M. (1996). Exploiting redundant measurement of dose and developmental outcome: New methods from the behavioral teratology of alcohol. *Developmental Psychology, 32,* 404–415.

Booth, A., & Edwards, J. N. (1989). Transmission of marital and family quality over the generations: The effect of parental divorce and unhappiness. *Journal of Divorce, 13,* 41–58.

Bootzin, R. R., Manber, R., Perlis, M. L., Salvio, M., & Wyatt, J. K. (1993). Sleep disorders. In P. B. Sutker & H. E. Adams (Eds.), *Comprehensive handbook of psychopathology* (2nd ed.). New York: Plenum.

Borden, M. E. (1998). Smart start: The parents' complete guide to preschool education. New York: Facts on File.

Bornstein, M. H. (Ed.). (2002). *Handbook of parenting: Vol. 1. Children and parenting* (2nd ed.). Mahwah, NJ: Erlbaum.

Bornstein, M. H., & Bradley, R. H. (2003). *Socioeconomic status, parenting, and child development.* Mahwah, NJ: Erlbaum.

Bornstein, M. H., Haynes, O. M., Azuma, H., Galperin, C., Maital, S., Ogino, M., et al. (1998). A cross-national study of self-evaluations and attributions in parenting: Argentina, Belgium, France, Israel, Italy, Japan, and the United States. *Developmental Psychology, 34,* 662–676.

Bornstein, M. H., Haynes, O. M., O'Reilly, A. W., & Painter, K. M. (1996). Solitary and collaborative pretense play in early childhood: Sources of individual variation in the development of representational competence. *Child Development, 67,* 2910–2929.

Bornstein, M. H., & Lamb, M. E. (1992a). *Development in infancy: An introduction.* New York: McGraw-Hill.

Bornstein, M. H., & Lamb, M. E. (1992b). *Developmental psychology: An advanced textbook.* Hillsdale, NJ: Erlbaum.

Bornstein, M. H., & Sigman, M. D. (1986). Continuity in mental development from infancy. *Child Development, 57,* 251–274.

Bornstein, M. H., & Tamis-LeMonda, C. S. (1989). Maternal responsiveness and cognitive development in children. In M. H. Bornstein (Ed.), *Maternal responsiveness: Characteristics and consequences.* San Francisco: Jossey-Bass.

Boston Samaritans. (1991). *Annual report.* Boston: Author.

Bosworth, K., Espelage, D. L., & Simon, T. R. (1999). Factors associated with bullying behavior in middle school students. *Journal of Early Adolescence, 19,* 341–362.

Botvin, G. J., Epstein, J. A., Schinke, S. P., & Diaz, T. (1994). Predictors of cigarette smoking among inner-city minority youth. *Journal of Developmental and Behavioral Pediatrics, 15,* 67–73.

Bouchard, C., Tremblay, A. Despres, J. P., Nadeau, A., Lupien, P. J., Theriault, J., et al. (1990). The response to long-term overfeeding in identical twins. *New England Journal of Medicine, 322,* 1477–1482.

Bouchard, T. J., Jr. (1994). Genes, environment, and personality. *Science, 264,* 1700–1701.

Bouchard, T. J., Jr. (1997, September–October). Whenever the twain shall meet. *Sciences,* 52–57.

Bouchard, T. J., Jr., & McGue, M. (1981). Familial studies of intelligence: A review. *Science, 264,* 1700–1701.

Bouchard, T. J., Jr., & Pedersen, N. (1999). Twins reared apart: Nature's double experiment. In M. C. La Buda & E. L. Grigorenko (Eds.), *On the way to individuality: Current methodological issues in behavioral genetics.* Commack, NY: Nova.

Boulton, M. J., & Smith, P. K. (1990). Affective bias in children's perceptions of dominance relationships. *Child Development, 61,* 221–229.

Bowen, D. J., Kahl, K., Mann, S. L., & Peterson, A. V. (1991). Descriptions of early triers. *Addictive Behaviors, 16,* 95–101.

Bowen, N. K., & Bowen, G. L. (1999). Effects of crime and violence in neighborhoods and schools on the school behavior and performance of adolescents. *Journal of Adolescent Research, 14,* 319–342.

Bower, B. (1985). The left hand of math and verbal talent. *Science News, 127,* 263.

Bower, T. G. R. (1977). *A primer of infant development.* San Francisco: Freeman.

Bowlby, J. (1951). Maternal care and mental health. *Bulletin of the World Health Organization, 3,* 355–534.

Boyatzis, C. J., Mallis, M., & Leon, I. (1999). Effects of game type of children's gender-based peer preferences: A naturalistic observational study. *Sex Roles, 40,* 93–105.

Boyd, G. M., Howard, J., & Zucker, R. A. (Eds.). (1995). *Alcohol problems among adolescents: Current directions in prevention research.* Hillsdale, NJ: Erlbaum.

Boylan, P. (1990). Induction of labor, complications of labor, and postmaturity. *Current Opinion in Obstetrics and Gynecology, 2,* 31–35.

Boysson-Bardies, B. de, Sagart, L., & Durand, C. (1984). Discernible differences in the babbling of infants according to target language. *Journal of Child Language, 11,* 1–15.

Boysson-Bardies, B. de, & Vihman, M. M. (1991). Adaptation to language: Evidence from babbling and first words in four languages. *Language, 67,* 297–307.

Braddock, O. (1993). Orientation- and motion-selective mechanisms in infants. In K. Simons (Ed.), *Early visual development: Normal and abnormal.* New York: Oxford University Press.

Bradley, R. H., & Caldwell, B. M. (1995). Caregiving and the regulation of child growth and development: Describing proximal aspects of caregiving systems. *Developmental Review, 15,* 38–85.

Brainerd, C. J., Reyna, V. F., & Brandse, E. (1995). Are children's false memories more persistent than their true memories? *Psychological Science, 6,* 359–364.

Branstetter, E. (1969). The young child's response to hospitalization: Separation anxiety or lack of mothering care? *American Journal of Public Health, 59,* 92–97.

Branta, C. F., Lerner, J. V., & Taylor, C. S. (Eds.). (1997). *Physical activity and youth sports: Social and moral issues.* Mahwah, NJ: Erlbaum.

Braza, F., Braza, P., Carreras, M. R., & Muñoz, J. M. (1997). Development of sex differences in preschool children: Social behavior during an academic year. *Psychological Reports, 80,* 179–188.

Brazelton, T. B. (1973). *The Neonatal Behavioral Assessment Scale.* Philadelphia: Lippincott.

Brazelton, T. B. (1983). *Infants and mothers: Differences in development* (Rev. ed.). New York: Dell.

Brazelton, T. B. (1990). Saving the bathwater. *Child Development, 61,* 1661–1671.

Brazelton, T. B. (1991). Discussion: Cultural attitudes and actions. In M. H. Bornstein (Ed.), *Cultural approaches to parenting.* Hillsdale, NJ: Erlbaum.

Brazelton, T. B. (1997). *Toilet training your child.* New York: Consumer Visions.

Brazelton, T. B., Christophersen, E. R., Frauman, A. C., Gorski, P. A., Poole, J. M., Stadtler, A. C. & Wright, C. L. (1999). Instruction, timeliness, and medical influences affecting toilet training. *Pediatrics, 103,* 1353–1358.

Brazelton, T. B., Nugent, J. K., & Lester, B. M. (1987). Neonatal Behavioral Assessment Scale. In J. D. Osofsky (Ed.), *Handbook of infant development* (2nd ed.) New York: Wiley.

Bredekamp, S. (Ed.). (1987). *Developmentally appropriate practice in early childhood programs serving children from birth through age 8.* Washington, DC: National Association for the Education of Young Children.

Bremer, J., & Rauch, P. K. (1998). Children and computers: Risks and benefits. *Journal of the American Academy of Child and Adolescent Psychiatry, 37,* 559–560.

Brent, D. A., Perper, J. A., Moritz, G., & Liotus, L. (1994). Familial risk factors for adolescent suicide: A case-control study. *Acta Psychiatrica Scandinavica, 89,* 52–58.

Bridges, J. S. (1993). Pink or blue: Gender-stereotypic perceptions of infants as conveyed by birth congratulations cards. *Psychology of Women Quarterly, 17,* 193–205.

Briere, J. N., Berliner, L., Bulkley, J., Jenny, C., & Reid, T. (Eds.). (1996). *The APSAC handbook on child maltreatment.* Thousand Oaks, CA: Sage.

Brislin, R. (1993). *Understanding culture's influence on behavior.* Fort Worth, TX: Harcourt.

Brody, J. E. (1994, February 2). Fitness and the fetus: A turnabout in advice. *New York Times,* p. C13.

Brody, J. E., & Benbow, C. P. (1987). Accelerative strategies: How effective are they for the gifted? *Gifted Child Quarterly, 3,* 105–110.

Brody, N. (1993). Intelligence and the behavioral genetics of personality. In R. Plomin & G. E. McClearn (Eds.), *Nature, nurture, and psychology.* Washington, DC: American Psychological Association.

Bronfenbrenner, U. (1989). Ecological systems theory. In R. Vasta (Ed.), *Six theories of child development.* Greenwich, CT: JAI Press.

Bronfenbrenner, U. (2000). Ecological theory. In A. Kazdin (Ed.), *Encyclopedia of psychology.* Washington, DC, and New York: American Psychological Association/Oxford University Press.

Bronfenbrenner, U., & Morris, P. (1998). The ecology of developmental processes. In W. Damon (Ed.), *Handbook of child psychology* (Vol. 1, 5th ed.). New York: Wiley.

Bronstein, P. (1999). Differences in mothers' and fathers' behaviors toward children: A cross-cultural comparison. In L. A. Peplau & S. C. De Bro (Eds.), *Gender, culture, and ethnicity: Current research about women and men.* Mountain View, CA: Mayfield.

Brooks, J., & Lewis, M. (1976). Infants' responses to strangers: Midget, adult, and child. *Child Development, 47,* 323–332.

Brooks-Gunn, J., Klebanov, P. K., & Duncan, G. J. (1996). Ethnic differences in children's intelligence test scores: Role of economic deprivation, home environment, and maternal characteristics. *Child Development, 67,* 396–408.

Brooks-Gunn, J., & Matthews, W. S. (1979). *He and she: How children develop their sex role identity.* Englewood Cliffs, NJ: Prentice Hall.

Brooks-Gunn, J., Petersen, A. C., & Compas, B. E. (1994). What role does biology play in childhood and adolescent depression? In I. M. Goodyear (Ed.), *Mood disorders in childhood and adolescence.* New York: Cambridge University Press.

Brooks-Gunn, J., & Reiter, E. (1990). The role of pubertal processes. In S. S. Feldman & G. R. Elliott (Eds.), *At the threshold: The developing adolescent.* Cambridge, MA: Harvard University Press.

Brown, A. L., & Campione, J. C. (1994). Guided discovery in a community of learners. In K. McGilly (Ed.), *Classroom lessons: Integrating cognitive theory and classroom practice.* Cambridge, MA: MIT Press.

Brown, A. L., & Ferrara, R. A. (1999). Diagnosing zones of proximal development. In P. Lloyd & C. Fernyhough (Eds.), *Lev Vygotsky: Critical assessments: The zone of proximal development* (Vol. 3). New York: Routledge.

Brown, B. (1990). Peer groups. In S. S. Feldman & G. R. Elliott (Eds.), *At the threshold: The developing adolescent.* Cambridge, MA: Harvard University Press.

Brown, J. D. (1998). *The self.* New York: McGraw-Hill.

Brown, J. L. (1987, June). Hunger in the U.S. *Scientific American,* 37–41.

Brown, J. L., & Pollitt, E. (1996, February). Malnutrition, poverty, and intellectual development. *Scientific American,* 38–43.

Brown, R. (1973). *A first language.* Cambridge, MA: Harvard University Press.

Brown, R., & Fraser, C. (1963). The acquisition of syntax. In C. N. Cofer & B. Musgrave (Eds.), *Verbal behavior and learning: Problems and processes.* New York: McGraw-Hill.

Browne, B. A. (1998). Gender stereotypes in advertising on children's television in the 1990s: A cross-national analysis. *Journal of Advertising, 27,* 83–96.

Brownell, C. (1986). Convergent developments: Cognitive-developmental correlates of growth in infant/toddler peer skills. *Child Development, 57,* 275–286.

Brownell, K. D., & Rodin, J. (1994). The dieting maelstrom: Is it possible and advisable to lose weight? *American Psychologist, 49,* 781–791.

Brownlee, S. (2002, January 21). Too heavy, too young. *Time,* 21–23.

Brownlee, S., Cook, G. G., & Hardigg, V. (1994, August 22). Tinkering with destiny. *U.S. News and World Report,* 58–65.

Bruck, M., & Ceci, S. J. (1999). The suggestibility of children's memory. *Annual Review of Psychology, 50,* 419–439.

Bruck, M., Ceci, S. J., & Francoeur, E. (2000). Children's use of anatomically detailed dolls to report genital touching in a medical examination: Developmental and gender comparisons. *Journal of Experimental Psychology: Applied, 6,* 74–83.

Bruck, M., Ceci, S. J., Francoeur, E., & Renick, A. (1995). Anatomically detailed dolls do not facilitate preschoolers' reports of a pediatric examination involving genital touching. *Journal of Experimental Psychology: Applied, 1,* 95–109.

Bruck, M., Ceci, S. J., & Hembrooke, H. (1998). Reliability and credibility of young children's reports: From research to policy and practice. *American Psychologist, 53,* 136–151.

Bryant, J., & Bryant, J. A. (Eds.). (2001). *Television and the American family* (2nd ed.). Mahwah, NJ: Erlbaum.

Brzezinski, M. (2002, August 14). *CBS Evening News* [Television broadcast]. New York: WCBS.

Buchanan, C. M., Eccles, J. S., & Becker, J. B. (1992). Are adolescents the victims of raging hormones? Evidence for activational effects of hormones on moods and behavior at adolescence. *Psychological Bulletin, 111,* 62–107.

Buchanan, C. M., Maccoby, E. E., & Dornbusch, S. M. (1996). *Adolescents after divorce.* Cambridge, MA: Harvard University Press.

Bukowski, W. M., & Cillessen, A. H. (Eds.). (1998). *Sociometry then and now: Building on six decades of measuring children's experiences with the peer group* (New Directions for Child and Adolescent Development No. 80). San Francisco: Jossey-Bass.

Bukowski, W. M., Sippola, L. K., & Newcomb, A. F. (2000). Variations in patterns of attraction to same- and other-sex peers during early adolescence. *Developmental Psychology, 36,* 147–154.

Bullinger, A. (1997). Sensorimotor function and its evolution. In J. Guimon (Ed.), *The body in psychotherapy.* Basel, Switzerland: Karger.

Bullock, C. J. (2000). Warriors and fathers: Once Were Warriors and the mythopoetic understanding of men's violence. In E. R. Barton (Ed.), *Mythopoetic perspectives of men's healing work: An anthology for therapists and others.* Westport, CT: Bergin & Garvey.

Bullock, J. (1988). Altering aggression in young children. *Early Childhood Education, 15,* 24–27.

Bullock, M. (1995, July–August). What's so special about a longitudinal study? *Psychological Science Agenda,* 9–10.

Burbules, N. C., & Linn, M. C. (1988). Response to contradiction: Scientific reasoning during adolescence. *Journal of Educational Psychology, 80,* 67–75.

Burn, S. M. (1996). *The social psychology of gender.* New York: McGraw-Hill.

Burnett, P. C. (1996). Gender and grade differences in elementary school children's descriptive and evaluative self-statements and self-esteem. *School Psychology International, 17,* 159–170.

Bushman, B. J. (1993). Human aggression while under the influence of alcohol and other drugs: An integrative research review. *Current Directions in Psychological Science, 2,* 148–152.

Bushman, B. J., & Geen, R. G. (1990). Role of cognitive-emotional mediators and individual differences in the effects of media violence on aggression. *Journal of Personality and Social Psychology, 58,* 156–163.

Buss, A. H., & Plomin, R. (1984). *Temperament: Early developing personality traits.* Hillsdale, NJ: Erlbaum.

Buss, K. A., & Goldsmith, H. H. (1998). Fear and anger regulation in infancy: Effects on the temporal dynamics of affective expression. *Child Development, 69,* 359–374.

Bussey, K. (1992). Lying and truthfulness: Children's definition, standards, and evaluative reactions. *Child Development, 63,* 1236–1250.

Bussey, K., & Bandura, A. (1992). Self-regulatory mechanisms governing gender development. *Child Development, 63,* 1236–1250.

Butterfield, E., & Siperstein, G. (1972). Influence of contingent auditory stimulation upon non-nutritional suckle. In J. Bosma (Ed.), *Oral sensation and perception: The mouth of the infant.* Springfield, IL: Thomas.

Butterworth, G. (1994). Infant intelligence. In J. Khalfa (Ed.), *What is intelligence? The Darwin College lecture series.* Cambridge, England: Cambridge University Press.

Button, E. (1993). *Eating disorders: Personal construct theory and change.* New York: Wiley.

Byard, R., & Krous, H. (1999). Suffocation, shaking, or sudden infant death syndrome: Can we tell the difference? *Journal of Paediatrics and Child Health, 35,* 432–433.

Byne, W., & Parsons, B. (1994, February). Biology and human sexual orientation. *Harvard Mental Health Letter,* 5–7.

Byrd, R. S., Weitzman, M., & Auinger, P. (1997). Increased behavior problems associated with delayed school entry and delayed school progress. *Pediatrics, 100,* 654–661.

Byrne, B. (2000). Relationships between anxiety, fear, self-esteem, and coping strategies in adolescence. *Adolescence, 35,* 201–215.

Cadinu, M. R., & Kiesner, J. (2000). Children's development of a theory of mind. *European Journal of Psychology of Education, 15,* 93–111.

Cai, Y., Reeve., J. M., & Robinson, D. T. (2002). Home schooling and teaching style: Comparing the motivating styles of home school and public school teachers. *Journal of Educational Psychology, 94,* 372–380.

Caldas, S. J., & Bankston, C. (1997). Effect of school population socioeconomic status on individual academic achievement. *Journal of Educational Research, 90,* 269–277.

Caldera, Y. M., & Sciaraffa, M. A. (1998). Parent–toddler play with feminine toys: Are all dolls the same? *Sex Roles, 39,* 657–668.

Campbell, F. A., Pungello, E. P., Miller-Johnson, S., Ramey, C. T., & Burchinal, M. (2001). The development of cognitive and academic abilities: Growth curves from an early childhood educational experiment. *Developmental Psychology, 37,* 231–242.

Campbell, J., Poland, M., Waller, J., & Ager, J. (1992). Correlates of battering during pregnancy. *Research in Nursing and Health, 15,* 219–226.

Campione, J., & Brown, A. L. (1987). Linking dynamic assessment with school achievement. In C. S. Lidz (Ed.), *Dynamic assessment.* New York: Guilford Press.

Campos, J. J., Langer, A., & Krowitz, A. (1970). Cardiac responses on the visual cliff in prelocomotor human infants. *Science, 170,* 196–197.

Camras, L. A., Malatesta, C., & Izard, C. E. (1991). The development of facial expressions in infancy. In R. S. Feldman & B. Rimé (Eds.), *Fundamentals of nonverbal behavior.* New York: Cambridge University Press.

Camras, L. A., Oster, H., Campos, J. J., Campos, R., Ujiie, T., Miyake, K., et al. (1998). Production of emotional facial expressions in European American, Japanese, and Chinese infants. *Developmental Psychology, 34,* 616–628.

Camras, L. A., & Sachs, V. B. (1991). Social referencing and caretaker expressive behavior in a day care setting. *Infant Behavior and Development, 14,* 27–36.

Canedy, D. (2001, March 3). Troubling label for Hispanics: "Girls most likely to drop out." *New York Times,* p. A1.

Canfield, R. L., Smith, E. G., Breznyak, M. P., & Snow, K. L. (1997). Information processing through the first year of life: A longitudinal study using the visual expectation paradigm. With commentary by R. N. Aslin, M. M. Hairth, T. S. Wass, & S. A. Adler. *Monographs of the Society for Research in Child Development, 62*(2, Serial No. 250).

Caplan, L. J., & Barr, R. A. (1989). On the relationship between category intensions and extensions in children. *Journal of Experimental Child Psychology, 47,* 413–429.

Cardon, L. R., & Fulker, D. W. (1993). Genetics of specific cognitive abilities. In R. Plomin & G. E. McClearn (Eds.), *Nature, nurture, and psychology.* Washington, DC: American Psychological Association.

Carlson, E., & Hoem, J. M. (1999). Low-weight neonatal survival paradox in the Czech Republic. *American Journal of Epidemiology, 149,* 447–453.

Carlson, J. S., & Wiedl, K. H. (1992). The dynamic assessment of intelligence. In C. Haywood & D. Tzuriel (Eds.), *Interactive assessment.* New York: Springer-Verlag.

Carmody, D. (1990, March 7). College drinking: Changes in attitude and habit. *New York Times.*

Carnegie Task Force on Meeting the Needs of Young Children. (1994). *Starting points: Meeting the needs of our youngest children.* New York: Carnegie Corporation.

Carpenter, S. (2000, October). Human Genome Project director says psychologists will play a critical role in the initiative's success. *Monitor on Psychology,* 14–15.

Carr, C. N., Kennedy, S. R., & Dimick, K. M. (1996). Alcohol use among high school athletes. *Prevention Researcher, 3,* 1–3.

Carr, J. (1995). *Down syndrome.* Cambridge, England: Cambridge University Press.

Carvajal, F., & Iglesias, J. (2000). Looking behavior and smiling in Down syndrome infants. *Journal of Nonverbal Behavior, 24,* 225–236.

Case, R. (1991). Stages in the development of the young child's first sense of self. *Developmental Review, 11,* 210–230.

Case, R., & Okamoto, Y. (1996). The role of central conceptual structures in the development of children's thought. *Monographs of the Society for Research in Child Development, 61,* v–265.

Caspi, A. (2000). The child is father of the man: Personality continuities from childhood to adulthood. *Journal of Personality and Social Psychology, 78,* 158–172.

Caspi, A., Henry, B., McGeen, R. O., Moffitt, T. E., & Silva, P. A. (1995). Temperamental origins of child and adolescent behavior problems: From age three to age fifteen. *Child Development, 66,* 55–68.

Caspi, A., & Moffitt, T. E. (1991). Individual differences are accentuated during periods of social change: The sample case of girls at puberty. *Journal of Personality and Social Psychology, 61,* 157–168.

Caspi, A., & Moffitt, T. E. (1993). *Continuity amidst change: A paradoxical theory of personality coherence.* Manuscript submitted for publication.

Cassel, W. S., Roebers, C. E. M., & Bjorklund, D. F. (1996). Developmental patterns of eyewitness responses to repeated and increasingly suggestive questions. *Journal of Experimental Child Psychology, 61,* 116–133.

Cassidy, J., & Berlin, L. J. (1994). The insecure/ambivalent pattern of attachment: Theory and research. *Child Development, 65,* 971–991.

Castles, A., Datta, H., Gayan, J., & Olson, R. K. (1999). Varieties of developmental reading disorder: Genetic and environmental influences. *Journal of Experimental Child Psychology, 72,* 73–94.

Catell, R. B. (1967). *The scientific analysis of personality.* Chicago: Aldine.

Catell, R. B. (1987). *Intelligence: Its structure, growth, and action.* Amsterdam: North-Holland.

Cauffman, E., & Steinberg, L. (1996). Interactive effects of mencheal status and dating on dieting and disordered eating among adolescent girls. *Developmental Psychology, 32,* 631–635.

Ceci, S. J., & Bruck, M. (1993). The suggestibility of the child witness: A historical review and synthesis. *Psychological Bulletin, 113,* 403–439.

Ceci, S. J., & Bruck, M. (1995). *Jeopardy in the courtroom.* Washington, DC: American Psychological Association.

Ceci, S. J,, & Huffman, M.L.C. (1997). How suggestible are preschool children? Cognitive and social factors. *Journal of the American Academy of Child and Adolescent Psychiatry, 36,* 948–958.

Celera Genomics: International Human Genome Sequencing Consortium (2001). Initial sequencing and analysis of the human genome. *Nature, 409,* 860–921.

Center for Communication and Social Policy, University of California. (1998). *National television violence study* (Vol. 2). Thousand Oaks, CA: Sage.

Center for Media and Public Affairs. (1995). Adaptation of analysis of violent content of broadcast and cable television stations on Thursday, April 7, 1995.

Centers for Disease Control and Prevention. (1997). *HIV/AIDS surveillance report* (Vol. 9, No. 2). Atlanta: Author.

Centers for Disease Control and Prevention. (1998). *Youth risk behavior surveillance—United States, 1997.* Atlanta: Author.

Chall, J. S. (1979). The great debate: Ten years later, with a modest proposal for reading stages. In L. B. Resnick & P. A. Weaver (Eds.), *Theory and practice of early reading.* Hillsdale, NJ: Erlbaum.

Chan, D. W. (1997). Self-concept and global self-worth among Chinese adolescents in Hong Kong. *Personality and Individual Differences, 22,* 511–520.

Chan, W. S., Chong, K. Y., Martinovich, C., Simerly, C., & Schatten, G. (2001). Transgenic monkeys produced by retroviral gene transfer into mature oocytes *Science, 291,* 309–312.

Chao, R. K. (1994). Beyond parental control and authoritarian parenting style: Understanding Chinese parenting through the cultural notion of training. *Child Development, 65,* 1111–1119.

Chao, R. K. (1996). Chinese and European American mothers' beliefs about the role of parenting in children's school success. *Journal of Cross-Cultural Psychology, 27,* 403–423.

Chen, C., & Stevenson, H. W. (1995). Motivation and mathematics achievement: A comparative study of Asian-American, Caucasian-American, and East Asian high school students. *Child Development, 66,* 1215–1234.

Chen, X., Hastings, P. D., Rubin, K. H., Chen, H., Cen, G., & Stewart, S. L. (1998). Child-rearing attitudes and behavioral inhibition in Chinese and Canadian toddlers: A cross-cultural study. *Developmental Psychology, 34,* 677–686.

Chen, Z., & Siegler, R. S. (2000). Intellectual development in childhood. In R. J. Sternberg (Ed.), *Handbook of intelligence.* New York: Cambridge University Press.

Cherlin, A. (1993). *Marriage, divorce, remarriage.* Cambridge, MA: Harvard University Press.

Children's Bureau. (1998). *Child maltreatment, 1996: Reports from the states of the National Child Abuse and Neglect Data System.* Washington, DC: U.S. Department of Health and Human Services.

Chin, J. (1994). The growing impact of the HIV/AIDS pandemic on children born to HIV-infected women. *Clinical Perinatology, 21,* 1–14.

Chira, S. (1994, July 10). Teenagers, in a poll, report worry and distrust of adults. *New York Times,* pp. 1, 16.

Chomsky, N. (1968). *Language and mind.* New York: Harcourt.

Chomsky, N. (1978). On the biological basis of language capacities. In G. A. Miller & E. Lennenberg (Eds.), *Psychology and biology of language and thought.* New York: Academic Press.

Chomsky, N. (1991). Linguistics and cognitive science: Problems and mysteries. In A. Kasher (Ed.), *The Chomskyan turn.* Cambridge, MA: Blackwell.

Chomsky, N. (1999). On the nature, use, and acquisition of language. In W. C. Ritchie & T. J. Bhatia (Eds.), *Handbook of child language acquisition.* San Diego: Academic Press.

Christopher, F. S. (1995). Adolescent pregnancy prevention. *Family Relations, 44,* 384–391.

Cicchetti, D. (1996). Child maltreatment: Implications for developmental theory and research. *Human Development, 39,* 18–39.

Cicchetti, D., & Beeghly, M. (Eds.). (1990). *Children with Down syndrome.* Cambridge, England: Cambridge University Press.

Cicchetti, D., & Toth, S. L. (1998). The development of depression in children and adolescents. *American Psychologist, 53,* 221–241.

Cipra, B. (1991). They'd rather switch than fight: Why college students transfer out of science and engineering majors. *Science, 254,* 370–372.

Ciricelli, V. G. (1995). *Sibling relationships across the life span.* New York: Plenum.

Clark, E. (1983). Meanings and concepts. In J. Flavell & E. Markham (Eds.), *Handbook of child psychology: Cognitive development* (Vol. 3). New York: Wiley.

Clark, J. E., & Humphrey, J. H. (Eds.). (1985). *Motor development: Current selected research.* Princeton, NJ: Princeton Book Company.

Clark, K. B., & Clark, M. P. (1947). Racial identification and preference in Negro children. In T. M. Newcomb & E. L. Hartley (Eds.), *Readings in social psychology.* New York: Holt, Rinehart & Winston.

Clark, R., Hyde, J. S., Essex, M. J., & Klein, M. H. (1997). Length of maternity leave and quality of mother–infant interactions. *Child Development, 68,* 364–383.

Clarke-Stewart, K. A. (1993). *Daycare.* Cambridge, MA: Harvard University Press.

Clarke-Stewart, K. A., & Friedman, S. (1987). *Child development: Infancy through adolescence.* New York: Wiley.

Clemetson, L. (1998, September). Our daughters, ourselves. *Newsweek* [special issue], 14–17.

Clifton, R. (1992). The development of spatial hearing in human infants. In L. A. Werner & E. W. Rubel (Eds.), *Developmental psychoacoustics.* Washington, DC: American Psychological Association.

Clinton, H. (1996). *It takes a village and other lessons children teach us.* New York: Touchstone.

Cnattingius, S., Berendes, H., & Forman, M. (1993). Do delayed childbearers face increased risks of adverse pregnancy outcomes after the first birth? *Obstetrics and Gynecology, 81,* 512–516.

Coats, E., & Feldman, R. S. (1995). The role of television in the socialization of nonverbal behavioral skills. *Basic and Applied Social Psychology, 17,* 327–341.

Cocaine before birth. (1998, December). *Harvard Mental Health Letter,* 1–4.

Coddington, R. D. (1984). Measuring the stressfulness of a child's environment. In J. H. Humphrey (Ed.), *Stress in childhood.* New York: American Mathematical Society.

Cohen, J. (1999). Nurture helps mold able minds. *Science, 283,* 1832–1833.

Cohen, P., Cohen, J., Kasen, S., Velez, C. N., Hartmark, C., Johnson, et al. (1993). An epidemiological study of disorders in late childhood and adolescence: I. Age- and gender-specific prevalence. *Journal of Child Psychology and Psychiatry and Allied Disciplines, 34,* 851–867.

Cohen, S., Tyrell, D. A., & Smith, A. P. (1993). Negative life events, perceived stress, negative affect, and susceptibility to the common cold. *Journal of Personality and Social Psychology, 64,* 131–140.

Cohen, S. E. (1995). Biosocial factors in early infancy as predictors of competence in adolescents who were born prematurely. *Journal of Developmental and Behavioral Pediatrics, 16,* 36–41.

Cohn, J. F., & Tronick, E. Z. (1988). Three-month-old infants' reactions to simulated maternal depression. *Child Development, 54,* 185–193.

Cohn, J. F., & Tronick, E. Z. (1989). Mother–infant face-to-face interaction: Influence is bidirectional and unrelated to periodic cycles in either partner's behavior. *Developmental Psychology, 24,* 386–392.

Colby, A., & Damon, W. (1987). Listening to a different voice: A review of Gilligan's *In a Different Voice.* In M. R. Walsh (Ed.), *The psychology of women.* New Haven, CT: Yale University Press.

Colby, A., & Kohlberg, L. (1987). *The measurement of moral adjudgment* (Vols. 1–2). New York: Cambridge University Press.

Cole, M. (1992). Culture in development. In M. H. Bornstein & M. E. Lamb (Eds.), *Developmental psychology: An advanced textbook* (3rd ed.). Hillsdale, NJ: Erlbaum.

Coleman, C. A., Friedman, A. G., & Burright, R. G. (1998). The relationship of daily stress and health-related behaviors to adolescents' cholesterol levels. *Adolescence, 33,* 447–460.

Coleman, J. (1961). *The adolescent society.* Glencoe, IL: Free Press.

Coley, R. L., & Chase-Lansdale, P. L. (1998). Adolescent pregnancy and parenthood: Recent evidence and future directions. *American Psychologist, 53,* 152–166.

Colino, S. (2002, February 26). Problem kid or label? *Washington Post,* p. HE01.

Collins, W. A., Gleason, T., & Sesma, A. (1997). Internalization, autonomy, and relationships: Development during adolescence. In J. E. Grusec & L. Kuczynski (Eds.), *Parenting and children's internalization of values: A handbook of contemporary theory.* New York: Wiley.

Collins, W. A., Maccoby, E. E., Steinberg, L., Hetherington, E. M., & Bornstein, M. H. (2000). Contemporary research on parenting: The case for nature and nurture. *American Psychologist, 55,* 218–232.

Colon, J. M. (1997). Assisted reproductive technologies. In M. L. Sipski & C. J. Alexander (Eds.), *Sexual function in people with disability and chronic illness: A health professional's guide.* Gaithersburg, MD: Aspen.

Coltrane, S., & Adams, M. (1997). Children and gender. In T. Arendell (Ed.), *Contemporary parenting: Challenges and issues. Understanding families* (Vol. 9). Thousand Oaks, CA: Sage.

Committee on Children, Youth and Families. (1994). *When you need child day care.* Washington, DC: American Psychological Association.

Committee to Study the Prevention of Low Birthweight. (1985). *Preventing low birthweight.* Washington, DC: National Academy Press.

Comstock, G., & Strasburger, V. C. (1990). Deceptive appearances: Television violence and aggressive behavior. *Journal of Adolescent Health Care, 11,* 31–44.

Condit, V. (1990). Anorexia nervosa: Levels of causation. *Human Nature, 1,* 391–413.

Condry, J. (1989). *The psychology of television.* Hillsdale, NJ: Erlbaum.

Condry, J., & Condry, S. (1976). Sex differences: A study of the eye of the beholder. *Child Development, 47,* 812–819.

Conklin, H. M., & Iacono, W. G. (2002). Schizophrenia: A neurodevelopmental perspective. *Current Directions in Psychological Science, 11,* 33–37.

Coons, S., & Guilleminault, C. (1982). Developments of sleep-wake patterns and non-rapid-eye-movement sleep stages during the first six months of life in normal infants. *Pediatrics, 69,* 793–798.

Cooper, B. (2001). Nature, nurture and mental disorder: Old concepts in the new millennium. *British Journal of Psychiatry, 178*(Suppl. 40), S91–S101.

Cooper, R. P., & Aslin, R. N. (1990). Preference for infant-directed speech in the first month after birth. *Child Development, 61,* 1584–1595.

Cooper, R. P., & Aslin, R. N. (1994). Developmental differences in infant attention to the spectral properties of infant-directed speech. *Child Development, 65,* 1663–1677.

Cooperative Institutional Research Program. (1990). *The American freshman: National norms for fall 1990.* Los Angeles: American Council on Education.

Cooperstock, M. S., Bakewell, J., Herman, A., & Schramm W. F. (1998). Effects of fetal sex and race on risk of very preterm birth in twins. *American Journal of Obstetrics and Gynecology, 179,* 762–765.

Corballis, M. C. (1999). The gestural origins of language. *American Scientist, 87,* 138–145.

Corballis, M. C. (2000). How laterality will survive the millennium bug. *Brain and Cognition, 42,* 160–162.

Corbin, C. (1973). *A textbook of motor development.* Dubuque, IA: Brown.

Coren, S., & Halpern, D. F. (1991). Left-handedness: A marker for decreased survival fitness. *Psychological Bulletin, 109,* 90–106.

Cormier, K., Mauk, C., & Repp, A. (1998). Manual babbling in deaf and hearing infants: A longitudinal study. In E. V. Clark (Ed.), *The proceedings of the twenty-ninth annual child language research forum.* Stanford, CA: Center for the Study of Language and Information.

Cornelius, M. D., Day, N. L., Richardson, G. A., & Taylor, P. M. (1999). Epidemiology of substance abuse during pregnancy. In P. J. Ott, R. E. Tarter, & R. T. Ammerman (Eds.), *Sourcebook on substance abuse: Etiology, epidemiology, assessment, and treatment.* Boston: Allyn & Bacon.

Corrigan, R. (1987). A developmental sequence of actor-object pretend play in young children. *Merrill-Palmer Quarterly, 33,* 87–106.

Couzin, J. (2002). Quirks of fetal environment felt decades later. *Science, 296,* 2167–2169.

Cox, M. J., Owen, M. T., Henderson, V. K., & Margand, N. A. (1992). Prediction of infant–father and infant–mother attachment. *Developmental Psychology, 28,* 474–483.

Crandall, C. S., Tsang, J., Goldman, S., & Pennington, J. T. (1999). Newsworthy moral dilemmas: Justice, caring, and gender. *Sex Roles, 40,* 187–209.

Cratty, B. (1979). *Perceptual and motor development in infants and children* (2nd ed.). Englewood Cliffs, NJ: Prentice Hall.

Cratty, B. (1986). *Perceptual and motor development in infants and children* (3rd ed.). Englewood Cliffs, NJ: Prentice Hall.

Crews, D. (1993). The organizational concept and vertebrates without sex chromosomes. *Brain, Behavior, and Evolution, 42,* 202–214.

Crick, N. R., Casas, J. G., & Ku, H. (1999). Relational and physical forms of peer victimization in preschool. *Developmental Psychology, 35,* 376–385.

Crockett, L. J., & Crouter, A. C. (Eds.). (1995). Pathways through adolescence: Individual development in relation to social contexts. Hillsdale, NJ: Erlbaum.

Cromwell, E. S. (1994). *Quality child care: A comprehensive guide for administrators and teachers.* Needham Heights, MA: Allyn & Bacon.

Crosby, W. (1991). Studies in fetal malnutrition. *American Journal of Diseases of Children, 145,* 871–876.

Cross, W. W., Jr. (1991). *Shades of black: Diversity in African-American identity.* Philadelphia: Temple University Press.

Crosscope-Happel, C., Hutchins, D. E., Getz, H. G., & Hayes, G. L. (2000). Male anorexia nervosa: A new focus. *Journal of Mental Health Counseling, 22,* 365–370.

Crowley, K., Callaman, M. A., Tenenbaum, H. R., & Allen, E. (2001). Parents explain more often to boys than to girls during shared scientific thinking. *Psychological Science, 12,* 258–261.

Crowley, M. (1997, October 20). Do kids need Prozac? *Newsweek,* 73–74.

Csibra, G., Davis, G., Spratling, M. W., & Johnson, M. H. (2000). Gamma oscillations and object processing in the infant brain. *Science, 290,* 1582–1584.

Csikszentmihalyi, M., & Larson, R. (1984). *Being adolescent: Conflict and growth in the teenage years.* New York: Basic Books.

Culbertson, J. L., & Gyurke, J. (1990). Assessment of cognitive and motor development in infancy and childhood. In J. H. Johnson & J. Goldman (Eds.), *Developmental assessment in clinical child psychology: A handbook.* New York: Pergamon Press.

Culp, A. M., Clyman, M. M., & Culp, R. E. (1995). Adolescent depressed mood, reports of suicide attempts, and asking for help. *Adolescence, 30,* 827–837.

Cummings, E. M., Iannotti, R. J., & Zahn-Waxler, C. (1989). Aggression between peers in early childhood: Individual continuity and developmental change. *Child Development, 60,* 887–895.

Currie, J., & Thomas, D. (1995). Does Head Start make a difference? *American Economic Review, 85,* 341–364.

Cynader, M. (2000). Strengthening visual connections. *Science, 287,* 1943–1944.

Dainton, M. (1993). The myths and misconceptions of the stepmother identity. *Family Relations, 42,* 93–98.

Daly, T., & Feldman, R. S. (1994). *Benefits of social integration for typical preschool children.* Unpublished manuscript.

Damon, W. (1977). *The social world of the child.* San Francisco: Jossey-Bass.

Damon, W. (1983). *Social and personality development.* New York: Norton.

Damon, W. (1988). *The moral child.* New York: Free Press.

Damon, W. (1995). *Greater expectations: Overcoming the culture of indulgence in America's homes and schools.* New York: Free Press.

Damon, W., & Hart, D. (1988). *Self-understanding in childhood and adolescence.* New York: Cambridge University Press.

Daniels, H. (Ed.). (1996). *An introduction to Vygotsky.* New York: Routledge.

Darroch, J. E., & Singh, S. (1999). *Why is teenage pregnancy declining? The roles of abstinence, sexual activity, and contraceptive use.* New York: Alan Guttmacher Institute.

Dasen, P. R. (1977). Are cognitive processes universal? A contribution to cross-cultural Piagetian psychology. In N. Warren (Ed.), *Studies in cross-cultural psychology* (Vol. 1). New York: Academic Press.

Dasen, P. R. (2000). Rapid social change and the turmoil of adolescence: A cross-cultural perspective. *World Psychology, 7,* 114–122.

Dasen, P. R., Inhelder, B., Lavallée, M., & Retschitzki, J. (1978). *Naissance de l'intelligence chez l'enfant baoulé de Côte d'Ivoire.* Berne: Huber.

Dasen, P. R., Ngini, L., & Lavallée, M. (1979). Cross-cultural training studies of concrete operations. In L. H. Eckenberger, W. J. Lonner, & Y. H. Poortinga (Eds.), *Cross-cultural contributions to psychology.* Amsterdam: Swets & Zeilinger.

Davidson, J. E. (1990). Intelligence re-created. *Educational Psychologist, 25,* 337–354.

Davies, P. T., & Cummings, E. M. (1994). Marital conflict and child adjustment: An emotional security hypothesis. *Psychological Bulletin, 116,* 387–411.

Davis, M., & Emory, E. (1995). Sex differences in neonatal stress reactivity. *Child Development, 66,* 14–27.

Davis-Floyd, R. E. (1994). The technocratic body: American childbirth as cultural expression. *Social Science and Medicine, 38,* 1125–1140.

Davis-Kean, P. E., & Sandler, H. M. (2001). A meta-analysis of measures of self-esteem for young children: A framework for future measures. *Child Development, 72,* 887–906.

De Angelis, T. (1994, December). What makes kids ready, set for school? *Monitor on Psychology,* 36–37.

De Casper, A. J., & Fifer, W. P. (1980). Of human bonding: Newborns prefer their mothers' voices. *Science, 208,* 1174–1176.

De Casper, A. J., & Prescott, P. (1984). Human newborns' perception of male voices: Preference, discrimination, and reinforcing value. *Developmental Psychobiology, 17,* 481–491.

De Casper, A. J., & Spence, M. J. (1986). Prenatal material speech influences newborns' perception of speech sounds. *Infant Behavior and Development, 9,* 133–150.

de Chateau, P. (1980). Parent–neonate interaction and its long-term effects. In E. G. Simmel (Ed.), *Early experiences and early behavior.* New York: Academic Press.

De Clercq, E. R. (1992). The transformation of American midwifery, 1975 to 1988. *American Journal of Public Health, 82,* 680–684.

De Cristofaro, J. D., & La Gamma, E. F. (1995). Prenatal exposure to opiates. *Mental Retardation and Developmental Disabilities Research Reviews, 1,* 177–182.

De Gelder, B. (2000). Recognizing emotions by ear and by eye. In R. D. Lane & L. Nadel (Eds.), *Cognitive neuroscience of emotion.* New York: Oxford University Press.

De Loache, J., & Gottlieb, A. (Eds.). (2002). *A world of babies.* Cambridge, England: Cambridge University Press.

de Mooij, M. K. (1998). *Global marketing and advertising: Understanding cultural paradoxes.* Thousand Oaks, CA: Sage.

de Villiers, P. A., & de Villiers, J. G. (1992). Language development. In M. H. Bornstein & M. E. Lamb (Eds.), *Developmental psychology: An advanced textbook.* Hillsdale, NJ: Erlbaum.

de Vries, M. W. (1984). Temperament and infant mortality among the Masai of East Africa. *American Journal of Psychiatry, 141,* 1189–1194.

de Vries, R. (1969). Constancy of generic identity in the years 3 to 6. *Monographs of the Society for Research in Child Development, 34*(3, Serial No. 127).

De Wolff, M. S., & van IJzendoorn, M. H. (1997). Sensitivity and attachment: A meta-analysis on parental antecedents of infant attachment. *Child Development, 68,* 571–591.

Deary, I. J., & Stough, C. (1996). Intelligence and inspection time. *American Psychologist, 51,* 599–608.

Deater-Deckard, K., & Dodge, K. A. (1997). Externalizing behavior problems and discipline revisited: Nonlinear effects and variation by culture, context, and gender. *Psychological Inquiry, 8,* 161–175.

Decarrie, T. G. (1969). A study of the mental and emotional development of the thalidomide child. In B. M. Foss (Ed.), *Determinants of infant behavior* (Vol. 4). London: Methuen.

Dejin-Karlsson, E., Hanson, B. S., Oestergren, P. O., Sjoeberg, N.O., & Marsal, K. (1998). Does passive smoking in early pregnancy increase the risk of small-for-gestational-age infants? *American Journal of Public Health, 88,* 1523–1527.

Delaney, C. H. (1995). Rites of passage in adolescence. *Adolescence, 30,* 891–897.

Demetriou, A., Shayer, M., & Efklides, A. (Eds.). (1993). *Neo-Piagetian theories of cognitive development: Implications and applications for education.* London: Routledge.

Demo, D. H., & Acock, A. (1991). The impact of divorce on children. In A. Booth (Ed.), *Contemporary families.* Minneapolis, MN: National Council on Family Relations.

Denmark, F. L., & Fernandez, L. C. (1993). Historical development of the psychology of women. In F. L. Denmark & M. A. Paludi (Eds.), *Psychology of women: A handbook of issues and theories.* Westport, CT: Greenwood Press.

Denny, F. W., & Clyde, W. A. (1983). Acute respiratory tract infections: An overview. In W. A. Clyde & F. W. Denny (Eds.), Workshop on acute respiratory diseases among children of the world. *Pediatric Research, 17,* 1026–1029.

Dent-Read, C., & Zukow-Goldring, P. (Eds.). (1997). *Evolving explanations of development: Ecological approaches to organism–environment systems.* Washington, DC: American Psychological Association.

Deutsch, M. (1967). *The disadvantaged child: Selected papers of Martin Deutsch and associates.* New York: Basic Books.

Deveny, K. (1994, December 5). Chart of kindergarten awards. *Wall Street Journal,* p. B1.

Devlin, B., Daniels, M., & Roeder, K. (1997). The heritability of IQ. *Nature, 388,* 468–471.

Di Franza, J. R., & Lew, R. A. (1995). Effect of maternal cigarette smoking on pregnancy complications and sudden infant death syndrome. *Journal of Family Practice, 40,* 385–394.

Di Lalla, L. F., Thompson, L. A., Plomin, R., Phillips, K., Fagan, J. F., Haith, M. M., et al. (1990). Infant predictors of preschool and adult IQ: A study of infant twins and their parents. *Developmental Psychology, 26,* 433–440.

Di Matteo, M. R., & Kahn, K. L. (1997). Psychosocial aspects of childbirth. In S. J. Gallant, G. P. Keita, & R. Royak-Schaler (Eds.), *Health care for women: Psychological, social, and behavioral influences.* Washington, DC: American Psychological Association.

Dick, D. M., & Rose, R. J. (2002). Behavior genetics: What's new? What's next? *Current Directions in Psychological Science, 11,* 70–74.

Dickenson, G. (1975). Dating behavior of black and white adolescents before and after desegregation. *Journal of Marriage and the Family, 37,* 602–608.

Diener, E., Suh, E. M., Lucas, R. E., & Smith, H. L. (1999). Subjective well-being: Three decades of progress. *Psychological Bulletin, 125,* 276–302.

Dietz, T. L. (1998). An examination of violence and gender role portrayals in video games: Implications for gender socialization and aggressive behavior. *Sex Roles, 38,* 425–442.

Dixon, R. A., & Lerner, R. M. (1999). History and systems in developmental psychology. In M. H. Bornstein & M. E. Lamb (Eds.), *Developmental psychology: An advanced textbook.* Mahwah, NJ: Erlbaum.

Dodge, K. A. (1985). A social information processing model of social competence in children. In M. Perlmutter (Ed.), *Minnesota Symposia on Child Psychology, 18,* 77–126.

Dodge, K. A., & Coie, J. D. (1987). Social information-processing factors in reactive and proactive aggression in children's peer groups. *Journal of Personality and Social Psychology, 53,* 1146–1158.

Dodge, K. A., & Crick, N. R. (1990). Social information-processing bases of aggressive behavior in children. *Personality and Social Psychology Bulletin, 16,* 8–22.

Dodge, K. A., Pettit, G. S., McClasky, C. L., & Brown, M. M. (1986). Social competence in children. *Monographs of the Society for Research in Child Development, 51*(2, Serial No. 213).

Dodge, K. A., & Price, J. M. (1994). On the relation between social information processing and socially competent behavior in early school-aged children. *Child Development, 65,* 1385–1397.

Dolcini, M. M., Coh, L. D., Adler, N. E., Millstein, S. G., Irwin, C. E., Kegeles, S. M., et al. (1989). Adolescent egocentrism and feelings of invulnerability: Are they related? *Journal of Early Adolescence, 9,* 409–418.

Dondi, M., Simion, F., & Caltran, G. (1999). Can newborns discriminate between their own cry and the cry of another newborn infant? *Developmental Psychology, 35,* 418–426.

Donlan, C. (1998). *The development of mathematical skills.* Philadelphia: Psychology Press.

Dornbusch, S. M., Carlsmith, J., Bushwall, S., Ritter, P. L., Leiderman, P., Hastorf, A., et al. (1985). Single parents, extended households, and the control of adolescents. *Child Development, 56,* 326–341.

Dornbusch, S. M., Ritter, P. L., & Steinberg, L. (1992). Differences between African Americans and non-Hispanic whites in the relation of family statuses to adolescent school performance. *American Journal of Education, 99,* 543–567.

Douglas, M. J. (1991). Potential complications of spinal and epidural anesthesia for obstetrics. *Seminars in Perinatology, 15,* 368–374.

Doussard-Roosevelt, J. A., Porges, S. W., Scanlon, J. W., Alemi, B., & Scanlon, K. B. (1997). Vagal regulation of heart rate in the prediction of developmental outcome for very low birthweight preterm infants. *Child Development, 68,* 173–186.

Douvan, E., & Adelson, J. (1966). *The adolescent experience.* New York: Wiley.

Downey, D. B. (2001). Number of siblings and intellectual development. *American Psychologist, 56,* 497–504.

Downey, G., Lebolt, A., Rincón, C., & Freitas, A. L. (1998). Rejection sensitivity and children's interpersonal difficulties. *Child Development, 69,* 1074–1091.

Doyle, R. (2000, June). Asthma worldwide. *Scientific American,* 28.

Drews, C. D., Murphy, C. C., Yeargin-Allsopp, M., & Decoufle, P. (1996). The relationship between idiopathic mental retardation and maternal smoking during pregnancy. *Pediatrics, 97,* 547–553.

Dromi, E. (1987). *Early lexical development.* Cambridge, England: Cambridge University Press.

Dromi, E. (1993). The development of prelinguistic communication: Implications for language evaluation. In N. J. Anastasiow & S. Harel (Eds.), *At-risk infants: Interventions, families, and research.* Baltimore: Brookes.

Dryfoos, J. G. (1990). *Adolescents at risk: Prevalence and prevention.* New York: Oxford University Press.

Du Bois, D. L., & Hirsch, B. J. (1990). School and neighborhood friendship patterns of blacks and whites in early adolescence. *Child Development, 61,* 524–536.

Du Breuil, S. C., Garry, M., & Loftus, E. F. (1998). Tales from the crib: Age regression and the creation of unlikely memories. In S. J. Lynn & K. M. McConkey (Eds.), *Truth in memory.* New York: Guilford Press.

Du Plessis, H. M., Bell, R., & Richards, T. (1997). Adolescent pregnancy: Understanding the impact of age and race on outcomes. *Journal of Adolescent Health, 20,* 187–197.

Duckitt, J. (1994). Conformity to social pressure and racial prejudice among white South Africans. *Genetic, Social, and General Psychology Monographs, 120,* 121–143.

Dukes, R., & Martinez, R. (1994). The impact of gender on self-esteem among adolescents. *Adolescence, 29,* 105–115.

Dulitzki, M., Soriano, D., Schiff, E., Chetrit, A., Mashiach, S., & Seidman, D. S. (1998). Effect of very advanced maternal age on pregnancy outcome and rate of cesarean delivery. *Obstetrics and Gynecology, 92,* 935–939.

Duncan, G. J., & Brooks-Gunn, J. (2000). Family poverty, welfare reform, and child development. *Child Development, 71,* 188–196.

Duncan, P., Ritter, P. L., Dornbusch, S. M., Gross, R. T., & Carlsmith, J. (1985). The effects of pubertal timing on body image, school behavior, and deviance. *Journal of Youth and Adolescence, 14,* 227–236.

Dunham, R. M., Kidwell, J. S., & Wilson, S. M. (1986). Rites of passage at adolescence: A ritual process paradigm. *Journal of Adolescent Research, 1,* 139–153.

Dunphy, D. C. (1963). The social structure of urban adolescent peer groups. *Society, 26,* 230–246.

Durik, A. M., Hyde, J. S., & Clark, R. (2000). Sequelae of cesarean and vaginal deliveries: Psychosocial outcomes for mothers and infants. *Developmental Psychology, 36,* 251–260.

Durkin, K., & Nugent, B. (1998). Kindergarten children's gender-role expectations for television actors. *Sex Roles, 38,* 387–402.

Durrant, J. E. (1999). Evaluating the success of Sweden's corporal punishment ban. *Child Abuse and Neglect, 23,* 435–448.

Dweck, C. S. (1991). Self-theories and goals: Their role in motivation, personality, and development. In R. Dienstbier (Ed.), *Nebraska symposium on motivation* (Vol. 36). Lincoln: University of Nebraska Press.

Dweck, C. S., & Bush, E. S. (1976). Sex differences in learned helplessness: I. Differential debilitation with peer and adult evaluators. *Developmental Psychology, 12,* 147–156.

Eagly, A. H., & Steffen, V. J. (1984). Gender stereotypes stem from the distribution of women and men into social roles. *Journal of Personality and Social Psychology, 46,* 735–754.

Eagly, A. H., & Steffen, V. J. (1986). Gender and aggressive behavior: A meta-analytic review of the social psychological literature. *Psychological Bulletin, 100,* 309–330.

Eakins, P. S. (Ed.). (1986). *The American way of birth.* Philadelphia: Temple University Press.

Early Head Start shows significant results for low income children and parents. (2001, January 12). *HHS News,* 5–7.

Eaton, M. J., & Dembo, M. H. (1997). Differences in the motivational beliefs of Asian American and non-Asian students. *Journal of Educational Psychology, 89,* 433–440.

Eaton, W. O., & Enns, L. R. (1986). Sex differences in human motor activity level. *Psychological Bulletin, 100,* 19–28.

Eaton, W. O., & Yu, A. P. (1989). Are sex differences in child motor activity level a function of sex differences in maturational status? *Child Development, 60,* 1005–1011.

Eberstadt, N. (1994). Why babies die in D.C. *Public Interest,* 3–16.

Ebstein, R. P., Novick, O., Umansky, R., Priel, B., Osher, Y., Blaine, D., et al. (1996). Dopamine D4 receptor (D4DR) exon III polymorphism associated with the human personality trait of novelty seeking. *Nature and Genetics, 12,* 78–80.

Eccles, J. S., Wigfield, A., Flanagan, C., Miller, C., Reuman, D., & Yee, D. (1989). Self-concepts, domain values, and self-esteem: Relations and changes at early adolescence. *Journal of Personality and Social Psychology, 57,* 283–310.

Ecenbarger, W. (1993, April). America's new merchants of death. *Reader's Digest,* 50.

Eckerman, C. O., & Oehler, J. M. (1992). Very low birthweight newborns and parents as early social partners. In S. L. Friedman & M. D. Sigman (Eds.), *The psychological development of low birthweight children.* Norwood, NJ: Ablex.

Edwards, C. P. (2000). Children's play in cross-cultural perspective: A new look at the Six Cultures study. *Cross-Cultural Research, 34,* 318–338.

Egan, S. K., & Perry, D. G. (1998). Does low self regard invite victimization? *Developmental Psychology, 34,* 299–309.

Egeland, B., & Farber, E. A. (1984). Infant–mother attachment: Factors related to its development and changes over time. *Child Development, 55,* 753–771.

Egeland, B., Pianta, R., & O'Brien, M. A. (1993). Maternal intrusiveness in infancy and child maladaptation in early school years. *Development and Psychopathology, 5,* 359–370.

Ehlers, C. L., Frank, E., & Kupfer, D. J. (1988). Social zeitgebers and biological rhythms: A unified approach to understanding the etiology of depression. *Archives of General Psychiatry, 45,* 948–952.

Eimas, P. D., Siqueland, E. R., Jusczyk, P., & Vigorito, J. (1971). Speech perception in infants. *Science, 171,* 303–306.

Einbinder, S. D. (2000). *A statistical profile of children living in poverty: Children under three and children under six.* Unpublished document from the National Center for Children in

Poverty. New York: Columbia University, School of Public Health.

Eisenberg, N., & Fabes, R. A. (1991). Prosocial behavior and empathy: A multimethod, developmental perspective. In M. S. Clark (Ed.), *Review of personality and social psychology* (Vol. 12). Newbury Park, CA: Sage.

Eisenberg, N., Fabes, R. A., Guthrie, I. K., & Reiser, M. (2000). Dispositional emotionality and regulation: Their role in predicting quality of social functioning. *Journal of Personality and Social Psychology, 78,* 136–157.

Eisenberg, N., Guthrie, I. K., Fabes, R. A., Reiser, M., Murphy, B. C., Holgren, R., et al. (1997). The relations of regulations and emotionality to resiliency and competent social functioning in elementary school children. *Child Development, 68,* 295–311.

Eisenberg, N., Guthrie, I. K., Murphy, B. C., Shepard, S. A., Cumberland, A., & Carlo, G. (1999). Consistency and development of prosocial dispositions: A longitudinal study. *Child Development, 70,* 1360–1372.

Eisenberg, N., Wolchik, S. A., Hernandez, R., & Pasternack, J. F. (1985). Parental socialization of young children's play: A short-term longitudinal study. *Child Development, 56,* 1506–1513.

Eisenberg, N., & Zhou, Q. (2000). Regulation from a developmental perspective. *Psychological Inquiry, 11,* 166–172.

Ekman, P., & O'Sullivan, M. (1991). Facial expression: Methods, means, and moues. In R. S. Feldman & B. Rimé (Eds.), *Fundamentals of nonverbal behavior.* New York: Cambridge University Press.

Elder, G. H., Jr. (1998). The life course as developmental theory. *Child Development, 69,* 1–12.

Elkind, D. (1967). Egocentrism in adolescence. *Child Development, 38,* 1025–1034.

Elkind, D. (1978). The children's reality: Three developmental themes. In S. Coren & L. M. Ward (Eds.), *Sensation and perception.* Hillsdale, NJ: Erlbaum.

Elkind, D. (1984). *All grown up and no place to go.* Reading, MA: Addison-Wesley.

Elkind, D. (1985). Egocentrism redux. *Developmental Review, 5,* 218–226.

Elkind, D. (1988). *Miseducation.* New York: Knopf.

Elkind, D. (1994). *A sympathetic understanding of the child: Birth to sixteen* (3rd ed.). Needham Heights, MA: Allyn & Bacon.

Ellis, L., & Engh, T. (2000). Handedness and age of death: New evidence on a puzzling relationship. *Journal of Health Psychology, 5,* 561–565.

Emery, R. E., & Laumann-Billings, L. (1998). An overview of the nature, causes, and consequences of abusive family relationships: Toward differentiating maltreatment and violence. *American Psychologist, 53,* 121–135.

Employment Policies Institute. (2000). *Correcting part-time misconceptions.* Washington, DC: Author.

Emslie, G. J., Rush, A. J., Weinberg, W. A., Kowatch, R. A., Hughes, C. W., Carmody, T., et al. (1997). Double-blind, randomized, placebo-controlled trial of fluoxetine in children and adolescents with depression. *Archives of General Psychiatry, 54,* 1031–1037.

Emslie, G. J., Walkup, J. T., Pliszka, S. R., & Ernst, M. (1999). Nontricyclic antidepressants: Current trends in children and adolescents. *Journal of the American Academy of Child and Adolescent Psychiatry, 38,* 517–528.

Endo, S. (1992). Infant–infant play from 7 to 12 months of age: An analysis of games in infant–peer triads. *Japanese Journal of Child and Adolescent Psychiatry, 33,* 145–162.

Endocrine Society. (2001). *The Endocrine Society and Lawson Wilkins Pediatric Endocrine Society call for further research to define precocious puberty.* Bethesda, MD: Author.

England, P., & McCreary, L. (1987). *Integrating sociology and economics to study gender and work.* Newbury Park, CA: Sage.

English, D. J. (1998). The extent and consequences of child maltreatment. *Future of Children, 8,* 39–51.

Englund, M. M., Levy, A. K., Hyson, D. M., & Sroufe, L. A. (2000). Adolescent social competence: Effectiveness in a group setting. *Child Development, 71,* 1049–1060.

Ennett, S. T., & Bauman, K. E. (1996). Adolescent social networks: School, demographic, and longitudinal considerations. *Journal of Adolescent Research, 11,* 194–215.

Epperson, S. E. (1988, September 16). Studies link subtle sex bias in schools with women's behavior in the workplace. *Wall Street Journal,* p. 19.

Epstein, K. (1993). The interactions between breastfeeding mothers and their babies during the breastfeeding session. *Early Child Development and Care, 87,* 93–104.

Erel, O., Oberman, Y., & Yirmiya, N. (2000). Maternal versus nonmaternal care and seven domains of children's development. *Psychological Bulletin, 126,* 727–747.

Erikson, E. H. (1963). *Childhood and society.* New York: Norton.

Erlandson, D. A., Harris, E. L., Skipper, B. L., & Allen, S. D. (1993). *Doing naturalistic inquiry: A guide to methods.* Newbury Park, CA: Sage.

Eron, L. D., & Huesmann, L. R. (1985). The control of aggressive behavior by changes in attitude, values, and the conditions of learning. In R. J. Blanchard & C. Blanchard (Eds.), *Advances in the study of aggression.* New York: Academic Press.

Erwin, P. (1993). *Friendship and peer relations in children.* Chichester, England: Wiley.

Espenschade, A. (1960). Motor development. In W. R. Johnson (Ed.), *Science and medicine of exercise and sports.* New York: Harper & Row.

Eveleth, P., & Tanner, J. (1976). *Worldwide variation in human growth.* New York: Cambridge University Press.

Everett, S. A., Warren, C. W., Santelli, J. S., Kann, L., Collins, J. L., & Kolbe, L. J. (2000). Use of birth control pills, condoms, and withdrawal among U.S. high school students. *Journal of Adolescent Health, 27,* 112–118.

Evinger, S. (1996, May). How to record race. *American Demographics,* 36–41.

Eyer, D. E. (1992). The bonding hype. In M. E. Lamb & J. B. Lancaster (Eds.), *Birth management: Biosocial perspectives.* Hawthorne, NY: Aldine de Gruyter.

Eyer, D. E. (1994). Mother–infant bonding: A scientific fiction. *Human Nature, 5,* 69–94.

Fabsitz, R. R., Carmelli, D., & Hewitt, J. K. (1992). Evidence for independent genetic influences on obesity in middle age. *International Journal of Obesity and Related Metabolic Disorders, 16,* 657–666.

Fagot, B. I. (1978). The influence of sex of child on parental reactions to toddler children. *Child Development, 49,* 459–465.

Fagot, B. I. (1991, April). *Peer relations in boys and girls from two to seven.* Paper presented at the biennial meeting of the Society for Research in Child Development, Seattle.

Fagot, B. I., & Hagan, R. (1991). Observation of parent reaction to sex-stereotyped behaviors: Age and sex effects. *Child Development, 62,* 617–628.

Fagot, B. I., & Leinbach, M. D. (1993). Gender-role development in young children: From discrimination to labeling. *Developmental Review, 13,* 205–224.

Faith, M. S., Johnson, S. L., & Allison, D. B. (1997). Putting the behavior into the behavior genetics of obesity. *Behavior Genetics, 27,* 423–439.

Falbo, T. (1992). Social norms and the one-child family: Clinical and policy implications. In F. Boer & J. Dunn (Eds.), *Children's sibling relationships.* Hillsdale, NJ: Erlbaum.

Fangman, J. J., Mark, P. M., Pratt, L., Conway, K. K., Healey, M. L., Oswald, J. W., et al. (1994). Prematurity prevention programs: An analysis of successes and failures. *American Journal of Obstetrical Gynecology, 170,* 744–750.

Fanshel, D., Finch, S. J., & Grundy, J. F. (1990). *Foster children in a life course perspective.* New York: Columbia University Press.

Fanshel, D., Finch, S. J., & Grundy, J. F. (1992). *Serving the urban poor.* Westport, CT: Praeger.

Fantz, R. L. (1961). The origin of form perception. *Scientific American,* 72–81.

Fantz, R. L. (1963). Pattern vision in newborn infants. *Science, 140,* 296–297.

Farel, A. M., Hooper, S. R., Teplin, S. W., Henry, M. M., & Kraybill, E. N. (1998). Very-low-birthweight infants at seven years: An assessment of the health and neurodevelopmental risk conveyed by chronic lung disease. *Journal of Learning Disabilities, 31,* 118–126.

Farhi, P. (1995, June 21). Turning the tables on TV violence. *Washington Post,* pp. F1, F2.

Farrar, M. J., & Goodman, G. S. (1992). Developmental changes in event memory. *Child Development, 63,* 173–187.

Farver, J. M., & Branstetter, W. H. (1994). Preschoolers' prosocial responses to their peers' distress. *Developmental Psychology, 30,* 334–341.

Farver, J. M., & Frosch, D. L. (1996). L.A. stories: Aggression in preschoolers' spontaneous narratives after the riots of 1992. *Child Development, 67,* 19–32.

Farver, J. M., Kim, Y. K., & Lee-Shin, Y. (1995). Cultural differences in Korean- and Anglo-American preschoolers' social interaction and play behaviors. *Child Development, 66,* 1088–1099.

Farver, J. M., & Lee-Shin, Y. (2000). Acculturation and Korean-American children's social and play behavior. *Social Development, 9,* 316–336.

Farver, J. M., Welles-Nystrom, B., Frosch, D. L., & Wimbarti, S. (1997). Toy stories: Aggression in children's narratives in the United States, Sweden, Germany, and Indonesia. *Journal of Cross-Cultural Psychology, 28,* 393–420.

Federal Interagency Forum on Child and Family Statistics. (2000). *America's children: Key national indicators of well-being, 2000.* Vienna, VA: Author.

Feldhusen, J. F., Haeger, W. W., & Pellegrino, A. S. (1989). A model training program in gifted education for school administrators. *Roeper Review, 11,* 209–214.

Feldman, R. S. (Ed.). (1982). *Development of nonverbal behavior in children.* New York: Springer-Verlag.

Feldman, R. S. (Ed.). (1992). *Applications of nonverbal behavioral theories and research.* Hillsdale, NJ: Erlbaum.

Feldman, R. S., Philippot, P., & Custrini, R. J. (1991). Social competence and nonverbal behavior. In R. S. Feldman & B. Rimé (Eds.), *Fundamentals of nonverbal behavior.* New York: Cambridge University Press.

Feldman, R. S., & Prohaska, T. (1979). The student as Pygmalion: Effect of student expectation on the teacher. *Journal of Educational Psychology, 4,* 485–493.

Feldman, R. S., & Rimé, B. (Eds.). (1991). *Fundamentals of nonverbal behavior.* New York: Cambridge University Press.

Feldman, R. S., & Theiss, A. J. (1982). The teacher and student as Pygmalions: The joint effects of teacher and student expectation. *Journal of Educational Psychology, 74,* 217–223.

Feldman, R. S., Tomasian, J., & Coats, E. J. (1999) Adolescents' social competence and nonverbal deception abilities: Adolescents with higher social skills are better liars. *Journal of Nonverbal Behavior, 23,* 237–249.

Feldman, R. S., Weller, A., Sirota, L., & Eidelman, A. I. (2002). Skin-to-skin contact (kangaroo care) promotes self-regulation in premature infants: Sleep–wake cyclicity, arousal modulation, and sustained exploration. *Developmental Psychology, 38,* 194–207.

Feldman, S. S., & Rosenthal, D. A. (1990). The acculturation of autonomy expectations in Chinese high schoolers residing in two Western nations. *International Journal of Psychology, 25,* 259–281.

Feng, T. (1993). Substance abuse in pregnancy. *Current Opinion in Obstetrics and Gynecology, 5,* 16–23.

Fenson, L., Dale, P. S., Reznick, J. S., Bates, E., Thal, D. J., & Pethick, S. J. (1994). Variability in early communicative development. *Monographs of the Society for Research in Child Development, 59*(5, Serial No. 242).

Fenwick, K., & Morrongiello, B. (1991). Development of frequency perception in infants and children. *Journal of Speech, Language Pathology, and Audiology, 15,* 7–22.

Fernald, A. (1984). The perceptual and affective salience of mothers' speech to infants. In L. Feagans, C. Garvey, & R. Golinkoff (Eds.), *The origins and growth of communication.* Norwood, NJ: Ablex.

Fernald, A. (1989). Intonation and communicative intent in mothers' speech to infants: Is the melody the message? *Child Development, 60,* 1497–1510.

Fernald, A., & Kuhl, P. K. (1987). Acoustic determinants of infant preference for motherese speech. *Infant Behavior and Development, 10,* 279–293.

Fernald, A., & Morikawa, H. (1993). Common themes and cultural variations in Japanese and American mothers' speech to infants. *Child Development, 64,* 637–656.

Fernald, A., Taeschner, T., Dunn, J., Papousek, M., Boysson-Bardies, B. de, & Fukui, I. (1989). A cross-language study of prosodic modifications in mothers' and fathers' speech to preverbal infants. *Journal of Child Language, 16,* 477–501.

Fernyhough, C. (1997). Vygotsky's sociocultural approach: Theoretical issues and implications for current research. In S. Hala (Ed.), *The development of social cognition.* Philadelphia: Psychology Press.

Festinger, L. (1954). A theory of social comparison processes. *Human Relations, 7,* 117–140.

Fetterman, D. M. (1998). Ethnography. In L. Bickman & D. J. Rog (Eds.), *Handbook of applied social research methods.* Thousand Oaks, CA: Sage.

Field, T. M. (1979). Games parents play with normal and high-risk infants. *Child Psychiatry and Human Development, 10,* 41–48.

Field, T. M. (1981). Infant gaze aversion and heart rate during face-to-face interactions. *Infant Behavior and Development, 4,* 307–313.

Field, T. M. (1982). Individual differences in the expressivity of neonates and young infants. In R. S. Feldman (Ed.), *Development of nonverbal behavior in children.* New York: Springer-Verlag.

Field, T. M. (1987). Interaction and attachment in normal and atypical infants. *Journal of Consulting and Clinical Psychology, 14,* 183–184.

Field, T. M. (Ed.). (1988). *Stress and coping across development.* Hillsdale, NJ: Erlbaum.

Field, T. M. (1990). *Infancy.* Cambridge, MA: Harvard University Press.

Field, T. M. (1995a). Infant massage therapy. In T. M. Field (Ed.), *Touch in early development.* Hillsdale, NJ: Erlbaum.

Field, T. M. (1995b). Massage therapy for infants and children. *Journal of Developmental and Behavioral Pediatrics, 16,* 105–111.

Field, T. M. (1999). Sucking and massage therapy reduce stress during infancy. In M. Lewis & D. Ramsay (Eds.), *Soothing and stress.* Mahwah, NJ: Erlbaum.

Field, T. M. (2000). Infant massage therapy. In C. H. Zeanah Jr. (Ed.), *Handbook of infant mental health* (2nd ed.). New York: Guilford Press.

Field, T. M. (2001). *Touch.* Cambridge, MA: MIT Press.

Field, T. M., Greenberg, R., Woodson, R., Cohen, D., & Garcia, R. (1984). Facial expression during Brazelton neonatal assessments. *Infant Mental Health Journal, 5,* 61–71.

Field, T. M., Harding, J., Yando, R., Gonzalez, K., Lasko, D., Bendell, D., et al. (1998). Feelings and attitudes of gifted students. *Adolescence, 39,* 331–342.

Field, T. M., & Roopnarine, J. L. (1982). Infant–peer interactions. In T. M. Field, A. C. Huston, H. Quay, & G. Finley (Eds.), *Review of human development.* New York: Wiley.

Field, T. M., & Walden, T. (1982). Perception and production of facial expression in infancy and early childhood. In H. Reese & L. Lipsitt (Eds.), *Advances in child development and behavior* (Vol. 16). New York: Academic Press.

Fields-Meyer, T. (1995, September 25). Having their say. *People,* 50–60.

Fifer, W. P. (1987). Neonatal preference for mother's voice. In N. A. Kasnegor, E. M. Blass, & M. A. Hofer (Eds.), *Perinatal development: A psychobiological perspective.* Orlando, FL: Academic Press.

Finkbeiner, A. K. (1996). *After the death of a child: Living with loss through the years.* New York: Free Press.

Finkelstein, D. L., Harper, D. A., & Rosenthal, G. E. (1998). Does length of hospital stay during labor and delivery influence patient satisfaction? Results from a regional study. *American Journal of Managed Care, 4,* 1701–1708.

Finkelstein, Y., Markowitz, M. E., & Rosen, J. F. (1998). Low-level lead-induced neurotoxicity in children: An update on central nervous system effects. *Brain Research Reviews, 27,* 168–176.

Fiore, S. M., & Schooler, J. W. (1998). Right hemisphere contributions to creative problem solving: Converging evidence for divergent thinking. In M. Beeman & C. Chiarello (Eds.), *Right hemisphere language comprehension: Perspectives from cognitive neuroscience.* Mahwah, NJ: Erlbaum.

First, J. M., & Cardenas, J. (1986). A minority view on testing. *Educational Measurement Issues and Practice, 5,* 6–11.

Fischer, K. W., & Hencke, R. W. (1996). Infants' construction of actions in context: Piaget's contributions to research on early development. *Psychological Science, 7,* 204–210.

Fischer, K. W., & Rose, S. P. (1995). Concurrent cycles in the dynamic development of brain and behavior. *Newsletter of the Society for Research in Child Development, 16.*

Fischgrund, J. E. (1996). Learners who are deaf or hard of hearing. In M. C. Wang, M. C. Reynolds, & H. J. Walberg (Eds.), *Handbook of special and remedial education: Research and practice* (2nd ed.). New York: Pergamon.

Fish, J. M. (Ed.). (2001). *Race and intelligence: Separating science from myth.* Mahwah, NJ: Erlbaum.

Fishbein, H. D., & Imai, S. (1993). Preschoolers select playmates on the basis of gender and race. *Journal of Applied Developmental Psychology, 14,* 303–316.

Fishel, E. (1993, September). Starting kindergarten. *Parents,* 165–169.

Fisher, C., & Tokura, H. (1996). Acoustic cues to grammatical structure in infant-directed speech: Cross-linguistic evidence. *Child Development, 67,* 3192–3218.

Fisher, J., Astbury, J., & Smith, A. (1997). Adverse psychological impact of obstetric interventions: A prospective longitudinal study. *Australian and New Zealand Journal of Psychiatry, 31,* 728–738.

Fishman, C. (1999, May). Watching the time go by. *American Demographics,* 56–57.

Fivush, R. (Ed.). (1995). *Long-term retention of infant memories.* Hillsdale, NJ: Erlbaum.

Fivush, R., Kuebli, J., & Clubb, P. A. (1992). The structure of events and event representations: A developmental analysis. *Child Development, 63,* 188–201.

Flavell, J. H. (1985). *Cognitive development* (2nd ed.). Englewood Cliffs, NJ: Prentice Hall.

Flavell, J. H. (1994). Cognitive development: Past, present, and future. In R. D. Parke, P. A. Ornstein, J. J. Rieser, & C. Zahn-Waxler (Eds.), *A century of developmental psychology.* Washington, DC: American Psychological Association.

Flavell, J. H. (1996). Piaget's legacy. *Psychological Science, 7,* 200–203.

Flavell, J. H., Flavell, E. R., & Green, F. L. (2001). Development of children's understanding of connections between thinking and feeling. *Psychological Science, 12,* 430–432.

Flavell, J. H., Green, F. L., & Flavell, E. R. (1995). The development of children's knowledge about attentional focus. *Developmental Psychology, 31,* 706–712.

Fleming, J. E., & Offord, D. R. (1990). Epidemiology of childhood depressive disorders: A critical review. *Journal of the American Academy of Child and Adolescent Psychiatry, 29,* 571–580.

Fletcher, A. C., Darling, N. E., Steinberg, L., & Dornbusch, S. M. (1995). The company they keep: Relation of adolescents' adjustment and behavior to their friends' perceptions of authoritative parenting in the social network. *Developmental Psychology, 31,* 300–310.

Flynn, C. P. (1998). To spank or not to spank: The effect of situation and age of child on support for corporal punishment. *Journal of Family Violence, 13,* 21–37.

Fogel, A. (1980). Peer- vs. mother-directed behavior in one- to three-month-old infants. *Infant Behavior and Development, 2,* 215–226.

Fogel, A., Nelson-Goens, G. C., Hsu, H., & Shapiro, A. F. (2000). Do different infant smiles reflect different positive emotions? *Social Development, 9,* 497–520.

Folkman, S., & Lazarus, R. S. (1980). An analysis of coping in a middle-aged community sample. *Journal of Health and Social Behavior, 21,* 219–239.

Folkman, S., & Lazarus, R. S. (1988). Coping as a mediator of emotion. *Journal of Personality and Social Psychology, 54,* 466–475.

Fortier, I., Marcoux, S., & Beaulac-Baillargeon, L. (1993). Relation of caffeine intake during pregnancy to intrauterine growth retardation and preterm birth. *American Journal of Epidemiology, 137,* 931–940.

Fowers, B. J., & Richardson, F. C. (1996). Why is multiculturalism good? *American Psychologist, 51,* 609–621.

Fox, N. F. (Ed.). (1994). *The development of emotion regulation: Biological and behavioral considerations.* Chicago: Society for Research in Child Development.

Fox, N. F., Kimmerly, N. L., & Schafer, W. D. (1991). Attachment to mother/attachment to father: A meta-analysis. *Child Development, 62,* 210–225.

Fraley, R. C. (2002). Attachment stability from infancy to adulthood: Meta-analysis and dynamic modeling of developmental mechanisms. *Personality and Social Psychology Review, 6,* 123–151.

Francasso, M. P., Lamb, M. E., Scholmerich, A., & Leyendecker, B. (1997). The ecology of mother–infant interaction in Euro-American and immigrant Central American families living in the United States. *International Journal of Behavioral Development, 20,* 207–217.

Franck, I., & Brownstone, D. (1991). *The parent's desk reference.* Englewood Cliffs, NJ: Prentice Hall.

Frankenburg, W. K., Dodds, J., Archer, P., Maschka, P., Edelman, N., & Shapiro, H. (1992a). *The Denver II training manual.* Denver, CO: Denver Developmental Materials.

Frankenburg, W. K., Dodds, J., Archer, P., Shapiro, H., & Bresnick, B. (1992b). The Denver II: A major revision and restandardization of the Denver Developmental Screening Test. *Pediatrics, 89,* 91–97.

Franzoi, S. L., Davis, M. H., & Vasquez-Suson, K. A. (1994). Two social worlds: Social correlates and stability of adolescent status groups. *Journal of Personality and Social Psychology, 67,* 462–473.

Freedman, D. G. (1979, January). Ethnic differences in babies. *Human Nature,* 15–20.

Freedman, R., Adler, L. E., & Leonard, S. (1999). Alternative phenotypes for the complex genetics of schizophrenia. *Biological Psychiatry, 45,* 551–558.

Freiberg, P. (1998, February). We know how to stop the spread of AIDS—so why can't we? *Monitor on Psychology, 32.*

Frenkel, L. D., & Gaur, S. (1994). Perinatal HIV infection and AIDS. *Clinics in Perinatology, 21,* 95–107.

Freud, S. (1920). *A general introduction to psychoanalysis.* New York: Boni & Liveright.

Freud, S. (1959). *Group psychology and the analysis of the ego.* London: Hogarth. (Original work published 1922)

Fried, P. A., & Watkinson, B. (1990). 36- and 48-month neurobehavioral follow-up of children prenatally exposed to marijuana, cigarettes, and alcohol. *Developmental and Behavioral Pediatrics, 11,* 49–58.

Friedman, H. S., Tucker, J. S., Schwartz, J. E., Martin, L. R., Tomlinson-Keasey, C., Wingard, D. L., et al. (1995). Childhood conscientiousness and longevity: Health behaviors and cause of death. *Journal of Personality and Social Psychology, 68,* 696–703.

Friend, R. M., & Neale, J. M. (1972). Children's perceptions of success and failure: An attributional analysis of the effects of race and social class. *Developmental Psychology, 7,* 124–128.

Fromberg, D. P., & Bergen, D. (1998). *Play from birth to twelve and beyond.* Levittown, PA: Garland.

Fuchs, D., & Fuchs, L. S. (1994). Inclusive schools movement and the radicalization of special education reform. *Exceptional Children, 60,* 294–309.

Fuligni, A. J. (1997). The academic achievement of adolescents from immigrant families: The roles of family background, attitudes, and behavior. *Child Development, 68,* 351–368.

Fuligni, A. J. (1998). The adjustment of children from immigrant families. *Current Directions in Psychological Science, 7,* 99–103.

Fuligni, A. J., Tseng, V., & Lam, M. (1999). Attitudes toward family obligations among American adolescents with Asian, Latin American, and European backgrounds. *Child Development, 70,* 1030–1044.

Furman, W., & Buhrmester, D. (1992). Age and sex differences in perceptions of networks of personal relationships. *Child Development, 63,* 103–115.

Furnham, A., & Weir, C. (1996). Lay theories of child development. *Journal of Genetic Psychology, 157,* 211–226.

Furstenberg, F. F., Jr., Brooks-Gunn, J., & Morgan, S. P. (1987). *Adolescent mothers in later life.* New York: Cambridge University Press.

Gable, S., & Lutz, S. (2000). Household, parent, and child contributions to childhood obesity. *Family Relations, 49,* 293–300.

Gadow, K. D., & Sprafkin, J. (1993). Television "violence" and children with emotional and behavioral disorders. *Journal of Emotional and Behavioral Disorders, 1,* 54–63.

Gaertner, S. L., Mann, J. A., Dovidio, J. F., Murrell, A. J., & Pomare, M. (1990). How does cooperation reduce intergroup bias? *Journal of Personality and Social Psychology, 59,* 692–704.

Gagnon, S. G., & Nagle, R. J. (2000). Comparison of the revised and original versions of the Bayley Scales of Infant Development. *School Psychology International, 21,* 293–305.

Galambos, N. L., & Dixon, R. A. (1984). Toward understanding and caring for latchkey children. *Child Care Quarterly, 13,* 116–125.

Gallagher, J. J. (1994). Teaching and learning: New models. *Annual Review of Psychology, 45,* 171–195.

Gallup, G. G., Jr. (1977). Self-recognition in primates: A comparative approach to the bidirectional properties of consciousness. *American Psychologist, 32,* 329–337.

Galper, A., Wigfield, A., & Seefeldt, C. (1997). Head Start parents' beliefs about their children's abilities, task values, and performances on different actives. *Child Development, 68,* 897–907.

Gans, J. (1990). *America's adolescents: How healthy are they?* Chicago: American Medical Association.

Garbarino, J. (1988). Preventing childhood injury: Developmental and mental health issues. *American Journal of Orthopsychiatry, 58,* 25–45.

Garbarino, J., & Asp, C. (1981). *Successful schools and competent students.* Lexington, MA: Lexington Books.

Garber, M. (1981). Malnutrition during pregnancy and lactation. In G. H. Bourne (Ed.), *World review of nutrition and dietetics* (Vol. 36). Basel, Switzerland: Karger.

Gardner, H. (1980). *Artful scribbles: The significance of children's drawings.* New York: Basic Books.

Gardner, H. (2000). *Intelligence reframed: Multiple intelligences for the 21st century.* New York: Basic Books.

Gardner, H., Krechevsky, M., Sternberg, R. J., & Okagaki, L. (1994). Intelligence in context: Enhancing students' practical intelligence for school. In K. McGilly (Ed.), *Classroom lessons: Integrating cognitive theory and classroom practice.* Cambridge, MA: MIT Press.

Gardner, R. M., Stark, K., Friedman, B. N., & Jackson, N. A. (2000). Predictors of eating disorder scores in children ages 6 through 14: A longitudinal study. *Journal of Psychosomatic Research, 49,* 199–205.

Garnefski, N., & Arends, E. (1998). Sexual abuse and adolescent maladjustment: Differences between male and female victims. *Journal of Adolescence, 21,* 99–107.

Garrity, C., Jens, K., & Porter, W. W. (1996, August). *Bully–victim problems in the school setting.* Paper presented at the annual meeting of the American Psychological Association, Toronto.

Gathercole, S. E. (1998). The development of memory. *Journal of Child Psychology and Psychiatry and Allied Disciplines, 39,* 3–27.

Gaulden, M. E. (1992). Maternal age effect: The enigma of Down syndrome and other trisomic conditions. *Mutation Research, 296,* 69–88.

Gauvain, M. (1998). Cognitive development in social and cultural context. *Current Directions in Psychological Science, 7,* 188–194.

Gavin, L. A., & Furman, W. (1996). Adolescent girls' relationships with mothers and best friends. *Child Development, 67,* 375–386.

Gazzaniga, M. S. (1983). Right-hemisphere language following brain bisection: A twenty-year perspective. *American Psychologist, 38,* 525–537.

Geary, D. C. (1996). International differences in mathematical achievement: Their nature, causes, and consequences. *Current Directions in Psychological Science, 5,* 133–137.

Geary, D. C. (1998). *Male, female: The evolution of human sex differences.* Washington, DC: American Psychological Association.

Geary, D. C., & Bjorklund, D. F. (2000). Evolutionary developmental psychology. *Child Development, 71,* 57–65.

Gelles, R. J. (1994). *Contemporary families.* Newbury Park, CA: Sage.

Gelles, R. J., & Cornell, C. (1990). *Intimate violence in families.* Beverly Hills, CA: Sage.

Gelman, D. (1994, April 18). The mystery of suicide. *Newsweek,* 44–49.

Gelman, R. (1972). Logical capacity of very young children: Number invariance rules. *Child Development, 43,* 75-90.

Gelman, R., & Baillargeon, R. (1983). A review of some Piagetian concepts. In P. H. Mussen (Ed.), *Handbook of child psychology: Vol 3. Cognitive development* (4th ed.). New York: Wiley.

Gelman, R., & Gallistel, C. R. (1978). *The child's understanding of number.* Cambridge, MA: Harvard University Press.

Gelman, S. A., & Kalish, C. W. (1993). Categories and causality. In R. Pasnak & M. L. Howe (Eds.), *Emerging themes in cognitive development: Vol. 2. Competencies.* New York: Springer-Verlag.

Genesee, F. (1994). Bilingualism. In V. S. Ramachandran (Ed.), *Encyclopedia of human behavior.* San Diego, CA: Academic Press.

Gergely, C., Bekkering, H., & Király, I. (2002). Rational imitation in preverbal infants. *Nature, 415,* 755.

Gerhardt, P. (1999, August 10). Potty training: How did it get so complicated? *Daily Hampshire Gazette,* p. C1.

Gerrish, C. J., & Mennella, J. A. (2000). Short-term influence of breastfeeding on the infants' interaction with the environment. *Developmental Psychobiology, 36,* 40–48.

Gesell, A. L. (1946). The ontogenesis of infant behavior. In L. Carmichael (Ed.), *Manual of child psychology.* New York: Harper.

Giant steps. (2000, May 8). *People,* 117.

Gibbs, N. (2002, April 15). Making time for a baby. *Time,* 48–54.

Gibson, E. J., & Walk, R. D. (1960). The "visual cliff." *Scientific American,* 64–71.

Gibson, M. A., & Bhachu, P. K. (1991). The dynamics of educational decision making: A comparative study of Sikhs in Britain and the United States. In M. A. Gibson & J. U. Ogbu (Eds.), *Minority status and schooling: A comparative study of immigrant and involuntary minorities.* New York: Garland.

Gilbert, L. A. (1994). Current perspectives on dual-career families. *Current Directions in Psychological Science, 3,* 101–105.

Gilbert, S. (2000). *Counseling for eating disorders.* Thousand Oaks, CA: Sage.

Gilbert, W. M., Nesbitt, T. S., & Danielsen, B. (1999). Childbearing beyond age 40: Pregnancy outcome in 24,032 cases. *Obstetrics and Gynecology, 93,* 9–14.

Gilligan, C. (1982). *In a different voice: Psychological theory and women's development.* Cambridge, MA: Harvard University Press.

Gilligan, C. (1987). Adolescent development reconsidered. In C. E. Irwin (Ed.), *Adolescent social behavior and health.* San Francisco: Jossey-Bass.

Gilligan, C., Brown, L. M., & Rogers, A. G. (1990). Psyche embedded: A place for body, relationships, and culture in personality theory. In A. I. Rabin, & R. A. Zucker (Eds). *Studying persons and lives.* New York: Springer.

Gilligan, C., Lyons, N. P., & Hammer, T. J. (Eds.). (1990). *Making connections.* Cambridge, MA: Harvard University Press.

Ginzberg, E. (1972). Toward a theory of occupational choice: A restatement. *Vocational Guidance Quarterly, 12,* 10–14.

Gladue, B. A. (1994). The biopsychology of sexual orientation. *Current Directions in Psychological Science, 3,* 150–154.

Glasgow, K. L., Dornbusch, S. M., Troyer, L., Steinberg, L., & Ritter, P. L. (1997). Parenting styles, adolescents' attributions, and educational outcomes in nine heterogeneous high schools. *Child Development, 68,* 507–529.

Gleason, J. B. (1987). Sex differences in parent–child interaction. In S. U. Philips, S. Steele, & C. Tanz (Eds.), *Language, gender, and sex in comparative perspective.* New York: Cambridge University Press.

Gleason, J. B., Perlmann, R. U., Ely, R., & Evans, D. W. (1991). The babytalk register: Parents' use of diminutives. In J. L. Sokolov, & C. E. Snow (Eds.), *Handbook of research in language development using CHILDES.* Hillsdale, NJ: Erlbaum.

Gleick, E., Reed, S., & Schindehette, S. (1994, October 24). The baby trap. *People,* 38–56.

Gleitman, L., & Landau, B. (1994). *The acquisition of the lexicon.* Cambridge, MA: Bradford.

Glick, P., Zion, C., & Nelson, C. (1988). What mediates sex discrimination in hiring decisions? *Journal of Personality and Social Psychology, 55,* 178–186.

Gogate, L. J., Bahrick, L. E., & Watson, J. D. (2000). A study of multimodal motherese: The role of temporal synchrony between verbal labels and gestures. *Child Development, 71,* 878–894.

Goldberg, J., Holtz, D., Hyslop, T., & Tolosa, J. E. (2002). Has the use of routine episiotomy decreased? Examination of episiotomy rates from 1983 to 2000. *Obstetrics and Gynecology, 99,* 395–400.

Goldsmith, H. H., & Gottesman, I. I. (1981). Origins of variation in behavioral style: A longitudinal study of temperament in young twins. *Child Development, 53,* 91–103.

Goldsmith, H. H., & Harman, C. (1994). Temperament and attachment: Individuals and relationships. *Current Directions in Psychological Science, 3,* 53–57.

Goldstein, A. (1994, August). Paper presented at the annual meeting of the American Psychological Association, Los Angeles.

Goleman, D. (1993, July 21). Baby sees, baby does, and classmates follow. *New York Times,* p. C10.

Goleman, D. (1995). *Emotional intelligence.* New York: Bantam.

Golinkoff, R. M. (1993). When is communication a "meeting of minds"? *Journal of Child Language, 20,* 199–207.

Golombok, S., & Fivush, R. (1994). *Gender development.* Cambridge, England: Cambridge University Press.

Golombok, S., & Tasker, F. (1996). Do parents influence the sexual orientation of their children? Findings from a longitudinal study of lesbian families. *Developmental Psychology, 32,* 3–11.

Gongla, P., & Thompson, E. H. (1987). Single-parent families. In M. B. Sussman & S. K. Steinmetz (Eds.), *Handbook of marriage and the family.* New York: Plenum.

Goode, E. (1999, January 12). Clash over when, and how, to toilet-train. *New York Times,* pp. A1, A17.

Goodlin-Jones, B. L., Burnham, M. M., & Anders, T. F. (2000). Sleep and sleep disturbances: Regulatory processes in infancy. In A. J. Sameroff & M. Lewis (Eds.), *Handbook of developmental psychopathology* (2nd ed.). New York: Kluwer.

Goodman, G. S., & Reed, R. S. (1986). Age differences in eyewitness testimony. *Law and Human Behavior, 10,* 317–332.

Goodman, J. C., & Nusbaum, H. C. (Eds.). (1994). *The development of speech perception.* Cambridge, MA: Bradford.

Goodstein, R., & Ponterotto, J. G. (1997). Racial and ethnic identity: Their relationship and their contribution to self-esteem. *Journal of Black Psychology, 23,* 275–292.

Goodwin, M. H. (1980). Directive-response speech sequences in girls' and boys' task activities. In S. McConnell-Ginet, R. Borker, & N. Furman (Eds.), *Women and language in literature and society.* New York: Praeger.

Goodwin, M. H. (1990). Tactical uses of stories: Participation frameworks within girls' and boys' disputes. *Discourse Processes, 13,* 33–71.

Goossens, F. A., & van IJzendoorn, M. H. (1990). Quality of infants' attachments to professional caregivers: Relation to infant–parent attachment and day-care characteristics. *Child Development, 61,* 832–837.

Gordon, B. N., Baker-Ward, L., & Ornstein, P. A. (2001). Children's testimony: A review of research on memory for past experiences. *Clinical Child and Family Psychology Review, 4,* 157–181.

Gordon, J. W. (1999). Genetic enhancement in humans. *Science, 283,* 2023–2024.

Gorman, K. S., & Pollitt, E. (1992). Relationship between weight and body proportionality at birth, growth during the first year of life, and cognitive development at 36, 48, and 60 months. *Infant Behavior and Development, 15,* 279–296.

Gortmaker, S. L., Must, A., Sobol, A. M., Peterson, K., Colditz, G. A., & Dietz, W. H. (1996). Television viewing as a cause of increasing obesity among children in the United States, 1896–1990. *Archives of Pediatrics and Adolescent Medicine, 150,* 356–362.

Goswami, U. (1998). *Cognition in children.* Philadelphia: Psychology Press.

Gottesman, I. I. (1991). *Schizophrenia genesis: The origins of madness.* New York: Freeman.

Gottesman, I. I. (1993). Origins of schizophrenia: Past as prologue. In R. Plomin & G. E. McClearn (Eds.), *Nature, nurture, and psychology.* Washington, DC: American Psychological Association.

Gottfredson, G. D., & Holland, J. L. (1990). A longitudinal test of the influence of congruence: Job satisfaction, competency utilization, and counterproductive behavior. *Journal of Counseling Psychology, 37,* 389–398.

Gottfried, A. E., & Gottfried, A. W. (Eds.). (1994). *Redefining families.* New York: Plenum.

Gottfried, A. W., Gottfried, A. E., Bathurst, K., & Guerin, D. W. (1994). *Early developmental aspects: The Fullerton Longitudinal Study.* New York: Plenum.

Gottlieb, G. (1991). Experimental canalization of behavioral development: Theory. *Developmental Psychology, 27,* 373–381.

Gottman, J. M. (1986). The world of coordinated play: Same- and cross-sex friendship in young children. In J. M. Gottman & J. G. Parker (Eds.), *Conversations of friends: Speculations on affective development.* Cambridge, England: Cambridge University Press.

Gottman, J. M. (1993). *What predicts divorce? The relationship between marital processes and marital outcomes.* Hillsdale, NJ: Erlbaum.

Gottman, J. M., & Katz, L. F. (1989). Effects of marital discord on young children's peer interaction and health. *Developmental Psychology, 25,* 373–381.

Gould, S. J. (1977). *Ontogeny and phylogeny.* Cambridge, MA: Harvard University Press.

Goyette-Ewing, M. (2000). Children's after-school arrangements: A study of self-care and developmental outcomes. *Journal of Prevention and Intervention in the Community, 20,* 55–67.

Graber, J. A., Brooks-Gunn, J., & Warren, M. P. (1995). The antecedents of menarcheal age: Heredity, family environment, and stressful life events. *Child Development, 66,* 346–359.

Graham, E. (1995, February 9). Leah: Life is all sweetness and insecurity. *Wall Street Journal,* p. B1.

Graham, S. (1986). An attributional perspective on achievement motivation and black children. In R. S. Feldman (Ed), *The social psychology of education: Current research and theory.* New York: Cambridge University Press.

Graham, S. (1990). Communicating low ability in the classroom: Bad things good teachers sometimes do. In S. Graham & V. S. Folkes (Eds.), *Attribution theory: Applications to achievement, mental health, and interpersonal conflict.* Hillsdale, NJ: Erlbaum.

Graham, S. (1992). "Most of the subjects were white and middle class": Trends in published research on African Americans in selected APA journals. *American Psychologist, 47,* 629–639.

Graham, S. (1994). Motivation in African Americans. *Review of Educational Research, 64,* 55–117.

Graham, S., & Harris, K. R. (1997). Whole language and process writing: Does one approach fit all? In J. W. Lloyd, E. J. Kameenui, & D. Chard (Eds.), *Issues in educating students with disabilities.* Mahwah, NJ: Erlbaum.

Grant, C. A., & Sleeter, C. E. (1986). Race, class, and gender in education research: An argument for integrative analysis. *Review of Educational Research, 56,* 195–211.

Grant, V. J. (1994). Sex of infant differences in mother–infant interaction: A reinterpretation of past findings. *Developmental Review, 14,* 1–26.

Grantham-McGregor, S., Ani, C., & Fernald, L. (2001). The role of nutrition in intellectual development. In R. J. Sternberg & E. L. Grigorenko (Eds.), *Environmental effects on cognitive abilities.* Mahwah, NJ: Erlbaum.

Grantham-McGregor, S., Powell, C., Walker, S., Chang, S., & Fletcher, P. (1994). The long-term follow-up of severely malnourished children who participated in an intervention program. *Child Development, 65,* 428–439.

Gratch, G., & Schatz, J. A. (1987). Cognitive development: The relevance of Piaget's infancy books. In J. D. Osofsky (Ed.), *Handbook of infant development* (2nd ed.). New York: Wiley.

Grattan, M. P., De Vos, E. S., Levy, J., & McClintock, M. K. (1992). Asymmetric action in the human newborn: Sex differences in patterns of organization. *Child Development, 63,* 273–289.

Gray-Little, B., & Hafdahl, A. R. (2000). Factors influencing racial comparisons of self-esteem: A quantitative review. *Psychological Bulletin, 126,* 26–54.

Greene, K., Krcmar, M., Walters, L. H., Rubin, D. L., & Hale, J. L. (2000). Targeting adolescent risk-taking behaviors: The contribution of egocentrism and sensation-seeking. *Journal of Adolescence, 23,* 439–461.

Greenfield, P. M. (1966). On culture and conservation. In J. S. Bruner, R. R. Olver, & P. M. Greenfield (Eds.), *Studies in cognitive growth.* New York: Wiley.

Greenfield, P. M. (1976). Cross-cultural research and Piagetian theory: Paradox and progress. In K. F. Riegel & J. A. Meacham (Eds.), *The developing individual in a changing world* (Vol. 1). The Hague, Netherlands: Mouton.

Greenfield, P. M. (1995, Winter). Culture, ethnicity, race, and development: Implications for teaching theory and research. *SRCD Newsletter,* 00–00.

Greenfield, P. M. (1997). You can't take it with you. Why ability assessments don't cross cultures. *American Psychologist, 52,* 1115–1124.

Greenglass, E. R., & Burke, R. J. (1991). The relationship between stress and coping among Type A's. *Journal of Social Behavior and Personality, 6,* 361–373.

Gregory, S. (1856). *Facts for young women.* Boston.

Grieser, T., & Kuhl, P. (1988). Maternal speech to infants in atonal language: Support for universal prosodic features in motherese. *Developmental Psychology, 24,* 14–20.

Griesler, P. C., & Kandel, D. B. (1998). Ethnic differences in correlates of adolescent cigarette smoking. *Journal of Adolescent Health, 23,* 167–180.

Griffith, D. R., Azuma, S. D., & Chasnoff, I. J. (1994). Three-year outcome of children exposed prenatally to drugs. *Journal of the American Academy of Child and Adolescent Psychiatry, 33,* 20–27.

Groome, L. J., Swiber, M. J., Atterbury, J. L., Bentz, L. S., & Holland, S. B. (1997). Similarities and differences in behavioral state organization during sleep periods in the perinatal infant before and after birth. *Child Development, 68,* 1–11.

Groopman, J. (1998, February 8). Decoding destiny. *New Yorker,* 42–47.

Gross, R. T., Spiker, D., & Haynes, C. W. (Eds.). (1997). *Helping low-birthweight, premature babies: The Infant Health and Development Program.* Stanford, CA: Stanford University Press.

Grossmann, K. E., Grossman, K., Huber, F., & Wartner, U. (1982). German children's behavior towards their mothers at 12 months and their fathers at 18 months in Ainsworth's Strange Situation. *International Journal of Behavioral Development, 4,* 157–181.

Groves, B., Zuckerman, B., Marans, S., & Cohen, D. (1993). Silent victims: Children who witness violence. *Journal of the American Medical Association, 269,* 262–264.

Grusec, J. E. (1982). Socialization processes and the development of altruism. In J. P. Rushton & R. M. Sorrentino (Eds.), *Altruism and helping behavior.* Hillsdale, NJ: Erlbaum.

Grusec, J. E. (1991). The socialization of altruism. In M. S. Clark (Ed.), *Prosocial behavior.* Newbury Park, CA: Sage.

Grusec, J. E., & Kuczynski, L. E. (Eds.). (1997). *Parenting and children's internalization of values: A handbook of contemporary theory.* New York: Wiley.

Grych, J. H., & Clark, R. (1999). Maternal employment and development of the father–infant relationship in the first year. *Developmental Psychology, 35,* 893–903.

Guasti, M. T. (2002). *Language acquisition: The growth of grammar.* Cambridge, MA: MIT Press.

Gur, R. C., Gur, R. E., Obrist, W. D., Hungerbuhler, J. P., Younkin, D., Rosen, A. D., et al. (1982). Sex and handedness differences in cerebral blood flow during rest and cognitive activity. *Science, 217,* 659–661.

Gur, R. E, & Chin, S. (1999). Laterality in functional brain imaging studies of schizophrenia. *Schizophrenia Bulletin, 25,* 141–156.

Guthrie, G., & Lonner, W. (1986). Assessment of personality and psychopathology. In W. Lonner & J. Berry (Eds.), *Field methods in cross-cultural research.* Newbury Park, CA: Sage.

Hack, M., Flannery, D. J., Schluchter, M., Cartar, L., Borawski, E., & Klein, N. (2002). Outcomes in young adulthood for very low birth weight infants. *New England Journal of Medicine, 346,* 149–157.

Haederle, M. (1999, January 18). Going too far? *People,* 101–103.

Hahn, C.-S., & Di Pietro, J. A. (2001). In vitro fertilization and the family: Quality of parenting, family functioning, and child psychosocial adjustment. *Developmental Psychology, 37,* 37–48.

Haight, W. L., Wang, X., Fung, H. H., Williams, K., & Mintz, J. (1999). Universal developmental and variable aspects of young children's play: A cross-cultural comparison of pretending at home. *Child Development, 70,* 1477–1488.

Haith, M. H. (1986). Sensory and perceptual processes in early infancy. *Journal of Pediatrics, 109,* 158–171.

Haith, M. H. (1991a). Gratuity, perception-action integration, and future orientation in infant vision. In F. S. Kessel, M. H. Bornstein, & A. J. Sameroff (Eds.), *Contemporary constructions of the child: Essays in honor of William Kessen.* Hillsdale, NJ: Erlbaum.

Haith, M. H. (1991b, April). *Setting a path for the '90s: Some goals and challenges in infant sensory and perceptual development.* Paper presented at the biennial meeting of the Society for Research in Child Development, Seattle.

Hales, K. A., Morgan, M. A., & Thurnau, G. R. (1993). Influence of labor and route of delivery on the frequency of respiratory morbidity in term neonates. *International Journal of Gynecology and Obstetrics, 43,* 35–40.

Halford, G. S., Maybery, M. T., O'Hare, A. W., & Grant, P. (1994). The development of memory and processing capacity. *Child Development, 65,* 1338–1356.

Hall, E. G., & Lee, A. M. (1984). Sex differences in motor performance of young children: Fact or fiction? *Sex Roles, 10,* 217–230.

Hall, G. S. (1916). *Adolescence.* New York: Appleton. (Original work published 1904)

Hallahan, D. P., Kauffman, J. M., & Lloyd, J. W. (2000). *Introduction to learning disabilities* (4th ed.). Needham Heights, MA: Allyn & Bacon.

Halliday, M. A. K. (1975). *Learning how to mean: Explorations in the development of language.* London: Arnold.

Hallinan, M. T., & Williams, R. A. (1989). Interracial friendship choices in secondary schools. *American Sociological Review, 54,* 67–78.

Halpern, L. F., MacLean, W. E., & Baumeister, A. A. (1995). Infant sleep–wake characteristics: Relation to neurological status and the prediction of developmental outcome. *Developmental Review, 15,* 255–291.

Halpern, S. H., Leighton, B. L., Ohlsson, A., Barrett, J. F. R., & Rice, A. (1998). Effect of epidural vs. parenteral opioid analgesia on the progress of labor. *Journal of the American Medical Association, 280,* 2105–2110.

Hamilton, C. (2000). Continuity and discontinuity of attachment from infancy through adolescence. *Child Development, 71,* 690–694.

Hamilton, G. (1998). Positively testing. *Families in Society, 79,* 570–576.

Hamm, J. V. (2000). Do birds of a feather flock together? The variable bases for African American, Asian American, and European American adolescents' selection of similar friends. *Developmental Psychology, 36,* 209–219.

Hammer, R. P. (1984). The sexually dimorphic region of the preoptic area in rats contains denser opiate receptor binding sites in females. *Brain Researcher, 308,* 172–176.

Hammersley, R. (1992). Cue exposure and learning theory. *Addictive Behaviors, 17,* 297–300.

Hammond, W. A., & Romney, D. M. (1995). Cognitive factors contributing to adolescent depression. *Journal of Youth and Adolescence, 24,* 667–683.

Hampson, J., & Nelson, K. (1993). The relation of maternal language to variation in rate and style of language acquisition. *Journal of Child Language, 20,* 313–342.

Hankin, B. L., & Abramson, L. Y. (2001). Development of gender differences in depression: An elaborated cognitive vulnerability–transactional stress theory. *Psychological Bulletin, 127,* 773–796.

Hanna, E., & Meltzoff, A. N. (1993). Peer imitation by toddlers in laboratory, home, and day-care contexts: Implications for social learning and memory. *Developmental Psychology, 29,* 701–710.

Harkness, S., & Super, C. M. (1985). The cultural context of gender segregation in children's peer groups. *Child Development, 56,* 219–224.

Harlow, H. F., & Zimmerman, R. R. (1959). Affectional responses in the infant monkey. *Science, 130,* 421–432.

Harmon, A. (1997, October 25). Internet's value in U.S. schools still in question. *New York Times,* p. 1A.

Harrell, J. S., Bangdiwala, S. I., Deng, S., Webb, J. P., & Bradley, C. (1998). Smoking initiation in youth: The roles of gender, race, socioeconomics, and developmental status. *Journal of Adolescent Health, 23,* 271–279.

Harrell, J. S., Gansky, S. A., Bradley C. B., & McMurray, R. G. (1997). Leisure time activities of elementary school children. *Nursing Research, 46,* 246–253.

Harris, H. W., Blue, H. C., & Griffin, E. H. (Eds.). (1995). *Racial and ethnic identity: Psychological development and creative expression.* New York: Routledge.

Harris, J. R. (1998). *The nurture assumption: Why children turn out the way they do.* New York: Free Press.

Harris, J. R. (2000). Socialization, personality development, and the child's environments: Comment on Vandell. *Developmental Psychology, 36,* 711–723.

Harris, K. M. (2000). The health status and risk behavior of adolescents in immigrant families. In D. J. Hernandez (Ed.), *Children of immigrants: Health, adjustment, and public assistance.* Washington, DC: National Academy Press.

Harris, L. K., Van Zandt, C. E., & Rees, T. H. (1997). Counseling needs of students who are deaf and hard of hearing. *School Counselor, 44,* 271–279.

Harris, M. J., & Rosenthal, R. (1986). Four factors in the mediation of teacher expectancy effects. In R. S. Feldman (Ed.), *The social psychology of education: Current research and theory.* New York: Cambridge University Press.

Harris, P. L. (1983). Infant cognition. In M. H. Haith & J. J. Campos (Eds.) & P. H. Mussen (Gen. Ed.), *Handbook of child psychology: Vol 2. Infancy and developmental psychobiology.* New York: Wiley.

Harris, P. L. (1987). The development of search. In P. Sallapatek & L. Cohen (Eds.), *Handbook of infant perception: From perception to cognition* (Vol. 2). Orlando, FL: Academic Press.

Hart, B., & Risley, T. R. (1995). *Meaningful differences in the everyday experience of young American children.* Baltimore: Brookes.

Hart, C. H., Yang, C., Nelson, D. A., Jin, S., Bazarskaya, N., & Nelson, L. (1998). Peer contact patterns, parenting practices, and preschoolers' social competence in China, Russia, and the United States. In P. Slee & K. Rigby (Eds.), *Peer relations amongst children: Current issues and future directions.* London: Routledge.

Hart, S. N., Brassard, M. R., & Karlson, H. (1996). Psychological maltreatment. In J. N. Briere, L. Berliner, J. Bulkley, C. Jenny, & T. Reid (Eds.), *The APSAC handbook on child maltreatment.* Thousand Oaks, CA: Sage.

Harter, S. (1990a). Identity and self-development. In S. S. Feldman & G. R. Elliott (Eds.), *At the threshold: The developing adolescent.* Cambridge, MA: Harvard University Press.

Harter, S. (1990b). Issues in the assessment of self-concept of children and adolescents. In A. La Greca (Ed.), *Through the eyes of a child.* Needham Heights, MA: Allyn & Bacon.

Hartup, W. W. (1983). Peer relations. In P. H. Mussen (Ed.), *Handbook of child psychology* (Vol. 4, 4th ed.). New York: Wiley.

Hartup, W. W., & Stevens, N. (1997). Friendships and adaptation in the life course. *Psychological Bulletin, 121,* 355–370.

Harvey, E. (1999). Short-term and long-term effects of early parental employment on children of the National Longitudinal Survey of Youth. *Developmental Psychology, 35,* 445–459.

Harvey, P. G., Hamlin, M. W., Kumar, R., & Delves, H. T. (1984). Blood lead, behavior, and intelligence test performance in preschool children. *Science of the Total Environment, 40,* 45–60.

Harwood, R. L., Miller, J. G., & Irizarry, N. L. (1995). *Culture and attachment: Perceptions of the child in context.* New York: Guilford Press.

Hasher, L., & Zacks, R. T. (1984). Automatic processing of fundamental information: The case of frequency of occurrence. *American Psychologist, 39,* 1372–1388.

Haskins, R. (1989). Beyond metaphor: The efficacy of early childhood education. *American Psychologist, 44,* 274–282.

Hauck, F. R. & Hunt, C. E. (2000). Sudden infant death syndrome in 2000. *Current Problems in Pediatrics, 30,* 237–261.

Hawton, K. (1986). *Suicide and attempted suicide among children and adolescents.* Newbury Park, CA: Sage.

Hayden, T. (1998, September 21). The brave new world of sex selection. *Newsweek,* 93.

Hayne, H., & Rovee-Collier, C. K. (1995). The organization of reactivated memory in infancy. *Child Development, 66,* 893–906.

Haynie, D. L., Nansel, T., Eitel, P., Crump, A. D., Saylor, K., Yu, K., et al. (2001). Bullies, victims, and bully-victims: Distinct groups of at-risk youth. *Journal of Early Adolescence, 21,* 29–49.

Hazell, P. (1993). Adolescent suicide clusters: Evidence, mechanisms and prevention. *Australian and New Zealand Journal of Psychiatry, 27,* 653–665.

Health Resources and Services Administration. (1993). *Child Health USA, 1993.* Washington, DC: U.S. Department of Health and Human Services.

Health Resources and Services Administration. (1998). *Child Health USA, 1998.* Washington, DC: U.S. Department of Health and Human Services.

Health Resources and Services Administration. (2001). *Child Health USA, 2001.* Washington, DC: U.S. Department of Health and Human Services.

Healy, P. (2001, March 3). Data on suicides set off alarm. *Boston Globe,* p. B1.

Heath, A. C. (1994, February). Winning at sports. *Parents,* 126–130.

Hebert, T. P. (1998). Gifted black males in an urban high school: Factors that influence achievement and underachievement. *Journal for the Education of the Gifted, 21,* 385–414.

Heckert, T. M., & Wallis, H. A. (1998). Career and salary expectations of college freshmen and seniors: Are seniors more realistic than freshmen? *College Student Journal, 32,* 334–339.

Heller, S., Larieu, J. A., D'Imperio, R., & Boris, N. W. (1999). Research on resilience to child maltreatment: Empirical considerations. *Child Abuse and Neglect, 23,* 321–338.

Hellman, P. (1987, November 23). Sesame street smart. *New York,* 49–53.

Hendrick, V., Altshuler, L. L., & Suri, R. (1998). Hormonal changes in the postpartum and implications for postpartum depression. *Psychosomatics, 39,* 93–101.

Henning-Stout, M. (1996). Gay and lesbian youths in schools. *Psychology Teacher Network, 6*, 2–4.

Henry, B., Caspi, A., Moffitt, T. E., & Silva, P. A. (1996). Temperamental and familial predictors of violent and nonviolent criminal convictions: Age 3 to 18. *Developmental Psychology, 32*, 614–623.

Henry, C. S., Stephenson, A. L., Hanson, M. F., & Hargett, W. (1993). Adolescent suicide and families: An ecological approach. *Adolescence, 28*, 291–308.

Hepper, P. G., Scott, D., & Shahidulla, S. (1993). Response to maternal voice. *Journal of Reproductive and Infant Psychology, 11*, 147–153.

Herbst, A. L. (1981). Diethylstilbestrol and other sex hormones during pregnancy. *Obstetrics and Gynecology, 58*, 355–405.

Herbst, A. L. (1994). The epidemiology of ovarian carcinoma and the current status of tumor markers to detect disease. *American Journal of Obstetrics and Gynecology, 170*, 1099–1105.

Herdt, G. H. (Ed.). (1998). *Rituals of manhood: Male initiation in Papua New Guinea*. Somerset, NJ: Transaction Books.

Herek, G. M. (1993). Sexual orientation and military service: A social science perspective. *American Psychologist, 48*, 538–549.

Hernandez-Reif, M., Field, T. M., Krasnegor, J., Martinez, E., Schwartzmann, M., & Mavunda, K. (1999). Children with cystic fibrosis benefit from massage therapy. *Journal of Pediatric Psychology, 24*, 175–181.

Herrnstein, R. J., & Murray, C. (1994). *The bell curve: Intelligence and class structure in American life*. New York: Free Press.

Hersch, P. (1999). *A tribe apart*. New York: Ballantine Books.

Hess-Biber, S. (1996). *Am I thin enough yet?* New York: Oxford University Press.

Hetherington, E. M., & Blechman, E. A. (Eds.). (1996). *Stress, coping, and resiliency in children and families*. Hillsdale, NJ: Erlbaum.

Hetherington, E. M., & Clingempeel, W. (1992). Coping with marital transitions: A family systems perspective. *Monographs of the Society for Research in Child Development, 57* (2–3, Serial No. 227).

Hetherington, E. M., & Kelly, J. (2002). *For better or worse: Divorce reconsidered*. New York: Norton.

Hetheringon, E. M., Stanley-Hagan, M., & Anderson, E. (1989). Marital transitions: A child's perspective. *American Psychologist, 44*, 303–312.

Hetherington, T. F., & Weinberger, J. (Eds.). (1993). *Can personality change?* Washington, DC: American Psychological Association.

Hewitt, B. (1997, December 15). A day in the life. *People*, 49–58.

Hewett, F. M., & Forness, S. R. (1974). *Education of exceptional learners*. Needham Heights, MA: Allyn & Bacon.

Hickok, G., Bellugi, U., & Klima, E. S. (2001, June). *Scientific American*, 58–65.

Highley, J. R., Esiri, M. M., McDonald, B., Cortina-Borja, M., Herron, B. M., & Crow, T. J. (1999). The size and fibre composition of the corpus callosum with respect to gender and schizophrenia: A post-mortem study. *Brian, 122*, 99–110.

Hines, M., & Kaufman, F. R. (1994). Androgen and the development of human sex-typical behavior: Rough-and-tumble play and sex of preferred playmates in children with congenital adrenal hyperplasi (CAH). *Child Development, 65*, 1042–1053.

Hingson, R., Heeren, T., Zakocs, R. C., Kopstein, A., & Wechsler, H. (2002). Magnitude of alcohol-related mortality and morbidity among U.S. college students ages 18–24. *Journal of Studies on Alcohol, 63*, 136–144.

Hirsch, H. V., & Spinelli, D. N. (1970). Visual experience modifies distribution of horizontally and vertically oriented receptive fields in cats. *Science, 168*, 869–871.

Hirshberg, L. (1990). When infants look to their parents: II. Twelve-month-olds' response to conflicting parental emotional signals. *Child Development, 61*, 1187–1191.

Hirshberg, L., & Svejda, M. (1990). When infants look to their parents: I. Infants' social referencing of mothers compared to fathers. *Child Development, 61*, 1175–1186.

Hirsh-Pasek, K., & Michnick-Golinkoff, R. (1995). *The origins of grammar: Evidence from early language comprehension*. Cambridge, MA: MIT Press.

Hocutt, A. M. (1996). Effectiveness of special education: Is placement the critical factor? *Future of Children, 6*, 77–102.

Hodges, E. V. E., Boivin, M., Vitaro, F., & Bukowski, W. M. (1999). The power of friendship: Protection against an escalating cycle of peer victimization. *Developmental Psychology, 35*, 94–101.

Hofferth, S. L., & Sandberg, J. F. (1998). *Changes in American children's time, 1981–1997*. Ann Arbor: University of Michigan, Institute for Social Research.

Hofferth, S. L., & Sandberg, J. F. (2001). How American children spend their time. *Journal of Marriage and the Family, 63*, 295–308.

Hoffman, D. L., & Novak, T. P. (1998). Bridging the racial divide on the Internet. *Science, 280*, 390–391.

Hoffman, L. W. (1989). Effects of maternal employment in the two-parent family. *American Psychologist, 44*, 283–292.

Hoffman, L. W. (1996). Progress and problems in the study of adolescence. *Developmental Psychology, 32*, 777–780.

Hoge, R. D. (1989). An examination of the giftedness construct. *Canadian Journal of Education, 14*, 6–17.

Hol, T., Van den Berg, C. L., Van Ree, J. M., & Spruijt, B. M. (1999). Isolation during the play period in infancy decreases adult social interactions in rats. *Behavioural Brain Research, 100*, 91–97.

Holahan, C. J., & Moos, R. H. (1987). Personal and contextual determinants of coping strategies. *Journal of Personality and Social Psychology, 52*, 946–955.

Holahan, C. J., & Moos, R. H. (1990). Life stressors, resistance factors, and improved psychological functioning: An extension of the stress resistance paradigm. *Journal of Personality and Social Psychology, 58*, 909–917.

Holden, G. W., & Miller, P. C. (1999). Enduring and different: A meta-analysis of the similarity in parents' child rearing. *Psychological Bulletin, 125*, 223–254.

Holland, J. L. (1973). *Making vocational choices: A theory of careers*. Englewood Cliffs, NJ: Prentice Hall.

Holland, J. L. (1987). Current status of Holland's theory of careers: Another perspective. *Career Development Quarterly, 36*, 24–30.

Holland, N. (1994, August). *Race dissonance: Implications for African American children*. Paper presented at the annual meeting of the American Psychological Association, Los Angeles.

Hollich, G. J., Hirsh-Pasek, K., Golinkoff, R. M., Brand, R. J., Brown, E. C., He, L., et al. (1990). *Leta Stetter Hollingworth: A biography*. Boston: Anker. (Original work published 1943)

Holmes, T. H., & Rahe, R. H. (1967). The Social Readjustment Scale. *Journal of Psychosomatic Research, 11*, 257–261.

Holowka, S., & Petitto, L. A. (2002). Left hemisphere cerebral specialization for babies while babbling. *Science, 297*, 1515.

Holroyd, R., & Sheppard, A. (1997). Parental separation: Effects on children, implications for services. *Child Care, Health and Development, 23*, 369–378.

Holtzman, N. A., Murphy, P. D., Watson, M. S., & Barr, P. A. (1997). Predictive genetic testing: From basic research to clinical practice. *Science, 278*, 602–604.

Holzman, L. (1997). *Schools for growth: Radical alternatives to current educational models*. Mahwah, NJ: Erlbaum.

Hood, B. M., Willen, J. D., & Driver, J. (1998). Adult's eyes trigger shifts of visual attention in human infants. *Psychological Science, 9*, 131–139.

Hopkins, B., & Westra, T. (1989). Maternal expectations of their infants' development: Some cultural differences. *Developmental Medicine and Child Neurology, 31*, 384–390.

Hopkins, B., & Westra, T. (1990). Motor development, maternal expectation, and the role of handling. *Infant Behavior and Development, 13*, 117–122.

Hoptman, M. J., & Davidson, R. J. (1994). How and why do the two cerebral hemispheres interact? *Psychological Bulletin, 116*, 195–219.

Hornik, R., & Gunnar, M. R. (1988). A descriptive analysis of infant social referencing. *Child Development, 59*, 626–634.

Houle, R., & Feldman, R. S. (1991). Emotional displays in children's television programming. *Journal of Nonverbal Behavior, 15*, 261–271.

Howe, M. J. A. (1997). *IQ in question: The truth about intelligence*. Thousand Oaks, CA: Sage.

Howe, M. L., & O'Sullivan, J. T. (1990). The development of strategic memory: Coordinating knowledge, metamemory, and resources. In D. F. Bjorklund (Ed.), *Children's strategies: Contemporary view of cognitive development*. Hillsdale, NJ: Erlbaum.

Howe, N., & Ross, H. S. (1990). Socialization, perspective-taking, and the sibling relationship. *Developmental Psychology, 26*, 160–165.

Howes, C. (1987). Social competence with peers in young children: Developmental sequences. *Developmental Review, 7*, 252–272.

Howes, C., Galinsky, E., & Kontos, S. (1998). Child care caregiver sensitivity and attachment. *Social Development, 7*, 25–36.

Howes, C., Unger, O., & Seidner, L. B. (1989). Social pretend play in toddlers: Parallels with social play and with solitary pretend. *Child Development, 60*, 77–84.

Hsu, L. K. G. (1990). *Eating disorders*. New York: Guilford Press.

Hubel, D. H., & Wiesel, T. N. (1979). Brain mechanisms of vision. *Scientific American*, 150–162.

Hudson, J. A., Sosa, B. B., & Shapiro, L. R. (1997). Scripts and plans: The development of preschool children's event knowledge and event planning. In S. L. Friedman & E. K. Scholnick (Eds.), *The developmental psychology of planning: Why, how, and when do we plan?* Mahwah, NJ: Erlbaum.

Huesmann, L. R. (1986). Psychological processes promoting the relations between exposure to media violence and aggressive behavior by the viewer. *Journal of Social Issues, 42*, 125–139.

Huesmann, L. R., Eron, L. D., Klein, R., Brice, P., & Fischer, P. (1983). Mitigating the imitation of aggressive behaviors by changing children's attitudes about media violence. *Journal of Personality and Social Psychology, 44*, 899–910.

Huesmann, L. R., Moise, J. F., & Podolski, C. (1997). The effects of media violence on the development of antisocial behavior. In D. M. Stoff, J. Breiling, & J. D. Maser (Eds.), *Handbook of antisocial behavior*. New York: Wiley.

Huff, C. O. (1999). Source, recency, and degree of stress in adolescence and suicide ideation. *Adolescence, 34*, 81–89.

Hughes, F. P. (1995). *Children, play, and development* (2nd ed.). Needham Heights, MA: Allyn & Bacon.

Hulanicka, B. (1999). Acceleration of menarcheal age of girls from dysfunctional families. *Journal of Reproductive and Infant Psychology, 17*, 119–132.

Human Genome Project. (1998). Currently available DNA genes test. Washington, DC: U.S. Department of Energy, Office of Biological and Environmental Research.

Hungerford, A., Brownell, C. A., & Campbell, S. B. (2000). Child care in infancy: A transactional perspective. In C. H. Zeanah Jr. (Ed), *Handbook of infant mental health* (2nd ed.). New York: Guilford Press.

Hunt, E., Streissguth, A. P., Kerr, B., & Olson, H. C. (1995). Mothers' alcohol consumption during pregnancy: Effects on spatial-visual reasoning in 14-year-old children. *Psychological Science, 6*, 339–342.

Hunt, M. (1974). *Sexual behaviors in the 1970s*. New York: Dell.

Hunt, M. (1993). *The story of psychology*. New York: Doubleday.

Hunter, J., & Mallon, G. P. (2000). Lesbian, gay, and bisexual adolescent development: Dancing with your feet tied together. In B. Greene, & G. L. Croom (Eds), *Education, research, and practice in lesbian, gay, bisexual, and transgendered psychology: A resource manual* (Vol. 5). Thousand Oaks, CA: Sage.

Huntsinger, C. S., Jose, P. E., Liaw, F., & Ching, W.-D. (1997). Cultural differences in early mathematics learning: A comparison of Euro-American, Chinese-American, and Taiwan-Chinese families. *International Journal of Behavioral Development, 21,* 371–388.

Huston, A. C. (Ed.). (1991). *Children in poverty: Child development and public policy*. Cambridge, England: Cambridge University Press.

Huston, A. C., & Wright, J. C. (1995). *The effects of educational television viewing of lower income preschoolers on academic skills, school readiness, and school adjustment 1 to 3 years later: Report to Children's Television Workshop*. Lawrence: University of Kansas, Department of Human Development, Center for Research on the Influences of Television on Children.

Hyde, J. S. (1994). *Understanding human sexuality* (5th ed.). New York: McGraw-Hill.

Hyde, J. S., Klein, M. H., Essex, M. J., & Clark, R. (1995). Maternity leave and women's mental health. *Psychology of Women Quarterly, 19,* 257–285.

Iacono, W. G., & Grove, W. M. (1993). Schizophrenia reviewed: Toward an integrative genetic model. *Psychological Science, 4,* 273–276.

Ialongo, N. S., Vaden-Kiernan, N., & Kellam, S. G. (1998). Early peer rejection and aggression: Longitudinal relations with adolescent behavior. *Journal of Developmental and Physical Disabilities, 10,* 199–213.

Illingworth, R. S. (1973). *Basic developmental screening: 0–2 years*. Oxford, England: Blackwell Scientific.

Ingersoll, E. W., & Thoman, E. B. (1999). Sleep–wake states of preterm infants: Stability, developmental change, diurnal variation, and relation with caregiving activity. *Child Development, 70,* 1–10.

International Labor Organization (1998). *Maternity leave policies*. Washington, DC: Author.

International Literacy Institute. (2001). *Literacy overview*. Retrieved from http://www.literacyonline.org/explorer/overview.html

Irwin, E. G. (1993). A focused overview of anorexia nervosa and bulimia: I. Etiological issues. *Archives of Psychiatric Nursing, 7,* 342–346.

Isay, R. A. (1990). *Being homosexual: Gay men and their development*. New York: Avon.

Izard, C. E., Frantauzzo, C. A., Castle, J. M., Haynes, O. M., Rayias, M. F., & Putnam, P. H. (1995). The ontogeny and significance of infants' facial expressions in the first 9 months of life. *Developmental Psychology, 31,* 997–1013.

Izard, C. E., & Malatesta, C. (1987). Perspectives on emotional development: I. Differential emotions theory of early emotional development. In J. D. Osofsky (Ed.), *Handbook of infant development*. New York: Wiley.

Jackson, L. A., Gardner, P. D., & Sullivan, L. A. (1992). Explaining gender differences in self-pay expectations: Social comparison standards and perceptions of fair pay. *Journal of Applied Psychology, 77,* 651–663.

Jacobsen, L., & Edmondson, B. (1993, August). Father figures. *American Demographics,* 22–27.

Jacobsen, T. (1999). Effects of postpartum disorders on parenting and on offspring. In L. J. Miller (Ed.), *Postpartum mood disorders*. Washington, DC: American Psychiatric Press.

Jacoby, L. L., & Kelley, C. M. (1992). A process-dissociation framework for investigating unconscious influences: Freudian slips, projective tests, subliminal perception, and signal detection theory. *Current Directions in Psychological Science, 1,* 174–179.

Jacoby, R., & Glauberman, N. (Eds.). (1995). *The bell curve debate*. New York: Times Books/Random House.

Jahoda, G. (1980). Theoretical and systematic approaches in mass-cultural psychology. In H. C. Triandis & W. W. Lambert (Eds.), *Handbook of cross-cultural psychology* (Vol. 1). Needham Heights, MA: Allyn & Bacon.

Jahoda, G. (1983). European "lag" in the development of an economic concept: A study in Zimbabwe. *British Journal of Developmental Psychology, 1,* 113–120.

Jahoda, G., & Lewis, I. M. (1988). *Acquiring culture: Cross-cultural studies in child development*. London: Croom Helm.

James, W. (1950). *The principles of psychology*. New York: Holt. (Original work published 1890)

Jamieson, D. W., Lydon, J. E., Stewart, G., & Zanna, M. P. (1987). Pygmalion revisited: New evidence for student expectancy effects in the classroom. *Journal of Educational Psychology, 79,* 461–466.

Janssens, J. M. A. M., & Dekovic, M. (1997). Child rearing, prosocial moral reasoning, and prosocial behaviour. *International Journal of Behavioural Development, 20,* 509–527.

Jeng, S. F., Yau, K.-I. T., & Teng, R.-J. (1998). Neurobehavioral development at term in very low birthweight infants and normal term infants in Taiwan. *Early Human Development, 51,* 235–245.

Jenkins, J. E. (1996). The influence of peer affiliation and student activities on adolescent drug involvement. *Adolescence, 31,* 297–306.

Jensen, A. (1969). How much can we boost IQ and scholastic achievement? *Harvard Educational Review, 39,* 101–123.

Jiao, S., Ji, G., & Jing, Q. (1996). Cognitive development of Chinese urban only children and children with siblings. *Child Development, 67,* 387–395.

Johnson, A. M., Wadsworth, J., Wellings, K., & Bradshaw, S. (1992). Sexual lifestyles and HIV risk. *Nature, 360,* 410–412.

Johnson, C. H., Vicary, J. R., Heist, C. L., & Corneal, D. A. (2001). Moderate alcohol and tobacco use during pregnancy and child behavior outcomes. *Journal of Primary Prevention, 21,* 367–379.

Johnson, J. L., Primas, P. J., & Coe, M. K. (1994). Factors that prevent women of low socioeconomic status from seeking prenatal care. *Journal of the American Academy of Nurse Practitioners, 6,* 105–111.

Johnson, M. H. (1998). The neural basis of cognitive development. In D. Kuhn & R. S. Siegler (Eds.), *Handbook of child psychology: Vol. 2. Cognition, perception, and language* (5th ed.). New York: Wiley.

Johnson, N. G., Roberts, M. C., & Worell, J. (Eds.). (1999). *Beyond appearance: A new look at adolescent girls*. Washington, DC: American Psychological Association.

Johnson, S. L., & Birch, L. L. (1994). Parents' and children's adiposity and eating style. *Pediatrics, 94,* 653–661.

Johnson, W., Emde, R. N., Pannabecker, B., Stenberg, C., & Davis, M. (1982). Maternal perception of infant emotion from birth through 18 months. *Infant Behavior and Development, 5,* 313–322.

Johnston, C. C. (1989). Pain assessment and management in infants. *Pediatrician, 16,* 16–23.

Johnston, L. D., Bachman, J. G., & O'Malley, P. M. (2000). *Monitoring the Future study*. Lansing: University of Michigan.

Jones, J. M. (1994). Our similarities are different: Toward a psychology of affirmative diversity. In E. J. Trickett, R. J. Watts, & D. Birman (Eds.), *Human diversity: Perspectives on people in context*. San Francisco: Jossey-Bass.

Joseph, R. (1999). Environmental influences on neural plasticity, the limbic system, emotional development, and attachment: A review. *Child Psychiatry and Human Development, 29,* 189–208.

Jost, H., & Songtag, L. (1944). The genetic factor in autonomic nervous system function. *Psychosomatic Medicine, 6,* 308–310.

Jusczyk, P. W. (1997). *The discovery of spoken language*. Cambridge, MA: MIT Press.

Jusczyk, P. W., & Hohne, E. A. (1997, September 26). Infants' memory for spoken words. *Science, 277,* 1894–1896.

Juvonen, J., & Graham, S. (Eds.). (2001). *Peer harassment in school: The plight of the vulnerable and victimized*. New York: Guilford Press.

Kagan, J. (1981). Universals in human development. In R. H. Munroe, R. L. Munroe, & B. B. Whiting (Eds.), *Handbook of crosscultural human development*. New York: Garland.

Kagan, J. (2000, October). Adult personality and early experience. *Harvard Mental Health Letter,* 4–5.

Kagan, J., Arcus, D., & Snidman, N. (1993). The idea of temperament: Where do we go from here? In R. Plomin & G. E. McClearn (Eds.), *Nature, nurture, and psychology*. Washington, DC: American Psychological Association.

Kagan, J., Arcus, D., Snidman, N., Feng, W. Y., Hendler, J., & Greene, S. (1994). Reactivity in infants: A cross-national comparison. *Developmental Psychology, 30,* 342–345.

Kagan, J., Kearsley, R., & Zelazo, P. R. (1978). *Infancy: Its place in human development*. Cambridge, MA: Harvard University Press.

Kagan, J., & Snidman, N. (1991). Infant predictors of inhibited and uninhibited profiles. *Psychological Science, 2,* 40–44.

Kahn, S., Zimmerman, G., Csikszentmihalyi, M., & Getzels, J. W. (1985). Relations between identity in young adulthood and intimacy at midlife. *Journal of Personality and Social Psychology, 49,* 1316–1322.

Kaiser Family Foundation. (2002). *Substance use and sexual health among teens and young adults in the U.S.* San Francisco: Author.

Kaitz, M., Meschulach-Sarfaty, O., Auerbach, J., & Eidelman, A. (1988). A reexamination of newborns' ability to imitate facial expressions. *Developmental Psychology, 24,* 3–7.

Kalichman, S. C. (1998). *Understanding AIDS, second edition: Advances in research and treatment*. Washington, DC: American Psychological Association.

Kalish, C. (1996). Causes and symptoms to preschoolers' conceptions of illness. *Child Development, 67,* 1647–1670.

Kaltiala-Heino, R., Rimpelae, M., Rantanen, P., & Rimpelae, A. (2000). Bullying at school: An indicator of adolescents at risk for mental disorders. *Journal of Adolescence, 23,* 661–674.

Kamhi, A. (1986). The elusive first word: The importance of the naming insight for the development of referential speech. *Journal of Child Language, 13,* 155–161.

Kantrowitz, B., & Wingert, P. (1990, Winter–Spring). Step by step. *Newsweek* [Special issue], 24–34.

Kantrowitz, B., & Wingert, P. (1999, May 10). How well do you know your kid? *Newsweek,* 36.

Kao, G. (2000). Psychological well-being and educational achievement among immigrant youth. In D. J. Hernandez (Ed.), *Children of immigrants: Health, adjustment, and public assistance*. Washington, D.C.: National Academy Press.

Kao, G., & Tienda, M. (1995). Optimism and achievement: The educational performance of immigrant youth. *Social Science Quarterly, 76,* 1–19.

Kaplan, H., & Dove, H. (1987). Infant development among the Ache of eastern Paraguay. *Developmental Psychology, 23,* 190–198.

Kaplan, R. M., Sallis, J. F., Jr., & Patterson, T. L. (1993). *Health and human behavior*. New York: McGraw-Hill.

Karmel, B. Z., Gardner, J. M., & Magnano, C. L. (1991). Attention and arousal in early infancy. In M. J. S. Weiss & P. R. Zelazo (Eds.), *Newborn attention: Biological constraints and the influence of experience*. Norwood, NJ: Ablex.

Karpov, Y. V., & Haywood, H. C. (1998). Two ways to elaborate Vygotsky's concept of mediation: Implications for instruction. *American Psychologist, 53,* 27–36.

Kates, E. (1995). Escaping poverty: The promise of higher education. *Social Policy Report, 9*, 1–21.

Katz, D. L. (2001). Behavior modification in primary care: The pressure system model. *Preventive Medicine, 32*, 66–72.

Katz, L. G. (1989, December). Beginners' ethics. *Parents*, 33–38.

Kauffman, J. M. (1993). How we might achieve the radical reform of special education. *Exceptional Children, 60*, 6–16.

Kaufmann, D., Gesten, E., Santa Lucia, R. C., Salcedo, O., Rendina-Gobioff, G., & Gadd, R. (2000). The relationship between parenting style and children's adjustment: The parents' perspective. *Journal of Child and Family Studies, 9*, 231–245.

Kavale, K. A., & Forness, S. R. (2000). History, rhetoric, and reality: Analysis of the inclusion debate. *Remedial and Special Education, 21*, 279–296.

Kazdin, A. E. (1990). Childhood depression. *Journal of Child Psychology and Psychiatry, 31*, 121–160.

Kazura, K. (2000). Fathers' qualitative and quantitative involvement: An investigation of attachment, play, and social interactions. *Journal of Men's Studies, 9*, 41–57.

Keating, D. P. (1980). Thinking processes in adolescence. In J. Adelson (Ed.), *Handbook of adolescent psychology*. New York: Wiley.

Keating, D. P. (1990). Adolescent thinking. In S. S. Feldman & G. R. Elliott (Eds.), *At the threshold: The developing adolescent*. Cambridge, MA: Harvard University Press.

Keating, D. P., & Clark, L. V. (1980). Development of physical and social reasoning in adolescence. *Developmental Psychology, 16*, 23–30.

Kecskes, I., & Papp, T. (2000). *Foreign language and mother tongue*. Mahwah, NJ: Erlbaum.

Keefer, B. L., Kraus, R. F., Parker, B. L., Elliot, R., & Patton, G. (1991). A state university collaboration program: Residents' prespectives. *Hospital and Community Psychiatry, 42*, 62–66.

Keel, P. K., Leon, G. R., & Fulkerson, J. A. (2000). Vulnerability to eating disorders in childhood and adolescence. In R. E. Ingram & J. M. Price, (Eds.) *Vulnerability to psychopathology: Risk across the life span*. New York: Guilford Press.

Kellam, S. G., Ling, X., Merisca, R., Brown, C. H., & Ialongo, N. S. (1998). The effect of the level of aggression in the first-grade classroom on the course and malleability of aggressive behavior into middle school. *Development and Psychopathology, 10*, 165–185.

Kellogg, R. (1970). Understanding children's art. In P. Cramer (Ed.), *Readings in developmental psychology today*. Del Mar, CA: CRM Books.

Kelly, G. (2001). *Sexuality today: A human perspective* (7th ed.). New York: McGraw-Hill.

Kemper, R. L., & Vernooy, A. R. (1994). Metalinguistic awareness in first graders: A qualitative perspective. *Journal of Psycholinguistic Research, 22*, 41–57.

Kempler, D., Van Lancker, D., Marchman, V., & Bates, E. (1999). Idiom comprehension in children and adults with unilateral brain damage. *Developmental Neuropsychology, 15*, 327–349.

Kenen, R., Smith, A. C. M., Watkins, C., & Zuber-Pittore, C. (2000). To use or not to use: The prenatal genetic technology/worry conundrum. *Journal of Genetic Counseling, 9*, 203–217.

Kerner, M., & Aboud, F. E. (1998). The importance of friendship qualities and reciprocity in a multi-racial school. *Canadian Journal of Research in Early Childhood Education, 7*, 117–125.

Kessen, W. (1979). The American child and other cultural inventions. *American Psychologist, 34*, 815–820.

Kidwell, J. S., Dunyam, R. M., Bacho, R. A., Pastorino, E., & Portes, P. R. (1995). Adolescent identity exploration: A test of Erikson's theory of transitional crisis. *Adolescence, 30*, 785–793.

Kiecolt-Glaser, J. K., & Glaser, R. (1986). Behavioral influences on immune function: Evidence for the interplay between stress and health. In T. M. Field, P. McCabe, & N. Schneiderman (Eds.), *Stress and coping* (Vol. 2). Hillsdale, NJ: Erlbaum.

Kiecolt-Glaser, J. K., & Glaser, R. (1991). Psychosocial factors, stress, disease, and immunity. In R. Ader, D. L. Felten, & N. Cohen (Eds.), *Psychoneuroimmunology*. San Diego, CA: Academic Press.

Kihlstrom, J. F. (1987). The cognitive unconscious. *Science, 237*, 1445–1452.

Kilborne, B. (1995). Of creatures large and small: Size anxiety, psychic size, shame, and the analytic situation. *Psychoanalytic Quarterly, 64*, 672–690.

Killen, M., & Hart, D. (Eds.). (1995). *Morality in everyday life: Developmental perspectives*. New York: Cambridge University Press.

Kim, K., & Smith, P. K. (1999). Family relations in early childhood and reproductive development. *Journal of Reproductive and Infant Psychology, 17*, 133–148.

Kim, K., Smith, P. K., & Palermiti, A. (1997). Conflict in childhood and reproductive development. *Evolution and Human Behavior, 18*, 109–142.

Kim, U., Triandis, H. C., Kagitçibais, Ç., Choi, S., & Yoon, G. (Eds.). (1994). *Individualism and collectivism: Theory, method, and applications*. Thousand Oaks, CA: Sage.

Kim, Y., & Stevens, J. H. (1987). The socialization of prosocial behavior in children. *Childhood Education, 63*, 200–206.

Kimball, J. W. (1983). *Biology* (5th ed.). Reading, MA: Addison-Wesley.

Kinsey, A. C., Pomeroy, W. B., & Martin, C. E. (1948). *Sexual behavior in the human male*. Philadelphia: Saunders.

Kitchener, R. F. (1996). The nature of the social for Piaget and Vygotsky. *Human Development, 39*, 243–249.

Klaczynski, P. A. (1997). Bias in adolescents' everyday reasoning and its relationship with intellectual ability, personal theories, and self-serving motivation. *Developmental Psychology, 33*, 273–283.

Klaus, H. M., & Kennell, J. H. (1976). *Maternal–infant bonding*. St. Louis, MO: Mosby.

Kling, K. C., Hyde, J. S., Showers, C. J., & Buswell, B. N. (1999). Gender differences in self-esteem: A meta-analysis. *Psychological Bulletin, 125*, 470–500.

Klinnert, M. D., McQuaid, E. L., & Gavin, L. A. (1997). Assessing the family asthma management system. *Journal of Asthma, 34*, 77–88.

Kmiec, E. B. (1999). Gene therapy. *American Scientist, 87*, 240–247.

Knecht, S., Deppe, M., Draeger, B., Bobe, L., Lohmann, H., Ringelstein, E. B., et al. (2000). Language lateralization in healthy right-handers. *Brain, 123*, 74–81.

Knight, K. (1994, March). Back to basics. *Essence*, 122–138.

Kochanska, G. (1997). Mutually responsive orientation between mothers and their young children: Implications for early socialization. *Child Development, 68*, 94–112.

Kochanska, G. (1998). Mother–child relationship, child fearfulness, and emerging attachment: A short-term longitudinal study. *Developmental Psychology, 34*, 480–490.

Kohlberg, L. (1966). A cognitive-developmental analysis of children's sex-role concepts and attitudes. In E. E. Maccoby (Ed.), *The development of sex differences*. Stanford, CA: Stanford University Press.

Kohlberg, L. (1969). Stage and sequence: The cognitive-developmental approach to socialization. In D. Goslin (Ed.), *Handbook of socialization theory and research*. Chicago: Rand McNally.

Kohlberg, L. (1975). Counseling and counselor education: A developmental approach. *Counselor Education and Supervision, 14*, 250–256.

Kohlberg, L. (1984). *The psychology of moral development: Essays on moral development* (Vol. 2). San Francisco: Harper & Row.

Kolata, G. (1998). *Clone: The road to Dolly and the path ahead*. New York: Morrow.

Kolb, B. (1989). Brain development, plasticity, and behavior. *American Psychologist, 44*, 1203–1212.

Kolb, B. (1995). *Brain plasticity and behavior*. Mahwah, NJ: Erlbaum.

Kopp, J., & Krakow, J. B. (1982). *Child development in the social context*. Reading, MA: Addison-Wesley.

Korkman, M., Autti-Raemoe, I., Koivulehto, H., & Granstroem, M. L. (1998). Neuropsychological effects at early school age of fetal alcohol exposure of varying duration. *Child Neuropsychology, 4*, 199–212.

Koroukian, S. M., Trisel, B., & Rimm, A. A. (1998). Estimating the proportion of unnecessary cesarean sections in Ohio using birth certificate data. *Journal of Clinical Epidemiology, 51*, 1327–1334.

Kotch, J. B., Browne, D. C., Dufort, V., & Winsor, J. (1999). Predicting child maltreatment in the first 4 years of life from characteristics assessed in the neonatal period. *Child Abuse and Neglect, 23*, 305–319.

Kotre, J., & Hall, E. (1990). *Seasons of life*. Boston: Little, Brown.

Kozulin, A., & Falik, L. (1995). Dynamic cognitive assessment of the child. *Current Directions in Psychological Science, 4*, 192–196.

Krantz, S. G. (1999). Conformal mappings. *American Scientist, 87*, 144.

Kraybill, E. N. (1998). Ethical issues in the care of extremely low birth weight infants. *Seminars in Perinatology, 22*, 207–215.

Kremar, M., & Greene, K. (2000). Connections between violent television exposure and adolescent risk taking. *Media Psychology, 2*, 195–217.

Kroger, J. (2000). *Identity development: Adolescence through adulthood*. Thousand Oaks, CA: Sage.

Kryter, K. D. (1983). Presbycusis, sociocusis, and nosocusis. *Journal of the Acoustical Society of America, 73*, 1897–1917.

Kuczynski, L., & Kochanska, G. (1990). Development of children's noncompliance strategies from toddlerhood to age 5. *Developmental Psychology, 26*, 398–408.

Kuhl, P. K., Andruski, J. E., Chistovich, I. A., Chistovich, L. A., Kozhevnikova, E. V., Ryskina, V. L., et al. (1997). Cross-language analysis of phonetic units in language addressed to infants. *Science, 277*, 684–686.

Kuhn, D. (2000). Metacognitive development. *Current Directions in Psychological Science, 9*, 178–181.

Kuhn, D., Garcia-Mila, M., Zohar, A., & Andersen, C. (1995). Strategies of knowledge acquisition. With commentary by S. H. White, D. Klahr, & S. M. Carver and a reply by D. Kuhn. *Monographs of the Society for Research in Child Development, 60*, 122–137.

Kupfersmid, J., & Wonderly, D. (1980). Moral maturity and behavior: Failure to find a link. *Journal of Youth and Adolescence, 9*, 249–261.

Kurtines, W. M., & Gewirtz, J. L. (1987). *Moral development through social interaction*. New York: Wiley.

La Fromboise, T., Coleman, H. L., & Gerton, J. (1993). Psychological impact of biculturalism: Evidence and theory. *Psychological Bulletin, 114*, 395–412.

Labouvie-Vief, G. (1980). Beyond formal operations: Uses and limits of pure logic in life-span development. *Human Development, 23*, 141–161.

Labouvie-Vief, G. (1986). Modes of knowledge and the organization of development. In M. L. Commons, L. Kohlberg, F. Richards, & J. Sinnott (Eds.), *Beyond formal operations: Vol. 3. Models and methods in the study of adult and adolescent thought*. New York: Praeger.

Ladd, G. W. (1983). Social networks of popular, average, and rejected children in social settings. *Merrill-Palmer Quarterly, 29*, 282–307.

Lafuente, M. J., Grifol, R., Segarra, J., & Soriano, J. (1997). Effects of the Firstart method of prenatal stimulation on psychomotor development: The first six months. *Pre- and Perinatal Psychology, 11,* 151–162.

Lamaze, F. (1970). *Painless childbirth: The Lamaze method.* Chicago: Regnery.

Lamb, M. E. (1977). The development of mother–infant and father–infant attachments in the second year of life. *Developmental Psychology, 13,* 637–648.

Lamb, M. E. (1982a). The bonding phenomenon: Misinterpretations and their implications. *Journal of Pediatrics, 101,* 555–557.

Lamb, M. E. (1982b). Paternal influences on early socioemotional development. *Journal of Child Psychology and Psychiatry and Allied Disciplines, 23,* 185–190.

Lamb, M. E. (Ed.). (1986). *The father's role: Applied perspectives.* New York: Wiley.

Lamb, M. E. (1987). Predictive implications of individual differences in attachment. *Journal of Consulting and Clinical Psychology, 55,* 817–824.

Lamb, M. E. (1994). Infant care practices and the application of knowledge. In C. B. Fisher & R. M. Lerner (Eds.), *Applied developmental psychology.* New York: McGraw-Hill.

Lamb, M. E., Morrison, D. C., & Malkin, C. M. (1987). The development of infant social expectations in face-to-face interaction. *Merrill-Palmer Quarterly, 33,* 241–254.

Lamb, M. E., Sternberg, R. J., Hwang, C. P., & Broberg, A. G. (Eds.). (1992). *Child care in context: Cross-cultural perspectives.* Hillsdale, NJ: Erlbaum.

Lambert, W. E., & Peal, E. (1972). The relation of bilingualism to intelligence. In A. S. Dil (Ed.), *Language, psychology, and culture* (3rd ed.). New York: Wiley.

Lamorey, S., Robinson, B. E., & Rowland, B. H. (1998). *Latchkey kids: Unlocking doors for children and their families.* Newbury Park, CA: Sage.

Lander, E. S., & Schork, N. J. (1994). Genetic dissection of complex traits. *Science, 265,* 2037–2048.

Landine, J., & Stewart, J. (1998). Relationship between metacognition, motivation, locus of control, self-efficacy, and academic achievement. *Canadian Journal of Counselling, 32,* 200–212.

Lane, W. K. (1976). The relationship between personality and differential academic achievement within a group of highly gifted and high achieving children. *Dissertation Abstracts International, 37*(5A), 2746.

Lang, A. A. (1999, June 13). Doctors are second-guessing the "miracle" of multiple births. *New York Times,* p. WH4.

Lanphear, B. P. (1998). The paradox of lead poisoning prevention. *Science, 281,* 1617–1618.

Lansford, J. E., & Parker, J. G. (1999). Children's interactions in triads: Behavioral profiles and effects of gender and patterns of friendships among members. *Developmental Psychology, 35,* 80–93.

Lanza, R. P., Cibelli, J. B., Faber, D., Sweeney, R. W., Henderson, B., Nevala, W., et al. (2001). Cloned cattle can be healthy and normal. *Science, 294,* 1893–1894.

Larson, R. W., Richards, M. H., Moneta, G., Holmbeck, G., & Duckett, E. (1996). Changes in adolescents' daily interactions with their families from ages 10 to 18: Disengagement and transformation. *Developmental Psychology, 32,* 744–754.

Larsson, B., & Melin, L. (1992). Prevalence and short-term stability of depressive symptoms in school children. *Acta Psychiatrica Scandinavica, 85,* 17–22.

Larwood, L., Szwajkowski, E., & Rose, S. (1988). Sex and race discrimination resulting from manager–client relationships: Applying the rational bias theory of managerial discrimination. *Sex Roles, 18,* 9–29.

Lattibeaudiere, V. H. (2000). An exploratory study of the transition and adjustment of former home-schooled students to college life. *Dissertation Abstracts International, 61A,* 2211.

Lau, S., & Kwok, L. K. (2000). Relationship of family environment to adolescents' depression and self-concept. *Social Behavior and Personality, 28,* 41–50.

Lauricella, T. (2001, November). The education of a home schooler. *Smart Money,* 115–121.

Laursen, B., Coy, K. C., & Collins, W. A. (1998). Reconsidering changes in parent–child conflict across adolescence: A meta-analysis. *Child Development, 69,* 817–832.

Laursen, B., Hartup, W. W., & Koplas, A. L. (1996). Toward understanding peer conflict. *Merrill-Palmer Quarterly, 42,* 76–102.

Lavelli, M., & Poli, M. (1998). Early mother–infant interaction during breast- and bottle-feeding. *Infant Behavior and Development, 21,* 667–683.

Le Vay, S. (1993). *The sexual brain.* Cambridge, MA: MIT Press.

Le Vine, R. E., Dixon, S., Le Vine, S., Richman, A., Leiderman, P. H., et al. (1994). *Child care and culture: Lessons from Africa.* New York: Cambridge University Press.

Leaper, C., Anderson, K. J., & Sanders, P. (1998). Moderators of gender effects on parents' talk to their children: A meta-analysis. *Developmental Psychology, 34,* 3–27.

Leary, W. E. (1996, November 20). U.S. rate of sexual diseases highest in developed world. *New York Times,* p. C1.

Leavitt, L. A., & Goldson, E. (1996). Biomedicine and developmental psychology: New areas of common ground. *Developmental Psychology, 32,* 387–389.

Leboyer, F. (1975). *Birth without violence.* New York: Knopf.

Lecanuet, J.-P., Granier-Deferre, C., & Busnel, M.-C. (1995). Human fetal auditory perception. In J.-P. Lecanuet, W. P. Fifer, N. A. Krasnegor, & W. P. Smotherman (Eds.), *Fetal development: A psychobiological perspective.* Hillsdale, NJ: Erlbaum.

Lecours, A. R. (1982). Correlates of developmental behavior in brain maturation. In T. Bever (Ed.), *Regressions in mental development.* Hillsdale, NJ: Erlbaum.

Lee, J. (1997). Never innocent: Breasted experiences in women's bodily narratives of puberty. *Feminism and Psychology, 7,* 453–474.

Lee, K., & Homer, B. (1999). Children as folk psychologists: The developing understanding of the mind. In A. Slater & D. Muir (Eds.), *The Blackwell reader in development psychology.* Malden, MA: Blackwell.

Lee, V. E., Loeb, S., & Lubeck, S. (1998). Contextual effects of prekindergarten classrooms for disadvantaged children on cognitive development: The case of Chapter 1. *Child Development, 69,* 479–494.

Lefkowitz, E. S., Sigman, M., & Au, T. K. (2000). Helping mothers discuss sexuality and AIDS with adolescents. *Child Development, 71,* 1383–1394.

Legerstee, M. (1998). Mental and bodily awareness in infancy: Consciousness of self-existence. *Journal of Consciousness Studies, 5,* 627–644.

Legerstee, M., Anderson, D., & Schaffer, A. (1998). Five- and eight-month-old infants recognize their faces and voices as familiar and social stimuli. *Child Development, 69,* 37–50.

Leitenberg, H., Detzer, M. J., & Srebnik, D. (1993). Gender differences in masturbation and the relation of masturbation experience in preadolescence and/or early adolescence to sexual behavior and sexual adjustment in young adulthood. *Archives of Sexual Behavior, 22,* 87–98.

Leiter, J., & Johnsen, M. C. (1997). Child maltreatment and school performance declines: An event-history analysis. *American Educational Research Journal, 34,* 563–589.

Lelwica, M., & Haviland, J. (1983). *Ten-week-old infants' reactions to mothers' emotional expressions.* Paper presented at the biennial meeting of the Society for Research in Child Development.

Lemery, K. S., Goldsmith, H. H., Klinnert, M. D., & Mrazek, D. A. (1999). Developmental models of infant and childhood temperament. *Developmental Psychology, 35,* 189–204.

Lemonick, M. D. (2000, October 30). Teens before their time. *Time,* 68–74.

Lenssen, B. G. (1973). Infants' reactions to peer strangers. *Dissertation Abstracts International, 33,* 60–62.

Leonard, C. M., Lombardino, L. J., Mercado, L. R., Browd, S. R., Breier, J. I., & Agee, O. F. (1996). Cerebral asymmetry and cognitive development in children: A magnetic resonance imaging study. *Psychological Science, 7,* 89–95.

Leonard, L. B. (1998). *Children with specific language impairment.* Cambridge, MA: MIT Press.

Lepore, S. J., Palsane, M. N., & Evans, G. W. (1991). Daily hassles and chronic strains: A hierarchy of stressors? *Social Science and Medicine, 33,* 1029–1036.

Lerner, R. M. (2002). *Concepts and theories of human development* (3rd ed.). Mahwah, NJ: Erlbaum.

Lerner, R. M., Fisher, C. B., & Weinberg, R. A. (2000). Toward a science for and of the people: Promoting civil society through the application of developmental science. *Child Development, 71,* 11–20.

Leslie, C. (1991, February 11). Classrooms of Babel. *Newsweek,* 56–57.

Levano, K. J., Cunningham, F. G., Nelson, S., Roark, M., Williams, M. L., Guzick, D., et al. (1986). A prospective comparison of selective and universal electronic fetal monitoring in 34,995 pregnancies. *New England Journal of Medicine, 315,* 615–619.

Levine, L. E., & Waite, B. M. (2000). Television viewing and attentional abilities in fourth- and fifth-grade children. *Journal of Applied Developmental Psychology, 21,* 667–679.

Levine, S. C., Huttenlocher, J., Taylor, A., & Langrock, A. (1999). Early sex differences in spatial skill. *Developmental Psychology, 35,* 940–949.

Leviton, A., Bellinger, D., Allred, E. N., Rabinowitz, M., Needleman, H., & Schoenbaum, S. (1993). Pre- and postnatal low-level lead exposure and children's dysfunction in school. *Environmental Research, 60,* 30–43.

Levy, D. H. (2000, August 20). Are you ready for the genome miracle? *Parade,* 8–10.

Levy, G. D., Barth, J. M., & Zimmerman, B. J. (1998). Associations among cognitive and behavioral aspects of preschoolers' gender role development. *Journal of Genetic Psychology, 159,* 121–126.

Lewin, T. (1995, May 11). Women are becoming equal providers: Half of working women bring home half the household income. *New York Times,* p. A14.

Lewinsohn, P. M., Roberts, R. E., Seeley, J. R., & Rohde, P. (1994). Adolescent psychopathology: II. Psychosocial risk factors for depression. *Journal of Abnormal Psychology, 103,* 302–315.

Lewinsohn, P. M., Rohde, P., & Seeley, J. R. (1994). Psychosocial risk factors for future adolescent suicide attempts. *Journal of Consulting and Clinical Psychology, 62,* 297–305.

Lewis, C., & Mitchell, P. (Eds.). (1994). *Children's early understanding of mind: Origins and development.* Hillsdale, NJ: Erlbaum.

Lewis, D. O., Yeager, C. A., Loveley, R., Stein, A., & Cobham-Portorreal, C. S. (1994). A clinical follow-up of delinquent males: Ignored vulnerabilities, unmet needs, and the perpetuation of violence. *Journal of the American Academy of Child and Adolescent Psychiatry, 33,* 518–528.

Lewis, M. (1998). *Altering fate: Why the past does not predict the future.* New York: Guilford Press.

Lewis, M., Feiring, C., & Rosenthal, S. (2000). Attachment over time. *Child Development, 71,* 707–720.

Lewis, T. E., & Phillipsen, L. C. (1998). Interactions on an elementary school playground: Variations by age, gender, race, group size, and playground area. *Child Study Journal, 28,* 309–320.

Lewkowicz, D. J., & Lickliter, R. (Eds.). (2002). *Conceptions of development: Lessons from the laboratory.* New York: Psychology Press.

Leyens, J. P., Camino, L., Parke, R. D., & Berkowitz, L. (1975). Effects of movie violence on aggression in a field setting as a function of group dominance and cohesion. *Journal of Personality and Social Psychology, 32,* 346–360.

Lickliter, R., & Bahrick, L. E. (2000). The development of infant intersensory perception: Advantages of a comparative convergent-operations approach. *Psychological Bulletin, 126,* 260–280.

Liebert, R. M., & Sprafkin, J. (1988). *The early window: Effects of television on children and youth* (3rd ed.). New York: Pergamon.

Lightfoot, C. (1997). *The culture of adolescent risk-taking.* New York: Guilford Press.

Lillard, A. (1998). Ethnopsychologies: Cultural variations in theories of mind. *Psychological Bulletin, 123,* 3–32.

Lillo-Martin, D. (1997). In support of the language acquisition device. In M. Marschark, P. Siple, D. Lillo-Martin, R. Campbell, & V. S. Everhart (Eds.), *Relations of language and thought: The view from sign language and deaf children.* New York: Oxford University Press.

Lindholm, K. J. (1991). Two-way bilingual/immersion education: Theory, conceptual issues, and pedagogical implications. In R. V. Padilla & A. Benavides (Eds.), *Critical perspectives on bilingual education research.* Tempe, AZ: Bilingual Review Press.

Lines, P. M. (2001). Home schooling. *ERIC Digest, EDO-EA-01–08,* 1–4.

Linn, M. C. (1997). Finding patterns in international assessments. *Science, 277,* 1743.

Linz, D. G., Donnerstein, E., & Penrod, S. (1988). Effects of long-term exposure to violent and sexually degrading depictions of women. *Journal of Personality and Social Psychology, 55,* 758–768.

Lipman, J. (1992, March 10). Surgeon General says it's high time Joe Camel quit. *Wall Street Journal,* pp. B1, B7.

Lipsitt, L. P. (1986). Learning in infancy: Cognitive development in babies. *Journal of Pediatrics, 109,* 172–182.

Liskin, L. (1985, November–December). Youth in the 1980s: Social and health concerns: 4. *Population Reports, 8.*

Litovsky, R. Y., & Ashmead, D. H. (1997). Development of binaural and spatial hearing in infants and children. In R. H. Gilkey & T. R. Andersen (Eds.), *Binaural and spatial hearing in real and virtual environments.* Mahwah, NJ: Erlbaum.

Little, T. D., & Lopez, D. F. (1997). Regularities in the development of children's causality beliefs about school performance across six sociocultural contexts. *Developmental Psychology, 33,* 165–175.

Livson, N., & Peskin, H. (1980). Perspectives on adolescence from longitudinal research. In J. Adelson (Ed.), *Handbook of adolescent psychology.* New York: Wiley.

Lloyd, B., & Duveen, G. (1991). Expressing social gender identities in the first year of school. *European Journal of Psychology of Education, 6,* 437–447.

Lobel, T. E., Bar-David, E., Gruber, R., Lau, S., & Bar-Tal, Y. (2000). Gender schema and social judgments: A developmental study of children from Hong Kong. *Sex Roles, 43,* 19–42.

Locke, J. L. (1983). *Phonological acquisition and change.* New York: Academic Press.

Locke, J. L. (1994). Phases in the child's development of language. *American Scientist, 82,* 436–445.

Loehlin, J. C. (1992). *Genes and environment in personality development.* Newbury Park, CA: Sage.

Loftus, E. F. (1997, September). Creating false memories. *Scientific American,* 71–75.

Lohr, S. (1995, June 18). The Net: It's hard to clean up. *New York Times,* sec. 4, p. 6.

Lohr, S. (1996, March 13). Plan to block censorship on Internet: Preemptory effort at self-policing. *New York Times,* p. D4.

Long, T., & Long, L. (1983). *Latchkey children.* New York: Penguin.

Lorenz, K. (1957). Companionship in bird life. In C. Scholler (Ed.), *Instinctive behavior.* New York: International Universities Press.

Lorenz, K. (1965). *Evolution and modification of behavior.* Chicago: University of Chicago Press.

Lorenz, K. (1966). *On aggression.* New York: Harcourt.

Lorenz, K. (1974). *Civilized man's eight deadly sins.* New York: Harcourt.

Lorenzo-Hernandez, J., & Ouiellette, S. C. (1998). Ethnic identity, self-esteem, and values in Dominicans, Puerto Ricans, and African Americans. *Journal of Applied Social Psychology, 28,* 2007–2024.

Lorion, R. P., Iscoe, I., De Leon, P. H., & Vanden Bos, G. R. (Eds.). (1996). *Psychology and public policy: Balancing public service and professional need.* Washington, DC: American Psychological Association.

Lourenco, O., & Machado, A. (1996). In defense of Piaget's theory: A reply to 10 common criticisms. *Psychological Review, 103,* 143–164.

Lowrey, G. H. (1986). *Growth and development of children* (8th ed.). Chicago: Year Book.

Lozoff, B., Wolf, A. W., & Davis, N. S. (1985). Sleep problems seen in pediatric practice. *Pediatrics, 75,* 477–483.

Lust, B., Suner, M., & Whitman, J. (Eds.). (1995). *Syntactic theory and first language acquisition.* Hillsdale, NJ: Erlbaum.

Luster, T., & McAdoo, H. P. (1994). Factors related to the achievement and adjustment of young African American children. *Child Development, 65,* 1080–1094.

Lykken, D. T., Bouchard, T. J., Jr., McGue, M., & Tellegen, A. (1993). Heritability of interests: A twin study. *Journal of Applied Psychology, 78,* 649–661.

Lyman, D. R. (1996). Early identification of chronic offenders: Who is the fledgling psychopath? *Psychological Bulletin, 120,* 209–234.

Lyman, D. R., Milich, R., Zimmerman, R., Novak, S. P., Logan, T. K., Martin, C., et al. (1999). Project DARE: No effects at 10-year follow-up. *Journal of Consulting and Clinical Psychology, 67,* 590–593.

Lyon, M. E., Benoit, M., O'Donnell, R. M., Getson, P. R., Silber, T., & Walsh, T. (2000). Assessing African American adolescents' risk for suicide attempts: Attachment theory. *Adolescence, 35,* 121–134.

Lysynchuk, L. M., Pressley, M. & Vye, N. J. (1990). Reciprocal teaching improves standardized reading-comprehension performance in poor comprehenders. *Elementary School Journal, 90,* 469–484.

Maccoby, E. E. (1980). *Social development: Psychological growth and the parent–child relationship.* New York: Harcourt.

Maccoby, E. E. (1990). The role of gender identity and gender constancy in sex-differentiated development. In D. Schrader (Ed.), *The legacy of Lawrence Kohlberg* (New Directions for Child Development, No. 47). San Francisco: Jossey-Bass.

Maccoby, E. E. (1999). *The two sexes: Growing up apart, coming together.* New York: Belknap.

MacDorman, M. F., Minino, A. M., Strobino, D. M., & Guyer, B. (2002). Annual summary of vital statistics, 2001. *Pediatrics, 110,* 1037–1052.

Mackey, M. C. (1990). Women's preparation for the childbirth experience. *Maternal–Child Nursing Journal, 19,* 143–173.

MacPhee, D., Kreutzer, J. C., & Fritz, J. J. (1994). Infusing a diversity perspective into human development courses. *Child Development, 65,* 699–715.

MacWhinney, B. (1991). Connectionism as a framework for language acquisition. In J. Miller (Ed.), *Research on child language disorders.* Austin, TX: Pro-Ed.

Mael, F. A. (1998). Single-sex and coeducational schooling: Relationships to socioemotional and academic development. *Review of Education Research, 68,* 101–129.

Mahoney, M. C., & James, D. M. (2000). Predictors of anticipated breastfeeding in an urban, low income setting. *Journal of Family Practice, 49,* 529–533.

Maiden, A. H. (1997). Celebrating a return to earth: Birth in indigenous aboriginal, Tibetan, Balinese, Basque and Cherokee cultures. *Pre- and Perinatal Psychology Journal, 11,* 251–264.

Mandel, D. R., Jusczyk, P. W., & Pisoni, D. B. (1995). Infants' recognition of the sound patterns of their own names. *Psychological Science, 6,* 314–317.

Mandler, J. M. (1990). A new perspective on cognitive development in infancy. *American Scientist, 78,* 236–243.

Mandler, J. M., & McDonough, L. (1994). Long-term recall of event sequences in infancy. *Journal of Experimental Child Psychology, 59,* 457–474.

Mangelsdorf, S., Gunnar, M., Kestenbaum, R., Lang, S., & Andreas, D. (1990). Infant proneness to distress temperament, maternal personality, and mother–infant attachment: Association and goodness of fit. *Child Development, 61,* 820–831.

Maratsos, M. P. (1983). Some current issues in the study of the acquisition of grammar. In P. H. Mussen (Ed.), *Handbook of child psychology* (Vol. 3, 4th ed.). New York: Wiley.

Marcia, J. E. (1966). Development and validation of ego identity status. *Journal of Personality and Social Psychology, 3,* 551–558.

Marcia, J. E. (1980). Identity in adolescence. In J. Adelson (Ed.), *Handbook of adolescent psychology.* New York: Wiley.

Marcus, G. F., Fijayan, S., Bandi Rao, S., & Vishon, P. M. (1999). Rule learning by seven-month-old infants. *Science, 283,* 77–80.

Markus, H. R., & Kitayama, S. (1991). Culture and the self: Implications for cognition, emotion, and motivation. *Psychological Review, 98,* 224–253.

Marlier, L., Schaal, B., & Soussignan, R. (1998). Neonatal responsiveness to the odor of amniotic and lacteal fluids: A test of perinatal chemosensory continuity. *Child Development, 69,* 611–623.

Marsh, H. W. (1990). Influences of internal and external frames of reference on the formation of math and English self-concepts. *Journal of Educational Psychology, 82,* 107–116.

Marsh, H. W., Craven, R., & Debus, R. (1998). Structure, stability, and development of young children's self-concepts: A multicohort, multioccasion study. *Child Development, 69,* 1030–1053.

Marsh, H. W., & Holmes, I. W. M. (1990). Multidimensional self-concepts: Construct validation of responses by children. *American Educational Research Journal, 27,* 89–118.

Marsh, H. W., & Parker, J. W. (1984). Determinants of student self-concept: Is it better to be a relatively large fish in a small pond even if you don't learn to swim as well? *Journal of Personality and Social Psychology, 47,* 213–231.

Marsh, H. W., & Shavelson, R. (1985). Self-concept: Its multifaceted, hierarchical structure. *Educational Psychologist, 20,* 107–123.

Marshall, E. (2000). Duke study faults overuse of stimulants for children. *Science, 289,* 721.

Martin, B. A. (1989). Gender differences in salary expectations. *Psychology of Women Quarterly, 13,* 87–96.

Martin, C. L. (1993). New directions for investigating children's gender knowledge. *Developmental Review, 13,* 184–204.

Martin, C. L. (2000). Cognitive theories of gender development. In T. Eckes & H. M. Trautner (Eds.), *The developmental social psychology of gender.* Mahwah, NJ: Erlbaum.

Martin, G. B., & Clark, R. D. (1982). Distress crying in neonates: Species and peer specificity. *Developmental Psychology, 18,* 3–9.

Martin, J. A., Maccoby, E. E., & Jacklin, C. N. (1981). Mothers' responsiveness to interactive bidding and nonbidding in boys and girls. *Child Development, 52,* 1064–1067.

Martin, J. A. & Park, M. M. (1999, September 14). Trends in twin and triplet births, 1980–1997. *National Vital Statistics Reports*, 1–17.

Martinez, R., & Dukes, R. L. (1991). Ethnic and gender differences in self-esteem. *Youth and Society, 22,* 318–338.

Marx, J. (1999). How stimulant drugs may calm hyperactivity. *Science, 283,* 1919–1920.

Marx, M. B., Garrity, T. F., & Bowers, F. R. (1975). The influence of recent life experience on the health of college freshmen. *Journal of Psychosomatic Research, 19,* 87–98.

Masataka, N. (1996). Perception of motherese in a signed language by 6-month-old deaf infants. *Developmental Psychology, 32,* 874–879.

Masataka, N. (1998). Perception of motherese in Japanese sign language by 6-month-old hearing infants. *Developmental Psychology, 34,* 241–246.

Masataka, N. (2000). The role of modality and input in the earliest stage of language acquisition: Studies of Japanese sign language. In C. Chamberlain (Ed.), *Language acquisition by eye.* Mahwah, NJ: Erlbaum.

Mash, E. J., & Barkley, R. A. (1998). *Treatment of childhood disorders* (2nd ed.). New York: Guilford Press.

Masling, J. M., & Bornstein, R. F. (Eds.). (1996). *Psychoanalytic perspectives on developmental psychology.* Washington, DC: American Psychological Association.

Mathew, A., & Cook, M. L. (1990). The control of reaching movements by young infants. *Child Development, 61,* 1238–1257.

Mathews, J. J., & Zadak, K. (1991). The alternative birth movement in the United States: History and current status. *Women and Health, 17,* 39–56.

Mathews, J. R., Friman, P. C., Barone, V. J., Ross, L. V., & Christophersen, E. R. (1987). Decreasing dangerous infant behaviors through parent instruction. *Journal of Applied Behavior Analysis, 20,* 165–169.

Matlin, M. M. (1987). *The psychology of women.* New York: Holt.

Matson, J. L., & Mulick, J. A. (Eds.). (1991). *Handbook of mental retardation* (2nd ed.). New York: Pergamon.

Matusov, E., & Hayes, R. (2000). Sociocultural critique of Piaget and Vygotsky. *New Ideas in Psychology, 18,* 215–239.

Mauthner, N. S. (1999). "Feeling low and feeling really bad about feeling low": Women's experiences of motherhood and postpartum depression. *Canadian Psychology, 40,* 143–161.

Maxfield, M. G., & Widom, C. S. (1996). The cycle of violence. *Archives of Pediatrics and Adolescent Medicine, 150,* 390–395.

Mayberry, R. I., & Nicoladis, E. (2001). Gesture reflects language development: Evidence from bilingual children. *Current Directions in Psychological Science, 9,* 192–195.

Mayer, J. D. (2001). Emotion, intelligence, and emotional intelligence. In J. P. Forgas (Ed.), *Handbook of affect and social cognition.* Mahwah, NJ: Erlbaum.

Mayer, J. D., Salovey, P., & Caruso, D. R. (2000). Emotional intelligence as zeitgeist, as personality, and as a mental ability. In R. Bar-On & J. D. A. Parker (Eds.), *The handbook of emotional intelligence: Theory, development, assessment, and application at home, school, and in the workplace.* San Francisco: Jossey-Bass.

Mayseless, O. (1996). Attachment patterns and their outcomes. *Human Development, 39,* 206–223.

McAuliffe, S. P., & Knowlton, B. J. (2001). Hemispheric differences in object identification. *Brain and Cognition, 45,* 119–128.

McCabe, M. (1984). Toward a theory of adolescent dating. *Adolescence, 19,* 159–169.

McCall, R. B. (1979). *Infants.* Cambridge, MA: Harvard University Press.

McCartney, K. (1984). Effect of quality of day care environment on children's language development. *Developmental Psychology, 20,* 244–260.

McCarty, M., & Ashmead, D. H. (1999). Visual control of reaching and grasping in infants. *Developmental Psychology, 35,* 620–631.

McClelland, D. C. (1993). Intelligence is not the best predictor of job performance. *Current Directions in Psychological Research, 2,* 5–8.

McCrae, R. R., Costa, P. T., Jr., Ostendorf, F., Angleitner, A., Hebíková, M., Avia, M. D., et al. (2000). Nature over nurture: Temperament, personality, and life span development. *Journal of Personality and Social Psychology, 78,* 173–186.

McDonald, M. A., Sigman, M., Espinosa, M. P., & Neumann, C. G. (1994). Impact of a temporary food shortage on children and their mothers. *Child Development, 65,* 404–415.

McGreal, D., Evans, B. J., & Burrows, G. D. (1997). Gender differences in coping following loss of a child through miscarriage or stillbirth: A pilot study. *Stress Medicine, 13,* 159–165.

McGue, M., Bouchard, T. J., Jr., Iacono, W., & Lykken, D. T. (1993). Behavioral genetics of cognitive ability: A life-span perspective. In R. Plomin & G. E. McClearn (Eds.), *Nature, nurture, and psychology.* Washington, DC: American Psychological Association.

McGuffin, P., Riley, B., & Plomin, R. (2001). Toward behavioral genomics. *Science, 291,* 1223–1249.

McKenna, J. J. (1983). Primate aggression and evolution: An overview of sociobiological and anthropological perspectives. *Bulletin of the American Academy of Psychiatry and the Law, 11,* 105–130.

McKenzie, R. B. (1997). Orphanage alumni: How they have done and how they evaluate their experience. *Child and Youth Care Forum, 26,* 87–111.

McWhirter, D. P., Sanders, S., & Reinisch, J. M. (1990). *Homosexuality, heterosexuality: Concepts of sexual orientation.* New York: Oxford University Press.

Mead, M. (1942). *Environment and education.* Symposium held in connection with the 50th anniversary celebration of the University of Chicago.

Mealey, L. (2000). *Sex differences: Developmental and evolutionary strategies.* Orlando, FL: Academic Press.

Meece, J. L. (1997). *Child and adolescent development for educators.* New York: McGraw-Hill.

Meece, J. L., & Kurtz-Costes, B. (2001). Introduction: The schooling of ethnic minority children and youth. *Educational Psychologist, 36,* 1–7.

Meeus, W. (1996). Studies on identity development in adolescence: An overview of research and some new data. *Journal of Youth and Adolescence, 25,* 569–598.

Mehler, J., & Dupoux, E. (1994). *What infants know: The new cognitive science of early development.* Cambridge, MA: Blackwell.

Mehran, K. (1997). Interferences in the move from adolescence to adulthood: The development of the male. In M. Laufer (Ed.), *Adolescent breakdown and beyond.* London: Karnac.

Meisels, S. J., & Plunkett, J. W. (1988). Developmental consequences of preterm birth: Are there long-term deficits? In P. B. Baltes, D. L. Featherman, & R. M. Lerner (Eds.), *Lifespan development and behavior* (Vol. 9). Hillsdale, NJ: Erlbaum.

Meiser, B., & Dunn, S. (2000). Psychological impact of genetic testing for Huntington's disease: An update of the literature. *Journal of Neurology, Neurosurgery and Psychiatry, 69,* 574–578.

Meltzoff, A. N. (1981). Imitation, intermodal coordination and representation in early infancy. In G. Butterworth (Ed.), *Infancy and epistemology.* Brighton, England: Harvester Press.

Meltzoff, A. N., & Moore, M. K. (1977). Imitation of facial and manual gestures by human neonates. *Science, 198,* 75–78.

Meltzoff, A. N., & Moore, M. K. (1989). Imitation in newborn infants: Exploring the range of gestures imitated and the underlying mechanisms. *Developmental Psychology, 25,* 954–962.

Meltzoff, A. N., & Moore, M. K. (1994). Imitation, memory, and the representation of persons. *Infant Behavior and Development, 17,* 83–99.

Meltzoff, A. N., & Moore, M. K. (1999). Persons and representation: Why infant imitation is important for theories of human development. In J. Nadel & G. Butterworth (Eds.), *Imitation in infancy.* New York: Cambridge University Press.

Mendelowitz, D. (1998). Nicotine excites cardiac vagal neurons via three sites of action. *Clinical and Experimental Pharmacology and Physiology, 25,* 453–456.

Mendelson, B. K., White, D. R., & Mendelson, M. J. (1996). Self-esteem and body esteem: Effects of gender, age, and weight. *Journal of Applied Developmental Psychology, 17,* 321–346.

Menella, J. (2000, June). *The psychology of eating.* Paper presented at the annual meeting of the American Psychological Society, Miami, FL.

Mercer, C. (1992). *Students with learning disabilities* (4th ed.). Columbus, OH: Merrill.

Mercer, J. R. (1973). *Labeling the mentally retarded.* Berkeley: University of California Press.

Meredith, H. V. (1971). Growth in body size: A compendium of findings on contemporary children living in different parts of the world. *Child Development and Behavior, 6,* 153–238.

Messinger, D. S. (2002). Positive and negative: Infant facial expressions and emotions. *Current Directions in Psychological Science, 11,* 1–6.

Messinger, D. S., & Fogel, A. (1998). Give and take: The development of conventional infant gestures. *Merrill-Palmer Quarterly, 44,* 566–590.

Meyer-Bahlburg, H. F. L., Ehrhardt, A. A., Rosen, L. R., Gruen, R. S., Veridiano, N. P., Vann, F. H., et al. (1995). Prenatal estrogens and the development of homosexual orientation. *Developmental Psychology, 31,* 12–21.

Meyerhoff, M. K., & White, B. L. (1986, September). Making the grade as parents. *Psychology Today,* 38–45.

Michael, R. T., Gagnon, J. H., Laumann, E. O., & Kolata, G. (1994). *Sex in America: A definitive survey.* Boston: Little, Brown.

Michel, G. L. (1981). Right-handedness: A consequence of infant supine head-orientation preference? *Science, 212,* 685–687.

Midlarsky, E., & Bryan, J. H. (1972). Affect expressions and children's imitative altruism. *Journal of Experimental Research in Personality, 6,* 195–203.

Mikhail, B. (2000). Prenatal care utilization among low-income African American women. *Journal of Community Health Nursing, 17,* 235–246.

Milerad, J., Vege, A., Opdal, S. H., & Rognum, T. O. (1998). Objective measurements of nicotine exposure in victims of sudden infant death syndrome and in other unexpected child deaths. *Journal of Pediatrics, 133,* 232–236.

Miller, C. A. (1987). A review of maternity care programs in western Europe. *Family Planning Perspectives, 19,* 207–211.

Miller, D. A., McCluskey-Fawcett, K., & Irving, L. (1993). Correlates of bulimia nervosa: Early family mealtime experiences. *Adolescence, 28,* 621–635.

Miller, J. L., & Eimas, P. D. (1995). Speech perception: From signal to word. *Annual Review of Psychology, 46,* 467–492.

Miller, K. J., & Mizes, J. S. (Eds.). (2000). *Comparative treatments for eating disorders.* New York: Springer.

Miller, N., & Brewer, M. (1984). *Groups in contact: The psychology of desegregation.* New York: Academic Press.

Miller, P. A., & Jansen op de Haar, M. A. (1997). Emotional, cognitive, behavioral, and temperament characteristics of high-empathy children. *Motivation and Emotion, 21,* 109–125.

Miller, P. H. & Seier, W. L. (1994). *Strategy utilization deficiencies in children: When, where, and why.* San Diego, CA: Academic Press.

Miller, P. H, Woody-Ramsey, J., & Aloise, P. A. (1991). The role of strategy effortfulness in strategy effectiveness. *Developmental Psychology, 27*, 738–745.

Miller, S. A. (1998). *Developmental research methods* (2nd ed.). Upper Saddle River, NJ: Prentice Hall.

Miller-Bernal, L. (1993). Single-sex versus coeducational environments: A comparison of women students' experiences at four colleges. *American Journal of Education, 102*, 23–54.

Mills, J. L. (1999). Cocaine, smoking, and spontaneous abortion. *New England Journal of Medicine, 340*, 380–381.

Mindell, J. A., & Cashman, L. (1995). Sleep disorders. In A. R. Eisen, C. A. Kearney, & C. E. Schaefer (Eds.), *Clinical handbook of anxiety disorders in children and adolescents.* Northvale, NJ: Aronson.

Minkowski, A. (1967). *Regional development of the brain in early life.* Oxford, England: Blackwell.

Minorities in Higher Education. (1995). *Annual status report on minorities in higher education.* Washington, DC: Author.

Mishra, R. C. (1997). Cognition and cognitive development. In J. W. Berry, P. R. Dasen, & T. S. Saraswathi (Eds.), *Handbook of cross-cultural psychology: Vol. 2. Basic processes and human development* (2nd ed.). Needham Heights, MA: Allyn & Bacon.

Mistretta, C. M. (1990). Taste development. In J. R. Coleman (Ed.), *Development of sensory systems in mammals.* New York: Wiley.

Mitchell, J. (1998). Memory and psychoanalysis. In P. Fara & K. Patterson (Eds.), *Memory: The Darwin College lectures.* New York: Cambridge University Press.

Mitchell, J., McCauley, E., Burke, P. M., & Moss, S. J. (1988). Phenomenology of depression in children and adolescents. *Journal of the American Academy of Child and Adolescent Psychiatry, 27*, 12–20.

Mitchell, P., & Riggs, K. (1999). *Children's reasoning and the mind.* Philadelphia: Psychology Press.

Mittendorf, R., Williams, M. A., Berkey, C. S., & Cotter, R. F. (1990). The length of uncomplicated human gestation. *Obstetrics and Gynecology, 75*, 73–78.

Mix, K. S., Huttenlocher, J., & Levine, S. C. (Eds.). (2001). *Quantitative development in infancy and early childhood.* New York: Oxford University Press.

Mix, K. S., Huttenlocher, J., & Levine, S. C. (2002). Multiple cues for quantification in infancy: Is number one of them? *Psychological Bulletin, 128*, 278–294.

Miyamoto, R. H., Hishinuma, E. S., Nishimura, S. T., Nahulu, L. B., Andrade, N. N., & Goebert, D. A. (2000). Variation in self-esteem among adolescents in an Asian/Pacific-Islander sample. *Personality and Individual Differences, 29*, 13–25.

Mizuta, I., Zahn-Waxler, C., Colre, P. M., & Hiruma, N. (1996). A cross-cultural study of preschoolers' attachment: Security and sensitivity in Japanese and U.S. dads. *International Journal of Behavioral Development, 19*, 141–159.

Moldin, S. O., & Gottesman, I. I. (1997). Genes, experience, and chance in schizophrenia: Positioning for the 21st century. *Schizophrenia Bulletin, 23*, 547–561.

Molfese, V. J., & Acheson, S. (1997). Infant and preschool mental and verbal abilities: How are infant scores related to preschool scores? *International Journal of Behavioral Development, 20*, 595–607.

Monaco, A. P. Enard, W., Przeworski, M., Fisher, S. E., Lai, C. S. L., Wiebe, V., et al. (2002). Molecular evolution of FOXP2, a gene involved in speech and language. *Nature, 418*, 869–872.

Mondloch, C. J., Lewis, T. L., Budreau, D. R., Maurer, D., Dannemiller, J. L., Stephens, B. R., et al. (1999). Face perception during early infancy. *Psychological Science, 10*, 419–422.

Money, J., & Ehrhardt, A. A. (1972). *Man and woman, boy and girl: The differentiation and dimorphism of gender identity from conception to maturity.* Baltimore: Johns Hopkins University Press.

Montemayor, R., Adams, G. R., & Gulotta, T. P. (Eds.). (1994). *Personal relationships during adolescence.* Newbury Park, CA: Sage.

Montgomery-Downs, H., & Thomas, E. B. (1998). Biological and behavioral correlates of quiet sleep respiration rates in infants. *Physiology and Behavior, 64*, 637–643.

Moon, C., Cooper, R. P., & Fifer, W. (1993). Two-day-olds prefer their native language. *Infant Behavior and Development, 16*, 495–500.

Moore, C. (1996). Theories of mind in infancy. *British Journal of Developmental Psychology, 14*, 19–40.

Moore, C. (1999). Gaze following and the control of attention. In P. Rochat (Ed.), *Early social cognition: Understanding others in the first months of life.* Mahwah, NJ: Erlbaum.

Moore, K. L. (1998). *Before we are born: Basic embryology and birth defects.* Philadelphia: Saunders.

Moores, D., & Meadow-Orlans, K. (1990). *Educational and developmental aspects of deafness.* Washington, DC: Gallaudet University Press.

Morelli, G. A., Rogoff, B., Oppenheim, D., & Goldsmith, D. (1992). Cultural variation in infants' sleeping arrangements: Questions of independence. Special section: Cross-cultural studies of development. *Developmental Psychology, 28*, 604–613.

Morgane, P., Austin-La France, R., Bronzino, J., Tonkiss, J., Diaz-Cintra, S., Cintra, L., et al. (1993). Prenatal malnutrition and development of the brain. *Neuroscience and Biobehavioral Reviews, 17*, 91–128.

Morice, A. (1998, February 27). Future moms, please note: Benefits vary. *Wall Street Journal,* p. 15.

Morrison, A. M., & von Gilnow, M. A. (1990). Women and minorities in management. *American Psychologist, 45*, 200–208.

Morrison, F. J. (1993). Phonological process in reading acquisition: Toward a unified conceptualization. *Developmental Review, 13*, 279–285.

Morrison, F. J., Smith, L., & Dow-Ehrensberger, M. (1995). Education and cognitive development: A natural experiment. *Developmental Psychology, 31*, 789–799.

Morse, R. M., & Flavin, D. K. (1992). The definition of alcoholism. *Journal of the American Medical Association, 268*, 1012–1014.

Mortensen, E. L., Michaelsen, K. F., Sanders, S. A., & Reinisch, J. M. (2002). The association between duration of breast feeding and adult intelligence. *Journal of the American Medical Association, 287*, 2365.

Moses, L. J., & Chandler, M. J. (1992). Traveler's guide to children's theories of mind. *Psychological Inquiry, 3*, 286–301.

Moshman, D., Glover, J. A., & Bruning, R. H. (1987). *Developmental psychology.* Boston: Little, Brown.

Mowry, B. J., Nancarrow, D. J., & Levinson, D. F. (1997). The molecular genetics of schizophrenia: An update. *Australian and New Zealand Journal of Psychiatry, 31*, 704–713.

Mueller, E., & Vandell, D. (1979). Infant–infant interactions. In J. Osofsky (Ed.), *Handbook of infant development.* New York: Wiley.

Mulvey, E. P., & Cauffman, E. (2001). The inherent limits of predicting school violence. *American Psychologist, 56*, 797–802.

Munakata, Y., McClelland, J. L., Johnson, M. H., & Siegler, R. S. (1997). Rethinking infant knowledge: Toward an adaptive process account of the successes and failures in object permanence tasks. *Psychological Review, 104*, 686–713.

Murray, B. (1996a, July). Getting children off the couch and onto the field. *Monitor on Psychology,* 42–43.

Murray, B. (1996b, January). Home schools: How do they affect children? *Monitor on Psychology,* 43.

Murray, J. A., Terry, D. J., Vance, J. C., Battistutta, D., & Connolly, Y. (2000). Effects of a program of intervention on parental distress following infant death. *Death Studies, 4*, 275–305.

Murray, L., & Cooper, P. J. (Eds.). (1997). *Postpartum depression and child development.* New York: Guilford Press.

Musick, J. (1993). *Young, poor, and pregnant: The psychology of teenage motherhood.* New Haven, CT: Yale University Press.

Mussen, P. H. (1969). Early sex-role development. In D. A. Goslin (Eds.), *Handbook of socialization theory and research.* Chicago: Rand McNally.

Mussen, P. H., & Jones, M. C. (1957). Self-conceptions, motivations, and interpersonal attitudes of late- and early-maturing boys. *Child Development, 28*, 243–256.

Myers, B. J., Britt, G. C., Lodder, D. E., Kendall, K. A., et al. (1992). Effects of cocaine exposure on infant development: A review. *Journal of Child and Family Studies, 1*, 393–415.

Myers, N. A., Clifton, R. K., & Clarkson, M. G. (1987). When they were very young: Almost-threes remember two years ago. *Infant Behavior and Development, 10*, 123–132.

Myklebust, B. M., & Gottlieb, G. L. (1993). Development of the stretch reflex in the newborn: Reciprocal excitation and reflex irradation. *Child Development, 64*, 1036–1045.

Nadeau, L., Boivin, M., Tessier, R., Lefebvre, F. & Robaey, P. (2001). Mediators of behavioral problems in 7-year-old children born after 24 to 28 weeks of gestation. *Journal of Developmental and Behavioral Pediatrics, 22*, 1–10.

Nadel, J., & Butterworth, G. (Eds.). (1999). *Imitation in infancy.* New York: Cambridge University Press.

Nakagawa, M., Lamb, M. E., & Miyaki, K. (1992). Antecedents and correlates of the Strange Situation behavior of Japanese infants. *Journal of Cross-Cultural Psychology, 23*, 300–310.

Nangle, D. W., & Erdley, C. A. (Eds.). (2001). *The role of friendship in psychological adjustment.* San Francisco: Jossey-Bass.

Nathanielsz, P. W. (1996). The timing of birth. *American Scientist, 84*, 562–569.

National Advisory Council on Alcohol Abuse and Alcoholism. (2002). *A call to action: Changing the culture of drinking at U.S. colleges.* Washington, DC: National Institute on Alcohol Abuse and Alcoholism.

National Center for Education Statistics. (1997). *Digest of education statistics, 1997.* Washington, DC: U.S. Government Printing Office.

National Center for Education Statistics. (2000a). *Digest of educational statistics, 2000.* Washington, DC: U.S. Government Printing Office.

National Center for Education Statistics. (2000b). *Dropout rates in the United States, 1999.* Washington, DC: U.S. Government Printing Office.

National Center for Education Statistics. (2001). *Time spent on homework and on the job (Indicator No. 21).* Retrieved from http://nces.ed.gov/programs/coe/2001/section3/ indicator21.asp

National Center for Health Statistics. (1993). *Health United States, 1992.* Washington, DC: Public Health Service.

National Center for Health Statistics. (1997). *Asthma conditions of children under 18.* Washington, DC: Public Health Service.

National Center for Health Statistics. (1998). *U.S. infant mortality rates by race of mother, 1975–1996.* Washington, DC: Public Health Service.

National Center for Health Statistics. (2000). *Health United States, 2000, with adolescent health chartbook.* Hyattsville, MD: Public Health Service.

National Center for Health Statistics. (2002). *National vital statistics report* (Vol. 50). Hyattsville, MD: Public Health Service.

National Center for Missing and Exploited Children. (1994). *Safety guidelines for children.* Alexandria, VA: Author. Retrieved from http://www.missingkids.com./html/ncmec_default_ec_internetsafty.html

National Center for Missing and Exploited Children. (2002). *Internet rules.* Alexandria, VA: Author. Retrieved from http://www.missingkids.com

National Center on Addiction and Substance Abuse. (2002). *National survey of American attitudes on substance abuse VII: Teens, parents, and siblings.* New York: Columbia University Press.

National Institute of Child Health and Human Development. (1997a). Child care in the first year of life. *Merrill-Palmer Quarterly, 43*, 340–360.

National Institute of Child Health and Human Development. (1997b). The effects of infant child care on infant–mother attachment security: Results of the NICHD study of early child care. *Child Development, 68*, 860–879.

National Institute of Child Health and Human Development. (1999). Child care and mother–child interaction in the first 3 years of life. *Developmental Psychology, 35*, 1399–1413.

National Institute of Child Health and Human Development. (2001a). Child care and children's peer interaction at 24 and 36 months: The NICHD study of early child care. *Child Development, 72*, 1478–1500.

National Institute of Child Health and Human Development. (2001b). Child care and family predictors of preschool attachment and stability from infancy. *Developmental Psychology, 37*, 847–862.

National Institute of Child Health and Human Development. (2002). Child-care structure_process_outcome: Direct and indirect effects of child-care quality on young children's development. *Psychological Science, 13*, 199–206.

National Institute on Alcohol Abuse and Alcoholism. (1990). *Alcohol and health.* Washington, DC: U.S. Government Printing Office.

National Longitudinal Study on Adolescent Health. (2000). *Teenage stress.* Chapel Hill, NC: Carolina Population Center.

National Research Council. (1991). *Caring for America's children.* Washington, DC: National Academy Press.

National Safety Council. (1989). *Accident facts* (1989 ed.). Chicago: Author.

Needleman, H. L., & Bellinger, D. (Eds.). (1994). *Prenatal exposure to toxicants: Developmental consequences.* Baltimore: Johns Hopkins University Press.

Needleman, H. L., Riess, J. A., Tobin, M. J., Biesecker, G. E., & Greenhouse, J. B. (1996). Bone lead levels and delinquent behavior. *Journal of the American Medical Association, 2755*, 363–369.

Neisser, U. (Ed.). (1999). *The rising curve: Long-term gains in IQ and related measures.* Washington, DC: American Psychological Association.

Neisser, U., Boodoo, G., Bourchard, T. J., Jr., Boykin, A. W., Brody, N., Ceci, S. J., et al. (1996). Intelligence: Knowns and unknowns. *American Psychologist, 51*, 77–101.

Nell, V. (2002). Why young men drive dangerously: Implications for injury prevention. *Current Directions in Psychological Science, 11*, 75–79.

Nelson, C. A. (1987). The recognition of facial expressions in the first two years of life: Mechanisms of development. *Child Development, 58*, 889–909.

Nelson, C. A. (1995). The ontogeny of human memory: A cognitive neuroscience perspective. *Developmental Psychology, 31*, 723–738.

Nelson, D. G. K., Jusczyk, P. W., Mandel, D. R., Myers, J., et al. (1995). The head-turn preference procedure for testing auditory perception. *Infant Behavior and Development, 18*, 111–116.

Nelson, K. (1981). Individual differences in language development: Implications for development and language. *Developmental Psychology, 17*, 170–187.

Nelson, K. (1986). *Event knowledge: Structure and function in development.* Hillsdale, NJ: Erlbaum.

Nelson, K. (1989). Remembering: A functional developmental perspective. In P. R. Solomon, G. R. Goethels, C. M. Kelley, & B. R. Stephens (Eds.), *Memory: An interdisciplinary approach.* New York: Springer-Verlag.

Nelson, K. (1992). Emergence of autobiographical memory at age 4. *Human Development, 35*, 172–177.

Nelson, K. (1996). *Language in cognitive development: Emergence of the mediated mind.* New York: Cambridge University Press.

Nelson, L. J., & Cooper, J. (1997). Gender differences in children's reactions to success and failure with computers. *Computers in Human Behavior, 13*, 247–267.

Nelson, T. O. (1994). Metacognition. In V. S. Ramachandran (Ed.), *Encyclopedia of human behavior* (Vol. 3). San Diego, CA: Academic Press.

Ness, R. B., Grisso, J. A., Hirschinger, N., Markovic, N., Shaw, L. M., Day, N. L., et al. (1999). Cocaine and tobacco use and the risk of spontaneous abortion. *New England Journal of Medicine, 340*, 333–339.

Nettles, S. M., & Pleck, J. H. (1990). Risk, resilience, and development: The multiple ecologies of black adolescents. In R. J. Haggerty, N. Garmezy, M. Rutter, & L. Sherrod (Eds.), *Risk and resilience in children: Developmental approaches.* New York: Cambridge University Press.

Newcomb, A. F., & Bagwell, C. L. (1995). Children's friendship relations: A meta-analytic review. *Psychological Bulletin, 117*, 306–347.

Newcombe, N., Drummey, A. B., & Lie, E. (1995). Children's memory for early experience. *Journal of Experimental Child Psychology, 59*, 337–342.

Ney, P. G., Fung, T., & Wickett, A. R. (1993). Child neglect: The precursor to child abuse. *Pre- and Perinatal Psychology Journal, 8*, 95–112.

Nguyen, L., & Frye, D. (1999). Children's theory of mind: Understanding of desire, belief and emotion with social referents. *Social Development, 8*, 70–92.

Nigg, J. T. (2001). Is ADHD a disinhibitory disorder? *Psychological Bulletin, 127*, 571–598.

Nihart, M. A. (1993). Growth and development of the brain. *Journal of Child and Adolescent Psychiatric and Mental Health Nursing, 6*, 39–40.

Nisbett, R. E. (1994, October 31). Blue genes. *New Republic,* 15.

Nisbett, R. E. (1998). Race, genetics, and IQ. In C. Jencks & M. Phillips (Eds.), *The black–white test score gap.* Washington, DC: Brookings Institution.

Nockels, R., & Oakeshott, P. (1999). Awareness among young women of sexually transmitted chlamydia infection. *Family Practice, 16*, 94.

Nolen-Hoeksema, S., & Girgus, J. S. (1994). The emergence of gender differences in depression during adolescence. *Psychological Bulletin, 115*, 424–443.

Norman, R. M. G., & Malla, A. K. (2001). Family history of schizophrenia and the relationship of stress to symptoms: Preliminary findings. *Australian and New Zealand Journal of Psychiatry, 35*, 217–223.

Nossiter, A. (1995, September 5). Asthma common and on rise in the crowded South Bronx. *New York Times,* pp. A1, B2.

Notzon, F. C. (1990). International differences in the use of obstetric interventions. *Journal of the American Medical Association, 263*, 3286–3291.

Nowak, M. A., Komarova, N. L., & Niyogi, P. (2001). Evolution of universal grammar. *Science, 291*, 114–116.

Nowak, R. (1994a). Genetic testing set for takeoff. *Science, 265*, 464–467.

Nowak, R. (1994b). Nicotine scrutinized as FDA seeks to regulate cigarettes. *Science, 263*, 1555–1556.

Nowicki, S., & Oxenford, C. (1989). The relation of hostile nonverbal communication styles to popularity in preadolescent children. *Journal of Genetic Psychology, 150*, 39–44.

NPD Group. (1998). *The reality of children's diet.* Port Washington, NY: Author.

Nugent, J. K., Lester, B. M., & Brazelton, T. B. (Eds.). (1989). *The cultural context of infancy: Vol. 1. Biology, culture, and infant development.* Norwood, NJ: Ablex.

Nyiti, R. M. (1982). The validity of "culture differences explanations" for cross-cultural variation in the rate of Piagetian cognitive development. In D. Wagner & H. Stevenson (Eds.), *Cultural perspectives on child development.* New York: Freeman.

O'Connor, M. J., Sigman, M., & Brill, N. (1987). Disorganization of attachment in relation to maternal alcohol consumption. *Journal of Consulting and Clinical Psychology, 55*, 831–836.

O'Neill, C. (1994, May 17). Exercise just for the fun of it. *Washington Post,* p. WH18.

O'Sullivan, J. T. (1993). Applying cognitive developmental principles in classrooms. In R. Pasnak & M. L. Howe (Eds.), *Emerging themes in cognitive development* (Vol. 2). New York: Springer-Verlag.

O'Toole, M. E. (2000). *The school shooter: A threat assessment perspective.* Washington, DC: Federal Bureau of Investigation.

Office of Juvenile Justice and Delinquency Prevention. (2002). *Juvenile justice facts and figures.* Retrieved from http://ojjdp.ncjrs.org/facts/facts.html

Office of the Surgeon General. (2001). *The Surgeon General's call to action to prevent and decrease overweight and obesity.* Rockville, MD: U.S. Department of Health and Human Services.

Ogbu, J. U. (1988). Black education: A cultural-ecological perspective. In H. P. McAdoo (Ed.), *Black families.* Beverly Hills, CA: Sage.

Ogbu, J. U. (1992). Understanding cultural diversity and learning. *Educational Researcher, 21*, 5–14.

Ogden, C. L., Kuczmarski, R. J., Flegal, K. M., Mei, Z., Guo, S., Wei, R., et al. (2002). Centers for Disease Control and Prevention 2000 growth charts for the United States: Improvements to the 1977 National Center for Health Statistics version. *Pediatrics, 109*, 45–60.

Oliver, M. B., & Hyde, J. S. (1993). Gender differences in sexuality: A meta-analysis. *Psychological Bulletin, 114*, 29–51.

Ollendick, T. H., Yang, B., King, N. J., Dong, Q., & Akande, A. (1996). Fears in American, Australian, Chinese, and Nigerian children and adolescents: A cross-cultural study. *Journal of Child Psychology and Psychiatry and Allied Disciplines, 37*, 213–220.

Oller, D. K., (1999). *The emergence of the speech capacity.* Mahwah, NJ: Erlbaum.

Oller, D. K., Eilers, R. E., Urbano, R., & Cobo-Lewis, A. B. (1997). Development of precursors to speech in infants exposed to two languages. *Journal of Child Language, 24*, 407–425.

Olson, J. M., Vernon, P. A., Harris, J. A., & Jang, K. L. (2001). The heritability of attitudes: A study of twins. *Journal of Personality and Social Psychology, 80*, 845–860.

Olweus, D. (1995). Bullying or peer abuse at school: Facts and intervention. *Current Directions in Psychological Science, 4*, 196–200.

Ono, Y. (1995, October 15). Ads do push kids to smoke, study suggests. *Wall Street Journal,* pp. B1–B2.

Onslow, M. (1992). Choosing a treatment program for early stuttering: Issues and future directions. *Journal of Speech and Hearing Research, 35*, 983–993.

Organization for Economic Cooperation and Development. (1998). *Education at a glance: OECD indicators, 1998.* Paris: Author.

Osborne, J. W. (1997). Race and academic disidentification. *Journal of Educational Psychology, 89*, 728–735.

Osofsky, J. D. (1995). The effects of exposure to violence on young children. *American Psychologist, 50*, 782–788.

Paikoff, R. L., & Brooks-Gunn, J. (1990). Physiological processes: What role do they play during the transition to adolescence? In R. Montemayor, G. R. Adams, & T. P. Gulotta (Eds.), *From childhood to adolescence: A transitional period?* Newbury Park, CA: Sage.

Painter, K. (1997, August 15). Doctors have prenatal tests for 450 genetic diseases. *USA Today,* pp. 1–2.

Palincsar, A. S., & Klenk, L. (1992). Fostering literacy learning in supportive contexts. *Journal of Learning Disabilities, 25*, 211–225, 229.

Paneth, N. S. (1995). The problem of low birth weight. *Future of Children, 5,* 19–34.

Panneton, R. K. (1985). *Prenatal auditory experience with melodies: Effects on postnatal auditory preferences in human newborns.* Unpublished doctoral dissertation, University of North Carolina, Greensboro.

Papousek, H., & Bernstein, P. (1969). The functions of conditioning stimulation in human neonates and infants. In A. Ambrose (Ed.), *Stimulation in early infancy.* New York: Academic Press.

Papousek, H., & Papousek, M. (1991). Innate and cultural guidance of infants' integrative competencies: China, the United States, and Germany. In M. H. Bornstein (Ed.), *Cultural approaches to parenting.* Hillsdale, NJ: Erlbaum.

Papps, F., Walker, M., Trimboli, A., & Trimboli, C. (1995). Parental discipline in Anglo, Greek, Lebanese, and Vietnamese cultures. *Journal of Cross-Cultural Psychology, 26,* 49–64.

Paris, J. (1999). *Nature and nurture in psychiatry: A predisposition–stress model of mental disorders.* Washington, DC: American Psychiatric Press.

Park, K. A., Lay, K., & Ramsay, L. (1993). Individual differences and developmental changes in preschoolers' friendships. *Developmental Psychology, 29,* 264–270.

Parke, R. D. (1990). In search of fathers: A narrative of an empirical journey. In I. Sigel & G. Brody (Eds.), *Methods of family research* (Vol. 1). Hillsdale, NJ: Erlbaum.

Parke, R. D. (1996). *New fatherhood.* Cambridge, MA: Harvard University Press.

Parke, R. D., & Sawin, D. B. (1980). The family in early infancy: Social interaction and attitudinal analyses. In F. A. Pedersen (Ed.), *The father–infant relationship: Observational studies in the family setting.* New York: Praeger.

Parmelee, A. H., Jr. (1986). Children's illnesses: Their beneficial effects on behavioral development. *Child Development, 57,* 1–10.

Parmelee, A. H., Jr., & Sigman, M. D. (1983). Prenatal brain development and behavior. In P. H. Mussen (Ed.), *Handbook of child psychology* (Vol. 2, 4th ed.). New York: Wiley.

Parmelee, A. H., Jr., Wenner, W., & Schulz, H. (1964). Infant sleep patterns from birth to 16 weeks of age. *Journal of Pediatrics, 65,* 572–576.

Parritz, R. H., Mangelsdorf, S., & Gunnar, M. R. (1992). Control, social referencing, and the infants' appraisal of threat. In S. Feinman (Ed.), *Social referencing and the social construction of reality in infancy.* New York: Plenum.

Parten, M. B. (1932). Social participation among preschool children. *Journal of Abnormal and Social Psychology, 27,* 243–269.

Pascalis, O., de Haan, M., & Nelson, C. A. (2002). Is face processing species-specific during the first year of life? *Science, 296,* 1321–1322.

Pascoe, J. M. (1993). Social support during labor and duration of labor: A community-based study. *Public Health Nursing, 10,* 97–99.

Patenaude, A. F., Guttmacher, A. E., & Collins, F. S. (2002). Genetic testing and psychology: New roles, new responsibilities. *American Psychologist, 57,* 271–282.

Patterson, C. J. (1994). Lesbians and gay families. *Current Directions in Psychological Science, 3,* 62–64.

Paus, T., Zijdenbos, A., Worsley, K., Collins, D. L., Blumenthal, J., Giedd, J. N., et al. (1999). Structural maturation of neural pathways in children and in adolescents: In vivo study. *Science, 283,* 1908–1911.

Pavis, S., Cunningham-Burley, S., & Amos, A. (1997). Alcohol consumption and young people: Exploring meaning and social context. *Health Education Research, 12,* 311–322.

Pavlov, I. P. (1927). *Conditioned reflexes.* London: Oxford University Press.

Paxton, S. J., Schutz, H. K., Wertheim, E. H., & Muir, S. L. (1999). Friendship clique and peer influences on body image concerns, dietary restraint, extreme weight-loss behaviors, and binge eating in adolescent girls. *Journal of Abnormal Psychology, 108,* 255–266.

Payne, J. S., Kauffman, J. M., Brown, G. B., & De Mott, R. M. (1974). *Exceptional children in focus.* Columbus, OH: Merrill.

Pear, R. (2000, March 19). Proposal to curb the use of drugs to calm the young. *New York Times,* p. 1.

Pedlow, R., Sanson, A., Prior, M., & Oberklaid, F. (1993). Stability of maternally reported temperament from infancy to 8 years. *Developmental Psychology, 29,* 998–1007.

Peisner-Feinberg, E. S., Burchinal, M. R., Clifford, R. M., Culkin, M. L., Howes, C., Kagan, S. L., et al. (2001). The relation of preschool child-care quality to children's cognitive and social developmental trajectories through second grade. *Child Development, 72,* 1534–1553.

Pelligrini, A. D., & Smith, P. K. (1998). Physical activity play: The nature and function of a neglected aspect of play. *Child Development, 69,* 577–598.

Peltonen, L., & McKusick, V. A. (2001). Dissecting the human disease in the postgenomic era. *Science, 291,* 1224–1229.

Pennisi, E. (2000). And the gene number is . . . ? *Science, 288,* 1146–1147.

Pennisi, E., & Vogel, G. (2000). Clones: A hard act to follow. *Science, 288,* 1722–1727.

Perlmann, R. Y., & Gleason, J. B. (1990, July). *Patterns of prohibition in mothers' speech to children.* Paper presented at the Fifth International Congress for the Study of Child Language, Budapest.

Perozzi, J. A., & Sanchez, M. C. (1992). The effect of instruction in L1 on receptive acquisition of L2 for bilingual children with language delay. *Language, Speech, and Hearing Services in Schools, 23,* 348–352.

Perry, C., & McIntire, W. G. (1995). Modes of moral judgment among early adolescents. *Adolescence, 30,* 707–715.

Petersen, A. C. (1988, September). Those gangly years. *Psychology Today,* 28–34.

Petersen, A. C. (2000). A longitudinal investigation of adolescents' changing perceptions of pubertal timing. *Developmental Psychology, 36,* 37–43.

Petersen, A. C., & Crockett, L. (1985). Pubertal timing and grade effects on adjustment. *Journal of Youth and Adolescence, 14,* 191–206.

Petersen, A. C., Sarigiani, P. A., & Kennedy, R. E. (1991). Adolescent depression: Why more girls? *Journal of Youth and Adolescence, 20,* 247–271.

Peterson, L. (1994). Child injury and abuse-neglect: Common etiologies, challenges, and courses toward prevention. *Current Directions in Psychological Science, 3,* 116–120.

Peterson, S., & Bainbridge, J. (1999). Teachers' gendered expectations and their evaluation of student writing. *Reading Research and Instruction, 38,* 255–271.

Petitto, L. A., & Marentette, P. F. (1991). Babbling in the manual mode: Evidence for the ontogeny of language. *Science, 251,* 1493–1496.

Petraitis, J., Flay, B. R., & Miller, T. Q. (1995). Reviewing theories of adolescent substance use: Organizing pieces in the puzzle. *Psychological Bulletin, 117,* 67–86.

Pettit, G. S., Bates, J. E., & Dodge, K. A. (1997). Supportive parenting, ecological context, and children's adjustment: A seven-year longitudinal study. *Child Development, 68,* 908–923.

Pfeiffer, S. I., & Stocking, V. B. (2000). Vulnerabilities of academically gifted students. *Special Services in the Schools, 16,* 83–93.

Phelan, P., Yu, H. C., & Davidson, A. L. (1994). Navigating the psychosocial pressures of adolescence: The voices and experiences of high school youth. *American Educational Research Journal, 31,* 415–447.

Phillips, D. A., Voran, M., Kisker, E., Howes, C., & Whitebook, M. (1994). Child care for children in poverty: Opportunity or inequity? *Child Development, 65,* 472–492.

Phillips, D. A., & Zimmerman, M. (1990). The developmental course of perceived competence and incompetence among competent children. In R. J. Sternberg & J. Kolligian (Eds.), *Competence considered.* New Haven, CT: Yale University Press.

Phillips, R. D., Wagner, S. H., Fells, C. A., & Lynch, M. (1990). Do infants recognize emotion in facial expressions? Categorical and "metaphorical" evidence. *Infant Behavior and Development, 13,* 71–84.

Phillips, S., King, S., & Du Bois, L. (1978). Spontaneous activities of female versus male newborns. *Child Development, 49,* 590–597.

Phinney, J. S., Ferguson, D. L., & Tate, J. D. (1997). Intergroup attitudes among ethnic minority adolescents: A causal model. *Child Development, 68,* 955–969.

Phinney, J. S., Lochner, B., & Murphy, R. (1990). Ethnic identity development and psychological adjustment in adolescence. In A. Stiffman & L. Davis (Eds.), *Advances in adolescent mental health: Vol. 5. Ethnic issues.* Greenwich, CT: JAI Press.

Piaget, J. (1932). *The moral judgment of the child.* New York: Harcourt.

Piaget, J. (1952). *The origins of intelligence in children.* New York: International Universities Press.

Piaget, J. (1954). *The construction of reality in the child* (Margaret Cook, Trans.). New York: Basic Books.

Piaget, J. (1962). *Play, dreams and imitation in childhood.* New York: Norton.

Piaget, J. (1983). Piaget's theory. In W. Kessen (Ed.) & P. H. Mussen (Series Ed.), *Handbook of child psychology: Vol 1. History, theory, and methods.* New York: Wiley.

Piaget, J., & Inhelder, B. (1958). *The growth of logical thinking from childhood to adolescence* (A. Parsons & S. Seagrin, Trans.). New York: Basic Books.

Piaget, J., Inhelder, B., & Szeminska, A. (1960). *The child's conception of geometry.* New York: Basic Books. (Original work published 1948)

Picard, E. M., Del Dotto, J. E., & Breslau, N. (2000). Prematurity and low birthweight. In K. O. Yeates & M. D. Ris (Eds.), *Pediatric neuropsychology: Research, theory, and practice.* New York: Guilford Press.

Pillay, A. L., & Wassenaar, D. R. (1997). Recent stressors and family satisfaction in suicidal adolescents in South Africa. *Journal of Adolescence, 20,* 155–162.

Pinker, S. (1994). *The language instinct.* New York: Morrow.

Pintney, R., Forlands, F., & Freedman, H. (1937). Personality and attitudinal similarity among classmates. *Journal of Applied Psychology, 21,* 48–65.

Pipp, S., Easterbrooks, M., & Brown, S. R. (1993). Attachment status and complexity of infants' self- and other-knowledge when tested with mother and father. *Social Development, 2,* 1–14.

Pipp-Siegel, S., & Foltz, C. (1997). Toddlers' acquisition of self/other knowledge: Ecological and interpersonal aspects of self and other. *Child Development, 68,* 69–79.

Plomin, R. (1994a). The genetic basis of complex human behaviors. *Science, 264,* 1733–1739.

Plomin, R. (1994b). *Genetics and experience: The interplay between nature and nurture.* Newbury Park, CA: Sage.

Plomin, R., & Caspi, A. (1998). DNA and personality. *European Journal of Personality, 12,* 387–407.

Plomin, R., & McClearn, G. E. (Eds.). (1993). *Nature, nurture, and psychology.* Washington, DC: American Psychological Association.

Plomin, R., & Rutter, M. (1998). Child development, molecular genetics, and what to do with genes once they are found. *Child Development, 69,* 1223–1242.

Poest, C. A., Williams, J. R., Witt, D. D., & Atwood, M. E. (1990). Challenge me to move: Large muscle development in young children. *Young Children, 45,* 4–10.

Pollitt, E. (1994). Poverty and child development: Relevance of research in developing countries to the United States. *Child Development, 65,* 283–295.

Pollitt, E., Golub, M., Gorman, K., Grantham-McGregor, S., Levitsky, D., Schürch, B., et al. (1996). A reconceptualization of the effects of undernutrition on children's biological, psychosocial, and behavioral development. *Social Policy Report, 10,* 1–22.

Pollitt, E., Gorman, K. S., Engle, P. L., Martorell, R., & Rivera, J. (1993). Early supplementary feeding and cognition: Effects over two decades. *Monographs of the Society for Research in Child Development, 58,* v–99.

Pomerleau, O. F., & Pomerleau, C. S. (1989). A biobehavioral perspective on smoking. In T. Ney & A. Gale (Eds.), *Smoking and human behavior.* New York: Wiley.

Ponton, L. E. (1999, May 10). Their dark romance with risk. *Newsweek,* 55–58.

Ponton, L. E. (2001). *The sex lives of teenagers: Revealing the secret world of adolescent boys and girls.* New York: Penguin Putnam.

Poole, D. A., & Lamb, M. E. (1998). *Investigative interviews of children: A guide for helping professionals.* Washington, DC: American Psychological Association.

Pope, A. W., & Bierman, K. L. (1999). Predicting adolescent peer problems and antisocial activities: The relative roles of aggression and dysregulation. *Developmental Psychology, 35,* 335–346.

Porges, S. W., & Lipsitt, L. P. (1993). Neonatal responsivity to gustatory stimulation: The gustatory–vagal hypothesis. *Infant Behavior and Development, 16,* 487–494.

Porter, F. L., Porges, S. W., & Marshall, R. E. (1988). Newborn pain cries and vagal tone: Parallel changes in response to circumcision. *Child Development, 59,* 495–515.

Porter, R. H., Bologh, R. D., & Malkin, J. W. (1988). Olfactory influences on mother–infant interactions. In C. K. Rovee-Collier & L. P. Lipsitt (Eds.), *Advances in infancy research* (Vol. 5). Norwood, NJ: Ablex.

Porter, R. H., & Winberg, J. (1999). Unique salience of maternal breast odors for newborn infants. *Neuroscience and Biobehavioral Reviews, 23,* 439–449.

Portes, A., & Rumbaut, R. (2001). *Legacies: The story of the immigrant second generation.* Berkeley: University of California Press.

Porzelius, L. K., Dinsmore, B. D., & Staffelbach, D. (2001). Eating disorders. In M. Hersen & V. B. Van Hasselt (Eds.), *Advanced abnormal psychology* (2nd ed.). New York: Kluwer/Plenum.

Poulin-Dubois, D., Serbin, L. A., Kenyon, B., & Derbyshire, A. (1994). Infants' intermodal knowledge about gender. *Developmental Psychology, 30,* 436–442.

Power, T. G. (1999). *Play and exploration in children and animals.* Mahwah, NJ: Erlbaum.

Power, T. G., & Parke, R. D. (1982). Play as a context for early learning: Lab and home analyses. In L. M. Laosa & I. E. Sigal (Eds.), *The family as a learning environment.* New York: Plenum.

Prechtl, H. F. R. (1982). Regressions and transformations during neurological development. In T. G. Bever (Ed.), *Regressions in mental development.* Hillsdale, NJ: Erlbaum.

Prentice, A. (1991). Can maternal dietary supplements help in preventing infant malnutrition? *Acta Paediatrica Scandinavica, 374*(Suppl.), 67–77.

Prescott, C., & Gottesman, I. I. (1993). Genetically mediated vulnerability to schizophrenia. *Psychiatric Clinics of North America, 16,* 245–267.

Pressley, M. (1987). Are keyword method effects limited to slow presentation rates? An empirically based reply to Hall and Fuson (1986). *Journal of Educational Psychology, 79,* 333–335.

Pressley, M., & Levin, J. R. (1983). *Cognitive strategy research: Psychological foundations.* New York: Springer-Verlag.

Pressley, M. & Schneider, W. (1997). *Introduction to memory development during childhood and adolescence.* Mahwah, NJ: Erlbaum.

Pressley, M., & Van Meter, P. (1993). Memory strategies: Natural development and use following instruction. In R. Pasnak & M. L. Howe (Eds.), *Emerging themes in cognitive development* (Vol. 2). New York: Springer-Verlag.

Price, D. W., & Goodman, G. S. (1990). Visiting the wizard: Children's memory for a recurring event. *Child Development, 61,* 664–680.

Price, R., & Gottesman, I. I. (1991). Body fat in identical twins reared apart: Roles for genes and environment. *Behavior Genetics, 21,* 1–7.

Prieto, S. L., Cole, D. A., & Tageson, C. W. (1992). Depressive self-schemas in clinic and nonclinic children. *Cognitive Therapy and Research, 16,* 521–534.

PRIMEDIA/Roper National Youth Survey. (1999). *Adolescents' view of society's ills.* Storrs, CT: Roper Center for Public Opinion Research.

Putnam, F. (1995, January). *Violence against children and the family.* Paper presented at a conference on violence against children in the family and the community, Los Angeles.

Pyryt, M. C., & Mendaglio, S. (1994). The multidimensional self-concept: A comparison of gifted and average-ability adolescents. *Journal for the Education of the Gifted, 17,* 299–305.

Pyszczynski, T., Greenberg, J., & La Prelle, J. (1985). Social comparison after success and failure: Biased search for information consistent with a self-servicing conclusion. *Journal of Experimental Social Psychology, 21,* 195–211.

Quinn, M. (1990, January 29). Don't aim that pack at us. *Time,* 60.

Quinn, P. C., & Eimas, P. D. (1996). *Perceptual organization and categorization in young infants.* Norwood, NJ: Ablex.

Quintana, C. (1998, May 17.) Riding the rails. *New York Times Magazine,* 22–24.

Rabain-Jamin, J., & Sabeau-Jouannet, E. (1997). Maternal speech to 4-month-old infants in two cultures: Wolof and French. *International Journal of Behavioral Development, 20,* 425–451.

Radetsky, P. (1994). Stopping premature births before it's too late. *Science, 266,* 1486–1488.

Radke-Yarrow, M., Zahn-Waxler, C., & Chapman, M. (1983). Children's prosocial dispositions and behavior. In E. M. Hetherington (Ed.), *Handbook of child psychology: Vol. 4. Socialization, personality, and social development.* New York: Wiley.

Radziszewska, B., & Rogoff, B. (1988). Influence of adult and peer collaborators on children's planning skills. *Developmental Psychology, 24,* 840–848.

Rahe, R. J., & Arthur, R. J. (1978). Life change and illness studies: Past history and future directions. *Human Stress, 4,* 3–15.

Ramey, C. T., & Ramey, S. L. (1998). Early intervention and early experience. *American Psychologist, 53,* 109–120.

Ramey, S. L. (1999). Head Start and preschool education. *American Psychologist, 54,* 344–346.

Ramsay, D. S. (1980). Onset of unimanual handedness in infants. *Infant Behavior and Development, 3,* 377–385.

Ramsey, P. G. (1995). Changing social dynamics in early childhood classrooms. *Child Development, 66,* 764–773.

Ranade, V. (1993). Nutritional recommendations for children and adolescents. *International Journal of Clinical Pharmacology, Therapy, and Toxicology, 31,* 285–290.

Randahl, G. J. (1991). A typological analysis of the relations between measured vocational interests and abilities. *Journal of Vocational Behavior, 38,* 333–350.

Rauch-Elnekave, H. (1994). Teenage motherhood: Its relationship to undetected learning problems. *Adolescence, 29,* 91–103.

Raymond, J. (2000). The world of the senses. *Newsweek* [Special issue: Your Child], 16–18.

Rayner, K., Foorman, B. R., Perfetti, C. A., Pesetsky, D., & Seidenberg, M. S. (2001). How psychological science informs the teaching of reading. *Psychological Science in the Public Interest, 2,* 31–74.

Rayner, K., Foorman, B. R., Perfetti, C. A., Pesetsky, D., & Seidenberg, M. S. (2002, March). How should reading be taught? *Scientific American,* 85–91.

Rayner, K., & Pollatsek, A. (Eds.). (1989). *The psychology of reading.* Englewood Cliffs, NJ: Prentice Hall.

Reddy, L. A., & Pfeiffer, S. I. (1997). Effectiveness of treatment of foster care with children and adolescents: A review of outcome studies. *Journal of the American Academy of Child and Adolescent Psychiatry, 36,* 381–588.

Redshaw, M. E. (1997). Mothers of babies requiring special care: Attitudes and experiences. *Journal of Reproductive and Infant Psychology, 15,* 109–120.

Reese, E., & Cox, A. (1999). Quality of adult book reading affects children's emergent literacy. *Developmental Psychology, 35,* 20–28.

Reese, H. W. (Ed.). (1987). *Advances in child development and behavior* (Vol. 20). New York: Academic Press.

Reid, K. J., Zeldow, M., Teplin, L. A., McClelland, G. M., Abram, K. A., & Zee, P. C. (2002). *Sleep habits of juvenile detainees in the Chicago area.* Paper presented at the annual meeting of the American Academy of Neurology, Denver.

Reifman, A. (2000). Revisiting *The Bell Curve. Psycoloquy, 11,* 99.

Reinis, S., & Goldman, J. M. (1980). *The development of the brain: Biological and functional perspectives.* Springfield, IL: Thomas.

Reis, H. T., Collins, W. A., & Berscheid, E. (2000). The relationship context of human behavior and development. *Psychological Bulletin, 126,* 844–872.

Reiss, I. L. (1960). *Premarital sexual standards in America.* New York: Free Press.

Reiss, M. J. (1984). Human sociobiology. *Zygon Journal of Religion and Science, 19,* 117–140.

Reissland, N. (1988). Neonatal imitation in the first hour of life: Observations in rural Nepal. *Developmental Psychology, 24,* 450–469.

Remafedi, G., French, S., Story, M., Resnick, M. D., & Blum, R. (1998). The relationship between suicide risk and sexual orientation: Results of a population-based study. *American Journal of Public Health, 88,* 57–60.

Repetti, R. L., Taylor, S. E., & Seeman, T. E. (2002). Risky families: Family social environments and the mental and physical health of offspring. *Psychological Bulletin, 128,* 330–366.

Reproductive Medicine Associates of New Jersey. (2002). *Older women and risks of pregnancy.* Princeton, NJ: American Society for Reproductive Medicine.

Reschly, D. J. (1996). Identification and assessment of students with disabilities. *Future of Children, 6,* 40–53.

Resnick, M. D., Bearman, P. S., Blum, R. W., Bauman, K. E., Harris, M. R., Jones, L., et al. (1997). Protecting adolescents from harm: Findings from the National Longitudinal Study on Adolescent Health. *Journal of the American Medical Association, 278,* 823–832.

Rest, J. R., Narvaez, D., Bebeau, M. J., & Thoma, S. J. (1999). *Postconventional moral thinking: A neo-Kohlbergian approach.* Mahwah, NJ: Erlbaum.

Reyna, V. F. (1997). Conceptions of memory development with implications for reasoning and decision making. In R. Vasta (Ed.), *Annals of child development: A research annual* (Vol. 12). London: Kingsley.

Ricciardelli, L. A. (1992). Bilingualism and cognitive development in relation to threshold theory. *Journal of Psycholinguistic Research, 21,* 301–316.

Ricciuti, H. N. (1993). Nutrition and mental development. *Current Directions in Psychological Science, 2,* 43–46.

Richards, M. H., & Duckett, E. (1991). Maternal employment and adolescents. In J. V. Lerner & N. Galambos (Eds.), *Employed mothers and their children.* New York: Garland.

Richards, M. H., & Duckett, E. (1994). The relationship of maternal employment to early adolescent daily experience with and without parents. *Child Development, 65,* 225–236.

Richards, M. P. M. (1996). The childhood environment and the development of sexuality. In C. J. K. Henry & S. J. Ulijaszek (Eds.), *Long-term consequences of early environment: Growth, development and the lifespan developmental perspective.* Cambridge, England: Cambridge University Press.

Richards, R., Kinney, D. K., Benet, M., & Merzel, A. P. C. (1990). Assessing everyday creativity: Characteristics of the lifetime creativity scales and validation with three large samples. *Journal of Personality and Social Psychology, 54,* 476–485.

Richardson, G. A., & Day, N. L. (1994). Detrimental effects of prenatal cocaine exposure: Illusion or reality? *Journal of the American Academy of Child and Adolescent Psychiatry, 33,* 28–34.

Richardson, V., & Champion, V. (1992). The relationship of attitudes, knowledge, and social support to breast-feeding. *Issues in Comprehensive Pediatric Nursing, 15,* 183–197.

Rief, S. F. (1995). *How to reach and teach ADD/ADHD children.* West Nyack, NY: Center for Applied Research in Education.

Rimm, S. B., & Lovance, K. J. (1992). The use of subject and grade skipping for the prevention and reversal of underachievement. *Gifted Child Quarterly, 36,* 100–105.

Ripple, C. H., Gilliam, W. S., Chanana, N., & Zigler, E. (1999). Will fifty cooks spoil the broth? The debate over entrusting Head Start to the states. *American Psychologist, 54,* 327–343.

Rizzo, T. A., Metzger, B. E., Dooley, S. L., & Cho, N. H. (1997). Early malnutrition and child neurobehavioral development: Insights from the study of children of diabetic mothers. *Child Development, 68,* 26–38.

Robbins, M. W. (1990, December 10). Sparing the child: How to intervene when you suspect abuse. *New York Times Magazine,* 42–53.

Roberts, R. D., Zeidner, M., & Matthews, G. (2001). Does emotional intelligence meet traditional standards for an intelligence? Some new data and conclusions. *Emotion, 1,* 196–231.

Roberts, R. E., Phinney, J. S., Masse, L. C., Chen, Y. R., Roberts, C. R., & Romero, A. (1999). The structure of ethnic identity of young adolescents from diverse ethnocultural groups. *Journal of Early Adolescence, 19,* 301–322.

Robertson, S. S. (1982). Intrinsic temporal patterning in the spontaneous movement of awake neonates. *Child Development, 53,* 1016–1021.

Robinson, J. P., & Bianchi, S. (1997, December). The children's hours. *American Demographics,* 20–23.

Robinson, N. M., Zigler, E., & Gallagher, J. J. (2000). Two tails of the normal curve: Similarities and differences in the study of mental retardation and giftedness. *American Psychologist, 55,* 1413–1421.

Rochat, P. (Ed.). *Early social cognition: Understanding others in the first months of life.* Mahwah, NJ: Erlbaum.

Rochat, P., & Goubet, N. (1995). Development of sitting and reaching in 5- and 6-month-old infants. *Infant Behavior and Development, 18,* 53–68.

Roche, T. (2000, November 13). The crisis of foster care. *Time,* 74–82.

Rodgers, J. L. (2001). What causes birth order intelligence patterns? The admixture hypothesis revived. *American Psychologist, 56,* 505–510.

Rodkin, P. C., Farmer, T. W., Pearl, R., & Van Acker, R, (2000). Heterogeneity of popular boys: Antisocial and prosocial configurations. *Developmental Psychology, 36,* 14–24.

Rodman, H., & Cole, C. (1987). A sense of control. In E. Hall (Ed.), *Growing and changing.* New York: Random House.

Roffwarg, H. P., Muzio, J. N., & Dement, W. C. (1966). Ontogenic development of the human sleep–dream cycle. *Science, 152,* 604–619.

Rogan, W. J., & Gladen, B. C. (1993). Breast-feeding and cognitive development. *Early Human Development, 31,* 181–193.

Rogler, L. H. (1999). Methodological sources of cultural insensitivity in mental health research. *American Psychologist, 54,* 424–433.

Rogoff, B. (1990). *Apprenticeship in thinking: Cognitive development in social context.* New York: Oxford University Press.

Rogoff, B. (1995). *Observing sociocultural activity on three planes: Participatory appropriation, guided participation, and apprenticeship.* New York: Cambridge University Press.

Rogoff, B., & Chavajay, P. (1995). What's become of research on the cultural basis of cognitive development? *American Psychologist, 50,* 859–877.

Rohner, R. P. (1998). Father love and child development: History and current evidence. *Current Directions in Psychological Science, 7,* 157–161.

Rolls, E. (2000). Memory systems in the brain. *Annual Review of Psychology, 51,* 599–630.

Romaine, S. (1994). *Bilingualism* (2nd ed.). London: Blackwell.

Rönkä, A., & Pulkkinen, L. (1995). Accumulation of problems in social functioning in young adulthood: A developmental approach. *Journal of Personality and Social Psychology, 69,* 381–391.

Roodenrys, S., Hulme, C., & Brown, G. (1993). The development of short-term memory span: Separable effects of speech rate and long-term memory. *Journal of Experimental Child Psychology, 56,* 431–442.

Roopnarine, J. L, (1992). Father–child play in India. In K. MacDonald (Ed.), *Parent–child play.* Albany: State University of New York Press.

Roopnarine, J. L., Johnson, J. E., & Hooper, F. H. (Eds.). (1994). *Children's play in diverse cultures.* Albany: State University of New York Press.

Rose, A. J., & Asher, S. R. (1999). Children's goals and strategies in response to conflicts within a friendship. *Developmental Psychology, 35,* 69–79.

Rose, S. A., & Feldman, J. F. (1995). Prediction of IQ and specific cognitive abilities at 11 years from infancy measures. *Developmental Psychology, 31,* 685–696.

Rose, S. A., & Feldman, J. F. (1997). Memory and speed: Their role in the relation of infant information processing to later IQ. *Child Development, 68,* 630–641.

Rose, S. A., Feldman, J. F., Wallace, I. F., & McCarton, C. (1991). Information processing at 1 year: Relation to birth status and developmental outcome during the first 5 years. *Developmental Psychology, 27,* 723–737.

Rose, S. A., & Ruff, H. A. (1987). Cross-modal abilities in human infants. In J. D. Osofsky (Ed.), *Handbook of infant development* (2nd ed.). New York: Wiley.

Rosen, D. (1997, March 25). The physician's perspective. *HealthNews,* 3.

Rosen, K. H. (1998). The family roots of aggression and violence: A life span perspective. In L. L'Abate (Ed.), *Family psychopathology: The relational roots of dysfunctional behavior.* New York: Guilford Press.

Rosen, K. S., & Burke, P. B. (1999). Multiple attachment relationships within families: Mothers and fathers with two young children. *Developmental Psychology, 35,* 436–444.

Rosen, W. D., Adamson, L. B., & Bakeman, R. (1992). An experimental investigation of infant social referencing: Mothers' messages and gender differences. *Developmental Psychology, 28,* 1172–1178.

Rosenstein, D., & Oster, H. (1988). Differential facial responses to four basic tastes in newborns. *Child Development, 59,* 1555–1568.

Rosenthal, A. (1996, January 10). In vitro child grows up. *New York Times,* pp. A1, B8.

Rosenthal, M. (1998). Women and infertility. *Psychopharmacology Bulletin, 34,* 307–308.

Rosenthal, R. (1987). Pygmalion effects: Existence, magnitude, and social importance. *Educational Researcher, 16,* 37–40.

Rosenthal, R. (1994). Interpersonal expectancy effects: A 30-year perspective. *Current Directions in Psychological Science, 3,* 176–179.

Rosenthal, R., & Jacobson, L. (1968). *Pygmalion in the classroom: Teacher expectation and pupils' intellectual development.* New York: Holt, Rinehart & Winston.

Rosenzweig, M. R., & Bennett, E. L. (1976). Enriched environments: Facts, factors, and fantasies. In L. Petrinovich & J. L. McGaugh (Eds.), *Knowing, thinking, and believing.* New York: Plenum.

Ross, R. K., & Yu, M. C. (1994). Breast feeding and breast cancer. *New England Journal of Medicine, 330,* 1683–1684.

Ross Laboratories. (1993). *Ross Laboratories' mothers' survey, 1992* [Unpublished data]. Columbus, OH. Abbott Laboratories USA.

Rosser, P. L., & Randolph, S. M. (1989). Black American infants: The Howard University normative study. In J. K. Nugent, B. M. Lester, & T. B. Brazelton (Eds.), *The cultural context of infancy: Vol. 1. Biology, culture, and infant development.* Norwood, NJ: Ablex.

Roth, D., Slone, M., & Dar, R. (2000). Which way cognitive development? An evaluation of the Piagetian and the domain-specific research programs. *Theory and Psychology, 10,* 353–373.

Rothbart, M. K., Ahadi, S. A., & Evans, D. E. (2000). Temperament and personality: Origins and outcomes. *Journal of Personality and Social Psychology, 78,* 122–135.

Rothbart, M. K., & Bates, J. E. (1998). Temperament. In N. Eisenberg (Ed.), *Handbook of child psychology: Vol. 3. Social, emotional, and personality development* (5th ed.) New York: Wiley.

Rothbart, M. K., Derryberry, D., & Hershey, K. (2000). Stability of temperament in childhood: Laboratory infant assessment to parent report at seven years. In V. J. Molfese & D. L. Molfese (Eds.), *Temperament and personality development across the life span.* Mahwah, NJ: Erlbaum.

Rothbaum, F., Weisz, J., Pott, M., Miyake, K., & Morelli, G. (2000). Attachment and culture: Security in the United States and Japan. *American Psychologist, 55,* 1093–1104.

Rovee-Collier, C. K. (1987). Learning and memory in infancy. In J. D. Osofsky (Ed.), *Handbook of infant development* (2nd ed.). New York: Wiley.

Rovee-Collier, C. K. (1993). The capacity for long-term memory in infancy. *Current Directions in Psychological Science, 2,* 130–135.

Rovee-Collier, C. K. (1999). The development of infant memory. *Current Directions in Psychological Science, 8,* 80–85.

Rovee-Collier, C. K., & Gerhardstein, P. (1997). The development of infant memory. In N. Cowan (Ed.), *The development of memory in childhood.* Philadelphia: Psychology Press.

Rovee-Collier, C. K., & Hayne, H. (1987). Reactivation and infant long-term memory. In H. W. Reese (Ed.), *Advances in child development and behavior* (Vol. 20). New York: Academic Press.

Rowe, D. C. (1994). *The effects of nurture on individual natures.* New York: Guilford Press.

Rowe, D. C. (1999). Heredity. In V. J. Derlega, B. A. Winstead, & W. H. Jones (Eds.), *Personality: Contemporary theory and research* (2nd ed.). Chicago: Nelson-Hall.

Roy, A., Nielsen, D., Rylander, G., Sarchiapone, M., & Segal, N. L. (1999). Genetics of suicide in depression. *Journal of Clinical Psychology, 60,* 12–17.

Rubenstein, A. J., Kalakanis, L., & Langlois, J. H. (1999). Infant preferences for attractive faces: A cognitive explanation. *Developmental Psychology, 35,* 848–855.

Rubin, D. H., Krasilnikoff, P. A., Leventhal, J. M., Weile, B., & Berget, A. (1986). Effects of passive smoking on birthweight. *Lancet, 315,* 415–417.

Rubin, K. H. (1998). Social and emotional development from a cultural perspective. *Developmental Psychology, 34,* 611–615.

Rubin, K. H., Fein, G., & Vandenberg, B. (1983). Play. In E. M. Hetherington (Ed.), *Handbook of child psychology: Vol. 4. Socialization, personality, and social development.* New York: Wiley.

Ruble, D. N. (1983). The development of social comparison processes and their role in achievementrelated self-actualization. In E. T. Higgins, D. N. Ruble, & W. W. Hartup (Eds.), *Social cognition and social development.* New York: Cambridge University Press.

Ruble, D. N., Boggiano, A. K., Feldman, N. S., & Loebl, J. H. (1989). Developmental analysis of the role of social comparison in self-evaluation. *Developmental Psychology, 16,* 105–115.

Ruble, D. N., & Brooks-Gunn, J. (1982). The experience of menarche. *Child Development, 53,* 1557–1566.

Ruda, M. A., Ling, Q.-D., Hohmann, A. G., Peng, Y. B., & Tachibana, T. (2000). Altered nociceptive neuronal circuits after neonatal peripheral inflammation. *Science, 289,* 628–630.

Ruff, H. A. (1989). The infant's use of visual and haptic information in the perception and recognition of objects. *Canadian Journal of Psychology, 43,* 302–319.

Ruffman, T., Perner, J., Naito, M., Parkin, L., & Clements, W. A. (1998). Older (but not younger) siblings facilitate false belief understanding. *Developmental Psychology, 34,* 161–174.

Rule, B. G., & Ferguson, T. J. (1986). The effects of media violence on attitudes, emotions, and cognitions. *Journal of Social Issues, 42,* 29–50.

Russell, G., & Radojevic, M. (1992). The changing role of fathers? Current understandings and future directions for research and practice. Special section: Attachment and the relationship the infant and caregivers. *Infant Mental Health Journal, 13,* 296–311.

Rust, J., Golombok, S., Hines, M., Johnston, K., Golding, J., & ALSPAC Study Team. (2000). The role of brothers and sisters in the gender development of preschool children. *Journal of Experimental Child Psychology, 77,* 292–303.

Rusting, R. (1990, March). Safe passage? *Scientific American,* 36.

Rutter, M., Bailey, A., Bolton, P., & Le Couteur, A. (1993). Autism: Syndrome definition and possible genetic mechanisms. In R. Plomin & G. E. McClearn, (Eds.), *Nature, nurture, and psychology.* Washington, DC: American Psychological Association.

Rutter, M., Dunn, J., Plomin, R., & Simonoff, E. (1997). Integrating nature and nurture: Implications of person–environment correlations and interactions for developmental psychopathology. *Development and Psychopathology, 9,* 335–364.

Ryan, A. S. (1997). The resurgence of breastfeeding in the United States. *Pediatrics, 99,* E12.

Rycek, R. F., Stuhr, S. L., McDermott, J., Benker, J., & Swartz, M. D. (1998). Adolescent egocentrism and cognitive functioning during late adolescence. *Adolescence, 33,* 745–749.

Saad, L. (2002, May 16). "Cloning" humans is a turnoff to most Americans. *Gallup News Service.* Retrieved from http://www.gallup.com

Saarni, C. (1999). *The development of emotional competence.* New York: Guilford Press.

Sacks, M. H. (1993). Exercise for stress control. In D. Goleman & J. Gurin (Eds.), *Mind–body medicine.* Yonkers, NY: Consumer Reports Books.

Sadker, M., & Sadker, D. (1994). *Failing at fairness: How America's schools cheat girls.* New York: Scribner.

Sagi, A. (1990). Attachment theory and research from a cross-cultural perspective. *Human Development, 33,* 10–22.

Sagi, A., Donnell, F., van IJzendoorn, M. H., Mayseless, O., & Aviezer, O. (1994). Sleeping out of home in a kibbutz communal arrangement: It makes a difference for infant–mother attachment. *Child Development, 65,* 992–1004.

Sagi, A., van IJzendoorn, M. H., Aviezer, O., Donnell, F., Koren-Karie, N., Joels, T., et al. (1995). Attachments in multiple-caregiver and multiple-infant environment: The case of the Israeli kibbutzim. *Monographs of the Society for Research in Child Development, 60,* 000–000.

Sagi, A., van IJzendoorn, M. H., & Kroonenberg, N. (1991). Primary appraisal of the Strange Situation: A cross-cultural analysis of preseparation episodes. *Developmental Psychology, 27,* 587–596.

Sagrestano, L. M., McCormick, S. H., Paikoff, R. L., & Holmbeck, G. N. (1999). Pubertal development and parent–child conflict in low-income, urban, African American adolescents. *Journal of Research on Adolescence, 9,* 85–107.

Salber, E. J., Freeman, H. E., & Abelin, T. (1968). Needed research on smoking: Lessons from the Newton study. In E. F. Borgatta & R. R. Evans (Eds.), *Smoking, health, and behavior.* Chicago: Aldine.

Sales, B. D., & Folkman, S. (Eds.). (2000). *Ethics in research with human participants.* Washington, DC: American Psychological Association.

Salmon, D. K. (1993, September). Getting through labor. *Parents,* 62–66.

Salthouse, T. A. (1984). Effects of age and skill in typing. *Journal of Experimental Psychology: General, 113,* 345–371.

Sanderson, C. A., & Cantor, N. (1995). Social dating goals in late adolescence: Implications for safer sexual activity. *Journal of Personality and Social Psychology, 68,* 1121–1134.

Sandler, B. (1994, January 31). First denial, then a near-suicidal plea: "Mom, I need your help." *People,* 56–58.

Sandoval, J., Frisby, C. L., Geisinger, K. F., Scheuneman, J. D., & Grenier, J. R. (Eds.). (1998). *Test interpretation and diversity: Achieving equity in assessment.* Washington, DC: American Psychological Association.

Sandyk, R. (1992). Melatonin and maturation of REM sleep. *International Journal of Neuroscience, 63,* 105–114.

Sanoff, A. P., & Minerbrook, S. (1993, April 19). Race on campus. *U.S. News and World Report,* 52–64.

Sanson, A., & di Muccio, C. (1993). The influence of aggressive and neutral cartoons and toys on the behavior of preschool children. *Australian Psychologist, 28,* 93–99.

Saudino, K., & McManus, I. C. (1998). Handedness, footedness, eyedness, and earedness in the Colorado Adoption Project. *British Journal of Developmental Psychology, 16,* 167–174.

Savage-Rumbaugh, E. S., Murphy, J., Sevcik, R. A., Brakke, K. E., Williams, S. L., & Rumbaugh, D. M. (1993). Language and comprehension in ape and child. *Monographs of the Society for Research in Child Development, 58*(3–4, Serial No. 233).

Savin-Williams, R. C., & Berndt, T. J. (1990). Friendship and peer relations. In S. S. Feldman & G. R. Elliott (Eds.), *At the threshold: The developing adolescent.* Cambridge, MA: Harvard University Press.

Savin-Williams, R. C., & Demo, D. (1983). Situational and transituational determinants of adolescent self-feelings. *Journal of Personality and Social Psychology, 44,* 824–833.

Sax, L. J., Astin, A. W., Korn, W. S， & Mahoney, K. M. (2000). *The American freshman: National norms for fall 2000.* Los Angeles: University of California, Higher Education Research Institute.

Saywitz, K. J., & Nathanson, R. (1993). Children's testimony and their perceptions of stress in and out of the courtroom. *Child Abuse and Neglect, 17,* 613–622.

Scariati, P. D., Grummer-Strawn, L. M., & Fein, S. B. (1997). A longitudinal analysis of infant morbidity and the extent of breastfeeding in the United States. *Pediatrics, 99,* E5.

Scarr, S. (1992). Developmental theories for the 1990s: Development and individual differences. *Child Development, 63,* 1–19.

Scarr, S. (1993). Biological and cultural diversity: The legacy of Darwin for development. *Child Development, 64,* 1333–1353.

Scarr, S. (1996). Child care research, social values, and public policy. *American Academy of Arts and Sciences Bulletin, 1,* 28–45.

Scarr, S. (1997). Why child care has little impact on most children's development. *Current Directions in Psychological Science, 6,* 143–147.

Scarr, S. (1998). American child care today. *American Psychologist, 53,* 95–108.

Scarr, S., & Carter-Saltzman, L. (1982). Genetics and intelligence. In R. J. Sternberg (Ed.), *Handbook of human intelligence.* New York: Cambridge University Press.

Scarr, S., Phillips, D., & McCartney, K. (1989). Working mothers and their families. *American Psychologist, 44,* 1402–1409.

Schanberg, S., Field, T. M., Kuhn, C., & Bartolome, J. (1993). Touch: A biological regulator of growth and development in the neonate. *Verhaltenstherapie, 3*(Suppl. 1), 15.

Schatz, M. (1994). *A toddler's life.* New York: Oxford University Press.

Schellenberg, E. G., & Trehub, S. E. (1996). Natural musical intervals: Evidence from infant listeners. *Psychological Science, 7,* 272–277.

Schemo, D. J. (2001, December 5). U.S. students prove middling on 32-nation test. *New York Times,* p. A21.

Schlegel, A., & Barry, H., III. (1991). *Adolescence: An anthropological inquiry.* New York: Free Press.

Schmitt, E. (2001, March 13). For 7 million people in census, one race category isn't enough. *New York Times,* pp. A1, A14.

Schneider, B. A., Atkinson, L., & Tardif, C. (2001). Child-parent attachment and children's peer relations: A quantitative review. *Developmental Psychology, 37,* 86–100.

Schneider, B. A., Bull, D., & Trehub, S. E. (1988). Binaural unmasking in infants. *Journals of the Acoustical Society of America, 83,* 1124–1132.

Schneider, B. A., Trehub, S. E., & Bull, D. (1980). High-frequency sensitivity in infants. *Science, 207,* 1003–1004.

Schneider, W., & Pressley, M. (1989). *Memory between two and twenty.* New York: Springer-Verlag.

Schneiderman, N. (1983). Animal behavior models of coronary hearty disease. In D. S. Kranz, A. Baum, & J. E. Singer (Eds.), *Handbook of psychology and health* (Vol. 3). Hillsdale, NJ: Erlbaum.

Schnur, E., & Belanger, S. (2000). What works in Head Start. In M. P. Kluger & G. Alexander (Eds.), *What works in child welfare.* Washington, DC: Child Welfare League of America.

Schofield, J. W., & Francis, W. D. (1982). An observational study of peer interaction in racially mixed "accelerated" classrooms. *Journal of Educational Psychology, 74,* 722–732.

Scholnick, E. K., Nelson, K., Gelman, S. A., & Miller, P. H. (1999). *Conceptual development: Piaget's legacy.* Mahwah, NJ: Erlbaum.

Schor, E. L. (1987). Unintentional injuries: Patterns within families. *American Journal of the Diseases of Children, 141,* 1280.

Schreiber, G. B., Robins, M., Striegel-Moore, R., Obarzanek, M., Morrison, J. A., & Wright, D. J. (1996). Weight modification efforts reported by black and white preadolescent girls: National Heart, Lung, and Blood Institute Growth and Health Study. *Pediatrics, 98,* 63–70.

Schuckit, M. A. (1999). New findings on the genetics of alcoholism. *Journal of the American Medical Association, 281,* 1875–1876.

Schulenberg, J. E., Asp, C. E., & Peterson, A. C. (1984). School from the young adolescent's perspective. *Journal of Early Adolescence, 4,* 107–130.

Schulman, M. (1991). *The passionate mind: Bringing up an intelligent and creative child.* New York: Free Press.

Schulman, M., & Mekler, E. (1994). *Bringing up a moral child: A new approach for teaching your child to be kind, just, and responsible.* Reading, MA: Addison-Wesley.

Schulman, P., Keith, D., & Seligman, M. (1993). Is optimism heritable? A study of twins. *Behavior Research and Therapy, 31,* 569–574.

Schultz, A. H. (1969). *The life of primates.* New York: Universe.

Schuster, C. S., & Ashburn, S. S. (1986). *The process of human development* (2nd. ed.). Boston: Little, Brown.

Schutt, R. K. (2001). *Investigating the social world: The process and practice of research.* Thousand Oaks, CA: Sage.

Schwartz, D., Dodge, K. A., Pettit, G. S., & Bates, J. E. (1997). The early socialization of aggressive victims of bullying. *Child Development, 68,* 665–675.

Schwartz, I. M. (1999). Sexual activity prior to coital interaction: A comparison between males and females. *Archives of Sexual Behavior, 28,* 63–69.

Schwebel, M., Maher, C. A., & Fagley, N. S. (Eds.). (1990). *Promoting cognitive growth over the life span.* Hillsdale, NJ: Erlbaum.

Scopesi, A., Zanobini, M., & Carossino, P. (1997). Childbirth in different cultures: Psychophysical reactions of women delivering in U.S., German, French, and Italian hospitals. *Journal of Reproductive and Infant Psychology, 15,* 9–30.

Scruggs, T. E., & Mastropieri, M. A. (1994). Successful mainstreaming in elementary science classes: A qualitative study of three reputational cases. *American Educational Research Journal, 31,* 785–811.

Sears, R. R. (1977). Sources of life satisfaction of the Terman gifted men. *American Psychologist, 32,* 119–129.

Segal, B. M., & Stewart, J. C. (1996). Substance use and abuse in adolescence: An overview. *Child Psychiatry and Human Development, 26,* 193–210.

Segal, J., & Segal, Z. (1992, September). No more couch potatoes. *Parents,* 32–39.

Segal, N. L. (1993). Twin, sibling, and adoption methods: Tests of evolutionary hypotheses. *American Psychologist, 48,* 943–956.

Segal, N. L. (2000). Virtual twins: New findings on within-family environmental influences on intelligence. *Journal of Educational Psychology, 92,* 188–194.

Segall, M. H., Dasen, P. R., Berry, J. W., & Poortinga, Y. H. (1990). *Human behavior in global perspective.* Needham Heights, MA: Allyn & Bacon.

Seidman, S. N., & Rieder, R. O. (1994). A review of sexual behavior in the United States. *American Journal of Psychiatry, 151,* 330–341.

Seifer, R., Schiller, M., & Sameroff, A. J. (1996). Attachment, maternal sensitivity, and infant temperament during the first year of life. *Developmental Psychology, 32,* 12–25.

Senghas, A., & Coppola, M. (2001). Children creating language: How Nicaraguan sign language acquired a spatial grammar. *Psychological Science, 12,* 323–328.

Seppa, N. (1996, December). Keeping schoolyards safe from bullies. *Monitor on Psychology, 41.*

Serbin, L. A., Poulin-Dubois, D., Colburne, K. A., Sen, M. G., & Eichstedt, J. A. (2001). Gender stereotyping in infancy: Visual preferences for and knowledge of gender-stereotyped toys in the second year. *International Journal of Behavioral Development, 25,* 7–15.

Serovich, J. M., & Greene, K. (1997). Predictors of adolescent risk-taking behaviors which put them at risk for contracting HIV. *Journal of Youth and Adolescence, 26,* 429–444.

Servin, A., Bohlin, G., & Berlin, L. (1999). Sex differences in 1-, 3-, and 5-year-olds' toy choice in a structured play session. *Scandinavian Journal of Psychology, 40,* 43–48.

Sesser, S. (1993, September 13). Opium war redux. *New Yorker,* 78–89.

Shafer, R. G. (1990, March 12). An anguished father recounts the battle he lost: Trying to rescue a teenage son from drugs. *People,* 81–83.

Shantz, C. U., & Hartup, W. W. (Eds.). (1995). *Conflict in child and adolescent development.* New York: Cambridge University Press.

Sharp, D. (1997, March 14). Your kids' education is at stake. *USA Weekend,* pp. 4–6.

Sharpe, R. (1994, July 18). Better babies: School gets kids to do feats at a tender age, but it's controversial. *Wall Street Journal,* pp. A1, A6.

Shavelson, R., Hubner, J. J., & Stanton, J. C. (1976). Self-concept: Validation of construct interpretations. *Review of Educational Research, 46,* 407–441.

Shaw, D. S., Winslow, E. B., & Flanagan, C. (1999). A prospective study of the effects of marital status and family relations on young children's adjustment among African American and European American families. *Child Development, 70,* 742–755.

Shaywitz, S. E. (1996, November). Dyslexia. *Scientific American,* 98–104.

Shaywitz, S. E., Shaywitz, B. A., Pugh, K. R., Fulbright, R. K., Skudlarski, P., Mencl, W. E., et al. (1999). Effect of estrogen on brain activation patterns in postmenopausal women during working memory tasks. *Journal of the American Medical Association, 281,* 1197–1202.

Shea, J. D. (1985). Studies of cognitive development in Papua New Guinea. *International Journal of Psychology, 20,* 33–61.

Shea, K. M., Wilcox, A. J., & Little, R. E. (1998). Postterm delivery: A challenge for epidemiologic research. *Epidemiology, 9,* 199–204.

Shealy, C. N. (1995). From Boys Town to Oliver Twist: Separating fact from fiction in welfare reform and out-of-home placement of children and youth. *American Psychologist, 50,* 565–580.

Sheets, R. H., & Hollins, E. R. (1999). *Racial and ethnic identity in school practices.* Mahwah, NJ: Erlbaum.

Sheingold, K., & Tenney, Y. J. (1982). Memory for a salient childhood event. In U. Neisser (Ed.), *Memory observed.* New York: Freeman.

Shepard, G. B. (1991). A glimpse of kindergarten—Chinese style. *Young Children, 47,* 11–15.

Shields, J. (1973). Heredity and psychological abnormality. In H. Eysenck (Ed.), *Handbook of abnormal psychology.* San Diego, CA: Edits.

Shiono, P. H., & Behrman, R. E. (1995). Low birth weight: Analysis and recommendations. *Future of Children, 5,* 4–18.

Short, R. J., & Talley, R. C. (1997). Rethinking psychology and the schools: Implications of recent national policy. *American Psychologist, 52,* 234–240.

Shriver, M. D., & Piersel, W. (1994). The long-term effects of intrauterine drug exposure: Review of recent research and implications for early childhood special education. *Topics in Early Childhood Special Education, 14,* 161–183.

Shrum, W., Cheek, N., Jr., & Hunter, S. M. (1988). Friendship in school: Gender and racial homophily. *Sociology of Education, 61,* 227–239.

Shucard, J., Shucard, D., Cummins, K., & Campso, J. (1981). Auditory evoked potentials and sex-related differences in brain development. *Brain and Language, 13,* 91–102.

Shurkin, J. N. (1992). *Terman's kids: The groundbreaking study of how the gifted grow up.* Boston: Little, Brown.

Shute, N. (1997, November 10). No more hard labor. *U.S. News and World Report,* 92–95.

Sieber, J. E. (1998). Planning ethically responsible research. In L. Bickman & D. J. Rog (Eds.), *Handbook of applied social research methods.* Thousand Oaks, CA: Sage.

Siegal, M. (1997). *Knowing children: Experiments in conversation and cognition* (2nd ed.). Philadelphia: Psychology Press.

Siegel, B. (1996). Is the emperor wearing clothes? Social policy and the empirical support for full inclusion of children with disabilities in the preschool and early elementary grades. *Social Policy Report, 10,* 2–17.

Siegel, L. S. (1989). A reconceptualization of prediction from infant test scores. In M. H. Bornstein & N. A. Krasnegor (Eds.), *Stability and continuity in mental development: Behavioral and biological perspectives.* Hillsdale, NJ: Erlbaum.

Siegler, R. S. (1994). Cognitive variability: A key to understanding cognitive development. *Current Directions in Psychological Science, 3,* 1–5.

Siegler, R. S. (1995). How does change occur?: A microgenetic study of number conservation. *Cognitive Psychology, 28,* 225–273.

Siegler, R. S. (1998). *Children's thinking* (3rd ed.). Upper Saddle River, NJ: Prentice Hall.

Siegler, R. S., & Ellis, S. (1996). Piaget on childhood. *Psychological Science, 7,* 211–215.

Siegler, R. S., & Richards, D. (1982). The development of intelligence. In R. J. Sternberg (Ed.), *Handbook of human intelligence.* New York: Cambridge University Press.

Sigman, M. D. (1995). Nutrition and child development: More food for thought. *Current Directions in Psychological Science, 4,* 52–55.

Sigman, M. D., Cohen, S. E., Beckwith, L., Asarnow, R., & Parmelee, A. H., Jr. (1992). The prediction of cognitive abilities at 8 and 12 years of age from neonatal assessments of preterm infants. In S. L. Friedman & M. D. Sigman (Eds.), *The psychological development of low birthweight children.* Norwood, NJ: Ablex.

Sigman, M. D., Neumann, C., Jansen, A. A. J., & Bwibo, N. (1989). Cognitive abilities of Kenyan children in relation to nutrition, family characteristics, and education. *Child Development, 60,* 1463–1474.

Signorella, M. L., Bigler, R. S., & Liben, L. (1993). Development differences in children's gender schemata about others: A meta-analytic review. *Developmental Review, 13,* 106–126.

Silbereisen, R., Peterson, A., Albrecht, H., & Krache, B. (1989). Maturational timing and the development of problem behavior: Longitudinal studies in adolescence. *Journal of Early Adolescence, 9,* 247.

Silver, L. B. (1999). *Attention deficit hyperactivity disorder: A clinical guide to diagnosis and treatment for health and mental health professionals.* Washington, DC: American Psychiatric Press.

Silverman, W. K., & Ginsburg, G. S. (1998). Anxiety disorders. In T. H. Ollendick & M. Hersen (Eds.), *Handbook of child psychopathology* (3rd ed.). New York: Plenum.

Silverstein, L. B., & Auerbach, C. F. (1999). Deconstructing the essential father. *American Psychologist, 54,* 397–407.

Silverthorn, P., & Frick, P. J. (1999). Developmental pathways to antisocial behavior: The delayed-onset pathway in girls. *Developmental and Psychopathology, 11,* 101–126.

Simcock, G., & Hayne, H. (2002). Breaking the barrier? Children fail to translate their preverbal memories into language. *Psychological Science, 13,* 225–231.

Simmons, R. (2002). *Odd girl out: The hidden culture of aggression in girls.* Orlando, FL: Harcourt.

Simmons, R., & Blyth, D. (1987). *Moving into adolescence.* Hawthorne, NY: Aldine de Gruyter.

Simon, T. J., Hespos, S. J., & Rochat, P. (1995). Do infants understand simple arithmetic? A replication of Wynn (1992). *Cognitive Development, 10,* 253–269.

Simons, K. (Ed.). (1993). *Early visual development: Normal and abnormal.* New York: Oxford University Press.

Singer, D. G., & Singer, J. L. (Eds.). (2000). *Handbook of children and the media.* Thousand Oaks, CA: Sage.

Singer, L. T., Arendt, R., Minnes, S., Farkas, K., & Salvator, A. (2000). Neurobehavioral outcomes of cocaine-exposed infants. *Neurotoxicology and Teratology, 22,* 653–666.

Singh, G. K., & Yu, S. M. (1995). Infant mortality in the United States: Trends, differentials, and projections, 1950 through 2010. *American Journal of Public Health, 85,* 957–964.

Singleton, L. C., & Asher, S. R. (1979). Racial integration and children's peer preferences. *Child Development, 50,* 936–941.

Skinner, B. F. (1957). *Verbal behavior.* New York: Appleton-Century-Crofts.

Skipper, J. K., & Nass, G. (1966). Dating behavior: A framework of analysis and an illustration. *Journal of Marriage and the Family, 28,* 412–420.

Slater, A., & Butterworth, G. (1997). Perception of social stimuli: Face perception and imitation. In G. Bremmer, A. Slater, & G. Butterworth (Eds.), *Infant development: Recent advances.* Philadelphia: Psychology Press.

Slater, A., & Johnson, S. P. (1998). Visual sensory and perceptual abilities of the newborn: Beyond the blooming, buzzing confusion. In F. Simon & G. Butterworth (Eds.), *The development of sensory, motor and cognitive capacities in early infancy: From perception to cognition.* Philadelphia: Psychology Press.

Slater, A., Mattock, A., & Brown, E. (1990). Size constancy at birth: Newborn infants' responses to retinal and real size. *Journal of Experimental Child Psychology, 49,* 314–322.

Slavin, R. E. (1995). Enhancing intergroup relations in schools: Cooperative learning and other strategies. In W. D. Hawley & A. W. Jackson (Eds.), *Toward a common destiny: Improving race and ethnic relations in America.* San Francisco: Jossey-Bass.

Sleek, S. (1997, June). Can "emotional intelligence" be taught in today's schools? *Monitor on Psychology,* 25.

Slobin, D. (1970). Universals of grammatical development in children. In G. Flores D'Arcais & W. Levelt (Eds.), *Advances in psycholinguistics.* New York: Elsevier.

Smetana, J. G. (1988). Concepts of self and social convention: Adolescents' and parents' reasoning about hypothetical and actual family conflicts. In M. Gunnar (Ed.), *21st Minnesota Symposium on Child Psychology.* Hillsdale, NJ: Erlbaum.

Smetana, J. G. (1989). Adolescents' and parents' reasoning about actual family conflict. *Child Development, 60,* 1052–1067.

Smetana, J. G. (1995). Parenting styles and conceptions of parental authority during adolescence. *Child Development 66,* 299–316.

Smetana, J. G., Yau, J., & Hanson, S. (1991). Conflict resolution in families with adolescents. *Journal of Research on Adolescence, 1,* 189–206.

Smith, M. (1990). Alternative techniques. *Nursing Times, 86,* 43–45.

Smith, P. K. (1978). A longitudinal study of social participation in preschool children: Solitary and parallel play reexamined. *Developmental Psychology, 12,* 517–523.

Smith, R. (1999, March). The timing of birth. *Scientific American,* 68–75.

Smotherman, W. P., & Robinson, S. R. (1996). The development of behavior before birth. *Developmental Psychology, 32,* 425–434.

Smuts, A. B., & Hagen, J. W. (1985). History of the family and of child development: Introduction to Part 1. *Monographs of the Society for Research in Child Development, 50*(4–5, Serial No. 211).

Snow, C. E. (1977). The development of conversation between mothers and babies. *Journal of Child Language, 4,* 1–22.

Snow, R. (1969). Unfinished Pygmalion. *Contemporary Psychology, 14,* 197–199.

Snowden, P. L., & Christian, L. G. (1999). Parenting the young gifted child: Supportive behaviors. *Roeper Review, 21,* 215–221.

Snyder, J., Horsch, E., & Childs, J. (1997). Peer relationships of young children: Affiliative choices and the shaping of behavior. *Journal of Clinical Child Psychology, 26,* 145–156.

Snyder, M. (1974). The self-monitoring of expressive behavior. *Journal of Personality and Social Psychology, 30,* 526–537.

Snyder, R. A., Verderber, K. S., Langmeyer, L., & Myers, M. (1992). A reconsideration of self- and organization-referent attitudes as "causes" of the glass ceiling effect. *Group and Organization Management, 17,* 260–278.

Socolar, R. R. S., & Stein, R. E. K. (1995). Spanking infants and toddlers: Maternal belief and practice. *Pediatrics, 95,* 105–111.

Socolar, R. R. S., & Stein, R. E. K. (1996). Maternal discipline of young children: Context, belief, and practice. *Developmental and Behavioral Pediatrics, 17,* 1–8.

Soken, N. H., & Pick, A .D. (1999). Infants' perception of dynamic affective expressions: Do infants distinguish specific expressions? *Child Development, 70,* 1275–1282.

Solomon, G. E. A., & Cassimatis, N. L. (1999). On facts and conceptual systems: Young children's integration of their understandings of germs and contagion. *Developmental Psychology, 35,* 113–126.

Solomon, R. C., & Serres, F. (1999). Effects of parental verbal aggression on children's self-esteem and school marks. *Child Abuse and Neglect, 23,* 339–351.

Sophian, C., Garyantes, D., & Chang, C. (1997). When three is less than two: Early developments in children's understanding of fractional quantities. *Developmental Psychology, 33,* 731–744.

Sorensen, K. (1992). Physical and mental development of adolescent males with Klinefelter syndrome. *Hormone Research, 37*(Suppl. 3), 55–61.

Sorensen, T., Nielsen, G., Andersen, P., & Teasdale, T. (1988). Genetic and environmental influences on premature death in adult adoptees. *New England Journal of Medicine, 318,* 727–732.

Sotos, J. F. (1997). Overgrowth: Section IV: Genetic disorders associated with overgrowth. *Clinical Pediatrics, 36,* 37–49.

Soussignan, R., Schaal, B., Marlier, L., & Jiang, T. (1997). Facial and autonomic responses to biological and artificial olfactory stimuli in human neonates: Reexamining early hedonic discrimination of odors. *Physiology and Behavior, 62,* 745–758.

Southern, W. T., Jones, E. D., & Stanley, J. C. (1993). Acceleration and enrichment: The context and development of program options. In K. A. Heller, F. J. Monks, & A. H. Passow (Eds.), *International handbook of research and development of giftedness and talent.* Oxford, England: Pergamon.

Spearman, C. (1927). *The abilities of man.* London: Macmillan.

Spelke, E. S. (1987). The development of intermodal perception. In P. Salapatek & L. Cohen (Eds.), *Handbook of infant perception* (Vol. 2). Orlando, FL: Academic Press.

Spelke, E. S. (1991). Physical knowledge in infancy: Reflections on Piaget's theory. In S. Carey & R. Gelman (Eds.), *The epigenesis of mind.* Hillsdale, NJ: Erlbaum.

Spencer, J. (2001). How to battle school violence. *MSNBC News.* Retrieved from http://www.msnbc.com/news/

Spencer, M. B. (1991). Identity, minority development of. In R. M. Lerner, A. C. Petersen, & J. Brooks-Gunn (Eds.), *Encyclopedia of adolescence* (Vol. 1). New York: Garland.

Spencer, M. B., & Dornbusch, S. M. (1990). Challenges in studying minority youth. In S. S. Feldman & G. R. Elliott (Eds.), *At the threshold: The developing adolescent.* Cambridge, MA: Harvard University Press.

Spencer, N. (2001). The social patterning of teenage pregnancy. *Journal of Epidemiology and Community Health, 55,* 5.

Spiegel, D. (1993). Social support: How friends, family, and groups can help. In D. Goleman & J. Gurin (Eds.), *Mind-body medicine.* Yonkers, NY: Consumer Reports Books.

Spira, A., Bajos, N., Bejin, A., Beltzer, N. (1992). AIDS and sexual behavior in France. *Nature, 360,* 407–409.

Springen, K. (2000). The circumcision decision. *Newsweek* [Special issue: *Your Child*], 50.

Springer, S. P., & Deutsch, G. (1989). *Left brain, right brain* (3rd ed.). New York: Freeman.

Squires, S. (1991, September 17). Lifelong fitness depends on teaching children to love exercise. *Washington Post,* p. WH16.

Sroufe, L. A. (1994). Pathways to adaptation and maladaptation: Psychopathology as developmental deviation. In D. Cicchetti (Ed.), *Developmental psychopathology: Past, present, and future.* Hillsdale, NJ: Erlbaum.

Sroufe, L. A. (1996). *Emotional development: The organization of emotional life in the early years.* New York: Oxford University Press.

Stack, D., & Muir, D. (1992). Adult tactile stimulation during face-to-face interactions modulates five-month-olds' affect and attention. *Child Development, 63,* 1509–1525.

Stacy, A. W., Sussman, S., Dent, C. W., Burton, D., et al. (1992). Moderators of peer social influence in adolescent smoking. *Personality and Social Psychology Bulletin, 18,* 163–172.

Stadtler, A. C., Gorski, P. A., & Brazelton, T. B. (1999). Toilet training methods, clinical interventions, and recommendations. *Pediatrics, 103,* 1359–1361.

Stanjek, K. (1978). Das Überreichen von Gaben: Funktion und Entwicklung in den ersten Lebensjahren. *Zeitschrift für Entwicklungpsychologie und Pädagogische Psychologie, 10,* 103–113.

Stanley, J. C., & Benbow, C. P. (1983). SMPY's first decade: Ten years of posing problems and solving them. *Journal of Special Education, 17,* 11–25.

Starfield, B. (1991). Childhood morbidity: Comparisons, clusters, and trends. *Pediatrics, 88,* 519–526.

Starfield, B., Katz, H., Gabriel, A., Livingston, G., Benson, P., Hankin, J., et al. (1984). Morbidity in childhood: A longitudinal view. *New England Journal of Medicine, 310,* 824–829.

Staub, E. (1977). A child in distress: The influence of nurturance and modeling on children's attempts to help. *Developmental Psychology, 5,* 124–133.

Staudenmeier, J. J., Jr. (1999). Children and computers. *Journal of the American Academy of Child and Adolescent Psychiatry, 38,* 5.

Stedman, L. C. (1997). International achievement differences: An assessment of a new perspective. *Educational Researcher, 26,* 4–15.

Steele, C. M. (1997). A threat in the air: How stereotypes shape intellectual identity and performance. *American Psychologist, 52,* 613–629.

Steele, C. M., & Aronson, J. (1995). Stereotype threat and the intellectual test performance of African Americans. *Journal of Personality and Social Psychology, 69,* 797–811.

Stein, J. A., Lu, M. C., & Gelberg, L. (2000). Severity of homelessness and adverse birth outcomes. *Health Psychology, 19,* 524–534.

Stein, J. H., & Reiser, L. W. (1994). A study of white middle-class adolescent boys' responses to "semenarche" (the first ejaculation). *Journal of Youth and Adolescence, 23,* 373–384.

Stein, Z., Susser, M., Saenger, G., & Marolla, F. (1975). *Famine and human development: The Dutch hunger winter of 1944–1945.* New York: Oxford University Press.

Steinberg, J. (1996, August 25). Why America's ever-fatter kids don't go to gym. *New York Times,* p. 14.

Steinberg, J. (1997, January 2). Turning words into meaning. *New York Times,* pp. B1–B2.

Steinberg, L. (1990). Autonomy, conflict, and harmony in the family relationship. In S. S. Feldman & G. R. Elliott (Eds.), *At the threshold: The developing adolescent.* Cambridge, MA: Harvard University Press.

Steinberg, L. (1993). *Adolescence.* New York: McGraw-Hill.

Steinberg, L., & Silverberg, S. (1986). The vicissitudes of autonomy in early adolescence. *Child Development, 57,* 841–851.

Steinberg, L., Dornbusch, S. M., & Brown, B. B. (1992). Ethnic differences in adolescent achievement: An ecological perspective. *American Psychologist, 47,* 723–729.

Steiner, J. E. (1979). Human facial expressions in response to taste and smell stimulation. *Advances in Child Development and Behavior, 13,* 257.

Steinhausen, H. C., & Spohr, H. L. (1998). Long-term outcome of children with fetal alcohol syndrome: Psychopathology, behavior, and intelligence. *Alcoholism: Clinical and Experimental Research, 22,* 334–338.

Sternberg, R. J. (1982). Reasoning, problems solving, and intelligence. In R. J. Sternberg (Ed.), *Handbook of human intelligence.* New York: Cambridge University Press.

Sternberg, R. J. (1985). *Beyond IQ: A triarchic theory of human intelligence.* New York: Cambridge University Press.

Sternberg, R. J. (1987). Liking versus loving: A comparative evaluation of theories. *Psychological Bulletin, 102,* 331–345.

Sternberg, R. J. (1990). *Metaphors of mind: Conceptions of the nature of intelligence.* New York: Cambridge University Press.

Sternberg, R. J. (1991). Theory-based testing of intellectual abilities: Rationale for the Sternberg Triarchic Abilities Test. In H. A. H. Rowe (Ed.), *Intelligence: Reconceptualization and measurement.* Hillsdale, NJ: Erlbaum.

Sternberg, R. J. (1995). For whom the bell curve tolls: A review of The Bell Curve. *Psychological Science, 6,* 257–261.

Sternberg, R. J. (1996). Educating intelligence: Infusing the triarchic theory into school instruction. In R. J. Sternberg & E. L. Grigorenko (Eds.), *Intelligence, heredity, and environment.* New York: Cambridge University Press.

Sternberg, R. J. (1997). Intelligence and lifelong learning: What's new and how can we use it? *American Psychologist, 52,* 1134–1139.

Sternberg, R. J. (2001, June). *Cultural approaches to intellectual and social competencies.* Symposium presented at the annual meeting of the American Psychological Society.

Sternberg, R. J., Conway, B. E., Ketron, J. L., & Bernstein, M. (1981). People's conceptions of intelligence. *Journal of Personality and Social Psychology, 41,* 37–55.

Sternberg, R. J., & Grigorenko, E. L. (Eds.). (1996). *Intelligence, heredity, and environment.* New York: Cambridge University Press.

Sternberg, R. J., & Grigorenko, E. L. (Eds.). (2002). *The general factor of intelligence: How general is it?* Mahwah, NJ: Erlbaum.

Sternberg, R. J., & Wagner, R. K. (1993). The *g*-centric view of intelligence and job performance is wrong. *Current Directions in Psychological Science, 2,* 1–5.

Stevenson, H. W., Chen, C., & Lee, S. Y. (1992). A comparison of the parent–child relationship in Japan and the United States. In L. L. Roopnarine & D. B. Carter (Eds.), *Parent–child socialization in diverse cultures.* Norwood, NJ: Ablex.

Stevenson, H. W., & Lee, S. Y. (1990). Contexts of achievement: A study of American, Chinese, and Japanese children. *Monographs of the Society for Research in Child Development, 55,* 1–123.

Stevenson, H. W., & Stigler, J. W. (1992). *The learning gap: Why our schools are failing and what we can learn from Japanese and Chinese education.* New York: Summit.

Steward, E. P. (1995). *Beginning writers in the zone of proximal development.* Hillsdale, NJ: Erlbaum.

Stice, E., Presnell, K., & Bearman, K. (2001). Relation of early menarche to depression, eating disorders, substance abuse, and comorbid psychopathology among adolescent girls. *Developmental Psychology, 37,* 608–619.

Stipek, D. J., & Hoffman, J. (1980). Development of children's performance-related judgments. *Child Development, 51,* 912–914.

Stolberg, S. G. (1998, April 3). Rise in smoking by young blacks erodes a success story in health. *New York Times,* p. A1.

Stolberg, S. G. (1999, August 8). Black mothers' mortality rate under scrutiny. *New York Times,* pp. 1, 18.

Stolberg, S. G. (2001, August 15). Researchers discount a caution in debate over cloned humans. *New York Times,* p. A18.

Storfer, M. (1990). *Intelligence and giftedness: The contributions of heredity and early environment.* San Francisco: Jossey-Bass.

Strauch, B. (1997, August 10). Use of antidepression medicine for young patients has soared. *New York Times,* pp. A1, A24.

Straus, M. A., & Gelles, R. J. (Eds.). (1990). *Physical violence in American families.* New Brunswick, NJ: Transaction.

Straus, M. A., & McCord, J. (1998). Do physically punished children become violent adults? In S. Nolen-Hoeksema (Ed.), *Clashing views on abnormal psychology.* Guilford, CT: Dushkin.

Streissguth, A. P. (1997). *Fetal alcohol syndrome: A guide for families and communities.* Baltimore: Brookes.

Streissguth, A. P., Randels, S. P., & Smith, D. F. (1991). A test-retest study of intelligence in patients with fetal alcohol syndrome: Implications for care. *Journal of the American Academy of Child and Adolescent Psychiatry, 30,* 584–587.

Strelau, J. (1998). *Temperament: A psychological perspective.* New York: Plenum.

Streri, A. O., & Spelke, E. S. (1988). Haptic perception of objects in infancy. *Cognitive Psychology, 20,* 1–23.

Striegel-Moore, R. H. (1997). Risk factors for eating disorders. In M. S. Jacobson, J. M. Rees, N. H. Golden, & C. E. Irwin (Eds.), *Adolescent nutritional disorders: Prevention and treatment.* New York: New York Academy of Sciences.

Sugarman, S. (1988). *Piaget's construction of the child's reality.* Cambridge, England: Cambridge University Press.

Sullivan, K. (2000). *The anti-bullying handbook.* New York: Oxford University Press.

Sullivan, M. W., Rovee-Collier, C. K., & Tynes, D. M. (1979). A conditioning analysis of infant long-term memory. *Child Development, 50,* 152–162.

Suls, J., & Wills, T. A. (Eds.). (1991). *Social comparison: Contemporary theory and research.* Hillsdale, NJ: Erlbaum.

Sulzer-Azaroff, B., & Mayer, R. (1991). *Behavior analysis and lasting change.* New York: Holt.

Sung, B. L. (1985). Bicultural conflicts in Chinese immigrant children. *Journal of Comparative Family Studies, 16,* 255–270.

Super, C. M. (1976). Environmental effects on motor development: A case of African infant precocity. *Developmental Medicine and Child Neurology, 18,* 561–576.

Super, C. M., & Harkness, S. (1982). The infant's niche in rural Kenya and metropolitan America. In L. Adler (Ed.), *Issues in cross-cultural research.* New York: Academic Press.

Suskind, R. (1994, September 24). Class struggle: Poor, black, and smart. *New York Times,* p. A1.

Suskind, R. (1999). *A hope in the unseen: An American odyssey from the inner city to the Ivy League.* New York: Broadway Books.

Susman-Stillman, A., Kalkose, M., Egeland, B., & Waldman, I. (1996). Infant temperament and maternal sensitivity as predictors of attachment security. *Infant Behavior and Development, 19,* 33–47.

Suzuki, L. A., & Valencia, R. R. (1997). Race-ethnicity and measured intelligence. *American Psychologist, 52,* 1103–1114.

Swanson, L. A., Leonard, L. B., & Gandour, J. (1992). Vowel duration in mothers' speech to young children. *Journal of Speech and Hearing Research, 35,* 617–625.

Swendsen, J. D., & Mazure, C. M. (2000). Life stress as a risk factor for postpartum depression: Current research and methodological issues. *Clinical Psychology: Science and Practice, 7,* 17–31.

Tajfel, H. (1982). *Social identity and intergroup relations.* Cambridge, England: Cambridge University Press.

Takahashi, K. (1986). Examining the Strange Situation procedure with Japanese mothers and 12-month-old infants. *Developmental Psychology, 22,* 265–270.

Takanishi, R., Hamburg, D. A., & Jacobs, K. (Eds.). (1997). *Preparing adolescents for the twenty-first century: Challenges facing Europe and the United States.* New York: Cambridge University Press.

Tamis-LeMonda, C. S., & Bornstein, M. H. (1993). Antecedents of exploratory competence at one year. *Infant Behavior and Development, 16,* 423–439.

Tamis-LeMonda, C. S., & Cabrera, N. (1999). Perspectives on father involvement: Research and policy. *Social Policy Report, 13,* 1–31.

Tamis-LeMonda, C. S., & Cabrera, N. (Eds.). (2002). *The handbook of father involvement: Multidisciplinary perspectives.* Mahwah, NJ: Erlbaum.

Tannen, D. (1991). *You just don't understand.* New York: Ballantine.

Tanner, J. M. (1972). Sequence, tempo, and individual variation in growth and development of boys and girls aged twelve to sixteen. In J. Kagan & R. Coles (Eds.), *Twelve to sixteen: Early adolescence.* New York: Norton.

Tanner, J. M. (1978). *Education and physical growth* (2nd ed.). New York: International Universities Press.

Tappan, M. B. (1997). Language, culture, and moral development: A Vygotskian perspective. *Developmental Review, 17,* 199–212.

Tardif, T. (1996). Nouns are not always learned before verbs: Evidence from Mandarin speakers' early vocabularies. *Developmental Psychology, 32,* 492–504.

Tate, D. C., Reppucci, N. D., & Mulvey, E. P. (1995). Violent juvenile delinquents: Treatment effectiveness and implications for future action. *American Psychologist, 50,* 777–781.

Tatum, B. (1997). *"Why are all the black kids sitting together in the cafeteria?" and other conversations about race.* New York: Basic Books.

Taylor, H. G., Klein, N., Minich, N. M., & Hack, M. (2000). Middle-school-age outcomes in children with very low birthweight. *Child Development, 71,* 1495–1511.

Taylor, S. E. (1991). *Health psychology* (2nd ed.). New York: McGraw-Hill.

Teerikangas, O. M., Aronen, E. T., Martin, R. P., & Huttunen, M. O. (1998). Effects of infant temperament and early intervention on the psychiatric symptoms of adolescents. *Journal of the American Academy of Child and Adolescent Psychiatry, 37,* 1070–1076.

Tegano, D. W., Lookabaugh, S., May, G. E., & Burdette, M. P. (1991). Constructive play and problem solving: The role of structure and time in the classroom. *Early Child Development and Care, 68,* 27–35.

Tellegen, A., Lykken, D. T., Bouchard, T. J., Jr., Wilcox, K. J., Segal, N. L., & Rich, S. (1988). Personality similarity in twins reared apart and together. *Journal of Personality and Social Psychology, 54,* 1031–1039.

Tenenbaum, H. R., & Leaper, C. (1998). Gender effects on Mexican-descent parents' questions and scaffolding during toy play: A sequential analysis. *First Language, 18,* 129–147.

Terman, D. L., Larner, M. B., Stevenson, C. S., & Behrman, R. E. (1996). Special education for students with disabilities: Analysis and recommendations. *Future of Children, 6,* 4–24.

Terman, L. M., & Oden, M. H. (1959). *The gifted group at midlife: Thirty-five-year follow-up of the superior child.* Stanford, CA: Stanford University Press.

Termin, N. T., & Izard, C. E. (1988). Infants' responses to their mothers' expressions of joy and sadness. *Developmental Psychology, 24,* 223–229.

Terry, D. (1994, December 12). When the family heirloom is homicide. *New York Times,* pp. A1, B7.

Terry, D. (2000, August, 11). U.S. child poverty rate fell as economy grew but is above 1979 level. *New York Times*, p. A10.

Tesman, J. R., & Hills, A. (1994). Developmental effects of lead exposure in children. *Social Policy Report, 8*, 1–17.

Tesser, A., Felson, R. B., & Suls, J. M. (Eds.). (2000). *Psychological perspectives on self and identity*. Washington, DC: American Psychological Association.

Tharp, R. G. (1989). Psychocultural variables and constants: Effects on teaching and learning in schools. *American Psychologist, 44*, 349–359.

Thelen, E. (1979). Rhythmical stereotypes in normal human infants. *Animal Behavior, 27*, 699–715.

Thelen, E. (1994). Three-month-old infants can learn task-specific patterns of interlimb coordination. *Psychological Science, 5*, 280–285.

Thiel de Bocanegra, H. (1998). Breast-feeding in immigrant women: The role of social support and acculturation. *Hispanic Journal of Behavioral Sciences, 20*, 448–467.

Thoma, S. J., & Rest, J. R. (1999). The relationship between moral decision making and patterns of consolidation and transition in moral judgment development. *Developmental Psychology, 35*, 323–334.

Thoman, E. B. (1990). Sleeping and waking states in infants: A functional perspective. *Neuroscience and Biobehavioral Review, 14*, 93–107.

Thoman, E. B., & Whitney, M. P. (1989). Sleep states of infants monitored in the home: Individual differences, developmental trends, and origins of diurnal cyclicity. *Infant Behavior and Development, 12*, 59–75.

Thoman, E. B., & Whitney, M. P. (1990). Behavioral states in infants: Individual differences and individual analyses. In J. Colombo & J. Fagen (Eds.), *Individual differences in infancy: Reliability, stability, prediction*. Hillsdale, NJ: Erlbaum.

Thomas, A., & Chess, S. (1977). *Temperament and development*. New York: Brunner/Mazel.

Thomas, A., & Chess, S. (1980). *The dynamics of psychological development*. New York: Brunner/Mazel.

Thomas, A., Chess, S., & Birch, H. G. (1968). *Temperament and behavior disorders in children*. New York: New York University Press.

Thomas, P. (1994, September 6). Washington's infant mortality rate, more than twice the U.S. average, reflects urban woes. *Wall Street Journal*, p. A14.

Thompson, R. A., & Limber, S. P. (1990). Social anxiety in infancy: Stranger and separation reactions. In H. Leitenberg (Ed.), *Handbook of social and evaluation anxiety*. New York: Plenum.

Thompson, R. A., & Nelson, C. A. (2001). Developmental science and the media. *American Psychologist, 56*, 5–15.

Thompson, W. C., Clarke-Stewart, K. A., & Lepore, S. J. (1997). What did the janitor do? Suggestive interviewing and the accuracy of children's accounts. *Law and Human Behavior, 21*, 405–426.

Thomson, J. A., Ampofo-Boateng, K., Lee, D. N., Grieve, R., Pitcairn, T. K., & Demetre, J. D. (1998). The effectiveness of parents in promoting the development of road-crossing skills in young children. *British Journal of Educational Psychology, 68*, 475–491.

Thornberry, T. P., & Krohn, M. D. (1997). Peers, drug use, and delinquency. In D. M. Stoff, J. Breiling, & J. D. Maser (Eds.), *Handbook of antisocial behavior*. New York: Wiley.

Thorne, B. (1986). Girls and boys together, but mostly apart. In W. W. Hartup & Z. Rubin (Eds.), *Relationships and development*. Hillsdale, NJ: Erlbaum.

Tincoff, R., & Jusczyk, P. W. (1999). Some beginnings of word comprehension in 6-month-olds. *Psychological Science, 10*, 172–175.

Tobin, J. J., Wu, D. Y. H., & Davidson, D. H. (1989). *Preschool in three cultures: Japan, China, and the United States*. New Haven, CT: Yale University Press.

Tobin-Richards, M. H., Boxer, A. M., & Petersen, A. C. (1983). The psychological significance of pubertal change: Sex differences in perceptions of self during early adolescence. In J. Brooks-Gunn & A. C. Petersen (Eds.), *Girls at puberty*. New York: Plenum.

Toch, T. (1995, January 2). Kids and marijuana: The glamour is back. *U.S. News and World Report*, 12.

Tomlinson-Keasey, C. (1985). *Child development: Psychological, sociological, and biological factors*. Homewood, IL: Dorsey.

Touwen, B. C. L. (1984). Primitive reflexes: Conceptual or semantic problem? In H. F. R. Prechtl (Ed.), *Continuity of neural functions from prenatal to postnatal life*. Philadelphia: Lippincott.

Trainor, L. J., Austin, C. M., & Desjardins, R. N. (2000). Is infant-directed speech prosody a result of the vocal expression of emotion? *Psychological Science, 11*, 188–195.

Treasure, J., & Tiller, J. (1993). The aetiology of eating disorders: Its biological basis. *International Review of Psychiatry, 5*, 23–31.

Trehub, S. E., Schneider, B. A., Morrongiello, B. A., & Thorpe, L. A. (1988). Auditory sensitivity in school-age children. *Journal of Experimental Child Psychology, 46*, 272–285.

Trehub, S. E., Schneider, B. A., Morrongiello, B. A., & Thorpe, L. A. (1989). Developmental changes in high-frequency sensitivity. *Audiology, 28*, 241–249.

Trehub, S. E., Thorpe, L. A., & Morrongiello, B. A. (1985). Infants' perception of melodies: Changes in a single tone. *Infant Behavior and Development, 8*, 213–223.

Tremblay, R. E. (2001). The development of physical aggression during childhood and the prediction of later dangerousness. In G. F. Pinard & L. Pagani (Eds.), *Clinical assessment of dangerousness: Empirical contributions*. New York: Cambridge University Press.

Triandis, H. C. (1995). *Individualism and collectivism*. Boulder, CO: Westview Press.

Troiano, R. P., Flegal, K. M., Kuczmarski, R. J., Campbell, S. M., & Johnson, C. L. (1995). Overweight prevalence and trends for children and adolescents. The National Health and Nutrition Examination Surveys, 1963–1992. *Archives of Pediatric and Adolescent Medicine, 10*, 1085–1091.

Tronick, E. Z. (1998). Dyadically expanded states of consciousness and the process of therapeutic change. *Infant Mental Health Journal, 19*, 290–299.

Tronick, E. Z., Thomas, R. B., & Daltabuit, M. (1994). The Quechua manta pouch: A caretaking practice for buffering the Peruvian infant against the multiple stressors of high altitude. *Child Development, 65*, 1005–1013.

Tsunoda, T. (1985). *The Japanese brain: Uniqueness and universality*. Tokyo: Taishukan.

Turner, J. C., & Onorato, R. S. (1999). Social identity, personality, and the self-concept: A self-categorizing perspective. In T. R. Tyler & R. M. Kramer (Eds.), *The psychology of the social self: Applied social research*. Mahwah, NJ: Erlbaum.

Turner, P. J., Gervai, J., & Hinde, R. A. (1993). Gender-typing in young children: Preferences, behavior and cultural differences. *British Journal of Developmental Psychology, 11*, 323–342.

Turner, M. E., Pratkanis, A. R., Probasco, P., & Leve, C. (1992). Threat, cohesion, and group effectiveness: Testing a social identity maintenance perspective on groupthink. *Journal of Personality and Social Psychology, 63*, 781–796.

Turner-Bowker, D. M. (1996). Gender stereotyped descriptors in children's picture books: Does "Curious Jane" exist in the literature? *Sex Roles, 35*, 461–488.

Twenge, J. M., & Campbell, W. K. (2001). Age and birth cohort differences in self-esteem: A cross-temporal meta-analysis. *Personality and Social Psychology Review, 5*, 321–344.

Twenge, J. M., & Crocker, J. (2002). Race and self-esteem: Meta-analyses comparing whites, blacks, Hispanics, Asians, and American Indians and comment on Gray-Little and Hafdahl (2000). *Psychological Bulletin, 128*, 371–408.

UNAIDS & World Health Organization. (2001). *Cases of AIDS around the world*. New York: United Nations.

UNESCO. (1998). *Compendium of statistics on illiteracy*. Paris: Author.

Unger, R., & Crawford, M. (1992). *Women and gender: A feminist psychology*. New York: McGraw-Hill.

Unger, R., & Crawford, M. (1999). *Women and gender: A feminist psychology* (4th ed.). New York: McGraw-Hill.

Ungrady, D. (1992, October 19). Getting physical: Fitness experts are helping shape up young America. *Washington Post*, p. B5.

United Nations. (1990). *Declaration of the world summit for children*. New York: Author.

U.S. Advisory Board on Child Abuse and Neglect. (1995). *A nation's shame: Fatal child abuse and neglect in the United States*. Washington, DC: Superintendent of Documents.

U.S. Bureau of the Census. (1990). *Current population reports*. Washington, DC: U.S. Government Printing Office.

U.S. Bureau of the Census. (1992). *Poverty in the United States, 1991*. Washington, D.C: U.S. Government Printing Office.

U.S. Bureau of the Census. (1994). Household statistics, 1993. *Current population reports*. Washington, DC: U.S. Government Printing Office.

U.S. Bureau of the Census. (1997). *Who's minding our preschoolers?* Washington, DC: U.S. Government Printing Office.

U.S. Bureau of the Census. (2000). *Current population reports*. Washington, DC: U.S. Government Printing Office.

U.S. Bureau of the Census. (2001a). *Living arrangements of children*. Washington, DC: U.S. Government Printing Office.

U.S. Bureau of the Census. (2001b). *Statistical abstract of the United States, 2001*. Washington, DC: U.S. Government Printing Office.

U.S. Department of Agriculture. (1999). *Dietary guidelines*. Washington, DC: U.S. Government Printing Office.

U.S. Department of Education, Office of Special Education and Rehabilitative Services. (1987). *Eighth annual report to Congress on the implementation of the Education of the Handicapped Act, 1986*. Washington, DC: U.S. Government Printing Office.

Urberg, K. A. (1982). The development of the concepts of masculinity and femininity in young children. *Sex Roles, 8*, 659–668.

Urberg, K. A., Degirmencioglu, S. M., & Pilgrim, C. (1997). Close friend and group influence on adolescent cigarette smoking and alcohol use. *Developmental Psychology, 33*, 834–844.

Vaillant, G. E., & Vaillant, C. O. (1981). Natural history of male psychological health: X. Work as a predictor of positive mental health. *American Journal of Psychiatry, 138*, 1433–1440.

van Balen, F. (1998). Development of IVF children. *Developmental Review, 18*, 30–46.

van Biema, D. (1995, December 11). Abandoned to her fate. *Time*, 32–36.

Van de Graaf, K. (2000). *Human anatomy* (5th ed.). New York: McGraw-Hill.

van der Veer, R., & Valsiner, J. (1991). *Understanding Vygotsky: A quest for synthesis*. Cambridge, MA: Blackwell.

van der Veer, R., & Valsiner, J. (Eds.). (1994). *The Vygotsky reader*. Cambridge, MA: Blackwell.

van Geert, P. (1998). A dynamic systems model of basic developmental mechanisms: Piaget, Vygotsky, and beyond. *Psychological Review, 105*, 634–677.

Van Riper, C. (1972). *Speech correction: Principles and methods*. Englewood Cliffs, NJ: Prentice Hall.

van't Spijker, A., & ten Kroode, H. F. (1997). Psychological aspects of genetic counseling: A review of the experience with Huntington's disease. *Patient Education and Counseling, 32*, 33–40.

Van Tassel-Baska, J. (1986). Effective curriculum and instructional models for talented students. *Gifted Child Quarterly, 30,* 164–169.

Van Tassel-Baska, J., Olszewski-Kubilius, P., & Kulieke, M. (1994). A study of self-concept and social support in advantaged and disadvantaged seventh- and eighth-grade gifted students. *Roeper Review, 16,* 186–191.

Vance, B., Hankins, N., & Brown, W. (1988). Ethnic and sex differences on the Test of Nonverbal Intelligence, Quick Test of Intelligence, and Wechsler Intelligence Scale for Children–Revised. *Journal of Clinical Psychology, 44,* 261–265.

VandeBerg, L.R., & Streckfuss, D. (1992). Prime-time television's portrayal of women and the world of work: A demographic profile. *Journal of Broadcasting and Electronic Media, 36,* 195–208.

Vandell, D. L. (2000). Parents, peer groups, and other socializing influences. *Developmental Psychology, 36,* 699–710.

Vargha-Khadem, F., Carr, L. J., Isaacs, E., Brett, E., Adams, C., & Mishkin, M. (1997). Onset of speech after left hemispherectomy in a nine-year-old boy. *Brain, 120,* 159–182.

Vaughn, V., McKay, R. J., & Behrman, R. (1979). *Nelson textbook of pediatrics* (11th ed.). Philadelphia: Saunders.

Vercellini, P., Zuliani, G., Rognoni, M., Trespidi, L., Oldani, S., & Cardinale, A. (1993). Pregnancy at forty and over: A case-control study. *European Journal of Obstetrics, Gynecology, and Reproductive Biology, 48,* 191–195.

Vereijken, C. M., Riksen-Walraven, J. M., & Kondo-Ikemura, K. (1997). Maternal sensitivity and infant attachment security in Japan: A longitudinal study. *International Journal of Behavioral Development, 21,* 35–49.

Vihman, M. M. (1991). Early syllables and the construction of phonology. In C. A. Ferguson, L. Menn, & C. Stoel-Gammon (Eds.), *Phonological development: Models, research, implications.* Hillsdale, NJ: Erlbaum.

Vincze, M. (1971). Examinations on the social contacts between infants and young children reared together. *Magyar Pszichologiai Szemle, 28,* 58–61.

Visscher, W. A., Bray, R. M., & Kroutil, L. A. (1999). Drug use and pregnancy. In R. M. Bray & M. E. Marsden (Eds.), *Drug use in metropolitan America.* Thousand Oaks, CA: Sage.

Vitaro, F., & Pelletier, D. (1991). Assessment of children's social problem-solving skills in hypothetical and actual conflict situations. *Journal of Abnormal Child Psychology, 19,* 505–518.

Vizmanos, B., & Marti-Henneberg, C. (2000). Puberty begins with a characteristic subcutaneous body fat mass in each sex. *European Journal of Clinical Nutrition, 54,* 203–206.

Vogel, G. (1997). Why the rise in asthma cases? *Science, 276,* 1645.

Volkow, N. D., Wang, G. J., Fowler, J. S., Logan, J., Gerasimov, M., Maynard, I., et al. (2001). Therapeutic doses of oral methylphenidate significantly increase extracellular dopamine in the human brain. *Journal of Neuroscience, 21,* 1–5.

Volling, B. L., & Belsky, J. (1992). The contribution of mother–child and father–child relationships to the quality of sibling interaction: A longitudinal study. *Child Development, 63,* 1209–1222.

Vondra, J. I., & Barnett, D. (1999). Atypical attachment in infancy and early childhood among children at developmental risk. *Monographs of the Society for Research in Child Development, 64*(Serial No. 258).

Vurpillot, E. (1968). The development of scanning strategies and their relation to visual differentiation. *Journal of Experimental Child Psychology, 6,* 632–650.

Vygotsky, L. S. (1997). *Educational psychology.* Delray Beach, FL: St. Lucie Press. (Original work published 1926)

Vygotsky, L. S. (1978). *Mind in society: The development of higher mental processes* (M. Cole, Ed.). Cambridge, MA: Harvard University Press. (Original works published 1930–1935)

Wachs, T. D. (1992). *The nature of nurture.* Newbury Park, CA: Sage.

Wachs, T. D. (1993). The nature–nurture gap: What we have here is a failure to collaborate. In R. Plomin & G. E. McClearn (Eds.), *Nature, nurture, and psychology.* Washington, DC: American Psychological Association.

Wachs, T. D. (1996). Known and potential processes underlying developmental trajectories in childhood and adolescence. *Developmental Psychology, 32,* 796–801.

Wade, N. (2001, October 4). Researchers say gene is linked to language. *New York Times,* p. A1.

Wagner, W.G., Smith, D., & Norris, W.R. (1988). The pschological adjustment of enuretic children: A comparison of two types. *Journal of Pediatric Psychology, 13,* 33–38.

Wahlsten, D., & Gottlieb, G. (1997). The invalid separation of effects of nature and nurture: Lessons from animal experimentation. In R. J. Sternberg & E. L. Grigorenko (Eds.), *Intelligence, heredity, and environment.* New York: Cambridge University Press.

Wakefield, M., Reid, Y., Roberts, L., Mullins, R., & Gillies, P. (1998). Smoking and smoking cessation among men whose partners are pregnant: A qualitative study. *Social Science and Medicine, 47,* 657–664.

Walden, T. A., & Baxter, A. (1989). The effect of context and age on social referencing. *Child Development, 60,* 1230–1240.

Walden, T. A., & Ogan, T. A. (1988). The development of social referencing. *Child Development, 59,* 1240–1249.

Walker, N. C., & O'Brien, B. (1999). The relationship between method of pain management during labor and birth outcomes. *Clinical Nursing Research, 8,* 119–134.

Walker-Andrews, A. S. (1997). Infants' perception of expressive behaviors: Differentiation of multimodal information. *Psychological Bulletin, 121,* 437–456.

Walker-Andrews, A. S., & Dickson, L. R. (1997). Infants' understanding of affect. In S. Hala (Ed.), *The development of social cognition: Studies in developmental psychology.* Philadelphia: Psychology Press.

Walker-Andrews, A. S., & Lennon, E. (1991). Infants' discrimination of vocal expressions: Contributions of auditory and visual information. *Infant Behavior and Development, 14,* 131–142.

Wallace, I. F., Rose, S. A., McCarton, C. M., Kurtzberg, D., & Vaughan, H. G., Jr. (1995). Relations between infant neurobehavioral performance and cognitive outcome in very low birthweight preterm infants. *Developmental and Behavioral Pediatrics, 16,* 309–317.

Wallerstein, J. S., & Blakeslee, S. (1989). *Second chances.* New York: Ticknor & Fields.

Wallerstein, J. S., Lewis, J. M., & Blakeslee, S. (2000). *The unexpected legacy of divorce.* New York: Hyperion.

Wallis, C. (1994, July 18). Life in overdrive. *Time,* 42–50.

Walsh, B. T., & Devlin, M. J. (1998). Eating disorders: Progress and problems. *Science, 280,* 1387–1390.

Walters, E., & Gardner, H. (1986). The theory of multiple intelligences: Some issues and answers. In R. J. Sternberg & R. K. Wagner (Eds.), *Practical intelligence.* New York: Cambridge University Press.

Walther, V. N. (1997). Postpartum depression: A review for perinatal social workers. *Social Work in Health Care, 24,* 99–111.

Wang, M. C., Reynolds, M. C., & Walberg, H. J. (Eds.). (1996). *Handbook of special and remedial education: Research and practice* (2nd ed.). New York: Pergamon.

Wang, Q. (2001). Culture effects on adults' earliest childhood recollection and self-description: Implication for the relation between memory and the self. *Journal of Personality and Social Psychology, 81,* 220–233.

Wang, Z. W., Black, D., Andreasen, N. C., & Crowe, R. R. (1993). A linkage study of chromosome 11q in schizophrenia. *Archives of General Psychiatry, 50,* 212–216.

Warin, J. (2000). The attainment of self-consistency through gender in young children. *Sex Roles, 42,* 209–231.

Warner, V., Weissman, M. M., Mufson, L., & Wickramaratne, P. J. (1999). Grandparents, parents, and grandchildren at high risk for depression: A three-generation study. *Journal of the American Academy of Child and Adolescent Psychiatry, 38,* 289–296.

Warren, C. W., Kann, L., Small, M. L., & Santelli, J. S. (1997). Age of initiating selected health-risk behaviors among high school students in the United States. *Journal of Adolescent Health, 21,* 225–231.

Warrick, P. (1991, October 30). What the doctors have to say. *Los Angeles Times,* p. E4.

Waterman, A. (1982). Identity development from adolescence to adulthood: An extension of theory and a review of research. *Developmental Psychology, 18,* 341–358.

Waters, E. (1978). The reliability and stability of individual differences in infant–mother attachment. *Child Development, 49,* 483–494.

Waters, E., Weinfield, N. S., & Hamilton, C. E. (2000). The stability of attachment security from infancy to adolescence and early adulthood: General discussion. *Child Development, 71,* 703–706.

Watson, A. C., Nixon, C. L., Wilson, A., & Capage, L. (1999). Social interaction skills and theory of mind in young children. *Developmental Psychology, 35,* 386–391.

Watson, J. B. (1925). *Behaviorism.* New York: Norton.

Watson, J. B., & Rayner, R. (1920). Conditioned emotional reactions. *Journal of Experimental Psychology, 3,* 1–14.

Watson, J. K. (2000). Theory of mind and pretend play in family context (false belief). *Dissertation Abstracts International, 60B,* 3599.

Waugh, E., & Bulik, C. M. (1999). Offspring of women with eating disorders. *International Journal of Eating Disorders, 25,* 123–133.

Webster, R. A., Hunter, M., & Keats, J. A. (1994). Peer and parental influences on adolescents' substance use: A path analysis. *International Journal of the Addictions, 29,* 647–657.

Wechsler, D. (1975). Intelligence defined and undefined. *American Psychologist, 30,* 135–139.

Wechsler, H., Lee, J. E., Kuo, M., Seibring, M., Nelson, T. F., & Lee, H. (2002). Trends in college binge drinking during a period of increased prevention efforts: Findings from 4 Harvard School of Public Health college alcohol study surveys, 1993–2001.

Wechsler, H., & Nelson, T. F. (2001). Binge drinking and the American college student: What's five drinks? *Psychology of Addictive Behaviors, 15,* 287–291.

Weed, K., Ryan, E. B., & Day, J. (1990). Metamemory and attributions as mediators of strategy use and recall. *Journal of Educational Psychology, 82,* 849–855.

Weigel, D. J., Devereux, P., Leight, G. K., & Ballard-Reisch, D. (1998). A longitudinal study of adolescents' perceptions of support and stress: Stability and change. *Journal of Adolescent Research, 13,* 158–177.

Weinberg, M. K., & Tronick, E. Z. (1996). Beyond the face: An empirical study of infant affective configurations of facial, vocal, gestural, and regulatory behaviors. *Child Development, 67,* 905–914.

Weinberg, R. A. (1989). Intelligence and IQ: Landmark issues and great debates. *American Psychologist, 44,* 98–104.

Weinberger, D. R. (2001, March 10). A brain too young for good judgment. *New York Times,* p. D1.

Weiner, B. (1985). *Human motivation.* New York: Springer-Verlag.

Weiner, B. (1994). Integrating social and personal theories of achievement striving. *Review of Educational Research, 64,* 557–573.

Weinfield, N. S., Sroufe, L. A., & Egeland, B. (2000). Attachment from infancy to early adulthood in a high-risk sample: Continuity, discontinuity, and their correlates. *Child Development, 71,* 695–702.

Weisinger, H. (1998 March 14). Tutored by television. *TV Guide,* 46–48.

Weiss, M. R., Ebbeck, V., & Horn. T. S. (1997). Children's self-perceptions and sources of physical competence information: A cluster analysis. *Journal of Sport and Exercise Psychology, 19,* 52–70.

Wellman, H. M., Cross, D., & Watson, J. (2001). Meta-analysis of theory-of-mind development: The truth about false belief. *Child Development, 72,* 655–684.

Wellman, H. M., & Gelman, S. A. (1992). Cognitive development: Foundational theories of core domains. *Annual Review of Psychology, 43,* 337–375.

Wells, A. S., & Crain, R. L. (1994). Perpetuation theory and the long-term effects of school desegregation. *Review of Educational Research, 64,* 531–555.

Wenar, C. (1994). *Developmental psychopathology: From infancy through adolescence* (3rd ed.). New York: McGraw-Hill.

Wenner, M. V. (1994). Depression, anxiety, and negative affectivity in elementary-aged learning disabled children. *Dissertation Abstracts International, 54*(9B), 4938.

Werner, E. E. (1972). Infants around the world: Cross-cultural studies of psychomotor development from birth to two years. *Journal of Cross-Cultural Psychology, 3,* 111–134.

Werner, E. E. (1993). Risk resilience and recovery: Perspectives from the Kauai Longitudinal Study. *Development and Psychopathology, 5,* 503–515.

Werner, E. E. (1995). Resilience in development. *Current Directions in Psychological Science, 4,* 81–85.

Werner, E. E., & Smith, R. S. (1992). *Overcoming the odds: High-risk children from birth to adulthood.* Ithaca, NY: Cornell University Press.

Werner, L. A., & Marean, G. C. (1996). *Human auditory development.* Boulder, CO: Westview Press.

Wertsch, J. V. (1999). The zone of proximal development: Some conceptual issues. In P. Lloyd & C. Fernyhough (Eds.), *Lev Vygotsky: Critical assessments: Vol. 3. The zone of proximal development.* New York: Routledge.

Wertsch, J. V., & Tulviste, P. (1992). L. S. Vygotsky and contemporary developmental psychology. *Developmental Psychology, 28,* 548–557.

Westen, D. (1990). Psychoanalytic approaches to personality. In L. A. Previn (Ed.), *Handbook of personality: Theory and research.* New York: Guilford Press.

Whalen, C. K., Jamner, L. D., Henker, B., Delfino, R. J., & Lozano, J. M. (2002). The ADHD spectrum and everyday life: Experience sampling of adolescent moods, activities, smoking, and drinking. *Child Development, 73,* 209–227.

Wheeldon, L. R. (1999). *Aspects of language production.* Philadelphia: Psychology Press.

Wheeler, G. (1998). The wake-up call we dare not ignore. *Science, 279,* 1611.

Whitaker, R. C., Wright, J. A., Pepe, M. S., Seidel, K. D., & Dietz, W. H. (1997). Predicting obesity in young adulthood from childhood and parental obesity. *New England Journal of Medicine, 337,* 869–873.

Whitbourne, S. K., Zuschlag, M. K., Elliot, L. B., & Waterman, A. S. (1992). Psychosocial development in adulthood: A 22-year sequential study. *Journal of Personality and Social Psychology, 63,* 260–271.

Whitehurst, G. J., & Fischel, J. E. (2000). Reading and language impairments in conditions of poverty. In D. V. M. Bishop & L. B. Leonard (Eds.), *Speech and language impairments in children: Causes, characteristics, intervention, and outcome.* Philadelphia: Psychology Press.

Whitelson, S. (1989, March). *Sex differences.* Paper presented at the annual meeting of the New York Academy of Science, New York.

Whiting, B. B., & Edwards, C. P. (1988). *Children of different worlds: The formation of social behavior.* Cambridge, MA: Harvard University Press.

Wickelgren, W. A. (1999). Webs, cell assemblies, and chunking in neural nets: Introduction. *Canadian Journal of Experimental Psychology, 53,* 118–131.

Wideman, M. V., & Singer, J. F. (1984). The role of psychological mechanisms in preparation for childbirth. *American Psychologist, 34,* 1357–1371.

Wigfield, A., Galper, A., Denton, K., & Seefeldt, C. (1999). Teachers' beliefs about former Head Start and non–Head Start first-grade children's motivation, performance, and future educational prospects. *Journal of Educational Psychology, 91,* 98–104.

Wilcox, A., Skjaerven, R., Buekens, P., & Kiely, J. (1995). Birth weight and perinatal mortality: A comparison of the United States and Norway. *Journal of the American Medical Association, 273,* 709–711.

Williams, B. C. (1990). Immunization coverage among preschool children: The United States and selected European countries. *Pediatrics, 86,* 1052–1056.

Williams, J. M., & Currie, C. (2000). Self-esteem and physical development in early adolescence: Pubertal timing and body image. *Journal of Early Adolescence, 20,* 129–149.

Willows, D. M., Kruk, R. S., & Corcos, E. (Eds.). (1993). *Visual processes in reading and reading disabilities.* Hillsdale, NJ: Erlbaum.

Wilmut, I. (1998). Cloning for medicine. *Scientific American,* 58–63.

Wilson, R. S. (1983). The Louisville twin study: Developmental synchronies in behavior. *Child Development, 54,* 298–316.

Windle, M. (1994). A study of friendship characteristics and problem behaviors among middle adolescents. *Child Development, 65,* 1764–1777.

Wineburg, S. S. (1987). The self-fulfillment of the self-fulfilling prophecy. *Educational Researcher, 16,* 28–37.

Winner, E. (1986, August). Where pelicans kiss seals. *Psychology Today,* 24–35.

Winner, E. (1989). Development in the visual arts. In W. Damon (Ed.), *Child development today and tomorrow.* San Francisco: Jossey-Bass.

Winner, E. (1997). *Gifted children: Myths and realities.* New York: Basic Books.

Winsler, A., Diaz, R. M., & Montero, I. (1997). The role of private speech in the transition from collaborative to independent task performance in young children. *Early Childhood Research Quarterly, 12,* 59–79.

Winter, G. (2001, August 24). Enticing third-world youth. *New York Times,* p. D1.

Witt, S. D. (1997). Parental influence on children's socialization to gender roles. *Adolescence, 32,* 253–259.

Wolf, A. M., Gortmaker, S. L., Cheung, L., & Gray, H. M. (1993). Activity, inactivity, and obesity: Racial, ethnic, and age differences among schoolgirls. *American Journal of Public Health, 83,* 1625–1627.

Wolff, P. H. (1963). Observations of the early development of smiling. In B. M. Foss (Ed.), *Determinants of infant behaviour* (Vol 4). London: Methuen.

Wolfner, G., Faust, D., & Dawes, R. M. (1993). The use of anatomically detailed dolls in sexual abuse evaluations: The state of the science. *Applied and Preventive Psychology, 2,* 1–11.

Women's Bureau, U.S. Department of Labor. (1998). *The median wages of women as a proportion of the wages that men receive.* Washington, DC: U.S. Government Printing Office.

Women's Bureau, U.S. Department of Labor. (2002). *Women's Bureau frequently asked questions.* Retrieved from http://www.dol.gov/wb/faq38.htm

Wong, B. Y. L. (1996). *The ABCs of learning disabilities.* San Diego, CA: Academic Press.

Wood, D., Bruner, J. S., & Ross, G. (1976). The role of tutoring in problem solving. *Journal of Child Psychology and Psychiatry and Allied Disciplines, 17,* 89–100.

Wood, J. (1989). Theory and research concerning social comparisons of personal attributes. *Psychological Bulletin, 106,* 231–248.

Wood, R. (1997). Trends in multiple births, 1938–1995. *Population Trends, 87,* 29–35.

Wood, W., Wong, F. Y., & Chachere, J. G. (1991). Effects of media violence on viewers' aggression in unconstrained social interaction. *Psychological Bulletin, 109,* 371–383.

Woolfolk, A. E. (1993). *Educational psychology* (5th ed.). Needham Heights, MA: Allyn & Bacon.

World Conference on Education for All. (1990). *World declaration on education for all and framework for action to meet basic learning needs.* New York: Author.

World Food Council. (1992). *The global state of hunger and malnutrition: 1992 report.* New York: Author.

World Food Summit. (2002). *The spectrum of malnutrition.* New York: United Nations.

World Health Organization & Centers for Disease Control and Prevention. (1999). *Marketing of cigarettes overseas.* Geneva/Atlanta: Authors.

Worobey, J., & Bajda, V. M. (1989). Temperament ratings at 2 weeks, 2 months, and 1 year: Differential stability of activity and emotionality. *Developmental Psychology, 25,* 257–263.

Wright, J. C., Huston, A. C., Murphy, K. C., St. Peters, M., Piñon, M., Scantlin, R., et al. (2001). The relations of early television viewing to school readiness and vocabulary of children from low-income families: The early window project. *Child Development, 72,* 1347–1366.

Wright, J. C., Huston, A. C., Reitz, A. L., & Piemyat, S. (1994). Young children's perceptions of television reality: Determinants and developmental differences. *Developmental Psychology, 30,* 229–239.

Wright, J. C., Huston, A. C., Truglio, R., Fitch, M., Smith, E., & Piemyat, S. (1995). Occupational portrayals on television: Children's role schemata, career aspirations, and perceptions of reality. *Child Development, 66,* 1706–1718.

Wright, R. (1995, March 13). The biology of violence. *New Yorker,* 68–77.

Wright, S. C., & Taylor, D. M. (1995). Identity and the language of the classroom: Investigation of the impact of heritage versus second-language instruction on personal and collective self-esteem. *Journal of Educational Psychology, 87,* 241–252.

Wyman, P. A., Cowen, E. L., Work, W. C., Hoyt-Meyers, L., Magnus, K. B., & Fagen, D. B. (1999). Caregiving and developmental factors differentiating young at-risk urban children showing resilient versus stress-affected outcomes: A replication and extension. *Child Development, 70,* 645–659.

Wynn, K. (1992). Addition and subtraction by human infants. *Nature, 358,* 749–750.

Wynn, K. (1995). Infants possess a system of numerical knowledge. *Current Directions in Psychological Science, 4,* 172–177.

Wynn, K. (2000). Findings of addition and subtraction in infants are robust and consistent: Reply to Wakeley, Rivera, and Langer. *Child Development, 71,* 1535–1536.

Yankee Group. (2001). *Teenage online activities.* Boston: Author.

Yardley, J. (2001, July 2). Child-death case in Texas raises penalty questions. *New York Times,* p. A1.

Yarrow, L. (1990, September). Does my child have a problem? *Parents,* 72.

Yarrow, M. R., Scott, P. M., & Waxler, C. Z. (1973). Learning concern for others. *Developmental Psychology, 8,* 240–260.

Yee, M., & Brown, R. (1994). The development of gender differentiation in young children. *British Journal of Social Psychology, 33,* 183–196.

Yell, M. L. (1995). The least restrictive environment mandate and the courts: Judicial activism or judicial restraint? *Exceptional Children, 61,* 578–581.

Yelland, G. W., Pollard, J., & Mercuri, A. (1993). The metalinguistic benefits of limited contact with a second language. *Applied Psycholinguistics, 14,* 423–444.

Young, H., & Ferguson, L. (1979). Developmental changes through adolescence in the spontaneous nomination of reference groups as a function of decision context. *Journal of Youth and Adolescence, 8,* 239–252.

Youniss, J. (1989). Parent–adolescent relationships. In W. Damon (Ed.), *Child development today and tomorrow.* San Francisco: Jossey-Bass.

Youniss, J., & Haynie, D. L. (1992). Friendship in adolescence. *Journal of Developmental and Behavioral Pediatrics, 13,* 59–66.

Yuill, N., & Perner, J. (1988). Intentionality and knowledge in children's judgments of actor's responsibility and recipient's emotional reaction. *Developmental Psychology, 24,* 358–365.

Zahn-Waxler, C., & Radke-Yarrow, M. (1990). The origins of empathic concern. *Motivation and Emotion, 14,* 107–130.

Zahn-Waxler, C., Robinson, J. L., & Emde, R. N. (1992). The development of empathy in twins. *Developmental Psychology, 28,* 1038–1047.

Zaidel, D. W. (1994). Worlds apart: Pictorial semantics in the left and right cerebral hemispheres. *Current Directions in Psychological Science, 3,* 5–8.

Zajonc, R. B. (2001). The family dynamics of intellectual development. *American Psychologist, 56,* 490–496.

Zanjani, E. D., & Anderson, W. F. (1999). Prospects for in utero human gene therapy. *Science, 285,* 2084–2088.

Zaporozhets, A. V. (1965). The development of perception in the preschool child. *Monographs of the Society for Research in Child Development, 30,* 82–101.

Zarbatany, L., Hartmann, D. P., & Rankin, D. B. (1990). The psychological functions of preadolescent peer activities. *Child Development, 61,* 1067–1080.

Zauszniewski, J. A., & Martin, M. H. (1999). Developmental task achievement and learned resourcefulness in healthy older adults. *Archives of Psychiatric Nursing, 13,* 41–47.

Zelazo, N. A., Zelazo, P. R., Cohen, K., & Zelazo, P. D. (1993). Specificity of practice effects on elementary neuromotor patterns. *Developmental Psychology, 29,* 686–691.

Zelazo, P. R. (1998). McGraw and the development of unaided walking. *Developmental Review, 18,* 449–471.

Zernike, K., & Petersen, M. (2001, August 19). Schools' backing of behavior drugs comes under fire. *New York Times,* pp. 1, 28.

Zeskind, P. S., & Ramey, D. T. (1981). Preventing intellectual and interactional sequels of fetal malnutrition: A longitudinal, transactional, and synergistic approach to development. *Child Development, 52,* 213–218.

Zhang, Y., Proenca, R., Maffel, M., Barone, M., Leopold, L., & Friedman, J. M. (1994). Positional cloning of the mouse obese gene and its human homologue. *Nature, 372,* 425–432.

Zigler, E. F. (1994, February). Early intervention to prevent juvenile delinquency. *Harvard Mental Health Newsletter,* 5–7.

Zigler, E. F., & Finn-Stevenson, M. (1995). The child care crisis: Implications for the growth and development of the nation's children. *Journal of Social Issues, 51,* 215–231.

Zigler, E. F., & Finn-Stevenson, M. (1999). Applied developmental psychology. In M. H. Bornstein & M. E. Lamb (Eds.), *Developmental psychology: An advanced textbook.* Mahwah, NJ: Erlbaum.

Zigler, E. F., & Gilman, E. (1998). The legacy of Jean Piaget. In G. A. Kimble & M. Wertheimer (Eds.), *Portraits of pioneers in psychology* (Vol. 3). Washington, DC: American Psychological Association.

Zigler, E. F., & Styfco, S. J. (1994). Head Start: Criticism in a constructive context. *American Psychologist, 49,* 127–132.

Zigler, E. F., Styfco, S. J., & Gilman, E. (1993). The national Head Start program for disadvantaged preschoolers. In E. Zigler & S. J. Styfco (Eds.), *Head Start and beyond: A national plan for extended childhood intervention.* New Haven, CT: Yale University Press.

Zillman, D. (1993). Mental control of angry aggression. In D. M. Wegner & J. W. Pennebaker (Eds.), *Handbook of mental control.* Englewood Cliffs, NJ: Prentice Hall.

Zito, J. M., Safer, D. J., dos Reis, S., Gardner, J. F., Boles, M., & Lynch, F. (2000). Trends in prescribing of psychotropic medications to preschoolers. *Journal of the American Medical Association, 283,* 1025–1030.

Credits

Photographs and Cartoons

Chapter 1 Page 2 Mark Tomalty, Masterfile Corporation; p. 3 AP/Wide World Photos; p. 7 The Image Works; p. 8 (top left) Claudio Vazquez; p. 8 (top right) Claudio Vazquez; p. 8 (bottom left) Claudio Vazquez; p. 8 (bottom right) Claudio Vazquez; p. 9 Lewis Hime, CORBIS; p. 11 Art Resource, N.Y.

Chapter 2 Page 20 Paul Eekhoff, Masterfile Corporation; p. 21 Julia Burke; p. 23 CORBIS; p. 25 Jon Erikson, Courtesy of the Library of Congress; p. 26 Getty Images Inc.—Hulton Archive Photos; p. 27 (left) Ken Heyman, Woodfin Camp & Associates; p. 27 (right) Picture Desk, Inc./Kobal Collection; p. 32 Daniel Wray, The Image Works; p. 33 Susan Ferguson; p. 34 Nina Leen, TimePix; p. 39 (left) Alexander Tsiaras, Stock Boston; p. 39 (right) Mary Kate Denny, PhotoEdit; p. 41 PhotoEdit; p. 43 (left) Jeff Greenberg, Index Stock Imagery, Inc.; p. 43 (right) M. Grecco. Stock Boston; p. 44 (left) Robert E Daemmrich, Getty Images Inc.—Stone Allstock; p. 44 (right) Laura Dwight, PhotoEdit; p. 47 George Shelley, Corbis/Stock Market.

Chapter 3 Page Howard Sochurek, The Stock Market; p. 54 Howard Sochurek, Corbis/Stock Market; p. 55 Keri Pickett, People/InStyle Syndication; p. 58 Aaron Haupt, Stock Boston; p. 59 Alfred Pasieka/Science Photo Library, Photo Researchers, Inc.; p. 62 CORBIS; p. 64 Bill Longcore, Photo Researchers, Inc.; p. 67 Jim Pickerell, The Image Works; p. 69 (left) AP/Wide World Photos; p. 69 (right) Jessica Boyatt Photographer; p. 74 Peter Glass, Peter Glass Photography; p. 76 The Cartoon Bank; p. 79 Sandra Scarr, Courtesy of Sandra Scarr, KinderCare Learning Centers, Inc., Alabama; p. 82 The Cartoon Bank; p. 83 Dr. Yorgos Nikas, Photo Researchers, Inc.; p. 84 Bradley R. Smith; p. 85 Photo Researchers, Inc.

Chapter 4 Page 94 David Muir, Masterfile Corporation; p. 95 Vince Messina, MetroHealth Medical Center; p. 97 (left) Michael Newman, PhotoEdit; p. 97 (right) Owen Franken, CORBIS; p. 101 Peter Byron, Photo Researchers, Inc.; p. 102 Lawrence Migdale, Stock Boston; p. 103 Charles Gupton, Stock Boston; p. 104 Mary Lou Singleton; p. 107 Ansell Horn, Phototake NYC; p. 114 Michael Newman, PhotoEdit; p. 117 Myrleen Ferguson, PhotoEdit; p. 119 Laura Dwight, Laura Dwight Photography; p. 121 Tiffany M. Field, Ph.D.

Chapter 5 Page 128 David Sharrock, Getty Images Inc.—Image Bank; p. 129 Bob Daemmrich, The Image Works; p. 135 (left) Comstock Images; p. 135 (right) Comstock Images; p. 137 Ed Bock, Corbis/Stock Market; p. 141 (left) Laura Elliott, Comstock Images; p. 141 (center) L. J. Weinstein, Woodfin Camp & Associates; p. 141 (right) Laura Dwight Photography; p. 143 (top and bottom) Laura Dwight, Laura Dwight Photography; p. 145 Nubar Alexanian, Woodfin Camp & Associates; p. 148 (right) Jose L. Pelaez, Corbis/Stock Market; p. 148 (right) Stuart Cohen, Comstock Images; p. 150 The Cartoon Bank; p. 151 Bob Daemmrich, The Image Works; p. 152 (all photos) Karen Kapoor, Getty Images Inc.—Stone Allstock; p. 155 Michael Newman, PhotoEdit; p. 156 Owen Franken, CORBIS; p. 157 Michelle Bridwell, PhotoEdit.

Chapter 6 Page 162 Jon Feingersh, Corbis/Stock Market; p. 163 PictureQuest; p. 165 CORBIS; p. 168 Elizabeth Crews, The Image Works; p. 171 Owen Franken, Stock Boston; p. 178 Peter Brandt, PictureQuest; p. 182 Dorothy Littell Greco, The Image Works; p. 183 Helen I. Shwe; p. 186 The Image Works; p. 187 Laura-Ann Petitto, Dartmouth College. From Holowka, S. and Petitto, L. A. (2002). Left Hemisphere Cerebral Specialization For Babies While Babbling. Science (August 30, 2002); p. 188 Laura-Ann Petitto, McGill University; p. 190 Myrleen Ferguson Cate, PhotoEdit; p. 192 Laura Dwight Photography.

Chapter 7 Page 198 Jack Reznicki, Corbis/Stock Market; p. 199 Jan Mueller Photography; p. 203 Gary Conner, PictureQuest; p. 206 Laura Dwight Photography; p. 208 Fredrik D. Bodin, Stock Boston; p. 210 (all photos) William Hamilton/Johns Hopkins University, Mary Ainsworth; p. 211 Mary Ainsworth, University of Virginia, Photo by Daniel Grogan; p. 212 Keith Brofsky, PictureQuest; p. 213 Ken Straitor, Corbis/Stock Market; p. 216 Robert S. Feldman; p. 218 Mark Andersen/RubberBall Productions, PictureQuest; p. 222 George Goodwin; p. 223 A. Ramey, PhotoEdit.

Chapter 8 Page 230 Peter Steiner, Corbis/Stock Market; p. 231 Antonia Reeve, Getty Images Inc.—Stone Allstock; p. 239 Laura Dwight Photography; p. 242 Chris Priest/Science Photo Library, Photo Researchers, Inc.; p. 243 G. Degrazia, Custom Medical Stock Photo, Inc.; p. 245 Frank Siteman; p. 247 Courtesy David Kurtz, Ph.D.; p. 249 (left) Charles Gupton, Stock Boston; p. 249 (right) Skjold Photographs; p. 252 Ellen Senisi, The Image Works.

Chapter 9 Page 258 Bill Varie, CORBIS; 259 Robert Harbison; p. 268 Esbin-Anderson, The Image Works; p. 270 Mike Derer, AP/Wide World Photos; p. 271 Felicia Martinez/PhotoEdit. Courtesy of Robert Solso; p. 282 Bruce Eric Kaplan, The Cartoon Bank; p. 284 Robert Recio Jr.; p. 285 The Cartoon Bank.

Chapter 10 Page 290 O'Brien Productions, CORBIS; p. 291 Myrleen Ferguson Cate, PhotoEdit; p. 293 The Image Works; p. 297 (top) Spencer Grant, Stock Boston; p. 297 (bottom) Myrleen Ferguson Cate, PhotoEdit; p. 300 J. Greenberg, The Image Works; p. 301 Arlene Collins; p. 304 Nancy Richmond, The Image Works; p. 307 Michelle Bridwell, PhotoEdit; p. 309 © 2002 The New Yorker Collection, M. Hamilton from cartoonbank.com. All Rights Reserved.; p. 311 Catherine Ursillo, Photo Researchers, Inc.; p. 314 Rick Kopstein.

Chapter 11 Page 320 Paul Barton, Corbis/Stock Market; p. 321 Lori Adamski Peek, Getty Images Inc.—Stone Allstock; p. 323 (top) Mary Kate Denny, PhotoEdit; p. 323 (bottom) Ken Heyman, Woodfin Camp & Associates; p. 324 © 2002 The New Yorker Collection, Eldon Dedini from cartoonbank.com. All Rights Reserved.; p. 327 Lester Sloan, Woodfin Camp & Associates; p. 330 Richard Hutchings, PhotoEdit; p. 331 David Young-Wolff, PhotoEdit; p. 338 Jose Azel, Aurora & Quanta Productions Inc.; p. 339 Elizabeth Crews Photography; p. 340 Valerie Patterson.

Chapter 12 Page 344 Jim Craigmyle, Masterfile Corporation; p. 345 Michelle Agins, New York Times Pictures, The New York Times; p. 348 David Lassman/Syracuse Newspapers, The Image Works; p. 350 Laura Dwight, Laura Dwight Photography; p. 352 Michael Newman, PhotoEdit; p. 353 Bob Daemmrich, The Image Works; p. 355 Bob Daemmrich, The Image Works; p. 360 Mark Richards, PhotoEdit; p. 361 Elizabeth Crews, Elizabeth Crews Photography; p. 362 B. Daemmrich, The Image Works; p. 365 CORBIS; p. 367 Laura Dwight, PhotoEdit; p. 375 Richard Hutchings, Photo Researchers, Inc.

Chapter 13 Page 380 Marc Vaughn, Masterfile Corporation; p. 381 Cary Wolinsky, Stock Boston; p. 383 (top) Robert Houser, Comstock Images; p. 383 (bottom) Myrleen Ferguson Cate, PhotoEdit; p. 387 Richard Lord, The Image Works; p. 388 Lew Merrim, Photo Researchers, Inc.; p. 390 Bob Daemmrich, The Image Works; p. 392 Bob Daemmrich, Stock Boston; p. 394 Richard Hutchings, PhotoEdit; p. 395 Jeff Greenberg, PhotoEdit; p. 401 Robert Brenner, PhotoEdit; p. 402 Phil Borden, PhotoEdit; p. 403 (left) CORBIS; p. 403 (right) Melchior DiGiacomo, Boys Town; p. 404 Universal Press Syndicate.

Chapter 14 Page 410 Tim Pannell, Masterfile Corporation; p. 411 Anna Palma; p. 413 (all photos) Ellen Senisi, The Image Works; p. 414 David Young-Wolff, PhotoEdit; p. 416 Tony Freeman, PhotoEdit; p. 418 B. Daemmrich, The Image Works; p. 419 Express Newspapers, Getty Images, Inc.—Liaison; p. 420 The Image Works; p. 423 Jonathan Nourok, PhotoEdit; p. 427 Arlene Collins; p. 428 Courtesy Doreen Branch.; p. 429 Michelle D. Bridwell, PhotoEdit; p. 431 (top) The Cartoon

Bank; p. 431 (bottom) Roger Mastroianni; p. 434 Michael A. Keller Studios LTD., Corbis/Stock Market.

Chapter 15 Page 438 David Schmidt, Masterfile Corporation; p. 439 Peter Byron, PhotoEdit; p. 442 (top) Bob Daemmrich, The Image Works; p. 442 (bottom) Bob Daemmrich, Stock Boston; p. 445 Christopher Brown, Stock Boston; p. 448 Photo by Jerry Bauer. Courtesy of Harvard Graduate School of Education.; p. 449 Lee Snider, The Image Works; p. 454 Porter Gifford, Getty Images, Inc.—Liaison; p. 456 Doug Menuez, Getty Images, Inc.—Photodisc; p. 458 Jose L. Pelaez, Corbis/Stock Market; p. 460 F. Pedrick, The Image Works; p. 463 Courtesy of Dr. Henry Klein; p. 465 Time Inc. Magazines/Sports Illustrated.

Chapter 16 Page 468 Copyright © Digital Vision; p. 469 Jeff Greenberg, PhotoEdit; p. 471 Jonathan Nourok, PhotoEdit; p. 472 Universal Press Syndicate; p. 473 Michael Newman, PhotoEdit; p. 475 D. Young Wolff, PhotoEdit; p. 476 Jonathan Nourok, PhotoEdit; p. 478 G & M David de Lossy, Getty Images Inc.—Image Bank; p. 481 Mary Kate Denny, PhotoEdit; p. 483 Keren Su, Stock Boston; p. 487 N. Richmond, The Image Works; p. 489 Lori Adamski Peek, Getty Images Inc.—Stone Allstock; p. 490 Ron Chapple, Getty Images, Inc.—Taxi; p. 491 Michael Newman, PhotoEdit; p. 496 Paula Lerner, Woodfin Camp & Associates; p. 497 Evan Johnson; p. 499 Anne Marie LaCorte.

Figures and Tables

Chapter 2 Figure 2-1: From Bronfenbrenner, U., & Morris, P. (1998). The ecology of developmental processes. In W. Damon (Ed.), *Handbook of child psychology.* (5th ed., Vol. 1). NY: Wiley. Copyright © 1998. Reprinted by permission of John Wiley & Sons, Inc.

Chapter 3 Figure 3-1: (a) Don W. Fawcett, Photo Researchers, Inc. (b) L. Willatt, E. Anglian Regional Genetics Srvc/Science Photo Library, Photo Researchers, Inc. (c) Peter Menzel, Stock Boston; Figure 3-2: Martin, J. A., & Park, M. M. (1999). Trends in twin and triplet births: 1980–1997. *National Vital Statistics Reports, 47,* 1–17; Figure 3-5: Figure 2-5 from J. W. Kimball, *Biology* (5th ed.) Copyright © 1984. Reprinted by permission of the McGraw-Hill Companies; Figure 3-6: Celera Genomics & International Humane Genome Sequencing Consortium, 2001; Figure 3-8: Figure 2-7 from T. J. Bouchard & M. McGue (1981). Familial studies of intelligence: A review. *Science, 264,* 1700–1701. Reprinted with permission of Dr. Matt McGue and Dr. Thomas Bouchard; Figure 3-9: From A. Tellegen et al. (1988). Personality similarity in twins reared apart and together. *Journal of Personality and Social Psychology, 54,* 1031–1039. Copyright © 1988 The American Psychological Association. Adapted with permission; Figure 3-10: Adapted from Schizophrenia Genesis by Irving I. Gottesman Copyright © 1991 by Irving I. Gottesman. Reprinted by permission of Henry Holt and company LLC; Figure 3-12: Adaptation of Figure depicting pregnancy odds. *Time* 4/15/02. Copyright © 2002 TIME, Inc. reprinted by permission; Figure 3-14: From K. L. Moore (1998). *Before we are born: Basic embryology and birth defects,* (5th ed.). Philadelphia: Saunders; Table 3-1: Reprinted permission from McGuffin, P., Riley, B., & Plomin, R. (2001, Feb. 16). Toward behavioral genomics. *Science, 291, 1232–1249.* Copyright © 2001 American Association for the Advancement of Science; Table 3-3: Human Genome Project (1998). National Human Genome Research Institute; Table 3-4: From Kagan, J. Arcus, D., Snidman, N. (1993). The idea of temperament. Where do we go from here? In Plomin, R. & McCleary, G. E. (eds.) *Nature, nurture and psychology. Washington, DC: American Psychological Association.* Copyright © 1993 The American Psychological Association. Adapted with permission.

Chapter 4 Figure 4-2: Adapted from Finkelstein, D. L., Harper, D. A., & Rosenthal, G. E. (1998). Does length of hospital stay during labor and delivery influence patient satisfaction? Results from a regional study." *American Journal of Managed Care, 4,* 1701–1708; Figure 4-3: National Center for Health Statistics (2001). *Health United States, 2000 with Adolescent Health Chartbook.* Hyattsville, MD: National Center for Health Statistics; Figure 4-4: From Infant and Child Health Studies Branch, (1997). *Survival rates of infants.* Washington, DC: National Center for Health Statistics; Figure 4-5: From F. C. Notzon (1990). International differences in the use of obstetric interventions. *Journal of the American Medical Association., 263 (23).* 3286–3291; Figure 4-6: From National Center for Health Statistics (1997).

U.S. infant mortality rates by race of mother: 1975–1996. Washington, DC; Public Health Service; Figure 4-7: Tiffany M. Field, Ph.D; Table 4-1: Adapted from Apgar, V. (1953). A proposal for a new method of evaluation in the newborn infant. *Current research in Anesthesia and Analgesia, 32,* 260. Used with permission of Lippincott, Wilkins & Williams; Table 4-2: Reprinted with permission from *Preventing low birth weight.* Copyright © 1985 by the National Academy of Sciences. Courtesy of the National Academy Press, Washington, DC; Table 4-3: Adapted from International Labor Organization (1998). *Maternity leave policies.* Washington, DC: International Labor Organization; Table 4-6: From Eckerman, C. O., & Oehler, J. M. (1992). Very low birth weight newborns and parents as early social partners. In Friedman, S. L. & Sigman, M. B., *The psychological development of low birth weight children.* Norwood, NJ: Ablex.

Chapter 5 Figure 5-1: From Cratty, B. J. (1979). *Perceptual and motor development in infants and children.* All rights reserved. Reprinted by permission of Allyn & Bacon; Figure 5-3: Bornstein, M. H., & Lamb, M. E. (eds.). (1992). Development psychology: An advanced textbook. p. 135. Hillsdale, NJ: Erlbaum; Figure 5-4: From *Human Anatomy, 5th edition,* by K. Van De Graaff, p. 339. Copyright © 2000 by The McGraw-Hill Companies, Inc; Figure 5-5: Reprinted by permission of the publishers from *Postnatal development of the human cerebral cortex,* Vols. I–VIII by J. L. Conel, Cambridge, Mass.: Harvard University Press, Copyright © 1939–1967 by the Presidents and Fellows of Harvard College; Figure 5-6: Reprinted from Roffwarg, H. P., Muzio, J. N., & Dement, W. C. (1966). Ontogenic development of the human sleep-dream cycle. *Science, 152,* 604–619. Copyright 1966 American Association for the Advancement of Science; Figure 5-7: National Institute for Child Health & Human Development (1997). SIDS deaths and infant sleep position; Figure 5-9: World Food Council. (1992). *The global state of hunger and malnutrition. 1992 Report.* Table 2, p. 8. New York: World Food Council; Figure 5-10: From: Einbinder, S.D. *A statistical profile of children living in poverty: Children under three and children under six.* New York, NY: National Center for Children in Poverty, Joseph L. Mailman School of Public Health, Columbia University; Figure 5-11: Reproduced with permission from *Pediatrics,* Vol. 99, Page 35. Copyright © 1997; Figure 5-12: Mark Richards, PhotoEdit; Figure 5-13: Adaptation used with permission of Alexander Semenoick. Original appeared in Fantz, R. L. (May, 1961). The origin of form perception. *Scientific American,* p. 72; Figure 5-14: One photo with four faces. From Pascalis, O. deHaan, M., & Nelson, C. A. (2002, May 17). Is face processing species specific during the first year of life? (Figure. 1, p. 1322) *Science, 296,* 1321–1322; Figure 5-15: Reprinted with permission from *Pediatrics,* Vol. 77, 657. Copyright © 1986; Table 5-2: Adapted from: Thoman, E. B., & Whitney, M. P. (1990). Behavioral states in infants: Individual differences and individual analyses. In J. Columbo, & J. Fagen (Eds.), *Individual differences in infancy: Reliability, stability, prediction.* Hillsdale, NJ: Erlbaum; Table 5-4: Reproduced with permission from *Pediatrics,* Vol. 89, 91–97. Copyright © 1992.

Chapter 6 Figure 6-4: David Sanders/Arizona Daily Star; Figure 6-5: Carolyn Rovee-Collier; Figure 6-6: Adapted from Bornstein, M. H. & Lamb, M. E. (1992). *Developmental psychology: An Advanced textbook.* Hillsdale, NJ: Erlbaum; Figure 6-7: Custom Medical Stock Photo, Inc; Figure 6-8: Gleason, J. B., Perlmann, R. Y., Ely, R., & Evans, D. W. (1991). The baby talk registry: Parents' use of diminutive. In J. L. Sokolov, & C. E. Snow (Eds.), Handbook of Research in Language Development using CHILDES. Hillsdale, NJ: Erlbaum; Table 6-3: From the *Bayley Scales of Infant Development.* Copyright © 1969 by The Psychological Corporation. Reproduced by permission. All rights reserved. "Bayley Scales of Infant Development" is a registered trademark of the Psychological Corporation; Table 6-4: Adapted from Benedict, H. (1979). Early lexical development: Comprehension and production. *Journal of Child Language, 6,* 183–200. Copyright © 1979. Reprinted by permission of Cambridge University Press; Table 6-6: Table 6-6 from B. G. Blount, B. G. (1982). Culture and the language of socialization: Parental speech. In D. A. Wagner & H. W. Stevenson (Eds.), *Cultural perspectives on child development.* San Francisco: Freeman. Copyright © by W.H. Freeman and Company. Used with permission.

Chapter 7 Figure 7-1: Courtesy of Dr. Carroll Izard; Figure 7-3: Adapted from Kagan, J., Kearsley, R. B., & Zelazo, P. R. (1978). *Intimacy, its place in Human Development,* pg, 107. Cambridge, MA: Harvard University Press. Copyright © 1978 by the Presidents and Fellows of Harvard College; Figure 7-4: Harlow Primate Laboratory/University of Wisconsin; Figure 7-5: Adapted from Bell, S. M., & Ainsworth, M. D.

(1972). Infant crying and maternal responsiveness. *Child Development, 43,* 1171–1190. Reprinted with the permission of The Society for Research in Child Development; Figure 7-5: Adapted from C. Tomlinson-Keasey, (1985). *Child Development: Psychological, sociological, and biological factors.* Homewood, IL: Dorsey. Used with permission of Dr. Carol Tomlinson-Keasey; Table 7-1: Adapted from Waters, E. (1978). The reliability and stability of individual differences in infant-mother attachment. *Child Development, 49,* 480–494. Reprinted with the permission of The Society for Research in Child Development; Table 7-2: Adapted from Thomas, A., Chess, S., & Birch, H. G. (1968). *Temperament and behavior disorders in children.* New York: New York University Press.

Chapter 8 Figure 8-2: Courtesy of Marcus E. Raichle, M.D.; Figure 8-3: From Fischer, K. W., & Rose, S. P. (1995). Concurrent cycles in the dynamic development of brain and behavior. *Newsletter of the Society for Research in Child Development,* p. 16. Reprinted with the permission of the Society for Research in Child Development; Figure 8-4: Elkind, D. (1978). The child's reality: Three developmental themes. In Coren, S., & Ward, L. M., Hillsdale, NJ: Erlbaum; Figure 8-6: From Zito, J. M., Safer, D. J., dosReis, S., Gardner, J. F., Boles, M., & Lynch, F. (2000). Trends in prescribing of psychotropic medications to preschoolers. *Journal of the American Medical Association, 283,* 1025–1030; Figure 8-7: From Needleman, H. L., Riess, J. A., Tobin, M. J., Biesecker, G. E., & Greenhouse, J. B. (1996, February 7). Bone lead levels and delinquent behavior. *Journal of the American Medical Association, 275,* 363–369; Figure 8-9: Laura Dwight Photography; Table 8-2: Adapted with permission from Charles C. Corbin, *A textbook of motor development.* Copyright © 1973 Times Mirror Higher Education Group, Inc., Dubuque, Iowa. All rights reserved. Used with permission of The McGraw-Hill Companies.

Chapter 9 Figure 9-2: Laura Dwight Photography; Figure 9-6: Adapted from: Berko, J. (1958). The child's learning of English morphology. *Word, 14,* 150–177; Figure 9-7: Hart, B., Risley, R. T. (1995). *Meaningful differences in the everyday experience of young American children.* Paul H. Brookes Publishing, P.O. Box 10624, Baltimore, MD 21285-0624; Figure 9-9: Based on Table 5-2, pg. 192 in Tobin J. J., Wu, D. Y. H., & Davidson, D. D. (1989). *Preschool in three cultures: Japan, China, and the United States.* New Haven, CT: Yale University Press. Reprinted with permission of Yale University Press; Figure 9-10: From Rideout, V. J., Foehr, U. G., Roberts, D. F., & Brodie, M. *(1999, November). Kids and media at the new millennium.* A Kaiser Family Foundation Report. Washington, DC: Henry J. Kaiser Family Foundation; Table 9-1: Poole, D., & Lamb, M. (1998). Investigative interviews of Children: A guide for helping professionals. Washington, DC: American Psychological Association Copyright © 1998 by the American Psychological Association. Adapted with permission; Table 9-3: Reuse, Table of growing speech capabilities from *The Language Instinct,* by Steven Pinker. Copyright © 1994 by Steven Pinker. Reprinted by permission of HarperCollins Publishers, Inc.

Chapter 10 Figure 10-1: Adapted from: Farver, J. M., Kim, Y. K., & Lee, Y. (1995). Cultural differences in Korean- and Anglo-American preschooler's interaction and play behaviors. *Child Development, 66,* 1088–1099. Reprinted with the permission of The Society for Research in Child Development, Inc.; Figure 10-2: Albert Bandura; Figure 10-3: Used with permission of the Center for Media and Public Affairs, Washington, DC.; Table 10-3: Baumrind, D. (1971). Current patterns of parental authority. *Developmental Psychology Monographs,* 4 (1, Pt. 2). Washington, DC: American Psychological Association Copyright © 1998 by the American Psychological Association. Adapted with permission.

Chapter 11 Figure 11-1: From Barrett, D. E., & Radke-Yarrow, M. (1985). Effects of nutritional supplementation on children's responses to novel, frustrating, and competitive situations. *American Journal of Clinical Nutrition, 42,* 102–120. Copyright © American Journal of Clinical Nutrition. American Society for Clinical Nutrition; Figure 11-4: From Cratty, B. J. (1979). *Perceptual and motor development in infants and children.* All rights reserved. Reprinted by permission of Allyn & Bacon; Figure 11-5: From Schor, E. L. (1987). Unintentional injuries: Patterns within families. *American Journal of the Diseases of Children, 141,* 1280. Used by Permission. American Medical Association; Table 11-1: These rules are from *Child Safety on the Information Highway* by Lawrence J. Magid. They are reprinted with permission of the National Center for Missing and Exploited Children (NCMEC).

Copyright © NCMEC 1994. All rights reserved. Table 11-2: Figure 2-5 from I. J. L. Meece, I. J. L. *Child and Adolescent Development for Educators,* pg. 400. Boston: McGraw-Hill Copyright © 1997. Reprinted by permission of the McGraw-Hill Companies.

Chapter 12 Figure 12-2: From Dasen, P., Ngini, L., & Lavallee, M. (1979). Cross-cultural training studies of concrete operations. In L. H. Eckenberger, W. J. Lonner, & Y. H. Poortinga (Eds.), *Cross-cultural contributions to psychology.* Amsterdam: Swets & Zeilinger. Used with permission; Figure 12-4: Copyright © UNESCO 1990. Reproduced by permission of UNESCO; Figure 12-7: Simulated items similar to those in the Wechsler Intelligence scale for Children: Third Edition. Copyright © 1990 by The Psychological Corporation. Reproduced by permission. All rights reserved. "Wechsler Intelligence Scale for Children" and "WISC-III" are registered trademarks of The Psychological Corporation; Table 12-1: Adapted from Chall, J. S. (1979). The great debate: Ten years later with a modest proposal for reading stages. In L. B. Resnick & P. A. Weaver (Eds.). *Theory and practice of early reading.* Hillsdale, NJ: Lawrence Erlbaum Associates; Table 12-2: Walters, E., & Gardner, H. (1986). The theory of multiple intelligences: Some issues and answers. In R. J. Sternberg & R. K. Wagner (eds.), Practical Intelligence. Cambridge University Press. Copyright © 1986. Reprinted with the permission of Cambridge University Press.

Chapter 13 Figure 13-1: From R. Shavelson, J. J. Hubner, & J. C. Stanton (1976). Self-concept: Validation of construct interpretations. *Review of Educational Research, 46,* 407–441; Figure 13-3: Adapted from Dodge, K. A. (1985). A social information processing model of social competence in children. In M. Perlmutter (Ed.), Minnesota Symposia on Child Psychology (Vol. 18), 77–126. Hillsdale, NJ: Erlbaum; Figure 13-4: From Hofferth, S., & Sandberg, J. F. (2001). How American children spend their time. *Journal of Marriage and the Family, 63,* 295–308; Figure 13-6: Adapted from Stevenson, H. W., & Lee, S. (1990). Contexts of achievement: A study of American, Chinese, and Japanese children. *Monographs of the Society for Research in Child Development. No. 221,* 55, Nos. 1–2. Reprinted with the permission of The Society for Research in Child Development, Inc.; Table 13-1: Adapted from Zarbatany, L., Haratmann, D. P., & Rankin, B. D. (1990). The psychological functions of preadolescent peer activities. *Child Development, 61,* 1067–1080. Reprinted with the permission of The Society for Research in Child Development, Inc.

Chapter 14 Figure 14-1: Cratty, B. J. *Perceptual and motor development in infants and children.* (2nd ed.). Copyright © 1986 by Allyn and Bacon. Reprinted/Adapted by permission; Figure 14-2: Adapted from Eveleth, P., & Tanner, J. (1976). Worldwide variation in human growth. New York: Cambridge University Press. Copyright © 1976. Reprinted with the permission of Cambridge University Press; Figure 14-3: Tanner, J. M. (1978). *Education and physical growth* (2nd ed.). New York: International Universities Press; Figure 14-6: Adapted from Wechsler, H., et al. (2002). Trends in College Binge Drinking During a Period of Increased Prevention Efforts Findings From 4 Harvard School of Public Health College Alcohol Study Surveys: 1993–2001. Used with permission of Henry Wechsler, Ph.D.; Figure 14-9: Reproduced with the permission of The Alan Guttmacher Institute, from The Alan Guttmacher Institute (AGI): *Sex and American's Teenagers,* New York, 1994; Table 14-1: Rahe, K. H., & Arthur, R. J. (1978). Life change and illness studies: Past history and future directions. *Human Stress, 4,* 3–15. Reprinted with permission of the Helen Dwight Reid Educational Foundation. Published by Heldref Publications, 1319 Eighteenth St., N.W., Washington, DC. 20036-1802; Table 14-2: Reprinted with the permission of Dr. Herbert Benson.

Chapter 15 Figure 15-1: Reprinted with permission of the Organization for Economic Cooperation and Development. Paris; Figure 15-2: Used with the permission of the Yankee Group; Figure 15-5: From Astin, A. W., Korn, W. S., & Berz, E. R. (1990). *The American freshman: National norms for Fall, 1990.* Los Angeles: Higher Education Research Institute, Graduate School of Education, UCLA; Table 15-1: Reprinted with permission of David A. Goslin, President, American Institute for Research, Washington, DC; Table 15-4: Reprinted with permission of Scribner, a Division of Simon & Schuster from *Failing at Fairness: How American's Schools Cheat Girls* by Myra & David Sadker. Copyright © 1994 by Myra Sadker and David Sadker.

Name Index

Abelin, T., 431
Able, E.L., 89
Aboud, F.E., 384, 395
Abram, K.A., 421
Abrams, D., 388
Abramson, L.Y., 415, 479
Achenbach, T.A., 165
Acheson, S., 180
Ackil, J.K., 269
Acocella, J., 328, 329
Acock, A., 400
Adams, C., 178
Adams, C.R., 452
Adams, G.R., 471, 482, 487
Adams, M., 221, 294
Adams, R.J., 119
Adamson, L., 89
Adamson, L.B., 204
Adelson, J., 494
Adler, N.E., 445
Adler, P., 394
Adler, P.A., 394
Adler, S.A., 177
Adolph, K.E., 143, 159
Agee, O.F., 235
Ager, J., 90
Ahadi, S.A., 218
Ainsworth, M.D.S., 142, 202, 209, 211, 215
Aitken, R.J., 81
Akande, A., 328
Akmajian, A., 185
Alan Guttmacher Institute, 85, 433, 434, 496
Albers, L.L., 113
Albrecht, H., 417
Alemi, B., 109
Ales, K.L., 87
Alessandri, S.M., 89
Allen, E., 272
Allen, J.P., 498
Allison, A.C., 65
Allison, D.B., 72, 325
Alloy, L.B., 328, 329
Allred, E.N., 243
Aloise, P.A., 271
Altemus, M., 149
Altshuler, L.L., 116
Amato, P.R., 400
Ambuel, B., 498
American Academy of Pediatrics, 106, 142, 149, 151, 157, 240, 244, 252, 285, 331, 333
American Association of University Women, 458
American Association on Mental Retardation, 374
American Cancer Society, 241
American College of Obstetricians and Gynecologists, 106
American Psychiatric Association, 252
Ammerman, R.T., 245
Amos, A., 429
Ampofo-Boateng, K., 333
Anand, K.J.S., 156
Anders, T.F., 138
Andersen, C., 350
Andersen, P., 74
Anderson, D., 206, 215
Anderson, E., 402
Anderson, K.J., 194, 221

Anderson, M., 368
Anderson, W.F., 69, 70
Andersson, T., 417
Andrade, N.N., 472
Andreas, D., 220
Andreasen, N.C., 78
Andrews, K., 89
Andruski, J.E., 193
Angier, N., 8
Angleitner, A., 71, 219
Ani, C., 147
Anisfeld, M., 214
Apgar, V., 99
Apostoleris, N.H., 394
Apter, A., 417
Archer, P., 144
Archer, S.L., 474
Arcus, D., 71, 72, 77
Ardila, A., 350
Arends, E., 480
Arendt, R., 89
Ariès, P., 11
Arlotti, J.P., 150
Armitage, P., 79
Arnett, J.J., 445, 484, 486
Aronen, E.T., 220
Aronson, E., 423
Aronson, J., 460
Arseneault, L., 109
Arthur, R.J., 422
Aseltine, R.H., 479
Asendorpf, J.B., 205
Ashburn, S.S., 234
Asher, S.R., 389, 392, 393, 395
Ashley, E., 350
Ashmead, D.H., 154, 159
Aslin, R.N., 152, 154, 194, 237
Asp, C.E., 450, 452
Astbury, J., 113
Astin, A.W., 458
Atkinson, L., 211
Atterbury, J.L., 85, 136, 137
Attie, I., 416
Atwood, M.E., 249
Au, T.K., 433
Auerbach, C.F., 212
Auerbach, J., 203
Auinger, P., 357
Austin, C.M., 123
Austin-La France, R., 86
Autti-Raemoe, I., 89
Aved, B.M., 115
Avia, M.D., 71, 219
Aviezer, O., 213
Axia, G., 156
Azar, B., 16, 188, 375
Azmitia, M., 351
Azuma, H., 305
Azuma, S.D., 88

Babad, E., 361
Bachman, J.G., 426, 427
Bacho, R.A., 475
Bader, A.P., 101
Bagwell, C.L., 390
Bahrick, L.E., 155, 158, 194
Bailey, A., 79
Bailey, J.M., 73

Baillargeon, R., 172, 266, 443
Bainbridge, J., 363
Bajda, V.M., 219
Bajos, N., 495
Bakeman, R., 89, 204
Baker-Ward, L., 270
Bakewell, J., 110
Balaban, M.T., 136
Ball, J.A., 102
Ballard-Reisch, D., 425
Bandi Rao, S., 175
Bandura, A., 298, 308, 311, 312, 329
Bangdiwala, S.I., 430
Bankston, C., 452
Barbaranelli, C., 329
Bar-David, E., 297
Barinaga, M., 14
Barkley, R.A., 328, 337, 338
Barnett, D., 211
Barnett, R.C., 398
Barone, M., 325
Barone, V.J., 243
Barr, H.M., 86, 88
Barr, P.A., 67, 70
Barr, R.A., 190
Barr, R.G., 89, 217
Barratt, M.S., 498
Barrett, D.E., 147, 234, 324
Barrett, J.F.R., 106
Barrett, M., 184
Barry, H., III, 486
Bar-Tal, Y., 297
Bartecchi, C.E., 431
Barth, J.M., 297
Bartolome, J., 158
Bashir, M., 79
Bates, E., 189, 191, 236, 276
Bates, J.E., 219, 281, 305, 395
Bathurst, K., 375
Battistutta, D., 113
Baudonniere, P., 205
Bauer, P.J., 177
Bauman, K.E., 484, 489
Bauman, K.J., 360
Baumeister, A.A., 138
Baumeister, R.F., 385
Baumrind, D., 304, 305
Baxter, A., 205
Bayley, N., 179, 180
Bazarskaya, N., 305
Beal, C.R., 354, 394, 395
Bearman, K., 415, 478
Bearman, P.S., 484, 498
Beaulac-Baillargeon, L., 90
Beautrais, A.L., 480
Bebeau, M.J., 448
Becahy, R., 431
Becker, J.B., 415
Beckwith, L., 180, 181
Beeghly, M., 64
Beeman, M.J., 235
Begley, S., 69, 106, 188, 291
Behrend, D.A., 191
Behrman, R., 58, 108, 374
Beilin, H., 274, 350
Bejin, A., 495
Bekkering, H., 216

Belanger, S., 284
Belgrad, S.L., 354
Belkin, L., 59
Bell, A., 496
Bell, R., 110
Bell, S.M., 142, 215
Belle, D., 400
Bellinger, D., 86, 243
Bellugi, U., 188
Belmont, J.M., 272
Belsky, J., 142, 211, 212, 220, 223, 281
Beltzer, N., 495
Bem, S., 298
Benbow, C.P., 296, 376
Bendell, D., 375
Bendersky, M., 89
Benedict, H., 185, 189
Benenson, J.F., 295, 394
Benini, F., 156
Benjamin, J., 76
Benker, J., 445
Bennett, A., 78
Bennett, D.S., 281
Bennett, E.L., 134
Benoit, D., 211
Benoit, M., 480
Benson, H., 424
Benson, P., 327
Bentz, L.S., 85, 136, 137
Berenbaum, S.A., 296, 496
Berendes, H., 87
Bergeman, C., 76
Bergen, D., 300
Bergen, J., 79
Berger, L., 400
Berget, A., 90
Berkey, C.S., 97
Berko, J., 276
Berkowitz, L., 310
Berlin, L., 210, 222
Berliner, L., 243
Berman, A.L., 479
Bernal, M.E., 295
Berndt, T.J., 487, 493, 494
Bernstein, G.A., 328
Bernstein, M., 365
Bernstein, N., 243
Bernstein, P., 121
Berrick, J.D., 402
Berry, J.W., 350, 442
Bersoff, D.M.N., 497
Berthenthal, B.I., 153
Berthier, N.E., 143
Bertoncini, J., 155
Besseghini, V.H., 329, 478
Best, C.T., 155
Betancourt, H., 8
Beth-Halachmi, N., 417
Bhachu, P.K., 387
Bianchi, S., 285
Bickham, D.S., 286
Bierman, K.L., 393, 492
Biesecker, G.E., 243
Bigelow, B.J., 390
Bigler, R.S., 294, 295, 395
Bijeljac-Babic, R., 155
Binet, A., 11, 365, 365–66
Bing, E.D., 102

549

Subject Index

SINGLE PC LICENSE AGREEMENT AND LIMITED WARRANTY

READ THIS LICENSE CAREFULLY BEFORE OPENING THIS PACKAGE. BY OPENING THIS PACKAGE, YOU ARE AGREEING TO THE TERMS AND CONDITIONS OF THIS LICENSE. IF YOU DO NOT AGREE, DO NOT OPEN THE PACKAGE. PROMPTLY RETURN THE UNOPENED PACKAGE AND ALL ACCOMPANYING ITEMS TO THE PLACE YOU OBTAINED THEM [[FOR A FULL REFUND OF ANY SUMS YOU HAVE PAID FOR THE SOFTWARE]]. THESE TERMS APPLY TO ALL LICENSED SOFTWARE ON THE DISK EXCEPT THAT THE TERMS FOR USE OF ANY SHAREWARE OR FREEWARE ON THE DISKETTES ARE AS SET FORTH IN THE ELECTRONIC LICENSE LOCATED ON THE DISK:

1. GRANT OF LICENSE and OWNERSHIP: The enclosed computer programs <<and data>> ("Software") are licensed, not sold, to you by Pearson Education, Inc. publishing as Prentice Hall ("We" or the "Company") and in consideration [[of your payment of the license fee, which is part of the price you paid]] [[of your purchase or adoption of the accompanying Company textbooks and/or other materials,]] and your agreement to these terms. We reserve any rights not granted to you. You own only the disk(s) but we and/or our licensors own the Software itself. This license allows you to use and display your copy of the Software on a single computer (i.e., with a single CPU) at a single location for academic use only, so long as you comply with the terms of this Agreement. You may make one copy for back up, or transfer your copy to another CPU, provided that the Software is usable on only one computer.

2. RESTRICTIONS: You may not transfer or distribute the Software or documentation to anyone else. Except for backup, you may not copy the documentation or the Software. You may not network the Software or otherwise use it on more than one computer or computer terminal at the same time. You may not reverse engineer, disassemble, decompile, modify, adapt, translate, or create derivative works based on the Software or the Documentation. You may be held legally responsible for any copying or copyright infringement that is caused by your failure to abide by the terms of these restrictions.

3. TERMINATION: This license is effective until terminated. This license will terminate automatically without notice from the Company if you fail to comply with any provisions or limitations of this license. Upon termination, you shall destroy the Documentation and all copies of the Software. All provisions of this Agreement as to limitation and disclaimer of warranties, limitation of liability, remedies or damages, and our ownership rights shall survive termination.

4. LIMITED WARRANTY AND DISCLAIMER OF WARRANTY: Company warrants that for a period of 60 days from the date you purchase this SOFTWARE (or purchase or adopt the accompanying textbook), the Software, when properly installed and used in accordance with the Documentation, will operate in substantial conformity with the description of the Software set forth in the Documentation, and that for a period of 30 days the disk(s) on which the Software is delivered shall be free from defects in materials and workmanship under normal use. The Company does not warrant that the Software will meet your requirements or that the operation of the Software will be uninterrupted or error-free. Your only remedy and the Company's only obligation under these limited warranties is, at the Company's option, return of the disk for a refund of any amounts paid for it by you or replacement of the disk. THIS LIMITED WARRANTY IS THE ONLY WARRANTY PROVIDED BY THE COMPANY AND ITS LICENSORS, AND THE COMPANY AND ITS LICENSORS DISCLAIM ALL OTHER WARRANTIES, EXPRESS OR IMPLIED, INCLUDING WITHOUT LIMITATION, THE IMPLIED WARRANTIES OF MERCHANTABILITY AND FITNESS FOR A PARTICULAR PURPOSE. THE COMPANY DOES NOT WARRANT, GUARANTEE OR MAKE ANY REPRESENTATION REGARDING THE ACCURACY, RELIABILITY, CURRENTNESS, USE, OR RESULTS OF USE, OF THE SOFTWARE.

5. LIMITATION OF REMEDIES AND DAMAGES: IN NO EVENT, SHALL THE COMPANY OR ITS EMPLOYEES, AGENTS, LICENSORS, OR CONTRACTORS BE LIABLE FOR ANY INCIDENTAL, INDIRECT, SPECIAL, OR CONSEQUENTIAL DAMAGES ARISING OUT OF OR IN CONNECTION WITH THIS LICENSE OR THE SOFTWARE, INCLUDING FOR LOSS OF USE, LOSS OF DATA, LOSS OF INCOME OR PROFIT, OR OTHER LOSSES, SUSTAINED AS A RESULT OF INJURY TO ANY PERSON, OR LOSS OF OR DAMAGE TO PROPERTY, OR CLAIMS OF THIRD PARTIES, EVEN IF THE COMPANY OR AN AUTHORIZED REPRESENTATIVE OF THE COMPANY HAS BEEN ADVISED OF THE POSSIBILITY OF SUCH DAMAGES. IN NO EVENT SHALL THE LIABILITY OF THE COMPANY FOR DAMAGES WITH RESPECT TO THE SOFTWARE EXCEED THE AMOUNTS ACTUALLY PAID BY YOU, IF ANY, FOR THE SOFTWARE OR THE ACCOMPANYING TEXTBOOK. BECAUSE SOME JURISDICTIONS DO NOT ALLOW THE LIMITATION OF LIABILITY IN CERTAIN CIRCUMSTANCES, THE ABOVE LIMITATIONS MAY NOT ALWAYS APPLY TO YOU.

6. GENERAL: THIS AGREEMENT SHALL BE CONSTRUED IN ACCORDANCE WITH THE LAWS OF THE UNITED STATES OF AMERICA AND THE STATE OF NEW YORK, APPLICABLE TO CONTRACTS MADE IN NEW YORK, AND SHALL BENEFIT THE COMPANY, ITS AFFILIATES AND ASSIGNEES. HIS AGREEMENT IS THE COMPLETE AND EXCLUSIVE STATEMENT OF THE AGREEMENT BETWEEN YOU AND THE COMPANY AND SUPERSEDES ALL PROPOSALS OR PRIOR AGREEMENTS, ORAL, OR WRITTEN, AND ANY OTHER COMMUNICATIONS BETWEEN YOU AND THE COMPANY OR ANY REPRESENTATIVE OF THE COMPANY RELATING TO THE SUBJECT MATTER OF THIS AGREEMENT. If you are a U.S. Government user, this Software is licensed with "restricted rights" as set forth in subparagraphs (a)-(d) of the Commercial Computer-Restricted Rights clause at FAR 52.227-19 or in subparagraphs (c)(1)(ii) of the Rights in Technical Data and Computer Software clause at DFARS 252.227-7013, and similar clauses, as applicable.

Should you have any questions concerning this agreement or if you wish to contact the Company for any reason, please contact in writing: Pearson Education, 1 Lake Street, Upper Saddle River, NJ 07458.

	PRENATAL PERIOD (conception to birth)	**INFANCY/TODDLERHOOD** (birth to 3 years)
Physical Development	*GERMINAL STAGE* (fertilization to 2 weeks) *EMBRYONIC STAGE* (2 to 8 weeks) *FETAL STAGE* (8 weeks to birth)	• Rapid height and weight gains. • Neurons grow and form interconnections in the brain. • Infants wiggle, push upward, sit up, crawl, and eventually walk. • Infants reach, grasp, and pick up small objects. • Vision is 20/20 by 6 months, with depth perception and recognition of patterns, faces, shapes, and colors. • Infants hear a wide range of frequencies.
Cognitive Development	• Intelligence is partly determined, and some psychological disorders may take root. • Cognitive functions can be affected by tobacco, alcohol and/or drug use by mother. 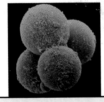	• Infants begin to understand object permanence and "experiment" with the physical world. • Use of representation and symbols begins. • Information-processing speed increases. • Language develops rapidly through babbling, holophrases, and telegraphic speech. 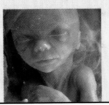
Social/Personality Development	• Some personality traits are partly determined genetically. • Drug and alcohol use by mothers can lead to problems in the child, including irritability and difficulty in dealing with multiple stimuli and in forming attachments.	• Infants exhibit different temperaments and activity levels. • Facial expressions appear to reflect emotions; facial expressions of others are understood. • Toddlers begin to feel empathy. • A style of attachment to others emerges. 

Theories & Theorists

Jean Piaget	Sensorimotor stage
Erik Erikson	Trust-vs.-mistrust stage (birth-1½ yrs.) Autonomy-vs.-shame-and-doubt stage (1½-3 yrs.)
Sigmund Freud	Oral and anal stages
Lawrence Kohlberg	Premoral period